ENGLISH THESAURUS

THE ULTIMATE WORD POWER COMPANION

ENGLISH THESAURUS

THE ULTIMATE WORD POWER COMPANION

ABBEYDALE PRESS

ENGLISH THESAURUS

This edition published in 2001
by Abbeydale Press
An imprint of Bookmart Limited
Desford Road, Enderby
Leicester LE9 5AD
England

ISBN 1-86147-023-1

Printed in Great Britain

CONTENTS

THESAURUS A–Z

ABBREVIATIONS

n noun
v vowel
pl n plural noun
adj adjective
adv adverb
prep preposition
inf informal

A

abandon *v* desert, ditch, forsake, forswear, jilt, leave behind, maroon, quit, relinquish, yield; depart from, evacuate, quit, vacate; cede, deliver, forgo, give up, renounce, resign, surrender, waive

abandon *n* careless, freedom, dash

abandoned *adj* depraved, derelict, deserted, discarded, dropped, forsaken, left, outcast, rejected, relinquished; corrupt, depraved, dissolute, lost, profligate, reprobate, shameful, sinful, unprincipled

abandonment *n* dereliction, desertion, forsaking, jilting, leaving

abashed *adj* ashamed, discomfited, disconcerted, embarrassed, humiliated, mortified, shamefaced

abate *v* die down, decrease, diminish, lessen, lower, moderate, reduce, relax, remove, slacken; deduct, mitigate, rebate, remit; allay, alleviate, appease, assuage, blunt, calm, compose, dull, moderate, mollify, pacify, qualify, quiet, quell, soften, soothe, tranquillize

abbey *n* cloister, convent, friary, monastery, nunnery, priory

abbreviate *v* abridge, clip, compress, condense, contract, cut, curtail, epitomize, précis, reduce, shorten

abbreviation *n* abridgement, compression, condensation, contraction, curtailment, cutting, reduction, shortened form

abdicate *v* abandon, cede, forgo, forsake, give up, quit, relinquish, renounce, retire, surrender, vacate, waive, yield

abduct *v* carry off, hold to ransom, kidnap, make off with, run away with, run off with, seize, snatch

aberration *n* departure, deviation, divergence, rambling, wandering; abnormality, anomaly, eccentricity, irregularity, peculiarity, singularity, unconformity; delusion, disorder, hallucination, illusion, instability

abhor *v* abominate, detest, dislike, hate, loathe, nauseate, recoil from, shrink from, shudder at

abhorrent *adj* abominable, detestable, disgusting, hateful, horrible, loathsome, nauseating, obnoxious, odious, offensive, repellent, repugnant, repulsive, revolting

abide *v* accept, bear, put up with, stand, stomach, suffer, tolerate; adhere to, agree to, comply with, conform to, follow, keep to, obey, observe, stand by, stick to

abiding *adj* changeless, constant, continuing, durable, enduring, lasting, permanent, stable, unchangeable

ability *n* ableness, adeptness, adroitness, aptitude, aptness, cleverness, dexterity, efficacy, efficiency, facility, ingenuity, knack, power, readiness, skill, strength, talent, vigour; competency, qualification; calibre, capability, capacity, faculty

ablaze *adj* afire, aflame, alight, blazing, burning, fiery, flaming, ignited, lighted, on fire; aglow, brilliant, flashing, gleaming, glowing, illuminated, incandescent, luminous, radiant, sparkling

able *adj* accomplished, adept, capable, clever, competent, expert, gifted, ingenious, masterly, proficient, qualified, skilled, strong, talented

abnormal *adj* aberrant, anomalous, atypical, bizarre, eccentric, erratic, exceptional, idiosyncratic, irregular, kinky, odd, peculiar, perverse, singular, strange, unexpected, unnatural, unusual, weird

abnormality *n* aberration, anomaly, atypicalness, bizarreness, deformity, deviation, eccentricity, exception, extraordinariness, flaw, irregularity, monstrosity, oddity, peculiarity, queerness, singularity, strangeness, uncommonness, unexpectedness, unnaturalness, untypicalness, unusualness, weirdness

abolish *v* abrogate, annul, axe, cancel, destroy, do away with, eliminate, end, eradicate, extinguish, invalidate, nullify, quash, put an end to, quash, repeal, rescind, revoke, stamp out, stop, terminate, wipe out

abolition *n* abrogation, annihilation, annulment, blotting out, cancellation, destruction, elimination, destruction, end, ending, eradiction, expunction, extermination, extinction, extirpation, invalidation, nullification, obliteration, over throw, overturning, quashing, repeal, repudiation, rescission, revcation, stamping out, subversion, suppression, termination, vitiation, voiding, wiping out, withdrawal

abominable *adj* abhorrent, contemptible, cursed, damnable, despicable, detestable, disgusting, execrable, foul, hateful, hellish, horrid, loathsome, nauseous, obnoxious, nefarious, odious; revolting, repugnant, repulsive; shabby, vile, wretched

abomination *n* abhorrence, antipathy, aversion, detestation, disgust, distaste, execration, hate, hatred, horror, loathing, odium, repugnance, revulsion

abortion *n* miscarriage, termination

abortive *adj* futile, fruitless, idle, immature, incomplete, ineffectual, inoperative, nugatory, profitless, unavailing, unsuccessful, useless, vain, worthless

abound *v* be alive with, be crawling with, be full of, be plentiful, crowd, flourish, increase, infest, luxuriate, overflow, proliferate, superabound, swarm, swell, teem, thrive

abounding *adj* abundant, bountiful, copious, filled, flourishing, flowing, flush, full, lavish, luxuriant, overflowing, plenteous, plentiful, profuse, prolific, rank, replete, rich, superabundant, teeming

about *prep* around, encircling, surrounding, round; near, concerning, referring to, regarding, relating to, relative to, respecting, touching, with regard to, with respect to; all over, over, through

about *adv* around, before; approximately, near, nearly

above *adj* above-mentioned, aforementioned, aforesaid, foregoing, preceding, previous, prior

above *adv* aloft, overhead; before, previously; of a higher rank

above *prep* higher than, on top of; exceeding, greater than, over;

beyond, superior to

aboveboard *adj* candid, frank, honest, open, straightforward, truthful, upright

aboveboard *adv* candidly, fairly, openly, sincerely

abrasive *adj* caustic, chafing, cutting, eroding, galling, grating, harsh, hurtful, irritating, nasty, rough, sharp, unpleasant

abreast *adv* acquainted, conversant, familiar, informed, in touch, knowledgeable, up to date

abridge *v* abbreviate, abstract, clip, compress, concentrate, condense, contract, curtail, cut, cut down, decrease, digest, diminish, epitomize, lessen, précis, reduce, shorten, summarize, synopsise

abroad *adv* beyond the sea, in foreign lands, out of the country, overseas

abrupt *adj* blunt, brisk, brusque, curt, direct, gruff, impolite, rough, rude, short, snappish, terse, uncivil, ungracious; hasty hurried, quick, rapid, sharp, sudden, swift, unexpected, unforeseen

absence *n* absenteeism, nonappearance, nonattendance; abstraction, distraction, inattention, musing, preoccupation, reverie; default, defect, deficiency, lack, omission, privation, want

absent *adj* abroad, away, elsewhere, gone, not present; abstracted, dreaming, inattentive, lost, musing, napping, preoccupied

absolute *adj* complete, entire, out right, perfect, pure, sheer, thorough, total, unqualified; actual, categorical, certain, decided, determinate, genuine, positive, real, unequivocal, unquestionable, veritable; authoritative, autocratic, despotic, dictatorial, full, sovereign, supreme, unbounded, unconditional, unlimited, unqualified, unrestricted

absolutely *adv* completely, definitely, entirely, fully, totally, utterly, wholly; actually, definitely, ownright, positively, really, surely, truly, unquestionably, unreservedly

absolution *n* acquitted, clearance, deliverance, discharge, forgiveness, liberation, pardon, release, remission, shrift, striving

absolve *v* acquit, clear, discharge, exempt, excuse, exonerate, forgive, free, liberate, let off, pardon, release, reprieve, set free, vindicate

absorb *v* appropriate, assimilate, drink in, imbibe, soak up; consume, destroy, devour, engorge, engulf, exhaust, swallow up, take up; arrest, engage, engross, fix, immense, occupy, rivet

absorbent *adj* absorbing, imbibing, penetrable, porous, receptive

absorbing *adj* captivating, engrossing, fascinating, gripping, intriguing, preoccupying, rivetting, spellbinding

abstain *v* avoid, cease, decline, deny yourself, desist, forbear, forgo, give up, go without, hold back, refrain, refuse, shun, stop, withhold

abstemious *adj* abstinent, austere, frugal, moderate, puritanical, self-denying, sober, sparing, temperate

abstinence *n* abstemiousness, avoidance, fast, moderation, restraint, self-denial, sobriety, teetotalism, temperance

abstract *v* detach, disengage,

dissociate, disunite, extract, isolate, remove, separate, take away, take out, withdraw

abstract *adj* abstruse, complex, conceptual, deep, general, isolated, obscure, theoretical; non-objective, non-representational abridgment, condensation, digest, excerpt, extract, outline, précis, résumé, selection, summary, synopsis

abstracted *adj* absent, absent-minded, dreaming, inattentive, lost, musing, preoccupied, refined, subtle

absurd *adj* crazy, daft, extravagant, fantastic, fatuous, foolish, idiotic, incongruous, ill-advised, ill-judged, irrational, ludicrous, nonsensical, nugatory, preposterous, ridiculous, self-annulling, senseless, silly, stupid, surreal, unreasonable, zany

absurdity *n* craziness, daftness, farce, farcicality, farcicalness, folly, foolishness, idiocy, illogicality, illogicalness, incongruity, irrationality, joke, ludicrousness, meaninglessness, nonsense, preposterous, ridiculousness, senselessness, silliness, stupidity, unreasonableness

abundant *adj* ample, bounteous, bountiful, copious, exuberant, fertile, flowing, flourishing, full, generous, great, huge, large, lavish, liberal, luxuriant, much, overflowing, plentiful, profuse, rampant, replete, rich, teeming, thick

abuse *v* betray, cajole, deceive, desecrate, dishonour, misapply, misemploy, misuse, pervert, pollute, profane, prostitute, violate, wrong; harm, hurt, ill-use, ill-treat, injure, maltreat, mishandle; berate, blacken, calumniate, curse, defame, disparage, lampoon, lash, malign, rebuke, revile, reproach, satirize, scold, swear, slander, traduce, upbraid, vilify

abuse *n* desecration, dishonour, ill-use, mis-use, perversion, pollution, profanation; cruelty, exploitation, ill-treatment, maltreatment, outrage; aspersion, defamation, disparage ment, insult, invective, obloquy, opprobrium, railing, rating, reviling, ribaldry, rudeness, scurrility, upbraiding, vilification, vituperation

abusive *adj* acrimonious, angry, calumnious, carping, censorous, condemnatory, contumelious, denunciatory, injurious, insulting, offensive, opprobrious, reproachful, reviling, ribald, rude, scornful, scurrilous, slanderous, vituperative

academic *adj* collegiate, educational, instructional, lettered, scholastic

academic *n* academician, classicist, doctor, don, fellow, pundit, savant, scholar, student, teacher, thinker, tutor

accede *v* accept, acquiesce, admit, agree, assent, comply, concede, concur, consent, endorse, grant, yield; assume, attain, come to, enter upon, inherit, succeed, succeed to

accelerate *v* dispatch, expedite, forward, go faster, hasten, hurry, pick up speed, precipitate, press on, quicken, speed up, spur on, step up, urge on

accent *n* acute, cedilla, circumflex, diacritic, grave, mark, sign, tilde, umlaut; beat, cadence, emphasis, force, pitch, rhythm, stress, timbre, tonality; articulation, enunciation, inflection, intonation, modulation, pronunciation, tone; accentuate, emphasize, stress, underline, underscore

accentuate *v* accent, emphasize, mark, point up, punctuate, stress; highlight, overemphasize, underline, underscore

accept *v* acquire, come by, derive, get, gain, obtain, receive, secure, take; accede to, acknowledge, acquiesce in, admit, agree to, approve, assent to, avow, embrace; estimate, construe, interpret, regard, value

acceptable *adj* agreeable, delightful, desirable, gratifying, pleasant, pleasing, pleasurable, welcome; adequate, admissible, all right, fair, moderate, OK, okay, passable, satisfactory, tolerable; be convinced, believe, credit, have faith, trust

access *v* broach, enter, open up

access *n* approach, avenue, entrance, entreé, entry, passage, right of way, way in; accessibility, admission, admittance, audience, interview; addition, accession, aggrandizement, enlargement, gain, increase, increment; attack, fit, onset, recurrence

accessible *adj* achievable, at hand, attainable, available, handy, near, nearby, obtainable, on hand, possible, reachable, ready; affable, approachable, available, conversable, cordial, friendly, informal; exposed, liable, open, subject, susceptible, vulnerable, wide open

accession *n* addition, augmentation, enlargement, extension, increase; succession

accessory *adj* abetting, additional, additive, adjunct, aiding, ancillary, assisting, contributory, helping, subsidiary, subordinate,supplemental

accessory *n* abettor, accomplice, assistant, confederate, helper, accompaniment, attendant, concomitant, detail, subsidiary

accident *n* calamity, casualty, condition, contingency, disaster, fortuity, incident, misadventure, miscarriage, mischance, misfortune, mishap; affection, alteration, chance, contingency, mode, modification, property, quality, state

accidental *adj* casual, chance, contingent, fortuitous, undesigned, unintended; adventitious, dispenable, immaterial, incidental, nonessential

acclaim *v* applaud, approve, celebrate, cheer, clap, commend, eulogize, exalt, extol, hail, honour, laud, praise, salute, welcome

acclaim *n* acclamation, applause, approbation, approval, celebration, cheering, clapping, commendation, eulogizing, exaltation, honour, laudation, plaudits, praise, welcome

acclimatize *v* accustom, adapt, adjust, condition, familiarize, habituate, inure, naturalize, season

accommodate *v* contain, furnish, hold, oblige, serve, supply; adapt, fit, suit; adjust, compose, harmonize, reconcile, settle

accommodation *n* board, digs, harbouring, house, housing, quartering, quarters, shelter, sheltering

accompany *v* attend, chaperon, convoy, escort, follow, go with

accomplice *n* abettor, accessory,

ally, assistant, associate, collaborator, colleague, confederate, friend, helper, henchman, mate, right-handman, sidekick, partner

accomplish *v* achieve, acquire, attain, bring about, bring off, carry off, complete, do, effect, execute, finish, fulfil, perform, perfect

accomplished *adj* able, adept, consummate, cultivated, expert, gifted, masterly, polished, practised, proficient, skillful, skilled, talented

accomplishment *n* achievement, act, attainment, bringing about, carrying out, completion, conclusion, consummation, coup, doing, effecting, execution, finishing, fulfilment, management, performance, production, realization; achievement, act, attainment, coup, deed, exploit, eat, stroke, success, triumph; ability, achievement, art, attainment, capability, gift, proficiency, skill, talent

according to *adj* as believed by, as maintained by as stated by, in the light of, on the authority of, on the authority of, on the report of; after, after the manner of, consistent with, in accordance with, in compliance with, in conformity with, in harmony with, in keeping with, in line with, in the manner of, obedient to

account *n* chronicle, description, detail, explanation, history, narration, narrative, portrayal, recital, record, relation, report, statement, story, tale, version; balance, balance sheets, bill, book, books, charge, computation, inventory, invoice, ledger, reckoning, register, score, statement, tally; basis, cause, consideration, ground, grounds, interest, motive, reason, regard, sake, score

account *v* appraise, assess, believe, calculate, compute, consider, count, deem, esteem, estimate, explain, gauge, hold, judge, rate, reckon, regard, think, value, weigh

accountability *n* answerability, chargeability, culpability, liability, responsibility

accountable *adj* amenable, answerable, charged with, liable, obligated obliged, responsible

account for *v* answer for, clarify, clear up, elucidate, explain, illuminate, justify, rationalize

accredit *n* appoint, authorize, certify, commission, depute, empower, endorse, entrust, guarantee, license, recognize, sanction, vouch for

accumulate *v* accrue, amass, assemble, build up, collect, cumulate, gather, grow, hoard, increase, pile up, stockpile, store

accumulation *n* aggregation, augmentation, build-up, collection, conglomeration, gathering, growth, heap, hoard, increase, mass, pile, stack, stock, stockpile, store, supply

accuracy *n* accurateness, authenticity, carefulness, closeness, correctness, exactitude, exactness, faithfulness, faultlessness, fidelity, meticulousness, niceness, nicety, precision, strictness, truth, truthfulness, veracity, verity

accurate *adj* authentic, careful, close, correct, exact, faithful, faultless, just, literal, meticulous, nice, precise, proper, regular, reliable, right, scrupulous, sound, spot-on, strict, true, truthful, unerring, veraciously

accusation *n* allegation, arraignment, attribution, blame, charge, citation, complaint, denunciation, impeachment, imputation, incrimination, indictment, recrimination, summons

accuse *v* allege, arraign, attribute, blame, censure, charge, cite, condemn, denounce, impeach, impute, incriminate, indict, recriminate, tax

accustom *v* acclimatize, acquaint, adapt, discipline, exercise, familiarize, habituate, inure, season, train

accustomed *adj* acclimatized, acquainted, adapted, disciplined, exercised, familiar, familiarized, given to habituated, in the habit of, inured, seasoned, trained, used; common, conventional, customary, established, everyday, expected, fixed, general, habitual, normal, ordinary, regular, routine, set, traditional, typical, usual

ache *n* discomfort, hurt, pain, pang, pound, smart, soreness, suffer, throb, twinge

ache *v* be painful, be sore, hurt, pound, smart, sting, throb

achieve *v* accomplish, acquire, attain, bring about, carry out, complete, consummate, do, earn, effect, execute, finish, fulfil, gain, get, obtain, perform procure, reach, realize, win

achievement *n* accomplishment, acquirement, attainment, completion, execution, fulfilment, performance, production, realization

acid *adj* acerbic, acidulous, acrid, biting, bitter, pungent, sharp, sour, tangy, tart, vinegarish, vinegary

acidity *n* acerbity, acidulousness, acridity, acridness, bitterness, pungency, sharpness, sourness, tartness, vinegariness, vinegarishness

acknowledge *n* accede, accept, acquiesce, admit, allow, concede, confess, declare, grant, own, profess, recognize, yield; answer to, return

acknowledgement *n* acceptance, accession, acquiescence, admission, allowing, confession, declaration, profession, realization, yielding; answer, appreciation, credit, gratitude, reaction, recognition, reply, response, return, thanks

acquaint *v* advise, announce, apprise of, disclose, divulge, enlighten, familiarize, inform, let someone know, notify, reveal, tell

acquaintance *n* associate, colleague, contact

acquiesce *v* accede, accept, agree, allow, approve, assent, bow to, comply, concur, conform, consent, give in, go along with, submit, yield

acquiescence *n* acceptance, accession, agreement, approval, assent, compliance, concurrence, conformity, consent, giving in obedience, submission, yielding

acquire *v* achieve, amass, attain, buy, collect, earn, gain, gather, get, obtain, pick up, procure, realize, receive, secure, win

acquisition *n* addition, buy, gain, possession, prize, property, purchase

acquisitive *adj* avaricious, avid, covetous, grabbing, grasping, greedy, predatory, rapacious

acquit *v* absolve, clear, deliver, discharge, exculpate, exonerate, fulfil, liberate, release, relieve, vindicate

acquittal *n* absolution, clearance, deliverance, discharge, exculpation, exoneration, freeing, liberation, release, relief, vindication

acrimonious *adj* acerbic, astringent, biting, bitter, caustic, censorious, churlish, crabbed, cutting, irascible, mordant, peevish, petulant, pungent, rancorous, sarcastic, severe, sharp, spiteful, splenetic, tart, testy, trenchant

act *n* accomplishment, achievement, action, blow, deed, doing, execution, exertion, exploit, feat, move, operation, performance, step, stroke, undertaking; bill, decree, edict, enactment, law, measure, ordinance, resolution, ruling, statute; performance, routine, show, sketch, turn

act *v* acquit, bear, behave, carry, carry out, comport, conduct, do, enact, execute, exert, function, go about, make, move, operate, perform, react, serve, strike, take effect, undertake, work; affect, assume, counterfeit, dissimulate, feign, imitate, perform, pose, posture, pretend, put on, seem, sham; act out, characterize, enact, impersonate, mime, mimic, perform, personate, personify, play, portray, represent, take the part of

act for *v* cover for, deputize for, fill in for, function in place of, replace, represent, serve, stand in for, substitute for, take the place of

acting *adj* deputy, interim, pro tem, provisional, stop gap, substitute, surrogate, temporary; (*Inf*) fill-in

acting *n* characterization, dramatics, enacting, impersonation, performance, performing, playing, portrayal, portraying, stagecraft, theatre; assuming, counterfeiting, dissimulation, feigning, imitating, imitation, imposture, play-acting, posing, posturing, pretence, pretending, putting on, seeming, shamming

action *n* accomplishment, achievement, act, blow, deed, exercise, exertion, exploit, feat, move, operation, performance, step, stroke, undertaking; activity, energy, force, liveliness, spirit, vigour, vim, vitality; battle, combat, conflict, fighting, warfare; case, cause, lawsuit, litigation, proceeding, prosecution

actions *pl n* bearing, behaviour, comportment, conduct, demeanour, deportment, manners, ways

active *adj* acting, astir, at work, doing, effectual functioning, in action, in force, in operation, moving, operative, running, stirring, working; animated, bustling, busy, engaged, full, hard-working, involved, occupied, on the go, on the move, strenuous; alert, animated, diligent, energetic, industrious, lively, nimble, on the go, quick, spirited, sprightly, spry, vibrant, vigorous, vital, vivacious

activity *n* action, activeness, animation, bustle, enterprise, exercise, exertion, hustle, labour, life, liveliness, motion, movement, stir, work; act, avocation, deed, endeavour, enterprise, hobby, interest, job, labour, occupation, pastime, project, pursuit, scheme, task, undertaking, venture, work

actor, actress *n* artist, artiste, dramatic, leading man, leading lady, performer, play-actor, player, star, starlet, supporting actor, Thespian, tragedian, trouper

actual *adj* absolute, bona fide, categorical, certain, concrete, corporeal, definite, factual, genuine, indisputable, indubitable, legitimate, physical, positive, real, substantial, tangible, true, undeniable, unquestionable, verified, veritable; current, existent, extant, live, living, present, prevailing

actually *adv* absolutely, as a matter of fact, essentially, indeed, in fact, in point of fact, in reality, in truth, literally, really, truly, veritably

acute *adj* alert, astute, canny, clever, discerning, discriminating, incisive, ingenious, insightful, intuitive, keen, observant, penetrating, perceptive, perspicacious, quick, sensitive, sharp, smart, subtle; cuspate, needle-shaped, peaked, pointed, sharp, sharpened; discerning, keen, sensitive

adamant *adj* determined, firm, fixed, immovable, inexorable, inflexible, insistent, intransigent, obdurate, resolute, rigid, set, stiff, stubborn, unbending, uncompromising, unrelenting, unshakable, unyielding

adapt *v* accommodate, adjust, alter, apply, change, comply, conform, familiarize, fashion, fit, habituate, harmonize, make, match, modify, prepare, qualify, remodel, shape, suit, tailor

adaptable *adj* adjustable, alterable, changeable, compliant, conformable, convertible, easy-going, flexible, malleable, modifiable, plastic, pliant, resilient, variable, versatile

adaptation *n* adjustment, alteration, change, conversion, modification, refitting, remodelling, reworking, shift, transformation, variation, version

add *v* adjoin, affix, amplify, annex, append, attach, augment, combine, enlarge by, include, increase by, supplement; add up, compute, count up, reckon, sum up, total; (*Inf*) tot up

addict *n* abuser, freak, user; (*Inf*) dope-fiend, junkie devotee, enthusiast, fan, follower

addicted *adj* absorbed, accustomed, dedicated, dependent, devoted, disposed, fond, habituated, inclined, obsessed, prone; (*Inf*) hooked

addiction *n* compulsion, craving, dependence, enslavement, habit, obsession

addition *n* accession, adding, adjoining, adjunct, affixing, amplification, annexation, attachment, augmentation, enlargement, extension, inclusion, increasing; addendum, additive, adjunct, affix, appendage, appendix, extension, extra, gain, increase, increment, supplement

additional *adj* added, affixed, appended, extra, fresh, further, increased, more, new, other, over-and-above, spare, supplementary

address *n* abode, domicile,

dwelling, home, house, location, lodging, place, residence, situation, where abouts; direction, inscription, superscription; discourse, disquisition, dissertation, harangue, lecture, oration, sermon, speech, talk; accost, apostrophize, approach, greet, hail, invoke, salute, speak to, talk to; discourse, give a speech, give a talk, lecture, orate

add up *v* add, compute, count, count up, reckon, sum up, total, tot up

adept *adj* able, accomplished, adroit, clever, dexterous, expert, masterful, masterly, practised, proficient, skilful, skilled, versed

adequate *adj* acceptable, ample, capable, commensurate, competent, enough, fair, mediocre, middling, passable, presentable, reasonable, requisite, satisfactory, sufficient, suitable, tolerable

adhere *v* attach, bind, bond, cement, cleave, cling, cohere, fasten, fix, glue, hold, fast, paste, stick, unite

adhesive *adj* adhering, attaching, clinging, cohesive, gluey, glutinous, gummy, holding, sticking, sticky, tacky, tenacious

adhesive *n* cement, glue, gum, mucilage, paste

adjacent *adj* abutting, adjoining, alongside, attached, beside, bordering, close, contiguous, near, neighbouring, next door, touching

adjoining *adj* abutting, adjacent, attached, bordering, connecting, contiguous, interconnecting, joined, joining, near, neighbouring, next, door, touching, verging

adjourn *v* break off, defer, delay, discontinue, interrupt, postpone, procrastinate, put off, recess, stay, suspend

adjournment *n* break, deferment, deferral, delay, discontinuation, interruption, pause, postponement, prorogation, putting off, recess, stay, suspension

adjudicate *v* adjudge, arbitrate, decide, determine, give a ruling judge, referee, settle, umpire

adjudication *n* arbitration, conclusion, decide ondecision, determina tion, finding, judging, judgment, pronouncement, ruling, settlement, umpiring, verdict

adjust *v* acclimatize, accommodate, accustom, adapt, alter, arrange, compose, dispose, fit, fix, harmonize, make conform, measure, modify, order, reconcile, rectify, redress, regulate, remodel, set, settle, suit, tune up

adjustable *adj* adaptable, alterable, flexible, malleable, modifiable, mouldable, movable, tractable

adjustment *n* adaptation, alteration, arrangement, arranging, fitting, fixing, modification, ordering, rectification, redress, regulation, remodelling, setting, tuning

ad-lib *v* extemporize, improvise, make up, speak impromptu, speak off the cuff

administer *v* conduct, control, direct, govern, manage, oversee, run, superintend, supervise

administration *n* administering, application, conduct, control, direction, dispensation, distribution, execution, governing, government, management, overseeing, performance, provision, running, superintendence, supervision; executive, governing body, government, management, ministry, regime

admirable *adj* commendable, creditable, estimable, excellent, exemplary, exquisite, fine, good, great, laudable, marvellous, praiseworthy, rare, superior, valuable, wonderful, worthy

admiration *n* adoration, affection, amazement, appreciation, approbation, approval, astonishment, awe, delight, esteem, pleasure, praise, regard, respect, surprise, veneration, wonder, wonderment

admire *v* adore, applaud, appreciate, approve, esteem, hero-worship, idolize, look up to, love, praise, prize, respect, revere, think highly of, value, venerate, wonder at, worship

admirer *n* beau, boyfriend, girl friend, lover, suitor, sweetheart, wooer; adherent, devotee, disciple, enthusiast, fan, follower, partisan, supporter, worshipper

admissible *adj* acceptable, allowable, allowed, passable, permissible, permitted, tolerable

admission *n* acceptance, access, admittance, entrance, entrée, entry, ingress, initiation, introduction; acknowledgment, admitting, affirmation, allowance, avowal, concession, confession, declaration, disclosure, divulgence, profession, revelation

admit *v* accept, allow, allow to enter, give access, initiate, introduce, let in, receive, take in; acknowledge, affirm, avow, concede, confess, declare, disclose, divulge, profess, reveal; agree, allow, grant, let, permit, recognise

adolescence *n* boyhood, girlhood, juvenescence, minority, teens, youth; boyishness, childishness, girlishness, immaturity, juvenility, puerility, youthfulness

adolescent *adj* boyish, girlish, growing, immature, juvenile, puerile, teenage, young, youthful

adolescent *n* juvenile, minor, teenager, youngster, youth

adopt *v* accept, appropriate, approve, assume, choose, embrace, endorse, espouse, follow, maintain, ratify, select, support, take on, take over, take up; foster, take in

adoption *n* acceptance, approbation, choice, embracing, endorsement, espousal, following, maintenance, ratification, selection, support, taking on, taking over, taking up; adopting, fosterage, fostering, taking in

adore *v* admire, bow to, cherish, dote on, esteem, exalt, glorify, honour, idolize, love, revere, reverence, venerate, worship

adorn *v* array, beautify, bedeck, deck, decorate, embellish, emblazon, enhance, enrich, garnish, grace, ornament, trim

adornment *n* accessory, decoration, embellishment, frill, frippery, ornament, trimming

adult *adj* full grown, full size, fully developed, fully grown, grown-up, mature, of age, ripe

adult *n* grown person, person of mature age

advance *v* accelerate, bring forward, bring up, come forward, elevate, go ahead, go forward, go on, hasten, move onward, move up, press on, proceed, progress, promote, send forward, send up, speed, upgrade; adduce, allege, cite, offer, present, proffer, put forward, submit, suggest; increase, lend pay beforehand, raise, supply on credit

advance *n* advancement, amelioration, betterment, breakthrough, furtherance, gain, growth, improvement, progress, promotion, step; appreciation, credit, deposit, down payment, increase in price, loan, prepayment, retainer

advances *pl n* approach, approaches, moves, overtures, proposals, proposition

advance *adj* beforehand, early, foremost, forward, in front, leading, prior

advanced *adj* ahead, avant-garde, extreme, foremost, forward, higher, late, leading, precocious, progressive

advantage *n* aid, ascendancy, asset, assistance, avail, benefit, blessing, boon, convenience, dominance, edge, gain, good, help, interest, lead, precedence, pre-eminence, profit, service, start, superiority, sway, upper hand, use, utility, welfare

advantageous *adj* dominant, dominating, favourable, superior, beneficial, convenient, helpful, of service, profitable, useful, valuable, worthwhile

adventure *n* chance, contingency, enterprise, experience, exploit, hazard, incident, occurrence, risk, speculation, undertaking, venture

adventurous *adj* adventuresome, audacious, bold, dangerous, daredevil, daring, enterprising, foolhardy, hazardous, headstrong, intrepid, rash, reckless, risky, temerarious, venturesome

adverse *adj* antagonistic, conflicting, contrary, detrimental, disadvantageous, hostile, inexpedient, inimical, injurious, inopportune, negative, opposing, opposite, reluctant, repugnant, unfavourable, unfortunate, unfriendly, unlucky, unpropitious, unwilling

adversity *n* affliction, bad luck, calamity, catastrophe, disaster, distress, hardship, hard times, ill-fortune, ill-luck, misery, misfortune, mishap, reverse, sorrow, suffering, trial, trouble, woe, wretchedness

advertise *v* advise, announce, apprise, blazon, declare, display, flaunt, inform, make known, notify, praise, proclaim, promote, promulgate, publicize, publish, puff, push; (*Inf*) plug, tout

advertisement *n* advert, announcement, bill, blurb, circular, commercial, display, notice, placard, poster, promotion, publicity; (*Inf*) ad

advice *n* admonition, caution, counsel, guidance, help, injunction, opinion, recommendation, suggestion, view

advisable *adj* appropriate, apt, desirable, expedient, fit, fitting, judicious; politic, profitable, proper, prudent, recommended, seemly, sensible, sound, suggested, suitable, wise

advise *v* admonish, caution, commend, counsel, enjoin, recommend, suggest, urge

adviser *n* aide, authority, coach, confidant, consultant, counsel, counsellor, guide, helper, lawyer, mentor, right-hand man, solicitor, teacher, tutor

advocate *v* advise, argue for, campaign for, champion, countenance, defend, encourage, favour, justify, plead for, press for, promote, propose, recommend, speak for, support, uphold, urge; (*Inf*) hold a brief for

advocate *n* apologist, apostle, backer, campaigner, champion, counsellor, defender, pleader, promoter, proponent, proposer, speaker, spokesman, supporter, upholder

affable *adj* amiable, amicable, approachable, benevolent, benign, civil, congenial, cordial, courteous, easy-going, friendly, genial, good-humoured, good-natured, gracious, kindly, mild, obliging, pleasant, sociable, urbane, warm

affair *n* activity, business, circumstance, concern, episode, event, happening, incident, interest, matter, occurrence, proceeding, project, question, subject, transaction, undertaking; amour, intrigue, liaison, relationship, romance

affect *v* act on, alter, bear upon, change, concern, impinge upon, influence, interest, involve, modify, prevail over, regard, relate to, sway, transform; adopt, aspire to, assume, contrive, counterfeit, feign, imitate, pretend, put on, sham, simulate

affectation *n* act, affectedness, appearance, artificiality, assumed, manners, façade, fakery, false display, insincerity, mannerism, pose, pretence, pretension, pretentiousness, sham, show, simulation, unnatural imitation

affected *adj* artificial, assumed, conceited, contrived, counterfeit, feigned, insincere, mannered, phoney, pompous, precious, pretended, pretentious, put-on, sham, simulated, spurious, stiff, studied, unnatural

affection *n* amity, attachment, care, desire, feeling, fondness, friendliness, good will, inclination, kindness, liking, love, passion, propensity, tenderness, warmth

affectionate *adj* attached, caring, devoted, doting, fond, friendly, kind, loving, tender, warm, warm-hearted

affiliate *v* associate with, coalesce, combine with, incorporate into, join with, unite with

affinity *n* alliance, analogy, closeness, compatibility, connection, correspondence, kinship, likeness, relation, relationship, resemblance, similarity; attraction, fondness, liking, penchant, rapport, sympathy

affirm *v* assert, asseverate, attest, aver, avouch, avow, certify, confirm, declare, maintain, pronounce, ratify, state, swear, testify

affirmation *n* assertion, asseveration, attestation, averment, avouchment, avowal, certification, confirmation, declaration, oath, pronouncement, ratification, statement, testimony

affirmative *adj* agreeing, approving, assenting, concurring, confirming, consenting, corroborative, favourable, positive

afflict *v* beset, bother, burden, cause suffering to, distress, grieve, harass, harm, hurt, oppress, pain, plague, rack, torment, torture, trouble, try, vex, worry, wound

affliction *n* distress, grief, hardship, misery, misfortune, ordeal, pain, scourge, sorrow, suffering, torment, trouble, woe, wretchedness

affluence *n* abundance, exuberance, fortune, opulence, plenty, profusion, prosperity, riches, wealth

affluent *adj* moneyed, opulent, prosperous, rich, wealthy, well-off; (*Inf*) loaded, well-heeled

afford *v* bear, spare, stand, sustain

affront *n* aspersion, indignity, insult, outrage, provocation, slight, slur, snub; (*Inf*) slap in the face

afraid *adj* alarmed, anxious, apprehensive, cowardly, faint-hearted, fearful, frightened, intimidated, nervous, reluctant, scared, suspicious, timid, timorous

afresh *adv* again, anew, once again, once more, over again

after *adv* afterwards, behind, below, following, later, subsequently, succeeding, thereafter; at the back, behind; in the rear

after *prep* behind, below, following, in the rear of; nearest, next to; in pursuit of, in search of, in quest of; despite, in spite of, notwithstanding, regardless of

after *adj* following, later, subsequent, succeeding

afterlife *n* afterworld, life after death, the hereafter

aftermath *n* after-effects, consequences, effects, results; end, end result, issue, outcome, upshot

again *adv* afresh, anew, another time, a second time, once more; also, besides, further more, in addition, moreover, on the contrary, on the other hand, a second time

against *prep* counter, hostile to, in contrast to, in defiance of, in opposition to, in the face of, opposed to, opposing, resisting, versus; abutting, close up to, facing, fronting, in contact with, on, opposite to, touching, upon

age *n* date, days, duration, epoch, era, generation, lifetime, period, span, time; advancing years, decline of life, dotage, majority, maturity, old age, senescence, senility, seniority; aeon, eternity, hours on end, lifetime, long time

age *v* decline, degenerate, deteriorate, grow older, look older, mature, mellow, ripen, wither

aged *adj* age-old, ancient, antiquated, antique, elderly, getting on, grey, hoary, old, senescent

agency *n* bureau, business, company, department, office, organization

agenda *n* list, plan, programme, schedule, scheme, timetable

agent *n* broker, deputy, emissary, envoy, factor, go-between, negotiator, representative, substitute, surrogate; spy; (*Inf*) mole, rep; agency, cause, force, instrument, means, power, vehicle; lawyer, solicitor; author, executor, performer; agency, cause, force, instrument, means, power, vehicle

agglomeration *n* accumulation, aggregate, collection, cluster, heap, jumble, hotchpotch, lump, pile

aggravate *v* compound, exacerbate,

exaggerate, heighten, increase, inflame, intensify, magnify, make worse, worsen; annoy, exasperate, irk, irritate, pester, provoke, tease, vex; (*Inf*) get on ones nerves

aggression *n* assault, attack, injury, invasion, offence, offensive, onslaught, raid

aggressive *adj* argumentative, belligerent, destructive, forceful, hostile, offensive, provocative, pugnacious, quarrelsome; (*Inf*) pushy

aggressor *n* assailant, assaulter, attacker, initiator, invader, provoker

aggrieved *adj* distressed, hurt, ill-used, injured, piqued, resentful, unhappy, upset, wronged; (*Inf*) peeved

aghast *adj* amazed, appalled, astounded, awestruck, flabbergasted, horrified, shocked, thunderstruck

agile *adj* active, acute, alert, brisk, clever, limber, lithe, lively, nimble, prompt, quick, quick-witted, sharp, sprightly, spry, supple, swift

agitate *v* beat, churn, convulse, disturb, rock, rouse, shake, stir, toss; alarm, arouse, confuse, disconcert, disquiet, distract, disturb, excite, ferment, fluster, incite, inflame, perturb, rouse, ruffle, stimulate, trouble, upset, work up, worry

agitation *n* churning, convulsion, disturbance, rocking, shake, shaking, stir, stirring, tossing, turbulence; alarm, arousal, clamour, commotion, confusion, discomposure, disquiet, distraction, disturbance, excitement, ferment, flurry, fluster, incitement, lather, outcry, stimulation, trouble, tumult, turmoil, upset, worry

agitator *n* agent provocateur, demagogue, firebrand, inciter, instigator, revolutionary, trouble maker

agnostic *n* disbeliever, doubter, doubting Thomas, questioner

ago *adv* formerly, in the past, in time gone by, since

agog *adv* avid, curious, eager, enthralled, expectant, impatient, keen

agonize *v* deliberate, fret, labour, struggle, suffer, worry, wrestle

agony *n* affliction, anguish, distress, misery, pain, pangs, suffering, throes, torment, torture, woe

agree *v* accede, acquiesce, admit, allow, assent, be of the same mind, comply, concede, concur, consent, engage, grant, permit, see eye to eye, settle; accord, answer, chime, coincide, conform, correspond, fit, get on, harmonize, match, square, suit, tally

agreeable *adj* acceptable, delight ful, enjoyable, gratifying, pleasant, pleasing, pleasurable, satisfying, to one's liking, to one's taste; acquiescent, amenable, approving, complying, concurring, consenting, in accord, responsive, sympathetic, well-disposed, willing

agreement *n* accord, accordance, affinity, analogy, compatibility, compliance, concert, concord, concurrence, conformity, congruity, consistency, correspondence, harmony, similarity, suitableness, union; arrangement, bargain, compact, contract, covenant, deal, pact, settlement, treaty, understanding

agriculture *n* agronomics, agronomy, cultivation, culture, farming, husbandry, tillage

aground *adv* ashore, beached, foundered, grounded, high and dry, on the rocks, stranded, stuck

ahead *adv* along, at an advantage, at the head, before, forwards, in advance, in front, in the foreground, in the lead, in the vanguard, leading, on onwards, to the fore, winning

aid *v* abet, assist, befriend, encourage, favour, help, lend a hand, promote, relieve, second, serve, subsidize, succour, support, sustain

aid *n* assistance, benefit, encourage ment, favour, help, relief, service, support; donation, gift, subsidy; aide, assistant, girl/man Friday, helper, second, supporter

aim *v* aspire, attempt, design, direct, endeavour, intend, level, mean, plan, point, propose, purpose, resolve, seek, set one's sights on, sight, strive, take aim, train, try, want, wish

aim *n* directing, pointing, training; line of sight; ambition, aspiration, course, design, desire, direction, end, goal, intent, intention, mark, object, objective, plan, proposal, purpose, resolve, scheme, target, wish

aimless *adj* chance, directionless, drifting, erratic, frivolous, futile, goalless, haphazard, pointless, purposeless, random, stray, undirected, unguided, unpredictable, vagrant, wayward

air *n* aerospace, atmosphere, heavens, sky; blast, breath, breeze, draught, puff, waft, whiff, wind, zephyr; ambience, appearance, atmosphere, aura, bearing, character, demeanour, effect, feeling, flavour, impression, look, manner, mood, quality, style, tome; circulation, display, dissemination, exposure, expression, publicity, utterance, vent, ventilation; aria, lay, melody, song, tune

air *v* aerate, expose, freshen, ventilate; broadcast, circulate, communicate, declare, disclose, display, disseminate, divulge, exhibit, expose, express, make known, make public, proclaim, publicize, reveal, tell, utter, ventilate, voice

airing *v* aerating, drying, freshening, ventilating; excursion, jaunt, outing, promenade, stroll, walk; circulation, communication, display, dissemination, exposure, expression, publicizing, publishing, utterance, venting, voicing

airless *adj* breathless, close, heavy, muggy, oppressive, stale, stifling, stuffy, suffocating, sultry, unventilated

airs *pl n* affectations, affectedness, arrogance, haughtiness, hauteur, pomposity, posing, posturing, pretensions, superciliousness; (*Inf*) swan

airtight *adj* closed, impermeable, sealed, shut tight; incontestable, incontrovertible, indisputable, irrefutable, unassailable

airy *adj* blowy, breezy, draughty, fresh, gusty, light, lofty, open, spacious, uncluttered, well ventilated, windy; aerial, delicate, flimsy, illusory, imaginary, immaterial, insubstantial, light, vaporous, visionary, weight-less, wispy; animated, blithe, buoyant, cheerful, cheery, gay, graceful, happy, high-spirited, light, lively, merry, nonchalant, sprightly

alarm *n* anxiety, apprehension, consternation, dismay, distress, fear, fright, nervousness, panic, scare, terror, trepidation, unease, uneasiness; alarm-bell, alert, bell, danger signal, distress signal, siren, warning

alarm *v* daunt, dismay, distress, frighten, give someone a turn, panic, scare, startle, terrify, unnerve; alert, arouse, signal, warn

alarmed *adj* anxious, apprehensive, concerned, dismayed, fearful, frightened, scary, terrifying

alarming *adj* daunting, dismaying, distressing, disturbing, dreadful, frightening, scaring, shocking, startling, terrifying, unnerving

alcoholic *n* bibber, dipsomaniac, drunk, drunkard, hard drinker, inebriate, tippler, toper; (*Inf*) boozer, wino

alert *adj* active, agile, attentive, brisk, careful, circumspect, heedful, lively, nimble, observant, on guard, on one's toes, on the lookout, on the watch, perceptive, quick, ready, spirited, vigilant, wary, watchful

alert *n* alarm, danger signal, emergency flare, mayday, red-alert, signal, siren, warning

alert *v* advise, alarm, forewarn, inform, notify, raise the alarm, signal, warn

alias *adv* also called, also known as, otherwise, otherwise known as

alias *n* assumed name, pen name, pseudonym, stage name

alibi *n* defence, excuse, explanation, justification, plea, pretext, reason

alien *adj* adverse, conflicting, contrary, estranged, exotic, extra-terrestrial, ET, foreign, inappropriate, incompatible, incongruous, not native, not naturalized, opposed, outlandish, remote, repugnant, separated, strange, unfamiliar, unatural, weird

alien *n* foreigner, newcomer, outsider, stranger

alight *v* come down, come to rest, descend, disembark, dismount, get down, get off, land, light, perch, settle, touch down

alight *adj* ablaze, aflame, aflame, blazing, burning, fiery, flaming, flaring, ignited, lighted, lit, on fire

alike *adj* akin, analogous, corresponding, duplicate, equal, equivalent, even, identical, parallel, resembling, similar, the same, twin, uniform

alive *adj* animate, breathing, having life, living, subsisting; active, existent, existing, extant, functioning, in existence, in force, operative, unquenched; (*Inf*) in the land of the living; active, alert, animated, awake, brisk, cheerful, eager, energetic, full of life, lively, quick, spirited, sprightly, spry, vigorous, vital, vivacious, zestful

all *adj* each, each and every, each one of, every, every bit of, every one of, every single; the complete, the entire, the sum of, the total of, the totality of, the whole of; complete, entire, full, greatest, perfect, total, utter

all *n* aggregate, entirety, everything, sum, sum total, total, total amount, utmost, whole

all *adv* altogether, completely, entirely, fully, totally, utterly, wholly

allay *v* alleviate, assuage, calm, diminish, lessen, pacify, quell, reduce, relieve, soothe

allegation *n* accusation, assertion, charge, claim

allege *v* accuse, assert, aver, contend, claim, declare, insist, maintain, profess, say, state, suggest

allegiance *n* adherence, devotion, duty, faithfulness, homage, loyalty, obedience

allegorical *adj* emblematic, figurative, metaphorical, parabolic, symbolic

allegory *n* apologue, fable, parable; analogy, metaphor, symbolism

allergic *adj* hypersensitive, sensitive, sensitized, susceptible; antipathy, aversion, disinclined, hostile, loath, opposed

allergy *n* allergic reaction, hypersensitivity, sensitivity, susceptibility; antagonism, antipathy, dislike, opposition

alley *n* alleyway, backstreet, lane, passage, passageway, pathway, walk

alliance *n* affiliation, affinity, agreement, association, coalition, combination, compact, concordat, confederacy, confederation, connection, federation, league, linked, marriage, pact, partnership, related, treaty, union

allied *adj* affiliated, amalgamated associated, bound, combined, confederate, connected, in league, joined, joint, kindred, leagued, linked, married, related, similar, unified, united, wed

allocate *v* allot, assign, distribute, earmark, give, give out, grant, set aside, share out; (*Inf*) dole out

allot *v* allocate, apportion, appropriate, assign, budget, designate, earmark, mete, set aside, share out

allotment *n* allocation, allowance, apportionment, appropriation, assign, distribute, grant, lot, measure, portion, quota, ration, share, stint; kitchen garden, patch, plot, tract

allow *v* acknowledge, acquiesce, admit, concede, confess, grant, own; approve, authorize, bear, brook, endure, give leave, let, permit, sanction, stand, suffer, tolerate; (*Inf*) put up with

allowance *n* allocation, allotment, amount, annuity, apportionment, grant, lot, measure, pension, portion, quota, ration, remittance, share, stint, stipend, subsidy; admission, concession, sanction, sufferance, toleration; concession, deduction, discount, rebate, reduction

allow for *v* arrange for, consider, foresee, keep in mind, make allowances for, make concessions for, make provision for, plan for, provide for, set aside for, take into account, take into consideration

all right *adj* acceptable, adequate, average, fair, OK, passable, satisfactory, standard, unobjectionable

all right *adv* acceptably, adequately,

passably, satisfactorily, unobjectionably, well enough

allude *v* cite, hint at, imply, mention, refer to, suggest, touch upon

allusion *n* casual remark, glance, hint, implication, indirect, reference, innuendo, insinuation, intimation, mention, reference, remark, suggestion

ally *n* abettor, accessory, accomplice, associate, coadjutor, collaborator, colleague, confederate, co-worker, friend, helper, partner

ally *v* affiliate, band together, combine, form an alliance, go into part nership, join, join forces, unite

almighty *adj* absolute, all-powerful, invincible, most high, omnipotent, supreme, unlimited

almost *adv* about, all but, approximately, as good as, close to, just about, nearly, not far from, not quite, on the brink of, practically, virtually, well-nigh

alone *adj* abandoned, apart, by itself, by oneself, deserted, desolate, detached, forlorn, forsaken, isolated, lonely, lonesome, only, separate, single, single-handed, sole, solitary, unaccompanied, unaided, unassisted, unattended, uncombined, unconnected, unescorted

aloof *adv* cold, cool, distant, haughty, inaccessible, indifferent, reserved, standoffish, unapproachable, unfriendly, unsociable

aloof *adj* chilly, cold, detached, distant, indifferent, remote, unfriendly, unsociable, unsympathetic

aloud *adv* audibly, clearly, distinctly, intelligibly, out loud, plainly

already *adv* before now, by now, previously

also *adv* additionally, along with, and, as well, as well as, besides, further, furthermore, in addition, including, into the bargain, moreover, on top of that, plus, too

alter *v* adapt, adjust, amend, change, convert, diversify, metamorphose, modify, recast, reform, remodel, reshape, revise, shift, transform, transmute, turn, vary

alteration *n* adaptation, adjustment, amendment, change, conversion, difference, diversification, metamorphosis, modification, reformation, remodelling, reshaping, revision, shift, transformation, transmutation, variance, variation

alternate *v* interchange, oscillate, rotate, substitute, take turns, vary

alternate *adj* alternating, every other, every second, interchanging, rotating, sequential

alternative *n* choice, option, preference, recourse, selection, substitute

alternative *adj* another, different, other, second

alternatively *adv* instead, otherwise

although *conj* albeit, despite the fact that, even if, even supposing, even though, notwithstanding, though, while

altogether *adv* absolutely, completely, fully, perfectly, quite, thoroughly, totally, utterly, wholly; all in all, all things considered, as a whole, by and large, collectively, generally, in general, in the main, in toto, on the whole; all told, everything included, in all, in sum, taken together

always *adv* consistently, regularly, repeatedly, unfailingly, without exception; constantly, eternally, forever, perpetually, repeatedly; come what may, in any case, in any event, no matter what

amalgamate *v* blend, combine, fuse, incorporate, integrate, intermingle, intermix, join, link, merge, mix, unify, unite

amass *v* accumulate, aggregate, assemble, collect, compile, gather, heap up, hoard, pile up, rake up, scrape together, store up; (*Inf*) stash away

amateur *n* dabbler, dilettante, layman, nonprofessional

amateurish *adj* bungling, clumsy, crude, incompetent, unskilled, unprofessional

amaze *v* astonish, astound, bewilder, confound, daze, dumb found, electrify, flabbergast, shock, stagger, startle, stun, stupefy, surprise; (*Inf*) bowl over

amazement *n* admiration, astonishment, bewilderment, confusion, marvel, perplexity, shock, stupefaction, surprise, wonder

ambassador *n* agent, attaché, consul, deputy, diplomat, emissary, envoy, legate, minister, plenipotentiary, representative

ambiguous *adj* abtruse, ambivalent, cryptic, doubtful, dubious, enigmatic, enigmatical, equivocal, inconclusive, indefinite, indeterminate, obscure, paradoxical, perplexing, puzzling, two-edged, uncertain, unclear, vague

ambition *n* aspiration, avidity, desire, drive, eagerness, enterprise, force, hankering, longing, striving, yearning, zeal; aim, aspiration, desire, dream, end, goal, hope, intent, objective, purpose, wish

ambitious *adj* aspiring, assertive, avid, designing, desirous, driving, eager, enterprising, forceful, go ahead, hankering after, hopeful, intent, longing, purposeful, striving, zealous; arduous, bold, challenging, demanding, difficult, exacting, formidable

ambivalent *adj* clashing, conflicting, doubtful, equivocal, hesitating, indecisive, irresolute, mixed, opposing, uncertain, vacillating

amble *verb* dawdle, ramble, stroll

ambush *n* ambuscade, concealment, cover, hiding, hiding place, lying in wait, retreat, shelter, trap, waylaying; ambuscade, lure, pitfall, snare, trap

ambush *v* attack, decoy, ensnare, entrap, lay a trap for, lie in wait for, trap, waylay

amenable *adj* accommodating, acquiescent, adaptable, agreeable, flexible, manageable, open, persuadable, pliant, responsive, susceptible, tractable; accountable, answerable, liable, responsible, subject

amend *v* adjust, alter, ameliorate, better, change, correct, enhance, fix, improve, mend, modify, rectify, reform, remedy, repair, revise, set right

amendment *n* addendum, addition, adjunct, adjustment, alteration, appendage, attachment, betterment, change, clarification correction, enhancement, fixing, improvement, mending, modification, rectification, remedy, repair, revision

amenity *n* advantage, convenience, facility, feature, resource, service; agreeableness, enjoyableness, niceness, pleasurableness

amiable *adj* charming, delightful, friendly, genial, good-humoured, good-natured, kind, kindly, lovable, obliging, pleasant, pleasing, sociable, sweet-tempered, winning, winsome

amicable *adj* amiable, civil, cordial, courteous, friendly, good-humoured, good-natured, harmonious, non-hostile, peaceable

amiss *adj* awry, defective, faulty, incorrect, out of order, unsatisfactory

ammunition *n* armaments, bombs, bullets, cartridges, explosives, grenades, gunpowder, material, missiles, munitions, pellets, powder, rounds, shells, shot, shot and shell; (*Inf*) ammo; ammo data, information, input; advantages, pointers

amnesty *n* dispensation, forgiveness, general pardon, immunity, pardon, remission, reprieve; absolution, dispensation, forgiveness, indulgence

among, amongst *prep* amid, amidst, in association with, in the middle of, in the midst of, in the thick of, midst, surrounded by, together with, with; between, to each of; included in, in the class of, in the company of, in the group of, in the number of, out of; by all of, by the joint action of, by the whole of, mutually, reciprocally, together, with one another

amount *v* degree, expanse, extent, lot, magnitude, mass, measure, number, quantity, size, supply, value, volume; addition, aggregate, entirety, extent, lot, measure, sum, sum total, total, whole

amount to *v* add up to, aggregate, become, come to, correspond to, develop into, equal, grow, make, mean, purport, run to, total

ample *adj* abounding, abundant, adequate, big, bountiful, broad, capacious, commodious, copious, enough, expansive, extensive, full, generous, great, large, lavish, liberal, more than enough, plentiful, plenty, profuse, rich, roomy, spacious, substantial, sufficient, unrestricted, voluminous, wide

amplify *v* boost, heighten, intensify, increase, magnify, make louder, strengthen; develop, elaborate on, enlarge on, expound, flesh out, go into details, say more about

amputate *v* chop off, cut off, dismember, lop off, remove, sever

amuse *v* beguile, charm, cheer, delight, divert, enliven, entertain, gladden, gratify, interest, occupy, please, recreate, regale; (*Inf*) tickle

amusement *n* beguilement, cheer, delight, diversion, enjoyment, entertainment, fun, gladdening, gratification, hilarity, interest, laughter, merriment, mirth, pleasing, pleasure, recreation, regalement, sport; distraction, diversion, entertainment, game, hobby, joke, lark, pastime, prank, recreation, sport

amusing *adj* cheerful, comical, delightful, diverting, droll, enjoyable, entertaining, facetious, funny, gladdening, gratifying, humorous, interesting, jocular, laughable, lively, merry, pleasant, witty

anaemic *adj* ashen, colourless, pale, pallid, weak; enervated, feeble, impotent, ineffectual, powerless

anaesthetic *n* analgesic, anodyne, narcotic, opiate, painkiller, sedative; general, local

anaesthetic *adj* anodyne, deadening, dulling, narcotic, opiate, painkilling, sedative, soporific

analogy *n* correlation, correspondence, homology, likeness, parallel, relation, resemblance, similarity

analyse *v* assay, decompose, estimate, evaluate, examine, fractionate, interpret, investigate, judge, test; dissect, enquire into, evaluate, interpret, investigate

analysis *v* assay, breakdown, dissection, dissolution, division, enquiry, examination, investigation, resolution, review, scrutiny; evaluation, finding, interpretation, judgment, opinion, study

analytical *adj* critical, detailed, diagnostic, enquiring, investigative, methodical, searching, systematic

anarchic *adj* chaotic, disorderly, lawless, rebellious, uncontrolled, undisciplined, unpredictable

anarchy *n* anarchism, chaos, disorder, lawless, rebellion

ancestor *n* forebear, forefather, forerunner, precursor, predecessor, progenitor

ancient *adj* aged, age-old, antediluvian, antiquated, antique, archaic, bygone, early, hoary, obsolete, old, olden, old-fashioned, out-moded, out-of-date, primeval, primordial, superannuated, timeworn

and *conj* along with, also, as well as, furthermore, in addition to, including, moreover, plus, together with

anecdote *n* reminiscence, short story, sketch, story, tale, yarn

angel *n* archangel, cherub, divine messenger, guardian spirit, seraph, spiritual being

anger *n* annoyance, antagonism, choler, displeasure, exasperation, fury, ill humour, ill temper, indignation, ire, irritability, irritation, outrage, passion, pique, rage, resentment, spleen, temper, vexation, wrath

anger *v* affront, annoy, antagonize, displease, enrage, exasperate, excite, fret, gall, incense, infuriate, irritate, madden, nettle, offend, outrage, pique, provoke, rile, vex

angle *n* bend, corner, crook, crotch, cusp, edge, elbow, intersection, knee, nook, point; approach, aspect, outlook, perspective, point of view, position, side, slant, stand point, viewpoint

angle *v* distort, skew, slant, slope, tilt, turncast; cast, fish, go fishing; aim, scheme, seek, solicit, try; (*Inf*) be after

angry *adj* annoyed, antagonized, choleric, displeased, enraged, exasperated, furious, heated, hot, ill-tempered, incensed, indignant, infuriated, irascible, irate, ireful, irritable, irritated, mad, nettled, outraged, passionate, piqued, provoked, raging, resentful, riled, splenetic, tumultuous, wrathful; (*Inf*) uptight

anguish *n* agony, distress, grief, heartbreak, misery, pain, sorrow,

suffering, torment, trauma
animal *n* beast, brute, creature
animal *adj* bestial, bodily, brutish, carnal, fleshly, gross, physical, sensual
animate *v* activate, embolden, encourage, energize, enliven, excite, fire, gladden, impel, incite, inspire, inspirit, instigate, invigorate, kindle, move, quicken, revive, rouse, spark, spur, stimulate, stir, urge, vitalize, vivify
animosity *n* acrimony, animus, antagonism, antipathy, bad blood, bitterness, enmity, hate, hatred, hostility, ill will, malevolence, malice, malignity, rancour, resentment, virulence
annihilate *v* abolish, destroy, eradicate, erase, exterminate, extinguish, extirpate, liquidate, nullify, obliterate, root out, wipe out
announce *v* advertise, broadcast, declare, disclose, divulge, give out, intimate, make known, proclaim, promulgate, propound, publish, report, reveal, tell
announcement *n* advertisement, broadcast, bulletin, communiqué, declaration, disclosure, divulgence, intimation, proclamation, promulgation, publication, report, revelation, statement
annoy *v* anger, badger, bedevil, bore, bother, displease, disturb, exasperate, harass, incommode, irk, irritate, madden, molest, nettle, peeve, pester, plague, provoke, rile, ruffle, tease, trouble, vex; (*Inf*) bug
annoyance *n* aggravation, anger, bedevilment, bother, displeasure, disturbance, exasperation, harassment, irritation, nuisance, provocation, trouble, vexation
annual *adj* once a year, yearly
anomaly *n* aberration, abnormality, departure, deviation, eccentricity, exception, incongruity, inconsistency, irregularity, oddity, peculiarity, rarity
anonymous *adj* incognito, innominate, nameless, unacknowledged, unattested, unauthenticated, uncredited, unidentified, unknown, unnamed, unsigned
answer *n* acknowledgment, comeback, defence, explanation, plea, reaction, refutation, rejoinder, reply, report, resolution, response, retort, return, riposte, solution, vindication
answer *v* acknowledge, explain, react, refute, rejoin, reply, resolve, respond, retort, return, solve
answerable *adj* accountable, amenable, chargeable, liable, responsible, subject, to blame
answer for *v* be accountable for, be answerable for, be chargeable for, be liable for, be responsible for, be to blame for; (*Inf*) take the rap for
antagonism *n* antipathy, competition, conflict, contention, discord, dissension, friction, hostility, opposition, rivalry
antagonize *v* alienate, anger, annoy, disaffect, estrange, insult, irritate, offend, repel; (*Inf*) rub up the wrong way
anthem *n* canticle, chant, chorale, hymn, psalm
anthology *n* collected works, collection, compendium, compilation, selection

anticipate *v* apprehend, await, count upon, expect, forecast, foresee, foretell, hope for, look for, look forward to, predict, prepare for; antedate, beat to it, forestall, intercept, prevent

anticipation *n* apprehension, awaiting, expectancy, expectation, foresight, forecast, forethought, hope, preconception, premonition, prescience, presentiment

anticlimax *n* bathos, comedown, disappointment, failure, flop, let-down, wash-out

antics *pl n* messing about, mischief, shenanigans, silliness, skylarking, tomfoolery, tricks

antidote *n* antitoxin, antivenom, countermeasure, cure, remedy

antipathy *n* abhorrence, animosity, animus, antagonism, aversion, bad blood, contrariety, disgust, dislike, distaste, enmity, hatred, hostility, ill will, incompatibility, loathing, opposition, rancour, repugnance, repulsion

antiquated *adj* aged, ancient, elderly, old; behind the times, dated, obsolete, old-fashioned, old hat, out-of-date, outmoded, out of the ark, passé

antique *adj* aged, ancient, elderly, old, superannuated; archaic, obsolete, old-fashioned, outdated

antique *n* bygone, heirloom, object of virtu, relic

antiquity *n* age, ancientness, elderliness, old age, oldness; ancient times, distant past, olden days, time immemorial

antiseptic *adj* aseptic, clean, germ-free, hygienic, pure, sanitary, sterile, uncontaminated, unpolluted

antiseptic *n* bactericide, disinfectant, germicide, purifier

antisocial *adj* alienated, asocial, misanthropic, reserved, retiring, uncommunicative, unfriendly, unsociable, withdrawn

anxiety *n* angst, apprehension, care, concern, disquiet, disquietude, distress, foreboding, fretfulness, misgiving, nervousness, restlessness, solicitude, suspense, tension, unease, uneasiness, watchfulness, worry

anxious *adj* apprehensive, careful, concerned, disquieted, distressed, disturbed, fearful, fretful, in suspense, nervous, overwrought, restless, solicitous, taut, tense, troubled, uneasy, unquiet, watchful, worried

apart *v* afar, alone, aloof, aside, away, by itself, by oneself, cut off, distant, distinct, divorced, excluded, independent, independently, isolated, piecemeal, separate, separated, separately, singly, to itself, to oneself, to one side; asunder, in bits, in pieces, into parts, to bits, to pieces

apart from *adv* aside from, besides, but, except for, excluding, not counting, other than, save

apartment *n* accommodation, chambers, compartment, flat, living quarters, penthouse, quarters, room, rooms, suite

apathetic *adj* cold, cool, emotionless, impassive, indifferent, insensible, listless, passive, phlegmatic, sluggish, stoic, stoical, torpid, unconcerned, unemotional, unfeeling, uninterested, unresponsive

apathy *n* coldness, coolness, emotionlessness, impassivity, passiveness, passivity, phlegm, sluggishness, stoicism, torpor, unconcern, unfeelingness, uninterestedness, unresponsiveness

apologetic *adj* contrite, penitent, regretful, remorseful, rueful, sorry

apologize *v* ask forgiveness, beg pardon, express regret, say one is sorry, say sorry

apology *v* acknowledgment, confession, defence, excuse, explanation, extenuation, justification, plea, vindication

appal *v* alarm, astound, daunt, disgust, dishearten, dismay, frighten, harrow, horrify, intimidate, outrage, petrify, scare, shock, terrify, unnerve

appalling *adj* alarming, astounding, awful, daunting, dire, disheartening, dismaying, dreadful, fearful, frightening, frightful, ghastly, grim, harrowing, hideous, horrible, horrid, horrific, horrifying, intimidating, petrifying, scaring, shocking, terrible, terrifying, unnerving

apparatus *n* appliance, contraption, device, equipment, gear, implements, machine, machinery, materials, means, mechanism, outfit, tackle, tools, utensils

apparent *adj* clear, conspicuous, discernible, distinct, evident, indubitable, manifest, marked, obvious, open, overt, patent, plain, understandable, unmistakable, visible

apparently *adv* it appears that, it seems that, on the face of it, ostensibly, outwardly, seemingly, speciously, superficially

apparition *n* appearance, manifestation, materialization, presence, vision, visitation, chimera, ghost, phantom, revenant, shade, spectre, spirit, visitant, wraith; (*Inf*) spook

appeal *n* adjuration, application, entreaty, invocation, petition, plea, prayer, request, solicitation, suit, supplication; allure, attraction, attractiveness, beauty, charm, engagingness, fascination, interestingness, pleasingness

appeal *v* adjure, apply, ask, beg, beseech, call, call upon, entreat, implore, petition, plead, pray, refer, request, resort to, solicit, sue, supplicate; allure, attract, charm, engage, entice, fascinate, interest, invite, please, tempt

appear *v* arise, arrive, attend, be present, come forth, come into sight, come into view, come out, come to light, crop up, develop, emerge, issue, loom, materialize, occur, surface, turn out, turn up; (*Inf*) show, show up; look, occur, seem, strike one as; be apparent, be clear, be evident, be manifest, be obvious, be patent, be plain; become available, be created, be developed, be invented, be published, come into being, come into existence, come out; act, be exhibited, come on, come on stage, enter, perform, play, play a part, take part

appearance *n* advent, appearing, arrival, coming, debut, emergence, introduction, presence, showing up, turning up; air, aspect, bearing, demeanour, expression face, figure, form, image, look, looks, manner; front, guise, illusion, image, impression, outward show, pretence, semblance

appease *v* calm down, mollify, pacify, placate, soften up, soothe

appendix *n* addendum, addition, adjunct, appendage, codicil, postscript, supplement

appetite *n* appetence, appetency, craving, demand, desire, hankering, hunger, inclination, liking, longing, passion, proclivity, propensity, relish, stomach, taste, willingness, yearning, zeal, zest

appetizing *adj* appealing delicious, inviting, mouthwatering, palatable, savoury, scrumptious, succulent, tasty, (*Inf*) tempting

applaud *v* acclaim, approve, cheer, clap, commend, compliment, encourage, eulogize, extol, laud, magnify, praise

applause *n* acclaim, acclamation, accolade, approbation, approval, cheering, cheers, commendation, eulogizing, hand, hand-clapping, laudation, ovation, plaudit, praise

appliance *n* apparatus, device, gadget, implement, instrument, machine, mechanism, tool

applicable *adj* apposite, appropriate, apropos, apt, befitting, fit, fitting, germane, pertinent, relevant, suitable, suited, to the point, to the purpose, useful

applicant *n* aspirant, candidate, claimant, inquirer, petitioner, postulant, suitor, suppliant

application *n* appositeness, exercise, function, germaneness, pertinence, practice, purpose, relevance, use, value; appeal, claim, inquiry, petition, request, requisition, solicitation, suit; assiduity, attention, attentiveness, commitment, dedication, diligence, effort, hard work, industry, perseverance, study

apply *v* administer, assign, bring into play, bring to bear, carry out, employ, engage, execute, exercise, implement, practise, put to use, use, utilize; appertain, be applicable, be appropriate, bear upon, be fitting, be relevant, fit, pertain, refer, relate, suit; anoint, bring into contact with, cover with lay on, paint, place, put on, smear, spread on, touch to; appeal, claim, inquire, make application, petition, put in, request, requisition, solicit, sue; address, be assiduous, be diligent, be industrious, commit, concentrate, dedicate, devote, direct, give, make an effort, pay attention, persevere, study, try, work hard; (*Inf*) buckle down

appoint *v* allot, arrange, assign, choose, decide, designate, determine, establish, fix, set, settle; assign, choose, commission, delegate, elect, install, name, nominate, select

appointed *v* allotted, arranged, assigned, chosen, decided, designated, determined, established, fixed, set, settled; assigned, chosen, commissioned, delegated, elected, installed, named, nominated, selected

appointment *n* arrangement, assignation, consultation, date, engagement, interview, meeting, rendezvous, session; assignment, berth, job, office, place, position, post, situation, station

apportion *v* allocate, allot, assign, deal, dispense, distribute, divide, dole out, measure out, mete out, parcel out, ration out, share

appraise *v* assess, cast your eye over, evaluate, judge, review; (*Inf*) size up

appreciable *adj* apparent, considerable, discernible, noticeable, signifiant, substantial

appreciate *v* be appreciative, be grateful for, be indebted, be obliged, be thankful for, give thanks for; acknowledge, be alive to, be aware of, comprehend, estimate, know, perceive, realize, recognize, sympathize with, take account of, understand; admire, cherish, enjoy, esteem, like, prize, rate highly, regard, relish, respect, savour, treasure, value; enhance, gain, grow, improve, increase, inflate, raise the value of, rise

appreciation *n* acknowledgement, gratefulness, gratitude, indebted ness, obligation, thankfulness, thanks; admiration, appraisal, assessment, awareness, cognizance, comprehension, enjoyment, esteem, estimation, knowledge, liking, perception, realization, recognition, regard, relish, respect, responsiveness, sensitivity, sympathy, understanding, valuation, enhancement, gain, growth, improvement, increase, inflation, rise; acclamation, criticism, critique, notice, praise, review, tribute

appreciative *adj* beholden, grateful, indebted, obliged, thankful; admiring, aware, cognizant, conscious, enthusiastic, in the know, knowledgeable, mindful, perceptive, pleased, regardful, respectful, responsive, sensitive, supportive, sympathetic, understanding

apprehend *v* arrest, capture, catch, seize, take, take prisoner; (*Inf*) collar, nick, pinch; appreciate, believe, comprehend, conceive, grasp, imagine, know, perceive, realize, recognize, think, understand

apprehension *n* alarm, anxiety, apprehensiveness, concern, disquiet, doubt, dread, fear, foreboding, misgiving, mistrust, premonition, suspicion, unease, uneasiness, worry; arrest, capture, catching, seizure, taking; awareness, comprehension, grasp, intellect, intelligence, knowledge, perception, understanding; belief, concept, conception, conjecture, idea, impression, notion, opinion, sentiment, thought, view

apprehensive *adj* afraid, alarmed, anxious, concerned, disquieted, doubtful, fearful, foreboding, mistrustful, suspicious, uneasy, worried

apprentice *n* beginner, learner, neophyte, novice, probationer, pupil, student, tyro

approach *n* access, advance, advent, arrival, avenue, coming, drawing near, entrance, nearing, passage, road, way; approximation, likeness, semblance; advance, appeal, application, invitation, offer, overture, proposal, proposition; attitude, course, manner, means, method, mode, *modus operandi*, procedure, style, technique, way

approach *v* advance, catch up, come close, come near, come to, draw near, gain on, meet, move towards, near, push forward, reach; appeal to, apply to, broach the matter with, make advances to, make a proposal to, make overtures to, sound out; approximate, be comparable to, be like, come close to, come near to, compare with, priate, pilfer, pocket, steal

appropriate *v* annex, arrogate, assume, commandeer, confiscate, expropriate, impound, pre-empt, seize, take, take over, take possession of; embezzle, filch, misappropriate, pilfer, pocket, steal

appropriate *adj* adapted, applicable, apposite, appurtenant, apropos, apt, becoming, befitting, belonging, congruous, correct, felicitous, fit, fitting, germane, meet, opportune, pertinent, proper, relevant, right, seemly, suitable, to the point, to the purpose, well-suited, well-timed

approval *n* acquiescence, agreement, assent, authorization, bless ing, compliance, concurrence, confirmation, consent, countenance, endorsement, imprimatur, leave, licence, mandate, permission, ratification, recommendation, sanction, validation; (*Inf*) OK; acclaim, admiration, applause, appreciation, approbation, commendation, esteem, favour, good opinion, liking, praise, regard, respect

approve *v* acclaim, admire, applaud, appreciate, be pleased with, commend, esteem, favour, have a good opinion of, like, praise, regard, highly, respect, think highly of; accede to accept, advocate, agree to, allow, assent to, authorize, bless, concur in, confirm, consent to, countenance, endorse, pass, permit, ratify, recommend, sanction, second, subscribe to, uphold, validate

approximate *adj* about, almost accurate, almost exact, close, near; estimated, inexact, loose, rough; approach, border on, come close, come near, reach, resemble, touch, verge on

approximately *adv* about, almost, around, circa, close to, generally, in the neighbourhood of, in the region of in the vicinity of, just about, loosely, more or less, nearly, not far off, relatively, roughly

approximation *n* ball park figure, conjecture, estimate, estimation, guess, guesswork, rough calculation, rough idea

apt *adj* applicable, apposite, appropriate, apropos, befitting, correct, fit, fitting, germane, meet, pertinent, proper, relevant, seemly, suitable, timely, to the point, to the purpose; disposed, given, inclined, liable, likely, of a mind, prone, ready; astute, bright, clever, expert, gifted, ingenious, intelligent, prompt, quick, sharp, skilful, smart, talented, teachable

aptitude *n* ability, faculty, flair, gift, knack, quickness, talent,

arbitrary *adj* capricious, chance,

discretionary, erratic, fanciful, inconsistent, optional, personal, random, subjective, unreasonable, whimsicle, wilful

arbitrate *v* adjudge, adjudicate, decide, determine, judge, pass judgement, referee, settle, sit in judgment, umpire

arbitration *n* adjudication, arbitrament, decision, determination, judgement, settlement

arbitrator *n* adjudicator, arbiter, judge, referee, umpire

arc *n* arch, bend, bow, crescent, curve, half-moon

arch *n* archway, curve, dome, span, vault

archaic *adj* ancient, behind the times, old, old fashioned, outdated, outmoded, passé

archetype *n* classic, exemplar, form, ideal, model, original, paradigm, pattern, prime example, prototype, standard

architect *n* designer, master builder, planner

archives *pl n* annals, chronicles, documents, papers, records, registers, rolls

ardent *adj* avid, eager, enthusiastic, fervent, fervid, fierce, fiery, hot, hot-blooded, impassioned, intense, keen, lusty, passionate, spirited, vehement, warm, warm blooded, zealous

ardour *n* avidity, devotion, eagerness, earnestness, enthusiasm, feeling, fervour, fierceness, fire, heat, intensity, keenness, passion, spirit, vehemence, warmth, zeal

arduous *adj* back breaking, burdensome, difficult, exhausting, fatiguing, formidable, gruelling, hard, harsh, heavy, laborious, onerous, painful, punishing, rigorous, severe, steep, strenuous, taxing, tiring, toilsome, tough, troublesome, trying

area *n* district, domain, locality, neighbourhood, patch, plot, realm, region, sector, sphere, stretch, territory, tract, zone; part, portion, section, sector; sunken space, yard

arena *n* amphitheatre, bowl, coliseum, field, ground, park, ring, stadium, stage; area, battlefield, battleground, domain, field, field of conflict, lists, province, realm, scene, scope, sector, sphere, territory, theatre

argue *v* altercate, bandy words, bicker, disagree, dispute, fall out, feud, fight, have an argument, quarrel, squabble, wrangle; assert, claim, contend, controvert, debate, discuss, dispute, expostulate, hold, maintain, plead, question, reason, remonstrate; demonstrate, denote, display, evince, exhibit, imply, indicate, manifest, point to, show, suggest

argument *n* altercation, bickering, clash, controversy, difference of opinion, disagreement, dispute, falling out, feud, fight, quarrel, row, squabble; assertion, claim, contention, debate, discussion, dispute, expostulation, plea, pleading, questioning, remonstrance; argumentation, case, defence, dialectic, grounds, line of reasoning, logic, polemic, reason, reasoning

argumentative *adj* belligerent,

combative, contentious, contrary, disputatious, litigious, opinionated, quarrelsome

arid *adj* barren, desert, dried up, dry, moistureless, parched, sterile, waterless

arise *v* appear, begin, come into being, come to light, commence, crop up, emanate, emerge, ensue, follow, happen, issue, occur, originate, proceed, result, set in, spring, start, stem; ascend, climb, lift, mount, move upward, rise, soar, tower

aristocracy *n* body of nobles, elite, gentry, nobility, noblesse, patricians, patriciate, peerage, ruling class, upper class

aristocrat *n* grandee, lady, lord, noble, nobleman, noblewoman, patrician, peer, peeress

aristocratic *adj* blue-blooded, elite, gentle, gentlemanly, highborn, lordly, noble, patrician, titled, upper-class, well-born

arm *n* appendage, limb, upper limb; bough, branch, department, detachment, division, extension, offshoot, projection, section, sector

arm *v* accoutre, array, deck out, equip, furnish, issue with, outfit, provide, rig, supply; mobilize, muster forces, prepare for war, take up arms

armed *v* accoutred, arrayed, carrying weapons, equipped, fitted out, forearmed, fortified, furnished, girded, guarded, in arms, prepared, primed, protected, provided, ready, rigged out, strengthened, supplied, under arms

armoured *adj* armour-plated, bombproof, bulletproof, fortified, protected, strengthened

arms *pl n* armaments, firearms, guns, instruments of war, ordnance, weaponry, weapons; blazonry, crest, escutcheon, heraldry, insignia

army *n* armed force, host, land forces, legions, military, military force, soldiers, soldiery, troops; array, horde, host, multitude, pack, swarm, throng, vast number

aroma *n* bouquet, fragrance, odour, perfume, redolence, savour, scent, smell

aromatic *adj* balmy, fragrant, odoriferous, perfumed, pungent, redolent, savoury, spicy, sweet-scented, sweet-smelling

around *prep* about, encircling, enclosing, encompassing, environing, on all sides of, on every side of, surrounding; about, approximately, circa, roughly

around *adv* about, all over, every where, here and there, in all directions, on all sides, throughout, to and fro; at hand, close, close at hand, close by, near, nearby, nigh

arouse *v* agitate, animate, awaken, call forth, enliven, excite, foment, foster, goad, incite, inflame, instigate, kindle, move, provoke, quicken, rouse, sharpen, spark, spur, stimulate, stir up, summon up, waken, warm, whet, whip up

arrange *v* align, array, class, classify, dispose, file, form, group, line up, marshal, order, organize, position, put in order, range, rank, set out, sort, systematize, tidy; (*Inf*) sort out; adjust, agree to, come to terms, compromise, contrive, devise, organize, plan, prepare, project, schedule, settle; adapt, instrument, orchestrate, score

arrangement *n* alignment, array, classification, design, display, disposition, form, grouping, line-up, marshalling, order, ordering, organization, ranging, structure, system; adaptation, instrumentation, interpretation, orchestration, score, version

array *n* arrangement, collection, display, disposition, exhibition, formation, line-up, marshalling, muster, order, parade, show, supply

arrest *n* apprehension, capture, detention, seizure

arrest *v* apprehend, bust, capture, catch, collar, detain, lay hold of, seize, take, take into custody, take prisoner

arrival *n* advent, appearance, arriving, coming, entrance, happening, occurrence, taking place

arrive *v* appear, attain, befall, come, enter, get to, happen, occur, reach, show up, take place, turn up

arrogance *n* bluster, conceit, conceitedness, contemptuousness, disdainfulness, haughtiness, hauteur, high-handedness, imperiousness, insolence, loftiness, lordiness, pomposity, pompousness, presumption, pretension, pretentiousness, pride, scornfulness, superciliousness, swagger, uppishness

arrogant *adj* assuming, blustering, cavalier, conceited, contemptuous, disdainful, haughty, high-handed, imperious, insolent, lordly, overbearing, pompous, presumptuous, pretentious, proud, scornful, supercilious, swaggering

arrow *n* bolt, dart, shaft; indicator, marker, pointer

arsenal *n* ammunition dump, armoury, arms depot, magazine, ordnance depot, stock, stockpile, store, storehouse, supply

art *n* adroitness, aptitude, artistry, craft, dexterity, expertise, facility, ingenuity, knack, knowledge, mastery, method, profession, skill, trade, virtuosity

artful *adj* adept, adroit, clever, crafty, cunning, deceitful, design ing, dexterous, foxy, ingenious, intriguing, masterly, politic, proficient, resourceful, scheming, sharp, shrewd, skilful, sly, smart, subtle, tricky, wily

article *n* commodity, item, object, piece, substance, thing, unit; composition, discourse, essay, feature, paper, piece, story, treatise

articulate *adj* clear, coherent, comprehensible, eloquent, expressive, fluent, intelligible, lucid, meaningful, understandable, vocal, well-spoken

articulate *v* enounce, enunciate, express, pronounce, say, speak, state, talk, utter, verbalize, vocalize, voice

artificial *adj* man-made, manufactured, non-natural, plastic, synthetic; bogus, counterfeit, fake, imitation, mock, phoney, sham, simulated, specious, spurious

artistic *adj* aesthetic, beautiful, creative, cultivated, cultured, decorative, elegant, exquisite, graceful, imaginative, ornamental, refined, sensitive, stylish, tasteful

as *conj* at the time that, during the time that, just as, when, while; in the manner that, in the way that, like; that which, what; because, considering that, seeing that, since; in the same manner with, in the same way that, like; for instance, like, such as; **as for** as regards, in reference to, on the subject of, with reference to, with regard to, with respect to; **as it were** in a manner of speaking, in a way, so to say, so to speak

as *prep* being, in the character of, in the role of, under the name of

ascend *v* climb, float up, fly up, go up, lift off, mount, move up, rise, scale, slope upwards, soar, take off, tower

ascent *n* ascending, ascension, clambering, climb, climbing, mounting, rise, rising, scaling, upward movement; acclivity, gradient, incline, ramp, rise, rising ground, upward slope

ascetic *v* abstemious, abstinent, austere, celibate, chaste, frugal, harsh, hermit-like, plain, puritanical, restrained, rigorous, self-denying, self-disciplined, severe, simple, spartan, strict, temperate

ascribe *v* assign, attribute, charge, credit, impute, put down, refer, set down

ashamed *adj* abashed, bashful, blushing, chagrined, conscience-stricken, crestfallen, discomfited, distressed, embarrassed, guilty, humbled, humiliated, mortified, prudish, reluctant, remorseful, shamefaced, sheepish, shy, sorry

aside *adv* alone, alongside, apart, away, beside, in isolation, in reserve, on one side, out of mind, out of the way, privately, separately, to one side, to the side

ask *v* inquire, interrogate, query, question, quiz; appeal, apply, beg, beseech, claim, crave, demand, entreat, implore, petition, plead, pray, request, seek, solicit, sue, supplicate; bid, invite, summon

asleep *adj/adv* dormant, dozing, fast asleep, napping, sleeping, slumbering, snoozing, sound asleep

aspect *n* air, appearance, attitude, bearing, condition, countenance, demeanour, expression, look, manner, mien; angle, facet, feature, side

asphixiate *v* choke, smother, stifle, strangle, strangulate, throttle

aspiration *n* aim, ambition, craving, desire, dream, eagerness, endeavour, goal, hankering, hope, longing, object, objective, wish, yearning

aspire *v* aim, be ambitious, be eager, crave, desire, dream, hanker, hope, long, pursue, seek, wish, yearn

aspiring *adj* ambitious, aspirant, eager, endeavouring, hopeful, longing, striving, wishful, would-be

assail *v* assault, attack, bombard, fall on, lay into, pelt, set upon; abuse, berate, blast, criticize, harangue, lambaste, malign, pillory, put down, revile, vilify

assassin *n* eliminator, executioner, hit man, killer, liquidator, murderer, slayer

assassinate *v* eliminate, hit, kill, liquidate, murder, slay

assault *n* aggression, attack, charge, incursion, invasion, offensive, onset, onslaught, storm, storming, strike

assault *v* assail, attack, beset, charge, fall upon, invade, lay into, set about, set upon, storm, strike at

assemble *v* accumulate, amass, bring together, call together, collect, come together, congregate, convene, convoke, flock, forgather, gather, marshal, meet, rally, round up, summon; build up, connect, construct, erect, fabricate, fit together, join, make, manufacture, piece together, put together, set up

assembly *n* accumulation, aggregation, assemblage, body, collection, company, conclave, conference, congregation, convocation, council, crowd, diet, flock, gathering, group, mass, meeting, multitude, rally, synod, throng; building up, connecting, construction, erection, fabrication, fitting, together, joining, manufacture, piecing together, putting, together, setting up

assent *n* acceptance, accession, accord, acquiescence, agreement, approval, compliance, concurrence, consent, permission, sanction

assent *v* accede, accept, acquiesce, agree, allow, approve, comply, concur, consent, fall in with, go along with, grant, permit, sanction, subscribe

assert *v* affirm, allege, asseverate, attest, aver, avouch, avow, contend, declare, maintain, predicate, profess, pronounce, state, swear

assertion *n* affirmation, allegation, argument, claim, contention, declaration, insistence, pronouncement, statement

assess *v* appraise, compute, determine, estimate, evaluate, fix, gauge, judge, rate, value, weigh; demand, evaluate, fix, impose, levy, rate, tax, value

assessment *n* appraisal, computation, determination, estimate, estimation, evaluation judgment, rating, valuation; charge, demand, duty, evaluation, fee, impost, levy, rate, rating, tariff, tax, taxation, toll, valuation

asset *n* advantage, aid, benefit, blessing, boon, help, resource, service

asset *pl n* capital, estate, funds, goods, holdings, means, money, possessions, property, reserves, resources, valuables, wealth

assign *v* appoint, choose, delegate, designate, name, nominate, select; allocate, apportion, consign, distribute, give, give out, grant, makeover

assignment *n* appointment, charge, commission, job, position, post, responsibility, task

assimilate *v* absorb, digest, incorporate, take in; adapt, conform with, fit in

assist *v* abet, aid, back, benefit, boost, collaborate, cooperate, expedite, facilitate, further, help, reinforce, relieve, serve, support, sustain, work with

assistance *n* abetment, aid, backing, benefit, collaboration, cooperation, help, reinforcement, relief, service, succour, support, sustenance

assistant *n* abettor, accessory,

accomplice, aider, ally, associate, auxiliary, backer, collaborator, colleague, confederate, helper, partner, second, supporter

associate *n* ally, collaborator, colleague, companion, comrade, confederate, co-worker, follower, friend, mate, partner

associate *v* affiliate, ally, combine, confederate, conjoin, connect, correlate, couple, identify, join, league, link, mix, pair, relate, unite

association *n* affiliate, ally, combine, confederate, conjoin, connect, correlate, couple, identify, join, league, link, mix, pair, relate, unite; affiliation, alliance, band, clique, club, coalition, combine, company, confederation, corporation, federation, group, league, organization, partnership, society, syndicate, union; blend, bond, combination, concomitance, connection, correlation, identification, joining, juxtaposition, linkage, linking, lumping together, mixing, mixture, pairing, relation, tie, union, yoking

assorted *adj* different, diverse, diversified, heterogeneous, miscellaneous, mixed, motley, sundry, varied, variegated, various

assortment *n* array, choice, collection, diversify, farrago, hotchpotch, jumble, medley, miscellany, mish mash, mixture, potpourri, selection, variety

assume *v* accept, believe, expect, fancy, guess, imagine, infer, presume, presuppose, suppose, surmise, suspect, take for granted, think; adopt, affect, counterfeit, feign, imitate, impersonate, mimic, pretend to, put on, sham, simulate; accept, acquire, attend to, begin, don, embark upon, embrace, enter upon, put on, set about, shoulder, take on, take over, take responsibility for, take up, undertake

assumed *adj* affected, bogus, counterfeit, fake, false, feigned, fictitious, imitation, made-up, make-believe, phoney, pretended, pseudonymous, sham, simulated, spurious

assumption *n* acceptance, belief, conjecture, expectation, fancy, guess, hypothesis, inference, postulate, postulation, premise, premiss, presumption, presupposition, supposition, surmise, suspicion, theory

assurance *n* affirmation, assertion, declaration, guarantee, oath, pledge, profession, promise, protestation, vow, word, word of honour; aggressiveness, assuredness, boldness, certainty, certitude, confidence, conviction, coolness, courage, faith, firmness, nerve, poise, positiveness, security, self-confidence, self-reliance, sureness

assure *v* comfort, convince, embolden, encourage, hearten, persuade, reassure, soothe; affirm, attest, certify, confirm, declare, confidently, give one's word to, guarantee, pledge, promise, swear, vow; clinch, complete, confirm, ensure, guarantee, make certain, make sure, seal, secure

astonish *v* amaze, astound, bewilder, confound, daze, dumbfound, flabbergast, stagger, stun, stupefy, surprise

astonishment *n* amazement, awe, bewilderment, confusion, consternation, stupefaction, surprise, wonder, wonderment

astounding *adj* amazing, astounding, awe-inspiring, bewildering, impressive, staggering, striking, surprising

astute *adj* adroit, artful, bright, calculating, canny, clever, crafty, cunning, discerning, foxy, insightful, intelligent, keen, knowing, penetrating, perceptive, politic, sagacious, sharp, shrewd, sly, subtle, wily

asylum *n* harbour, haven, preserve, refuge, retreat, safety, sanctuary, shelter; hospital, institution, mental hospital, psychiatric hospital; (*Inf*) loony bin

atheism *n* disbelief, freethinking, godlessness, heathenism, infidelity, irreligion, nonbelief, paganism, scepticism, unbelief

atheist *n* disbeliever, freethinker, heathen, infidel, irreligionist, nonbeliever, pagan, sceptic, unbeliever

athlete *n* competitor, contender, contestant, games player, gymnast, player, runner, sportsman, sportswoman

athletic *adj* able-bodied, active, brawny, energetic, fit, herculean, muscular, powerful, robust, sinewy, strapping, strong, sturdy, vigorous

athletic *pl n* contests, exercised, games of strength, gymnastics, races, sorts, track and field events

atmosphere *n* aerosphere, air, heavens, sky; air, ambience, aura, character, climate, environment, feel, feeling, flavour, mood, quality, spirit, surroundings, tone

atrocious *adj* barbaric, brutal, cruel, diabolical, fiendish, flagrant, heinous, infamous, infernal, inhuman, monstrous, nefarious, ruthless, savage, vicious, villainous, wicked

atrocity *n* abomination, act of savagery, barbarity, brutality, crime, cruelty, enormity, evil, horror, monstrosity, outrage, villainy

attach *v* add adhere, affix, annex, append, bind, connect, couple, fasten, fix, join, link, make fast, secure, stick, subjoin, tie, unite

attached *adj* affectionate, devoted, fond of, full of regard for, possessive

attachment *n* adapter, bond, clamp, connection, connector, coupling, fastener, fastening, joint, junction, link, tie

attack *n* aggression, assault, charge, foray, incursion, inroad, invasion, offensive, onset, onslaught, raid, rush, strike; abuse, blame, calumny, censure, criticism, denigration, impugnment, vilification; access, bout, convulsion, fit, paroxysm, seizure, spasm, spell, stroke; embolden, encourage, hearten, persuade, reassure, soothe; affirm, attest, certify, confirm, declare, confidently, give one's word to, guarantee, pledge, promise, swear, vow; clinch, complete, confirm, ensure, guarantee, make certain, make sure, seal, secure

attack *v* assail, assault, charge, fall upon, invade, lay into, raid, rush, set about, set upon, storm, strike at; abuse, berate, blame, censure, criticize, impugn, malign, revile, vilify

attain *v* accomplish, achieve, acquire, arrive at, bring off, complete, earn, effect, fulfil, gain, get, grasp, obtain, procure, reach, realize, reap, secure, win

attempt *n* assault, attack, bid, effort, endeavour, essay, experiment, go, shot, trial, try, undertaking, venture

attempt *v* endeavour, essay, experiment, seek, strive, tackle, take on, try, try one's hand at, undertake, venture; (*Inf*) have a crack at

attend *v* appear, be at, be here, be present, be there, frequent, go to, haunt, make one, put in an appearance, show oneself, show up, turn up, visit; follow, hear, hearken, heed, listen, look on, mark, mind, note, notice, observe, pay attention, pay heed, regard, take to heart, watch; **attend to** apply oneself to, concentrate on, devote oneself to, get to work on, look after, occupy oneself with, see to, take care of; accompany, chaperon, companion, convoy, escort, guard, squire, usher

attendance *n* audience, crowd, gate, house, number present, turnout

attendant *n* aide, assistant, auxiliary, chaperon, companion, custodian, escort, flunky, follower, guard, guide, helper, lackey, menial, servant, steward, underling, usher, waiter

attention *n* concentration, consideration, contemplation, deliberation, heed, heedfulness, intentness, mind, scrutiny, thinking, thought, thoughtfulness; awareness, consciousness, consideration, notice, observation, recognition, regard; care, concern, looking after, ministration, treatment

attentive *adj* alert, awake, careful, concentrating, heedful, intent, listening, mindful, observant, regardful, studious, watchful

attitude *n* approach, disposition, frame of mind, mood, opinion, outlook, perspective, point of view, position, posture, stance, standing, view; air, aspect, bearing, carriage, condition, demeanour, manner, pose, position, posture, stance

attract *v* allure, appeal to, bewitch, captivate, charm, decoy, draw, enchant, endear, engage, entice, fascinate, incline, induce, interest, invite, lure, pull, tempt

attraction *n* allure, appeal, attractiveness, bait, captivation, charm, draw, enchantment, endearment, entice ment, fascination, inducement, interest, invitation, lure, magnetism, pull, temptation, temptingness

attractive *adj* agreeable, alluring, appealing, beautiful, captivating, charming, comely, engaging, enticing, fair, fascinating, fetching, good-looking, gorgeous, handsome, interesting, inviting, lovely, magnetic, pleasant, pleasing, prepossessing, pretty, seductive, tempting, winning, winsome

attribute *n* aspect, character, characteristic, facet, feature, idiosyncrasy, indication, mark, note, peculiarity, point, property, quality, quirk, sign, symbol, trait, virtue

attribute *v* apply, ascribe, assign, blame, charge, credit, impute, lay at the door of, put down to, refer, set down to, trace to

audacious *adj* adventurous, bold, brave, courageous, daredevil, daring, dauntless, death-defying, enterprising, fearless, intrepid, rash, reckless, risky, valiant, venturesome

audacity *n* adventurousness, audaciousness, boldness, bravery, courage, daring, dauntlessness, enterprise, fearlessness, intrepidity, nerve, pluck, rashness, reckless ness, valour, venturesomeness; (*Inf*) guts, spunk; cheek, defiance, disrespectfulness, effrontery, forwardness, gall, impertinence, impudence, insolence, nerve, pertness, presumption, rudeness, shameless ness

audible *adj* clear, detectable, discernible, distinct, hearable, perceptible

audience *n* assemblage, assembly, congregation, crowd, gallery, gathering, house, listeners, on lookers, spectators, turnout, viewers; consultation, hearing, interview, meeting, reception

audit *n* book-keeping, check, examination, inspection, monitoring, review, scrutiny

audit *v* check, examine, go through, inspect, monitor, oversee, review, scrutinize

auspicious *adj* bright, encouraging, favourable, felicitous, fortunate, happy, hopeful, lucky, opportune, promising, propitious, prosperous, rosy, timely

austere *adj* cold, exacting, forbidding, formal, grave, grim, hard, harsh, inflexible, rigorous, serious, severe, solemn, stern, stiff, strict, stringent, unfeeling, unrelenting; abstemious, abstinent, ascetic, chaste, continent, economical, exacting, puritanical, rigid, self-denying, self-disciplined, sober, solemn, strict, unrelenting

austerity *n* belt-tightening, frugality, hardship, poverty, recession, straitened circumstances

authentic *adj* accurate, actual, authoritative, bona fide, certain, dependable, factual, faithful, genuine, legitimate, original, pure, real, reliable, true, trustworthy, valid, veritable

authenticity *n* accuracy, actuality, authoritativeness, certainty, dependability, factualness, faithfulness, genuineness, legitimacy, purity, realness, reliability, trustworthiness, truth, truthfulness, validity, veritableness, verity

author *n* architect, composer, creator, designer, doer, fabricator, father, founder, framer, initiator, inventor, maker, mover, originator, parent, planner, prime mover, producer, writer

authoritarian *adj* absolute, autocratic, despotic, dictatorial, disciplinarian, doctrinaire, dogmatic, domineering, harsh, imperious, rigid, severe, strict, tyrannical, unyielding

authority *n* ascendancy, charge, command, control, domination, dominion, force, government, influence, jurisdiction, might, power, prerogative, right, rule, strength, supremacy, sway, weight; authorization, justification, licence, permission, permit, sanction, warrant; arbiter, bible, connoisseur, expert, judge, master, professional, scholar, specialist, textbook

authorize *v* accredit, commission, empower, enable, entitle, give authority; accredit, allow, approve, confirm, countenance, give authority for, give leave, license, permit, ratify, sanction, vouch for, warrant

autocratic *adj* authoritarian, despotic, dictatorial, dominant, domineering, imperious, tyrannical, undemocratic

automatic *adj* automated, mechanical, mechanized, robot, self-acting, self-moving, self-propelling; habitual, mechanical, perfunctory, routine, unconscious

autonomy *n* free, independent, self-determining, self-governing, self-ruling, sovereign

auxiliary *adj* accessory, aiding, ancillary, assisting, emergency, helping, reserve, secondary, subsidiary, substitute, supplementary, supporting

available *n* accessible, applicable, at hand, at one's disposal, attainable, convenient, free, handy, obtainable, on hand, on tap, ready, ready for use, to hand, vacant

avalanche *n* landslide, landslip, snow-slide, snow-slip; barrage, deluge, flood, inundation, torrent

avaricious *n* acquisitive, close-fisted, covetous, grasping, greedy, mean, miserable, miserly, niggardly, parsimonious, penurious, rapacious, stingy

avenge *v* even the score for, get even for, punish, repay, requite, retaliate, revenge, take satisfaction for, take vengeance

avenue *n* access, alley, approach, boulevard, channel, course, drive, driveway, entrance, entry, pass, passage, path, pathway, road, route, street, thoroughfare, way

average *n* common run, mean, medium, midpoint, norm, normal, par, rule, run, run of the mill, standard

average *adj* common, commonplace, fair, general, indifferent, mediocre, middling, moderate, normal, not bad, ordinary, passable, regular, standard, tolerable, typical, undistinguished, unexceptional, usual; intermediate, mean, median, medium, middle

averse *adj* antipathetic, backward, disinclined, hostile, ill-disposed, indisposed, inimical, loath, opposed, reluctant, unfavourable, unwilling

avert *v* avoid, prevent, stop, turn aside, turn away,

avid *adj* ardent,devoted, eager, enthusiastic, fanatical, fervent, intense, keen, passionate, zealous

avoid *v* avert, bypass, circumvent, dodge, elude, escape, eschew, evade, fight shy of, keep aloof from, keep away from, prevent, refrain from, shirk, shun, sidestep, steer clear of

avoidable *adj* escapable, preventable, unnecessary

await *v* abide, anticipate, expect, look for, look forward to, stay for, wait for; attend, be in readiness for, be in store for, be prepared for, be ready for, wait for

awake *v* alert, alive, aroused, attentive, awakened, aware, conscious, heedful, not sleeping, observant, on guard, on the alert, on the lookout, vigilant, wakeful, waking, watchful, wide-awake

awaken *v* activate, alert, animate, arouse, awake, call forth, enliven, excite, fan, incite, kindle, provoke, revive, rouse, stimulate, stir up, vivify, wake

award *n* adjudication, allotment, bestowal, conferment, conferral, decision, decree, endowment, gift, order, presentation; decoration, gift, grant, prize, trophy, verdict

award *v* accord, adjudge, allot, apportion, assign, bestow, confer, decree, distribute, endow, gift, give, grant, present, render

aware *adj* acquainted, alive to, appreciative, apprised, attentive, cognizant, conscious, conversant, enlightened, familiar, informed, knowing, knowledgeable, mindful, sensible, sentient, wise

awareness *n* acquaintance, appreciation, attention, cognizance, consciousness, enlightenment, familiarity, knowledge, mindfulness, perception, realization, recognition, sensibility, sentience, understanding

away *adv* abroad, elsewhere, from here, from home, hence, off; apart, at a distance, far, remote; aside, out of the way, to one side

away *adj* abroad, absent, elsewhere, gone, not at home, not here, not present, not there, out

awe *n* admiration, adoration, amazement, fear, wonder

awesome *adj* amazing, astonishing, awe-inspiring, incredible, magnificent, marvellous, stupendous, unbelievable, wonderful

awful *adj* alarming, appalling, deplorable, dire, distressing, dreadful, fearful, frightful, ghastly, gruesome, harrowing, hideous, horrendous, horrible, horrific, horrifying, nasty, shocking, terrible, tremendous, ugly, unpleasant, unsightly

awfully *adv* badly, disgracefully, disreputably, dreadfully, inadequately, reprehensibly, shoddily, unforgivably, unpleasantly, wickedly, woefully, wretchedly

awkward *adj* all thumbs, artless, blundering, bungling, clownish, clumsy, coarse, gauche, gawky, graceless, ill-bred, inelegant, inept, inexpert, lumbering, oafish, rude, skill-less, stiff, uncoordinated, uncouth, ungainly, ungraceful, unpolished, unrefined, unskilful, unskilled; cumbersome, difficult, inconvenient, troublesome, unhandy, unmanageable, unwieldy; annoying, difficult, disobliging, exasperating, hard to handle, intractable, irritable, perverse, prickly, stubborn, troublesome, trying, unhelpful, unpredictable, vexing

awkwardness *n* artlessness, clownishness, clumsiness, coarseness, gaucheness, gawkiness, gracelessness, ill-breeding, inelegance, ineptness, inexpertness, maladroitness, oafishness, rudeness, skillessness, stiffness, uncoordination, ungainliness, unskilfulness, unskilledness; cumbersomeness, difficulty, inconvenience, troublesomeness, unhandiness, unmanageability, unwieldiness; delicacy, difficulty, discomfort, embarrassment, inconvenience, inopportuneness, painfulness, perplexingness, thorniness, unpleasantness, untimeliness; disobligingness, intractability, irritability perversity, prickliness, stubbornness, touchiness, uncooperativeness, unhelpfulness, unpredictability

axe *n* abolish, dismiss, do away with, fire, get rid of, make redundant, remove repeal, sack

axiom *n* adage, aphorism, apophthegm, dictum, fundamental, gnome, maxim, postulate, precept, principle, truism

axiomatic *adj* absolute, accepted, apodictic, assumed, certain, fundamental, given, granted, indubitable, manifest, presupposed, self-evident, understood, unquestioned; aphoristic, apophthegmatic, epigrammatic, gnomic, pithy, terse

axis *n* arbor, axis, mandrel, pin, pivot, rod, shaft, spindle

B

baby *n* babe, bairn, child, infant, newborn child

baby *v* coddle, cosset, indulge, molly-coddle, pamper, spoil

baby *adj* diminutive, dwarf, little, midget, miniature, minute, pygmy, small, tiny, wee

babyish *adj* baby, childish, foolish, immature, infantile, juvenile, namby-pamby, puerile, silly, sissy, spoiled

back *v* abet, advocate, assist, champion, countenance, encourage, endorse, favour, finance, sanction, second, side with, sponsor, subsidise, support, sustain, underwrite; backtrack, go back, move back, regress, retire, retreat, reverse, turn tail, withdraw

back *n* backside, end, far end, hindpart, hindquarters, posterior, rear, reverse, stern, tail end

back *adj* end, hind, posterior, rear, tail

backer *n* advocate, angel, benefactor, patron, promoter, punter, second, sponsor, subscriber, supporter, underwriter, well-wisher

backfire *v* boomerang, disappoint, fail, flop, miscarry, rebound, recoil

background *n* breeding, circumstances, credentials, culture, education, environment, experience, grounding, history, milieu, preparation, qualifications, tradition, upbringing

backing *n* abetment, accompaniment, advocacy, aid, assistance, championing, encouragement, endorsement, funds, grant, moral support, patronage, sanction, seconding, sponsorship, subsidy, support

backlash *n* backfire, boomerang, counteraction, counterblast, kickback, reaction, recoil, repercussion, resentment, resistance, response, retaliation, retroaction

backlog *n* accumulation, build-up, excess, hoard, reserve, reserves, resources, stock, supply

back out *v* abandon, cancel, chicken out, give up, go back on, recant, resign, retreat, withdraw

backslider *n* apostate, deserter, recidivist, recreant, renegade, reneger, turncoat

back up *v* aid, assist, bolster, confirm, corroborate, reinforce, substantiate, support

back up *n* reinforcement, reserve, second, stand by, stand in for, substitute

backward *adj* bashful, diffident, disinclined, hesitating, indisposed late, loath, reluctant, shy, sluggish, tardy, unwilling, wavering; behind, behindhand, dense, dull, retarded, slow, stupid, subnormal, underdeveloped, undeveloped

backward *adv* aback, in reverse, rearward

bad *adj* defective, deficient, erroneous, fallacious, faulty, imperfect, inadequate, incorrect, inferior, poor, substandard, unsatisfactory; damaging, dangerous, deleterious, detrimental, harmful, hurtful, injurious, ruinous, unhealthy; base, corrupt, criminal, delinquent, evil, immoral, mean, sinful, vile, villainous, wicked, wrong; disobedient, mischievous, naughty, unruly; decayed, mouldy, off, putrid, rancid, rotten, sour, spoiled; ailing, diseased, ill, sick, unwell; adverse, discouraged, distressed, gloomy, grim, troubled, unfortunate, unpleasant

badge *n* brand, device, emblem, identification, insignia, mark, sign, stamp, token

badger *v* annoy, bait, bother, harangue, hector, pester, persecute, tease, torment, trouble, vex, worry

badly *adv* carelessly, defectively, erroneously, faultily, imperfectly, inadequately, incorrectly, ineptly, poorly, shoddily, wrongly; unfavourably, unfortunately; criminally, evilly, immorally, improperly, shamefully, unethically, wickedly

baffle *v* amaze, astound, bewilder, confound, confuse, daze, disconcert, dumbfound, elude, flummox, mystify, nonplus, perplex, puzzle, stump, stun; balk, check, defeat, foil, frustrate, hinder, thwart, upset

bag *v* acquire, capture, catch, gain, get, kill, land, shoot, take, trap

baggage *n* accoutrements, bags, belongings, equipment, gear, impedimenta, luggage, paraphernalia, suitcases, things

baggy *adj* billowing, bulging, droopy, floppy, ill-fitting, loose, oversize, roomy, sagging, seated, slack

bail *n* bond, guarantee, guaranty, pledge, security, surety, warranty

bail *v* dip, drain off, ladle, scoop

bail out *v* aid, help, relieve, rescue; escape, quit, retreat, withdraw

bait *n* allurement, attraction, bribe, decoy, enticement, inducement, lure, snare, temptation

bait *v* annoy, gall, harass, harry, irk, irritate, needle, persecute, provoke, tease, torment, worry

bake *v* cook; burn, desiccate, dry, parch, scorch, sear

balance *v* level, match, parallel, poise, stabilize, steady; adjust, compensate for, counteract, counterbalance, counterpoise, equalize, equate, make up for, neutralize, offset

balance *n* correspondence, equilibrium, equity, equivalence, evenness, liberation, parity, symmetry, uniformity; composure, equanimity, poise, self-control, stability, steadiness; difference, excess, remainder, residue, rest, surplus

bald *adj* baldheaded, baldpated, depilated, glabrous, hairless; bare, barren, bleak, exposed, naked, stark, treeless, uncovered

bale *see* BAIL

balk *v* demur, dodge, evade, flinch, hesitate, jib, recoil, refuse, resist, shirk, shrink from; baffle, bar, check, counteract, defeat, disconcert, foil, forestall, frustrate, hinder, obstruct, prevent, thwart

ball *n* drop, globe, globule, orb, pellet, sphere, spheroid

ballast *n* balance, counterbalance, counterweight, equilibrium, sandbag, stability, stabilizer, weight

ballet *n* arabesque, chassé, contretemps, glissade, glissée, jeté, pas de

basque, pas de chat, pas de deaux, piqué, pirouette, plié, saut, sissonne, soubresaut, temps, tours en l'air
balloon *n* airship, blimp, dirigible, hot air balloon, montgolfier, Zeppelin
balloon *v* billow, blow up, fill out, inflate, puff out, swell out
ballot *n* election, poll, polling, vote, voting
balm *n* cream, lotion, ointment
balmy *adj* clement, mild, summery, temperate
bamboozle *v* cheat, deceive, defraud, fool, hoax, swindle, trick
ban *v* banish, bar, debar, disallow, exclude, forbid, interdict, outlaw, prohibit, proscribe, restrict, suppress
ban *n* boycott, censorship, embargo, interdiction, prohibition, proscription, restriction, stoppage, suppression, taboo
banal *adj* bland, clichéd, commonplace, everyday, hackneyed, humdrum, old hat, meaningless, ordinary, pedestrian, platitudinous, stale, stereotyped, stock, threadbare, tired, trite, unimaginative, unoriginal, vapid
band *n* bandage, belt, binding, bond, chain, cord, fetter, fillet, ligature, manacle, ribbon, shackle, strap, strip, tie; assembly, association, body, clique, club, company, coterie, crew, gang, horde, party, society, troop, combo, ensemble, group, orchestra
bandage *n* compress, dressing, gauze, plaster
bandage *v* bind, cover, dress, swathe
bandit *n* brigand, crook, freebooter, gangster, gunman, highwayman, hijacker, marauder, outlaw, pirate, racketeer, robber, thief
bang *n* boom, burst, clang, clap, clash, detonation, explosion, peal, pop, shot, thud, thump; blow, box, bump, clatter, crash, hammer, knock, pound, pummel, rap, strike
banish *v* deport, drive away, eject, evict, exclude, excommunicate, exile, expatriate, expel, ostracize, outlaw, shut out, transport; ban, cast out, discard, dislodge, dismiss, dispel, eliminate, eradicate, oust, remove, shake off
banishment *n* deportation, exile, expatriation, expulsion, proscription, transportation
banisters *pl n* balustrade, handrail, rail, railing; balusters
bank *n* accumulation, depository, fund, hoard, repository, reserve, reservoir, savings, stock, stockpile, store, storehouse; banking, embankment, heap, mass, mound, pile, ridge; brink, edge, margin, shore, side; array, file, group, line, rank, row, sequence, series, succession, tier, train
bank *v* deal with, deposit, keep, save, transact business with; amass, heap, mass, mound, pile, stack; camber, cant, incline, pitch, slant, slope, tilt, tip
bank on *v* assume, count on, depend on, rely on, trust
bankrupt *v* broke, cleaned out, depleted, destitute, exhausted, failed, impoverished, insolvent, lacking, ruined, spent
banner *n* colours, flag, pennant, placard, standard, streamer
banquet *n* dinner, dinner party, feast, meal, formal dinner, repast
banter *n* chaff, gossip, idle chat,

joking, joshing, small talk, teasing

baptism *n* christening, immersion, purification, sprinkling; beginning, debut, dedication, initiation, introduction, launching, rite of passage

bar *n* batten, crosspiece, paling, pole, rail, rod, shaft, stake, stick; barricade, barrier, deterrent, hindrance, impediment, obstacle, obstruction, rail, stop; canteen, counter, inn, pub, public house, saloon, tavern; (Inf) boozer; bench, court, courtroom, dock, law court; body of lawyers, counsel, court, judgment

bar *v* barricade, bolt, fasten, latch, lock, secure; ban, exclude, forbid, hinder, keep out, obstruct, prevent, prohibit, restrain

barb *n* point, prong, quill, spike, thorn

barbarian *n* boor, brute, hooligan, lout, lowbrow, monster, ruffian, savage, vandal; bigot, ignoramus, illiterate, philistine

barbaric *adj* primitive, rude, uncivilized, wild; brutal, coarse, cruel, savage, vulgar

barbecue *n* outdoor meal, party, picnic; (*Inf*) barbie

barbecue *v* broil, charcoal, grill

bare *adj* denuded, exposed, naked, nude, peeled, shorn, stripped, unclad, unclothed, uncovered, undressed; barren, blank, empty, lacking, mean, open, poor, scanty, scarce, unfurnished, vacant, void, wanting

barefaced *adj* audacious, bold, brash, brazen, impudent, insolent; blatant, flagrant, manifest, naked, obvious, palpable, patent, transparent, unconcealed

barely *adv* by the skin of your teeth, hardly, just, only just, scarcely

bargain *n* agreement, arrangement, business, compact, contract, convention, engagement, negotiation, pact, pledge, promise, stipulation, transaction, treaty, understanding; discount, giveaway, good buy, good deal, good value, reduction, snip

bargain *v* agree, contract, covenant, negotiate, promise, stipulate, transact; barter, buy, deal, haggle, sell, trade, traffic

bark *v* bay, growl, howl, snarl, woof, yap, yelp; bawl, bluster, scream, screech, shout, shriek, thunder, yell; abrade, excoriate, flay, rub, scrape, shave, skin, strip

bark *n* casing, coating, cortex, covering, crust, husk, rind, skin

barmy *adj* crazy, daft, dippy, foolish, idiotic, insane, odd, silly, stupid

barn *n* byre, outbuilding, outhouse, shed, shelter; mews, stables

baron *n* aristocrat, lord, noble, nobleman, peer; captain of industry, executive, financier, industrialist, magnate, tycoon

baroque *adj* bizarre, convoluted, decorated, elaborate, embellished, extravagant, flamboyant, florid, fussy, grotesque, ornate, ostentatious, overdecorated, showy

barracks *pl n* billet, camp, casern, fort, garrison; quarters

barrage *n* battery, bombardment, broadside, cannonade, curtain of fire, fusillade, gunfire, salvo, shelling, volley; abundance, avalanche, burst, deluge, flood, hail, mass, onslaught, plethora, profusion, storm, stream, torrent

barrel *n* butt, cask, firkin, hogshead,

keg, tank, tub, tun, vat

barren *adj* childless, infecund, infertile, sterile, unprolific; arid, desert, desolate, dry, empty, uncultivable, unfruitful, unproductive, waste; boring, fruitless, futile, lacklustre, prosaic, stale, uninteresting, unrewarding, useless, vapid, valueless, worthless

barricade *n* bar, barrier, blockade, bulwark, fence, obstacle, obstruction, palisade, rampart, roadblock, stockade

barricade *v* bar, blockade, close up, defend, fence in, fortify, obstruct

barrier *n* bar, barricade, blockade, boundary, ditch, fence, fortification, obstacle, obstruction, railing, rampart, stop, wall; check, difficulty, drawback, handicap, hindrance, hurdle, impediment, limitation, obstacle, restriction, stumbling block

barrister *n* counsel, professional pleader; advocate; attorney

barter *n* bargain, beatdown, exchange, haggle, sell, swap, trade, trade-off, trafficking

base *n* bed, bottom, foot, foundation, groundwork, pedestal, rest, stand, support; basis, core, essence, essential, fundamental, heart, key, origin, principle, root, source; camp, centre, home, post, settlement, starting point, station

base *v* build, construct, depend, derive, establish, fasten, form, found, ground, hinge, rest, root, station; install, locate, place, post, situate

baseless *adj* groundless, unconfirmed, uncorroborated, unfounded, ungrounded, unjustifiable, unjustified, unsubstantiated, unsupported

basement *n* cellar, crypt, garden flat, vault

bashful *adj* abashed, backward, blushing, confused, constrained, coy, demure, diffident, easily embarrassed, hesitant, nervous, overmodest, reserved, reticent, retiring, self-effacing, self-conscious, shame faced, sheepish, shrinking, shy, timid, timorous

basic *adj* central, elementary, essential, fundamental, indispensable, inherent, intrinsic, key, necessary, primary, radical, rudimentary, underlying, vital; bottom, ground, lowest, lowest-level, starting, without commission; plain, simple, sparse, spartan, unadorned, without frills

basics *pl n* core, essentials, facts, fundamentals, hard facts, necessaries, practicalities, principles, realities, rudiments; *(Inf)* brass tacks, nitty-gritty, nuts and bolts

basin *n* container, receptacle, vessel; bowl, dish, pan; bed, channel

basis *n* back-up, base, bottom, foot ing, foundation, ground, ground work, reasoning, support; core, essence, fundamental point, premise, principal constituent, main ingredient, starting-point; condition, position, procedure, status

bask *v* laze, lie, loll, lounge, relax, sunbathe; delight, enjoy, rejoice in, relish, revel, savour, take pleasure

basket *n* container, receptacle; creel, hamper, pannier, punnet

bass *adj* deep-pitched, deep-toned, low-pitched, low-toned, resonant, sonorous

bastard *n* illegitimate child, love

child, natural son/daughter; black guard, cad, rascal, scoundrel, villain

bastard *adj* illegitimate, natural; adulterated, alloyed, artificial, counterfeit, fake, false, hybrid, imperfect, impure, inferior, irregular, sham, spurious

bastion *n* bulwark, citadel, defence, fastness, fortress, garrison, keep, mainstay, parapet, prop, rampart, rock, stronghold, support, tower of strength

batch *n* accumulation, aggregation, amount, assemblage, bunch, collection, crowd, group, lot, mass, pack, quantity, set

bath *n* bath-tub, hip-bath, sauna, sitz-bath, steam bath, tub, whirlpool bath; dip, douche, shower, soak, soaping

bath *v* bathe, clean, douse, scrub down, shower, soak, soap, sponge, wash

bathe *v* clean, cleanse, cover, dunk, flood, immerse, moisten, rinse, soak, steep, suffuse, wash, wet; take a dip; envelope, suffuse

bathe *n* dip, swim, wash

bathos *n* anticlimax, let-down; sentimentality

baton *n* bar, club, mace, rod, staff, stick, truncheon, wand

battalion *n* army, brigade, company, contingent, detachment, division, forces, garrison, legion, platoon regiment, section, squadron, troops, unit; crowd, herd, horde, host, multitude, protesters, throng

batten *n* bar, board, bolt, clamp, strip

batten *v* fasten, fix, secure

batter *v* abuse, assault, bash, beat, belabour, break, buffet, hit, lash, pelt, pound, pummel, smash, smite, strike, thrash, wallop; bruise, crush, deface, demolish, destroy, disfigure, harm, hurt, injure, mangle, mar, maul, ruin, shatter, shiver, smash, spoil, wound

battery *n* assault, attack, beating, grievous bodily harm, mayhem, mugging, onslaught, physical violence, striking, thrashing, thumping; artillery, cannon, cannonry, gun emplacements

battle *n* affray, armed conflict, attack, campaign, clash, collision, combat, confrontation, contest, crusade, encounter, engagement, fight, fray, hostilities, meeting, mêlée, skirmish, tussle, warfare

battle *v* combat, contend, feud, fight, strive, struggle, war; labour, push, struggle; argue, bicker, disagree, feud, quarrel, wrangle

battleaxe *n* dragon, fury, harridan, martinet, shrew, stramullion, tartar, termagant, virago

battle-cry *n* rallying call, war cry, war whoop; catchword, catchphrase, motto, shibboleth, slogan, watchword

battlefield *n* battlefront, battleground, battle stations, combat zone, field of battle, field of operations, front, theatre of war

battlement *n* balustrade, barbican, batizan, bulwark, fortification, parapet, rampart; breastwork, circum vallation, crenellation, outwork

battleship *n* capital ship, cruiser, gunboat, man-of-war, warship

batty *adj* eccentric, foolish, idiotic, insane, odd, queer, silly, stupid

bauble *n* bagatelle, bibelot, gewgaw, gimcrack, kickshaw, knick-knack, plaything, toy, trifle, trinket

bawdy *adj* blue, coarse, crude, dirty, disgusting, filthy, gross, indecent, indelicate, lascivious, lecherous, lewd, licentious, naughty, obscene, pornographic, purient, racy, risqué, rude, smutty, salacious, steamy

bawl *v* bellow, call, cry out, howl, roar, scream, screech, shout, yell, whoop, vociferate

bay *n* arm, basin, bight, cove, firth, gulf, harbour, indentation, inlet, natural harbour, sound; alcove, niche, nook, opening, recess; bark, baying, cry, howl, ululation

bay *v* bark, bellow, clamour, cry, growl, howl, roar, yelp

bazaar *n* exchange, market, market place, mart, souk; bring-and-buy, fair, fête, sale of work

be *v* be alive, breathe, exist, inhabit, live; abide, continue, endure, last, obtain, persist, prevail, remain, stand, stay, survive

beach *n* coast, coastline, lido, littoral, margin, plage, sands, seaboard, seashore, seaside, shingle, shore, strand, water's edge

beachcomber *n* accumulator, collector, forager, gatherer, scavenger; hobo, scrounger, tramp, vagrant, wanderer

beached *adj* abandoned, aground, ashore, grounded, high and dry, marooned, stranded, wrecked

beacon *n* beam, bonfire, flare, lighthouse, pharos, rocket, sign, signal, signal fire, smoke signal, warning light, watchtower

bead *n* ball, globule, oval, pellet, pill, spheroid; blob, bubble, dew drop, dot, drop, droplet, glob, teardrop

beak *n* bill, mandible, nib; nose, proboscis, snout; bow, prow, ram, rostrum, stem

beam *n* board, girder, joist, lath, plank, rafter, spar, support, timber; bar, emission, flare, gleam, glimmer, glint, glow, radiation, ray, shaft, streak

beam *v* broadcast, emit, glare, gleam, glitter, glow, radiate, shine, transmit; grin, laugh, smile

bear *v* bring, carry, convey, fetch, haul, move, take, tote, transport; carry, spread, transmit; display, exhibit, show; abide, admit, allow, brook, endure, permit, put up with, stomach, suffer, tolerate, undergo; beget, breed, bring forth, develop, engender; generate, give, give forth, produce, provide, yield; shoulder, support, sustain, uphold; endure, experience, go through, put up with, suffer, support, tolerate, weather; cherish, entertain, harbour, have, hold, possess; bend, curve, deviate, diverge, fork, go, move, turn; authenticate, confirm, corroborate, endorse, give credence to, justify, prove, ratify, support, verify, vindicate; carry on, cope, endure, grin and bear, manage, persevere, withstand; be patient with, endure, make allowances for, put up with, suffer, tolerate

bear *n* American black, Asiatic black, brown, cinnamon, giant panda, grizzly, Himalayan black, honey, Kodiak, musquaw, polar, sloth, red panda, spectacled, sun

bearable *adj* admissible, endurable, manageable, passable, supportable, sustainable, tolerable

beard *n* bristle, designer stubble, facial hair, five o'clock shadow, stubble, whiskers; beaver, full beard, goatee, imperial, sideboards, sideburns, side-whiskers

bearded *adj* bewhiskered, bristly, bushy, hairy, hirsute, stubbly, whiskered, unshaven,

bear down *v* burden, compress, encumber, push, strain, weigh down

bearer *n* agent, carrier, conveyor, courier, messenger, porter, runner, servant; beneficiary, consignee, payee

bearing *n* air, aspect, attitude, behaviour, carriage, demeanour, deportment, gait, manner, mien, posture; course, direction; connection, pertinence, relation, relevance, significance; location, orientation, position, situation, track, way, whereabouts

bear out *v* confirm, corroborate, endorse, justify, prove, substantiate, support, uphold, vindicate

bear with *v* be patient, forbear, make allowances, put up with, suffer, tolerate, wait

beast *n* animal, brute, creature; barbarian, fiend, monster, ogre, sadist, savage, swine

beastly *adj* barbarous, bestial, brutal, brutish, coarse, cruel, depraved, inhuman, monstrous, repulsive, sadistic, savage; awful, disagreeable, foul, horrible, mean, nasty, rotten, terrible, unpleasant, vile

beat *v* bang, batter, break, bruise, buffet, cane, chastise, cudgel, cuff, drub, flay, flog, hit, knock, lash, maul, pelt, pound, pummel, punch, smack, slap, strike, thrash, whip; best, conquer, defeat, excel, outdo, outrun, outstrip, overcome, overwhelm, subdue, surpass, vanquish; flap, flutter, quiver, tremble, vibrate; blend, mix, stir, whip, whisk; break against, dash, lap, strike, wash; conquer, defeat, overpower, quash, rout, trounce, vanquish

beat *n* blow, lit, lash, punch, shake, slap, strike, swing, thump; flutter, palpitation, pulsation, pulse, throb; accent, cadence, measure, metre, rhythm, stress, time; circuit, course, orbit, path, rounds, route, way

beat *adj* exhausted, fatigued, spent, tired, wearied, worn out

beaten *adj* bested, defeated, disappointed, disheartened, frustrated, overcome, overwhelmed, quashed, thwarted, trounced, vanquished; blended, foamy, frothy, mixed, stirred, whipped, whisked

beatific *adj* blessed, blissful, celestial, heavenly, paradisical; blissful, ecstatic, glad, happy, joyful, rapturous

beating *n* battering, hitting, striking, thrashing; corporal punishment; conquest, defeat, downfall, overthrow; palpating, pulse, pulsing, throb; dashing, striking

beatitude *n* blessedness, bliss, ecstasy, divine rapture, exaltation, sainthood, supreme happiness

beau *n* admirer, boyfriend, escort, fiancé, lover, partner, significant other, suitor; cavalier, coxcomb, dandy, fop, gallant, popinjay

beautiful *adj* alluring, appealing, attractive, charming, comely, delightful, elegant, exquisite, fair, fine, good looking, gorgeous, graceful, handsome, lovely, pleasing, radiant, ravishing, stunning, winsome

beautify *v* adorn, array, bedeck, deck, decorate, embellish, enhance, garnish, gild, glamorize, grace, ornament, prettify, preen, smarten

beauty *n* allure, artistry, attractiveness, bloom, charm, comeliness, elegance, exquisiteness, fairness, glamour, grace, handsomeness, loveliness, seemliness, symmetry; belle, charmer, goddess

becalmed *adj* at a standstill, halt, marooned, motionless, stranded

because *conj* as, by reason of, by virtue of, in that, on account of, owing to, since, thanks to

beckon *v* bid, call, gesticulate, gesture, motion, nod, signal, summon, wave at; attract, call, coax, draw, entice, lure, tempt

become *v* alter into, be transformed into, be converted into, change into, come to be, develop into, evolve into, grow into, mature into, metamorphose into, ripen into, turn into, turn out to be; embellish, enhance, fit, flatter, grace, harmonize, ornament, set off, suit; befell, happen to

becoming *adj* attractive, chic, comely, elegant, enhancing, flattering, graceful, handsome, lovely, neat, pretty, stylish, tasteful; appropriate, apt, decent, fitting, proper, seemly, suitable, worthy; compatible with, consistent with, congruous with

bed *n* bedstead, berth, bunk, cot, couch, divan; area, border, garden, patch, plot, row, strip; base, basis, foundation, substructure, substratum, support

bed *v* bury, embed, establish, fix into, found, implant, inlay, insert, set; seduce, spend the night with; plant out, set in beds; go to bed, have a nap, settle down; put to bed, say goodnight to, settle down, tuck in

bedazzle *v* amaze, astound, bewilder, blind, captivate, confuse, dazzle, enchant, overwhelm, stun

bedeck *v* adorn, array, decorate, embellish, festoon, garnish

bedevil *v* afflict, annoy, beset, distress, frustrate, irritate, irk, pester, plague, torture, worry

bedlam *n* chaos, clamour, commotion, disarray, disorder, furore, hubbub, hullabaloo, noise, pandemonium, tumult, turmoil, uproar

bedraggled *adj* dirty, dishevelled, drenched, dripping wet, messy, muddy, muddied, saturated, soaking wet, soaking, soggy, soiled, stained, unkempt, untidy

bedridden *adj* confined, confined to bed, flat on one's back, housebound incapacitated

bedrock *n* bed, bottom, foundation, rock bed, solid foundation, substratum, substructure; lowest point, nadir, rock bottom

beef *n* brawn, bulk, burliness, heftiness, muscle, muscularity, physique, powerfulness, robustness, strength; complaint, criticism, grievance, griping, grousing, grumble, objection, protestation

beefy *adj* brawny, burly, heavy, hefty, hulking, muscular, powerful, robust, solid, stocky, strapping, strong, thickset,

beer *n* ale, bitter, bottled, brown ale, canned, draught, keg, lager, lite, mild, pale ale, porter, real ale, shandy, stout, strong ale

befall *v* arise, chance, come about, come to pass, crop up, ensue, fall, follow, happen, materialize, occur, result, supervene, take place, transpire

befitting *adj* appropriate, apt, becoming, decorous, fit, fitting, proper, right, seemly, suitable

before *adv* earlier, formerly, hitherto, in the past, previously, sooner; ahead, in advance, in front, in the lead

before *prep* earlier than, in advance of, in front of, in the presence of, in the sight of, previous to, prior to, under the nose of

beforehand *adv* ahead of time, already, before, before now, earlier, in advance, in anticipation, in readiness, previously, sooner

befriend *v* advise, aid, assist, back, benefit, encourage, favour, keep an eye on, help, look after, patronize, make friends with, protect, side with, stand by, succour, support, sustain, uphold, welcome

befuddled *adj* bewildered, confused, dazzed, fuddled, groggy, muddled, numbed, stunned; dazed, drunk, drunken, inebriated, stupefied

beg *v* beseech, crave, desire, entreat, implore, importune, petition, plead with, pray, request, solicit, supplicate; ask for, cadge, call for alms, scrounge, seek charity, solicit charity, sponge from

beget *v* engender, father, generate, procreate, sire, spawn; bring about, cause, bring to pass, create, effect, engender, give rise to, occasion, produce, result in

beggar *n* cadger, derelict, down and out, mendicant, pauper, scrounger, sponger, supplicant, tramp, vagabond, vagrant; bloke, creature, fellow, individual, person

beggar *v* bankrupt, impoverish, make poor, pauperize, reduce to poverty

begin *v* commence, embark on, get ahead with, inaugurate, initiate, instigate, institute, prepare, set about, set in motion, set on foot, start; get going, go ahead; appear, arise, come into existence, crop up, emerge, dawn, happen, occur, originate

beginner *n* amateur, apprentice, cub, fledgling, fresher, freshman, initiate, learner, neophyte, novice, novitiate, pupil, raw recruit, recruit, starter, student, tenderfoot, trainee

beginning *n* birth, commencement, conception, dawn, emergence, inauguration, inception, initiation, onset, opening, origin, outset, preface, prelude, rise, rudiments, source, start, starting point

begrudge *v* be jealous, be reluctant, be stingy, envy, grudge, resent

beguile *v* attract, bewitch, charm, delight, enchant, please, seduce

behalf *n* in the interest of, in the name of, in place of, representing; for the good of, on account of, in support of

behave *v* act, function, operate, perform, run, work; act correctly, conduct oneself properly, mind one's manners

behaviour *n* actions, bearing, carriage, comportment, conduct, demeanour, deportment, manner, manners, ways; action, functioning, operation, performance

behead *v* decapitate, guillotine

behest *n* charge, command, decree, directive, edict, mandate, request, ruling, wish

behind *prep* after, at the back of, at the rear of, following, later than; at the bottom of, causing, initiating, instigating, responsible for; backing, for, in agreement, in the side of, supporting

behind *adv* after, afterwards, follow ing, in the wake of, next, subsequently; behindhand, in arrears, in debt, overdue

behold *v* consider, contemplate, discern, eye, look at, observe, perceive, regard, scan, survey, view, watch, witness

beige *adj* biscuit, buff, coffee, neutral, oatmeal, sand

being *n* actuality, animation, existence, life, living, reality; entity, essence, nature, soul, spirit, substance; animal, beast, body, creature, human being, individual, living thing, mortal, thing

belated *adj* behindhand, behind time, delayed, late, overdue, tardy

belch *v* break wind, bring up wind, burp, hiccough; discharge, emit, give off, give out, issue, spew out, vent

beleaguered *adj* beseiged, blockaded, encircled, hemmed in, surrounded, under attack, under seige

belief *n* admission, assent, assurance, confidence, conviction, credit, feeling, impression, judgment, notion, opinion, persuasion, presumption, reliance, theory, trust, view; credence, creed, doctrine, dogma, faith, ideology, principles

believe *v* accept, be certain of, be convinced of, count on, credit, depend on, have faith in, hold, place confidence in, presume true, rely on, swear by, trust; assume, conjecture, consider, gather, guess, imagine, judge, maintain, postulate, presume, reckon, speculate, suppose, think

believer *n* adherent, convert, devotee, disciple, follower, proselyte, supporter, upholder, zealot

belittle *v* decry, deprecate, depreciate, detract from, minimize, play down, scoff at, sneer at

belligerent *adj* aggressive, antagonistic, argumentative, militant, quarrelsome, pugnacious, quick-tempered

bellow *v* bawl, call out, howl, scream, screech, shout, shriek, yell

belong ***to*** *v* to be at the disposal of, be held by, be owned by, be the property of; be affiliated to, be allied to, be a member of, be associated with, be included in; attach to, be connected with, be fitting, be part of, fit, go with, pertain to, relate to

belongings *pl n* accoutrements, chattels, effects, gear, goods, paraphernalia, personal property, possessions, stuff, things

beloved *n* admired, adored, cherished, darling, dear, dearest, loved, pet, precious, revered, treasured, worshipped

below *adv* beneath, down, lower, under, underneath;

below *prep* inferior, lesser than, subject, subordinate, unworthy of

belt *n* band, cummerband, girdle, girth, sash, waistband; conveyor, fan; area, district, extent, region, stretch, tract; band, line, stria, stripe; bang, blow, punch, smack, thump

belt *v* bind, encircle, encompass, fasten, gird, tie; birch, cane, flagelate, flail, flog, lash, scourge, strap, thrash, thump, whip; bang, batter, beat, pound, pummel, punch, smack

bemoan *v* deplore, lament, mourn, regret, grieve for, repent, rue, sorrow for, weep over

bemused *adj* absent-minded, astonished, bewildered, confused, dazed, engrossed, fuddled, muddled, perplexed, preoccupied, puzzled, stunned, stupefied

bench *n* form, long seat, pew, seat, settle, stall; board, counter, table, trestle table, workbench; bar, court, courtroom, judge, judiciary, magistrate, tribunal

benchmark *n* criterion, gauge, model, norm, pattern, touchstone, yardstick

bend *v* bow, buckle, contort, crook, crouch, curve, deflect, diverge, flex, incline, incurvate, lean, stoop, swerve, turn, twist, veer, warp

bend *n* angle, arc, bow, corner, crook, curve, hook, loop, turn, twist, zigzag

beneath *adv* below, in a lower place, underneath

beneath *prep* below, inferior to, less than, lower than, unbefitting, under neath, unworthy of

benediction *n* blessing, grace, prayer, thanksgiving; blessedness, bliss, favour, grace

benefactor *n* backer, donor, helper, patron, philanthropist, promoter, subsidizer, sympathizer, well-wisher

beneficial *adj* advantageous, benign, favourable, gainful, healthy, helpful, obliging, profitable, promising, rewarding, salubrious, salutary, serviceable, useful, valuable, wholesome

beneficiary *n* assignee, heir, inheritor, payee, receiver, recipient

benefit *n* advantage, aid, asset, assistance, avail, betterment, blessing, boon, favour, gain, good, help, interest, profit; allowance, insurance money, sick pay, social security payment, unemployment benefit

benefit *v* advance, advantage, aid, ameliorate, assist, avail, better, enhance, further, good to, help, improve, profit, promote, serve

benevolence *n* altruism, charity, generosity, goodness, humanity, humanitarianism, kindness, philanthropism

bent *adj* angled, arched, bowed, crooked, curved, hunched, stooped, twisted; corrupt, crooked, dishonest, fraudulent; gay, homosexual

bent on *adj* determined, disposed, fixed, inclined, insistent, predisposed, resolved, set

bequest *n* bequeathal, bestowal, dower, endowment, estate, gift, heritage, inheritance, legacy, settlement, trust

berate *v* castigate, censure, criticize, chide, harangue, lambaste, rebuke, reprimand, reprove, scold

bereavement *n* deprivation, loss; decease, demise, passing

bereft of *adj* cut off from, deprived of, destitute, devoid of, lacking, minus, parted from

berserk *adj* amok, crazed, crazy, enraged, frantic, frenzied, hysterical, insane, mad, maniacal, manic, rabid, raging, raving, uncontrollable, unrestrainable, violent, wild

berth *n* bed, billet, bunk, cot, hammock; anchorage, dock, harbour, haven, mooring, pier, port, tie up, quay, wharf

berth *v* anchor, dock, land; accommodate, house, lodge, put up, shelter, sleep

beseech *v* adjure, ask, beg, call upon, crave, entreat, implore, importune, invoke, petition, plead, pray, solicit, sue, supplicate

beset *v* attack, bother, harass, plague, trouble, worry

beside *prep* abreast of, adjacent to, alongside, at the side of, close to, near, nearby, neighbouring, next door to, next to, overlooking

besides *adv* also, as well, further, furthermore, in addition, moreover, otherwise, too, what's more

besiege *v* beleaguer, beset, blockade, confine, encircle, encompass, environ, hedge in, hem in, invest, lay siege to, shut in, surround

best *adj* chief, excellent, finest, first, first-class, first-rate, foremost, high est, leading, most excellent, outstanding, perfect, pre-eminent, principal, superlative, supreme, top, worthiest, unsurpassed; (*Inf*) ace, crack; advantageous, apt, correct, golden, most fitting, right; greatest, largest, most

best *adv* advantageously, attractively, excellently, most fortunately; extremely, greatly, most highly

best *n* choice, cream, elite, favourite, finest, first, pick, prime, top

bestial *adv* animal, barbaric, barbarous, beastlike, beastly, brutal, brutish, carnal, depraved, gross, inhuman, low, savage, sensual, sordid, vile

bestow *v* accord, allot, apportion, award, commit, confer, donate, entrust, give, grant, honour with, impart, lavish, present, render to

bet *n* ante, gamble, hazard, long shot, pledge, risk, speculation, stake, venture, wager

bet *v* chance, gamble, hazard, pledge, put money on, risk, speculate, stake, venture, wager

betray *v* be disloyal, break one's promise, break with, inform on; blurt out, disclose, divulge, expose, lay bare, let slip, manifest, reveal, show, tell, tell on, uncover, unmask; abandon, desert, forsake, jilt, walk out on

betrayal *n* deception, disloyalty, double-cross, duplicity, falseness, perfidy, treachery, treason, trickery, unfaithfulness; blurting out, disclosure, divulgence, giving away, revelation, telling

better *adj* bigger, excelling, finer, fitter, greater, higher-quality, larger, more appropriate, preferable, superior, surpassing, worthier; cured, fitter, fully recovered, healthier, improving, less ill, mending, more healthy, on the mend, progressing, recovering, stronger, well; bigger, greater

better *adv* in a more excellent manner, in a superior way, more advantageously, to a greater degree

between *prep* amidst, among, halfway, in the middle of, mid

bewail *v* bemoan, cry over, deplore, express sorrow, grieve for, keen, lament, moan, mourn, regret, repent, rue, wail, weep over

beware *v* avoid, be careful, guard against, heed, look out, mind, refrain from, shun, steer clear of, take heed, watch out

bewilder *v* baffle, befuddle, bemuse, confound, confuse, daze, mix up, mystify, perplex, puzzle, stupefy

bewitch *v* allure, attract, beguile, captivate, charm, enchant, enrapture, entrance, fascinate, hypnotize, spellbind

beyond *prep* above, apart from, at a distance, away from, before, farther, out of range, out of reach, over, past, remote, superior to, yonder

bias *n* bent, bigotry, favouritism, inclination, intolerance, leaning, narrow-mindedness, one-sideness, partiality, penchant, predilection, predisposition, prejudice, proclivity, proneness, propensity, tendency, turn, unfairness

biased *adj* distorted, embittered, jaundiced, one-sided, partial, predisposed, prejudiced, slanted, swayed, warped, weighted

bicker *v* argue, disagree, dispute, fall out, fight, quarrel, row, scrap, spar, squabble, wrangle

bid *v* offer, proffer, propose, submit, tender; call, greet, say, tell, wish; ask, call, charge, command, desire, direct, enjoin, instruct, invite, require, solicit, summon, tell

bid *n* advance, amount, offer, price, proposal, proposition, submission, sum, tender; attempt, effort, endeavour, try, venture

bidding *n* behest, call, charge, command, demand, direction, injunction, instruction, invitation, order, request, summons

big *adj* bulky, colossal, considerable, enormous, extensive, gigantic, great, huge, hulking, immense, large, massive, prodigious, sizable, spacious, substantial, vast, voluminous; eminent, important, influential, leading, main, momentous, paramount, powerful, prime, principal, prominent, serious, significant, valuable, weighty; altruistic, benevolent, generous, gracious, heroic, magnani mous, noble, princely, unselfish; arrogant, boastful, bragging, conceited, haughty, inflated, proud

bigot *n* chauvinist, dogmatist, fanatic, homophobic, racist, sexist

bill *n* account, charges, invoice, note of charge, reckoning, score, statement, tally; advertisement, broadsheet, bulletin, circular, handout, leaflet, notice, poster; measure, piece of legislation, projected law, proposal; beak, mandible, neb, nib

bill *v* charge, debit, figure, invoice, reckon, record

billet *n* accommodation, barracks, housing, living quarters, lodging, quarters

billet *v* accommodate, berth, quarter, station
billow *n* breaker, crest, roller, surge, swell, tide, wave; cloud, deluge, flood, outpouring, rush
billow *v* balloon, belly, puff up, rise up, roll, surge, swell
bind *v* attach, fasten, glue, hitch, lash, paste, rope, secure, stick, strap, tie, truss, wrap; compel, constrain, engage, force, necessitate, obligate, oblige, prescribe, require; confine, detain, hamper, hinder, restrain, restrict; bandage, cover, dress, encase, swathe, wrap; border, edge, finish, hem, trim
binding *adj* compulsory, conclusive, imperative, indissoluble, irrevocable, mandatory, necessary, obligatory, unalterable
biography *n* account, life, life story, memoir, memoirs, profile
birth *n* childbirth, confinement, delivery, nativity, parturition; beginning, emergence, fountainhead, genesis, origin, rise, source, start; ancestry, background, blood, breeding, derivation, descent, extraction, family, forebears, genealogy, heritage, origin, line, lineage, nobility, noble, extraction, parentage, pedigree, race, stock, strain
bisect *v* bifurcate, cross, cut across, cut in half, cut in two, divide in two, halve, intersect, separate, split, split down the middle
bit *n* atom, chip, chunk, crumb, flake, fragment, grain, hunk, iota, jot, lump, mite, morsel, mouthful, part, particle, piece, portion, scrap, segment, shred, slice, sliver, small piece, speck, trace, whit
bitchy *adj* backbiting, catty, cruel, malicious, mean, nasty, snide, spiteful, vicious, vindictive
bite *v* champ, chew, clamp, crunch, crush, cut, gnaw, hold, masticate, munch, nibble, nip, pierce, pinch, seize, snap, tear, wound
bite *n* itch, nip, pinch, prick, smarting, sting, tooth marks, wound; food, light meal, morsel, mouthful, piece, snack; edge, kick, piquancy, punch, pungency, spice, spiciness
biting *adj* bitter, cold, cutting, freezing, harsh, nipping, penetrating, piercing, stinging; acid, bitter, caustic, cutting, mordant, sarcastic, scathing, sharp, stinging, withering
bitter *adj* acid, acrid, astringent, sharp, sour, tart, unsweetened, vinegary; acrimonious, begrudging, crabbed, embittered, hostile, morose, resentful, sore, sour, sullen
bitterness *n* acerbity, acidity, sharpness, sourness, tartness, vinegariness; animosity, grudge, hostility, pique, rancour, resentment
bizarre *adj* abnormal, comical, curious, eccentric, extraordinary, fantastic, freakish, ludicrous, odd, offbeat, outlandish, peculiar, queer, ridiculous, strange, unusual, weird; (*Inf*) oddball, off-the-wall, wacky, way-out
black *adj* coal-black, dark, dusky, ebony, inky, jet, murky, pitchy, raven, sable, starless, stygian, swarthy; atrocious, dark, depressing, dismal, distressing, doleful, funereal, gloomy, hopeless, horrible, lugubrious, melancholy, mournful, ominous, pessimistic, sad, sombre; bad, devilish, diabolic,

evil, foul, heinous, iniquitous, nefarious, villainous, wicked;

black *v* ban, bar, blacklist, boycott

blacken *v* befoul, begrime, besmudge, cloud, darken, grow black, make black, smudge, soil; calumniate, decry, defame, defile, denigrate, dishonour, malign, slander, smear, smirch, stain, sully, taint, tarnish, traduce, vilify

blacklist *v* ban, bar, boycott, debar, exclude, expel, ostracize, preclude, proscribe, reject, repudiate, snub, vote against

black magic *n* black art, diabolism, necromancy, sorcery, voodoo, witchcraft, wizardry

blackmail *n* bribe, exaction, extortion, intimidation, milking, ransom

blackout *n* coma, faint, loss of consciousness, oblivion, swoon, unconsciousness; power cut, power failure

black sheep *n* disgrace, dropout, outcast, prodigal, renegade, reprobate, wastrel

blame *n* accountability, culpability, fault, guilt, incrimination, liability, onus, responsibility; accusation, castigation, censure, charge, complaint, condemnation, criticism, recrimination, reproach, reproof

blame *v* accuse, admonish, censure, charge, chide, condemn, criticize, disapprove, express disapprobation, find fault with, hold responsible, indict, reprehend, reproach, reprove, take to task, upbraid

blameless *adj* above suspicion, clean, faultless, guiltless, immaculate, impeccable, innocent, in the clear, irreproachable, not to blame, perfect, stainless, unblemished, unoffending, unspotted, unsullied, untarnished, upright, virtuous

bland *adj* boring, dull, flat, flavourless, humdrum, insipid, mediocre, mild, monotonous, neutral, nondescript, safe, tasteless, tedious, uncontroversial, undistinctive, unexciting, uninspiring, uninteresting, vapid, weak; affable, amiable, congenial, courteous, friendly, gentle, gracious, smooth, suave, unemotional, urbane

blank *adj* bare, clean, clear, empty, plain, spotless, uncompleted, unfilled, unmarked, vacant, void, white; at a loss, bewildered, confounded, confused, disconcerted, dumbfounded, expressionless, muddled, nonplussed, perplexed, puzzled, uncomprehending

blank *n* emptiness, empty space, gap, nothingness, space, vacancy, vacuity, vacuum, void

blanket *n* afghan, bedcover, cover, coverlet, rug, spread, throw; carpet, cloak, coat, coating, covering, envelope, film, layer, mantle, sheet, wrapper, wrapping

blanket *v* cloak, cloud, coat, conceal, cover, eclipse, hide, mask, obscure, suppress, surround

blare *v* blast, boom, clamour, clang, honk, hoot, peal, resound, roar, scream, sound out, toot, trumpet

blasé *adj* apathetic, bored, indifferent, lukewarm, nonchalant, offhand, unenthusiastic, uninterested, unmoved

blasphemous *adj* godless, impious, irreligious, irreverent, profane, sacrilegious, ungodly, unholy

blasphemy *n* cursing, desecration, execration, impiety, impiousness, indignity, irreverence, profanation, profaneness, profanity, sacrilege, swearing

blast *n* blow, draught, gale, rush, storm; bellow, blare, boom, clang, honk, peal, screech, toot, wail; blowing up, detonation, discharge, eruption, explosion; attack, castigation, criticism, outburst, rebuke, reprimand, reproof

blast *v* blare, boom, roar; blow, demolish, explode, ruin, shatter; blight, crush, dash, destroy, kill, mar, ruin, shrivel, spoil, wreck, wither; attack, berate, criticize, rebuke, reprimand; discharge, let fly

blatant *adj* bald, barefaced, brazen, conspicuous, flagrant, flaunting, glaring, naked, obtrusive, obvious, ostentatious, outright, overt, prominent, pronounced, shameless, sheer, unmitigated

blaze *n* bonfire, conflagration, fire, flame, flames, holocaust; beam, brilliance, flare, flash, glare, gleam, glitter, glow, light, radiance; burst, eruption, flare-up, outbreak, rush, storm, torrent

blaze *v* be ablaze, burn, burst into flames, catch fire; beam, flare, flash, glare, glitter; blow up, boil, explode, smoulder; blast, discharge, fire, let fly

blazon *v* advertise, broadcast, proclaim, publish, trumpet

bleak *adj* arid, bare, barren, chilly, cold, desolate, exposed, gaunt, open, raw, unsheltered, waste, weatherbeaten, windswept, windy; cheerless, comfortless, depressing, discouraging, disheartening, dismal, dreary, gloomy, grim, hopeless, joyless, miserable, sombre, unpromising, wretched

blemish *n* birthmark, blot, blotch, bruise, blur, defect, discolouration, disfigurement, disgrace, dishonour, fault, flaw, imperfection, mark, naevus, patch, scar, smudge, speck, spot, stain, taint

blench *v* cower, flinch, quail, quiver, shrink, shudder, tremble

blend *v* amalgamate, coalesce, combine, compound, fuse, intermix, meld, merge, mingle, mix, synthesize, unite; complement, fit, go well, go with, harmonize, suit

blend *n* alloy, amalgam, amalgamation, combination, composite, compound, concoction, fusion, homogenization, meld, mingling, mix, mixture, synthesis, union

bless *v* anoint, consecrate, dedicate, exalt, extol, give thanks to, glorify, hallow, invoke happiness on, laud, magnify, ordain, praise, sanctify, thank; bestow, endow, favour, give, grace, grant, provide grace; ask God's favour; give benediction for, invoke happiness

blessed *adj* adored, beatified, divine, hallowed, holy, revered, sacred, sanctified; endowed, favoured, fortunate, granted, lucky

blessing *n* benediction, benison, commendation, consecration, dedication, grace, invocation, thanksgiving; approbation, approval, backing, concurrence, consent, favour, good wishes, leave, permission, regard, sanction, support; advantage, benefit, boon, bounty, favour, gain, gift, godsend, good fortune, help, kindness, profit, service, windfall

blight *n* canker, decay, disease, fungus, infestation, mildew, pest, pestilence, rot

blight *v* blast, destroy, injure, nip in the bud, ruin, shrivel, taint with mildew, wither; annihilate, crush, dash, destroy, disappoint, frustrate, kill, mar, nullify, ruin, spoil, wreck

blind *adj* destitute of vision, eyeless, sightless, stone-blind, unseeing, unsighted, visionless; careless, heedless, ignorant, inattentive, inconsiderate, indifferent, indiscriminate, injudicious, insensitive, morally darkened, neglectful, oblivious, prejudiced, thoughtless, unaware of, unconscious of, uncritical, undiscerning, unmindful of, unobservant, unreasoning; hasty, impetuous, irrational, mindless, rash, reckless, senseless, uncontrollable, uncontrolled, unthinking, violent, wild

blind *n* camouflage, cloak, cover, façade, feint, front, mask, masquerade, screen, smoke screen

bliss *n* beatitude, blessedness, blissfulness, delight, ecstasy, elation, euphoria, gladness, happiness, heaven, joy, paradise, pleasure, rapture

blissful *adj* delighted, ecstatic, elated, enchanted, enraptured, euphoric, happy, heavenly, in ecstasies, joyful, joyous, rapturous, wonderful

blithe *adj* animated, buoyant, carefree, cheerful, cheery, debonair, gladsome, happy, jaunty, lighthearted, merry, mirthful, sprightly, sunny, vivacious

blitz *n* assault, attack, blitzkrieg, bombardment, bombing, offensive, onslaught, raid, strike

blizzard *n* blast, gale, snowstorm, squall, storm, tempest

bloated *adv* dilated, distended, enlarged, full, inflated, puffed up, swollen

blob *n* ball, bead, dad, dollop, drop, globule, lump, mass

block *n* bar, brick, cake, chunk, cube, hunk, ingot, lump, mass, piece, rectangle, square, wedge; bar, barrier, blockage, hindrance, impediment, jam, obstacle, obstruction, prevent, stoppage

block *v* bung up, choke, clog, close, obstruct, plug, stop up; arrest, bar, check, deter, halt, hinder, impede, prevent, obstruct, stop, thwart

blockade *n* barricade, barrier, closure, encirclement, hindrance, impediment, obstacle, obstruction, restriction, siege, stoppage

blockage *n* bar, barrier, bung, clog, impediment, jam, obstacle, obstruction, occlusion, plug, stopper

blond *adj* fair, fair-haired, flaxen, golden, golden-haired

blood *n* gore, lifeblood, vital fluids; ancestry, birth, consanguinity, descendants, descent, extraction, family, genealogy, kindred, kinship, lineage, noble, relations

bloodshed *n* blood bath, bloodletting, butchery, carnage, gore, killing, massacre, murder, slaughter, slaying, violence, war

bloodthirsty *adj* barbaric, barbarous, brutal, cruel, ferocious, inhuman, murderous, ruthless, sadistic, savage, vicious, violent, warlike

bloody *adj* bleeding, blood-soaked, blood-splattered, blood-stained, gaping, gory, raw, unstaunched; cruel, ferocious, fierce, sanguinary, savage

bloom *n* blossom, bud, efflorescence, flower, opening; beauty, blush, flourishing, flush, freshness, glow, health, lustre, perfection, prime, radiance, rosiness, vigour

bloom *v* blossom, blow, bud, burgeon, open, sprout

blossom *n* bloom, bud, floret, flower, flowers

blossom *v* bloom, burgeon, flower; bloom, develop, flourish, get on well, grow, mature, progress, prosper, succeed, thrive

blot *n* blotch, mark, patch, smear, smudge, speckle, splodge, spot, stain; blemish, blur, defect, disgrace, fault, flaw, spot, stain, taint

blow *v* blast, breathe, exhale, fan, huff, pant, puff, waft; flow, rush, stream, whirl, whisk; bear, buffet, drive, fling, flutter, sweep, waft, whirl, whisk; blare, mouth, pipe, play, sound, toot, trumpet, vibrate

blow *n* blast, draught, flurry, gale, gust, puff, strong breeze, tempest, wind; bang, bash, belt, knock, punch, rap, smack, stroke, thump, whack; affliction, bolt from the blue, bombshell, calamity, catastrophe, comedown, disappointment, disaster, jolt, misfortune, reverse, setback, shock, upset

blow up *v* bloat, distend, enlarge, expand, fill, inflate, puff up, pump up, swell; blast, bomb, burst, detonate, dynamite, explode, go off, rupture, shatter; enlarge, exaggerate, heighten, magnify, overstate

blue *adj* azure, cerulean, cobalt, cyan, indigo, navy, sapphire, sky blue, turquoise, ultramarine; dejected, depressed, despondent, dismal, downcast, down-hearted, fed up, gloomy, glum, low, melancholy, miserable, sad, unhappy; (*Inf*) down in the dumps

blueprint *n* design, draft, layout, outline, pattern, pilot scheme, plan, project, prototype, scheme, sketch

bluff *v* con, deceive, defraud, delude, fake, feign, hoax, humbug, lie, mislead, pretend, sham, take in, trick

bluff *n* bluster, boast, braggadocio, bragging, bravado, deceit, deception, fake, feint, fraud, humbug, idle boast, lie, mere, show, pretence, sham, show, subterfuge

bluff *adj* blunt, candid, direct, frank, open, outspoken, plain-spoken; abrupt, acclivitous, perpendicular, sheer, steep, sudden

blunder *n* error, fault, *faux pas*, gaffe, inaccuracy, mistake, oversight, slip; (*Inf*) boo-boo, bloomer, clanger, cock-up, howler, slip-up

blunder *v* err, make a mistake; (*Inf*) blow it, slip up, screw up; falter, flounder, lurch, stumble; botch, bungle, make a mess of, mismanage

blunt *adj* dull, dulled, edgeless, pointless, rounded, unsharpened; bluff, brusque, discourteous, explicit, forthright, frank, impolite, outspoken, plain spoken, rude, straightforward, tactless, trenchant, uncivil, unpolished

blur *v* becloud, bedim, befog, cloud, darken, dim, fog, make hazy, make indistinct, make vague, mask, mist-up, obscure, soften, steam up, veil; blot, smear, smudge, spot, stain;

blur *n* blear, blurredness, cloudiness, confusion, dimness, fog, haze, indistinctness, obscurity

blurt out *v* babble, blab, cry, disclose, exclaim, let out, let slip, reveal, say; (*Inf*) spill the beans

blush *v* colour, crimson, flush, go pink, redden, turn red, turn scarlet

bluster *v* boast, brag, bulldoze, bully, domineer, hector, rant, roar, roister, storm, swagger, swell, vaunt

bluster *n* bluff, boasting, bombast, bragging, bravado, crowing, swaggering

board *n* beam, panel, piece of timber, plank, slat, timber; daily meals, food, meals, provisions, victuals; advisers, advisory group, body, committee, conclave, council, directorate, directors, panel, trustees

board *v* embark, embus, enplane, enter, entrain, go aboard, go on board, mount; accommodate, feed, house, lodge, put up, quarter, room, take in

boast *v* blow one's own trumpet, bluster, brag, crow, exaggerate, puff, show off, strut, swagger, vaunt; be proud of, congratulate oneself on, exhibit, flatter oneself, possess, pride oneself on, exhibit, flatter oneself, possess, pride oneself on, show off; (*Inf*) talk big

boast *n* avowal, brag, vaunt; gem, joy, pride, pride and joy, source of pride, treasure

boastful *adj* bragging, cocky, conceited, crowing, egotistical, puffed-up, swaggering, vainglorious, vaunting

bodily *adv* carnal, corporeal, fleshly, material, physical

body *n* build, figure, flesh, form, frame, physique, shape, torso, trunk; cadaver, carcass, corpse, dead body, relics, remains; bulk, essence, main part, mass, material, matter, substance; association, authority, band, collection, committee, company, confederation, congress, corporation, group, organization, society; crowd, horde, majority, mass, mob, multitude, throng

bog *n* fen, marsh, marshland, mire, morass, moss, peat bog, quagmire, slough, swamp, wetland

bogus *adj* artificial, counterfeit, dummy, fake, false, forged, fraudulent, imitation, make believe, mock, phoney, pseudo, quasi, sham, spurious

bohemian *adj* alternative, artistic, avant-garde, eccentric, exotic, left-bank, nonconformist, offbeat, original, unconventional, unorthodox

boil *v* bubble, cook, heat, simmer, stew; agitate, bubble, churn, effervesce, fizz, foam, froth, seethe; angry, explode, fume, furious, indignant, rage, rant, rave; (*Inf*) blow a fuse, blow one's top, fly off the handle, go off at the deep end, go up the wall, hit the roof

boiling *adj* baking, blistering, roasting, scorching, searing, sweltering, torrid, very hot; fuming, furious, incensed, indignant, infuriated, irate, seething; (*Inf*) mad

boisterous *adj* active, bouncy, clamorous, disorderly, exuberant, frisky, impetuous, lively, loud, noisy, obstreperous, riotous, rollicking, romping, rowdy, rumbustious, spirited, unrestrained, unruly, uproarious, vociferous, wild; blustery, breezy, gusting, raging, rough, squally, stormy, turbulent

bold *adj* adventurous, audacious, brave, confident, courageous, daring, dauntless, enterprising, fearless, gallant, heroic, intrepid, lionhearted, valiant, valorous; bright, colourful, conspicuous, eye-catching, flashy, forceful, lively, loud, prominent, pronounced, showy, spirited, striking, strong, vivid; barefaced, brash, brazen, cheeky, forward, immodest, impudent, saucy

bolshie *adj* annoying, awkward, difficult, stubborn, unhelpful

bolster *n* cushion, pad, pillow, support; aid, assist, boost, buoy up, hold up, reinforce, strengthen, support

bolt *n* bar, catch, fastener, latch, lock, sliding bar; peg, pin, rivet, rod; bound, dart, dash, escape, flight, rush, spring, sprint; arrow, dart, missile, projectile, shaft, thunderbolt

bolt *v* bar, fasten, latch, lock, secure; cram, devour, gobble, gorge, gulp, guzzle, stuff, swallow whole, wolf; abscond, bound, dart, dash, escape, flee, fly, hurtle, jump, leap, make a break, run, run for it, rush, spring

bomb *n* bombshell, charge, device, explosive, grenade, mine, missile, projectile, rocket, shell, torpedo

bomb *v* attack, blitz, blow up, bombard, destroy, shell, strafe, torpedo

bombard *v* assault, attack, blitz, bomb, cannonade, pepper, fire at, fusillade, pound, shell, strafe

bombast *n* affectedness, bluster, braggadocio, euphuism, grandiloquence, magniloquence, ostentation, pretentiousness, rant, rodomontade, turgidity, verbosity

bona fide *adj* actual, authentic, genuine, honest, lawful, legal, legitimate, real, sound, sterling, true; (*Inf*) kosher

bonanza *n* boon, bonus, godsend, run of luck, windfall

bond *n* band, binding, chain, cord, fastening, fetter, ligature, link, manacle, shackle, tie; affiliation, affinity, attachment, connection, ligature, link, nexus, relation, tie, union; agreement, compact, contract, covenant, guarantee, obligation, pledge, promise, word

bond *v* bind, connect, fasten, fix together, fuse, glue, gum, paste

bondage *n* captivity, enslavement, oppression, serfdom, servitude, slavery, thraldom

bonus *n* benefit, boon, bounty, commission, dividend, extra, gain, gift, gratuity, honorarium, perk, plus, premium, prize, reward, tip

book *n* manual, opus, publication, roll, scroll, textbook, title, tome, tract, treatise, volume, work; album, diary, exercise book, jotter, notebook, pad

book *v* arrange for, bill, charter, engage, line up, make reservations, organize, procure, programme, reserve, schedule

boom *v* bang, blast, crash, explode,

resound, reverberate, roar, roll, rumble, thunder; develop, expand, flourish, gain, grow, increase, intensify, prosper, spurt, strengthen, succeed, swell, thrive

boom *n* bang, blast, burst, clap, crash, explosion, roar, rumble, thunder; advance, boost, development, expansion, gain, growth, improvement, increase, jump, push, spurt, upsurge, upswing, upturn

boomerang *v* backfire, come back, rebound, return, reverse, ricochet

boon *n* advantage, benefaction, benefit, blessing, donation, favour, gain, good thing, grant, gratuity, perk, requisite, present, windfall

boon *adj* best, close, favourite, inseparable, intimate, special

boor *n* barbarian, lout, oaf, philistine, rough

boost *n* encouragement, help, hype, improvement, inspiration, praise, promotion, shot in the arm, stimulus, uplift; heave, hoist, lift, push, raise, shove, thrust; addition, expansion, improvement, increase, increment, jump, rise; advertisement, promotion, publicity, write-up

boost *v* add to, advance, amplify, assist, develop, expand, facilitate, foster, further, help, increase, promote, raise; elevate, heave, help, hoist, lift, raise; advertise, praise, promote, write up

boot *v* kick, knock; dismiss, eject, expel, kick out, oust, sack, throw out; load, make ready, prepare

booth *n* counter, stall, stand; cubicle, compartment, enclosure

booty *n* haul, loot, pillage, plunder, spoil; pickings, profits, spoils, takings, winnings; *(Inf)* swag

bordello *n* brothel, house of ill repute, house of prostitution, whorehouse

border *n* bound, boundary, bounds, brim, brink, confine, confines, edge, hem, limit, limits, lip, margin, rim, skirt, verge; borderline, boundary, frontier, line, march

borderline *adj* ambivalent, doubtful, equivocal, indecisive, indefinite, indeterminate, inexact, marginal, unclassifiable

bore *v* burrow, drill, gouge out, mine, penetrate, perforate, pierce, sink, tunnel; annoy, be tedious, bother, exhaust, fatigue, jade, pall on, pester, end to sleep, tire, trouble, vex, wear out, weary, worry

bore *n* borehole, calibre, diameter, drill hole, guage, hole, shaft, tunnel; bother, dullard, dull person, nuisance, pest, tiresome person, wearisome talker; (*Inf*) pain in the neck

boredom *n* apathy, doldrums, dullness, ennui, flatness, irksomeness, monotony, sameness, tediousness, tedium, weariness

boring *adj* dead, dull, flat, humdrum, insipid, monotonous, repetitious, routine, stale, tedious, tiresome, tiring, unexciting, uninteresting, unvaried, wearisome

borrow *v* cadge, scrounge, take and return, take on loan, use temporarily; acquire, adopt, appropriate, copy, filch, grab, imitate, obtain, pilfer, pirate, plagiarize, purloin, simulate, steal, take, use, usurp

bosom *n* breast, bust, chest; (*Inf*) boobs, bristols, knockers, tits; affections, being, centre, core, emotions, feelings, heart, sentiments, soul, spirit, sympathies

bosom *adj* boon, cherished, close, confidential, faithful, intimate, thick as thieves, very dear

boss *n* administrator, chief, controller, director, employer, executive, foreman, head, leader, manager, master, overseer, owner, superintendent, supervisor

boss *v* administrate, command to, control, domineer, in charge of, head, manage, order about, preside, run, supervise

bossy *adj* authoritarian, autocratic, despotic, dictatorial, overbearing

botch *v* blunder, bungle, butcher, cobble, fumble, mar, mend, mess, mismanage, muff, patch, spoil; (*Inf*) cock up, foul up, louse up, make a hash of, mess up, screw up

bother *v* alarm, annoy, concern, dismay, distress, disturb, harass, inconvenience, irritate, molest, nag, pester, plague, provoke, put out, torment, upset, vex, worry

bother *n* aggravation, annoyance, bustle, difficulty, flurry, fuss, inconvenience, irritation, molestation, nuisance, perplexity, pest, problem, strain, trouble, vexation, worry

bottle *n* carafe, decanter, demijohn, flagon, flask, pitcher; boldness, bravery, confidence, courage, daring, nerve, pluck; (*Inf*) pluck, spunk

bottleneck *n* blockage, congestion, constriction, hold up, jam, narrowing, obstruction

bottom *n* base, basis, bed, deepest part, depths, floor, foot, foundation, groundwork, lowest part, pedestal, support; (*Inf*) backside, bum; lower side, sole, underneath, underside

bottom *adj* base, basement, basic, fundamental, ground, last, lowest, undermost

bottomless *adj* deep, fathomless, immeasurable; boundless, inexhaustable, infinite, unlimited

bough *n* branch, limb, twig

boulder *n* rock, stone

boulevard *n* avenue, broad road, drive, promenade, roadway, thoroughfare

bounce *v* back, bob, bound, bump, jounce, jump, leap, rebound, recoil, resile, ricochet, spring back, thump

bounce *n* bound, elasticity, give, rebound, recoil, resilience, spring, springiness; animation, dynamism, energy, life, liveliness, pep, vigour, vitality, vivacity

bound *adj* cased, fastened, fixed, pinioned, secured, tied, tied up; certain, destined, doomed, fated, sure; beholden, committed, compelled, constrained, duty-bound, forced, obligated, obliged, pledged, required

bound *v* bob, bounce, caper, frisk, gambol, hurdle, jump, leap, pounce, prance, skip, spring, vault

bound *n* bounce, jump, hop, hurdle, leap, spring, vault; bob, caper, curvet, dance, frisk, frolic, gambol, prance, skip

bound *n* circumscribe, cramp, define, delimit, demarcate, restrict, restrain, straiten; circumscribe, encircle, enclose, hem in, surround, wall in; abut, adjacent to, adjoin, be next to, border

boundary *n* barrier, border, borderline, bounds, brink, confines, edges, extremity, fringes, frontier, limits, march, margins, perimeter, periphery, precinct, termination, verge

boundless *adj* endless, illimitable, immeasurable, immense, incalculable, inexhaustible, infinite, limitless, measureless, never ending, unbounded, unconfined, unending, unlimited, untold, vast

bountiful *adj* abundant, ample, bounteous, copious, exuberant, lavish, luxuriant, plenteous, plentiful, prolific; beneficent, bounteous, generous, liberal, magnanimous, munificent, open-handed, princely, unstinting

bounty *n* bonus, gratuity, premium, recompense, remuneration, reward

bouquet *n* bunch, buttonhole, chaplet, corsage, garland, nosegay, posy, spray, wreath; aroma, fragrance, odour, perfume, redolence, scent, smell

bourgeois *adj* middle-class, propertied, property-owning; capitalistic, materialistic, money-oriented

bout *n* battle, boxing match, competition, contest, encounter, engagement, fight, match, set-to, struggle; attack, fit, spell, paroxysm

bovine *adj* cattle-like, cow-like; dense, dim-witted, doltish, slow, stupid, thick

bow *v* bend, bob, droop, genuflect, incline, make obeisance, nod, stoop; accept, acquiesce, nod, stoop; comply, concede, defer, give in, relent, submit, surrender, yield

bow *n* bending, bob, genuflexion, inclination, nod, obeisance, salaam

bowdlerize *v* blue-pencil, censor, expurgate

bowel *n* colon, intestine, large intestine, small intestine

bowels *pln* entrails, guts, intestines, viscera; belly, core, depths, inside, interior; (*Inf*) innards, insides

box *n* bin, carton, case, casket, chest, coffer, container, crate, pack, package, portmanteau, receptacle, trunk; cabin, compartment, cubicle, enclosure, kiosk, hut; cuff, slap, punch, thump

box *v* bundle up, package, wrap; fight, grapple, spar; batter, cuff, buffet, knock, hit, pummel, slap, strike, thump; (*Inf*) belt, clout, slug, whack, whop

boxer *n* fighter, prizefighter, sparing partner

boy *n* fellow, junior, kid, lad, school boy, stripling, whippersnapper, youngster, youth; garçon, page, servant, waiter

boycott *v* avoid, ban, bar, black, blacklist, debar, embargo, exclude, ostracize, outlaw, prohibit, proscribe, refrain from, refuse, reject, spurn

boyfriend *n* admirer, beau, date, follower, lover, man, steady, suitor, swain, sweetheart, toy boy, young man

bracing *adj* brisk, chilly, cool, crisp, energizing, exhilarating, fortifying, fresh, healthful, health-giving, invigorating, lively, refreshing, restorative, reviving, rousing, stimulating, strengthening, tonic, vigorous, vitalizing

bracket *n* buttress, prop, support; angle bracket, brace, parenthesis, round bracket, square bracket; category, class, classification, division, grade, group, order, section, set

brackish *adj* bitter, briny, impure, saline, undrinkable, unsavoury

brag *v* bluster, boast, crow, show off

braggart *n* bluster, boaster, brag, braggadocio, fanfaronade, gasconader

braid *v* entwine, intertwine, interweave, plait, twist, wind

braid *n* tape, thread, twine, yarn; pigtail, plait

brain *n* cerebral matter, encephalon; head, intellect, intelligence, wit; powers of reasoning; genius, thinker, intellect, intellectual, mastermind, mind, polymath, pundit, sage; (*Inf*) egghead, Einstein, highbrow

brainless *adj* foolish, idiotic, inept, mindless, senseless, stupid, thoughtless, unintelligent, witless

brainwashing *n* conditioning, indoctrination, persuasion

brake *n* check, constraint, control, curb, rein, restraint

brake *v* check, decelerate, halt, moderate, reduce speed, slacken, slow, stop

branch *n* arm, bough, limb, offshoot, prong, ramification, shoot, spray, sprig; chapter, department, division, local office, office, part, section, subdivision, subsection, wing; feeder, subsiduary, tributary

branch *v* bifurcate, divaricate, divide, fork, subdivide; diverge, separate; depart from, deviate from, diverge from, go off at a tangent to; broaden, diversify, expand, extend, open up, spread out, widen

brand *n* kind, line, label, registered trade mark, trade name, trade mark; kind, sort, style, type, variety; earmark, identification, marker; blot, slur, stain, stigma, taint

brand *v* burn in, mark, scorch, stamp; engrave, fix, impress, imprint, print; denounce, discredit, disgrace, mark, stigmatize, taint

brandish *v* display, exhibit, flaunt, flourish, parade, raise, shake, show off, swing, wave, wield

brash *adj* aggressive, audacious, brazen, cheeky, cocky, forward, impertinent, impudent, insolent; careless, hasty, heedless, impetuous, impulsive, rash, reckless; garish, gaudy, ostentatious, tasteless, tawdry

brassy *adj* bold, brash, cheeky, flashy, forward, garish, self-assertive, showy; brass, metallic; blaring loud, noisy, raucous, piercing, shrill, thundering

bravado *n* arm, audacity, bluster, boast, boastfulness, bombast, brag, swagger, swaggering, vaunting

brave *adj* audacious, bold, courageous, daring, dauntless, fearless, gallant, game, heroic, intrepid, mettlesome, plucky, resolute, undaunted, valiant, valorous; fine, ostentatious, showy, spectacular, splendid

brave *n* fighter, fighting man, soldier, warrior

brave *v* bear, challenge, confront, defy, endure, put up with, stand up to, suffer

bravery *n* audacity, boldness, bravura, courage, daring, dauntless ness, doughtiness, fearlessness, for titude, gallantry, gameness, grit, hardihood, hardiness, heroism, indomitability, intrepidity, mettle, pluck, pluckiness, spirit, valour

brawl *n* affray, altercation, argument, battle, broil, clash, commotion, disagreement, disorder, dispute, fight, fracas, fray, mêlée, quarrel, row, rumpus, scuffle, squabble, tumult, uproar, wrangle

brawl *v* altercate, argue, battle, clash, dispute, fight, quarrel, scuffle, tussle, wrangle, wrestle

brawn *n* burliness, heftiness, might, muscle, muscularity, physical strength, physique, robustness

bray *v* hee-haw, neigh, whinny

brazen *adj* audacious, brash, brassy, cheeky, defiant, forward, impudent insolent, pert, presumptious, saucy, shameless, unashamed

breach *n* aperture, break, chasm, cleft, rack, fissure, gap, hole, opening, rent, rift, rupture, split; contravention, disobedience, infraction, infringement, noncompliance, nonobservance, offence, transgression, trespass, violation

breach *v* burst through, make a gap in, open up, rupture, split; contravene, defy, disobey, flaunt, infringe, transgress against, violate

bread *n* brown bread, white bread; aliment; diet, fare, food, necessities, nourishment, nutriment, provisions, subsistence, sustenance, viands, victuals; cash, finance, funds; (*Inf*) dibs, dosh, dough, shekels, spondulicks, tin

breadth *n* beam (of a ship), broadness, latitude, span, spread, thickness, wideness, width; broad mindedness, freedom, latitude, liberality, open-mindedness, openness, permissiveness; compass, degree, dimensions, expanse, immensity, magnitude, scale, spread, volume

break *v* batter, burst, crack, crash, demolish, destroy, disintegrate, divide, fracture, fragment, part, rend, separate, sever, shatter, shiver, smash, snap, splinter, split, tear; breach, contravene, disobey, infringe, transgress, violate; become damaged, be unusable, cease to operate; cow, cripple, demoralize, dispirit, enervate, enfeeble, impair, incapacitate, subdue, tame, undermine, weaken; beat, better, exceed, excel, go beyond, outdo, outstrip, surpass, top; appear, burst out, come forth suddenly, emerge, erupt, happen, occur; dash, escape, flee, fly, get away, run away; discontinue, give up, pause, rest, stop, take a break; cushion, diminish, lessen, moderate; collide with, crash, dash, hit, hurl

break *n* breach, chasm, cleft, crack, division, fissure, fracture, gap, gash, hole, opening, rent, rift, rupture, schism, split, tear; halt, hiatus, interlude, intermission, interruption, interval, lacuna, let-up, lull, pause, respite, rest, stop, suspension; coffee break, tea break, supper break; holiday, recess, time off, vacation; advantage, chance, gain, opening, opportunity, stroke of luck; alteration, change, variation

breakable *adj* brittle, crumbly, delicate, destructible, flimsy, fragile, frail, frangible, friable, insubstantial, jerry-built

breakdown *n* collapse, crackup, disintegration, disruption, failure, malfunctioning, mishap, seizing up, stoppage; analysis, categorization, classification, detailed list, diagnosis, dissection, itemization, segregation, separation; caving in, disintegration, going to pieces, loss of control, nervous breakdown

breaker *n* billow, comber, roller, surf, wave; white horses

break-in *n* breaking and entering, burglary, house-breaking, unlawful entry; robbery, theft

break-in *v* barge in, push one's way in; butt in, interfere, interrupt, intervene, intrude; break and enter, burgle, commit burglary, rob; condition, initiate, prepare, show the ropes to, tame, train; accustom, get used to, habituate

breakneck *adj* dangerous, fast, rapid, reckless, speedy, swift

breakthrough *n* advance, development, discovery, find, gain, improvement, invention, leap, progress, quantum leap, step forward

break-up *n* adjourn, cessation, collapse, disband, dismantle, disperse, disrupt, dissolve, divide, divorce, end, founder, part, scatter, separate, severance, split up, stop, suspend, terminate

breakwater *n* barrier, embankment, groyne, jetty, mole, sea wall

breath *n* air, animation, breathing, exhalation, expiration, gasp, gulp, inhalation, pant, respiration, wheeze; aroma, odour, smell, vapour, whiff; animation, life force, vital force; faint breeze, flutter, gust, puff, sigh, slight movement, waft, zephyr; hint, murmur, suggestion, suspicion, trace, undertone, whisper

breathe *v* draw in, gasp, gulp, inhale and exhale, pant, puff, respire, wheeze; be alive, have life, live; impart, imbue with, inject, instil, transfuse; articulate, express, murmur, say, sigh, voice, whisper; augur, betoken, express, indicate, intimate, manifest, suggest; blow, murmur, sigh, whisper

breather *n* break, halt, interval, pause, respite, rest, stop; breath of air, fresh air

breathless *adj* choking, exhausted, gasping, gulping, out of breath, panting, puffing, short-winded, spent, wheezing, winded; agog, all agog, anxious, astounded, avid, eager, excited, flabbergasted, on tenterhooks, open-mouthed, thunderstruck, with bated breath

breathtaking *adj* amazing, astonishing, astounding, awe-inspiring, awesome, exciting, heart-stirring, impressive, magnificent, moving, overwhelming, spectacular, stunning, thrilling

breed *v* bear, beget, bring forth, engender, generate, give birth, hatch, multiply, originate, procreate, produce, propagate, reproduce; bring up, cultivate, develop, discipline, educate, foster, instruct, nourish, nurture, raise, rear, train; arouse, bring about, cause, create, generate, give rise to, induce, occasion, originate, stir up

breed *n* brand, class, extraction, family, ilk, kind, line, lineage, pedigree, progeny, race, sort, species, stamp, stock, strain, type, variety; extraction, lineage, pedigree, race, stock; brand, class, kind, strain, type, variety

breeding *n* ancestry, cultivation, development, education, generation, lineage, multiplying, nurture, raising, rearing, reproduction, training, upbringing; civility, conduct, courtesy, cultivation, culture, gentility, manners, polish, refinement, urbanity

breeze *n* air, breath of wind, current of air, draught, flurry, gentle wind, gust, light wind, puff of air, waft, whiff, zephyr; land breeze, onshore breeze, sea breeze

breeze *v* drift, glide, flit, sail, sally, stroll, sweep

breezy *adj* airy, blowy, blustery, fresh, gusty, squally; blithe, buoy ant, casual, cheery, cheerful, easy-going, frisky, free and easy, lively, sparkling, spirited, sunny, vivacious; (*Inf*) bright-eyed and bushy-tailed

brevity *n* brachyolgy, conciseness, concision, condensation, crispness, curtness, economy of language, pithiness, succinctness, terseness; briefness, ephemerality, impermanence, shortness, transience, transitoriness

brew *v* boil, ferment, infuse, make beer, prepare by fermentation, seethe, soak, steep, stew; breed, concoct, contrive, develop, devise, excite, foment, form, gather, hatch, plan, plot, project, scheme, start, stir up; be in the offing, be threatening, gather, gather force, form, loom

brew *n* ale, beer, beverage, liquor, tea; infusion, preparation

bribe *n* allurement, carrot, corrupting gift, enticement, graft, incentive, inducement, lure, reward for treachery; (*Inf*) backhander, boodle, bung, graft, hush money, kickback, protection money, sweetner; (*Inf*) payola

bribe *v* buy off, corrupt, get at, influence by gifts, reward, square, suborn; (*Inf*) bung, fix, give a back hander, grease/oil the palm of, sweetener

bribery *n* buying off, corruption, graft, inducement, protection, subornation

bric-à-brac *n* baubles, bibelots, curios, gewgaws, knick-knacks, ornaments, trinkets

bridal *adj* conjugal, connubial, marital, matrimonial, nuptial

bridge *n* arch, flyover, overpass, span, viaduct; band, bonding, bond, connection, cord, link, tie

bridge *v* arch over, attach, bind, connect, couple, cross, cross over, extend across, go over, join, link, reach across, span, traverse, unite

bridle *n* halter; check, control, restraint

bridle *v* check, constrain, control, curb, govern, keep control of, keep in check, hold back, master, moderate, repress, restrain, subdue; bristle, draw oneself up, feel one's hackles rise, get angry

brief *adj* compendious, compressed, concise, condensed, crisp, curt, epigrammatic, laconic, limited, pithy, pointed, short, sparing, succinct, terse, thumbnail, to the point; ephemeral, fading, fast, fleeting, fugacious, hasty, impermanent, little, momentary, passing, quick, short, short-lived, swift, temporary, transient, transitory; abrupt, blunt, brusque, curt, sharp, short, surly

brief *n* abstract, digest, epitome, outline, precise, résumé, sketch, summary, synopsis; argument, case, contention, data, defence, demonstration, evidence, proof; briefing, data, directions, guidance, intelligence, instructions, preparation, priming

brief *v* advise, explain, fill in, give a rundown, guide, inform, instruct, prepare, prime

briefing *n* conference, directions, guidance, information, instruction, instructions, meeting, preamble, preparation, priming, rundown

briefly *adv* abruptly, briskly, casually, concisely, cursorily, curtly, economically, fleetingly, hastily, hurriedly, in a few words, in a nut shell, in brief, in outline, in passing, momentarily, precisely, quickly, shortly, temporarily, tersely

brigade *n* association, band, body, contingent, crew, force, group, organization, outfit, party, section, squad, team

brigand *n* bandit, criminal, desperado, freebooter, gangster, highwayman, marauder, outlaw, pirate, plunderer, ruffian, robber

bright *adj* beaming, blazing, brilliant, dazzling, effulgent, flashing, gleaming, glistening, glittering, glowing, incandescent, illuminated, intense, luminous, lustrous, phosphorescent, radiant, scintillating, shimmering, shining, sparkling, twinkling, vivid; clear, clement, cloudless, fair, sunny, pleasant, translucent, transparent, unclouded; bold, brilliant, glowing, intense, rich, vivid; acute, astute, aware, brainy, brilliant, clever, ingenious, intelligent, inventive, keen, proficient, quick, quick-witted, resourceful, sharp, smart; auspicious, encouraging, excellent, favourable, fortunate, golden, good, hopeful, lucky, optimistic, promising, propitious, prosperous; buoyant, cheerful, genial, glad, happy, jolly, joyful, lively, merry, sparky, vivacious

brighten *v* clear up, enliven, gleam, glow, illuminate, illumine, irradiate, light up, lighten, make brighter, shine; become cheerful, buoy up, cheer, cheer up, enliven, encourage, gladden, hearten, make happy, perk up

brilliance, brilliancy *n* beam, blaze, brightness, dazzle, effulgence, flash, gleam, glitter, intensity, luminosity, lustre, radiance, refulgence, resplendence, sheen, sparkle, vividness; aptitude, braininess, cleverness, distinction, éclat, excellence, genus, greatness, inventiveness, talent, wisdom; glamour, grandeur, illustriousness, lustre, magnificence, pomp, resplendence, splendidness, splendour

brilliant *adj* ablaze, beaming, bright, coruscating, dazzling, effulgent, gleaming, glittering, glossy, intense, luminous, lustrous, radiant, refulgent, resplendent, scintillating, shining, sparkling, vivid; celebrated, eminent, exceptional, famous, glorious, illustrious, magnificent, outstanding, splendid, superb; accomplished, acute, astute, brainy, bright, cerebral, clever, discerning, educated, erudite, expert, gifted, impressive, intellectual, intelligent, inventive, learned, masterly, penetrating, precocious, profound, quick, remarkable, resourceful, scholarly, smart, talented

brim *n* border, brink, circumference, edge, lip, margin, rim, skirt, verge; projecting edge, shield, shade, visor

brim *v* be filled up, be filled to the top, be full to capacity, be full to the top, overflow, run over, well over

brimful *adj* brimming, filled, flush, full, running over

bring *v* accompany, bear, carry, conduct, convey, deliver, escort, fetch, gather, guide, import, lead, take, transfer, transport, usher; cause, contribute to, create, effect, engender, inflict, occasion, produce, result in, wreak

bring about *v* accomplish, achieve, bring to pass, cause, compass, create, effect, effectuate, generate, give rise to, make happen, manage, occasion, occur, produce, realize

bring down *v* cause to fall, cut, lower, reduce; cause to fall, lay low, overthrow, pull down; cast down, depress, make desolate, sadden

bring up *v* breed, develop, educate, form, nurture, raise, rear, support, teach, train

brink *n* border, boundary, brim, edge, fringe, frontier, limit, lip, margin, point, rim, skirt, threshold, verge

brisk *adj* active, agile, alacritous, alert, animated, bustling, busy, energetic, fast, hectic, lively, nimble, no-nonsense, quick, rapid, speedy, spirited, sprightly, spry, swift, vigorous, vivacious; biting, bracing, crisp, energizing, exhilarating, fresh, invigorating, refreshing; (*Inf*) nippy

bristle *n* barb, designer stubble, hair, prickle, spine, stubble, thorn, whiskers; be angry, be infuriated, be maddened, bridle, flare up, rage, see red, seethe

brittle *adj* breakable, crisp, crumbling, crumbly, delicate, fragile, frail, frangible, friable, shatterable, shivery

broach *v* bring up, mention, propose, propound, put forward, suggest, submit; open, start, uncork; draw off, pierce, puncture, tap

broad *adj* ample, beamy, boundless, capacious, expansive, extensive, generous, large, roomy, spacious, vast, voluminous, wide, widespread; all-embracing, catholic, comprehensive, encyclopedic, far-reaching, general, global, inclusive, nonspecific, sweeping, undetailed, universal, unlimited, wide; broad-minded, free-thinking, just, liberal, open, permissive, progressive, tolerant, unbiased, unpredjudiced

broadcast *v* air, beam, cable, put on the air, radio, relay, show, telecast, televise, transmit; advertise, announce, circulate, disseminate, make public, proclaim, promulgate, publish, report, spread; disperse, scatter, sow, strew

broadcast *n* programme, radio/television show, show, telecast, transmission

broaden *v* add to, amplify, augment, become broader, develop, enlarge, expand, extend, fatten, increase, make wider, open up, spread, stretch, supplement, swell, widen

broad-minded *adj* catholic, cosmopolitan, dispassionate, flexible, forebearing, free-thinking, indulgent, just, liberal, open-minded, permissive, progressive, responsive, tolerant, unbiased, unbigoted, undogmatic, unprejudiced

broadside *n* barrage, cannonade, salvo; abuse, assault, attack, battering, censure, criticism, diatribe, harangue, onslaught

brochure *n* advertisement, booklet, circular, folder, handbill, hand-out, leaflet, mailshot, pamphlet

broiling *adj* boiling, burning hot, blistering, blistering/searing hot, hot, roasting, scorching

broke *adj* bankrupt, destitute, flat-broke, impecunious, impoverished, indigent, moneyless, penniless, poverty-stricken, ruined, stony-broke; (*Inf*) bust, cleaned out, skint, strapped for cash

broken *adj* burst, cracked, demolished, destroyed, fractured, fragmented, rent, ruptured, separated, severed, shattered, shivered, smashed, snapped, splintered, torn; perforated, split; pierced, punctured; bust, defective, exhausted, feeble, imperfect, inoperative, kaput, non-functioning, out of order, ruined, rundown, spent, weak; disconnected, discontinuous, discouraged, dispirited, disturbed, erratic, fragmentary, incomplete, intermittent, interrupted, spasmodic; beaten, browbeaten, crippled, crushed, defeated, demoralized, dishonoured, humbled, oppressed, overpowered, subdued, tamed, vanquished; contravened, disobeyed, disregarded, flaunted, ignored, infracted, infringed, transgressed, violated; disjointed, faltering, halted, hesitating, imperfect, stammering, stumbling

broken-down *adj* broken, collapsed, dilapidated, in disrepair, inoperative, not functioning, not in working order, old, out of commission, out of order, worn out; (*Inf*) bust, clapped out, kaput, on the blink

broken-hearted *adj* crestfallen, desolate, despairing, devastated, forlorn, grief-stricken heartbroken, inconsolable, miserable, mourning, overwhelmed, prostrated, sorrowing, woeful, wretched

broker *n* agent, broker-dealer, dealer, factor, go-between, insurance broker, intermediary, middleman, negotiator, stockbroker

brooch *n* breast-pin, clip, pin, tie-clip, tie-pin

brood *v* agonize, dwell upon, fret, meditate, mope, mull over, muse, ponder, repine, ruminate, sulk, think upon, worry; cover young, hatch eggs, incubate eggs

brood *n* breed, chicks, children, clutch, family, hatch, infants, issue, litter, nest, offspring, progeny, young, youngsters

brook *n* beck, burn, rill, rivulet, runnel, stream, streamlet, watercourse

brother *n* relation, relative, sibling; associate, colleague, companion, compeer, comrade, confrère, fellow member, partner; cleric, friar, monk,

regular, religious; (*Inf*) mate, pal
brotherhood *n* brotherliness, camaraderie, companionship, comradeship, *espirit de corps*, fellowship, fraternalism, friendliness, kinship; alliance, affiliation, association, clan, clique, club, coalition, community, consortium, coterie, fraternity, guild, league, lodge, society, union
brotherly *adj* affectionate, altruistic, amicable, benevolent, charitable, cordial, fraternal, friendly, kind, kindly, neighbourly, philanthropic, sympathetic
brow *n* forehead, temple; eyebrows; apex, brink, crown, peak, summit, top
browbeat *v* badger, bulldoze, bully, coerce, cow, domineer, dragoon, hector, intimidate, lord it over, oppress, overawe, overbear, threaten, tyrannize
brown *adj* bay, roan, sorrel; brick, bronze, bronzed, browned, brunette, chestnut, chocolate, coffee, cocoa, dark, dun, dusky, ginger, hazel, rust, tawny, umber; browned, sunburnt, tan, tanned, toasted
brown *v* fry, grill, sauté, seal, sear
browned off *adj* bored, fed up, discontented, discouraged, disgruntled, disheartened, weary
browse *v* dip into, examine cursorily, flip through, glance at, have a look, leaf through, look round, look through, peruse, scan, skim, survey, thumb through, window shop; crop, eat, feed, graze, nibble, pasture
bruise *v* blacken, blemish, contuse, crush, damage, deface, discolour, injure, mar, mark, pound, pulverize
bruise *n* black and blue mark, blemish, contusion, discolouration, injury, mark, swelling
brunt *n* burden, force, full force, impact, pressure, shock, strain, stress, thrust; consequences, repercussions
brush *n* besom, broom, sweeper; clash, conflict, confrontation, encounter, fight, fracas, scrap, skirmish, slight engagement, tussle; brushwood, bushes, copse, scrub, shrubs, thicket, undergrowth, underwood
brush *v* buff, clean, paint, polish, sweep, wash; caress, contact, flick, glance, graze, kiss, scrape, stroke, sweep, touch
brush aside *v* disregard, dismiss, ignore, shrug off, sweep aside
brush off *v* cold-shoulder, deny, disdain, dismiss, disown, ignore, refuse, reject, repudiate, scorn, slight, snub, spurn
brush up *v* cram, go over, polish up, read up, refresh one's memory, relearn, revise, study
brusque *adj* abrupt, bluff, blunt, caustic, churlish, curt, discourteous, gruff, hasty, outspoken, plain-spoken, rude, sharp, short, terse
brutal *adj* barbarous, bloodthirsty, callous, cruel, ferocious, heartless, inhuman, merciless, pitiless, remorseless, ruthless, savage, uncivilized, vicious; animal, beastly, bestial, brute, brutish, carnal, coarse, crude, sensual
brute *n* animal, beast, creature, wild animal; barbarian, devil, fiend, monster, ogre, sadist, savage,

swine; boor, churl, dolt, oaf

bubble *n* air cavity, bead, blister, blob, drop, droplet, globule, vesicle; delusion, dream, chimera, fantasy, illusion

bubble *v* effervesce, fizz, foam, froth, percolate, seethe, sparkle, spume; boil, percolate, seethe, simmer; brim over, be filled

bubbly *adj* carbonated, effervescent, fizzy, foamy, frothy, sparkling, sudsy; animated, bouncy, boyant, bubbling, ebullient, effervescent, elated, excited, happy, lively, merry, scintillating, vivacious

buccaneer *n* corsair, free-booter, pirate, sea rover, Viking

buck up *v* hasten, hurry/speed up, hurry, make haste, rush; perk up, rally, take heart; cheer up, enliven, gladden, make happier

bucket *n* can, pail, pitcher, scuttle

buckle *n* catch, clasp, clip, fastener, fastener, fastening, hasp; bulging, contorted, curved, distorted, kinked, warped

buckle *v* catch, clasp, clip, close, fasten, hook, secure, strap, tie; bend, bulge, cave in, collapse, contorted, crumpled, curved, distorted, fold, twisted, warped

bucolic *adj* agricultural, country, pastoral, rural, rustic

bud *n* burgeon, embryo, flowerlet, floret, germ, shoot, sprout

bud *v* burst forth, develop, germinate, grow, pullulate, send out shoots, shoot, sprout

budding *adj* beginning, burgeoning, developing, embryonic, fledgling, flowering, germinal, growing, incipient, nascent, potential

budge *v* dislodge, give way, inch, move, propel, push, remove, roll, shift, slide, stir; bend, change, convince, give way, influence, persuade, sway, yield

budget *n* allocation, allotment, allowance, quota, ration; blueprint, estimate, financial plan, statement

budget *v* allocate, apportion, plan, ration, schedule; allow, plan, save, set aside, set aside money

buff *adj* beige, sandy, straw-coloured, yellowish, yellowish-brown

buff *v* burnish, polish, rub, rub up, shine, smooth

buff *n* addict, admirer, aficionado, devotee, enthusiast, expert, fan

buffer *n* bulwark, bumper, cushion, fender, guard, intermediary, safe-guard, screen, shield, shock absorber

buffet *v* bang, batter, beat, box, bump, clobber, cuff, flail, hit, knock, pound, pummel, push, rap, shove, slap, strike, thump, wallop, whack

buffet *n* café, caféteria, counter, refreshment stall, salad bar, snack bar; cold meal, cold table, self-service, smorgasbord; bang, battering, blow, box, bump, clout, cuff, jab, jolt, knock, poke, push, rap, shove, slap, smack, thump, thwack, wallop, whack

bug *n* flea, insect, mite; bacterium, disease, germ, infection, micro-organism, virus; craze, fad, fixation, mania, obsession, passion; defect, error, failing, fault, flaw, gremlin, imperfection, obstruction; listening device, phone-tap, tap, wire-tap

bug *v* phone-tap, wire-tap; eaves-drop on, listen in, spy, tap; anger, annoy, exasperate, inflame, irk, irritate, provoke, try one's patience

bugbear *n* abomination, anathema, bane, bogey, dread, hate, horror, nightmare, pet hate

build *v* assemble, construct, erect, fabricate, form, make, manufacture, put up, raise; base, begin, develop, establish, formulate, found, inaugurate, initiate, institute, originate, set up, start

build *n* body, figure, form, frame, physique, shape, structure

building *v* domicile, dwelling, edifice, fabric, house, pile, structure; architecture, construction, erection, fabricating, railing

build up *v* develop, establish, expand; boost, increase, strengthen; advertise, promote, publicize; augment, develop, escalate, improve, increase, intensify, strengthen; escalate, get stronger

build up *n* accumulation, development, enlargement, escalation, expansion, gain, growth, increase; accretion, accumulation, heap, mass, pile, stack, stockpile, store; advertising, publicity

built in *adj* incorporated, integral, integrated; essential, in-built, included, incorporated, inherent, inseparable, intensification, intrinsic

bulge *n* bump, lump, projection, prominence, protrusion, protuberance, swelling; augmentation, boost, intensification, increase, rise, surge

bulge *v* bag, balloon up/out, belly, bloat, dilate, distend, enlarge, expand, jut out, project, protrude, puff out, sag, stand out, stick out, swell, swell out

bulk *n* ampleness, amplitude, bigness, dimensions, immensity, largeness, magnitude, mass, massiveness, size, substance, volume, weight; better part, body, generality, greater part, lion's share, main part, major part, majority, mass, most, nearly all, plurality, preponderance

bulk *v* augment, expand, fill out, make larger, make thicker, pad out, stretch out

bulky *adj* big, colossal, enormous, heavy, huge, hulking, immense, large, ponderous, substantial, vast, voluminous, weighty; chubby, fat, obese, plump, portly, stout, thickset, tubby; awkward, awkward-shaped, cumbersome, unmanageable, unwieldy

bulldoze *v* demolish, flatten, level, raze; drive, force, propel, push, shove; bludgeon, browbeat, bully, coerce, cow, dragoon, intimidate, railroad, steam-roller

bullet *n* ball, dumdum bullet, missile, pellet, plastic bullet, projectile, rubber bullet, shot, slug

bulletin *n* account, announcement, communication, communiqué, dispatch, flash, message, newsflash, news report, notification, report, statement; broadsheet, leaflet, listings, newsletter, newspaper, pamphlet

bullish *adj* assured, cheerful, confident, hopeful, improving, optimistic, positive, sanguine

bully *n* browbeater, bully-boy, coercer, intimidator, oppressor, persecutor, ruffian, thug, tormentor, tough, tyrant

bully *v* browbeat, bulldoze, coerce, domineer, persecute, pressure, pressurize, tyrannize; (*Inf*) push around, strong-arm

bully *adj* admirable, excellent, fine, first-rate, very good; (*Inf*) A1, wicked

bulwark *n* bastion, buttress, defence, embankment, fortification, mole, outwork, partition, rampart, redoubt; defence, guard, mainstay, safeguard, support; defendant, protector

bumble *v* babble, mumble, mutter, ramble, stutter; blunder, flounder about, lurch, stumble

bumbling *adj* awkward, blundering, botching, bungling, clumsy, foolish, incompetent, inefficient, inept, lumbering, muddled, stumbling

bump *v* bang, collide with, crash into, hit, injure, knock, slam, smash into, strike; bounce, jar, jerk, jolt, jostle, jounce, rattle, shake; budge, dislodge, move, shift

bump *n* bang, blow, collision, crash, hit, impact, jar, jolt, knock, rap, shock, smash, thud, thump; bulge, contusion, hump, injury, intumescence, lump, node, nodule, protuberance, swelling, tumescence; bulge, hump, knob, knot

bump into *n* chance upon, collide with, come across, encounter, happen upon, light upon, meet, meet up with, run across, run into, smash into; come across, encounter, happen upon, meet by chance, meet up with, run into

bumper *adj* abundant, big, bountiful, excellent, exceptional, large, massive, unusual

bumpkin *n* boor, clod-hopper, country bumpkin, lout, oaf, peasant

bumptious *adj* arrogant, cocky, conceited, forward, full of oneself, over bearing, pompous, presumptuous, puffed up, self-arrogant, self-assertive, self-important, self-opinionated

bunch *n* assortment, batch, bouquet, bundle, clump, cluster, collection, heap, lot, mass, number, parcel, pile, quantity, sheaf, spray, stack, tuft

bunch *v* assemble, bundle, cluster, collect, congregate, cram together, crowd, flock, group, herd, huddle, mass, pack

bundle *n* accumulation, assortment, batch, bunch, collection, group, heap, mass, pile, quantity, stack; bag, bale, box, carton, crate, pack, package, packet, pallet, parcel, roll

bundle *v* bale, bind, fasten, pack, package, palletize, tie, tie together, tie up, truss, wrap

buoy *n* beacon, float, guide, marker, signal

buoyant *adj* afloat, floatable, floating, light, weightless; animated, blithe, bouncy, breezy, bright, carefree, cheerful, debonair, happy, jaunty, joyful, light-hearted, lively, sunny, sparky, vivacious

burden *n* affliction, anxiety, care, clog, encumbrance, grievance, load, millstone, obstruction, onus, responsibility, sorrow, strain, stress, trial, trouble, weight, worry

burden *v* bother, encumber, handicap, load, oppress, overload, overwhelm, saddle with, strain, tax, weigh down, worry

bureau *n* desk, writing desk; agency, branch, department, division, office, service

bureaucracy *n* administration, authorities, civil service, corridors of power, directorate, government, ministry, officialdom, officials, the system

bureaucrat *n* administrator, apparatchik, civil servant, functionary, mandarin, minister, office holder, officer, official, public servant

burglar *n* cat burglar, filcher, house breaker, picklock, pilferer, robber, sneak thief, thief

burial *n* burying, entombment, exequies, funeral, inhumation, interment, obsequies, sepulture

buried *v* coffined, consigned to the grave, entombed, interred, laid to rest; dead and buried, dead and gone, in the grave, long gone, pushing up the daisies, six feet under; covered, forgotten, hidden, repressed, sunk in, oblivion, suppressed; caught up, committed, concealed, concentrating, devoted, engrossed, hidden, private, sequestered, tucked away; concentrating, devoted, engrossed, immersed, intent, lost, occupied, preoccupied, rapt

burlesque *n* caricature, mock, mockery, parody, satire, end-up, travesty

burlesque *v* ape, caricature, exaggerate, imitate, lampoon, make fun of, mock, parody, ridicule, satirize, send up, travesty

burly *adj* beefy, big, brawny, bulky, hefty, hulking, muscular, powerful, stocky, stout, strapping, strong, sturdy, thickset, well-built

burn *v* be ablaze, be on fire, blaze, flame, flare, flash, flicker, glow, smoke; brand, calcine, char, ignite, incinerate, kindle, light, parch, reduce to ashes, scorch, set on fire, shrivel, singe, toast, wither

burning *adj* blazing, fiery, flaming, flashing, gleaming, glowing, hot, illuminated, scorching, smouldering; all-consuming, ardent, eager, earnest, fervent, fervid, frantic, frenzied, impassioned, intense, passionate, vehement, zealous

burrow *n* den, hole, lair, retreat, shelter, tunnel

burrow *v* delve, dig, excavate, hollow out, scoop out, tunnel

burst *v* blow up, break, crack, disintegrate, explode, fly open, fragment, puncture, rend, asunder, rupture, shatter, shiver, split, tear apart

burst *n* bang, blast, blasting, blowout, blow up, breach, break, crack, discharge, explosion, rupture, split

bury *v* consign to the grave, entomb, inearth, inhume, inter, lay to rest, sepulchre; conceal, cover, cover up, enshroud, hide, secrete, shroud, stow away; drive in, embed, engulf, implant, sink, submerge

bush *n* hedge, plant, shrub, shrubbery, thicket; backwoods, brush, scrub, scrubland, woodland

business *n* calling, career, craft, employment, function, job, line, occupation, profession, pursuit, trade, vocation, work; company, concern, corporation, enterprise, establishment, firm, organization, venture; bargaining, commerce, dealings, industry, manufacturing, merchandising, selling, trade, trading, transaction

businesslike *adj* correct, efficient, matter-of-fact, methodical, orderly, organized, practical, professional, regular, routine, systematic, thorough, well-ordered, workaday

businessman *n* capitalist, commercial intermediary, employer, entrepreneur, executive, financier, industrialist, merchant, middleman, promoter, tradesman, tycoon

bust *n* bosom, breast, chest, torso

bust *v* break, crack, fracture, rupture; bankrupt, break, impoverish, ruin; arrest, capture, catch, raid, seize

bustle *v* bestir, dash, flutter, fuss, hasten, hurry, rush, scamper, scramble, scurry, stir, tear

bustle *n* activity, ado, agitation, commotion, excitement, flurry, fuss, haste, hurry, pother, stir, tumult

busy *adj* active, assiduous, brisk, diligent, employed, engaged, engrossed, hard at work, industrious, in harness, occupied, on duty, persevering, slaving, working; active, energetic, exacting, full, hectic, hustling, lively, on the go, restless, strenuous, tireless, tiring

but *conj* further, however, moreover, nevertheless, on the contrary, on the other hand, still, yet

but *prep* bar, barring, except, excluding, notwithstanding, save, with the exception of, without

but *adv* just, merely, only, simply, singly, solely

but *conj* further, however, nevertheless, still, yet

butcher *n* meat merchant, meat retailer, meat seller; bloodshedder, homicidal maniac, killer, murderer, serial killer, slaughterer, slayer

butcher *v* carve, clean, cut, cut up, dress, joint, prepare, slaughter; assassinate, cut down, destroy, exterminate, kill, liquidate, massacre, put to the sword, slaughter, slay; bodge, botch, destroy, mess up, mutilate, ruin, spoil, wreck

butt *n* haft, handle, hilt, shaft, shank, stock; end, remnant, stub, tail-end, bottom, buttocks; dupe, laughing stock, mark, object, point, scapegoat, subject, target, victim; barrel, cask, pipe

butt *v* buck, buffet, bump, bunt, jab, knock, poke, prod, punch, push, ram, shove, thrust; abut, conjoin, join, meet; interfere, interrupt, intrude, put one's oar in; (*Inf*) stick one's nose into

buttress *n* abutment, reinforcement, pier, prop, stanchion, support; cornerstone, mainstay, pillar, sustainer, upholder

buttress *v* back up, brace, defend, prop up, shore up, strengthen, support, uphold, underpin

buy *v* acquire, get, invest in, obtain, pay for, procure, purchase, shop for

buy *n* acquisition, bargain, deal, purchase

buzz *n* buzzing, drone, hiss, hum, humming, murmur, sibilation, whir, whirring, whisper; purr, purring, ring, ringing; chitchat, gossip, hearsay, news, report, scandal, whisper

buzz *v* be active, be busy, be bustling; bustle, dash, hurry, rush; chatter, gossip, natter, spread rumours, tattle; purr, reverberate, ring; drone, hiss, hum, murmur, whirr, whisper

by *prep* along, alongside, beside, by way of, close to, in front of, near, next to, over, past, via; through, through the agency of, under the aegis of; at, before, no later than; as a result, because of, through

by *adv* aside, at hand, away, beyond, close, handy, in reach, near, past, to one side

by and by *adv* eventually, presently

bygone *adj* ancient, antiquated, dead, departed, extinct, forgotten, former, lost, obsolete, of old, of yore, olden, one-time, outmoded, passé, past, previous

by-law, bye-law *n* local regulation, regulation, rule, statute

bypass *n* alternative route, circuitous route, detour, ring road, roundabout way

bypass *v* go round, make a detour round, pass round; avoid, evade, circumvent, find a way round, get round; avoid, circumvent, go over the head of, ignore, miss out, pass over

bystander *n* beholder, eyewitness, gaper, looker-on, observer, onlooker, passer-by, spectator, viewer, watcher, witness

byword *n* catchword, embodient of, example of, motto, personification of, slogan; adage, aphorism, apophthegm, maxim, proverb

C

cab *n* hackney, hackney carriage, minicab, taxi, taxicab; cabin, compartment, cubicle, cubbyhole, quarters

cabaret *n* floorshow, entertainment, show; club, disco, discotheque, nightclub, nightspot

cabbage *n* Chinese, green, red, savoy, white, winter; couch potato

cabin *n* berth, chalet, cot, cottage, crib, hovel, hut, lodge, shack, shanty, shed; bothy; berth, compartment, deckhouse, quarters, room

cabinet *n* case, chiffonier, closet, commode, cupboard, dresser, escritoire, locker; administration, assembly, council, counsellors, ministers, ministry, senate

cable *n* cord, cordage, line, rope, wire; cablegram, telegram, telegraph, telemessage, wire

cable *v* radio, telegraph, wire

cache *n* hiding-place, hole, secret place

cachet *n* admiration, approval, distinction, respect, prestige, stature

cackle *v* clack, cluck, squawk; chortle, chuckle, giggle, laugh, snigger, tee-hee; blab, blather, chatter, jabber, prattle

cacophony *n* caterwauling, discord, grating, jarring, rasping, stridency

cad *n* double-crosser, knave, rascal, rat, rogue, scoundrel; (*Inf*) bounder, heel, rotter

cadaver *n* carcass, corpse, dead body, remains; (*Inf*) stiff

cadaverous *adj* ashen, corpse-like, death-like, emaciated, gaunt, ghostly, haggard, hollow-eyed, skeletal, wan

cadence *n* beat, cadency, lilt, measure, metre, rhythmical flow, swing, tempo

café *n* bistro, cafeteria, coffee bar, coffee shop, lunchroom, restaurant, snack bar, tearoom, teashop, wine bar

cage *n* coop, enclosure, lock-up, pen, pound; corral; aviary, birdcage, hen coop, mew, sheep pen

cage *v* confine, coop, coop up, corral, fence in, hem in, immure, impound, imprison, incarcerate, lock up, mew, pen, restrain, restrict, shut in

cagey *adj* careful, cautious, guarded, non-commital, secretive, shrewd, wily

cajole *v* beguile, coax, decoy, dupe, entice, entrap, flatter, humour, inveigle, jolly, lure, manoeuvre, mislead, seduce, tempt, wheedle; (*Inf*) butter up, soft soap, sweet talk

cake *n* bun, pastry; bar, block, cube, chunk, loaf, lump, mass, slab

cake *v* bake, coagulate, dry, harden, ossify, solidify, thicken; coat, cover, encrust, plaster

calamity *n* adversity, affliction, cataclysm, catastrophe, disaster, distress, downfall, hardship, misadventure, mischance, misfor tune, mishap, reverse, ruin, scourge, tragedy, trial, tribulation, woe, wretchedness

calculate *v* adjust, compute, consider, count, determine, enumerate, estimate, figure, gauge, judge, rate, reckon, value, weigh, work out

calculation *n* answer, computation, estimate, estimation, figuring, forecast, judgment, reckoning, result

calibre *n* bore, diameter, gauge, measure; ability, capacity, capability, competence, distinction, endow ment, excellence, faculty, force, gifts, merit, parts, quality, scope, stature, strengths, talent, worth

call *v* announce, arouse, awaken, cry, cry out, exclaim, hail, halloo, proclaim, roar, rouse, shout, shriek, waken, yell; assemble, bid, collect, contact, convene, convoke, gather, invite, muster, phone, rally, ring up, summon, telephone; christen, denominate, describe as, designate, dub, entitle, label, name, style, term

call *n* cry, hail, scream, shout, signal, whoop, yell; announcement, appeal, command, demand, invitation, notice, order, plea, request, summons, supplication, visit

call for *v* demand, entail, involve, necessitate, need, occasion, require, suggest

call off *v* check, hold back, order away, order off, rein in, stop; cancel, countermand, postpone, rescind, revoke

call on *v* go and see, pay a visit, visit; (*Inf*) drop in on, look in on, look up; appeal to, ask, entreat, invoke, request, urge

calling *n* business, career, employment, life's work, line, métier, mission, occupation, profession, province, pursuit, trade, vocation, walk of life, work

callous *adj* apathetic, case-hardened, cold, hard-bitten, hardened, hardhearted, heartless, indifferent, insensate, insensible, insensitive, inured, obdurate, soulless, thick-skinned, torpid, uncaring, unfeeling, unresponsive, unsusceptible, unsympathetic; hard, hardened, leathery, thickened

callow *adj* adolescent, immature, inexperienced, naive, undeveloped, unsophisticated

calm *adj* balmy, halcyon, mild, pacific, peaceful, placid, quiet, restful, serene, smooth, still, tranquil, windless; collected, composed, cool, dispassionate, equable, impassive, imperturbable, relaxed, sedate, self-possessed, undisturbed, unemotional, unexcitable, unexcited, unmoved, unruffled

calm *n* harmony, peace, quietude, repose, restfullness, serenity, stillness, tranquillity; composure, coolness, equability, poise, sangfroid, self-control; (*Inf*) cool

calm *v* allay, alleviate, appease, assuage, hush, lull, mollify, pacify, placate, quieten, relax, soothe, tranquillize; die down, quieten, settle down, still

calmness *n* calm, composure, equability, hush, motionless, peace, peacefulness, placidity, quiet, repose, restfulness, serenity, smooth ness, stillness, tranquillity; composure, cool, coolness, dispassion, equanimity, impassivity, imperturability, poise, self-possession

camaraderie *n* affinity, brotherliness, closeness, companionship, comradeship, fellowship, friend-

ship, sociability
camouflage *n* blind, cloak, concealment, cover, disguise, façade, false front, front, guise, mask, masquerade, mimicry, protective colouring, screen, subterfuge
camouflage *v* cloak, conceal, cover up, disguise, hide, mask, obfuscate, obscure, screen, veil
camp *n* bivouac, camping ground, camp site, cantonment, encampment, tents; cabal, clique, coterie, faction, group, party, sect, set
camp *v* encamp, pitch camp, pitch tents, set up camp; behave affectedly, ham it, lay it on, overact, over do it, spread it on thick
camp *adj* affected, artificial, effeminate, homosexual, mannered, posturing, studied
campaign *n* attack, battle, crusade, drive, expedition, movement, offensive, operation, push, war; action, battle plan, course of action, manoeuvre, promotion, set of action, strategy
campaign *v* agitate, battle, crusade, fight, strive, struggle, work
can *n* container, receptacle, tin
can *v* bottle, preserve, tin
canal *n* channel, race, watercourse, waterway; conduit, duct, pipe, tube
cancel *v* abolish, abort, abrogate, annul, blot out, call off, countermand, cross out, declare null and void, declare void, delete, do away with, efface, eliminate, erase, expunge, invalidate, negate, nullify, obliterate, quash, repeal, repudiate, rescind, retract, revoke, set aside
cancer *n* growth, malignancy; carcinoma, melanoma, metastasis, sarcoma; blight, canker, corruption, disease, pestilence, plague, scourge, sickness
candid *adj* bluff, blunt, brusque, fair, forthright, frank, free, guileless, impartial, ingenuous, just, open, outspoken, plain, sincere, straightforward, truthful, unbiased, unequivocal, unprejudiced
candidate *n* applicant, aspirant, claimant, competitor, contender, contestant, entrant, nominee, possibility, runner, office seeker, solicitant, suitor
candour *n* artlessness, bluntness, brusqueness, directness, fairness, forthrightness, frankness, guilelessness, honesty, impartiality, ingenuousness, naïveté, openness, outspokenness, simplicity, sincerity, straightforwardness, truthfulness, unequivocalness
cane *n* alpenstock, reed, rod, shepherd's crook, shoot, staff, stave, stick, walking stick
cane *v* beat, flog, hit, scourge, strap, strike, thrash; (*Inf*) tan one's back side; defeat, put to rout, rout, vanquish, thrash, trounce
canker *n* abcess, blister, lesion, running sore, ulcer, ulceration
cannibal *n* anthropophagite, maneater, people eater; barbican, savage, wild man
cannon *n* field gin, gun, mounted gun; (*Inf*) big gun
canny *adj* acute, artful, astute, careful, cautious, circumspect, clever, discerning, judicious, knowing, penetrating, perspicacious, prudent, sagacious, sensible, sharp, shrewd, subtle, thrifty, wise, worldly-wise

canon *n* benchmark, convention, criterion, exemplar, formula, measure, model, pattern, precept, principle, ruling, standard, yardstick
canopy *n* awning, baldachin, cover, sunshade, tarpaulin, tester
cant *n* argot, jargon, lingo, patter, slang, terminology; humbug, hypocrisy, insincerity, lip service, pretence, pseudo-piety, sanctimony, sanctimonious, sham holiday; angle, inclination, slope, tilt
cant *v* angle, lean, overturn, slant, slope, tilt
cantankerous *adj* abrupt, bad-tempered, brusque, crabby, curt, difficult, grumpy, ill-natured, irritable, short-tempered, surly, testy, touchy; (*Inf*) cranky, crotchety, grouchy
canter *n* amble, dogtrot, easy, gait, gallop, jog, lope, saunter, trot
canvass *v* analyse, campaign, convince, drum up support, electioneer, enquire into, examine, explore, find out, inspect, investigate, look into, persuade, poll, scan, scrutinize, sift, solicit, solicit votes, study; air, argue, debate, dispute, ventilate
canvass *n* examination, investigation, poll, scrutiny, survey, tally
canyon *n* abyss, chasm, gorge, gulf, gully, ravine, valley
cap *n* bonnet, hat, headgear; (*Inf*) lid; bung, cork, lid, plug, stopper, top; apex, crest, peak, pinnacle, summit
cap *v* beat, better, complete, cover, crown, eclipse, exceed, excel, finish, outdo, outstrip, overtop, surpass, top, transcend; include, pick, select; curb, keep within bounds
capability *n* ability, accomplishment, adeptness, aptitude, capacity, competence, effectiveness, efficiency, experience, facility, faculty, means, potential, potentiality, power, proficiency, qualifications, skill, smartness, talent, wherewithal; flair, forte, gift, knack, strong point
capable *adj* able, accomplished, adapted, adept, adequate, apt, clever, competent, effective, efficient, experienced, fitted, gifted, intelligent, masterly, practised, proficient, qualified, skilful, smart, suited, susceptible, talented
capacious *adj* ample, broad, comfortable, commodious, comprehensive, expansive, extended, extensive, generous, immense, large, liberal, roomy, sizeable, spacious, substantial, vast, voluminous, wide
capacity *n* ampleness, amplitude, compass, dimensions, extent, magnitude, proportions, range, room, scope, size, space, volume; ability, accomplishment, aptitude, aptness, brains, capability, cleverness, competence, competency, efficiency, facility, faculty, forte, genius, gift, intelligence, power, proficiency, readiness, strength; appointment, function, job, office, position, post, province, role, service, sphere
cape *n* cloak
cape *n* chersonese, head, headland, jess, peninsula, point, promontory, tongue
caper *v* bounce, bound, cavort, dance, frisk, frolic, gambol, hop, jump, leap, prance, romp, skip, spring
caper *n* cavorting, dancing, frisking,

frolics, gambolling,

capital *adj* cardinal, central, chief, controlling, essential, foremost, important, leading, main, major, overruling, paramount, pre-eminent, primary, prime, principal, prominent, vital; excellent, fine, first, prime, splendid, superb

capital *n* centre of administration, first city, seat of government; capital letter, majuscule, uncial; cash, finance, finances, financing, funds, hard cash, investment, liquid assets, means, money, principal, property, reserves, resources, stock, wealth, wherewithal, working capital

capitalism *n* free enterprise, private enterprise, *laissez-faire*, private enterprise, private ownership, privatized industries

capitalist *n* banker, financier, investor, moneyman, tycoon; nabob, plutocrat; loadsamoney, yuppie

capitalize *v* back, finance, fund, provide backing for, sponsor

capitalize on *v* cash in on, exploit, make the most of, profit from, put to advantage, take advantage of

capitulate *v* accede, come to terms, give in, give up, relent, submit, succumb, surrender, yield

capsize *v* invert, keel over, over turn, tip over, turn over, upset

captain *n* boss, chief, chieftain, commander, head, leader, master, number one, officer, pilot, skipper

captivate *v* allure, attract, beguile, bewitch, charm, dazzle, enamour, enchant, enrapture, enslave, ensnare, enthral, entrance, fascinate, hypnotize, infatuate, lure, mesmerize, seduce, win

captive *n* bondservant, convict, detainee, hostage, internee, prisoner of war, slave

captive *adj* caged, confined, enslaved, ensnared, imprisoned, incarcerated, locked up, penned, restricted, subjugated

captivity *v* bondage, confinement, custody, detention, duress, enthrallment, imprisonment, incarceration, internment, restraint, servitude, slavery, thraldom, vassalage

capture *v* apprehend, arrest, bag, catch, secure, seize, take, take into custody, take prisoner; (*Inf*) collar

capture *n* apprehension, arrest, catch, imprisonment, seizure, taking, taking captive, trapping

car *n* auto, automobile, machine, motor, motorcar, vehicle

carcass *n* body, cadaver, corpse, corse, dead body, framework, hulk, remains, shell, skeleton

cardinal *n* capital, central, chief, essential, first, foremost, fundamental, greatest, highest, important, key, leading, main, paramount, pre-eminent, primary, prime, principal

care *n* affliction, anxiety, burden, concern, disquiet, hardship, interest, perplexity, pressure, responsibility, trouble, vexation, woe, worry; attention, carefulness, caution, circumspection, consideration, direction, forethought, heed, management, meticulousness, pains, prudence, regard, vigilance, watchfulness; charge, control, custody, guardianship, keeping, manage ment, ministration, protection, supervision, ward

career *n* calling, employment, life

work, livelihood, occupation, pursuit, vocation
care for *v* attend, foster, look after, mind, minister to, nurse, protect, provide for, tend, watch over; be fond of, desire, enjoy, find congenial, like, love, prize, take to, want
careful *adj* accurate, attentive, cautious, chary, circumspect, conscientious, discreet, fastidious, heedful, painstaking, precise, prudent, punctilious, scrupulous, thoughtful, thrifty; alert, concerned, judicious, mindful, particular, protective, solicitous, vigilant, wary, watchful
careless *adj* absent-minded, cursory, forgetful, hasty, heedless, incautious, inconsiderate, indiscreet, negligent, perfunctory, regardless, remiss, thoughtless, unconcerned, unguarded, unmindful, unthinking; inaccurate, irresponsible, lackadaisical, neglectful, offhand, slap dash, slipshod; (*Inf*) sloppy
caress *v* cuddle, embrace, fondle, hug, kiss, nuzzle, pet, stroke
caress *n* cuddle, embrace, fondling, hug, kiss, pat, stroke
caretaker *n* concierge, curator, custodian, janitor, keeper, porter, superintendent, warden, watchman
cargo *n* baggage, consignment, contents, freight, goods, lading, load, merchandise, shipment, tonnage, ware
caricature *n* burlesque, cartoon, distortion, farce, lampoon, mimicry, parody, pasquinade, satire, travesty
caricature *v* burlesque, distort, lampoon, mimic, mock, parody, ridicule, satirize
carnival *n* celebration, fair, festival, fiesta, gala, holiday, jamboree, jubilee, Mardi Gras, merry making, revelry
carriage *n* carrying, conveyance, conveying, delivery, freight, transport, transportation; cab, coach, conveyance, vehicle; air, bearing, behaviour, comportment, conduct, demeanour, deportment, gait, manner, mien, posture, presence
carry *v* bear, bring, conduct, convey, fetch, haul, lift, lug, move, relay, take, transfer, transmit, transport; bear, hold up, maintain, shoulder, stand, suffer, support, sustain, underpin, uphold
carry on *v* continue, endure, keep going, last, maintain, perpetuate, persevere, persist
carry out *v* accomplish, achieve, carry through, consummate, discharge, effect, execute, fulfil, implement, perform, realize
carton *n* box, case, container, pack, package, packet
cartoon *n* animated cartoon, animated film, animation, caricature, comic strip, lampoon, parody, satire, sketch; (*Inf*) takeoff
cartridge *n* charge, round, shell
carve *v* chip, chisel, cut, divide, engrave, etch, fashion, form, grave, hack, hew, incise, indent, mould, sculpt, sculpture, slash, slice, whittle
cascade *n* avalanche, cataract, deluge, falls, flood, fountain, outpouring, shower, torrent, waterfall
case *n* baggage, bin, box, briefcase, bureau, cabinet, canister, capsule, carton, cartridge, casing, casket, chest, chiffonier, coffer, compact,

container, covering, crate, cupboard, envelope, folder, holder, housing, jacket, luggage, receptacle, sheath, shell, suitcase, tray, trunk, wrapping; circumstances, condition, context, contingency, dilemma, event, phenomenon, plight, position, predicament, situation, state; example, happening, illustration, instance, occasion, occurrence, specimen; action, cause, dispute, lawsuit, legal cause, legal dispute, legal proceedings, proceedings, process, suit, trial; invalid, patient, sick person, sufferer, victim

cash *n* banknotes, bullion, capital, change, coin, coinage, currency, finance, funds, investment capital, money, notes, payment, ready money, resources, wherewithal; (*Fml*) specie

cashier *n* accountant, bank clerk, banker, bursar, clerk, controller, purser, teller, treasurer

casino *n* gambling club, gambling den, gambling house

cask *n* barrel, firkin, hogshead, keg, pipe, tun, vat, vessel

casket *n* box, case, chest, coffer, container, receptacle; coffin, pall, sarcophagus; (*Inf*) wooden overcoat

cast *v* chuck, discard, drive, drop, fling, hurl, impel, launch, let fly, lob, pitch, project, sling, throw, thrust, toss; discard, get rid of, let drop, let fall, peel off, slough off, throw off; direct, send out, shoot, turn; diffuse, emit, give off, radiate send out, shed, spread out; create, form; bestow, confer, give, grant, impart, throw; enter, record, register, vote; fashion, form, model, mould, sculpt; allot, appoint, assign, choose, name, pick, select; actors, characters, company, *dramatis personae*, players, troupe

cast *n* fling, hurl, lob, pitch, shy, throw, toss; kind, nature, sort, stamp, type; figure, form, mould, shape; defect, squint, twist

cast down *v* defect, deject, depress, desolate, discourage, dishearten, dispirit

caste *v* class, grade, grading, place, position, social class, social order, standing, station, status

castigate *v* admonish, berate, censure, chasten, chastise, chide, criticize, discipline, dress down, haul over the coals, punish, rebuke, reprimand, reproach, scold, take to task, upbraid

castle *n* chateau, citadel, donjon, fastness, fortress, keep, hold, mansion, palace, peel, stronghold, tower

casual *adj* accidental, chance, contingent, fortuitous, impromptu, incidental, irregular, occasional, random, serendipitous, spontaneous, unanticipated, uncertain, unexpected, unforeseen, unintentional, unpremeditated; apathetic, blasé, cursory, indifferent, informal, insouciant, lackadaisical, lukewarm, nonchalant, offhand, perfunctory, pococurante, relaxed, unceremonious, unconcerned, unthinking; irregular, part-time, temporary; cursory, desultory, hasty, hurried, shallow, superficial

casualty *n* loss, sufferer, victim

catalogue *n* directory, gazetteer, index, inventory, list, record, register, roll, roster, schedule

catastrophe *n* adversity, affliction, blow, calamity, cataclysm, devastation, disaster, failure, fiasco, ill, mischance, misfortune, mishap, reverse, tragedy, trial, trouble; (*Inf*) meltdown

catch *v* apprehend, arrest, capture, clutch, ensnare, entangle, entrap, grab, grasp, grip, lay hold of, seize, snare, snatch, take; detect, discover, expose, find out, surprise, take unawares, unmask

catch *n* bolt, clasp, clip, fastener, hasp, hook, hook and eye, latch, sneck, snib; disadvantage, draw back, fly in the ointment, hitch, snag, stumbling block, trap, trick

catching *adj* communicable, contagious, infectious, infective, transferable, transmittable

categorical *adj* absolute, direct, downright, emphatic, explicit, express, positive, unambiguous, unconditional, unequivocal, unqualified, unreserved

category *n* class, classification, department, division, grade, grouping, head, heading, list, order, rank, section, sort, type

cater *v* furnish, outfit, provide, provision, purvey, supply, victual

cattle *n* beasts, bovines, cows, kine, livestock, neat, stock

catty *adj* backbiting, ill-natured, malevolent, malicious, mean, rancorous, snide, spiteful, venomous; (*Inf*) bitchy

cause *n* agent, beginning, creator, genesis, mainspring, maker, origin, originator, prime mover, producer, root, source, spring; account, agency, aim, basis, consideration, end, grounds, incentive, inducement, motivation, motive, object, purpose, reason

cause *v* begin, bring about, compel, create, effect, engender, generate, give rise to, incite, induce, lead to, motivate, occasion, precipitate, produce, provoke, result in

caustic *adj* acrid, astringent, biting, burning, corroding, corrosive, keen, mordant

caution *n* alertness, care, carefulness, circumspection, deliberation, discretion, forethought, heed, heedfulness, prudence, vigilance, watchfulness; admonition, advice, counsel, injunction, warning

caution *v* admonish, advise, tip off, urge, warn

cautious *adj* alert, cagey, careful, chary, circumspect, discreet, guarded, heedful, judicious, prudent, tentative, vigilant, wary, watchful

cave *n* cavern, cavity, den, grotto, hollow

cavern *n* cave, hollow, pothole

cavity *n* crater, dent, gap, hole, hollow, pit

cease *v* break off, bring to an end, conclude, culminate, desist, die away, discontinue, end, fail, finish, halt, leave off, refrain, stay, stop, terminate

ceaseless *adj* constant continual, continuous, endless, eternal, everlasting, incessant, indefatigable, interminable, never-ending, non-stop, perennial, perpetual, unending, unremitting, untiring

celebrate *v* bless, commemorate, commend, drink to, eulogize, exalt, extol, glorify, honour, keep, laud,

observe, perform, praise, proclaim, publicize, rejoice, reverence, solemnize, toast
celebrated *adj* acclaimed, distinguished, eminent, famed, famous, glorious, illustrious, lionized, notable, outstanding, popular, pre-eminent, prominent, renowned, revered, well-known
celebration *n* carousal, festival, festivity, gala, jollification, jubilee, junketing, merrymaking, party, revelry
celebrity big name, dignitary, lion, luminary, name, personality, star, superstar, VIP; (*Inf*) celeb
cell *n* cavity, chamber, compartment, cubicle, dungeon, stall
cement *v* attach, bind, bond, cohere, combine, glue, gum, join, plaster, seal, solder, stick together, unite, weld
cemetery *n* burial ground, churchyard, God's acre, graveyard, necropolis
censure *v* abuse, berate, blame, castigate, chide, condemn, criticize, denounce, rebuke, reprehend, reprimand, reproach, reprove, scold, upbraid
censure *n* blame, castigation, condemnation, criticism, disapproval, dressing, obloquy, rebuke, remonstrance, reprehension, reprimand, reproach, reproof, stricture; (*Inf*) down
central *adj* chief, essential, focal, fundamental, inner, interior, key, main, mean, median, mid, middle, primary, principal
centre *n* bull's-eye, core, crux, focus, heart, hub, mid, middle, midpoint, nucleus, pivot
ceremonial *adj* formal, liturgical, ritual, ritualistic, solemn, stately
ceremonial *n* ceremony, formality, rite, ritual, solemnity
ceremony *n* commemoration, function, observance, parade, rite, ritual, service, show, solemnities
certain *adj* assured, confident, convinced, positive, satisfied, sure; ascertained, conclusive, incontrovertible, indubitable, irrefutable, known, plain, true, undeniable, undoubted, unequivocal, unmistakable, valid; decided, definite, established, fixed, settled
certainty *n* assurance, authoritativeness, certitude, confidence, conviction, faith, indubitableness, inevitability, positiveness, sureness, trust, validity
certificate *n* authorization, credentials, diploma, document, licence, testimonial, voucher, warrant
certify *v* ascertain, assure, attest, authenticate, aver, avow, confirm, corroborate, declare, endorse, guarantee, notify, show, testify, validate, verify, vouch, witness
chain *v* bind, confine, enslave, fetter, handcuff, manacle, restrain, shackle, tether, trammel, unite
chain *n* bond, coupling, fetter, link, manacle, shackle, union; concatenation, progression, sequence, series, set, string, succession, train
challenge *v* accost, arouse, beard, brave, call out, claim, confront, dare, defy, demand, dispute, impugn, investigate, object to, provoke, question, require, stimulate, sum-

mon, tax, test, throw down the gauntlet, try

chamber *n* apartment, bedroom, cavity, compartment, cubicle, enclosure, hall, hollow, room

champion *n* backer, challenger, conqueror, defender, guardian, hero, patron, protector, title holder, upholder, victor, vindicator, warrior, winner

chance *n* liability, likelihood, occasion, odds, opening, opportunity, possibility, probability, prospect, scope, time; accident, casualty, coincidence, contingency, destiny, fate, fortuity, fortune, luck, misfortune, peril, providence; gamble, hazard, jeopardy, risk, speculation, uncertainty

chance *v* befall, betide, come about, come to pass, fall out, happen, occur; endanger, gamble, go out on hazard, jeopardize, risk, stake, try, venture, wager; (*Inf*) a limb

change *v* alter, convert, diversify, fluctuate, metamorphose, moderate, modify, mutate, reform, remodel, reorganize, restyle, shift, transform, transmute, vacillate, vary, veer; alternate, barter, convert, displace, exchange, interchange, remove, replace, substitute, swap, trade, transmit

change *n* alteration, difference, innovation, metamorphosis, modification, mutation, permutation, revolution, transformation, transition, transmutation, vicissitude; conversion, exchange, interchange, substitution, trade

changeable *adj* capricious, change ful, chequered, erratic, fickle, fitful, fluid, inconstant, irregular, kaleidoscopic, mercurial, mobile, mutable, protean, shifting, uncertain, unpredictable, unreliable, unsettled, unstable, unsteady, vacillating, variable, versatile, volatile, wavering

channel *n* canal, chamber, conduit, duct, fluting, furrow, groove, gutter, main, passage, route, strait

channel *v* conduct, convey, direct, guide, transmit

chant *n* carol, chorus, melody, psalm, song

chant *v* carol, chorus, croon, descant, intone, recite, sing, warble

chaos *n* anarchy, bedlam, confusion, disorder, disorganization, entropy, lawlessness, pandemonium, tumult

chapter *n* clause, division, episode, part, period, phase, section, stage, topic

character *n* attributes, bent, calibre, cast, complexion, constitution, disposition, individuality, kidney, make-up, marked traits, nature, personality, quality, reputation, temper, temperament, type; honour, integrity, rectitude, strength, uprightness; card, eccentric, oddity, original; part, persona, portrayal, role

characteristic *adj* distinctive, distinguishing, idiosyncratic, individual, peculiar, representative, singular, special, specific, symbolic, symptomatic, typical

characteristic *n* attribute, faculty, feature, idiosyncrasy, mark, peculiarity, property, quality, quirk, trait

charge *v* accuse, arraign, blame, impeach, incriminate, indict, involve; bid, command, enjoin, exhort, instruct, order, require

charge *n* accusation, allegation, imputation, indictment; assault, attack, onset, onslaught, rush, sortie; burden, care, concern, custody, duty, office, responsibility, safekeeping, trust, ward; amount, cost, damage, expenditure, expense, outlay, payment, price, rate

charity *n* alms-giving, assistance, benefaction, contributions, donations, endowment, fund, gift, hand-out, philanthropy, relief

charm *v* allure, attract, beguile, bewitch, cajole, captivate, delight, enamour, enchant, enrapture, entrance, fascinate, mesmerize, please, win, win over

charm *n* allure, allurement, appeal, attraction, desirability, enchantment, fascination, magic, magnetism, sorcery, spell

charming *adj* appealing, attractive, bewitching, captivating, delectable, delightful, engaging, eyecatching, fetching, irresistible, lovely, pleasant, pleasing, seductive, winning, winsome

chart *n* blueprint, diagram, graph, map, plan, table, tabulation

chart *v* delineate, draft, graph, map out, outline, plot, shape, sketch

charter *n* bond, concession, contract, deed, document, franchise, indenture, licence, permit, prerogative, privilege, right

chase *v* course, drive, drive away, expel, follow, hound, hunt, pursue, put to flight, run after, track

chaste *adj* austere, decent, decorous, elegant, immaculate, incorrupt, innocent, modest, moral, neat, pure, quiet, refined, restrained, simple, unaffected, uncontaminated, undefiled, unsullied, vestal, virginal, virtuous, wholesome

chat *n* chatter, gossip, heart-to-heart, natter, talk

chat *v* chatter, gossip, natter, talk

chatter *n/v* babble, blather, chat, gossip, jabber, natter, prate, prattle, tattle, twaddle; (*Inf*) chin wag, natter

cheap *adj* bargain, cut-price, economical, economy, inexpensive, keen, low-cost, low-priced, reasonable, reduced, sale; common, inferior, paltry, poor, second-rate, shoddy, tatty, tawdry, worthless; base, contemptible, despicable, low, mean, sordid, vulgar

cheat *v* beguile, con, deceive, defraud, double-cross, dupe, fleece, fool, hoax, hoodwink, mislead, swindle, take for a ride, thwart, trick, victimize; baffle, check, defeat, deprive, foil, frustrate, prevent, thwart;

cheat *n* examination, inspection, investigation, research, scrutiny, test; constraint, control, curb, damper, hindrance, impediment, inhibition, limitation, obstruction, restraint, stoppage

cheer *v* animate, brighten, buoy up, cheer up, comfort, console, elate, elevate, encourage, enliven, exhilarate, gladden, hearten, incite, inspirit, solace, uplift, warm; acclaim, applaud, clap, hail, hurrah

cheer *n* animation, buoyancy, cheerfulness, comfort, gaiety, gladness, glee, hopefulness, joy, liveliness, merriment, merry-making, mirth, optimism, solace

cheerful *adj* animated, blithe, bright, buoyant, cheery, contented, enlivening, enthusiastic, gay, glad, gladsome, happy, hearty, jaunty, jolly, joyful, light-hearted, lightsome, merry, optimistic, pleasant, sparkling, sprightly, sunny

cheerless *adj* austere, bleak, comfortless, dark, defected, depressed, desolate, despondent, disconsolate, dismal, dolorous, drab, dreary, dull, forlorn, gloomy, grim, joyless, melancholy, miserable, mournful, sad, sombre, sorrowful, sullen, unhappy, woebegone, woeful

cherish *v* care for, cleave to, cling to, comfort, cosset, encourage, entertain, foster, harbour, hold dear, nourish, nurse, nurture, prize, shelter, support, sustain, treasure

chest *n* box, case, casket, coffer, crate, strongbox, trunk

chew *v* bite, champ, crunch, gnaw, grind, masticate, munch

chief *adj* capital, cardinal, central, especial, essential, foremost, grand, highest, key, leading, main, most important, outstanding, paramount, predominant, pre-eminent, premier, prevailing, primary, prime, principal, superior, supreme, uppermost, vital

chief *n* boss, captain, chieftain, commander, director, governor, head, leader, lord, manager, master, principal, ringleader, ruler, superintendent, suzerain

chiefly *adv* above all, especially, essentially, in general, in the main, mainly, mostly, on the whole, predominantly, primarily, principally, usually

child *n* babe, baby, bairn, brat, chit, descendant, infant, issue, juvenile, little one, minor, nursling, off spring, progeny, suckling, toddler, tot, wean, youngster

childhood *n* boyhood, girlhood, immaturity, infancy, minority, schooldays, youth

childlike *adj* artless, credulous, guileless, ingenuous, innocent, naive, simple, trustful, trusting, unfeigned

chill *adj* biting, bleak, chilly, cold, freezing, frigid, raw, sharp, wintry;

chill *v* congeal, cool, freeze, refrigerate

chilly *adj* blowy, breezy, brisk, cool, crisp, draughty, fresh, nippy, penetrating, sharp; frigid, hostile, unfriendly, unresponsive, unsympathetic, unwelcoming

chip *n* dent, flake, flaw, fragment, nick, notch, paring, scrap, scratch, shard, shaving, sliver, wafer

chivalrous *adj* bold, brave, courageous, courteous, courtly, gallant, gentlemanly, heroic, highminded, honourable, intrepid, knightly, magnanimous, true, valiant

chivalry *n* courage, courtesy, courtliness, gallantry, gentlemanliness, knight errantry, knighthood, politeness

choice *n* alternative, discrimination, election, option, pick, preference, say, selection, variety;

choice *adj* best, crucial, dainty, elect, elite, excellent, exclusive, exquisite, hand-picked, nice, precious, prime, prize, rare, select, special, superior, uncommon, unusual, valuable

choke *v* asphyxiate, bar, block, clog, close, congest, constrict, dam, obstruct, occlude, overpower, smother, stifle, stop, strangle, suffocate, suppress, throttle

choose *v* adopt, cull, designate, desire, elect, espouse, fix on, opt for, pick, predestine, prefer, see fit, select, settle upon, single out, take, wish

chore *n* burden, duty, errand, job, task

chorus *n* choir, choristers, ensemble, singers, vocalists; burden, refrain, response, strain

christen *v* baptize, call, designate, dub, name, style, term, title

chronicle *n* account, annals, diary, history, journal, narrative, record, register, story

chronicle *v* enter, narrate, put on record, record, recount, register, relate, report, set down, tell

chuck *v* cast, discard, fling, heave, hurl, pitch, shy, sling, throw, toss

churlish *adj* boorish, brusque, crabbed, harsh, ill-tempered, impolite, loutish, morose, oafish, rude, sullen, surly, uncivil, unmannerly, vulgar

cinema *n* films, motion pictures, movies, pictures; (*Inf*) big screen, flicks

circle *n* band, circumference, coil, cordon, cycle, disc, globe, lap, loop, orb, perimeter, periphery, revolution, ring, round, sphere, turn; area, bounds, circuit, compass, domain, enclosure, field, orbit, province, range, realm, region, scene, sphere; assembly, class, clique, club, company, coterie, crowd, fellowship, fraternity, group, society

circle *v* belt, circumnavigate, circumscribe, coil, compass, curve, encircle, enclose, encompass, envelop, gird, hem in, pivot, revolve, ring, rotate, surround, tour, whirl

circuit *n* area, compass, course, journey, orbit, perambulation, revolution, round, route, tour, track

circulate *v* broadcast, diffuse, disseminate, distribute, issue, make known, promulgate, propagate, publicize, publish, spread

circulation *n* currency, dissemination, distribution, spread, transmission, vogue; circling, flow, motion, rotation

circumference *n* border, boundary, bounds, circuit, edge, extremity, fringe, limits, outline, perimeter, periphery, rim, verge

circumstance *n* accident, condition, contingency, detail, element, event, fact, factor, happening, incident, item, occurrence, particular, position, respect, situation

circumstances *pl n* life style, means, position, resources, situation, state, state of affairs, station, status, times

cite *v* adduce, advance, allude to, enumerate, evidence, extract, mention, name, quote, specify

citizen *n* burgess, burgher, denizen, dweller, freeman, inhabitant, ratepayer, resident, subject, townsman

city *n* conurbation, megalopolis, metropolis, municipality

civil *adj* civic, domestic, home, interior, municipal, political; accommodating, affable, civilized, complaisant, courteous, courtly, obliging, polished, polite, refined, urbane, well-bred, well-mannered

civilization *n* advancement, cultivation, culture, development, education, enlightenment, progress, refinement, sophistication; community, nation, people, polity, society

civilize *v* cultivate, educate, enlighten, humanize, improve, polish, refine, sophisticate, tame

claim *v* allege, ask, assert, call for, challenge, collect, demand, exact, hold, insist, maintain, need, pick up, profess, require, take, uphold

claim *n* affirmation, allegation, application, assertion, call, demand, petition, pretension, privilege, protestation, request, requirement, right, title

clan *n* band, brotherhood, clique, coterie, faction, family, fraternity, gens, group, house, race, sect, sept, set, society, sodality, tribe

clap *v* acclaim, applaud, cheer

clarify *v* clear up, elucidate, explain, illuminate, make plain, resolve, simplify, throw light on

clarity *n* clearness, comprehensibility, definition, explicitness, intelligibility, limpidity, lucidity, obviousness, precision, simplicity, transparency

clash *v* conflict, cross swords, feud, grapple, quarrel, war, wrangle

clash *n* brush, collision, conflict, confrontation, difference of opinion, disagreement, fight; (*Inf*) showdown

clasp *v* attack, clutch, concatenate, connect, embrace, enfold, fasten, grapple, grasp, grip, hold, hug, press, seize, squeeze

clasp *n* brooch, buckle, catch, clip, fastener, fastening, grip, hasp, hook, pin, press stud, snap

class *n* caste, category, classification, collection, denomination, department, division, genre, genus, grade, group, grouping, kind, league, order, rank, set, sort, species, sphere, status, type, value

classic *adj* best, consummate, finest, first-rate, masterly; archetypal, definitive, exemplary, ideal, master, model, paradigm, prototype, standard

classical *adj* chaste, elegant, harmonious, pure, refined, restrained, symmetrical, understated, well-proportioned; Attic, Augustan, Grecian, Greek, Hellenic, Latin, Roman

classification *n* analysis, arrangement, cataloguing, categorization, codification, grading, sorting, taxonomy

classify *v* arrange, catalogue, categorize, codify, dispose, distribute, file, grade, pigeonhole, rank, sort, systematize, tabulate

clause *n* article, chapter, condition, paragraph, part, passage, section; heading, item, point, provision, proviso, specification, stipulation

claw *n* chela, nail, nipper, pincer, talon, tentacle, unguis

clean *adj* faultless, flawless, fresh, hygienic, immaculate, laundered, pure, sanitary, spotless, unblemished, unsoiled, unspotted, unstained, unsullied, washed; chaste, decent, exemplary, good, honourable, innocent, moral, pure, respectable, undefiled, upright, virtuous

clean *v* bath, cleanse, deodorize, disinfect, do up, dust, launder, lave, mop, purge, purify, rinse, sanitize, scour, scrub, sponge, swab, sweep, vacuum, wash, wipe

clear *adj* bright, cloudless, fair, fine, halcyon, light, luminous, shining, sunny, unclouded, undimmed; apparent, articulate, audible, beyond doubt, beyond question, coherent, comprehensible, conspicuous, definite, distinct, evident, explicit, express, incontrovertible, intelligible, irrefutable, lucid, manifest, obvious, palpable, patent, perceptible, plain, pronounced, recognizable, sure, unambiguous, unequivocal, unmistakable, unquestionable; empty, free, open, smooth, unhampered, unhindered, unimpeded, unlimited, unobstructed; certain, convinced, decided, definite, positive, resolved, satisfied, sure

clear *v* clean, cleanse, erase, purify, refine, sweep away, tidy, wipe; break up, brighten, clarify, lighten; absolve, acquit, excuse, exonerate, justify, vindicate, jump, leap, miss, pass over, vault

clear-cut *v* definite, explicit, plain, precise, specific, straightforward, unambiguous, unequivocal

clearly *adv* beyond doubt, distinctly, evidently, incontestably, incontrovertibly, markedly, obviously, openly, undeniably, undoubtedly

clear up *v* answer, clarify, elucidate, explain, resolve, solve, straighten out, unravel; order, rearrange, tidy

clergyman *n* chaplain, cleric, curate, divine, father, man of God, man of the cloth, minister, padre, parson, pastor, priest, rabbi, rector, vicar

clever *adj* able, adroit, apt, astute, brainy, bright, canny, capable, cunning, deep, dexterous, discerning, expert, gifted, ingenious, intelligent, inventive, keen, knowing, knowledgeable, quick, rational, resourceful, sagacious, sensible, shrewd, skilful, smart, talented, witty

client *n* applicant, buyer, consumer, customer, dependant, patient, patron, shopper

clientele *n* business, clients, customers, following, market, patronage, regulars, trade

cliff *n* bluff, crag, escarpment, face, overhang, precipice, rock face, scar, scarp

climate *n* clime, country, region, temperature, weather; ambience, disposition, feeling, mood, temper, tendency, trend

climax *n* acme, apogee, culmination, head, height, highlight, highspot, peak, summit, top, zenith

climb *v* ascend, clamber, mount, rise, scale, shin up, soar, top

cling *v* adhere, attach to, be true to, clasp, cleave to, clutch, embrace, fasten, grasp, grip, hug, stick, twine round

clip *v* crop, curtail, cut, cut short, pare, prune, shear, shorten, snip, trim; attach, fasten, fix, hold, pin, staple; box, cuff, hit, punch, smack, wallop; (*Inf*) clout; dash, gallop, go fast, go like lightning, race, rush, whip along, zoom

cloak *v* camouflage, conceal, cover, disguise, hide, mask, obscure, screen, veil

cloak *n* blind, cape, coat, cover, front, mantle, mask, pretext, shield, wrap

clog *v* block, burden, congest, dam up, hamper, hinder, impede, jam, obstruct, occlude, shackle, stop up

close *v* bar, bolt, fasten, latch, padlock, secure, slam, shut; block, choke, clog, confine, cork, fill, obstruct, occlude, plug, seal, secure, shut, shut up, stop up; adjourn, agree, bring to an end, cease, clinch, complete, conclude, culminate, discontinue, end, establish, finish, fix, mothball, seal, settle, shut down, terminate, wind up; dwindle, grow smaller, lessen, narrow, reduce; clench, clutch one another, come together, connect, couple, grapple, grip, join, unite

close *adj* adjacent, adjoining, approaching, at hand, handy, hard by, imminent, impending, near, nearby, neighbouring, nigh; compact, congested, cramped, cropped, crowded, dense, impenetrable, jampacked, packed, short, solid, thick, tight; attached, confidential, dear, devoted, familiar, inseparable, intimate, loving; airless, confined, fuggy, heavy, humid, muggy, oppressive, stale, stifling, stuffy, suffocating, sweltering, thick, unventilated; illiberal, mean, mingy, miserly, near, niggardly, parsimonious, penurious, stingy, tight-fisted, ungenerous; alert, assiduous, attentive, concentrated, detailed, dogged, intense, keen, painstaking, rigorous, searching, vigilant

close *n* cessation, completion, conclusion, end, finale, finish, termination, wind-up; courtyard, cul-de-sac, enclosure, piazza, quadrangle

closet *n* cabinet, cupboard, locker, storage room, wardrobe

closet *adj* concealed, furtive, secret, undisclosed, unrevealed

closet *v* cloister, confine, isolate, seclude, sequester, shut away

cloth *n* dry goods, fabric, material, stuff, textiles

clothe *v* accoutre, apparel, array, attire, bedizen, caparison, cover, deck, drape, dress, endow, enwrap, equip, fit out, garb, habit, invest, outfit, rig, robe, swathe

clothing *n* apparel, attire, costume, dress, ensemble, garb, garments, habits, outfit, raiment, vestments, vesture, wardrobe, wear

cloud *n* billow, darkness, fog, gloom, haze, mist, murk, nebula, nebulosity, obscurity, vapour

cloud *v* becloud, darken, dim, eclipse, obfuscate, obscure, over cast, overshadow, shade, shadow, veil

cloudy *adj* blurred, confused, dark, dim, dismal, dull, dusky, emulsified, gloomy, hazy, indistinct, leaden, lowering, muddy, murky, nebulous, obscure, opaque, overcast, sombre, sullen, sunless

clown *n* buffoon, comedian, comic, dolt, fool, harlequin, humourist, jester, joker, merry andrew, pierrot, prankster, punchinello; dolt, fool, half-wit, idiot, nitwit; (*Inf*) clot, dope

clown *v* act foolishly, fool, jest, joke, mess about; (*Inf*) mess, muck about

club *n* bat, bludgeon, cosh, cudgel, stick, truncheon; association, circle, clique, company, fraternity, group, guild, lodge, order, set, society, sodality, union

clue *n* evidence, hint, indication, inkling, intimation, lead, pointer, sign, suggestion, suspicion, tip, trace

clumsy *adj* awkward, blundering, bumbling, bungling, gauche, gawky, heavy, ill-shaped, inept, inexpert, lumbering, maladroit, ponderous, uncoordinated, uncouth, ungainly, unhandy, unskilful, unwieldy; (*Inf*) butter-fingered

cluster *n* assemblage, batch, bunch, clump, collection, gathering, group, knot

cluster *v* assemble, bunch, collect, flock, gather, group

clutch *v* catch, clasp, cling to, embrace, fasten, grab, grapple, grasp, grip, seize, snatch

clutch *n* hatching, incubation, nest, set, setting

coach *n* bus, car, carriage, charabanc, vehicle; instructor, teacher, trainer, tutor

coach *v* cram, drill, instruct, prepare, train, tutor

coalition *v* affiliation, alliance, amalgam, amalgamation, association, bloc, combination, compact, confederacy, confederation, conjunction, fusion, integration, league, merger, union

coarse *adj* boorish, brutish, coarse-grained, foul-mouthed, gruff, loutish, rough, rude, uncivil

coarseness *n* bawdiness, boorish ness, crudity, earthiness, indelicacy, offensiveness, poor taste, ribaldry, roughness, smut, smuttiness, uncouthness, unevenness

coast *n* beach, border, coastline, littoral, seaboard, seaside, shore, strand

coast *v* cruise, drift, freewheel, get by, glide, sail, taxi

coat *n* fleece, fur, hair, hide, pelt, skin, wool; coating, covering, layer, overlay

coat *v* apply, cover, plaster, smear, spread

coax *v* allure, beguile, cajole, decoy, entice, flatter, inveigle, persuade, prevail upon, soothe, talk into, wheedle

cocky *adj* arrogant, brash, cocksure, conceited, egotistical, lordly, swaggering, swollen-headed, vain

code *n* cipher, cryptograph; canon, convention, custom, ethics, etiquette, manners, maxim, regulations, rules, system

coil *v* convolute, curl, entwine, loop, snake, spiral, twine, twist, wind, wreathe, writhe

coincide *v* accident, chance, eventuality, fluke, fortuity, happy, accident, luck, stroke of luck

cold *adj* arctic, biting, bitter, bleak, brumal, chill, chilly, cool, freezing, frigid, frosty, frozen, gelid, icy, inclement, raw, wintry; chilled, chilly, freezing, numbed, shivery; aloof, apathetic, cold-blooded, dead, distant, frigid, glacial, indifferent, inhospitable, lukewarm, passionless, phlegmatic, reserved, spiritless, standoffish, stony, undemonstrative, unfeeling, unmoved, unresponsive, unsympathetic

cold *n* chill, chilliness, coldness, frigidity, frostiness, iciness, inclemency

collaborate *v* cooperate, coproduce, join forces, participate, team up, work together

collaborator *n* associate, colleague, confederate, co-worker, partner, team-mate

collapse *v* break down, cave in, come to nothing, crack up, crumple, fail, faint, fall, fold, founder, give way, subside

collapse *n* breakdown, cave-in, disintegration, downfall, exhaustion, failure, faint, prostration, subsidence

colleague *n* aider, ally, assistant, associate, auxiliary, coadjutor, collaborator, companion, comrade, confederate, confrère, fellow worker, helper, partner, team-mate, workmate

collect *v* accumulate, aggregate, amass, assemble, gather, heap, hoard, save, stockpile; assemble, cluster, congregate, convene, converge, flock together, rally

collected *adj* calm, composed, confident, cool, placid, poised, self-possessed, serene, together, unperturbable, unperturbed, unruffled

collection *n* accumulation, anthology, compilation, congeries, heap, hoard, mass, pile, set, stockpile, store; assemblage, assembly, assortment, cluster, company, congregation, convocation, crowd, gathering, group; alms, contribution, offering, offertory

collide *v* clash, come into collision, conflict, crash, meet head-on

collision *n* accident, bump, crash, impact, pile-up, smash; (*Inf*) prang

colony *n* community, dependency, dominion, outpost, possession, province, satellite, state, settlement, territory

colossal *adj* elephantine, enormous, gargantuan, gigantic, ginormous, herculean, huge, immense, mammoth, massive, monstrous, monumental, mountainous, prodigious, titanic, vast

colour *n* colourant, coloration, complexion, dye, hue, paint, pigment, pigmentation, shade, tincture, tinge, tint; animation, bloom, blush, brilliance, flush, glow, liveliness, rosiness, ruddiness, vividness

colour *v* colourwash, dye, paint, stain, tinge, tint; disguise, distort, embroider, exaggerate, falsify, garble, gloss over, misrepresent, pervert, prejudice, slant, taint; blush, burn, crimson, flush, go crimson, redden

colourful *adj* bright, brilliant, intense, kaleidoscopic, motley, multicoloured, psychedelic, rich, variegated, vibrant, vivid; characterful, distinctive, graphic, interesting, lively, picturesque, rich, stimulating, unusual, vivid

colourless *adj* characterless, dreary, insipid, lacklustre, tame, uninteresting, unmemorable, vacuous, vapid

column *n* calvacade, file, line, list, procession, queue, rank, row, string, train; caryatid, obelisk, pilaster, pillar, post, shaft, support, upright

coma *n* black-out, drowsiness, insensibility, lethargy, oblivion, somnolence, stupor, torpor, trance, unconsciousness

comb *v* arrange, dress, groom, untangle; go through with a fine-tooth comb, hunt, rake, ransack, rummage, recur, re-enter, return

combat *n* action, battle, conflict, contest, encounter, engagement, fight, skirmish, struggle, war, warfare

combination *n* amalgam, amalgamation, blend, coalescence, composite, connection, mix, mixture; alliance, association, cabal, cartel, coalition, combine, compound, confederacy, confederation, consortium, conspiracy, federation, merger, syndicate, unification, union

combine *v* amalgamate, associate, bind, blend, bond, compound, connect, cooperate, fuse, incorporate, integrate, join, link, marry, merge, mix, pool, put together, synthesize, unify, unite

come *v* advance, appear, approach, arrive, become, draw near, enter, happen, materialize, move, near, occur, originate, reach, show up, turn out; appear, arrive, attain, enter, materialize, reach; fall, happen, occur, take place; arise, emanate, emerge, end up, flow, issue, originate, result, turn out; extend, reach; (*Inf*) show up

come about *v* arise, befall, come to pass, happen, occur, result, take place, transpire

come across *v* bump into, chance upon, discover, encounter, find, happen upon, hit upon, light upon, meet, notice, stumble upon, unearth

comeback *n* rally, rebound, recovery, resurgence, return, revival, triumph

come back *v* reappear, recur, re-enter, return

comedown *n* anticlimax, blow, decline, deflation, demotion, disappointment, humiliation, letdown, reverse

comedy *n* chaffing, drollery, facetiousness, farce, fun, hilarity, humour, jesting, joking, light entertainment, sitcom, slapstick, wisecracking, witticisms

come in *v* appear, be published, be divulged, be issued, be released, be reported, revealed; conclude, end, result, terminate

come through *v* accomplish, achieve, prevail, succeed, triumph; endure, survive, weather the storm, withstand

comfort *v* alleviate, assuage, cheer, commiserate with, compassionate, console, ease, encourage, enliven, gladden, hearten, inspirit, invigorate, reassure, refresh, relieve, solace, soothe, strengthen;

comfort *n* aid, alleviation, cheer, compensation, consolation, ease, encouragement, enjoyment, help, relief, satisfaction, succour, support; coziness, creature, comforts, ease, luxury, opulence, snugness, wellbeing

comfortable *adj* adequate, agreeable, ample, commodious, convenient, cosy, delightful, easy, enjoy able, homely, loose, loosefitting, pleasant, relaxing, restful, roomy, snug; affluent, prosperous, well-off, well-to-do

comic *adj* amusing, comical, droll,

facetious, farcical, funny, humorous, jocular, joking, light, rich, waggish, witty

coming *adj* approaching, at hand, due, en route, forthcoming, future, imminent, impending, in store, in the wind, near, next, nigh

coming *n* accession, advent, approach, arrival

command *v* bid, charge, compel, demand, direct, enjoin, order, require; control, dominate, govern, head, lead, manage, reign over, rule, supervise, sway

command *n* behest, bidding, commandment, decree, direction, directive, edict, fiat, injunction, instruction, mandate, order, precept, requirement, ultimatum

commander *n* boss, captain, chief, C in C, CO, commander-in-chief, commanding officer, director, head, leader, officer, ruler

commanding *adj* advantageous, controlling, decisive, dominant, dominating, superior

commemorate *v* celebrate, honour, immortalize, keep, memorialize, observe, pay tribute to, remember, salute, solemnize

commemoration *n* ceremony, honouring, memorial service, observance, remembrance, tribute

commence *v* begin, embark on, enter upon, inaugurate, initiate, open, originate, start

commend *v* acclaim, applaud, approve, compliment, eulogize, extol, praise, recommend, speak highly of

comment *v* animadvert, interpose, mention, note, observe, opine, point out, remark, say; annotate, criticize, elucidate, explain, interpret

comment *n* animadversion, observation, observation, remark, statement; annotation, commentary, criticism, elucidation, explanation, exposition, illustration, note

commentary *n* analysis, critique, description, exegesis, explanation, narration, notes, review, treatise, voice-over

commentator *n* commenter, reporter, special, correspondent, sportscaster

commerce *n* business, mercantile, profit-making, sales, trade, trading

commission *n* appointment, authority, charge, duty, employment, errand, function, mandate, mission, task, allowance, brokerage, compensation, cut, fee, percentage; board, body of commissioners, commissioners, committee, delegation, deputation, representative

commission *v* appoint, authorize, contract, delegate, depute, empower, engage, nominate, order, select, send

commit *v* carry out, do, enact, execute, perform, perpetrate

commitment *n* duty, engagement, liability, obligation, responsibility, tie; assurance, guarantee, pledge, promise, undertaking, vow, word

common *adj* average, commonplace, conventional, customary, daily, everyday, familiar, frequent, general, habitual, humdrum, obscure, ordinary, plain, regular, routine, run-of-the-mill, simple, standard, stock, usual; accepted, general, popular, prevailing, prevalent, universal, widespread; coarse, inferior, low, pedestrian, plebeian, stale, trite, undistinguished, vulgar

commotion *n* ado, agitation, bustle, disorder, disturbance, excitement, ferment, furore, fuss, perturbation, racket, riot, rumpus, to-do, tumult, turmoil, uproar

communal *adj* collective, communistic, community, general, joint, neighbourhood, public, shared

communicate *v* acquaint, announce, be in contact, be in touch, connect, convey, correspond, declare, disclose, disseminate, divulge, impart, inform, make known, pass on, phone, proclaim, publish, report, reveal, ring up, signify, spread, transmit, unfold

communication *n* connection, contact, conversation, correspondence, dissemination, intercourse, link, transmission; announcement, disclosure, dispatch, information, intelligence, message, news, report, statement, word

communism *n* Bolshevism, collectivism, Marxism, socialism, state socialism

community *n* association, body politic, brotherhood, company, district, general public, locality, people, populace, population, public, residents, society, state

compact *adj* close, compressed, condensed, dense, firm, impenetrable, impermeable, pressed together, solid, thick; brief, compendious, concise, epigrammatic, laconic, pithy, pointed, succinct, terse, to the point

companion *n* accomplice, ally, associate, colleague, comrade, confederate, consort, crony, friend, mate, partner; complement, counterpart, fellow, match, mate, twin

companionship *n* amity, camaraderie, company, comradeship, conviviality, fellowship, fraternity, friendship, rapport, togetherness

company *n* assemblage, assembly, band, body, circle, collection, community, concourse, convention, coterie, crew, crowd, ensemble, gathering, group, league, party, set, throng, troop, troupe, turnout; association, business, concern, corporation, establishment, firm, house, partnership, syndicate

compare with *v* balance, collate, contrast, juxtapose, set against, weigh

comparison *n* collation, contrast, distinction, juxtaposition, analogy, comparability, correlation, likeness, resemblance, similarity

compartment *n* alcove, bay, berth, booth, carrel, carriage, cell, chamber, cubbyhole, cubicle, locker, niche, pigeonhole, section

compassion *n* charity, clemency, commiseration, compunction, condolence, fellow, feeling, heart, humanity, kindness, mercy, sorrow, sympathy, tenderness

compel *v* coerce, constrain, dragoon, drive, enforce, exact, force, impel, make, necessitate, oblige, restrain, squeeze, urge; (*Inf*) bulldoze

compensation *n* amends, atonement, damages, indemnification, indemnity, payment, recompense, reimbursement, remuneration, reparation, requital, restitution, reward, satisfaction

compete *v* be in the running, challenge, contend, contest, emulate, fight, pit oneself against, rival, strive, struggle, vie

competent *adj* able, adapted, adequate, appropriate, capable, clever, endowed, equal, fit, pertinent, proficient, qualified, sufficient, suitable

competition *n* contention, contest, emulation, one-upmanship, opposition, rivalry, strife, struggle; championship, contest, event, puzzle, quiz, tournament

competitor *n* adversary, antagonist, challenger, competition, contestant, emulator, opponent, opposition, rival

compile *v* accumulate, amass, anthologize, collect, cull, garner, gather, marshal, organize, put together

complacent *adj* contented, gratified, pleased, pleased with oneself, satisfied, self-assured, self-contented, self-righteous, self-satisfied, serene, smug, unconcerned

complain *v* bemoan, bewail, carp, deplore, find fault, fuss, grieve, gripe, groan, grouse, growl, grumble, lament, moan, whine; (*Inf*) bellyache

complaint *n* accusation, annoyance, charge, criticism, dissatisfaction, fault-finding, grievance, gripe, grouse, grumble, lament, moan, plaint, remonstrance, trouble, wail; affliction, ailment, disease, disorder, illness, indisposition, malady, sickness, upset

complete *adj* all, entire, faultless, full, intact, integral, plenary, unabridged, unbroken, undivided, unimpaired, whole; accomplished, achieved, concluded, ended, finished; absolute, consummate, perfect, thorough, thoroughgoing, total, utter

complete *v* accomplish, achieve, cap, close, conclude, crown, discharge, do, end, execute, fill in, finalize, finish, fulfil, perfect, perform, realize, round off, settle, terminate

completely *adv* absolutely, altogether, down to the ground, entirely, from beginning to end, fully, heart and soul, hook, line and sinker, in full, perfectly, quite, solidly, thoroughly, totally, utterly, wholly

complex *adj* circuitous, complicated, convoluted, intricate, involved, knotty, mingled, mixed, tangled, tortuous

complicate *v* confuse, entangle, interweave, involve, make intricate, muddle, snarl up

complicated *adj* complex, convoluted, elaborate, interlaced, intricate, involved, labyrinthine; difficult, perplexing, problematic, puzzling, troublesome

complication *n* combination, complexity, confusion, entanglement, intricacy, mixture, web

compliment *n* admiration, bouquet, commendation, congratulations, courtesy, eulogy, favour, flattery, honour, praise, tribute

compliment *v* commend, congratulate, extol, felicitate, flatter, laud, pay tribute to, praise, salute, sing the praises of, speak highly of, wish joy to

comply *v* abide by, accede, accord, acquiesce, adhere to, agree to, conform to, consent to, defer, discharge, follow, fulfil, obey, observe, perform, respect, satisfy, submit, yield

component *n* constituent, element, ingredient, item, part, piece, unit

compose *v* build, compound, comprise, constitute, construct, fashion, form, make, make up, put together

composition *n* arrangement, configuration, constitution, design, form, formation, layout, make-up, organization, structure; creation, essay, exercise, literary work, opus, piece, study, work, writing

composure *n* aplomb, calm, calmness, collectedness, cool, coolness, dignity, ease, equanimity, imperturbability, placidity, poise, sedateness, self-assurance, self-possession, serenity, tranquillity

compound *v* amalgamate, blend, coalesce, combine, concoct, fuse, intermingle, mingle, mix, synthesize, unite

compound *n* alloy, amalgam, blend, combination, composite, composition, conglomerate, fusion, medley, mixture, synthesis

compound *adj* complex, composite, conglomerate, intricate, multiple, not simple

comprehend *v* apprehend, assimilate, conceive, discern, fathom, grasp, know, make out, perceive, see, take in, understanding

compress *v* abbreviate, compact, concentrate, condense, constrict, contract, cram, crowd, crush, press, shorten, squash, squeeze, summarize, wedge

comprise *v* be composed of, com prehend, consist of, contain, embrace, encompass, include, take in

compromise *v* adjust, agree, arbitrate, compose, compound, concede, give and take, meet halfway, settle, strike a balance

compromise *n* accommodation, accord, adjustment, agreement, concession, half measures, middle ground, settlement, trade-off

compulsive *adj* besetting, compelling, driving, irresistible, obsessive, overwhelming, uncontrollable, urgent

compulsory *adj* binding, forced, imperative, mandatory, obligatory, required, requisite

comrade *n* ally, associate, buddy, colleague, companion, compatriot, compeer, confederate, co-worker, crony, fellow, friend, partner; (*Inf*) mate, pal

conceal *v* bury, camouflage, cover, disguise, dissemble, hide, keep, dark, keep secret, mask, obscure, screen, secrete, shelter

conceit *n* arrogance, complacency, egotism, narcissism, pride, self-importance, self-love, swagger, vainglory, vanity

conceited *adj* arrogant, bigheaded, cocky, egotistical, immodest, narcissistic, overweening, puffed up, self-important, stuck up, swollen-headed, vain, vainglorious

conceivable *adj* believable, credible, imaginable, possible, thinkable

conceive *v* appreciate, apprehend, believe, comprehend, envisage, fancy, grasp, imagine, realize, suppose, understand; contrive, create, design, develop, devise, form, formulate, produce, project, purpose, think up

concentrate *v* be engrossed in, consider closely, focus attention on, give all one's attention to, put one's mind to rack one's brains; bring to bear, centre, cluster, converge, focus

concentrated *adj* deep, hard, intense, intensive; boiled down, condensed, evaporated, reduced, rich, thickened, undiluted

concept *n* abstraction, conception, conceptualization, hypothesis, idea, image, impression, notion, theory, view

concern *v* affect, apply to, bear on, be relevant to, interest, involve, pertain to, regard, touch; bother, disquiet, distress, disturb, make anxious, make uneasy, perturb, trouble, worry

concern *n* affair, business, charge, deportment, field, interest, involvement, job, matter, mission, occupation, responsibility, task, transaction; anxiety, apprehension, attention, burden, care, consideration, disquiet, disquietude, distress, heed, responsibility, solicitude, worry; company, corporation, enterprise, establishment, firm, house, organization

concerned *adj* active, implicated, interested, involved, mixed up, privy to; anxious, bothered, distressed, disturbed, exercised, troubled, uneasy, upset, worried

concerning *prep* about, apropos of, as regards, as to, in the matter of, in the subject of, re, regarding, relating to, respecting, touching, with reference to

concise *adj* brief, compact, compendious, compressed, condensed, epigrammatic, laconic, pithy, short, succinct, summary, synoptic, terse, to the point

conclude *v* bring down the curtain, cease, close, come to an end, complete, draw to a close, end, finish, round off, terminate, wind up; assume, decide, deduce, gather, infer, judge, reckon, sum up, suppose, surmise

conclusion *n* close, completion, end, finale, finish, result, termination; consequence, culmination, issue, outcome, result, upshot; agreement, conviction, decision, deduction, inference, judgment, opinion, resolution, settlement, verdict

conclusive *adj* clinching, convincing, decisive, definitive, final, irrefutable, ultimate, unanswerable, unarguable

concrete *adj* actual, definite, explicit, factual, material, real, sensible, specific, substantial, tangible

condemn *v* blame, censure, damn, denounce, disapprove, reprehend, reproach, reprobate, reprove, upbraid; convict, damn, doom, pass sentence on, proscribe, sentence

condemnation *n* blame, censure, denouncement, denunciation, disapproval, reproach, reprobation, reproof, stricture; conviction, damnation, doom, judgment, proscription, sentence

condense *v* abbreviate, abridge, compact, compress, concentrate, contract, curtail, encapsulate, epitomize, shorten, summarize

condensed *adv* abridged, compressed, concentrated, curtailed, shortened, shrunken, slimmed down, summarized

condescend *v* be courteous, bend, come down off one's high horse, deign, humble oneself, demean-oneself, lower oneself, see fit, stoop, submit, unbend, vouchsafe; patronize, talk, down to

condescending *adj* disdainful, lofty, lordly, patronizing, snobbish, supercilious, superior

condition *n* case, circumstances, plight, position, predicament, shape, situation, state, state of affairs; arrangement, article, demand, limitation, modification, prerequisite, provision, qualification, requirement, requisite, restriction, rule, stipulation, terms; fettle, fitness, health, kilter, order, shape, trim

condition *v* accustom, adapt, educate, equip, habituate, inure, make ready, prepare, tone up, train, work out

conditional *n* contingent, dependent, limited, provisional, qualified, subject to, with reservations

conditions *pl n* circumstances, environment, milieu, situation, surroundings, way of life

conduct *n* administration, control, direction, guidance, leadership, management, organization, running, supervision

conduct *v* administer, carry on, control, direct, govern, handle, lead, manage, organize, preside over, regulate, run, supervise

conduct *n* attitude, bearing, behaviour, carriage, comportment, demeanour, deportment, manners, mien, ways

confederacy *n* alliance, bund, coalition, compact, confederation, conspiracy, covenant, federation, league, union

confer *v* consult, converse, deliberate, discourse, parley, talk

conference *n* colloquium, congress, consultation, convention, convocation, discussion, forum, meeting, seminar, symposium, teach-in

confess *v* acknowledge, admit, allow, blurt out, come clean, concede, confide, disclose, divulge, grant, make a clean breast of, own, own up, recognize; affirm, assert, attest, aver, confirm, declare, evince, manifest, profess, prove, reveal

confession *n* acknowledgment, admission, avowal, disclosure, divulgence, exposure, revelation, unbosoming

confide *v* admit, breathe, confess, disclose, divulge, impart, reveal, whisper

confidence *n* belief, credence, dependence, faith, reliance, trust, aplomb, assurance, boldness, courage, firmness, nerve, self-possession, self-reliance; **in confidence** between you and me, confidentially, in secrecy, privately

confident *adj* certain, convinced, counting on, positive, satisfied, secure, sure; assured, bold, dauntless, fearless, self-assured, self-reliant

confidential *adj* classified, intimate, off the record, private, privy, secret

confine *v* bind, bound, cage, circumscribe, enclose, hem in, hold back, immure, imprison, incarcerate, intern, keep, limit, repress, restrain, restrict, shut-up

confirm *v* assure, buttress, clinch, establish, fix, fortify, reinforce, settle, strengthen; approve, authenticate, bear out, corroborate, endorse, ratify, sanction, substantiate, validate, verify

confirmation *n* authentication, corroboration, evidence, proof, substantiation, testimony, validation, verification; acceptance, agreement, approval, assent, endorsement, ratification, sanction

confirmed *adj* chronic, habitual, hardened, ingrained, inured, inveterate, long established, rooted, seasoned

conflict *n* battle, clash, collision, combat, contention, contest, encounter, engagement, fight, fracas, strife, war, warfare; antagonism, difference, disagreement, discord, dissension, divided loyalties, friction, hostility, interference, opposition, strife, variance

conflict *v* be at variance, clash, collide, combat, contend, contest, differ, disagree, fight, interfere, strive, struggle

confuse *v* baffle, bemuse, bewilder, darken, mystify, obscure, perplex, puzzle; abash, addle, demoralize, discomfit, discompose, disconcert, discountenance, disorient, embarrass, fluster, mortify, nonplus, shame, throw off balance, upset

confusion *n* befuddlement, bemuse ment, bewilderment, disorientation, mystification, perplexity, puzzle ment; bustle, chaos, clutter, commotion, disarrangement, disorder, disorganization, hotchpotch, jumble, mess, muddle, shambles, tangle, turmoil, untidiness, upheaval

congenial *adj* adapted, agreeable, companionable, compatible, complaisant, favourable, fit, friendly, genial, kindly, kindred, like-minded, pleasant, pleasing, suitable, sympathetic, well-suited

congested *adj* blocked-up, clogged, crammed, crowded, jammed, over crowded, overfilled, overflowing, packed, stuffed, stuffed-up, teeming

congratulate *v* compliment, felicitate, wish joy to

congratulations best wishes, compliments, felicitations, good wished, greetings

congregate *v* assemble, collect, come together, concentrate, convene, converge, convoke, flock, for gather, gather, mass, meet, muster, rally, rendezvous, throng

congregation *n* assembly, brethren, crowd, fellowship, flock, host, laity, multitude, parish, parishioners, throng

congress *n* assembly, chamber of deputies, conclave, conference, convention, convocation, council, delegates, diet, legislative, assembly, legislature, meeting, parliament, representative

connect *v* affix, ally, associate, cohere, combine, couple, fasten,

join, link, relate, unite
connected *adv* affiliated, akin, allied, associated, banded together, bracketed, combined, coupled, joined, linked, related, united
connection *n* alliance, association, attachment, coupling, fastening, junction, link, tie, union; affinity, association, bond, commerce, communication, correlation, correspondence, intercourse, interrelation, link, marriage, relation, relationship, relevance, tie-in; acquaintance, ally, associate, contact, friend, sponsor
connoisseur *n* aficionado, appreciator, arbiter, authority, cognoscente, devotee, expert, judge, savant, specialist
conquer *v* beat, checkmate, crush, defeat, discomfit, get the better of, humble, master, overcome, overpower, overthrow, prevail, quell, rout, subdue, subjugate, succeed, surmount, triumph, vanquish
conqueror *n* champion, conquistador, defeater, hero, lord, master, subjugator, vanquisher, victor, winner
conquest *n* defeat, discomfiture, mastery, overthrow, rout, triumph, vanquishment, victory; acquisition, annexation, appropriation, coup, invasion, occupation, subjection, subjugation, takeover
conscience *n* moral sense, principles, scruples, sense of right and wrong, still small voice
conscientious *adj* careful, diligent, exact, faithful, meticulous, painstaking, particular, punctilious, thorough
conscious *adj* alert, alive to, awake, aware, cognizant, percipient, responsive, sensible, sentient; calculated, deliberate, intentional, knowing, premeditated, rational, reasoning, reflective, responsible, self-conscious, studied, wilful
consciousness *n* apprehension, awareness, knowledge, realization, recognition, sensibility
consecrate *v* dedicate, devote, exalt, hallow, ordain, sanctify, set apart, venerate
consecutive *adj* chronological, following, in sequence, in turn, running, sequential, seriatim, succeeding, successive, uninterrupted
consent *v* accede, acquiesce, agree, allow, approve, assent, comply, concede, concur, permit, yield
consent *n* acquiescence, agreement, approval, assent, compliance, concession, concurrence, permission, sanction
consequence *n* effect, end, event, issue, outcome, repercussion, result, upshot
conservation *n* custody, economy, guardianship, husbandry, maintenance, preservation, protection, safeguarding, safekeeping, saving, upkeep
conservative *adj* cautious, conventional, die-hard, guarded, hidebound, middle-of-the-road, moderate, quiet, reactionary, right-wing, sober, tory, traditional
conserve *v* hoard, husband, keep, nurse, preserve, protect, save, store up, take care of, use sparingly; (*Inf*) go easy on
consider *v* chew over, cogitate,

consult, contemplate, deliberate, discuss, examine, meditate, mull over, muse, ponder, reflect, revolve, ruminate, study, think about, turn over in one's mind, weigh; bear in mind, care for, keep in view, make allowance for, reckon with, regard, remember, respect, take into account

considerable *adj* abundant, ample, appreciable, comfortable, goodly, great, large, lavish, marked, much, noticeable, plentiful, reasonable, sizable, substantial, tidy, tolerable; distinguished, important, influential, noteworthy, renowned, significant, venerable

considerate *adj* attentive, charitable, circumspect, concerned, discreet, forbearing, kind, kindly, mindful, obliging, patient, tactful, thoughtful, unselfish

consideration *n* analysis, attention, cogitation, contemplation, deliberation, discussion, examination, reflection, regard, review, scrutiny, study, thought; concern, considerateness, friendliness, kindliness, kindness, respect, solicitude, tact, thoughtfulness

considering *prep* all in all, all things considered, insomuch as, in the light of, in view of

consignment *n* batch, delivery, goods, shipment

consist *v* be composed of, be made up of, amount to, comprise, contain, embody, include, incorporate, involve

consistent *adj* constant, dependable, persistent, regular, steady, true to type, unchanging, undeviating

consolation *n* alleviation, assuagement, cheer, comfort, ease, easement, encouragement, help, relief, solace, succour, support

console *v* assuage, calm, cheer, comfort, encourage, express sympathy for, relieve, solace, soothe

consolidate *v* fortify, reinforce, secure, stabilize, strengthen

conspicuous *adj* apparent, clear, discernible, easily seen, evident, manifest, noticeable, obvious, patent, perceptible, visible

conspiracy *n* cabal, collusion, confederacy, intrigue, league, machination, plot, scheme, treason

conspire *v* cabal, confederate, contrive, devise, hatch treason, intrigue, machinate, manoeuvre, plot, scheme

constant *adj* continual, even, firm, fixed, habitual, immutable, invariable, permanent, perpetual, regular, stable, steadfast, steady, unalterable, unbroken, uniform, unvarying; ceaseless, continual, continuous, endless, eternal, everlasting, incessant, interminable, never-ending, nonstop, perpetual, persistent, relentless, sustained, uninterrupted, unrelenting, unremitting

constantly *adv* all the time, always, continually, continuously, endlessly, everlastingly, incessantly, interminably, invariably, morning, noon and night, night and day, nonstop, perpetually, persistently, relentlessly

consternation *n* alarm, amazement, anxiety, awe, bewilderment, confusion, dismay, distress, dread, fear, fright, horror, panic, shock,

terror, trepidation
constituent *adj* basic, component, elemental, essential, integral
constituent *n* component, element, essential, factor, ingredient, part, principle, unit
constitute *v* compose, comprise, create, enact, establish, fix, form, found, make, make up, set up
constitution *n* composition, establishment, formation, organization
constrain *v* bind, coerce, compel, drive, force, impel, necessitate, oblige, pressure, pressurize, urge
constraint *n* coercion, compulsion, force, necessity, pressure, restraint; check, curb, damper, deterrent, hindrance, limitation, restriction
construct *v* assemble, build, compose, create, design, elevate, engineer, erect, establish, fabricate, fashion, form, formulate, found, frame, make, manufacture, organize, put up, raise, set up, shape
construction *n* assembly, building, composition, creation, edifice, erection, fabric, fabrication, figure, form, formation, shape, structure
constructive *adj* helpful, positive, practical, productive, useful, valuable
consult *v* ask, ask advice of, commune, compare notes, confer, consider, debate, deliberate, interrogate, question, refer to, take counsel, turn to
consultant *n* adviser, authority, specialist
consultation *n* appointment, conference, council, deliberation, dialogue, discussion, examination, hearing, interview, meeting, session
consume *v* absorb, deplete, dissipate, drain, eat up, employ, exhaust, expend, finish up, fritter away, lavish, lessen, spend, squander, use, use up, utilize, vanish, waste, wear out
consumer *n* buyer, customer, purchaser, shopper, user
contact *n* approximation, contiguity, junction, juxtaposition, touch, union; acquaintance, connection
contact *v* approach, call, communicate with, get in touch with, get hold of, phone, reach, ring, speak to, write to
contain *v* accommodate, enclose, have capacity for, hold, incorporate, seat
container *n* holder, receptacle, repository, vessel
contemplate *v* brood over, consider, deliberate, meditate, meditate on, mull over, muse over, observe, ponder, reflect upon, turn over in one's mind, study; aspire to, consider, design, envisage, expect, foresee, have in view, intend, mean, plan, propose, think of
contemporary *adj* coetaneous, coeval, coexistent, coexisting, concurrent, contemporaneous, synchronous; current, in fashion, latest, modern, present, recent, ultramodern, up-to-date
contemporary *n* compeer, fellow, peer
contempt *n* condescension, contumely, derision, disdain, disregard, disrespect, mockery, neglect, scorn, slight
contend *v* clash, compete, contest, cope, emulate, grapple, jostle,

litigate, skirmish, strive, struggle, vie; affirm, allege, argue, assert, aver, avow, debate, dispute, hold, maintain

content *n* burden, gist, ideas, matter, subject matter, substance, text, theme; amount, proportion, quantity; capacity, size, volume; contentment, happiness, pleasure, satisfaction

content *adj* agreeable, at ease, at peace, cheerful, comfortable, complacent, contented, fulfiled, glad, gratified, pleased, satisfied, serene, tranquil willing to accept

content *v* appease, be fulfilled, be gratified, delight, gladden, gratify, humour, indulge, mollify, pacify, placate, please, reconcile, satisfy, soothe, suffice

contented *adj* at ease, at peace, cheerful, comfortable, complacent, content, glad, gratified, happy, pleased, satisfied, serene, thankful

contentment *n* cheerfulness, comfort, complacency, content, content edness, ease, equanimity, fulfilment, gladness, gratification, happiness, peace, pleasure, repletion, satisfaction, serenity

contents *pl n* constituents, elements, ingredients, load; chapters, divisions, subject matter, subjects, themes, topics

contest *n* competition, game, match, tournament, trial

contest *v* compete, contend, fight, fight over, strive, vie; argue, call into a question, challenge, debate, dispute, doubt, litigate, object to, oppose, question

contestant *n* aspirant, candidate, competitor, contender, entrant, participant, player, rival

context *n* background, connection, frame of reference, framework, relation

continual *adj* constant, continuous, endless, eternal, everlasting, frequent, incessant, interminable, perpetual, recurrent, regular, repeated, repetitive, unceasing, uninterrupted, unremitting

continually *adv* all the time, always, constantly, endlessly, eternally, everlastingly, forever, incessantly, interminably, nonstop, persistently, repeatedly

continuation *n* addition, extension, furtherance, postscript, sequel, supplement

continue *v* abide, carry on, endure, last, live on, persist, remain, rest, stay, stay on, survive

continuity *n* cohesion, connection, flow, interrelationship, progression, sequence, succession, whole

continuous *adj* connected, constant, continued, extended, prolonged, unbroken, unceasing, undivided, uninterrupted

contract *v* abbreviate, abridge, compress, condense, confine, constrict, curtail, dwindle, epitomize, lessen, narrow, purse, reduce, shrink, shrivel, tighten, wither, wrinkle; agree, arrange, bargain, bond, commission, commitment, compact, concordat, convention, covenant, engagement, pact, settle ment, stipulation, treaty, understanding

contradict *v* be at variance with, belie, challenge, contravene, controvert, counter, counteract, deny, dis-

pute, impugn, negate, oppose
contradiction *n* conflict, confutation, contravention, denial, incongruity, inconsistency, negation, opposite
contradictory *adj* antagonistic, antithetical, conflicting, contrary, discrepant, incompatible, inconsistent, irreconcilable, opposed, opposite, paradoxical, repugnant
contrary *adj* adverse, antagonistic, clashing, contradictory, counter, discordant, hostile, inconsistent, inimical, opposed, opposite, paradoxical
contrast *n* comparison, contrariety, difference, differentiation, disparity, dissimilarity, distinction, divergence, foil, opposition
contrast *v* compare, differ, differentiate, distinguish, oppose, set in opposition, set off
contribute *v* add afford, bestow, donate, furnish, give, provide, subscribe, supply
contribution *n* addition, bestowal, donation, gift, grant, input, offering, subscription
contributor *n* backer, bestower, conferrer, donor, giver, patron, subscriber, supporter; correspondent, freelance, freelancer, journalist, reporter
contrite *adj* chastened, conscience-stricken, humble, in sackcloth and ashes, penitent, regretful, remorseful, repentant, sorrowful, sorry
contrive *v* concoct, construct, create, design, devise, engineer, fabricate, frame, improvise, invent
contrived *adj* artificial, elaborate, forced, laboured, overdone, planned, recherché, strained, unnatural
control *v* boss, call the tune, command, conduct, direct, dominate, govern, have charge of, lead, manage, manipulate, oversee, pilot, reign over, rule, steer, superintend, supervise; bridle, check, constrain, contain, curb, hold back, limit, master, rein in, repress, restrain, subdue
control *n* authority, charge, command, direction, discipline, government, guidance, management, rule, supervision, supremacy; brake, check, curb, limitation, regulation, restraint
controversial *adj* at issue, contented, contentious, controvertible, debatable, disputable, disputed, open to question, under discussion
controversy *n* altercation, argument, contention, debate, discussion, dispute, dissension, polemic, quarrel, squabble, strife, wrangle, wrangling
convene *v* assemble, bring together, call, come together, congregate, convoke, gather, meet, muster, rally, summon
convenience *n* accessibility, appropriateness, availability, fitness, handiness, opportuneness, serviceability, suitability, usefulness, utility
convenient *adj* adapted, appropriate, beneficial, commodious, fit, fitted, handy, helpful, labour-saving, opportune, seasonable, serviceable, suitable, suited, timely, useful, well-timed; accessible, at hand, available, handy, nearby, within reach
convention *n* assembly, conference,

congress, convocation, council, delegates, meeting, representatives; code, custom, etiquette, formality, practice, propriety, protocol, tradition, usage

converge *v* coincide, combine, come together, concentrate, focus, gather, join, meet, merge, mingle

conversation *n* chat, colloquy, communication, communion, confabulation, conference, converse, dialogue, discourse, discussion, exchange, gossip, intercourse, talk

converse *n* antithesis, contrary, observe, opposite, other side of the coin, reverse

conversion *n* change, metamorphosis, transfiguration, transformation, transmutation; adaptation, alteration, modification, reconstruction, remodelling, reorganization; change of heart, rebirth, reformation, regeneration

convert *v* alter, change, interchange, metamorphose, transform, transmute, transpose, turn; adapt, apply, appropriate, modify, remodel, reorganize, restyle, revise

convey *v* bear, bring, carry, conduct, fetch, forward, grant, guide, move, send, support, transmit, transport

convict *v* condemn, find guilty, imprison, pronounce guilty, sentence

convict *n* con, criminal, culprit, felon, jailbird, malefactor, prisoner

conviction *n* assurance, certainty, certitude, confidence, earnestness, fervour, firmness, reliance

convince *v* assure, bring round, gain the confidence of, persuade, prevail upon, prove to, satisfy, sway, win over

cool *adj* chilled, chilling, chilly, coldish, nippy, refreshing; calm, collected, composed, deliberate, dispassionate, imperturbable, level-headed, placid, quiet, relaxed, self-controlled, self-possessed, serene, unemotional, unexcited, unruffled; (*Inf*) laid-back; aloof, apathetic, distant, frigid, incurious, indifferent, lukewarm, offhand, reserved, standoffish, uncommunicative, unconcerned, unenthusiastic, unfriendly, uninterested, unresponsive, unwelcoming

cool *v* chill, cool off, freeze, lose heat, refrigerate; abate, allay, assuage, calm, dampen, lessen, moderate, quiet, temper

cooperate *v* bet, aid, assist, collaborate, combine, concur, conduce, conspire, contribute, coordinate, help, join forces, pool resources, pull together, work together

cooperation *n* assistance, collaboration, combined, effort, concert, concurrence, give-and-take, helpfulness, participation, responsiveness, teamwork, unity

cooperative *adj* accommodating, helpful, obliging, responsive, supportive

coordinate *v* correlate, harmonize, integrate, match, mesh, organize, relate, synchronize, systematize

cope *v* carry on, get by, hold one's own, make the grade, manage, rise to the occasion, struggle through, survive; **cope with** contend, deal, dispatch, encounter, grapple, handle, struggle, tangle, tussle, weather, wrestle

copious *adj* abundant, ample, bounteous, bountiful, extensive, exuberant, full, generous, lavish, liberal, luxuriant, overflowing, plenteous, plentiful, profuse, rich, superabundant

copy *n* archetype, carbon copy, counterfeit, duplicate, facsimile, fake, fax, forgery, image, imitation, likeness, model, pattern, photocopy, print, replica, replication, represen tation, reproduction, transcription

copy *v* counterfeit, duplicate, photo copy, replicate, reproduce, transcribe; ape, echo, emulate, follow, follow suit, follow the example of, imitate, mimic, mirror, parrot, repeat, simulate

cord *n* line rope, string, twine

cordial *adj* affable, affectionate, agreeable, cheerful, earnest, friendly, genial, heartfelt, hearty, invigorating, sociable, warm, welcoming, wholehearted

core *n* centre, crux, essence, gist, heart, kernel, nub, nucleus, pith

corner *n* angle, bend, crook, joint; cavity, cranny, hideaway, hide-out, hole, niche, nook, recess, retreat

corner *v* bring to bay, run to earth, trap

corny *adj* banal, commonplace, dull, feeble, hackneyed, maudlin, old-fashioned, old hat, sentimental, stale, stereotyped, trite

corpse *n* body, cadaver, carcass, remains

correct *v* adjust, amend, cure, emend, improve, rectify, redress, reform, regulate, remedy, right; admonish, chasten, chastise, chide, discipline, punish, reprimand, reprove

correct *adj* accurate, equitable, exact, faultless, flawless, just, precise, regular, right, strict, true

correction *n* adjustment, alteration, amendment, improvement, modification, rectification, righting; admonition, castigation, chastisement, discipline, punishment, reformation, reproof

correctly *adv* accurately, perfectly, precisely, properly, right, rightly

correctness *n* accuracy, exactitude, exactness, faultlessness, fidelity, preciseness, precision, regularity, truth

correspond *v* accord, agree, be consistent, coincide, complement, conform, correlate, fit, harmonize, match, square, tally; communicate, exchange letters, keep in touch, write

correspondence *n* agreement, analogy, coincidence, comparability, comparison, concurrence, conformity, congruity, correction, fitness, harmony, match, relation, similarity; communication, letters, mail, post, writing

correspondent *n* letter writer, pen friend; contributor, journalist, reporter, special correspondent

corresponding *adj* analogous, answering, complementary, correlative, correspondent, equivalent, identical, interrelated, matching, reciprocal, similar, synonymous

corridor *n* aisle, hallway, passage, passageway

corrode *v* canker, consume, corrupt, deteriorate, eat away, erode, gnaw, oxidise, rust, waste, wear away

corrosive *adj* acrid, biting, caustic, consuming, corroding, erosive, virulent, wasting, wearing

corrupt *adj* bribable, dishonest, fraudulent, rotten, shady, unethical, unprincipled, unscrupulous, venal

corrupt *v* bribe, buy off, debauch, demoralize, deprave, entice, fix, lure, pervert, square, suborn, subvert

corrupt *adj* adulterated, altered, contaminated, decayed, defiled, distorted, doctored, falsified, infected, polluted, putrescent, putrid, rotten, tainted

corruption *n* breach of trust, bribery, bribing, crookedness, demoralization, dishonesty, extortion, fiddling, fraud, graft, jobbery, profiteering, shadiness, shady dealings, unscrupulousness, venality; baseness, decadence, degeneration, degradation, depravity, evil, immorality, impurity, iniquity, perversion, profligacy, sinfulness, turpitude, vice, viciousness, wickedness

cosmetic *adj* beautifying, non-essential, superficial, surface, touching-up

cosmopolitan *adj* broad-minded, catholic, open-minded, sophisticated, universal, urbane, well-travelled, worldly, worldly-wise

cost *n* amount, charge, damage, expenditure, expense, figure, outlay, payment, price, rate, worth; damage, deprivation, detriment, expense, harm, hurt, injury, loss, penalty, sacrifice, suffering

cost *v* come to, command a price of, sell at, set back

costly *adj* dear, excessive, exorbitant, expensive, extortionate, highly-priced, steep, stiff, valuable; gorgeous, lavish, luxurious, opulent, precious, priceless, rich, splendid, sumptuous

costume *n* apparel, attire, clothing, dress, ensemble, garb, livery, national dress, outfit, robes, uniform

cosy *adj* comfortable, cuddled up, homely, intimate, secure, sheltered, snug, snuggled down, tucked up, warm

council *n* assembly, board, cabinet, chamber, committee, conclave, conference, congress, convention, convocation, diet, governing, body, ministry, panel, parliament, synod

counsel *n* admonition, advice, caution, consideration, consultation, deliberation, direction, forethought, guidance, information, recommendation, suggestion, warning; advocate, attorney, barrister, lawyer, legal adviser, solicitor

counsel *v* admonish, advise, advocate, caution, exhort, instruct, recommend, urge, warn

count *v* add up, calculate, cast up, check, compute, enumerate, estimate, number, reckon, score, tally, tot up; carry weight, enter into consideration, matter, rate, signify, tell, weigh

counter *adv* against, at variance with, contrarily, contrariwise, conversely, in defiance of, versus

counter *adj* adverse, against, conflicting, contradictory, contrary, contrasting, obverse, opposed, opposing, opposite

counter *v* answer, hit back, meet, offset, parry, resist, respond, retaliate, return, ward off

counterbalance *n* balance, compensate, counterpoise, countervail, make up for, offset, set off

counterfeit *v* copy, fabricate, fake, feign, forge, imitate, impersonate, pretend, sham, simulate

counterfeit *adj* bogus, copied, faked, false, feigned, forged, fraudulent, imitation, sham, simulated, spurious

counterfeit *n* copy, fake, forgery, fraud, imitation, reproduction, sham

counterpart *n* complement, copy, correlative, duplicate, equal, fellow, match, mate, opposite, number, supplement, tally, twin

countless *adj* endless, immeasurable, legion, limitless, measureless, multitudinous, myriad, numberless, uncounted, untold

count on *v* bank on, believe, depend on, lean on, pin one's faith on, reckon on, rely on, take for granted, take on trust, trust

country *n* commonwealth, kingdom, nation, people, realm, sovereign state, state; fatherland, homeland, motherland, nationality, native land; land, part, region, terrain, territory; citizenry, citizens, community, electors, grass roots, inhabitants, nation, people, populace, public, society, voters; backwoods, countryside, farmland, green belt, outback, out doors, provinces, rural areas, sticks, the back of beyond, the middle of nowhere, wide open spaces

count up *v* add reckon up, sum, tally, total

coup *n* accomplishment, action, deed, exploit, feat, manoeuvre, masterstroke, stratagem, stroke, stroke of genius, stunt

couple *n* brace, duo, item, pair, twain, twosome

couple *v* buckle, clasp, conjoin, connect, hitch, join, link, marry, pair, unite, wed, yoke

courage *n* boldness, bravery, daring, dauntlessness, fearlessness, firm ness, fortitude, gallantry, grit, guts, hardihood, heroism, intrepidity, mettle, nerve, pluck, resolution, valour

courageous *adj* audacious, bold, brave, daring, dauntless, fearless, gallant, hardy, heroic, indomitable, intrepid, plucky, resolute, valiant, valorous

course *n* advance, advancement, continuity, development, flow, furtherance, march, movement, order, progress, progression, sequence, succession, unfolding; channel, direction, line, orbit, passage, path, road, route, tack, track, trail, trajectory, way; duration, lapse, passage, passing, sweep, term, time; behaviour, conduct, manner, method, mode, plan, policy, procedure, programme, regimen; cinder track, circuit, lap, race, racecourse, round; classes, course of study, curriculum, lectures, programme, schedule, studies; **of course** certainly, definitely, indubitably, naturally, obviously, undoubtedly, without a doubt

court *n* cloister, courtyard, piazza, plaza, quad, quadrangle, square, yard; hall, manor, palace; attendants, cortege, entourage, retinue, royal household, suite, train; bar, bench, court of justice, lawcourt, seat of judgment, tribunal

court *v* chase, date, go out with, go steady with, keep company with, make love to, pay court to, pay one's addresses to, pursue, run after, serenade, set one's cap at, sue, take out, walk out with, woo; cultivate, fawn upon, flatter, pander to seek, solicit

courteous *adj* affable, attentive, ceremonious, civil, courtly, elegant, gallant, gracious, mannerly, polished, polite, refined, respectful, urbane, well-bred, well-mannered

courtesy *n* affability, civility, courteousness, courtliness, elegance, gallantness, gallantry, good breeding, good manners, graciousness, polish, politeness, urbanity

courtier *n* attendant follower, henchman, liegeman, pursuivant, squire, train-bearer

courtyard *n* area, enclosure, peristyle, playground, quad, quadrangle, yard

covenant *n* arrangement, bargain, commitment, compact, concordat, contract, convention, pact, promise, stipulation, treaty, trust; bond, deed

cover *v* camouflage, cloak, conceal, cover up, curtain, disguise, eclipse, enshroud, hide, hood, house, mask, obscure, screen, secrete, shade, shroud, veil; defend, guard, protect, reinforce, shelter, shield, watch over

cover *n* cloak, cover-up, disguise, façade, front, mask, obscure, screen, smoke screen, veil, window-dressing; camouflage, concealment, defence, guard, hiding place, protection, refuge, sanctuary, shelter, shield, undergrowth, woods; double for, fill in for, relieve, stand in for, substitute, take over; describe, detail, investigate, narrate, recount, relate, report, tell of, write up

cover *n* compensation, indemnity, insurance, payment, protection, reimbursement

covering *n* blanket, casing, clothing, coating, cover, housing, layer, overlay, protection, shelter, top, wrap, wrapper, wrapping

covering *adj* accompanying, descriptive, explanatory, introductory

cover up *v* conceal, cover one's tracks, feign ignorance, hide, hush up, keep dark, keep secret, keep silent about, repress, suppress

covet *v* aspire to begrudge, crave, desire, envy, hanker after, have one's eye on, long for, lust after, thirst for, yearn for

covetous *adj* acquisitive, avaricious, close-fisted, envious, grasp ing, greedy, jealous, mercenary, rapacious, yearning

coward *n* craven, faint-heart, renegade, skulker, sneak; (*Inf*) scaredy-cat

cowardly *adj* base, chicken, craven, dastardly, faint-hearted, fearful, gutless, pusillanimous, scared, shrinking, soft, spineless, timorous, weak, weak-kneed, white-livered

cower *v* cringe, crouch, draw back, fawn, flinch, grovel, quail, shrink, skulk, sneak, tremble, truckle

coy *adj* arch, backward, bashful, coquettish, demure, evasive, flirtatious, kittenish, modest, overmodest, prudish, reserved, retiring, self-effacing, shrinking, shy, skittish, timid

crack *v* break, burst, chip, chop, cleave, crackle, craze, fracture, rive, snap, splinter, split

crack *n* breach, break, chink, chip, cleft, cranny, crevice, fissure, fracture, gap, interstice, rift, burst, clap, crash, explosion, pop, report, snap;

crack *v* break down, collapse, give way, go to pieces, lose control, succumb, yield

crack *n* attempt, go, opportunity, stab, try

crack *adj* choice, elite, excellent, first-class, first-rate, hand-picked, superior; (*Inf*) ace

crack up *v* break down, collapse, come apart at the seams, go berserk, go out of one's mind, have a break down; (*Inf*) go off one's rocker, go to pieces

craft *n* ability, aptitude, art, artistry, cleverness, dexterity, expertise, expertness, ingenuity, knack, skill, technique, workmanship; artfulness, artifice, contrivance, craftiness, cunning, deceit, duplicity, guile, ruse, scheme, shrewdness, stratagem, subterfuge, subtlety, trickery, wiles; business, calling, employment, handicraft, handiwork, line, occupation, pursuit, trade, vocation, work; aircraft, barque, boat, plane, ship, spacecraft, vessel

craftsman *n* artificer, artisan, maker, master, skilled worker, smith, technician, wright

crafty *adj* artful, astute, calculating, canny, cunning, deceitful, designing, devious, duplicitous, foxy, fraudulent, guileful, insidious, knowing, scheming, sharp, shrewd, sly, subtle, tricky, tricky, wily

cram *v* compact, compress, crowd, crush, fill to overflowing, force, jam, overcrowd, overfill, pack, pack in, press, ram, shove, squeeze, stuff

cramp *v* check, circumscribe, clog, confine, constrain, encumber, hamper, hamstring, handicap, hinder, impede, inhibit, obstruct, restrict, shackle, thwart

cramp *n* ache, contraction, convulsion, crick, pain, pang, shooting pain, spasm, stiffness, stitch, twinge

cramped *adj* awkward, circumscribed, closed in, confined, congested, crowded, hemmed in, jammed in, narrow, overcrowded, packed, restricted, squeezed, uncomfortable

cranny *n* breach, chink, cleft, crack, crevice, fissure, gap, hole, interstice, nook, opening

crash *n* bang, boom, clang, clash, clatter, clattering, din, racket, smash, smashing, thunder

crash *v* come a cropper, dash, fall, fall headlong, give way, hurtle, lurch, overbalance, pitch, plunge, precipitate oneself, sprawl, topple; bang, bump, collide, drive into, have an accident, hit, hurtle into, plough into, run together, wreck

crash *n* bankruptcy, collapse, debacle, depression, downfall, failure, ruin, smash

crate *n* box, case, container, packing case, tea chest

crate *v* box, case, encase, enclose, pack, pack up

crave *v* be dying for, cry out for, desire, hanker after, long for, lust after, need, pant for, pine for, require, sigh for, thirst for, want, yearn for; ask, beg, beseech, entreat, implore, petition, plead for, pray for, seek, solicit, supplicate

crawl *v* advance slowly, creep, drag, go on all fours, inch, move at a snails, pace, move on hands and knees, pull oneself along, slither, worm one's way, wriggle, writhe; abase oneself, cringe, fawn, grovel, humble oneself, toady, truckle

craze *n* enthusiasm, fad, fashion, infatuation, mania, mode, novelty, passion, preoccupation, rage, the latest thing, trend, vogue

crazy *adj* berserk, crazed, delirious, demented, deranged, idiotic, insane, lunatic, mad, maniacal, mental, of unsound mind, touched, unbalanced, unhinged; bizarre, eccentric, fantastic, odd, outrageous, peculiar, ridiculous, silly, strange, weird

creak *v* grate, grind, groan, rasp, scrape, scratch, screech, squeak, squeal

cream *n* cosmetic, emulsion, essence, liniment, lotion, oil, ointment, paste, salve, unguent; best, elite, flower, pick, prime

crease *v* corrugate, crimp, crinkle, crumple, double up, fold, pucker, ridge, ruck up, rumple, screw up, wrinkle

crease *n* bulge, corrugation, fold, groove, line, overlap, pucker, ridge, ruck, tuck, wrinkle

create *v* beget, bring into being, coin, compose, concoct, design, develop, devise, form, formulate, generate, give birth to, give life to, hatch, initiate, invent, make originate, produce, spawn

creation *n* conception, formation, generation, genesis, making, procreation, siring; constitution, develop ment, establishment, formation, foundation, inception, institution, laying down, origination, production, setting up; achievement, concept, concoction, handiwork, invention, production

creative *adj* artistic, clever, fertile, gifted, imaginative, ingenious, inspired, inventive, original, productive, stimulating, visionary

creator *n* architect, author, begetter, designer, father, framer, God, initiator, inventor, maker, originator, prime mover

creature *n* animal beast, being, brute, dumb, animal, living thing, lower animal, quadruped

credentials *pl n* attestation, authorization, card, certificate, deed, diploma, docket, letter of recommendation, letters of credence, licence, missive, passport, recommendation, reference, testament, testimonial, title, voucher, warrant

credibility *n* believability, believe ableness, integrity, plausibility, reliability, tenability, trustworthiness

credible *adj* believable, conceivable, imaginable, likely, plausible, possible, probable, reasonable, supposable, tenable, thinkable

credit *n* acclaim, acknowledgement, approval, commendation, fame, glory, honour, kudos, merit, praise, recognition, thanks, tribute

credit with *v* accredit, ascribe to, assign to, attribute to, chalk up to, impute to, refer to; accept, bank on, believe, buy, depend on, fall for, have faith in rely on, swallow, trust

creditable *n* admirable, commendable, deserving, estimable, exemplary, honourable, laudable, meritorious, praiseworthy, reputable, respectable, worthy

credulity *n* blind faith, credulousness, gullibility, naiveté, silliness, simplicity, stupidity

creed *n* articles of faith, belief, canon, catechism, confession, credo, doctrine, dogma, persuasion, principles, profession, tenet

creek *n* bay, bight, cove, firth, inlet

creep *v* crawl, crawl on all fours, glide, insinuate, slither, squirm, worm, wriggle, writhe; approach, unnoticed, skulk, slink, sneak, steal, tiptoe; crawl, dawdle, drag, edge, inch, proceed at a snail's pace

crescent *n* half-moon, meniscus, new moon, old moon, sickle, sickle-shaped

crest *n* apex, crown, head, height, highest point, peak, pinnacle, ridge, summit, top

crestfallen *adj* chapfallen, dejected, depressed, despondent, disappointed, disconsolate, discouraged, disheartened, downcast, downhearted

crevice *n* chink, cleft, crack, cranny, fissure, fracture, gap, hole, interstice, opening, rent, rift, slit, split

crew *n* hands, company, complement, company, corps, gang, party, posse, squad, team, working party

crib *v* pass off as one's own work, pilfer, pirate, plagiarize, purloin, steal; (*Inf*) cheat

crime *n* atrocity, fault, felony, malfeasance, misdeed, misdemeanour, offence, outrage, transgression, trespass, unlawful act, violation, wrong

criminal *n* con, con man, convict, crook, culprit, delinquent, evildoer, felon, jailbird, lawbreaker, malefactor, offender, sinner, transgressor;

criminal *adj* bent, corrupt, crooked, culpable, felonious, illegal, illicit, immoral, indictable, iniquitous, lawless, nefarious, peccant, unlawful, unrighteous, vicious, villainous, wicked, wrong

cripple *v* debilitate, disable, enfeeble, hamstring, incapacitate, lame, maim, mutilate, paralyse, weaken

crippled *adj* bedridden, deformed, disabled, enfeebled, handicapped, housebound, incapacitated, laid up, lame, paralysed

crisis *n* climacteric, climax, confrontation, critical point, crunch, crux, culmination, height, moment of truth, point of no return, turning point; catastrophe, critical, situation, dilemma, dire straits, disaster, emergency, exigency, extremity, meltdown, mess, plight, predicament, quandary, strait, trouble

crisp *adj* brittle, crispy, crumbly, crunchy, firm, fresh, unwilted; bracing, brisk, fresh, invigorating, refreshing; brief, brusque, clear, incisive, pithy, short, succinct, tart, terse

criterion *n* bench mark, canon, gauge, measure, norm, principle, proof, rule, standard, test, touch stone, yardstick

critic *n* analyst, arbiter, authority, commentator, connoisseur, expert, expositor, judge, pundit, reviewer; attacker, carper, caviller, censor, censurer, detractor, fault-finder, knocker, reviler, vilifier

critical *adj* captious, carping, cavilling, censorious, derogatory, disapproving, disparaging, fault-finding, nagging, niggling; accurate, analytical, diagnostic, discerning, discriminating, fastidious, judicious, penetrating, perceptive, precise; all-important, crucial, dangerous, deciding, decisive, grave, high-priority, momentous, perilous, pivotal, precarious, pressing, psychological, risky, serious, urgent, vital

criticism animadversion, bad press, censure, critical remarks, disapproval, disparagement, fault-finding, stricture; analysis, appraisal, appreciation, assessment, comment, commentary, critique, elucidation, evaluation, judgement, notice, review; (*Inf*) flak, knocking, panning

criticize *v* animadvert on, carp, censure, condemn, disapprove of, disparage, excoriate, find fault with, give a bad press, nag at, pass strictures upon, pick to pieces, slate (*Inf*)

crook *n* criminal, racketeer, robber, rogue, shark, swindler, thief, villain; (*Inf*) cheat

crooked *adj* anfractuous, bent, bowed, crippled, curved, deformed, deviating, disfigured, distorted, hooked, irregular, meandering, misshapen, out of shape, tortuous, twisted, twisting, warped, winding, zigzag; angled, askew, asymmetric, at an angle, awry, lopsided, off-centre, slanted, slanting, squint, tilted, to one side, uneven, unsymmetrical; corrupt, crafty, criminal, deceitful, dishonest, dishonourable, dubious, fraudulent, illegal, knavish, nefarious, questionable, shifty, treacherous, underhand, unlawful, unprincipled, unscrupulous; (*Inf*) bent, shady

crop *n* fruits, gathering, harvest, produce, reaping, season's growth, vintage, yield

crop *v* clip, curtail, cut, lop, mow, pare, prune, reduce, shear, shorten, snip, top, trim

crop up *v* appear, arise, emerge, happen, occur, spring up, turn up

cross *adj* angry, annoyed, cantankerous, captious, churlish, crusty, fretful, grouchy, grumpy, ill-humoured, ill-tempered, impatient, in a bad mood, irascible, irritable, out of humour, peevish, pettish, petulant, put out, querulous, short, snappish, snappy, splenetic, sullen, surly, testy, vexed, waspish

cross *v* bridge, cut across, extend over, ford, meet, pass over, ply, span, traverse, zigzag; crisscross, intersect, intertwine, lace, lie athwart of; blend, crossbreed, cross-fertilize, cross-pollinate, hybridize, interbreed, intercross, mix, mongrelize

cross *n* crucifix, rood; crossing, crossroads, intersection, junction; amalgam, blend, combination, crossbreed, cur, hybrid, hybridization, mixture, mongrel

cross *adj* crosswise, intersecting, oblique, transverse

cross-examine *v* catechize, interrogate, pump, question, quiz; (*Inf*) grill

cross out *v* blue-pencil, cancel, delete, eliminate, strike out

crouch *v* bend down, bow, duck, hunch, kneel, squat, stoop

crow *v* bluster, boast, brag, exult, flourish, gloat, glory in, strut, swagger, triumph, vaunt

crowd *n* army, assembly, company, concourse, flock, herd, horde, host, mass, mob, multitude, pack, press, rabble, swarm, throng, troupe; attendance, audience, gate, house, spectators

crowd *v* cluster, congregate, cram, flock, forgather, gather, huddle, mass, muster, press, push, stream, surge, swarm, throng

crowded *adj* busy, congested, cramped, crushed, full, huddled, jam-packed, mobbed, overflowing, packed, populous, swarming, teeming, thronged

crown *n* chaplet, circlet, coronal, coronet, diadem, tiara; bays, distinction, garland, honour, kudos, laurels, laurel, wreath, prize, trophy; emperor, empress, king, monarch, monarchy, queen, rex, royalty, ruler, sovereign, sovereignty

crown *v* adorn, dignify, festoon, honour, invest, reward; be the climax of, cap, complete, consummate, finish, fulfil, perfect, put the finishing touch to, round off, surmount, terminate, top

crucial *adj* central, critical, decisive, pivotal, psychological, searching, testing, trying

crude *adj* boorish, coarse, crass, dirty, gross, indecent, lewd, obscene, smutty, tactless, tasteless, uncouth, unpolished, unprepared, unprocessed, unrefined; clumsy, makeshift, out line, primitive, rough, rough-hewn, rude, rudimentary, sketchy, undeveloped, unfinished, unformed, unpolished

crudity *n* coarseness, crudeness, impropriety, indecency, indelicacy, lewdness, loudness, lowness, obscenity, obtrusiveness, smuttiness, vulgarity

cruel *n* atrocious, barbarous, bitter, bloodthirsty, brutal, brutish, callous, cold-blooded, depraved, excruciating, ferocious, fierce, flinty, grim, hard, hard-hearted, harsh, heartless, hellish, implacable, inclement, inexorable, inhuman, inhumane, malevolent, painful, poignant, ravening, raw, relentless, remorseless, sadistic, sanguinary, savage, severe, spiteful, unfeeling, unkind, unnatural, vengeful, vicious; merciless, pitiless, ruthless, unrelenting

cruelty *n* barbarity, bestiality, blood thirstiness, brutality, brutishness, callousness, depravity, ferocity, fiendishness, hard-heartedness, harshness, heartlessness, inhumanity, mercilessness, murderousness, ruthlessness, sadism, savagery, severity, spite, spitefulness, venom, viciousness

cruise *v* coast, sail, voyage

cruise *n* boat trip, sail, sea trip, voyage

crumb *n* atom, bit, grain, mite, morsel, particle, scrap, shred, sliver, snippet, soupçon, speck

crumble *v* bruise, crumb, crush, fragment, granulate, grind, pound, powder, pulverize, triturate; break up, collapse, come to dust, decay, decompose, degenerate, deteriorate, disintegrate, fall apart, go to pieces, moulder, perish, tumble down

crumple *v* crease, crush, pucker, rumple, screw up, wrinkle, break down, cave in, collapse, fall, give way, go to pieces

crusade *v* campaign, cause, drive, holy war, jihad, movement, push

crush *v* bray, bread, bruise, comminute, compress, contuse, crease, crumble, crumple, crunch, mash, pound, pulverize, rumple, smash, squeeze, wrinkle; conquer, extinguish, overcome, overpower, over whelm, put down, quell, stamp out, subdue, vanquish

crush *n* congestion, crowd, huddle, jam; fancy, infatuation, liking, love, passion; (*Inf*) pash

crust *n* caking, coat, coating, concretion, covering, film, incrustation, layer, outside, scab, shell, skin, surface

cry *v* bawl, bewail, blubber, boohoo, greet, howl one's eyes out, keen, lament, mewl, pule, shed tears, snivel, sob, wail, weep, whimper, whine, yowl; (*Inf*) whinge

cry *n* bawling, blubbering, crying, howl, keening, lament, lamentation, snivel, snivelling, sob, sobbing, sorrowing, wailing, weep, weeping; bawl, bellow, call, call out, ejaculate, exclaim, hail, halloo, holler, howl, roar, scream, screech, shout, shriek, sing out, vociferate, whoop, yell

cry off *v* back out, beg off, excuse oneself, quit, withdraw, withdraw from

cub *n* offspring, whelp, young; beginner, fledgling, lad, learner, puppy, recruit, tenderfoot, trainee, whippersnapper, youngster; (*Inf*) babe

cue *n* catchword, hint, key, nod, prompting, reminder, sign, signal, suggestion

culminate *v* climax, close, come to a climax, come to a head, conclude, end, end up, finish, rise to a crescendo, terminate; (*Inf*) wind up

culprit *n* criminal, delinquent, evildoer, felon, guilty, party, malefactor, miscreant, offender, person responsible, rascal, sinner, transgressor, wrongdoer

cult *n* body, church, clique, denomination, faction, faith, following, party, religion, school, sect; admiration, craze, devotion, idolization, reverence, veneration, worship

cultivate *v* bring under cultivation, dig, farm, fertilize, harvest, plant, plough, prepare, tend, till, work; ameliorate, better, bring on, cherish, civilize, develop, discipline, elevate, enrich, foster, improve, polish, promote, refine, train

cultivation *n* advancement, advocacy, development, encouragement, enhancement, fostering, further ance, help, nurture, patronage, promotion, support

cultural *adj* artistic, broadening, civilizing, developmental, edifying, educational, educative, elevating, enlightening, enriching, humane, humanizing, liberal, liberalizing

culture *n* civilization, customs, life style, mores, society, stage of development, the arts, way of life, accomplishment, breeding, education, elevation, enlightenment, erudition, gentility, good taste, improvement, polish, politeness, refinement, urbanity

cultured *adj* accomplished, advanced, educated, enlightened, erudite, genteel, highbrow, knowledgeable, polished, refined, scholarly, urbane, versed, well-bred, well-informed, well-read

cumbersome *adj* awkward, bulky, burdensome, clumsy, cumbrous, embarrassing, heavy, incommodious, inconvenient, oppressive, unmanageable, unwieldy, weighty; (*Inf*) hefty

cunning *adj* artful,astute, canny, crafty, devious, foxy, guileful, knowing, sharp, shifty, shrewd, subtle, tricky, wily

cunning *n* artfulness, astuteness, craftiness, deceitfulness, deviousness, foxiness, guile, shrewdness, slyness, trickery, wiliness

curb *v* bite back, bridle, check, constrain, contain, control, hinder, impede, inhibit, moderate, muzzle, repress, restrain, restrict, retard, subdue, suppress

curb *n* brake, bridle, check, control, deterrent, limitation, rein, restraint

cure *v* alleviate, correct, ease, heal, help, make better, mend, rehabilitate, relieve, remedy, restore, restore to health

cure *n* alleviation, antidote, corrective, healing, medicine, panacea, recovery, remedy, restorative, specific, treatment;

cure *v* dry, kipper, pickle, preserve, salt, smoke

curiosity *n* inquisitiveness, interest, (*Inf*) nosiness; celebrity, freak, marvel, novelty, oddity, phenomenon, rarity, sight, spectacle, wonder

curious *adj* inquiring, inquisitive, interested, puzzled, questioning, searching; inquisitive, meddling, nosy, peeping, peering, prying; bizarre, exotic, extraordinary, marvellous, mysterious, novel, odd, peculiar, puzzling, quaint, queer, rare, singular, strange, unconventional, unexpected, unique, unorthodox, unusual, wonderful

curl *v* bend, coil, convolute, corkscrew, crimp, crinkle, crisp, curve, entwine, frizz, loop, meander, ripple, spiral, turn, twine, twirl, twist, wind, wreathe, writhe

currency *n* bills, coinage, coins, medium of exchange, money, notes

current *adj* accepted, circulating, common, common knowledge, customary, general, going around, in circulation, in progress, in the air, in the news, ongoing, popular, present, prevailing, prevalent, rife, widespread; contemporary, fashionable, in, in fashion, invogue, now, present-day, up-to-date, up-to-the-minute; (*Inf*) sexy, trendy

current *n* course, draught, flow, jet, progression, river, stream, tide

curse *n* blasphemy, expletive, oath, obscenity, swearing, swear word; anathema, ban, denunciation, evil eye, excommunication, execration, imprecation, jinx, malediction; affliction, bane, burden, calamity, cross, disaster, evil, misfortune, ordeal, plague, scourge, torment, tribulation, trouble, vexation

curse *v* be foul mouthed, blaspheme, cuss, swear, take the Lord's name in vain, use bad language; accurse, anathematize, damn, excommunicate, execrate, fulminate, imprecate

cursed *adj* accursed, bedevilled, blighted, cast out, confounded, damned, doomed, excommunicate, execrable, foredoomed, ill-fated, star-crossed, unholy, unsanctified, villainous; abominable, damnable, detestable, devilish, fell, fiendish, hateful, infamous, infernal, loathsome, odious, pernicious, pestilential, vile

curt *adj* abrupt, blunt, brief, brusque, concise, gruff, offhand, pithy, rude, sharp, short, snappish, succinct, summary, tart, terse, unceremonious, uncivil, ungracious

curtail *v* abbreviate, abridge, contract, cut, cut back, cut short, decrease, dock, lessen, lop, pare down, reduce, retrench, shorten, trim, truncate

curtain *n* drape, hanging

curtain *v* conceal, drape, hide, screen, shroud, shut off, shutter, veil

curve *v* arc, arch, bend, bow, coil, hook, inflect, spiral, swerve, turn, twist, wind

curve *n* arc, bend, camber, curvature, half-moon, loop, trajectory, turn

curved *adj* arced, arched, bent, bowed, crooked, humped, rounded, serpentine, sinuous, sweeping, turned, twisted

custody *n* arrest, confinement, detention, durance, duress, imprisonment, incarceration

custom *n* habit, habitude, manner, mode, procedure, routine, way, wont

customary *adj* accepted, accustomed, acknowledged, common, confirmed, conventional, established, everyday, familiar, fashionable, general, habitual, normal, ordinary, popular, regular, routine, traditional, usual, wonted

customer *n* buyer, client, consumer, habitué, patron, prospect, purchaser, regular, shopper

customs *pl n* duty, import charges, tariff, taxes, toll

cut *v* chop, sleave, divide, gash, incise, lacerate, nick, notch, penetrate, pierce, score, sever, slash, slice, slit, wound; carve, chip, chisel, shop, engrave, fashion, form, saw, sculpt, sculpture, shape, whittle; contract, cut back, decrease, ease up on, lower, rationalize, reduce, slash, slim; abbreviate, abridge, condense, curtail, delete, edit out, excise, precis, shorten; gash, graze, groove, incision, laceration, nick, rent, rip, slash, slit, stroke, wound; cutback, decrease, decrement, diminution, economy, fall, lowering, reduction, saving

cutback *v* cut decrease, economy, lessening, reduction, retrenchment

cut down *v* fell, hew, level, lop, raze

cut in *v* break in, butt in, interpose, interrupt, intervene, intrude; (*Inf*) move in

cut off *v* disconnect, intercept, interrupt, intersect; isolate, separate, sever

cut out *v* cease, delete, extract, give up, refrain from, remove, sever, stop

cut-price *adj* bargain, cheap, reduced, sale

cut short *v* abort, break off, bring to an end, check, halt, interrupt, leave unfinished, postpone, stop, terminate

cutting *adj* biting, bitter, chill, keen, numbing, penetrating, piercing, raw, sharp, stinging

cut up *v* carve, chop, dice, divide, mince, slice; injure, knife, lacerate, slash, wound

cycle *n* aeon, age, circle, era, period, phase, revolution, rotation, round (of years)

cynic *n* doubter, misanthrope, misanthropist, pessimist, sceptic, scoffer

cynical *adj* contemptuous, derisive, distrustful, ironic, misanthropic, misanthropical, mocking, pessimistic, sarcastic, sardonic, sceptical, scoffing, scornful, sneering, unbelieving

D

dab *n* blot, pat, press, smudge, touch,
daft *adj* absurd, crazy, dim-witted feeble-minded, idiotic, insane, mad, ridiculous, silly, simple, stupid; (*Inf*) batty, bonkers, crackers, not all there, mental, nutty; besotted, infatuated with, obsessed by
daily *adj* diurnal, each day, everyday, quotidian; common, commonplace, day-to-day, everyday, ordinary, regular, routine
daily *adv* constantly, day after day, day by day, every day, habitual, often, once a day, per diem, regularly
dainty *adj* charming, delicate, elegant, exquisite, fine, graceful, neat, petite, pretty, refined
dale *n* coomb, dell, glen, vale, valley
dam *n* barrage, barrier, embankment, hindrance, obstruction, wall
dam *v* barricade, block, block up, check, choke, confine, hold back, hold in, obstruct, restrict
damage *n* destruction, detriment, devastation, harm, hurt, impairment, injury, loss, mischief, mutilation, suffering; **damages** compensation, fine, indemnity, reimbursement, reparation, restitution, satisfaction
damage *v* abuse, deface, harm, hurt, impair, incapacitate, injure, mar, mutilate, ruin, spoil, tamper with, weaken, wreck
damaging *adj* deleterious, detrimental, disadvantageous, harmful, hurtful, injurious, prejudicial, ruinous
damn *v* against, blast, castigate, censure, condemn, criticize, denounce, denunciate, excoriate, inveigle; abuse, anathematize, blaspheme, curse, execrate, imprecate, revile, swear; condemn, doom, sentence
damn *n* brass farthing, hoot, iota, jot, tinker's curse, two hoots, whit
damned *adj* anathematized, condemned, cursed, doomed, infernal, lost, reprobate, unhappy; confounded, despicable, detestable, hateful, infamous, infernal, loathsome, revolting
damp *n* dankness, darkness, dew, drizzle, fog, humidity, mist, moisture, muzziness, vapour
damp *adj* clammy, dank, dewy, dripping, drizzly, humid, misty, moist, muggy, sodden, soggy, sopping, vaporous, wet; dampen, moisten, wet; allay, check, chill, cool, curb, dash, deaden, deject, depress, diminish, discourage, dispirit, dull, inhibit, moderate, restrain, stifle
dance *v* bob up and down, caper, frolic, gambol, hop, jig, pirouette, prance, rock, romp, skip, spin, sway, swing, twirl
dance *n* ball, dancing party, disco, discotheque, social
danger *n* endangerment, hazard, insecurity, instability, jeopardy, menace, peril, precariousness, risk, threat, venture
dangerous *adj* alarming, break

neck, exposed, hazardous, insecure, menacing, nasty, perilous, precarious, risky, threatening, treacherous, ugly, unchancy, unsafe, vulnerable

dangle *v* droop, flap, hang, hang down, sway, swing, trail; brandish, entice, flaunt, flourish, lure, swing tantalize, tempt, wave

dapper *adj* smart, smartly well-dressed, well-turned out,

dappled *adj* blotched, flecked, marked, mottled, pied, piebald, pinto spotted,

dare *v* confront, defy, goad, provoke, taunt, throw down the gauntlet; adventure, brave, endanger, gamble, hazard, make bold, presume, risk, stake, venture

dare *n* challenge, defiance, goad, provocation, taunt, ultimatum

daredevil *adj* adventurous, audacious, bold, courageous, dauntless, fearless, hair-brained, heedless, intrepid, incautious, madcap, rash, undaunted

daredevil *n* adventurer, desperado, exhibitionist, mad cap, stunt man; (*Inf*) stunt man

daring *adj* adventurous, audacious, bold, brave, daredevil, fearless, impulsive, intrepid, plucky, rash, reckless, valiant, venturesome; (*Inf*) game

daring *n* audacity, boldness, bottle, bravery, courage, fearlessness, grit, guts, intrepidity, nerve, rashness, spirit, temerity; (*Inf*) balls, guts, spunk

dark *adj* black, brunette, dark-haired dark-skinned, dusky, ebony, jet-black, sable, swarthy; cloudy, dim, dingy, foggy, indistinct, murky, overcast, pitch-black, pitchy, shadowy, shady, sunless, unlit; abstruse, arcane, concealed, cryptic, deep, enigmatic, hidden, mysterious, mystic, obscure, occult, puzzling, recondite, secret; bleak, cheerless, dismal, doleful, drab, gloomy, grim, joyless, morbid, morose, mournful, sombre; angry, dour, forbidding, frowning, glowering, glum, ominous, scowling, sulky, sullen, threatening

dark *n* darkness, dimness, dusk, gloom, murk, murkiness, obscurity, semi-darkness; evening, night, night-fall, night-time, twilight

darkness *n* blackness, dark, dim ness, dusk, duskiness, gloom, murk, murkiness, nightfall, obscurity, shade, shadowiness, shadows; ignorance, unenlightenment

darling *n* beloved, dear, dearest, love, sweetheart, true love; apple of one's eye, blue-eyed boy, fair-haired boy, favourite, pet, spoiled child

darling *adj* adored, beloved, cherished, dearest, precious, prized, treasured, valued

darn *v* cobble up, mend, patch, repair, sew up, stitch

darn *n* mend, patch, reinforcement, repair

dart *n* bolt, bound, dash, flash, flit, fly, race, run, rush, scoot, shoot, spring, sprint, start, tear, whistle, whiz

dash *v* break, crash, destroy, shatter, shiver, smash, splinter; cast, fling, hurl, slam, sling, throw; bolt, bound, dart, fly, haste, hasten, hurry, race, run, rush, speed, spring, sprint, tear;

abash, chagrin, confound, dampen, disappoint, discomfort, discourage

dash *n* brio, flair, flourish, panache, spirit, style, verve, vigour, vivacity

dashing *adj* bold, daring, dazzling, debonair, dynamic, exuberant, gallant, lively, plucky, spirited, swashbuckling; chic, elegant, fashionable, flamboyant, jaunty, smart, sporty stylish

data *pl n* details, documents, facts, figures, information, input, materials, statistics; (*Inf*) info

date *n* age, epoch, era, period, stage, time; appointment, assignation, engagement, meeting, rendezvous, tryst

date *v* belong to, come from, originate in,

dated *adj* antiquated, archaic, obsolete, old-fashioned, old hat, out, outdated, outmoded, out of date, passé, unfashionable, untrendy

daub *v* besmear, coat, cover, paint, plaster, smear, spatter; (*Inf*) slap on

daub *n* blot, blotch, patch, smudge, splotch

daunt *v* alarm, appal, cow, dismay, frighten off, intimidate, overawe, scare, subdue, terrify

dawdle *v* dally, delay, dilly-dally, fritter away, hang about, idle, lag, loaf, loiter, move at a snail's pace, potter, trail, waste time

dawn *n* aurora, cock crow, crack of dawn, dawning, daybreak, daylight, morning, sunrise, sunup; advent, arrival, beginning, birth, emergence, inception, onset, origin, rise

dawn *v* break, brighten, gleam, grow, light, lighten; appear, commence, develop, emerge, originate, rise, start, unfold; come to mind, cross one's mind, hit, register, strike

day *n* appointed day, broad daylight, daylight, daylight hours, daytime, full day, twenty-four hours, working day; date, particular day, point in time, set time, time

daybreak *n* break of day, dawn, first light, sunrise

daydream *n* dream, imagining, musing, reverie, stargazing, vision, wool-gathering; castle in the air, dream, fancy, fantasy, figment of the imagination, fond hope, pipe-dream, wishful thinking

daydream *v* dream, envision, fancy, fantasise, hallucinate, imagine, muse, stargaze

daylight *n* light of day, natural light, sunlight, sunshine; broad daylight, daylight hours, daytime; full view, openness, public attention

daze *v* benumb, bewilder, muddle, numb, paralyse, shock, stun, stupefy; amaze, astonish, astound, befog, bewilder, blind, confuse, dazzle, dumbfound, flabbergast, perplex, stagger, startle, surprise

daze *n* bewilderment, confusion, distraction, shock, stupor, trance, trancelike state

dazed *adj* baffled, bemused, bewildered, confused, disorientated, dizzy, fuddled, light-headed, muddled, nonplussed, numbed, perplexed, punch-drunk, shocked, staggered, stunned, stupefied, woozy

dazzle *v* bedazzle, blind, blur, confuse, daze, overpower; amaze, astonish, awe, bowl over, dumbfound, fascinate, hypnotize, impress, overawe, overwhelm, stagger, strike dumb, stupefy; (*Inf*) bowl over, take one's breath away

dazzle *n* brightness, brilliance, flash, gleam, glitter, glory, magnificence, splendour, sparkle; (*Inf*) pizzazz, razzle-dazzle, razzmatazz

dead *adj* deceased, defunct, departed, extinct, gone, inanimate, late, lifeless, passed away, perished; apathetic, callous, cold, dull, frigid, glassy, glazed, indifferent, inert, lukewarm, numb, paralysed, spiritless, torpid, unresponsive, wooden; boring, dead-and-alive, dull, flat, insipid, stale, tasteless, uninteresting, vapid

deadlock *n* cessation, dead heat, draw, full stop, halt, impasse, stalemate, standoff, standstill, tie

deadly *adj* baleful, baneful, dangerous, death-dealing, deathly, destructive, fatal, lethal, malignant, mortal, noxious, pernicious, poisonous, venomous; cruel, grim, implacable, mortal, ruthless, savage, unrelenting; accurate, effective, exact, on target, precise, sure, true, unerring, unfailing

deaf *adj* hard of hearing, stone deaf, without hearing; indifferent, oblivious, unconcerned, unhearing, unmoved

deafening *adj* booming, dinning, ear-piercing, ear-splitting, intense, overpowering, piercing, resounding, ringing, thunderous

deaf *adj* bargain, buy and sell, do business, negotiate, sell, stock, trade, traffic, treat

deaf *n* agreement, arrangement, bargain, buy, contract, pact, transaction, understanding

deaf *v* allot, apportion, assign, bestow, dispense, distribute, divide, dole out, give, mete out, reward, share

dealer *n* chandler, marketer, merchandiser, merchant, trader, tradesman, wholesaler

dear *adj* beloved, cherished, close, darling, esteemed, familiar, favourite, intimate, precious, prized, respected, treasured; at a premium, costly, expensive, high-priced, overpriced, pricey

dear *n* angel, beloved, darling, loved one, precious, treasure

dearly *adv* extremely, greatly, profoundly, very much

death *n* bereavement, cessation, decease, demise, departure, dissolution, dying, end, exit, expiration, loss, passing, quietus, release; annihilation, destruction, downfall, eradication, extermination, extinction, finish, grave, obliteration, ruin, ruination, undoing

deathless *adj* eternal, everlasting, immortal, imperishable, incorruptible, timeless, undying

deathly *adj* cadaverous, deathlike, gaunt, ghastly, grim, haggard, pale, pallid, wan; deadly, extreme, fatal, intense, mortal, terrible

debase *v* abase, cheapen, degrade, demean, devalue, disgrace, dishonour, drag down, humble, humiliate, lower, reduce, shame

debatable *adj* arguable, borderline, controversial, disputable, doubtful, dubious, in dispute, moot, open to question, problematical, questionable, uncertain, undecided, unsettled

debate *v* argue, contend, contest, controvert, discuss, dispute, question, wrangle

debate *n* altercation, argument, contention, controversy, discussion, disputation, dispute, polemic; cogitation, consideration, deliberation, meditation, reflection

debris *n* bits, brash, detritus, dross, fragments, litter, pieces, remains, rubbish, rubble, ruins, waste, wreck, wreckage

debt *n* arrears, bill, claim, commitment, debit, due, duty, liability, obligation, score

debtor *n* borrower, defaulter, insolvent, mortgagor

debunk *n* cut down to size, deflate, disparage, expose, lampoon, mock, puncture, ridicule, show up

debut *n* beginning, bow, coming out, entrance, first appearance, inauguration, initiation, introduction, launching, presentation

decadent *adj* corrupt, debased, debauched, decaying, declining, degenerate, degraded, depraved, dissolute, immoral, self-indulgent

decay *v* atrophy, crumble, decline, degenerate, deteriorate, disintegrate, dissolve, dwindle, moulder, shrivel, sink, spoil, wane, waste away, wear way, wither; corrode, decompose, mortify, perish, putrefy, rot

deceased *adj* dead, defunct, departed, expired, finished, former, gone, late, lifeless, lost

deceit *n* artifice, cheating, chicanery, craftiness, cunning, deceitfulness, deception, dissimulation, double-dealing, duplicity, fraud, fraudulence, guile, hypocrisy, imposition, pretence, slyness, treachery, trickery, underhandedness

deceitful *adj* counterfeit, crafty, deceiving, deceptive, designing, dishonest, disingenuous, double-dealing, duplicitous, fallacious, false, fraudulent, guileful, hypocritical, illusory, insincere, knavish, sneaky, treacherous, tricky, two-faced, underhand, untrustworthy

deceive *v* beguile, betray, cheat, con, cozen, delude, disappoint, double-cross, dupe, ensnare, entrap, fool, hoax, hoodwink, impose upon, mislead, outwit, swindle, trick

decency *n* appropriateness, civility, correctness, courtesy, decorum, etiquette, fitness, good form, good manners, modesty, propriety, respectability, seemliness

decent *adj* appropriate, becoming, befitting, chaste, comely, decorous, delicate, fit, fitting, modest, nice, polite, presentable, proper, pure, respectable, seemly, suitable

deception *n* craftiness, cunning, deceit, deceitfulness, deceptiveness, dissimulation, duplicity, fraud, fraudulence, guile, hypocrisy, imposition, insincerity, legerdemain, treachery, trickery

deceptive *adj* ambiguous, deceitful, delusive, dishonest, fake, fallacious, false, fraudulent, illusory, misleading, mock, specious, spurious, unreliable

decide *v* adjudge, adjudicate, choose, come to a conclusion, commit oneself, conclude, decree, determine, elect, end, make a decision, purpose, reach a decision, resolve, settle

decipher *v* construe, crack decode,

deduce, explain, figure out, interpret, make out, read, reveal, solve, understand, unfold, unravel

decision *n* arbitration, conclusion, finding, judgment, outcome, resolution, result, ruling, sentence, settlement, verdict

decisive *adj* absolute, conclusive, critical, crucial, definite, definitive, fateful, final, influential, momentous, positive, significant; decided, determined, firm, forceful, incisive, resolute, strong-minded, trenchant

deck *v* adorn, array, attire, beautify, bedeck, clothe, decorate, dress, embellish, festoon, garland, grace, ornament, trim

declaim *v* harangue, hold forth, lecture, orate, perorate, proclaim, rant, recite, speak; (*Inf*) spiel

declaration *n* acknowledgement, affirmation, assertion, attestation, averment, avowal, deposition, disclosure, protestation, revelation, statement, testimony; announcement, edict, manifesto, notification, propclamation, profession, promulgation, pronouncement, pronunciamento

declare *v* affirm, announce, assert, attest, aver, avow, certify, claim, confirm, maintain, proclaim, profess, pronounce, state, swear, testify, validate

decline *v* avoid, deny, forgo, refuse, refect, say 'no', send one's regrets, turn down; decrease, diminish, dwindle, ebb, fade, fail, fall, fall off, flag, lessen, shrink, sink, wane

decline *n* abatement, diminution, down turn, dwindling, falling off, lessening, recession, slump

decorate *v* adorn, beautify, bedeck, deck, embellish, enrich, grace, ornament, trim; colour, furbish, paint, paper, renovate, wallpaper; cite, honour, pin a medal on

decoration *n* adornment, beautification, elaboration, embellishment, enrichment, garnishing, ornamentation, trimming; arabesque, bauble, curlicue, falderal, flounce, flourish, frill, furbelow, garnish, ornament, scroll, spangle, trimmings, trinket; award, badge, colours, emblem, garter, medal, order, ribbon, star

decorum *n* behaviour, breeding, courtliness, decency, deportment, dignity, etiquette, gentility, good grace, good manners, gravity, politeness, propriety, protocol, respectability, seemliness

decoy *n* attraction, bait, ensnare ment, enticement, inducement, lure, pretence, trap

decoy *v* allure, bait, deceive, ensnare, entice, entrap, lure, seduce, tempt

decrease *v* abate, contract, curtail, cut down, decline, diminish, drop, dwindle, ease, fall off, lessen, lower, peter out, reduce, shrink, slacken, subside, wane

decrease *n* abatement, contraction, cutback, decline, diminution, down turn, dwindling, ebb, falling off, lessening, loss, reduction, shrinkage, subsidence

decree *n* act, command, dictum, edict, enactment, law, mandate, order, ordinance, precept, proclamation, regulation, ruling, statute

decree *v* adjudge, command, decide, determine, dictate, direct, enact, lay down, mandate, ordain, order, pre scribe, proclaim, pronounce, rule; judgement, ruling, verdict; findings

decrepit *adj* aged, crippled, debilitated, doddering, effete, feeble, frail, incapacitated, infirm, superannuated, wasted, weak

dedicate *v* commit, devote, give over to, pledge, surrender

deduce *v* conclude, derive, draw, gather, glean, infer, reason, take to mean, understand

deduct *v* decrease by, knock off, reduce by, remove, subtract, take away, take from, take off, take out, withdraw

deduction *n* assumption, conclusion, consequence, corollary, finding, inference, reasoning, result; abatement, allowance, decrease, diminution, discount, reduction, subtraction, withdrawal

deed *n* achievement, act, action, exploit, fact, feat, performance, reality, truth

deep *adj* abyssal, bottomless, broad, far, profound, unfathomable, wide, yawning; extreme, grave, great, intense, profound; bass, booming, full-toned, low, low-pitched, resonant, sonorous

deep *adv* deeply, far down, far into, late

default *n* absence, defect, deficiency, dereliction, failure, fault, lack, lapse, neglect, non-payment, omission, want

default *v* bilk, defraud, dodge, evade, fail, neglect, rat, swindle

defeat *v* beat, conquer, crush, overpower, overthrow, overwhelm, quell, repulse, rout, subdue, subjugate, vanquish

defeat *n* beating, conquest, debacle, overthrow, repulse, rout, trouncing, vanquishment

defect *n* blemish, blotch, error, failing, fault, flaw, foible, imperfection, mistake, spot, taint, want

defect *v* abandon, apostatize, break faith, change sides, desert, go over, rebel, revolt, tergiversate; (*Inf*) walk out on

defective *adj* deficient, faulty, flawed, imperfect, inadequate, incomplete, insufficient, not working, out of order, scant, short

defence *n* armament, cover, deterrence, guard, immunity, protection, resistance, safeguard, security, shelter; apologia, apology, argument, excuse, exoneration, explanation, extenuation, justification, plea, vindication; alibi, case, declaration, denial, plea, pleading, rebuttal, testimony

defend *v* cover, fortify, guard, deep safe, preserve, protect, safeguard, screen, secure, shelter, shield, ward off, watch over; assert, champion, endorse, espouse, justify, maintain, plead, speak up for, stand by, stand up for, support, sustain, uphold, vindicate

defender *n* bodyguard escort, guard, protector; advocate, champion, patron, sponsor, supporter, vindicator

defer *v* adjourn, delay, hold over, postpone, procrastinate, prorogue, protract, put off, put on ice, set aside, shelve, suspend, table; accede, acquiesce, bow, capitulate,

defiance *n* challenge, confrontation,

contempt, contumacy, disobedience, disregard, insolence, insubordination, opposition, provocation, rebelliousness, recalcitrance, spite

deficiency *n* defect, demerit, failing, fault, flaw, frailty, imperfection, shortcoming, weakness

deficit *n* arrears, default, deficiency, loss, shortage, shortfall

define *v* characterize, describe, designate, detail, determine, explain, expound, interpret, specify, spell out

definite *adj* clear, clear-cut, clearly, defined, determined, exact, explicit, express, fixed, marked, obvious, particular, precise, specific

definitely *adv* absolutely, beyond any doubt, categorically, certainly, clearly, decidedly, easily, far and away, finally, indubitably, obviously, plainly, positively, surely, undeniably, unequivocally, unmistakably, unquestionably, without doubt, without fail, without question

definition *n* clarification, description, elucidation, explanation, exposition, statement of meaning

deflate *n* collapse, contract, empty, exhaust, flatten, puncture, shrink, void; chasten, dash, debunk, disconcert, dispirit, humble, humiliate, mortify, squash, take the wind out of someone's sails; (*Inf*) put down

deflect *v* bend, deviate, diverge, glance off, ricochet, shy, sidetrack, slew, swerve, turn, turn aside, twist, veer, wind

defraud *v* beguile, bilk, cheat, cozen, delude, dupe, embezzle, fleece, outwit, pilfer, rob, swindle, trick

deft *adj* able, adept, adroit, agile, clever, dexterous, expert, handy, neat, nimble, proficient, skilful

defy *v* beard, brave, challenge, confront, contemn, dare, despise, disregard, face, flout, hurl, defiance at, provoke, scorn, slight, spurn

degenerate *adj* base, corrupt, debased, debauched, decadent, degenerated, degrade, depraved, deteriorated, dissolute, fallen, immoral, low, mean, perverted

degenerate *v* decay, decline, decrease, deteriorate, fall off, lapse, regress, retrogress, rot, sink, slip, worsen

degrade *v* cheapen, corrupt, debase, demean, deteriorate, discredit, disgrace, dishonour, humble, humiliate, impair, injure, pervert, shame, vitiate

degree *n* class, grade, level, order, position, rank, standing, station, status; calibre, extent, intensity, level, measure, proportion, quality, quantity, range, rate, ratio, scale, scope, severity, standard

dejected *adj* blue, cast down, crestfallen, depressed, despondent, disconsolate, disheartened, dismal, doleful, down, downcast, down hearted, gloomy, glum, low, low-spirited, melancholy, miserable, morose, sad, woebegone, wretched

delay *v* defer, hold over, postpone, procrastinate, prolong, protract, put off, shelve, stall, suspend, table, temporize

delay *n* deferment, postponement, procrastination, stay, suspension; check, detention, hindrance, hold-up, impediment, interruption, interval, obstruction, setback, stoppage

delegate *n* agent, ambassador,

commissioner, deputy, envoy, legate, representative, vicar

delegation *n* commission, contingent, deputation, embassy, envoys, legation, mission

delete *v* blot out, blue-pencil, cancel, cross out, cut out, dele, edit, edit out, efface, erase, expunge, obliterate, remove, rub out, strike out

deliberate *v* cogitate, consider, consult, debate, discuss, meditate, mull over, ponder, reflect, think, weigh

deliberate *adj* calculated, conscious, considered, designed, intentional, planned, prearranged, premeditated, purposeful, studied, thoughtful, wilful

deliberation *n* calculation, care, carefulness, caution, circumspection, cogitation, consideration, coolness, forethought, meditation, prudence, purpose, reflection, speculation, study, thought, wariness

delicacy *n* accuracy, daintiness, elegance, exquisiteness, fineness, lightness, nicety, precision, subtlety; discrimination, fastidiousness, finesse, purity, refinement, sensibility, sensitiveness, sensitivity, tact, taste; dainty, luxury, relish, savoury, titbit, treat

delicate *adj* ailing, debilitated, flimsy, fragile, frail, sickly, slender, slight, tender, weak; accurate, deft, detailed, minute, precise, skilled; considerate, diplomatic, discreet, sensitive, tactful; critical, difficult, precarious, sensitive, ticklish, touchy

delicately *adv* carefully, daintily, deftly, elegantly, exquisitely, fastidiously, finely, gracefully, lightly, precisely, sensitively, skillfully, softly, subtly, tactfully

delicious *adj* ambrosial, appetising, choice, dainty, delectable, luscious, mouthwatering, nectareous, palatable, savoury, tasty; (*Inf*) scrumptious

delight *n* ecstasy, enjoyment, felicity, gladness, gratification, happiness, joy, pleasure, rapture, transport

delight *v* amuse, charm, cheer, divert, enchant, gratify, please, ravish, rejoice, satisfy, thrill

delightful *adj* agreeable, amusing, captivating, charming, congenial, delectable, enchanting, engaging, enjoyable, entertaining, fascinating, gratifying, heavenly, pleasant, pleasing, pleasurable, rapturous, ravishing, thrilling

deliver *v* bear, bring, carry, cart, convey, distribute, transport; cede, commit, give up, grant, hand over, make over, relinquish, resign, surrender, transfer, turn over, yield; acquit, discharge, emancipate, free, liberate, loose, ransom, redeem, release, rescue, save

delivery *n* consignment, conveyance, dispatch, distribution, handing over, surrender, transfer, transmission, transmittal; deliverance, escape, liberation, release, rescue

delude *v* bamboozle, beguile, cheat, cozen, deceive, dupe, fool, hoax, hoodwink, impose on, lead up the garden path, misguide, mislead, trick

deluge *n* cataclysm, downpour, flood, inundation, overflowing, spate, torrent

de luxe *adj* choice, costly, elegant, exclusive, expensive, grand, luxurious, opulent, palatial, plush, rich, select, special, splendid, sumptuous, superior

demand *v* ask, challenge, inquire, interrogate, question, request; call for, cry out for, involve, necessitate, need, require, take, want

demand *n* bidding, charge, inquiry, interrogation, order, question, request, requisition

demanding *adj* challenging, difficult, exacting, exhausting, exigent, hard, taxing, tough, trying, wearing

demeanour *n* air, bearing, behaviour, carriage, comportment, conduct, deportment, manner, mien

democracy *n* commonwealth, government by the people, representative government, republic

democratic *adj* autonomous, egalitarian, popular, populist, representative, republican, self-governing

demolish *v* bulldoze, destroy, dismantle, flatten, knock down, level, overthrow, pulverise, raze, ruin, tear down; annihilate, defeat, destroy, overthrow, overturn, undo, wreck

demonstrable *adj* attestable, axiomatic, certain, evident, evincible, incontrovertible, indubitable, irrefutable, obvious, palpable, positive, provable, self-evident, undeniable, unmistakable, verifiable

demonstrate *v* display, establish, evidence, evince, exhibit, indicate, manifest, prove, show, testify to; describe, explain, illustrate, make clear, show how, teach; march, parade, picket, protest, rally

demonstration *n* affirmation, confirmation, display, evidence, exhibition, expression, illustration, manifestation, proof, substantiation, testimony, validation; description, explanation, exposition, presentation, test, trial; march, mass lobby, parade, picket, protest, rally, sit-in

demure *adj* decorous, diffident, grave, modest, reserved, reticent, retiring, sedate, shy, sober, staid, unassuming

den *n* cave, cavern, haunt, hideout, hole, lair, shelter; cloister, cubbyhole, hideaway, retreat, sanctuary, sanctum, snuggery, study

denial *n* adjuration, contradiction, disavowal, disclaimer, dismissal, dissent, negation, prohibition, rebuff, refusal, rejection, renunciation, repudiation, repulse, retraction, veto

denomination *n* belief, communion, creed, persuasion, religious group, school, sect; grade, size, unit, value

denote *v* betoken, designate, express, imply, import, indicate, mark, mean, show, signify, typify

denounce *v* accuse, arraign, attack, brand, castigate, censure, condemn, declaim against, decry, denunciate, impugn, proscribe, revile, stigmatise, vilify

dense *adj* close, close-knit, compact, compressed, condensed, heavy, impenetrable, opaque, solid, substantial, thick, thickset

dent *n* chip, concavity, crater, depression, dimple, dip, hollow, impression, indentation, pit

dent *v* depress, dint, gouge, hollow, imprint, make a dent in, make concave, press in, push in

deny *v* contradict, disagree with,

disprove, gainsay, oppose, rebuff, refute; abjure, disavow, discard, disclaim, disown, recant, renounce, repudiate, revoke

depart *v* absent, decamp, disappear, escape, exit, go, go away, leave, migrate, quit, remove, retire, retreat, set forth, start out, take leave, vanish, withdraw

department *n* district, division, province, region, sector; branch, bureau, division, office, section, station, subdivision, unit; area, domain, function, line, province, realm, responsibility, speciality, sphere

departure *n* exit, exodus, going, going away, leave-taking, leaving, removal, retirement, withdrawal; branching out, change, difference, innovation, novelty, shift

depend *v* bank on, build upon, calculate on, confide in, count on, lean on, reckon on, rely upon, trust in, turn to; be based on, be contingent on, be determined by, be subject to, be subordinate to, hang on, hinge on, rest on, revolve around

dependent *adj* counting on, defenceless, helpless, immature, reliant, relying on, vulnerable, weak; conditional, contingent, depending, determined by, liable to, relative, subject to

deplete *v* bankrupt, consume, decrease, drain, empty, evacuate, exhaust, expend, impoverish, lessen, milk, reduce, use up

deplorable *adj* calamitous, dire, disastrous, distressing, grievous, heartbreaking, lamentable, melancholy, miserable, pitiable, regrettable, sad, unfortunate, wretched; blameworthy, disgraceful, dishonourable, disreputable, execrable, opprobrious, reprehensible, scandalous, shameful

deplore *v* bemoan, bewail, grieve for, lament, mourn, regret, rue, sorrow over; abhor, censure, condemn, denounce, deprecate, disapprove of, object to

depose *v* break, cashier, degrade, demote, dethrone, dismiss, displace, downgrade, oust, remove from office

deposit *v* drop, lay, locate, place, precipitate, put, settle, sit down

deposit *n* down payment, install ment, money, part payment, pledge, retainer, security, stake, warranty

depot *n* depository, repository, storehouse, warehouse; bus station, garage, terminus

depraved *adj* abandoned, corrupt, debased, debauched, degenerate, degraded, dissolute, evil, immoral, lascivious, lewd, licentious, perverted, profligate, shameless, sinful, vicious, vile, wicked

depreciate *v* decrease, deflate, devaluate, devalue, lessen, lose value, lower, reduce

depreciation *n*deflation, depression, devaluation, drop, fall, slump; belittlement, deprecation, derogation, detraction, disparagement, pejoration

depress *v* cast down, chill, damp, daunt, deject, desolate, discourage, dishearten, dispirit, make despondent, oppress, sadden, weigh down

depressed *adj* blue, crestfallen, dejected, despondent, discouraged, dispirited, down, downcast, dow-hearted, fed up, glum, low, low-spirited, melancholy, moody, morose, pessimistic, sad, unhappy

depressing *adj* black, bleak, daunt ing, dejecting, depressive, discouraging, disheartening, dismal, dispiriting, distressing, dreary, gloomy, heartbreaking, hopeless, melancholy, sad, saddening, sombre

depression dejection, despair, despondency, dolefulness, downheartedness, gloominess, hopelessness, low spirits, melancholia, melancholy, sadness, the blues; economic decline, hard times, inactivity, lowness, recession, slump, stagnation

deprive *v* bereave, despoil, divest, expropriate, rob, strip, wrest

deprived *adj* bereft, denuded, destitute, disadvantaged, forlorn, in need, in want, lacking, necessitous, needy, poor

depth *n* abyss, deepness, drop, extent, measure, profoundness, profundity; **depths** abyss, bowels of the earth, deepest, furthest, innermost, most intense, remotest part, middle, midst, slough of despond

deputation *n* commission, delegates, delegation, deputies, embassy, envoys, legation

deputise *v* act for, stand in for, take the place of, understudy

deputy *n* agent, ambassador, commissioner, delegate, legate, lieutenant, nuncio, proxy, representative, second-in-command, substitute, surrogate, vicegerent

deranged *adj* berserk, crazed, crazy, delirious, demented, distracted, frantic, frenzied, insane, irrational, lunatic, mad, maddened, unbalanced, unhinged

derelict *adj* abandoned, deserted, dilapidated, discarded, forsaken, neglected, ruined

deride *v* chaff, contemn, detract, disdain, disparage, flout, gibe, insult, jeer, knock, mock, ridicule, scoff, scorn, sneer, taunt

derivation *n* ancestry, basis, beginning, descent, etymology, foundation, genealogy, origin, root, source

derive *v* collect, deduce, draw, elicit, extract, follow, gain, gather, get, glean, infer, obtain, procure, receive, trace

descend *v* alight, dismount, drop, fall, go down, move down, plummet, plunge, swoop; ancestry, extraction, family tree, genealogy, heredity, lineage, origin, parentage

describe *v* characterise, define, depict, detail, explain, express, illustrate, narrate, portray, recount, relate, report, specify, tell

description *n* account, characterisation, delineation, depiction, detail, explanation, narration, narrative, portrayal, report, representation, sketch

desert *n* solitude, waste, wasteland, wilderness, wilds

desert *adj* arid, bare, barren, desolate, infertile, lonely, solitary, uncultivated, uninhabited, unproductive, untilled, waste, wild

desert *v* abandon, abscond, betray, decamp, defect, forsake, give up, jilt, leave, leave high and dry, leave in the lurch, leave stranded, maroon, quit, rat, relinquish, renounce, resign, run out on, strand, throw over, vacate; (*Inf*) walk out on

deserter *n* absconder, apostate, defector, escapee, fugitive, renegade, runaway, traitor, truant

deserve *v* be entitled to, be worthy of, earn, gain, justify, merit, procure, rate, warrant, win

deserved *adj* appropriate, condign, due, earned, fair, fitting, just, justifiable, justified, meet, merited, proper, right, rightful, suitable, warranted, well-earned

design *v* delineate, describe, draft, draw, outline, plan, sketch, trace; conceive, create, fabricate, fashion, invent, originate, think up; aim, contrive, destine, devise, intend, make, mean, plan, project, propose, purpose, scheme, tailor;

design *n* blueprint, delineation, draft, drawing, model, outline, plan, scheme, sketch; aim, end, goal, intent, intention, meaning, object, objective, point, purport, purpose, target, view

designation *n* denomination, description, epithet, label, mark, name, title

designer *n* architect, artificer, couturier, creator, deviser, inventor, originator, stylist

desirable *adj* advantageous, advisable, agreeable, beneficial, covetable, eligible, enviable, good, pleasing, preferable, profitable, worthwhile; adorable, alluring, attractive, fascinating, fetching, seductive; (*Inf*) sexy

desire *v* aspire to, covet, crave, desiderate, fancy, hanker after, long for, set one's heart on, want, wish for, yearn for; ask, entreat, importune, petition, request, solicit

desire *n* appetite, aspiration, craving, hankering, longing, need, want, wish, yearning; appetite, concupiscence, lasciviousness, lechery, libido, lust, lustfulness, passion

desist *v* abstain, break off, cease, discontinue, end, forbear, give over, give up, have done with, leave off, pause, refrain from, stop, suspend

desolate *adj* bare, barren, bleak, desert, dreary, ruined, solitary, unfrequented, uninhabited, waste, wild; abandoned, bereft, cheerless, comfortless, companionless, defected, depressing, despondent, disconsolate, dismal, downcast, forlorn, forsaken, gloomy, lonely, melancholy, miserable, wretched

desolation *n* destruction, devastation, havoc, ravages, ruin, ruination

despair *v* despond, give up, lose heart, lose hope

despair *n* anguish, dejection, depression, desperation, despondency, disheartenment, gloom, hopelessness, melancholy, misery, wretchedness

despairing *adj* anxious, brokenhearted, dejected, depressed, desperate, despondent, disconsolate, downcast, frantic, grief-stricken, hopeless, inconsolable, melancholy, miserable, suicidal, wretched

desperate *adj* audacious, dangerous, daring, death-defying, determined, foolhardy, frantic, furious, hasty, hazardous, headstrong, impetuous, madcap, precipitate, rash, reckless, risky, violent, wild; despairing, despondent, forlorn, hopeless, inconsolable, irrecoverable, irremediable, irretrievable, wretched

desperately *adv* badly, dangerously, gravely, perilously, seriously, severely

despise *v* abhor, contemn, deride, detest, disdain, disregard, flout, loathe, look down on, neglect, revile, scorn, slight, spurn, undervalue

despite *prep* against, even with, in contempt of, in defiance of, in spite of, in the face of, in the teeth of, notwithstanding, regardless of, undeterred by

despondent *adj* blue, dejected, depressed, despairing, disconsolate, discouraged, disheartened, dispirited, doleful, down, downcast, downhearted, gloomy, glum, hopeless, in despair, low, lowspirited, melancholy, miserable, morose, sad, sorrowful, wretched

despotism *n* absolutism, autarchy, autocracy, dictatorship, monocracy, oppression, totalitarianism, tyranny

destination *n* harbour, haven, journey's end, landing-place, resting-place, station, stop, terminus

destined *adj* bound, certain, designed, doomed, fated, foreordained, ineluctable, inescapable, inevitable, intended, meant, ordained, predestined, unavoidable

destiny *n* cup, divine decree, doom, fate, fortune, karma, kismet, lot, portion

destitute *adj* distressed, down and out, impecunious, impoverished, indigent, insolvent, moneyless, necessitous, needy, on one's uppers, penniless, penurious, poor, poverty-stricken; (*Inf*) on the breadline

destroy *v* annihilate, blow to bits, break down, crush, demolish, desolate, devastate, dismantle, dispatch, eradicate, extinguish, extirpate, gut, kill, ravage, raze, ruin, shatter, slay, smash, torpedo, waste, wipe out, wreck

destruction *n* annihilation, crushing, demolition, devastation, downfall, end, eradication, extermination, extinction, havoc, liquidation, massacre, overthrow, overwhelming, ruin, ruination, shattering, slaughter, undoing, wreckage, wrecking

destructive *adj* baleful, baneful, calamitous, cataclysmic, catastrophic, damaging, deadly, deleterious, detrimental, devastating, fatal, harmful, hurtful, injurious, lethal, noxious, pernicious, ruinous

detach *v* cut off, disconnect, disengage, disentangle, disjoin, disunite, divide, free, isolate, loosen, remove, segregate, separate, sever, tear off, uncouple, unfasten, unhitch

detachment *n* aloofness, coolness, indifference, remoteness, unconcern

detail *n* aspect, component, count, element, fact, factor, feature, item, particular, point, respect, specific, technicality

detail *v* allocate, appoint, assign, charge, commission, delegate, detach, send

detailed *adj* circumstantial, comprehensive, elaborate, exact, exhaustive, full, intricate, itemized, meticulous, minute, particular, particularized, specific, thorough

detain *v* check, delay, hinder, hold

up, impede, keep, keep back, retard, slow up, stay, stop; arrest, confine, hold, intern, restrain

detect *v* ascertain, catch, descry, distinguish, identify, note, notice, observe, recognize, scent, spot; catch, disclose, discover, expose, find, reveal, track down, uncover, unmask

detective *n* CID, constable, copper, investigator, private eye, private investigator; (*Inf*) sleuth

detention *n* confinement, custody, delay, hindrance, holding back, imprisonment, incarceration, keeping in, quarantine, restraint, withholding

deter *v* caution, check, damp, daunt, debar, discourage, dissuade, frighten, hinder, inhibit from, intimidate, prevent, prohibit, put off, restrain, stop, talk out of

deteriorate *v* corrupt, debase, decline, degenerate, degrade, deprave, depreciate, go to pot, impair, injure, lower, slump, spoil, worsen; be the worse for wear, crumble, decay, decline, decompose, disintegrate, ebb, fade, fall apart, lapse, weaken, wear away

determination *n* backbone, constancy, conviction, dedication, doggedness, drive, firmness, fortitude, indomitability, perseverance, persistence, resoluteness, resolution, resolve, single-mindedness, steadfastness, tenacity, willpower

determine *v* arbitrate, conclude, decide, end, finish, fix upon, ordain, regulate, settle, terminate; ascertain, certify, check, detect, discover, find out, learn, verify, work out

determined *adj* bent on, constant, dogged, firm, fixed, intent, persevering, persistent, purposeful, resolute, set on, single-minded, steadfast, strong-minded, strong-willed, tenacious, unflinching, unwavering

deterrent *n* check, curb, defensive, measures, determent, discouragement, disincentive, hindrance, impediment, obstacle, restraint

detest *v* abhor, abominate, despise, dislike intensely, execrate, feel aversion, feel disgust, feel hostility, feel repugnance towards, hate, loathe, recoil from

detour *n* bypass, byway, circuitous, route, deviation, diversion, indirect, course, roundabout way

detract *v* devaluate, diminish, lessen, lower, reduce, take away from

detriment *n* damage, disadvantage, disservice, harm, hurt, impairment, injury, loss, mischief, prejudice

detrimental *adj* adverse, baleful, damaging, deleterious, destructive, disadvantageous, harmful, inimical, injurious, mischievous, pernicious, prejudicial, unfavourable

devastate *v* demolish, desolate, despoil, destroy, lay waste, level, pillage, plunder, ravage, raze, ruin, sack, spoil, waste, wreck

devastating *adj* caustic, cutting, deadly, destructive, effective, incisive, keen, mordant, overpower ing, overwhelming, ravishing, sardonic, satirical, savage, stunning, trenchant, withering

develop *v* advance, cultivate, evolve, flourish, foster, grow, mature, progress, promote, prosper, ripen; amplify, augment, broaden, dilate upon, elaborate, enlarge, expand, unfold, work out; be a direct result of, break out, come about, ensue, follow, happen, result

development *n* advance, advancement, evolution, expansion, growth, improvement, increase, maturity, progress, progression, spread, unfolding, unravelling; change, circumstance, event, happening, incident, issue, occurrence, outcome, phenomenon, result, situation, turn of events, upshot

deviate *v* avert, bend, deflect, depart, differ, digress, diverge, drift, err, part, stray, swerve, turn, turn aside, vary, veer, wander

deviation *n* aberration, alteration, change, deflection, departure, digression, discrepancy, disparity, divergence, fluctuation, inconsistency, irregularity, shift, variance

device *n* apparatus, appliance, contraption, contrivance, gadget, gimmick, implement, instrument, invention, tool, utensil; artifice, design, dodge, expedient, gambit, improvisation, manoeuvre, plan, ploy, project, purpose, ruse, scheme, shift, stratagem, strategy, stunt, trick, wile

devil *n* archfiend, Beelzebub, Belial, Clootie, demon, fiend, Lucifer, Prince of Darkness, Satan; beast, brute, demon, monster, ogre, rogue, savage, terror, villain

devious *adj* calculating, crooked, deceitful, dishonest, double-dealing, evasive, indirect, insidious, insincere, not straight-forward, scheming, sly, surreptitious, treacherous, tricky, underhand, wily

devise *v* arrange, conceive, concoct, construct, contrive, design, dream up, form, formulate, frame, imagine, invent, plan, plot, prepare, project, scheme, think up, work out

devoid *adj* barren, bereft, deficient, denuded, destitute, empty, free from, lacking, vacant, void, wanting, without

devote *v* allot, apply, appropriate, assign, commit, concern oneself, consecrate, dedicate, enshrine, give, occupy oneself, pledge, reserve, set apart

devoted *adj* ardent, caring, committed, concerned, constant, dedicated, devout, faithful, fond, loving, loyal, staunch, steadfast, true

devour *v* bolt, consume, cram, dispatch, eat, gobble, gorge, gulp, guzzle, polish off, stuff, swallow, wolf

devout *adj* godly, holy, orthodox, pious, prayerful, pure, religious, irreverent, saintly

dexterity *n* adroitness, artistry, deftness, effortlessness, expertise, facility, finesse, handiness, knack, mastery, neatness, nimbleness, proficiency, skill, smoothness, touch

diagnose *v* analyse, determine, distinguish, identify, interpret, investigate, pinpoint, pronounce, recognize

diagnosis *n* analysis, examination, investigation, scrutiny; conclusion, interpretation, judgement, opinion, pronouncement

diagonal *adj* angled, catercornered, cornerways, cross, crossways, crosswise, oblique, slanting

diagonally *adv* aslant, at an angle, cornerwise, crosswise, obliquely, on the bias, on the cross

diagram *n* chart, drawing, figure, layout, outline, plan, representation, sketch

dialect *n* accent, idiom, jargon, language, localism, patois, pronunciation, provincialism, speech, tongue, vernacular

dialogue *n* colloquy, communication, confabulation, conference, conversation, converse, discourse, discussion, duologue, interlocution; co-versation, lines, script, spoken part

diary *n* appointment book, chronicle, daily record, day-to-day- account, engagement book, journal

dictate *v* read out, say, speak, transmit, utter; command, decree, direct, enjoin, impose, lay down, ordain, order, prescribe, pronounce

dictator *n* absolute ruler, autocrat, despot, oppressor, tyrant

diction *n* expression, language, phraseology, phrasing, style, usage, vocabulary, wording; articulation, delivery, elocution, enunciation, fluency, inflection, intonation, pronunciation, speech

dictionary *n* concordance, encyclopedia, glossary, lexicon, vocabulary, wordbook

die *v* breathe one's last, decease, depart, expire, finish, give up the ghost, hop the twig, pass away, perish; decay, decline, disappear, dwindle, ebb, end, fade, lapse, pass, sink, subside, vanish, wane, wilt, wither; break down, fade out, fail, fizzle out, halt, lose power, peter out, run down, stop

die-hard *n* fanatic, intransigent, old fogy, reactionary, ultraconservative, zealot

die-hard *adj* dyed-in-the-wool, immovable, inflexible, intransigent, reactionary, ultraconservative, uncompromising

diet *n* abstinence, dietary, fast, regime, regimen; aliment, comestibles, commons, edible, fare, food, nourishment, nutriment, provisions, rations, subsistence, sustenance, viands, victuals

diet *v* abstain, eat sparingly, fast, loose weight, reduce, slim

differ *v* be dissimilar, be distinct, contradict, contrast, depart form, diverge, run counter to, stand apart, vary

difference *n* alteration, change, contrast, deviation, differentiation, discrepancy, disparity, dissimilarity, distinction, distinctness, divergence, diversity, unlikeness, variation, variety; distinction, exception, idiosyncrasy, particularity, peculiarity, singularity; argument, clash, conflict, contention, contrariety, contretemps, controversy, debate, disagreement, discordance, dispute, quarrel, strife, tiff, wrangle

different *adj* altered, at odds, at variance, changed, clashing, contrasting, deviating, discrepant, disparate, dissimilar, divergent, diverse, inconsistent, opposed, unlike; assorted, divers, diverse, manifold, many, miscellaneous, multifarious, numerous, several, some, sundry, varied, various

differentiate *v* contrast, discern, discriminate, distinguish, make a distinction, distinguish, make a distinction, mark off, separate, set off, tell apart

difficult *adj* arduous, burdensome, demanding, formidable, hard, laborious, onerous, painful, strenuous, toilsome, uphill, wearisome; demanding, fastidious, fractious, fussy, hard to please, intractable, obstreperous, perverse, refractory, rigid, tiresome, troublesome, trying, unaccommodating, unamenable, unmanageable

difficulty *n* arduousness, awkward ness, hardship, laboriousness, labour, pain, painfulness, strain, strenuousness, tribulation; deep water, dilemma, distress, embarrassment, hot water, mess, perplexity, pickle, plight, predicament, quandary, straits, trial, trouble

diffident *adj* backward, bashful, constrained, distrustful, doubtful, hesitant, insecure, meek, modest, reluctant, reserved, self-conscious, self-effacing, sheepish, shrinking, shy, suspicious, timid, timorous, unassertive, unassuming, unobtrusive, unsure, withdrawn

dig *v* break up, burrow, delve, excavate, gouge, grub, hoe, hollow out, mine, penetrate, pierce, quarry, scoop, till, tunnel, turn over; delve, dig down, go into, investigate, probe, research, search

dig *n* jab, poke, prod, punch, thrust; crack, cutting remark, gibe, insult, jeer, quip, sneer, taunt, wisecrack

dig *v* absorb, assimilate, concoct, dissolve, incorporate, macerate; absorb, assimilate, con, consider, contemplate, grasp, master, meditate, ponder, study, take in, understand

dignified *adj* august, decorous, distinguished, exalted, formal, grave, honourable, imposing, lofty, lordly, noble, reserved, solemn, stately, upright

dignitary *n* bigwig, notability, notable, personage, pillar of society, public figure, VIP, worthy

dignity *n* courtliness, decorum, grandeur, gravity, hauteur, loftiness, majesty, mobility, propriety, solemnity, stateliness

digress *v* be diffuse, depart, deviate, diverge, drift, expatiate, get off the point, go off at a tangent, ramble, stray, turn aside, wander

dilapidated *adj* battered, broken-down, crumbling, decayed, decrepit, fallen in, falling apart, gone to rack and ruin, in ruins, neglected, ramshackle, rickety, ruined, ruinous, rundown, shabby, shaky, tumble down, uncared for, worn-out

dilemma *n* difficulty, embarrassment, fix, jam, mess, perplexity, plight, predicament, problem, puzzle, quandary, strait, tight corner

diligence *n* activity, application, assiduity, assiduousness, attention, attentiveness, care, constancy, earnestness, heedfulness, industry, intentness, laboriousness, perseverance, sedulousness

diligent *adj* active, assiduous, attentive, busy, careful, conscientious, constant, earnest, hard-working, indefatigable, industrious, laborious, painstaking, persevering, persistent, sedulous, studious, tireless

dilute *v* adulterate, cut, make

thinner, thin, water down, weaken

dim *adj* caliginous, cloudy, dark, dusky, grey, overcast, poorly lit, shadowy, tenebrous; bleary, blurred, faint, fuzzy, ill-defined, indistinct, obscured, shadowy, unclear; dense, dull, fade, lower, obscure, tarnish, turndown

diminish *v* abate, contract, curtail, cut, decrease, lessen, lower, reduce, retrench, shrink, weaken

diminutive *adj* bantam, little, midget, mini, miniature, minute, petite, pocket, pygmy, small, tiny, undersized, wee

din *n* babel, clamour, clangour, clash, clatter, commotion, crash, hubbub, hullabaloo, noise, outcry, pandemonium, racket, row, shout, uproar

dingy *adj* bedimmed, colourless, dark, dim, dirty, discoloured, drab, dreary, dull, dusky, faded, gloomy, grimy, murky, obscure, seedy, shabby, soiled, sombre, tacky

dinner *n* banquet, blowout, collation, feast, main meal, meal, refection, repast, spread

dip *v* bathe, douse, duck, dunk, immerse, plunge, rinse, souse; ladle, scoop, spoon

dip *n* douche, drenching, ducking, immersion, plunge, soaking; bathe, dive, plunge, swim; concoction, dilution, infusion, mixture, preparation, solution, suspension, basin, concavity, depression, hole, hollow, incline, slope; decline, fall, lowering, sag, slip, slump

diplomacy *n* international negotiation, statecraft, statesmanship; artfulness, craft, delicacy, discretion, finesse, savoir faire, skill, subtlety, tact

diplomat *n* conciliator, go-between, mediator, moderator, negotiator, politician, public, relations expert, tactician

diplomatic *adj* adept, discreet, polite, politic, prudent, sensitive, subtle, tactful

dire *adj* alarming, appalling, awful, calamitous, cataclysmic, catastrophic, cruel, disastrous, horrible, horrid, ruinous, terrible, woeful; dismal, dreadful, fearful, gloomy, grim, ominous, portentous

direct *v* administer, advise, conduct, control, dispose, govern, guide, handle, lead, manage, mastermind, oversee, preside over, regulate, rule, run, superintend, supervise; bid, charge, command, dictate, enjoin, instruct, order; guide, indicate, lead, point in the direction of, point the way, show

direct *adj* candid, frank, honest, man-to-man, matter-of-fact, open, outspoken, plain-spoken, sincere, straight, straightforward; absolute, blunt, categorical, downright, explicit, express, plain, point-blank, unambiguous, unequivocal; non-stop, not crooked, shortest, straight, through, unbroken, undeviating, uninterrupted

direction *n* administration, charge, command, control, government, guidance, leadership, management, order, oversight, superintendence, supervision; aim, bearing, course, line, path, road, route, track, way

directly *adv* by the shortest, route, exactly, in a beeline, precisely, straight, unswerving, without deviation; candidly, face-to-face, honestly, in person, openly, personally, plainly, point-blank, straightforwardly, truthfully, unequivocally, without prevarication

director *n* administrator, boss, chairman, chief, controller, executive, governor, head, leader, manager, organizer, principal, producer, supervisor

dirt *n* dust, excrement, filth, grime, impurity, mire, muck, mud, slime, smudge, stain, tarnish; clay, earth, loam, soil

dirty *adj* begrimed, filthy, foul, grimy, grubby, messy, mucky, muddy, nasty, polluted, soiled, sullied, unclean; corrupt, crooked, dishonest, fraudulent, illegal, treacherous, unfair, unscrupulous, unsporting

disability *n* affliction, ailment, complaint, defect, disablement, disorder, handicap, impairment, infirmity, malady

disable *v* cripple, damage, debilitate, enfeeble, hamstring, handicap, immobilize, impair, incapacitate, paralyse, prostrate, put out of action, render inoperative, unfit, unman, weaken

disabled *adj* bedridden, crippled, handicapped, incapacitated, infirm, lame, maimed, mangled, mutilated, paralysed, weak, weakened, wrecked

disadvantage *n* damage, detriment, disservice, harm, hurt, injury, loss, prejudice

disagree *v* be discordant, be dissimilar, conflict, contradict, counter, depart, deviate, differ, diverge, run counter to, vary; argue, bicker, clash, contend, contest, debate, differ, dispute, dissent, fall out, have words, object, oppose, quarrel, take issue with wrangle

disagreeable *adj* bad-tempered, brusque, churlish, contrary, cross, difficult, disobliging, ill-natured, irritable, nasty, peevish, rude, surly, unfriendly, ungracious, unlikable, unpleasant

disagreement *n* difference, discrepancy, disparity, dissimilarity, dissimilitude, divergence, diversity, incompatibility, incongruity, unlikeness, variance; altercation, argument, clash, conflict, debate, difference, discord, dispute, dissent, division, falling out, misunderstanding, quarrel, squabble, strife, wrangle

disappear *v* be lost to view, depart, drop out of sight, ebb, escape, evanesce, fade away, flee, fly, go pass, recede, retire, vanish from sight, wane, withdraw; cease, cease to be known, die out, dissolve, end, evaporate, expire, fade, leave no trace, melt away, pass away, perish, vanish

disappearance *n* departure, desertion, disappearing, disappearing trick, eclipse, evanescence, evaporation, fading, flight, going, loss, melting, passing, vanishing, vanish ing point

disappoint *v* chagrin, dash, deceive, delude, disenchant, disgruntle, dishearten, disillusion, dismay, dissatisfy, fail, let down, sadden, vex

disappointed *adj* balked, cast down, depressed, despondent, discontented, discouraged, disenchanted, disgruntled, disillusioned, dissatisfied, distressed, down-hearted, foiled, frustrated, let down, saddened, thwarted, upset

disappointment *n* chagrin, discontent, discouragement, disenchantment, disillusionment, displeasure, dissatisfaction, distress, failure, frustration, ill-success, mortification, regret, unfulfilment

disapproval *n* censure, condemnation, criticism, denunciation, deprecation, disapprobation, displeasure, dissatisfaction, objection, reproach

disapprove *v* blame, censure, condemn, deplore, deprecate, discountenance, dislike, find unacceptable, frown on, look down one's nose at, object to, refect, take exception to; disallow, set aside, spurn, turn down, veto

disarrange *v* confuse, derange, discompose, disorder, disorganize, disturb, jumble, mess, scatter, shake, shuffle, unsettle, untidy

disarray *n* confusion, discomposure, disharmony, dismay, disorder, disorderliness, disorganization, disunity, indiscipline, unruliness, upset; chaos, clutter, dishevelment, jumble, mess, mix-up, muddle, shambles, tangle, untidiness

disaster *n* accident, act of God, adversity, blow, calamity, cataclysm, catastrophe, misadventure, mischance, misfortune, mishap, reverse, ruin, ruination, stroke, tragedy, trouble

disastrous *adj* adverse, calamitous, cataclysmic, catastrophic, destructive, detrimental, devastating, dire, dreadful, fatal, hapless, harmful, ill-fated, ill-starred, ruinous, terrible, tragic, unfortunate, unlucky, unpropitious, untoward

disbelief *n* distrust, doubt, dubiety, incredulity, mistrust, scepticism, unbelief

discard *v* abandon, cast aside, dispense with, dispose of, drop, dump, get rid of, jettison, reject, relinquish, remove, repudiate, scrap, shed, throw away

discharge *v* absolve, acquit, allow to go, clear, exonerate, free, liberate, pardon, release, set free

discharge *n* acquittal, clearance, exoneration, liberation, pardon, release, remittance; blast, burst, detonation, discharging, explosion, firing, fusillade, report, salvo, shot, volley

discharge *v* cashier, discard, dismiss, eject, expel, fire, give, the sack, oust, remove, sack; detonate, explode, fire, let off, set off, shoot; accomplish, carry out, do, execute, fulfil, observe, perform; clear, honour, meet, pay, relieve, satisfy, settle, square up

disciple *n* adherent, apostle, believer, catechumen, convert, devotee, follower, learner, partisan, proselyte, pupil, student, supporter, votary

disciplinarian *n* authoritarian, despot, drill sergeant, hard master, martinet, stickler, strict, teacher, taskmaster, tyrant

discipline *v* drill, exercise, method, practice, regiment, regulation, training; conduct, control, orderliness, regulation, restraint, self-control, strictness; castigation, chastisement, correction, punishment

discipline *v* break in, bring up, check control, drill, educate, exercise, form, govern, instruct, inure, prepare, regulate, restrain, train

disclose *v* broadcast, communicate, confess, divulge, impart, leak, let slip, make known, make public, publish, relate, reveal, spill the beans about, tell, unveil, utter

discolour *v* fade, mar, mark, rust, soil, stain, streak, tarnish, tinge

discomfort *n* ache, annoyance, disquiet, distress, hardship, hurt, inquietude, irritation, malaise, nuisance, pain, soreness, trouble, uneasiness, unpleasantness, vexation

disconcert *v* abash, agitate, bewilder, discompose, disturb, flurry, fluster, nonplus, perplex, perturb, put out of countenance, ruffle, take aback, throw off balance, trouble, unbalance, unsettle, upset, worry

disconcerting *adj* alarming, awkward, baffling, bewildering, bothersome, confusing, dismaying, distracting, disturbing, embarrassing, off-putting, perplexing, upsetting

disconnect *v* cut off, detach, disengage, divide, part, separate, sever, take apart, uncouple

disconsolate *adj* crushed, dejected, desolate, despairing, forlorn, gloomy, grief-stricken, heartbroken, hopeless, inconsolable, melancholy, miserable, sad, unhappy, woeful, wretched

discontinue *v* abandon, break off, cease, drop, end, finish, give up, halt, interrupt, leave off, pause, put an end to, quit, refrain from, stop, suspend, terminate

discord *n* clashing, conflict, contention, difference, disagreement, discordance, dispute, dissension, disunity, division, friction, incompatibility, lack of concord, opposition, rupture, strife, variance, wrangling; cacophony, din, disharmony, dissonance, harshness, jangle, jarring, racket, tumult

discount *v* brush off, disbelieve, disregard, ignore, leave out of account, overlook, pass over; deduct, lower, mark down, rebate, reduce, take off

discount *n* abatement, allowance, concession, cut, cut price, deduction, drawback, percentage, rebate, reduction

discourage *v* abash, awe, cast down, cow, damp, dampen, dash, daunt, deject, demoralize, depress, dishearten, dismay, dispirit, frighten, intimidate, overawe, put a damper on, scare, unman, unnerve

discouraged *adj* crestfallen, dashed, daunted, deterred, disheartened, dismayed, dispirited, downcast, down in the mouth, glum, pessimistic, put off

discouragement *n* dejection, depression, despair, despondency, disappointment, discomfiture, dismay, downheartedness, hopelessness, loss of confidence, low spirits, pessimism

discourse *n* chat, communication, conversation, converse, dialogue, discussion, speech, talk

discourse *v* confer, converse, debate, declaim, discuss, expatiate, hold forth, speak, talk

discourteous *adj* abrupt, bad-mannered, boorish, brusque, curt, disrespectful, ill-bred, ill-mannered, impolite, insolent, offhand, rude, uncivil, uncourteous, ungentlemanly, ungracious, unmannerly

discover *v* bring to light, come across, come upon, locate, turn up, uncover, unearth; ascertain, descry, detect, determine, discern, disclose, espy, find out, learn, notice, perceive, realize, recognize, reveal, see, spot, turn up, uncover

discovery *n* ascertainment, detection, disclosure, espial, exploration, finding, introduction, locating, location, origination, revelation, uncovering; bonanza, breakthrough, coup, find, findings, godsend, innovation, invention, secret

discreet *adj* careful, cautious, circumspect, considerate, diplomatic, discerning, guarded, judicious, politic, prudent, reserved, sagacious, sensible, tactful, wary

discrepancy *n* conflict, contrariety, difference, disagreement, discordance, disparity, dissimilarity, dissonance, divergence, incongruity, inconsistency, variance, variation

discretion *n* acumen, care, carefulness, caution, circumspection, consideration, diplomacy, discernment, good sense, heedfulness, judgement, judiciousness, maturity, prudence, sagacity, tact, wariness

discriminate *v* disfavour, favour, show bias, show prejudice, single out, treat as inferior, treat differently, victimize; assess, differentiate, discern, distinguish, draw a distinction, evaluate, segregate, separate, sift, tell the difference

discriminating *adj* acute, astute, critical, cultivated, discerning, fastidious, keen, particular, refined, selective, sensitive, tasteful

discrimination *n* bias, bigotry, favouritism, inequity, intolerance, prejudice, unfairness

discuss *v* argue, confer, consider, consult with, converse, debate, deliberate, examine, exchange views on, get together, reason about, review, sift, talk about, thrash out, ventilate, weigh up the pros and cons

discussion *n* analysis, argument, colloquy, confabulation, conference, consideration, consultation, conversation, debate, deliberation, dialogue, discourse, examination, exchhange, review, scrutiny, symposium

disdain *n* arrogance, contempt, contumely, derision, dislike, haughtiness, hauteur, indifference, scorn, sneering, snobbishness, superciliousness

disease *n* affliction, ailment, complaint, condition, disorder, ill health, illness, indisposition, infection, infirmity, malady, sickness, upset

diseased *adj* ailing, infected, rotten, sick, sickly, tainted, unhealthy, unsound, unwell, unwholesome

disembark *v* alight, arrive, get off, go ashore, land, step out of

disentangle *v* detach, disconnect, disengage, extricate, free, loose, separate, sever, unfold, unravel, unsnarl, untangle, untwist

disfavour *n* disapprobation, disapproval, dislike, displeasure

disfigure *v* blemish, damage, deface, deform, disfeature, distort, injure, maim, make ugly, mar, mutilate, scar

disgrace *n* baseness, degradation, dishonour, disrepute, ignominy, infamy, odium, opprobrium, shame; aspersion, blemish, blot, defamation, reproach, scandal, slur, stain, stigma; contempt, discredit, disesteem, disfavour, obloquy

disgrace *v* abase, bring shame upon, defame, degrade, discredit, disfavour, dishonour, disparage, humiliate, reproach, shame, slur, stain, stigmatize, sully, taint

disgraceful *adj* blameworthy, contemptible, degrading, detestable, discreditable, dishonourable, disreputable, infamous, low, mean, opprobrious, scandalous, shameful, shocking, unworthy

disgruntled *adj* annoyed, discontented, displeased, dissatisfied, grumpy, irritated, malcontent, peeved, peevish, petulant, put out, sulky, sullen, testy, vexed

disguise *v* camouflage, cloak, conceal, cover, hide, mask, screen, secrete, shroud, veil; deceive, dissemble, dissimulate, fake, falsify, fudge, gloss over, misrepresent

disguise *n* camouflage, cloak, costume, cover, mask, screen, veil

disgust *v* cause aversion, displease, fill with loathing, nauseate, offend, outrage, put off, repel, revolt, sicken, turn one's stomach

disgust *n* abhorrence, abomination, antipathy, aversion, detestation, dislike, distaste, hatefulness, hatred, loathing, nausea, repugnance, repulsion, revulsion

disgusting *adj* abominable, destestable, distasteful, foul, gross, grotty, hateful, loathsome, nasty, nauseating, nauseous, objectionable, obnoxious, odious, offensive, repellent, repugnant, revolting, shame less, sickening, stinking, vile, vulgar

dish *n* bowl, plate, platter, salver; fare, food, recipe

dishearten *v* cast down, crush, damp, dampen, dash, daunt, deject, depress, deter, discourage, dismay, dispirit, put a damper on

dishonest *adj* bent, cheating, corrupt, crafty, crooked, deceitful, deceiving, deceptive, designing, disreputable, double-dealing, false, fraudulent, guileful, lying, perfidious, swindling, treacherous, unfair, unprincipled, unscrupulous, untrustworthy, untruthful

dishonesty *n* cheating, chicanery, corruption, craft, criminality, crookedness, deceit, duplicity, falsehood, falsity, fraud, fraudulence, graft, improbity, mendacity, perfidy, sharp practice, stealing, treachery, trickery, wiliness

dishonour *v* abase, blacken, corrupt, debase, debauch, defame, degrade, discredit, disgrace, shame, sully

dishonour *n* abasement, degradation, discredit, disfavour, disgrace, disrepute, ignominy, infamy, obloquy, odium, opprobrium, reproach, scandal, shame

dishonourable *adj* base, contemptible, despicable, discreditable, disgraceful, ignoble, ignominious, infamous, scandalous, shameful

disillusioned *adj* disabused, disappointed, disenchanted, enlightened, indifferent, out of love, sadder and wiser, undeceived

disinclination *n* alienation, antipathy, aversion, demur, dislike, hesitance, hesitancy, lack of desire, lack of enthusiasm, loathness, objection, opposition, reluctance, repugnance, resistance, unwillingness

disinclined *adj* apathetic, averse, balking, hesitating, indisposed, loath, not in the mood, opposed, reluctant, resistant, unwilling

disinfect *v* clean, cleanse, decontaminate, deodorize, fumigate, purify, sanitize, sterilize

disinfectant *n* antiseptic, germicide, sanitizer, sterilizer

disinherit *v* cut off, cut off without a penny, disown, dispossess, oust, repudiate

disintegrate *v* break apart, break up, crumble, disunite, fall apart, fall to pieces, reduce to fragments, separate, shatter, splinter

disinterested *adj* candid, detached, dispassionate, equitable, even-handed, free from self-interest, impartial, impersonal, neutral, outside, unbiased, uninvolved, unprejudiced, unselfish

dislike *n* animosity, animus, antagonism, antipathy, aversion, detestation, disapprobation, disapproval, disgust, disinclination, distaste, enmity, hatred, hostility, loathing, repugnance

dislike *v* abhor, abominate, be averse to, despise, detest, disapprove, disfavour, disrelish, hate, loathe, object to, scorn, shun

disloyal *adj* apostate, disaffected, faithless, false, perfidious, seditious, subversive, traitorous, treacherous, treasonable, two-faced, unfaithful, unpatriotic, untrustworthy

disloyalty *n* betrayal of trust, breach of trust, breaking of faith, deceitfulness, double-dealing, falseness, falsity, inconstancy, infidelity, perfidy, treachery, treason, unfaithfulness

dismal *adj* black, bleak, cheerless, dark, depressing, despondent, dolorous, dreary, forlorn, funereal, gloomy, gruesome, lonesome, lowering, lugubrious, melancholy, sad, sombre, sorrowful

dismay *v* affright, alarm, appal, distress, fill with consternation, frighten, horrify, paralyse, scare, terrify, unnerve

dismay *n* agitation, alarm, anxiety, apprehension, consternation, distress, dread, fear, fright, horror, panic, terror, trepidation

dismiss *v* axe, cashier, discharge, fire, give notice to, lay off, oust, remove, sack, send packing; disband, disperse, dissolve, free, let go, release, send away

dismissal *n* adjournment, end, freedom to depart, permission to go, release; discharge, expulsion, notice, removal, the sack

disobedience *n* indiscipline, infraction, insubordination, mutiny, noncompliance, nonobservance, recalcitrance, revolt, unruliness, waywardness

disobedient *adj* contrary, contumacious, defiant, disorderly, forward, insubordinate, intractable, mischievous, naughty, noncompliant, nonobservant, obstreperous, refractory, undisciplined, unruly, wayward, wilful

disobey *v* contravene, defy, disregard, flout, go counter to, ignore, infringe, overstep, rebel, refuse to obey, resist, transgress, violate

disorderly *adj* chaotic, confused, disorganized, indiscriminate, irregular, jumbled, messy, unsystematic, untidy; boisterous, disruptive, indisciplined, lawless, obstreperous, rebellious, refractory, riotous, rowdy, stormy, tumultuous, turbulent, ungovernable, unlawful, unmanageable, unruly

disown *v* abandon, abnegate, cast off, deny, disallow, disavow, disclaim, disinherit, refuse to acknowledge, reject, renounce, repudiate, turn one's back on

dispassionate *adj* calm, collected, composed, cool, imperturbable, moderate, quiet, serene, sober, temperate, unemotional, unexcitable, unexcited, unmoved, unruffled

dispatch *v* conclude, discharge, dispose of, expedite, finish, make short work of, perform, settle

dispatch *n* account, bulletin, communication, document, instruction, item, letter, message, missive, news, piece, report, story

dispense *v* allocate, allot, apportion, assign, deal out, disburse, distribute, dole out, mete out, share; administer, apply, carry out, direct, discharge, enforce, execute, implement, operate, undertake

disperse *v* broadcast, circulate, diffuse, disseminate, dissipate, distribute, scatter, spread, strew; break up, disappear, disband, dismiss, dispel, dissolve, rout, scatter, send off, separate, vanish

dispirited *adj* crestfallen, dejected, depressed, despondent, discouraged, disheartened, down, gloomy, glum, in the doldrums, low, morose, sad

displace *v* derange, disarrange, disturb, misplace, move, shift, transpose; crowd out, oust, replace, succeed, supersede, supplant, take the place of

display *v* betray, demonstrate, disclose, evidence, evince, exhibit, expose, manifest, open, open to view, present, reveal, show, unveil; expand, extend, model, open out, spread out, stretch out, unfold, unfurl

display *n* array, demonstration, exhibition, exposition, exposure, manifestation, presentation, revelation, show; flourish, ostentation, pageant, parade, pomp, show, spectacle

displease *v* aggravate, anger, annoy, disgust, dissatisfy, exasperate, gall, incense, irk, irritate, nettle, offend, pique, provoke, rile, upset, vex

displeasure *n* anger, annoyance, disapprobation, disapproval, disfavour, disgruntlement, dislike, distaste, indignation, irritation, offence, pique, resentment, vexation, wrath

disposal *n* clearance, discarding, ejection, jettisoning, parting, with relinquishment, removal, riddance, scrapping, throwing away; arrangement, array, dispensation, disposition, distribution, grouping, placing, position

dispose *v* adjust, arrange, array, determine, distribute, fix, group, marshal, order, place, put, range, rank, regulate, set, settle, stand

dispose of *v* deal with decide, determine, end, finish, settle; bestow, give, make over, part with, sell, transfer; destroy, discard, dump, get rid of, jettison, scrap, throw out, unload

disposition *n* character, constitution, make-up, nature, spirit, temper, temperament

disproportion *n* asymmetry, discrepancy, disparity, imbalance, inadequacy, inequality, insufficiency, lopsidedness, unevenness, unsuitableness

disproportionate *adj* excessive, incommensurate, inordinate, out of proportion, too much, unbalanced, unequal, uneven, unreasonable

disprove *v* confute, contradict, controvert, discredit, expose, give the lie to, invalidate, negate, prove false, rebut, refute

dispute *v* altercate, argue, brawl, clash, contend, debate, discuss, quarrel, squabble, wrangle; challenge, contest, contradict, controvert, deny, doubt, impugn, question

dispute *n* altercation, argument, brawl, conflict, disagreement, discord, disturbance, feud, friction, quarrel, strife, wrangle

disqualification *n* disability, incapacitation, unfitness; debarment, disenablement, disentitlement, elimination, exclusion, incompetence, ineligibility, rejection

disqualify *v* disable, incapacitate, invalidate, unfit; debar, declare, ineligible, disentitle, preclude, prohibit, rule out

disquiet *n* alarm, angst, anxiety, concern, disquietude, distress, disturbance, fear, foreboding, fretfulness, nervousness, restlessness, trouble, uneasiness, unrest, worry

disregard *v* brush aside, discount, disobey, ignore, make light of, neglect, overlook, pass over, take no notice of; brush off, contempt, despise, disdain, disparage, snub

disreputable *adj* base, contemptible, derogatory, discreditable, disgraceful, dishonourable, disorderly, ignominious, infamous, louche, low, mean, notorious, opprobrious, scandalous, shameful, shocking, unprincipled, vicious, vile

disrepute *n* bad reputation, discredit, disesteem, disfavour, disgrace, dishonour, ignominy, ill favour, ill-repute, infamy, notoriety, obloquy, shame, unpopularity

disrespect *n* contempt, discourtesy, dishonour, disregard, impertinence, impoliteness, impudence, incivility, insolence, irreverence, lack of respect, rudeness, unmannerliness

disrupt *v* agitate, confuse, disorder, disorganize, disturb, spoil, throw into disorder, upset

dissatisfaction *n* annoyance, chagrin, disappointment, discomfort, discontent, dislike, dismay, displeasure, distress, exasperation, frustration, irritation, regret, resentment, unhappiness

dissatisfied *adj* disappointed, discontented, disgruntled, displeased, fed up, frustrated, not

satisfied, unfulfilled, ungratified, unhappy, unsatisfied
dissect *v* anatomize, cut up, dismember, lay open
disseminate *v* broadcast, circulate, diffuse, disperse, dissipate, distribute, proclaim, promulgate, propagate, publicize, publish, scatter, sow, spread
dissension *n* conflict, conflict of opinion, contention, difference, disagreement, discord, discordance, dispute, dissent, friction, quarrel, strife, variance
dissent *v* decline, differ, disagree, object, protest, refuse, withhold assent
dissent *n* difference, disagreement, discord, dissension, dissidence, nonconformity, objection, opposition, refusal, resistance
dissertation *n* critique, discourse, disquisition, essay, exposition, thesis, treatise
disservice *n* bad turn, disfavour, harm, ill turn, injury, injustice, unkindness, wrong
dissident *adj* differing, disagreeing, discordant, dissentient, dissenting, heterodox, nonconformist
dissident *n* agitator, dissenter, protestor, rebel, recusant
dissimilar *adj* different, disparate, divergent, diverse, heterogeneous, mismatched, not alike, not capable of comparison, not similar, unlike, unrelated, various
dissipate *v* burn up, consume, deplete, expend, fritter away, indulge oneself, lavish, misspend, run through, spend, squander, waste
dissociate *v* break off, disband, disrupt, part company, quit; detach, disconnect, distance, divorce, isolate, segregate, separate, set apart
dissolute *adj* abandoned, corrupt, debauched, degenerate, depraved, dissipated, immoral, lax, lewd, libertine, licentious, loose, profligate, rakish, unrestrained, vicious, wanton, wild
dissolution *n* breaking, up, disintegration, division, divorce, parting, resolution, separation
dissolve *v* deliquesce, flux, fuse, liquefy, melt, soften, thaw; crumble, decompose, diffuse, disappear, disintegrate, disperse, dissipate, dwindle, evanesce, evaporate, fade, melt away, perish, vanish, waste away
dissuade *v* advise against, deter, discourage, disincline, divert, expostulate, persuade not to do, put off, talk out of, urge not to, warn
distance *n* absence, extent, gap, interval, lapse, length, range, reach, remoteness, remove, separation, space, span, stretch, width
distance *v* dissociate, oneself, put in proportion, separate oneself
distant *adj* abroad, afar, far, far-flung, far-off, outlying, remote, removed; aloof, ceremonious, cold, cool, formal, haughty, reserved, restrained, reticent, standoffish, stiff, unapproachable, unfriendly, withdrawn
distaste *n* abhorrence, antipathy, aversion, detestation, disfavour, disgust, disinclination, dislike, displeasure, disrelish, dissatisfaction, horror, loathing, repugnance, revulsion

distasteful *adj* abhorrent, disagreeable, displeasing, loathsome, nauseous, objectionable, obnoxious, offensive, repugnant, repulsive, undesirable, uninviting, unpalatable, unpleasant, unsavoury

distil *v* condense, draw out, evaporate, express, extract, press out, purify, rectify, refine, sublimate, vaporize

distinct *adj* apparent, clear, clearcut, decided, definite, evident, lucid, manifest, marked, noticeable, obvious, palpable, patent, plain, recognizable, sharp, unambiguous, unmistakable, well-defined; detached, different, discrete, dissimilar, individual, separate, unconnected

distinction *n* differentiation, discernment, discrimination, penetration perception, separation; contrast, difference, differential, division, separation; account, celebrity, consequence, credit, eminence, excellence, fame, greatness, honour, importance, merit, name, note, prominence, quality, rank, renown, reputation, repute, superiority, worth

distinguish *v* ascertain, decide, determine, differentiate, discriminate, judge, tell apart, tell between, tell the difference; discern, know, make out, perceive, pick out, recognize, see, tell; celebrate, dignify, honour, immortalize, make famous, signalize

distort *v* bend, buckle, contort, deform, disfigure, misshape, twist, warp, wrench, wrest; bias, colour, falsify, garble, misrepresent, pervert, slant, twist

distract *v* divert, draw away, sidetrack, turn aside; agitate, bewilder, confound, confuse, derange, discompose, disconcert, disturb, harass, madden, perplex, puzzle, torment, trouble

distraction *n* abstraction, agitation, bewilderment, commotion, confusion, discord, disorder, disturbance; amusement, beguilement, diversion, entertainment, pastime, recreation

distress *n* affliction, agony, anguish, anxiety, desolation, discomfort, grief, heartache, misery, pain, sadness, sorrow, suffering, torment, torture, woe, worry, wretchedness

distress *v* afflict, agonize, bother, disturb, grieve, harass, harrow, pain, perplex, sadden, torment, trouble, upset, worry, wound

distressing *v* affecting, afflicting, distressful, disturbing, grievous, heart-breaking, hurtful, lamentable, painful, sad, upsetting, worrying

distribute *v* administer, allocate, allot, apportion, assign, deal, dispense, dispose, divide, dole out, give, measure out, mete, share

distribution *n* allocation, allotment, apportionment, dispensation, division, dole, partition, sharing, dealing, delivery, handling, mailing, marketing, trading, transport, transportation

district *n* area, community, locality, neighbourhood, parish, quarter, region, sector, vicinity, ward

distrust *v* be sceptical of, be suspicious, of, be wary of, disbelieve, mistrust, question, suspect, wonder about

distrust *n* disbelief, doubt, lack of faith, misgiving, mistrust, qualm, question, scepticism, suspicion, wariness

disturb *v* bother, butt in on, disrupt, interfere with, interrupt, intrude on, pester, rouse, startle; agitate, alarm, annoy, confound, discompose, distract, distress, excite, fluster, harass, perturb, ruffle, shake, trouble, unsettle, upset, worry

disturbance *n* agitation, annoyance, bother, confusion, derangement, disorder, distraction, hindrance, interruption, intrusion, molestation, perturbation, upset; bother, brawl, commotion, disorder, fracas, fray, riot, tumult, turmoil, uproar

disuse *n* abandonment, decay, desuetude, discontinuance, idleness, neglect, non-employment, nonuse

ditch *n* channel, drain, dyke, furrow, gully, moat, trench, watercourse

ditch *v* dig, drain, excavate, gouge, trench; abandon, discard, dispose of, drop, get rid of, jettison, scrap, throw out, throw overboard

dither *v* faff about, falter, haver, hesitate, oscillate, teeter, vacillate, waver

dive *v* descend, dip, disappear, drop, duck, fall, go underwater, jump, leap, nose-dive, pitch, plummet, plunge, submerge, swoop

dive *n* dash, header, jump, leap, lunge, nose dive, plunge, spring

diverge *v* bifurcate, branch, divaricate, divide, fork, part, radiate, separate, split, spread

diverse *adj* assorted, diversified, miscellaneous, of every description, several, sundry, varied, various; different, differing, discrete, disparate, dissimilar, distinct, divergent, separate, unlike, varying

diversion *n* alteration, change, deflection, departure, detour, deviation, digression, variation; amusement, beguilement, delight, distraction, enjoyment, entertainment, game, gratification, pastime, play, pleasure, recreation, relaxation, sport

diversity *n* assortment, difference, dissimilarity, distinctiveness, divergence, diverseness, diversification, medley, multiplicity, range, unlikeness, variance, variegation, variety

divert *v* avert, deflect, redirect, switch, turn aside

divide *v* bisect, cleave, cut, detach, disconnect, part, partition, segregate, separate, sever, shear, split, subdivide, sunder; allocate, allot, apportion, deal out, dispense, distribute, dole out, measure out, portion, share

dividend *n* bonus, cut, extra, gain, plus, portion share, surplus

divine *adj* angelic, celestial, godlike, heavenly, holy, mystical, saintly, seraphic, spiritual, superhuman, supernatural, transcendental, transmundane; beautiful, excellent, glorious, marvellous, perfect, splendid, superlative, wonderful

divine *v* apprehend, conjecture, deduce, discern, foretell, guess, hypothesize, infer, intuit, perceive, prognosticate, suppose, surmise, suspect, theorize, understand

divinity *n* deity, divine nature, godhead, godhood, godliness, holiness, sanctity; daemon, deity, genius, god, goddess, guardian spirit, spirit; religion, religious studies, theology

divisible *adj* dividable, fractional, separable, splittable

division *n* bisection, cutting up, detaching, dividing, partition, separation, splitting up; allotment, apportionment, distribution, sharing, border, boundary, demarcation, divide, divider, dividing, line, partition; branch, class, compartment, department, group, head, part, portion, section, sector, segment

divorce *n* annulment, breach, break, decree, dissolution, disunion, rupture, separation, severance

divorce *v* annul, disconnect, dissociate, dissolve, disunite, divide, part, separate, sever, split up, sunder

divulge *v* betray, communicate, confess, declare, disclose, exhibit, expose, impart, leak, let slip, make known, proclaim, promulgate, publish, reveal, tell, uncover

dizzy *adj* faint, giddy, light-headed, off balance, reeling, shaky, stagger ing, swimming, vertiginous, wobbly; (*Inf*) woozy

do *v* accomplish, achieve, act, carry out, complete, conclude, discharge, end, execute, perform, produce, transact, undertake, work; answer, be adequate, be enough for, be of use, be, sufficient, pass muster, satisfy, serve, suffice, suit; adapt, render, translate, transpose; bear oneself, behave, carry oneself; fare, get along, get on, make out, man age, proceed; bring about, cause, create, effect, produce; cheat, cozen, deceive, defraud, dupe, fleece, hoax, swindle, trick

do *n* affair, event, function, gathering, occasion, party

docile *adj* amenable, biddable, compliant, ductile, manageable, obedient, pliant, submissive, teachable, tractable

dock *n* harbour, pier, quay, waterfront, wharf

dock *v* anchor, berth, drop anchor, land, moor, put in, tie up

doctor *n* general practitioner, GP, medic, medical practitioner, physician

doctor *v* apply medication, to, give medical treatment to, treat; botch, cobble, fix, mend, patch up, repair; alter, change, disguise, falsify, fudge, misrepresent, pervert, tamper with

doctrine *n* article, article of faith, belief, canon, concept, conviction, creed, dogma, opinion, precept, principle, teaching, tenet

document *n* certificate, instrument, legal form, paper, record, report

document *v* authenticate, back up, certify, cite, corroborate, detail, give weight to, instance, particularize, substantiate, support, validate, verify

dodge *v* dart, duck, shift, side-step, turn aside; avoid, deceive, elude, equivocate, evade, fend off, fudge, get out of, hedge, parry, shirk, shuffle, trick

dodge *n* contrivance, device, feint, machination, ploy, ruse, scheme, stratagem, subterfuge, trick, wile

dog *n* bitch, canine, cur, hound, man's best friend, mongrel, pup, puppy, tyke

dog *v* haunt, hound, plague, pursue, shadow, track, trail, trouble

dogged *adj* determined, firm, indefatigable, obstinate, persevering, persistent, pertinacious, resolute, single-minded, staunch, steadfast, steady, stubborn, tenacious, unflagging, unshakable, unyielding

dogma *n* article, article of faith, belief, credo, creed, doctrine, opinion, precept, principle, teachings, tenet

dogmatic *adj* arbitrary, arrogant, assertive, categorical, dictatorial, doctrinaire, downright, emphatic, imperious, magisterial, obdurate, opinionated, overbearing, peremptory

doldrums *pl n* apathy, blues, boredom, depression, dullness, dumps, ennui, gloom, inertia, lassitude, listlessness, malaise, stagnation, tedium, torpor

dole *n* allowance, alms, benefit, donation, gift, grant, gratuity, modicum, parcel, pittance, portion, quota, share

dole out *v* administer, allocate, allot, apportion, assign, deal, dispense, distribute, divide, give, hand out, mete, share

domestic *adj* domiciliary, family, home, household, private; domesticated, house, housetrained, pet, tame, trained; indigenous, internal, native, not foreign

dominant *adj* ascendant, assertive, authoritative, commanding, controlling, governing, leading, presiding, ruling, superior, supreme

dominate *v* control, direct, domineer, govern, have the upper hand over, have the whip hand over, keep under one's thumb, lead, master, monopolize, overbear, rule, tyrannize; bestride, loom over, overlook, stand head and shoulders above, stand over, survey, tower above

domination *n* ascendancy, authority, command, control, influence, mastery, power, rule, superiority, supremacy, sway

domineer *v* bluster, boss around, browbeat, bully, hector, intimidate, lord over, menace, overbear, ride roughshod over, swagger, threaten, tyrannize

dominion *n* ascendancy, authority, command, control, domination, government, jurisdiction, mastery, power, rule, sovereignty, supremacy, sway

don *v* clothe oneself in, dress in, get into, pull on, put on, slip on

donate *v* bequeath, bestow, con tribute, gift, give, make a gift of, present, subscribe; (*Inf*) chip in

donation *n* alms, benefaction, boon, contribution, gift, grant, gratuity, largess, offering, present, subscription

done *adj* accomplished, completed, concluded, consummated, ended, executed, finished, over, perfected, realized, terminated, through; cooked, cooked sufficiently, ready; depleted, exhausted, finished, spent, used up; acceptable, conventional, proper

donor *n* almsgiver, benefactor, contributor, donator, giver, philanthropist

doom *n* catastrophe, death, destiny, destruction, downfall, fate, fortune, lot, portion, ruin

doom *v* condemn, consign, damn, decree, destine, foreordain, judge, predestine, sentence, threaten

doomed *adj* bedevilled, bewitched, condemned, cursed, fated, hopeless, ill-fated, ill-omened, luckless, star-crossed

door *n* doorway, egress, entrance, entry, exit, ingress, opening

dope *n* drugs, narcotic, opiate

dormant *adj* asleep, comatose, fallow, hibernating, inactive, inert, inoperative, latent, quiescent, sleeping, sluggish, slumbering, suspended, torpid

dose *n* dosage, draught, drench, measure, portion, potion, prescription, quantity

dot *n* atom, circle, dab, fleck, full stop, iota, jot, mark, mite, mote, point, speck, spot

dotage *n* decrepitude, feebleness, imbecility, old age, second childhood, senility, weakness

dote on *v* admire, adore, hold dear, idolize, lavish affection on, prize, treasure

double *adj* binate, coupled, doubled, dual, duplicate, in pairs, paired, twice, twin, twofold

double *v* duplicate, enlarge, fold, grow, increase, magnify, multiply, plait, repeat

double-cross *v* betray, cheat, defraud, hoodwink, mislead, swindle, trick; (*Inf*) two-time

doubt *v* discredit, distrust, fear, lack confidence, in, misgive, mistrust, query, question, suspect; be dubious, be uncertain, demur, fluctuate, hesitate, scruple, vacillate, waver

doubt *n* apprehension, disquiet, distrust, fear, incredulity, lack of faith, misgiving, mistrust, qualm, scepticism, suspicion; ambiguity, confusion, difficulty, dilemma, perplexity, problem, quandary

doubtful *adj* ambiguous, debatable, dubious, equivocal, hazardous, inconclusive, indefinite, indeterminate, obscure, precarious, problematic, questionable, unclear, unconfirmed, unsettled, vague; distrustful, hesitating, in two minds, irresolute, perplexed, sceptical, suspicious, tentative, uncertain, unconvinced, undecided, unresolved, unsettled, unsure, vacillating, wavering

doubtless *adv* assuredly, certainly, clearly, indisputably, of course, precisely, surely, truly, undoubtedly, unquestionably, without doubt; apparently, most likely, ostensibly, presumably. probably, seemingly, supposedly

dour *adj* dismal, dreary, forbidding, gloomy, grim, morose, sour, sullen, unfriendly

dowdy *adj* dingy, drab, frowzy, frumpish, frumpy, ill-dressed, old-fashioned, slovenly, unfashionable

do without *v* abstain from, dispense with, forgo, get along without, give up, manage without

down *adj* blue, defected, depressed, disheartened, downcast, low, miserable, sad, unhappy

down and out *adj* derelict, destitute, impoverished, penniless, ruined

downcast *adj* cheerless, crestfallen, daunted, dejected, depressed, despondent, disappointed, disconsolate, discouraged, disheartened, dismayed, dispirited, miserable, sad, unhappy

downfall *n* breakdown, collapse, comedown, debacle, descent, destruction, disgrace, fall, overthrow, run, undoing

downgrade *v* degrade, demote, humble, lower in rank; (*Inf*) take down a peg

downhearted *adj* blue, chapfallen, crestfallen, defected, depressed, despondent, discouraged, disheartened, dismayed, dispirited, downcast, low-spirited, sad, sorrowful, unhappy

downpour *n* cloudburst, deluge, flood, inundation, rainstorm, torrential rain

down-to-earth *adj* common-sense, hard-headed, matter-of-fact, mundane, no-nonsense, plain-spoken, practical, realistic, sane, sensible, unsentimental

downward *adj* declining, descending, earthward, heading down, sliding, slipping

doze *v* catnap, crop off, drowse, nap, nod, sleep, sleep lightly, slumber, snooze

drab *adj* cheerless, colourless, dingy, dismal, dreary, dull, flat, gloomy, grey, lacklustre, shabby, sombre, uninspired, vapid

draft *v* compose, delineate, design, draw, draw up, formulate, outline, plan, sketch

draft *n* abstract, delineation, outline, plan, preliminary form, rough, sketch, version

drag *v* draw, hale, haul, lug, pull, tow, trail, tug, yank

drain *v* bleed, draw off, dry, empty, evacuate, milk, pump off, remove, tap, withdraw; consume, deplete, dissipate, empty, exhaust, sap, strain, tax, use up, weary

drain *n* channel, conduit, culvert, ditch, duct, outlet, pipe, sewer, sink, trench, watercourse; depletion, drag, exhaustion, expenditure, reduction, sap, strain, withdrawal

drama *n* dramatization, play, show, stage play, stage show, theatrical piece; acting, dramatic art, dramaturgy, stagecraft, theatre, Thespian art; crisis, dramatics, excitement, histrionic, scene, spectacle, theatrics, turmoil

dramatic *adj* dramaturgic, dramaturgical, theatrical, Thespian; breathtaking, climactic, electrifying, emotional, exciting, melodramatic, sensational, startling, sudden, suspenseful, tense, thrilling

dramatist *n* dramaturge, playwright, screen-writer, script-writer

dramatize *v* act, exaggerate, lay it on, make a performance of, overdo, overstate, play-act, play to the gallery

drastic *adj* desperate, dire, extreme, forceful, harsh, radical, severe, strong

draught *n* current, flow, influx, movement, puff; cup, dose, drench, drink, potion, quantity

draw *v* drag, haul, pull, tow, tug; delineate, depict, design, map out, mark out, outline, paint, portray, sketch, trace; allure, attract, bring forth, call forth, elicit, engage, entice, evoke, induce, influence, invite, persuade; attenuate, elongate, extend, lengthen, stretch;

breathe in, drain, inhale, inspire, puff, pull, respire, suck; compose, draft, formulate, frame, prepare, write

draw *n* allure, attraction, enticement, lure, magnetism, pull; dead heat, deadlock, impasse, stalemate, tie; lottery, raffle, sweepstake

drawback *n* defect, deficiency, detriment, difficulty, disadvantage, fault, flaw, fly in the ointment, handicap, hindrance, hitch, impediment, imperfection, nuisance, obstacle, snag, stumbling block, trouble

drawing *n* cartoon, delineation, depiction, illustration, outline, picture, portrayal, representation, sketch, study

drawn *adj* fatigued, fraught, haggard, harassed, harrowed, pinched, sapped, strained, stressed, taut, tense, tired, worn

draw out *v* drag out, extend, lengthen, make longer, prolong, prolongate, protract, spin out, stretch, string out

dread *v* anticipate with horror, cringe at, fear, have cold feet, quail, shrink from, shudder, tremble

dread *n* affright, alarm, apprehension, aversion, awe, dismay, fear, fright, horror, terror, trepidation

dreadful *adj* alarming, appalling, awful, dire, distressing, fearful, formidable, frightful, ghastly, grievous, hideous, horrendous, horrible, monstrous, shocking, terrible, tragic, tremendous

dream *n* daydream, delusion, fantasy, hallucination, illusion, imagination, pipe dream, reverie, speculation, trance, vagary, vision; ambition, aspiration, design, desire, gal, hope, notion, wish

dream *v* build castle, in the air, conjure up, daydream, envisage, fancy, fantasize, hallucinate, have dreams, imagine, stargaze, think, visualize

dreamy *adj* chimerical, dreamlike, fantastic, intangible, misty, phantasmagoric, phantasmagorical, shadowy, unreal; absent, abstracted, daydreaming, faraway, in a reverie, musing, pensive, preoccupied, with one's head in the clouds

dreary *adj* bleak, cheerless, comfortless, depressing, dismal, doleful, downcast, drear, forlorn, gloomy, glum, joyless, lonely, lonesome, melancholy, mournful, sad, solitary, sombre, sorrowful, wretched; boring, colourless, drab, dull, humdrum, lifeless, monotonous, routine, tedious, uneventful, uninteresting, wearisome

dregs *pl n* deposit, draff, dross, grounds, lees, residue, residuum, scourings, scum, sediment, trash, waste

drench *v* drown, duck, flood, imbrue, inundate, saturate, soak, souse, steep, wet

dress *n* costume, ensemble, frock, garment, get-up, gown, outfit, robe, suit; apparel, attire, clothes, clothing, costume, garb, garments, guise, habiliment, raiment, togs, vestment

dress *v* attire, change, clothe, don, garb, put on, robe, slip on; bandage, bind up, plaster, treat

dressmaker *n* couturier, modiste, seamstress, swing woman, tailor

dress up *v* beautify, do oneself up,

embellish, gild, improve, titivate

dribble *n* drip, drop, fall in drops, leak, ooze, run, seep, trickle

drift *v* be carried along, coast, float, go, meander, stray, waft, wander

drill *v* coach, discipline, exercise, instruct, practise, rehearse, teach, train; bore, penetrate, perforate, pierce, puncture, sink in

drill *n* discipline, exercise, instruction, practice, preparation, repetition, training; bit, borer, boring-tool, gimlet, rotary tool

drink *v* absorb, drain, gulp, guzzle, imbibe, partake of, quaff, sip, suck, sup, swallow, swig, swill, wash down; carouse, go on a binge, indulge, pub-crawl, revel, tipple, tope, wassail; (*Inf*) booze

drink *n* beverage, liquid, potion, refreshment, thirst quencher; alcohol, booze, liquor, spirits; (*Inf*) the bottle

drip *v* dribble, drizzle, drop, exude, filter, plop, splash, sprinkle, trickle

drip *n* dribble, dripping, drop, leak, trickle

drive *v* herd, hurl, impel, propel, push, send, urge; direct, go, guide, handle, manage, motor, operate, ride, steer, travel

drive *n* excursion, hurl, jaunt, journey, outing, ride, run, spin, trip, turn; ambition, effort, energy, enterprise, get-up-and-go, initiative, motivation, pressure, push (*Inf*) vigour

driving *v* compelling, dynamic, energetic, forceful, galvanic, sweeping, vigorous, violent

drizzle *n* fine rain, Scotch mist

drizzle *v* rain, shower, spit with rain, spray, sprinkle

droll *adj* amusing, clownish, comic, comical, diverting, eccentric, entertaining, farcical, funny, humorous, jocular, laughable, ludicrous, odd, quaint, ridiculous, risible, waggish, whimsical

droop *v* bend, dangle, drop, fall down, hang, sag, sink

drop *n* bead, bubble, driblet, drip, droplet, globule, pearl, tear; dab, dash, mouthful, nip, pinch, shot, sip, spot, taste, tot, trace, trickle; cut, decline, decrease, deterioration, downturn, fall-off, lowering, reduction, slump

drop *v* decline, depress, descend, diminish, dive, droop, fall, lower, plummet, plunge, sink, tumble; abandon, cease, desert, discontinue, forsake, give up, leave, quit, relinquish, remit, terminate

drop out *v* abandon, back out, forsake, give up, leave, quit, renege, stop, withdraw

drought *n* aridity, dehydration, dryness, dry spell, dry weather, parchedness

drove *n* collection, company, crowd, flock, gathering, herd, horde, mob, multitude, press, swarm, throng

drown *v* deluge, drench, engulf, flood, go down, go under, immerse, inundate, sink, submerge, swamp

drudge *n* dogsbody, factotum, hack, maid, menial, plodder, servant, skivvy, slave, toiler, worker

drudgery *n* chore, donkey-work, hack work, hard work, labour, menial labour, skivvying, slavery, slog, sweat, sweated labour, toil

drug *n* medicament, medication,

medicine, physic, poison, remedy; dope, narcotic, opiate, stimulant

drug *v* administer a drug, dose, medicate, treat

drunk *adj* bacchic, drunken, fuddled, inebriated, intoxicated, maudlin, merry, pickled, tipsy, under the influence; (*Inf*) canned, legless, loaded, merry, pickled, pie-eyed, pissed, plastered, sloshed, soaked, stewed, tanked up, tiddly

drunk *n* alcoholic, dipsomaniac, drunkard, inebriate, intoxicated, sot, tippler, toper; (*Inf*) alky, boozer, lush, soak, wino

drunkenness *n* alcoholism, bibulousness, dipsomania, inebriety, insobriety, intemperance, intoxication, sottishness, tipsiness

dry *adj* arid, barren, dehydrated, desiccated, dried up, juiceless, moistureless, parched, sapless, thirsty, torrid, waterless; boring, dreary, dull, monotonous, plain, tedious, tiresome, uninteresting

dry *v* dehumidify, dehydrate, desiccate, drain, make dry, parch, sear

dual *adj* binary, coupled, double, duplex, duplicate, matched, paired, twin, twofold

dubious *adj* doubtful hesitant, sceptical, uncertain, unconvinced, undecided, unsure, wavering; ambiguous, debatable, doubtful, equivocal, indefinite, indeterminate, obscure, problematical, unclear, unsettled; questionable, shady, suspect, suspicious, undependable, unreliable, untrustworthy

duck *v* bend, bob, bow, crouch, dodge, drop, lower, stoop; (*Inf*) avoid, dodge, escape, evade, shirk, shun, sidestep

due *adj* in arrears, outstanding, owed, owing, payable, unpaid; appropriate, becoming, bounden, deserved, fit, fitting, just, justified, merited, obligatory, proper, requisite, right, rightful, suitable, well-earned; expected, expected to arrive, scheduled

due *adv* dead, direct, directly, exactly, straight, undeviatingly

duel *n* affair of honour, single combat; clash, competition, contest, encounter, engagement, fight, rivalry

dues *pl n* charge, charges, fee, levy

dull *adj* dense, dim, dim-witted, doltish, slow, stolid, stupid, thick, unintelligent; apathetic, blank, callous, dead, empty, heavy, indifferent, insensible, insensitive, lifeless, listless, passionless, slow, sluggish, unresponsive, unsympathetic, vacuous; boring, commonplace, dreary, dry, flat, humdrum, monotonous, plain, prosaic, run-of-the-mill, tedious, tiresome, unimaginative, uninteresting, vapid; cloudy, dim, dismal, gloomy, leaden, opaque, overcast, turbid

duly *adv* accordingly, appropriately, befittingly, correctly, decorously, deservedly, fittingly, properly, rightfully, suitably; at the proper time, on time, punctually

dumb *adj* at a loss for words, inarticulate, mum, mute, silent, soundless, speechless, tongue-tied, voiceless, wordless

dummy *n* figure, form, lay figure, manikin, mannequin, model; copy, counterfeit, duplicate, imitation, sham, substitute

dummy *adj* artificial, bogus, fake,

false, imitation, mock, phoney, sham, simulated
dump *v* deposit, drop, fling down, let fall, throw down
dump *n* coup, junk yard, refuse heap, rubbish heap, rubbish tip, tip; (*Inf*) hole, hovel, mess, pigsty, shack, shanty, slum
dungeon *n* cage, cell, donjon, lock up, oubliette, prison, vault
duplicate *adj* corresponding, identical, matched, matching, twin, twofold
duplicate *n* carbon copy, clone, copy, double, facsimile, fax, likeness, lookalike, match, mate, photocopy, Photostat, replica, reproduction, twin
duplicate *v* clone, copy, double, echo, fax, photocopy, repeat, replicate, reproduce, Xerox (*Trademark*)
durable *adj* abiding, constant, dependable, enduring, fast, firm, fixed, hard-wearing, lasting, long-lasting, permanent, persistent, reliable, resistant, sound, stable, strong, sturdy, substantial, tough
dusk *n* dark, evening, eventide, gloaming, nightfall, sundown, sunset, twilight
dusky *adj* dark, dark-complexioned, dark-hued, sable, swarthy
dust *n* fine fragments, grime, grit, particles, powder, powdery, dirt; dirt, earth, ground, soil
dusty *adj* dirty, grubby, sooty, unclean, undusted, unswept
dutiful *adj* compliant, conscientious, deferential, devoted, docile, filial, obedient, punctilious, respectful, reverential, submissive
duty *n* assignment, business, calling, charge, engagement, function, mission, obligation, office, onus, province, responsibility, role, service, task, work; customs, due, excise, impost, levy, tariff, tax, toll; **off duty** at leisure, free, off, off work, on holiday
dwarf *n* bantam, homunculus, Lilliputian, manikin, midget, pygmy, Tom Thumb
dwarf *adj* baby, bonsai, diminutive, dwarfed, miniature, petite, pocket, small, tiny, undersized
dwarf *v* dim, diminish, dominate, minimize, overshadow, tower above
dwell *v* abide, establish oneself, inhabit, lie, lodge, quarter, remain, reside, rest, settle, sojourn, stay, stop
dwelling *n* abode, domicile, dwelling house, establishment, habitation, home, house, lodging, quarters, residence
dye *n* colorant, colour, colouring, pigment, stain, tinge, tint
dye *v* colour, pigment, stain, tincture, tinge, tint
dying *adj* at death's door, ebbing, expiring, fading, failing, final, going, in extremis, moribund, mortal, passing, perishing, sinking
dynamic *adj* active, driving, electric, energetic, forceful, go-ahead, high-powered, lively, magnetic, powerful, vigorous, vital, zippy
dynasty *n* ascendancy, dominion, empire, government, house, regime, rule, sovereignty, sway

E

each *adj* every
each *pron* each and every one, each one, every one, one and all
each *adv* apiece, for each, from each, individually, per capita, per head, per person, respectively, singly, to each
eager *adj* agog, anxious, ardent, athirst, avid, earnest, enthusiastic, fervent, fervid, greedy, hot, hungry, impatient, intent, keen, longing, raring, vehement, yearning, zealous
early *adj* advanced, forward, premature, untimely
early *adv* ahead of time, beforehand, betimes, in advance, in good time, prematurely, too soon
earn *v* bring in, collect, draw, gain, get, gross, make, net, obtain, procure, realize, reap, receive; acquire, attain, be entitled to, be worthy of, deserve, merit, rate, warrant, win
earnest *adj* close, constant, determined, firm, fixed, grave, intent, resolute, resolved, serious, sincere, solemn, stable, staid, steady, thoughtful
earnings *pl n* emolument, gain, income, pay, proceeds, profits, receipts, remuneration, return, reward, salary, stipend, takings, wages
earth *n* globe, orb, planet, sphere, terrestrial, sphere, world; clay, clod, dirt, ground, land, loam, mould, sod, soil, topsoil, turf
earthenware *n* ceramics, crockery, crocks, pots, pottery, terracotta
earthly *adj* mundane, sublunary, tellurian, telluric, terrene, terrestrial, worldly; human, material, mortal, non-spiritual, profane, secular, temporal, worldly
ease *n* affluence, calmness, comfort, content, contentment, enjoyment, happiness, leisure, peace, peace of mind, quiet, quietude, relaxation, repose, rest, restfulness, serenity, tranquillity
ease *v* abate, allay, alleviate, appease, assuage, calm, comfort, disburden, lessen, lighten, mitigate, moderate, mollify, pacify, palliate, quiet, relax, relent, relieve, slacken, soothe, still, tranquillize
easily *adv* comfortably, effortlessly, facilely, readily, simply, smoothly, with ease, without difficulty, without trouble
easy *adj* clear, effortless, facile, light, no bother, not difficult, no trouble, painless, simple, smooth, straightforward, uncomplicated, undemanding; (*Inf*) a piece of cake
easygoing *adj* amenable, calm, carefree, casual, complacent, easy, even-tempered, flexible, happy-go-lucky, indulgent, insouciant, laid-back, lenient, liberal, mild, moderate, nonchalant, permissive, placid, relaxed, serene, tolerant, unconcerned, uncritical, undemanding, unhurried
eat *v* chew, consume, devour, gobble, ingest, munch, swallow; break bread, dine, feed, have a meal, take food, take nourishment

eavesdrop *v* listen in, monitor, over hear; tap (*Inf*) bug, snoop, spy

ebb *v* abate, fall away, fall back flow back, go out, recede, retire, retreat, retrocede, sink, subside, wane, withdraw; decay, decline, decrease, degenerate, deteriorate, diminish, drop, dwindle, fade away, fall away, flag, lessen, peter out, shrink, sink, slacken, weaken

eccentric *adj* aberrant, abnormal, anomalous, bizarre, capricious, erratic, freakish, idiosyncratic, irregular, odd, outlandish, peculiar, quirky, singular, strange, uncommon, unconventional, weird, whimsical

eccentricity *n* aberration, abnormality, anomaly, bizarreness, caprice, capriciousness, foible, freakishness, idiosyncrasy, irregularity, noncon formity, oddity, oddness, outlandishness, peculiarity, quirk, singularity, strangeness, unconventionality, waywardness, weirdness, whimsicality, whimsicalness

ecclesiastic *n* churchman, clergyman, cleric, divine, holy man, man of the cloth, minister, parson, priest

echo *v* repeat, resound, reverberate

echo *n* answer, repetition, reverberation; copy, imitation, mirror image, parallel, reflection, reiteration, reproduction, ringing

eclipse *v* blot out, cloud, darken, dim, extinguish, obscure, overshadow, shroud, veil

eclipse *n* darkening, dimming, extinction, obscuration, occultation, shading, decline, diminution, failure, fall loss

economic *adj* business, commercial, financial, industrial, mercantile, trade; money-making, productive, profitable, profitmaking, remunerative, solvent, viable; budgetary, financial, fiscal, material, monetary, pecuniary

economical *adj* cost-effective, efficient, money-saving, sparing, time-saving, unwasteful, work-saving; careful, economizing, frugal, prudent, saving, scrimping, sparing, thrifty

economize *v* be economical, be frugal, be sparing, cut back, husband, retrench, save, scrimp, tighten one's belt

economy *n* frugality, husbandry, parsimony, providence, prudence, restraint, retrenchment, saving, sparingness, thrift, thriftiness

ecstasy *n* bliss, delight, elation, enthusiasm, euphoria, exaltation, fervour, frenzy, joy, rapture, ravishment, rhapsody, seventh heaven, trance, transport

ecstatic *adj* blissful, delirious, elated, enraptured, enthusiastic, entranced, euphoric, fervent, frenzied, in exaltation, in transports of delight, joyful, joyous, on cloud nine, overjoyed, rapturous, rhapsodic, transported

eddy *n* counter-current, counterflow, swirl, vortex, whirlpool

eddy *v* swirl, whirl

edge *n* border, bound, boundary, brim, brink, contour, fringe, limit, line, lip, margin, outline, perimeter, periphery, rim, side, threshold, verge; acuteness, animation, bite, effectiveness, force, incisiveness, interest, keenness, point, pungency, sharpness, sting, urgency, zest

edible *adj* comestible, digestible, eatable, esculent, fit to eat, good, harmless, palatable, wholesome

edict *n* act, command, decree, dictate, dictum, enactment, fiat, injunction, law, mandate, manifesto, order, ordinance, proclamation, pronouncement, pronunciamento, regulation, ruling, statute

edit *v* adapt, annotate, censor, check, condense, correct, emend, polish, redact, rephrase, revise, rewrite

edition *n* copy, impression, issue, number, printing, programme, version, volume

educate *v* civilize, coach, cultivate, develop, discipline, drill, edify, enlighten, exercise, foster, improve, indoctrinate, inform, instruct, mature, rear, school, teach, train, tutor

education *n* breeding, civilization, coaching, cultivation, culture, development, discipline, drilling, edification, enlightenment, erudition, improvement, indoctrination, instruction, knowledge, nurture, scholarship, schooling, teaching, training, tuition, tutoring

eerie *adj* awesome, creepy, fearful, frightening, ghostly, mysterious, scary, spectral, strange, uncanny, unearthly, uneasy, weird

effect *n* aftermath, conclusion, consequence, event, fruit, issue, outcome, result, upshot; **in effect** actually, effectively, essentially, for practical purposes, in actuality, in fact, in reality, in truth, really, to all intents and purposes, virtually; **take effect become law,** become operative, become valid, begin, come into force, produce results, work

effect *v* accomplish, achieve, actuate, bring about, carry out, cause, complete, consummate, create, effectuate, execute, fulfil, give rise to, initiate, make, perform, produce

effective *adj* able, active, adequate, capable, competent, effectual, efficacious, efficient, energetic, operative, productive, serviceable, useful; active, actual, current, in effect, in execution, in force, in operation, operative, real

effects *pl n* belongings, chattels, furniture, gear, goods, movables, paraphernalia, possessions, property, things, trappings

effervesce *v* bubble, ferment, fizz, foam, froth, sparkle

effervescent *adj* bubbling, bubbly, carbonated, fermenting, fizzing, fizzy, foaming, foamy, frothing, frothy, sparkling; animated, bubbly, buoyant, ebullient, enthusiastic, excited, exhilarated, exuberant, gay, in high spirits, irrepressible, lively, merry, vital, vivacious; (*Inf*) zingy

efficacious *adj* active, adequate, capable, competent, effective, effectual, efficient, energetic, operative, potent, powerful, productive, serviceable, successful, useful

efficiency *n* ability, adeptness, capability, competence, economy, effectiveness, efficacy, power, productivity, proficiency, readiness, skilfulness, skill

efficient *adj* able, adept, businesslike, capable, competent, deft, economic, effective, effectual, organized, powerful, productive, proficient, ready, skilfull, streamlined, well-organized, workmanlike

effort *n* application, endeavour, energy, exertion, force, labour, pains, power, strain, stress, stretch, striving, struggle, toil, trouble, work

effortless *adj* easy, facile, painless, simple, smooth, uncomplicated, undemanding, untroublesome

effusion *n* discharge, effluence, efflux, emission, gush, outflow, outpouring, shedding, stream

effusive *adj* demonstrative, ebullient, enthusiastic, expansive, extravagant, exuberant, free-flowing, fulsome, gushing, lavish, overflowing, profuse, talkative, unreserved, unrestrained, wordy

egocentric *adj* egoistic, egoistical, egotistic, egotistical, self-centred, selfish

egoism *n* egocentricity, egomania, egotism, narcissism, self absorption, self-centredness, self-importance, self-interest, selfishness, self-love, self-regard, self-seeking

egotist *n* bighead, blowhard, boaster, braggadocio, braggart, egoist, egomaniac, self-admirer, swaggerer

eject *v* cast out, discharge, disgorge, emit, expel, spew, spout, throw out, vomit; discharge, dislodge, dismiss, get rid of, oust, throw out

elaborate *adj* careful, detailed, exact, intricate, laboured, minute, painstaking, perfected, precis, skilful, studied, thorough; complex, complicated, decorated, detailed, extravagant, fancy, fussy, involved, ornamented, ornate, ostentatious, showy

elaborate *v* add detail, amplify, complicate, decorate, develop, devise, embellish, enhance, enlarge, expand, flesh out, garnish, improve, ornament, polish, produce, refine, work out

elapse *v* glide by, go, go by, lapse, pass, pass by, roll by, slide by, slip away, slip by

elastic *adj* ductile, flexible, plastic, pliable, pliant, resilient, rubbery, springy, stretchable, stretchy, supple, yielding

elated *adj* animated, blissful, cheered, delighted, ecstatic, elevated, euphoric, excited, exhilarated, exultant, gleeful, in high spirits, joyful, joyous, jubilant, overjoyed, proud, puffed up, roused

elbow *n* angle, bend, corner, joint, turn

elbow *v* bump, crowd, hustle, jostle, knock, nudge, push, shoulder, shove

elder *adj* ancient, earlier born, first-born, older, senior

elder *n* older person, senior

elect *v* appoint, choose, decide upon, designate, determine, opt for, pick, pick out, prefer, select, settle on, vote

election *n* appointment, choice, choosing, decision, determination, judgment, preference, selection, vote, voting

elector *n* chooser, constituent, selector, voter

electric *adj* charged, dynamic, exciting, rousing, stimulating, stirring, tense, thrilling

electrify *v* amaze, animate, astonish, astound, excite, fire, galvanize, invigorate, jolt, rouse, shock, startle, stimulate, stir, take one's breath away, thrill

elegance *n* beauty, courtliness, dignity, gentility, grace, gracefulness, grandeur, luxury, polish, politeness, refinement, sumptuousness

elegant *adj* artistic, beautiful, chic, choice, comely, courtly, cultivated, delicate, exquisite, fashionable, fine, genteel, graceful, handsome, luxurious, modish, nice, polished, refined, stylish, sumptuous, tasteful

element *n* basis, component, constituent, essential factor, factor, feature, hint, ingredient, member, part, section, subdivision, trace, unit

elementary *adj* clear, easy, plain, rudimentary, simple, straightforward, uncomplicated; basic, elemental, fundamental, initial, introductory, original, primary, rudimentary

elements *n* basics, essentials, foundations, fundamentals, principles, rudiments

elevate *v* heighten, hoist, lift, lift up, raise, uplift, upraise; advance, aggrandize, exalt, prefer, promote, upgrade

elevation *n* altitude, height; acclivity, eminence, height, hill, hillock, mountain, rise, rising ground; exaltedness, grandeur, loftiness, nobility, nobleness, sublimity

elicit *v* bring forth, bring out, bring to light, call forth, cause, derive, draw out, educe, evoke, evolve, exact, extort, extract, give rise to, obtain, wrest

eligible *adj* acceptable, appropriate, desirable, fit, preferable, proper, qualified, suitable, suited, worthy

eliminate *v* cut out, dispose, of, do away with, eradicate, expel, exterminate, get rid of, remove, stamp out, take out

elite *n* aristocracy, best, cream, elect, flower, gentry, high society, nobility, pick, upper class

elocution *n* articulation, declamation, delivery, diction, enunciation, oratory, pronunciation, public speaking, rhetoric, speech, speech making, utterance, voice production

elope *v* abscond, bolt, decamp, disappear, escape, leave, run away, run off, slip away, steal away

eloquence *n* expression, expressive ness, fluency, forcefulness, oratory, persuasiveness, rhetoric, way with words

eloquent *adj* articulate, fluent, forceful, graceful, moving, persuasive, silver-tongued, stirring, well-expressed

elsewhere *adv* abroad, absent, away, hence, in another place, not here, not present, somewhere else

elucidate *v* annotate, clarify, clear up, explain, explicate, expound, gloss, illuminate, illustrate, interpret, make plain, shed light upon, spell out, unfold

elude *v* avoid, circumvent, dodge, duck, escape, evade, flee, get away from, outrun, shirk, shun

elusive *adj* difficult to catch, shifty, slippery, tricky

emaciated *v* atrophied, attenuate, attenuated, cadaverous, gaunt, haggard, lank, lean, meagre, pinched, scrawny, skeletal, thin, undernourished, wasted

emanate *v* arise, come forth, derive, emerge, flow, issue, originate, proceed, spring, stem

emancipate *v* deliver, discharge,

disencumber, disenthral, enfranchise, free, liberate, manumit, release, set free, unchain, unfetter, unshackle

emancipation *n* deliverance, discharge, enfranchisement, freedom, liberation, liberty, manumission, release

embargo *n* ban, bar, barrier, blockage, check, hindrance, impediment, interdict, interdiction, prohibition, proscription, restraint, restriction, stoppage

embark *v* board ship, go aboard, put on board, take on board, take ship; begin, broach, commence, engage, enter, initiate, launch, lunge into, set about, set out, start, take up, undertake

embarrass *v* abash, chagrin, confuse, discomfit, discompose, disconcert, discountenance, distress, fluster, mortify, put out of countenance, shame, show up

embarrassing *adj* awkward, blushmaking, compromising, discomfiting, disconcerting, distressing, humiliating, mortifying, sensitive, shameful, shaming, touchy, tricky, uncomfortable

embarrassment *n* awkwardness, bashfulness, chagrin, confusion, discomfort, discomposure, distress, humiliation, mortification, self-consciousness, shame; difficulty, dilemma, entanglement, mess, plight, predicament; (*Inf*) bind, fix, pickle, quandary, scrape

embellish *v* adorn, beautify, bedeck, deck, decorate, dress up, elaborate, embroider, enhance, enrich, exaggerate, festoon, garnish, gild, grace, ornament, varnish

embezzle *v* abstract, appropriate, defalcate, filch, have one's hand in the till, misapply, misappropriate, misuse, peculate, pilfer, purloin, steal

embitter *v* alienate, anger, disaffect, disillusion, envenom, make bitter, poison, sour

emblem *n* badge, crest, device, figure, image, insignia, mark, representation, sigil, sign, symbol, token, type

embrace *v* canoodle, clasp, cuddle, encircle, enfold, grasp, hold, hug, seize, squeeze, accept, adopt, avail oneself of, espouse, grab, make use of, receive, seize, take up, welcome

embrace *n* clasp, clinch, cuddle, hug, squeeze

embroil *v* complicate, compromise, confound, confuse, disorder, disturb, encumber, enmesh, ensnare, entangle, implicate, incriminate, involve, mire, mix up, muddle, perplex, trouble

embryo *n* beginning, germ, nucleus, root, rudiment

emend *v* amend, correct, edit, improve, rectify, redact, revise

emerge *v* appear, arise, become visible, come forth, come into view, come out, come up, emanate, issue, proceed, rise, spring up, surface; become apparent, become common knowledge, become known, come out, come to light, come to the fore, crop up, develop, get around, materialize, transpire, turn up

emergency *n* crisis, danger, difficulty, exigency, extremity, necessity, pass, pinch, plight, predicament,

quandary, scrape, strait
emigrate *v* migrate, move, move abroad, remove
eminence *n* celebrity, dignity, distinction, esteem, fame, greatness, illustriousness, importance, notability, note, pre-eminence, prestige, prominence, rank, renown, reputation, repute, superiority
eminent *adj* celebrated, conspicuous, distinguished, elevated, esteemed, exalted, famous, grand, great, high, illustrious, important, notable, noted, noteworthy, outstanding, paramount, pre-eminent, prestigious, prominent, renowned, signal, superior, well-known
emission *n* diffusion, discharge, ejaculation, ejection, emanation, exhalation, exudation, issuance, issue, radiation, shedding, transmission, utterance, venting
emit *v* breathe forth, cast out, diffuse, discharge, eject, emanate, exhale, exude, give off, give out, give vent to, issue, radiate, send forth, send out, throw out, transmit, utter, vent
emotion *n* agitation, ardour, excitement, feeling, fervour, passion, perturbation, sensation, sentiment, vehemence, warmth
emotional *adj* demonstrative, excitable, feeling, hot-blooded, passionate, responsive, sensitive, sentimental, susceptible, temperamental, tender, warm; ardent, enthusiastic, fervent, fervid, fiery, impassioned, passionate, roused, stirred, zealous
emphasis *n* accent, accentuation, attention, decidedness, force, importance, impressiveness, insistence, intensity, moment, positiveness, power, pre-eminence, priority, prominence, significance, strength, stress, underscoring, weight
emphasize *v* accent, accentuate, dwell on, give priority to, highlight, insist on, lay stress on, play up, press home, put the accent on, stress, underline, underscore, weight
emphatic *adj* absolute, categorical, certain, decided, definite, direct, distinct, earnest, energetic, forceful, forcible, important, impressive, insistent, marked, momentous, positive, powerful, pronounced, resounding, significant, striking, strong, telling, unequivocal, unmistakable, vigorous
empire *n* commonwealth, domain, imperium, kingdom, realm
employ *v* commission, engage, enlist, hire, retain, take on; engage, fill, keep busy, make use of, occupy, spend, take up, use up
employed *v* active, busy, engaged, in a job, in employment, in work, occupied, working
employee *n* hand, job-holder, staff member, wage-earner, worker, workman
employer *n* boss, business, company, establishment, firm, gaffer, organization, outfit, owner, patron, proprietor
employment *n* engagement, enlistment, hire, retaining, taking on; application, exercise, exertion, use, utilization; avocation, business, calling, craft, employ, job, line, occupation, profession, pursuit, service, trade, vocation, work
empower *v* allow, authorize, commission, delegate, enable, entitle,

equip, give power to, give strength to, license, permit, qualify, sanction, warrant

emptiness *n* bareness, blankness, desertedness, desolation, destitution, vacancy, vacuum, void, waste; cheapness, hollowness, idleness, insincerity, triviality, trivialness

empty *adj* bare, blank, clear, deserted, desolate, destitute, hollow, unfurnished, uninhabited, unoccupied, untenanted, vacant, void, waste; aimless, banal, bootless, frivolous, fruitless, futile, hollow, inane, ineffective, meaningless, purposeless, senseless, silly, unreal, unsatisfactory, unsubstantial, vain, valueless, worthless; absent, blank, expressionless, unintelligent, vacant, vacuous

empty *v* clear, consume, deplete, discharge, drain, dump, evacuate, exhaust, gut, pour out, unburden, unload, use up, vacate, void

enable *v* allow, authorize, capacitate, commission, empower, facilitate, fit, license, permit, prepare, qualify, sanction, warrant

enact *v* authorize, command, decree, establish, legislate, ordain, order, pass, proclaim, ratify, sanction

enamoured *adj* bewitched, captivate, charmed, enchanted, enraptured, entranced, fascinated, fond, infatuated, in love, smitten, swept off one's feet, taken, wild about

enchant *v* beguile, bewitch, captivate, cast a spell on, charm, delight, enamour, enrapture, enthral, entrance, fascinate, hypnotize, make spellbound, mesmerize, spellbind

enchanting *adj* alluring, appealing, attractive, bewitching, captivating, charming, delightful, endearing, entrancing, fascinating, lovely, pleasant, ravishing, winsome

enclose *v* bound, circumscribe, cover, encase, encircle, encompass, environ, fence, hedge, hem in, pen. shut in, wall in, wrap; include, insert, put in, send with

encompass *v* circle, circumscribe, encircle, enclose, envelop, environ, girdle, hem in, ring, surround; bring about, cause, contrive, devise, effect, manage

encounter *v* bump into, chance upon, come upon, confront, experience, face, happen on, meet, run across, run into; attack, clash with, combat, come into conflict with, contend, cross swords with, do battle with, engage, fight, grapple with, strive, struggle

encounter *n* chance meeting, meeting, rendezvous; battle, brawl, brush, clash, combat, conflict, confrontation, contest, dispute, engagement, scuffle, skirmish

encourage *v* animate, buoy up, cheer, comfort, console, embolden, hearten, incite, inspire, rally, reassure, rouse, stimulate

encouragement *n* advocacy, aid, boost, cheer, consolation, favour, help, incitement, inspiration, inspiritment, promotion, reassurance, stimulation, stimulus, succour, support, urging

encouraging *adj* bright, cheerful, cheering, comforting, good, heartening, hopeful, promising, reassuring, rosy, satisfactory, stimulating

encroach *v* appropriate, arrogate,

impinge, infringe, intrude, invade, make inroads, overstep, trench, trespass, usurp

end *n* bound, boundary, edge, extent, extreme, extremity, limit, point, terminus, tip; attainment, cessation, close, closure, completion, conclusion, consequence, consummation, culmination, denouement, ending, expiration, expiry, finale, finish, issue, outcome, resolution, result, stop, termination, upshot, wind-up; aim, aspiration, design, drift, goal, intent, intention, object, objective, point, purpose, reason; annihilation, death, demise, destruction, dissolution, doom, extermination, extinction, ruin, ruination

end *v* break off, bring to an end, cease, close, complete, conclude, culminate, discontinue, dissolve, expire, fade away, finish, peter out, resolve, stop, terminate; (*Inf*) wind up; annihilate, destroy, extinguish, put an end to,

endanger *v* compromise, hazard, imperil, jeopardize, put at risk, put in danger, risk, threaten

endeavour *n* aim, attempt, effort, enterprise, essay, go, shot, trial, try, undertaking, venture

endeavour *v* aim, aspire, attempt, do one's best, essay, have a go, labour, make an effort, strive, struggle, take pains, try, undertake

ending *n* catastrophe, cessation, close, completion, conclusion, consummation, culmination, denouement, end, expiration, finale, finish, resolution, termination

endless *adj* boundless, ceaseless, constant, continual, eternal, everlasting, immortal, incessant, infinite, interminable, limitless, measureless, perpetual, unbounded, unbroken, undying, unending, uninterrupted, unlimited; interminable, monotonous, overlong; continuous, unbroken, undivided, whole

endorse *v* advocate, affirm, approve, authorize, back, champion, confirm, favour, ratify, recommend, sanction, subscribe to, support, sustain, vouch for, warrant

endow *v* award, bequeath, bestow, confer, donate, endue, enrich, favour, finance, fund, furnish, give, grant, invest, leave, make over, provide, settle on, supply, will

endurance *n* bearing, fortitude, patience, perseverance, persistence, pertinacity, resignation, resolution, stamina, staying, power, strength, submission, sufferance, tenacity, toleration

endure *v* bear, brave, cope with, experience, go through, stand, stick it out, suffer, support, sustain, take it, undergo, weather, withstand; bide, allow, bear, brook, countenance, permit, put up with, stand, stick, stomach, submit to, suffer, swallow, take, patiently, tolerate

enemy *n* adversary, antagonist, competitor, foe, hostile party, opponent, rival, the opposition, the other side; competition, opposition

energetic *adj* active, animate, brisk, determined, dynamic, forceful, forcible, high-powered, indefatigable, lively, potent, powerful, spirited, strenuous, strong, tireless, vigorous; (*Inf*) zippy

energize *v* activate, arouse, goad, prompt, rouse, stimulate, spur on

energy *n* activity, animation, ardour, drive, efficiency, exertion, fire, force, forcefulness, go, intensity, life, liveliness, pluck, power, spirit, stamina, strength, strenuousness, verve, vigour, vim, vitality, vivacity, zeal, zest

enforce *v* administer, apply, carry out, coerce, compel, constrain, exact, execute, implement, impose, insist on, oblige, prosecute, put in force, put into, effect, reinforce, require, urge

engage *v* appoint, commission, employ, enlist, enroll, hire, retain, take on; bespeak, book, charter, hire, lease, prearrange, rent, reserve, secure; absorb, busy, engross, grip, involve, occupy, preoccupy, tie up; attack, combat, come to close quarters with, encounter, fall on, fight with, five battle, to, join battle with, meet, take on; activate, apply, bring into operation, energize, set going, switch, on; dovetail, interact, interconnect, interlock, join, mesh

engaged *adj* affianced, betrothed, espoused, pledged, plighted, promised, spoken for; busy, in conference, occupied, unavailable; booked, in use, reserved

engagement *n* appointment, business, employment, hire, job, post, situation, work; booking, charter, lease, rent, reservation; betrothal, marriage pledge; absorption, preoccupation; agreement, bond, compact, contract, oath, obligation, pact, pledge, promise, stipulation, undertaking, vow, word; arrangement, assignation, commitment, date, interview, meeting, rendezvous, tryst; action, battle, clash, combat, conflict, confrontation, contest, encounter, fight, hostilities, struggle, warfare

engineer *n* architect, contriver, designer, deviser, director, inventor, manager, manipulator, originator, planner, schemer

engineer *v* bring about, cause, concoct, contrive, control, create, devise, effect, encompass, manage, manoeuvre, mastermind, originate, plan, plot, scheme; (*Inf*) wangle

engrave *v* carve, chase, chisel, cut, etch, grave, inscribe

engrossed *adj* absorbed, captivated, caught up, deep, enthralled, fascinated, gripped, immersed, intent, intrigued, lost, preoccupied, rapt, riveted

enjoy *v* appreciate, be entertained by, be pleased with, delight in, like, rejoice in, relish, revel in, take joy in, take pleasure in; avail oneself of, be blessed with, experience, have, have the use of, own, possess, reap the benefits of, use

enjoyable *adj* agreeable, amusing, delectable, delicious, delightful, entertaining, gratifying, pleasant, pleasing, pleasurable, satisfying, to one's liking

enjoyment *n* amusement, delectation, delight, diversion, entertainment, fun, gladness, gratification, gusto, happiness, indulgence, joy, pleasure, recreation, relish, satisfaction, zest

enlarge *v* add to, amplify, augment, broaden, diffuse, dilate, distend, elongate, expand, extend, grow, heighten, increase, inflate, lengthen, magnify, make larger, multiply, stretch, swell, wax, widen

enlighten *v* advise, apprise, cause to understand, civilize, counsel, edify, educate, inform, instruct, make ware, teach

enlist *v* engage, enroll, enter, gather, join, join up, muster, obtain, procure, recruit, register, secure, sign up, volunteer

enliven *v* animate, brighten, buoy up, cheer, cheer up, excite, exhilarate, fire, gladden, hearten, inspire, inspirit, invigorate, pep up, perk up, quicken, rouse, spark, stimulate, vitalize, vivify, wake up

enmity *n* acrimony, animosity, animus, antagonism, antipathy, aversion, bad blood, bitterness, hate, hatred, hostility, ill will, malevolence, malice, malignity, rancour, spite, venom

enormity *n* atrociousness, atrocity, depravity, disgrace, evilness, heinousness, monstrousness, nefariousness, outrageousness, turpitude, viciousness, vileness, villainy, wickedness

enormous *adj* astronomic, colossal, excessive, gargantuan, gigantic, gross, huge, immense, jumbo, mammoth, massive, monstrous, mountainous, prodigious, titanic, tremendous, vast

enough *adj* abundant, adequate, ample, plenty, sufficient

enough *adv* abundantly, adequately, amply, fairly, moderately, passably, reasonably, satisfactorily, sufficiently, tolerably

enquire see **inquire**

enquiry see **inquiry**

enrage *n* aggravate, anger, annoy, exasperate, incense, incite, inflame, infuriate, irk, irritate, livid, madden, make one's blood, oil, make one see red, make one's hackles rise, provoke

en route *adv* in transit, on the way, on the road

ensue *v* arise, attend, be consequent on, befall, come after, come next, derive, flow, follow, issue, proceed, result, stem, succeed, supervene, turn up

entail *v* bring about, call for, cause, demand, encompass, give rise to, impose, involve, lead to, necessitate, occasion, require, result in

entangle *v* catch, compromise, embroil, enmesh, ensnare, entrap, foul, implicate, involve, knot, mat, mix up, ravel, snag, snare, tangle, trammel, trap; bewilder, complicate, confuse, jumble, mix up, muddle, perplex, puzzle, snarl, twist

enter *v* arrive, come into, insert, introduce, make an entrance, pass into, penetrate, pierce; become a member of, begin, commence, commit oneself to, embark upon, enlist, enroll, join, participate in, set about, set out on, sign up, start, take part in, take up; inscribe, list, log, note, record, register, set down, take down; offer, present, proffer, put forward, register, submit, tender

enterprise *n* adventure, effort, endeavour, essay, operation, plan, programme, project, undertaking, venture; activity, adventurousness, alertness, audacity, boldness, daring, dash, drive, eagerness, energy, enthusiasm, initiative, push, readiness, resource, resourcefulness, spirit, vigour, zeal; business, company, concern, establishment, firm, operation

enterprising *adj* active, adventurous, alert, audacious, bold, daring, dashing, eager, energetic, enthusiastic, intrepid, keen, ready, resourceful, spirited, stirring, venturesome, vigorous, zealous

entertain *v* amuse, charm, cheer, delight, divert, occupy, please, recreate, regale; accommodate, be host to, harbour, have company, have guests, lodge, put up, show, hospitality to, treat

entertainment *n* amusement, cheer, distraction, diversion, enjoyment, fun, good time, leisure, activity, pastime play, pleasure, recreation, satisfaction, sport, treat

enthusiasm *n* ardour, avidity, devotion, eagerness, earnestness, excitement, fervour, frenzy, interest, keenness, passion, relish, vehemence, warmth, zeal, zest

enthusiast *n* admirer, aficionado, devotee, fan, fanatic, follower, lover, supporter, zealot

enthusiastic *adj* ardent, avid, devoted, eager, earnest, ebullient, excited, exuberant, fervent, fervid, forceful, hearty, keen, lively, passionate, spirited, unqualified, unstinting, vehement, vigorous, warm, wholehearted, zealous

entice *v* allure, attract, beguile, cajole, coax, decoy, draw, inveigle, lead on, lure, persuade, prevail, on, seduce, tempt, wheedle

entire *adj* complete, full, gross, total, unbroken, whole; absolute, outright, thorough, unreserved; intact, perfect, undamaged, unimpaired, unmarked

entirely *adv* absolutely, altogether, completely, fully, in every respect, perfectly, thoroughly, totally, unreservedly, utterly, wholly, without exception, without reservation

entitle *v* accredit, allow, authorize, empower, enable, enfranchise, fit for, license, make eligible, permit, qualify for, warrant; call, characterize, christen, denominate, designate, dub, label, name, style, term, title

entrance *n* access, avenue, door, doorway, entry, gate, ingress, inlet, opening, passage, portal, way in; appearance, arrival, coming in, entry, ingress, inlet, opening, passage, portal, way in; appearance, arrival, coming in, entry, ingress, introduction; access, admission, admittance, entrée, entry, ingress, permission to enter

entrance *v* bewitch, captivate, charm, delight, enchant, enrapture, enthral, fascinate, gladden, ravish, spellbind, transport

entrant *n* beginner, convert, initiate, neophyte, newcomer, new member, novice, probationer, tyro; candidate, competitor, contestant, entry, participant, player

entrust *v* assign, authorise, charge, commend, commit, confide, consign, delegate, deliver, give custody of, hand over, invest, trust, turn over

entry *n* appearance, coming in, entering, entrance, initiation, introduction; access, avenue, door, doorway, entrance, gate, ingress, inlet, opening, passage, passageway, portal, way in; access, admission, entrance, entree, free passage, permission, to enter; attempt, candidate, competitor, contestant, effort, entrant, participant, player, submission

envelop *v* blanket, cloak, conceal, cover, embrace, encase, encircle, enclose, encompass, enfold, engulf, enwrap, hide, obscure, sheathe, shroud, surround, swaddle, swathe, veil, wrap

envelope *n* case, casing, coating, cover, covering, jacket, sheath, shell, skin, wrapper, wrapping

enviable *adj* advantageous, blessed, covetable, desirable, favoured, fortunate, lucky, much to be desired, privileged

envious *adj* begrudging, covetous, green-eyed, green with envy, grudging, jaundiced, jealous, malicious, resentful, spiteful

environment *n* atmosphere, back ground, conditions, context, domain, element, habitat, locale, medium, milieu, scene, setting, situation, surroundings, territory

envoy *n* agent, ambassador, courier, delegate, deputy, diplomat, emissary, intermediary, legate, messenger, minister, plenipotentiary, representative

envy *n* covetousness, enviousness, grudge, hatred, jealousy, malice, malignity, resentfulness, resentment, spite, the green-eyed monster

envy *v* be envious, begrudge, be jealous, covet, grudge, resent

epidemic *adj* general, pandemic, prevailing, prevalent, rampant, rife, sweeping, wide-ranging, wide spread

epidemic *n* contagion, growth, out break, plague, rash, spread, upsurge, wave

epigram *n* aphorism, quip, witticism

epilogue *n* afterword, coda, concluding speech, conclusion, postscript

episode *n* adventure, affair, business, circumstance, event, experience, happening, incident, matter, occurrence; chapter, installment, part, passage, scene, section

epistle *n* communication, letter, message, missive, note

epitome *n* archetype, embodiment, essence, exemplar, personification, quintessence, representation, type, typical, example

equable *adj* agreeable, clam, composed, easy-going, even tempered, imperturbable, level-headed, placid, serene, temperate, unexcitable, unflappable, unruffled; consistent, constant, even, regular, smooth, stable, steady, temperate, tranquil, unchanging, uniform, unvarying

equal *adj* alike, commensurate, equivalent, identical, like, proportionate, tantamount, the same, uniform; balanced, corresponding, egalitarian, even, evenly balanced, evenly matched, evenly proportioned, level pegging, matched, regular, symmetrical, uniform, unvarying; able, adequate, capable, competent, fit, good enough, ready, strong enough, suitable, up to

equal *n* brother, compeer, counter part, equivalent, fellow, match, mate, parallel, peer, rival, twin

equal *v* amount to, be equivalent to, come to, correspond to, make, total; be tantamount to, emulate, equate with, match, measure up to, parallel, rival, vie with; achieve, be level with, come up to, measure up to, reach

equality *n* balance, coequality, correspondence, egalitarianism, equal opportunity, equatability, equivalence, evenness, fairness, identity, likeness, parity, sameness, similarity, uniformity

equate *v* agree, balance, be commensurate with, compare, correspond, equalize, liken, make equal, match, offset, pair, parallel, square, tally, think of together

equation *n* agreement, balancing, comparison, correspondence, equality, equalization, equating, equivalence, likeness, match, pairing, parallel

equilibrium *n* balance, counterpoise, equipoise, evenness, rest, stability, steadiness, symmetry; calm, calmness, collectedness, composure, coolness, equanimity, poise, self-possession, serenity, stability, steadiness

equip *v* accoutre, arm, array, attire, deck out, dress, endow, fit out, fit up, furnish, kit out, outfit, prepare, provide, rig, stock, supply

equipment *n* accoutrements, apparatus, appurtenances, baggage, equipage, furnishings, furniture, gear, materiel, outfit, paraphernalia, rig, stuff, supplies, tackle, tools

equivalence *n* agreement, alike ness, conformity, correspondence, equality, evenness, identity, interchangeableness, likeness, match, parallel, parity, sameness, similarity, synonymy

equivalent *adj* alike, commensurate, comparable, correspondent, corresponding, equal, even, homologous, interchangeable, of a kind, same, similar, synonymous, tantamount

equivocal *adj* ambiguous, ambivalent, doubtful, dubious, evasive, indefinite, indeterminate, misleading, oblique, obscure, prevaricating, questionable, suspicious, uncertain, vague

era *n* aeon, age, cycle, date, day, days, epoch, generation, period, stage, time

eradicate *v* abolish, annihilate, deracinate, destroy, efface, eliminate, erase, expunge, exterminate, extinguish, extirpate, obliterate, remove, root out, stamp out, uproot, weed out, wipe out

erect *adj* elevated, firm, perpendicular, pricked-up, raised, rigid, standing, stiff, straight, upright, vertical

erect *v* build, construct, elevate, lift, mount, pitch, put up, raise, rear, set up, stand up

erode *v* abrade, consume, corrode, destroy, deteriorate, disintegrate, eat away, grind down, spoil, wear down

err *v* be inaccurate, be incorrect, be in error, blunder, go astray, go wrong, make a mistake, misapprehend, miscalculate, misjudge, mistake; (*Inf*) slip up

errand *n* charge, commission, job, message, mission, task

erratic *adj* aberrant, abnormal, capricious, changeable, desultory, eccentric, fitful, inconsistent, irregular, shifting, unpredictable, unreliable, unstable, variable, wayward

erroneous *adj* amiss, fallacious, false, faulty, flawed, inaccurate, incorrect, inexact, invalid, mistaken, spurious, unfounded, unsound, untrue, wrong

error *n* bloomer, blunder, delusion, erratum, fallacy, fault, flaw, inaccuracy, misapprehension, miscalculation, misconception, mistake, over sight, slip, solecism

erudite *adj* cultivated, cultured, educated, knowledgeable, learned, lettered, literate, scholarly, well-educated, well-read

erupt *v* be ejected, belch forth, blow up, break out, burst forth, burst into, burst out, discharge, explode, flare up, gush, pour forth, spew forth, spit out, spout, throw off, vent, vomit

eruption *n* discharge, ejection, explosion, flare up, outbreak, outburst, sally, venting

escalate *v* amplify, ascend, be increased, enlarge, expand, extend, grow, heighten, increase, intensify, magnify, mount, raise, rise, step up

escapade *n* adventure, antic, caper, fling, mischief, prank, romp, scrape, spree, stunt, trick; (*Inf*) lark

escape *v* abscond, bolt, break free, decamp, flee, fly, get away, make one's escape, make one's getaway, run away, skip, slip away; avoid, circumvent, dodge, duck, elude, evade, pass, shun, slip; discharge, drain, emanate, flow, gush, issue, leak, pour forth, seep, spurt;

escape *n* bolt, break, break-out, decampment, flight, getaway; avoid ance, circumvention, elusion, evasion; discharge, drain, effluence, efflux, emanation, emission, gush, leak, leakage, outflow, outpour, seepage, spurt

escort *n* bodyguard, company, convoy, cortege, entourage, guard, protection, retinue, safeguard, train

escort *v* accompany, chaperon, conduct, convoy, defend, guard, guide, lead, partner, protect, shepherd, squire, usher

especially *adv* chiefly, conspicuously, exceptionally, extraordinarily, mainly, markedly, notably, out standingly, principally, remarkably, signally, specially, strikingly, supremely, uncommonly, unusually

essay *n* article, composition, discourse, disquisition, dissertation, paper, piece, tract

essence *n* being, core, crux, entity, heart, kernel, life, lifeblood, meaning, nature, pith, principle, quiddity, quintessence, significance, soul, sprit, substance; concentrate, distillate, elixir, extract, spirits, tincture

essential *adj* crucial, important, indispensable, necessary, needed, requisite, vital; basic, cardinal, constitutional, elemental, elementary, fundamental, inherent, innate, intrinsic, key, main, principal

essential *n* basic, fundamental, must, necessity, prerequisite, principle, requisite, rudiment, *sine* *qua non,* vital part

establish *v* base, constitute, create, decree, enact, ensconce, entrench, fix, form, found, ground, implant, inaugurate, install, institute, organize, plant, root, secure, settle, set up, start

establishment *n* business, company, concern, corporation, enterprise, firm, house, institute, institution, organization, outfit, structure, system; **the Establishment** bureaucracy, established order, institutionalized authority, officialdom, ruling class, the powers that be, the system

estate *n* area, domain, holdings, lands, manor, piece of land, property; land, region, tract; development; assets, belongings, effects, fortune, possessions, resources, wealth; caste, class, rank, status; condition, position, situation, state

esteem *v* admire, be fond of, cherish, honour, like, love, prize, regard highly, respect, revere, reverence, think highly of, treasure, value, venerate

esteem *n* admiration, consideration, credit, estimation, good opinion, honour, regard, respect, reverence, veneration

estimate *v* appraise, assess, calculate roughly, evaluate, gauge, guess, judge, number, reckon, value; assess, believe, conjecture, consider, form an opinion, guess, judge, rank, rate, reckon, surmise, think

estimate *n* appraisal, appraisement, approximate calculation, assessment, evaluation, guess, judgment, reckoning, valuation

estuary *n* bay, cove, creek, firth, fjord, inlet, river mouth

et cetera, etcetera *adv* and others, and so forth, and so on, and the like, and the rest, et al.; (*Inf*) and what have you

eternal *adj* abiding, ceaseless, constant, deathless, endless, everlasting, immortal, infinite, interminable, never-ending, perennial, perpetual, sempiternal, timeless, unceasing, undying, unending, unremitting, without end

ethical *adj* conscientious, correct, decent, fair, fitting, good, honest, honourable, just, moral, principled, proper, right, righteous, upright, virtuous

ethics *pl n* conscience, moral code, morality, moral philosophy, moral values, principles, rules of conduct, standards

etiquette *n* civility, code, convention, courtesy, customs, decorum, formalities, good behaviour, manners, politeness, politeness, propriety, protocol, rules, usage

evacuate *v* abandon, clear, decamp, depart, desert, forsake, leave, move out, pull out, quit, relinquish, remove, vacate, withdraw

evade *v* avoid, circumvent, decline, dodge, duck, elude, escape, escape the clutches of, get away form, shirk, shun, sidestep, steer clear of

evaluate *v* appraise, assay, assess, calculate, estimate, gauge, judge, rank, rate, reckon, size up, value, weigh

evaporate *v* dehydrate, desiccate, dry, dry up, vaporize; dematerialize,

disappear, dispel, disperse, dissipate, dissolve, evanesce, fade, fade away, melt, melt away, vanish
evasion *n* artifice, avoidance, circumvention, cop-out, cunning, dodge, elusion, equivocation, escape, evasiveness, excuse, fudging, obliqueness, pretext, prevarication, ruse, shift, shirking, shuffling, sophism, sophistry, subterfuge, trickery; (*Inf*) waffle
eve *n* day before, night before, vigil
even *adj* flat, flush, horizontal, level, parallel, plane, plumb, smooth, steady, straight, true, uniform; calm, composed, cool, equable, equanimous, even-tempered, impeturbable, peaceful, placid, serene, stable, steady, tranquil, undisturbed, unexcitable, unruffled, well-balanced; balanced, equitable, fair, fair and square, impartial, just, unbiased, unprejudiced
even *adv* all the more, much, still, yet
event *n* adventure, affair, business, circumstance, episode, experience, fact, happening, incident, matter, milestone, occasion, occurrence
eventful *adj* active busy, consequential, critical, crucial, decisive, exciting, fateful, full, historic, important, lively, memorable, momentous, notable, noteworthy, remarkable, significant
eventually *adv* after all, at the end of the day, finally, in the course of time, in the end, in the long run, one day, some day, some time, sooner or later, ultimately, when all is said and done
ever *adv* at all, at any time, by any chance, in any case, on any occasion; always, at all times, constantly, continually, endlessly, eternally, everlastingly, evermore, for ever, incessantly, perpetually, relentlessly, to the end of time, unceasingly, unendingly
everlasting *adj* abiding, deathless, endless, eternal, immortal, imperishable, indestructible, infinite, interminable, never-ending, perpetual, timeless, undying
evermore *adv* always, eternally, ever, for ever, in perpetuum, to the end of time
everyday *adj* accustomed, common, common or garden, commonplace, conventional, customary, dull, familiar, frequent, habitual, informally, mundane, ordinary, routine, run-of-the-mill, stock, unexceptional, unimaginative, usual, wonted, workaday
evict *v* chuck out, dislodge, dispossess, eject, expel, oust, put out, remove, show the door, throw on to the streets, throw out, turn out
evidence *n* affirmation, attestation, averment, confirmation, corroboration, data, declaration, demonstration, deposition, grounds, indication, manifestation, mark, proof, sign, substantiation, testimony, token, witness
evident *adj* apparent, clear, conspicuous, incontestable, incontrovertible, indisputable, manifest, notice able, obvious, palpable, patent, perceptible, plain, tangible, unmistakable, visible
evidently *adj* apparently, from all appearances, it appears, it seems, it

would seem ostensibly, outwardly, seemingly, to all appearances; clearly, plainly, unmistakably, without question

evil *adj* bad, base, corrupt, depraved, heinous, immoral, iniquitous, maleficent, malevolent, malicious, malignant, nefarious, reprobate, sinful, vicious, vile, villainous, wicked, wrong

evil *n* badness, baseness, corruption, curse, depravity, heinousness, immorality, iniquity, maleficence, malignity, sin, sinfulness, turpitude, vice, viciousness, villainy, wickedness, wrong, wrongdoing;

evil *adj* baneful, calamitous, catastrophic, deleterious, destructive, detrimental, dire, disastrous, harmful, hurtful, inauspicious, injurious, mischievous, painful, pernicious, ruinous, sorrowful, unfortunate, unlucky, woeful

evoke *v* arouse, awaken, call excite, give rise to, induce, recall, rekindle, stimulate, stir up, summon up; call forth,educe, elicit, produce, provoke

evolution *n* development, enlarge ment, evolvement, expansion, growth, increase, maturation, progress, progression, unfolding, unrolling, working out

evolve *v* develop, disclose, educe, elaborate, enlarge, expand, grow, increase, mature, open, progress, unfold, unroll, work out

exact *adj* accurate, careful, correct, definite, explicit, express, faithful, faultless, identical, literal, methodical, orderly, particular, precise, right, specific, true, unequivocal, unerring, veracious, very; careful, exacting, meticulous, painstaking, punctilious, rigorous, scrupulous, severe, strict

exact *v* call for, claim, command, compel, demand, extort, extract, force, impose, insist upon, require, squeeze, wrest, wring

exactly *adv* accurately, carefully, correctly, definitely, explicitly, faithfully, faultlessly, literally, methodically, precisely, rigorously, scrupulously, severely, strictly, truly, truthfully, unequivocally, unerringly, veraciously; absolutely, bang, explicitly, expressly, indeed, in every respect, just, particularly, precisely, quite, specifically

exactness *n* accuracy, carefulness, correctness, exactitude, faithfulness, faultlessness, nicety, orderliness, painstakingness, preciseness, precision, promptitude, regularity, rigorousness, rigour, scrupulousness, strictness, truth, unequivocalness, veracity

exaggerate *v* amplify, embellish, embroider, emphasize, enlarge, exalt, hyperbolize, inflate, lay it on thick, magnify, overdo, overemphasize, overestimate, overstate

exaggeration *n* amplification, embellishment, emphasis, enlargement, exaltation, excess, extravagance, hyperbole, inflation, magnification, overemphasis, overestimation, overstatement, pretension, pretentiousness

exalt *v* advance, aggrandize, dignify, elevate, ennoble, honour, promote, raise, upgrade

exalted *adj* august, dignified, elevated, eminent, grand, high, high-ranking, honoured, lofty, prestigious

examination *n* analysis, assay, catechism, checkup, exploration, inquiry, inquisition, inspection, interrogation, investigation, observation, perusal, probe, questioning, quiz, research, review, scrutiny, search, study, survey, test, trial

examine *v* analyse, appraise, assay, check, check out, consider, explore, go over, inspect, investigate, look over, peruse, ponder, pore over, probe, review, scan, scrutinize, sift, study, survey, take stock of, test, vet, weigh

example *n* case, case in point, exemplification, illustration, instance, sample, specimen; **for example** as an illustration, by way of illustration, e.g., for instance, to cite an instance, to illustrate

exasperate *v* anger, annoy, embiter, enrage, exacerbate, excite, gall, get, incense, inflame, infuriate, irk, irritate, madden, nettle, pique, provoke, rankle, rouse, try the patience of, vex; (*Inf*) aggravate, bug, peeve, rile

exasperation *n* aggravation, anger, annoyance, exacerbation fury, ire, irritation, passion, pique, provocation, rage, vexation, wrath

excavate *v* burrow, cut, delve, dig, dig out, dig up, gouge, hollow, mine, quarry, scoop, trench, tunnel, uncover, unearth

exceed *v* beat, be superior to, better, cap, eclipse, excel, go beyond, outdistance, outdo, outreach, outrun, outshine, outstrip, overtake, pass, surmount, surpass, top, transcend

excel *v* beat, be superior, better, eclipse, exceed, go beyond, outdo, outrival, outshine, pass, surmount, surpass, top, transcend

excellence *n* distinction, eminence, fineness, goodness, greatness, high quality, merit, perfection, preeminence, purity, superiority, supremacy, transcendence, virtue, worth

excellent *adj* admirable, brilliant, capital, champion, choice, distinguished, estimable, exemplary, exquisite, fine, first-class, first-rate, good, great, meritorious, notable, noted, outstanding, prime, select, sterling, superb, superior, superlative, tiptop, worthy

except *prep* apart from, bar, barring, besides, but, excepting, excluding, exclusive of, leaving out, omitting, other than, save, saving, with the exception of

except *v* bar, exclude, leave out, pass over, omit, rule out

exception *n* anomaly, departure, deviation, freak, inconsistency, irregularity, oddity, peculiarity, quirk, special case

exceptional *adj* excellent, extraordinary, marvellous, outstanding, phenomenal, prodigious, remarkable, special, superior

excess *n* glut, leftover, overabundance, overdose, overflow, overload, plethora, remainder, superabundance, superfluity, surfeit, surplus, too much; debauchery, dissipation, dissoluteness, exorbitance, extravagance, immoderation, intemperance, overindulgence, prodigality, unrestraint

excess *adj* extra, leftover, redundant, remaining, residual, spare, superfluous, surplus, too much

excessive *adj* disproportionate, enormous, exaggerated, exorbitant, extravagant, extreme, immoderate, inordinate, intemperate, needless, overdone, overmuch, prodigal, profligate, superfluous, too much, unconscionable, undue, unreasonable

exchange *v* bandy, barter, change, commute, convert into, interchange, reciprocate, swap, switch, trade, truck

exchange *n* barter, dealing, interchange, *quid pro quo*, reciprocity, substitution, swap, switch, tit for tat, trade, traffic, truck

excitable *adj* edgy, emotional, hasty, highly strung, hot-headed, hot-tempered, irascible, mercurial, nervous, passionate, quick-tempered, sensitive, susceptible, temperamental, testy, touchy, uptight, violent, volatile

excite *v* agitate, animate, arouse, awaken, discompose, disturb, electrify, elicit, evoke, fire, foment, galvanize, incite, inflame, inspire, instigate, kindle, move, provoke, quicken, rouse, stimulate, stir up, thrill, titillate, waken, whet

excitement *n* action, activity, ado, adventure, agitation, animation, commotion, discomposure, elation, enthusiasm, ferment, fever, flurry, furore, heat, kicks, passion, perturbation, thrill, tumult, warmth

exciting *adj* electrifying, exhilarating, inspiring, intoxicating, moving, provocative, rip-roaring, rousing, sensational, stimulating, stirring, thrilling, titillating

exclaim *v* call call out, cry, cry out, declare, ejaculate, proclaim, shout, utter, vociferate, yell

exclamation *n* call, cry, ejaculation, expletive, interjection, outcry, shout, utterance, vociferation, yell

exclude *v* ban, bar, blackball, debar, disallow, embargo, forbid, interdict, keep out, ostracize, prohibit, proscribe, refuse, shut out, veto; count out, eliminate, except, ignore, leave out, omit, pass over, preclude, reject, repudiate, rule out set aside

exclusive *adj* aristocratic, chic, choice, clannish, cliquish, closed, discriminative, elegant, fashionable, limited, narrow, private, restricted, restrictive, select, selfish, snobbish; confined, limited, peculiar, restricted, unique

excommunicate *v* anathematize, ban, banish, cast out, denounce, eject, exclude, expel, proscribe, remove, repudiate, unchurch

excursion *n* airing, day trip, expedition, jaunt, journey, outing, pleasure trip, ramble, tour, trip

excuse *v* absolve, acquit, bear with exculpate, exonerate, extenuate, forgive, indulge, make allowances for, overlook, pardon, pass over, tolerate, turn a blind eye to, wink at; absolve, discharge, exempt, free, let off, liberate, release, relieve, spare

excuse *n* apology, cover-up, defence, escape, evasion, explanation, fabrication, front, grounds, justification, mitigating circumstances, mitigation, mitigating circumstances, mockery, pitiful example, plea, poor substitute, pretence, pretext, reason, subterfuge, travesty, vindi cation; (*Inf*) cop out

execute *v* behead, crucify, decapitate, electrocute, guillotine, hand, kill, put before a firing squad, put to death, send to the electric chair, send to the gas chamber, shoot, stone to death; accomplish, achieve, administer, bring off, carry out, do, effect, engineer, implement, perform, put into effect; perform, stage

execution *n* accomplishment, achievement, administration, carrying, out, completion, consummation, discharge, effect, enactment, enforcement, implementation, operation, performance, prosecution, realization, rendering; capital punishment, hanging, killing

executive *n* administrator, director, manager, official; administration, directorate, directors, government, hierarchy, leadership, management

executive *adj* administrative, controlling, decision-making, directing, governing, managerial

exemplary *adj* admirable, commendable, correct, estimable, excellent, good, honourable, ideal, laudable, meritorious, model, praiseworthy, punctilious, sterling

exemplify *v* demonstrate, depict, display, embody, evidence, exhibit, illustrate, instance, manifest, represent, serve as an example of, show

exempt *v* absolve, discharge, except, excuse, exonerate, free, grant, immunity, let off, liberate, release, relieve, spare

exempt *adj* absolved, clear, discharged, excepted, excused, favoured, free, immune, liberated, not liable, not subject, privileged, released, spared

exercise *v* apply, bring to bear, employ, enjoy, exert, practise, put to use, use, utilize, wield; discipline, drill, habituate, inure, practise, train, work out

exercise *n* action, activity, discipline, drill, drilling, effort, labour, toil, training, work, work-out; drill, lesson, practice, problem, schooling, schoolwork, task, work

exert *v* bring into play, bring to bear, employ, exercise, expend, make use of, put forth, use, utilize, wield

exertion *n* action, application, attempt, effort, employment, endeavour, exercise, industry, labour, pains, strain, stretch, struggle, toil, trial, use, utilization

exhaust *v* bankrupt, cripple, debilitate, disable, drain, enervate, enfeeble, fatigue, impoverish, prostrate, sap, tire, tire out, weaken, wear out; consume, deplete, dissipate, expend, finish, run through, spend, squander, use up, waste; drain, dry, empty, strain, void

exhausted *adj* all in, beat, crippled, dead, dead beat, dead tired, debilitated, disabled, dog-tired, done in, drained, enervated, enfeebled, fatigued, jaded, knackered, out on one's feet, prostrated, ready to drop, sapped, spent, tired out, wasted, weak, worn out; at an end, consumed, depleted, dissipate, done, expended, finished, gone, spent, squandered, used up, wasted

exhausting *adj* arduous, backbreaking, crippling, debilitating, difficult, draining, enervating, fatiguing, gruelling, hard, laborious, punishing, sapping, strenuous, taxing, testing, tiring

exhibit *v* air, demonstrate, disclose, display, evidence, evince, expose, express, flaunt, indicate, make clear, manifest, offer, parade, present, put on view, reveal, show

exhibit *n* demonstration, display, exhibition, illustration, model, presentation, show, viewing

exhort *v* admonish, advise, beseech, bid, call upon, caution, counsel, encourage, enjoin, entreat, goad, incite, persuade, press, spur, urge, warn

exile *n* banishment, deportation, expatriation, expulsion, ostracism, proscription, separation; deportee, expatriate, outcast, refugee

exile *v* banish, deport, drive out, eject, expatriate, expel, ostracize, oust, proscribe

exist *v* abide, be, be extant, be living, be present, breathe, continue, endure, happen, last, live, obtain, occur, prevail, remain, stand, survive

existence *n* actuality, animation, being, breath, continuance, continuation, duration, endurance, life, subsistence, survival

exit *n* door, egress, gate, outlet, passage, out, vent, way out

expand *v* amplify, augment, bloat, blow up, broaden, develop, dilate, distend, enlarge, extend, fatten, fill out, grow, heighten, increase, inflate, lengthen, magnify, multiply, prolong, protract, swell, thicken, wax, widen

expanse *n* area, breadth, extent, field, plain, range, space, stretch, sweep, tract

expansive *adj* affable, communicative, easy, effusive, free, friendly, garrulous, genial, loquacious, open, outgoing, sociable, talkative, unreserved, warm

expect *v* assume, believe, calculate, conjecture, forecast, foresee, imagine, presume, reckon, suppose, surmise, think, trust; anticipate, await, bargain for, contemplate, envisage, hope for, look ahead to, look for, look forward to, predict, watch for

expectation *n* assumption, assurance, belief, calculation, confidence, conjecture, forecast, likelihood, presumption, probability, supposition, surmise, trust

expediency, expedience *n* advantageousness, advisability, appropriateness, aptness, benefit, convenience, desirability, effectiveness, fitness, helpfulness, judiciousness, meetness, opportunism, practicality, pragmatism, profitability, properness, propriety, propitiousness, prudence, suitability, timeliness, usefulness, utilitarianism, utility

expedient *adj* advantageous, advisable, appropriate, beneficial, convenient, desirable, effective, fit, helpful, judicious, meet, opportune, politic, practical, pragmatic, profitable, proper, prudent, suitable, useful, utilitarian, worthwhile

expedition *n* enterprise, excursion, exploration, journey, mission, quest, safari, tour, trek, trip, undertaking, voyage

expel *v* belch, cast out, discharge, dislodge, drive out, eject, remove, spew, throw out; ban, banish, bar, blackball, discharge, dismiss, drum out, evict, exclude, exile, expatriate, oust, proscribe, send packing, throw out, turf out

expend *v* consume, disburse, dissipate, employ, exhaust, fork out, go through, pay out, spend, use up; (*Inf*), lay out, shell out

expendable *adj* dispensable, inessential, nonessential, replaceable, unimportant, unnecessary

expenditure *n* application, charge, consumption, cost, disbursement, expense, outgoings, outlay, output, payment, spending, use

expense *n* charge, consumption, cost, disbursement, expenditure, loss, outlay, output, payment, sacrifice, spending, toll, use

expensive *adj* costly, dear, excessive, exorbitant, extravagant, high-priced, inordinate, lavish, overpriced, rich, steep, stiff

experience *n* contact, doing, evidence, exposure, familiarity, involvement, knowledge, observation, participation, practice, proof, training, trial, understanding; adventure, affair, encounter, episode, event, happening, incident, occurrence, ordeal, test, trial

experience *v* apprehend, become familiar with, behold, encounter, endure, face, feel, go through, have, know, live through, meet, observe, participate in, perceive, sample, sense, suffer, sustain, taste, try, undergo

experienced *adj* accomplished, adept, capable, competent, expert, familiar, knowledgeable, master, practised, professional, qualified, seasoned, skilful, tested, trained, tried, veteran, well-versed

experiment *n* assay, attempt, examination, experimentation, investigation, procedure, proof, research, test, trial, trial and error, trial run, venture

experiment *v* assay, examine, investigate, put to the test, research, sample, test, try, verify

experimental *adj* empirical, exploratory, pilot, preliminary, probationary, provisional, speculative, tentative, test, trial, trial-and-error

expert *n* ace, adept, authority, connoisseur, dab hand, master, past master, pro, professional, specialist, virtuoso, wizard

expert *adj* able, adept, adroit, apt, clever, deft, dexterous, experienced, facile, handy, knowledgeable, master, masterly, practised, professional, proficient, qualified, skilful, skilled, trained, virtuoso

expertise *n* ableness, adroitness, aptness, cleverness, command, deftness, dexterity, expertness, facility, judgment, knack, knowledge, masterliness, mastery, proficiency, skilfulness, skill

expire *v* cease, close, come to an, end, conclude, end, finish, lapse, run out, stop, terminate; decease, depart, die, kick the bucket, pass away, perish

explain *v* clarify, clear up, define, demonstrate, describe, disclose, elucidate, explicate, expound, illustrate, interpret, make clear, resolve, solve, teach unfold

explanation *n* clarification,

definition, demonstration, description, elucidation, explication, exposition, illustration, interpretation, resolution; account, answer, cause, excuse, justification, meaning, mitigation, motive, reason, sense, significance, vindication

explicit *adj* absolute, categorical, certain, clear, definite, direct, distinct, exact, express, frank, open, outspoken, patent, plain, positive, precise, specific, state, straightforward, unambiguous, unequivocal, unqualified, unreserved

explode *v* blow up, burst, detonate, discharge, erupt, go off, set off, shatter, shiver; belie, debunk, discredit, disprove, give the lie to, invalidate, refute, repudiate

exploit *n* accomplishment, achievement, adventure, attainment, deed, feat, stunt

exploit *v* abuse, impose upon, manipulate, milk, misuse, play on, take advantage of

exploration *n* analysis, examination, inquiry, inspection, investigation, probe, research, scrutiny, search, study

explore *v* analyse, examine, inquire into, inspect, investigate, look into, probe, prospect, research, scrutinize, search

explosion *n* bang, blast, burst, clap, crack, detonation, discharge, outburst, report

explosive *adj* unstable, volatile; fiery, stormy, touchy, vehement, violent

exponent *n* advocate, backer, champion, defender, promoter, propagandist, proponent, spokesman, spokeswoman, supporter, upholder

expose *v* display, exhibit, make obvious, manifest, present, put on view, reveal, show, uncover, unveil; betray, bring to light, denounce, denude, detect, disclose, divulge, lay bare, let out, make known, reveal, show, up, smoke out, uncover, unearth, unmask; (*Inf*) blow the whistle on, pull the plug on, spill the beans on

exposé *v* disclosure, divulgence, exposure, revelation

exposed *adj* bare, exhibited, laid bare, made manifest, made public, on display, on show, on view, revealed, shown, unconcealed, uncovered, unveiled; open, open to the elements, unprotected, unsheltered

exposure *n* baring, display, exhibition, manifestation, presentation publicity, revelation, showing, uncovering, unveiling; airing, betrayal, denunciation, detection, disclosure, divulgence, divulging, exposé, revelation, unmasking

expound *v* describe, elucidate, explain, explicate, illustrate, interpret, set forth, spell out, unfold

express *v* articulate, assert, asseverate, communicate, couch, declare, enunciate, phrase, pronounce, put, put across, put into words, say, speak, state, tell, utter, verbalize, voice, word

express *adj* clearcut, especial, particular, singular, special; direct, fast, high-speed, nonstop, quick, rapid, speedy, swift

expression *n* announcement, assertion, asseveration, communication, declaration, enunciation, mention, pronouncement, speaking, statement, utterance, verbalization, voicing; demonstration, embodiment, exhibition, indication, manifestation, representation, show, sign, symbol, token, choice of words, delivery, diction, emphasis, execution, intonation, language, phraseology, phrasing, speech, style, wording; idiom, locution, phrase, term, turn of phrase, word

expressly *adv* especially, exactly, intentionally, on purpose, particularly, precisely, purposely, specially, specifically

expulsion *n* banishment, debarment, discharge, dislodgment, dismissal, ejection, eviction, exclusion, exile, expatriation, extrusion, proscription, removal

exquisite *adj* beautiful, dainty, delicate, elegant, fine, lovely, precious; attractive, beautiful, charming, comely, lovely, pleasing, striking

extend *v* carry on, continue, drag out, draw out, elongate, lengthen, make longer, prolong, protract, spin out, spread out, stretch, unfurl, unroll; add to, amplify, augment, broaden, develop, dilate, enhance, enlarge, expand, increase, spread, supplement, widen

extension *n* addendum, addition, adjunct, annexe, appendage, appendix, branch, ell, supplement, wing

extensive *adj* all-inclusive, broad, capacious, commodious, comprehensive, expanded, extended, far-flung, far-reaching, general, great, huge, large, large-scale, lengthy, long, pervasive, prevalent, protracted, spacious, sweeping, thorough, universal, vast, voluminous, wholesale, wide, widespread

extent *n* bounds, compass, play, range, reach, scope, sphere, sweep; amount, amplitude, area, breadth, bulk, degree, duration, expanse, expansion, length, magnitude, measure, quantity, size, stretch, term, time, volume, width

exterior *n* appearance, aspect, coating, covering, façade, face, finish, outside, shell, skin, surface

exterior *adj* external, outer, outer most, outside, outward, superficial, surface

exterminate *v* abolish, annihilate, destroy, eliminate, eradicate, extirpate

external *adj* apparent, exterior, outer, outermost, outside, outward, superficial, surface, visible

extinct *adj* dead, defunct, gone, lost, vanished

extinction *n* abolition, annihilation, death, destruction, dying out, eradication, excision, extermination, extirpation, obliteration, oblivion

extinguish *v* blow out, douse, put out, quench, smother, snuff out, stifle; abolish, annihilate, destroy, eliminate, end, eradicate, erase, expunge, exterminate, extirpate, kill, obscure, remove, suppress, wipe out

extol *v* acclaim, applaud, celebrate, commend, cry up, eulogize, exalt, glorify, laud, magnify, panegyrize, pay tribute to, praise, sing the praises of

extort *v* blackmail, bleed, bully, coerce, exact, extract, force, squeeze, wrest, wring

extra *adj* accessory, added, additional, ancillary, auxiliary, fresh, further, more, new, other, supplemental, supplementary

extra *n* accessory, addendum, addition, adjunct, affix, appendage, appurtenance, attachment, bonus, complement, extension, supernumerary, supplement

extra *adv* especially, exceptionally, extraordinarily, extremely, particularly, remarkably, uncommonly, unusually

extract *v* draw, extirpate, pluck out, pull, pull out, remove, take out, uproot, withdraw, elicit, evoke, exact, gather, get, glean, obtain, reap, wrest, wring

extract *n* concentrate, decoction, distillate, distillation, essence, juice; abstract, citation, clipping, cutting, excerpt, passage, quotation, selection

extraction *n* drawing out, pulling out, removal, uprooting; extortion, wresting; distillation, expressing, separation, squeezing

extradite *v* banish, deport, exile, expel, outlaw

extraordinary *adj* amazing, bizarre, curious, exceptional, fantastic, marvellous, odd, outstanding, particular, peculiar, phenomenal, rare, remarkable, singular, special, strange, surprising, uncommon, unfamiliar, unheard-of, unique, unprecedented, unusual, unwonted, weird, wonderful

extravagance *n* improvidence, lavishness, overspending, profligacy, profusion, squandering, waste, wastefulness

extravagant *adj* excessive, improvident, imprudent, lavish, prodigal, profligate, spendthrift, wasteful; costly, excessive, exorbitant, expensive, extortionate, inordinate, over priced, steep; (*Inf*), unreasonable

extreme *adj* acute, great, greatest, high, highest, intense, maximum, severe, supreme, ultimate, utmost, uttermost, worst; faraway, far-off, farthest, final, last, most distant, outermost, remotest, terminal, ultimate, utmost, uttermost

extreme *n* acme, apex, apogee, boundary, climax, consummation, depth, edge, end, excess, extremity, height, limit, maximum, minimum, nadir, pinnacle, pole, termination, top, ultimate, zenith

extremely *adv* acutely, awfully, exceedingly, exceptionally, excessively, extraordinarily, greatly, highly, inordinately, intensely, markedly, quite, severely, terribly, to the extreme, ultra, uncommonly, unusually, utterly, very

extremity *n* acme, apex, apogee, border, bound, boundary, brim, brink, edge, end, extreme, frontier, limit, margin, maximum, minimum, nadir, pinnacle, pole, rim, terminal, termination terminus, tip, top, ultimate, verge, zenith; **extremities** fingers and toes, hands and feet, limbs

extricate *v* clear, deliver, disembar rass, disengage, disentangle, free, get out, get off the hook, liberate, release, relieve, remove, rescue, withdraw, wriggle out of

exuberance *n* animation, buoyancy, cheerfulness, eagerness, ebullience, effervescence, energy, enthusiasm, excitement, exhilaration, high spirits, life, liveliness, spirit, sprightliness, vigour, vitality, vivacity, zest; abundance, copiousness, lavishness, lushness, luxuriance, plenitude, profusion, rankness, richness, superabundance, teemingness

exuberant *adj* animated, buoyant, cheerful, eager, ebullient, effervescent, elated, energetic, enthusiastic, excited, exhilarated, full of life, high-spirited, in high spirits, lively, sparkling, spirited, sprightly, vigorous, vivacious, zestful; abundant, copious, lavish, lush, luxuriant, overflowing, plenteous, plentiful, profuse, rank, rich, superabundant, teeming

exult *v* be delighted, be elated, be in high spirits, be joyful, be jubilant, be overjoyed, celebrate, jubilate, jump for joy, make merry, rejoice

eye *n* eyeball, optic, orb; appreciation, discernment, discrimination, judgment, perception, recognition, taste; (*Inf*) peeper ; **keep an eye on** guard, keep in view, keep under surveillance, look after, look out for, monitor, observe, pay attention to, regard, scrutinize, supervise, survey, watch, watch over; **see eye to eye** accord, agree, back, be in unison, coincide, concur, fall in, get on, go along, harmonize, jibe, subscribe to; **up to one's eyes** busy, caught up, engaged, flooded out, fully occupied, inundated, overwhelmed, up to here, up to one's elbows, wrapped up in

eye *v* contemplate, gaze at, glance at, have a look at, inspect, look at, peruse, regard, scan, scrutinize, stare at, study, survey, view, watch

eyesight *n* observation, perception, range of vision, sight, vision

eyesore *n* atrocity, blemish, blight, blot, disfigurement, disgrace, horror, mess, monstrosity, sight, ugliness

eyewitness *n* bystander, looker-on, observer, onlooker, passer-by, spectator, viewer, watcher, witness

F

fabric *n* cloth, material, stuff, textile, web; constitution, construction, foundations, frame-work, infrastructure, make-up, organization, structure

fabulous *adj* amazing, astounding, breathtaking, fictitious, incredible, legendary, phenomenal, unbelievable; apocryphal, fantastic, imaginary, invented, made-up, mythical, unreal

façade *n* appearance, exterior, face, front, frontage, guise, mask, pretence, semblance, show, veneer

face *n* clock, countenance, features, lineaments, physiognomy, visage; (*Inf*) dial, mug; appearance, aspect, expression, frown, grimace, look, pout, scowl, smirk; **face to face** confronting, eyeball to eyeball, in confrontation, opposite; **on the face of it** apparently, at first sight, seem ingly, to all appearances, to the eye

face *v* be confronted by, brave, come up against, confront, cope with, deal with, defy, encounter, experience, meet, oppose; be opposite, front onto, give towards, look onto, overlook

facet *n* angle, aspect, face, part, phase, plane, side, slant, surface

facetious *adj* amusing, comical, droll, flippant, frivolous, funny, humorous, jesting, jocose, jocular, merry, playful, pleasant, tongue in cheek, unserious, waggish, witty

face up to *v* accept, acknowledge, come to terms with, confront, cope with, deal with, meet head on

facile *adj* adept, adroit, dexterous, easy, effortless, fluent, light, proficient, quick, ready, simple, skilful, smooth, uncomplicated

facilitate *v* assist the progress of, ease, expedite, forward, further, help, make easy, promote, smooth the path of, speed up

facility *n* ability, adroitness, dexterity, ease, efficiency, effortlessness, expertness, fluency, gift, knack, proficiency, quickness, readiness, skilfulness, skill, smoothness, talent

facing *adj* fronting, opposite, partnering

facsimile *n* carbon, carbon copy, copy, duplicate, fax, photocopy, print, replica, reproduction, transcript

fact *n* act, deed, event, happening, incident, occurrence, performance; actuality, certainty, gospel, naked truth, reality, truth; **in fact** actually, indeed, in point of fact, in reality, in truth, really, truly

faction *n* bloc, cabal, camp, caucus, clique, coalition, combination, confederacy, contingent, coterie, division, gang, ginger, group, group, junta, lobby, minority, party, pressure group, section, sector, set, splinter group

factor *n* aspect, cause, circumstance, component, consideration, determinant, element, influence, item, part, point, thing

factory *n* manufacturing building, mill, plant, works; foundry

facts *pl n* data, details, information, the lowdown, the whole story

factual *adj* accurate, authentic, circumstantial, close, correct, credible, exact, faithful, genuine, literal, matter-of-fact, objective, precise, real, sure, true, true-to-life, unadorned, unbiased, veritable

faculty *n* branch of learning, department, discipline, profession, school, teaching staff; authorization, licence, prerogative, privilege, right

fad *n* affectation, craze, fancy, fashion, mania, mode, rage, trend, vogue, whim

fade *v* blanch, bleach, blench, dim, discolour, dull, grow dim, lose colour, lose lustre, pale, wash out; decline, die away, die out, diminish, disappear, disperse, dissolve, droop, dwindle, ebb, etiolate, evanesce, fail, fall, flag, languish, melt away, perish, shrivel, vanish, vanish into thin air, wane, waste away, wilt, wither

fail *v* be defeated, be found lacking, be in vain, be unsuccessful, break down, come to grief, come to naught, come to nothing, fall, fall short, fall short of, fall through, founder, go astray, go down, meet with disaster, miscarry, misfire, miss, not make the grade, run aground, turn out badly; abandon, break one's word, desert, disappoint, for get, forsake, let down, neglect, omit

failing *n* blemish, blind spot, defect, deficiency, draw back, error, failure, fault, flaw, foible, frailty, imperfection, lapse, miscarriage, misfortune, shortcoming, weakness

failure *n* abortion, breakdown, collapse, defeat, downfall, fiasco, frustration, lack of success, miscarriage, overthrow, wreck; black sheep, disappointment, incompetent, loser, no-good, nonstarter; default, deficiency, dereliction, neglect, negligence, nonobservance, nonperformance, nonsuccess, omission, remissness, shortcoming, stoppage; decay, decline, deterioration, failing, loss; bankruptcy, crash, downfall, insolvency, ruin

faint *adj* bleached, delicate, dim, distant, dull, faded, faltering, feeble, hazy, hushed, ill-defined, indistinct, light, low, muffled, muted, obscure, soft, subdued, thin, vague, whispered; frail, remote, slight, unenthusiastic, weak; dizzy, drooping, enervated, exhausted, faltering, fatigued, giddy, languid, lethargic, lightheaded, muzzy, vertiginous; (*Inf*) woozy

faint *v* black out, collapse, fade, fail, flake out, languish, lose consciousness, pass out, weaken

fair *adj* above board, according to the rules, clean, disinterested, dispassionate, equal, equitable, even-handed, honest, honourable, impartial, just, lawful, legitimate, objective, on the level, proper, square, trustworthy, unbiased, unprejudiced, upright; blond, blonde, fair-haired, light, light-complexioned, tow-headed; adequate, all right, average, decent, mediocre, middling, moderate, not bad, OK, passable, reasonable, respectable, satisfactory, tolerable; beauteous, beautiful, bonny, comely, handsome, lovely, pretty, well-favoured

fair *n* bazaar, carnival, expo, exposition, festival, gala, market, show

fairly *adv* adequately, moderately, pretty well, quite, rather, reasonably, somewhat, tolerably; deservedly, equitably, honestly, impartially, justly, objectively, properly, without fear

fairness *n* decency, disinterestedness, equitableness, equity, impartiality, justice, legitimacy, rightfulness, uprightness

fairy *n* brownie, elf, hob, leprechaun, pixie, Robin Goodfellow, sprite

fairy tale *n* folk tale, romance; fabrication, fantasy, fiction, invention, lie, tall story, untruth; (*Inf*) cock-and-bull story

faith *n* assurance, confidence, conviction, credence, credit, dependence, reliance, trust; allegiance, constancy, faithfulness, fealty, infidelity, loyalty, truth, truthfulness

faithful *n* attached, constant, dependable, devoted, loyal, reliable, staunch, steadfast, true, true-blue, trusty, truthful, unswerving, unwavering; accurate, close, exact, just, precise, strict, true

faithless *adj* disloyal, doubting, false, fickle, inconstant, perfidious, traitorous, treacherous, unbelieving, unfaithful, unreliable, untrue, untrustworthy, untruthful

fake *v* affect, assume, copy, counter feit, fabricate, feign, forge, pretend, put on, sham, simulate

fake *n* charlatan, copy, forgery, fraud, hoax, imitation, impostor, mountebank, reproduction, sham

fall *v* be precipitated, cascade, collapse, crash, descend, dive, drop, drop down, go head over heels, keel over, nose-dive, pitch, plummet, plunge, settle, sink, stumble, subside, topple, trip, trip over, tumble; abate, become lower, decline, decrease, depreciate, diminish, dwindle, ebb, fall off, flag, go down, lessen, slump, subside; be overthrown, be taken, capitulate, give in, give way, go out of office, pass into enemy hands, resign, succumb, surrender, yield

fall *n* descent, dive, droop, nose dive, plummet, plunge, slip, spill, tumble; cut, decline, decrease, diminution, dip, drop, dwindling, falling off, lessening, lowering, reduction, slump; capitulation, collapse, death, defeat, destruction, downfall, failure, overthrow, resignation, ruin, surrender; declivity, descent, downgrade, incline, slant, slope

fallacy *n* casuistry, deceit, deception, delusion, error, falsehood, faultiness, flaw, illusion, inconsistency, misapprehension, misconception, mistake, sophism, sophistry, untruth

fall apart *v* break up, crumble, disband, disintegrate, disperse, dissolve, fall to bits, go to pieces, lose, cohesion, shatter

fall back on *v* call upon, employ, have recourse to, make use, of, press into service, resort to

fall behind *v* be in arrears, drop back, get left behind, lag, lose one's place, trail

fallible *adj* erring, frail, ignorant, imperfect, mortal, prone to error, uncertain, weak

fall out *v* altercate, argue, clash, differ, disagree, fight, quarrel, squabble

fallow *adj* dormant, idle, inactive, inert, resting, uncultivated, undeveloped, unplanted, untilled, unused

false *adj* concocted, erroneous, faulty, fictitious, improper, inaccurate, incorrect, inexact, invalid, mistaken, unfounded, unreal, wrong, lying, mendacious, truthless, unreliable, unsound, untrue, untrustworthy, untruthful; artificial, bogus, counterfeit, ersatz, fake, feigned, forged, imitation, mock, pretended, sham, simulated, spurious, synthetic

falsehood *n* deceit, deception, dishonesty, dissimulation, inveracity, mendacity, perjury, prevarication, untruthfulness; fabrication, fib, fiction, lie, mistatement, story, untruth

falsify *v* alter belie, counterfeit, distort, doctor, fake, forge, garble, misrepresent, mistake, pervert, tamper with

falter *v* break hesitate, shake, speak haltingly, stammer, stumble, stutter, totter, tremble, vacillate, waver

fame *n* celebrity, credit, eminence, glory, honour, illustriousness, name, prominence, public esteem, renown, reputation, repute, stardom

familiar *adj* accustomed, common, conventional, customary, domestic, everyday, frequent, household, mundane, ordinary, recognizable, repeated, routine, stock, well-known; **familiar with** abreast of, acquainted with, at home with, aware of, conscious of, conversant with, introduced, knowledgeable, no stranger to, on speaking terms with, versed in, well up in; amicable, chummy, close, confidential, cordial, easy, free, free-and-easy, friendly, informal, intimate, near, open, relaxed, unceremonious, unconstrained, unreserved

familiarity *n* acquaintance, acquaintanceship, awareness, experience, grasp, understanding; absence of reserve, closeness, ease, fellowship, freedom, friendliness, friendship, informality, intimacy, naturalness, openness, sociability, unceremoniousness

family *n* brood, children, descendants, household, issue, kin, off spring, one's nearest and dearest, one's own flesh and blood, people, progeny, relations, relatives

famine *n* death, destitution, hunger, scarcity, starvation

famous *adj* acclaimed, celebrated, conspicuous, distinguished, eminent, excellent, far-famed, glorious, honoured, illustrious, legendary, much-publicized, notable, noted, prominent, remarkable, renowned, signal, well-known

fanatic *n* activist, addict, bigot, devotee, enthusiast, extremist, militant, visionary, zealot

fancy *v* be inclined to think, believe, conceive, conjecture, guess, imagine, infer, reckon, suppose, surmise, think, think likely; be attracted to, crave, desire, dream of, hanker after, have a yen for, long for, relish, wish for, would like, yearn for

fancy *adj* baroque, decorated, decorative, elaborate, elegant, embellished, extravagant, fanciful, intricate, ornamental, ornamented, ornate

fantastic *adj* comical, eccentric, exotic, fanciful, freakish, grotesque, imaginative, odd, outlandish, peculiar, phantasmagorical, quaint, queer, rococo, strange, unreal, weird, whimsical

far *adv* afar, a good way, a great distance, a long way, deep, miles; considerably, decidedly, extremely, greatly, incomparably, much; **so far** thus far, to date, until now, up to now, up to the present

far *adj* distant, faraway, far-flung, far-off, far removed, long, outlying, out-of-the-way, remote, removed

farce *n* broad comedy, buffoonery, burlesque, comedy, satire, slapstick, absurdity, joke, mockery, nonsense, parody, ridiculousness, sham, travesty

fare *n* charge, passage money, price, ticket money, transport cost; commons, diet, eatables, food, meals, menu, provisions, rations, sustenance, table, victuals

fare *v* do, get along, get on, make out, manage, prosper

farewell *int* adieu, *adios*, *Auf Wiedersehen*, cheerio, ciao, goodbye, leave-taking, parting, send-off, so long, valediction; (*Inf*) see you later

farewell *n* adieu, departure, farewell, goodbye, going away, parting

far-fetched *adj* doubtful, dubious, fantastic, hard to swallow, implausible, improbable, incredible, preposterous, strained, unbelievable, unconvincing, unlikely, unnatural, unrealistic

farm *n* acreage, acres, croft, farmstead, grange, holding, homestead, land, plantation, ranch

farm *v* bring under, cultivation, cultivate, operate, plant, practise husbandry, till the soil, work

far-reaching *adj* broad, extensive, important, momentous, pervasive, significant, sweeping, widespread

fascinate *v* absorb, allure, beguile, bewitch, captivate, charm, delight, enamour, enchant, engross, enrapture, enravish, enthral, entrance, hold spellbound, hypnotize, infatuate, intrigue, mesmerize, rivet, spell bind, transfix

fascination *n* allure, attraction, charm, enchantment, glamour, lure, magic, magnetism, pull, sorcery, spell

fashion *n* convention, craze, custom, fad, latest, latest style, look, mode, prevailing taste, rage, style, trend, usage, vogue; attitude, demeanour, manner, method, mode, style, way;

fashion *v* construct, contrive, create, design, forge, form, make, manufacture, mould, shape, work

fashionable *adj* à la mode, all the go, all the rage, chic, current, customary genteel, hip, in vogue, latest, modern, modish, popular, prevailing, smart, stylish, trendsetting, up-to-date, up-to-the-minute, usual

fast *adj* accelerated, brisk, fleet, flying, hasty, hurried, mercurial, nippy, quick, rapid, speedy, swift, winged; dissipated, dissolute, extravagant, gadabout, giddy, immoral, intemperate, licentious, loose, profligate, promiscuous, rakish, reckless, self-indulgent, wanton, wild

fast *adv* apace, hastily, hell for leather, hurriedly, in haste, like a flash, posthaste, presto, quickly, rapidly, speedily, swiftly, with all haste; extravagantly, intemperately, loosely, promiscuously, rakishly, recklessly, wildly

fast *v* abstain, deny oneself, go hungry, go without food, practise abstention, refrain from food

fast *n* abstinence, fasting

fasten *v* affix, anchor, attach, bind, bolt, chain, connect, fix, grip, join, lace, link, lock, make fast, make firm, seal, secure, tie, unite

fat *adj* beefy, corpulent, elephantine, fleshy, gross, heavy, obese, overweight, plump, podgy, portly, rotund, solid, stout, tubby; adipose, fatty, greasy, oily, oleaginous, suety

fat *n* adipose tissue, blubber, bulk, cellulite, corpulence, fatness, flab, flesh, obesity, overweight, paunch, weight problem

fatal *adj* deadly, destructive, final, incurable, killing, lethal, malignant, mortal, pernicious, terminal; bale ful, baneful, calamitous, catastrophic, disastrous, lethal, ruinous

fate *n* chance, destiny, divine, will, fortune, kismet, nemesis, predestination, providence; end, future, issue, outcome, upshot

fated *adj* destined, doomed, foreordained, ineluctable, inescapable, inevitable, marked down, predestined, pre-elected, preordained, sure, written

fateful *adj* critical, crucial, decisive, important, portentous, significant

father *n* begetter, dad, pater, paterfamilias, patriarch, sire; ancestor, forebear, forefather, predecessor, progenitor; abbé, confessor, curé, padre, pastor, priest

father *v* beget, get, procreate, sire

fatherly *adj* affectionate, benevolent, benign, forbearing, indulgent, kind, kindly, paternal, patriarchal, protective, supportive, tender

fatigue *v* drain, drain of energy, exhaust, jade, overtire, tire, weaken, wear out, weary

fatigue *n* debility, ennui, heaviness, languor, lethargy, listlessness, overtiredness, tiredness

fault *n* blemish, defect, deficiency, drawback, failing, flaw, imperfection, infirmity, lack, shortcoming, snag, weakness, weak point; delinquency, frailty, lapse, misconduct, misdeed, misdemeanour, offence, peccadillo, sin, transgression, trespass, wrong

fault-finding *adj* captious, carping, censorious, critical, hypercritical, pettifogging

faultless *adj* accurate, classic, correct, exemplary, faithful, flawless, foolproof, impeccable, model, perfect, unblemished; above reproach, blameless, guiltless, immaculate, innocent, irreproachable, pure, sinless, spotless, stainless, unblemished, unspotted, unsullied

faulty *adj* bad, blemished, broken, damaged, defective, erroneous, fallacious, flawed, impaired, imperfect, imprecise, inaccurate, incorrect, invalid, malfunctioning, not working, out of order, unsound, weak, wrong

favour *n* approbation, approval, backing, bias, championship, esteem, favouritism, friendliness, good opinion, good will, grace, kindness, kind regard, partiality, patronage, support; benefit, boon, courtesy, good turn, indulgence, kindness, obligement, service

favourable *adj* advantageous, appropriate, auspicious, beneficial, convenient, encouraging, fair, fit, good, helpful, hopeful, opportune, promising, propitious, suitable, timely

favourably *adv* advantageously, auspiciously, conveniently, fortunately, opportunely, profitably, to one's advantage, well

favourite *adj* best-loved, choice, dearest, esteemed, favoured, preferred

favourite *n* beloved, choice, darling, dear, idol, pet, pick, preference, teacher's pet, the apple of one's eye

fawn *v* be obsequious, be servile, bow and scrape, court, crawl, creep, cringe, dance attendance, flatter, grovel, ingratiate oneself, kneel, pay court, truckle

fear *n* alarm, apprehensiveness, awe, consternation, cravenness, dismay, dread, fright, horror, panic, qualms, terror, timidity, tremors, trepidation; bogey, bugbear, horror, nightmare, phobia, spectre

fear *v* apprehend, be afraid, dare not, dread, have a horror of, have a phobia about, have qualms, live in dread of, shake in one's shoes, shudder at, take fright, tremble at

fearful *adj* afraid, alarmed, anxious, apprehensive, diffident, faint-hearted, frightened, hesitant, intimidated, jittery, jumpy, nervous, nervy, panicky, scared, shrinking, tense, timid, timorous, uneasy; appaling, atrocious, awful, dire, distressing, dreadful, frightful, grievous, grim, hideous, horrendous, horrible, horrific, monstrous, shocking, terrible, unspeakable

fearless *adj* bold, brave, confident, courageous, daring, gallant, heroic, indomitable, intrepid, plucky, unafraid, valiant, valorous

feasible *adj* achievable, attainable, likely, possible, practicable, realizable, reasonable, viable, workable

feast *n* banquet, barbecue, carousal, carouse, dinner, entertainment, festive board, jollification, junket, repast, revels, treat; (*Inf*) spread

feat *n* accomplishment, achievement, act, attainment, deed, exploit, performance

feather *n* down, pinion, plumage, plumule, quill

feathery *adj* downy, feathered, fleecy, fluffy, plumes; feather-like, gossamer-like, light as a feather, unsubstantial,

feature *n* aspect, attribute, characteristic, facet, factor, hall-mark, mark, peculiarity, point, property, quality, trait; article, column, comment item, piece, report, story

feature *v* accentuate, call attention to, emphasize, give prominence to, headline, play up, present, promote, set off, spotlight, star

federation *n* alliance, amalgamation, association, coalition, combination, confederacy, co-partnership, entente, federacy, league, syndicate, union

fed up with (*Inf*) annoyed, blue, bored, brassed off, browned-off, depressed, discontented, dismal, dissatisfied, down, gloomy, glum, sick and tired of, tired of, weary of

fee *n* account, bill, charge, compensation, emolument, hire, honorarium, pay, payment, recompense, remuneration, reward, toll

feeble *adj* debilitated, delicate, doddering, effete, enervated, enfeebled, etiolated, exhausted, failing, faint, frail, infirm, languid, powerless, puny, sickly, weak, weakened

feebleness *n* debility, delicacy, effeteness, enervation, etiolation, exhaustion, frailness, frailty, incapacity, infirmity, lack of strength, languor, lassitude, sickliness, weak ness

feed *v* cater for, nourish, provide for, provision, supply, sustain, victual, wine and dine; **feed on** devour, eat, exist on, fare, graze, live on, nurture, partake of, pasture, subsist, take nourishment

feel *v* caress, finger, fondle, handle, manipulate, maul, paw, run one's hands over, stroke, touch; be aware of, be sensible of, endure, enjoy, experience, go through, have, have a sensation of, know, notice, observe, perceive, suffer, take to heart, under go; explore, fumble, grope, sound, test, try; be convinced, feel in one's bones, have a hunch, have the impression, intuit, sense; believe, be of the opinion that, consider, deem, hold, judge, think; appear, resemble, seem, strike one as; **feel like** could do with, desire, fancy, feel inclined, feel the need for, feel up to, have the inclination, want

feeling *adj* feel, perception, sensation, sense, sense of touch, touch; apprehension, consciousness, hunch, idea, impression, inkling, notion, presentiment, sense, suspicion; inclination, instinct, opinion, point of view, view

feelings *pl n* ego, emotions, self-esteem, sensitivities, susceptibilities

fell *v* cut, cut down, demolish, flatten, floor, hew, knock down, level, prostrate, raze, strike down

fellow *n* boy, chap, character, customer, individual, man, person; associate, colleague, companion, compeer, comrade, co-worker, equal, friend, member, partner, peer; (*Inf*) bloke

fellowship *n* amity, brotherhood, camaraderie, communion, companionability, companionship, familiarity, fraternization, intercourse, intimacy, kindliness, sociability

feminine *adj* delicate, gentle, girlish, graceful, ladylike, modest, soft, tender, womanly

fen *n* bog, holm, marsh, morass, quagmire, slough, swamp

fence *n* barbed wire, barricade, barrier, defence, guard, hedge, paling, palisade, railings, rampart, shield, stockade, wall; **fence in** bound, circumscribe, confine, coop, defend, encircle, enclose, fortify, guard, hedge, pen, protect, restrict, secure, separate, surround

ferment *v* boil, brew, bubble, concoct, effervesce, foam, froth, heat, leaven, rise, seethe, work; agitate, boil, excite, fester, foment, heat, incite, inflame, provoke, rouse, seethe, smoulder, stir up

ferment *n* agitation, commotion,

disruption, excitement, fever, frenzy, furore, glow, heat, hubbub, imbroglio, state of unrest, stew, stir, tumult, turbulence, turmoil, unrest, uproar

ferocious *adj* feral, fierce, predatory, rapacious, ravening, savage, violent, wild

ferocity *n* barbarity, bloodthirstiness, brutality, cruelty, ferociousness, fierceness, inhumanity, rapacity, ruthlessness, savageness, savagery, viciousness, wildness

ferry *n* ferryboat, packet, packet boat

ferry *v* carry, chauffeur, convey, run, ship, shuttle, transport

fertile *adj* abundant, fat, fecund, flowering, flowing with milk and honey, fruitful, generative, luxuriant, plenteous, plentiful, productive, prolific, rich, teeming, yielding

fertility *n* abundance, fecundity, fruitfulness, luxuriance, productiveness, richness

fervent, fervid *adj* animated, ardent, devout, eager, earnest, ecstatic, emotional, enthusiastic, excited, fiery, heartfelt, impassioned, intense, vehement, warm, zealous

fervour *n* animation, ardour, eagerness, earnestness, enthusiasm, excitement, fervency, intensity, passion, vehemence, warmth, zeal

festival *n* anniversary, commemoration, feast, fiesta, holiday, holy day, saint's day; carnival, celebration, entertainment, festivities, field day, gala, jubilee, treat

festive *adj* back-slapping, carnival, celebratory, cheery, convivial, festal, gala, gay, gleeful, happy, hearty, holiday, jolly, jovial, joyful, joyous, jubilant, light-hearted, merry, mirthful, sportive

festoon *v* array, bedeck, beribbon, deck, decorate, drape, garland, hang, swathe, wreathe

fetch *v* bring, carry, conduct, convey, deliver, escort, get, go for, lead, obtain, retrieve, transport; draw forth, elicit, give rise to, produce; bring in, earn, go for, make, realize, sell for, yield

feud *n* argument, bad blood, bickering, broil, conflict, contention, disagreement, discord, dissension, enmity, estrangement, faction, falling out, grudge, hostility, quarrel, rivalry, strife, vendetta

feud *v* be at daggers drawn, be at odds, bicker, brawl, clash, contend, dispute, duel, fall out, quarrel, row, squabble, war

fever *n* agitation, delirium, ecstasy, excitement, ferment, fervour, flush, frenzy, heat, intensity, passion, restlessness, turmoil, unrest

few *adj* hardly any, inconsiderable, infrequent, insufficient, meagre, negligible, not many, rare, scant, scanty, scarce, scarcely any, scattered, sparse, sporadic, thin

few *pron* handful, scarcely any, scattering, small number, some

fiancé, fiancée *n* betrothed, bride-to-be, intended, prospective, spouse, wife-to-be, husband-to-be

fiasco *n* catastrophe, debacle, disaster, failure, flap, mess, rout, ruin; (*Inf*) washout

fib *n* fiction, lie, prevarication, story, untruth, white lie; (*Inf*) whopper

fibre *n* fibril, filament, pile, staple, strand, texture, thread

fibre *n* essence, nature, quality, spirit, substance

fickle *adj* blowing hot and cold, capricious, changeable, faithless, fitful, flighty, inconstant, irresolute, mercurial, mutable, quick-silver, unfaithful, unpredictable, unstable, unsteady, vacillating, variable, volatile

fiction *n* fable, fantasy, legend, myth, novel, romance, story, story telling, tale, work of imagination; (*Inf*) yarn; concoction, fabrication, falsehood, fancy, fantasy, figment of the imagination, imagination, improvisation, invention, lie, tall story, untruth; (*Inf*) cock and bull story

fictitious *adj* apocryphal, artificial, assumed, bogus, counterfeit, fabricated, false, fanciful, feigned, imaginary, imagined, improvised, invented, made-up, make-believe, mythical, spurious, unreal, untrue

fidelity *n* allegiance, constancy, dependability, devotedness, devotion, faith, faithfulness, fealty, integrity, lealty, loyalty, staunchness, true-heartedness, trustworthiness; accuracy, adherence, closeness, correspondence, exactitude, exactness, faithfulness, preciseness, precision, scrupulousness

fidget *v* bustle, chafe, fiddle, fret, juggle, jitter, move restlessly, squirm, twitch, worry; (*Inf*) have ants in one's pants

fidgety *adj* impatient, jerky, jumpy, nervous, on edge, restive, restless, twitchy, uneasy

field *n* grassland, green, meadow, pasture; area, area of activity,

field *v* catch, pick up, retrieve, return, stop

fiend *n* demon, devil, evil spirit, hellhound; (*Inf*) addict, enthusiast, fanatic, freak, maniac

fierce *adj* barbarous, brutal, cruel, dangerous, fell, feral, ferocious, fiery, menacing, murderous, passionate, savage, threatening, tigerish, truculent, uncontrollable, untamed, vicious, wild

fight *v* assault, battle, bear arms against, box, brawl, carry on war, clash, close, combat, come to blows, conflict, contend, cross swords, do battle, engage, exchange blows, feud, go to war, grapple, joust, spar, struggle, take the field, tilt, tussle, wage war, war, wrestle; contest, defy, dispute, make a stand against, oppose, resist, stand up to, strive, struggle, withstand; argue, bicker, dispute, fall out, squabble, wrangle; carry on, conduct, engage in, prosecute, wage

fight *n* action, affray, altercation, battle, bout, brawl, brush, clash, combat, conflict, contest, dispute, dissension, dogfight, duel, encounter, engagement, exchange of blows, fracas, fray, hostilities, joust, riot, tow, scuffle, skirmish, sparring match, struggle, tussle, war

fighter *n* fighting man, man-at-arms, soldier, warrior; boxer, prize fighter, pugilist

fighting *adj* aggressive, argumentative, bellicose, belligerent, combative, contentious, disputatious, hawkish, martial, militant, pugnacious, truculent, warlike

fight off *v* beat off, keep at bay,

repel, repress, repress, repulse, resist, stave off, ward off

figure *n* character, cipher, digit, number, numeral, symbol; amount, cost, price, sum, total, value; form, outline, shadow, shape, silhouette; body, build, frame, physique, proportions, shape, torso; celebrity, character, dignitary, force, leader, notability, notable, personage, personality, presence, somebody, worthy

figurehead *n* cipher, dummy, front man, leader in name only, man of straw, mouthpiece, name, nonentity, puppet, titular head, token

figure out *v* calculate, compute, reckon, work out; comprehend, decipher, fathom, make head or tail of, make out, resolve, see, understand

file *v* abrade, burnish, furbish, polish, rasp, refine, rub, rub down, scrape, shape, smooth

file *n* case, data, documents, dossier, folder, information, portfolio

file *v* document, enter, pigeonhole, put in place, record, register, slot in

fill *v* brim over, cram, crowd, furnish, glut, gorge, inflate, pack, pervade, replenish, sate, satiate, satisfy, stock, store, stuff, supply, swell

fill in *v* answer, complete, fill out, fill up; deputize, replace, represent, stand in, sub, substitute, take the place of

filling *n* contents, filler, innards, inside, insides, padding, stuffing, wadding

filling *adj* ample, heavy, satisfying, square, substantial

film *n* coat, coating, covering, dusting, gauze, integument, layer, membrane, pellicle, scum, skin, tissue; flick, motion picture, movie

film *v* photograph, shoot, take, video, videotape

filter *v* clarify, filtrate, purify, refine, screen, sieve, sift, strain, winnow

filter *n* gauze, membrane, mesh, riddle, sieve, strainer

filth *n* carrion, contamination, defilement, dirt, dung, excrement, excreta, faeces, filthiness, foul matter, foulness, garbage, grime, muck, nastiness, ordure, pollution, putrefaction, putrescence, refuse, sewage, slime, sludge, squalor, uncleanness; corruption, dirty-mindedness, impurity, indecency, obscenity, pornography, smut, vileness, vulgarity

filthy *adj* dirty, faecal, feculent, foul, nasty, polluted, putrid, scummy, slimy, squalid, unclean, vile; begrimed, black, blackened, grimy, grubby, miry, mucky, muddy, mud-encrusted, smoky, sooty, unwashed; bawdy, coarse, corrupt, depraved, dirty-minded, foul, impure, indecent, lewd, licentious, obscene, pornographic, smutty, suggestive

final *adj* closing, concluding, end, eventual, last, last-minute, latest, terminal, terminating, ultimate; absolute, conclusive, decided, decisive, definite, definitive, determinate, finished, incontrovertible, irrevocable, settled

finale *n* climax, close, conclusion, culmination, denouement, final curtain, final scene, finish, last act; (*Inf*) wind up

finalize *v* agree on, clinch, complete,

conclude, decide, settle, tie up, work out; (*Inf*) wrap up

finally *adv* at last, at length, at long last, at the last, at the last moment, eventually, in the end, in the long run, lastly, ultimately, when all is said and done

finance *n* accounts, banking, business, commerce, economics, financial affairs, investment, money, money management

finance *v* back, bankroll, float, fund, guarantee, pay for, provide, security for, set up in business, subsidize, support, underwrite

finances *pl n* affairs, assets, capital, cash, financial, condition, funds, money, resources, wherewithal

financial *adj* budgeting, economic, fiscal, monetary, money, pecuniary

find *v* catch sight of, chance upon, come across, come up with, descry, discover, encounter, espy, expose, ferret out, hit, upon, lay one's hand on, light upon, locate, meet, recognize, run to earth, spot, stumble upon, track down, turn up, uncover, unearth; get back recover, regain repossess, retrieve;

find *n* acquisition, asset, bargain, catch, discovery, good buy

find out *v* detect, discover, learn, note, observe, perceive, realize

fine *adj* accomplished, admirable, beautiful, choice, excellent, exceptional, exquisite, first-class, first-rate, great, magnificent, masterly, ornate, outstanding, rare, select, showy, skilful, splendid, superior, supreme; balmy, bright, clear, clement, cloudless, dry, fair, pleasant, sunny; dainty, delicate, elegant, expensive, exquisite, fragile, quality; abstruse, acute, critical, discriminating, fastidious, hairsplitting, intelligent, keen, minute, nice, precise, quick, refined, sensitive, sharp, subtle, tasteful, tenuous; clear, pure, refined, solid, sterling, unadulterated, unalloyed, unpolluted; acceptable, agreeable, all right, convenient, good, OK, satisfactory, suitable

fine *v* amerce, mulct, penalize, punish

fine *n* amercement, damages, forfeit, penalty, punishment

finesse *n* adeptness, adroitness, artfulness, cleverness, craft, delicacy, diplomacy, discretion, polish, quickness, skill, sophistication, subtlety, tact; artifice, bluff, feint, manoeuvre, ruse, stratagem, trick, wile

finger *v* feel, fiddle with, handle, manipulate, maul, meddle with, play about with touch, toy with

finish *v* accomplish, achieve, bring to a close, carry through, cease, close, complete, conclude, culminate, deal with, discharge, do, end, execute, finalize, fulfil, get done, get out of the way, make short work of, put the finishing touches to, round off, stop, terminate, wrap up; elaborate, perfect, polish, refine; coat, face, gild, lacquer, polish, smooth off, stain, texture, veneer, wax; **finish off** administer, annihi late, best, bring down, defeat, destroy, dispose of, drive to the wall, exterminate, get rid of, kill, overcome, overpower, put an end to, ruin, worst

finish *n* cessation, close, closing,

completion conclusion, culmination, end, ending, finale, last stage, termination, winding up; annihilation, bankruptcy, death, defeat, end, end of the road, liquidation, ruin; cultivation, culture, elaboration, perfection, polish, refinement; appearance, grain, lustre, patina, polish, shine, smoothness, surface, texture

finite *adj* bounded, circumscribed, conditioned, delimited, demarcated, limited, restricted, subject to limitations, terminable

fire *n* blaze, combustion, conflagra tion, flames, inferno; barrage, bombardment, cannonade, flak, fusillade, hail, salvo, shelling, sniping, volley; **on fire** ablaze, aflame, alight, blaz ing, burning, fiery, flaming, in flames; ardent, eager, enthusiastic, excited, inspired, passionate

fire *v* enkindle, ignite, kindle, light, put a match to, set ablaze, set aflame, set alight, set fire to, set on fire; detonate, discharge, eject, explode, hurl, launch, let off, loose, pull the trigger, set off, shell shoot, touch off

firm *adj* close-grained, compact, compressed, concentrate, congealed, dense, hard, inelastic, inflexible, jelled, jellified, rigid, set, solid, solidified, stiff, unyielding; anchored, braced, cemented, embedded, fast, fastened, fixed, immovable, motionless, rivetted, robust, rooted, secure, secured, stable, stationary, steady, strong, sturdy, taut, tight, unfluctuating, unmoving, unshakable; adamant, constant, definite, fixed, inflexible, obdurate, resolute, resolved, set on, settled, staunch, steadfast, strict, true, unalterable, unbending, unfaltering, unflinching, unshakable, unshaken, unswerving, unwavering, unyielding

firm *n* association, business, company, concern, conglomerate, corporation, enterprise, house, organization, outfit, partnership

firmly *adv* enduringly, immovably, like a rock, motionlessly, securely, steadily, tightly, unflinchingly, unshakably; determinedly, resolutely, staunchly, steadfastly, strictly, through thick and thin, unchangeably, unwaveringly, with a rod of iron, with decision

firmness *n* compactness, density, fixedness, hardness, inelasticity, inflexibility, resistance, rigidity, solidity, stiffness; immovability, soundness, stability, steadiness, strength, tautness, tensile strength, tension, tightness; constancy, fixedness, fixity of purpose, inflexibility, obduracy, resolution, resolve, staunchness, steadfastness, strength of will, strictness

first *adj* chief, foremost, head, highest, leading, pre-eminent, prime, principal, ruling; earliest, initial, introductory, maiden, opening, original, premier, primeval, primitive, primordial, pristine; basic, cardinal, elementary, fundamental, key, primary, rudimentary

first *adv* at the beginning, at the outset, before all else, beforehand, firstly, initially, in the first place, to begin with, to start with

first-rate *adj* admirable, elite, excellent, exceptional, exclusive, first class, outstanding, prime, second to none, superb, superlative, tiptop, top; (*Inf*) topnotch, tops

fissure *n* breach, break, chink, cleavage, cleft, crack, cranny, crevice, fault, fracture, gap, hole, interstice, opening, rent, rift, rupture, slit, split

fit *adj* able, adapted, adequate, appropriate, apt, becoming, capable, competent, convenient, correct, deserving, equipped, expedient, fitted, fitting, good enough, prepared, proper, qualified, ready, right seemly, suitable, trained, well-suited, worthy; able bodied, hale, healthy, in good condition, in good shape, in good trim, robust, strapping, toned up, trim, well

fit *v* accord, agree, be consonant, belong, concur, conform, correspond, go interlock, join, match, meet, suit, tally; adapt, adjust, alter, arrange, dispose, fashion, modify, place, position, shape

fitful *adj* broken, desultory, disturbed, erratic, flickering, fluctuating, haphazard, impulsive, intermittent, irregular, spasmodic, sporadic, unstable, variable

fitness *n* adaptation, applicability, appropriateness, aptness, competence, eligibility, pertinence, preparedness, propriety, qualifications, readiness, seemliness, suitability; good condition, good health, health, robustness, strength, vigour

fitting *adj* appropriate, becoming, correct, decent, decorous, desirable, proper, right, seemly, suitable

fitting *n* accessory, attachment, component, connection, part, piece, unit

fix *v* anchor, embed, establish, implant, install, locate, place, plant, position, root, set, settle; attach, bind, cement, connect, couple, fasten, glue, link, make fast, pin, secure, stick, tie; agree on, appoint, arrange, arrive at, conclude, decide, define, determine, establish, limit, name, resolve, set, settle, specify

fix *n* difficult situation, difficulty, dilemma, embarrassment, mess, plight, predicament, quandary, tick lish situation; (*Inf*) bind, hole, jam, pickle, scrape, spot

fixed *adj* anchored, attached, established, immovable, made fast, permanent, rigid, rooted, secure, set; agreed, arranged, decided, definite, established, planned, resolved, settled

fix up *v* agree on, arrange, fix, organize, plan, settle, sort out

flabbergast *v* amaze, astonish, astound, bowl over, confound, daze, disconcert, dumbfound, non-plus, overcome, overwhelm, render, speechless, speechless, staggered, strick dumb, stun

flag *v* abate, decline, die, droop, ebb, fade, fail, faint, fall, fall off, feel the pace, languish, peter out, pine, sag, sink, slump, succumb, taper off, wane, weaken, weary, wilt

flag *n* banderole, banner, colours, ensign, gonfalon, jack, pennant, pennon, standard, streamer

flagrant *adj* arrant, atrocious, awful, barefaced, blatant, bold, brazen, crying, dreadful, egregious, enormous, flagitious, flaunting, glaring, heinous, immodest, infamous, notorious, open, ostentatious, out-and-out, outrageous, scandalous, shameless, undisguised

flail *v* beat, thrash, thresh, windmill

flair *n* ability, accomplishment, aptitude, faculty, feel, genius, gift, knack, mastery, talent; chic, dash, discernment, elegance, panache, style, stylishnesss, taste

flamboyant *adj* baroque, elaborate, extravagant, florid, ornate, ostentatious, over the top, rich, rococo, showy, theatrical; brilliant, colourful, dashing, dazzling, exciting, glamorous, swashbuckling

flame *v* blaze, burn, flare, flash, glare, glow, shine, sparkle

flame *n* blaze, conflagration; brightness, gleam, glow; fire, light; affection, ardour, eagerness, enthusiasm, fervency, fervour, fire, intensity, keenness, passion, warmth; beau, beloved, boyfriend, girlfriend, lover, partner, sweetheart

flaming *adj* ablaze, afire, blazing, brilliant, burning, fiery, glowing, ignited, in flames, raging, red, red-hot; angry, ardent, aroused, frenzied, hot, impassioned, intense, raging, scintillating, vehement, vivid

flank *n* haunch, loin, quarter, thigh; side, wing

flank *v* be situated along, border, bound, edge, fringe, skirt

flannel *n* blarney, evasion, equivocation, flattery, nonsense, rubbish; (*Inf*) baloney, rot, sweet talk, waffle

flannel *v* be evasive, equivocate, hedge, prevaricate, talk blarney, use flattery; (*Inf*) butter up, soft-soap

flap *v* agitate, beat, flail, flutter, shake, swing, swish, thrash, thresh, vibrate, wag, wave

flap *n* apron, cover, fly, fold, lapel, lappet, overlap, skirt, tab, tail

flare *v* blaze, burn up, dazzle, flicker, flutter, glare, waver

flash *v* blaze, coruscate, flare, flicker, glare, gleam, glint, glisten, glitter, light, scintillate, shimmer, sparkle, twinkle; bolt, dart, dash, fly, race, shoot, speed, sprint, streak, sweep, whistle, zoom

flash *n* blaze, burst, coruscation, dazzle, flare, flicker, gleam, ray, scintillation, shaft, shimmer, spark, sparkle, streak, twinkle; instant, jiffy, moment, second, shake, split second, trice, twinkling, twinkling of an eye; instant, jiffy, moment, second, shake, split second, trice, twinkling, twinkling of an eye

flashy *adj* cheap, cheap and nasty, flamboyant, flaunting, garish, gaudy, glittery, glitzy, in poor taste, jazzy, loud, meretricious, ostentatious, showy, tasteless, tawdry, tinselly

flat *adj* even, horizontal, level, levelled, low, planar, plane, smooth, unbroken, laid low, lying full length, outstretched, prostrate, reclining, recumbent, supine; boring, dead, dull, flavourless, insipid, jejune, lacklustre, lifeless, monotonous, pointless, prosaic, spiritless, stale, tedious, uninteresting, vapid, watery, weak

flat *n* apartment, rooms; (*Inf*) pad

flatness *n* evenness, horizontality, levelness, smoothness, uniformity; dullness, emptiness, insipidity, monotony, staleness, tedium, vapidity

flatten *v* compress, even out, iron out, level, plaster, raze, roll, smooth off, squash, trample

flatter *v* blandish, butter up, cajole, compliment, court, fawn, flannel, humour, inveigle, lay it on thick, praise, puff, softsoap, sweet-talk, wheedle

flattering *adj* adulatory, complimentary, fawning, fulsome, gratifying, honeyed, honey-tongued, ingratiating, laudatory, sugary

flattery *n* adulation, blandishment, blarney, cajolery, false praise, fawning, fulsomeness, honeyed words, obsequiousness, servility, sycophancy, toadyism

flavour *n* aroma, essence, extract, flavouring, odour, piquancy, relish, savour, seasoning, smack, tang, taste, zest, zing

flavour *v* ginger up, imbue, infuse, lace, leaven, season, spice

flaw *n* blemish, defect, disfigure ment, failing, fault, imperfection, speck, spot, weakness, weak spot; breach, break, cleft, crack, crevice, fissure, fracture, rent, rift, scission, split, tear

flawed *adj* blemished, broken, chipped, cracked, damaged, defective, erroneous, faulty, imperfect, unsound

fleck *n* mark, speckle, spot

fleck *v* dot, mark, mottle, freckle, speckle, sprinkle, streak

flee *v* abscond, avoid, beat a hasty retreat, bolt, cut and run, decamp, depart, escape, fly, get away, leave, make a quick exit, make off, make oneself scarce, make one's escape, make one's getaway, run away, scarper, take flight, take to one's heels, vanish

fleet *n* argosy, armada, flotilla, naval force, navy, sea power, squadron, task force, vessels, warships

fleet *adj* fast, like the wind, nimble, quick, speedy, swift-footed

fleeting *adj* brief, ephemeral, evanescent, flitting, flying, fugacious, fugitive, here today gone tomorrow, momentary, passing, short, short-lived, temporary, transient, transitory

flesh *n* body, brawn, fat, fatness, food, meat, tissue, weight; animality, body, human nature, physicality, physical, nature, sensuality

flexible *adj* bendable, ductile, elastic, limber, lithe, mouldable, plastic, pliable, pliant, springy, stretchy, supple, tensile, whippy, willowy, yielding; adaptable, adjustable, discretionary, open, variable; amenable, biddable, complaisant, compliant, docile, gentle, manageable, responsive, tractable

flexibility *n* adaptability, adjustability, complaisance, elasticity, pliability, pliancy, resilience, springiness, tensility

flicker *v* blink, flare, flash, flutter, glimmer, glint, glitter, quiver, sparkle, twinkle, vibrate, waver,

flight *n* flying, mounting, soaring, winging; journey, trip, voyage; bevy, cloud, covey, flock, formation, skein, squadron, swarm, unit, wing; migration; absconding, departure, escape, exit, exodus, fleeing, departure, getaway, retreat, running away; aviation, aerial navigation; aeronautics; journey, shuttle; (*Inf*) plane trip; flight of stairs, staircase, stairs

flimsy *adj* delicate, fragile, frail, insubstantial, make-shift, rickety, shaky, shallow, slight, superficial, unsubstantial; feeble, frivolous, implausible, inadequate, poor, thin, transparent, trivial, unconvincing, unsatisfactory, weak

flinch *v* baulk, blench, cower, cringe, draw back, duck, flee, quail, recoil, retreat, shirk, shrink, shy away, start, swerve, wince, withdraw

fling *v* cast, catapult, heave, hurl, jerk, let fly, pitch, precipitate, propel, send, shy, sling, throw, toss

flippant *adj* cheeky, disrespectful, frivolous, glib, impertinent, impudent, irreverent, offhand, pert, rude, saucy, superficial

flirt *v* chat up, coquet, dally, lead on, make advances, make eyes at, philander

flirt *n* coquette, heart-breaker, philanderer, tease, trifler, wanton

float *v* be on the surface, lie on the surface, be buoyant, displace water, hang, hover, poise, rest on water, stay afloat; bob, drift, glide, move gently, sail, slide, slip along; get going, launch, promote, push off, set up

floating *adj* afloat, buoyant, buoyed up, nonsubmersible, ocean-going, sailing, swimming, unsinkable; fluctuating, free, migratory, mov able, unattached, uncommitted, unfixed, variable, wandering

flock *v* collect, congregate, converge, crowd, gather, group, herd, huddle, mass, throng, troop

flock *n* colony, drone, flight, gaggle, herd, skein; assembly, bevy, collection, company, congregation, convoy, crowd, gathering, group, herd, host, mass, multitude, throng

flog *v* beat, castigate, chastise, flagellate, flay, lash, scourge, thrash, trounce, whack, whip; dive, oppress, overexert, overtax, overwork, punish, push, strain, tax

flood *v* brim over, deluge, drown, immerse, inundate, overflow, pour over, submerge, swamp; engulf, flow, gush, overwhelm, rush, surge, swarm, sweep; choke, fill, glut, oversupply, saturate

flood *n* deluge, downpour, flash flood, freshet, inundation, overflow, spate, tide, torrent; abundance, flow, glut, multitude, outpouring, profusion, rush, stream, torrent

floor *n* deck, level, stage, storey, tier

floor *v* fell, ground, knock down, prostrate; baffle, beat, bewilder, bowl over, bring up short, confound, conquer, defeat, discomfit, disconcert, dumbfound, knock down, nonplus, overthrow, perplex, prostrate, puzzle, stump; (*Inf*) throw

flop *v* dangle, droop, sag; fail, fall flat, founder, go down like a lead balloon, miss the mark

flop *n* debacle, disaster, failure, fiasco, loser; (*Inf*) dud, lemon, no-hoper, washout

florid *adj* blowzy, flushed, high-coloured, rubicund, ruddy; baroque, busy, embellished, euphuistic, figurative, flamboyant, flowery, fussy, grandiloquent, high-flown, ornate,

overelaborate, purple, verbose
flounder *v* be in the dark, blunder, fumble, grope, muddle, plunge, struggle, stumble, thrash, toss, tumble, wallow
flourish *v* bear fruit, be in one's prime, be successful, be vigorous, bloom, blossom, boom, burgeon, develop, do well, flower, get ahead, get on, go up in the world, grow, grow fat, increase, prosper, succeed, thrive
flourish *n* brandishing, dash, display, fanfare, parade, shaking, show, showy, gesture, twirling, wave
flourishing *adj* blooming, burgeoning, doing well, going strong, in the pink, in top form, lush, luxuriant, mushrooming, on the up, prospering, rampant, successful, thriving
flow *v* circulate, course, glide, gush, move, pour, purl, ripple, roll, run, rush, slide, surge, sweep, swirl, whirl
flower *n* bloom, blossom, efflorescence; best, choicest part, cream, elite, freshness, greatest point, height, pick, vigour
flower *v* bloom, blossom, blow, burgeon, effloresce, flourish, mature, open, unfold
flowery *adj* baroque, embellished, euphuistic, fancy, figurative, florid, high-flown, ornate, overwrought, rhetorical
flowing *adj* continuous, cursive, easy, fluent, smooth, unbroken, uninterrupted
fluctuate *v* alter, alternate, change, ebb and flow, go up and down, hesitate, oscillate, rise and fall, seesaw, shift, swing, undulate, vacillate, vary, veer, waver
fluency *n* articulateness, assurance, command, control, ease, facility, glibness, readiness, slickness, smoothness, volubility
fluent *adj* articulate, easy, effortless, facile, flowing, glib, natural, ready, smooth, smooth-spoken, voluble, well-versed
fluid *adj* aqueous, flowing, in solution, liquefied, liquid, melted, molten, running, runny, watery; adaptable, adjustable, changeable, flexible, floating, fluctuating, indefinite, mercurial, mobile, mutable, protean, shifting
fluid *n* liquid, liquor, solution
flurry *n* ado, agitation, bustle, commotion, disturbance, excite ment, ferment, flap, fluster, flutter, furore, fuss, hurry, stir, to-do, tumult, whirl
flush *v* blush, burn, colour, colour up, crimson, flame, glow, go red, redden, suffuse
flush *n* bloom, blush, colour, freshness, glow, redness, rosiness
flush *adj* even, flat, level, plane, square, true; abundant, affluent, full, generous, lavish, liberal, overflowing, prodigal
flush *adv* even with, hard against, in contact with, level with, squarely, touching
fluster *v* agitate, bother, bustle, confound, confuse, disturb, excite, flurry, heat, hurry, make nervous, perturb, ruffle, throw off balance, upset; (*Inf*) hassle, rattle
fluster *n* agitation, bustle, commotion, disturbance, dither, flurry, flutter, furore, perturbation, ruffle,

turmoil; (*Inf*) flap, state

flutter *v* agitate, bat, beat, flap, flicker, flit, flitter, fluctuate, hover, palpitate, quiver, ripple, ruffle, shiver, tremble, vibrate, waver

flutter *n* palpitation, quiver, quiver ing, shiver, shudder, tremble, tremor, twitching, vibration

fly *v* flit, flutter, hover, mount, sail, soar, take to the air, take wing, wing; aviate, be at the controls, control, manoeuvre, operate, pilot; display, flap, float, flutter, show, wave; elapse, flit, glide, pass, pass swiftly, roll on, run its course, slip away; bolt, career, dart, dash, hasten, hurry, race, rush, scamper, scoot, shoot, speed, sprint, tear, whiz (*Inf*) be off like a shot, zoom

flying *adj* brief, fleeting, fugacious, hasty, hurried, rushed, short-lived, transitory; express, fast, fleet, mercurial, mobile, rapid, speedy, winged

foam *n* bubbles, froth, head, lather, spray, spume, suds

foam *v* boil, bubble, effervesce, fizz, froth, lather

focus *n* bull's eye, centre, centre of activity, centre of attraction, core, cynosure, focal point, headquarters, heart, hub, meeting place, target

foe *n* adversary, antagonist, enemy, foeman, opponent, rival

fog *n* gloom, miasma, mist, murk, murkiness, smog; (*Inf*) peasouper

foggy *adj* blurred, brumous, cloudy, dim, grey, hazy, indistinct, misty, murky, nebulous, obscure, smoggy, soupy, vaporous

foil *v* baffle, balk, check, checkmate, circumvent, counter, defeat, disappoint, elude, frustrate, nip in the bud, nullify, outwit, put a spoke in someone's wheel, stop, thwart

foil *n* antithesis, background, complement, contrast, setting, striking difference

foil *v* baffle, baulk, check, checkmate, counter, frustrate, thwart

fold *v* bend, crease, crumple, dog-ear, double, double over, gather, intertwine, overlap, pleat, tuck, turn under

fold *n* bend, crease, double thick ness, folded, portion, furrow, knife-edge, layer, overlap, pleat, turn, wrinkle

fold *v* do up, enclose, enfold, entwine, envelop, wrap, wrap up

folder *n* binder, envelope, file, portfolio

folk *n* clan, ethnic group, family, kin, kindred, people, race, tribe

follow *v* come after, come next, step into the shoes of, succeed, supersede, supplant, take the place of; chase, dog, hound, hunt, pursue, run after, shadow, stalk, tail, track, trail; act in accordance with, be guided by, comply, conform, give allegiance to, heed, mind, note, obey, observe, regard, watch

follower *n* adherent, admirer, apostle, backer, believer, convert, devotee, disciple, fan, fancier, habitué, partisan, pupil, representative, supporter, votary, worshipper

following *adj* coming, consequent, consequential, ensuing, later, next, specified, subsequent, succeeding, successive

folly *n* absurdity, daftness, fatuity, foolishness, idiocy, imbecility, imprudence, indiscretion, irrationality, lunacy, madness, nonsense, preposterousness, rashness, recklessness, silliness, stupidity

fond *adj* adoring, affectionate, amorous, caring, devoted, doting, indulgent, loving, tender, warm

fondle *v* caress, cuddle, dandle, pat, pet, stroke

fondly *adv* affectionately, dearly, indulgently, lovingly, possessively, tenderly, with affection

fondness *n* attachment, fancy, liking, love, partiality, penchant, predilection, preference, soft spot, susceptibility, taste, weakness

food *n* aliment, board, bread, chow, comestible, commons, cooking, cuisine, diet, eatables, edibles, fare, foodstuffs, larder, meat, menu, nourishment, nutriment, nutrition, provender, provisions, rations, refreshment, stores, subsistence, sustenance, table, viands, victuals

fool *n* ass, blockhead, dunce, halfwit, idiot, ignoramus, illiterate, jackass, loon, mooncalf, moron, nincompoop, ninny, nitwit, numskull, silly, simpleton; buffoon, clown, comic, harlequin, jester, motley, pierrot, punchinello; (*Inf*) dimwit, imbecile, twit

fool *v* bamboozle, beguile, bluff, cheat, deceive, delude, dupe, hoax, hoodwink, make a fool of, mislead play a trick on, put one over on, take in, trick; act the fool, cut capers, feign, jest, joke, make believe, pretend, tease

foolhardy *adj* adventurous, bold, hotheaded, impetuous, imprudent, incautious, irresponsible, madcap, precipitate, rash, reckless, temerarious, venturesome, venturous

foolish *adj* absurd, ill-advised, ill-considered, ill-judged, imprudent, incautious, indiscreet, injudicious, nonsensical, senseless, short-sighted, silly, unintelligent, unreasonable, unwise; brainless, crazy, doltish, fatuous, half-witted, harebrained, idiotic, imbecilic, ludicrous, mad, moronic, ridiculous, senseless, silly, simple, stupid, weak, witless

foolishly *adv* absurdly, idiotically, ill-advisedly, imprudently, incautiously, indiscreetly, injudiciously, like a fool mistakenly, short-sightedly, stupidly, unwisely, without due consideration

foolishness *n* absurdity, folly, imprudence, inanity, indiscretion, irresponsibility, silliness, stupidity, weakness

foolproof *adj* certain, guaranteed, infallible, never-failing, safe, unas sailable, unbreakable; (*Inf*) sure-fire

footing *n* basis, establishment, foothold, foundation, ground, groundwork, installation, settlement

footstep *n* footfall, step, tread; footmark, footprint, trace, track

forage *n for cattle* feed, fodder, food, foodstuffs, herbage, pasturage, provender; assault, foray, incursion, invasion, plundering, raid, ravaging

forbear *v* abstain, avoid, cease, decline, desist, eschew, hold back, keep from, omit, pause, refrain, resist the temptation to, restrain oneself, stop, withhold

forebearance *n* indulgence, leniency,

lenity, long-suffering, merciful, mild, moderate, patient, tolerant

forbid *v* ban, debar, disallow, exclude, hinder, inhibit, interdict, outlaw, preclude prohibit, proscribe, rule out, veto

forbidden *adj* banned, outlawed, out of bounds, prohibited, proscribed, taboo, verboten, vetoed

force *n* dynamism, energy, impact, impulse, life, might, momentum, muscle, potency, power, pressure, stimulus, strength, stress, vigour; coercion, compulsion, constraint, duress, enforcement, pressure, violence; (*Inf*) arm-twisting; cogency, effect, effectiveness, efficacy, influence, persuasiveness, power, strength, validity, weight; (*Inf*) bite, drive, emphasis, fierceness, intensity, persistence, vehemence, vigour

force *v* bring pressure to bear upon, coerce, compel, constrain, drive, impel, impose, make, necessitate, obligate, oblige, overcome, press, press-gang, pressure, pressurize, urge; (*Inf*) strong-arm; blast, break, open, prise, propel, push, thrust, use violence on, wrench, wrest; drag, exact, extort, wring

forced *adj* compulsory, conscripted, enforced, involuntary, mandatory, obligatory, slave, unwilling; affected, artificial, contrived, false, insincere, laboured, stiff, strained, unnatural, wooden

forceful *n* cogent, compelling, convincing, dynamic, effective, persuasive, pithy, potent, powerful, telling, vigorous, weighty

forcible *adj* active, cogent, compelling, effective, efficient, energetic, forceful, impressive, mighty, potent, powerful, strong, telling, valid, weighty

forbear *v* ancestor, father, forefather, forerunner, predecessor, progenitor

foreboding *n* anxiety, apprehension, apprehensiveness, chill, dread, fear, misgiving, premonition, presentiment

forecast *v* anticipate, augur, calculate, divine, estimate, foresee, foretell, plan, predict, prognosticate, prophesy

forecast *n* anticipation, conjecture, foresight, forethought, guess, out look, planning, prediction, prognosis, projection, prophecy

forefather *n* ancestor, father, forebear, forerunner, predecessor, primogenitor, procreator, progenitor

foregoing *adj* above, antecedent, anterior, former, preceding, previous, prior

foreign *adj* alien, borrowed, distant, exotic, external, imported, outlandish, outside, overseas, remote, strange, unfamiliar, unknown

foreigner *n* alien, immigrant, incomer, newcomer, outlander, stranger

foremost *adj* chief, first, front, headmost, highest, inaugural, initial, leading, paramount, pre-eminent, primary, prime, principal, supreme

forerunner *n* ancestor, announcer, envoy, forebear, foregoer, harbinger, herald, precursor, predecessor, progenitor, prototype

foresee *v* anticipate, divine, envisage, forebode, forecast, foretell, predict, prophesy

foreshadow *v* adumbrate, augur, betoken, bode, forebode, imply, indicate, portend, predict, prefigure, presage, promise, prophesy, signal

foresight *n* anticipation, care, caution, circumspection, farsighted ness, forethought, precaution, premeditation, preparedness, prescience, prevision, provision, prudence

foretell *v* adumbrate, augur, bode, forebode, forecast, foreshadow, foreshow, forewarn, portend, predict, presage, prognosticate, prophesy, signify, soothsay

forethought *n* anticipation, farsightedness, foresight, precaution, providence, provision, prudence

forewarn *v* admonish, advise, alert, apprise, caution, dissuade, give fair warning, put on guard, put on the qui vive, tip off

forfeit *n* amercement, damages, fine, forfeiture, loss, mulct, penalty

forfeit *v* be deprived of, be stripped of, give up, lose, relinquish, renounce, surrender

forge *v* coin, copy, counterfeit, fake, falsify, feign, imitate

forget *v* leave behind, lose sight of, omit, overlook

forgive *v* absolve, accept some one's apology, acquit, bear no malice, condone, excuse, exonerate, let bygones be bygones, pardon, remit

forgiving *adj* clement, compassionate, forbearing, humane, lenient, magnanimous, merciful, mild, soft-hearted, tolerant

forgo *v* abandon, abjure, cede, do without, give up, leave alone, relinquish, renounce, resign, sacrifice, surrender, waive, yield

forgotten *adj* blotted out, buried, bygone, consigned to oblivion, left behind, left out, lost, obliterated, omitted, past, past recall unremembered

forlorn *adj* abandoned, bereft, cheer less, comfortless, deserted, desolate, destitute, disconsolate, forgotten, forsaken, friendless, helpless, homeless, hopeless, lonely, lost, miserable, pathetic, pitiable, pitiful, unhappy, woebegone, wretched

form *v* assemble, bring about, build, concoct, construct, contrive, create, devise, establish, fabricate, fashion, forge, found, invent, make, manufacture, model, mould, pro duce, put together, set up, shape; arrange, combine, design, dispose, draw up, frame, organize, pattern, plan, think up

form *n* appearance, cast, configuration, construction, cut, fashion, formation, model, mould, pattern, shape, structure; format, framework, harmony, order, orderliness, organization, plan, proportion, structure, symmetry; application, document, paper, sheet

formal *adj* approved, ceremonial, explicit, express, fixed, lawful, legal, methodical, official, pre scribed, regular, rigid, ritualistic, set, solemn, strict

formality *n* ceremony, convention, conventionality, custom, form, gesture, matter of form, procedure, red tape, rite, ritual; ceremonious ness, correctness, decorum, etiquette, politesse, protocol, punctilio

formation *n* accumulation, compilation, composition, constitution, crystallization, development, establishment, evolution, forming, generation, genesis, manufacture, organization, production; arrangement, configuration, design, disposition, figure, grouping, patter, rank, structure

former *adj* ancient, bygone, departed, long ago, long gone, of yore, old, old-time, past; above, aforementioned, aforesaid, first mentioned, foregoing, preceding

formerly *adv* already, at one time, before, heretofore, lately, once, previously

formidable *adj* appaling, dangerous, daunting, dismaying, dreadful, fearful, frightful, horrible, intimidating, menacing, shocking, terrifying, threatening; arduous, challenging, colossal, difficult, mammoth, onerous, overwhelming, staggering, toilsome

formula *n* form of words, formulary, rite, ritual, rubric; blueprint, method, modus, operandi, precept, prescription, principle, procedure, recipe, rule, way

formulate *v* codify, define, detail, express, frame, give form to, particularize, set down, specify, systematize

forsake *v* abandon, cast off, desert, disown, jettison, jilt, leave, leave in the lurch, quit, repudiate, throw over

forsaken *adj* abandoned, cast off, deserted, destitute, disowned, for lorn, friendless, ignored, isolated, jilted, left behind, left in the lurch, lonely, marooned, outcast, solitary

fort *n* blockhouse, cam, castle, citadel, fastness, fortification, fortress, garrison, redoubt, station, stronghold

forth *adv* ahead, away, forward, into the open, onward, out, out of concealment, outward

forthcoming *adj* approaching, coming, expected, future, imminent, impending, prospective; chatty, communicative, expansive, free, informative, open, sociable, talkative, unreserved

forthright *adj* above-board, blunt, candid, direct, frank, open, outspoken, plain-spoken, straightforward, straight from the shoulder

forthwith *adv* at once, directly, immediately, instantly, quickly, right away, straightaway, without delay

fortification *n* bastion, bulwark, castle, citadel, defence, fastness, fort, fortress, keep, protection, stronghold

fortify *v* brace, cheer, confirm, embolden, encourage, hearten, invigorate, reassure, stiffen, strengthen, sustain

fortress *n* castle, citadel, fastness, fort, redoubt, stronghold

fortunate *adj* born with a silver spoon in one's mouth, bright, favoured, golden, happy, having, a charmed life, in luck, lucky, prosperous, rosy, sitting pretty, success ful, well-off

fortunately *adv* by a happy chance, by good luck, happily, luckily providentially

fortune *n* affluence, gold mine, opulence, possessions, property, prosperity, riches, treasure, wealth; accident, chance, contingency, destiny, fate, fortuity, luck, . providence

forward *adj* advanced, advancing, early, forward-looking, onward, precocious, premature, progressive, well-developed

forward *adv* ahead, forth,on, onward

forwar *v* advance, aid, assist, back, encourage, expedite, favour, foster, further, hasten, help, hurry, promote, speed, support

foster *v* cultivate, encourage, feed, foment, nurture, promote, stimulate, support, uphold, bring up, mother, nurse, raise, rear, take care of; accommodate, cherish, entertain, harbour, nourish, sustain

foul *adj* contaminated, dirty, disgusting, fetid, filthy, grotty, impure, loathsome, malodorous, mephitic, nasty, nauseating, noisome, offensive, polluted, putrid, rank, repulsive, revolting, rotten, squalid, stinking, sullied, tainted, unclean; bad, blustery, disagreeable, foggy, murky rainy, rough, stormy, wet, wild

foul *v* begrime, besmear, besmirch, contaminate, defile, dirty, pollute, smear, soil, stain, sully, taint

found *v* bring into being, constitute, construct, create, endow, erect, establish, fix, inaugurate, institute, organize, originate, plant, raise, settle, set up, start

foundation *n* base, basis, bedrock, bottom, footing, groundwork, substructure, underpinning; endowment, establishment, inauguration, institution organization, setting up, settlement

founder *n* architect, author, beginner, benefactor, builder, constructor, designer, establisher, father, framer, generator, initiator, institutor, inventor, maker, organizer, originator, patriarch

founder *v* be lost, go down, go to the bottom, sink, submerge

fountain *n* font, fount, jet, reservoir, spout, spray, spring, well

foyer *n* antechamber, anteroom, entrance hall, lobby, reception, area, vestibule

fracas *n* affray, aggro, brawl, disturbance, donnybrook, fight, free-for-all, melee, quarrel, riot, row, rumpus, scrimmage, scuffle, trouble, uproar

fractious *adj* awkward, captious, crabby, cross, fretful, froward, irritable, peevish, pettish, petulant, querulous, recalcitrant, refractory, testy, touchy, unruly

fracture *n* breach, break, cleft, crack, fissure, gap, opening, rent, rift, rupture, schism, split

fracture *v* break, crack, rupture, splinter, split

fragile *adj* breakable, brittle, dainty, delicate, feeble, fine, flimsy, frail, frangible, infirm, slight, weak

fragment *n* bit, chip, fraction, morsel, part, particle, piece, portion, remnant, scrap, shiver, sliver

fragmentary *adj* bitty, broken, disconnected, discrete, disjointed, incoherent, incomplete, partial, piecemeal, scattered, scrappy, sketchy, unsystematic

fragrance *n* aroma, balm, bouquet, fragrancy, perfume, redolence, scent, smell, sweet odour

fragrant *n* ambrosial, aromatic, balmy, odoriferous, odorous, perfumed, redolent, sweet-scented, sweet-smelling

frail *adj* breakable, brittle, decrepit, delicate, feeble, flimsy, fragile, frangible, infirm, insubstantial, puny, slight, tender, unsound, vulnerable, weak wispy

frailty *n* fallibility, feebleness, frailness, infirmity, peccability, puniness, susceptibility, weakness

frame *v* assemble, build, constitute, construct, fabricate, fashion, forge, form, institute, invent, make, manufacture, model, mould, put together, set up; block out, compose, conceive, concoct, contrive, cook up, devise, draft, draw up, form, formulate, hatch, map out, plan, shape, sketch; case, enclose, mount, surround

frame *n* casing, construction, fabric, form, framework, scheme, shell, structure, system; anatomy, body, build, carcass, morphology, physique, skeleton; mount, mounting, setting

framework *n* core, fabric, foundation, frame, form of reference, groundwork, plan, schema, shell, skeleton, structure, the bare bones

frank *adj* artless, blunt, candid, direct, downright, forthright, free, honest, ingenuous, open, outright, outspoken, plain, plain-spoken, sincere, straightforward, straight from the shoulder, transparent, truthful, unconcealed, undisguised, unreserved, unrestricted

frantic *adj* berserk, beside oneself, distracted, distraught, fraught, frenetic, frenzied, furious, hectic, mad, overwrought, raging, raving, uptight, wild

fraternity *n* association, brotherhood, camaraderie, circle, clan, club, companionship, company, comradeship, fellowship, guild, kinship, league, set, union

fraud *n* artifice, cheat, chicane, chicanery, craft, deceit, deception, duplicity, guile, hoax, humbug, imposture, sharp practice, spurious ness, stratagems, swindling, treachery, trickery; bluffer, charlatan, cheat, counterfeit, double-dealer, fake, forgery, hoax, hoaxer, impostor, mountebank, pretender, quack, sham, swindler

fraudulent *adj* counterfeit, crafty, criminal, deceitful, deceptive, dishonest, double-dealing, duplicitous, false, knavish, sham, spurious, swindling, treacherous

fray *v* become threadbare, chafe, fret, rub, wear, wear away, wear thin

freak *n* aberration abnormality abortion, anomaly, grotesque, malformation, monster, monstrosity, mutant, oddity, sport, teratism, wierdo

freak *adj* aberrant, abnormal, atypical, bizarre, erratic, exceptional, fortuitous, odd, queer, unaccountable, unexpected, unforeseen, unparalleled, unpredictable, unusual

free *adj* complimentary, for free, for nothing, free of charge, gratis, gratuitous, on the house, unpaid, without charge; at large, at liberty, footloose, independent, liberated, loose, off the hook, on the loose, uncommitted, unconstrained, unen gaged, unfettered, unrestrained; able, allowed, clear, disengaged, lose, open, permitted, unattached, unengaged, unhampered, unimpeded, unobstructed, unregulated, unrestricted; **free of** above, beyond, deficient in, devoid of, exempt from, immune to, not liable to, safe from, unaffected by, unencumbered by, untouched by, without; autarchic, autonomous, democratic, emancipated, independent, self-governing, self-ruling, sovereign; at leisure available, empty, extra, idle, not tied down, spare, unemployed, uninhabited, unoccupied, unused, vacant; big, bounteous, bountiful, charitable, eager, generous, hospitable, lavish, liberal, munificent, open-handed, prodigal, unsparing, unstinting, willing; **free and easy** casual, easy-going, informal, laid-back, lenient, liberal, relaxed, toler ant, unceremonious

free *adv* at no cost, for love, gratis, without charge; abundantly, copiously, freely, idly, loosely

free *v* deliver, discharge, disenthrall, emancipate, let go, loose, release, set at liberty, set free, uncage, unfetter, unleash, untie; clear, cut loose, deliver, disengage, disentangle exempt, extricate, ransom, redeem, relieve, rescue, rid, unburden, undo, unshackle

freedom *n* autonomy, deliverance, emancipation, home rule, independence, liberty, manumission, release, self-government;exemption, immunity, impunity, privilege; ability, carte blanche, discretion, elbowroom, facility, flexibility, free rein, latitude, leeway licence, opportunity, play, power, range, scope

freely *adv* of one's own accord, of one's own free will, spontaneously, voluntarily, willingly, without prompting; candidly, frankly, openly, plainly, unreservedly, without, reserve; as you, please, unchallenged, without let, without, restraint; abundantly, amply, bountifully, copiously, extravagantly, lavishly, liberally, like water, open-handedly, unstintingly, with a free hand

freeze *v* benumb, chill, congeal, glaciate, harden, ice over, stiffen; fix, hold up, inhibit, peg, stop, suspend

freezing *adj* arctic, biting, bitter, chill, chilled, cutting, frost-bound, frosty, glacial, icy, numbing, penetrating, polar, raw, siberian, wintry

freight *n* bales, bulk, burden, cargo, consignment, contents, goods, haul, lading, load, merchandise, payload, tonnage

frenzied *adj* agitated, all het up, convulsive, distracted, distraught, excited, feverish, frantic, frenetic, furious, hysterical, mad, maniacal, rabid, uncontrolled, wild

frequent *adj* common, constant, continual, customary, everyday, familiar, habitual, incessant, numerous, persistent, recurrent, recurring, reiterate, repeated, usual

frequent *v* attend, be a regular customer of, be found at, haunt, patronize, resort, visit

frequently *adv* commonly, custom arily, habitually, many a time, many times, much, not infrequently, often, over and over again, repeatedly, thick and fast, very often

fresh *adj* different, latest, modern, modernistic, new, new-fangled, novel, original, recent, this season's, unconventional, unusual, up-to-date; added, additional, auxiliary, extra, further, more, other, renewed, supplementary; bracing, bright, brisk, clean, clear, cool, crisp, invigorating, pure, refreshing, sparkling, stiff, sweet, unpolluted; blooming, clear, fair, florid, glow ing, good, hardy, healthy, rosy, ruddy, wholesome; artless, callow, green, inexperienced, natural, new, raw, uncultivated, untrained, untried, youthful

freshen *v* enliven, freshen up, liven up, refresh, restore, revitalize, rouse, spruce up, titivate

fret *v* affront, agonize, anguish, annoy, brood, chagrin, goad, grieve, harass, irritate, lose sleep over, provoke, ruffle, torment, upset, worry

friction *n* abrasion, attrition, chafing, erosion, fretting, grating, irritation, rasping, resistance, rubbing, scraping, wearing away

friend *n* alter ego, boon companion, bosom friend, companion, comrade, confidant, crony, familiar, intimate, mate, pal, partner, playmate, soulmate

friendliness *adj* affability, amiability, companionability, congeniality, conviviality, geniality, kindliness, mateyness, neighbourliness, open arms, sociability, warmth

friendly *adj* affable, affectionate, amiable, amicable, attached, attentive, auspicious, beneficial, benevolent, benign, chummy, close, clubby, companionable, comradely, conciliatory, confiding, convivial, cordial, familiar, favourable, fond, fraternal, genial, good, helpful, intimate, kind, kindly, matey, neighbourly, on good terms, on visiting, terms, outgoing, peaceable, propitious, receptive, sociable, sympathetic, thick, welcoming, well-disposed

friendship *n* affection, affinity, alliance, amity, attachment, benevolence, closeness, concord, familiarity, fondness, friendliness, good-fellowship, good will, harmony, intimacy, love, rapport, regard

fright *n* alarm, apprehension, cold sweat, consternation dismay, dread, fear, fear and trembling, horror, panic, quaking, scare, shock, terror, the shivers, trepidation

frighten *v* affright, alarm, appal, cow, daunt, dismay, freeze one's blood, intimidate, petrify, scare, scare stiff, scare the living daylights out of someone, shock, startle, terrify, terrorise, throw, into a fright, throw into a panic, unman, unnerve

frightful *adj* alarming, appaling, awful, dire, dread, dreadful, fearful, ghastly, grim, grisly, gruesome, harrowing, hideous, horrendous, horrible, horrid, lurid, macabre, petrifying, shocking, terrible, terrifying, traumatic, unnerving, unspeakable

frigid *adj* arctic, chill, cold, cool, frost-bound, frosty, frozen, gelid, glacial, hyperboreal, icy Siberian, wintry; aloof, austere, cold-hearted, forbidding, formal, icy, lifeless, passionless, passive, repellent, rigid, stiff, unapproachable, unbending, unfeeling, unloving, unresponsive

frills *pl n* additions, affectations, bits and pieces, decorations, dressing up, embellishment, extras, fanciness, fandangles, finery, frilliness, frippery, fuss, mannerisms, nonsense, ornamentation, ostentation, superfluities, tomfoolery, trimmings

fringe *n* binding, border, edging, hem, tassle, trimming; borderline, edge, limits, march, marches, margin, outskirts, perimeter, periphery

frisk *v* bounce, caper, cavort, curvet, dance, frolic, gambol, hop, jump, play, prance, rollick, romp, skip, sport, trip

fritter away *v* dally away, dissipate, fool away, idle, misspend, run through, spend like water, squander, waste

frivolity *n* childishness, flightiness, flippancy, flummery, folly, frivolousness, fun, gaiety, giddiness, jest, levity, light-heartedness, lightness, nonsense, puerility, shallow ness, silliness, superficiality, trifling, triviality

frivolous *adj* childish, dizzy, empty-headed, flighty, flippant, foolish, giddy, idle, ill-considered, juvenile, light-minded, nonserious, puerile, silly, superficial

frolic *v* caper, cavort, cut capers, frisk, gambol, lark, make merry, play, rollick, romp, sport

frolic *n* antic, escapade, gambado, gambol, game, lark, prank, revel, romp, spree; amusement, drollery, fun, fun and games, gaiety, high jinks, merriment, sport; (*Inf*) sky-larking

front *n* anterior, exterior, façade, face, facing, foreground, forepart, frontage, obverse; beginning, fore, forefront, frontline, head, lead, top, van, vanguard; blind, cover, disguise, mask, pretext, show; **in front** ahead, before, first, in advance, in the lead, in the van, leading, preceding, to the fore

front *adj* first, foremost, head, lead, leading, topmost

front *v* face, look over, overlook

frontier *n* borderland, borderline, bound, boundary, confines, edge, limit, marches, perimeter, verge

frosty *adj* chilly, cold, frozen, ice-capped, icicled, icy, rimy, wintry; discouraging, frigid, off-putting, standoffish, unenthusiastic, unfriendly, unwelcoming

frown *v* give a dirty look, glare, glower, knit one's brows, look daggers, lower, scowl; **frown upon** disapprove of, discountenance, discourage, dislike, look askance at, not take kindly to, show, disapproval, take a dim view of, view with disfavour

frozen *adj* arctic, chilled, chilled to the marrow, frigid, frosted, ice-bound, ice-cold, ice-covered, icy, numb; fixed, pegged, petrified, rooted, stock-still, stopped, suspended, turned to stone

frugal *adj* abstemious, careful, cheesparing, economical, meagre, niggardly, parsimonious, penny-wise, provident, prudent, saving, sparing, thrifty

fruit *n* crop, harvest, produce, product, yield; advantage, benefit, consequence, effect, outcome, profit, result, return, reward

fruitful *adj* fecund, fertile, fructiferous; abundant, copious, flush, plenteous, plentiful, productive, profuse, prolific, rich, spawning

fruitless *adj* abortive, barren, boot less, futile, idle, ineffectual, in vain, pointless, profitless, to no avail, to no effect, unavailing, unfruitful, unproductive, unprofitable, unprolific, unsuccessful, useless, vain

frustrate *v* baffle, balk, block, check, circumvent, confront, counter, defeat, disappoint, foil, forestall, inhibit, neutralize, nullify, render null and void, stymie, thwart

frustrated *adj* disappointed, discontented, discouraged, disheartened, embittered, foiled, irked, resentful

fuel *n* coal, diesel oil, kerosene, paraffin, petrol, wood; fodder, food, nourishment, sustenance; ammunition, encouragement, goading, incitement, material, means, nourishment, provocation, stimulus

fuel *v* charge, fire, power, stoke up; encourage, fan, goad, incite, inflame, stimulate

fugitive *n* deserter, escapee, refugee, runaway; (*Inf*) AWOL, on the run

fulfil *v* accomplish, achieve, answer, bring to completion, carry out, complete, comply with, conclude, conform to, discharge, effect, execute, fill, finish, implement, keep, meet, obey, observe, perfect, perform, realise, satisfy; attain, consummate, realize; answer, comply with, conform to, meet, obey, observe

fulfilment *n* accomplishment, achievement, attainment, carrying out, completion, consummation, crowning, discharge, discharging, effecting, end, implementation, observance, perfection, realization

full *adj* brimful, brimming, complete,entire, filled, gorged, intact, loaded, replete, sated, satiated, satisfied, saturated, stocked, sufficient; abundant, adequate, ample, broad, comprehensive, copious, detailed, exhaustive, extensive, generous, maximum, plenary, plenteous, plentiful, thorough, unabridged; chock-a-block, chock-full, crammed, crowded, in use, jammed, occupied, packed, taken

full-grown *adj* adult, developed, full-fledged, grown-up, in one's prime, marriageable, mature, nubile, of age, ripe

fullness *n* broadness, completeness, comprehensiveness, entirety, extensiveness, plenitude, totality, vastness, wealth, wholeness

full-scale *adj* all-encompassing, all-out, comprehensive, exhaustive, extensive, full-dress, in-depth, major, proper, sweeping, thorough, thoroughgoing, wide-ranging

fully *adv* absolutely, altogether, completely, entirely, every inch, from first to last, heart and soul, in all respects, intimately, perfectly, positively, thoroughly, totally, utterly, wholly; abundantly, adequately, comprehensively, plentifully, satisfactorily, sufficiently

fulsome *adj* adulatory, cloying, excessive, extravagant, fawning, gross, immoderate, ingratiating, inordinate, insincere, nauseating, overdone, saccharine, sickening, sycophantic, unctuous

fumble *v* botch, bungle, misfield, mishandle, mismanage, muff, spoil; (*Inf*) make a hash of

fume *v* boil, chafe, get hot under the collar, rage, rant, rave, seethe, smoulder, storm

fumes *pl n* effluvium, exhalation, exhaust, gas, haze, miasma, pollution, reek, smog, smoke, stench, vapour

fumigate *v* clean out, cleanse, disinfect, purify, sanitate, sanitize, sterilize

fun *n* amusement, cheer, distraction, diversion, enjoyment, entertainment, frolic, gaiety, good time, jollification, jollity, joy, junketing, living it up, merriment, merrymaking, mirth, pleasure, recreation, romp, sport, treat

function *n* activity, business, capacity, charge, concern, duty, employment, exercise, job, mission, occupation, office, operation, part, post, province, purpose, responsibility, role, situation, task;

function *v* act, act the part of, behave, be in commission, be in operation, be in running order, do duty, go officiate, operate, perform, run, serve, serve one's turn, work

function *n* affair, do, gathering, reception, social occasion

functional *adj* hard-wearing, operative, practical, serviceable, useful, utilitarian, utility, working

fund *n* capital, endowment, foundation, kitty, pool, reserve, stock, store, supply; hoard, mine, repository, reserve, reservoir, source, storehouse, treasury, vein

fund *v* capitalize, endow, finance, float, pay for, promote, stake, subsidize, support

fundamental *adj* basic, cardinal, central, constitutional, crucial, elementary, essential, first, important, indispensable, integral, intrinsic, key, necessary, organic, primary, prime, principal, rudimentary, underlying, vital

funds *pl n* bread, capital, cash, finance, hard cash, money, ready money, resources, savings, the ready, the wherewithal

funeral *n* burial, cremation, entombment, inhumation, interment; exequies, funeral rites, obsequies

funereal *adj* black, dark, drab; depressing, dismal, dreary, gloomy, grave, lugubrious, melancholy, solemn, sombre

fungus *n* mildew, mould, mushroom, rust, toadstool; parasite, saprophyte

funny *adj* absurd, amusing, a scream, comic, comical, diverting, droll, entertaining, facetious, farcical, hilarious, humorous, hysterical, jocose, jocular, jolly, laughable, ludicrous, rich, ridiculous, riotous, risible, side-splitting, silly, slapstick, waggish, witty; (*Inf*) killing; curious, dubious, mysterious, odd, peculiar, perplexing, puzzling, queer, remarkable, strange, suspicious, unusual, weird

furious *adj* angry, beside oneself, boiling, enraged, frantic, frenzied, fuming, incensed, infuriated, in high dudgeon, livid, mad, maddened, on the warpath, raging, up in arms, wrathful; (*Inf*) boisterous, foaming at the mouth, hot under the collar, livid, up in arms; fierce, intense, stormy, tempestuous, unrestrained, vehement, violent, wild

furnish *n* appoint, decorate, equip, fit, outfit, provide, provision, rig, stock, store, supply; afford, bestow, endow, give, grant, offer, present, provide, reveal, supply

furniture *n* appliances, appointments, chattels, effects, equipment, fittings, furnishings, goods, household goods, movable, property, movables, possessions, things

furrow *n* channel, corrugation, crease, crow's-foot, fluting, groove, hollow, line, rut, seam, trench, wrinkle

further *adj* additional, extra, fresh, more, new, other, supplementary

further *adv* additionally, also, as well as, besides, furthermore, in addition, moreover, on top of, over and above, to boot, what's more, yet

further *v* advance, aid, assist, champion, contribute to, encourage, expedite, facilitate, forward, foster, hasten, help, lend support to, patronize, promote, push, speed, succour, work for

furtherance *n* advancement, elevation, promotion; (*Inf*) step-up; aid ing, assisting, backing, forwarding, furthering

furthermore *adv* additionally, as well, besides, further, in addition, into the bargain, moreover, not to mention, to boot, too, what's more

furthest *adj* extreme, farthest, furthest away, furthermost, most distant, most remote, outermost, outmost, remotest, ultimate, uttermost

furtive *adj* clandestine, cloaked, conspiratorial, covert, hidden, secret, secretive, skulking, slinking, sly, sneaking, sneaky, stealthy, surreptitious, underhand, under the table

fury *n* anger, frenzy, furore, impetuosity, ire, madness, passion, rage, wrath; ferocity, fierceness, force, intensity, power, savagery, severity, tempestuousness, turbulence, vehemence, violence

fuse *v* amalgamate, blend, combine, compound, intermingle, intermix, unite, join, merge, solder; dissolve, liquefy, melt, melt down, smelt

fuss *n* ado, agitation, bother, bustle, commotion, confusion, excitement, fidget, flap, flurry, fluster, flutter, hurry, palaver, pother, stir, storm in a teacup, to-do, upset, worry; altercation, argument, bother, complaint, difficulty, display, furore, hassle, objection, row, squabble, trouble, unrest, upset

fuss *v* bustle, chafe, fidget, flap, fret, fume, get in a stew, get worked up, labour over, niggle, take pains, worry; (*Inf*) be in a stew, get in a flap, get worked up over nothing; complain; (*Inf*) kick up a fuss; annoy, disturb, irritate, nag, pester

fussy *adj* choosy, dainty, difficult, discriminating, exacting, faddish, faddy, fastidious, finicky, hard to please, nit-picking, old-maidish, old-womanish, overparticular, particular, pernickety, squeamish

futile *adj* abortive, barren, bootless, empty, forlorn, fruitless, hollow, ineffectual, in vain, nugatory, profitless, sterile, to no avail, unavailing, unproductive, unprofitable, unsuccessful, useless, vain, valueless, worthless

future *n* expectation, hereafter, outlook, prospect, time to come

future *adj* approaching, coming, destined, eventual, expected, fated, forthcoming, impending, in the offing, later, prospective, subsequent, to be, to come, ultimate, unborn

fuzzy *adj* befuddled, bleary, blurred, indefinite, indistinct, misty, out of focus, unclear, unfocused; befuddled, blurred, confused, muddled, foggy, misty, shadowy

G

gad *v* flit about, meander, ramble, roam, rove, run around, stray, travel about, wander

gadget *n* appliance, contraption, contrivance, device, gimmick, invention, novelty, thing, tool

gag *v* curb, muffle, muzzle, quiet, silence, stifle, still, stop up, suppress, throttle

gaiety *n* animation, blitheness, blithesomeness, cheerfulness, effervescence, elation, exhilaration, glee, good humour, high spirits, hilarity, jollity, joviality, joyousness, light-heartedness, liveliness, merriment, mirth, sprightliness, vivacity

gaily *adv* blithely, cheerfully, glee fully, happily, joyfully, light-heartedly, merrily

gain *v* achieve, acquire, advance, attain, bag, build up, capture, collect, enlist, gather, get, glean, harvest, improve, increase, net, obtain, pick up, procure, profit, realize, reap, secure, win, win over; acquire, bring in, clear, earn, get, make, net, obtain, produce, realize, win, yield

gain *n* accretion, achievement, acquisition, advance, advancement, advantage, attainment, benefit, dividend, earnings, emolument, growth, headway, improvement, income, increase, increment, lucre, proceeds, produce, profit, progress, return, rise, winnings, yield

gainful *adj* advantageous, beneficial, financially rewarding, lucrative, paying, profitable, rewarding, worthwhile, useful

gait *n* bearing, carriage, pace, step, stride, tread, walk

gala *n* carnival, celebration, festival, festivity, fete, jamboree, pageant, party

galaxy *n* constellation, stars, the heavens; brilliant gathering, illustrious group

gale *n* blast, cyclone, hurricane, squall, storm, tempest, tornado, typhoon

gallant *adj* bold, brave, courageous, daring, dashing, dauntless, doughty, fearless, game, heroic, high-spirited, honourable, intrepid, lion-hearted, manful, manly, mettlesome, noble, plucky, valiant, valorous; attentive, chivalrous, courteous, courtly, gentlemanly, gracious, magnanimous, noble, polite

gallant *n* admirer, beau, boyfriend, escort, lover, paramour, suitor, wooer

gallantry *n* audacity, boldness, bravery, courage, courageousness, daring, dauntlessness, fearlessness, heroism, intrepidity, manliness, mettle, nerve, pluck, prowess, spirit, valiance, valour

galling *adj* aggravating, annoying, bitter, bothersome, exasperating, harassing, humiliating, irksome, irritating, nettlesome, plaguing, provoking, rankling, vexatious, vexing

gallop *v* bolt, career, dart, dash, fly, hasten, hurry, race, run, rush, scud, shoot, speed, sprint, tear along, zoom

gamble *v* back, bet, game, make a bet, play, punt, stake, try one's luck, wager; back, chance, hazard, risk, speculate, stake, take a chance, venture

gamble *n* chance, leap in the dark, lottery, risk, speculation, uncertainty, venture; bet, flutter, punt, wager,

gambol *v* caper, cavort, curvet, cut a caper, frisk, frolic, hop, jump, prance, rollick, skip

game *n* amusement, distraction, diversion, entertainment, frolic, fun, jest, joke, lark, merriment, pastime, play, recreation, romp, sport; competition, contest, event, match, meeting, round, tournament; chase, prey, quarry, wild animals

game *adj* bold, brave, courageous, dauntless, dogged, fearless, gallant, heroic, intrepid, persevering, persistent, plucky, resolute, spirited, unflinching, valiant, valorous

gamut *n* complete scale, complete sequence, entire area, entire range, whole series, whole spectrum

gang *n* band, circle, clique, club, company, coterie, crew, crowd, group, herd, horde, lot, mob, pack, party, ring, set, shift, squad, team, troupe

gangster *n* bandit, brigand, crook, desperado, gang member, racketeer, robber, ruffian, thug, tough

gap *n* blank, breach, break, chink, cleft, crack, cranny, crevice, discontinuity, divide, hiatus, hole, interlude, intermission, interruption, interstice, interval, lacuna, lull, opening, pause, recess, rent, rift, space, vacuity, void

gape *v* gawk, gawp, goggle, stare, wonder; crack, open, split, yawn

gaping *adj* broad, cavernous, great, open, vast, wide, wide open, yawning

garbage *n* bits and pieces, debris, detritus, junk, litter, odds and ends, rubbish, scraps

garble *v* confuse, jumble, mix up; corrupt, distort, doctor, falsify, misinterpret, misquote, misreport, misrepresent, misstate, mistranslate, mutilate, pervert, slant, tamper with, twist

garish *adj* brassy, brummagem, cheap, flash, flashy, flaunting, gaudy, glaring, glittering, loud, meretricious, raffish, showy, tasteless, tawdry, vulgar

garland *n* bays, chaplet, coronal, crown, festoon, honours, laurels, wreath

garments *pl n* apparel, array, articles of clothing, attire, clothes, clothing, costume, dress, duds, garb, gear, habiliment, habit, outfit, robes, togs, uniform, vestments, wear

garner *v* accumulate, amass, assemble, collect, deposit, gather, hoard, husband, lay in, put by, reserve, save, stockpile, store, stow away, treasure

garnish *v* adorn, beautify, bedeck, deck, decorate, embellish, enhance, grace, ornament, set off, trim

garrison *n* armed force, command, detachment, troops, unit; base, camp, encampment, fort, fortification, fortress, post, station, stronghold

gash *v* cleave, cut, gouge, incise,

lacerate, rend, slash, slit, split, tear, wound

gash *n* cleft, cut, gouge, incision, laceration, rent, slash, slit, split, tear, wound

gasp *v* blow, catch one's breath, choke, fight for breath, gulp, pant, puff

gasp *n* blow, ejaculation, exclamation, gulp, pant, puff

gate *n* access, barrier, door, door way, egress, entrance, exit, gateway, opening, passage, portal

gather *v* accumulate, amass, assemble, bring together, collect, congregate, convene, flock, forgather, garner, group, heap, hoard, marshal, mass, muster, pile up, round up, stack up, stockpile; assume, be led to believe, conclude, deduce, draw, hear, infer, learn, make, surmise, understand; crop, cull, garner, glean, harvest, pick, pluck, reap, select

gathering *n* assemblage, assembly, company, conclave, concourse, congregation, congress, convention, convocation, crowd, flock, group, knot, meeting, muster, party, rally, throng, turnout

gauche *adj* awkward, clumsy, graceless, ignorant, ill-bred, ill-mannered, inelegant, inept, insensitive, lacking in social graces, mal - adroit, tactless, uncultured, unpolished, unsophisticated

gaudy *adj* bright, brilliant, Brummagem, flash, flashy, florid, garish, gay, glaring, loud, meretricious, ostentatious, raffish, showy, taste less, tawdry, vulgar; (*Inf*) flash

gauge *v* ascertain, calculate, check, compute, count, determine, measure, weigh; adjudge, appraise, assess, estimate, evaluate, guess, judge, rate, reckon, value

gauge *n* basis, criterion, example, exemplar, guide, guideline, indicator, measure, meter, model, pattern, rule, sample, standard, test, touchstone, yardstick; bore, capacity, degree, depth, extent, height, magnitude, measure, scope, size, span, thickness, width

gaunt *adj* angular, attenuated, bony, cadaverous, emaciated, haggard, lank, lean, meagre, pinched, rawboned, scraggy, scrawny, skeletal, skinny, spare, thin, wasted

gawky *adj* awkward, clownish, clumsy, gauche, loutish, lumbering, lumpish, maladroit, oafish, uncouth, ungainly

gay *adj* animated, blithe, carefree, cheerful, debonair, glad, gleeful, happy, hilarious, insouciant, jolly, jovial, joyful, joyous, light-hearted, lively, merry, sparkling, sunny, vivacious; bright, brilliant, colourful, flamboyant, flashy, fresh, garish, gaudy, rich, showy, vivid

gaze *v* contemplate, gape, look, look fixedly, regard, stare, view, watch, wonder

gaze *n* fixed look, look, stare

gear *n* cog, cogwheel, gearwheel, toothed wheel; accessories, accoutrements, apparatus, equipment, harness, instruments, outfit, paraphernalia, rigging, supplies, tackle, tools, trappings; baggage, belongings, effects, kit, luggage, stuff, things

gem *n* jewel, precious stone,

semiprecious stone, stone; flower, jewel, masterpiece, pearl, pick, prize, treasure

general *adj* accepted, broad, common, extensive, popular, prevailing, prevalent, public, universal, wide spread; accustomed, conventional, customary, everyday, habitual, normal, ordinary, regular, typical, usual; approximate, ill-defined, imprecise, inaccurate, indefinite, inexact, loose, undetailed, unspecific, vague

generally *adv* almost always, as a rule, by and large, conventionally, customarily, for the most part, habitually, in most cases, mainly, normally, on average, on the whole, ordinarily, regularly, typically, usually; commonly, extensively, popularly, publicly, universally, widely

generate *v* beget, breed, bring about, cause, create, engender, form, give rise to, initiate, make, originate, procreate, produce, propagate, spawn, whip up

generation *n* begetting, breeding, creation, engenderment, formation, genesis, origination, procreation, production, propagation, reproduction; age, day, days, epoch, era, period, time, times

generosity *n* beneficence, benevolent, bounteous, bountiful, charitable, free, hospitable, kind, lavish, liberal, munificent, open-handed, princely, ungrudging, unstinting; big-hearted, disinterested, good, high-minded, lofty, magnanimous, noble, unselfish

genial *adj* affable, agreeable, amiable, cheerful, cheery, congenial, convivial, cordial, easygoing, enlivening, friendly, glad, good-nature, happy, hearty, jolly, jovial, joyous, kind, kindly, merry, pleasant, sunny, warm, warm-hearted

genius *n* adept, brain, expert, intellect, maestro, master, master-hand, master-mind, virtuoso; ability, aptitude, bent, brilliance, capacity creative power, endowment, faculty, flair, gift, inclination, knack, propensity, talent, turn

genteel *adj* aristocratic, civil, courteous, courtly, cultivated, cultured, elegant, fashionable, formal, gentlemanly, ladylike, mannerly, polished, polite, refined, respectable, stylish, urbane, well-bred, well-mannered

gentility *n* civility, courtesy, courtliness, cultivation, culture, decorum, elegance, etiquette, formality, good breeding, good manners, mannerliness, polish, politeness, propriety, refinement, respectability, urbanity

gentle *adj* amiable, benign, bland, compassionate, dove-like, humane, kind, kindly, lenient, meek, merciful, mild, pacific, peaceful, placid, quiet, soft, sweet-tempered, tender; balmy, calm, clement, easy, light, low, mild, moderate, muted, placid, quiet, serene, slight, smooth, soft, soothing, temperate, tranquil, untroubled

gentlemanly *adj* civil, civilized, courteous, cultivated, gallant, genteel, gentlemanlike, honourable, mannerly, noble, obliging, polished, polite, refined, reputable, suave, urbane, well-bred, well-mannered

genuine *adj* actual, authentic, bona fide, honest, legitimate, natural, original, pure, real, sound, sterling, true, unadulterated, unalloyed, veritable

germ *n* bacterium, bug, microbe, micro-organism, virus; beginning, bud, cause, embryo, origin, root, rudiment, seed, source, spark

germinate *v* bud develop, generate, grow, originate, pullulate, shoot, sprout, swell, vegetate

gesture *n* action, gesticulation, indication, motion, sign, signal

gesture *v* gesticulate, indicate, motion, sign, signal, wave

get *v* achieve, acquire, attain, bag, bring, come by, come into possession of, earn, fall heir to, fetch, gain, glean, inherit, make, net, obtain, pick up, procure, realize, reap, receive, secure, succeed to, win; arrest, capture, collar, grab, lay hold of, seize, take, trap; become, come to be, grow, turn, wax; arrive, come, make it, reach, arrange, contrive, fix, manage, succeed, wangle; coax, convince, induce, influence, persuade, prevail upon, sway, talk into, wheedle, win over

get across *v* communicate, convey, get over, impart, make clear, put over, transmit

get along *v* agree, be compatible, be friendly, get on, harmonize, hit it off; cope, develop, fare, make out, manage, progress, shift

get around *v* bypass, circumvent, outmanoeuvre, outwit; (*Inf*) outsmart; coax, convert, persuade, prevail upon, sway, talk round, wheedle, win over; (*Inf*) cajole; circulate, socialize, travel, visit

get at *v* acquire, attain, come to grips with, gain access to, get, get hold of, reach; hint, imply, intend, lead up to, mean, suggest; annoy, attack, blame, carp, criticize, find fault with, irritate, nag, pick on, taunt

get down *v* alight, bring down, climb down, descend, disembark, dismount, get off, lower, step down

get off *v* alight, depart, descend, disembark, dismount, escape, exit, leave

get on *v* ascend, board, climb, embark, mount; advance, cope, fare, get along, make out, manage, progress, prosper, succeed; agree, be compatible, be friendly, concur, get along, harmonize, hit it off

get over *v* cross, ford, get across, pass, pass over, surmount, traverse; come round, get better, mend, pull through, recover from, revive, survive, communicate, convey, get across, impart, make clear, make understood

get-up *n* apparel, clothes, clothing, dress, garments; (*Inf*) rig-out

ghastly *adj* ashen, cadaverous, deathlike, deathly pale, dreadful, frightful, grim, grisly, gruesome, hideous, horrendous, horrible, horrid, livid, loathsome, pale, pallid, repellent, shocking, spectral, terrible, terrifying, wan

ghost *n* apparition, manes, phan tasm, phantom, revenant, shade, soul, spectre, spirit, spook, wraith

ghostly *adj* eerie, ghostlike, illusory, insubstantial, phantasmal, phantom, spectral, spooky, supernatural, uncanny, unearthly, weird, wraithlike

giant *n* behemoth, colossus, leviathan, monster, titan

giant *adj* colossal, elephantine, enormous, gargantuan, gigantic, huge, immense, jumbo, large, mammoth, monstrous, prodigious, titanic, vast

gibberish *n* babble, balderdash, blather, double talk, drivel, gabble, jabber, jargon, mumbo jumbo, nonsense, prattle, twaddle

gibe, jibe *v* deride, flout, jeer, make fun of, mock, poke fun at, ridicule, scoff, scorn, sneer, taunt, twit

gibe, jibe *n* crack, cutting remark, derision, dig, jeer, mockery, ridicule, sarcasm, scoffing, sneer, taunt

giddiness *n* dizziness, faintness, light-headedness, vertigo

giddy *n* dizzy, dizzying, faint, light-headed, reeling, unsteady, vertiginous

gift *n* benefaction, bequest, bonus, boon, bounty, contribution, donation, grant, gratuity, largess, legacy, offering, present; ability, aptitude, attribute, bent, capability, capacity, endowment, faculty, flair, genius, knack, power, talent, turn

gift *v* bestow, confer, contribute, donate,

gifted *adj* able, accomplished, adroit, brilliant, capable, clever, expert, ingenious, intelligent, masterly, skilled, talented

gigantic *adj* colossal, elephantine, enormous, gargantuan, giant, herculean, huge, immense, mammoth, monstrous, prodigious, stupendous, titanic, tremendous, vast

giggle *v* cackle, chortle, chuckle, laugh, snigger, titter, twitter; (*Inf*) ha-ha, tee-hee

gimmick *n* contrivance, device, dodge, gadget, gambit, ploy, scheme, stratagem, stunt, trick

gird *v* belt, bind, girdle; blockade, encircle, enclose, encompass, enfold, engird, environ, hem in, pen, ring, surround

girdle *n* band, belt, cincture, cummerbund, fillet, sash, waistband

girdle *v* bind, bound, encircle, enclose, encompass, engird, environ, gird, hem, ring, surround

girl *n* bird, daughter, female child, lass, lassie, maiden, miss, wench

girth *n* bulk, circumference, measure, size

gist *n* core, drift, essence, force, idea, import, marrow, meaning, nub, pith, point, quintessence, sense, significance, substance

give *v* accord, administer, allow, award, bestow, commit, confer, consign, contribute, deliver, donate, entrust, furnish, grant, hand out, make over, permit, present, provide, supply, vouchsafe; demonstrate, display, evidence,indicate, manifest, offer, proffer, provide, set forth, show; allow, cede, concede, devote, grant, hand over, lend, relinquish, surrender, yield

give away *v* betray, disclose, divulge, expose, inform on, leak, let out, let slip, reveal, uncover; (*Inf*) blow the whistle on, grass on, rat on; bestow, donate, gift

give in *v* admit defeat, capitulate, collapse, comply, concede, quit, submit, surrender, yield
give off *v* discharge, emit, exhale, exude, produce, release, send out, smell of, throw out, vent
give up *v* abandon, capitulate, cease, cede, cut out, desist, despair, forswear, hand over, leave off, quit, relinquish, renounce, resign, stop, surrender, throw in the towel, waive
glad *adj* blithesome, cheerful, chuffed, contented, delighted, gay, gleeful, gratified, happy, jocund, jovial, joyful, overjoyed, pleased, willing
gladden *v* cheer, delight, elate, enliven, exhilarate, gratify, hearten, please, rejoice
gladly *adv* cheerfully, freely, gaily, gleefully, happily, jovially, joyfully, joyously, merrily, readily, willingly, with good grace, with pleasure
gladness *n* animation, blitheness, cheerfulness, delight, felicity, gaiety, glee, happiness, high spirits, hilarity, jollity, joy, joyousness, mirth, pleasure
glamorous *adj* alluring, attractive, beautiful, bewitching, captivating, charming, dazzling, elegant, enchanting, entrancing, exciting, fascinating, glittering, glossy, lovely, prestigious, smart
glamour *n* allure, appeal, attraction, beauty, bewitchment, charm, enchantment, fascination, magnetism, prestige, ravishment, witchery
glance *v* gaze, glimpse, look, peek, peep, scan, view
glance *n* brief look, gander, glimpse, look, peek, peep, quick look, squint, view; flash, gleam, glimmer, glint, reflection, sparkle, twinkle; allusion, passing mention, reference
glare *v* frown, give a dirty look, glower, look daggers, lower, scowl, stare angrily
glare *n* angry stare, black look, dirty look, frown, glower, lower, scowl; blaze, brilliance, dazzle, flame, flare, glow
glaring *adj* audacious, blatant, conspicuous, egregious, flagrant, gross, manifest, obvious, open, outrageous, outstanding, overt, patent, rank, unconcealed, visible
glasses *pl n* bifocals, binoculars, eyeglasses, field-glasses, lorgnette, monocle, opera-glasses, pince-nez, spectacles, sun-glasses
glassy *adj* clear, glossy, icy, shiny, slick, slippery, smooth, transparent
glaze *v* burnish, coat, enamel, furbish, gloss, lacquer, polish, varnish
glaze *n* coat, enamel, finish, gloss, lacquer, lustre, patina, polish, shine, varnish
gleam *n* beam, flash, glimmer, glow, ray, sparkle
gleam *v* coruscate, flare, flash, glance, glimmer, glint, glisten, glitter, glow, scintillate, shimmer, shine, sparkle
glee *n* cheerfulness, delight, elation, exhilaration, exuberance, exultation, fun, gaiety, gladness, hilarity, jocularity, jollity, joviality, joy, joyfulness, joyousness, liveliness, merriment, mirth, sprightliness, triumph, verve
gleeful *adj* cheerful, cock-a-hoop,

delighted, elated, exuberant, exultant, gay, gratified, happy, jocund, jovial, joyful, joyous, jubilant, merry, mirthful, overjoyed, pleased, triumphant

glib *adj* artful, easy, fast-talking, fluent, garrulous, insincere, plausible, quick, ready, slick, slippery, smooth, smooth-tongued, suave, talkative, voluble

glide *v* coast, drift, float, flow, fly, roll, run, sail, skate, skim, slide, slip, soar

glimmer *v* blink, flicker, gleam, glisten, glitter, glow, shimmer, shine, sparkle, twinkle

glimmer *n* blink, flicker, gleam, glow, ray, shimmer, sparkle, twinkle

glimpse *n* brief view, glance, look, peek, peep, quick look, sight, sighting, squint

glimpse *v* catch sight of, descry, espy, sight, spot, spy, view

glint *v* flash, gleam, glimmer, glitter, shine, sparkle, twinkle

glint *n* flash, gleam, glimmer, glitter, shine, sparkle, twinkle, twinkling

glisten *v* coruscate, flash, glance, glare, gleam, glimmer, glint, glitter, scintillate, shimmer, shine, sparkle, twinkle

glitter *v* coruscate, flare, flash, glare, gleam, glimmer, glint, glisten, scintillate, shimmer, shine, sparkle, twinkle

glitter *n* beam, brightness, brilliance, flash, glare, gleam, lustre, radiance, scintillation, sheen, shimmer, shine, sparkle

gloat *v* crow, exult, glory, relish, revel in, rub it in, triumph, vaunt

global *adj* international, pandemic, planetary, universal, world, worldwide; all-encompassing, all-inclusive, all-out, comprehensive, encyclopedic, exhaustive, general, thorough, total, unbounded, unlimited

globe *n* ball, earth, orb, planet, round, sphere, world

globule *n* bead, bubble, drop, droplet, particle, pearl, pellet

gloom *n* blackness, cloud, cloudiness, dark, darkness, dimness, dullness, dusk, duskiness, gloominess, murk, murkiness, obscurity, shade, shadow, twilight; blues, dejection, depression, desolation, despair, despondency, downheartedness, low spirits, melancholy, misery, sadness, sorrow, unhappiness, woe

gloomy *adj* black, crepuscular, dark, dim, dismal, dreary, dull, dusky, murky, obscure, overcast, shadowy, sombre, tenebrous; bad, black, cheerless, comfortless, depressing, disheartening, dispiriting, dreary, joyless, sad, saddening, sombre; blue, chapfallen, cheerless, crestfallen, dejected, despondent, dismal, dispirited, down, downcast, downhearted, down in the mouth, glum, in low, spirits, melancholy, miserable, moody, morose, pessimistic, sad, saturnine, sullen

glorify *v* add lustre to, adorn, aggrandize, augment, dignify, elevate, enhance, ennoble, illuminate, immortalize, lift up, magnify, panegyrize, praise, sing the praises of

glorious *adj* celebrated, distinguished, elevated, eminent, excellent, famed, famous, grand, honoured, illustrious, magnificent, majestic, noble, noted, renowned, sublime, triumphant; (*Inf*) delight ful, enjoyable, excellent, fine, great, heavenly, marvellous, pleasurable, splendid, wonderful

glory *n* celebrity, dignity, distinction, eminence, exaltation, fame, honour, illustriousness, immortality, kudos, praise, prestige, renown; adoration, benediction, blessing, gratitude, homage, laudation, praise, thanksgiving, veneration, worship; grandeur, greatness, magnificence, majesty, nobility, pageantry, pomp, splendour, sublimity, triumph

glory *v* boast, crow, exult, gloat, pride oneself, relish, revel, take delight, triumph

gloss *n* brightness, brilliance, burnish, gleam, lustre, polish, sheen, shine, varnish, veneer; annotation, comment, commentary, elucidation, explanation, footnote, interpretation, note, scholium, translation

gloss *v* camouflage, conceal, cover up, disguise, hide, mask, smooth over, veil; (*Inf*) whitewash

glossy *adj* bright, brilliant, burnished, glassy, glazed, lustrous, polished, sheeny, shining, shiny, silken, silky, sleek, smooth

glow *n* burning, gleam, glimmer, incandescence, light, luminosity, phosphorescence; brightness, brilliance, effulgence, radiance, splendour, vividness; ardour, earnestness, enthusiasm, excite ment, fervour, gust, impetuosity, intensity, passion, vehemence, warmth

glow *v* brighten, burn, gleam, glimmer, redden, shine, smoulder; be suffuse, blush, colour, fill, flush, radiate, thrill, tingle

glower *v* frown, give a dirty look, glare, look daggers, lower, scowl

glowing *adj* aglow, beaming, bright, flaming, florid, flushed, lambent, luminous, red, rich, ruddy, suffused, vibrant, vivid, warm

glue *n* adhesive, cement, gum, mucilage, paste

glue *v* affix, agglutinate, cement, fix, gum, paste, seal, stick

glum *adj* chapfallen, churlish, crabbed, crestfallen, crusty, dejected, doleful, down, gloomy, gruff, grumpy, ill-humoured, low, moody, morose, pessimistic, saturnine, sour, sulky, sullen, surly

glut *n* excess, overabundance, oversupply, saturation, superabundance, superfluity, surfeit, surplus

glutinous *adj* adhesive, glue-like, gummy, mucous, viscous, tacky

gluttony *n* gormandizing, gourmandism, greed, greediness, pigishness, rapacity, voraciousness, voracity

gnaw *v* bite, chew, munch, nibble, worry; consume, devour, eat away, erode, fret, wear away

go *v* advance, decamp, depart, fare, journey, leave, make for, move, move out, pass, proceed, repair, set off, travel, withdraw; function, move, operate, perform, run, work; develop, eventuate, fall out, fare, happen, proceed, result, turn out, work out; die, expire, give up the ghost, pass away, perish; elapse, expire, flow, lapse, pass, slip away;

go *n* attempt, bid, effort, essay, shot,

stab, try, turn; (*Inf*) whirl

goad *n* impetus, incentive, incitement, irritation, motivation, pressure, spur, stimulation, stimulus, urge

goad *v* annoy, arouse, drive, egg on, exhort, harass, hound, impel, incite, instigate, irritate, lash, prick, prod, prompt, propel, spur, stimulate, sting, urge, worry

goal *n* aim, ambition, design, destination, end, intention, limit, mark, object, objective, purpose, target

go along *v* acquiesce, agree, assent, concur, cooperate, follow

go away *v* decamp, depart, exit, leave, move out, recede, withdraw

go back *v* return, revert

gobble *v* bolt, cram, devour, gorge, gulp, guzzle, stuff, swallow, wolf

go-between *n* agent, broker, dealer, factor, intermediary, liaison, mediator, medium, middleman

go by *v* elapse, exceed, flow on, move onward, pass, proceed; adopt, be guided by, follow, heed, judge from, observe, take as guide

god-forsaken *adj* abandoned, backward, bleak, deserted, desolate, dismal, dreary, forlorn, gloomy, lonely, neglected, remote, wretched

godless *adj* atheistic, depraved, evil, impious, irreligious, profane, ungodly, unprincipled, unrighteous, wicked

godly *adj* devout, god-fearing, good, holy, pious, religious, righteous, saintly

godsend *n* blessing, boon, manna, stroke of luck, windfall

go into *v* analyse, consider, delve into, discuss, examine, inquire into, investigate, look into, probe, pursue, review, scrutinize, study

gone *v* elapsed, ended, finished, over, past; absent, astray, away, lacking, lost, missing, vanished; dead, deceased, defunct, departed, extinct, no more; consumed, done, finished, spent, used up

good *adj* acceptable, admirable, agreeable, capital, choice, commendable, crucial, excellent, fine, first-class, first-rate, great, pleasant, pleasing, positive, precious, satisfactory, splendid, superior, tiptop, valuable, worthy; admirable, estimable, ethical, exemplary, honest, honourable, moral, praiseworthy, right, righteous, trustworthy, upright, virtuous, worthy; able, accomplished, adept, adroit, capable, clever, competent, dexterous, efficient, expert, first-rate, proficient, reliable, satisfactory, serviceable, skilled, sound, suitable, talented, thorough, useful; authentic, bona fide, dependable, genuine, honest, legitimate, proper, real, reliable, sound, true, trustworthy, valid; decorous, dutiful, obedient, polite, proper, well-behaved; adequate, ample, complete, entire, extensive, full, large, long, sizable, solid, substantial, sufficient

good *n* advantage, avail, behalf, benefit, gain, interest, profit, service, use, usefulness, welfare, well-being, worth; excellence, goodness, merit, morality, right, righteousness, uprightness, virtue, worth

goodbye *inter* adieu, farewell, leave-taking, parting

good-for-nothing *n* black sheep, idler, layabout, ne'er-do-well, profligate, rapscallion, scapegrace, waster

good-for-nothing *adj* feckless, idle, irresponsible, useless, worthless

good-humoured *adj* affable, amiable, cheerful, congenial, genial, good-tempered, happy, pleasant

good-looking *adj* attractive, comely, fair, handsome, personable, pretty, well-favoured

good-natured *adj* agreeable, benevolent, friendly, good-hearted, helpful, kind, kindly, tolerant, well-disposed, willing to please

goodness *n* excellence, merit, quality, superiority, value, worth; beneficence, benevolence, friendliness, generosity, good will, graciousness, humaneness, kind-heartedness, kindliness, kindness, mercy, obligingness; honesty, honour, integrity, merit, morality, probity, rectitude, righteousness, uprightness, virtue

goods *pl n* appurtenances, belongings, chattels, effects, furnishings, furniture, gear, movables, paraphernalia, possessions, property, things, trappings; commodities, merchandise, stock, stuff, wares

goodwill *n* amity, benevolence, favour, friendliness, friendship, heartiness, kindliness, zeal

go off *v* blow up, detonate, explode, fire; (*Inf*) go bad, go stale, rot

go on *v* continue, endure, happen, last, occur, persist, proceed, stay

go out *v* depart, exit, leave; die out, expire, fade out

go over *v* examine, inspect, rehearse, reiterate, review, revise, study; peruse, read, scan, skim

gorge *n* canyon, cleft, clough, defile, fissure, pass, ravine

gorge *v* bolt, cram, devour, feed, fill, glut, gobble, gormandize, gulp, guzzle, overeat, raven, sate, satiate, stuff, surfeit, swallow, wolf

gorgeous *adj* beautiful, brilliant, dazzling, elegant, glittering, grand, luxuriant, magnificent, opulent, ravishing, resplendent, showy, splendid, stunning, sumptuous, superb

gossamer *adj* airy, delicate, diaphanous, fine, flimsy, gauzy, light, sheer, silky thin, transparent

gossip *n* blether, chitchat, hearsay, idle talk, prattle, scandal, small talk, tittle-tattle; babbler, blatherskite, blether, busybody, chatterer, gossipmonger, prattler, quidnunc, scandalmonger, tattler, telltale

gossip *v* blather, blether, chat, gabble, jaw, prattle, tattle

go through *v* bear, brave, endure, experience, suffer, tolerate, undergo, withstand; consume, exhaust, squander, use; check, examine, explore, hunt, look, search

govern *v* administer, be in power, command, conduct, control, direct, guide, hold sway, lead, manage, order, oversee, pilot, reign, rule, steer, superintend, supervise; decide, determine, guide, influence, rule, sway, underlie

government *n* administration, authority, dominion, execution, governance, law, polity, rule, sovereignty, state, statecraft;

administration, executive, ministry, powers-that-be, regime; authority, command, control, direction, domination, guidance, management, regulation, restraint, superintendence, supervision, sway

governor *n* administrator, boss, chief, commander, controller, director, executive, head, leader, manager, overseer, ruler, superintendent, supervisor

go with *v* accompany, agree, blend, complement, concur, correspond, fit, harmonize, match, suit

go without *v* abstain, be denied, be deprived of, deny oneself, do without, go short, lack, want

gown *n* costume, dress, frock, garb, garment, habit, robe

grab *v* bag, capture, catch, clutch, grasp, grip, latch on to, nab, pluck, seize, snap up, snatch, take hold of

grace *n* attractiveness, beauty, charm, comeliness, ease, elegance, finesse, gracefulness, loveliness, pleasantness, poise, polish, refinement, shapeliness, tastefulness; benefaction, beneficence, benevolence, favour, generosity, goodness, goodwill, kindliness, kindness; breeding, consideration, cultivation, decency, decorum, etiquette, mannerliness, manners, propriety, tact; charity, clemency, compassion, forgiveness, indulgence, leniency, lenity, mercy, pardon, quarter, reprieve; benediction, blessing, prayer, thanks, thanksgiving

grace *v* adorn, beautify, deck, decorate, dignify, distinguish, elevate, embellish, enhance, enrich, favour, garnish, glorify, honour, ornament

graceful *adj* agile, beautiful, becoming, charming, comely, easy, elegant, fine, flowing, natural, pleasing, smooth, symmetrical, tasteful

gracious *adj* accommodating, affable, amiable, beneficent, benevolent, benign, charitable, chivalrous, civil, compassionate, considerate, cordial, courteous, courtly, friendly, hospitable, indulgent, kind, kindly, lenient, loving, merciful, mild, obliging, pleasing, polite, well-mannered

grade *n* brand, category, class, condition, degree, echelon, group, level, mark, notch, order, place, position, quality, rank, rung, size, stage, station, step

grade *v* arrange, brand, class, classify, evaluate, group, order, range, rank, rate, sort, value

gradient *n* acclivity, bank, declivity, grade, hill, incline, rise, slope

gradual *adj* continuous, even, gentle, graduated, moderate, piecemeal, progressive, regular, slow, steady, successive, unhurried

gradually *adv* bit by bit, by degrees, drop by drop, evenly, gently, little by little, moderately, piece by piece, piecemeal, progressively, slowly, steadily, step by step, unhurriedly

graduate *v* calibrate, grade, mark off, measure out, proportion, regulate

grain *n* cereals, corn; grist, kernel, seed

grand *adj* ambitious, august, dignified, elevated, eminent, exalted, fine, glorious, grandiose, great, haughty, illustrious, imposing, impressive, large, lofty, lordly, luxurious, magnificent, majestic, monumental, noble, opulent, ostentatious, palatial, pompous, pretentious, princely, regal, splendid, stately, striking, sublime, sumptuous; admirable, excellent, fine, first-class, first-rate, marvellous, splendid, superb, very good, wonderful

grandeur *n* augustness, dignity, greatness, importance, loftiness, magnificence, majesty, nobility, pomp. splendour, state, stateliness, sublimity

grandiose *adj* affected, ambitious, bombastic, extravagant, flamboyant, high-flown, ostentatious, pompous, pretentious, showy

grant *v* accede to, accord, acknowledge, admit, agree to, allocate, allot, allow, assign, award, bestow, cede, concede, confer, consent to, donate, give, impart, permit, present, vouchsafe, yield

grant *n* admission, allocation, allotment, allowance, award, benefaction, bequest, boon, bounty, concession, donation, endowment, gift, resent, subsidy

grasp *v* catch, clasp, clinch, clutch, grab, grapple, grip, hold, seize, snatch; catch the drift, of, catch, on, comprehend, follow, get, realize, see, take in, understand

grasp *n* clasp, clutches, embrace, grip, hold, possession, tenure; awareness, comprehension, knowledge, mastery, perception, realization, understanding

grasping *adj* acquisitive, avaricious, close-fisted, covetous, greedy, mean, miserly, niggardly, rapacious, selfish, stingy, tightfisted, usurious, venal

grate *v* creak, grind, rasp, rub, scrape, scratch; annoy, chafe, exasperate, fret, gall, get one down, irk, irritate, jar, nettle, peeve, rankle, rub one up the wrong way, set one's teeth on edge, vex; (*Inf*) get on one's nerves

grateful *adj* appreciative, beholden, indebted, obliged, thankful

gratify *v* cater to, delight, favour, fulfil, give pleasure, gladden, humour, indulge, please, recompense, requite, satisfy, thrill

gratitude *n* appreciation, gratefulness, indebtedness, obligation, recognition, sense of obligation, thankfulness, thanks

gratuitous *adj* complimentary, free, spontaneous, unasked-for, unpaid, unrewarded, voluntary

grave *n* burying place, crypt, last resting place, mausoleum, pit, sepulchre, tomb, vault

grave *adj* dignified, dour, dull, earnest, gloomy, grim-faced, heavy, leaden, long-faced, muted, quiet, sedate, serious, sober, solemn, sombre, staid, subdued, thoughtful, unsmiling; acute, critical, crucial, dangerous, exigent, hazardous, important, life-and-death, momentous, of great, consequence, perilous, pressing, serious, severe, significant, threatening, urgent, vital, weighty

graveyard *n* boneyard, burial ground, cemetery, charnel house, churchyard, necropolis

gravity *n* acuteness, consequence, exigency, hazardousness, importance, moment, momentousness, perilousness, pressingness, seriousness, severity, significance, urgency, weightiness

greasy *adj* fatty, oily, slick, slimy, slippery; fawning, glib, grovelling, ingratiating, oily, slick, smooth, sycophantish, toadying, unctuous

great *adj* big, bulky, colossal, enormous, extensive, gigantic, huge, immense, large, mammoth, prodigious, stupendous, tremendous, vast, voluminous; extended, lengthy, long, prolonged, protracted; capital, chief, grand, leading, main, major, paramount, primary, principal, prominent, superior; considerable, decided, excessive, extravagant, extreme, grievous, high, inordinate, prodigious, pronounced, strong; consequential, critical, crucial, grave, heavy, important, momentous, serious, significant, weighty; celebrated, distinguished, eminent, exalted, excellent, famed, famous, glorious, illustrious, notable, noteworthy, outstanding, prominent, remarkable, renowned, superlative, talented; august, chivalrous, dignified, distinguished, exalted, fine, glorious, grand, heroic, high-minded, idealistic, impressive, lofty, magnanimous, noble, princely, sublime; active, devoted, enthusiastic, keen, zealous; able, adept, adroit, expert, good, masterly, proficient, skilful, skilled; (*Inf*) admirable, excellent, fantastic, fine, first-rate, good, marvellous, terrific, wonderful

greatly *adv* abundantly, by leaps and bounds, by much, considerable, enormously, exceedingly, extremely, highly, hugely, immensely, markedly, mightily, much, notably, powerfully, remarkable, tremendously, vastly, very much

greatness *n* bulk, enormity, hugeness, immensity, largeness, length, magnitude, mass, prodigiousness, size, vastness; gravity, heaviness, import, importance, moment, momentousness, seriousness, significance, urgency, weight; celebrity, distinction, eminence, fame, glory, grandeur, illustriousness, lustre, not, renown

greed, greediness *n* edacity, esurience, gluttony, gormandizing, hunger, insatiableness, ravenousness, voracity; acquisitiveness, avidity, covetousness, craving, cupidity, desire, eagerness, graspingness, longing, rapacity, selfishness

greedy *adj* edacious, esurient, gluttonous, gormandizing, hoggish, hungry, insatiable, piggish, ravenous, voracious; acquisitive, avaricious, avid, covetous, craving, desirous, eager, grasping, hungry, impatient, rapacious, selfish

green *adj* blooming, budding, flourishing, fresh, grassy, leafy, new, undecayed, verdant, verdurous; fresh, immature, new, raw, recent, unripe

green *n* common, grass, grassplot, greensward, lawn, sward, turf, village green

greenhouse *n* conservatory, glasshouse, hothouse

green light *n* approval, assent, blessing, consent, go ahead, permission, warranty (*Inf*) thumbs up

greet *n* accost, address, compliment, hail, meet, nod to, receive, salute, tip one's hat to, welcome

greeting *n* address, hail, reception, salutation, salute, welcome

grey *adj* ashen, bloodless, colourless, livid, pale, pallid, wan; cheerless, cloudy, dark, depressing, dim, dismal, drab, dreary, dull, foggy, gloomy, misty, murky, overcast, sunless; aged, ancient, elderly, experienced, hoary, mature, old, venerable

grief *n* affliction, agony, anguish, bereavement, dejection, distress, grievance, heartache, heartbreak, misery mournfulness, mourning, pain, regret, remorse, sadness, sorrow, suffering, trial, tribulation, trouble, woe

grievance *n* affliction complaint, damage, distress, grief, hardship, injury, injustice, resentment, sorrow, trial, tribulation, trouble, unhappiness, wrong

grieve *v* ache, bemoan, bewail, complain, deplore, lament, mourn, regret, rue, sorrow, suffer, wail, weep; afflict, agonize, break the heart of, crush, distress, hurt, injure, make one's heart bleed, pain, sadden, wound

grievous *adj* afflicting, calamitous, damaging, distressing, dreadful, grave, harmful, heavy, hurtful, injurious, lamentable, oppressive, painful, severe, wounding; appalling, atrocious, deplorable, dreadful, egregious, flagrant, glaring, heinous, intolerable, lamentable, monstrous, offensive, outrageous, shameful, shocking, unbearable

grim *adj* cruel, ferocious, fierce, forbidding, formidable, frightful, ghastly, gruesome, harsh, hideous, horrible, horrid, implacable, merciless, morose, relentless, resolute, ruthless, severe, shocking, sinister, stern, sullen, surly, terrible, unrelenting, unyielding

grimace *n* face, frown, mouth, scowl, sneer, wry face

grime *n* dirt, filth, smut, soot

grimy *adj* begrimed, besmeared, besmirched, dirty, filthy, foul, grubby, smutty, soiled, sooty, unclean

grind *v* abrade, comminute, crush, granulate, grate, kibble, levigate, mill, pound, powder, pulverize, triturate; gnash, grate, grit, scrape

grind *n* drudgery, hard work, labour, task, toil; (*Inf*) chore, fag, sweat

grip *n* clasp, purchase; clutches, comprehension, control, domination, grasp, hold, influence, keeping, mastery, perception, possession, power, tenure, understanding

grip *v* clasp, clutch, grasp, hold, latch, on to, seize, take, hold, of; catch, up, compel, engross, enthral, entrance, fascinate, hold, involve, mesmerize, rivet, spellbind

gripe *v* complain, groan, grumble, object, protest, whine

gripping *adj* compelling, compulsive, engrossing, enthralling, entrancing, exciting, fascinating, rivetting, spellbinding, thrilling, (*Inf*) unputdownable

grisly *adj* abominable, appaling, awful, dreadful, frightful, ghastly, grim, gruesome, hideous, horrible, horrid, macabre, shocking, sickening, terrible, terrifying

grit *n* dust, gravel, pebbles, sand; backbone, courage, determination, doggedness, fortitude, gameness, hardihood, mettle, nerve, perseverance, pluck, resolution, spirit, tenacity, toughness

groan *n/v* cry, moan, sigh, whine

groggy *adj* befuddled, confused, dazed, dizzy, faint, muzzy, punch drunk, reeling, shaky, staggering, stunned, stupefied, unsteady, weak, wobbly

groom *n* equerry, hostler, stableboy, stableman

groom *v* arrange, clean, dress, freshen up, get up, preen, primp, put in order, smarten up, spruce up, tidy, turn out; coach, drill, educate, instruct, make, ready, nurture, pre pare, prime, ready, school, teach, train, tutor

groove *n* channel, cut, cutting, flute, furrow, gutter, hollow, indentation, rebate, rut, score, trench

grope *v* cast about, feel, finger, fish, flounder, fumble, grabble, scrabble, search

gross *adj* big, bulky, corpulent, dense, fat, great, heavy, hulking, large, lumpish, massive, obese, overweight, thick; aggregate, before deductions, before tax, entire, total, whole; coarse, crude, improper, impure, indecent, indelicate, lewd, low, obscene, offensive, ribald, rude, sensual, smutty, unseemly, vulgar; boorish, callous, coarse, crass, dull, ignorant, imperceptive, insensitive, tasteless, uncultured, undiscriminating, unfeeling, unrefined, unsophisticated

grotesque *adj* absurd, bizarre, deformed, distorted, extravagant, fanciful, fantastic, freakish, incongruous, ludicrous, malformed, misshapen, odd, outlandish, preposterous, ridiculous, strange, unnatural, weird, whimsical

ground *n* clod, dirt, dry, land, dust, earth, field, land, loam mould, sod, soil, terra firma, terrain, turf

groundless *adj* baseless, chimerical, empty, false, idle, illusory, imaginary, unauthorized, uncalled for, unfounded, unjustified, unprovoked, unsupported, unwarranted

groundwork *n* base, basis, cornerstone, footing, foundation, fundamentals, preliminaries, preparation, spadework, underpinnings

group *n* aggregation assemblage, association, band, batch, bunch, category, circle, class, clique, clump, cluster, collection, company, congregation coterie, crowd, faction, formation, gang, gathering, organization, pack, party, set, troop

group *v* arrange, assemble, associate, assort, bracket, class, classify, dispose, gather, marshal, order, organize, put together, range, sort

grouse *v* complain, groan, moan, protest, whinge; (*Inf*) bellyache, bitch

grouse *n* grievance, grumble, moan, objection,

grow *v* develop, enlarge, expand, extend, fill out, get bigger, get taller, heighten, increase, multiply, spread, stretch, swell, thicken, widen; develop, flourish, germinate, shoot, spring up, sprout, vegetate; advance, expand, flourish, improve, progress, prosper, succeed, thrive; breed, cultivate, farm, nurture, produce, propagate, raise

growl *v* bark, howl, snarl, yelp

grown-up *adj* adult, fully-grown, mature, of age

growth *n* aggrandizement, augmentation, development, enlargement, evolution, expansion, extension, growing, heightening, increase, multiplication, proliferation, stretching, thickening, widening; crop, cultivation, development, germination, produce, production, shooting, sprouting, vegetation; advance, advancement, expansion, improvement, progress, prosperity, rise, success

grubby *adj* besmeared, dirty, filthy, frowzy, grimy, mean, messy, mucky, scruffy, seedy, shabby, slovenly, smutty, soiled, sordid, squalid, unkempt, untidy, unwashed

grudge *n* animosity, animus, antipathy, aversion, bitterness, dislike, enmity, grievance, hard feelings, hate, ill will, malevolence, malice, pique, rancour, resentment, spite, venom

grudge *v* begrudge, be reluctant, complain, covet, envy, hold, back, mind, resent, stint

gruelling *adj* arduous, backbreak ing, brutal, crushing, demanding, difficult, exhausting, fatiguing, fierce, grinding, hard, harsh, laborious, punishing, sever, stiff, strenuous, taxing, tiring, trying

gruesome *adj* abominable, awful, fearful, ghastly, grim, grisly, hideous, horrendous, horrible, horrid, horrific, horrifying, loathsome, macabre, repugnant, repulsive, shocking, spine-chilling, terrible

gruff *adj* bad-tempered, bearish, blunt, brusque, churlish, crabbed, crusty, curt, discourteous, grouchy, grumpy, ill-humoured, ill-natured, impolite, rough, rude, sour, sullen, surly, uncivil, ungracious, unmannerly

grumble *v* carp, complain, find fault, grouse, moan, repine, whine; (*Sl*) bellyache

grumble *n* complaint, grievance, grouse, moan, objection

guarantee *n* assurance, bond, certainty, collateral, covenant, earnest, guaranty, pledge, promise, security, surety, undertaking, warranty, word, word of honour

guarantee *v* answer for, assure, certify, ensure, insure, maintain, make certain, pledge, promise, protect, secure, stand behind, swear, vouch for, warrant

guard *v* cover, defend, escort, keep, mind, oversee, patrol, police, preserve, protect, safeguard, save, screen, secure, shelter, shield, supervise, tend, watch, watch over;

guard *n* custodian, defender, look out, picket, protector, sentinel, sentry, warder, watch, watchman; buffer, bulwark, bumper, defence, pad, protection, rampart, safeguard, screen, security, shield; attention, care, caution, heed, vigilance, wariness, watchfulness

guardian *n* attendant, champion, curator, custodian, defender, escort, guard, keeper, preserver, protector,

trustee, warden, warder
guess *v* conjecture, estimate, fathom, hypothesize, penetrate, predict, solve, speculate, work out
guess *n* conjecture, feeling, hypothesis, judgment, notion, prediction, reckoning, speculation, supposition, surmise, suspicion, theory
guesswork *n* conjecture, estimate, hypothesis, judgement, presumption, reckoning, speculation, supposition; (*Inf*) guesstimate
guest *v* boarder, caller, company, lodger, visitant, visitor
guidance *n* advice, auspices, conduct, control, counsel, counselling, direction, government, help, instruction, intelligence, leadership, management, teaching
guide *v* accompany, attend, conduct, convoy, direct, escort, lead, pilot, shepherd, show the way, steer, usher; command, control, direct, handle, manage, manoeuvre, steer; advise, counsel, educate, govern, influence, instruct, oversee, regulate, rule, superintend, supervise, sway, teach, train
guide *n* adviser, attendant, chaperon, cicerone, conductor, controller, counsellor, director, escort, leader, mentor, monitor, pilot, steersman, teacher, usher; catalogue, directory, guidebook, handbook, instructions, key, manual
guild *n* association, brotherhood, club, company, corporation, fellow ship, raternity, league, lodge, order, organization, society, union
guile *n* art, artfulness, artifice, cleverness, craft, craftiness, cunning, deceit, deception, duplicity, gamesmanship, knavery, ruse, sharp, practice, slyness, treachery, trickery, trickiness, wiliness
guilt *n* blame, blameworthiness, criminality, culpability, delinquency, guiltiness, iniquity, misconduct, responsibility, sinfulness, wicked ness, wrong, wrongdoing; bad conscience, contrition, disgrace, dishonour, guiltiness, guilty, conscience, infamy, regret, remorse, self-condemnation, self-reproach, shame, stigma
guiltless *adj* blameless, clear, immaculate, impeccable, innocent, irreproachable, pure, sinless, spotless, unimpeachable, unsullied, untainted, untarnished
guilty *adj* at fault, blameworthy, convicted, criminal, culpable, delinquent, erring, evil, felonious, iniquitous, offending, reprehensible, responsible, sinful, to blame, wicked, wrong
gulf *n* bay, blight, sea inlet; abyss, breach, chasm, cleft, gap, opening, rent, rift, separation, split, void, whirlpool
gullible *adj* born yesterday, credulous, easily taken in, foolish, green, innocent, naive, silly, simple, trustting, unsceptical, unsophisticated, unsuspecting
gulp *v* bolt, devour, gobble, guzzle, knock back, quaff, swallow, swill, wolf
gulp *n* draught, mouthful, swallow; (*Inf*) swig
gum *n* adhesive, cement, exudate, glue, mucilage, paste, resin
gumption *n* ability, acumen, astuteness, cleverness, commonsense,

discernment, enterprise, horse sense, initiative, mother wit, resourcefulness, sagacity, shrewd ness, spirit

gurgle *v* babble, bubble, burble, crow, lap, murmur, plash, purl, ripple, splash

gurgle *n* babble, murmur, purl, ripple

gush *v* burst, cascade, flood, flow, jet, pour, run, rush, spout, spurt, stream

gush *n* burst, cascade, flood, flow, jet, outburst, outflow, rush, spout, spurt, stream, torrent

gust *n* blast, blow, breeze, flurry, gale, puff, rush, squall

gusto *n* appetite, appreciation, brio, delight, enjoyment, enthusiasm, exhilaration, fervour, liking, pleasure, relish, savour, verve, zeal, zest

guts *pl n* audacity, backbone, boldness, courage, daring, forcefulness, grit, hardihood, mettle, nerve, pluck, spirit, willpower

gutter *n* channel, conduit, ditch, drain, duct, pipe, sluice, trench, trough, tube

guttural *adj* deep, gravelly, gruff, hoarse, husky, low, rasping, tough, thick, throaty

guy *n* chap, fellow, lad, male, man, person, youth; (*Inf*) bloke, chap; effigy, figure, representation

guy *v* caricature, make fun of, mock, poke fun at, ridicule, send up, sneer at

gypsy *n* didcoi, rambler, Romany, rover, traveler, tzigane, wanderer; (*Inf*) tinker, transient, vagrant

H

habit *n* bent, custom, disposition, manner, mannerism, practice, proclivity, propensity, quirk, tendency, way; convention, custom, mode, practice, routine, rule, second nature, usage, wont; apparel, dress, garb, garment, habiliment, riding dress

habitation *n* abode, domicile, dwelling, dwelling house, home, house, living, quarters, lodging, quarters, residence

habitual *adj* accustomed, common, customary, familiar, fixed, natural, normal, ordinary, regular, routine, standard, traditional, usual, wonted

hack *v* chop, cut, gash, hew, kick, lacerate, mangle, mutilate, notch, slash

hack *adj* banal, mediocre, pedestrian, poor, stereotyped, tired, undistinguished, uninspired, unoriginal

hack *n* Grub Street writer, literary hack, penny-a-liner, scribbler; drudge, plodder, slave

hackneyed *adj* banal, chichéd, common, commonplace, over worked, pedestrian, run-of-the-mill, stale, stereotyped, stock, threadbare, timeworn, tired, trite, unoriginal, worn-out

hag *n* bedlam, crone, fury, harridan, shrew, termagant, virago, vixen, witch

haggard *adj* careworn, drawn, emaciated, gaunt, ghastly, hollow-eyed, pinched, shrunken, thin, wan, wasted, wrinkled

haggle *v* bargain, barter, beat down, chaffer, dicker, higgle, palter; bicker, dispute, quarrel, squabble, wrangle

hail *n* barrage, batter, beat down upon, bombard, pelt, rain, rain down on, shower, storm, volley; frozen rain, hailstones, sleet

hail *v* acclaim, acknowledge, applaud, cheer, exalt, glorify, greet, honour, salute, welcome; call, flag down, make a sign to, wave down; be a native of, come from, originate in; batter, bombard, pelt, pepper, rain down, shower, volley

hair *n* head of hair, locks, mane, mop, shock, tresses

hair-raising *adj* alarming, blood-curdling, breathtaking, creepy, exciting, frightening, horrifying, petrifying, scary, shocking, spine-chilling, startling, terrifying, thrilling

halcyon *adj* calm, gentle, peaceful, placid, serene, still, stormless, temperate, tranquil, windless; blissful, carefree, flourishing, golden, joyous, prosperous, thriving

hale *adj* able-bodied, blooming, fit, flourishing, healthy, hearty, in fine fettle, in the pink, robust, sound, strong, vigorous, well

half *n* bisection, division, equal part, fifty per cent, fraction, hemisphere, portion, section

half *adj* divided, fractional, halved, incomplete, limited, moderate, par tial

half *adv* after a fashion, all but, barely,

inadequately, incompletely, in part, partially, partly, pretty nearly, slightly

half-baked *adj* ill-conceived, ill-judged, poorly planned, premature, short-sighted, undeveloped; (*Inf*) crackpot; brainless, foolish, green, ignorant, immature, inexperienced, senseless, silly, stupid, wet behind the ears; (*Inf*) dim-witted, dopey, half-witted

half-hearted *adj* apathetic, cool, indifferent, lacklustre, listless, lukewarm, neutral, passive, perfunctory, spiritless, tame, unenthusiastic, uninterested

halfway *adv* midway, in the middle, to the midpoint; almost, just about, nearly, incompletely, moderately, nearly, partially, partly, in some measure; establish a middle ground with, give and take with, meet halfway, reach a compromise with; (*Inf*) go fifty-fifty with, go halvers with

halfway *adj* central, equidistant, intermediate, mean, medial, median, mid, middle, midway

halfwit *n* dunce, dunderhead, fool, numbskull; (*Inf*) crackpot, dim-wit, imbecile, moron, nitwit, nut

halfwitted *adj* barmy, crazy, doltish, dull-witted, feeble-minded, foolish, half-baked, idiotic, moronic, silly, simple, simple-minded, stupid; (*Inf*) barmy, batty, cracked, crackpot, crazy, dim-witted, imbecile, moron, nitwitted, nutty

hall *n* corridor, entrance hall, entry, foyer, hallway, lobby, passage, passageway, vestibule; assembly room, auditorium, chamber, church hall, concert hall, conference hall, meeting place

halt *v* break off, call it a day, cease, close down, come to an end, desist, draw up, pull up, rest, standstill, stop, wait; arrest, block, bring to an end, check, curb, cut short, end, hold, back, impede, obstruct, stem, terminate; be defective, falter, hobble, limp, stumble; be unsure, boggle, dither, haver, hesitate, pause, stammer, swither, think twice, waver

halt *n* arrest, break, breathing space, cessation, close, desistance, discontinue, end, hiatus, impasse, interlude, interruption, interval, pause, rest, respite, stand, standstill, time out stop, stopping, stoppage, termination

halting *adj* awkward, faltering, hesitant, imperfect, laboured, stammering, stumbling, stuttering

halve *v* bisect, cut in half, divide equally, reduce by fifty per cent, share equally, split in two

hammer *v* bang, beat, club, drive, hit, knock, strike, tap; bear out, fabricate, fashion, forge, from, make, mould, shape; batter, beat, bludgeon, club, cudgel, hit, pound, pummel, slap, strike, thrash, trounce; (*Inf*) beat, clobber; drudge, grind away, keep on, labour, plod away, slog away; (*Inf*) beaver away, plug away, stick at; accomplish, bring to a finish, carry through, complete, effect, negotiate, produce, resolve, settle, sort out, work out,

hammer *n* beetle, claw-hammer, gavel, mallet, sledgehammer

hamper *v* bind, cramp, curb, embarrass, encumber, entangle, fetter, frustrate, hamstring, handicap, hinder, hold up, impede, interfere with, obstruct, prevent, restrain, restrict, slow down, thwart, trammel

hand *n* fist, palm, paw; agency, direction, influence, part, participation, share; aid, assistance, help, support; artificer, artisan, craftsman, employee, hired man, labourer, operative, worker, workman; **in hand** in order, receiving attention, under control; available for use, in reserve, put by, ready

hand *v* deliver, hand over, pass; aid, assist, conduct, convey, give, guide, help, lead, present, transmit

handbill *n* advertisement, brochure, bulletin, circular, leaflet, notice, pamphlet; (*Inf*) junk mail

handbook *n* guide, guidebook, instruction book, manual

handcuff *v* fetter, manacle, shackle

hand down *v* bequeath, give, grant, pass on, transfer, will

handful *n* few, small number, small quantity, smattering, sprinkling

handicap *n* barrier, block, curb, check, disadvantage, drawback, encumbrance, hindrance, impediment, limitation, millstone, obstacle, restriction, shortcoming, stumbling block; defect, disability, impairment

handicap *v* block, bridle, check, curb, constrain, hold back, limit, restrict, trammel

handicraft *n* art, artisanship, craft, craftmanship, handiwork, skill, workmanship

handiwork *n* achievement, artefact, creation, design, invention, product, production, result

handle *n* grip, haft, handgrip, helve, hilt, knob, shaft, stock

handle *v* feel, finger, fondle, grasp, hold, maul, pick up, poke, touch; control, direct, guide, manage, manipulate, manoeuvre, operate, steer, use, wield; administer, conduct, cope with, deal with, manage, supervise, take care of, treat

hand-outs *pl n* alms, charity, dole, gifts; bulletin, circular, free sample, leaflet, literature, mailshot, pamphlet, press release

hand out *v* deal out, disburse, dish-out, dispense, disseminate, distribute, give out, mete

hand over *v* deliver, donate, fork out, present, release, surrender, transfer, turn over, yield

hand-picked *adj* choice, elect, élite, select, specially chosen

handsome *adj* admirable, attractive, becoming, comely, elegant, fine, good-looking, gorgeous, graceful, majestic, personable, stately, well-proportioned

handsomely *adv* abundantly, amply, bountifully, generously, liberally, magnanimously, munificently, plentifully, richly

handwriting *adj* calligraphy, chirography, fist, hand, longhand, penmanship, scrawl, script

handy *adj* accessible, at hand, available, close, convenient, near, near by, within reach; convenient, easy to use, helpful, manageable, neat, practical, serviceable, useful, user-friendly; adept, adroit, clever, deft, dexterous, expert, nimble, proficient, ready, skilful, skilled

hang *v* be pendent, dangle, depend,

droop, incline, suspend; execute, gibbet, sent to the gallows, string up; adhere, cling, hold, rest, stick; attach, cover, deck, decorate, drape, fasten, fix, furnish

hang about *adj* dally, linger, loiter, roam, tarry, waste time

hang back *adj* be backward, be reluctant, demur, hesitate, hold back, recoil

hanger-on *n* dependant, follower, flunkey, freeloader, lackey, leech, minion, parasite, retainer, sponger, sycophant

hanging *adj* dangling, drooping, flapping, flopping, floppy, loose, pendent, suspended, swinging, unattached, unsupported

hank *n* coil, length, loop, piece, roll, skein

hankering *n* craving, desire, hunger, itch, longing, pining, thirst, urge, wish, yearning

haphazard *adj* accidental, arbitrary, chance, random; aimless, careless, casual, disorderly, disorganized, hit or miss, indiscriminate, slapdash, slipshod, unmethodical, unsystematic

happen *v* appear, arise, come about, come to ass, crop up, develop, ensue, eventuate, follow, materialize, occur, present itself, result, take place; become of, befall, betide; chance, fall out, have the fortune to be, supervene, turn out

happening *n* accident, adventure, affair, case, chance, episode, event, experience, incident, occasion, occurrence, phenomenon, proceeding, scene

happily *adv* agreeably, contentedly, delightedly enthusiastically, freely, gladly, heartily, willingly, with pleasure; blithely, cheerfully, gaily, gleefully, joyfully, joyously, merrily; auspiciously, favourably, fortunately, luckily, opportunely, propitiously, providentially, seasonably, appropriately, aptly, felicitously, gracefully, successfully

happiness *n* beatitude, blessedness, bliss, cheer, cheerfulness, cheeriness, contentment, delight, ecstasy, elation, enjoyment, exuberance, felicity, gaiety, gladness, high, spirits, joy, jubilation, light-heartedness, merriment, pleasure, prosperity, satisfaction, wellbeing

happy *adj* blessed, blest, blissful, blithe, cheerful, content, contented, delighted, ecstatic, elated, glad, gratified, jolly, joyful, joyous, jubilant, merry, overjoyed, over the moon, pleased, sunny, thrilled

happy-go-lucky *adj* blithe, care free, casual, devil-may-care, easygoing, heedless, improvident, insouciant, irresponsible, light-hearted, nonchalant, unconcerned, untroubled

harangue *n* address, diatribe, declamation, exhortation, homily, lecture, sermon, speech, talk, tirade

harass *v* annoy, badger, bait, beleaguer, bother, disturb, exasperate, exhaust, fatigue, harry, hound, perplex, persecute, pester, plague, tease, tire, torment, trouble, vex, weary, worry

harbour *n* anchorage, destination, haven, port; asylum, covert, haven, refuge, retreat, sanctuary, sanctum, security shelter

harbour *v* conceal, hide, lodge, protect, provide, refuge, relieve, secrete, shelter, shield

hard *adj* compact, dense, firm, impenetrable, inflexible, rigid, rocklike, solid, stiff, stony, strong, tough, unyielding; arduous, backbreaking, burdensome, exacting, exhausting, fatiguing, formidable, laborious, rigorous, strenuous, toilsome, tough, uphill, wearying; baffling, complex, complicated, difficult, intricate, involved, knotty, perplexing, puzzling, tangled, thorny, unfathomable, callous, cold, cruel, exacting, grim, hardhearted, harsh, implacable, obdurate, pitiless, ruthless, severe, strict, stubborn, unkind, unrelenting, unsympathetic

hard *adv* energetically, fiercely, forcefully, forcibly, heavily, intensely, powerfully, severely, sharply, strongly, vigorously, violently; assiduously, determinedly, diligently, doggedly, earnestly, industriously, intently, persistently, steadily, strenuously, untiringly; agonizingly, badly, distressingly, harshly, painfully, severely, with difficulty; bitterly, hardly, keenly, rancorously, reluctantly, resentfully, slowly, sorely

hard-core *adj* dedicated, die-hard, extreme, intransigent, obstinate, staunch, steadfast, stubborn; blatant, explicit, obscene; (*Inf*) full-frontal

harden *v* anneal, bake, cake, freeze, set, solidify, stiffen; brace, buttress, fortify, gird, indurate, nerve, reinforce, steel, strengthen, toughen

hardened *adj* chronic, fixed, habitual, incorrigible, inveterate, irredeemable, reprobate, set, shameless; accustomed, habituated, inured, seasoned, toughened

hard-headed *adj* astute, cool, level-headed, practical, pragmatic, realistic, sensible, shrewd, tough, unsentimental

hard-hearted *adj* callous, cold, cruel, hard, heartless, indifferent, inhuman, insensitive, intolerant, merciless, pitiless, stony, uncaring, unfeeling, unkind, unsympathetic

hardly *adv* almost not, barely, by no means, faintly, infrequently, just, not at all, not quite, no way, only, only just, scarcely, with difficulty

hardship *n* adversity, affliction, austerity, burden, calamity, destitution, difficulty, fatigue, grievance, labour, misery, misfortune, need, oppression, persecution, privation-suffering, toil, torment, trial, tribulation, trouble, want

hard-wearing *adj* durable, resilient, rugged, stout, strong, tough, well-made

hard-working *adj* assiduous, busy, conscientious, diligent, energetic, indefatigable, industrious, sedulous, zealous

hardy *adj* firm, fit, hale, healthy, hearty, in fine fettle, lusty, robust, rugged, sound, stalwart, stout, strong, sturdy, tough, vigorous

harm *n* abuse, damage, detriment, disservice, hurt, ill, impairment, injury, loss, mischief, misfortune

harm *v* abuse, blemish, damage, hurt, ill-treat, ill-use, impair, injure, maltreat, mar, molest, ruin, spoil, wound

harmful *adj* baleful, baneful, damaging, deleterious, destructive, detrimental, disadvantageous, evil, hurtful, injurious, noxious, pernicious

harmless *adj* gentle, innocent, innocuous, innoxious, inoffensive, nontoxic, not dangerous, safe, unobjectionable

harmonious *adj* agreeable, compat ible, concordant, congruous, consonant, coordinated, correspondent, dulcet, euphonious, harmonic, harmonizing, matching, mellifluous, melodious, musical, sweet-sounding, tuneful

harmony *n* accord, agreement, amicability, amity, compatibility, concord, conformity, consensus, cooperation, friendship, food will, like-mindedness, peace, rapport, sympathy, unanimity, understanding, unity; euphony, melodiousness, melody, tune, tunefulness

harness *n* equipment, gear, tack, tackle, trappings

harness *v* couple, hitch up, put in harness, saddle, yoke; apply, channel, control, employ, exploit, make productive, mobilize, render useful, turn to account, utilize

harsh *adj* coarse, croaking, crude, discordant, dissonant, glaring, grating, guttural, jarring, rasping, raucous, rough, strident, unmelodious; abusive, austere, bitter, bleak, brutal, comfortless, cruel, dour, grim, hard, pitiless, punitive, relentless, ruthless, sever, sharp, stern, stringent, unfeeling, unkind, unpleasant, unrelenting

harshness *n* acerbity, acrimony, asperity, austerity, bitterness, brutality, churlishness, coarseness, crudity, hardness, ill-temper, rigour, roughness, severity, sourness, sternness

harvest *n* harvesting, harvest-time, ingathering, reaping; crop, produce, yield

hash *n* confusion, hotchpotch, jumble, mess, mishandle, mishmash, mix-up, muddle, shambles; (*Inf*) screw up; cannabis, ganja, hemp, marihuana, marijuana; (*Inf*) grass, pot

haste *n* alacrity, briskness, celerity, dispatch, expedition, fleetness, nimbleness, promptitude, quickness, rapidity, rapidness, speed, swiftness, urgency, velocity; bustle, hastiness, helter-skelter, hurry, hustle, impetuosity, precipitateness, rashness, recklessness, rush

hasten *v* bolt, dash, fly, haste, hurry, make haste, race, run, rush, scurry, scuttle, speed, sprint, tear along

hastily *adv* apace, double-quick, fast, fleet, hurried, prompt, rapid, speedy, swift, urgent; foolhardy, headlong, heedless, impetuous, impulsive, indiscreet, precipitate, rash, reckless, thoughtless, unduly quick

hatch *v* breed, bring forth, brood, incubate, conceive, concoct, contrive, cook up, design, devise, dream up, plan, plot, project, scheme, think up

hate *v* abhor, abominate, be hostile to, be repelled by, be sick of, despise, detest, dislike, execrate, have an aversion, to loathe, recoil from

hate *n* abhorrence, abomination,

animosity, animus, antagonism, antipathy, aversion, detestation, dislike, enmity, execration, hatred, hostility, loathing, odium

hateful *adj* abhorrent, abominable, despicable, detestable, disgusting, execrable, forbidding, foul, heinous, horrible, loathsome, obnoxious, odious, offensive, repellent, repugnant, repulsive, revolting, vile

hatred *n* abomination, animosity, antagonism, antipathy, aversion, detestation, dislike, enmity, execration, hate, ill will, odium, repugnance, revulsion

haughty *adj* arrogant, assuming, conceited, contemptuous, disdainful, high, imperious, lofty, overweening, proud, scornful, snobbish, supercilious

haul *v* drag, draw, hale, heave, lug, pull, tow, trail, tug

haul *n* booty, catch, find, gain, harvest, loot, spoils, takings, yield

haunt *v* visit, walk; beset, come back, obsess, plague, possess, prey on, recur, stay with, torment, trouble; frequent, hang around, repair, resort, visit

haunt *n* den, gathering place, hang out, meeting place, rendezvous, resort, stamping ground

haunting *adj* disturbing, eerie, evocative, indelible, nostalgic, persistent, poignant, recurrent, recurring, unforgettable

have *v* hold, keep, obtain, occupy, own, possess, retain; accept, acquire, gain, procure, receive; compreise, contain, embrace, include, incorporate, take in; encounter, experience, go through, meet, put up with, tolerate; ask, bid, command, direct, give orders to, request, tell; abide, endure, enjoy, experience, feel, meet with, suffer, sustain, undergo; **have to** be bound, be compelled, be forced, be obliged, have got to, must, ought, should

haven *n* anchorage, harbour, port, roads; asylum, refuge, retreat, sanctum, shelter

haversack *n* backpack, kitbag, knapsack, rucksack, satchel

havoc *n* carnage, damage, desolation, despoliation, destruction, devastation, rack and ruin, ravages, ruin, slaughter, waste, wreck; chaos, confusion, disorder, disruption, mayhem; (*Inf*) shambles

hawk *v* cry, doorstep, market, peddle, sell, tout

hazardous *adj* dangerous, difficult, fraught with danger, insecure, perilous, precarious, risky, unsafe

haze *n* cloud, dimness, film, fog, mist, obscurity, smog, smokiness, steam, vapour

hazy *adj* blurry, cloudy, dim, dull, faint, foggy, misty, nebulous, obscure, overcast, smoky, veiled; fuzzy, ill-defined, indefinite, indistinct, loose, muddled, muzzy, nebulous, uncertain, unclear, vague

head *n* cranium, crown, pate, skull; boss, captain, chief, chieftain, commander, director, headmaster, headmistress, head teacher, leader, manager, master, principal, superintendent, supervisor; apex, crest, crown, height, peak, pitch, summit, tip, top, vertex, ability, aptitude, brain, brains, capacity, faculty, flair, intellect, intelligence, mentality, mind, talent, thought, understanding; branch, category, class, department, division, heading, section, subject, topic

head *adj* arch, chief, first, foremost, front, highest, leading, main, pre-eminent, premier, prime, principal, supreme, topmost

head *v* be first, cap, crown, lead, lead the way, precede, top; be in charge of, command, control, direct, govern, guide, lead, manage, rule, run, supervise

headache *n* migraine; bane, bother, bugbear, inconvienience, pest, trouble, vexation

heading *n* caption, headline, name, rubric, title; category, class, division, section

headlong *adj* breakneck, dangerous, hasty, impetuous, impulsive, inconsiderate, precipitate, reckless, thoughtless

headlong *adv* hastily, heedlessly, helter-skelter, hurriedly, pell-mell, precipitately, rashly, thoughtlessly, wildly

headstrong *adj* contrary, foolhardy, forward, heedless, imprudent, impulsive, intractable, mulish, obstinate, perverse, pig-headed, rash, reckless, self-willed, stubborn, ungovernable, unruly, wilful

headway *n* advance, improvement, progress, progression, way

heal *v* cure, make well, mend, regenerate, remedy, restore, treat; alleviate, ameliorate, compose, conciliate, harmonize, patch up, reconcile, settle, soothe

health *n* fitness, good condition, haleness, healthiness, robustness, salubrity, soundness, strength, vigour, wellbeing

healthy *adj* active, blooming, fit, flourishing, hale, hale and hearty, hardy, hearty, in fine form, in good condition, in the pink, physically fit, robust, sound, strong, sturdy, vigorous, well

heap *n* accumulation, aggregation, collection, hoard, lot, mass, mound, mountain, pile, stack, stockpile, store; (*Inf*) lashings, loads, oodles, pots, stacks, tons

heap *v* accumulate, amass, augment, bank, collect, gather, hoard, increase, lay by, mound, pile, set aside, stack, stockpile, store up

hear *v* catch, eavesdrop, give attention, heed, listen in, listen to, over hear; ascertain, be informed, be told of, discover, find out, gather, learn, pick up, understand; (*Inf*) get wind of; ajudicate, consider, examine, inquire into, investigate, judge, try

hearing *n* audition, auditory, ear, perception, audience, audition, chance to speak, interview; auditory range, earshot, hearing distance, range, reach, sound; inquiry, investigation, review, trial

hearsay *n* buzz, gossip, idle talk, mere talk, report, rumour, talk, talk of the town, tittle-tattle, word of mouth

heart *n* affection, benevolence, compassion, concern, humanity, love, pity, tenderness, understand ing; boldness, bravery, courage, fortitude, mettle, mind, nerve, pluck, purpose, resolution, spirit, sill; central, part, centre, core, crux, essence, hub, kernel, marrow, middle, nucleus, pith, quintessence, root; **by heart** by memory, by rote, off pat, pat, word for word

heartbreaking *adj* agonizing, bitter, desolating, disappointing, distress ing, grievous, heart-rending, pitiful, poignant, sad, tragic

heartbroken *adj* brokenhearted, crestfallen, crushed, dejected, desolate, despondent, disappointed, disconsolate, disheartened, dispirited, downcast, grieved, heartsick, miserable

heartfelt *adj* ardent, cordial, deep, devout, earnest, fervent, genuine, hearty, honest, profound, sincere, unfeigned, warm, wholehearted

heartless *adj* brutal, callous, cold, cold-blooded, cold-hearted, cruel, hard, hardhearted, harsh, inhuman, merciless, pitiless, uncaring, unfeeling, unkind

heart-to heart *adj* dejected, depressed, despondent, disappointed, downcast, heavy-hearted

heart-to-heart *n* cosy chat

heart-warming *adj* cheerful, cheering, encouraging, gladdening, moving, touching, uplifting; gratifying, pleasing, rewarding, satisfying

hearty *adj* affable, ardent, back-slapping, cordial, eager, ebullient, effusive, enthusiastic, exuberant, friendly, generous, genial, jovial, unreserved, warm; active, energetic, hale, hardy, healthy, robust, sound, strong, vigorous, well

heat *n* calefaction, fever, fieriness, high temperature, hotness, hot spell, sultriness, swelter, torridity, warmness, warmth; agitation, ardour, earnestness, excitement, fever, impetuosity, intensity, passion, violence, zeal

heat *v* become warm, chafe, cook, flush, glow, grow hot, make hot, reheat, warm up; animate, arouse, enrage, excite, impassion, inflame, inspirit, rouse, stimulate, stir, warm

heated *adj* angry, bitter, excited, fierce, fiery, frenzied, furious, impassioned, intense, passionate, raging, stormy, tempestuous, vehement, violent

heathen *n* agnostic, atheist, disbeliever, heretic, infidel, pagan, sceptic

heathen *adj* barbarian, barbourous, brutish, savage, uncivilized

heave *v* drag up, elevate, haul, heft, hoist, lever, lift, pull, raise, tug; cast, fling, hurl, pitch, send, sling, throw, toss

heaven *n* Avalon, bliss, dreamland, ecstasy, Eden, enchantment, fairyland, felicity, happiness, happy hunting-ground, nirvana, paradise, rapture, seventh heaven, sheer bliss, transport, utopia

heavenly *adj* alluring, beautiful, blissful, celestial, delightful, entrancing, exquisite, lovely, rapturous, ravishing, sublime, wonderful; (*Inf*) divine, glorious,

heaviness *n* gravity, heftiness, ponderousness, weight; arduousness, burdensomeness, grievousness, onerousness, oppressiveness, severity, weightiness; deadness, dullness, languor, numbness, sluggishness, torpor

heavy *adj* bulky, hefty, massive, ponderous, portly, weighty; awkward, burdensome, cumbersome, difficult, grievous, hard, harsh, intolerable, laborious, onerous, oppressive, severe, tedious, vexatious, wearisome; apathetic, drowsy, dull, inactive, indolent, inert, listless, slow, sluggish, stupid, torpid, wooden, burdened, encumbered, laden, loaded, oppressed, weighted; bulky, corpulent, fat, overweight, obese, paunchy, portly, stout, tubby; dense, solid, thick; boggy, clogged, difficult, miry, muddy; abundant, copious, profuse, superabundant; intense, serious, severe; boring, tedious, uninteresting; rough, tempestuous, squally, turbulent, wild; cloudy, dark, dreary, dull, gloomy, grey, louring, overcast,

heckle *v* bait, barrack, disrupt, interrupt, jeer, pester, shout down, taunt

hectic *adj* animated, boisterous, chaotic, excited, fevered, feverish, flurrying, flustering, frantic, frenetic, frenzied, furious, heated, riotous, tumultuous, turbulent, wild

hector *v* badger, bait, browbeat, bully, coerce, intimidate, menace, provoke, threaten, torment,

hedge *n* hedgerow, quickset; barrier, boundary, protection, screen, windbreak; cover, guard, insurance cover, safeguard

hedge *v* border, edge, enclose, fence, surround; block, confine, hem in, hinder, obstruct, restrict; beg the question, be noncommittal, dodge, duck, equivocate, evade, prevaricate, quibble, sidestep, temporize

heed *n* attention, care, caution, consideration, ear, heedfulness, mind, note, notice, regard, respect, thought, watchfulness;

heed *v* attend, bear in mind, be guided by, consider, follow, give ear to, listen, to, mark, mind, note, obey, observe, pay attention to, regard, take notice of, take to heart

heel *n* crust, end, remainder, rump, stub, stump, **down at heel** dowdy, impoverished, out at elbows, run-down, seedy, shabby, slipshod, slovenly, worn

height *n* altitude, elevation, high ness, loftiness, stature, tallness; apex, apogee, crest, crown, elevation, hill, mountain, peak, pinnacle, summit, top, vertex, zenith; acme, dignity, eminence, exaltation, grandeur, loftiness, prominence

heighten *v* add to, aggravate, amplify, augment, enhance, improve, increase, intensify, magnify, sharpen, strengthen

hell *n* Abaddon, abode of the damned, abyss, bottomless pit, fire and brimstone, hellfire, infernal regions, inferno, lower world, nether world, underworld; affliction, agony, anguish, martyrdom, misery, nightmare, ordeal, suffering, torment, trial, wretchedness

hellish *adj* damnable, damned, demoniacal, devilish, diabolical, fiendish, infernal

help *v* abet, aid, assist, back, befriend, cooperate, lend a hand, promote, relieve, save, second, serve, stand by, succour, support; alleviate, ameliorate, cure, facilitate, heal, improve, relieve, remedy, restore

help *n* advice, aid, assistance, avail, benefit, cooperation, guidance, helping, hand, service, support, use, utility

helper *n* abettor, adjutant, aide, aider, ally, assistant, attendant, auxiliary, coadjutor, collaborator, colleague, deputy, helpmate, mate, partner, right-hand man, second, subsidiary, supporter

helpful *adj* advantageous, beneficial, constructive, favourable, fortunate, practical, productive, profitable, serviceable, timely, useful; accommodating, beneficent, benevolent, caring, considerate, cooperative, friendly, kind, neighbourly, supportive, sympathetic

helping *n* piece, plateful, portion, ration, serving

helpless *adj* abandoned, defence less, dependent, destitute, exposed, forlorn, unprotected, vulnerable; debilitated, disabled, feeble, impotent, incapable, incompetent, infirm, paralysed, powerless, unfit, weak

hem *n* border, edge, fringe, margin, trimming

herald *n* bearer of tidings, crier, messenger; forerunner, harbinger, indication, omen, precursor, sign, signal, token

herd *n* assemblage, collection, crowd, crush, drove, flock, horde, mass, mob, multitude, pack, press, swarm, throng

herd *v* assemble, associate, collect, congregate, flock, gather, huddle, muster, rally, round up

hereafter *adv* after this, from now on, from this day forth, hence, henceforth, henceforward, in future

hereafter *n* heaven, immortality, life after death, life to come, next world, paradise, the after-life, the after-world, the beyond

hereditary *adj* congenital, family, genetic, inborn, inbred, inherent, inheritable, innate, transmissible; ancestral, bequeathed, family, handed down, transferred, willed

heresy *n* apostasy, dissidence, error, heterodoxy, iconoclasm, impiety, revisionism, schism, unorthodoxy

heretic *n* apostate, dissenter, dissident, nonconformist, renegade, revisionist, schismatic, sectarian, separatist

heritage *n* background, history, tradition; bequest, birthright, endowment, estate, inheritance, legacy, lot, patrimony, portion, share, tradition; ancestry, birth, bloodline, descent, dynasty, extraction, lineage

hermit *n* anchoress, anchorite, ancress, eremite, monk, pillarist, pillar-saint, recluse, solitary, stylite

hermitage *n* asylum, haven, hideaway, reuge, retreat, sanctuary

hero *n* cavalier, celebrity, champion, conqueror, exemplar, great man, idol, knight, man of the hour, paladin, popular figure, shining example, star, superstar, victor; lead actor, leading man, male lead, principal male character, protagonist; ideal man, ideal woman, idol, popular figure; (*Inf*) heart-throb

heroic *adj* bold, brave, chivalrous, courageous, daring, dauntless, doughty, fearless, gallant, intrepid, lion-hearted, stout-hearted, undaunted, valiant, valorous

heroine *n* celebrity, goddess, ideal, woman of the hour; diva, female lead, lead actress, leading lady, paragon, prima donna, principal female character, protagonist, shining example

heroism *n* boldness, bravery, chivalry, courage, courageousness, daring, fearlessness, fortitude, gallantry, intrepidity, lion-heartedness, manliness, mettle, prowess, spirit, valour, virililty

hesitant *adj* diffident, doubtful, half-hearted, halting, hanging back, hesitating, indecisive, irresolute, lacking confidence, oscillating, reluctant, sceptical, shilly-shallying, shy, stalling, timid, uncertain, unsure, vacillating, wavering

hesitate *v* be uncertain, delay, dither, doubt, hang back, hesitate, pause, shilly-shally, stall, swither, vacillate, wait, waver; (*Inf*) dilly-dally

hesitation *v* cunctation, delay, doubt, dubiety, hesitancy, indecision, irresolution, stalling, uncertainty, vacillation; disinclination, misgivings, qualms, reluctance, unwillingness

hew *v* axe, chop, cut, fell, hack, lop, prune, saw, sever, split, trim; carve, chip, chisel, fashion, form, make, model, sculpt, sculpture, shape, smooth, whittle

heyday *n* bloom, crowning point, culmination, flowering, peak, peak of perfection, pink, pinnacle, prime, prime of life, salad days

hiatus *n* blank, break, discontinuity, gap, interruption, lacuna; aperature, breach, cavity, cleft, fissure, foramen, opening

hidden *adj* abstruse, arcane, clandestine, close, concealed, covered, covert, cryptic, dark, hermetic, hermetical, masked, mysterious, mystic, mystical, obscure, occult, recondite, secret, shrouded, ulterior, unrevealed, unseen, veiled

hide *v* cache, conceal, cover one's tracks, go into hiding, go to ground, go underground, lie low, secrete, stash, take cover; (*Inf*) hole up; camouflage, cloak, cloud, conceal, cover, darken, disguise, eclipse, mask, obscure, obstruct, screen, shelter, shroud, veil

hide *n* coat, fleece, fur, pelt, skin

hideaway *n* cache, den, hermitage, hiding-place, lair, refuge, retreat, shelter

hidebound *adj* bigoted, conservative, conventional, fundamentalist, intolerant, intractable, narrow, narrow-minded, orthodox, prejudiced, reactionary, rigid, set, set in one's ways, strait-laced, ultraconservative, uncompromising

hideous *adj* disgusting, ghastly, grim, grisly, grotesque, gruesome, macabre, monstrous, repellant, repulsive, revolting, ugly, unsightly; abominable, appalling, contemptible, foul, frightening, heinous, horrific, horrifying, monstrous, odius, outrageous, terrifying

hiding *n* battering, beating, caning, drubbing, flogging, spanking, thrashing, thumping, whipping; (*Inf*) larruping, lathering, licking, tanning, walloping, whaling

hierarchy *n* class system, grading, ranking, pecking, social order

hieroglyphics *pl n* cipher, code, cryptogram, cryptograph, shorthand

high *adj* elevated, lofty, soaring, steep, tall, towering; excessive, extraordinary, extreme, great, intensified, sharp, strong; chief, distinguished, eminent, exalted, high-ranking, important, influential, leading, main, powerful, principal, ruling, superior; arch, chief, consequential, costly, dear, exorbitant, expensive, high-priced, inflated, stiff; (*Inf*) steep; extreme, forceful, potent, powerful, sharp, strong, vigorous; acute, high-pitched, penetrating, piercing, piping, sharp, shrill, soprano, strident, treble; extravagant, grand, high-living, lavish, luxurious, prodigal, rich; boisterous, cheerful, ecstatic, elated, happy, jolly, overexcited; delirious, drugged, hallucinating, intoxicated; (*Inf*) freaked out, on a trip, spaced out, stoned, tripping, turned on; going bad, going off, rotting, smelling, tainted; (*Inf*) ponging, niffy, whiffy

high *adv* aloft, altitude, at great height, far up, high up, way up

high *n* apex, height, peak, summit, top, zenith

highbrow *n* aesthete, intellectual, mastermind, savant, scholar; (*Inf*) bookworm, brain-box, brain, egghead

highbrow *adj* bookish, cultivated, cultured, deep, genius, high-browed, intellectual, mastermind, sophisticated; (*Inf*) brainy

high-class *adj* choice, elegant, élite, first-rate, luxurious, posh, superior, up market, upper class; (*Inf*) classy, super, super-duper

high-flown *adj* bombastic, elaborate, exaggerated, extravagant, florid, grandiloquent, ornate, overblown, overdone, pretentious

high-handed *adj* arbitrary, arrogant, autocratic, despotic, dictatorial, domineering, haughty. imperious, inconsiderate, lordly, oppressive, overbearing, peremptory, selfwilled, tyrannical, wilful; (*Inf*) bossy

highland *n* mountainous region, hilly country, plateau, ridge, tableland, uplands,

highlight *n* best part, climax, cynosure, feature, focal point, focus, high point, high spot, main feature, memorable part, peak, outstanding feature

highlight *v* accent, accentuate, bring home, bring to the fore, emphasize, feature, focus attention on, give prominence to, place emphasis on, play up, point upset off, show up, spotlight, stress, underline

highly *adv* certainly, decidedly, eminently, exceptionally, extraordinarily, extremely, greatly, immensely, supremely, to a great extent, tremendously, vastly, very, very much; admiringly, appreciatively, enthusiastically, favourably, warmly, well

highly-strung *adv* edgy, excitable, irritable, neurotic, nervous, overwrought, stressed, temperamental, wound up

high-powered *adj* aggressive, driving, dynamic, effective, energetic, enterprising, fast-track, forceful, go-ahead, go-getting, highly capable, vigorous

high-spirited *adj* active, animated, boisterous, bold, bouncy, daring, dashing, ebullient, effervescent, energetic, exuberant, frolicsome, full of life, fun-loving, gallant, lively, spirited, vibrant, vital, vivacious

high spirits *pl n* animation, boisterousness, bounciness, dynamism, exhilaration, exuberance, liveliness, vitality, vivacity

hijack *v* car-jack, commandeer, expropriate, seize, skyjack, steal, take over

hike *v* back-pack, ramble, tramp, trek, walk, wander

hike *n* march, ramble, tramp, trek, trudge, walk

hilarious *adj* a great laugh, amusing, animated, comic, comical, convivial, entertaining, exhilarated, funny, gay, happy, humorous, jolly, jovial, joyful, joyous, merry, mirth ful, noisy, rollicking, side-splitting, sparkling, uproarious, witty, zany

hilarity *n* amusement, boisterousness, cheerfulness, comedy, conviviality, exhilaration, exuberance, gaiety, glee, high spirits, jollification, jollity, joviality, joyousness, laughter, levity, merriment, mirth

hill *n* brae, elevation, eminence, fell, heights, high land, hillock, hilltop, hummock, knoll, mound, mount, prominence, ridge, tor; acclivity, gradient, incline, rise, slope; drift, heap, mound, mountain, pile

hillock *n* barrow, hummock, knob, knoll

hilt *n* grip, haft, handle, hold, shaft; all the way, completely, entirely, fully, totally, wholly

hinder *v* abort, arrest, baffle, baulk, block, check, curb, debar, defer, delay, deter, encumber, foil, forstall, frustrate, hamper, hamstring, handicap, hold back, hold up, impede, inhibit, interfere with, interrupt, obstruct, oppose, prevent, retard, slow down, stop, stymie, thwart, trammel

hindrance *n* bar, barrier, check, debarment, deterrent, difficulty, drag, drawback, encumbrance, handicap, hitch, impediment, interference, interruption, limitation, obstacle, obstruction, restraint, restriction, snag, stoppage, stumbling-block, trammel

hinge *v* be contingent on, be subject to, centre on, depend, hang on, pivot on, rest on, revolve around, turn on

hint *n* allusion, clue, implication, indication, inkling, innuendo, insinuation, intimation, mention, reminder, suggestion, tip-off, word to the wise; advice, help, pointer, suggestion, tip; breath, dash, speck, suggestion, suspicion, taste, tinge, touch, trace, undertone, whiff, whisper

hint *v* allude, cue, imply, indicate, insinuate, intimate, let it be known, mention, prompt, signal, suggest, tip-off

hire *v* appoint, commission, employ, engage, enlist, sign up, take on; charter, engage, lease, let, rent

hire *n* charge, cost, earnings, fee, pay, price, renumeration, salary, stipend, wage; lease, rent, rental

hiss *n* buzz, hissing, sibilance, sibilation, wheeze, whistle; boo, catcall, clamour, contempt, derision, hoot, jeer; (*Inf*) raspberry

hiss *v* rasp, shrill, sibilate, wheeze,

whirr, whistle, whiz; boo, catcall, condemn, damn, decry, deride, hoot, jeer, mock, revile, ridicule, scorn, taunt; (*Inf*) blow raspberries

historian *n* annalist, antiquarian, archivist, biographer, chronicler, historiographer, palaeographer

historic *adj* celebrated, consequential, epoch-making, extraordinary, famous, important, memorable, momentous, notable, outstanding, red-letter, remarkable, significant

history *v* account, annals, autobiography, biography, chronicle, memoirs, narration, narrative, recapitulation, recital, records, relation, saga, story, study; background, experiences, fortunes; antiquity, bygones, days of old, former times, yesterday

hit *v* bang, batter, beat, box, cuff, flog, hammer, knock, lob, pound, punch, slap, smack, strike, swat, thrash, thump; (*Inf*) biff, clobber, clout, sock, wallop, whack; bang into, bump, clash with, collide with, crash against, meet head-on, run into, smash into

hit *n* beating, blow, box, bump, clash, collision, cuff, impact, knock, punch, rap, shot, slap, smack, stroke, thump; (*Inf*) bashing, belt ing, clout, swipe, wallop; sellout, sensation, smash, success, triumph, winner

hitch *v* attach, bind, connect, couple, fasten, harness, join, make fast, tether, tie, unite, yoke; hike up, jerk up, pull up; (*Inf*) yank up; hitch a lift, hitch-hike, thumb a lift

hitch *n* barrier, catch, check, delay, difficulty, drawback, hindrance, hold-up, impediment, mishap, obstacle, obstruction, problem, snag, stoppage, stumbling-block, trouble

hitherto *adv* before, beforehand, heretofore, previously, so far, thus far, till now, until now, up to now

hit-or-miss *adj* aimless, careless, casual, cursory, disorganized, haphazard, off-hand, perfunctory, random

hoard *n* accumulation, cache, fund, heap, mass, pile, reserve, stockpile, store, supply, treasure trove; (*Inf*) stash

hoard *v* accumulate, aggregation, amass, buy up, cache, collect, conglomeration, deposit, garner, gather, hive, lay up, put away, put by, save, squirrel away, stash away, stockpile, store, stow away, treasure

hoarse *adj* croaky, discordant, grating, gravelly, growling, gruff, guttural, harsh, husky, rasping, raucous, rough, throaty

hoax *n* cheat, deception, fraud, imposture, jest, joke, practical joke, prank, ruse, swindle, trick; (*Inf*) con, fast one, scam, spoof

hobble *v* falter, limp, reel, shuffle, stagger, totter

hobby *n* activity, amusement, diversion, game, leisure pursuit, occupation, pastime, recreation, relaxation, sideline, sport

hoist *v* elevate, erect, heave, hike up, jack up, lift, raise, upraise

hoist *n* capstan, crane, elevator, jack, lift, pulley, tackle, winch

hold *v* adhere, clasp, cleave, clinch, cling to, clutch, cradle, embrace, enfold, fondle, grasp, grip, hold on to, hug; have, keep, own, possess, retain; arrest, bind, confine, curb, detain, imprison, restrain, stay, stop, suspend; assume, believe, consider, deem, entertain, esteem, judge, maintain, presume, reckon, regard, think, view; continue, endure, last, persevere, persist, remain, resist, stay, wear; assemble, call, carry on, celebrate, conduct, convene, have, officiate at, preside over, run, solemnize; bear, brace, carry, prop, shoulder, support, sustain, take; accommodate, comprise, contain, have a capacity for, seat, take

hold *n* clasp, clutch, grasp, grip; anchorage, foothold, footing, leverage, prop, purchase, stay, support, vantage; ascendancy, authority, control, dominion, grip, power; dominance, influence, mastery, sway; (*Inf*) clout, pull; deferment, delay, pause, postpone ment

holder *n* bearer, custodian, incumbent, keeper, occupant, owner, possessor, proprietor, purchaser; case, casing, container, cover, housing, receptacle, sheath, stand

hold forth *v* declaim, descant, discourse, harangue, lecture, orate, preach, speak, speechify; (*Inf*) spiel, spout

hold off *v* avoid, defer, delay, keep from, postpone, put off, refrain; fend off, keep off, rebuff, repel, repulse, stave off

hold out *v* extend, give, offer, present, proffer; carry on, continue, endure, hang on, last, persevere, persist, proffer, stand fast, withstand

hold-up *n* bottleneck, delay, difficulty, hitch, obstruction, setback, snag, stoppage, traffic jam, trouble, wait

hold-up *v* delay, detain, hinder, impede, retard, set back, slow down, stop; brace, buttress, jack up, prop, shore up, support, sustain

hole *n* aperture, breach, break, crack, fissure, gap, gash, notch, opening, orifice, outlet, perforation, puncture, rent, slit, space, split, tear, vent; cave, cavern, chamber, crater, depression, dip, dug-out, excavation, hollow, mine, pit, scoop, shaft, defect, discrepancy, error, fallacy, fault, flaw, inconsistency, loophole; burrow, covert, earth, den, lair, nest, set, shelter; hovel, slum; (*Inf*) dive, dump, joint; cell, dungeon, prison; crack, discrepancy, error, fallacy, fault, flaw, inconsistency; dilemma, mess, muddle, plight, predicament, tangle, trouble; (*Inf*) fix, jam, hot water, pickle, scrape

hole *v* gash, lacerate, perforate, pierce, puncture, spike, stab

holiday *n* break, leave, recess, sabbatical, time off, vacation; anniversary, bank holiday, carnival day, celebration, feast, festival, festivity, gala, public holiday, saint's day

holiness *n* blessedness, divineness, divinity, godliness, goodness, piety, purity, righteousness, sacredness, saintliness, sanctity, virtuousness

hollow *adj* empty, not solid, unfilled, vacant, void; cavernous, concave, deep-set, depressed, indented, sunken; deep, dull, expressionless, flat, low, muffled, muted, reverberant, rumbling, sepulchral, toneless; empty, fruitless, futile, meaningless, pointless, specious, unavailing, useless, vain, worthless

hollow *n* basin, bowl, cave, cavern, cavity, concavity, crater, cup, den, dent, depression, dimple, excavation, hole, indentation, pit, trough; bottom, dale, dell, dingle, glen, valley

holocaust *n* annihilation, conflagration, fire, inferno; butchery, carnage, ethnic cleansing, extermination, genocide, massacre, mass murder, slaughter

holy *adj* devout, divine, faithful, god-fearing, godly, hallowed, pious, pure, religious, righteous, saintly, sublime, virtuous

home *n* abode, domicile, dwelling, dwelling place, habitation, house, residence; birth-place, family, fireside, hearth, homestead, home town, household; abode, element, environment, habitat, habitation, haunt, home ground, range, stamping ground, territory; **at home** available, in, present; at ease, comfortable, familiar, relaxed; entertaining, giving a party, receiving; **at home in, on** *or* **with** conversant with, familiar with, knowledgeable, proficient, skilled, well-versed

homeland *n* country of origin, fatherland, mother country, motherland, native land

homespun *adj* artless, coarse, homely, home-made, inelegant, plain, rough, rude, rustic, unpolished, unsophisticated

homicidal *adj* deadly, death-dealing, ethal, maniacal, mortal, murderous

homicide *n* bloodshed, killing, manslaughter, murder, slaying

homily *n* address, discourse, lecture, lesson, oration, preaching, sermon, speech, talk

homogeneous *adj* akin, alike, analogous, cognate, comparable, consistent, identical, kindred, similar, uniform, unvarying

honest *adj* conscientious, decent, ethical, high-minded, honourable, law-abiding, reliable, reputable, scrupulous, trustworthy, trusty, truthful, upright, veracious, virtuous; equitable, fair, fair and square, impartial, just; candid, direct, forth right, frank, ingenuous, open, out right, plain, sincere, straightforward, undisguised, unfeigned

honestly *adv* by fair means, cleanly, ethically, honourably, in good faith, lawfully, legally, legitimately, with clean hands; candidly, frankly, in all sincerity, in plain English, plainly, straight out, to one's face, truth fully; (*Inf*) on the level

honesty *n* faithfulness, fidelity, honour, incorruptibility, integrity, morality, probity, rectitude, reputability, scrupulousness, straightness, trustworthiness, truthfulness, uprightness, veracity, virtue

honour *v* credit, dignity, distinction, elevation, esteem, fame, glory, high standing, prestige, rank, renown, reputation, repute; acclaim, accolade, adoration, commendation, deference, homage, kudos, praise, recognition, regard, respect, reverence, tribute, veneration; decency, fairness, goodness, honesty, integrity, morality, principles, probity, rectitude, righteousness, trustworthiness, uprightness; compliment, credit, favour, pleasure, privilege, source of pride; chastity, innocence, modesty, purity, virginity, virtue

honour *v* admire, adore, appreciated, esteem, exalt, glorify, hallow, prize, respect, revere, reverence, value, venerate, worship

honourable *adj* ethical, fair, high-minded, honest, just, moral, principled, true, trustworthy, trusty, upright, upstanding, virtuous; distinguished, eminent, great, illustrious, noble, notable, noted, prestigious, renowned, venerable

honours *pl n* adornments, awards, decorations, dignities, distinctions, laurels, titles

hook *n* catch, clasp, fastener, hasp, holder, link, lock, peg; noose, snare, springe, trap

hook *v* catch, clasp, fasten, fix, hasp, secure; catch, enmesh, ensnare, entrap, snare, trap

hooligan *n* casual, delinquent, lager lout, rowdy, ruffian, tough, vandal, yob

hoop *n* band, circlet, girdle, loop, ring, wheel

hoot *n* call, cry, toot; boo, catcall, hiss, jeer, yell

hoot *v* boo, catcall, condemn, decry, denounce, execrate, hiss, howl, down, jeer, yell at; cry, scream, shout, shriek, toot, whoop, yell

hop *v* bound, caper, dance, jump, leap, skip, spring, vault

hop *n* bounce, bound, jump, leap, skip, spring, step, vault

hope *n* ambition, anticipation, assumption, belief, confidence, desire, dream, expectancy, expectation, faith, longing

hope *v* anticipate, aspire, await, believe, contemplate, count on, desire, expect foresee, long, look forward to, rely, trust

hopeful *adj* anticipating, assured, buoyant, confident, expectant, looking forward to, optimistic, sanguine; auspicious, bright, cheerful, encouraging, heartening, promising, propitious, reassuring, rosy

hopefully *adv* confidently, expectantly, optimistically, sanguinely; all being well, conceivably, expectedly, feasibly, probably

hopeless *adj* defeatist, dejected, demoralized, despairing, desperate, despondent, disconsolate, downhearted, forlorn, in despair, pessimistic, woebegone; helpless, incurable, irremediable, irreparable, irreversible, lost, past remedy, remediless; forlorn, futile, impossible, impracticable, pointless, unachievable, unattainable, useless, vain

horde *n* band, crew, crowd, drove, gang, host, mob, multitude, pack, press, swarm, throng, troop

horizon *n* field of vision, skyline, vista; compass, perspective, prospect, purview, range, realm, scope, sphere, stretch

horrible *adj* abhorrent, abominable, appalling, awful, dreadful, fearful, frightful, ghastly, grim, grisly, gruesome, heinous, hideous, horrid, loathsome, repulsive, revolting, shameful, shocking, terrible, terrifying; awful, cruel, disagree able, dreadful, ghastly, mean, nasty, terrible, unkind, unpleasant

horrid *adj* awful, disagreeable, disgusting, dreadful, horrible, nasty, offensive, terrible, unpleasant; abominable, alarming, appalling, formidable, frightening, hair-raising, harrowing, hideous, horrific, odious, repulsive, revolting, shocking, terrifying, terrorizing

horrify *v* affright, alarm, frighten, intimidate, petrify, scare, terrify, terrorize; appal, disgust, dismay, outrage, shock, sicken

horror *n* alarm, apprehension, awe, consternation, dismay, dread, fear, fright, panic, terror; abhorrence, abomination, antipathy, aversion, detestation, disgust, hatred, loathing, repugnance, revulsion

horseplay *n* buffoonery, capers, clowning, fooling around, high jinks, pranks, romping, rough-and-tumble, skylarking, tomfoolery; (*Inf*) monkey business, shenanigans

hospitable *adj* amicable, bountiful, cordial, friendly, generous, genial, gracious, kind, liberal, sociable, welcoming

hospitality *n* cheer, conviviality, cordiality, friendliness, heartiness, hospitableness, neighbourliness, sociability, warmth, welcome

host *n* entertainer, innkeeper, hotelier, hotel keeper, landlord, master of ceremonies, proprietor; entertainer, party-giver; anchorman, anchorwoman, compère, master of ceremonies, MC, presenter; army, array, drove, horde, legion, multitude, myriad, swarm, throng

host *v* compère, introduce, present

hostage *n* captive, gage, pawn, pledge, prisoner, security, surety

hostile *adj* antagonistic, bellicose, belligerent, contrary, ill-disposed, inimical, malevolent, opposed, opposite, rancorous, unkind, warlike; adverse, alien, inhospitable, unfriendly, unpropitious, unsympathetic, unwelcoming

hostilities *pl n* conflict, fighting, state of war, war, warfare

hostility *n* abhorrence, animosity, animus, antagonism, antipathy, aversion, detestation, enmity, hatred, ill will, malevolence, malice, opposition, resentment, unfriendliness

hot *adj* blistering, boiling, burning, fiery, flaming, heated, piping hot, roasting, scalding, scorching, searing, steaming, sultry, sweltering, torrid, warm; acrid, biting, peppery, piquant, pungent, sharp, spicy

hotchpotch *n* clutter, conglomeration, farrago, gallimaufry, hash, jumble, medley, mess, miscellany, mishmash, mixture, podrida, pot-pourri

hotfoot *adv* fast, hastily, helter-skelter, hurriedly, post-hate, quickly, rapidly, speedily, swiftly

hotheaded *adj* excitable, fiery, foolhardy, hasty, hot-tempered, impetuous, implusive, rash, reckless, short-tempered, unruly, volatile, wild

hound *v* chase, drive, give chase, hunt, hunt down, pursue

house *n* abode, building, domicile, dwelling, edifice, habitation, home, residence; family, household, ménage; ancestry, clan, dynasty, family tree, kindred, line, lineage, race, tribe; business, company, concern, establishment, firm, organization, partnership; hotel, inn, public house, tavern

house *v* accommodate, billet, board, domicile, harbour, lodge, put up, quarter, take in

household *n* family, home, house, ménage

housing *n* accommodation, dwellings, homes, houses

hovel *n* cabin, den, hole, hut, shack, shanty, shed

hover *v* be suspended, drift, float, flutter, fly, hang, poise; hang about, linger, wait nearby

however *adv* after all, anyhow, be that as it may, but, nevertheless, nonetheless, notwithstanding, on the other hand, still, though, yet

howl *n* bay, bellow, clamour, cry, groan, hoot, outcry, roar, scream, shriek, ululation, wail, yelp, yowl

howl *v* bellow, cry, cry out, lament, roar, scream, shout, shriek, ululate, wail, weep, yell, yelp

huddle *n* confusion, crowd, disorder, heap, jumble, mass, mess, muddle; conference, discussion, meeting, powwow

huddle *v* cluster, converge, crowd, flock, gather, press, throng; crouch, cuddle, curl up, hunch up, make oneself small, nestle, snuggle

hue *n* colour, dye, shade, tincture, tinge, tint, tone; aspect, cast, complexion, light; baloo, brouhaha, clamour, commotion, furore, hulla baloo, much ado, outcry, racket, uproar

hug *v* clasp, cuddle, embrace, enfold, hold close, squeeze, take in one's arms; cling to, follow closely, keep close, stay near

hug *n* bear hug, clasp, embrace, squeeze

huge *adj* bulky, colossal, enormous, extensive, gargantuan, giant, gigantic, great, immense, large, mammoth, massive, mega, monumental, mountainous, prodigious, stupendous, titanic, tremendous, vast

hulk *n* derelict, frame, hull, shell, shipwreck, wreck

hull *n* body, casing, covering, frame, framework, skeleton; husk, peel, pod, rind, shell, shuck, skin

hum *v* buzz, drone, drone, murmur, purr, throb, vibrate; bustle, croon, mumble, sing, thrum, whir, whis per; be active, be busy, bustle, buzz, move quickly, pulsate, pulse, stir, vibrate

hum *n* buzz, drone, murmur, purr, throb, vibration, whirr

human *adj* anthropoid, fleshly, manlike, mortal; approachable, compassionate, considerate, fallible, forgivable, humane, kind, kindly, natural, understandable, understanding, vulnerable

human *n* child, man, woman; human being, individual, living soul, mortal

humane *adj* benevolent, benign, charitable, clement, compassionate, forbearing, forgiving, gentle, good, good-natured, kind, kind-hearted, kindly, lenient, merciful, mild, sympathetic, tender, understanding

humanities *pl n* classical languages, classical literature, classics, classical studies, liberal arts

humanity *n* humankind, human race, man, mankind, flesh, mortals, people, *Homo sapiens*; flesh and blood, human nature, mortality; benevolence, compassion, gentleness, goodness, goodwill, kind-heartedness, kindness, leniency, mercy, sympathy, tenderness, tolerance, understanding

humble *adj* meek, modest, self-effacing, submissive, unassuming, unostentatious, unpretentious; common, commonplace, insignificant, low, low-born, lowly, mean, modest, obscure, ordinary, plebeian, poor, simple, undistinguished, unimportant, unpretentious

humbug *n* bluff, cheat, deceit, deception, dodge, feint, fraud, hoax, imposition, imposture, ruse, sham, swindle, trick, trickery, wile; charlatan, cheat, con man, faker, impostor, quack, swindler, trickster

humdrum *adj* boring, common place, dreary, dull, monotonous, mundane, ordinary, repetitious, routine, tedious, tiresome, uneventful, uninteresting, unvaried, wearisome

humid *adj* clammy, damp, dank, moist, muggy, steamy, sticky, sultry, watery, wet

humiliate *v* abase, abash, bring low, chagrin, chasten, crush, debase, degrade, discomfit, disgrace, embarrass, humble, make someone eat humble pie, mortify, shame, subdue

humility *n* diffidence, humbleness, lack of pride, lowliness, meekness, modesty, self-abasement, servility, submissiveness, unpretentiousness

humourist *n* comedian, comic, droll, eccentric, funny man, jester, joker, wag, wit

humorous *adj* amusing, comic, comical, entertaining, facetious, farcical, funny, hilarious, jocose, jocular, laughable, ludicrous, merry, playful, pleasant, side-splitting, waggish, whimsical, witty

humour *n* amusement, comedy, drollery, facetiousness, fun, funniness, jocularity, ludicrousness, wit; comedy, farce, jesting, jests, jokes, joking, pleasantry, wit, witticisms, wittiness; disposition, frame of mind, mood, spirits, temper; bent, bias, fancy, freak, mood, propensity, quirk, vagary, whim

humour *v* accommodate, cosset, favour, flatter, go along with, gratify, indulge, mollify, pamper, placate, soothe, spoil

hump *n* bulge, bump, hunch, knob, lump, mound, projection, protrusion, protuberance, swelling

hunch *n* feeling, idea, impression, inkling, intuition, premonition, presentiment, suspicion

hunger *n* appetite, emptiness, esurience, famine, hungriness, ravenousness, starvation, voracity; appetence, appetite, craving, desire, greediness, itch, lust, yearning

hunger *v* crave, desire, hanker, itch, long, pine, starve, thirst, want, wish, yearn

hungry *adj* empty, famished, famishing, hollow, ravenous, sharpset, starved, starving, voracious; athirst, avid, covetous, craving, desirous, eager, greedy, keen, yearning

hunk *n* block, chunk, gobbet, lump, mass, piece, slab, wedge

hunt *v* chase, gun for, hound, pursue, stalk, track, trail; ferret about, forage, go in quest of, look, look high and low, rummage, through, scour, search, seek, try to find

hurdle *n* chase, hunting, investigation, pursuit, quest, search; barricade, barrier, fence, hedge, wall; barrier, complication, difficulty, handicap, hindrance, impediment, obstacle, obstruction, snag, stumbling block

hurl *v* cast, fire, fling, heave, launch, let fly, pitch, project, propel, send, shy, sling, throw, toss

hurricane *n* cyclone, gale, storm, tempest, tornado, typhoon, windstorm

hurried *adj* breakneck, brief, cursory, hasty, hectic, perfunctory, precipitate, quick, rushed, short, slapdash, speedy, superficial, swift

hurry *v* dash, fly, lose no time, make haste, rush, scoot, scurry, step on it; accelerate, expedite, goad, hasten, hustle, push on, quicken, speed, urge; (*Inf*) get a move on

hurry *n* bustle, celerity, commotion, dispatch, expedition, flurry, haste, precipitation, promptitude, quickness, rush, speed, urgency

hurt *v* bruise, damage, disable, harm, impair, injure, mar, spoil, wound; ache, be sore, be tender, burn, pain, smart, sting, throb; afflict, aggrieve, annoy, cut to the quick, distress, grieve, pain, sadden, sting, upset, wound

hurt *n* discomfort, distress, pain, pang, soreness, suffering; bruise, sore, wound

hush *v* mute, muzzle, quieten, shush, silence, still, suppress; allay, appease, calm, compose, mollify, soothe

hush *n* calm, peace, peacefulness, quiet, silence, stillness, tranquillity

husky *adj* croaking, croaky, gruff, guttural, harsh, hoarse, rasping, raucous, rough, throaty

hustle *v* bustle, crowd, elbow, force, haste, hasten, hurry, impel, jog, jostle, push, rush, shove, thrust

hut *n* cabin, den, hovel, refuge, shanty, shed, shelter

hygiene *n* cleanliness, hygienics, sanitary measures, sanitation

hygienic *adj* aseptic, clean, disinfected, germ-free, healthy, pure, salutary, sanitary, sterile

hypnotize *v* mesmerize, put in a trance, put to sleep; entrance, fascinate, magnetize, spellbind

hypocrisy *n* cant, deceit, deceitfulness, deception, dissembling, duplicity, falsity, imposture, insincerity, Pharisaism, pretence, sanctimoniousness, speciousness, two-facedness

hypocrite *n* charlatan, deceiver, dissembler, fraud, Holy willie, impostor, Pecksniff, pharisee, pretender, Tartuffe, whited sepulchre

hypocritical *adj* canting, deceitful, deceptive, dissembling, duplicitous, false, fraudulent, hollow, insincere, Janus-faced, pharisaical, sanctimonious, specious, spurious, two-faced

hypothesis *n* assumption, axiom, conjecture, postulate, premise, premise, presumed, proposition, postulate, speculation, supposition, theorem, theory, thesis

hypothetical *adj* academic, assumed, conjectural, imaginary, putative, speculative, supposed, theoretical

hysteria *n* agitation, delirium, frenzy, hysterics, loss of control, loss of reason, madness, outburst of agita tion, panic, panic attack, unreason able; (*Inf*) the screaming habdabs

hysterical *adj* agitated, berserk, beside oneself, convulsive, crazed, delirious, distracted, distraught, frantic, frenzied, in a panic, mad, out of control, overwrought, raving, uncontrollable; amusing, comical, farcical, hilarious, side-splitting, unfunny, uproarious, very funny, wildly amusing

I

icy *adj* arctic, biting, bitter, chill, chilling, chilly, cold, freezing, frost-bound, frosty, frozen over, glacial, ice-cold, polar, raw, rimy, Siberian, slippery; aloof, cold, cool, distant, frigid, frosty, hostile, indifferent, reserved, reticent, steely, stony, unfriendly, unwelcoming

idea *n* abstraction, concept, conception, conclusion, fancy, impression, judgment, perception, thought, understanding; belief, conviction, doctrine, interpretation, notion, opinion, teaching, view, viewpoint

ideal *n* archetype, criterion, epitome, example, exemplar, last word, model, nonpareil, paradigm, paragon, pattern, perfection, prototype, standard, standard of perfection

ideal *adj* archetypal, classic, complete, consummate, model, optimal, perfect, quintessential, supreme; abstract, conceptual, hypothetical, intellectual, mental, theoretical, transcendental

idealist *n* dreamer, perfectionist, romantic, Utopian, visionary

identical *adj* alike, corresponding, duplicate, equal, equivalent, indistinguishable, interchangeable, like, matching, selfsame, similar, the same, twin

identification *n* cataloguing, classifying, establishment of identity, labelling, naming, pin pointing, recognition, single out, spotting; credentials, ID, letters of introduction, papers

identify *v* catalogue, classify, diagnose, distinguish, discern, label, make out, name, pick out, pinpoint, place, put one's finger on, recognize, single, out, spot, tag

identity *n* distinctiveness, existence, individuality, oneness, particularity, personality, self, self-hood, singularity, uniqueness

ideology *n* creed, credo, doctrine, dogma, teaching, theory; beliefs, opinion, tenets

idiocy *n* abject, absurdity, asinity, craziness, cretinism, fatuity, fatuousness, foolishness, imbecility, inanity, insanity, lunacy, senselessness, stupidity, tomfoolery

idiom *n* expression, locution, phrase, set phrase, turn, of phrase; jargon, language, mode of expression, parlance, patois, phraseology, speech, style, talk, usage, vernacular

idiosyncrasy *n* affectation, characteristic, eccentricity, feature, habit, mannerism, oddity, peculiarity, personal trait, quality, quirk, singularity, trick

idiot *n* ass, blockhead, cretin, dimwit, dunderhead, fool, halfwit, imbecile, mooncalf, moron, nincompoop, nitwit, pillock, simpleton

idiotic *adj* absurd, asinine, crazy, daft, fatuous, foolhardy, foolish, halfwitted, hare-brained, imbecile, imbecilic, inane, insane, lunatic, moronic, senseless, stupid, unintelligent; (*Inf*) daft, dumb

idle *adj* dronish, indolent, loafing, slothful, sluggish; inactive, inoperative, mothballed, unused; inactive, jobless, out of action, out of work, redundant, unemployed; (*Inf*) on the dole; empty, unoccupied, vacant, unfilled; baseless, foundationless, groundless; foolish, insignificant, meaningless, shallow, superficial, trifling, trivial; fruitless, futile, frivolous, ineffectual, meaningless, pointless; frivolous, insubstantial, nugatory, worthless

idle *v* coast, drift, fritter, laze, loaf, mark time, potter, shirk, sit back and do nothing, saunter, shirk, slack, slow down, stroll, vegetate, waste; (*Inf*) rest on one's oars, take it easy; tick over

idol *n* deity, effigy, false god, god, graven, icon, image, likeness, pagan symbol; darling, favourite, hero, heroine, pet, superstar; (*Inf*) pin-up

idolize *v* admire, adore, apotheosize, bow down before, deify, dot upon, exalt, glorify, hero-worship, look up to, love, revere, reverence, venerate, worship, worship to excess

idyll *n* Garden of Eden, heaven-on-earth, honeymoon, paradise, perfect time, Shangri-La

iffy *adj* doubtful, uncertain, undecide, unresolved, unsettled, unsure; (*Inf*) up in the air; dubious, hesitant, tentative

ignite *v* burn, burst into flames, catch fire, fire, flare up, inflame, kindle, light, set alight, set fire to, take fire, touch off

ignominious *adj* abject, base, despicable, discreditable, disgraceful, dishonourable, disreputable, humiliating, indecorous, infamous, inglorious, mortifying, scandalous, shameful, sorry, undignified; contemptible, despicable, low, offensive, revolting, vile, wicked

ignominy *n* discredit, disgrace, dishonour, humiliation, infamy, mortification, scandal, stigma

ignorance *n* benightedness, blindness, denseness, illiteracy, lack of education, mental darkness, stupidity, thickness, unenlightenment, unintelligence; greenness, inexperience, innocence, unawareness

ignorant *adj* benighted, blind to, dense, inexperienced, innocent, in the dark about, oblivious, unaware, unconscious, unenlightened, unfamiliar, uninformed, uninitiated, unknowing, unschooled, unwitting; green, illiterate, naive, unaware, uncultivated, uneducated, unknowledgeable, unlearned, unlettered, unread, untaught, untrained, untutored

ignore *v* be oblivious to, bury one's head in the sand, cold-shoulder, disregard, give the cold shoulder to, neglect, overlook, pass over, pay no attention to, refect, shut one's eyes to, take no notice of, turn a blind eye to, turn a deaf ear to, turn one's back on

ill *adj* ailing, diseased, indisposed, infirm, off-colour, queasy, queer, seedy, sick, under the weather, unhealthy, unwell, valetudinarian; bad, damaging, deleterious, detrimental, evil, foul, harmful, iniquitous, injurious, ruinous, unfortunate, unlucky, vile, wicked, wrong; disturbing, foreboding, inauspicious, ominous, sinister, threatening, unfavourable, unhealthy, unlucky, unpromising, unpropitious, unwholesome

ill *n* affliction, harm, hurt, injury, misery, misfortune, pain, trial, tribulation, trouble, unpleasantness, woe; ailment, complaint, disease, disorder, illness, indisposition, infirmity, malady, malaise, sickness; abuse, badness, cruelty, damage, depravity, destruction, evil, ill-usage, malice, mischief, suffering, wickedness

ill *adv* badly, hard, inauspiciously, poorly, unfavourably, unfortunately, unluckily

ill-advised *adj* foolhardy, foolish, ill-considered, ill-judged, impolitic, imprudent, inappropriate, incautious, indiscreet, injudicious, misguided, overhasty, rash, reckless, short-sighted, thoughtless, unseemly, unwise, wrong-headed

ill-assorted *adj* incompatible, incongruous, mismatched, unsuited

ill-bred *adj* bad-mannered, boorish, churlish, coarse, crass, crude, discourteous, ill-mannered, impolite, indelicate, rude, uncouth, ungentlemanly, unladylike, unseemly, vulgar

ill-defined *adj* blurred, dim, fuzzy, indistinct, nebulous, shadowy, unclear, vague

ill-disposed *adj* antagonistic, averse, contrary, hostile, opposing, unfriendly, unsympathetic

illegal *adj* actionable, banned, black-market, bootleg, criminal, felonious, forbidden, illicit, lawless, outlawed, prohibited, proscribed, unauthorized, unconstitutional, under the counter, unlawful, unlicensed, unofficial, wrongful

illegality *n* crime, criminality, felony, illegitimacy, illicitness, lawlessness, unlawfulness, wrong, wrongness

illegible *adj* crabbed, faint, hard to make out, hieroglyphic, indecipherable, obscure, scrawled, undecipherable, unreadable

illegitimate *adj* illegal, illicit, improper, unauthorized, unconstitutional, unlawful, unsanctioned; bastard, born on the wrong side of the blanket, born out of wedlock, fatherless, natural, spurious

ill-fated *adj* blighted, doomed, hapless, ill-omened, ill-starred, luckless, star-crossed, unfortunate, unhappy, unlucky

ill feeling *n* animosity, animus, antagonism, bad blood, bitterness, disgruntlement, dissatisfaction, enmity, frustration, hard feelings, hostility, ill will, indignation, offence, rancour, resentment

ill-founded *adj* baseless, empty, groundless, idle, unjustified, unproven, unreliable, unsubstantiated, unsupported

illicit *adj* black-market, bootleg, contraband, criminal, felonious, illegal, illegitimate, prohibited, unauthorized, unlawful, unlicensed; clandestine, forbidden, furtive, guilty, immoral, improper, wrong

illiterate *adj* benighted, ignorant, uncultured, uneducated, unlettered, untaught, untutored

ill-mannered *adj* badly behaved, boorish, churlish, coarse, discourteous, ill-behaved, ill-bred, impolite, insolent, loutish, rude, uncivil, uncouth, unmannerly

illness *n* affliction, ailment, attack,

complaint, disability, disease, disorder, ill health, indisposition, infirmity, malady, malaise, poor health, sickness

illogical *adj* absurd, fallacious, faulty, inconclusive, inconsistent, incorrect, invalid, irrational, meaningless, senseless, sophistical, specious, spurious, unreasonable, unscientific, unsound

ill-treat *v* abuse, damage, handle roughly, harass, harm, harry, ill-use, injure, knock about, maltreat, mishandle, misuse, oppress, wrong

illuminate *v* brighten, illumine, irradiate, light, light up; clarify, clear up, elucidate, enlighten, explain, give insight into, instruct, make clear, shed light on

illuminating *adj* enlightening, explanatory, helpful, informative, instructive, revealing

illumination *n* awareness, clarification, edification, enlightenment, insight, inspiration, instruction, perception, revelation, understanding

illusion *n* chimera, daydream, fantasy, figment of the imagination, hallucination, mirage, mockery, semblance, will-o'-the-wisp; deception, delusion, error, fallacy, false impression, fancy, misapprehension, misconception

illusory *adj* apparent, beguiling, chimerical, deceitful, deceptive, delusive, fallacious, false, hallucinatory, misleading, mistaken, seeming, sham, unreal, untrue

illustrate *v* bring home, clarify, demonstrate, elucidate, emphasize, exemplify, exhibit, explain, instance, interpret, make clear, make plain, point up, show; adorn, decorate, depict, draw, ornament, picture, sketch

illustration *n* analogy, case, case in point, clarification, demonstration, elucidation, example, exemplification, explanation, instance, interpretation, specimen; adornment, decoration, figure, picture, plate, sketch

illustrious *adj* brilliant, celebrated, distinguished, eminent, exalted, famed, famous, glorious, great, noble, notable, noted, prominent, remarkable, renowned, resplendent, signal, splendid

ill will *n* acrimony, animosity, animus, antagonism, antipathy, aversion, bad blood, dislike, enmity, envy, grudge, hard feelings, hatred, hostility, malevolence, malice, no love lost, rancour, resentment, spite, unfriendliness, venom

image *n* appearance, effigy, figure, icon, idol, likeness, picture, portrait, reflection, representation, statue; conceit, concept, conception, figure, idea, impression, mental picture, perception, trope

imaginable *adj* believable, comprehensible, conceivable, credible, likely, plausible, possible, supposable, thinkable, under the sun, within the bounds of possibility

imaginary *adj* assumed, chimerical, dreamlike, fancied, fanciful, fictional, fictitious, hallucinatory, hypothetical, ideal, illusive, illusory, imagined, invented, legendary, made-up, mythological, non-existent, phantasmal, shadowy, supposed, suppositious, unreal, unsubstantial, visionary

imagination *n* creativity, enterprise, fancy, ingenuity, insight, inspiration, invention, inventiveness, originality, resourcefulness, vision, wit, wittiness

imaginative *adj* clever, creative, dreamy, enterprising, fanciful, fantastic, ingenious, inspired, inventive, original, poetical, visionary, vivid, whimsical

imagine *v* conceive, conceptualize, conjure up, create, devise, envisage, fantasize, frame, invent, picture, plan, project, scheme, see in the mind's eye, think of, think up, visualize

imbecile *n* bungler, cretin, dolt, dotard, fool, halfwit, idiot, moron, thickhead

imbecile *adj* asinine, fatuous, feeble-minded, foolish, idiotic, imbecilic, inane, ludicrous, moronic, simple, stupid, thick, witless

imbue *v* charge, fill, impregnate, ingrain, inject, instil, permeate

imitate *v* affect, ape, burlesque, caricature, copy, counterfeit, do an impression of, duplicate, echo, emulate, follow, follow in the footsteps of, follow suit, impersonate, mimic, mirror, mock, parody, personate, repeat, simulate, travesty; (*Inf*) spoof

imitation *n* aping, copy, counterfeit, counterfeiting, duplication, echoing, likeness, mimicry, resemblance, simulation; fake, forgery, impersonation, impression, mockery, parody, reflection, replica, reproduction, sham, substitution, takeoff, travesty;

imitation *adj* artificial, dummy, ersatz, man-made, mock, repro, reproduction, sham, simulated, synthetic; (*Inf*) phoney

imitator *n* aper, copier, echo, epigone, follower, impersonator, impressionist, mimic, parrot, shadow; (*Inf*) copycat

immaculate *adj* clean, impeccable, neat, neat as a new pin, spick-and-span, spruce, trim, unexceptionable; above, reproach, faultless, flawless, guiltless, incorrupt, innocent, perfect, pure, sinless, spotless, stainless, unblemished, uncontaminated, undefiled, unpolluted, unsullied, untarnished, virtuous

immaterial *adj* a matter of indifference, extraneous, impertinent, inapposite, inconsequential, inconsiderable, inessential, insignificant, irrelevant, of little account, of no consequence, of no importance, trifling, trivial, unimportant, unnecessary

immature *adj* adolescent, crude, green, imperfect, premature, raw, undeveloped, unfinished, unfledged, unformed, unripe, unseasonable, untimely, young; babyish, callow, childish, inexperienced, infantile, jejune, juvenile, puerile; (*Inf*) wet behind the ears

immediate *adj* instant, instantaneous; adjacent, close, contiguous, direct, near, nearest, next, primary, proximate, recent

immediately *adv* at once, directly, forthwith, instantly, now, promptly, right away, right now, straight away, this instant, this very minute, unhesitatingly, without delay, without hesitation

immense *adj* colossal, elephantine, enormous, extensive, giant, gigantic, great, huge, illimitable, immeasurable, infinite, interminable, large, mammoth, massive, monstrous, monumental, prodigious, stupendous, titanic, tremendous, vast

immigrant *n* incomer, newcomer, settler

imminent *adj* at hand, brewing, close, coming, fast-approaching, forthcoming, gathering, impending, in the air, in the offing, looming, menacing, near, on the horizon, on the way, threatening

immobile *adj* at a standstill, at rest, fixed, frozen, immobilized, immotive, immovable, like a statue, motionless, rigid, rivetted, rooted, stable, static, stationary, stiff, still, stock-still, stolid, unmoving

immobilize *v* bring to a standstill, cripple, disable, freeze, halt, lay up, paralyse, put out of action, render inoperative, stop, transfix

immoderate *adj* egregious, enormous, exaggerated, excessive, exorbitant, extravagant, extreme, inordinate, intemperate, profligate, uncalled-for, unconscionable, uncontrolled, undue, unjustified, unreasonable, unrestrained, unwarranted, wanton

immoral *adj* abandoned, bad, corrupt, debauched, degenerate, depraved, dishonest, dissolute, evil, impure, indecent, iniquitous, lewd, licentious, nefarious, obscene, of easy virtue, pornographic, profligate, reprobate, sinful, unchaste, unethical, unprincipled, vicious, vile, wicked, wrong

immortal *adj* abiding, constant, death-defying, deathless, endless, enduring, eternal, everlasting, imperishable, incorruptible, indestructible, lasting, perennial, perpetual, sempiternal, timeless, undying, unfading

immortal *n* god, goddess, olympian; genius, great, hero, paragon

immovable *adj* fast, firm, fixed, immutable, jammed, rooted, secure, set, stable, stationary, stuck, unbudgeable; adamant, constant, impassive, inflexible, resolute, steadfast, unchangeable, unimpressionable, unshakable, unwavering, unyielding

immune *adj* clear, exempt, free, insusceptible, invulnerable, let off, not affected, not liable, not subject, protected, resistant, safe, unaffected

immunity *n* amnesty, charter, exemption, exoneration, franchise, freedom, indemnity, invulnerability, liberty, licence, prerogative, privilege, release, right

impact *n* bang, blow, bump, collision, concussion, contact, crash, force, jolt, knock, shock, smash, stroke, thump

impair *v* blunt, damage, debilitate, decrease, deteriorate, diminish, enervate, enfeeble, harm, hinder, injure, lessen, mar, reduce, spoil, undermine, vitiate, weaken, worsen

impart *v* communicate, convey, disclose, discover, divulge, make known, pass on, relate, reveal, tell

impartial *adj* detached, disinterested, equal, equitable, even-handed, fair, just, neutral, nondiscriminating, nonpartisan, objective, open-minded, unbiased, unprejudiced, without fear/favour

impasse *n* blind alley, dead end, dead lock, stalemate, standoff, standstill

impassioned *adj* animated, ardent, blazing, excited, fervent, fervid, fiery, furious, glowing, heated, inflamed, inspired, intense, passionate, rousing, stirring, vehement, violent, vivid, warm, worked up

impatience *n* haste, hastiness, heat, impetuosity, intolerance, irritability, irritableness, quick temper, rashness, shortness, snappiness, vehemence, violence

impatient *adj* abrupt, brusque, curt, demanding, edgy, hasty, hot-tempered, indignant, intolerant, irritable, quick-tempered, snappy, sudden, testy, vehement, violent; agog, athirst, chafing, eager, fretful, headlong, impetuous, restless, straining at the leash

impeach *v* accuse, arraign, blame, censure, charge, criminate, denounce, implicate, indict, tax

impeccable *adj* above suspicion, blameless, exact, exquisite, faultless, flawless, immaculate, incorrupt, innocent, irreproachable, perfect, precise, pure, sinless, stainless, unblemished, unerring, unimpeachable

impede *v* bar, block, brake, check, clog, curb, delay, disrupt, hamper, hinder, hold up, obstruct, restrain, retard, slow, stop, thwart; (*Inf*) throw a spanner in the works

impediment *n* bar, barrier, block, check, clog, curb, defect, difficulty, encumbrance, hindrance, obstacle, obstruction, snag, stumbling block

impel *v* actuate, chivy, compel, constrain, drive, force, goad, incite, induce, influence, inspire, instigate, motivate, move, oblige, power, prod, prompt, propel, push, require, spur, stimulate, urge

impending *adj* approaching, at hand, brewing, close, coming, forthcoming, gathering, hovering, imminent, in the offing, looming, menacing, near, nearing, on the horizon, threatening

imperative *adj* compulsory, crucial, essential, exigent, indispensable, insistent, obligatory, pressing, urgent, vital

imperceptible *adj* faint, fine, gradual, impalpable, inappreciable, inaudible, indiscernible, indistinguishable, infinitesimal, insensible, invisible, microscopic, minute, shadowy, slight, small, subtle, tiny, undetectable, unnoticeable

imperfect *adj* broken, damaged, defective, deficient, faulty, flawed, immature, impaired, incomplete, inexact, limited, partial, patchy, rudimentary, sketchy, undeveloped, unfinished

imperfection *n* blemish, defect, deficiency, failing, fallibility, fault, flaw, foible, frailty, inadequacy, incompleteness, infirmity, insufficiency, peccadillo, shortcoming, stain, taint, weakness, weak point

imperial *adj* kingly, majestic, princely, queenly, regal, royal, sovereign; august, exalted, grand, great, high, imperious, lofty, magnificent, noble, superior, supreme

imperil *v* endanger, expose, hazard, jeopardize, risk

impersonal *adj* aloof, bureaucratic, businesslike, cold, detached, dispassionate, formal, inhuman, neutral, remote

impersonate *v* act, ape, burlesque, caricature, do an impression of, enact, imitate, masquerade as, mimic, parody, pass oneself off as, personate; (*Inf*) take off

impertinence *n* assurance, audacity, boldness, brazenness, disrespect, effrontery, forwardness, impudence, incivility, insolence, pertness, presumption, rudeness; (*Inf*) nerve

impertinent *adj* bold, brazen, cheeky, discourteous, disrespectful, forward, impolite, impudent, insolent, interfering, pert, presumptuous, rude, uncivil, unmannerly

impetuous *adj* ardent, eager, fierce, furious, hasty, headlong, impassioned, impulsive, passionate, precipitate, rash, spontaneous, spur-of-the-moment, unbridled, unplanned, unpremeditated, unreflecting, unrestrained, unthinking, vehement, violent

impetus *n* catalyst, goad, impulse, impulsion, incentive, motivation, push, spur, stimulus; energy, force, momentum, power

impish *adj* devilish, elfin, mischievous, prankish, puckish, rascally, roguish, sportive, waggish

implant *v* inculcate, infix, infuse, inseminate, instil, sow

implement *n* agent, apparatus, appliance, device, gadget, instrument, tool, utensil

implement *v* bring about, carry out, complete, effect, enforce, execute, fulfil, perform, put into action, realize

implicate *v* associate, compromise, concern, embroil, entangle, imply, include, incriminate, inculpate, involve, mire, tie up with

implication *n* association, connection, entanglement, incrimination, involvement; conclusion, inference, innuendo, meaning, overtone, resumption, ramification, significance, signification, suggestion

implicit *adj* contained, implied, inferred, inherent, latent, tacit, taken for granted, undeclared, understood, unspoken

implied *adj* hinted at, implicit, indirect, inherent, insinuated, suggested, tacit, undeclared, unexpressed, unspoken, unstated

implore *v* beg, beseech, conjure, crave, entreat, go on bended knee to, importune, plead with, pray, solicit, supplicate

imply *v* connote, give to understand, hint, insinuate, intimate, signify, suggest; betoken, denote, entail, evidence, import, include, indicate, involve, mean, point to, presuppose

impolite *adj* bad-mannered, boorish, churlish, discourteous, disrespect ful, ill-bred, ill-mannered, indecorous, indelicate, insolent, loutish, rough, rude, uncivil, ungallant, ungentlemanly, ungracious, unladylike, unmannerly, unrefined

importance *n* concern, consequence, import, interest, moment, momentousness, significance, substance, value, weight; distinction, eminence, esteem, influence, mark, pre-eminence, prestige, prominence, standing, status, usefulness, worth

important *adj* far-reaching, grave, large, material, meaningful, momentous, of substance, primary, salient, serious, signal, significant, substantial, urgent, weighty; eminent, foremost, high-level, high-ranking, influential, leading, notable, noteworthy, of not, outstanding, powerful, pre-eminent, prominent, seminal

impose *v* decree, establish, exact, fix, institute, introduce, lay, levy, ordain, place, promulgate, put, set

imposing *adj* august, commanding, dignified, effective, grand, impressive, majestic, stately, striking

imposition *n* application, decree, introduction, laying on, levying, promulgation; encroachment, intrusion, liberty, presumption

impossible *adj* beyond one, beyond the bounds of possibility, hopeless, impracticable, inconceivable, not to be thought of, out of the question, unachievable, unattainable, unobtainable, unthinkable

impostor *n* charlatan, cheat, deceiver, fake, fraud, hypocrite, impersonator, pretender, quack, rogue, sham, trickster

impotence *n* disability, enervation, feebleness, frailty, helplessness, inability, inadequacy, incapacity, incompetence, ineffectiveness, inefficacy, inefficiency, infirmity, paralysis, powerlessness, uselessness, weakness

impotent *adj* disabled, emasculate, enervated, feeble, frail, helpless, incapable, incapacitated, incompetent, ineffective, infirm, nerveless, paralysed, powerless, unable, unmanned, weak

impoverished *adj* bankrupt, destitute, distressed, impecunious, indigent, in reduced circumstances, necessitous, needy, on one's uppers, penurious, poverty-stricken, ruined, straitened

impracticable *adj* impossible, out of the question, unachievable, unattainable, unfeasible, unworkable; awkward, impractical, inapplicable, inconvenient, unserviceable, unsuitable, useless

impractical *adj* impossible, impracticable, inoperable, nonviable, unrealistic, unserviceable, unworkable, visionary, wild; idealistic, romantic, starry-eyed, unbusinesslike, unrealistic, visionary

imprecise *adj* ambiguous, blurred, round the edges, careless, equivocal, estimated, fluctuating, hazy, ill-defined, inaccurate, indefinite, indeterminate, inexact, inexplicit, loose, rough, sloppy, vague, wide of the mark

impress *v* affect, excite, influence, inspire, make an impression, move, stir, strike, sway, touch

impression *n* effect, feeling, impact, influence, reaction, sway; belief, concept, conviction, fancy, feeling, funny feeling, hunch, idea, memory, notion, opinion, recollection, sense, suspicion; imitation, impersonation, parody; (*Inf*) send up, take-off

impressive *adj* affecting, exciting, forcible, moving, powerful, stirring, touching

imprint *n* impression, indentation,

mark, print, sign, stamp
imprint *v* engrave, establish, etch, fix, impress, print, stamp
imprison *v* confine constrain, detain, immure, incarcerate, intern, jail, lock up, put away, put under lock and key, send to prison
imprisonment *n* confinement, custody, detention, duress, incarceration, internment
improbability *n* doubt, doubtful ness, dubiety, uncertainty, unlikelihood
improbable *adj* doubtful, dubious, fanciful, far-fetched, implausible, questionable, unbelievable, uncertain, unconvincing, unlikely, weak
impromptu *adj* ad-lib, extemporaneous, extempore, extemporized, improvised, offhand, spontaneous, unpremeditated, unprepared, unrehearsed, unscripted, unstudied
improper *adj* impolite, indecent, indecorous, indelicate, off-colour, smutty, suggestive, unbecoming, unfitting, unseemly, untoward, vulgar; abnormal, erroneous, false, inaccurate, incorrect, irregular, wrong
impropriety *n* bad taste, immodesty, incongruity, indecency, indecorum, unsuitability, vulgarity; blunder, faux pas, gaffe, gaucherie, mistake, slip, solecism
improve *v* advance, ameliorate, amend, augment, better, correct, face-lift, help, mend, polish, rectify, touch up, upgrade; develop, enhance, gain strength, increase, look up, make strides, perk, up, pick up, progress, rally, reform, rise, take a turn; (*Inf*) for the better
improvement *n* advancement, amelioration, amendment, augmentation, betterment, correction, face-lift, gain, rectification; advance, development, enhancement, furtherance, increase, progress, rally, recovery, reformation, rise, upswing
improvise *v* ad-lib, coin, extemporize, invent, play it by ear; concoct, contrive, devise, make do, throw, together
imprudent *adj* careless, foolhardy, foolish, heedless, ill-advised, ill-considered, ill-judged, impolitic, improvident, incautious, inconsiderate, indiscreet, injudicious, irresponsible, overhasty, rash, reckless, temerarious, unthinking, unwise
impudence *n* assurance, audacity, boldness, brazenness, bumptiousness, effrontery, impertinence, insolence, pertness, presumption, rudeness, shamelessness; (*Inf*) backchat, brass neck, cheek, face, lip, nerve, sauciness
impudent *adj* audacious, bold, bold-faced, brazen, bumptious, cheeky, forward, fresh, immodest, impertinent, insolent, pert, presumptuous, rude, shameless; (*Inf*) saucy
impulse *n* catalyst, force, impetus, momentum, movement, pressure, push, stimulus, surge, thrust
impulsive *adj* devil-may-care, emotional, hasty, headlong, impetuous, instinctive, intuitive, passionate, precipitate, quick, rash, spontaneous, unconsidered, unpredictable, unpremeditated
impure *adj* admixed, adulterated, alloyed, debased, mixed, unrefined;

contaminated, defiled, dirty, filthy, foul, infected, polluted, sullied, tainted, unclean, unwholesome, vitiated

impurity *n* admixture, adulteration, mixture; befoulment, contamination, defilement, dirtiness, filth, foulness, infection, pollution, taint, uncleanness

impute *v* accredit, ascribe, assign, attribute, credit

inability *n* disability, disqualification, impotence, inadequacy, incapability, incapacity, incompetence, ineptitude, powerlessness

inaccessible *adj* impassable, out of reach, out of the way, remote, unapproachable, unattainable, unreachable

inaccurate *adj* careless, defective, discrepant, erroneous, faulty, imprecise, incorrect, in error, inexact, mistaken, out, unfaithful, unreliable, unsound, wide, of the mark, wild, wrong

inactive *adj* abeyant, dormant, idle, immobile, inert, inoperative, job less, kicking, one's heels, latent, mothballed, out of service, out of work, unemployed, unoccupied, unused

inadequate *adj* defective, deficient, faulty, imperfect, incommensurate, incomplete, insubstantial, insufficient, meagre, niggardly, scanty, short, sketchy, skimpy, sparse; found wanting, inapt, incapable, incompetent, not up to scratch, unequal, unfitted, unqualified

inadmissible *adj* immaterial, improper, inappropriate, incompetent, irrelevant, unacceptable, unallowable, unqualified, unreasonable

inadvisable *adj* ill-advised, impolitic, imprudent, inexpedient, injudicious, unwise

inane *adj* asinine, devoid of intelligence, empty, fatuous, frivolous, futile, idiotic, imbecilic, mindless, puerile, senseless, silly, stupid, trifling, unintelligent, vacuous, vain, vapid, worthless

inanimate *adj* cold, dead, defunct, extinct, inactive, inert, insensate, insentient, lifeless, quiescent, soulless, spiritless

inapplicable *adj* inapposite, inappropriate, inapt, irrelevant, unsuitable, unsuited

inappropriate *adj* disproportionate, ill-fitted, ill-suited, ill-timed, improper, incongruous, malapropos, out of place, tasteless, unbecoming, unbefitting, unfit, unfitting, unseemly, unsuitable, untimely

inapt *adj* ill-fitted, ill-suited, inapposite, inappropriate, infelicitous, unsuitable, unsuited; awkward, clumsy, dull, gauche, incompetent, inept, inexpert, maladroit, slow, stupid

inarticulate *adj* blurred, incoherent, incomprehensible, indistinct, muffled, mumbled, unclear, unintelligible; dumb, mute, silent, speechless, tongue-tied, unspoken, unuttered, unvoiced, voiceless, wordless; faltering, halting, hesitant, poorly spoken

inattentive *adj* absent-minded, careless, distracted, distrait, dreamy, heedless, inadvertent, neglectful, negligent, preoccupied, regardless, remiss, thoughtless, unheeding, unmindful, unobservant, vague

inaudible *adj* indistinct, low, mumbling, out of, earshot, stifled, unheard

inaugurate *v* begin, commence, get under way, initiate, institute, introduce, launch, originate, set in motion, set up, usher in; induct, install, instate, invest

inauguration *n* initiation, institution, launch, launching, opening, setting up

incalculable *adj* boundless, countless, endless, enormous, immense, incomputable, inestimable, infinite, innumerable, limitless, measureless, numberless, uncountable, untold, vast, without number

incapable *adj* feeble, inadequate, incompetent, ineffective, inept, inexpert, insufficient, not equal to, not up to, unfit, unfitted, unqualified, weak

incapacitated *adj* crippled, disabled, disqualified, immobilized, laid up, paralysed, unfit

incapacity *n* disqualification, feebleness, impotence, inability, inadequacy, incapability, incompetency, ineffectiveness, powerlessness, unfitness, weakness

incautious *adj* careless, hasty, heedless, ill-advised, ill-judged, improvident, imprudent, impulsive, inconsiderate, indiscreet, injudicious, negligent, precipitate, rash, reckless, thoughtless, unguarded, unthinking, unwary

incentive *n* bait, encouragement, enticement, goad, impetus, impulse, inducement, lure, motivation, motive, spur, stimulant, stimulus

incessant *adj* ceaseless, constant, continual, continuous, endless, eternal, everlasting, interminable, never-ending, nonstop, perpetual, persistent, relentless, unbroken, unceasing, unending, unrelenting, unremitting

incident *n* adventure, circumstance, episode, event, fact, happening, matter, occasion, occurrence; brush, clash, commotion, confrontation, contretemps, disturbance, mishap, scene, skirmish

incidental *adj* accidental, casual, chance, fortuitous, odd, random

incipient *adj* beginning, commencing, developing, embryonic, inceptive, inchoate, nascent, originating, starting

incision *n* cut, gash, notch, opening, slash, slit

incisive *adj* acute, keen, penetrating, perspicacious, piercing, trenchant; acid, biting, caustic, cutting, mordant, sarcastic, sardonic, satirical, severe, sharp

incite *v* agitate for, animate, drive, egg on, encourage, excite, foment, goad, impel, inflame, instigate, prompt, provoke, put up to, rouse, set on, spur, stimulate, stir up, urge, whip up

incitement *n* agitation, encouragement, goad, impetus, impulse, inducement, instigation, motivation, motive, prompting, provocation, spur, stimulus

incivility *n* bad manners, boorishness, discourteousness, discourtesy, disrespect, ill-breeding, impoliteness, rudeness, unmannerliness

inclement *adj* bitter, boisterous,

foul, harsh, intemperate, rigorous, rough, severe, stormy, tempestuous

inclination *n* affectation, aptitude, bent, bias, desire, disposition, fancy, fondness, leaning, liking, partiality, penchant, predilection, predisposition, prejudice, proclivity, proneness, propensity, stomach, taste, tendency, turn, turn of mind, wish

incline *v* be disposed, bias, influence, persuade, predispose, prejudice, sway, tend, turn; bend, bevel, cant, deviate, diverge, lean, slant, slope, tend, tilt, tip, veer

include *v* comprehend, comprise, contain, cover, embody, embrace, encompass, incorporate, involve, subsume, take in, take into account

inclusion *n* addition, incorporation, insertion

inclusive *adj* across-the board, all-embracing, all in, all together, blanket, comprehensive, full, general, global, overall, sweeping, umbrella, without exception

incognito *adj* camouflaged, concealed identity, disguised, sailing under false colours, under an assumed name

incoherent *adj* confused, disconnected, disjointed, disordered, inarticulate, inconsistent, jumbled, loose, muddled, rambling, stammering, stuttering, unconnected, uncoordinated, unintelligible, wandering, wild

income *n* earnings, gains, interest, means, pay, proceeds, profits, receipts, revenue, salary, takings, wages

incomparable *adj* beyond compare, inimitable, matchless, paramount, peerless, superlative, supreme, transcendent, unequalled, unmatched, unparalleled, unrivalled

incompatible *adj* antagonistic, antipathetic, conflicting, contradictory, discordant, discrepant, disparate, ill-assorted, incongruous, inconsistent, inconsonant, irreconcilable, mismatched, uncongenial, unsuitable, unsuited

incompetent *adj* bungling, floundering, incapable, incapacitated, ineffectual, inept, inexpert, insufficient, skill-less, unable, unfit, unfitted, unskilful, useless

incomplete *adj* broken, defective, deficient, fragmentary, imperfect, insufficient, lacking, partial, short, unaccomplished, undeveloped, undone, unexecuted, unfinished, wanting

incomprehensible *adj* above one's head, baffling, beyond grasp, enigmatic, impenetrable, inconceivable, inscrutable, mysterious, obscure, opaque, perplexing, puzzling, unfathomable, unimaginable, unintelligible, unthinkable

inconceivable *adj* beyond belief, impossible, incomprehensible, incredible, not to be thought of, out of the question, unbelievable, unheard of, unimaginable, unknowable, unthinkable

inconclusive *adj* ambiguous, indecisive, indeterminate, open, uncertain, unconvincing, undecided, unsettled, vague

incongruous *adj* absurd, conflict ing, contradictory, contrary, disconsonant, discordant, extraneous, improper, inappropriate, inapt, incoherent, incompatible, inconsistent, out of keeping, out of place, unbecoming, unsuitable, unsuited

inconsiderate *adj* careless, indelicate, insensitive, intolerant, rude, self-centred, selfish, tactless, thoughtless, uncharitable, ungracious, unkind, unthinking

inconsistency *n* contrariety, disagreement, discrepancy, disparity, divergence, incompatibility, incongruity, inconsonance, paradox, variance

inconsistent *adj* at odds, at variance, conflicting, contradictory, contrary, discordant, discrepant, incoherent, incompatible, in conflict, incongruous, irreconcilable, out of step; capricious, changeable, erratic, fickle, inconstant, irregular, unpredictable, unstable, unsteady, variable

inconspicuous *adj* camouflaged, hidden, insignificant, modest, muted, ordinary, plain, quiet, retiring, unassuming, unnoticeable, unobtrusive, unostentatious

inconvenience *n* annoyance, awkwardness, bother, difficulty, disadvantage, disruption, disturbance, drawback, fuss, hindrance, nuisance, trouble, uneasiness, upset, vexation

inconvenient *adj* annoying, awkward, bothersome, disadvantageous, disturbing, embarrassing, inopportune, tiresome, troublesome, unseasonable, unsuitable, untimely, vexatious

incorporate *v* absorb, amalgamate, assimilate, blend, coalesce, combine, consolidate, embody, fuse, include, integrate, merge, mix, subsume, unite

incorrect *adj* erroneous, false, faulty, flawed, improper, inaccurate, inappropriate, inexact, mistaken, out, specious, unfitting, unsuitable, untrue, wrong

incorrigible *adj* hardened, hopeless, incurable, intractable, inveterate, irredeemable, unreformed

increase *v* add to, advance, aggrandize, amplify, augment, boost, build up, develop, dilate, enhance, enlarge, escalate, expand, extend, grow, heighten, inflate, intensify, magnify, mount, multiply, proliferate, prolong, raise, snowball, spread, strengthen, swell, wax

increase *n* addition, augmentation, boost, development, enlargement, escalation, expansion, extension, gain, growth, increment, intensification, rise, upsurge, upturn

incredible *adj* absurd, beyond belief, far-fetched, implausible, impossible, improbable, inconceivable, preposterous, unbelievable, unimaginable, unthinkable

incredulous *adj* disbelieving, distrustful, doubtful, doubting, dubious, mistrustful, sceptical, suspicious, unbelieving, unconvinced

incriminate *v* accuse, arraign, blacken the name of, blame, charge, impeach, implicate, inculpate, indict, involve, point the finger at, stigmatize

incumbent *adj* binding, compelling, compulsory, mandatory, necessary, obligatory; lounging, lying, reclining, reposing, resting

incumbent *n* functionary, occupier,

office-holder, official

incur *v* arouse, bring upon oneself, contract, draw, earn, experience, expose oneself to, gain, induce, lay oneself open to, liable to, meet with, provoke

incurable *adj* dyed-in-the-wool, hopeless, incorrigible, inveterate; fatal, inoperable, irrecoverable, irremediable, remediless, terminal

indebted *adj* beholden, grateful, in debt, obligated, obliged, under an obligation

indecency *n* bawdiness, coarseness, crudity, foulness, grossness, immodesty, impropriety, impurity, indecorum, indelicacy, lewdness, licentiousness, obscenity, outrageousness, pornography, smut, smuttiness, unseemliness, vileness, vulgarity

indecent *adj* blue, coarse, crude, dirty, filthy, foul, gross, immodest, improper, impure, indelicate, lewd, licentious, pornographic, salacious, scatological, smutty, vile

indecision *n* ambivalence, doubt, hesitancy, hesitation, indecisiveness, irresolution, uncertainty, vacillation, wavering

indecisive *adj* doubtful, faltering, hesitating, irresolute, tentative, uncertain, undecided, undetermined, vacillating, wavering

indeed *adv* absolutely, actually, certainly, doubtlessly, in fact, in point of fact, in reality, in truth, positively, really, strictly, surely, to be sure, truly, undeniably, undoubtedly, veritably

indefensible *adj* faulty, inexcusable, insupportable, unforgivable, unjustifiable, unpardonable, untenable, unwarrantable, wrong

indefinite *adj* ambiguous, confused, doubtful, equivocal, evasive, general, ill-defined, imprecise, indeterminate, indistinct, inexact, loose, obscure, uncertain, unclear, undefined, undetermined, unfixed, unknown, unlimited, unsettled, vague

indelible *adj* enduring, indestructible, ineffaceable, ineradicable, inexpungible, inextirpable, lasting, permanent

indelicate *adj* blue, coarse, crude, embarrassing, gross, immodest, improper, indecent, indecorous, low, obscene, off-colour, offensive, risqué, rude, suggestive, tasteless, unbecoming, unseemly, untoward, vulgar

independence *n* autarchy, autonomy, freedom, home-rule, liberty, non-alignment, self-determination, self-government, self-legislation, self-reliance, self-rule, self-sufficiency, separation, sovereignty; (*Inf*) standing on one's own feet; bold, free-thinking, individualistic, liberated, unconventional, unfettered, unrestrained

independent *adj* absolute, free, liberated, separate, unconnected, unconstrained, uncontrolled, unrelated

independently *adv* alone, autonomously, by oneself, individually, on one's own, separately, solo, unaided

indescribable *adj* beggaring, description, beyond description, beyond words, incommunicable, indefinable, ineffable, inexpressible, unutterable

indestructible *adj* abiding, durable, enduring, everlasting, immortal, imperishable, incorruptible, indelible, indissoluble, lasting, nonperishable, permanent, unbreakable, unfading

indeterminate *adj* imprecise, inconclusive, indefinite, inexact, uncertain, undefined, undetermined, unfixed, unspecified, unstipulated, vague

index *n* clue, guide, indication, mark, sign, symptom, token; director, forefinger, hand, indicator, needle, pointer

indicate *v* bespeak, be symptomatic of, betoken, denote, evince, imply, manifest, point to, reveal, show, signify, suggest; (*Inf*) add up to

indication *n* clue, evidence, explanation, forewarning, hint, index, inkling, intimation, manifestation, mark, note, omen, portent, sign, signal, suggestion, symptom, warning

indicator *n* display, gauge, guide, index, mark, marker, meter, pointer, sign, signal, signpost, symbol

indictment *n* accusation, allegation, charge, impeachment, prosecution, summons

indifference *n* absence of feeling, aloofness, apathy, callousness, carelessness, coldness, coolness, detachment, disregard, heedlessness, inattention, lack of interest, negligence, stoicalness, unconcern

indifferent *adj* aloof, apathetic, callous, careless, cold, cool, detached, distant, heedless, impervious, inattentive, regardless, uncaring, unconcerned, unimpressed, uninterested, unmoved, unresponsive, unsympathetic; average, fair, mediocre, middling, moderate, ordinary, passable, perfunctory, undistinguished, uninspired

indignant *adj* angry, annoyed, disgruntled, exasperated, furious, heated, in a huff, incensed, irate, provoked, resentful, riled, scornful, wrathful

indignation *n* anger, exasperation, fury, pique, rage, resentment, righteous, anger, scorn, umbrage, wrath

indirect *adj* backhanded, circuitous, circumlocutory, crooked, devious, long-drawn-out, meandering, oblique, periphrastic, rambling, roundabout, tortuous, wandering, winding, zigzag

indiscreet *adj* foolish, hasty, heedless, ill-advised, ill-considered, ill-judged, impolitic, imprudent, incautious, injudicious, naive, rash, reckless, tactless, undiplomatic, unthinking, unwise

indiscriminate *adj* aimless, careless, desultory, general, random, sweeping, uncritical, undiscriminating, unmethodical, unselective, unsystematic, wholesale

indispensable *adj* crucial, essential, imperative, key, necessary, needed, needful, requisite, vital

indisposed *adj* ailing, confined to bed, ill, sick, unwell; (*Inf*) laid up, poorly

indisputable *adj* absolute, beyond doubt, certain, evident, incontestable, incontrovertible, indubitable, irrefutable, positive, sure, unassailable, undeniable, unquestionable

indistinct *adj* ambiguous, bleary, blurred, confused, dim, doubtful, faint, fuzzy, hazy, ill-defined, indefinite, indeterminate, indiscernible, indistinguishable, misty, muffled, obscure, out of focus, shadowy, unclear, undefined, unintelligible, vague, weak

indistinguishable *adj* alike, identical, same, twin

individual *adj* characteristic, discrete, distinct, distinctive, exclusive, identical, idiosyncratic, own, particular, peculiar, personal, personalized, proper, respective, separate, several, single, singular, special, specific, unique

individual *n* being, body, character, creature, mortal, party, person, personage, soul, type, unit

individuality *n* character, discreteness, distinction, distinctiveness, originality, peculiarity, personality, separateness, singularity, uniqueness

indomitable *adj* bold, invincible, resolute, staunch, steadfast, unbeatable, unconquerable, unflinching, untameable, unyielding

indubitable *adj* certain, evident, incontestable, incontrovertible, indisputable, irrefutable, obvious, sure, unarguable, undeniable, undoubted, unquestionable, veritable

induce *v* actuate, convince, draw, encourage, get, impel, incite, influence, instigate, move, persuade, press, prevail upon, prompt, talk into

inducement *n* attraction, bait, cause, consideration, encouragement, impulse, incentive, incitement, influence, lure, motive, reward, spur, stimulus, urge

indulge *v* cater to, give way to, gratify, pander to, regale, satiate, satisfy, treat oneself to, yield to

indulgence *n* excess, fondness, immoderation, intemperance, intemperateness, kindness, leniency, pampering, partiality, permissive ness, profligacy, profligateness, spoiling; courtesy, forbearance, good will, patience, tolerance, understanding

indulgent *adj* compliant, easy-going, favourable, fond, forbearing, gentle, gratifying, kind, kindly, lenient, liberal, mild, permissive, tender, tolerant, understanding

industrious *adj* active, assiduous, busy, conscientious, diligent, energetic, hard-working, laborious, persevering, persistent, productive, purposeful, sedulous, steady, tireless, zealous

industry *n* business, commerce, commercial, enterprise, manufacturing, production, trade; activity, application, assiduity, determination, diligence, effort, labour, perseverance, persistence, tirelessness, toil, vigour, zeal

ineffective *adj* barren, bootless, feeble, fruitless, futile, idle, impotent, inadequate, ineffectual, inefficacious, inefficient, unavailing, unproductive, useless, vain, weak, worthless

ineffectual *adj* abortive, bootless, emasculate, feeble, fruitless, futile, idle, impotent, inadequate, incompetent, ineffective, inefficacious, inefficient, inept, lame, powerless, unavailing, useless, vain, weak

inefficient *adj* disorganized, feeble, incapable, incompetent, ineffectual, inefficacious, inept, inexpert, slipshod, sloppy, wasteful, weak

ineligible *adj* disqualified, incompetent, objectionable, ruled out, unacceptable, undesirable, unequipped, unfit, unfitted, unqualified, unsuitable

inept *adj* awkward, bumbling, bungling, clumsy, gauche, incompetent, inexpert, maladroit, unhandy, unskilful, unworkmanlike

inequality *n* bias, difference, disparity, disproportion, diversity, imparity, irregularity, lack of balance, preferentiality, prejudice, unevenness

inert *adj* dead, dormant, dull, idle, immobile, inactive, inanimate, indolent, lazy, leaden, lifeless, motionless, passive, quiescent, slack, slothful, sluggish, slumberous, static, still, torpid, unmoving, unreactive, unresponsive

inertia *n* apathy, deadness, disinclination to move, drowsiness, dullness, idleness, immobility, inactivity, indolence, languor, lassitude, laziness, lethargy, listlessness, passivity, sloth, sluggishness, stillness, stupor, torpor, unresponsiveness

inescapable *adj* certain, destined, fated, ineluctable, ineludible, inevitable, inexorable, sure, unavoidable

inevitable *adj* assured, certain, decreed, destined, fixed, ineluctable, inescapable, inexorable, necessary, ordained, settled, sure, unavoidable, unpreventable

inexcusable *adj* indefensible, inexpiable, outrageous, unforgivable, unjustifiable, unpardonable, unwarrantable

inexpensive *adj* bargain, budget, cheap, economical, low-cost, low-priced, modest, reasonable

inexperienced *adj* amateur, callow, fresh, green, immature, new, raw, unaccustomed, unacquainted, unfamiliar, unfledged, unpractised, unschooled, unseasoned, unskilled, untrained, untried, unused, unversed

inexpert *adj* amateurish, awkward, bungling, clumsy, inept, maladroit, skilless, unhandy, unpractised, unprofessional, unskilful, unskilled, unworkmanlike

inexplicable *adj* baffling, beyond comprehension, enigmatic, incomprehensible, inscrutable, insoluble, mysterious, mystifying, strange, unaccountable, unfathomable, unintelligible

infallible *adj* faultless, impeccable, omniscient, perfect, unerring, unimpeachable; certain, dependable, foolproof, reliable, sure, trustworthy, unbeatable, unfailing

infamous *adj* abominable, atrocious, base, detestable, disgraceful, dishonourable, disreputable, egregious, flagitious, hateful, heinous, ignominious, ill-famed, iniquitous, loathsome, monstrous, nefarious, notorious, odious, opprobrious, outrageous, scandalous, scurvy, shameful, shocking, vile, villainous, wicked

infancy *n* babyhood, early childhood; beginnings, cradle, dawn, early stages, emergence, inception, origins, outset, start

infant *n* babe, baby, child, little one, neonate, newborn child, suckling, toddler, tot

infantile *adj* babyish, childish, immature, puerile, tender, weak, young

infatuated *adj* beguiled, besotted, bewitched, captivated, carried away, enamoured, enraptured, fascinated, head over heels in love with, inflamed, intoxicated, obsessed, possessed, smitten, spellbound, swept off one's feet, under the spell of

infect *v* affect, blight, contaminate, corrupt, defile, influence, poison, pollution, septicity, virus

infectious *adj* catching, communicable, contagious, contaminating, corrupting, defiling, infective, pestilential, poisoning, polluting, spreading, transmittable, virulent, vitiating

infer *v* conclude, conjecture, deduce, derive, gather, presume, read between the lines, surmise, understand

inference *n* assumption, conclusion, conjecture, consequence, corollary, deduction, presumption, reading, surmise

inferior *adj* junior, lesser, lower, menial, minor, secondary, subordinate, subsidiary, under, underneath

inferiority *n* badness, deficiency, imperfection, inadequacy, insignificance, meanness, mediocrity, shoddiness, unimportance, worthlessness

infertile *adj* barren, infecund, non-productive, sterile, unfruitful, unproductive

infest *v* beset, flood, invade, overrun, penetrate, permeate, ravage, swarm, throng

infiltrate *v* creep in, filter through, insinuate oneself, penetrate, percolate, permeate, pervade, work one's way into

infinite *adj* absolute, all-embracing, bottomless, boundless, enormous, eternal, everlasting, illimitable, immeasurable, immense, inestimable, inexhaustible, interminable, limitless, measureless, never-ending, numberless, perpetual, stupendous, total, unbounded, uncounted, untold, vast, wide, without end, without number

infinity *n* boundlessness, endlessness, eternity, immensity, infinitude, perpetuity, vastness

infirm *adj* ailing, debilitated, decrepit, doddering, doddery, enfeebled, failing, feeble, frail, lame, weak

inflame *v* agitate, anger, arouse, embitter, enrage, exasperate, excite, fire, foment, heat, ignite, impassion, incense, infuriate, intoxicate, kindle, madden, provoke, rile, rouse, stimulate

inflamed *adj* angry, chafing, festering, fevered, heated, hot, infected, red, septic, sore, swollen

inflammable *adj* combustible, flammable, incendiary

inflate *v* aerate, aggrandize, amplify, balloon, bloat, blow up, boost, dilate, distend, enlarge, escalate, exaggerate, expand, increase, puff up, pump, swell

inflation *n* aggrandizement, blowing

up, distension, enhancement, enlargement, escalation, expansion, extension, increase, intensification, puffiness, rise, spread, swelling, tumefaction

inflection *n* accentuation, bend, bow, crook, curvature, intonation, modulation; conjugation, declension

inflexible *adj* adamant, brassbound, dyed-in-the-wool, firm, fixed, hard and fast, immovable, immutable, implacable, inexorable, intractable, iron, obdurate, obstinate, relentless, resolute, rigorous, set, set in one's ways, steadfast, steely, strict, stringent, stubborn, unadaptable, unbending, unchangeable, uncompromising, unyielding

inflict *v* administer, apply, deliver, exact, impose, levy, visit, wreak

influence *n* agency, ascendancy, authority, control, credit, direction, domination, effect, guidance, magnetism, master, power, pressure, rule, spell, sway, weight; connections, good offices, hold, importance, leverage, power, prestige, weight

influence *v* act upon, affect, arouse, bias, control, count, direct, dispose, guide, impel, impress, incite, incline, induce, instigate, lead to believe, manipulate, modify, move, persuade, predispose, prompt, rouse, sway

inform *v* acquaint, advise, apprise, communicate, enlighten, give someone to understand, instruct, leak to, let know, make conversant with, notify, send word to, teach, tell, tip off

informal *adj* casual, colloquial, cosy, easy, familiar, natural, relaxed, simple, unceremonious, unconstrained, unofficial

information *n* advice, blurb, counsel, data, facts, inside story, instruction, intelligence, knowledge, material, message, news, notice, report, tidings, word; (*Inf*) lowdown

informed *adj* abreast, acquainted, briefed, conversant, enlightened, erudite, expert, familiar, in the know, knowledgeable, learned, posted, primed, reliable, up, up-to-date, versed, well-read

informer *n* accuser, betrayer, grass, sneak, stool pigeon

infrequent *adj* few and far between, occasional, rare, sporadic, uncommon, unusual

infringe *v* break, contravene, disobey, transgress, violate

infuriate *v* anger, be like a red rag to a bull, enrage, exasperate, get one's back up, incense, irritate, madden, make one's blood boil, make one's hackles rise, pique, provoke, raise one's hackles, rile, vex; (*Inf*) make one see red

infuriating *adj* aggravating, annoying, exasperating, galling, irritating, maddening, mortifying, pestilential, provoking, vexatious

ingenious *adj* adroit, bright, brilliant, clever, crafty, creative, dexterous, fertile, inventive, masterly, original, ready, resourceful, shrewd, skilful, subtle

ingenuous *adj* artless, candid, childlike, frank, guileless, honest, innocent, naive, open, plain, simple, sincere, trustful, trusting, unreserved, unsophisticated, unstudied

ingratitude *n* thanklessness, unappreciativeness, ungratefulness
ingredient *adj* component, constituent, element, part
inhabit *v* abide, dwell, live, lodge, make one's home, occupy, people, populate, possess, reside, take up residence in, tenant
inhabitant *n* aborigine, citizen, denizen, dweller, indigene, indweller, inmate, native, occupant, occupier, resident, tenant
inhabited *v* colonized, developed, held, occupied, peopled, populated, settled, tenanted
inherit *v* accede to be bequeathed, be left, come into fall heir to, succeed to
inheritance *n* bequest, birthright, heritage, legacy, patrimony
inhibit *v* arrest, bar, bridle, check, constrain, curb, debar, discourage, forbid, frustrate, hinder, hold back, impede, obstruct, prevent, prohibit, restrain, stop
inhibition *n* bar, check, embargo, hindrance, interdict, mental blockage, obstacle, prohibition, reserve, restraint, restriction, reticence, self-consciousness, shyness
inhospitable *adj* cool, uncongenial, unfriendly, ungenerous, unkind, unreceptive, unsociable, unwelcoming, xenophobic; bare, barren, bleak, desolate, empty, forbidding, hostile, lonely, sterile, unfavourable, uninhabitable
inhuman *adj* animal, barbaric, barbarous, bestial, brutal, cold-blooded, cruel, diabolical, fiendish, heartless, merciless, pitiless, remorseless, ruthless, savage, unfeeling, vicious
inhumane *adj* brutal, cruel, heartless, pitiless, uncompassionate, unfeeling, unkind, unsympathetic
initial *adj* beginning, commencing, early, first, inaugural, inceptive, inchoate, incipient, introductory, opening, primary
initially *adv* at first, at the outset, at the start, first, firstly, in the begin ning, in the early stages, originally, primarily, to begin with
initiate *v* begin, break the ice, commence, get under way, inaugurate, institute, launch, lay the foundations of, open, originate, pioneer, set going, set in motion, set the ball rolling, start; coach, familiarize with indoctrinate, induct, instate, instruct, introduce, invest, teach, train
initiative *n* advantage, beginning, commencement, first move, first step, lead
inject *v* inoculate, jab, vaccinate; bring in, infuse, insert, instil, interject, introduce
injunction *n* admonition, command, dictate, exhortation, instruction, mandate, order, precept, ruling
injure *v* abuse, blemish, blight, break, damage, deface, disable, harm, hurt, ill, injustice, mischief, ruin, spoil, tarnish, undermine, vitiate, weaken, wound, wrong
injustice *n* bias, discrimination, favouritism, inequality, inequity, iniquity, one-sidedness, oppression, partiality, partisanship, prejudice, unfairness, unjustness, unlawfulness
inland *adj* domestic, interior, internal, upcountry

inlet *n* bay, bight, cove, creek, entrance, ingress, loch, passage, sea

innate *adj* congenital, connate, constitutional, essential, inborn, inbred, indigenous, ingrained, inherent, inherited, instinctive, intrinsic, intuitive, native, natural

inner *adj* central, essential, inside, interior, internal, intestinal, inward, middle

innermost *adj* basic, buried, central, deep, deepest, essential, intimate, personal, private, secret

innocence *n* blamelessness, chastity, clean hands, guiltlessness, incorruptibility, probity, purity, righteousness, sinlessness, stainlessness, uprightness, virginity, virtue; artlessness, credulousness, naiveté, simplicity, unsophistication, unworldliness

innocent *adj* blameless, clear, faultless, guiltless, honest, in the clear, not guilty, uninvolved, unoffending; chaste, immaculate, impeccable, incorrupt, pristine, pure, righteous, sinless, spotless, stainless, unblemished, unsullied, upright, virgin, virginal; artless, childlike, credulous, frank, guileless, gullible, ingenuous, naive, open, simple, unsuspicious, unworldly; (*Inf*) wet behind the ears

innovation *n* alteration, change, departure, introduction, modernism, modernization, newness, novelty, variation

innuendo *n* allusion, aspersion, hint, implication, imputation, inkling, insinuation, intimation, overtone, suggestion, whisper

innumerable *adj* beyond number, countless, incalculable, infinite, many, multitudinous, myriad, numberless, numerous, unnumbered, untold

inoffensive *adj* harmless, humble, innocent, innocuous, innoxious, mild, neutral, nonprovocative, peaceable, quiet, retiring, unobjectionable, unobtrusive, unoffending

inopportune *adj* ill-chosen, ill-timed, inappropriate, inauspicious, inconvenient, malapropos, mistimed, unfavourable, unfortunate, unpropitious, unseasonable, unsuitable, untimely

inordinate *adj* disproportionate, excessive, exorbitant, extravagant, immoderate, intemperate, preposterous, unconscionable, undue, unreasonable, unrestrained, unwarranted

inquest *n* inquiry, inquisition, investigation, probe

inquire *v* examine, explore, inspect, investigate, look into make inquiries, probe, scrutinize, search

inquiry *n* examination, exploration, inquest, interrogation, investigation, probe, research, scrutiny, search study, survey

inquisition *n* cross-examination, examination, inquest, inquiry, investigation, question, quizzing

inquisitive *adj* curious, inquiring, intrusive, peering, probing, prying, questioning, scrutinizing; (*Inf*) snooping

insane *adj* crazed, crazy, demented, deranged, mad, mentally, disordered, mentally ill, of unsound mind, out of one's mind, unhinged

insanitary *adj* contaminated, dirtied, dirty, disease-ridden, feculent, filthy, impure, infected, infested, insalubrious, noxious, polluted, unclean, unhealthy, unhygienic

insanity *n* aberration, craziness, delirium, dementia, frenzy, madness, mental disorder, mental illness

insatiable *adj* gluttonous, greedy, insatiate, intemperate, quenchless, rapacious, ravenous, unappeasable, unquenchable, voracious

inscribe *v* carve, cut, engrave, etch, impress, imprint; address, dedicate

inscription *n* dedication, engraving, label, legend, lettering, saying, words

inscrutable *adj* blank, deadpan, enigmatic, impenetrable, unreadable; hidden, incomprehensible, inexplicable, mysterious, undiscoverable, unexplainable, unfathomable, unintelligible; (*Inf*) poker-faced

insecure *adj* afraid, anxious, uncertain, unconfident, unsure; built upon sand, flimsy, frail insubstantial, loose, on thin ice, precarious, rickety, rocky, shaky, unreliable, unsound, unstable, unsteady, weak, wobbly

insensible *adj* anaesthetized, benumbed, dull, inert, insensate, numbed, senseless, stupid, torpid

insensitive *adj* callous, crass, hardened, immune, imperceptive, impervious to, indifferent, non-reactive to, obtuse, oblivious to, tactless, thick-skinned, tough, uncaring, unconcerned, unfeeling, unresponsive, unsusceptible

inseparable *adj* conjoined, inalienable, indissoluble, indivisible, inseverable; bosom, close, devoted, intimate

insert *n* embed, enter, implant, infix, interject, interpolate, interpose, introduce, place, put, set, stick in, tuck in, work in

insertion *n* addition implant, inclusion, insert, inset, interpolation, introduction supplement

inside *n* contents, inner part, interior; **insides** belly, bowels, entrails, guts, innards, internal organs, stomach, viscera, vitals

inside *adv* indoors, into the building, under cover, within

inside *adj* inner, innermost, interior, internal, intramural, inward; classified, confidential, esoteric, private, priveledged, privy, secret

insidious *adj* artful, crafty, crooked, cunning, deceitful, deceptive, designing, disingenuous, duplicitous, guileful, intriguing, slick, sly, smooth, sneaking, stealthy, subtle, surreptitious, treacherous, tricky, wily

insight *n* acumen, awareness, comprehension, discernment, intuition, intuitiveness, judgment, observation, penetration, perception, perspicacity, understanding, vision

insignia *n/pl n* badge, crest, decoration, distinguishing mark, earmark, emblem, ensign, symbol

insignificant *adj* flimsy, immaterial, inconsequential, inconsiderable, irrelevant, meagre, meaningless, minor, negligible, nondescript, nonessential, nugatory, of no account, paltry, petty, scanty, trifling, trivial, unimportant, unsubstantial

insincere *adj* deceitful, deceptive, devious, dishonest, disingenuous, dissembling, dissimulating, double-dealing, duplicitous, evasive, faithless, false, hollow, hypocritical, lying, mendacious, pretended, unfaithful, untrue, untruthful

insinuate *v* allude, hint, imply, indicate, intimate, suggest; infiltrate, infuse, inject, instil, introduce

insinuation *n* allusion, aspersion, hint, implication, innuendo, slur, suggestion

insipid *adj* anaemic, baal, bland, characterless, colourless, drab, dry, dull, flat, jejune, lifeless, limp, pointless, prosaic, prosy, spiritless, stale, stupid, tame, tedious, trite, unimaginative, uninteresting, vapid, weak, wearisome; bland, flavourless, savourless, tasteless, unappetizing, watered down, watery

insist *v* be firm, brook no refusal, demand, lay down the law, not take no for an answer, persist, require, stand firm, stand one's ground, take a stand, urge; assert, asseverate, aver, claim, contend, hold, maintain, reiterate, repeat, swear, urge, vow

insistent *adj* demanding, dogged, emphatic, exigent, forceful, importunate, incessant, peremptory, persevering, persistent, pressing, unrelenting, urgent

insolence *n* abuse, audacity, boldness, contemptuousness, contumely, disrespect, effrontery, impertinence, impudence, incivility, insubordination, offensiveness, pertness, rudeness, uncivility

insolent *adj* abusive, bold, brazen-faced, contemptuous, impertinent, impudent, insubordinate, insulting, pert, rude, saucy, uncivil

insoluble *adj* baffling, impenetrable, indecipherable, inexplicable, mysterious, mystifying, obscure, unaccountable, unfathomable, unsolvable

insolvent *adj* bankrupt, failed, gone bust, in receivership, in the hands of the receivers, on the rocks, ruined

insomnia *n* insomnolence, restlessness, sleeplessness, wakefulness

inspect *v* audit, check, examine, go over, investigate, look over, oversee, scan, scrutinize, search, superintend, supervise, survey, vet

inspection *n* check, checkup, examination, investigation, look-over, review, scan, scrutiny, search, superintendence, supervision, surveillance, survey

inspector *n* censor, checker, critic, examiner, investigator, overseer, scrutineer, scrutinizer, superintendent, supervisor

inspiration *n* arousal, awakening, encouragement, influence, muse, spur, stimulus

inspire *v* animate, be responsible for, encourage, enliven, galvanize, hearten, imbue, influence, infuse, inspirit, instil, spark off, spur, stimulate

inspired *adj* brilliant, dazzling, enthralling, exciting, marvellous, memorable, outstanding, supreme, thrilling, wonderful

instability *n* capriciousness, changeableness, disequilibrium, fickleness, fitfulness, fluctuation, fluidity, frailty, imbalance, impermanence, inconstancy, insecurity, irresolution, mutability, oscillation, precariousness, restlessness, shakiness, transience, unpredictability, unsteadiness, vacillation, variability, volatility, wavering, weakness

install *v* fix, lay, lodge, place, position, put in, set up, station; establish, inaugurate, induct, instate, institute, introduce, invest, set up

installation *n* inauguration, induction, instatement, investiture; equipment, machinery, plant, system

instalment *n* chapter, division, episode, part, portion, repayment, section

instance *n* case, case in point, example, illustration, occasion, occurrence, precedent, situation, time

instance *v* adduce, cite, mention, name, quote, specify

instant *n* flash, moment, second, split second, trice, twinkling; (*Inf*) jiffy, two shakes of a lamb's tail

instant *adj* direct, immediate, instantaneous, prompt, quick, split-second, urgent

instantaneous *adj* direct, immediate, instant, on-the-spot

instantly *adv* at once, directly, forth with, immediately, instantaneously, now, on the spot, right away, right now, straight away, there and then, this, minute, without delay

instead *adv* alternatively, in preference to, on second thoughts, preferably, rather than, substitute for

instigate *v* actuate, bring about, encourage, foment, impel, incite, influence, initiate, kindle, move, persuade, prompt, provoke, rouse, set on, spur, start, stimulate, stir up, urge, whip up

instil *v* engender, engraft, imbue, implant, impress, inculcate, infix, infuse, insinuate, introduce

instinct *n* aptitude, faculty, feeling, gift, impulse, intuition, knack, natural, inclination, predisposition, proclivity, sixth sense, talent, tendency, urge

instinctive *adj* automatic, inborn, inherent, innate, instinctual, intuitional, intuitive, involuntary, mechanical, native, natural, reflex, spontaneous, unlearned, unpremeditated, unthinking, visceral

institute *v* appoint, begin, bring into being, commence, constitute, enact, establish, fix, found, induct, initiate, install, introduce, invest, launch, ordain, organize, originate, pioneer, put into operation, set in motion, settle, set up, start

institute *n* academy, association, college, conservatory, foundation, guild, institution, school, seat of learning, seminary, society

institution *n* constitution, creation, enactment, establishment, formation, foundation, initiation, introduction, investiture, investment, organization; academy, college, establishment, foundation, hospital, institute, school, seminary, society, university; convention, custom, law, practice, ritual, rule, tradition

instruct *v* bid, charge, command,

direct, enjoin, order, tell; coach, discipline, drill, educate, enlighten, ground, guide, inform, school, teach, train, tutor

instruction *n* apprenticeship, coaching, discipline, drilling, education, enlightenment, grounding, guidance, information, preparation, schooling, teaching, training, tuition, tutelage

instructions *pl n* advice, directions, guidance, information, key, orders, recommendations, rules

instructor *n* adviser, coach, demonstrator, exponent, guide, master, mentor, mistress, pedagogue, preceptor, school-master, school-mistress, teacher, trainer, tutor

instrument *n* apparatus, appliance, contraption, contrivance, device, gadget, implement, mechanism, tool, utensil

instrumental *adj* active, assisting, auxiliary, conducive, contributory, helpful, helping, influential, involved, of help, subsidiary, useful

insubordinate *adj* contumacious, defiant, disobedient, disorderly, fractious, insurgent, mutinous, rebellious, recalcitrant, refractory, riotous, seditious, turbulent, undisciplined, ungovernable, unruly

insubordination *n* defiance, disobedience, indiscipline, insurrection, mutinousness, mutiny, rebellion, recalcitrance, revolt, riotousness, sedition, ungovernability

insufferable *adj* detestable, dreadful, enough to test the patience of a saint, impossible, insupportable, intolerable, more than flesh and blood can stand, outrageous, past bearing, too much, unbearable, unendurable, unspeakable

insufficient *adj* deficient, inadequate, incapable, incommensurate, incompetent, lacking, short, unfitted, unqualified

insular *adj* blinkered, circumscribed, closed, contracted, cut off, illiberal, inward-looking, isolated, limited, narrow, narrow-minded, parish-pump, parochial, petty, prejudiced, provincial

insulate *v* close off, cocoon, cushion, cut off, isolate, protect, sequester, shield, wrap up in cotton wool; cover, encase, enwrap, envelop, heatproof, pad, seal, shockproof, soundproof, wrap

insult *n* abuse, affront, aspersion, contumely, indignity, insolence, offence, outrage, rudeness, slap in the face, slight, snub

insult *v* abuse, affront, call names, give offence to, injure, offend, outrage, revile, slander, slight, snub

insurance *n* assurance, cover, coverage, guarantee, indemnification, indemnity, protection, provision, safeguard, security, warranty

insure *v* assure, cover, guarantee, indemnify, underwrite, warrant

intact *adj* all in one piece, complete, entire, perfect, scatheless, sound, together, unbroken, undamaged, undefiled, unharmed, unhurt, unimpaired, uninjured, unscathed, untouched, unviolated, virgin, whole

integral *adj* basic, component, constituent, elemental, essential, fundamental, indispensable, intrinsic, necessary, requisite;

complete, entire, full, intact, undivided, whole

integrate *v* accommodate, amalgamate, assimilate, blend, coalesce, combine, fuse, harmonize, incorporate, intermix, join, knit, merge, mesh, unite

integrity *n* candour, goodness, honesty, honour, incorruptibility, principle, probity, purity, rectitude, righteousness, uprightness, virtue

intellect *n* brains, intelligence, judgment, mind, reason, sense, understanding

intellectual *adj* bookish, cerebral, highbrow, intelligent, mental, rational, scholarly, studious, thoughtful

intellectual *n* academic, highbrow, thinker

intelligence *n* acumen, alertness, aptitude, brain-power, brightness, capacity, cleverness, comprehension, discernment, intellect, mental aptitude, mind, penetration, perception, quickness, reason, understanding; advice, data, disclosure, facts, findings, information, knowledge, news, notice, notification, reports, rumour, tidings, tip-off, word; observation, spying, surveillance

intelligent *adj* acute, alert, apt, bright, clever, discerning, enlightened, instructed, knowing, penetrating, perspicacious, quick, quick-witted, rational, sharp, smart, thinking, well-informed

intelligible *adj* clear, comprehensible, distinct, lucid, open, plain, understandable

intend *v* aim, be resolved, contemplate, determine, have in mind, mean, meditate, plan, propose, purpose, scheme

intense *adj* acute, agonizing, close, concentrated, deep, excessive, exquisite, extreme, fierce, forceful, great, harsh, intensive, powerful, profound, protracted, sever, strained; ardent, burning, consuming, eager, earnest, energetic, fanatical, fervent, fervid, fierce, forcible, heightened, impassioned, keen, passionate, speaking, vehement

intensify *v* add to, aggravate, boost, concentrate, deepen, emphasize, enhance, escalate, exacerbate, heighten, increase, magnify, quicken, redouble, reinforce, set off, sharpen, strengthen, whet; (*Inf*) add fuel to the flames

intensity *n* ardour, concentration, depth, earnestness, emotion, energy, excess, extremity, fanaticism, fervency, fervour, fierceness, fir, force, intenseness, keenness, passion, potency, power, severity, strain, strength, tension, vehemence, vigour

intensive *adj* all-out, comprehensive, concentrated, demanding, exhaustive, in-depth, thorough, thoroughgoing

intent *adj* absorbed, alert, attentive, committed, concentrated, determined, eager, earnest, engrossed, fixed, industrious, intense, occupied, piercing, preoccupied, rapt, resolute, resolved, steadfast, steady, watchful, wrapped up

intention *n* aim, design, end, end in view, goal, idea, intent, meaning, object, objective, point, purpose, scope, target, view

intentional *adj* calculated, deliberate, designed, done on purpose, intended, meant, planned, prearranged, preconcerted, premeditated, purposed, studied, wilful

intercept *v* arrest, block, catch, check, cut off, deflect, head off, interrupt, obstruct, seize, stop, take

interchangeable *adj* commutable, equivalent, exchangeable, identical, reciprocal, synonymous, the same, transposable

intercourse *n* association, commerce, communication, communion, connection, contact, converse, correspondence, dealings, intercommunication, trade, traffic, truck; carnal knowledge, coition, coitus, congress, copulation, intimacy, love-making, sexual act, sexual intercourse, sexual relations

interest *n* affection, attention, attentiveness, attraction, concern, curiosity, notice, regard, suspicion, sympathy; concern, consequence, importance, moment, note, relevance, significance, weight; activity, pastime, preoccupation, pursuit, relaxation; advantage, benefit, gain, good, profit

interest *v* amuse, arouse one's curiosity, attract, divert, engross, fascinate, hold the attention of, intrigue, move, touch; affect, concern, engage, involve

interested *adj* affected, attentive, attracted, curious, drawn, excited, fascinated, intent, keen, moved, responsive, stimulated; biased, concerned, implicated, involved, partisan, predisposed, prejudiced

interesting *adj* absorbing, amusing, appealing, attractive, compelling, curious, engaging, engrossing, entertaining, gripping, intriguing, pleasing, provocative, stimulating, suspicious, thought-provoking, unusual

interfere *v* butt in, get involved, intermeddle, intervene, intrude, meddle, tamper

interference *n* intermeddling, intervention, intrusion, meddlesomeness, meddling, prying; clashing, collision, conflict, impedance, obstruction, opposition

interior *adj* inner, inside, internal, inward; central, inland, remote, upcountry; hidden, inner, intimate, mental, personal, private, secret, spiritual

interior *n* centre, heartland, upcountry

interlude *n* break, breathing space, delay, episode, halt, hiatus, intermission, interval, pause, respite, rest, spell, stop, stoppage, wait

intermediate *adj* halfway, in between, intermediary, interposed, intervening, mean, mid, middle, midway, transitional

intermittent *adj* broken, discontinuous, fitful, irregular, occasional, periodic, punctuated, recurrent, recurring, spasmodic, sporadic,

internal *adj* inner, inside, interior, intimate, private, subjective

international *adj* cosmopolitan, ecumenical, global, intercontinental, universal, worldwide

interpose *v* come between, intercede, interfere, intermediate, intervene, intrude, mediate, step in; insert, interject, interrupt, introduce,

interpret *v* adapt, clarify, construe,

decipher, decode, define, elucidate, explain, explicate, expound, make sense of, paraphrase, read, render, solve, spell out, take, throw light on, translate, understand

interpretation *n* analysis, clarification, construction, diagnosis, elucidation, exegesis, explanation, explication, exposition, expounding, meaning, performance, portrayal, reading, rendering, rendition, sense, signification, understanding, version; deciphering, decoding; paraphrase, transcription, translation, transliteration; depiction, presentation, enactment, execution

interpreter *n* annotator, commentator, exponent, performer, portrayer, scholiast, transcriber, translator

interrogate *v* ask, catechize, cross-examine, cross-question, enquire, examine, give the third degree to, grill, inquire, investigate, probe, pump, question, quiz; (*Inf*) put the screws on

interrogation *n* catechization, cross-examination, cross-questioning, enquiry, examination, grilling, inquiry, inquisition, probing, questioning

interrupt *v* barge in, break, break in, break off, bring to a standstill, check, cut, cut off, cut short, delay, disconnect, discontinue, disjoin, disturb, disunite, divide, halt, heckle, hinder, hold up, interfere, intrude, lay aside, leave off, obstruct, postpone, punctuate, separate, sever, stay, stop, suspend; (*Inf*) butt in on, chime in on, chip in, muscle in on

interruption *n* break, cessation, disconnection, discontinuance, disruption, dissolution, disturbance, disuniting, division, halt, hiatus, hindrance, hitch, impediment, intrusion, obstacle, obstruction, pause, separation, severance, stop, stoppage, suspension

intersection *n* criss-crossing, crossing, crossroads, interchange, junction, meeting, road junction, roundabout; (*Inf*) spaghetti junction

interval *n* break, delay, distance, gap, hiatus, interim, interlude, intermission, interspace, meantime, meanwhile, opening, pause, period, playtime, rest, season, space, spell, term, time, wait

intervene *v* arbitrate, intercede, interfere, interpose oneself, intrude, involve oneself, mediate; (*Inf*) step in, take a hand

intervention *n* agency, intercession, interference, interposition, intrusion, mediation

interview *n* audience, conference, consultation, dialogue, evaluation, meeting, oral examination, press conference, talk

interview *v* examine, interrogate, question, sound out, talk to

intimacy *n* closeness, confidence, confidentiality, familiarity, fraternization, understanding

intimate *adj* bosom, cherished, close, confidential, dear, friendly, innermost, near, nearest and dearest, warm; confidential, personal, private, privy, secret, thorough; (*Inf*) comfy, cosy, thick; friendly, informal, snug, warm

intimate *n* bosom, friend, close friend, comrade, confidant, confidante, companion, crony, familiar, friend, mate, pal

intimate *v* allude, announce, communicate, declare, drop a hint, hint, impart, imply, indicate, inform, insinuate, let it be known, make known, remind, signal, state, suggest, tell, warn

intimately *adv* affectionately, closely, confidentially, confidingly, familiarly, personally, tenderly, very well, warmly; fully, in detail, inside out, through and through, thoroughly, to the core, very well

intimidate *v* affright, alarm, appal, browbeat, bully, coerce, cow, daunt, dishearten, dismay, dispirit, frighten, overawe, scare, scare off, subdue, terrify, terrorize, threaten; (*Inf*) lean on, twist someone's arm

intimidation *n* browbeating, bullying, coercion, fear, menaces, pressure, terror, terrorization, threats; (*Inf*) arm-twisting

intolerable *adj* beyond bearing, excruciating, impossible, insufferable, insupportable, more than flesh and blood can stand, not to be borne, painful, unbearable, unendurable

intolerant *adj* bigoted, chauvinistic, dictatorial, dogmatic, fanatical, illiberal, impatient, narrow, narrow-minded, one-sided, prejudiced, racialist, racist, small-minded, uncharitable, xenophobic

intoxicated *adj* befuddled, blind drunk, drunk, drunk as a lord, drunken, fuddled, high, inebriated, merry, plastered, smashed, sozzled, stewed, the worse for drink, tight, tipsy, under the influence

intoxication *n* drunkenness, inebriation, inebriety, insobriety, tipsiness

intrepid *adj* audacious, bold, brave, courageous, daring, dauntless, doughty, fearless, gallant, heroic, lion-hearted, nerveless, plucky, resolute, stalwart, stouthearted, unafraid, undaunted, unflinching, valiant, valourous

intricate *adj* baroque, complex, complicated, convoluted, difficult, elaborate, fancy, involved, knotty, labyrinthine, obscure, perplexing, rococo, sophisticated, tangled, tortuous

intrigue *v* arouse the curiosity of, attract, charm, fascinate, interest, pique, rivet, tickle one's fancy, titillate; connive, conspire, machinate, manoeuvre, plot, scheme

intrigue *n* cabal, chicanery, collusion, conspiracy, double-dealing, knavery, machination, manipulation, manoeuvre, plot, ruse, scheme, sharp, practice, trickery, wile; affair, amour, intimacy, liaison, romance

intriguing *adj* absorbing, beguiling, compelling, diverting, exciting, fascinating, interesting, tantalizing, titillating

intrinsic *adj* basic, built-in, central, congenital, constitutional, elemental, essential, fundamental, genuine, inborn, inbred, inherent, native, natural, real, true, underlying

introduce *v* acquaint, do the honours, familiarize, make known, make the introduction, present; begin, bring in, commence, establish, found, inaugurate, initiate, institute, launch, organize, pioneer, set up, start, usher in; announce, lead into, lead off, open, preface

introduction *n* baptism, debut,

establishment, first, acquaintance, inauguration, induction, initiation, institution, launch, pioneering, presentation; commencement, exordium, foreword, into, lead-in, opening, opening passage, opening, remarks, overture, preamble, preface, preliminaries, prelude, proem, prolegomena, prole gomenon, prologue

introductory *adj* early, elementary, first, inaugural, initial, initiatory, opening, precursory, prefatory, preliminary, preparatory, startling

intrude *v* butt in, encroach, infringe, interfere, interrupt, meddle, obtrude, push in, thrust oneself forward, trespass, violate

intruder *n* burglar, housebreaker, infiltrator, interloper, invader, prowler, raider, squatter, thief, trespasser; (*Inf*) gate-crasher

intrusion *n* encroachment, infringement, interference, interruption, invasion, trespass, violation

intuition *n* discernment, hunch, insight, instinct, perception, presentiment, sixth sense

invade *v* assail, assault, attack, burst in, descend upon, encroach, infringe, make inroads, occupy, raid, violate

invader *n* aggressor, alien, attacker, looter, plunderer, raider, trespasser

invalid *adj* ailing, bedridden, disabled, feeble, frail, ill, infirm, sick, sickly, valetudinarian, weak

invalid *adj* baseless, fallacious, false, ill-founded, illogical, inoperative, irrational, not binding, nugatory, null, null and void, unfounded, unscientific, unsound, untrue, void, worthless

invaluable *adj* beyond price, costly, inestimable, precious, priceless, valuable

invariable *adj* changeless, consistent, constant, fixed, immutable, inflexible, regular, rigid, set, unalterable, unchangeable, unchanging, unfailing, uniform, unvarying, unwavering

invasion *n* aggression, assault, attack, foray, incursion, inroad, irruption, offensive, onslaught, raid

invent *v* coin, come up with, conceive, contrive, create, design, devise, discover, dream up, formulate, imagine, improvise, originate, think up; (*Inf*) cook up

invention *n* contraption, contrivance, creation, design, development, device, discovery, gadget; (*Inf*) brainchild; deceit, fabrication, fake, falsehood, fantasy, fiction, figment of someone's imagination, forgery, lie, prevarication, sham, story, untruth, yarn

inventive *adj* creative, fertile, gifted, imaginative, ingenious, innovative, inspired, original, resourceful

inventor *n* architect, author, coiner, creator, designer, father, framer, maker, originator

inventory *n* account, catalogue, checklist, description, file, list, record, register, roll, roster, schedule, statement, stock book, tally

inverse *adj* contrary, converse, inverted, opposite, reverse, reversed, transposed

invert *v* capsize, introvert, overset, overturn, reverse, transpose, turn inside out, turn turtle, turn upside down, upset, upturn

invest *v* advance, devote, lay out, put in, sink, spend; endow, endue, provide, supply; beleaguer, beset, besiege, enclose, lay siege to, surround

investigate *v* consider, enquire into, examine, explore, go into, inquire into, inspect, look into, make enquiries, probe, put to the test, scrutinize, search, sift, study

investigation *n* analysis, enquiry, examination, exploration, fact finding, hearing, inquest, inquiry, inspection, probe, research, review, scrutiny, search, study, survey

investigator *n* examiner, detective, private eye, researcher, reviewer, sleuth

investment *n* asset, investing, speculation, transaction, venture

inveterate *adj* chronic, confirmed, deep-dyed, deep-rooted, deep-seated, deep-set, die-hard, dyed-in-the-wool, entrenched, established, habitual, hard-core, hardened, incorrigible, incurable, ineradicable, ingrained, long-established, long-standing, obstinate

invigorate *v* animate, brace, buck up energize, enliven, exhilarate, fortify, freshen, galvanize, harden, liven up, nerve, pep up, perk up, put new heart into, quicken, refresh, rejuvenate, revitalize, stimulate, strengthen

invincible *adj* impregnable, indestructible, indomitable, inseparable, insuperable, invulnerable, unassailable, unbeatable, unconquerable, unsurmountable, unyielding

invisible *adj* imperceptible, indiscernible, out of sight, unperceivable, unseen; concealed, disguised, hidden, inappreciable, inconspicuous, infinitesimal, microscopic

invitation asking, begging, bidding, call, request, solicitation, summons, supplication; allurement, challenge, coquetry, enticement, incitement, inducement, open door, overture, provocation, temptation; (*Inf*) invite

invite *v* ask, beg, bid, call, request, request the pleasure of someone's company, solicit, summon; allure, ask for, attract, bring on, court, draw, encourage, entice, lead, leave the door open to, provoke, solicit, tempt, welcome

inviting *adj* alluring, appealing, attractive, beguiling, captivating, delightful, engaging, enticing, fascinating, intriguing, magnetic, mouthwatering, pleasing, seductive, tempting, warm, welcoming, winning

invoke *v* adjure, appeal to, beg, beseech, call upon, conjure, entreat, implore, petition, pray, solicit, supplicate

involuntary *adj* compulsory, forced, obligatory, reluctant, unwilling

involve *v* entail, imply, mean, necessitate, presuppose, require; affect, associate, compromise, concern, connect, draw in, implicate, incriminate, inculpate, touch; absorb, bind, commit, engage, engross, grip, hold, preoccupy, rivet, wrap up

invulnerable *adj* insensitive; impenetrable, impregnable, invincible, safe, secure, unassailable, undefeatable

inward *adj* entering, inbound, incoming, inflowing, ingoing, inpouring, penetrating; confidential, hidden, inmost, inner, innermost, inside, interior, internal, personal, private, privy, secret

irksome *adj* aggravating, annoying, boring, bothersome, burdensome, disagreeable, exasperating, irritating, tedious, tiresome, troublesome, uninteresting, unwelcome, vexatious, vexing, wearisome

iron *adj* adamant, cruel, hard, heavy, immovable, implacable, indomitable, inflexible, obdurate, rigid, robust, steel, steely, strong, tough, unbending, unyielding

ironic *adj* double-edged, mocking, ridiculing, sarcastic, sardonic, satirical, scoffing, scornful, sneering, wry; incongruous, paradoxical

iron out *v* clear up, eliminate, eradicate, erase, expedite, get rid of, harmonize, put right, reconcile, resolve, settle, simplify, smooth over, sort out, straighten out, unravel

irony *n* mockery, sarcasm, satire; contrariness, incongruity, paradox

irrational *adj* absurd, crazy, foolish, illogical, injudicious, nonsensical, preposterous, silly, unreasonable, unreasoning, unsound, unthinking, unwise

irregular *adj* desultory, disconnected, eccentric, erratic, fitful, fluctuating, haphazard, intermittent, non-uniform, occasional, out of order, patchy, random, shifting, spasmodic, sporadic, uncertain, unmethodical, unpunctual, unsteady, unsystematic, variable, wavering; asymmetrical, broken, bumpy, craggy, crooked, elliptic, elliptical, holey, jagged, lopsided, lumpy, pitted, ragged, rough, serrated, unequal, uneven, unsymmetrical

irregular *n* guerrilla, mercenary, partisan, resistance fighter, underground fighter, volunteer

irregularity *n* asymmetry, bumpiness, lack of symmetry, lopsidedness, lumpiness, non-uniformity, patchiness, raggedness, roughness, unevenness; aberration, abnormality, anomaly, breach, deviation, eccentricity, freak, malfunction, malpractice, oddity, peculiarity, singularity, unconventionality, unorthodoxy

irrelevant *adj* beside the point, extraneous, immaterial, impertinent, inapplicable, inapposite, inappropriate, inapt, inconsequent, neither here nor there, unconnected, unrelated

irreparable *adj* beyond repair, incurable, irrecoverable, irremediable, irreplaceable, irretrievable, irreversible

irrepressible *adj* boisterous, bubbling over, buoyant, ebullient, effervescent, insuppressible, uncontainable, uncontrollable, unmanageable, unquenchable, unrestrainable, unstoppable

irreproachable *adj* beyond reproach, blameless, faultless, guiltless, impeccable, inculpable, innocent, irreprenhensible, perfect, pure, unblemished, unimpeachable

irresistible *adj* compelling, imperative, overmastering, overpowering, overwhelming, potent, urgent; alluring, beckoning, enchanting, fascinating, ravishing, seductive, tempting

irresponsible *adj* careless, feather-brained, flighty, giddy, hare-brained, harum-scarum, ill-considered, immature, reckless, scatter-brained, shiftless, thoughtless, undependable, unreliable, untrustworthy, wild

irreverent *adj* cheeky, contemptuous, derisive, disrespectful, flipant, iconoclastic, impertinent, impious, impudent, mocking, saucy, tongue-in-cheek

irreversible *adj* final, incurable, irreparable, irrevocable, unalterable

irrevocable *adj* changeless, fated, fixed, immutable, invariable, irremediable, irretrievable, irreversible, predestined, predetermined, settled, unalterable, unchangeable, unreversible

irrigate *v* flood, inundate, moisten, water, wet

irritable *adj* bad-tempered, cantankerous, choleric, crabbed, crabby, cross, dyspeptic, exasperated, fiery, fretful, hasty, hot, ill-humoured, ill-tempered, irascible, out of humour, oversensitive, peevish, petulant, prickly, snappish, snappy, snarling, tense, testy, touchy

irritate *v* aggravate, anger, annoy, bother, drive one up the wall, enrage, exasperate, fret, harass, incense, inflame, infuriate, nettle, offend, pester, provoke, raise one's hackles, ruffle, try one's patience, vex; aggravate, chafe, fret, inflame, intensify, pain, rub

irritating *adj* aggravating, annoying, displeasing, disquieting, disturbing, galling, infuriating, irksome, maddening, nagging, pestilential, pro voking, thorny, troublesome, trying, upsetting, vexatious, worrisome

irritation *n* anger, annoyance, crossness, displeasure, exasperation, ill-humour, ill temper, impatience, indignation, irritability, resentment, shortness, snappiness, testiness, vexation, wrath

isolate *v* cut off, detach, disconnect, divorce, insulate, quarantine, segregate, separate, sequester, set apart

isolated *adj* backwoods, hidden, incommunicado, lonely, off the beaten track, outlying, out-of-the-way, remote, retired, secluded, unfrequented

isolation *n* aloofness, detachment, disconnection, exile, insularity, insulation, loneliness, quarantine, remoteness, retirement, seclusion, segregation, self-sufficiency, separation, solitude, withdrawal

issue *n* affair, argument, concern, controversy, matter, matter of contention, point, point in question, problem, question, subject, topic; copy, edition, impression, installment, number, printing; children, descendants, heirs, offspring, progeny, scions

issue *v* announce, broadcast, circulate, deliver, distribute, emit, give out, promulgate, publish, put in circulation, put out, release; arise, be a consequence of, come forth, emanate, emerge, flow, originate, proceed, rise, spring, stem

itch *v* crawl, irritate, prickle, tickle, tingle; ache, burn, crave, hanker, hunger, long, lust, pant, pine, yearn

itch *n* irritation, itchiness, prickling, tingling; craving, desire, hankering, hunger, longing, lust, passion, restlessness, yearning, yen

item *n* article, aspect, component, consideration, detail, entry, matter, particular, point, thing, account, article, bulletin, dispatch, feature, not, notice, paragraph, piece, report

itemize *v* detail, document, enumerate, inventory, list, number, record, register, set out, specify, tabulate

iterate *v* dwell on, emphasize, harp on about, press one's point, repeat, restate, stress, underscore

itinerant *adj* gypsy, journeying, migratory, nomadic, rambling, roaming, roving, travelling, wandering

itinerary *n* circuit, course, journey, line, programme, route, schedule, timetable, tour, travel arrangements, travel plan; daybook, diary, log, logbook, record

J

jab *v* box, bump, dig, elbow, lunge, nudge, poke, prod, punch, stab, tap, thrust

jab *n* dig, nudge, poke, prod, punch, stab

jabber *v* babble, chatter, gabble, gibber, prattle, ramble

jack (up) *v* elevate, hike up, hoist, lift, raise; boost, escalate, increase, inflate, push up, put up

jacket *n* case, casing, coat, covering, envelope, folder, sheath, skin, wrapper, wrapping

jackpot *n* award, bonanza, kitty, pool, pot, prize, reward, winnings

jaded *adj* exhausted, fatigued, spent, tired, tired-out, weary; bored, cloyed, dulled, glutted, gorged, sated, satiated, surfeited, tired; (*Inf*) bushed, done in, pooped

jagged *adj* barbed, broken, cleft, craggy, enticulate, indented, notched, pointed, ragged, ridged, rough, serrated, snaggy, spiked, toothed, uneven

jail, gaol *n* borstal, detention, lock up, penitentiary, prison, reformatory; (*Inf*) clink, inside, nick

jail, gaol *v* confine, detain, immure, impound, imprison, incarcerate, intern, lock up, put away, send down

jailer, gaoler *n* captor, guard, keeper, warden, warder

jam *v* cram, crowd, crush, force, pack, press, ram, squeeze, stuff, throng, wedge; block, cease, clog, congest, halt, obstruct, stall, stick

jam *n* crowd, crush, horde, mass, mob, multitude, pack, press, swarm, throng; bind, dilemma, hole, plight, predicament, quandary, scrape, strait, trouble

jamb *n* doorjamb, doorpost, pillar, post, upright

jamboree *n* carnival, celebration, festival, festivity, fête, get together, jubilee, merrymaking, party, rally; (*Inf*) beanfeast, rave-up, shindig

jangle *v* chime, clank, clash, clatter, jingle, rattle, vibrate; disturb, grate on, jar on, irritate

jangle *n* cacophony, clank, clink, clangour, clash, din, dissonance, jar, jarring, racket, rattle, reverberation, stridor

janitor *n* caretaker, concierge, custodian, doorkeeper, porter

jar *n* carafe, container, crock, flagon, flask, jamjar, jug, pitcher, pot, receptacle, urn, vase, vessel

jar *v* bicker, clash, contend, disagree, interfere, oppose, quarrel, wrangle; agitate, convulse, disturb, grate, irritate, jerk, jolt, offend, rasp, rattle, screech, rock, shake, vibrate; annoy, clash, discompose, disturb, grate, grind, irk, irritate, nettle, upset, vex; conflict, be at odds, be at variance, be in opposition

jargon *n* argot, cant, dialect, idiom, parlance, patois, slang, tongue, usage

jaunt *n* airing, excursion, expedition, outing, promenade, ramble, stroll, tour, trip

jaunty *adj* airy, breezy, buoyant, carefree, dapper, gay, high-spirited, lively, perky, self-confident, showy, smart, sparky, sprightly, spruce, trim

jealous *adj* covetous, desirous, emulous, envious, green, green-eyed, grudging, intolerant, invidious, resentful, rival

jealousy *n* covetousness, distrust, doubt, envy, green-eyed monster, heart-burning, ill-will, insecurity, mistrust, possessiveness, resentment, spite, suspicion

jeer *v* banter, barrack, boo, contemn, deride, flout, gibe, heckle, hector, hiss, mock, ridicule, scoff, sneer, taunt, tease

jeopardize *v* chance, endanger, expose, gamble, hazard, imperil, lay open to danger, menace, risk, stake, threaten, venture

jeopardy *n* danger, endangerment, hazard, insecurity, liability, menace, peril, precariousness, risk, threat, venture, vulnerability

jerk *v* bounce, bump, jolt, jump, lurch, pluck, pull, shake, throw, thrust, tremble, tug, tweak, twitch, wrench, yank; say curtly, snap,

jerk *n* bump, jar, start; dimwit, dope, fool, idiot, rogue, scoundrel; (*Inf*) creep, heel, nerd

jerry-built *adj* cheap, defective, faulty, flimsy, insubstantial, ramshackle, rickety, shoddy

jersey *n* jumper, pullover, sweater, top; (*Inf*) woolly

jest *n* banter, fun, hoax, jape, joke, play, pleasantry, prank, quip, sally, sport, wisecrack, witticism

jest *v* banter, chaff, deride, gibe, jeer, joke, kid, mock, quip, scoff, sneer, tease

jester *n* comedian, comic, humorist, joker, quipster, wag, wit; buffoon, clown, fool, harlequin, madcap, mummer, pantaloon, prankster, zany

jet *n* flow, fountain, gush, spout, spray, spring, stream; atomizer, nose, nozzle, rose, spout, sprayer, sprinkler

jet *v* flow, gush, issue, rush, shoot, spew, spout, squirt, stream, surge

jettison *v* abandon, discard, dump, eject, expel, heave, scrap, throw overboard, unload

jetty *n* breakwater, dock, groyne, mole, pier, quay, wharf

jewel brilliant, gemstone, ornament, precious stone, trinket; (*Inf*) rock; charm, find, gem, humdinger, masterpiece, paragon, pearl, prize, rarity, treasure, wonder

jiffy *n* flash, instant, minute, moment, second, split second, trice; (*Inf*) two shakes of a lamb's tail

jig *v* bob, bounce, caper, jiggle, jounce, prance, shake, skip, twitch, wiggle, wobble

jingle *v* chime, clatter, clink, jangle, rattle, ring, tinkle, tintinnabulate

jingle *n* clang, clangour, clink, rattle, reverberation, ringing, tinkle; chorus, ditty, doggerel, limerick, melody, song, tune

jinx *n* black magic, curse, evil eye, nemesis, plague, voodoo

jinx *v* bewitch, curse

job *n* affair, assignment, charge, chore, concern, contribution, duty, enterprise, errand, function, pursuit, responsibility, role, stint, task, undertaking, venture, work; activity, business, calling, capacity, career, craft, employment, function, livelihood, occupation, office, position, post, profession, situation, trade, vocation

jocular *adj* amusing, comical, droll, facetious, frolicsome, funny, humorous, jesting, jocose, jocund, joking, jolly, jovial, playful, roguish, sportive, teasing, waggish, whimsical, witty

jog *v* activate, arouse, nudge, prod, prompt, push, remind, shake, stimulate, stir, suggest; canter, dogtrot, lope, run, trot; lumber, plod, traipse, tramp, trudge

join *v* accompany, add, adhere, annex, append, attack, cement, combine, connect, couple, fasten, knit, link, marry, splice, tie, unite, yoke; affiliate with, associate, with, enlist, enroll, enter, sign up

joint *n* articulation, connection, hinge, intersection, junction, juncture, knot, nexus, node, seam, union

joint *adj* collective, combined, communal, concerted, consolidated, cooperative, joined, mutual, shared, united

jointly *adv* as one, collectively, in common, in conjunction, in league, in partnership, mutually, together, unitedly

joke *n* frolic, fun, jape, jest, lark, play, pun, quip, quirk, sally, sport, whimsy, wisecrack, witticism, yarn

joke *v* banter, chaff, deride, frolic, gambol, jest, mock, quip, ridicule, taunt, tease

jolly *adj* blithesome, carefree, cheerful, convivial, festive, frolicsome, funny, gay, gladsome, hilarious, jocund, jovial, joyful, joyous, jubilant, merry, mirthful, playful, sportive, sprightly

jolt *v* jar, jerk, jog, jostle, knock, push, shake, shove; astonish, discompose, disturb, perturb, stagger, startle, stun, surprise, upset

jolt *n* bump, jar, jerk, jog, jump, lurch, quiver, shake, start; blow, bolt from the blue, bombshell, reversal, setback, shock, surprise, thunderbolt

jostle *v* bump, butt, crowd, elbow, hustle, jog, joggle, jolt, press, push, scramble, shake, shove, squeeze, throng, thrust

journal *n* chronicle, daily, gazette, magazine, monthly, newspaper, paper, periodical, record, register, review, tabloid, weekly; chronicle, commonplace book, daybook, diary, log, record

journalist *n* broadcaster, columnist, commentator, contributor, correspondent, hack, newsman, newspaperman, pressman, reporter, stringer

journey *n* excursion, expedition, jaunt, odyssey, outing, passage, peregrination, pilgrimage, progress, ramble, tour, travel, trek, trip, voyage

jovial *adj* airy, animated, blithe, buoyant, cheery, convivial, cordial, gay, glad, happy, hilarious, jocose, jocund, jolly, jubilant, merry, mirthful

joy *n* bliss, delight, ecstasy, elation, exaltation, exultation, felicity, festivity, gaiety, gladness, glee, hilarity, pleasure, rapture, ravishment, satisfaction, transport

joyful *adj* blithesome, delighted, elated, enraptured, glad, gladsome, gratified, happy, jocund, jolly, jovial, jubilant, light-hearted, merry, pleased, satisfied

joyless *adj* cheerless, dejected, depressed, dismal, dispirited, down cast, dreary, gloomy, miserable, sad, unhappy

jubilant *adj* elated, enraptured, euphoric, excited, exuberant, exultant, glad, joyous, overjoyed, rejoicing, rhapsodic, thrilled, triumphal, triumphant

judge *n* adjudicator, arbiter, arbitrator, moderator, referee, umpire; appraiser, arbiter, assessor, authority, connoisseur, critic, evaluator, expert; justice, magistrate

judge *v* adjudge, adjudicate, arbitrate, ascertain, conclude, decide, determine, discern, distinguish, mediate, referee, umpire; appraise, appreciate, assess, consider, criticize, esteem, estimate, evaluate, examine, rate, review, value

judgment *n* acumen, common sense, discernment, discrimination, good sense, intelligence, penetration, percipience, perspicacity, prudence, sagacity, sense, shrewdness, taste, understanding, wisdom; arbitration, award, conclusion, decision, decree, determination, finding, order, result, ruling, sentence, verdict; appraisal, assessment, belief, conviction, deduction, diagnosis, estimate, finding, opinion, valuation, view

judicial *adj* judiciary, juridical, legal, official

judicious *adj* acute, astute, careful, cautious, circumspect, considered, diplomatic, discerning, discreet, discriminating, enlightened, expedient, informed, politic, prudent, rational, reasonable, sagacious, sage, sane, sapient, sensible, shrewd, skilful, sober, sound, thoughtful, well-advised, well-judged, wise

jug *n* carafe, container, crock, decanter, ewer, jar, pitcher, receptacle, urn, vessel

juggle *v* alter, change around, fake, falsify, manipulate, rig, tamper with

juice *n* extract, fluid, liquid, liquor, nectar, sap, secretion, serum

juicy *adj* lush, moist, sappy, succulent, watery; colourful, interesting, provocative, racy, risqué, sensational, spicy, suggestive, vivid

jumble *v* confound, confuse, disarrange, dishevel, disorder, disorganize, entangle, mistake, mix, muddle, shuffle, tangle

jumble *n* chaos, clutter, confusion, disarrangement, disarray, disorder, farrago, gallimaufry, hodgepodge, hotchpotch, litter, medley, mess, miscellany, mishmash, mixture, muddle

jump *v* bounce, bound, caper, clear, gambol, hop, hurdle, leap, skip, spring, vault; avoid, digress, evade, miss, omit, overshoot, skip, switch

jump *n* bound, buck, caper, hop, leap, skip, spring, vault; advance, augmentation, boost, increase, increment, rise, upsurge, upturn

jumper *n* jersey, pullover, sweater

jumpy *adj* agitated, anxious, apprehensive, fidgety, nervous, on edge, restless, shaky, tense, timorous

junction *n* alliance, combination,

connection, coupling, joint, juncture, linking, seam, union

junior *adj* inferior, lesser, lower, minor, secondary, subordinate, younger

junk *n* bric-à-brac, cast-offs, clutter, debris, garbage, leavings, leftovers, litter, oddments, odds and ends, refuse, rejects, remnants, rubbish, rummage, scrap, trash, waste

jurisdiction *n* authority, command, control, dominion, influence, power, prerogative, rule, say, sway

just *adj* blameless, conscientious, decent, equitable, fair, fair minded, good, honest, honourable, impartial, lawful, pure, right, righteous, unbiased, upright, virtuous; appropriate, apt, condign, deserved, due, fitting, justified, legitimate, merited, proper, reasonable, rightful, suitable, well-deserved

just *adv* absolutely, completely, entirely, exactly, perfectly, precisely; hardly, lately, only now, recently, scarcely

justice *n* equity, fairness, honesty, impartiality, integrity, justness, law, legality, legitimacy, reasonableness, rectitude, right; amends, compensation, correction, penalty, recompense, redress, reparation

justifiable *adj* acceptable, defensible, excusable, fit, lawful, legitimate, proper, reasonable, right, sound, tenable, understandable, valid, vindicable, warrantable, well-founded

justification *n* absolution, apology, approval, defence, exculpation, excuse, exoneration, explanation, extenuation, plea, rationalization, vindication

justify *v* absolve, acquit, approve, confirm, defend, establish, exculpate, excuse, exonerate, explain, legalize, legitimize, maintain, substantiate, support, sustain, uphold, validate, vindicate, warrant

juvenile *n* adolescent, boy, child, girl, infant, minor, youth

K

kaleidoscope *adj* psychedelic, variegated; changeable, fluid, mobile, mutable, variable, varying

keel *n* bottom, bottom side, under side; boat, craft, ship, vessel

keen *adj* ardent, avid, devoted to, eager, earnest, ebullient, enthusiastic, fervid, fierce, fond of, impassioned, intense, zealous; acid, acute, biting, caustic, cutting, edged, finely honed, incisive, penetrating, piercing, pointed, razorlike, sardonic, satirical, sharp, tart, trenchant

keenness *n* ardour, avidity, avidness, diligence, eagerness, earnestness, ebullience, enthusiasm, fervour, impatience, intensity, passion, zeal, zest

keep *v* conserve, control, hold, maintain, possess, preserve, retain; accumulate, amass, carry, deal in, deposit, furnish, garner, heap, hold, pile, place, stack, stock, store, trade in; care for, defend, guard, look after, maintain, manage, mind, operate, protect, safeguard, shelter, shield, tend, watch over; board, feed, foster, maintain, nourish, nurture, provide for, provision, subsidize, support, sustain, victual; adhere to, celebrate, commemorate, comply with, fulfil, hold, honour, obey, observe, perform, respect, ritualize, solemnize

keep *n* board, food, livelihood, living, maintenance, means, nourishment, subsistence, support; castle, citadel, donjon, dungeon, fastness, stronghold, tower

keep back *v* check, constrain, control, curb, delay, hold back, limit, prohibit, restrain, restrict, retard, withhold

keeper *n* attendant, caretaker, curator, custodian, defender, gaoler, governor, guard, guardian, jailer, overseer, preserver, steward, superintendent, warden, warder

keeping *n* aegis, auspices, care, charge, custody, guardianship, keep, maintenance, patronage, possession, protection, safekeeping, trust

keepsake *n* emblem, favour, memento, relic, remembrance, reminder, souvenir, symbol, token

keep up *v* balance, compete, contend, continue, emulate, keep pace, maintain, match, persevere, preserve, rival, sustain, vie

key *n* latchkey, opener; answer, clue, cue, explanation, guide, indicator, interpretation, lead, means, pointer, sign, solution, translation

key *adj* basic, chief, crucial, decisive, essential, fundamental, important, leading, main, major, pivotal, principal

keynote *n* centre, core, essence, gist, heart, kernel, marrow, pith, substance, theme

kick *v* boot, punt

kick *n* force, intensity, pep, power, punch, pungency, snap, sparkle, strength, tang, verve, vitality, zest

kid *n* baby, bairn, boy, child, girl, infant, lad, little one, stripling, teenager, tot, youngster, youth

kid *v* bamboozle, beguile, cozen,

delude, fool, hoax, hoodwink, jest, joke, mock, plague, pretend, ridicule, tease, trick

kidnap *v* abduct, capture, hijack, hold to ransom, remove, seize, steal

kill *v* annihilate, assassinate, butcher, destroy, dispatch, do away with, eradicate, execute, exterminate, extirpirate, liquidate, massacre, murder, neutralize, obliterate, slaughter, slay, waste; cancel, cease, deaden, defeat, extinguish, halt, quash, quell, ruin, scotch, smother, stifle, still, stop, suppress, veto

killer *n* assassin, butcher, cutthroat, destroyer, executioner, exterminator, gunman, liquidator, murderer, slaughterer, slayer; (*Inf*) hit-man

killing *n* bloodshed, carnage, execution, extermination, fatality, homicide, manslaughter, massacre, murder, slaughter, slaying

killjoy *n* dampener, spoilsport; (*Inf*) party-pooper, wet blanket

kin *n* affinity, blood, connection, consanguinity, extraction, kinship, lineage, relationship, stock

kind *n* brand, breed, class, family, genus, ilk, race, set, sort, species, variety

kind *adj* affectionate, amiable, amicable, beneficent, benevolent, benign, bounteous, charitable, clement, compassionate, congenial, considerate, cordial, courteous, friendly, generous, gentle, good, gracious, humane, indulgent, kind-hearted, kindly, lenient, loving, mild, neighbourly, obliging, philanthropic, propitious, sympathetic, tenderhearted, thoughtful, understanding

kindle *v* fire, ignite, inflame, light, set fire to

kindly *adj* beneficial, benevolent, benign, compassionate, cordial, favourable, genial, gentle, good-natured, hearty, helpful, kind, mild, pleasant, polite, sympathetic, warm

kindly *adv* agreeably, cordially, graciously, politely, tenderly, thoughtfully

kindness *n* affection, amiability, beneficence, benevolence, charity, clemency, compassion, decency, fellow feeling, generosity, gentle ness, goodness, good will, grace, hospitality, humanity, indulgence, kindliness, magnanimity, patience, philanthropy, tenderness, tolerance, understanding; aid, assistance, benefaction, bounty, favour, generosity, good deed, help, service

kindred *n* family, kin, people, relations, relatives

kindred *adj* cognate, connected, consanguineous, related; allied, corresponding, matching, resembling, similar

king *n* crowned head, emperor, majesty, monarch, overlord, prince, ruler, sovereign

kingdom *n* dominion, dynasty, empire, monarchy, realm, reign, sovereignty; commonwealth, county, division, nation, province, state, territory, tract

kink *n* bend, coil, corkscrew, crimp, entanglement, frizz, knot, tangle, twist, wrinkle; crotchet, eccentricity, fetish, foible, idiosyncrasy, quirk, singularity, vagary, whim

kinky *adj* bent, coiled, curled, twisted;

crimped, curly, frizzed; bizarre, eccentric, odd, quirky, strange, unconventional, weird; abnormal, degenerate, depraved, deviant, lascivious, lewd, licentious, masochistic, sadistic, unatural

kinksfolk *n* kin, kindred, family, relations, relatives

kiosk *n* bookstall, booth, counter, news-stand, refreshments kiosk, stall, stand, telephone kiosk

kiss *v* brush the lips against, greet, greet with the lips, osculate, salute, (*Inf*) canoodle, neck, peck, smooch, snog; brush against, caress, glance off, graze

kit *n* accoutrements, apparatus, effects, equipment, gear, implements, instruments, outfit, paraphernalia, provisions, rig, supplies, tackle, tools, trappings, utensils

kit *v* arm, accoutre, deck out, equip, fit out, fix up, furnish, outfit, provide, supply

kitchen *n* bakehouse, cookhouse, galley, kitchenette, scullery

knack *n* ability, adroitness, aptitude, bent, capacity dexterity, expertise, expertness, facility, flair, forte, genius, gift, handiness, ingenuity, propensity, quickness, skilfulness, skill, talent, trick

kneel *v* bow, bow down, curtsy, genuflect, get down on one's knees, kowtow, make obeisance, stoop

knell *v* announce, chime, herald, peal, resound, ring, sound, toll

knell *n* chime, peal, ringing, sound, toll

knickers *pl n* bikini briefs, bloomers, briefs, camiknickers, Directoire knickers, drawers, lingerie, pants, panties, smalls, underwear

knick-knack *n* bagatelle, bauble, bibelot, bric-à-brac, gewgaw, gimcrack, kickshaw, ornament, plaything, trifle, trinket

knife *n* blade, cutter, cutting tool

knife *v* bayonet, cut, impale, lacerate, pierce, run through, slash, stab

knit *v* affix, ally, bind, crochet, connect, contract, draw in, draw together, fasten, furrow, gather in, heal, interlace, intertwine, join, link, loop, mend, secure, tie, unite, weave, wrinkle

knob *n* buss, bulk, bump, bunch, door-handle, knot, knurl, lump, nub, projection, protrusion, protuberance, snag, stud, swell, swelling, tumour

knock *v* buffet, clap, cuff, hit, punch, rap, slap, smack, smite, strike, thump, thwack; (*Inf*) clip, clout, whack; bang, crash, jolt, smash, thud; censure, critiscism, condemnation, fault-finding; (*Inf*) panning, lambasting; failure, misfortune, rejection, reversal, set-back

knock *n* blow, box, clip, clout, cuff, hammering, punch, rap, slap, smack, thump

knockout *n* *coup de grâce*, finishing blow; (*Inf*) KO; coup, sensation, smash hit, success, triumph, winner

knot *v* bind, complicate, entangle, knit, lash, loop, secure, tether, tie

knot *n* bond, bow, braid, connection, joint, ligature, loop, rosette, tie, twist; gnarl, knur, knob, lump, node, nodule, protuberance; bunch, cluster, company, gatheing, mob, pack, throng

know *v* apprehend, comprehend,

experience, fathom, feel certain, learn, notice, perceive, realize, recognize, see, undergo, understand; associate with, be acquainted with, be familiar with, fraternize with, have dealings with, have knowledge of, recognize; differentiate, discern, distinguish, identify, make out, perceive, recognize, see, tell

knowing *adj* astute, clever, competent, discerning, experienced, expert, intelligent, qualified, skilful, well-informed

knowledge *n* education, enlightenment, erudition, instruction, intelligence, learning, scholarship, schooling, science, tuition, wisdom; ability, apprehension, cognition, comprehension, consciousness, discernment, grasp, judgment, recognition, understanding

knowledgeable *adj* acquainted, aware, cognizant, conscious, conversant, experienced, familiar, understanding, well-informed; (*Inf*) in the know

known *adj* acknowledged, admitted, avowed, celebrated, common, confessed, familiar, famous, manifest, noted, obvious, patent, plain, popular, published, recognized, well-known

L

label *n* docket, marker, sticker, tag, tally, ticket; brand, company, mark, trademark

label *v* docket, mark, stamp, sticker, tag, tally; brand, call, characterize, class, classify, define, describe, designate, identify, name

laborious *adj* arduous, difficult, fatiguing, hard, heavy, strenuous, tedious, wearisome; assiduous, careful, diligent, meticulous, painstaking, scrupulous

labour *n* industry, toil, work; employees, hands, labourers, workers, work force, workmen; donkey-work, drudgery, effort, exertion, industry, pains, painstaking, toil, travail; childbirth, contractions, delivery, labour pains, pains, parturition, throes

labour *v* dwell on, elaborate, overdo, overemphasise, strain

laboured *adj* awkward, difficult, forced, heavy, stiff, strained

labourer *n* blue-collar worker, drudge, hand labouring man, manual worker, unskilled worker, working man, workman

labyrinth *n* convolution, entanglement, jungle, maze, network, warren; complication, enigma, problem, puzzle, tangle

lace *n* filigree, meshwork, netting, tatting; bootlace, cord, shoelace, string, thing, tie, twine

lace *v* bind, close, do up, fasten, secure, thread, twine; compress, confine, constrict, squeeze; band streak, striate, stripe; blend, flavour, fortify, stiffen, strengthen; (*Inf*) spike

lacerate *v* claw, cut, cut open, gash, hurt, jag, maim, mangle, mutilate, rend, rip, slash, tear, wound; afflict, crucify, distress, harrow, hurt, torment, torture, wound

lachrymose *adj* crying, dolorous, mournful, sobbing, weeping, woeful

lack *n* absence, dearth, deficiency, deprivation, destitution, insufficiency, need, paucity, privation, scantiness, scarcity, shortage, shortcoming, shortness, want

lack *v* be deficient, in, be lacking in, be short of, be without, miss, need, require, want

lackadaisical *adj* apathetic, dull, enervated, half-hearted, idel, indifferent, indolent, inert, languid, languorous, lazy, lethargic, limp, listless, lukewarm, sluggish, spiritless, uninterested, unenthusiastic

lackey *n* camp follower, doormat, flatterer, flunkey, hanger-on, minion, parasite, pawn, puppet, stooge, sycophant; equerry, footman, manservant, steward

lacking *adj* defective, deficient, flawed, impaired, inadequate, missing, needing, wanting, without

lacklustre *adj* boring, dim, drab, dry, dull, flat, leaden, lifeless, lustreless, muted, prosaic, sombre, unimaginative, uninspired, vapid

laconic *adj* abrupt, blunt, brief, concise, crut, short, succinct, terse; quiet, reticent, silent; uncommunicative, untalkative

lad *n* boy, fellow, guy, juvenile, kid, schoolboy, stripling, youngster, youth; (Inf) bloke, chap, little shaver

laden *adj* burdened, charged, encumbered, fraught, full, hampered, heavily-laden, loaded, oppressed, taxed, weighed down, weighted

ladylike *adj* courtly, cultured, decorous, elegant, genteel, modest, polite, proper, refined, respectable, well-bred

lag *v* be behind, dawdle, delay, drag, drag one's feet, hang back, idle, linger, loiter, saunter, straggle, tarry, trail

laid-back *adj* at ease, casual, easygoing, free and easy, informal, leisurely, nonchalant, relaxed, unhurried; (*Inf*) unflappable

laid-up *adj* ailing, bedridden, disabled, housebound, immobilized, incapacitated, out of action, sick

lair *n* cave, hollow, tunnel; den hideaway, refuge, retreat, sanctum, sanctuary, snug, study

lame *adj* crippled, defective, disabled, game, handicapped, hobbling, limping; feeble, flimsy, inadequate, insufficient, poor, thin, unconvincing, unsatisfactory, weak

lament *v* bemoan, bewail, complain, deplore, grieve, mourn, regret, sorrow, wail, weep

lament *n* complaint, keening, lamentation, moan, moaning, plaint, ululation, wail, wailing

lamentable *adj* deplorable, distressing, grievous, mournful, regrettable, sorrowful, tragic, unfortunate, woeful; low, meagre, mean, miserable, pitiful, poor, unsatisfactory

lampoon *n* burlesque, caricature, parody, pasquinade, satire, skit, squib, take off

lampoon *v* burlesque, caricature, make fun of, mock, parody, pasquinade, ridicule, satirize, send up, squib, take off

land *n* dry land, earth, ground, terrafirma; dirt, ground, loam, soil; acres, estate, grounds, property, real property, realty; country, district, fatherland, motherland, nation, province, region, territory, tract

land *v* alight, arrive, berth, come to rest, debark, disembark, dock, touch down

landlord *n* host, hotelier, hotelkeeper, innkeeper

landmark *n* feature, monument; crisis, milestone, turning point, watershed

landscape *n* countryside, outlook, panorama, prospect, scene, scenery, view, vista

language *n* communication, conversation, converse, discourse, expression, interchange, parlance, speech, talk, utterance, verbal expression, verbalization, vocalization, words; argot, cant, colloquialism, dialect, idiom, jargon, lingua, franca, mother tongue, native tongue, patois, patter, speech, provincialism, terminology, tongue, vernacular, vocabulary; diction, expression, phraseology, phrasing, style, wording; bureaucratese, journalese, legalese, medicalese, newspeak; (*Inf*) lingo; diction, expression, phrasing, rhetoric, style, terminology, vocabulary, wording

languid *adj* debilitated, drooping,

faint, feeble, flagging, languorous, limp, pining, sickly, weak, weary; indifferent, lackadaisical, lazy, listless, spiritless, unenthusiastic, uninterested; apathetic, dull, heavy, inactive, inert, lethargic, sluggish, torpid

languish *v* decline, droop, fade, fail, faint, flag, sicken, waste, weaken, wilt, wither

lank *adj* dull, lifeless, limp, long, lustreless, straggling; attenuated, emaciated, gaunt, lanky, lean, raw-boned, scraggy, scrawny, skinny, slender, slim, spare, thin

lap *n* knee, knees; comfort, protection, refuge, safety, secureness; charge, job, responsibility, task; circle, circuit, course, distance, loop, orbit, round, tour

lap *v* cover, encase, enfold, envelop, fold, swaddle, swathe, turn, twist, wind, wrap; beat splash, wash; drink up, lick up, sip sup

lapse *n* error, failing, fault, indiscretion, mistake, negligence, omission, oversight, slip

lapse *v* decline, degenerate, deteriorate, drop, fail, fall, sink, slide, slip; become obsolete, become void, end, expire, run out, stop, terminate

larceny *n* burglary, misappropriation, pilfering, robbery, stealing; (*Inf*) nicking

larder *n* cooler, pantry, scullery, still-room, storeroom

large *adj* big, bulky, colossal, considerable, enormous, gargantuan, giant, gigantic, goodly, great, high, huge, immense, king-size, man-size, massive, monumental, out-size, prodigious, sizable, stupendous, substantial, vast; (*Inf*) jumbo, whopping; ample, burly, fat, heavy, hefty, heavy-set, thick-set; abundant, broad, capacious, comprehensive, copious, corpulent, extensive, full, generous, grand, grandiose, liberal, obese, plentiful, roomy, spacious, sweeping, wide; far-reaching, wide-ranging

largely *adv* as a rule, by and large, chiefly, considerably, extensively, generally, mainly, mostly, predominantly, primarily, principally, to a great extent, widely

lark *n* antic, caper, escapade, fling, frolic, fun, gambol, game, jape, mischief, prank, revel, rollick, romp, skylark, spree

lash *n* blow, bullwhip, cat-o'-nine-tails, hit, horsewhip, scourge, stripe, stroke, swipe, whip

lash *v* beat, birch, chastise, flagellate, flog, hammer, scourge, strike, thrash, whip; beat, buffet, dash, drum, hit, knock, pound, smack, strike; berate, castigate, chise, condemn, criticize, harangue, rebuke, scold; (*Inf*) lambaste, pitch into; bind, fasten, joint, make fast, rope, secure, strap, tether, tie

lass *n* damsel, girl, maid, maiden, miss, schoolgirl, young woman; (*Inf*) bird, chick

last *adj* aftermost, at the end, hindmost, rearmost; latest, most recent; closing, concluding, extreme, final, furthest, remotest, terminal, ultimate, utmost

last *adv* after, behind, bringing up the rear, in the end, in the rear

last *v* abide, carry on, continue, endure, hold on, hold out, keep,

keep on, persist, remain, stand up, survive, wear

lasting *adj* abiding, continuing, deep-rooted, durable, enduring, indelible, lifelong, long-standing, long-term, perennial, permanent, perpetual, unceasing, undying, unending

latch *n* bar, bolt, catch, clamp, fastening, hasp, hook, lock

late *adj* behind, behindhand, belated, delayed, last-minute, overdue, slow, tardy, unpunctual; advanced, fresh, modern, new, recent; dead, deceased, defunct, departed, ex-, former, old, past, preceding, previous

lately *adv* in recent times, just now, latterly, not long ago, of late, recently

lateness *n* advanced hour, belatedness, delay, late date, retardation, tardiness, unpunctuality

later *adv* after, afterwards, by and by, in a while, in time, later on, next, subsequently, thereafter

latest *adj* current, fashionable, in, modern, most recent, newest, now, up-to-date, up-to-the-minute; (*Inf*) with it

lather *n* bubbles, foam, froth, soap, soapsuds, suds

latitude *n* breadth, compass, extent, range, reach, room, scope, space, span, spread, sweep, width; elbowroom, freedom, indulgence, laxity, leeway, liberty, licence, play, unrestrictedness

latter *adj* closing, concluding, last, last-mentioned, later, latest, modern, recent, second

lattice *n* fretwork, grating, grid, grille, latticework, mesh, network, openwork, reticulation, tracery, trellis, web

laudable *adj* admirable, commend able, creditable, estimable, excellent, meritorious, of note, praise worthy, worthy

laugh *v* be in stitches, chortle, chuckle, giggle, guffaw, roar with laughter, snigger, split one's sides, titter; (*Inf*) be convulsed; **laugh at** belittle, deride, jeer, lampoon, make a mock of, make fun of, mock, ridicule, scoff at, taunt; (*Inf*) take the mickey out of

laugh *n* chortle, chuckle, giggle, guffaw, roar, snigger, titter; (*Inf*) belly laugh

laughable *adj* absurd, derisive, derisory, ludicrous, nonsensical, preposterous, ridiculous, worthy of scorn

laughter *n* amusement, glee, hilarity, merriment, mirth

launch *v* cast, discharge, dispatch, fire, project, propel, send off, set afloat, set in motion, throw; begin, commence, embark upon, inaugurate, initiate, instigate, introduce, open, start

lavatory *n* bathroom, cloakroom, convenience, Gents, Ladies, latrine, loo, powder room, toilet, washroom, water closet, WC

lavish *adj* abundant, copious, exuberant, lush, luxuriant, opulent, plentiful, profuse, prolific, sumptuous; bountiful, effusive, free, generous, liberal, munificent, open-handed, unstinting

law *n* charter, code, constitution, jurisprudence; act, code, command, commandment, covenant, decree, edict, enactment, order, ordinance, rule, statute

law-abiding *adj* compliant, dutiful, good, honest, honourable, lawful, obedient, orderly, peaceable, peaceful

lawbreaker *n* convict, criminal, culprit, felon

lawful *adj* allowable, authorized, constitutional, just, legal, legalized, legitimate, licit, permissible, proper, rightful, valid, warranted

lawless *adj* anarchic, chaotic, disorderly, insubordinate, insurgent, mutinous, rebellious, reckless, riotous, seditious, ungoverned, unrestrained, unruly, wild

lawsuit *n* action, argument, case, cause, contest, dispute, litigation, proceedings, prosecution, suit, trial

lawyer *n* advocate, attorney, barrister, counsel, counsellor, legal adviser, solicitor

lax *adj* careless, casual, easy-going, lenient, neglectful, negligent, overindulgent, remiss, slack, slipshod

lay *v* deposit, establish, leave, place, plant, posit, put, set, set down, settle, spread; arrange, dispose, locate, organize, position, set out; bear, deposit, produce, allocate, slot, ascribe, assign, attribute, charge, impute; concoct, contrive, design, devise, hatch, plan, plot, prepare, work out; bet, gamble, give odds, hazard, risk, stake, wager

lay *adj* laic, laical, non-clerical, secular; amateur, inexpert, non-professional, non-specialist

layabout *n* beachcomber, good-for-nothing, idler, laggard, loafer, lounger, ne'er-do-well, shirker, vagrant, wastrel; (*Inf*) couch potato

layer *n* bed, ply, row, seam, stratum, thickness, tier

layman *n* amateur, lay person, non-professional, outsider

lay-off *n* discharge, dismissal, drop, let go, make redundant, oust, pay off, unemployment

lay on *v* cater, furnish, give, provide, supply

layout *n* arrangement, design, draft, formation, geography, outline, plan

lay out *v* arrange, design, display, exhibit, plan, spread out

laziness *n* dilatoriness, donothingness, faineance, faineancy, idleness, inactivity, indolence, lackadaisicalness, slackness, sloth, slothfulness, slowness, sluggishness, tardiness

lazy *adj* idle, inactive, indolent, inert, remiss, shiftless, slack, slothful, slow, workshy; drowsy, languid, languorous, lethargic, sleepy, slow-moving, sluggish, somnolent, torpid

lead *v* conduct, escort, guide, pilot, precede, show the way, steer, usher; cause, dispose, draw, incline, induce, influence, persuade, prevail, prompt; command, direct, govern, head, manage, preside over, supervise; be ahead, come first, exceed, excel, outdo, outstrip, surpass, transcend; experience, have, live, pass, spend, undergo

lead *n* advance, advantage, cutting, edge, edge, first place, margin, precedence, primacy, priority, start, supremacy, van, vanguard; direction, example, guidance, leadership, model; clue, guide, hint, indication, suggestion, tip, trace; leading role, principal, protagonist, star part, title role

leader *n* boss, captain, chief, chieftain, commander, conductor, counsellor, director, guide, head, number one, principal, ringleader, ruler, superior

leadership *n* administration, direction, directorship, domination, guidance, management, running, superintendency; authority, command, control, influence, initiative, pre-eminence, supremacy, sway

leading *adj* chief, dominant, first, foremost, governing, greatest, highest, main, number one, outstanding, pre-eminent, primary, principal, ruling, superior

leaf *n* blade, bract, flag, frond, needle, pad; folio, page, sheet

leaflet *n* advert, bill, booklet, brochure, circular, handbill, mailshot, pamphlet

league *n* alliance, association, band, coalition, combination, combine, compact, confederacy, confederation, consortium, federation, fellowship, fraternity, group, guild, partnership, union

leak *n* aperture, break, chink, crack, crevice, cut, fissure, gash, hole, opening, puncture, rift, slit; discharge, drip, escape, leakage, leaking, oozing, percolation, seepage; disclosure, divulgence

leak *v* discharge, drip, escape, exude, ooze, pass, percolate, seep, spill, trickle; disclose, divulge, give away, let slip, let the cat out of the bag, make, known, make public, pass on, reveal, tell; (*Inf*) spill the beans

lean *v* be supported, prop, recline, repose, rest; bend, incline, slant, slope, tilt, tip

lean *adj* angular, bony, emaciated, gaunt, lank, rangy, scraggy, scrawny, skinny, slender, slim, spare, thin, unfatty, wiry; bare, barren, inadequate, infertile, meagre, pitiful, poor, scanty, sparse, unfruitful, unproductive

leaning *n* aptitude, bent, bias, disposition, inclination, liking, partiality, penchant, predilection, proclivity, proneness, propensity, taste, tendency

leap *v* bounce, bound, caper, cavort, frisk, gambol, hop, jump, skip, spring, vault; hasten, hurry, hurtle; escalate, mount, rise up, rocket, sky-rocket, soar

leap *n* bound, caper, frisk, hop, jump, skip, spring, vault

learn *v* acquire, attain, become able, grasp, imbibe, master, pick up; commit to memory, get off pat, word-perfect, learn by heart, memorize; ascertain, detect, determine, discern, discover, find out, gain, gather, hear, understand

learned *adj* academic, cultured, erudite, experienced, expert, highbrow, intellectual, lettered, literate, scholarly, skilled, versed, well-informed, well-read

learner *n* apprentice, beginner, neophyte, novice, tyro; disciple, pupil, scholar, student

learning *n* acquirements, attainments, culture, education, erudition, information, knowledge, letters, literature, lore, research, scholarship, schooling, study, tuition, wisdom

lease *v* charter, hire, let, loan, rent

least *adj* feeblest, fewest, last, lowest, meanest, minimum, minutest, poorest, slightest, smallest, tiniest

leave *v* abandon, decamp, depart, desert, disappear, do a bunk, exit, forsake, go, go away, move, pull out, quit, relinquish, retire, set out, withdraw; abandon, cease, desert, desist, drop, evacuate, forbear, give up, refrain, relinquish, renounce, stop, surrender; allot, assign, cede, commit, consign, entrust, give over, refer; bequeath, demise, devise, hand down, transmit, will

leave *n* allowance, authorization, concession, consent, dispensation, freedom, liberty, permission, sanction; furlough, holiday, leave of absence, sabbatical, time off, vacation

leave out *v* bar, cast aside, count out, disregard, except, exclude, ignore, neglect, omit, overlook, refect

lecture *n* address, discourse, disquisition, harangue, instruction, lesson, speech, talk

lecture *v* address, discourse, expound, give a talk, harangue, hold forth, speak, talk, teach; admonish, berate, castigate, censure, chide, rate, reprimand, reprove, scold; (*Inf*) tell off

lecture *n* castigation, censure, chiding, dressing-down, rebuke, reprimand, reproof, scolding

leeway *n* elbowroom, latitude, margin, play, room, scope, space

left-handed *adj* awkward, cack-handed, careless, clumsy, fumbling, gauche, maladroit

leg *n* limb, lower limb, member; brace, prop, support, upright; lap, part, portion, section, segment, stage, stretch

legacy *n* bequest, estate, gift, heirloom, inheritance; birthright, endowment, heritage, inheritance, patrimony, throwback, tradition

legal *adj* allowable, allowed, authorized, constitutional, lawful, legalized, legitimate, licit, permissible, proper, rightful, sanctioned, valid

legalize *v* allow, approve, authorize, decriminalize, legitimate, legitimatize, license, permit, sanction, validate

legend *n* fable, fiction, folk, tale, myth, narrative, saga, story; caption, device, inscription, motto

legendary *adj* apocryphal, fabled, fabulous, fanciful, fictitious, mythical, romantic, storied, traditional

legible *adj* clear, decipherable, distinct, easily read, easy to read, neat, plain, readable

legion *n* army, brigade, company, division, force, troop; drove, horde, host, mass, multitude, myriad, number, throng

legion *adj* countless, multitudinous, myriad, numberless, numerous, very many

legislate *v* codify, constitute, enact, establish, make laws, ordain, pass laws, prescribe, put in force

legislation *n* codification, enactment, lawmaking, prescription, regulation; act, bill, charter, law, measure, regulation, ruling, statute

legislative *adj* congressional, judicial, juridical, jurisdictive, law-giving, lawmaking, ordaining, parliamentary

legitimate *adj* acknowledged, authentic, authorized, genuine, lawful, legal, licit, proper, real, rightful, sanctioned, statutory, true

leisure *n* breathing space, ease, freedom, free time, holiday, liberty, opportunity, pause, quiet, recreation, relaxation, respite, rest, retirement, spare moments, spare time, time off, vacation

leisurely *adj* comfortable, easy, gentle, lazy, relaxed, restful, slow, unhurried

lend *v* accommodate one with, advance, loan; add, afford, bestow, confer, contribute, furnish, give, grant, impart, present, provide, supply

length *n* distance, extent, longitude, measure, reach, span; duration, period, space, span, stretch, term

lengthen *v* continue, draw out, elongate, expand, extend, increase, make longer, prolong, protract, spin out, stretch

lengthy *adj* diffuse, drawn out, extended, interminable, lengthened, long, long-drawn-out, long-winded, overlong, prolonged, protracted, tedious, verbose, very long

leniency *n* clemency, compassion, forbearance, gentleness, indulgence, lenity, mercy, mildness, moderation, tenderness, tolerance

lenient *adj* clement, compassionate, forbearing, forgiving, gentle, indulgent, kind, merciful, mild, sparing, tender, tolerant

less *adj* shorter, slighter, smaller; inferior, minor, secondary, subordinate

less *adv* barely, little, meagrely, to a smaller extent

lessen *v* abate, abridge, contract, curtail, decrease, de-escalate, degrade, die down, diminish, dwindle, ease, erode, grow less, impair, lighten, lower, minimize, moderate, narrow, reduce, shrink, slacken, slow down, weaken, wind down

lesser *adj* inferior, less important, lower, minor, secondary, slighter, subordinate, under

lesson *n* class, coaching, instruction, period, schooling, teaching, tutoring; deterrent, example, exemplar, message, model, moral, precept

let *v* allow, authorize, give leave, give permission, give the go-ahead, grant, permit, sanction, suffer, tolerate, warrant; hire, lease, rent

let-down *n* disappoint, disenchant, disillusion, dissatisfy, fail, fall short, leave in the lurch, leave stranded

lethal *adj* baneful, dangerous, deadly, deathly, destructive, devastating, fatal, mortal, murderous, noxious, pernicious, poisonous, virulent

lethargic *adj* apathetic, comatose, debilitated, drowsy, dull, enervated, heavy, inactive, indifferent, inert, languid, lazy, listless, sleepy, slothful, slow, sluggish, somnolent, stupefied, torpid

lethargy *adj* apathy, drowsiness, dullness, inaction, indifference, inertia, languor, lassitude, listlessness, sleepiness, sloth, slowness, sluggishness, stupor, torpidity, torpor

let in *v* admit, allow to enter, give access to, greet, include, incorporate, receive, take in, welcome

let off *v* detonate, discharge, emit, explode, exude, fire, give off, leak, release; absolve, discharge, dispense, excuse, exempt, exonerate, forgive, pardon, release, spare

let out *v* emit, give vent to, produce; discharge, free, let go, liberate, release; betray, disclose, leak, let fall, let slip, make known, reveal

letter *n* character, sign, symbol; acknowledgment, answer, communication, dispatch, epistle, line, message, missive, note, reply

let-up *n* abatement, break, cessation, interval, lessening, lull, pause, recess, remission, respite, slackening

let-up *n* abate, decrease, diminish, ease up, moderate, slacken, stop, subside

level *adj* consistent, even, flat, horizontal, plain, plane, regular, smooth, uniform; aligned, balanced, commensurate, comparable, equivalent, even, flush, in line, level-pegging, neck and neck, on a line, on a par, proportionate; calm, constant, equable, even, even-tempered, stable, steady

level *v* even off, flatten, make flat, plane, smooth, tear down, lay low, pull down, raze, smooth, tear down, wreck

level *n* altitude, elevation, height, vertical position; bed, floor, layer, storey, stratum, zone

level-headed *adj* balanced, calm, collected, composed, cool, dependable, even-tempered, reasonable, sane, self-possessed, sensible, steady, together; (*Inf*) unflappable

lever *n* bar, crowbar, handle, handspike, jemmy

lever *v* force, jemmy, move, prise, pry, purchase, raise

levy *v* charge, collect, demand, exact, gather, impose, tax

levy *n* assessment, collection, exaction, gathering, imposition

lewd *adj* bawdy, blue, dirty, impure, indecent, lascivious, libidinous, licentious, loose, lustful, obscene, pornographic, profligate, salacious, smutty, unchaste, vile, vulgar, wanton, wicked

liability *n* accountability, answerability, culpability, duty, obligation, onus, responsibility; arrear, debit, debt, indebtedness, obligation; burden, disadvantage, drag, drawback, encumbrance, handicap, hindrance, impediment, inconvenience, millstone, nuisance; (*Inf*), minus

liable *adj* accountable, amenable, answerable, bound, chargeable, obligated, responsible; exposed, open, subject, susceptible, vulnerable

liaison *n* communication, connection, contact, go-between, hook-up, interchange, intermediary; affair, amour, entanglement, illicit romance, intrigue, love affair, romance

liar *n* fabricator, falsifier, fibber, perjurer, prevaricator; (*Inf*) storyteller

libel *n* aspersion, calumny,

defamation, denigration, obloquy, slander, smear, vituperation

libel *v* blacken, calumniate, defame, derogate, drag someone's name through the mud, malign, revile, slander, slur, smear, traduce, vilify

libellous *adj* aspersive, calumniatory, calumnious, defamatory, derogatory, false, injurious, malicious, maligning, scurrilous, slanderous, untrue, vilifying, vituperative

liberal *adj* advanced, humanistic, latitudinarian, libertarian, progressive, radical, reformist; (*Inf*) right on; altruistic, beneficent, bounteous, bountiful, charitable, free-handed, generous, kind, open-handed, open-hearted, unstinting; abundant, ample, bountiful, copious, handsome, lavish, munificent, plentiful, profuse, rich

liberality *n* altruism, beneficence, benevolence, bounty, charity, free-handedness, generosity, kindness, largess, munificence, open-handedness, philanthropy; breadth, broad-mindedness, candour, catholicity, impartiality, latitude, liberalism, libertarianism, magnanimity, permissiveness, progressivism, toleration

liberate *v* deliver, discharge, disenthral, emancipate, free, let loose, let out, manumit, redeem, release, rescue, set free

liberation *n* deliverance, emancipation, enfranchisement, freedom, freeing, liberating, liberty, manumission, redemption, release, unfettering, unshackling

libertine *n* debauchee, lecher, profligate, rake, reprobate, roue, seducer, sensualist, voluptuary, womanizer

liberty *n* autonomy, emancipation, freedom, immunity, independence, liberation, release, self-determination, sovereignty; authorization, carte blanche, dispensation, exemption, franchise, freedom, leave, licence, permission, prerogative, privilege, right, sanction

licence *n* authority, authorization, carte blanche, certificate, charter, dispensation, entitlement, exemption, immunity, leave, liberty, permission, permit, privilege, right, warrant; abandon, anarchy, disorder, excess, immoderation, impropriety, indulgence, irresponsibility, lawlessness, laxity, profligacy, unruliness

License *v* accredit, allow, authorize, certify, commission, empower, permit, sanction, warrant

licentious *adj* abandoned, debauched, disorderly, dissolute, immoral, impure, lascivious, lax, lewd, libertine, libidinous, lubricous, lustful, profligate, promiscuous, sensual, uncontrollable, uncontrolled, uncurbed, unruly, wanton

lick *v* brush, lap, taste, tongue, touch, wash

lie *v* dissimulate, equivocate, fabricate, falsify, fib, forswear, oneself, invent, misrepresent, perjure, prevaricate, tell a lie, tell untruths

lie *n* deceit, fabrication, falsehood, falsification, falsity, fib, fiction, invention, mendacity, prevarication, untruth, white lie

lie *v* be prone, be prostrate, be

recumbent, be supine, couch, loll, lounge, recline, repose, rest, sprawl, stretch out; be, be buried, be found, be interred, be located, belong, be placed, be situated, exist, extend, remain

life *n* animation, being, breath, entity, growth, sentence, viability, vitality; being, career, continuance, course, duration, existence, lifetime, span, time; human, human being, individual, mortal, person, soul; autobiography, biography, career, confessions, history, life story, memoirs, story; behaviour, conduct, lifestyle, way of life; activity, animation, brio, energy, high spirits, liveliness, sparkle, spirit, verve, vigour, vitality, vivacity, zest; (*Inf*) get-up-and-go , go, oomph

lifeless *adj* cold, dead, deceased, defunct, extinct, inanimate, inert; comatose, dead to the world, in a faint, inert, insensate, insensible, out cold, out for six, unconscious

lifelike *adj* authentic, exact, faithful, graphic, natural, photographic, real, realistic, true-to-life, undistorted, vivid

lifelong *adj* constant, deep-rooted, enduring, for all one's life, for life, lasting, lifetime, long-lasting, long-standing, perennial, permanent, persistent

lift *v* bear aloft, buoy up, draw up, elevate, hoist, pick up, raise, raise high, rear, upheave, uplift, upraise; annul, cancel, countermand, end, relax, remove, rescind, revoke, stop, terminate; ascend, be dispelled, climb, disappear, disperse, dissipate, mount, rise, vanish

lift *n* car ride, drive, ride, run, transport; boost, encouragement, fillip, pick-me-up, reassurance, uplift; (*Inf*) shot in the arm

light *n* blaze, brightness, brilliance, effulgence, flash, glare, glean, glint, glow, illumination, incandescence, lambency, luminescence, luminosity, lustre, phosphorescence, radiance, ray, refulgence, scintillation, shine, sparkle; beacon, bulb, candle, flare, lamp, lantern, lighthouse, start, taper, torch, windowpane; broad day, cockcrow, dawn, daybreak, daylight, daytime, morning, sun, sunbeam, sunrise, sunshine; example, exemplar, guiding light, model, paragon, shining example; flame, lighter, match; **bring to light** disclose, discover, expose, reveal, show, uncover, unearth, unveil; **come to light** appear, be disclosed, be discovered, be revealed, come out, transpire, turn up; **in the light of** bearing in mind, because of, considering, in view of, taking into account, with knowledge of

light *adj* aglow, bright, brilliant, glowing, illumination, luminous, lustrous, shining, sunny, well-lighted, well-lit: bleached, blond, faded, fair, light-hued, light-toned, pale, pastel; airy, buoyant, delicate, easy, flimsy, imponderous, insubstantial, lightsome, light weight, portable, slight, soft, weak; inconsequential, inconsiderable, insignificant, minute, scanty, slight, small, thin, tiny, trifling, trivial, unsubstantial, wee; easy, effortless, manageable, moderate, simple, undemanding, unexacting, untaxing; (*Inf*) cushy; agile, airy, graceful, light-footed, lithe, nimble, sprightly, sylph-like; amusing, diverting, entertaining, frivolous, funny, gay, humorous, light-hearted, pleasing, superficial, trifling, trivial, witty; airy, animated, blithe, carefree, cheerful, cheery, fickle, frivolous, gay, lively, merry, sunny; digestible, frugal, modest, not heavy, not rich, restricted, small

light *v* fire, ignite, inflame, kindle, set a match to; brighten, clarify, floodlight, flood with light, illuminate, illumine, irradiate, lighted, light up, put on, switch on, turn on; animate, brighten, cheer, irradiate, lighten

lighten *v* become light, brighten, flash, gleam, illuminate, irradiate, light up, make bright, shine; disburden, ease, make lighter, reduce in weight, unload; alleviate, ameliorate, assuage, ease, facilitate, lessen, mitigate, reduce, relieve

light-headed *adj* featherbrained, fickle, flighty, flippant, foolish, frivolous, giddy, inane, shallow, silly, superficial, trifling; (*Inf*) bird-brained, rattle-brained

light-hearted *adj* blithe, bright, carefree, cheerful, effervescent, frolicsome, gay, glad, gleeful, happy-go-lucky, insouciant, jocund. jolly, jovial, joyful, joyous, merry, playful, sunny, untroubled; (*Inf*) upbeat

lightweight *adj* inconsequential, insignificant, of no account, paltry, petty, slight, trifling, trivial, unimportant, worthless

like *adj* akin, alike, allied, analogues, approximating, cognate, corresponding,equivalent, identical, parallel, relating, resembling, same, similar

like *v* be fond of, be keen on, be partial to, delight in, enjoy, love, relish, revel in; (*Inf*) adore, dig, go for; admire, appreciate, approve, cherish, esteem, hold dear, prize, take to; (*Inf*) take a shine to

likeable *adj* agreeable, amiable, appealing, attractive, charming, engaging, friendly, genial, nice, pleasant, pleasing, sympathetic, winning, winsome

likelihood *n* chance, good chance, liability, likeliness, possibility, probability, prospect, reasonableness, strong possibility

likely *adj* anticipated, apt, disposed, expected, in a fair way, inclined, liable, on the cards, possible, probable, prone, tending, to be expected

likely *adv* doubtlessly, in all probability, no doubt, presumable, probably; (*Inf*) like as not, like enough

liken *n* compare, equate, juxtapose, match, parallel, relate, set beside,

likeness *n* affinity, correspondence, resemblance, similarity, similitude; copy, counterpart, delineation, depiction, effigy, facismile, image, model, photograph, picture, portrait, replica, representation, reproduction, study

liking *n* affection, affinity, appreciation, attraction, bent, bias, desire, fondness, inclination, love, partiality, penchant, predilection, preference, proneness, propensity, soft spot, stomach, taste, tendency, weakness

limb *n* appendage, arm, extension, extremity, leg, member, part, wing

limelight *n* attention, celebrity, fame, glare of publicity, prominence, public eye, publicity, public notice, recognition, stardom, the spotlight

limit *n* bound, breaking point, cutoff point, deadline, end, end point, furthest bound, greatest extent, termination, the bitter end, ultimate, utmost; border, boundary, confines, edge, end, extent, frontier, perimeter, periphery, precinct; ceiling, check, curb, limitation, maximum, obstruction, restraint, restriction

limit *v* bound, check, circumscribe, confine, curb, delimit, demarcate, fix, hem in, hinder, ration, restrain, restrict, specify

limitation *n* block, check, condition, constraint, control, curb, disadvantage, drawback, impediment, obstruction, qualification, reservation, restraint, restriction, snag

limited *adj* bounded, checked, circumscribed, confined, constrained, controlled, curbed, defined, finite, fixed, hampered, hemmed in, restricted

limitless *adj* boundless, countless, endless, illimitable, immeasurable, immense, inexhaustible, infinite, measureless, never-ending, numberless, unbounded, unceasing, undefined, unending, unlimited, untold, vast

limp *v* falter, hobble, hop, shamble, shuffle

limp *adj* drooping, flabby, flacid, flexible, floppy, lax, limber, loose, pliable, relaxed, slack, soft

line *n* band, bar, channel, ash, groove, mark, rule, score, scratch, streak, stripe, stroke, underline; crease, crow's-foot, furrow, mark, wrinkle; border, borderline, boundary, demarcation, edge, frontier, limit, mark; configuration, contour, features, figure, outline, profile, silhouette; cable, cord, filament, silhouette; cable, cord, filament, rope, strand, string, thread, wire; axis, course, direction, path, route, track, trajectory; approach, avenue, belief, course, course of action, ideology, method, policy, position, practice, procedure, scheme, system; activity, area, business, calling, department, employment, field, forte, interest, job, occupation, profession, province, pursuit, specialization, trade, vocation; column, file, procession, queue, rank, row, sequence, series; ancestry, breed, family, lineage, race, stock, strain, succession; card, letter, message, note, postcard, report, word; **draw the line** lay down the law, object, prohibit, put one's foot down, restrict, set a limit

line *v* crease, cut, draw, furrow, inscribe, mark, rule, score, trace, underline; border, bound, edge, fringe, rank, rim, skirt, verge

line-up *n* arrangement, array, row, selection, team

line up *v* fall in, form ranks, queue up; assemble, come up with, lay on, obtain, organize, prepare, procure, produce, secure

linger *v* hang around, loiter, remain, stay, stop, tarry, wait; abide, continue, endure, persist

lingering *adj* dragging, long-drawn-out, persistent, protracted, remaining, slow

link *n* component, constituent, division, element, member, part, piece; association, attachment, bond; association, attachment, bond, connection, joint, knot, relationship, tie, tie-up, vinculum

link *v* attach, bind, connect, couple, fasten, join, tie, unite, yoke; associate, bracket, connect, identify, relate

liquid *n* fluid, juice, liquor, solution

liquid *adj* aqueous, flowing, fluid, liquefied, melted, molten, running, runny, thawed, wet; bright, brilliant, clear, limpid, shining, translucent, transparent; dulcet, fluent, mellifluent, mellifluous, melting, smooth, soft, sweet; convertible, negotiable

liquidate *v* clear, discharge, honour, pay, pay off, settle, square; abolish, annul, cancel, dissolve, terminate; cash, convert to cash, realize, sell off, sell up; annihilate, destroy, dispatch, do away with, eliminate, exterminate, finish off, get rid of, kill, murder, remove, silence, (*Inf*) blow away, bump off, do in, rub out, wipe out

liquor *n* alcohol, drink, grog, intoxicant, spirits, strong drink; (*Inf*) booze, hard stuff, hooch

list *n* catalogue, directory, file, index, inventory, invoice, listing, record, register, roll, schedule, series, syllabus, tabulation, tally; cant, leaning, slant, tilt

list *v* bill, book, catalogue, enrol, enter, enumerate, file, index, itemize, note, prepare, procure, preoduce, secure; cant, careen, heel, heel over, incline, lean, tilt, tip

listen *v* attend, be all ears, be attentive, give ear, hang on someone's words, hark, hear, keep one's ears open, lend an ear; (*Inf*) pin back one's ears, prick up one's ears; concentrate, do as one is told, give heed to, heed, mind, obey, observe, pay attention, take notice

listless *adj* apathetic, enervated, heavy, impassive, inattentive, indif ferent, indolent, inert, languid, languishing, lethargic, lifeless, limp, lymphatic, mopish, sluggish, spiritless, supine, torpid, vacant

literal *adj* accurate, close, exact, faithful, strict, verbatim, word for word; actual, bona fide, genuine, gospel, plain, real, simple, true, unexaggerated, unvarnished

literally *adv* actually, exactly, faithfully, plainly, precisely, really, simply, strictly, to the letter, truly, verbatim, word for word

literary *adj* bookish, erudite, formal, learned, lettered, literate, scholarly, well-read

literate *adj* cultivated, cultured, educated, erudite, informed, knowledgeable, learned, lettered, scholarly, well-informed, well-read

literature *n* belles-lettres, letters, lore, writings, written works

lithe *adj* flexible, limber, lissom, loose-jointed, loose-limbed, pliable, pliant, supple

litigation *n* action, case, contending, disputing, lawsuit, process, prosecution

litter *n* debris, detritus, fragments,

garbage, muck, refuse, rubbish, shreds; clutter, confusion, disarray, disorder, jumble, mess, scatter, untidiness; brood, family, offspring, progeny, young; bedding, couch, floor cover, mulch, straw bed; palanquin, stretcher

litter *v* clutter, derange, disarrange, disorder, mess up, scatter, strew

little *adj* diminutive, dwarf, elfin, infinitesimal, Lilliputian, mini, miniature, minute, petite, pygmy, short, slender, small, tiny, wee; babyish, immature, infant, junior, undeveloped, young; hardly any, insufficient, meagre, scant, skimpy, small, sparse; brief, fleeting, hasty, passing, short, short-lived, inconsiderable, insignificant, minor, negligible, paltry, trifling, trivial, unimportant; base, cheap, illiberal, mean, narrow-minded, petty, small-minded

little *adv* barely, hardly, not much, not quite, only just; hardly ever, not often, rarely, scarcely, seldom

live *v* be, be alive, breathe, draw breath, exist, have life; be permanent, be remembered, last, persist, prevail, remain alive; **live in** abide, dwell, inhabit, lodge, occupy, reside, settle, stay; (*Inf*) hang out; abide, continue, earn a living, endure, fare, feed, get along, lead, make ends meet, pass, remain, subsist, support oneself, survive

live *adj* alive, animate, breathing, existent, living, vital; active, burning, controversial, current, hot, pertinent, pressing, prevalent, topical, unsettled, vital; active, alert, brisk, dynamic, earnest, energetic, lively, sparky, vigorous, vivid, wide-awake

livelihood *n* employment, income, job, living, maintenance, means, means of support, occupation, source of income, subsistence, sustenance, work

liveliness *n* activity, animation, boisterousness, briskness, dynamism, energy, gaiety, quickness, smartness, spirit, sprightliness, vitality, vivacity

lively *adj* active, agile, alert, brisk, chirpy, energetic, keen, nimble, perky, quick, sprightly, spry, vigorous; (*Inf*) chipper, full of beans, full of pep; animated, blithe, blithe some, cheerful, frisky, frolicsome, gay, merry, sparkling, sparky, spirited, vivacious; astir, bustling, busy, buzzing, crowded, eventful, moving, stirring; bright, colourful, exciting, forceful, invigorating, racy, refreshing, stimulating, vivid

liven *v* animate, brighten, enliven, perk up, put life into, rouse, stir, vitalize, vivify; (*Inf*) buck up, hot up, pep up

livid *adj* angry, black-and-blue, bruised, contused, discoloured, purple; ashen, blanched, bloodless, doughy, greyish, leaden, pale, pal lid, pasty, wan, waxen; angry, beside oneself, boiling, enraged, exasperated, fuming, furious, incensed, indignant, infuriated, outraged; (*Inf*) mad

living *adj* active, alive, animated, breathing, existing, lively, strong, vigorous, vital; (*Inf*) in the land of the living

living *n* animation, being, existence, existing, life, subsistence; job, livelihood, maintenance, occupation, support, subsistence, sustenance, work

load *n* bale, cargo, consignment, freight, ladin, shipment; affliction, burden, encumbrance, incubus, millstone, onus, oppression, pressure, trouble, weight, worry

load *v* cram, fill, freight, heap, lade, pack, pile, stack, stuff; burden, encumber, hamper, oppress, saddle with trouble, weigh down, worry; charge, make ready, prepare to fire, prime

loaded *adj* burdened, charged, freighted, full, laden, weighted; biased, distorted, weighted; at the ready, charged, primed, ready to shoot ; affluent, moneyed, rich, wealthy, well-off, well-to-do; (*Inf*) flush, rolling, well-heeled

loan *n* accommodation, advance, allowance, credit, mortgage

loathing *n* abhorrence, abomination. antipathy, aversion, detestation, disgust, execration, hatred, horror, odium, repugnance, repulsion, revulsion

loathsome *adj* abhorrent, abominable, detestable, disgusting, execrable, hateful, horrible, nasty, nauseating, obnoxious, odious, offensive, repugnant, repulsive, revolting, vile

lobby *n* corridor, entrance hall, foyer, hall, hallway, passage, passageway, porch, vestibule; pressure group

lobby *v* bring pressure to bear, campaign for, exert influence, influence, persuade, press for, pressure, promote, push for, solicit votes, urge; (*Inf*) pull strings

local *adj* community district, neighbourhood, parish, provincial, regional; confined, limited, narrow, parish pump, parochial, provincial, restricted, small-town

local *n* character, inhabitant, local yokel, native, resident; (*Inf*) neighbourhood pub

locality *n* area, district, neighbourhood, region, vicinity; (*Inf*) neck of the woods

locate *v* come across, detect, discover, find, lay one's hands on, pin down, pin point, run to earth, track down, unearth

location *n* bearings, locale, locus, place, point, position, site, situation, spot, venue, whereabouts

lock *n* bolt, clasp, fastening, padlock

lock *v* bolt, close, fasten, latch, seal, secure, shut

lodge *n* cabin, chalet, cottage, gatehouse, house, hunting lodge, hut, shelter; assemblage, association, branch, chapter, club, group, society

lodge *v* accommodate, billet, board, entertain, harbour, put up, quarter, room, shelter, sojourn, stay, stop; become fixed, catch, come to rest, imbed, implant, stick

lodger *n* boarder, guest, paying guest, PG, resident, roomer, tenant

lodging *n* bode, accommodation, apartments, boarding, dwelling, habitation, quarters, residence, rooms, shelter; (*Inf*) digs

lofty *adj* elevated, high, raised, sky-high, soaring, tall, towering; dignified, distinguished, elevated, exalted, grand, illustrious, imposing, majestic, noble, renowned, stately, sublime, superior; arrogant, condescending, disdainful, haughty, lordly, patronizing, proud, supercilious; (*Inf*) high and mighty, snotty, toffee-nosed

log *n* block, bole, chunk, piece of timber, stump, trunk; account, chart, daybook, journal, listing, logbook, record, tally

log *v* book, chart, make a note of, note, record, register, report, set down, tally

logic *n* good reason, good sense, reason, sense, sound judgment; chain of thought, coherence, connection, link, rationale, relationship

logical *adj* clear, cogent, coherent, consistent, deducible, pertinent, rational, reasonable, relevant, sound, valid, well-organized

loiter *v* dally, dawdle, delay, hang about or around, idle, lag, linger, loaf, loll, saunter, skulk, stroll; (*Inf*) dilly-dally

lone *adj* by oneself, deserted, isolated, lonesome, one, only, separate, separated, single, sole, solitary, unaccompanied

loneliness *n* aloneness, deserted ness, desolation, dreariness, forlornness, isolation, lonesomeness, seclusion, solitariness, solitude

lonely *adj* abandoned, companionless, destitute, estranged, forlorn, forsaken, friendless, lonesome, out cast; alone, by oneself, isolated, lone, rejected, single, solitary, withdrawn; barren, deserted, desolate, isolated, out-of-the-way, remote, secluded, sequestered, solitary, unfrequented, uninhabited; (*Inf*) off the beaten track

long *adj* elongated, expanded, extended, extensive, far reaching, lengthy, spread out, stretched

long *v* covet, crave, desire, dream of, hanker, hunger, itch, lust, pine, want, wish, yearn

longing *n* ambition, aspiration, coveting, craving, desire, hankering, hungering, itch, thirst, urge, wish, yearning; (*Inf*) yen

long-standing *adj* abiding, enduring, established, fixed, long-established, long-lasting, long-lived, time-honoured

long-suffering *adj* easygoing, forbearing, forgiving, patient, resigned, stoical, tolerant, uncomplaining

long-winded *adj* diffuse, discursive, garrulous, lengthy, long-drawn-out, overlong, prolix, prolonged, rambling, repetitious, tedious, verbose, wordy

look *v* consider, contemplate, examine, eye, feast one's eyes upon, gaze, glance, inspect, observe, peep, regard, scan, scrutinize, see, study, survey, view, watch; (*Inf*) check out, take a gander at; appear, display, evidence, exhibit, look like, make clear, manifest, present, seem, seem to be, show, strike one as; forage, hunt, search, seek

look *n* examination, gaze, glance, glimpse, inspection, observation, peek, review, sight, squint, survey, view; (*Inf*) eyeful, once over, squiz; air, appearance, aspect, bearing, cast, complexion, countenance, demeanour, effect, expression, face, fashion, guise, manner, semblance

look after *v* attend to, care for, guard, keep an eye on, mind, nurse, protect, sit with, supervise, take care of, take charge of, tend, watch

look down on *v* contemn, despise, disdain, hold, in contempt, misprize, scorn, sneer, spurn, treat with contempt; (*Inf*) look down one's nose at, turn one's nose up at

look forward to *v* anticipate, await, count on, count the days until, expect, hope for, long for, look for, wait for

look into *v* check out, delve into, examine, explore, follow up, go into, inquire about, inspect, investigate, look over, make queries, probe, research, scrutinize, study

lookout *n* guard, qui vive, readiness, vigil, watch; guard, sentinel, sentry, vedette, watchman; beacon, citadel, observation post, post, tower, watchtower

look out *v* be alert, be careful, be on guard, be on the qui vive, be vigilant, keep an eye out, keep one's eyes open, pay attention, watch out; (*Inf*) keep one's eyes peeled,

loom *v* appear, become visible, be imminent, bulk, emerge, hover, impend, menace, take shape, threaten

loop *n* bend, circle, coil, convolution, curl, curve, eyelet, hoop, kink, loophole, noose, ring, spiral, twirl, twist, wind round

loophole *n* aperture, gap, knothole, opening, slot; ambiguity, avoidance, escape, escape clause, escape route, evasion, excuse, let-out, means of escape, means of evasion, ommission, plea, pretence, pretext, subterfuge

loose *adj* floating, free, insecure, movable, released, unattached, unbound, unconfined, unfastened, unfettered, unrestricted, unsecured, untied, wobbly; baggy, easy, hanging, loosened, not fitting, not tight, relaxed, slack, slackened, sloppy; diffuse, disconnected, disordered, ill-defined, imprecise, inaccurate, indefinite, indistinct, inexact, rambling, random, vague; abandoned, debauched, disreputable, dissipated, dissolute, fast, immoral, lewd, libertine, licentious, profligate, promiscuous, unchaste, wanton

loose *v* detach, disconnect, disengage, ease, free, let go, liberate, loosen, release, set free, slacken, unbind, undo, unfasten, unleash, unloose, untie

loosen *v* detach, let out, separate, slacken, unbind, undo, unloose, unstick, untie, work free, work loose; deliver, free, let go, liberate, release, set free

loot *n* booty, goods, haul, plunder, prize, spoils, swag

lopsided *adj* askew, asymmetrical, awry, cockeyed, crooked, disproportionate, off balance, one-sided, out of shape, out of true, squint, tilting, unbalanced, unequal, uneven, warped

lord *n* commander, governor, king, leader, liege, master, monarch, overlord, potentate, prince, ruler, seigneur, sovereign, superior; earl, noble, nobleman, peer, viscount

lore *n* beliefs, doctrine, experience, folk-wisdom, mythos, saws, sayings, teaching, traditional wisdom, traditions, wisdom

lose *v* be deprived of, displace, drop, fail to keep, forget, mislay, mis place. miss, suffer loss; capitulate, default fail, fall short, forfeit, miss, yield; (*Inf*) lose out on, pass up; be defeated, be the loser, be worsted, come to grief, get the worst of, lose out, suffer defeat; (*Inf*) come a cropper, take a licking

loser *n* also-ran, failure, underdog, (*Inf*) dud, flop, lemon, no-hoper, washout

loss *n* bereavement, deprivation, disappearance, failure, forfeiture, losing, privation, squandering, waste; cost, damage, defeat, destruction, detriment, disadvantage, harm, hurt, impairment, injury, ruin

lost *adj* disappeared, forfeited, mislaid, misplaced, missed, missing, strayed, vanished, wayward; adrift, astray, at sea, disoriented, off-course, off-track; baffled, bewildered, confused, helpless, ignorant, mystified, perplexed, puzzled; (*Inf*) clueless; absent, absorbed, abstracted, distracted, dreamy, engrossed, entranced, preoccupied, rapt, spellbound, taken up; bygone, dead, extinct, forgotten, gone, lapsed, obsolete, out-of-date, past, unremembered; abandoned, corrupt, damned, depraved, dissolute, fallen, irreclaimable, licentious, profligate, unchaste, wanton

lot *n* assortment, batch, collection, consignment, crowd, group, quantity, set; (*Inf*) bunch; accident, chance, destiny, doom, fate, fortune, hazard, plight, portion; allowance, parcel, part, percentage, piece, portion, quota, ration, share; (*Inf*) cut; abundance, a great deal, large amount, numbers, plenty, quantities, scores; (*Inf*) heaps, loads, masses, oceans, oddles, piles, reams, stacks

lotion *n* balm, cream, embrocation, liniment, slave, solution

lottery *n* draw, raffle, sweepstake; chance, gamble, hazard, risk, venture; (*Inf*) toss-up

loud *adj* blaring, blatant, boisterous, booming, clamorous, deafening, ear-piercing, eat splitting, forte, high-sounding, noisy, obstreperous, piercing, resounding, rowdy, sonorous, stentorian, strident, strong, thundering, tumultuous, turbulent, vehement, vociferous; brassy, flamboyant, flashy, garish, gaudy, glaring, lurid, ostentatious, showy, tasteless, tawdry, vulgar; brash, brazen, coarse, crass, crude, offensive, raucous, vulgar; (*Inf*) loud-mouthed

lounge *v* laze, lie about, loaf, loiter, loll, recline, relax, saunter, sprawl; (*Inf*) take it easy

lout *n* bear, bumpkin, clod, clumsy, idiot; (*Inf*) dolt, gawk, lubber, lummox, oaf, yahoo, yob, yobbo

lovable *adj* adorable, amiable, attractive, captivating, charming, cuddly, delightful, enchanting, endearing, engaging, likeable, lovely, pleasing, sweet, winning, winsome; (*Inf*) fetching

love *v* adore, adulate, be attached to, be in love with, cherish, dote on, have affection for, hold dear, idolize, prize, think the world of, treasure, worship; appreciate, delight in, desire, enjoy, fancy, have a weakness for, like, relish, savour, take pleasure in; caress, cuddle, embrace, fondle, kiss, pet; (*Inf*) canoodle, neck

love *n* adoration, adulation, affection, amity, ardour, attachment, devotion, fondness, friendship, infatuation, liking, passion, rapture, regard, tenderness, warmth

lovely *adj* admirable, adorable, amiable, attractive, beautiful, charming, comely, exquisite, graceful, handsome, pretty, sweet, winning; agreeable, captivating, delightful, enchanting, engaging, enjoyable, gratifying, nice, pleasant, pleasing

lover *n* admirer, beau, beloved, boyfriend, fiance, fiance, girlfriend, inamorata, inamorata, mistress, paramour, partner, suitor, sweetheart, toy boy; (*Inf*) fancy man, fancy woman, flame

loving *adj* affectionate, amorous, ardent, cordial, dear, demonstrative, devoted, doting, fond, friendly, kind, solicitous, tender, warm, warm-hearted

low *v* little, short, small, squat, stunted; deep, depressed, ground-level, low-lying, shallow, subsided, sunken; depleted, insignificant, little, meagre, paltry, reduced, scant, small, sparse, trifling; deficient, inadequate, inferior, low-grade, mediocre, poor, puny, second-rate, shoddy, substandard, worthless; coarse, common, crude, disgraceful, dishonourable, disreputable, gross, ill-bred, obscene, rough, rude, unbecoming, undignified, unrefined, vulgar; humble, lowborn, lowly, meek, obscure, plain, plebeian, poor, simple, unpretentious; blue, dejected, depressed, despondent, disheartened, down, downcast, forlorn, gloomy, glum, miserable, morose, sad, unhappy; (*Inf*) brassed off, down in the dumps, fed up; gentle, hushed, muffled, muted, quiet, soft, subdued, whispered; cheap, economical, inexpensive, moderate, modest, reasonable; abject, base, contemptible, dastardly, degraded, depraved, despicable, ignoble, mean, menial, nasty, scurvy, servile, sordid, unworthy, vile, vulgar

lower *adj* inferior, junior, lesser, low-level, minor, secondary, second-class, smaller, subordinate, under

lower *v* depress, drop, fall, let down, make lower, sink, submerge, take down; abase, belittle, condescend, debase, degrade, deign, demean, devalue, disgrace, downgrade, humble, humiliate, stoop

loyal *adj* attached, constant, dependable, devoted, dutiful, faithful, patriotic, staunch, steadfast, tried and true, true, true-blue, truehearted, trustworthy, trusty, unswerving, unwavering

loyalty *n* allegiance, constancy, dependability, devotion, faithfulness, fealty, fidelity, patrionism, reliability, staunchness, steadfastness, true-heartedness, trueness, trustiness, trustworthiness

lubricate *v* grease, make slippery, make smooth, moisturize, oil, oil the wheels, smear, smooth the way

lucid *adj* clear, clear-cut, comprehensible, crystal-clear, distinct, evident, explicit, intelligible, limpid, obvious, pellucid, plain, transparent; beaming, bright, brilliant, effulgent, gleaming, luminous, radiant, resplendent, shining; clear, crystalline, diaphanous, glassy, limpid, pellucid, pure, translucent, transparent

luck *n* accident, chance, destiny, fate, fortuity, fortune, hazard; advantage, blessing, fluke, godsend, good fortune, good luck, prosperity, serendipity, stroke, success, windfall; (*Inf*) break

luckily *adv* favourably, fortunately, happily, opportunity, propitiously, providentially

lucky *adv* advantageous, blessed, charmed, favoured, fortunate, prosperous, serendipitous, successful

lucrative *adv* advantageous, fat, fruitful, gainful, high income, money-making, paying, productive, profitable, remunerative, well-paid

ludicrous *adj* absurd, burlesque, comic, comical, crazy, droll, farcical, funny, incongruous, laughable, nonsensical, odd, outlandish, preposterous, ridiculous, silly, zany

luggage *n* baggage, bags, cases, gear, impedimenta, paraphernalia, suitcases, things, trunks

lukewarm *adj* apathetic, cold, cool, half-hearted, indifferent, laodicean, phlegmatic, unconcerned, unenthusiastic, uninterested, unresponsive

lull *v* allay, calm, compose, hush, lullaby, pacify, quell, quiet, rock to sleep, soothe, still, subdue, tranquillize

lull *n* calm, calmness, hush, pause, quiet, respite, silence, stillness, tranquillity; (*Inf*) let-up

lumber *n* castoffs, clutter, discards, jumble, junk, refuse, rubbish, trash, trumpery, white elephants

lumbering *adj* awkward, blundering, bovine, bumbling, clumsy, elephantine, heavy, heavy-footed, hulking, lubberly, overgrown, ponderous, ungainly, unwieldy

luminous *adj* bright, brilliant, glow ing, illuminated, lighted, lit, luminescent, lustrous, radiant, resplendent, shining, vivid

lump *n* ball, bunch, cake, chunk, clod, cluster, dab, gob, gobbet, group, hunk, mass, nugget, piece, spot, wedge; bulge, bump, growth, protrusion, protuberance, swelling, tumescence, tumour

lump *v* agglutinate, aggregate, batch, bunch, coalesce, collect, combine, conglomerate, consolidate, group, mass, pool, unite

lunacy *n* dementia, derangement, idiocy, insanity, madness, mania, psychosis; aberration, absurdity, craziness, folly, foolhardiness, foolishness, idiocy, imbecility, madness, senselessness, stupidity, tomfoolery

lunatic *adj* absurd, crack-brained, crazy, daft, demented, deranged, foolish, illogical, inane, insane, irrational, ludicrous, mad, maniacal, preposterous, psychotic, senseless, stupid, unhinged, unreasonable; (*Inf*) barmy, bonkers, nuts

lunatic *n* imbecile, madman, maniac, psychopath; (*Inf*) basket case, head-banger, headcase, loony, nutcase, nutter, psycho, screwball

lunge *n* charge, cut, jab, pass, pounce, spring, stab, swing, swipe, thrust

lunge *v* bound, charge, cut, dash, dive, fall upon, hit at, jab, leap, pitch into, plunge, poke, pounce, set upon, stab, strike at, thrust

lure *v* allure, attract, beckon, decoy, draw, ensnare, entice, inveigle, invite, lead on, seduce, tempt

lure *n* allurement, attraction, bait, decoy, enticement, inducement, magnet, temptation; (*Inf*) carrot, come-on

lurid *adj* exaggerated, graphic, melodramatic, sensational, shocking, startling, unrestrained, vivid; disgusting, ghastly, gory, grim, grisly, gruesome, macabre, revolting, savage, violent

lurk *v* conceal oneself, crouch, go furtively, hide, lie in wait, move with stealth, prowl, skulk, slink, sneak, snoop

luscious *adj* appetizing, delectable, delicious, honeyed, juicy, mouth-watering, palatable, rich, savoury, succulent, sweet, toothsome; (*Inf*) scrumptious, yummy

lush *n* abundant, dense, flourishing, green, lavish, overgrown, prolific, rank, teeming, verdant

lust *n* carnality, concupiscence, lasciviousness, lechery, lewdness, libido, licentiousness, pruriency, salaciousness, sensuality, wantonness; (*Inf*) randiness, the hots; appetence, appetite, avidity, covetousness, craving, cupidity, desire, greed, longing, passion, thirst

lust *v* be consumed with desire for, covet, crave, desire, hunger for, hunger after, need, slaver over, want, yearn; (*Inf*) lech after

lustre *n* burnish, gleam, glint, glitter, gloss, glow, sheen, shimmer, shine, sparkle; brightness, brilliance, dazzle, lambency, luminousness, radiance, resplendence; distinction, fame, glory, honour, illustriousness, prestige, renown

lusty *adj* brawny, energetic, hale, healthy, hearty, in fine fettle, powerful, Ramboesque, robust, rugged, stalwart, stout, strapping, strong, sturdy, vigorous, virile; (*Inf*) red-blooded

luxurious *adj* comfortable, costly, deluxe, expensive, lavish, magnificent, opulent, rich, splendid, sumptuous, well-appointed; (*Inf*) plush, ritzy

luxury *n* affluence, hedonism, opulence, richness, splendour, sumptuousness, voluptuousness; bliss, comfort, delight, enjoyment, gratification, indulgence, pleasure, satisfaction, wellbeing; extra, extravagance, frill, indulgence, non-essential, treat

lying *n* deceit, dishonesty, dissimulation, double-dealing, duplicity, fabrication, falsity, fibbing, guile, mendacity, perjury, prevarication, untruthfulness

lying *adj* deceitful, dishonest, dissembling, double-dealing, false, guile ful, mendacious, perfidious, treacherous, two-faced, untruthful

M

machine *n* apparatus, appliance, contraption, contrivance, device, engine, instrument, mechanism, tool; agency, machinery, organization, party, structure, system; (*Inf*) setup

machinery *n* apparatus, equipment, gear, instruments, mechanism, tackle, tools, works; agency, channels, machine, organization, procedure, structure, system

mad *adj* aberrant, crazed, delirious, demented, deranged, distracted, frantic, frenzied, insane, lunatic, non compos mentis, off one's head, of unsound mind, psychotic, rabid, raving, unbalanced, unhinged, unstable; absurd, foolhardy, foolish, imprudent, irrational, ludicrous, nonsensical, preposterous, senseless, unreasonable, unsafe, unsound, wild; (*Inf*) bananas, barmy, batty, bonkers, crackers, crazy, cuckoo, daft, flaky, loony, loopy, mental, nuts, nutty, off one's chump, off one's nut, off one's rocker, off one's trolley, round the bend, screwy

madden *v* annoy, craze, derange, drive one crazy, round the twist, enrage, exasperate, get one's hackles, up, incense, inflame, infuriate, irritate, make one's blood boil, make one's hackles rise, provoke, raise one's hackles, unhinge, upset, vex; (*Inf*) make one see red

made-up *adj* fabricated, false, fictional, imaginary, invented, make-believe, mythical, specious, trumped-up, unreal, untrue

madly *adv* crazily, deliriously, dementedly, distractedly, frantically, frenziedly, hysterically, insanely, rabidly; absurdly, foolishly, irrationally, ludicrously, nonsensically, senselessly, unreasonable, wildly; energetically, excitedly, furiously, hastily, hurriedly, quickly, rapidly, recklessly, speedily, violently, wildly

madness *n* aberration, craziness, delusion, dementia, derangement, distraction, insanity, lunacy, mania, mental illness, psychopathy, psychosis; absurdity, folly, foolhardiness, foolishness, nonsense, preposterousness, wildness; anger, exasperation, frenzy, fury, ire, rage, raving, wildness, wrath; ardour, craze, enthusiasm, fanaticism, fondness, infatuation, keenness, passion rage, zeal; abandon, agitation, excitement, frenzy, furore, intoxication, riot, unrestraint, uproar

magazine *n* journal, pamphlet, paper, periodical; ammunition, dump, arsenal, depot, store, store house, warehouse

magic *n* black art, enchantment, necromancy, occultism, sorcery, sortilege, spell, theurgy, witchcraft, wizardry; conjuring, hocus-pocus, illusion, jiggery-pokery jugglery, legerdemain, prestitation, sleight of hand, tricker; allurement, charm, enchantment, fascination, glamour, magnetism, power

magic *adj* bewitching, charismatic, charming, enchanting, entrancing, fascinating, magnetic, marvellous, miraculous, sorcerous, spellbinding

magistrate *n* bailie, JP, judge, justice, justice of the peace, provost

magnanimous *adj* beneficent, big, big-hearted, bountiful, charitable, free, generous, great-hearted, handsome, high-minded, kind, kindly, munificent, noble, open-handed, selfless, ungrudging, unselfish, unstinting

magnate *n* baron, captain of industry, chief, leader, mogul, notable, plutocrat, tycoon, VIP; aristocrat, baron, bashaw, grandee, magnifico, merchant, noble, notable, personage, prince; (*Inf*) aristo, big cheese, big noise, big shot, big wheel, big wig, fat cat, Mr. Big

magnetic *adj* alluring, attractive, captivating, charismatic, charming, enchanting, entrancing, fascinating, hypnotic, irresistible, mesmerizing, seductive

magnetism *n* allure, appeal, attraction, attractiveness, captivatingness, charisma, charm, draw, drawing power, enchantment, fascination, hypnotism, magic, mesmerism, power, pull, seductiveness, spell

magnificence *n* brilliance, glory, gorgeousness, grandeur, luxuriousness, luxury, majesty, nobility, opulence, pomp, resplendence, splendour, stateliness, sublimity, sumptuousness

magnificent *adj* august, brilliant, elegant, elevated, exalted, excellent, fine, glorious, gorgeous, grand, grandiose, imposing, impressive, lavish, luxurious, majestic, noble, opulent, outstanding, princely, regal, resplendent, rich, splendid, stately, sublime, sumptuous, superb, superior, transcendent

magnify *v* aggrandize, amplify, augment, blow up, boost, build up, deepen, dilate, enlarge, expand, heighten, increase, intensify; aggravate, blow up, blow up out of all proportion, dramatize, enhance, exaggerate, inflate, make a mountain out of a molehill, overdo, overemphasize, overestimate, overplay, overrate, overstate

magnitude *n* consequence, eminence, grandeur, greatness, importance, mark, moment, note, significance, weight; amount, amplitude, bigness, bulk, capacity, dimensions, enormity, expanse, extent, hugeness, immensity, intensity, largeness, mass, measure, proportions, quantity, size, space, strength, vastness, volume

maid *n* damsel, girl, lass, lassie, maiden, miss, wench; housemaid, maidservant, servant, serving-maid

maiden *n* damsel, girl, lass, lassie maid, miss, virgin, wench

maiden *adj* chaste, intact, pure, undefiled, unmarried, unwed, virgin, virginal; first, inaugural, initial, intiatory, introductory; fresh, new, unbroached, untapped, untried, unused

mail *n* correspondence, letters, packages, parcels, post; post, postal service, postal system

mail *v* dispatch, forward, post, send, send by post

maim *v* cripple, disable, hamstring, hurt, impair, incapacitate, injure, lame, mangle, mar, mutilate, put out of action, wound

main *adj* capital, cardinal, central, chief, critical, crucial, essential, foremost, head, leading, necessary, outstanding, paramount, particular, predominant, pre-eminent, premier, primary, prime, principle, special, supreme, vital

main *n* cable, channel, conduit, duct, line, pipe

mainly *adv* above all, chiefly, first and foremost, for the most part, generally, in general, in the main, largely, mostly, most of all, on the whole, overall, predominantly, primarily, principally, substantially, to the greatest extent, usually

mainstay *n* anchor, backbone, bulwark, buttress, chief support, linchpin, pillar, prop

maintain *v* care for, carry on, conserve, continue, finance, keep, keep up, look after, nurture, perpetuate, preserve, prolong, provide, retain, supply, support, sustain, take care of, uphold; affirm, allege, assert, asseverate, aver, avow, claim, contend, declare, hold, insist, profess, state; advocate, argue for, back, champion, defend, fight for, justify, plead for, stand by, take up the cudgels for, uphold, vindicate

maintenance *n* care, carrying-on, conservation, continuance, continuation, keeping, nurture, perpetuation, preservation, prolongation, preservation, prolongation, provision, repairs, retainment, supply, support, sustainment, sustention, upkeep; aliment, alimony, allowance, food, keep, livelihood, living subsistence, support, sustenance, upkeep

majestic *adj* august, awesome, dignified, elevated, exalted, grand, grandiose, imperial, imposing, impressive, kingly, lofty, magnificent, monumental, noble, pompous, princely, regal, royal, splendid, stately, sublime, superb

majesty *n* augustness, awesomeness, dignity, exaltedness, glory, grandeur, imposingness, impressiveness, kingliness, loftiness, magnificence, nobility, pomp, queenliness, royalty, splendour, state, stateliness, sublimity

major *adj* better, bigger, chief, elder, greater, higher, larger, leading, main, most, senior, superior, supreme, uppermost

majority *n* best part, bulk, greater number, mass, more, most, plurality, preponderance, superiority; adult hood, manhood, maturity, seniority, womanhood

make *v* assemble, build, compose, constitute, construct, create, fabricate, fashion, forge, from, frame, manufacture, mould, originate, produce, put together, shape, synthesize; accomplish, beget, bring about, cause, create, effect, engender, generate, give rise to, lead to, occasion, produce; cause, co-oerce, compel, constrain, dragoon, drive, force, impel, induce, oblige, press, pressurize, prevail upon, require; appoint, assign, create, designate, elect, install, invest, nominate, ordain; draw up, enact, establish, fix, form, frame, pass; add up to, amount to, compose, constitute, embody form, represent; calculate, estimate gauge, judge, reckon, suppose, think; acquire, clear, earn, gain, get, net, obtain, realize, secure, tale in, win

make *n* brand, build, character, composition, constitution, construction, cut, designation, form, kind, make-up, mark, model, shape, sort, structure, style, type, variety

make-believe *n* charade, dream, fantasy, imagination, play-acting, pretence, unreality

make do *v* cope, get by, improvise, manage, muddle through, scrape along, scrape by

make off *v* abscond, beat a hasty retreat, bolt, clear out, cut and run, decamp, flee, fly, make away, run away, run off, run for it, take to one's heels

make out *v* descry, detect, discern, discover, distinguish, espy, perceive, recognize, see; comprehend, decipher, fathom, follow, grasp, perceive, realize, see, understand, work out; complete, draw up, fill in, fill out, inscribe, write out

maker *n* author, builder, constructor, director, fabricator, framer, manufacturer, producer

makeshift *adj* expedient, make-do, provisional, rough and ready, stopgap, substitute, temporary

makeshift *n* expedient, shift, stop gap, substitute

make-up *n* blusher, cosmetics, eye brow pencil, eye-liner, eye-shadow, foundation, greasepaint, lipstick, lip gloss, maquillage, powder, rouge; (*Inf*) face paint, war paint; arrangement, assembly, composition, con figuration, constitution, construction, form, format, formation, organization, structure; character, disposition, humour, make, mould, nature, personality, stamp, temper, temperament; (*Inf*) what makes someone tick

make up *n* compose, comprise, constitute, form; coin, compose, concoct, construct, create, devise, dream up, fabricate, formulate, frame, hatch, invent, originate, trump up, write; (*Inf*) cook up, complete, fill, meet, supply; bury the hatchet, forgive and forget, make a truce, make peace, mend fences, settle differences, shake hands; concoct, mix, prepare, put together; decide, determine, resolve

maladjusted *adj* alienated, disturbed, estranged, neurotic, unstable

malady *n* affliction, ailment, complaint, disease, disorder, ill, illness, indisposition, infirmity, sickness

male *adj* manful, manlike, manly, masculine, virile

malevolence *n* hate, hatred, ill will, malice, maliciousness, malignity, rancour, spite, spitefulness, vengefulness, vindictiveness

malevolent *adj* baleful, evil-minded, hostile, ill-natured, malignant, pernicious, rancorous, spiteful, vengeful, vicious, vindictive

malfunction *v* break down, develop a fault, fail, go wrong

malfunction *n* breakdown, defect, failure, fault, flaw, glitch, impairment

malice *n* animosity, animus, bad blood, bitterness, enmity, evil intent, hate, hatred, ill will, malevolence, maliciousness, malignity, rancour, spite, spitefulness, spleen, vengefulness, venom, vindictiveness

malicious *adj* baleful, bitter, evil-minded, hateful, ill-disposed, ill-natured, injurious, malevolent, malignment, mischievous, pernicious, rancorous, resentful, spiteful, vengeful, vicious; (*Inf*) bitchy, catty

malign *adj* bad, baleful, baneful, deleterious, destructive, evil, harmful, hostile, hurtful, injurious, malevolent, malignant, pernicious, vicious, wicked

malign *v* abuse, calumniate, defame, denigrate, derogate, disparage, harm, injure, libel, revile, run down, slander, smear, speak ill of, traduce, vilify

malignant *n* baleful, bitter, destructive, evil, harmful, hostile, hurtful, inimical, injurious, malevolent, malicious, malign, pernicious, spiteful, vicious; cancerous, non-benign; deadly, fatal, lethal, life-threatening, uncontrollable, virulent

malpractice *n* abuse, dereliction, misbehaviour, misconduct, mismanagement, negligence

maltreat *v* abuse, bully, damage, harm, hurt, ill-treat, injure, manhandle roughly, mistreat

man *n* gentleman, male; adult, being, body, human, human being, individual, one, person, personage, somebody, soul; *Homo sapiens*, humanity, humankind, human race, mankind, mortals, people; attendant, employee, follower, hand, hireling, manservant, retainer, servant, soldier, subject, subordinate, valet, vassal, worker, workman; (*Inf*) bloke, chap, guy

man *v* crew, fill, furnish with men, garrison, occupy, people staff

manage *v* administer, be in charge of, command, concert, conduct, direct, govern, manipulate, oversee, preside over, rule, run, superintend, supervise; accomplish, arrange, bring about, bring off, contrive, cope with, deal with, effect, engineer, succeed; control, dominate, govern, guide, handle, influence, manipulate, operate, pilot, ply, steer, train, use, wield

manageable *adj* amenable, compliant, controllable, convenient, docile, easy, governable, handy, submissive, tamable, tractable, user-friendly, wieldy

management *n* administration, board, directorate, directors, employers, executives; (*Inf*) bosses

manager *n* administrator, comptroller, conductor, controller, director, executive, governor, head, organizer, overseer, proprietor, superintendent, supervisor; (*Inf*) boss, gaffer

mandatory *adj* binding, compulsory, obligatory, required, requisite

mangle *v* butcher, cripple, crush, cut, deform, destroy, disfigure, distort, hack, lacerate, maim, mar, maul, mutilate, rend, ruin, spoil, tear, wreck

mangy *adj* dirty, filthy, grungy, mean, moth-eaten, scabby, seedy, shabby, shoddy, squalid

manhandle *v* handle roughly, knock about, maul, paw, pull, push, rough up; carry, haul, heave, hump, lift, manoeuvre, pull, push, shove, tug

manhood *n* bravery, courage, determination, firmness, fortitude, hardihood, manfulness, manliness, masculinity, maturity, mettle, resolution, spirit, strength, valour, virility

mania *n* aberration, craziness, delirim, dementia, derangement, disorder, frenzy, insanity, lunacy, madness

maniac *n* lunatic, madman, madwoman, psychopath

manifest *v* demonstrate, exhibit, indicate; confirm, corroborate, establish, substantiate, show, verify

manifest *adj* apparent, clear, conspicuous, distinct, evident, glaring, noticeable, obvious, open, palpable, patent, plain, unmistakable, visible

manifestation *n* appearance, demonstration, disclosure, display, exhibition, exposure, expression, indication, instance, mark, materialization, revelation, show, sign, symptom, token

manifold *adj* abundant, assorted, copius, diverse, diversified, many, multifarious, multifold, multiple, multiplied, multitudinous, numerous, varied, various

manipulate *v* employ, handle, operate, ply, use, wild, work; conduct, control, direct, engineer, guide, influence, manoeuvre, negotiate, steer

mankind *n Homo sapiens*, humanity, humankind, human race, man, people

manly *adj* bold, brave, courageous, daring, dauntless, fearless, gallant, hardy, heroic, macho, male, manful, masculine, muscular, noble, powerful, Ramboesque, resolute, robust, stout-hearted, strapping, strong, valiant, valorous, vigorous, virile, well-built; (*Inf*) butch

man-made *adj* artificial, imitation, manufactured, simulated, synthetic, synthesized; (*Inf*) plastic

manner *n* air, appearance, aspect, bearing, behaviour, comportment, conduct, demeanour, deportment, look, presence, tone; approach, custom, fashion, form, genre, habit, line, means, method, mode, practice, procedure, process, routine, style, tack, tenor, usage, way, wont

mannerism *n* characteristic, foible, habit, idiosyncrasy, peculiarity, quirk, trait, trick

mannerly *adj* civil, civilized, courteous, decorous, genteel, gentle manly, gracious, ladylike, polished, polite, refined, respectful, well-behaved, well-bred, well-mannered

manners *pl n* bearing, behaviour, breeding, carriage, comportment, conduct, demeanour, deportment; ceremony, courtesy, decorum, etiquette, formalities, good form, posh, politeness, politesse, proprieties, protocol, refinement, social graces, the done thing

manoeuvre *n* action, artifice, dodge, intrigue, machination, move, movement, plan, plot, ploy, ruse, scheme, stratagem, subterfuge, tactic, trick

manoeuvre *v* contrive, devise, engineer, intrigue, machinate, manage, manipulate, plan, plot, pull strings, scheme; direct, drive, guide, handle, navigate, negotiate, pilot, steer; deployment, exercise

mansion *n* abode, dwelling, habitation, hall, manor, residence, seat, villa

manual *adj* done by hand, hand-operated, human, physical

manual *n* bible, guide, guidebook, handbook, instructions, workbook

manufacture *v* assemble, build, compose, construct, create, fabricate, forge, form, make, mass-produce, mould, process, produce, put together, shape, turn out

manufacture *n* assembly, construction, creating, fabrication, making, mass-production, produce, production

manure *n* compost, droppings, dung, excrement, fertilizer, guano, muck, ordure

many *adj* abundant, copius, countless, frequent, innumerable, manifold, multifarious, multifold, multitudinous, myriad, numerous, profuse, sundry, varied, various; (*Inf*) umpteen

mar *v* blemish, blight, blot, damage, deface, detract from, disfigure, harm, hurt, impair, injure, maim, mangle, mutilate, ruin, scar, spoil, stain, sully, taint, tarnish, vitiate

march *v* file, footslog pace, parade, stalk, stride, strut, tramp, tread, walk;

march *n* hike, routemarch, tramp, trek, walk; demonstration, parade, procession

margin *n* border, bound, boundary, brim, brink, confine, edge, limit, perimeter, periphery, rim, side, verge; allowance, compass, elbow room, extra, latitude, leeway, play, room, scope, space, surplus

marginal *adj* bordering, borderline, on the edge, peripheral

marine *adj* maritime, nautical, naval, ocean-going, oceanic, pelagic, saltwater, sea, seafaring, seagoing, thalassic

mariner *n* bluejacket, hand, Jack Tar, navigator, sailor, salt, sea dog, seafarer, seafaring man, seaman; (*Inf*) limey, matelot, tar

marital *adj* conjugal, connubial, married, matrimonial, nuptial, spousal, wedded

maritime *adj* marine, nautical, naval, oceanic, sea, seafaring

mark *n* blemish, blot, blotch, bruise, dent, impression, line, nick, pock, scar, spot, stain, streak; badge, blaze, brand, characteristic, device, earmark, emblem, evidence, feature, hallmark, impression, incision, index, indication, label, note, print, proof, seal, sign, stamp, symbol, symptom, token, aim, end, goal, object, objective, purpose, target; footmark, footprint, sign, trace, track, trail, vestige

mark *v* blemish, blot, blotch, brand, bruise, dent, impress, imprint, nick, scar, scratch, smudge, splotch, stain, streak; brand, characterize, identify, label, stamp; attend, mind, note, notice, observe, pay attention, pay heed, regard, remark, watch

marked *adj* apparent, clear, considerable, conspicuous, decided, distinct, evident, manifest, notable, noted, noticeable, obvious, out standing, patent, prominent, pronounced, remarkable, salient, signal, striking

market *n* bazaar, fair, mart
market *v* offer for sale, retail, sell, vend
maroon *v* abandon, cast ashore, cast away, desert, leave, strand; (*Inf*) high and dry
marriage *n* espousal, match, matrimony, nuptials, wedding, wedding ceremony, wedlock; alliance, amalgamation, association, confederation, coupling, link, merger, union
married *adj* joined one, united, wed, wedded; (*Inf*) hitched, spliced; conjugal, connubial, husbandly, marital, matrimonial, nuptial, spoussal, wifely
marrow *n* core, cream, essence, gist, heart, kernel, pith, quick, quintessence, soul, spirit, substance
marry *v* become man and wife, espouse, take to wife, wed; (*Inf*) get hitched, get spliced, take the plunge, tie the knot, walk down the aisle; ally, bond, join, knit, link, match, merge, splice, tie, unify, unite, yoke
marsh *n* bog, fen, morass, moss, quagmire, slough, swamp
marshal *v* align, arrange, array, assemble, collect, deploy, dispose, draw up, gather, group, line up, muster, order, organize, rank
marshy *adj* boggy, fenny, miry, quaggy, spongy, swampy, water logged, wet
marvel *v* be amazed, be awed, be filled with surprise, gape, gaze, goggle at, wonder
marvel *n* amazing, genius, miracle, phenomenon, portent, prodigy, whiz; (*Inf*) wonder
marvellous *adj* amazing, astonishing, astounding, breathtaking, extraordinary, miraculous, phenomenal, prodigious, remarkable, singular, stupendous, wondrous
masculine *adj* male, manful, manly, mannish, virile; bold, brave, gallant, hardy, macho, muscular, powerful, Ramboesque, resolute, robust, stout-hearted, strapping, strong, vigorous, well-built; (*Inf*) butch
mass *n* block, chunk, concretion, hunk, lump, piece; aggregate, body, collection, entirety, sum, sum total, totality, whole; accumulation, aggregation, assemblage, batch, bunch, collection, combination, conglomeration, heap, load, lot, pile, quantity, stack; assemblage, band, body, crowd, group, horde, host, lot, mob, number, throng, troop;(Inf) bunch; body, bulk, greater part, lion's share, majority, preponderance; bulk, dimension, greatness, magnitude, size
mass *adj* extensive, general, indiscriminate, large-scale, pandemic, popular, wholesale, widespread
mass *v* accumulate, amass, assemble, collect, congregate, forgather, gather, mob, muster, rally, swarm, throng
massacre *n* annihilation, blood bath, butchery, carnage, extermina tion, holocaust, killing, mass slaughter, murder, slaughter
massacre *v* annihilate, blow away, butcher, cut to pieces, exterminate, kill, mow down, slaughter, slay, wipe out
massage *n* acupressure, kneading, manipulation, palpation, pummel

ing, rubbing, rub-down; acupressure, aromatherapy, reflexology, shiatsu

massage *v* knead, manipulate, rub, rub down

massive *adj* big, bulky, colossal, enormous, extensive, gargantuan, gigantic, great, heavy, hefty, huge, hulking, immense, imposing, impressive, mammoth, monster, monumental, ponderous, solid, substantial, titanic, vast, weighty; (*Inf*) ginormous, mega, whacking, whopping

master *n* captain, chief, commander, controller, director, employer, governor, head, lord, manager, overlord, overseer, owner, principle, ruler, skipper, superintendent; (*Inf*) big cheese, boss, top dog; adept, doyen, expert, genius, grandmaster, maestro, pastmaster, virtuoso, wizard; (*Inf*) ace, dab hand, pro

master *adj* adept, expert, masterly, proficient, skilful, skilled; (*Inf*) crack

master *v* acquire, become proficient in, grasp, learn; bridle, check, conquer, curb, defeat, overcome, overpower, quash, quell, subdue, subjugate, suppress, tame, triumph over, vanquish; (*Inf*) get clued up on, get the hang of

masterful *adj* adept, adroit, clever, consummate, deft, dexterous, excellent, expert, exquisite, fine, finished, first-rate, masterly, skilful, skilled, superior, superlative, supreme; (*Inf*) crack; arrogant, authoritative, despotic, dictatorial, domineering, high-handed, imperious, magisterial, peremptory, self-willed, tyrannical; (*Inf*) bossy

masterly *adj* adept, adroit, clever, consummate, dexterous, excellent, expert, exquisite, fine, finished, first-rate, masterful, skilful, skilled, superior, superlative, supreme; (*Inf*) crack

masterpiece *n chef d'oeuvre*, classic, creation, jewel, *magnum opus*, master work, *pièce de résistance, tour de force*

mastery *n* command, comprehension, familiarity, grasp, knowledge, understanding; ability, acquirement, attainment, cleverness, deftness, dexterity, expertise, finesse, proficiency, prowess, skill, virtuosity; (*Inf*) know-how

match *n* bout, competition, contest, game, test, trial; competitor, counterpart, equal, equivalent, peer, rival; copy, double, duplicate, equal, lookalike, replica, twin; affiliation, alliance, combination, couple, duet, marriage, pair, pairing, partnership, union; (*Inf*) dead ringer, item, spitting image

match *v* ally, combine, couple, join, link, marry, mate, pair, unite, yoke; accompany, accord, adapt, agree, blend, coordinate, correspond, fit, go with; compare, compete, contend, emulate, equal, measure up to, oppose, pit against, rival, vie

matching *adj* analogous, comparable, coordinating, corresponding, double, duplicate, equal, equivalent, identical, like, paired, parallel, same, toning, twin

matchless *adj* consummate, exquisite, incomparable, inimitable, peerless, perfect, superlative, supreme, unequalled, unique, unmatched, unparalleled, unrivalled, unsurpassed

mate *n* better half, husband, partner, spouse, wife; comrade, crony, friend; (*Inf*) buddy, china, chum, pal; assistant, helper, subordinate

mate *v* breed, copulate, couple, pair; marry, match, wed; couple, join, match, pair, yoke

material *n* body, constituents, element, matter, stuff, substance; data, evidence, facts, information, notes, work; cloth, fabric, stuff

material *adj* bodily, concrete, corporeal, fleshly, nonspiritual, palpable, physical, substantial, tangible, worldly; consequential, essential, grave, important, indispensable, serious, significant, vital, weighty

materialize *v* appear, come about, come into being, come to pass, happen, occur, take place, take shape, turn up

matrimonial *adj* conjugal, connubial, hymeneal, marital, married, nuptial, spousal, wedded, wedding

matrimony *n* marital rites, marriage, nuptials, wedding ceremony, wedlock

matter *n* body, material, stuff, substance; affair, business, concern, episode, event, incident, issue, occurrence, proceeding, question, situation, subject, thing, topic, transaction; consequence, import, importance, moment, note, significance, weight

matter *v* be important, be of consequence, carry weight, count, have influence, make a difference, mean something, signify

matter-of-fact *v* deadpan, down-to-earth, dry, dull, emotionless, flat, lifeless, mundane, plain, prosaic, sober, unembellished, unimaginative, unsentimental, unvarnished

mature *adj* adult, complete, fit, full-blown, full-grown, fully-fledged, grown, grown-up, matured, mellow, of age, perfect, prepared, ready, ripe, ripened, seasoned

mature *v* age, become adult; bloom, come of age, develop, grow up, maturate, mellow, perfect, reach adulthood, ripen, season

maturity *n* adulthood, completion, experience, full bloom, full growth, fullness, majority, manhood, maturation, matureness, perfection, ripeness, wisdom, womanhood

maul *v* abuse, handle roughly, ill-treat, manhandle, molest, paw; batter, beat, claw, knock about, lacerate, mangle, pummel, rough up, thrash; (*Inf*) beat up

maxim *n* adage, aphorism, apophthegm, axiom, byword, gnome, motto, proverb, rule, saw, saying

maximum *n* apogee, ceiling, crest, extremity, height, mot, peak, pinnacle, summit, top, upper limit, utmost, uttermost, zenith

maximum *adj* greatest, highest, maximal, most, paramount, supreme, topmost, utmost

maybe *adv* it could be, perhaps, possibly

mayhem *n* chaos, commotion, confusion, destruction, disorder, fracas, havoc, trouble, violence

maze *n* convolutions, intricacy, labyrinth, meander; bewilderment, confusion, imbroglio, mesh, perplexity, puzzle, snarl, tangle, uncertainty, web

meadow *n* field, grassland, ley, pasture

meagre *adj* deficient, exiguous, inadequate, insubstantial, little, paltry, poor, puny, scanty, scrimpy, short, skimpy, slender, slight, small, spare, sparse

mean *v* betoken, connote, convey, denote, drive at, express, hint at, imply, indicate, purport, represent, say. signify, spell, stand for, suggest, symbolize; aim, aspire, contemplate, design, desire, have in mind, intend, plan, propose, purpose, set out, want, wish

mean *adj* beggarly, close, mercenary, miserly, niggardly, parsimonious, penny-pinching, penurious, selfish stingy, tight, tight-fisted, ungenerous; (*Inf*) mingy; abject, base, callous, contemptible, degenerate, degraded, despicable, disgraceful, dishonourable, hard-hearted, ignoble, low-minded, narrow-minded, petty, scurvy, shabby, shameful, sordid, vile, wretched; beggarly, down-at-heel, grungy, insignificant, miserable, paltry, petty, poor, run-down, scruffy, seedy. shabby, sordid, squalid, tawdry, wretched; (*Inf*) near

mean *n* average, balance, compromise, happy medium, median, middle, middle course,midway, mid-point, norm

mean *adj* average, intermediate, medial, median, medium, middle, middling, normal, standard

meander *v* ramble, snake, stray, stroll, turn, wander, wind, zigzag

meander *n* bend, coil, curve, loop, turn, twist, zigzag

meaning *n* connotation, denotation, drift, explanation, gist, implication, import, interpretation, message, purpot, sense, signification, substance, upshot, value; aim, design, end, goal, idea, intention, object, plan, point, purpose, trend; effect, efficacy, force, point, thrust, use, usefulness, validity, value, worth

meaningful *adj* important, material, purposeful, relevant, serious, significant, useful, valid, worthwhile; eloquent, expressive, meaning, pointed, pregnant, speaking, suggestive

meaningless *adj* aimless, empty, futile, hollow, inane, inconsequential, insignificant, insubstantial, nonsensical, nugatory, pointless, purposeless, senseless, trifling, trivial, useless, vain, valueless, worthless

means *pl n* agency, avenue, channel, course, expedient, instruction, measure, medium, method, mode, process, way; affluence, capital, estate, fortune, funds, income, money, property, resources, riches, substance, wealth, wherewithal

measurable *adj* assessable, computable, determinable, gaugeable, material, mensurable, perceptible, quantifiable, quantitative, significant

measure *n* allotment, allowance, amount, amplitude, capacity, degree, extent, magnitude, portion, proportion, quantity, quota, range, ration, reach, scope, share, size; gauge, metre, rule, scale, yardstick;

method, standard, system; criterion, example, model, norm, standard, system; criterion, example, model, norm, standard, test, touchstone, yardstick; act, action, course, deed, expedient, manoeuvre, means, procedure, proceeding, step; act, bill, enactment, law, resolution, statute; beat, cadence, foot, metre, rhythm, verse

measure *v* appraise, assess, calculate, calibrate, compute, determine, estimate, evaluate, gauge, judge, mark out, quantify, rate, size, sound, survey, value, weigh

measurement *n* appraisal, assessment, calculation, calibration, computation, estimation, evaluation, judgement, mensuration, metage, survey, valuation

measure up to *v* be adequate, be capable, be equal to, be fit, be suitable, be suited, come up to standard, compare, equal, fit or fill the bill, fulfil the expectations, match, meet, rival; (*Inf*) come up to scratch, cut the mustard, make the grade

mechanical *adj* automated, automatic, machine-driven; automatic, cold, cursory, dead, emotionless, habitual, impersonal, instinctive, involuntary, lacklustre, lifeless, machine-like, matter-of-fact, perfunctionory, routine, spiritless, unconscious, unfeeling, unthinking

mechanism *n* apparatus, appliance, contrivance, device, instrument, machine, structure, system, tool; agency, execution, functioning, means, medium, method, operation, performance, procedure, process, system, technique, workings

meddle *v* butt in, interfere, intermeddle, interpose, intervene, intrude, pry, put one's oar in, tamper; (*Inf*) stick one's nose in

mediate *v* act as middleman, arbitrate, bring to an agreement, bring to terms, conciliate, intercede, interpose, intervene, make peace between, moderate, reconcile, referee, resolve, restore, harmony, settle, umpire; (*Inf*) step in

medicine *n* cure, drug, medicament, medication, physic, remedy

medieval *adj* antiquated, antique, archaic, old fashioned, primitive, unenlightened

mediocre *adj* average, common place, indifferent, inferior, insignificant, mean, medium, middling, ordinary, passable, pedestrian, run-of-the-mill, second-rate, tolerable, undistinguished, uninspired; (*Inf*) fair to middling, so-so

meditate *v* be in a brown study, cogitate, consider, contemplate, deliberate, muse, ponder, reflect, ruminate, study, think

medium *adj* average, fair, intermediate, mean, medial, median, mediocre, middle, middling, midway

medium *n* average, centre, compromise, mean, middle, middle course, middle ground, middle path, middle way, midpoint; agency, avenue, channel, form, instrument, means, mode, organ, vehicle, way

medley *n* assortment, confusion, farrago, gallimaufry, hodgepodge, hotchpotch, jumble, *mélange,* miscellany, mishmash, mixture, olio, pastiche, patchwork, potpourri, salmagundi; (*Inf*) mixed bag, omnium-gatherum

meek *adj* deferential, docile, forbearing, gentle, humble, long-suffering, mild, modest, patient, peaceful, soft, submissive, unassuming, unpretentious, yielding; acquiescent, compliant, resigned, spineless, spiritless, tame, timid, unresisting, weak; (*Inf*) weak-kneed, wimpish, wimpy

meet *v* bump into, chance on, come across, confront, contact, encounter, find, happen on, run across, run into; abut, adjoin, come together, connect, converge, cross, intersect, join, link, touch, unite; answer, carry out, come up to, comply, cope with, discharge, equal, fulfil, gratify, handle, match, measure up, perform, satisfy; assemble, collect, come together, congregate, convene, forgather, gather, muster, rally

meeting *n* assignation, confrontation, encounter, engagement, introduction, rendezvous, tryst; assemble, audience, company, conclave, conference, congregation, convention, convocation, gathering, meet, powwow, rally, reunion, session; (*Inf*) get-together; concourse, confluence, conjunction, convergence, crossing, intersection, junction, union

melancholy *n* blues, dejection, depression, despondency, gloom, gloominess, low spirits, misery, pensiveness, sadness, sorrow, unhappiness, woe

melancholy *adj* blue, dejected, depressed, despondent, disconsolate, dismal, dispirited, doleful, down, downcast, downhearted, gloom, glum, heavy-hearted, joyless, low, low-spirited, lugubrious, melancholic, miserable, moody, mournful, pensive, sad, sombre, sorrowful, unhappy, woebegone, woeful; (*Inf*) down in the dumps, down in the mouth

mellow *adj* delicate, full-flavoured, juicy, mature, perfect, rich, ripe, soft, sweet, well-matured; dulcet, full, mellifluous, melodious, rich, rounded, smoothe, sweet, tuneful, well-tuned; cheerful, cordial, elevated, expansive, genial, half-tipsy, happy, jolly, jovial, merry relaxed

mellow *v* develop, improve, mature, perfect, ripen, season, soften, sweeten

melodious *adj* concordant, dulcet, euphonious, harmonious, melodic, musical, silvery, sweet-sounding, sweet-toned, tuneful

melodramatic *adj* blood-and-thunder, extravagant, histrionic, over-dramatic, over-emotional, sensational, stagy, theatrical; (*Inf*) hammy

melody *n* air, descant, music, refrain, song, strain, theme, tune

melt *v* deliquesce, diffuse, dissolve, flux, fuse, liquefy, soften, thaw; disarm, mollify, relax, soften, touch

member *n* associate, fellow, representative; appendage, arm, component, constituent, element, extremity, leg, limb, organ, part, portion

memoir *n* account, biography, essay, journal, life, monograph, narrative, record, record, register

memoirs *pl n* autobiography, diary, experiences, journals, life, life story, memories, recollections, reminiscences

memorable *adj* catchy, celebrated, distinguished, extraordinary, famous, historic, illustrious, important, impressive, momentous, notable, noteworthy, remarkable, signal, significant, striking, unforgettable

memorial *adj* commemorative, monumental

memorial *n* cairn, memento, monument, plaque, record, remembrance, souvenir

memorize *v* commit to memory, get by heart, learn, learn by heart, learn by rote, remember

memory *n* recall, recollection, remembrance, reminiscence, retention; commemoration, honour, remembrance

menace *v* alarm, bode ill, browbeat, bully, frighten, impend, intimidate, loom, lour, lower, terrorize, threaten, utter threats to

menace *n* commination, intimidation, scare, threat, warning; danger, hazard, jeopardy, peril

menacing *adj* alarming, dangerous, frightening, intimidating, intimidatory, looming, louring, lowering, minacious, minatory, ominous, threatening

mend *v* cure, darn, fix, heal, patch, rectify, refit, reform, remedy, renew, renovate, repair, restore, retouch; ameliorate, amend, better, correct, emend, improve, rectify, reform, revise

mend *n* darn, patch, repair, stitch

menial *adj* boring, dull, humdrum, low-status, routine, unskilled

mental *adj* cerebral, intellectual

mentality *n* brainpower, brains, comprehension, intellect, intelligence quotient, IQ, mental age, mind, rationality, understanding, wit; attitude, cast of mind, character, disposition, frame of mind, make-up, outlook, personality, psychology, turn of mind, way of thinking; (*Inf*) grey matter

mentally *adv* in one's head, intellectually, in the mind, inwardly, psychologically, rationally, subjectively

mention *v* acknowledge, adduce, allude to, bring up, broach, call attention to, cite, communicate, declare, disclose, divulge, hint at, impart, intimate, make known, name, point out, recount, refer to, report, reveal, speak about, speak of, state, tell, touch upon

mention *n* acknowledgment, citation, recognition, tribute; allusion, announcement, indication, notification, observation, reference, remark

mercenary *adj* acquisitive, avaricious, bribable, covetous, grasping, greedy, sordid, venal; bought, hired, paid, venal; (*Inf*) money-grabbing

mercenary *n* *condottiere,* freelance, hired soldier, soldier of fortune

merchandise *n* commodities, goods, produce, products, staples, stock, stock in trade, truck, vendibles, wares

merchant *n* broker, dealer, distributor, retailer, salesman, seller, shopkeeper, trader, tradesman, trafficker, vendor, wholesaler

merciful *adj* beneficent, benignant, clement, compassionate, forbearing, forgiving, generous, gracious, humane, kind, lenient, liberal, mild, pitying, soft, sparing, sympathetic, tender-hearted

merciless barbarous, callous, cruel, hard, hard-hearted, harsh, heartless, implacable, inexorable, inhumane, pitiless, relentless, ruthless, severe, unappeasable, unfeeling, unforgiving, unmerciful, unpitying, unsparing, unsympathetic

mercy *n* benevolence, charity, clemency, compassion, favour, forbearance, forgiveness, grace, kindness, leniency, pity, quarter; blessing, boon, godsend, piece of luck, relief

mere *adj* absolute, bare, common, complete, entire, nothing more than, plain, pure, pure and simple, sheer, simple, stark, unadulterated, unmitigated, unmixed, utter

merge *v* amalgamate, be swallowed up by, become lost in, blend, coalesce, combine, consolidate, converge, fuse, incorporate, intermix, join, meet, met, melt into, mingle, mix, tone with, unite

merger *n* amalgamation, coalition, combination, consolidation, fusion, incorporation, union

merit *n* advantage, asset, excellence, good, goodness, integrity, quality, strong point, talent, value, virtue, worth, worthiness; claim, credit, desert, due, right

merit *v* be entitled to, be worthy of, deserve, earn, have a claim to, have a right to, have coming to one, incur, rate, warrant

merriment *n* amusement, conviviality, festivity, frolic, fun, gaiety, glee, hilarity, jocularity, jollity, joviality, laughter, levity, liveliness, merry-making, mirth, revelry, sport

merry *adj* blithe, blithesome, carefree, cheerful, convivial, festive, frolicsome, fun-loving, gay, glad, gleeful, happy, jocund, jolly, joyful, joyous, light-hearted, mirthful, rollicking, sportive, vivacious; amusing, comic, comical, facetious, funny, hilarious, humorous, jocular, mirthful

mesh *n* net, netting, network, plexus, reticulation, tracery, web; entanglement, snare, tangle, toils, trap, web

mesh *v* catch, enmesh, ensnare, entangle, net, snare, tangle, trap; combine, come together, connect, coordinate, dovetail, engage, fit together, harmonize, interlock, knit

mess *n* botch, chaos, clutter, confusion, dirtiness, disarray, disorder, disorganization, jumble, litter, mishmash, shambles, turmoil, untidiness; (*Inf*) hash; difficulty, dilemma, imbroglio, mix-up, muddle, perplexity, plight, predicament; (*Inf*) fine kettle of fish, fix, jam, pickle, stew

mess *v* befoul, besmirch, botch, bungle, clutter, dirty, disarrange, dishevel, foul, litter, muddle, pol lute, scramble; (*Inf*) make a hash of, muck up

message *n* bulletin, communication, communiqué, dispatch, intimation, letter, memorandum, missive, note, notice, tidings, word; idea, import, meaning, moral, point, purport, theme

messenger *n* agent, bearer, carrier, courier, delivery boy, emissary, envoy, errand-boy, go-between, harbinger, herald, runner

messy *adj* chaotic, cluttered, confused, dirty, dishevelled, disordered, disorganized, grubby, littered, muddled, shambolic, sloppy, slovenly, unkempt, untidy

metaphor *n* allegory, analogy, emblem, figure of speech, image, symbol, trope

method *n* approach, arrangement, course, fashion, form, manner, mode, modus, operandi, plan, practice, procedure, process, programme, routine, rule, scheme, style, system, technique, way; design, form, order, orderness, organization, pattern, planning, purpose, regularity, structure. system

methodical *adj* businesslike, deliberate, disciplined, efficient, meticulous, neat, ordered, orderly, organized, painstaking, planned, precise, regular, structured, systematic, tidy, well-regulated

meticulous *adj* details, exact, fastidious, fussy, microscopic, painstaking, particular, perfectionist, precise, punctilious, scrupulous, strict, thorough

microscopic *adj* imperceptible, infinitesimal, invisible, minuscule, minute, negligible, tiny

midday *n* noon, noonday, noontide, noontime, twelve noon, twelve o'clock

middle *adj* central, halfway, inner, inside, intermediate, intervening, mean, medial, median, medium, mid

middle *n* centre, focus, halfway point, heart, inside, mean, midpoint, midsection, midst, thick

middling *adj* adequate, all right, average, fair, indifferent, mediocre, medium, moderate, modest, OK, okay, ordinary, passable, run-of-the-mill, tolerable, unexceptional, unremarkable; (*Inf*) so-so

midget *n* dwarf, gnome, homuncule, homunculus, manikin, pygmy, Tom Thumb; (*Inf*) shrimp

midst *n* bosom, centre, core, depths, heart, hub, interior, middle, nucleus, thick

might *n* ability, capability, capacity, efficacy, efficiency, energy, force, potency, power, prowess, puissance, strength, sway, valour, vigour; (*Inf*) clout

mighty *adj* doughty, forceful, hardy, indomitable, lusty, manful, potent, powerful, puissant, Ramboesque, robust, stalwart, stout, strapping, strong, sturdy, vigorous

migrant *n* drifter, emigrant, gypsy, immigrant, itinerant, nomad, rover, tinker, transient, traveller, vagrant, wanderer

migrate *v* drift, emigrate, journey, move, roam, rove, shift, travel, trek, voyage, wander

migration *adj* emigration, journey, movement, roving, shift, travel, trek, voyage, wandering

migratory *adj* gypsy, itinerant, migrant, nomadic, peripatetic, roving, shifting, transient, travelling, unsettled, vagrant, wandering

mild *adj* amiable, balmy, bland, calm, clement, compassionate, docile, easy, easy-going, equable, forbearing, forgiving, gentle, indulgent, kind, meek, mellow, merciful, moderate, pacific, peaceable, placid, pleasant, serene, smooth, soft, temperate, tender, tranquil, warm

mildness *n* blandness, calmness, clemency, docility, forbearance, gentleness, indulgence, kindness, leniency, lenity, meekness, mellowness, moderation, placidity, smoothness, softness, temperateness, tenderness, tranquillity, warmth

militant *adj* active, aggressive, assertive, combative, Ramboesque, vigorous; belligerent, combating, contending, embattled, fighting, in arms, warring

military *adj* armed, martial, soldierlike, soldierly, warlike

military *n* armed forces, army, forces, services

mill *n* factory, foundry, plant, shop, works; crusher, grinder

mime *n* dumb show, gesture, mummery, pantomime

mime *v* act out, gesture, pantomime, represent, simulate

mimic *v* ape, caricature, imitate, impersonate, parody; (*Inf*) take off

mimic *n* caricaturist, copycat, imitator, impersonator, impressionist, parodist, parrot

mind *n* intellect, intelligence, mentality, ratiocination, reason, sense, spirit, understanding, wits; memory, recollection, remembrance; (*Inf*) brains, grey matter; brain, head, imagination, psyche; bent, desire, disposition, fancy, inclination, intention, leaning, notion, purpose, tendency, urge, will, wish; attention, concentration, thinking, urge, will, wish; attention, concentration, thinking, thoughts; **make up one's mind** choose, come to a decision, decide, determine, reach a decision, resolve; **bear in mind** be cognizant of, be mindful of, remember, take note of **mind**

mind *v* be affronted, be bothered, care, disapprove, dislike, look askance at, object, resent, take offense; adhere to, attend, comply with, follow, heed, listen to, mark, note, notice, obey, observe, pay attention, pay heed to, regard, respect, take heed, watch; be sure, ensure, make certain; attend to, guard, have charge of, keep an eye on, look after, take care of, tend watch

mindful *adj* alert, alive to, attentive, ware, careful, chary, cognizant, conscious, heedful, regardful, respectful, sensible, thoughtful, wary, watchful

mine *n* coalfield, colliery, deposit, excavation, lode, pit, shaft, vein; abundance, fund, hoard, reserve, source, stock, store, supply, treasury, wealth

mine *v* delve, dig for, dig up, excavate, extract, hew, quarry, unearth

mingle *v* alloy, amalgamate, blend, coalesce, combine, commingle, compound, fuse, intermingle, intermix, interweave, join, marry, merge, mix, unite; associate with, circulate, consort, fraternize, hang about, hang around, hobnob, socialize

miniature *adj* baby, diminutive, dwarf, Lilliputian, little, midget, mini, minuscule, minute, pocket, pygmy, reduced, scaled-down, small, tiny, toy, wee

minimal *adj* least, least possible, littlest, minimum, nominal, slightest, smallest, token

minimize *v* abbreviate, attenuate, curtail, decrease, diminish, miniaturize, prune, reduce, shrink; belittle, decry, deprecate, depreciate, discount, disparage, make light, make little of, play down, underes timate, underrate

minimum *n* bottom, depth, least, lowest, nadir, slightest

minimum *adj* least, least possible, littlest, lowest, minimal, slightest, smallest

minister *n* chaplain, churchman, clergyman, cleric, divine, ecclesiastic, padre, parson, pastor, preacher, priest, rector, vicar; administrator, ambassador, cabinet member, delegate, diplomat, envoy, executive, office-holder, official, plenipotentiary

minister *v* accommodate, administer, answer, attend, be solicitous of, cater to, pander to, serve, take care of, tend

ministry *n* administration, cabinet, council, government, holy orders, the church, the priesthood, the pulpit

minor *adj* inconsequential, inconsiderable, inferior, insignificant, junior, lesser, light, negligible, paltry, petty, secondary, slight, small. smaller, subordinate, trifling, trivial, unimportant

mint *adj* brand-new, excellent, first-class, fresh, perfect, unblemished, undamaged, untarnished

mint *v* cast, coin, make, produce, punch, stamp, strike

minute *n* flash, instant, moment, second; (*Inf*) jiffy, shake, tick, trice

minute *adj* diminutive, fine, infinitesimal, Lilliputian, little, microscopic, miniature, minuscule, slender, small, tiny

minutes *pl n* memorandum, notes, proceedings, record, transactions, transcript

minx *n* coquette, flirt, hoyden, hussy, jade, tomboy, wanton

miracle *n* marvel, phenomenon, prodigy, thaumaturgy, wonder

miraculous *adj* amazing, astonishing, astounding, extraordinary, incredible, inexplicable, magical, marvellous, phenomenal, preternatural, prodigious, superhuman, supernatural, thaumaturgic, unaccountable, unbelievable, wonderful, wondrous

mirage *n* hallucination, illusion, optical, illusion, phantasm

mire *n* bog, marsh, morass, quagmire, swamp

mirror *n* glass, looking-glass, reflector, speculum; copy, double, image, likeness, reflection, replica, representation, twin

mirror *v* copy, depict, echo, emulate, follow, reflect, represent, show

mirth *n* amusement, cheerfulness, festivity, frolic, fun, gaiety, gladness, glee, hilarity, jocularity, jollity, joviality, joyousness, laughter, levity, merriment, merrymaking, pleasure, rejoicing, revelry, sport

misappropriate *v* embezzle, misapply, misspend, misuse, peculate, pocket, steal, swindle, thieve; misapply, misuse

misbehaviour *n* bad behaviour, impropriety, incivility, indiscipline, insubordination, mischief, misconduct, misdeeds, misdemeanour, naughtiness, rudeness; (*Inf*) acting up, carrying on, monkey business

miscalculate *v* blunder, calculate wrongly, err, go wrong, make a mistake, misjudge, overestimate, overrate, slip up, underestimate, underrate

miscellaneous *adj* assorted, confused, diverse, diversified, farraginous, heterogenous, indiscriminate, jumbled, many, mingles, mixed, motley, multifarious, multiform, promiscuous, sundry, varied, various

mischance *n* accident, bad luck, calamity, contretemps, disaster, ill chance, ill fortune, ill luck, infelicity, misadventure, misfortune, mishap; (*Inf*) bad break

mischief *n* devilment, impishness, misbehaviour, naughtiness, pranks, roguery, roguishness, trouble, way wardness; (*Inf*) monkey business, shenanigans; damage, detriment, disadvantage, disruption, evil, harm, hurt, injury, misfortune, trouble

mischievous *adj* arch, bad, badly behaved, exasperating, frolicsome, impish, naughty, playful, puckish, rascally, roguish, sportive, teasing, troublesome, vexatious, wayward; bad, damaging, deleterious, destructive, detrimental, evil, harmful, hurtful, injurious, malicious, malignant, pernicious, sinful, spiteful, troublesome, vicious, wicked

misconception *n* delusion, error, fallacy, misapprehension, misconstruction, mistaken belief, misunderstanding, wrong idea; (*Inf*) wrong end of the stick

misconduct *n* delinquency, dereliction, immorality, impropriety, malpractice, misbehaviour, misdemeanor, mismanagement, naughtiness, rudeness, transgression, unethical behaviour, wrong doing

misdemeanour *n* fault, infringe ment, misbehaviour, misconduct, misdeed, offense, peccadillo, transgression, trespass

miser *n* churl, curmudgeon, niggard, penny-pincher, Scrooge, skinflint; (*Inf*) cheapskate, screw

miserable *adj* afflicted, brokenhearted, crestfallen, dejected, depressed, desolate, despondent, disconsolate, distressed, doleful, down, downcast, forlorn, gloomy, heartbroken, melancholy, mournful, sorrowful, unhappy, woebegone, wretched; (*Inf*) down in the mouth; destitute, impoverished, indigent, meagre, needy, penniless, poor, poverty-stricken, scanty; abject, bad, contemptible, deplorable, despicable, detestable, disgraceful, lamentable, low, mean, pathetic, piteous, pitiable, scurvy, shabby, shameful, sordid, sorry, squalid, vile, worthless, wretched

miserly *adj* avaricious, beggarly, close, close-fisted, covetous, grasping, illiberal, mean, near, niggardly, parsimonious, penny-pinching, penurious, sordid, stingy, tight-fisted, ungenerous

misery *n* agony, anguish, depression, desolation, despair, discomfort, distress, gloom, grief, hardship, melancholy, sadness, sorrow, suffering, torment, torture, unhappiness, woe, wretchedness; affliction, bitter pill, burden, calamity, catastrophe, curse, disaster, load, misfortune, ordeal, sorrow, trial, tribulation, trouble, woe

misfire *v* fail, fail to go off, fall through, go wrong, miscarry; (*Inf*) bite the dust, go phut, go up in smoke

misfit *n* eccentric, fish out of water, nonconformist, square peg in a round hole; (*Inf*) oddball, weirdo

misfortune *n* bad luck, evil fortune, hard luck, ill luck, infelicity; accident, adversity, affliction, blow, calamity, disaster, evil chance, failure, hardship, harm, loss, misadventure, mischance, misery, mishap, reverse, setback, stroke of bad luck, tragedy, trial, tribulation, trouble

misgiving *n* anxiety, apprehension, distrust, doubt, hesitation, qualm, reservation, scruple, suspicion, uncertainty. unease, worry

misguided *adj* deluded, erroneous, foolish, ill-advised, imprudent, injudicious, labouring under a delusion *or* misapprehension, misled, misplaced, mistaken, uncalled-for, unreasonable, unwarranted, unwise

mishandle *v* botch, bungle, make a mess of, misdirect, misgovern, mismanage, muff; (*Inf*) foul up, make a hash of, make a pig's ear of, mess up, screw up

mishap *n* accident, adversity, bad luck, calamity, contretemps, disaster, evil chance, evil fortune, hard luck, ill fortune, ill luck, infelicity, misadventure, mischance, misfortune

misinform *v* deceive, give someone wrong information, misdirect, misguide, mislead; (*Inf*) give some one a bum steer

misinterpret *v* distort, falsify, get wrong, misapprehend, misconceive, misconstrue, misjudge, misread, misrepresent, mistake, misunderstand, pervert

mislead *n* beguile, bluff, deceive, delude, fool, hoodwink, lead astray, misdirect, misguide, misinform, pull the wool over someone's eyes; (*Inf*) lead up the garden path, take for a ride

misleading *adj* ambiguous, casuistical, confusing, deceitful, deceptive, delusive, delusory, disingenuous, evasive, false, illusory, sophistical, specious, spurious, unstraightforward; (*Inf*) tricky

mismanage *v* be incompetent, be inefficient, botch, bungle, make a mess of, maladminister, mess up, misconduct, misdirect, misgovern, mishandle; (*Inf*) make a hash of

misquote *v* distort, falsify, garble, mangle, misreport, misrepresent, misstate, muddle, pervert, quote out of context, take out of context, twist

misrepresent *v* belie, disguise, distort, falsify, garble. misinterpret, misstate, pervert, twist

misrule *n* bad government, maladministration, misgovernment, mismanagement; anarchy, chaos, confusion, disorder, lawlessness, tumult, turmoil

miss *v* avoid, be late for, blunder, err, escape, evade, fail, fail to grasp, fail to notice, forego, lack, leave out, let go, let slip, lose, miscarry, mistake, omit, overlook, pass over, pass up, skip, slip, trip; feel the loss of, hunger for, long for, need, pine for, want, wish, yearn for

miss *n* blunder, error, failure, fault, loss, mistake, omission, oversight, want; damsel, girl, lass, maid, maiden, schoolgirl, spinster, young lady

misshapen *adj* contorted, crippled, crooked, deformed, distorted, grotesque, ill-made, ill-proportioned malformed, twisted, ugly, ungainly, unshapely, unsightly, warped, wry

missile *n* projectile, rocket, weapon

missing *adj* absent, astray, gone, lacking, left behind, left out, lost, mislaid, misplaced, not present, nowhere to be found, unaccounted for, wanting

mission *n* aim, assignment, business, calling, charge, commission, duty, errand, goal, job, office, operation, purpose, pursuit, quest, task, trust, undertaking, vocation, work; commission, delegation, deputation, embassy, legation, ministry, task force

missionary *n* apostle, converter, evangelist, preacher, propagandist, proselytizer

mist *n* cloud, condensation, dew, drizzle, film, fog, haar, haze, smog, smur, spray, steam, vapour

mistake *n* blunder, erratum, error, error of judgement, false move, fault, faux pas, gaffe, inaccuracy, miscalculation, misconception, misstep, misunderstanding, oversight, slip, solecism, misconceive, misconstrue, misinterpret, misjudge, misread, misunderstand; (*Inf*) bloomer, boob, boo-boo, clanger, goof, howler, slip up

mistaken *adj* erroneous, fallacious, false, faulty, inaccurate, inappropriate, incorrect, in the wrong, labouring under a misapprehension, misguided, misinformed, misled, off target, off the mark, unfounded, unsound, wide off the mark, wrong; (*Inf*) barking up the wrong tree

mistress *v* concubine, girlfriend, inamorata, kept woman, lady-love, live-in lover, lover, paramour, partner; (*Inf*) fancy woman, floozy

mistrust *v* apprehend, beware, be wary of, distrust, doubt, fear, have doubts about, suspect

mistrust *n* apprehension, distrust, doubt, dubiety, fear, misgiving, scepticism, suspicion, uncertainty, wariness

misty *adj* bleary, blurred, cloudy, dark, dim, foggy, fuzzy, hazy, indistinct, murky, nebulous, obscure, opaque, overcast, unclear, vague

misunderstand *v* get the wrong idea about, misapprehend, misconceive, misconstrue, mishear, misinterpret, misjudge, missread, miss- the point of, mistake; the wrong end of the stick

misunderstanding *n* error, false

impression, misapprehension, misconception, misconstruction, misinterpretation, misjudgment, misreading, mistake, mix-up, wrong-idea

misuse *n* abuse, barbarism, corruption, desecration, dissipa tion, malapropism, misapplication, misemployment, misusage, perversion, profanation, solecism, squandering, waste

misuse *v* abuse, corrupt, desecrate, dissipate, misapply, misemploy, pervert, profane, prostitute, squander, waste

mitigate *v* abate, allay, appease, assuage, blunt, calm, check, diminish, dull, ease. extenuate, lessen, lighten, moderate, modify, mollify, pacify, palliate, placate, quiet, reduce the force of, remit, soften, soothe, subdue, take the edge off, temper, tone down, tranquillize, weaken

mix *v* alloy, amalgamate, associate, blend, coalesce, combine, commingle, commix, compound, cross, fuse, incorporate, intermingle, interweave, join, jumble, merge, mingle, put together, unite; associate, come together, consort, fraternize, hob nob, join, mingle, socialize; (*Inf*) hang out

mixed *adj* alloyed, amalgamated, blended, combined, composite, compound, fused, incorporated, joint, mingled, united; assorted, cosmopolitan, diverse, diversified, heterogeneous, miscellaneous, motley, varied; ambivalent, equivocal, indecisive, uncertain

mixture *n* admixture, alloy, amalgam, amalgamation, association, assortment, blend, brew, combine, composite, compound, concoction, conglomeration, cross, fusion, hotchpotch, jumble, medley, *mélange,* miscellany, mix, potpourri, salmagundi, union, variety

mix-up *n* confusion, disorder, jumble, mess, mistake, misunderstanding, muddle, snarl-up, tangle

moan *n* groan, lament, lamentation, sigh, sob, sough, wail, whine

moan *v* bemoan, bewail, deplore, grieve, groan, keen, lament, mourn, sigh, sob, sough, whine

mob *n* assemblage, body, collection, crowd, drove, flock, gang, gathering, herd, horde, host, mass, multitude, pack, press, swarm, throng

mob *v* crowd around, jostle, overrun, set upon, surround, swarm around

mobile *adj* ambulatory, itinerant, locomotive, migrant, motile, movable, moving, peripatetic, portable, travelling, wandering; animated, changeable, ever-changing, expressive

mobilize *v* activate, animate, call to arms, call up, get or make ready, marshal, muster, organize, prepare, put in motion, rally, ready

mock *v* chaff, deride, flout, insult, jeer, laugh at, laugh to scorn, make fun of, poke fun at, ridicule, scoff, scorn, show contempt for, sneer, taunt, tease; (*Inf*) take the mickey out of

mock *n* banter, derision, gibe, jeer ing, mockery, ridicule, scorn, sneer, sneering; counterfeit, fake, forgery, fraud, imitation, phoney, sham

mock *adj* artificial, bogus, counterfeit, dummy, ersatz, fake, faked, false, feigned, forged, fraudulent, imitation, phoney, pretended, pseudo; (*Inf*) sham, spurious

mockery *n* contempt, contumely, derision, disdain, disrespect, gibes, insults, jeering, ridicule, scoffing, scorn; burlesque, caricature, deception, farce, imitation, lampoon, laughing, stock, mimicry, parody, pretence, send-up, sham, spoof take-off, travesty

mocking *adj* contemptuous, contumelious, derisive, derisory, disdainful, disrespectful, insulting, irreverent, sarcastic, sardonic, satiric, satirical, scoffing, scornful, taunting

model *n* copy, dummy, facsimile, image, imitation, miniature, mock-up, replica, representation; archetype, design, epitome, example, exemplar, gauge, ideal, lodestar, mould, original, paradigm, paragon, pattern, prototype, standard, type; poser, sitter, subject; mannequin

model *v* base, carve, cast, design, fashion, form, mould, pattern, plan, sculpt, shape; display, show off, sport, wear

model *adj* archetypal, illustrative, prototypal, standard, typical; ideal, perfect

moderate *adj* calm, controlled, cool, deliberate, equable, gentle, judicious, limited, middle-of-the-road, mild, modest, peaceable, reasonable, restrained, sober, steady, temperate

moderate *v* abate, allay, appease, assuage, calm, control, curb, decrease, diminish, lessen, mitigate, modulate, pacify, play down, quiet, regulate, repress, restrain, soften, subdue, tame, temper, tone down

moderately *adv* fairly, gently, in moderation, passably, quite, rather, reasonably, slightly, somewhat, to a degree, tolerably, to some extent, within limits, within reason

moderation *n* calmness, composure, coolness, equanimity, fairness, judiciousness, justice, justness, mildness, moderateness, reasonableness, restraint, sedateness, temperance

modern *adj* contemporary, current, fresh, late, latest, new, newest, new fangled, novel, present, present-day, recent, twentieth-century, twenty-first century, up-to-date, up-to-the-minute, with-it; (*Inf*) latest gizmo

modernize *v* bring into the twentieth century, bring into the twenty-first century, bring up to date, face-lift, make over, rejuvenate, remake, remodel, renew, renovate, revamp, update

modest *adj* bashful, blushing, coy, demure, diffident, discreet, humble, meek, quiet, reserved, reticent, retiring, self-conscious, self-effacing, shy, simple, unassuming, unpretentious; fair, limited, middling, moderate, ordinary, small, unexceptional

modesty *n* bashfulness, coyness, decency, demureness, diffidence, discreetness, humbleness, humility, lack of pretension, meekness, propriety, quietness, reserve, reticence, self-effacement, shyness, simplicity, timidity, unobtrusiveness, unpretentiousness

modicum *n* crumb, dab, fragment, grain, iota, jot, little bit, pinch, speck, tinge, touch; (*Inf*) teeny bit

modification *n* adjustment, alteration, change, modulation, mutation, qualification, refinement, reformation, restriction, revision, variation

modify *v* adapt, adjust, alter, change, convert, recast, redo, refashion, reform, remodel, reorganize, reshape, revise, rework, transform, vary

moist *adj* clammy, damp, dampish, dank, dewy, dripping, drizzly, humid, not dry, rainy, soggy, wet, wettish

moisten *v* bedew, damp, dampen, humidify, lick, moisturize, soak, water wet

moisture *n* damp, dampness, dankness, dew, humidity, liquid, perspiration, sweat, water, wateriness, wetness

molest *v* abuse, afflict, annoy, badger, beset, bother, disturb, harass, harry, hector, irritate, persecute, pester, plague, tease, torment, upset, vex, worry; (*Inf*) bug

moment *n* flash, instant, minute, no time, second, split second, trice, twinkling; (*Inf*) jiffy, shake, tick; hour, instant, juncture, point, point in time, stage, time, two shakes, two shakes of a lamb's tail

momentous *adj* consequential, critical, crucial, decisive, earthshaking, fateful, grave, historic, important, pivotal, serious, significant, vital, weighty

momentum *n* drive, energy, force, impetus, power, propulsion, push, strength, thrust

monarch *n* crowned head, emperor, empress, king, potentate, prince, princess, queen, ruler, sovereign

monastery *n* abbey, cloister, convent, friary, house, nunnery, priory, religious community

monastic *adj* ascetic, austere, celibate, cloistered, cloistral, coeno bitic, contemplative, conventual, eremitic, hermit-like, monachal, monkish, recluse, reclusive, secluded, sequestered, withdrawn

monetary *adj* budgetary, capital, cash, financial, fiscal, pecuniary

money *n* banknotes, capital, cash, coin, currency, funds, hard cash, legal tender, riches, specie, the wherewithal, wealth; (*Inf*) bread, dosh, dough, loot, lolly, mazuma, moolah, readies, the ready, spondulix

mongrel *n* cross, crossbreed, halfbreed, hybrid, mixed breed

mongrel *adj* bastard, crossbreed, half-breed, hybrid, of mixed breed

monitor *n* guide, invigilator, overseer, prefect, supervisor, watchdog

monitor *v* check, follow, keep an eye on, keep track of, observe, oversee, record, scan, supervise, survey, watch

monk *n* abbot, brother, friar, monastic, prior, religious

monkey *n* primate, simian; devil, imp, mischief maker, rascal, rogue, scamp

monkey *v* fiddle, fool, interfere, meddle, mess, play, tamper, tinker, trifle

monologue *n* harangue, lecture, sermon, soliloquy, speech

monopolize *v* control, corner, corner the market in, dominate, engross, exercise a monopoly of, keep to oneself, take over, take up; (*Inf*) hog

monotonous *adj* all the same, boring, colourless, droning, dull, flat, humdrum, plodding, repetitious, repetitive, soporific, tedious, tiresome, toneless, unchanging, uniform, uninflected, unvaried, wearisome; (*Inf*) samey

monster *n* barbarian, beast, bogeyman, brute, demon, devil, fiend, ogre, savage, villain

monster *adj* Brobdingnagian, colossal, enormous, gargantuan, giant, gigantic, ginormous, huge, immense, mammoth, massive, monstrous, prodigious, stupendous, titanic, tremendous, vast; (*Inf*) ginormous, jumbo, mega, whopping

monstrous *adj* abnormal, dreadful, enormous, fiendish, freakish, frightful, grotesque, gruesome, hellish, hideous, horrendous, horrible, miscreated, obscene, teratoid, terrible, unnatural; atrocious, cruel, devilish, diabolical, disgraceful, egregious, evil, fiendish, foul, heinous, horrifying, infamous, inhuman, intolerable, loathsome, odious, outrageous, satanic, scandalous, shocking, vicious, villainous; colossal, elephantine, enormous, gargantuan, giant, gigantic, great, huge, immense, mammoth, massive, prodigious, stupendous, titanic, towering, tremendous, vast; (*Inf*) ginormous, jumbo, mega, whopping

monument *n* cairn, cenotaph, commemoration, gravestone, headstone, marker, mausoleum, memorial, obelisk, pillar, shrine, statue, tombstone

monumental *adj* awe-inspiring, awesome, classic, enduring, enormous, epoch-making, historic, immortal, important, lasting, majestic, memorable, outstanding, prodigious, significant, stupendous, unforgettable

mood *n* disposition, frame of mind, humour, spirit, state of mind, temper, tenor, vein; bad temper, blues, depression, doldrums, fit of pique, low spirits, melancholy, sulk, the sulks; (*Inf*) dumps, grumps

moody *adj* angry, broody, cantankerous, crabbed, crabby, crestfallen, cross, crusty, curt, dismal, doleful, dour, downcast, frowning, gloomy, glum, huffish, huffy, ill-humoured, ill-tempered, in a huff, in the doldrums, introspective, irascible, irritable, lugubrious, melancholy, miserable, mopish, mopy, morose, offended, pensive, petulant, piqued, sad, saturnine, short tempered, splenetic, sulky, sullen, temperamental, testy, touchy, waspish, wounded; (*Inf*) crotchety, down in the dumps, down in the mouth, out of sorts

moon *n* satellite

moon *v* daydream, idle, languish, mooch, mope, waste time

moor *n* fell, grouse moor, heath, moorland, muir

moor *v* anchor, berth, dock, fasten, fix, lash, make fast, secure, tie up

mop up *v* clean, mop, soak up, sponge, swab, wash, wipe

moral *adj* ethical; blameless, chaste, decent, ethical, good, high-minded, honest, honourable, incorruptible, innocent, just, meritorious, noble, principled, proper, pure, right, righteous, upright, upstanding, virtuous

moral *n* lesson, meaning, message, point, significance

morale *n* cheerfulness, confidence, heart, hopefulness, mettle, self-confidence, self-esteem, spirit, temper

morality *n* chastity, decency, ethicality, ethicalness, goodness, honesty, integrity, justice, principle, rectitude, righteousness, rightness, uprightness, virtue

morals *pl n* behaviour, conduct, ethics, habits, integrity, manners, morality, mores, principles, scruples, standards

moratorium *n* embargo, freeze, halt, postponement, respite, stay

morbid *adj* brooding, ghoulish, gloomy, grim, melancholy, pessimistic, sick, sombre, unhealthy, unwholesome; dreadful, ghastly, grisly, gruesome, hideous, horrid, macabre

more *adj* added, additional, extra, fresh, further, new, other, spare, supplementary

more *adv* better, further, longer, to a greater extent

moreover *adv* additionally, also as well, besides, further, furthermore, in addition, into the bargain, like wise, to boot, too, what is more

morning *n* a.m., break of day, dawn, daybreak, forenoon, sunrise

moron *n* ass, blockhead, cretin, dolt, dunce, dunderhead, fool, halfwit, idiot, imbecile, mental defective, nincompoop, numskull, simpleton, thickhead; (*Inf*) airhead, bonehead, dickhead, dimwit, dope, dummy, muttonhead, nurd, pillock, plonker, tosser

morose *adj* blue, churlish, crabbed, crabby, cross, crusty, depressed, dour, down, gloomy, glum, gruff, ill-humoured, ill-natured, ill-tempered, in a bad mood, low, melancholy, miserable, moody, mournful, perverse, pessimistic, saturnine, sour, sulky, sullen, surly, taciturn; (*Inf*) down in the dumps, grouchy

morsel *n* bite, crumb, fraction, fragment, grain, mouthful, nibble, part, piece, scrap, segment, slice, snack, soupçon, tad, taste, titbit

mortal *adj* corporeal, earthly, ephemeral, human, impermanent, passing, sublunary, temporal, transient, worldly; deadly, death-dealing, destructive, fatal, killing, lethal, murderous, terminal

mortal *n* being, body, earthling, human, human being, individual, man, person, woman

mortality *n* ephemerality, humanity, impermanence, temporality, transience; bloodshed, carnage, death, destruction, fatality, killing, loss of life

mortified *v* abashed, affronted, annoyed, ashamed, chagrined, chastened, confounded, crushed, deflated, discomfited, displeased, embarrassed, humbled, humiliated, put down, put to shame, rendered speechless, shamed, vexed; (*Inf*) made to eat humblepie, put out

mostly *adv* above all, almost entirely,

as a rule, chiefly, customarily, for the most part, generally, largely, mainly, most often, on the whole, particularly, predominantly, primarily, principally, usually

mother *n* birth mother, matriarch, surrogate mother; (*Inf*) ma, mater, mom, mum, mummy, old lady

mother *adj* connate, inborn, innate, native, natural

mother *v* bear, bring forth, drop, give birth to, produce; care for, cherish, nurse, nurture, protect, raise, rear, tend

motherly *adj* affectionate, caring, comforting, fond, gentle, kind, loving, maternal, protective, sheltering, tender, warm

motion *n* action, change, flow, kinetics, locomotion, mobility, motility, move, movement, passage, passing, progress, travel; proposal, proposition, recommendation, submission, suggestion

motion *v* beckon, direct, gesticulate, gesture, nod, signal, wave

motionless *adj* at a standstill, at rest, calm, fixed, frozen, halted, immobile, inanimate, inert, lifeless, paralysed, standing, static, stationary, still, stock-still, transfixed, unmoved, unmoving

motivate *v* actuate, arouse, bring, cause, draw, drive, give incentive to, impel, indure, inspire, inspirit, instigate, lead, move, persuade, prompt, provoke, set on, stimulate, stir, trigger

motivation *n* ambition, desire, drive, hunger, inspiration, interest, wish

motive *n* cause, design, grounds, incentive, inticement, inducement, influence, inspiration, intention, mainspring, motivation, object, occasion, purpose, rationale, reason, spur, stimulus, thinking

motley *adj* assorted, disparate, dissimilar, diversified, heterogeneous, mingled, miscellaneous, mixed, unlike, varied

mottled *adj* blotchy, brindled, chequered, dappled flecked, freckled, marbled, piebald, pied, speckled, spotted, stippled, streaked, tabby, variegated

motto *n* adage, byword, cry, formula, gnome, maxim, precept, proverb, rule, saw, saying, slogan, watch word

mould *n* cast, die, form, matrix, pattern, shape; brand, build, configuration, construction, cut, design, fashion, form, format, frame, kind, line, make, pattern, shape, structure, style

mould *v* carve, cast, construct, create, fashion, forge, form, make, model, sculpt, shape, stamp, work

mouldy *adj* bad, blighted, decaying, fusty, mildewed, musty, rotten, rotting, spoiled, stale

mound *n* barrow, drift, heap, pile, stack; bank, dune, embankment, hill, hillock, hummock, knoll, rise

mount *v* ascend, clamber up, climb, escalade, go up, make one's way up, scale; bestride, climb onto, climb up on, get astride, get up on, jump on; arise, ascend, rise, soar, tower; accumulate, build, escalate, row, increase, intensify, multiply, pile up, swell; display, frame, set, set off; exhibit, get up, prepare, produce, put on stage

mount *n* backing, base, fixture, foil, frame, mounting, setting, stand, support; horse, steed

mountain *n* alp, ben, elevation, eminence, fell, height, mount, Munro, peak, pinnacle; abundance, mound, stack; (*Inf*) ton; excess, surfeit, surplus

mountainous *adj* alpine, high, highland, hilly, lofty, rocky, soaring, steep, towering, upland

mourn *v* bemoan, bewail, deplore, grieve, keen, lament, miss, rue, sorrow, wail, wear black, weep

mournful *adj* afflicting, calamitous, deplorable, distressing, grievous, lamentable, melancholy, painful, piteous, plaintive, sad, sorrowful, tragic, unhappy, woeful

mourning *n* bereavement, grief, grieving, keening, lamentation, weeping, woe

mouth *n* jaws, lips, maw, muzzle; (*Inf*) chops, gob, kisser, trap; aperture, cavity, crevice, door, entrance, gateway, inlet, lips, opening, orifice, rim; **down in the mouth** blue, crestfallen, dejected, depressed, disheartened, dispirited, down, down, downcast, in low spirits, melancholy, miserable, sad, unhappy; (*Inf*) down in the dumps

move *v* advance, budge, change position, drift, go, march, proceed, progress, shift, stir, walk; carry, change, shift, switch, transfer, transport, transpose; change residence, flit, flitting, go away, leave, migrate, move house, quit, relocate, remove; activate, drive, impel, motivate, operate, propel, push, set going, shift, shove, start, turn; actuate, affect, agitate, cause, excite, give rise to, impel, impress, incite, induce, influence, inspire, instigate, lead, make an impression on, motivate, persuade, prompt, rouse, stimulate, touch, urge advocate, propose, put forward, recommend, suggest, urge

move *n* act, action, deed, manoeuvre, measure, motion, ploy, shift, step, stratagem, stroke, turn

movement *n* act, action, activity, advance, agitation, change, development, displacement, exercise, flow, gesture, manoeuvre, motion, move, moving, operation, progress, progression, shift, steps, stir, stir ring, transfer; campaign, crusade, drive, faction, front, group, grouping, organization, party; division, part, passage, section; beat, cadence, measure, metre, pace, rhythm, swing, tempo

moving *adj* affecting, arousing, emotional, emotive, exciting, impelling, impressive, inspiring, pathetic, persuasive, poignant, stirring, touching

mow *v* crop, cut, scythe, shear, trim

much *adj* abundant, a lot of, ample, considerable, copious, great, plenteous, plenty of, sizeable, substantial

much *adv* a great deal, a lot, considerably, decidedly, exceedingly, frequently, greatly, indeed, often, regularly

muck *n* droppings, dung, excrement, faeces, guano, manure; dirt, filth, grime, mud, slime, sludge; (*Inf*) gunge, gunk; botch, bungle, mar, mess, ruin, spoil

mud *n* clay, dirt, mire, ooze, silt, sludge

muddle *v* confuse, disarrange, disorder, disorganize, jumble, make a mess of, mess, mix up, scramble, spoil, tangle; befuddle, bewilder, confound, confuse, daze, disorient, perplex, stupefy

muddle *n* chaos, clutter, confusion, daze, disarray, disorder, disorganization, jumble, mess, mix-up, perplexity, plight, predicament, tangle

muddy *adj* bespattered, boggy, dirty, grimy, marshy, miry, mucky, mud-caked, quaggy, soiled, swampy

muffle *v* cloak, conceal, cover, disguise, envelop, hood, mask, shroud, swaddle, swathe, wrap up

muffled *adj* dim, dull, faint, indistinct, muted, stifled, strangled, subdued, suppressed

mug *n* beaker, cup, flagon, jug, pot, tankard, toby jug

muggy *adj* clammy, close, damp, humid, moist, oppressive, sticky, stuffy, sultry

mull *v* consider, contemplate, deliberate on, examine, ponder, reflect, study, think about, view

multiple *adj* collective, manifold, many, multitudinous, numerous, several, sundry, various

multiply *v* accumulate, augment, breed, build up, expand, extend, increase, proliferate, propagate, reproduce, spread

multitude *n* army, assemblage, assembly, collection, concourse, congregation, crowd, great number, horde, host, legion, lot, mass, mob, myriad, sea, swarm, throng; (*Inf*) lots

munch *v* chew, chomp, crunch, eat, masticate

mundane *adj* banal, commonplace, day-to-day, everyday, humdrum, ordinary, prosaic, routine, workaday

municipal *adj* borough, city, civic, community, public, town, urban

murder *n* assassination, bloodshed, butchery, carnage, homicide, killing, manslaughter, massacre, slaying

murder *v* assassinate, blow away, butcher, destroy, dispatch, do to death, kill, massacre, slaughter, slay, take the life of; (*Inf*) bump off, do in, eliminate, hit, rub out, waste

murderer *n* assassin, butcher, cutthroat, homicide, killer, slaughterer, slayer; (*Inf*) hit man

murderous *adj* barbarous, bloodthirsty, bloody, brutal, cruel, deadly, death-dealing, destructive, devastating, fatal, ferocious, lethal, sanguinary, savage, slaughterous, withering

murky *adj* cheerless, cloudy, dark, dim, dismal, dreary, dull, dusky, foggy, gloomy, grey, impenetrable, misty, nebulous, obscure, overcast

murmur *n* babble, buzzing, drone, humming, mumble, muttering, purr, rumble, undertone, whisper, whispering

murmur *v* babble, buzz, drone, hum, mumble, mutter, purr, rumble, speak in an undertone, whisper

muscle *n* muscle tissue, sinew, tendon, threw; brawn, force, forcefulness, might, potency, power, stamina, strength, sturdiness, weight; (*Inf*) clout

muscular *adj* athletic, brawny, lusty, powerful, powerfully built,

Ramboesque, robust, sinewy, stalwart, strapping, strong, sturdy, vigorous, well-knit; (*Inf*) beefy, husky

muse *v* be in a brown study, be lost in thought, brood, cogitate, consider, contemplate, deliberate, dream, meditate, mull over, ponder, reflect, ruminate, speculate, think, think over, weigh

mushroom *n* chanterelle, fungus, ink-cap, morel

mushroom *v* boom, burgeon, burst forth, flourish, prosper, spring up, sprout, thrive

musical *adj* dulcet, euphonious, harmonious, lilting, lyrical, melodic, melodious, sweet-sounding, tuneful

must *n* duty, essential, fundamental, imperative, necessary thing, necessity, obligation, prerequisite, requirement, requisite; fungus, mildew, mould, mustiness

muster *v* assemble, call together, call up, collect, come together, congregate, convene, convoke, enrol, gather, group, marshal, meet, mobilize, rally, round up, summon;

muster *n* assemblage, assembly, collection, concourse, congregation, convention, convocation, gathering, meeting, mobilization, rally, roundup

musty *adj* airless, dank, decayed, fusty, mildewed, mildewy, mouldy, old, smelly, stale, stuffy

mute *adj* aphasiac, aphasic, aphonic, dumb, mum, silent, speechless, unexpressed, unspeaking, unspoken, voiceless, wordless

mute *v* dampen, deaden, lower, moderate, muffle, soften, soft-pedal, subdue, tone down, turn down

mutilate *v* amputate, butcher, cripple, cut to pieces, cut up, damage, disable, disfigure, dismember, hack, injure, lacerate, lame, maim, mangle

mutinous *adj* contumacious, disobedient, insubordinate, insurgent, rebellious, refractory, revolutionary, riotous, seditious, subversive, turbulent, ungovernable, unmanageable, unruly; (*Inf*) bolshie

mutiny *n* defiance, disobedience, insubordination, insurrection, rebellion, refusal to obey orders, resistance, revolt, revolution, riot, rising, stroke, uprising

mutiny *v* be insubordinate, defy authority, disobey, revel, refuse to obey orders, resist, revolt, rise up, strike

mutter *v* complain, grouch, grouse, grumble, mumble, murmur, rumble

mutual *adj* common, communal, correlative, interactive, interchange able, interchanged, joint, reciprocal, reciprocated, requited, returned, share

muzzle *n* jaw, mouth; nose, snout; bridle, gag, restraint

muzzle *v* censor, gag; choke, curb, restrain, silence, stifle, suppress

myriad *n* army, horde, host, legion, mass, multitude, scores, sea, swarm, throng; (*Inf*) oodles, millions, thousands, zillions

mysterious *adj* abstruse, arcane, baffling, concealed, covert, cryptic, curious, dark, enigmatic, furtive, hidden, impenetrable, incomprehensible, inexplicable, inscrutable, insoluble, mystical, mystifying, obscure, perplexing, puzzling, recondite, secret, secretive, sphinx-like, strange, uncanny, unfathomable, unknown, veiled, weird

mystery *n* conundrum, enigma, problem, puzzle, question, riddle, secrecy, secret

mystify *v* baffle, befog, bewilder, confound, confuse, elude, escape, perplex, puzzle, stump; (*Inf*) bamboozle, beat

myth *n* allegory, fable, fairy story, fiction, folk tale, legend, parable, saga, story, tradition

mythical *adj* allegorical chimerical, fabled, fabulous, fairy-tale, legendary, mythological, storied; fabricated, fanciful, fantasy, fictitious, imaginary, invented, made-up, make-believe, nonexistent, pretended, unreal, untrue; (*Inf*) pretend

mythology *n* folklore, folk tales, legend, lore, mythos, myths, stories, tradition

N

nadir *n* bottom, depths, lowest level, minimum, rock-bottom, zero; (Inf) the pits

nag *v* annoy, badger, berate, chivvy, goad, harass, harry, henpeck, irritate, pester, plague, provoke, scold, torment, upbraid, vex, worry

nag *n* harpy, scold, shrew, tartar, termagant, virago

nail *v* attach, beat, fasten, fix, hammer, join, pin, secure, tack

naive *adj* artless, candid, childlike, confiding, frank, guileless, ingenuous, innocent, jejune, natural, open, simple, trusting, unaffected, unpretentious, unsophisticated, unworldly

naivety *n* artlessness, candour, frankness, guilelessness, inexperience, ingeniousness, innocence, naturalness, openness, simplicity

naked *adj* bare, denude, disrobed, divested, exposed, nude, stripped, unclothed, unconcealed, uncovered, undraped, undressed; defenceless, helpless, insecure, unarmed, unguarded, unprotected, vulnerable; (*Inf*) in one's birthday suit, in the altogether, in the buff, starkers

name *n* alias, appellation, congomen, denomination, designation, epithet, family name, label, nickname, pet name, pseudonym, sobriquet, style, surname, tag, title; (*Inf*) handle, moniker; big name, celebrity, dignitary, megastar, star, VIP; (*Inf*) big shot, bigwig; eminence, esteem, fame, honour, note, praise, prestige, renown, repute, reputation

name *v* baptize, call, christen, denominate, dub, entitle, label, style, term; appoint, choose, cite, classify, commission, designate, give, identify, mention, nominate, pick, select, specify

named *adj* baptized, called, christened, denominated, dubbed, entitled, dubbed, entitled, known as, labelled, styled, termed

nameless *adj* anonymous, innominate, undesignated, unnamed, untitled; incognito, obscure, undistinguished, unheard-of, unknown, unsung; abominable, horrible, indescribable, ineffable, inexpressible, unmentionable, unspeakable, unutterable

namely *adv* i.e., specifically, that is to say, to wit, viz

narrate *v* chronicle, describe, detail, recite, recount, rehearse, relate, repeat, report, set forth, tell, unfold

narration *n* description, explanation, reading, recital, rehearsal, relation, story telling, telling, voice-over in film or tape

narrative *n* account, chronicle, detail, history, report, statement, story, tale

narrator *n* annalist, author, bard, chronicler, commentator, raconteur, reciter, relater, reporter, storyteller, writer

narrow *adj* circumscribed, close, confined, constricted, contracted, cramped, incapacious, limited, meagre, near, pinched, restricted, scanty, straitened, tight; biased, bigoted, dogmatic, illiberal, intolerant, narrow-minded, partial, prejudiced, reactionary, small-minded

narrow *v* circumscribe, constrict, diminish, limit, reduce, simplify, straiten, tighten

narrowly *adv* barely, by a whisper *or* hair's-breadth, just, only just, scarcely

narrow-minded *adj* biased, bigoted, conservative, hidebound, illiberal, insular, intolerant, opinionated, parochial, petty, prejudiced, provincial, reactionary, short-sighted, small-minded, strait-laced

nastiness *n* defilement, dirtiness, filth, filthiness, foulness, impurity, pollution, squalor, uncleanliness; indecency, licentiousness; obscenity, pollution, pornography, ribaldry, smuttiness; (*Inf*) porn; disagreeableness, malice, meanness, offensiveness, spitefulness, unpleasantness

nasty *adj* dirty, disagreeable, disgusting, filthy, foul, horrible, loathsome, malodorous, mephitic, nauseating, noisome, objectionable, obnoxious, odious, offensive, polluted, repellent, repugnant, sickening, unappetizing, unpleasant, vile; (*Inf*) grotty; blue, foul, gross, impure, indecent, lascivious, lewd, licentious, obscene, pornographic, ribald, smutty; abusive, annoying, bad-tempered, despicable, disagreeable, distasteful, malicious, mean, spiteful, unpleasant, vicious, vile

nation *n* commonwealth, community, country, people, population, race, realm, society, state, tribe

national *adj* civil, countrywide, governmental, nationwide, public, state, widespread; domestic, internal, social

nationalism *n* allegiance, chauvinism, fealty, jingoism, loyalty, nationality, patriotism

nationality *n* birth, ethnic group, nation, race

native *adj* built-in, congenital, endemic, hereditary, inborn, inbred, indigenous, ingrained, inherent, inherited, innate, instinctive, intrinsic, inveterate, natal, natural; genuine, original, real; domestic, home, home-grown, home-made, indigenous, local, mother, vernacular

native *n* aborigine, autochthon, citizen, countryman, dweller, inhabitant, national, resident

natural *adj* common, everyday, legitimate, logical, normal, ordinary, regular, typical, usual; characteristic, congenital, essential, inborn, indigenous, inherent, innate, instinctive, intuitive, natal, native; artless, candid, frank, genuine, ingenuous, open, real, simple, spontaneous, unaffected, unpretentious, unsophisticated, unstudied

nature *n* attributes, character, complexion, constitution, essence, features, make-up, quality, traits; category, description, kind, sort, species, style, type, variety; cosmos, creation, earth, environment, universe, world; disposition, humour, mood, outlook, temper, temperament; country, countryside, landscape, natural history, scenery

naughty *adj* annoying, bad, disobedient, exasperating, fractious, impish, misbehaved, mischievous, perverse, playful, refractory, roguish, sinful, teasing, wayward, wicked, worthless

nausea *n* airsickness, biliousness, carsickness, gagging, morning sickness, motion sickness, queasiness, retching, seasickness, sickness, squeamishness, vomiting; (*Inf*) throwing up; abhorrence, aversion, detestation, disgust, loathing, repugnance, revulsion

nauseate *v* disgust, horrify, offend, repel, repulse, revolt, sicken, turn one's stomach; (*Inf*) gross out

nautical *adj* marine, maritime, naval, oceanic, seafaring, seagoing, yachting

naval *adj* marine, maritime, nautical, oceanic

navigable *adj* clear, negotiable, passable, traversable, unobstructed

navigate *v* cross, cruise, direct, drive, guide, handle, journey, manoeuvre, pilot, plan, plot, sail, skipper, steer, voyage

navigation *n* cruising, helmsman ship, pilotage, sailing, seamanship, steering, voyaging

navvy *n* labourer, manual worker, workman

navy *n* armada, fleet, flotilla

near *adj* adjacent, adjoining, alongside, at close quarters, beside, bordering, close, close by, contiguous, nearby, neighbouring, nigh, touching; approaching, forthcoming, imminent, impending, in the offing, looming, near-at-hand, next; (*Inf*) on the cards; akin, allied, attached, connected, dear, familiar, intimate, related

nearby *adj* adjacent, adjoining, convenient, handy, neighbouring

nearly *adv* about, all but, almost, approaching, approximately, as good as, closely, just about, not quite, practically, roughly, virtually, well-nigh

nearness *n* accessibility, availability, closeness, contiguity, handiness, juxtaposition, propinquity, proximity, vicinity; immediacy, imminence

neat *adj* accurate, dainty, fastidious, methodical, nice, orderly, shipshape, smart, spick-and-span, spruce, straight, systematic, tidy, trim, uncluttered; adept, adroit, agile, apt, clever, deft, dexterous, efficient, effortless, elegant, expert, graceful, handy, nimble, practiced, precise, skilful, stylish, well-judged; pure, straight, diluted, unmixed

neatness *n* accuracy, daintiness, fastidiousness, methodicalness, niceness, nicety, orderliness, niceness, nicety, orderliness, plainness, simplicity, smartness, spruceness, straightness, tidiness, trimness; adeptness, adroitness, agility, aptness, cleverness, deftness, dexterity, ease, efficiency, effortlessness, elegance, expertness, felicity, grace, gracefulness, handiness, nimbleness, pithiness, preciseness, precision, skilfulness, skill, style, stylishness, wit

necessarily *adv* accordingly, automatically, axiomatically, by definition, certainly, compulsorily, consequently, incontrovertibly, ineluctably, inevitably, inexorably, irresistibly, like it or not, naturally, of course, of necessity, perforce, undoubtedly, willy-nilly

necessary *adj* compulsory, *de rigueur*, essential, imperative, indispensable, mandatory, needed, needful, obligatory, required, requisite, vital; certain, fated, inescapable, inevitable, preordained

necessitate *v* call for, coerce, compel, constrain, demand, force, impel, make necessary, oblige, require

necessity *n* demand, exigency, indispensability, need, needfulness, requirement; desideratum, essential, fundamental, necessary, need, prerequisite, requirement, requisite, *sine qua non*, want; certainty, destiny, fate, inevitability

née *adj* born, formerly, previously

need *v* call for, demand, have occasion for, lack, miss, necessitate, require, want

need *n* longing, requisite, want, wish; depravation, destitution, distress, extremity, impecuniousness, inadequacy, indigence, insufficiency, lack, neediness, paucity, penury, poverty, privation, shortage; emergency, exigency, necessity, obligation, urgency, want; demand, desideratum, essential, requirement, requisite

needful *adj* essential, necessary, needed, required

needless *adj* causeless, dispensable, excessive, expendable, gratuitous, groundless, non-essential, pointless, redundant, superfluous, uncalled-for, undesired, unnecessary, unwanted, useless

needy *adj* deprived, destitute, disadvantaged, impecunious, impoverished, indignant, on the breadline, penniless, poor, poverty-stricken, underprivileged

negate *v* abrogate, annul, cancel, countermand, invalidate, neutralize, nullify, repeal, rescind, retract, reverse, revoke, void, wipe out

negation *n* antithesis, antonym, contradiction, contrary, converse, counterpart, denial, disavowal, disclaimer, inverse, opposite, rejection, renunciation, reverse

negative *adj* contradictory, contrary, denying, dissenting, opposing, recusant, refusing, rejecting, resisting; annulling, counteractive, invalidating, neutralizing, nullifying; antagonistic, colourless, contrary, cynical, gloomy, jaundiced, neutral, pessimistic, uncooperative, unenthusiastic, uninterested, unwilling, weak

negative *n* contradiction, denial, refusal

neglect *v* contemn, disdain, disregard, ignore, leave alone, overlook, pass by, rebuff, scorn, slight, spurn; be remiss, evade, forget, let slide, omit, pass over, procrastinate, shirk, skimp

neglect *n* disdain, disregard, disrespect, needlessness, inattention, indifference, slight, unconcern; carelessness, default, dereliction, failure, forgetfulness, laxity, laxness, neglectfulness, negligence, oversight, remissness, slackness, slovenliness

neglected *adj* abandoned, derelict, overgrown

negligent *adj* careless, cursory,

disregardful, forgetful, heedless, inadvertent, inattentive, indifferent, neglectful, nonchalant, offhand, regardless, remiss, slack, thoughtless, unmindful, unthinking

negligible *adj* imperceptible, inconsequential, insignificant, minor, minute, petty, small, trifling, trivial unimportant

negotiate *v* adjudicate, arbitrate, arrange, bargain, conciliate, confer, consult, contract, deal, debate, discuss, handle, manage, mediate, parley, settle, transact, work out

negotiation *n* arbitration, bargaining, debate, diplomacy, discussion, mediation, transaction; *(Inf)* wheeling and dealing

neighbourhood *n* community, confines, district, environs, locale, locality, precincts, proximity, purlieus, quarter, region, surroundings, vicinity

neighbouring *adj* abutting, adjacent, adjoining, bordering, connecting, contiguous, near, nearby, nearest, next, surrounding

nerve *n* bravery, coolness, courage, daring, determination, endurance, energy, fearlessness, firmness, force, fortitude, gameness, hardihood, intrepidity, mettle, might, luck, resolution, spirit, steadfastness, vigour, will; *(Inf)* balls, bottle, grit, guts, spunk; audacity, boldness, brazenness, effrontery, gall, impertinence, impudence, insolence, temerity; *(Inf)* brass, brass neck, cheek, sauce

nerves *pl n* anxiety, fretfulness, imbalance, nervousness, strain, stress, tension, worry

nervous *adj* agitated, anxious, apprehensive, edgy, excitable, fearful, fidgety, flustered, hesitant, highly strung, hysterical, jumpy, neurotic, on edge, ruffled, shaky, tense, timid, timorous, uneasy, weak, worried; *(Inf)* hyper, jittery, nervy, uptight

nest *n* haunt, hideaway, refuge, resort, retreat, shelter, snuggery; *(Inf)* hide-out, hidey-hole; burrow, den, eyrie, form, lair, lodge, nest, set; assemblage, cluster, group

nest egg *n* cache, reserve, savings

nestle *v* cuddle up, curl up, huddle together, nuzzle, snuggle

net *n* lacework, lattice, mesh, netting, network, openwork, reticulum, tracery, web

net *v* bag, capture, catch, enmesh, ensnare, entangle, trap; *(Inf)* nab

net, nett *adj* after taxes, clear, final, take-home; closing, conclusive, final

net, nett *v* accumulate, bring in, clear, earn, gain, make, realize, reap

network *n* arrangement, channels, circuitry, complex, convolution, grid, grill, interconnections, labyrinth, maze, mesh, net, nexus, organization, plexus, structure, system, tracks, web

neurosis *n* abnormality, affliction, derangement, deviation, instability, maladjustment, mental disturbance, mental illness, obsession, phobia, psychological or emotional disorder

neurotic *adj* abnormal, anxious, compulsive, disordered, distraught, disturbed, maladjusted, manic, nervous, obsessive, over-sensitive, unhealthy, unstable; *(Inf)* hyper

neuter *v* castrate, dress, emasculate, geld, spay; (*Inf*) doctor, fix

neutral *adj* disinterested, dispassionate, even-handed, impartial, indifferent, nonaligned, nonbelligerent, noncombatant, noncommittal, nonpartisan, sitting on the fence, unaligned, unbiased, uncommitted, undecided, uninvolved, unprejudiced, without favour

neutralize *v* cancel, compensate for, counteract, counterbalance, frustrate, invalidate, negate, nullify, offset, undo

never-ending *adj* boundless, ceaseless, constant, continual, continuous, eternal, everlasting, incessant, interminable, nonstop, perpetual, persistent, relentless, unbroken, unceasing, unchanging, uninterrupted, unremitting

nevertheless *adv* but, even so, however, nonetheless, notwithstanding, regardless, still, yet

new *adj* advanced, contemporary, current, different, fresh, latest, modern, modernistic, modish, newfangled, novel, original, recent, state-of-the-art, topical, ultramodern, unfamiliar, unknown, unused, unusual, up-to-date, virgin; added, extra, more, supplementary; altered, changed, improved, modernized, redesigned, renewed, restored

newcomer *n* alien, arrival, beginner, foreigner, immigrant, incomer, novice, outsider, parvenu, settler, stranger; (*Inf*) Johnny-come-lately

newly *adv* anew, freshly, just, lately, latterly, recently

news *n* account, advice, bulletin, communiqué, disclosure, dispatch, exposé, gossip, hearsay, information, intelligence, leak, news-flash, release, report, revelation, rumour, scandal, statement, story, tidings, word

next *adj* consequent, ensuing, following, later, subsequent, succeeding; adjacent, adjoining, closest, nearest, neighbouring

next *adv* afterwards, closely, follow ing, later, subsequently, thereafter

nice *adj* agreeable, amiable, attractive, charming, commendable, courteous, delightful, friendly, good, kind, likable, pleasant, pleasurable, polite, prepossessing, refined, well-mannered; dainty, fine, neat, tidy, trim; accurate, careful, critical, delicate, discriminating, exact, exacting, fastidious, fine, meticulous, precise, rigorous, scrupulous, strict, subtle

niche *v* alcove, corner, hollow, nook, opening, recess; calling, job, place, position, vocation; (*Inf*) slot

nick *v* chip, cut, damage, dent, mark, notch, scar, score, scratch, snick

nickname *n* diminutive, epithet, familiar name, label, pet name, sobriquet; (*Inf*) handle, moniker

niggardly *adj* avaricious, frugal, grudging, mean, mercenary, miserly, parsimonious, penny-pinching, penurious, sordid, sparing, stingy, tightfisted, ungenerous

niggle *v* carp, cavil, criticize, find fault, fuss; annoy, irritate, rankle, worry

night *n* dark, darkness, dead of night, hours of darkness, night-time,

nightfall *n* crepuscule, dusk, evening, eventide, gloaming, sundown, sunset, twilight

nightmare *n* bad dream, hallucination; horror, ordeal, torment, tribulation

nil *n* duck, love, naught, nihil, none, nothing, zero; (*Inf*) zilch

nimble *adj* active, agile, alert, brisk, deft, dexterous, lively, proficient, prompt, quick, quick-witted, ready, smart, sprightly, spry, swift; (*Inf*) nippy

nip *v* bite, catch, clip, compress, grip, nibble, pinch, snag, snap, squeeze, sting, tweak, twitch; cut off, dock, lop, snip; dart, dash, hurry, rush

nip *n* dram, draught, drop, finger, mouthful, portion, sip, soupçon, sup, swallow, taste; (*Inf*) peg, shot

nippy *adj* biting, chilly, nipping, sharp, stinging

nirvana *n* bliss, joy, peace, serenity, tranquillity; heaven, paradise; enlightenment, oblivion

nitty-gritty *n* basics, centre, core, crux, essence, essentials, facts, fundamentals, gist, heart of the matter, quintessence, reality, substance; (*Inf*) brass tacks, nuts and bolts

nobility *n* aristocracy, elite, high society, lords, nobles, patricians, peerage, ruling class, upper class; dignity, eminence, excellence, grandeur, greatness, illustriousness, loftiness, magnificence, majesty, nobleness, stateliness, sublimity, superiority, worthiness; honour, incorruptibility, integrity, upright ness, virtue

noble *n* aristocrat, lady, lord, nobleman, noblewoman, peer

noble *adj* aristocrat, blue-blooded, highborn, lordly, patrician, titled; august, dignified, distinguished, elevated, eminent, excellent, grand, great, imposing, impressive, lofty, splendid, stately; (*Inf*) A1, top-notch; generous, honourable, magnanimous, upright, virtuous, worthy

nocturnal *adj* night, nightly, night-time, of the night

nod *v* acknowledge, bob, bow, dip, duck, gesture, indicate, salute, signal; agree assent, concur, show, agreement; be sleepy, doze, droop, drowse, nap, sleep, slump

node *n* bulge, bump, growth, lump, nodule, protuberance, swelling,

noise *n* babble, blare, clamour, clatter, commotion, cry, din, fracas, hubbub, loud sound, outcry, pandemonium, racket, row, sound, talk, tumult, uproar

noisy *adj* blaring, blasting, boisterous, cacophonous, chattering, clamourous, deafening, ear-splitting, loud, obstreperous, piercing, riotous, rowdy, strident, tumultuous, turbulent, uproarious, vociferous

nomad *n* drifter, itinerant, migrant, rambler, rover, vagabond, wanderer

nominal *adj* formal, ostensible, pretended, professed, puppet, purported, self-styled, so-called, supposed, theoretical, titular; symbolic, token; minimal, trivial

nominate *v* appoint, assign, choose, commission, designate elect, elevate, empower, name, present propose, recommend, select, submit, suggest, term

nomination *n* appointment, choice, designation, election, proposal, recommendation, selection, suggestion

nominee *n* aspirant, candidate, contestant, entrant, favourite, protégé, runner

nonchalant *adj* airy, apathetic, blasé, calm, careless, casual, collected, cool, detached, dispassionate, indifferent, insouciant, offhand, unconcerned, unemotional, unper turbed; (*Inf*) laid-back

non-committal *adj* ambiguous, careful, cautious, circumspect, discreet, equivocal, evasive, guarded, indefinite, neutral, politic, reserved, tactful, temporizing, tentative, unrevealing, vágue, wary

nonconformist *adj* dissenter, dissentient, eccentric, heretic, iconoclast, individualist, maverick, protester, radical, rebel

nondescript *adj* characterless, commonplace, dull, featureless, indeterminate, mousy, ordinary, unclassifiable, unclassified, undistinguished, unexceptional, uninspiring, uninteresting, unmemorable, unremarkable, vague; (*Inf*) common-or-garden

none *pro* nil, nobody, no-one, no part, not a bit, not any, nothing, not one, zero

nonentity *n* cipher, mediocrity, nobody, small fry, unimportant person; (*Inf*) lightweight

non-essential *adj* dispensable, excessive, expendable, extraneous, inessential, peripheral, superfluous, unimportant, unnecessary

nonetheless *adv* despite that, even so, however, in spite of that, nevertheless, yet

non-existent *adj* chimerical, fancied, fictional, ficticious, hallucinatory, hypothetical, illusory, imaginary, imagined, insubstantial, legendary, missing, mythical, unreal

nonsense *n* absurdity, balderdash, blather, bombast, drivel, fatuity, folly, foolishness, gibberish, inanity, jest, ludicrousness, ridiculousness, rot, rubbish, senselessness, silliness, stuff, stupidity, trash, twaddle, waffle; (*Inf*) bosh, bull, bunk, bunkum, claptrap, crap, double Dutch, flannel, gobbledegook, mumbo-jumbo, poppycock, tosh, tripe

nonstop *adj* ceaseless, constant, continuous, direct, endless, incessant, interminable, relentless, steady, unbroken unending, unfaltering, uninterrupted, unremitting

nonstop *adv* ceaselessly, constantly, continuously, directly, endlessly, incessantly, interminable, relentlessly, unfalteringly, uninterruptedly, unremittingly, without stopping

nook *n* alcove, cavity, corner, cranny, crevice, cubbyhole, gap, hide-out, inglenook, niche, opening, recess, retreat; den, hideaway, refuge, retreat, shelter

norm *n* average, benchmark, criterion, mean, measure, model, pattern, rule, standard, type, yardstick

normal *adj* accustomed, acknowledged, average, common, conventional, habitual, natural, ordinary, popular, regular, routine, run-of-the-mill, standard, typical, usual

nosedive *v* dive, drop, fall, plunge

nosedive *n* dive, get worse, go down, plunge, plummet, worsen

nostalgia *n* homesickness, longing, pining, regret, regretfulness, remembrance, reminiscence, wistfulness, yearning

nostalgic *adj* emotional, homesick, longing, maudlin, regretful, sentimental, wistful

nosy *adj* curious, eavesdropping, intrusive, meddlesome, prying

notable *adj* celebrated, conspicuous, distinguished, eminent, evident, extraordinary, famous, manifest, marked, memorable, noteworthy, noticeable, notorious, outstanding, pre-eminent, pronounced, rare, remarkable, renowned, striking, uncommon, unusual, well-known

notable *n* celebrity, dignitary, notability, personage, VIP, worthy; (*Inf*) celeb, megastar

notation *n* characters, code, script, signs, symbols, system

notch *n* cleft, cut, incision, indentation, mark, nick, score

note *n* annotation, comment, communication, epistle, gloss, jotting, letter, memo, memorandum, message, minute, record, remark, reminder; indication, mark, sign, symbol, token; heed, notice, observation, regard

note *v* denote, designate, indicate, mark, mention, notice, observation, regard; observe, perceive, record, register, remark, see

noted *adj* acclaimed, celebrated, conspicuous, distinguished, eminent, famous, illustrious, notable, notorious, prominent, recognized, renowned, well-known

noteworthy *adj* exceptional, extraordinary, important, notable, outstanding, remarkable, significant, unusual

nothing *n* bagatelle, cipher, emptiness, naught, nobody, nonentity, nonexistence, nothingness, nought, nullity, trifle, void, zero

notice *v* detect, discern, distinguish, heed, mark, mind, note, observe, perceive, remark, see, spot

notice *n* cognizance, consideration, heed, note, observation, regard; advice, announcement, communication, instruction, intelligence, intimation, news, notification, order, warning; advertisement, comment, criticism, poster, review, sign

noticeable *adj* appreciable, clear, conspicuous, distinct, evident, manifest, observable, obvious, perceptible, plain, striking, unmistakable

notification *n* advice, alert, announcement, declaration, information, intelligence, message, notice, notifying, publication, statement, telling, warning

notify *v* acquaint, advise, alert, announce, appraise, declare, inform, publish, tell, warn

notion *n* apprehension, belief, concept, conception, idea, impression, inkling, judgment, knowledge, opinion, sentiment, understanding, view; caprice, desire, fancy, impulse, inclination, whim, wish

notoriety *n* dishonour, disrepute, infamy, obloquy, opprobrium, scandal

notorious *adj* dishonourable, disreputable, infamous, opprobrious, scandalous; blatant, flagrant, glaring, obvious, open, overt, patent, undisputed

notwithstanding *prep* although, despite, however, nevertheless, nonetheless, though, yet

nought *n* naught, nil, nothing, nothingness, zero

nourish *v* attend, feed, furnish, nurse, nurture, supply, sustain, tend

nourishing *adj* alimentative, beneficial, healthful, health-giving, nutritious, nutritive, wholesome

nourishment *n* aliment, diet, food, nutriment, nutrition, sustenance, viands, victuals

novel *adj* different, fresh, innovative, new, original, rare, singular, strange, uncommon, unfamiliar, unusual

novel *n* fiction, narrative, romance, story, tale

novelty *n* freshness, innovation, newness, oddity, originality, strangeness, surprise, unfamiliarity, uniqueness; bagatelle, bauble, curiosity, gadget, gimcrack, gimmick, knick-knack, memento, souvenir, trifle, trinket

novice *n* amateur, apprentice, beginner, convert, greenhorn, learner, neophyte, newcomer, novitiate, probationer, proselyte, pupil, tiro; (*Inf*) rookie

now *adv* at once, immediately, instantly, presently, promptly, straightaway, without delay

nucleus *n* basis, centre, core, focus, heart, kernel, marrow, nub, pith, pivot

nude *adj au naturel*, bare, disrobed, exposed, naked, stark-naked, stripped, unclad, unclothed, uncovered, undraped, undressed; (*Inf*) in one's birthday suit, in the altogether, in the buff, in the raw, naked as the day one was born, mother naked, starkers, without a stitch on

nudge *v* bump, dig, elbow, jog, poke, prod, push, shove, touch

nudity *n* bareness, dishabille, nakedness, nudism, undress

nugget *n* chunk, clump, hunk, lump, mass, piece

nuisance *n* annoyance, bore, bother, inconvenience, infliction, irritation, offence, pest, plague, trouble, vexation

numb *adj* benumbed, dead, deadened, frozen, immobilized, insensible, insensitive, paralysed, stupefied, torpid, unfeeling

numb *v* benumb, deaden, dull, freeze, immobilize, paralyse, stun, stupefy

number *n* character, count, digit, figure, integer, numeral, sum, total, unit; aggregate, amount, collection, company, crowd, horde, many, multitude, quantity, throng; copy, edition, imprint, issue, printing

number *v* account, add, calculate, compute, count, enumerate, include, reckon, tell, total

numbness *n* deadness, dullness, insensibility, insensitivity, paralysis, stupefaction, torpor, unfeelingness

numeral *n* character, cipher, digit, figure, integer, number, symbol

numerous *adj* abundant, copious, many, plentiful, profuse, several

nunnery *n* abbey, cloister, convent, house, monastery

nurse *v* care for, look after, minister to, tend, treat; breast-feed, feed, nourish, nurture, suckle, wet-nurse;

cherish. cultivate, encourage, foster, harbour, keep alive, preserve, promote, succour, support

nurture *n* diet, food, nourishment;

nurture *v* feed, nourish, nurse, support, sustain, tend; bring up, cultivate, develop, discipline, educate, instruct, rear, school, train

nutrition *n* food, nourishment, nutriment, sustenance

nutritious *adj* alimental, alimentative, beneficial, health-giving, invigorating, nourishing, nutritive, strengthening, wholesome

nuts and bolts *pl n* basics, essentails, fundamentals, practicalities; (*Inf*) nitty-gritty

O

oasis *n* haven, island, refuge, resting place, retreat, sanctuary, sanctum

oath *n* affirmation, avowal, bond, pledge, promise, sworn, statement, vow, word; blasphemy, curse, expletive, imprecation, malediction, profanity, strong language, swear-word; (*Inf*) cuss

obedience *n* accordance, acquiescence, agreement, compliance, conformability, deference, docility, dutifulness, duty, observance, respect, reverence, submission, submissiveness, subservience, tractability

obedient *adj* acquiescent, amenable, biddable, compliant, deferential, docile, duteous, dutiful, law-abid ing, observant, regardful, respectful, submissive, subservient, tractable, under control, well-trained, yielding

obese *adj* corpulent, Falstaffian, fat, fleshy, gross, heavy, outsize, over weight, paunchy, plump, podgy, portly, roly-poly, rotund, stout, tubby; (*Inf*) well-upholstered

obey *v* abide by, act upon, adhere to, be ruled by, carry out, comply, conform, discharge, do what is expected, embrace, execute, follow, fulfil, heed, keep, mind, observe, perform, respond, serve; bow to, come to heel, do what one is told, get into line, give in, give way, submit, surrender to, take orders from, toe the line, yield; (*Inf*) knuckle under

object *n* article, body, entity, fact, item, phenomenon, reality, thing; aim, butt, focus, recipient, target, victim; design, end, end in view, end purpose, goal, idea, intent, intention, motive, objective, point, purpose, reason

object *v* argue, against, demur, expostulate, oppose, protest, raise objections, take exception

objection *n* cavil, censure, counter-argument, demur, doubt, exception, opposition, protest, remonstrance, scruple; (*Inf*) niggle

objectionable *adj* abhorrent, deplorable, dislikable, displeasing, distasteful, exceptionable, indecorous, insufferable, intolerable, noxious, obnoxious, offensive, regrettable, repugnant, unacceptable, undesirable, unpleasant, unseemly, unsociable

objective *adj* detached, disinterested, dispassionate, equitable, even-handed, fair, impartial, impersonal, judicial, just, open-minded, unbiased, uncoloured, unemotional, uninvolved, unprejudiced

objective *n* aim, ambition, aspiration, design, end, end in view, goal, intention, mark, object, purpose, target

obligation *n* accountability, accountableness, burden, charge, compulsion, duty, liability, must, onus, requirement, responsibility, trust

obligatory *adj* binding, coercive, compulsory, *de rigueur*, enforced, essential, imperative, mandatory, necessary, required, requisite, unavoidable

oblige *v* bind, coerce, compel, constrain, force, impel, make, necessitate, obligate, require; accommodate, benefit, do someone a favour, favour, gratify, indulge, please, put oneself out for, serve

obliging *adj* accommodating, agree able, amiable, civil, complaisant, considerate, cooperative, courteous, eager to please, friendly, good-natured, helpful, kind, polite, willing

oblique *n* angled, aslant, at an angle, inclined, slanted, slanting, sloped, sloping, tilted

obliterate *v* annihilate, blot out, cancel, delete, destroy, destroy root and branch, efface, eradicate, erase, expunge, extirpate, root out, wipe off the face of the earth, wipe out

oblivion *n* abeyance, disregard, forgetfulness, insensibility, neglect, obliviousness, unawareness, unconsciousness; blackness, darkness, eclipse, extinction, limbo, nothingness, obscurity, void

oblivious *adj* blind, careless, deaf, disregardful, forgetful, heedless, ignorant, inattentive, insensible, neglectful, negligent, regardless, unaware, unconcerned, unconscious, unmindful, unobservant

obnoxious *adj* adherent, abominable, detestable, disagreeable, disgusting, dislikable, foul, hateable, hateful, horrid, insufferable, loathsome, nasty, nauseating, objectionable, odious, offensive, repellent, reprehensible. repugnant, repulsive, revolting, sickening, unpleasant

obscene *adj* bawdy, blue, coarse, dirty, disgusting, filthy, foul, gross, immodest, immoral, improper, impure, indecent, led, licentious, loose, offensive, pornographic, prurient, ribald, salacious, scabrous, shameless, smutty, suggestive, unchaste, unwholesome

obscenity *n* bawdiness, blueness, coarseness, dirtiness, filthiness, foulness, grossness, immodesty, impurity, lewdness, licentiousness, pornography, prurience, salacity, smuttiness, suggestiveness, vileness; four-letter word, impropriety, indecency, indelicacy, profanity, smut, swearword, vulgarism

obscure *adj* abstruse, ambiguous, arcane, concealed, confusing, cryptic, deep, doubtful, enigmatic, esoteric, hazy, hidden, incomprehensible, indefinite, intricate, involved, mysterious, occult, opaque, recondite, unclear, vague; blurred, clouded, cloud, dim, dusky, faint, gloomy, indistinct, murky, obfuscated, shadowy, shady, sombre, tenebrous, unlit, veiled

obscure *v* conceal, cover, disguise, hide, muddy, obfuscate, screen, throw a veil over, veil; adumbrate, bedim, befog, block, block out, blur, cloak, cloud, darken, dim, dull, eclipse, mask, overshadow, shade, shroud

obscurity *n* abstruseness, ambiguity, complexity, impenetrableness, incomprehensibilty, intricacy, reconditeness, vagueness; darkness, dimness, dusk, duskiness, gloom, haze, haziness, indistinctness, murkiness, shadowiness, shadows, inconspicuousness, ingloriousness, insignificance, lowliness, namelessness, nonrecognition, unimportance

observance *n* adherence to, attention, carrying out, celebration, compliance, discharge, fulfilment, heeding, honouring, notice, observation, performance; ceremonial, ceremony, custom, fashion, form, formality, practice, rite, ritual, service, tradition

observant *adj* alert, attentive, eagle-eyed, heedful, mindful, obedient, perceptive, quick, sharp-eyed, submissive, vigilant, watchful, wide-awake

observation *n* attention, cognition, consideration, examination, experience, information, inspection, knowledge, monitoring, notice, review scrutiny, study, surveillance, watching

observe *v* detect, discern, discover, espy, note, notice, perceive, see, spot, witness; contemplate, keep under observation, look at, monitor, pay attention to, regard, scrutinize, study, survey, view, watch; (*Inf*) keep an eye on; animadvert, comment, declare, mention, note, opine, remark, say, state, abide by, adhere to, comply, conform to, follow, fulfil, heed, honour, keep, mind, obey, perform, respect; celebrate, commemorate, keep, remember, solemnize

observer *n* beholder, bystander, commentator, eyewitness, looker-on, onlooker, spectator, spotter, viewer, watcher, witness

obsessive *adj* besetting, compulsive, consuming, fixed, gripping, haunting, tormenting, unforgettable

obsolescent *adj* ageing, declining, dying out, on the decline, on the wane, on the way out, past its prime, waning; (*Inf*) not with it

obsolete *adj* anachronistic, ancient, antediluvian, antiquated, antique, archaic, bygone, dated, *démodé,* discarded, disused, extinct, musty, old, old-fashioned, old hat, outmoded, out of date, out of fashion, outworn, passé, superannuated, *vieux jeu;* (*Inf*) out of the ark

obstacle *n* bar, barrier, check, difficulty, hindrance, hitch, hurdle, impediment, interference, interruption, obstruction, snag, stumbling block

obstinate *adj* contumacious, determined, dogged, firm, headstrong, immovable, inflexible, intractable, intransigent, mulish, opinionated, persistent, pertinacious, perverse, pig-headed, recalcitrant, refractory, self-willed, steadfast, strong minded, stubborn, tenacious, unyielding, wilful

obstruct *v* arrest, bar, barricade, block, bring to a standstill, check, choke, clog, cumber, curb, cut off, frustrate, get in the way of, hamper, hamstring, hide, hinder, hold up, impede, inhibit, interfere with, interrupt, mask, obscure, prevent, restrict, retard, shield, shut off, slow down, stop, thwart, trammel

obstruction *n* bar, barricade, barrier, blockage, check, difficulty, hindrance, impediment, snag, stop, stoppage, trammel

obstructive *adj* awkward, blocking, delaying, hindering, inhibiting, preventative, restrictive, stalling, uncooperative, unhelpful

obtain *v* achieve, acquire, attain, come by, earn, gain, get hold of, get ones hands on, procure, secure

obtrusive *adj* forward, importunate, interfering, intrusive, meddling, nosy, officious, prying; (*Inf*) pushy

obvious *adj* apparent, clear, clear as a bell, conspicuous, distinct, evident, indisputable, manifest, much in evidence, noticeable, open, overt, palpable, patent, perceptible, plain, pronounced, recognizable, self-evident, self-explanatory, straight forward, transparent, unconcealed, undeniable, undisguised, unmistakable, unsubtle, visible; (*Inf*) plain as the nose on your face, right under one's nose, staring one in the face, sticking out a mile

occasion *n* chance, convenience, incident, moment, occurrence, opening, opportunity, time; affair, celebration, event, experience, happening, occurrence; call, cause, excuse, grounds, inducement, influence, justification, motive, prompting, provocation, reason

occasional *adj* casual, desultory, incidental, infrequent, intermittent, irregular, odd, rare, sporadic, uncommon

occasionally *adv* at intervals, at times, every now and then, every so often, from time to time, irregularly, now and again, off and on, on and off, once in a while, on occasion, periodically, sometimes

occupant *n* addressee, denizen, holder, incumbent, indweller, inhabitant, inmate, lessee, occupier, resident, tenant, user

occupation *n* activity, business, calling, craft, employment, job, line of work, post, profession, pursuit, trade, vocation, walk of life, work; control, holding, occupancy, possession, residence, tenancy, tenure, use; conquest, foreign rule, invasion, seizure, subjugation

occupied *adj* busy, employed, engaged, working; engaged, full, in use, taken, unavailable; (*Inf*) hard at it, tied up

occupy *v* absorb, amuse, busy, divert, employ, engage, engross, entertain, hold the attention of, immerse, interest, involve, keep busy or occupied, monopolize, preoccupy, take up, tie up; capture, garrison, hold, invade, keep, over run, seize, take over, take possession of

occur *v* arise, befall, betide, chance, come about, eventuate, happen, materialize, result, take place; (*Inf*) crop up, turn up

occurrence *n* adventure, afar, circumstance, episode, event, happening, incident, instance, proceeding, transaction

odd *adj* abnormal, atypical, bizarre, curious, deviant, different, eccentric, exceptional, extraordinary, fantastic, freak, freakish, funny, irregular, outlandish, out of the ordinary, peculiar, quaint, queer, rare, remarkable, singular, strange, uncanny, uncommon, unconventional, unusual, weird, whimsical; leftover, lone, remaining, single, solitary, spare, surplus, unconsumed, uneven, unmatched, unpaired; (*Inf*) freaky, kinky

oddity *n* abnormality, anomaly, eccentricity, freak, idiosyncrasy, irregularity, peculiarity, phenomenon, quirk, rarity; (*Inf*) kink

odds *pl n* advantage, allowance, edge, lead, superiority; balance, chances, likelihood, probability; difference, disparity, dissimilarity, distinction

odious *adj* abhorrent, abominable, detestable, disgusting, execrable, foul, hateful, horrible, horrid, loathsome, obnoxious, offensive, repellent, repugnant, repulsive, revolting, unpleasant, vile

odour *n* aroma, bouquet, essence, fragrance, perfume redolence, scent, smell, stench, stink

off *adj* absent, cancelled, finished, gone, inoperative, postponed, unavailable; bad, below par, disappointing, disheartening, displeasing, low-quality, mortifying, poor, quiet, slack, substandard, unrewarding, unsatisfactory; bad, decomposed, high, mouldy, rancid, rotten, sour, turned

off and on *adv* every now and again, every once in a while, from time to time, intermittently, now and then, occasionally, on and off, sometimes, sporadically

offbeat *adj* bizarre, Bohemian, eccentric, hippy, idiosyncratic, novel, *outré,* strange, uncommon, unconventional, unorthodox, unusual, weird; (*Inf*) far-out, freaky, kinky, oddball, wayout

offence *n* breach of conduct, crime, delinquency, fault lapse, misdeed, misdemeanour, peccadillo, sin, transgression, trespass, wrong, wrongdoing; anger, annoyance, displeasure, hard feelings, huff, indignation, needle, pique, resentment, umbrage, wounded, feelings, wrath

offend *v* affront, annoy, disgruntle, displease, fret, gall, give offence, hurt someone's feelings, insult, irritate, outrage, pain, pique, provoke, rile, slight, snub, upset, vex, wound; (*Inf*) miff, put someone's back up, tread on someone's toes; be disagreeable to, disgust, nauseate, repel, repulse, sicken; (*Inf*) turn someone off

offender *n* criminal, crook, culprit, delinquent, lawbreaker, malefactor, miscreant, sinner, transgressor, wrongdoer

offensive *adj* abusive, annoying, detestable, discourteous, displeasing, disrespectful, embarrassing, impertinent, insolent, insulting, irritating, objectionable, rude, uncivil, unmannerly; abominable, detestable, disagreeable, disgusting, grisly, loathsome, nasty, nauseating, noisome, obnoxious, odious, repellent, revolting, sickening, unpalatable, unpleasant, unsavoury, vile; aggressive, attacking, invading

offensive *v* attack, drive, onslaught; (*Inf*) push

offer *v* bid, extend, give, hold out, proffer, put on the market, put under the hammer, put up for sale, tender; afford, furnish, make available, place at someone's disposal, present, provide, show; advance, extend, move, propose, put fort, put forward, submit, suggest; be at someone's service, come forward, offer one's services, volunteer

offer *n* attempt, bid, endeavour, essay, overture, proposal, proposition, submission, suggestion, tender

offering *n* contribution, donation, gift, oblation, present, sacrifice, subscription, widow's mite

offhand *adj* abrupt, aloof, brusque, careless, casual, cavalier, couldn't care less, curt, glib, informal, offhanded, perfunctory, inceremonious, unconcerned, uninterested; (*Inf*) take it or leave it

office *n* appointment, business, capacity, charge, commission, duty, employment, function, obligation, occupation, place, post, responsibility, role, service, situation, station, trust, work

officer *n* agent, appointee, bureaucrat, dignitary, executive, functionary, office-holder, official, public servant, representative

official *adj* accredited, authentic, authoritative, authorized, bona fide, certified, endorsed, ex cathedra, ex-officio, formal, legitimate, licensed, proper, sanctioned; (*Inf*) straight from the horses mouth

official *n* agent, bureaucrat, executive, functionary, office bearer, officer, representative

officiate *v* chair, conduct, manage, oversee, preside, serve, superintend; (*Inf*) emcee

officious *adj* bustling, dictatorial, forward, impertinent, inquisitive, interfering, intrusive, meddlesome, meddling, mischievous, obtrusive, opinionated, overbusy, overzealous, self-important; (*Inf*) pushy

off-load *v* disburden, discharge, dump, get rid of, jettison, shift, take off, transfer, unburden, unload, unship

off-putting *adj* daunting, discomfiting, disconcerting, discouraging, dismaying, dispiriting, disturbing, formidable, frustrating, intimidating, unnerving, unsettling, upsetting

offset *v* balance out, cancel out, compensate for, counteract, counterbalance, counterpoise, countervail, make up for, neutralize

offshoot *n* adjunct, appendage, branch, by-product, development, limb, outgrowth, spin-off, sprout

often *adv* again and again, frequently, generally, many a time, over and over again, repeatedly, time after time, time and again

oil *v* grease, lubricate

old *adj* advanced in years, aged, ancient, decrepit, elderly, full of years, grey, grey-haired, grizzled, hoary, mature, past one's prime, patriarchal, senescent, senile, venerable; (*Inf*) getting on, over the hill; antediluvian, antiquated, antique, cast-off, crumbling, dated, decayed, done, hackneyed, obsolete, old-fashioned, outdated, outmoded, out of date, passé, stale, superannuated, timeworn, unfashionable, unoriginal, worn-out; aboriginal, antique, archaic, bygone, early, immemorial, of old, of yore, original, primeval, primitive, primordial, pristine, remote; age-old, experienced, familiar, hardened, long-established, of long standing, practised, skilled, time-honoured, traditional, versed, veteran, vintage

old-fashioned *adj* ancient, antiquated, archaic, behind the times, dated, dead, *démodé,* fusty, musty, obsolescent, obsolete, oldfangled, old-fogyish, old hat, old time, outdated, outmoded, out of date, out of style, passé, past, superannuated, unfashionable; (*Inf*) not with it, out of the ark, square

omen *n* augury, foreboding, foretoken, indication, portent, premonition, presage, prognostic, prognostication, sign, straw in the wind, warning, writing on the wall

ominous *adj* baleful, dark, fateful, foreboding, inauspicious, menacing, minatory, portentous, premonitory, sinister, threatening, unpromising, unpropitious

omission *n* default, exclusion, failure, forgetfulness, gap, lack, leaving out, neglect, non-inclusion, over sight

omit *v* disregard, drop, eliminate, exclude, fail, forget, give something a miss, leave out, leave something undone, let something slide, miss out, neglect, overlook, pass over, skip

once *adv* at one time, formerly, in the old days, in the past, in times gone by, in times past, long ago, once upon a time, previously; **at once** directly, forthwith, immediately, instantly, now, rightaway, straight away, this very minute, without delay, without hesitation; at the same time, simultaneously, together

one-sided *adj* biased, coloured, discriminatory, inequitable, lopsided, partial, partisan, prejudiced, unequal, unfair, unjust

onlooker *n* bystander, eyewitness, looker-on, observer, spectator, viewer, watcher, witness

only *adv* at most, barely, exclusively, just, merely, purely, simply

only *adj* exclusive, individual, lone, one and only, single, sole, solitary, unique

onslaught *n* assault, attack, blitz, charge, offensive, onrush, onset

ooze *v* bleed, discharge, drain, dribble, drip, drop, emit, escape, exude, filter, leach, leak, overflow with, percolate, seep strain, sweat, weep

opaque *adj* clouded, cloudy, dim, dull, filmy, hazy, impenetrable, lustreless, muddied, muddy, murky, obfuscated, turbid

open *adj* agape, ajar, expanded, extended, gaping, revealed, spread out, unbarred, unclosed, uncovered, unfastened, unfolded, unfurled, unlocked, unobstructed, unsealed, yawning; airy, bare, clear, exposed, extensive, free, navigable, not built-up, passable, rolling, spacious, sweeping, uncluttered, uncrowded, unenclosed, unfenced, unsheltered, wide, wide-open; accessible, available, free, general, nondiscriminatory, public, unconditional, unengaged, unoccupied, unqualified, unrestricted, vacant; apparent, avowed, barefaced, blatant, clear, conspicuous, downright, evident, flagrant, frank, manifest, noticeable, obvious, overt, lain, unconcealed, undisguised, visible; arguable, debatable, moot, undecided, unresolved, unsettled, up in the air, yet to be decided; artless, candid, fair, frank, guileless, honest, ingenious, innocent, natural, sincere, transparent, unreserved; exposed, undefended, unfortified, unprotected

open *v* begin, begin business, commence, get the ball rolling, inaugurate, initiate, launch, put up one's plate, set in motion, set up shop, start; (*Inf*) kickoff; clear, crack, throw wide, unbar, unblock, unclose, uncork, uncover, undo, unfaste, unlock, unseal, untie, unwrap; expand, spread out, unfold, unfurl, unroll

open-air *adj* alfresco, outdoor

opening *n* aperture, breach, break, chink, cleft, crack, fissure, gap, hole, interstice, orifice, perforation, rent, rupture, slot, space, split, vent; chance, occasion, opportunity, place, vacancy; beginning, birth, commencement, dawn, inauguration, inception, initiation, launch, launch ing, onset, outset, start; (*Inf*) break, kickoff, look-in

opening *adj* beginning, commencing, early, first, inaugural, initial, initiatory, introductory, maiden, primary

open-minded *adj* broad, broad minded, catholic, dispassionate, enlightened, fee, impartial, liberal, reasonable, receptive, tolerant, unbiased, undogmatic, unprejudiced

operate *v* act, be in action, function, go, perform, run, work

operation *n* action, affair, course, exercise, motion, movement, performance, procedure, process, use, working; in operation; effective, functioning, going, in action, in force, operative; activity, agency, effect, effort, force, influence, instrumentality, manipulation; affair, business, deal, enterprise, proceeding, transaction, undertaking; assault, campaign, exercise, manoeuvre

operational *adj* functional, going, in working order, operative, prepared, ready, useable, viable, workable, working

operator *n* conductor, driver, handler, mechanic, operative, practitioner, skilled employee, technician, worker

opinion *n* assessment, belief, conception, conjecture, estimation, feeling, idea, impression, judgment, mid, notion, persuasion, point of view, sentiment, theory, view

opinionated *adj* adamant, biased, bigoted, bull-headed, cocksure, dictatorial, doctrinaire, dogmatic, inflexible, open-minded, receptive, tolerant, unbiased, unbigoted, unprejudiced

opponent *n* adversary, antagonist, challenger, competitor, contestant, disputant, dissentient, enemy, foe, opposer, rival, the opposition

opportune *adj* advantageous, appropriate, apt, auspicious, convenient, favourable, felicitous, fit, fitting, fortunate, happy, lucky, proper, propitious, seasonable, suitable, timely, well-timed

opportunity *n* chance, convenience, hour, moment, occasion, opening, scope, time; (*Inf*) break, look-in

oppose *v* bar, check, combat, confront, contradict, counter, counterattack, defy, face, fight, fly in the face of, hinder, obstruct, prevent, resist, speak against, stand up to, take a stand against, take issue with, take on, thwart, withstand

opposed *v* against, antagonistic, antipathetic, antithetical, at daggers drawn, clashing, conflicting, contrary, dissentient, hostile, incompatible, inimical, in opposition, opposing, opposite; (*Inf*) anti

opposite *adj* corresponding, facing, fronting; adverse, antagonistic, antithetical, conflicting, contradictory, contrary, contrasted, diametrically, opposed, different, differing, diverse, hostile, inconsistent, inimical, irreconcilable, opposed, reverse, unlike

opposite *n* antithesis, contradiction, contrary, converse, inverse, reverse, the other extreme; (*Inf*) the other side of the coin

opposition *n* antagonism, competition, contrariety, counteraction, disapproval, hostility, obstruction, obstructiveness, prevention, resistance, unfriendliness; antagonist, competition, foe, opponent, other side, rival

oppress *v* afflict, burden, depress, dispirit, harass, lie or weigh heavy upon, sadden, take the heart out of, torment, vex; abuse, crush, harry, maltreat, overpower, overwhelm, persecute, rule with an iron hand, subdue, subjugate, suppress, trample, underfoot, tyrannize over, wrong

oppression *n* abuse, brutality, calamity, cruelty, hardship, harshness, injury, injustice, iron hand, maltreatment, misery, persecution, severity, subjection, suffering, tyranny

oppressive *adj* brutal, burdensome, cruel, despotic, grinding, harsh, heavy, inhuman, onerous, overbearing, overwhelming, repressive, severe, tyrannical, unjust; airless, close, heavy, muggy, overpowering, stifling, stuffy, suffocating, sultry, torrid

oppressor *n* autocrat, bully, despot, harrier, intimidator, iron hand, persecutor, scourge, slavedriver, taskmaster, tormentor, tyrant

opt for *v* choose, decide on, elect, make a selection, pump for, prefer; (*Inf*) go for

optimistic *adj* assured, bright, buoyant, buoyed up, cheerful, confident, encouraged, expectant, hopeful, positive, sanguine

optimum *adj* best, choicest, flawless, highest, ideal, most favourable or advantageous, optimal, peak, perfect, superlative; (*Inf*) A1

option *n* alternative, choice, election, preference, selection

optional *adj* discretionary, elective, extra, noncompulsory, open, possible, up to the individual, voluntary

oracle *n* augur, Cassandra, prophet, seer, sibyl, soothsayer; answer, augury, divination, divine utterance, prediction, prognostication, prophecy, revelation, vision

oral *adj* spoken, verbal, viva, voice, vocal

orator *n* Cicero, declaimer, lecturer,

public speaker, rhetorician, speaker, spellbinder; (*Inf*) spieler

oratory *n* declamation, elocution, eloquence, grandiloquence, public speaking, rhetoric, speechifying, speech-making; (*Inf*) spieling

orbit *n* circle, circumgyration, course, cycle, ellipse, path, revolution, rotation, track, trajectory; ambit, compass, course, domain, influence, range, reach, scope, sphere, sphere of influence, sweep

orbit *v* circle, circumnavigate, encircle, revolve around

ordain *v* anoint, appoint, call, consecrate, destine, elect, frock, invest, nominate; fate, foreordain, intend, predestine, predetermine; decree, dictate, enact, enjoin, fix, lay down, legislate, order, prescribe, pronounce, rule, set, will

ordeal *n* affliction, agony, anguish, nightmare, suffering, teat torture, trial, tribulations, troubles

order *n* arrangement, harmony, method, neatness, orderliness, organization, pattern, plan, propriety, regularity, symmetry, system, tidiness; arrangement, array, categorization, classification, codification, disposal, disposition, grouping, lay out, line, line-up, ordering, place ment, progression, sequence, series structure, succession; (*Inf*) setup; calm, control, discipline, law, law and order, peace, quiet, tranquillity; caste, class, degree, grade, hierarchy, position, rank, status; breed, cast, class, family, genre, genus, ilk, kind, sort, species, subclass, taxonomic group, tribe, type; (*Inf*) pecking order; behest, command, decree, dictate, direction, directive, injunction, instruction, law, mandate, ordinance, precept, regulation, rule, stipulation; (*Inf*) say-so; application, booking, commission, request, requisition, reservation; association, brotherhood, community, company, fraternity, guild, league, lodge, organization, sect, sisterhood, society, sodality, union

order *v* adjure, bid, charge, command, decree, direct, enact, enjoin, instruct, ordain, prescribe, require; apply for, authorize, book, call for, contract for engage, prescribe, request, reserve. send away for; adjust, align, arrange, catalogue, class, classify, conduct, control, dispose, group, lay out, manage, marshal, neaten, organize, put to rights, regulate, set in order, sort out, systematize

orderly *adj* business-like, in order, methodical, neat, regular, scientific, shipshape, systematic, systemized, tidy, trim, well-organized, well-regulated; (*Inf*) in apple-pie order; controlled, decorous, disciplined, law-abiding, nonviolent, peaceable, quiet, restrained, well-behaved

ordinary *adj* accustomed, common, customary, established, everyday, habitual, humdrum, normal, prevailing, quotidian, regular, routine, settled, standard, stock, typical, usual, wanted; (*Inf*) common or garden; conventional, familiar, homespun, household, humble, modest, plain, prosaic, run-of-the-mill, simple, unmemorable, unpretentious, unremarkable, workaday; average, commonplace, fair, indifferent, inferior, mean, mediocre, pedestrian, second-rate, stereotyped, undistinguished, unexceptional, uninspired, unremarkable

organ *n* device, implement, instrument, tool; element, member, part, process, structure, unit; agency, channel, forum, journal, means, medium, mouthpiece, newspaper, paper, periodical, publication, vehicle, voice

organism *n* animal, being, body, creature, entity, living thing, structure

organization *n* assembling, assembly, construction, coordination, disposal, formation, forming formulation, making, management, methodology, organization, planning, regulation, running, standardization, structuring; arrangement, chemistry, composition, configuration, conformation, constitution, design, format, framework, grouping, make-up, method, organism, pattern, plan, structure, system, unity, whole; association, body, combine, company, concern, confederation, consortium, corporation, federation, group, institution, league, syndicate; (*Inf*) outfit

orgy *n* bacchanal, bacchanalia, debauch, revel, revelry, Saturnalia; bout, excess, indulgence, overindulgence, splurge, spree, surfeits; (*Inf*) binge

origin *n* base, basis, cause, derivation, *fons et origo*, fountain, fountainhead, occasion, provenance, root, roots, source, spring, welspring; beginning, birth, commencement, creation, dawning, early stages, emergence, fountain, genesis, inauguration, inception, launch, origination, outset, start

original *adj* aboriginal, autochthonous, commencing, earliest, early, embryonic, first, infant, initial, introductory, opening, primary, primitive, primordial, pristine, rudimentary, starting; creative, fertile, fresh, imaginative, ingenious, innovative, innovatory, inventive, new, novel, resourceful, seminal, unconventional, unprecedented, untried, unusual; archtypal, authentic, first, first-hand, genuine, master, primary, prototypical

origin *n* archetype, master, model, paradigm, pattern, precedent, prototype, standard, type

originality *n* boldness, break with tradition, cleverness, creativeness, creative spirit, creativity, daring, freshness, imagination, imaginativeness, individuality, ingenuity, innovation, innovativeness, inventiveness, new ideas, newness, novelty, resourcefulness, unconventionality, unorthodoxy

originate *v* arise, be born, begin, come, derive, emanate, emerge, flow, issue, proceed, result, rise, spring, start, stem; bring about, conceive, create, develop, discover, evolve, form, formulate, generate, give birth to, inaugurate, initiate, institute, introduce, invent, launch, pioneer, produce, set in motion

ornament *n* accessory, adornment, bauble, decoration, embellishment, frill, furbelow, garnish, gewgaw, knick-knack, trimming, trinket;

flower, honour, jewel, leading light, pride, treasure

ornamental *adj* attractive, beautifying, decorative, embellishing, for show, showy

ornate *adj* aureate, baroque, beautiful, bedecked, busy, convoluted, decorated, elaborate, elegant, fancy, florid, flowery, fussy, grandiose, ornamented, ostentatious, overelaborate, pompous, rococo

orthodox *adj* accepted, approved, conformist, conventional, correct, customary, doctrinal, established, official, received, sound, traditional, true, well-established; (*Inf*) kosher

ostensible *adj* alleged, apparent, avowed, exhibited, manifest, outward, plausible, pretended, professed, purported, seeming, so-called, specious, superficial, supposed

ostentation *n* affection, boasting, display, exhibitionism, flamboyance, flashiness, flaunting, flourish, pageantry, parade, pomp, pretension, pretentiousness, show, showiness, vaunting, window-dressing; (*Inf*) showing off, swank

ostentatious *adj* boastful, conspicuous, crass, dashing, extravagant, flamboyant, flashy, flaunted, gaudy, loud, obtrusive, pompous, pretentious, showy, sombre, van; (*Inf*) flash, swanky

other *adj* added, additional, alternative, auxiliary, extra, further, more, spare, supplementary; contrasting, different, dissimilar, distinct, diverse, remaining, separate, unrelated, variant

otherwise *adv* differently, if not, in other respects, in other ways, or else, or then

out *adj* impossible, not allowed, riled out, unacceptable; (*Inf*) not on; abroad, absent, away, elsewhere, gone, not at home, outside

outbreak *n* burst, epidemic, eruption, explosion, flare-up, flash, out burst, rash, spasm, upsurge

outcast *n* castaway. derelict. displaced person, exile, leper, pariah, *persona non grata*, refugee, reprobate, untouchable, vagabond, wretch

outcome *n* aftereffect, aftermath, conclusion, consequence, end, end result, issue, result, upshot; (*Inf*) payoff

outcry *n* clamour, commotion, complaint, cry, exclamation, howl, hue and cry, hullabaloo, noise, outburst, protest, scream, screech, uproar, yell

outdated *adj* antiquated, antique, archaic, *démodé,* obsolete, old-fashioned, outmoded, out of date, out of fashion, passé, unfashionable; (*Inf*) behind the times

outdoor *adj* alfresco, open-air, out-of-doors, outside

outer *adj* exposed, exterior, external, outlying, outside, outward, peripheral, remote, superficial, surface

outfit *n* accoutrements, clothes, costume, ensemble, garb, gear, kit, suit, trappings; (*Inf*) get-up, rigout, togs

outfit *v* accoutre, appoint, equip, fit out, furnish, kit out, provision, stock, supply, turn out

outgoing *adj* departing, ex-, former, last, late, leaving, past, retiring, with-drawing; affable, affectionate, communicative, demonstrative, easygoing, extrovert, friendly, genial, gregarious, sociable, talka tive, unreserved

outgoings *pl n* costs, expenditure, expenses, outlay, overheads

outing *n* excursion, expedition, jaunt, pleasure trip, trip; (*Inf*) spin

outlandish *adj* alien, barbarous, bizarre, eccentric, exotic, fantastic, foreign, freakish, grotesque, outré, preposterous, queer, strange, unheard-of, weird; (*Inf*) far-out

outlaw *n* bandit, brigand, desperado, fugitive, highwayman, marauder, outcast, pariah, robber

outlaw *v* ban, banish, bar, condemn, disallow, embargo, exclude, forbid, interdict, make illegal, prohibit, proscribe, put a price on someone's head

outlay *n* cost, disbursement, expenditure, expenses, investment, outgoings, spending

outlet *n* avenue, channel, duct, egress, exit, means of expression, opening, orifice, release, safety, valve, vent, way out

outline *n* draft, drawing, frame, framework, layout, lineaments, plan, rough, skeleton, sketch, tracing; bare facts, main features, recapitulation, résumé, rough idea, rundown, sketch, summary, synopsis, thumbnail; configuration, contour, delineation, figure, form, profile, shape, silhouette

outline *v* adumbrate, delineate, draft, plan, rough out, sketch in, summarize, trace

outlook *n* angle, attitude, frame of mind, perspective, point of view, slant, standpoint, viewpoint, views; expectations, forecast, future, prospect

output *n* achievement, manufacture, product, production, productivity, yield

outrage *n* atrocity, barbarism, enormity, evil, inhumanity; abuse, affront, desecration, indignity, injury, insult, offence, profanation, rape, ravishing, shock, violation, violence; anger, fury, hurt, indignation, resentment, shock, wrath

outrage *v* affront, incense, infuriate, madden, make one's blood boil, offend, scandalize, shock

outrageous *adj* abominable, atrocious, barbaric, beastly, egregious, flagrant, heinous, horrible, infamous, inhuman, iniquitous, nefarious, scandalous, shocking, unspeakable, villainous, violent, wicked; disgraceful, excessive, exorbitant, extravagant, immoderate, offensive, preposterous, scandalous, shocking, unreasonable; (*Inf*) steep

outright *adj* absolute, arrant, complete, consummate, downright, out-and-out, perfect pure, thorough, thoroughgoing, total, unconditional, undeniable, unmitigated, unquali fied, utter, wholesale; definite, direct, flat, straightforward, unequivocal, unqualified

outright *adv* absolutely, completely, explicitly, openly, overtly, straightforwardly, thoroughly, to the full, without hesitation, without restraint; at once, cleanly, immediately, instantaneously, instantly, on the spot, straight away, there and then, without more ado

outset *n* beginning, commencement, early days, inauguration, inception, onset, opening, start, starting point; (*Inf*) kickoff

outside *adj* exterior, external, extramural, extraneous, extreme, out, outdoor, outer, outermost, outward, surface; distant, faint, marginal, negligible, remote, slight, slim, small, unlikely

outside *n* exterior, façade, face, front, skin, surface, topside

outskirts *pl n* borders, boundary, edge, environs, faubourgs, periphery, purlieus, suburbia, suburbs, vicinity

outspoken *adj* abrupt, blunt, candid, direct, explicit, forthright, frank, free, free-spoken, open, plain-spoken, round, unceremonious, undissembling, unequivocal, unreserved

outstanding *adj* celebrated, distinguished, eminent, excellent, exceptional, great, important, impressive, meritorious, pre-eminent, special, superior, superlative, well-known; arresting, conspicuous, eye-catching, marked, memorable, notable, noteworthy, prominent, salient, signal, striking; due, ongoing, open, owing, payable, pending, remaining, uncollected, unpaid, unresolved, unsettled

outward *adj* apparent, evident, exterior, external, noticeable, observable, obvious, ostensible, outer, outside, perceptible, superficial, surface, visible

outweigh *v* cancel out, compensate for, eclipse, make up for, outbalance, overcome, override, predominate, preponderate, prevail over, take precedence over, tip the scales

outwit *v* cheat, circumvent, deceive, defraud, dupe, get the better of, make a fool of, outfox, outjockey, outmanoeuvre, outthink, swindle; (*Inf*) outsmart, put one over on, run rings round, take in

ovation *n* acclaim, acclamation, applause, cheering, cheers, clapping, laudation, plaudits, tribute

over *adv* ancient history, at an end, by, bygone, closed, completed, concluded, dead, done with, ended, finished, gone, no more, past, terminated; extra, in addition, in excess, left over, remaining, superfluous, surplus, unused

over *prep* above, on, on top of, superior to, upon; above, exceeding, in excess of, more than; around, everywhere, throughout

overall *adj* all-embracing, blanket, complete, comprehensive general, global, inclusive, long-range, long-term, total, umbrella

overbalance *v* capsize, keel over, lose one's balance, lose one's footing, overset, overturn, slip, take a tumble, tip over, topple over, tumble, turn turtle, upset

overbearing *v* arrogant, autocratic, cavalier, despotic, dictatorial, dogmatic, domineering, haughty, high-handed, imperious, lordly, magisterial, officious, oppressive, overweening, peremptory, supercilious, superior, tyrannical; (*Inf*) bossy

overcast *adj* clouded, clouded over, cloudy, darkened, dismal, dreary, dull, grey, hazy, leaden, lowering, murky, sombre, sunless, threatening

overcharge *v* cheat, fleece, short-change, surcharge; (*Inf*) diddle, do, rip off

overcome *v* beat, best, be victorious, conquer, crush, defeat, get the better of, master, overpower, overthrow, overwhelm, prevail, render incapable, rise above, subdue, subjugate, surmount, survive, triumph over, vanquish, weather, worst; (*Inf*) come out on top, lick

overcrowded *adj* choked, congested, crammed full, jam-packed, like the Black Hole of Calcutta, overloaded, overpopulated, packed out, swarming

overdo *v* be intemerate, belabour, carry too far, exaggerate, gild the lily, go to extremes, not know when to stop, overindulge, overplay, overreach, overstate, overuse, over work, run, riot; (*Inf*) do to death, go overboard, lay it on thick

overdone *adj* beyond all bounds, exaggerated, excessive, fulsome, immoderate, inordinate, overelaborate, preposterous, too much, undue, unnecessary; burnt, burnt to a cinder, charred, dried up, over cooked, spoiled

overdue *adj* behindhand, behind schedule, behind time, belated, late, long delayed, owing, tardy, unpunctual; (*Inf*) not before time

overemphasize *v* belabour, blow up out of all proportion, lay too much stress on, make something out of nothing, make too much of, overdramatize, overstress; (*Inf*) make a big thing of, make a mountain out of a molehill

overflow *v* cover, deluge, drown, flood, inundate, soak submerge, swamp

overflow *n* discharge, flash flood, flood, flooding, inundation, over abundance, spilling over, surplus

overflowing *adj* abounding, bountiful, brimful, copious, plentiful, profuse, rife, superabundant, swarm ing, teeming, thronged

overhaul *v* check, examine, inspect, recondition, re-examine, repair, restore, service, survey; (*Inf*) do up; catch up with, draw level with, get ahead of, overtake, pass

overhaul *n* check, checkup, examination, going-over, inspection, reconditioning, service; (*Inf*) going-over

overhead *adv* above, aloft, atop, in the sky, on high skyward, up above, upward

overhead *adj* aerial, overhanging, roof, upper

overheads *pl n* burden, disbursement, expenditure, expenses, operating costs, running costs

overjoyed *adj* delightful, deliriously happy, elated, euphoric, happy as a lark, happy as a sandboy, in raptures, joyful, jubilant, rapturous, thrilled, tickled pink, transported; (*Inf*) on cloud nine

overload *v* encumber, oppress, overburden, overcharge, overtax, strain, weigh down; (*Inf*) saddle with

overlook *v* disregard, fail to notice, forget, ignore, leave out of consideration, leave undone, miss, neglect, omit, pass, slight, slip up on; condone, disregard, excuse, for give, let bygones be bygones, let one off with, let pass, let ride, make allowances for, pardon, turn a blind eye to

overpower *v* beat, conquer, crush, defeat, get the upper hand over, immobilize, knock out, master, overcome, overthrow, overwhelm, quell, subdue, subjugate, vanquish

overrate *v* assess too highly, exaggerate, make too much of, overestimate, overpraise, overprize, oversell, overvalue, rate too highly, think *or* expect too much of, think too highly of

overriding *adj* central, chief, compelling, determining, dominant, final, focal, major, number one, overruling, paramount, pivotal, predominant, prevailing, primary, prime, principal, ruling, supreme, ultimate

overrule *v* alter, annul, cancel, countermand, disallow, invalidate, make null and void, nullify, out vote, override, overturn, recall, repeal, rescind, reverse, revoke, rule against, set aside, veto

overseer *n* chief, foreman, manager, master, superintendent, superior, supervisor; (*Inf*) boss, gaffer, super

overshadow *v* dominate, dwarf, eclipse, excel, leave in the shade, outshine outweigh, put in the shade, render insignificant by comparison, rise above, steal the limelight from, surpass, take the precedence over, throw into the shade, tower above, transcend, upstage; adumbrate, becloud, bedim, cloud, darken, dim, obfuscate, obscure, veil

oversight *n* blunder, carelessness, delinquency, error, fault, inattention, lapse, laxity, mistake, neglect, omission, slip; administration, care, charge, control, custody, direction, handling, inspection, keeping, management, superintendence, supervision, surveillance

overtake *v* catch up with, do better than draw level with, get past, leave behind, outdistance, outdo, outstrip, overhaul, pass

overthrow *v* abolish, beat, bring down, conquer, crush, defeat, depose, dethrone, do away with master, oust, overcome overpower, overwhelm, subdue, subjugate, topple, unseat, vanquish; bring to ruin, demolish, destroy, knock down level, overturn, put an end to, raze, ruin, subvert, upend, upset

overthrow *n* defeat, deposition, destruction, dethronement, discomfiture, dispossession, downfall, end, fall, ousting, prostration, rout, ruin, subjugation, subversion, suppression, undoing unseating

overture *n* advance, approach, conciliatory move, invitation, offer, opening move, proposal, proposition, signal, tender

overturn *v* capsize, keel over, knock over, overbalance, reverse, spill, tip over, topple, tumble, upend, upset, upturn; abolish, annul, bring down, countermand, depose, destroy, invalidate, overthrow, repeal, rescind, reverse, set aside, unseat

overwhelm *v* bury, crush, deluge, engulf, flood, inundate, snow under, submerge, swamp; confuse, devastate, overcome, overpower, prostrate, render speechless, stagger; (*Inf*) bowl over, knock someone for six

overwhelming *adj* breathtaking, crushing, devastating, invincible, irresistible, overpowering, shattering, stunning, towering, uncontrollable, vast, vastly superior

overwork *v* be a slave driver or hard taskmaster to, burden, burn the midnight oil, drive into the ground, exhaust, exploit, fatigue, oppress, overstrain, overtax, overuse, prostrate, strain, wear out, weary, work one's fingers to the bone

overwrought *adj* agitated, beside oneself, distracted, excited, frantic, keyed up, on edge, overexcited, overworked, stirred, tense; (*Inf*) in a state, in a tizzy, strung up, uptight, worked-up, wound-up

owing *adj* due, outstanding, overdue, owed, payable, unpaid, unsettled

own *adj* individual, particular, personal, private

own *n* **on one's own** alone, by one self, by one's own efforts, independently, isolated, left to one's own devise, off one's own bat, on one's tod, singly, standing on one's own two feet, unaided unassisted; **hold one's own** compete, keep going, keep one's end up, keep one's head above water, maintain one's position

own *v* be in possession of, be responsible for, enjoy, have, hold, keep, possess, retain; **own up to** admit, confess, make a clean breast of, tell the truth about; (*Inf*) come clean about; acknowledge, admit, allow, allow to be valid, avow, concede, confess, disclose, grant, recognize; (*Inf*) go along with

owner *n* holder, landlord, lord, master, mistress, possessor, proprietor, proprietress, proprietrix

ownership *n* dominion, possession, proprietary rights, proprietoryship, right of possession, title

P

pace *n* gait, measure, step, stride, tread, walk; momentum, motion, movement, progress, rate, speed, tempo, time, velocity

pace *v* march, patrol, pound, stride, walk back and forth, walk up and down; count, determine, mark out measure, step

pack *n* back pack, bale, bundle, burden, kit, kitbag, knapsack, load, package, packet, parcel, rucksack, truss; assemblage, band, bunch, collection, company, crew, crowd, deck, drove, flock, gang, group, herd, lot, mob, set, troop

pack *v* batch, bundle, burden, load, package, packet, store, stow; charge, compact, compress, cram, crowd, fill, jam, mob, press, ram, stuff, tamp, throng, wedge

package *n* box, carton, container, packet, parcel; amalgamation, combination, entity, unit, whole

package *v* batch, box, pack, packet, parcel up, wrap, wrap up

packed *adj* brimful, chock-a-block, chock-full, congested, cram-full, crammed, crowded, filled, full, jammed, jam-packed, loaded to the gunwales, overflowing, overloaded, packed like sardines, seething, swarming

packet *n* bag, carton, container, package, wrapper, wrapping

pact *n* agreement, alliance, arrange ment, bargain, compact, concord, concordat, contract, convention, covenant, deal, league, protocol, treaty, understanding

pad *n* buffer, cushion, stiffening, stuffing, wad; block, jotter, notepad, tablet, writing pad; foot, paw, sole

pad *v* cushion, fill, line, pack, protect, shape, stuff; **pad out** amplify, augment, eke out, elaborate, fill out, flesh out, inflate, lengthen, protract, spin out, stretch

padding *n* filling, packing, stuffing, wadding

paddle *n* oar, scull, sweep

paddle *v* oar, propel, pull, punt, row, scull; dabble, plash, plunge, slop, splash about, stir, wade

paddock *n* corral, enclosure, field, meadow, pen, yard

pagan *n* atheist, disbeliever, heathen, idolater, infidel, non-believer, polytheist, unbeliever

pagan *adj* atheistic, heathen, heathenish, idolatrous, infidel, irreligious, polytheistic

page *n* folio, leaf, recto, sheet, side, verso; episode, epoch, era, event, incident, stage, time; attendant, bellboy, bellhop, footboy, page-boy, servant, squire

page *v* announce, call, call out, preconize, seek, send for, summon; foliate, paginate

pageant *n* display, extravaganza, parade, procession, ritual, show, spectacle, tableau

pain *n* ache, cramp, discomfort, hurt, irritation, pang, smarting, soreness, spasm, suffering, tender ness, throb, trouble, twinge; affliction, agony, anguish, bitterness, distress, grief, heartache, misery, suffering, torment, torture, tribulation, vexation, woe, wretchedness

pain *v* ache, chafe, discomfort, harm, hurt, inflame, injure, smart, sting, throb; afflict, aggrieve, agonize, cut to the quick, disquiet, distress, grieve, hurt, sadden, torment, torture, vex, worry, wound

pained *adj* aggrieved, anguished, distressed, hurt, injured, offended, reproachful, stung, unhappy, upset, worried, wounded; (*Inf*) miffed

painful *adj* afflictive, disagreeable, distasteful, distressing, grievous, saddening, unpleasant, aching, agonizing, excruciating, harrowing, hurting, inflamed, raw, smarting, sore, tender, throbbing; arduous, difficult, hard, laborious, severe, tedious, troublesome, trying, vexatious

painkiller *n* anaesthetic, analgesic, anodyne, drug, palliative, remedy, sedative

painless *adj* easy, effortless, fast, no trouble, pain-free, quick, simple, trouble-free

pains *pl n* assiduousness, bother, care, diligence, effort, industry, labour, special attention, trouble

painstaking *adj* assiduous, careful, conscientious, diligent, earnest, extracting, hard-working, industrious, meticulous, persevering, punctilious, scrupulous, sedulous, strenuous, thorough

paint *n* colour, colouring, decorate, distemper, dye, emulsion, gloss, pigment, stain, tint, whitewash; oil, oil-paint, water-colour; greasepaint, make-up

paint *v* catch a likeness, delineate, depict, describe, draw, evoke, figure, picture, portray, recount, represent, sketch; apply, coat, colour, cover, daub, decorate, slap on

pair *n* brace, combination, couple, doublet, duo, match, matched set, span, twins, two of a kind, twosome, yoke

pair *v* bracket, couple, join, marry, match, match up, mate, par off, put together, team, twin, wed, yoke

palatial *adj* de luxe, grand, illustrious, imposing, luxurious, magnificent, majestic, opulent, plush, regal, spacious, splendid, stately, sumptuous; (*Inf*) posh

pale *adj* anaemic, ashen, ashy, bleached, bloodless, colourless, faded, light, pallid, pasty, sallow, wan, washed-out, white, whitish; dim, faint, feeble, inadequate, poor, thin, weak

paltry *adj* base, beggarly, contemptible, derisory, despicable, inconsiderable, insignificant, low, meagre, mean, minor, miserable, petty, pitiful, poor, puny, slight, small, sorry, trifling, trivial, unimportant, worthless, wretched; (*Inf*) piddling

pamper *v* baby, cater to one's every whim, coddle, cosset, fondle, ratify, humour, indulge, mollycoddle, pet, spoil

pamphlet *n* booklet, brochure, circular, folder, leaflet, tract

pan *n* casserole, container, fish-kettle, frying pan, pot, pressure cooker, saucepan, skillet, vessel, wok

pan *v* censure, criticize, flay, knock, roast; (*Inf*) knock, rubbish, slag off, slam, slate; search for, sift for; follow, scan, sweep, track

panacea *n* cure-all, elixir, nostrum, sovereign remedy, universal cure

panache *n* a flourish, *brio,* dash, élan, flair, flamboyance, spirit, style, swagger, verve, zest; (*Inf*) pizzazz

pancake *n* blini, crêpe, drop scone, tortilla

pandemic *adj* extensive, global, prevalent, rampant, rife, universal, widespread

pandemonium *n* bedlam, chaos, clamour, commotion, confusion, din, hubbub, hue and cry, hullabaloo, racket, rumpus, tumult, turmoil, uproar; (*Inf*) ruckus, ruction

pang *n* ache, agony, anguish, discomfort, distress, gripe, pin, prick, spasm, stab, sting, stitch, twinge, wrench

panic *n* agitation, alarm, consternation, dismay, fear, fright, horror, hysteria, scare, terror

panorama *n* bird's-eye view, prospect, scenery, scenic view, view, vista; overall picture

pant *v* blow, breathe, gasp, heave, huff, palpitate, puff, throb, wheeze

paper *n* assignment, certificate, deed, document, instrument, record; archive, diaries, documents, dossier, file, letters, record; daily, gazette, journal, news, newspaper, organ, weekly; (*Inf*) rag; article, dissertation, essay, report, study, thesis

paper *v* cover with paper, decorate, hang, line, paste up, wallpaper; **paper over** camouflage, conceal, disguise, gloss over, hide, white wash

papers *v* legal document; ID, identification papers, identity card; documents, files, letters, records

par *n* average, level, mean, median, norm, standard, usual

parable *n* allegory, exemplum, fable, lesson, moral tale, story

parade *n* array, cavalcade, ceremony, column march, pageant, procession, review, spectacle, train; array, display, exhibition, flaunting, ostentation, pomp, show, spectacle

parade *v* defile, march, process; air, brandish, display, exhibit, flaunt, make a show of, show; (*Inf*) show off, strut, swank, swagger, vaunt

paradise *n* bliss, delight, felicity, heaven, seventh heaven, Shangri-La, utopia

paradox *n* absurdity, ambiguity, anomaly, contradiction, enigma, inconsistency, mystery, oddity, puzzle

paragon *n* apotheosis, archetype, criterion, cynosure, epitome, exemplar, ideal, jewel, masterpiece, model, nonpareil, paradigm, pattern, prototype, quintessence, standard

paragraph *n* clause, item, notice, part, passage, portion, section, subdivision

parallel *adj* aligned, alongside, coextensive, equidistant, side by side; akin, analogous, complementary, correspondent, corresponding, like, matching, resembling, similar, uniform

parallel *n* analogue, complement, corollary, counterpart, duplicate, equal, equivalent, likeness, match, twin; analogy, comparison, correlation, correspondence, likeness, parallelism, resemblance, similarity

paralyse *v* cripple, debilitate, disable, incapacitate, lame; anaesthetize, arrest, benumb, freeze, halt, immobilize, numb, petrify, stop dead, stun, stupefy, transfix

paralysis *adj* immobility, incapacity, palsy; arrest, breakdown, halt, shutdown, stagnation, standstill, stoppage

paramount *adj* capital, cardinal, chief, dominate, eminent, first, foremost, main, outstanding, predominant, pre-eminent, primary, prime, principle, superior, supreme

paraphernalia *pl n* accoutrements, apparatus, appurtenances, baggage, belongings, effects, equipage, equipment, gear, impedimenta, material, stuff, tackle, things, trappings; (*Inf*) clobber

parasite *n* bloodsucker, cadger, drone, freeloader, hanger-on, leech, scrounger; (*Inf*) sponger

parcel *n* bundle, carton, pack, package, packet; **parcel up** do up, pack, pack, package, tie up, wrap

parched *adj* arid, dehydrated, dried up, dry, scorched, shrivelled, thirsty, waterless, withered

pardon *v* absolve, acquit, amnesty, condone, exculpate, excuse, exonerate, forgive, free, liberate, overlook, release, remit, reprieve; (*Inf*) let off

pardon *n* absolution, acquittal, allowance, amnesty, condonation, discharge, excuse, exoneration, for giveness, grace, indulgence, mercy, release, remission, reprieve

pardonable *adj* allowable, condon able, excusable, forgivable, minor, not serious, permissible, under standable, venial

parent *v* begetter, father, guardian, mother, procreator, progenitor, sire

parentage *n* ancestry, birth, derivation, decent, extraction, family, line, lineage, origin, paternity, pedigree, race, stock

parish *n* church, churchgoers, community, congregation, flock, fold, parishioners

park *n* estate, garden, grounds, parkland, pleasure garden, recreation ground, woodland

parliament *n* assembly, congress, convocation, council, diet, legislature, senate

parliamentary *adj* congressional, deliberative, governmental, lawgiving, lawmaking, legislative

parlour *n* best room, drawing room, front room, lounge, reception room, sitting room

parody *n* burlesque, caricature, imitation, lampoon, satire, skit; (*Inf*) send-up, spoof, takeoff

parody *v* burlesque, caricature, lampoon, mimic, poke fun at, satirize, travesty; (*Inf*) do a takeoff of, send up, spoof, take off

parry *v* block, deflect, fend off, hold at bay, rebuff, repel, repulse, stave off, ward off; avoid, circumvent, dodge, evade, fence, fight shy of, shun, sidestep; (*Inf*) duck

part *n* bit, fraction, fragment, lot, particle, piece, portion, scrap, section, sector, segment, share, slice; branch, component, constituent, department, division, element, ingredient, limb, member, module, organ, piece, unit; behalf, cause, concern, faction, interest, party, side; bit, business, capacity, charge, duty, function, involvement, office, pace, responsibility, role, say, share task, work; character, lines, role; **in good part** cheerfully, cordially, good-naturedly, well, without offence; **in part** a little, in some measure, partially, partly, slightly, somewhat, to a certain extent, to some degree

part *v* break, cleave, come apart, detach, disconnect, disjoin, dismantle, disunite, divide, rend, separate, server, split, tear; break, cleave, come apart, detach, disconnect, disjoin, dismantle, disunite, divide, rend, separate, sever, split, tear; break up, depart, go, go away, go their separate ways, leave, part company, quit, say goodbye, separate, split up, take one's leave, withdraw

partake *v* engage, enter into, join in, participate, share, take part; consume, drink, eat, share in, take

partial *adj* fragmentary, imperfect, incomplete, limited, uncompleted, unfinished; biased, discriminatory, influenced, interested, one-sided, partisan, predispose, prejudiced, tendentious, unfair, unjust

partiality *n* bias, favouritism, partisanship, predisposition, preference, prejudice; affinity, fondness, inclination, liking, love, penchant, predilection, predisposition, preference, proclivity, taste, weakness

participant *n* associate, contributor, member, partaker, participator, party, shareholder

participate *v* be a participant, be a party, engage in, enter into, get in on the act, have a hand in, join in, partake, perform, share, take part

particle *n* atom, bit, crumb, grain, iota, jot, mite, molecule, mote, piece, scrap, shred, speck, tittle, whit

particular *adj* distinct, exact, express, peculiar, precise, special, specific; especial, exceptional, marked, notable, noteworthy, remarkable, singular, uncommon, unusual; critical, dainty, demanding, discriminating, exacting fastidious, finicky, fussy, meticulous, overnice; (*Inf*) choosy, pernickety, picky

particular *n* circumstance, detail, fact, feature, item, specification

particularly *adv* decidedly, especially, exceptionally, markedly, notably, outstandingly, peculiarly, singularly, surprisingly, uncommonly, unusually

parting *n* adieu, departure, farewell, going, goodbye, leave-taking, valediction; breaking, detachment, divergence, division, partition rift, rupture, separation, split

partisan *n* adherent, backer, champion, devotee, disciple, follower, stalwart, supporter, upholder, votary

partisan *adj* biased, factional, interested, one-sided, partial, prejudiced, sectarian, tendentious

partisan *n* guerrilla, irregular, resistance, fighter, underground fighter

partition *n* breaking up, dividing, division, segregation, separation, severance, splitting up, subdivision; barrier, divider, dividing wall, room divider, fence, screen, screen wall

partition *v* apportion, cut up, divide, parcel out, portion, section, segment, separate, share, split up, subdivide

partly *adv* halfway, incompletely, in part, in some measure, not fully, partially, relatively, slightly, some what, to a certain extent, up to a certain point

partner *n* accomplice, ally, associate, bedfellow, collaborator, colleague, companion, comrade, confederate, co-worker, helper, mate, participant, team-mate; bedfellow, consort, helpmate, husband, mate, spouse, wife

partnership *n* alliance, association, combine, company, conglomerate, cooperative, corporation, form, house society, union

party *n* at-home, celebration, festivity, function, gathering, reception, social, social gathering, soirée; (*Inf*) bash, do, get-together, knees-up, rave-up, shindig; band, body, company, crew, detachment, gang, gathering, group, squad, team, unit; alliance, association, cabal, clique, coalition, combination, confederacy, coterie, faction, grouping, league, set, side; individual, person, somebody, someone

pass *v* depart, elapse, flow, go, go by, lapse, leave, move, move onwards, proceed, roll, run; beat, exceed, excel, go beyond, outdistance, outdo, outstrip, surmount, surpass, transcend; answer, do, get through, graduate, pass muster, qualify, succeed, suffice, suit; (*Inf*) come up to scratch; befall, come up, develop, happen, occur, take place; convey, deliver, exchange, give, hand, kick, let have, reach, send, throw, transfer, transmit; accept, adopt, approve, authorize, decree, enact, establish, legislate, ordain, ratify, sanction, validate

pass *n* canyon, col, defile, gap, gorge, narow road, ravine; authorization, identification, licence, passport, permission, permit, safe-conduct, ticket, warrant

passable *adj* acceptable, adequate, admissible, allowable, all right, average, fair, fair enough, mediocre, middling, moderate, not too bad, ordinary, presentable, tolerable, unexceptional; (*Inf*) so-so

passage *n* avenue, channel, course, lane, opening, path, road, route, thoroughfare, way; corridor, doorway, entrance, entrance hall, exit, hall, hallway, lobby, passageway, vestibule; clause, excerpt, extract, paragraph, piece, quotation, reading, section, sentence, text, verse; crossing, journey, your, trek, trip, voyage; allowance, authorization, freedom, permission, right, safe-conduct, visa, warrant

passé *adj* antiquated, dated, obsolete, out of date, out of fashion,

passenger *n* fare, hitchhiker, pillion rider, traveller

passing *adj* brief, ephemeral, fleeting, momentary, short, short-lived, temporary, transient, transitory; casual, cursory, glancing, hasty, quick, shallow, short, slight, superficial

passion *n* animation, ardour, eagerness, emotion, excitement, feeling, fervour, fire, heat, intensity, joy, rapture, spirit, transport, warmth, zeal, zest; adoration, affection, ardour, attachment, concupiscence, desire, fondness, infatuation, itch, keenness, love, lust; craving, craze, enthusiasm, fancy, fascination, idol, infatuation, mania, obsession; anger, fit, frenzy, fury, indignation, ire, outburst, paroxysm, rage, resentment, storm, vehemence, wrath

passionate *adj* amorous, ardent, aroused, desirous, erotic, hot, loving, lustful, sensual, wanton; (*Inf*) sexy; animated, ardent, eager, emotional, enthusiastic, excited, fervent, fervid, fierce, frenzied, heartfelt, impassioned, impetuous, impulsive, intense, strong, vehement, warm, wild, zealous

passive *adj* acquiescent, complaint, docile, enduring, inactive, inert, lifeless, long-suffering, nonviolent, patient, quiescent, receptive, resigned, submissive, unassertive, uninvolved, unresisting

past *adj* accomplished, completed, done, elapsed, ended, extinct, finished, forgotten, gone, over, over and done with, spent; ancient, bygone, early, erstwhile, foregoing, former, late, long-ago, olden, preceding, previous, prior, recent

past *n* background, experience, history, life, past life

past *adv* across, beyond, by, on, over

pastel *adj* delicate, light, muted, pale, soft, soft-hued

pastime *n* activity, amusement, distraction, diversion, entertainment, game, hobby, leisure, play, recreation, relaxation, sport

pastoral *adj* Arcadian, bucolic, country, georgic, idyllic, rural, rustic, simple; clerical, ecclesiastical, ministerial, priestly

pastry *n* pie, pasty, patty, quiche, tart, vol-au-vent,

pasture *n* grass, grassland, grazing, grazing land, meadow, pasturage

pat *v* caress, dab, fondle, pet, slap, stroke, tap, touch

pat *n* clap, dab, light blow, slap, stroke, tap

patch *n* piece of material, reinforcement; bit, scrap, shred, small piece, spot, stretch, area, ground, land, plot, tract

patch *v* cover, fix, mend, reinforce, repair, sew up

patchy *adj* bitty, erratic, fitful, irregular, random, sketchy, spotty, uneven, variable, varying

patent *adj* apparent, blatant, clear, conspicuous, downright, evident, flagrant, glaring, indisputable, manifest, obvious, open, palpable, transparent, unconcealed, unequivocal, unmistakable

patent *n* copyright, invention, licence

path *n* footpath, footway, pathway, towpath, track, trail, walkway; direction, passage, procedure, road, route, track, walk, way

pathetic *adj* affecting, distressing, heartbreaking, heart-rending, melting, moving, pitiable, plaintive, poignant, sad, tender, touching

pathos *n* pitiableness, pitifulness, plaintiveness, poignancy, sadness

patience *n* calmness, composure, equanimity, even temper, forbearance, imperturbability, restraint, serenity, sufferance, tolerance, toleration; (*Inf*) cool; constancy, diligence, endurance, fortitude, long-suffering, perseverance, persistence, resignation, stoicism, submission

patient *adj* calm, composed, enduring, long-suffering, persevering, persistent, philosophical, quiet, resigned, self-possessed, serene, stoical, submissive, uncomplaining, untiring; accommodating, even-tempered, forbearing, forgiving, indulgent, lenient, mild, tolerant, understanding

patient *n* case, invalid, sick person, sufferer

patriot *n* chauvinist, flagwaving, jingo, lover of one's country, loyalist, nationalist

patriotic *adj* chauvinistic, flagwaving, jingoistic, loyal, nationalistic

patrol *n* guarding, policing, protecting, rounds, safeguarding, vigilance, watching; garrison, guard, patrolman, sentinel, watch, watchman

patrol *v* cruise, guard, inspect, keep guard, keep watch, make the rounds, police, pound, range, safeguard, walk the beat

patron *n* advocate, backer, benefactor, champion, defender, friend, guardian, helper, philanthropist, protector, sponsor, supporter; (*Inf*) angel; buyer, client, customer, frequenter, habitué, shopper

patronage *n* aid, assistance, backing, benefaction, championship, encouragement, help, promotion, sponsorship, support; business, clientele, commerce, custom, trade, trading, traffic

patronizing *adj* condescending, contemptuous, disdainful, gracious, haughty, lofty, snobbish, stooping, supercilious, superior; (*Inf*) toffee-nosed

pattern *n* arrangement, decoration, decorative design, design, device, figure, motif, ornament; arrange ment, method, order, orderliness, plan, sequence, system; kind, shape, sort, style, type, variety; design, diagram, guide, instructions, original, plan, stencil, template; archetype, criterion, cynosure, example, exemplar, guide, model, norm, original, paradigm, paragon, prototype, sample, specimen, standard

pattern *v* copy, emulate, follow, form, imitate, model, mould, order, shape, style

pauper *n* bankrupt, beggar, down-and-out, have-not, indigent, insolvent, mendicant, poor person

pause *v* break, cease, delay, deliberate, desist, discontinue, halt, hesitate, interrupt, rest, stop briefly, take a break, wait, waver; (*Inf*) have a breather

pause *n* break, caesura, cessation, delay, discontinuance, gap, halt, hesitation, interlude, intermission, interruption, interval, lull, respite, rest, stay, stoppage, wait; (*Inf*) breather, let-up

pawn *v* deposit, hazard, mortgage, pledge, stake, wager; (*Inf*) hock, pop

pay *v* clear, compensate, discharge, foot, give, honour, liquidate, meet, offer, recompense, reimburse, remit, remunerate, render, requite, reward, settle, square up; be advantageous, benefit, be worthwhile, repay, serve; bestow, extend, give, grant, present, proffer, render; bring in produce, profit, return, yield; (*Inf*) cough up

pay *n* allowance, compensation, earnings, emoluments, fee, hire, income, payment, recompense, reimbursement, remuneration, reward, salary, stipend, takings, wages

payable *v* clear, compensate, discharge, foot, give, honour, liquidate, meet, offer, recompense, reimburse, remit, renumerate, render, requite, reward, settle, square up; (*Inf*) cough up; be advantageous, benefit, be worthwhile, repay, serve; bestow, extend, give, grant, present, proffer, render; bring in produce, profit, return, yield

payable *n* allowance, compensation, earnings, emoluments, fee, hire, income, payment, recompense, reimbursement, renumeration, reward, salary, stipend, takings, wages

payable *adj* due, mature, obligatory, outstanding, owed, owing, receivable, to be paid

pay back *v* get one's own back, reciprocate, recompense, retaliate, settle a score; (*Inf*) get even with

payment *n* defrayal, discharge, out lay, paying, remittance, settlement; earnings, fee, hire, remuneration, reward, wage

pay off *v* discharge, dismiss, fire, lay off, let go; (*Inf*) sack; clear, discharge, liquidate, pay in full, settle, square; be effective, be profitable, be successful, succeed, work

pay out *v* disburse, expend, spend; (*Inf*) cough up, fork out, lay out, shell out

peace *n* accord, agreement, amity, concord, harmony; armistice, cessation of hostilities, conciliation, pacification, treaty, truce; calm, composure, contentment, placidity, relaxation, repose, serenity; calm, calmness, hush, peacefulness, quiet, quietude, repose rest, silence, stillness, tranquillity

peaceable *adj* amiable, amicable, conciliatory, dovish, friendly, gently, inoffensive, mild, nonbelligerent, pacific, peaceful, peace-loving, placid, unwarlike; balmy, calm, peaceful, quiet, restful, serene, still, tranquil, undisturbed

peaceful *adj* amicable, at peace, free from strife, friendly, harmonious, nonviolent, on friendly terms, on good terms, without hostility; calm, gentle, placid, quiet, restful, serene, still, tranquil undisturbed unruffled, untroubled; conciliatory, pacific, peaceable, peace-loving, placatory, unwarlike

peak *n* aiguille, apex, brow, crest, pinnacle, point, summit, tip, top; acme, apogee, climax, crown, culmination, high point, maximum point, ne plus ultra, zenith

peak *v* be at its height, climax, come to a head, culminate, reach its highest point, reach the zenith

peal *n* blast, carillon, chime, clamour, clang, clap, crash, resounding, roar, rumble, sound, tintinnabulation

peal *n* chime, crack, crash, resonate, resound reverberate, ring, roar, roll, rumble, sound, tintinnabulate, toll

peasant *n* agricultural worker, countryman, rustic, son of the soil; boor, churl, country bumpkin, lout, provincial, yokel

peculiar *adj* abnormal, bizarre, curious, eccentric, exceptional, extraordinary, far-out freakish, funny, odd, offbeat, outlandish, out-of-the-way, quaint, queer, singular, strange, uncommon, unconventional, unusual, weird; (*Inf*) far-out

peculiarity *n* abnormality, bizarreness, eccentricity, foible, freakishness, idiosyncrasy, mannerism, oddity, odd trait, queerness, quirk

pedantic *adj* abstruse, academic, bookish, didactic, donnish, erudite, formal, fussy, hairsplitting, overnice, particular, pedagogic, pompous, precise, priggish, punctilious, scholastic, schoolmasterly, sententious, stilted; (*Inf*) nit-picking

pedestal *n* base, dado, foot, foundation, mounting, pier, plinth, stand, support

pedestrian *n* footslogger, foot-traveller, walker

pedestrian *adj* banal, boring, commonplace, dull, flat, humdrum, mediocre, mundane, ordinary, plodding, prosaic, run-of-the-mill, unimaginative, uninspired, uninteresting

pedigree *n* ancestry, blood, breed, derivation, decent, extraction, family, family tree, genealogy, heritage, line, lineage, race, stock

peek *v* glance, look, peep, peer, snatch a glimpse, sneak a look, spy, squint, take a gander at; (*Inf*) take a look

peel *v* decorticate, desquamate, flake off, pare, scale, skin, strip of

peer *v* look closely, squint

peer *n* aristocrat, baron, count, duke, earl, lord, marquess, marquis, noble, nobleman, patrician, viscount; (*Inf*) aristo; coequal, compeer, confrère, equal, fellow, like, match

peerless *adj* beyond, compare, excellent, incomparable, matchless, nonpareil, outstanding, second to none, superlative, unequalled, unique, unmatched, unparalleled, unrivalled, unsurpassed

peevish *adj* acrimonious, cantanker ous, captious, childish, churlish, crabbed, cross, crusty, fractious, fretful, grumpy, ill-natured, ill-tempered, irritable, pettish, petulant, querulous, short-tempered, snappy, splenetic, sulky, sullen, surly, testy, touchy, waspish; (*Inf*) crotchety, ratty, whingeing

pelt *v* assail, batter, beat, belabour, bombard, cast, hurl, pepper, pummel, shower, sling, strike, thrash, throw; (*Inf*) wallop

pen *n* ball-point, felt-tip, fountain-pen, marker; coop, corral, enclosure, fold, hutch, sty

pen *v* commit to paper, compose, draft, draw up, jot down, write; cage, confine, coop up, enclose, fence in, hedge, hem in, hurdle, mew up, shut in

penal *adj* corrective, disciplinary, penalizing, punitive, retributive

penalize *v* castigate, correct, discipline, handicap, impose a penalty on, inflict a handicap on, punish, put at a disadvantage

penalty *n* disadvantage, fine, forfeit, forfeiture, handicap, mulct, price, punishment, retribution; disadvantage, drawback, handicap, obstacle, snag

penance *n* atonement, mortification, penalty, punishment, reparation, sackcloth and ashes

penchant *n* affinity, bent, bias, desire, disposition, fancy, fondness, inclination, leaning, liking, love, partiality, passion, predilection, predisposition, proclivity, proneness, propensity, soft spot, taste, tendency, turn, weakness

pencil *v* compose, draft, jot down, pen, scribble down; draw, outline, sketch, trace

pendent *adj* dangling, hanging, suspended,

pending *prep* awaiting, until, waiting for; during, in the course of, throughout

pending *adj* awaiting, uncertain, undecided, unresolved, unsettled, up in the air; (*Inf*) on the back burner, approaching, coming, forthcoming, imminent, impending, in the balance, in the offing

penetrate *v* bore, enter, go through, perforate, pierce, prick, probe, stab; diffuse, enter, get in, infiltrate, permeate, pervade, seep, suffuse

penetration *n* entrance, entry, incision, inroad, invasion, perforation, piercing, puncturing; acuteness, astuteness, discernment, insight, keenness, perception, perspicacity, sharpness, shrewdness, wit

penniless bankrupt, destitute, impecunious, impoverished, indigent, moneyless, necessitous, needy, on one's uppers, penurious, poor, poverty-stricken, ruined, with out a penny to one's name; (*Inf*) broke, cleaned out, skint, stony broke, strapped for cash

pension *n* allowance, annuity, benefit, old-age pension, retirement pension, superannuation; allowance, benefit, support, welfare

pensive *adj* cogitative, contemplative, dreamy, grave, meditative, melancholy, mournful, musing, preoccupied, reflective, ruminative, sad, serious, sober, solemn, sorrow ful, thoughtful, wistful; (*Inf*) blue

people *n* human beings, humanity, humans, mankind, men and women, mortals, persons; citizens, clan, community, family, folk, inhabitants, action, population, public, race, tribe; commonalty, crowd, general, public, grass roots, hoi polloi, masses, mob, multitude, plebs, populace, rabble, rank and file, the herd

people *v* colonize, inhabit, occupy, populate, settle

perceive *v* be aware of, behold, descry, discern, discover, distinguish, espy, make out, note, notice, observe, recognize, remark, see, spot

perceptible *adj* apparent, appreciable, clear, conspicuous, detectable, discernable, distinct, evident, noticeable, observable, obvious, palpable, perceivable, recognizable, tangible, visible

perception *n* apprehension, awareness, conception, consciousness, discernment, feeling, grasp, impressio, insight, notion, observation, recognition, sensation, sense, taste, understanding

perceptive *adj* cute, alert, astute, aware, discerning, insightful, intuitive, observant, penetrating, percipient, perspicacious, quick, responsive, sensitive, sharp

perch *n* branch, pole, post, resting place, roost

perch *v* alight, balance, land, rest, roost, settle, sit on

percipient *adj* astute, discerning, intuitive, perceptive, sensitive, shrewd, understanding

percolate *v* drain, drip, filter, seep; filtrate, sieve, strain

perennial *adj* abiding, chronic, constant, continual, continuing, enduring, incessant, inveterate, lasting, lifelong, persistent, recurrent, unchanging

perfect *adj* absolute, complete, completed, consummate, entire, finished, full, out-and-out, sheer, unadulterated, unalloyed, unmitigated, utter, whole; blameless, excellent, faultless, flawless, idea, immaculate, impeccable, pure, splendid, spotless, sublime, superb, superlative, supreme, unblemished, unmarred, untarnished

perfect *v* accomplish, achieve, carry out, complete, consummate, effect, finish, fulfil, perform, realize

perfection *n* accomplishment, achievement, achieving, completion, consummation, evolution, fulfilment, realization; completeness, exactness, excellence, exquisiteness, faultlessness, integrity, maturity, perfectness, precision, purity, sublimity, superiority, wholeness; acme, crown, ideal, paragon

perform *v* accomplish, achieve, act, bring about, carry out, complete, comply with, discharge, do, effect, execute, fulfil, function, observe, pull off, satisfy, transact, work; appear as, depict, enact, play, present, produce, put on, render, represent, stage

performance *n* accomplishment, achievement, act, carrying out, completion, conduct, consummation, discharge, execution, exploit, feat, fulfilment, work; acting, appearance, exhibition, interpretation, play, portrayal, presentation, production, representation, show; (*Inf*) gig

performer *n* actor, actress, artiste, play-actor, player, Thespian, trouper

perfume *n* aroma, attar, balminess, bouquet, cologne, essence, fragrance, incense, odour, redolence, scent, smell, sweetness

perfunctory *adj* automatic, careless, cursory, heedless, inattentive, indifferent, mechanical, negligent, offhand, routine, sketchy, slipshod, slovenly, stereotyped, superficial, unconcerned, unthinking, wooden

perhaps *adv* as the case may be, conceivably, feasibly, for all one knows, it may be, maybe, possibly

peril *n* danger, exposure, hazard, insecurity, jeopardy, menace, pitfall, risk, uncertainty, vulnerability

perimeter *n* ambit, border, border - line, boundary, bounds, circumference, confines, edge, fringe, frontier, limits, margin, outer limits, periphery

period *n* interval, season, space, span, spell, stretch, term, time, while; aeon, age, days, epoch, era; conclusion, end, finis, finish, halt, stop; full stop, point, stop; menses, menstruation, menstrual flow; (*Inf*) the curse

periodical *n* journal, magazine, monthly, organ, paper, publication, quarterly, review, serial, weekly

perish *v* be killed, be lost, decease, die, expire, lose ones life, pass away; be destroyed, collapse, decline, disappear, fall, go under, vanish; decay, decompose, disintegrate, moulder, rot, waste, wither

perishable *adj* decaying, decomposable, destructible, easily, spoilt, liable to rot, short-lived, unstable

perjury *n* bearing false witness, false oaths, false statement, false swearing, forswearing, giving false testimony, lying under oath, oath breaking, violation of an oath, wilful falsehood

permanence *n* constancy, continuance, continuity, dependability, durability, duration, endurance, finality, fixedness, fixity, immortality, indestructibility, lastingness, permanency, perpetuity, stability, survival

permanent *adj* abiding, constant, durable, enduring, everlasting, fixed, immutable, imperishable, indestructible, invariable, lasting, long-lasting, perennial, perpetual, persistent, stable, steadfast, unchanging, unfading

permeate *v* charge, diffuse, throughout, fill, filter through, imbue, impregnate, infiltrate, pass through, penetrate, percolate, pervade, saturate, seep through, soak through, spread throughout

permissible *adj* acceptable, admissible, allowable, all right, authorized, lawful, legal, legitimate, licit, permitted, proper, sanctioned; (*Inf*) kosher, legit, OK

permission *n* allowance, approval, assent, authorization, consent, dispensation, freedom, green light, leave, liberty, licence, permit, sanction, sufferance, tolerance; (*Inf*) go-ahead

permissive *adj* acquiescent, easy going, forbearing, free, indulgent, latitudinarian, lax, lenient, liberal, open-minded, tolerant

permit *v* admit, agree, allow, authorize, consent, empower, enable, endorse, endure, give leave, grant, let, license, sanction, suffer, tolerate, warrant

permit *n* authorization, liberty, licence, pass, passport, permission, sanction

perpendicular *adj* at right angles to, on end, plumb, straight, upright, vertical

perpetrate *v* be responsible for, bring about, carry out, commit, do, effect, enact, execute, inflict, perform, wreak

perpetual *adj* abiding, endless, enduring, eternal, everlasting, immortal, infinite, lasting, never-ending, perennial, permanent, unchanging, undying, unending

perpetuate *v* continue, eternalize, immortalize, keep alive, keep going, keep up, maintain, reserve, sustain

perplex *v* baffle, befuddle, beset, bewilder, confound, confuse, dumbfound, mix up, muddle, mystify, nonplus, puzzle, stump; complicate, encumber, entangle, involve, jumble, mix up, snarl up, tangle, thicken

persecute *v* afflict, distress, dragoon, harass, hound, hunt, illtreat, injure, maltreat, martyr, molest, oppress, pursue, torment, torture, pester, tease, vex, worry

perseverance *n* constancy, dedication, determination, diligence, doggedness, endurance, indefatigability, persistence, pertinacity, purposefulness, resolution, sedulity, stamina, steadfastness, tenacity

persevere *v* be determined, be resolved, carry on, continue, endure, go on, hang on, hold fast, keep going, keep on, maintain, persist, pursue, remain, stand firm, stick at; (*Inf*) hold on, plug away

persist *v* be resolute, continue, insist, persevere, stand firm; abide, carry on, continue, endure, keep up, last, linger, remain; (*Inf*) hold on

persistence *n* constancy, determination, diligence, doggedness, endurance, grit, indefatigability, perseverance, pertinacity, pluck, resolution, stamina, steadfastness, tenacity, tirelessness

persistent *adj* assiduous, determined, dogged, enduring, fixed, immovable, indefatigable, obdurate, obstinate, persevering, pertinacious, resolute, steadfast, steady, stubborn, tenacious, tireless, unflagging

person *n* being, body, human, human being, individual, living soul, soul

personal *adj* exclusive, individual, intimate, own, particular, peculiar, private, privy, special

personality *n* character, disposition, identity, individuality, make-up, nature, psyche, temper, temperament, traits; celebrity, famous-name, household name, notable, personage, star, well-known face, well-known person

personally *adv* alone, by oneself, independently, in person, in the flesh, on one's own, solely; individualistically, individually, privately, specially, subjectively

personification *n* embodiment, image, incarnation, likeness, portrayal, recreation, representation, semblance

personify *v* body forth, embody, epitomize, exemplify, express, incarnate, mirror, represent, symbolize, typify

personnel *n* employees, helpers, human resources, liveware, members, men and women, people, staff, workers, workforce

perspective *n* angle, attitude, broad view, context, frame of reference, objectivity, outlook, overview, proportion, relation, relative, importance, relativity, way of looking; outlook, panorama, prospect, scene, view, vista

perspire *v* be damp, be wet, drip, exude, glow, pour with sweat, secrete, sweat, swelter

persuade *v* actuate, advise, allure, coax, counsel, entice, impel, incite, induce, influence, inveigle, prevail upon, prompt, sway, talk into, urge, win over; (*Inf*) bring round

persuasion *n* blandishment, cajolery, conversion, enticement, exhortation, inducement, influencing, inveiglement, wheedling; cogency, force, persuasiveness, potency, power; (*Inf*) pull; belief, certitude, conviction, credo, creed, faith, firm belief, fixed opinion, tenet, views

persuasive *adj* cogent, compelling, convincing, credible, effective, eloquent, forceful, impelling, impressive, inducing influential, logical, moving, plausible, sound, telling, touching, valid, weighty, winning

pertain *v* appertain, apply, be appropriate, bear on, befit, belong, be part of, be relevant, concern, refer, regard, relate

pertinent *adj* admissible, *ad rem*, applicable, apposite, appropriate, apropos, apt, fit, fitting, germane, material, pat, proper, relevant, suitable, to the point, to the purpose

perturb *v* agitate, alarm, bother, discompose, disconcert, discounte nance, disquiet, disturb, fluster, ruffle, trouble, unsettle, upset, vex, worry

peruse *v* browse, check, examine, inspect, look through, read, run one's eye over, scan, scrutinize, study

pervade *v* affect, charge, diffuse, extend, fill, imbue, infuse, overspread, penetrate, percolate, permeate, spread through, suffuse

pervasive *adj* common, extensive, general, inescapable, omnipresent, permeating, pervading, prevalent, rife, ubiquitous, universal, widespread

perverse *adj* abnormal, contradictory, contrary, delinquent, depraved, deviant, disobedient, forward, improper, incorrect, miscreant, rebellious, refractory, troublesome, unhealthy, unmanageable, unreasonable; contrary, contumacious, cross gained, dogged, headstrong, intractable, intransigent, obdurate, wilful, wrong-headed; contrary, mulish, obstinate, pigheaded, stubborn, unyielding, wayward

pervert *v* abuse, distort, falsify, garble, misconstrue, misinterpret, misrepresent, misuse, twist, warp; corrupt, debase, debauch, degrade, deprave, desecrate, initiate, lead astray, subvert

pervert *n* debauchee, degenerate, deviant, weirdo

perverted *adj* aberrant, abnormal, corrupt, debased, debauched, depraved, deviant, distorted, evil, immoral, impaired, misguided, sick, twisted, unhealthy, unnatural, vicious, vitiated, warped, wicked; (*Inf*) kinky

pessimism *n* cynicism, dejection, depression, despair, despondency, distrust, gloom, gloominess, gloomy outlook, glumness, hopelessness, melancholy

pessimist *n* cynic, defeatist, doomster, killjoy, melancholic, misanthrope, prophet of doom, worrier; (*Inf*) gloom merchant, wet blanket

pessimistic *adj* bleak, cynical, dark, dejected, depressed, despairing, despondent, distrustful, downhearted, fatalistic, foreboding, gloomy, glum, hopeless, melancholy, misanthropic, morose, resigned, sad

pest *n* annoyance, bane, bore, bother, irritation, nuisance, thorn in one's flesh, trial, vexation; (*Inf*) pain, pain in the neck; bane, blight, bug, curse, epidemic, infection, pestilence, plague, scourge

pester *v* annoy, badger, bedevil, bother, chivvy, disturb, fret, get at, get on someone's nerves, harass, harry, irk, nag, pick on, plague, torment, worry; (*Inf*) bug, drive one up the wall, hassle, rile

pet *n* apple of one's eye, darling, favourite, idol, jewel, treasure; (*Inf*) blue-eyed boy

pet *adj* cherished, dearest, dear to one's heart, favoured, favourite, particular, preferred, special

pet *v* baby, coddle, cosset, mollycoddle, pamper, spoil; caress, fondle, pat, stroke

peter out *v* come to nothing, die out, dwindle, ebb, evaporate, fade, fail, give out, run dry, run our, stop, taper off, wane

petition *n* address, appeal, application, entreaty, invocation, memorial, plea, prayer, request, round robin, solicitation, suit, supplication

petition *v* adjure, appeal, ask, beg, beseech, call, upon, crave, entreat, plead, pray, press, solicit, sue, supplicate, urge

petty *adj* contemptible, inconsiderable, inessential, inferior, insignificant, little, negligible, paltry, slight, small, trifling, trivial, unimportant; (*Inf*) measly, piddling; cheap, grudging, mean, mean-minded, shabby, small-minded, spiteful, stingy, ungenerous

petulant *adj* bad-tempered, captious, cavilling, crabbed, cross, crusty, fault-finding, fretful, illhumoured, impatient, irritable, moody, peevish, perverse, pouting, querulous, snappish, sour, sulky, sullen, ungracious, waspish

phantom *n* apparition, chimera, ghost, phantasm, revenant, shade, spectre, spirit; (*Inf*) spook

phase *n* aspect, chapter, condition, development, juncture, period, point, position, stage, state, step, time

phase out *v* close, deactivate, dispose of gradually, ease off, eliminate, pull out, remove, replace, run down, taper off, terminate, wind down, withdraw; (*Inf*) wind up

phenomenal *adj* exceptional, extraordinary, fantastic, marvellous, miraculous, outstanding, prodigious, remarkable, sensational, singular, uncommon, unique, unparalleled, unusual, wondrous

phenomenon *n* circumstance, episode, event, fact, happening, incident, occurrence; exception, marvel, miracle, nonpareil, prodigy, rarity, sensation, sight, spectacle, wonder

philanthropist *n* alms-giver, altruist, benefactor, contributor, donor, giver, humanitarian, patron

philistine *n* barbarian, boor, bourgeois, Goth, ignoramus, lout, lowbrow, vulgarian, yahoo

philistine *adj* anti-intellectual, boorish, bourgeois, crass, ignorant, lowbrow, tasteless, uncultivated, uncultured, uneducated, unrefined

philosopher *n* dialectician, logician, metaphysician, sage, seeker of the truth, theorist, thinker, wise man

philosophical *adj* abstract, erudite, learned, logical, rational, sagacious, theoretical, thoughtful, wise; calm, collected, composed, cool, impassive, imperturbable, patient, resigned, serene, stoical, tranquil, unruffled

philosophy *n* aesthetics, knowledge, logic, metaphysics, rationalism, reason, reasoning, thinking, thought, wisdom; attitude to life, basic idea, beliefs, convictions, doctrine, ideology, principle, tenets, thinking, values, viewpoint, worldview

phobia *n* aversion, detestation, dislike, distaste, dread, fear, hatred, horror, irrational fear, loathing, obsession, overwhelming, anxiety, repulsion, terror; (*Inf*) hang-up, thing

phone *n* telephone; (*Inf*) blower; call, give someone a call, give someone a ring, make a call, ring, ring up, telephone; (*Inf*) bell, buzz, get on the blower; give someone a bell; give someone a buzz, give someone a tinkle

phoney *adj* affected, assumed, bogus, counterfeit, fake, false, forged, imitation, put-on, sham, spurious, trick; (*Inf*) pseudo

phoney *n* counterfeit, fake, faker, forgery, fraud, humbug, impostor, pretender, sham

photograph *n* image, likeness, picture, print, shot, slide, snapshot, transparency; (*Inf*) photo, snap

photograph *v* capture on film, film, get a shot of, record, shoot, take, take a picture of, take someones picture; (*Inf*) snap

phrase *n* expression, group of words, idiom locution, motto, remark, saying, tag, utterance, way of speaking

phrase *v* couch, express, formulate, frame, present, put, put into words, say, term, utter, voice, word

physical *adj* bodily, carnal, corporal, corporeal, earthly, fleshly, incarnate, mortal, somatic, unspiritual; material, natural, palpable, real, sensible, solid, substantial, tangible, visible

physique *n* body, build, constitution, figure, form, frame, make-up, shape, structure

pick *v* choose, decide upon, elect, fix upon, hand-pick, mark out, opt for, select, settle upon, sift out, singe out, sort out; collected, cull, cut, gather, harvest, pluck, pull

pick *n* choice, choosing, decision, option, preference, selection; choicest, *créme de la créme*, elect, elite, flower, pride, prize, the best, the cream, the tops

pick up *v* gather, grasp, hoist, lift, raise, take up, uplift; buy, come across, find, garner, happen upon, obtain, purchase; gain, gain ground, improve, mend, perk up, rally, recover, take a turn for the better; (*Inf*) get better; call for, collect, get, give someone a lift, go to get, uplift; acquire, learn, master; (*Inf*) get the hang of

picnic *n* alfresco meal, excursion, *fête champêtre*, outdoor meal, outing

pictorial *adj* expressive, graphic, illustrated, picturesque, representational, scenic, striking, vivid

picture *n* delineation, drawing, effigy, engraving, illustration, image, likeness, painting, photograph, portrait, portrayal, print, representation, similitude, sketch; account, depiction, description, image, impression, re-creation, report; carbon copy, copy, double, duplicate, image, likeness, living image, lookalike, replica, twin; (*Inf*) dead ringer, ringer, spitting image; film, motion picture, movie; (*Inf*) flick

picture *v* conceive of, envision, image, see, see in the mind's eye, visualize

picturesque *adj* attractive, beautiful, charming, colourful, graphic, pretty, quaint, scenic, striking, vivid

piece *n* allotment, bit, chunk, division, fraction, fragment, length, morsel, mouthful, part, portion, quantity, scrap, section, segment, share, shred, slice; article, composition, creation, item, production, study, work, work of art; (*Inf*) bit

pier *n* jetty, landing place, prome nade, quay, wharf; buttress, column, pile, piling, pillar, post, support, upright

pierce *v* bore, drill, enter, penetrate, perforate, prick, probe, puncture, run through, spike, stab, stick into, transfix

piety *n* devotion, devoutness, dutifulness, duty, faith, godliness, grace holiness, piousness, religion, reverence, sanctity, veneration

pig *n* boar, grunter, hog, piggy, piglet, porker, shoat, sow, swine

pigeonhole *n* compartment, cubbyhole, cubicle, locker, niche, place, section

pigeonhole *v* defer, file, postpone, put off, shelve

pigheaded *adj* bull-headed, contrary, cross-grained, dense, froward, inflexible, mulish, obstinate, perverse, self-willed, stiff-necked, stubborn, stupid, unyielding, wilful, wrongheaded

pile *n* accumulation, assemblage, assortment, collection, heap, hoard, mass, mound mountain, stack, stockpile; building, edifice, erection, structure

pile *v* accumulate, amass, assemble, collect, gather, heap, hoard, load up mass, stack, store

pile-up *n* accident, collision, crash, multiple collision, smash; (*Inf*) smash-up

pilgrim *n* crusader, hajji, palmer, traveller, wanderer, wayfarer

pilgrimage *n* crusade, excursion, expedition, hajj, journey, mission, tour, trip

pillage *v* despoil, loot, maraud, plunder, raid, ransack, ravage, rife, rob, sack, spoliate, strip

pillage *n* depredation, devastation, marauding, plunder, rapine, robbery, sack, spoliation

pillar *n* column, pier, pilaster, piling, post, prop, shaft, stanchion, support, upright; leader, mainstay, rock, supporter, tower of strength, upholder, worthy; (*Inf*) leading light

pilot *n* airman, aviator, captain, conductor, coxswain, director, flier, guide, helmsman, leader, navigator, steersman

pilot *v* conduct, control, direct, drive, fly, guide, handle, lead, manage, navigate, operate, shepherd, steer

pilot *adj* experimental, model, test, trial

pin *v* affix, attach, fasten, fix, join, secure; fix, hold down, hold fast, immobilize, pinion, press, restrain

pinch *v* compress, grasp, nip, press, squeeze, tweak; chafe, confine, cramp, crush, hurt, pain

pinch *n* nip, squeeze, tweak; bit, dash, jot, mite, small, quantity, soupçon, speck, taste; crisis, difficulty, emergency, exigency, hardship, necessity, oppression, pass, plight, predicament, pressure, strait, stress

pin down *v* compel, constrain, force, make, press, pressurize; bind, confine, constrain, fix, hold, hold down, immobilize, nail down, tie down

pink *adj* flesh, flushed, reddish, rose, roseate, rosy, salmon

pinnacle *n* acme, apex, apogee, crest, crown eminence, height, meridian, peak, summit, top, vertex, zenith

pinpoint *v* define, distinguish, get a fix on, home in on, identify, locate, spot

pioneer *n* colonist, colonizer, explorer, frontiersman, settler; developer, founder, founding, father, innovator, leader, trailblazer

pioneer *v* create, develop, discover, establish, initiate, instigate, institute, invent, launch, lay the groundwork, map out, open up, originate, prepare, show the way, start, take the lead

pious *adj* dedicated, devoted, devout, God-fearing, godly, holy, religious, reverent, righteous, saintly, spiritual; goody-goody, holier than thou, hypocritical, pietistic, religiose, sanctimonious, self-righteous, unctuous

pipe *n* conduit, conveyor, duct, hose, line, main, passage, pipeline, tube; briar, clay, meerschaum; fife, horn, tooter, whistle, wind instrument

pipe *v* cheep, peep, play, sing, sound, tootle, trill, tweet, twitter, warble, whistle

piquant *adj* biting, highly-seasoned, peppery, pungent, savoury, sharp, spicy, stinging, tangy, tart, zesty; (*Inf*) with a kick

pique *n* annoyance, displeasure, grudge, huff, hurt feelings, irritation, offence, resentment, umbrage, vexation, wounded pride; (*Inf*) miff

pique *v* affront, annoy, displease, gall, incense, irk, irritate, mortify, nettle offend, provoke, put out, rile, sting, vex, wound; (*Inf*) get, miff, peeve, put someone's nose out of joint

piracy *n* buccaneering, freebooting, hijacking, infringement, plagiarism, rapine, robbery at sea, stealing, theft

pirate *n* buccaneer, corsair, filibuster, freebooter, marauder, raider, rover, sea, robber, sea rover, seawolf; infringer, plagiarist, plagiarizer; (*Inf*) cribber

pirate *v* appropriate, borrow, copy, plagiarize, poach, reproduce, steal; (*Inf*) crib, lift

pit *n* abyss, cavity, chasm, coal-mine, crater, dent, depression, dimple, excavation, gulf, hole, hollow, indentation, mine, pockmark, pothole, trench

pitch *v* cast, chuck, fling, heave, hurl, launch, sling, throw, toss; (*Inf*) bung, chuck, lob; erect, fix, locate, place, plant, put up, raise, settle, set up, station

pitch *n* angle, cant, dip, gradient, incline, slope, steepness, tilt; degree, height, highest point, level, point, summit; harmonic, modulation, sound, timbre, tone; line, patter, sales talk; (*Inf*) spiel; field of play, ground, sports field; (*Inf*) park

piteous *adj* affecting, deplorable, distressing, doleful, grievous, heartbreaking, heart-rending, lamentable, miserable, mournful, moving, pathetic, pitiable, pitiful, plaintive, poignant, sad, sorrowful, woeful, wretched

pitfall *n* catch, danger, difficulty, drawback, hazard, peril, snag, trap

pith *n* core, crux, essence, gist, heart, heart of the matter, kernel, marrow, meat, nub, point, quintessence, salient point, the long and short of it; consequence, depth, force, import, importance, matter, moment, power, significance, strength, substance, value, weight

pitiful *adj* deplorable, distressing, grievous, heartbreaking, heartrending, lamentable, miserable, pathetic, piteous, pitiable, sad, woeful, wretched; abject, base, beggarly, contemptible, despicable, inadequate, insignificant, low, mean, miserable, paltry, scurvy, shabby, sorry, vile, worthless

pitiless *adj* brutal, callous, cold-blooded, cold-hearted, cruel, hardhearted, harsh, heartless, implacable, inexorable, inhuman, merciless, relentless, ruthless, uncaring, unfeeling, unmerciful, unsympathetic

pittance *n* allowance, drop, mite, modicum, portion, ration, slave wages, trifle; (*Inf*) chicken feed, peanuts

pity *n* charity, clemency, commiseration, compassion, condolence, fellow, feeling, forbearance, kindness, mercy, sympathy, tenderness, understanding

pity *v* bleed for, commiserate with, condole with, feel for, feel sorry for, grieve for, have compassion for, sympathize with, weep for

pivot *n* axis, axle, fulcrum, spindle, swivel; centre, focal point, heart, hinge, hub, kingpin

pivot *v* revolve, rotate, spin, swivel, turn, twirl; be contingent, depend, hang, hinge, rely, revolve round, turn

placard *n* advertisement, affiche, bill, poster, public notice, sticker

placate *v* appease, assuage, calm, conciliate, humour, mollify, pacify, propitiate, satisfy, soothe, win over

place *n* area, location, locus, point, position, site, situation, spot, station, venue, whereabouts; city, district, hamlet, locale, locality, neighbourhood, quarter, region, town, vicinity, village; grade, position, rank, station, status; appointment, employment, job, position, post; accommodation, berth, billet, room, space, stead; affair, charge, concern, duty, function, prerogative, responsibility, right, role; take place; befall, betide, come about, come to go on, happen, occur, transpire

place *v* deposit, dispose, establish, fix, install, lay, locate, plant, position, put, rest, set settle, situate, stand, station; arrange, class, classify, grade, group, order, rank, sort; allocate, appoint, assign, charge, commission, entrust, give

placid *adj* calm, collected, compose, cool, equable, even, even-tempered, gentle, halcyon, imperturbable, mild, peaceful, quiet, self-possessed, serene, still, tranquil, undisturbed, unexcitable, unmoved, unruffled, untroubled

plague *n* contagion, disease, epidemic, infection pandemic, pestilence; affliction, bane, blight, calamity, cancer, curse, evil, scourge, torment, trial; annoyance, bother, irritant, nuisance, pest, problem, thorn in one's flesh, vexation; (*Inf*) aggravation, pain

plague *v* afflict, annoy, badger, bedevil, bother, disturb, fret, harass, harry, haunt, molest, pain, persecute, pester, tease, torment, torture, trouble, vex; (*Inf*) hassle

plain *adj* apparent, clear, comprehensible, distinct, evident, legible, lucid, manifest, obvious, patent, transparent, unambiguous, understandable, unmistakable, visible; artless, blunt, candid, direct, downright, forthright, frank, guileless, honest, ingenuous, open, outspoken, sincere, straightforward; common-commonplace, everyday, frugal, homely, lowly, modest, ordinary, simple, unaffected, unpretentious, workaday; austere, bare, basic, discreet, modest, muted, pure, restrained, severe, simple, Spartan, stark, unadorned, unembellished, unornamented, unpatterned, unvarnished; ill-favoured, not beautiful, not striking, ordinary, ugly, unalluring, unattractive, unlovely, unprepossessing; even, flat, level, plane, smooth

plain *n* flatland, grassland, lowland, open country, plateau, prairie, steppe, tableland

plain-spoken *adj* blunt, candid, direct, downright, explicit, forthright, frank, open, outright, outspoken, straightforward, unequivocal

plaintive *adj* disconsolate, doleful, grief-stricken, grievous, heart-rending, melancholy, mournful, pathetic, piteous, pitiful, rueful, sad, sorrow ful, wistful, woebegone, woeful

plan *n* contrivance, design, device, idea, method, plot, procedure, programme, project, proposal, proposition, scenario, scheme, strategy, suggestion, system; blueprint, chart, delineation, diagram, drawing, illustration, layout, map, representation, scale drawing, sketch

plan *v* arrange, concoct, contrive, design, develop, devise, draft, formulate, frame, invent, line up, organize, outline, plot, prepare, represent, scheme, schedule, think out; aim, contemplate, envisage, foresee, intend, mean, propose, purpose

plane *n* flat surface, level surface; condition, degree, footing, level, position, rank, stage, stratum; aircraft, jet jumbo jet; airplane

plane *adj* even, flat, flush, horizontal, level, plain, regular, smooth, uniform

plant *n* bush, flower, herb, shrub, vegetable, weed; factory, foundry, mill, shop, works, yard; apparatus, equipment, gear, machinery

plant *v* implant, put in the ground, scatter, seed, set out, sow, transplant

plaster *n* gypsum, mortar, plaster of Paris, stucco; adhesive plaster, bandage, dressing, Elastoplast (*Trademark*), sticking plaster

plaster *v* bedaub, besmear, coat, cover, daub, overlay, smear, spread

plastic *adj* ductile, fictile, flexible, mouldable, pliable, pliant, soft, supple

plate *n* dish, platter; course, dish, helping, portion, serving; layer, panel, sheet, slab

plateau *n* highland, mesa, table, tableland, upland

platform *n* dais, podium, rostrum, stage, stand

platitude *n* banality, bromide, cliché, commonplace, hackneyed saying, inanity, stereotype, trite remark, truism

plausible *adj* believable, colourable, conceivable, credible, fair-spoken, glib, likely, persuasive, possible, probable, reasonable, smooth, smooth-talking, smooth-tongued, specious, tenable

play *v* amuse oneself, caper, engage in games, entertain oneself, frisk, frolic, gambol, have fun, revel, romp, sport, trifle; be in a team, challenge, compete, contend against, participate rival, take on, take part, view with; act, act on the part of, execute, impersonate, perform, personate, portray, represent, take the part of; play by ear; ad lib, extemporize, improvise, rise to the occasion, take it as it comes; play for time delay, filibuster, hang fire, procrastinate, stall, temporize; (*Inf*) drag one's feet

play *n* comedy, drama, dramatic piece, entertainment, farce, masque, performance, piece, radio play, show, soap opera, stage show, television drama, tragedy; amusement, caper, diversion, entertain ment, frolic, fun, gambol, game, jest, pastime, prank, recreation, romp, sort; foolery, fun, humour, jest, joking, prank, sport, teasing; (*Inf*) lark

playboy *n* gay dog, ladies' man, man about town, philanderer, pleasure seeker, rake, roué, socialite, womanizer; (*Inf*) lady-killer, lover boy

player *n* competitor, contestant, participant, sportsman, sports woman, team member; actor, actress, entertainer, performer, Thespian, trouper; artist, instrumentalist, musician, music maker, performer, virtuoso

playful *adj* cheerful, coltish, frisky, frolicsome, gay, impish, joyous, kittenish, lively, merry, mischievous, puckish, rollicking, spirited, sportive, sprightly, vivacious

playmate *n* companion, comrade, friend, neighbour, playfellow; (*Inf*) chum, pal

plaything *n* amusement, bauble, game, gewgaw, gimcrack, pastime, toy, trifle, trinket

plea *n* appeal begging, entreaty, intercession, overture, petition, prayer, request, suit, supplication

plead *v* appeal to, ask, beg, beseech, crave, entreat, implore, importune, petition, request, solicit, supplicate; adduce, allege, argue, assert, maintain, put forward, use as an excuse

pleasant *adj* acceptable, agreeable, musing, delectable, delightful, enjoyable, fine, gratifying, lovely, nice, pleasing, pleasurable, refreshing, satisfying, welcome; affable, agreeable, amiable, charming, cheerful, cheery, congenial, engaging, friendly, genial, good-humour, likable, nice

please *v* amuse, charm, cheer, content, delight, entertain, give pleasure to, gladden, gratify, humour, indulge, rejoice, satisfy, suit, tickle, tickle pink

pleased *adj* contented, delightful, euphoric, glad, gratified, happy, in high spirits, satisfied, thrilled, tickled pink; (*Inf*) chuffed, over the moon, pleased as punch

pleasing *adj* agreeable, amiable, amusing, attractive, charming, delightful, engaging, enjoyable, entertaining, gratifying, likable, pleasurable, polite, satisfying, winning

pleasure *n* amusement, bliss, comfort, contentment, delectation, delight, diversion, ease, enjoyment, gladness, gratification, happiness, joy, recreation, satisfaction, solace

pledge *n* assurance, covenant, oath, promise, undertaking, vow, warrant, word, word of honour; bail, bond, collateral, deposit, earnest, gage, guarantee, paw, security, surety; health, toast

pledge *v* contract, engage, give one's word, promise, swear, undertake, vouch

plentiful *adj* abundant, ample, complete, copious, generous, inexhaustible, infinite, lavish, liberal, overflowing, plenteous, profuse

plenty *n* abundance, enough, fund, good deal, great deal, mass, masses, mine, mountains, plethor, quantities, quantity, store, sufficiency, volume; (*Inf*) heaps, lots, oodles, piles, stacks; abundance, affluence, copiousness, fertility, fruitfulness, luxury, opulence, plenitude, plenteousness, plentifulness, profusion, prosperity, wealth

pliable *adj* bendable, bendy, ductile, flexible, limber, lithe, malleable, plastic, pliant, supple; adaptable, compliant, docile, easily led, impressionable, influenceable, manageable, persuadable, pliant, receptive, responsive, susceptible, tractable, yielding

plight *n* case, circumstances, condition, difficulty, dilemma, extremity, perplexity, predicament, situation, state, straits, trouble; (*Inf*) hole, jam, pickle, scrape, spot

plod *v* clump, drag, lumber, slog, tramp, tread, trudge; (*Inf*) stomp

plot *n* cabal, conspiracy, intrigue,

machination, plan, scheme, stratagem; action, narrative, outline, scenario, story, story line, subject, theme, thread

plot *v* cabal, collude, conspire, contrive, hatch, intrigue, machinate, manoeuvre, plan, scheme; calculate, chart, compute, draft, draw, locate, map, mark, outline; brew, conceive, concoct, contrive, design, devise, frame, hatch, imagine, lay, project; (*Inf*) cook up

plot *n* allotment, area, ground, lot, parcel, patch, tract

plough *v* break ground, cultivate, dig, furrow, ridge, till, turn over

pluck *v* collect, draw, gather, harvest, pick, pull out, pull off; finger, pick, plunk, strum, thrum, twang

plucky *adj* bold, brave, courageous, daring, doughty, game, gritty, hardy, heroic, intrepid, mettlesome, spirited, undaunted, unflinching, valiant; (*Inf*) gutsy, spunky

plug *n* bung, cork, spigot, stopper, stopple; advertisement, good word, mention, publicity, puff, push; (*Inf*) advert, hype

plug *v* block, bun, choke, close, cork, cover, fill, pack, seal, stop, stopper, stopple, stop up, stuff; build up, mention, promote, publicize, puff, push, write up; (*Inf*) advertise, hype

plumb *n* lead, plumb, bob, plummet, weight

plumb *adv* perpendicularly, up and down, vertically; bag, exactly, precisely, slap; (*Inf*) spot-on

plumb *v* delve, explore, fathom, gauge, go into, measure, penetrate, probe, search, sound, unravel

plump *adj* burly, buxom, chubby, corpulent, dumpy, fat, fleshy, full, obese, podgy, portly, rolypoly, rotund, round, stout, tubby, well-covered; (*Inf*) beefy, well-upholstered

plunder *v* despoil, devastate, loot, pillage, raid, ransack, ravage, rifle, rob, sack, spoil, steal, strip

plunder *n* booty, ill-gotten gains, loot, pillage, prey, prize, rapine, spoils; (*Inf*) swag

plunge *v* cast, descend, dip, dive, douse, drop, fall, go down, immerse, jump, nosedive, pitch, plummet, sink, submerge, swoop, throw, tumble

plunge *n* descent, dive, drop, fall, immersion, jump, submersion, swoop

plus *prep* added to, and, coupled with, with the addition of

plus *adj* added, additional, extra, positive, supplementary

poach *v* appropriate, encroach, hunt illegally, infringe, intrude, plunder, rob, steal, steal game, trespass

pocket *n* bag, compartment, hollow, pouch, receptacle, sack

pocket *adj* abridged, compact, concise, little, miniature, portable, small; (*Inf*) pint-sized, potted

poem *n* lyric, ode, rhyme, song, sonnet, verse

poet *n* bard, balladmonger, lyricist, rhymer, versifier

poetic *adj* elegiac, lyric, lyrical, metrical, rhythmical, songlike

poetry *n* metrical composition, poems, rhyme, rhyming, verse

poignant *adj* affecting, agonizing, bitter, distressing, heartbreaking, heart-rending, intense, moving, painful, pathetic, sad, touching, upsetting; acute, biting, caustic, keen, penetrating, piercing, pointed, sarcastic

point *n* dot, full stop, mark, period, speck, stop; location, place, position, site, spot, stage, station; apex, end, nib, prong, sharp end, spike, spur, summit, tine, tip, top; bill, bluff, cape, foreland, head, headland, ness promontory; circumstance, condition, degree, extent, position, stage; instant, juncture, moment, time, very minute; aim, design, end, goal, intent, intention, motive, object, objective, purpose, reason, use, usefulness, utility; burden, core, crux, drift, essence, gist, heart, import, main idea, marrow, matter, meaning, nub, pith, proposition, question, subject, text, theme, thrust; aspect, attribute, characteristic, peculiarity, property, quality, respect, side, trait; score, tally, unit; **beside the point** immaterial, incidental, inconsequential, irrelevant, not to the purpose, off the subject, out of the way, pointless, unimportant, without connection; **to the point** applicable, appropriate, apropos, apt, brief, fitting, germane, pertinent, pithy, pointed, relevant, short, suitable, terse

point *v* bespeak, call attention to, denote, designate, direct, indicate, show, signify

point-blank *adj* abrupt, blunt, categorical, direct, downright, explicit, express, plain, straight-from-the-shoulder, unreserved

point-blank *adv* bluntly, brusquely, candidly, directly, explicitly, forthrightly, frankly, openly, plainly, straight, straightforwardly

pointer *n* guide, hand, indicator, needle; advice, caution, hint, information, recommendation, suggestion, tip, warning

pointless *adj* absurd, aimless, fruitless, futile, inane, ineffectual, irrelevant, meaningless, nonsensical, senseless, silly, stupid, unavailing, unproductive, unprofitable, useless, vague, vain, worthless

point-out *v* allude to, bring up, call attention to, identify, indicate, mention, remind, reveal, show, specify

poise *n* aplomb, assurance, calmness, composure, coolness, dignity, elegance, equanimity, equilibrium, grace, presence, presence of mind, sang-froid, savoir-faire, self-possession, serenity; (*Inf*) cool

poise *v* balance, float, hang, hang in midair, hang suspended, hold, hover, position, support, suspend

poised *adj* calm, collected, composed, dignified, graceful, nonchalant, self-confident, self-possessed, serene, suave, unruffled, urbane; (*Inf*) together; all set, in the wings, on the brink, prepared, ready, standing by, waiting

poisonous *adj* deadly, fatal, lethal, mephitic, mortal, noxious, toxic, venomous, virulent; corruptive, evil, malicious, noxious, pernicious, pestiferous, pestilential, vicious

poke *v* butt, dig, elbow, hit, jab, nudge, prod, punch, push, shove, stab stick, thrust; **poke fun at** chaff, jeer, make a mock of, make fun of, mock, ridicule, tease; (*Inf*) rib, send up, take the mickey, take the piss

poke *n* butt, dig, hit, jab, nudge, prod, punch, thrust

pole *n* bar, mast, pillar, post, rod, shaft, spar, staff, stanchion, standard, stick, support, upright

police *n* constabulary, law enforcement agency, police force; (*Inf*) boys in blue, fuzz, the law, the Old Bill

police *v* control, guard, keep in order, keep the peace, patrol, protect, regulate, watch

policeman, policewoman *n* constable, PC, police officer, WPC; (*Inf*) bobby, bogey, cop, copper, flatfoot, fuzz, peeler, pig, rozzer

policy *n* action, approach, code, course, custom, guideline, line, plan, practice, procedure, programme, protocol, rule, scheme, stratagem, theory

polish *v* brighten, buff, burnish, clean, furbish, rub, shin, smooth, wax; brush up, correct, cultivate, emend, enhance, finish, improve, perfect, refine, touch up

polish *n* brightness, brilliance, finish, glaze, gloss, lustre, sheen, smoothness, sparkle, veneer; varnish, wax; elegance, finesse, finish, grace, politeness, refinement, style, suavity, urbanity; (*Inf*) class

polished *adj* bright, burnished, furbished, glassy, gleaming, glossy, shining, slippery, smooth; civilized, courtly, cultivated, elegant, finished, genteel, polite, refined, sophisticated, urbane, well-bred; accomplished, adept, expert, faultless, fine, flawless, impeccable, masterly, outstanding, professional, skilful, superlative

polite *adj* affable, civil, complaisant, courteous, deferential, gracious, mannerly, obliging, respectful, well-behaved, well-mannered

politician *n* legislator, Member of Parliament, MP, office bearer, public servant, statesman; (*Inf*) politico

politics *n* affairs of state, civics, government, government policy, political science, polity, statecraft, statesmanship

poll *n* figures, returns, tally, vote, voting; ballot, canvass, census, count, Gallup Poll, public opinion poll, sampling, survey

pollute *v* adulterate, befoul, contaminate, dirty, foul, infect, make filthy, mar, poison, soil, spoil, stain, taint; besmirch, corrupt, debase, debauch, defile, deprave, desecrate, dishonour, profane, sully, violate

pompous *v* affected, arrogant, bloated, grandiose, imperious, magisterial, ostentatious, overbearing, pontifical, portentous, pretentious, puffed up, self important, showy, supercilious, vainglorious; boastful, bombastic, flatulent, fustian, grandiloquent, high-flown, inflated, magniloquent, orotund, overblown, turgid, windy

ponder *v* brood, cerebrate, cogitate, consider, contemplate, deliberate, examine, excogitate, give thought to, meditate, mull over, muse, puzzle over, reflect, ruminate, study, think, weigh

pool *n* fish pool, lake, mere, pond, puddle, splash, tarn, water hole; swimming bath, swimming pool; collective, combine, consortium, group, syndicate, team, trust; bank, funds, jackpot, kitty, pot, stakes

pool *v* amalgamate, combine, join forces, league, merge, put together, share

poor *adj* badly off, destitute, impecunious, impoverished, indigent, in need, in want, necessitous, needy, on one's beam-end, on one's uppers, on the rocks, penniless, penurious, poverty stricken; (*Inf*) broke, hard up, skint, stony-broke; deficient, exiguous, inadequate, incomplete, insufficient, lacking, meagre, miserable, niggardly, pitiable, reduced, scanty, skimpy, slight, sparse, straitened; below par, faulty, feeble, inferior, lowgrade, mediocre, rubbishy, second-rate, shabby, shoddy, sorry, substandard, unsatisfactory, valueless, weak, worthless; (*Inf*) rotten; bad, bare, barren, deplete, exhausted, fruitless, impoverished, infertile, sterile, unfruitful, unproductive; hapless, ill-fated luckless, miserable, pathetic, pitiable, unfortunate, unhappy, unlucky, wretched; humble, insignificant, lowly, mean, modest, paltry, plain, trivial

pop *v* bang, burst, crack, explode, go off, report, snap; insert, push, put, shove, slip, stick, thrust, tuck

pop *n* bang, burst, crack, explosion, noise, report

populace *n* commonalty, crowd, general public, hoi polloi, inhabitants, masses, mob, multitude, people, rabble, throng

popular *adj* accepted, approved, celebrated, famous, fashionable, favoured, favourite, in, in demand, in favour, liked, sought-after, well-liked; common, conventional, current, general, prevailing, public, standard, stock, ubiquitous, universal, widespread

popularity *n* acceptance, acclaim, adoration, approval, celebrity, currency, esteem, fame, favour, idolization, lionization, recognition, regard, renown, reputation, repute, vogue

populate *v* colonize, inhabit, live in, occupy, people,settle

population *n* citizenry, community, denizens, folk, inhabitants, natives, people, populace, residents, society

pore *v* brood, contemplate, dwell on, examine, go over, peruse, ponder, read, scrutinize, study

port *n* anchorage, harbour, haven, roads, roadstead, seaport

portable *adj* compact, convenient, easily carried, handy, light, lightweight, manageable, movable, portative

portend *v* adumbrate, augur, bespeak, betoken, bode, foreshadow, foretell, foretoken, forewarn, harbinger, herald, indicate, omen, point to, predict, presage, prognosticate, promise threaten, warn of

porter *n* baggage attendant, bearer, carrier; caretaker, concierge, doorman, gatekeeper, janitor

portion *n* bit, fraction, fragment, morsel, part, piece, scrap, section, segment; allocation, allotment, allowance, division, lot, measure, parcel, quantity, quota, ration, share; helping, piece, serving; cup, destiny, fate, fortune, lot, luck

portrait *n* image, likeness, painting, photograph, picture, portraiture, representation, sketch

portray *v* delineate, depict, draw, figure, illustrate, limn, paint, picture, render, represent, sketch; charcterize, depict, describe, paint a mental picture of, put in words

pose *v* arrange, model, position, sit, sit for; **pose as** feign, impersonate, masquerade as, pass oneself off as, pretend to be, profess to be, sham; affect, attitudeinize, posture, put on airs, strike an attitude; (*Inf*) show off; advance, posit, present, propound, put, put forward, set, state, submit

pose *n* attitude, bearing, position, posture, stance; act, affectation, air, attitudinizing, façade, front, mannerism, masquerade, posturing, pretence, role

poser *n*conundrum, enigma, knotty point, problem, puzzle, question riddle, tough one, vexed question; (*Inf*) brain-teaser

position *n* area, bearings, locale, locality, location, place, point, post, reference, site, situation, spot, station, whereabouts; arrangement, attitude, disposition, pose, posture, stance; angle, attitude, belief, opinion, outlook, point of view, slant, stance, stand, standpoint, view, viewpoint; circumstances, condition, pass, plight, predicament, situation, state, straits; caste, class, consequence, importance, place, prestige, rank, reputation, standing, station, stature, status; capacity, duty, employment, function, job, occupation, office, place, post, role, situation; (*Inf*) berth, billet

position *v* arrange, array, dispose, fix, lay out, locate, place, put, set, settle, stand; (*Inf*) stick

positive *adj* absolute, actual, affirmative, categorical, certain, clear, clear-cut, conclusive, concrete, decisive, definite, direct, explicit, express, firm, incontrovertible, indisputable, real, unequivocal, unmistakable; assured, certain, confident, convinced, sure; assertive, cocksure, decided, dogmatic, emphatic, firm, forceful, opinionated, peremptory, resolute, stubborn; beneficial, constructive, effective, efficacious, forward looking, helpful, practical, productive, progressive, useful; absolute, complete, consummate, out-and-out, perfect, rank, thorough, thoroughgoing, unmitigated, utter

possess *v* be pleased with, be born with, be endowed with, enjoy, have, have to ones name, hold, own; acquire, control, dominate, hold, occupy, seize, take over, take possession of

possessed *adj* bedevilled, berserk, bewitched, consumed, crazed, cursed, demented, enchanted, frenetic, frenzied, hag-ridden, haunted, maddened, obsessed, raving, under a spell

possession *n* control, custody, hold, occupancy, occupation, own ership, proprietorship, tenure, title; assets, belongings, chattels, effects, estate, goods and chattels, property,

things, wealth
possibility *n* feasibility, likelihood, plausibility, potentiality, practicability, workableness; chance, hazard, hope, liability, likelihood, odds, probability, prospect, risk
possible *adj* conceivable, credible, hypothetical, imaginable, likely, potential; attainable, doable, feasible, practicable, realizable, viable, within reach, workable; (*Inf*) on; hopeful, likely, potential, probable, promising
post *n* column, newel, pal, palisade, picket, pillar, pole, shaft, standard, stock, support, upright; appointment, assignment, employ ment, job, office, place, position, situation; (*Inf*) berth, billet; collection, delivery, mail, postal service
post *v* advertise, affix, announce, display, make known, pin up, proclaim, promulgate, publicize, publish, put up, stick up; assign, establish, locate, place, position, put, situate, station; dispatch, mail, send, transmit
poster *n* advertisement, *affiche,* announcement, bill, notice, placard, public notice, sticker; (*Inf*) advert
posterity *n* children, descendants, family, heirs, issue, offspring, progeny, scions, seed; future, future generations, succeeding generations
postpone *v* adjourn, defer, delay, hold over, put back, put off, shelve, suspend, table
postscript *n* addition, afterthought, afterword, appendix, PS, supplement
postulate *v* advance, assume, hypothesize, posit, predicate, presuppose, propose, put forward, suppose, take for granted, theorize
posture *n* attitude, bearing, carriage, disposition, pose, position, set, stance
posture *v* affect, attitudinize, do for effect, make a show, pose, put on airs, try to attract attention; (*Inf*) show off
potent *adj* efficacious, forceful, mighty, powerful, puissant, strong, vigorous
potential *adj* budding, dormant, embryonic, future, hidden, inherent, latent, likely, possible, promising, undeveloped, unrealized
potential *n* ability, aptitude, capability, capacity, possibility, potentiality, power, the makings, wherewithal; (*Inf*) what it takes
potter *v* dabble, fribble, fitter, mess about, poke along, tinker; (*Inf*) fiddle
pouch *n* bag, container, pocket, purse, sack
pounce *v* ambush, attack, bound onto, dash at, drop, fall upon, jump, leap at, snatch, spring, strike, swoop, take by surprise, take unaware
pounce *n* assault, attack, bound, jump, leap, spring, swoop
pound *v* batter, beat, belabour, hammer, pelt, pummel, strike, thrash, thump; (*Inf*) clobber; bruise, comminute, crush, powder, pulverize, triturate
pour *v* decant, let flow, spill, splash; course, emit, flow, gush, jet, run, rush, spew, spout, spurt, stream; come down in torrents, rain, rain heavily, sheet, teem; (*Inf*) bucket

down, rain cats and dogs; crowd, flood, stream, swarm, throng

pout *v* glower, look petulant, look sullen, lower, make a moue, mope, pull a long face, purse one's lips, sulk, turn down the corners of one's mouth

poverty *n* beggary, destitution, distress, hand-to-mouth existence, hardship, indigence, insolvency, necessitousness, necessity, need, pauperism, pennilessness, penury, privation, want; dearth, deficiency, insufficiency, lack, paucity, scarcity, shortage; aridity, bareness, barrenness, deficiency, infertility, meagreness, poorness, sterility, unfruitfulness

powder *n* dust, fine, grains, loose particles, pounce, talc

powder *v* crush, granulate, grind, pestle, pound, pulverize; cover, dredge, dust, scatter, sprinkle, strew

power *n* ability, capability, capacity, competence, competency, faculty, potential; brawn, energy, force, forcefulness, intensity, might, muscle, potency, strength, vigour, weight; ascendancy, authority, command, control, dominance, domination, dominion, influence, mastery, rule, sovereignty, supremacy, sway; authority, authorization, licence, prerogative, privilege, right, warrant

powerful *adj* energetic, mighty, potent, robust, stalwart, strapping, strong, sturdy, vigorous; authoritative, commanding, controlling, dominant, influential, prevailing, puissant, sovereign, supreme; cogent, compelling, convincing, effective, effectual, forceful, forcible, impressive, persuasive, telling, weighty

powerless *adj* debilitated, disabled, etiolated, feeble, frail, helpless, impotent, incapable, incapacitated, ineffectual, infirm, paralysed, prostrate, weak; defenceless, dependent, disenfranchised, disfranchised, ineffective, subject, tied, unarmed, vulnerable

practicability *n* advantage, feasibility, operability, possibility, practicality, use, usefulness, value, viability, workability

practicable *adj* achievable, attainable, doable, feasible, performable, possible, viable, within the realm of possibility, workable

practical *adj* applied, efficient, empirical, experimental, factual, functional, pragmatic, realistic, utilitarian; businesslike, down-to-earth, everyday, hard-headed, matter-of-fact, mundane, ordinary, realistic, sensible, workaday; accomplished, efficient, experience, proficient, qualified, seasoned, skilled, trained, veteran, working

practically *adv* all but, almost, basically, close to, essentially, fundamentally, in effect, just about, nearly, to all intents and purposes, very nearly, virtually, well-nigh; nearly, matter-of-factly, rationally, realistically, reasonably, sensibly, unsentimentally, with common sense

practice *n* custom, habit, method, mode, praxis, routine, rule, system, tradition, usage, use, usual, procedure, way, wont; discipline, drill, exercise, preparation, rehearsal, repetition, study, training, work-out; business, career, profession, vocation, work

practise *v* discipline, drill, exercise, go over, go through, polish, prepare, rehearse, repeat, study, train, warm up, work out; apply, carry out, do, follow, live up to, observe, perform, put into practice; carry on, engage in, ply, pursue, specialize in, undertake, work at

praise *n* acclaim, acclamation, accolade, applause, approbation, approval, cheering, commendation, compliment, congratulation, encomium, eulogy, good word, kudos, laudation, ovation, panegyric, plaudit, tribute; adoration, devotion, glory, homage, thanks, worship

praise *v* acclaim, admire, applaud, approve, cheer, compliment, congratulate, cry up, eulogize, extol, honour, laud, pay tribute to, sing the praises of; adore, bless, exalt, give thanks to, glorify, pay homage to, worship

pray *v* adjure, ask, beg, beseech, call upon, crave, cry for, entreat, implore, importune, invoke, petition, plead, request, solicit, sue, supplicate, urge

prayer *n* communion, devotion, invocation, litany, orison, supplication; appeal, entreaty, petition, plea, request, suit, supplication

preach *v* address, deliver a sermon, evangelize, exhort, orate; admonish, advocate, exhort, harangue, lecture, moralize, sermonize, urge

preacher *n* clergyman, evangelist, minister, missionary, parson, revivalist

precarious *adj* dangerous, doubtful, dubious, hazardous, insecure, perilous, risky, shaky, slippery, touch and go, tricky, uncertain, unreliable, unsafe, unsettled, unstable, unsteady, unsure; (*Inf*) chancy, dicey, dodgy, hairy

precaution *n* insurance, preventative measure, protection, provision, safeguard, safety measure; anticipation, care, caution, circumspection, foresight, forethought, providence, prudence, wariness

precede *v* antecede, antedate, come first, forerun, go ahead of, go before, head, herald, introduce, lead, pave the way, preface, take precedence, usher

precedent *n* antecedent, authority, criterion, example, exemplar, instance, model, paradigm, pattern, previous example, prototype, standard

precinct *n* bound, boundary, confine, enclosure, limit; area, district, quarter, section, sector, zone

precious *adj* adored, beloved, cherished, darling, dear, dearest, favourite, idolized, loved, prized, treasured, valued; choice, costly, dear, expensive, exquisite, fine, high-priced, inestimable, invaluable, priceless, prized, rare, recerché, valuable

precipice *n* bluff, brink, cliff, cliff face, crag, height, rock face, sheer drop, steep

precipitate *v* accelerate, advance, bring on, dispatch, expedite, further, hasten, hurry, press, push forward, quicken, speed up, trigger;

precipitate *adj* breakneck, headlong, plunging, rapid, rushing, swift, violent; abrupt, brief, quick, sudden, unexpected, without warning

precise *adj* absolute, accurate, actual, clear-cut, correct, definite, exact, explicit, express, fixed, literal, particular, specific, strict, unequivocal

precisely *adv* absolutely, accurately, bang correctly, exactly, just, just so, literally, neither more nor less, square, squarely, strictly; (*Inf*) plumb, slap, smack

precision *n* accuracy, care, correctness, definiteness, exactitude, exactness, fidelity, meticulousness, nicety, particularity, preciseness, rigour

preclude *v* check, debar, exclude, forestall, hinder, inhibit, make impossible, make impracticable, obviate, prevent, prohibit, put a stop to, restrain, rule out, stop

precocious *adj* advanced, ahead, bright, developed, forward, quick, smart

precursor *n* forerunner, harbinger, herald, messenger, usher, vanguard

predatory *adj* carnivorous, hunting, predacious, rapacious, raptorial, ravening

predecessor *n* antecedent, forerunner, precursor, previous job holder

predetermined *adj* agreed, arranged in advance, decided before-hand, fixed, prearranged, preplanned, set, settled, set up; (*Inf*) cut and dried

predicament *n* corner, dilemma, emergency, mess, pinch, plight, quandary, situation, state; (*Inf*) fix, hole, jam, pickle, scrape, spot

predict *v* augur, divine, forebode, forecast, foresee, foretell, portend, presage, prognosticate, prophesy, soothsay

predictable *adj* anticipated, calculable, certain, expected, foreseeable, forseen, likely, reliable, sure, (*Inf*) sure-fire

prediction *n* augury, divination, forecast, prognosis, prognostication, prophecy, soothsaying

predisposed *adj* agreeable. amenable, given to, inclined, liable, minded, prone, ready, subject, susceptible, willing

predominant *adj* ascendant, capital, chief, controlling, dominant, important, leading, main, paramount, preponderant, prevailing, prevalent, primary, prime, principal, prominent, ruling, sovereign, superior, supreme, top-priority

preface *n* exordium, foreword, introduction, preamble, preliminary, prelude, proem, prolegomenon, prologue

preface *v* begin, introduce, launch, lead up to, open, precede, prefix

prefer *v* adopt, be partial to, choose, desire, elect, fancy, favour, go for, incline towards, like better, opt for, pick, plump for, select, single out, wish, would rather, would sooner

preferable *adj* best, better, choice, chosen, favoured, more, desirable, more eligible, superior, worthier

preferably *adv* as a matter of choice, by choice, first, in preference, much rather, much sooner, rather, sooner, willingly

preference *n* choice, desire, election, favourite, first choice, option, partiality, pick, predilection, selection, top of the list; advantage, favoured treatment, favouritism, first place, precedence, pride of place, priority

prejudge *v* anticipate, forejudge, jump to conclusions, make a hasty assessment, presume, presuppose

prejudice *n* bias, jaundiced, eye, partiality, preconceived notion, preconception, prejudgment, warp; bigotry, chauvinism, discrimination, injustice, intolerance, narrow-mindedness, racism, sexism, unfairness; damage, detriment, disadvantage, harm, hurt, impairment, loss, mischief

prejudice *v* bias, colour, distort, influence, jaundice, poison, predispose, prepossess, slant, sway, warp; damage, harm, hinder, hurt, impair, injure, mar, spoil, undermine

preliminary *adj* exploratory, first, initial, introductory, opening, pilot, precursory, prefatory, preparatory, prior, qualifying, test, trial

preliminary *n* beginning, first round, foundation, groundwork, initiation, introduction, opening, preamble, preface, prelims, prelude, preparation, start

prelude *n* beginning, commence ment, curtain-raiser, exordium, foreword, introduction, overture, preamble, preface, preliminary, preparation, proem, prolegomenon, prologue, start; (*Inf*) intro

premature *adj* abortive, early, embryonic, forward, green, immature, incomplete, predeveloped, raw, undeveloped, unfledged, unripe, unseasonable, untimely; hasty, ill-considered, ill-timed, impulsive, inopportune, overhasty, precipitate, rash, too soon, untimely; (*Inf*) previous

premeditated *adj* aforethought, calculated, conscious, considered, contrived, deliberate, intended, intentional, planned, prepense, studied, wilful

premier *n* chancellor, head of government, PM, prime minister

premier *adj* arch, chief, first, foremost, head, highest, leading, main, primary, prime, principal, top; earliest, first, inaugural, initial, original

première *n* debut, first night, first performance, first showing, opening

premises *pl n* building, establishment, place, property, site

premiss, premise *n* argument, assertion, assumption, ground, hypothesis, postulate, postulation, presupposition, proposition, supposition. thesis

premium *n* bonus, boon, bounty, fee, perquisite, prize, recompense, remuneration, reward; appreciation, regard, stick, store, value

premonition *n* apprehension, feeling, feeling in one's bones, foreboding, forewarning, hunch, idea, intuition, misgiving, omen, portent, presage, presentiment, sign, suspicion, warning; (*Inf*) funny feeling

preoccupation *n* absence of mind, absent-mindedness, absorption, abstraction, brown study, daydreaming, engrossment, immersion, inattentiveness, musing, oblivion, pensiveness, prepossession, reverie

preoccupied *n* absent-minded, absorbed, abstracted, caught up in, distracted, distrait, engrossed, faraway, heedless, immersed, in a brown study, intent, lost in, lost in thought, oblivious, rapt, taken up, unaware, wrapped up

preparation *n* development, getting ready, groundwork, preparing, putting in order; alertness, anticipation, expectation, foresight, precaution, preparedness, provision, readiness, safeguard; composition, compound, concoction, medicine, mixture, tincture; homework, revision, schoolwork, study; (*Inf*) prep, swotting

preparatory *adj* basic, elementary, introductory, opening, prefatory, preliminary, preparative, primary

prepare *v* adapt, adjust, anticipate, arrange, coach, dispose, form, groom, make provision, make ready, plan, practise, prime, put in order, train, warm up; brace, fortify, gird, ready steel, strengthen; assemble, concoct, construct, contrive, draw up, fashion, fix up, make, produce, put together, turn out; (*Inf*) get up

prepared *adj* all set, arranged, fit, in order, in readiness, planned, primed, ready, set; able, disposed, inclined, minded, of a mind, predisposed, willing

preposterous *adj* absurd, asinine, bizarre, crazy, excessive, exorbitant, extravagant, extreme, foolish, impossible, incredible, insane, irrational, laughable, ludicrous, monstrous, nonsensical, out of the question, outrageous, ridiculous, senseless, shocking, unreasonable, unthinkable

prerequisite *adj* called for, essential, imperative, indispensable, mandatory, necessary, needful, obligatory, of the essence, required, requisite, vital

prerequisite *n* condition, essential, imperative, must, necessity, precondition, qualification, requirement, requisite, sine qua non

prescribe *v* appoint, assign, command, decree, dictate, direct, enjoin, fix, impose, lay down, ordain, order, require, rule, set, specify, stipulate

prescription *n* drug, medicine, mixture, preparation, remedy

presence *n* attendance, being, companionship, company, existence, habitation, inhabitance, occupancy, residence; closeness, immediate, circle, nearness, neighbourhood, propinquity, proximity, vicinity; air, appearance, aspect, aura, bearing carriage, compart ment, demeanour, ease, personality, poise, self-assurance

present *adj* contemporary, current, existent, existing, extant, immediate, instant, present-day, accounted for, at hand, available, here, in attendance, near, nearby, ready, there, to hand

present *n* here and now, now, present moment, the time being, this day and age

present *v* acquaint with, introduce, made known; demonstrate, display, exhibit, give, mount, put before the public, put on, show, stage; adduce, advance, declare, expound, extend, hold out, introduce, offer, pose, produce, proffer, put forward, raise, recount, relate, state, submit, suggest, tender

present *n* benefaction, boon, bounty, donation, endowment, favour, gift, grant, gratuity, largess, offering, (*Inf*) prezzie

presentation *n* award, bestowal, conferral, donation, giving, investiture, offering; appearance, arrangement, delivery, exposition, production, rendition, staging, submission; demonstration, display, exhibition, performance, production, representation, show

presently *n* before long, by and by, in a minute, in a moment, in a short while, shortly, soon; (*Inf*) pretty soon

preservation *n* conservation, defence, keeping, maintenance, perpetuation, protection, safeguarding, safekeeping, safety, salvation, security, storage, support, upholding

preserve *v* care for, conserve, defend, guard, keep, protect, safeguard, save, secure, shelter, shield

preserve *n* area, domain, field, realm, specialism, sphere

preside *v* administer, be at the head of, be in authority, chair, conduct, control, direct, govern, head, lead, manage, officiate, run, supervise

press *v* bear down on, compress, condense, crush, depress, force down, jam, mash, push, reduce, squeeze, stuff; calender, finish, flatten, iron, mangle, out the creases in, smooth, steam; clasp, crush, embrace, encircle, enfold, fold in one's arms, hold close, hug, squeeze; compel, constrain, demand, enforce, enjoin, force, insist on; beg, entreat, exhort, implore, importune, petition, plead, pressurize, sue, supplicate, surge; cluster, crowd, flock, gather, hasten, herd, hurry, mill, push, rush, seethe, surge, swarm, throng

press *n* **the press** Fleet Street, fourth estate, journalism, news, media, newspapers, the papers; columnists, correspondents, gentlemen of the press, journalists, newsmen, photographers, pressmen, reporters

pressure *n* compressing, compression, crushing, force, heaviness, squeezing, weight; coercion, compulsion, constraint, force, influence, obligation, power, sway

prestige *n* authority, cachet, celebrity, credit, distinction, eminence, esteem, fame, honour, importance, influence, kudos, regard, renown, reputation, standing, stature, status, weight

presume *v* assume, believe, conjecture, infer, posit, postulate, presuppose, suppose, surmise, take for granted, take it, think

presumption *n* assurance, audacity, boldness, effrontery, forwardness, impudence, insolence, presumptuousness, temerity; (*Inf*) brass, brass neck, cheek, gall, nerve

pretence *n* acting, charade, deceit, deception, fabrication, fakery, faking, falsehood, feigning, invention, make-believe, sham, simulation, subterfuge, trickery; affection, appearance, artifice, display, façade, posing, posturing, pretentiousness, show, veneer

pretend *v* affect, allege, assume, counterfeit, dissemble, dissimulate, fake, falsify, feign, impersonate, make out, pass oneself of as, profess, put on, sham, simulate; act, make up, play, play the part of, suppose

pretension *n* aspiration, assertion, assumption, claim, demand, pretence, profession; affectation, airs, conceit, hypocrisy, ostentation, pomposity, pretentiousness, self-importance, show, showiness, snobbery, snobbishness, vainglory, vanity

pretentious *adj* affected, assuming, bombastic, conceited, exaggerated, extravagant, flaunting, grandiloquent, grandiose, highfalutin, high-sounding, hollow, inflated, magniloquent, mannered, ostentatious, over-ambitious, pompous, puffed up, showy, snobbish, specious, vainglorious; (*Inf*) high-flown

pretext *n* affectation, alleged reason, appearance, cloak, cover, device, excuse, guise, mask, ploy, pretence, red herring, ruse, semblance, show, simulation, veil

pretty *adj* appealing, attractive, beautiful, bonny, charming, comely, cute, fair, good-looking, graceful, lovely, personable

pretty *adv* moderately, quite, rather, reasonably, somewhat; (*Inf*) fairly, kind of

prevail *v* be victorious, carry the day, gain mastery, overcome, over rule, prove superior,succeed, triumph, win; abound, be current (prevalent, widespread), exist generally, obtain, predominate, preponderate; **prevail upon** bring round, convince, dispose, incline, induce, influence, persuade, prompt, sway, talk into, win over

prevailing *adj* common, current, customary, established, fashionable, general, in style, in vogue, ordinary, popular, prevalent, set, usual, widespread

prevaricate *v* beat about the bush, beg the question, cavil, deceive, dodge, equivocate, evade, give a false colour to, hedge, lie, palter, quibble, shift, shuffle, stretch the truth, tergiversate

prevent *v* anticipate, avert, avoid, balk, bar, bock, check, counteract, defend against, foil, forestall, frustrate, hamper, head off, hinder, impede, inhibit, intercept, nip in the bud, obstruct, obviate, preclude, restrain, stave off, stop, thwart, ward off

prevention *n* anticipation, avoidance, deterrence, elimination, forestalling, obviation, precaution, preclusion, prophylaxis, safeguard, thwarting; bar, check, deterrence, frustration, hindrance, impediment, interruption, obstacle, obstruction, stoppage

preventive, preventative *adj* hampering, hindering, impeding, obstructive

preventive, preventative *n* block, hindrance, impediment, obstacle, obstruction

previous *adj* antecedent, anterior,

earlier, erstwhile, ex-, foregoing, former, one-time, past, preceding, prior, quondam, sometime

previously *adv* at one time, a while ago, before, beforehand, earlier, formerly, heretofore, hitherto, in advance, in anticipation, in days gone by, in the past, once, then, until now

prey *n* game, kill, quarry; dupe, fall, guy, mark, victim; target; (*Inf*) mug

price *n* amount, asking price, assessment, bill, charge, cost, estimate, expenditure, expense, fac-value, fee, figure, outlay, payment, rate, valuation, value, worth; consequences, cost, penalty, sacrifice, toll; (*Inf*) damage

price *v* assess, cost, estimate, evaluate, put a price on, rate, value

priceless *adj* beyond price, cherished, costly, dear, expensive, incalculable, incomparable, inestimable, invaluable, irreplaceable, precious, prized, rare, rich, treasured, worth a king's ransom

prick *v* bore, jab, lance, perforate, pierce, pink, punch, puncture, stab; bite, itch, prickle, smart, sting, tingle

prick *n* cut, gash, hole, perforation, pinhole, puncture, wound

prickly *adj* barbed, brambly, briery, bristly, spiny, thorny; crawling, itchy, pricking, prickling, scratchy, smarting, stinging, tingling

pride *n amour-propre,* dignity, ego, honour, self-esteem, self-respect, self-worth; arrogance, conceit, egotism, haughtiness, hauteur, hubris, loftiness, morgue, presumption, pretension, pretentiousness, self-importance, self-love, smugness, snobbery, superciliousness, vainglory, vanity; (*Inf*) bigheadedness; boast, gem, jewel, pride and joy, prize, treasure; best, choice, cream, elite, flower, glory, pick

pride *v* be proud of, boast, brag, congratulate oneself, crow, exult, flatter oneself, glory in, pique, plume, preen, revel in, take pride, vaunt

priest *n* churchman, clergyman, cleric, curate, divine, ecclesiastic, father, father confessor, holy man, man of God, man of the cloth, minister, padre; (*Inf*) vicar

prim *adj* demure, fastidious, formal, fussy, particular, precise, priggish, proper, prudish, puritanical, stiff, strait-laced; (*Inf*) old-maidish, prissy, schoolmarmish, starchy

primarily *adv* above all, basically, chiefly, especially, essentially, for the most part, fundamentally, generally, mainly, mostly on the whole, principally

primary *adj* best, capital, cardinal, chief, dominant, first, greatest, highest, leading, main, paramount, prime, principal, top; basic, beginning, elemental, essential, fundamental, radical, ultimate, underlying

prime *adj* best, capital, choice, excellent, first-class, first-rate, grade A, highest, quality, select, selected, superior, top; basic, earliest, fundamental, original, primary, underlying; chief, leading, main, predominant, pre-eminent, primary, principal, ruling, senior

prime *n* best days, bloom, flower, full flowering, height, heyday, maturity, peak, perfection, zenith

prime *v* break in, coach, fit, get ready, groom, make ready, prepare, train; brief, clue up, give someone the lowdown inform, notify, tell; (*Inf*) fill in, gen up

primitive *adj* earliest, early, elementary, first, original, primary, primeval, primordial, pristine; barbarian, barbaric, crude, rough, rude, rudimentary, savage, simple, uncivilized, uncultivated, undevel oped, unrefined

prince *n* lord, monarch, potentate, ruler, sovereign

principal *adj* capital, cardinal, chief, controlling, dominate, essential, first, foremost, highest, key, leading, main, most important, paramount, pre-eminent, primary, prime, strongest

principal *n* chief, director, head, leader, master, ruler, superintendent; dean, director, headmaster, headmistress, head teacher, master, rector; assets, capital, capital funds, money; (*Inf*) boss, head

principally *adv* above all, chiefly, especially, first and foremost, for the most part, in the main, mainly, mostly, particularly, predominantly, primarily

principle *n* assumption, axiom, canon, criterion, dictum, doctrine, dogma, ethic, formula, fundamental, golden rule, law, maxim, moral law, precept, proposition, rule, standard, truth, verity; attitude, belief, code, credo, ethic, morality, opinion, tenet, theory; conscience, ethics, honour, integrity, morals, probity, rectitude, righteousness, scruples, sense of duty, sense of honour, uprightness

print *v* engrave, go to press, impress, imprint, issue, mark, publish, run off, stamp; (*Inf*) put to bed

print *n* book, magazine, newspaper, newsprint, periodical, printed matter, publication, typescript; copy, engraving, photograph, picture, reproduction; (*Inf*) photo

priority *n* first concern, greater importance, precedence, pre-eminence, preference, prerogative, rank, right of way, seniority, superiority, supremacy, the lead

prison *n* confinement, dungeon, gaol, glasshouse, jail, penitentiary (*Inf*) can, clink, cooler, glasshouse, jug, quod, slammer, stir

prisoner *n* convict, jailbird; captive, detainee, hostage, internee; (*Inf*) con, lag

privacy *n* isolation, privateness, retirement, retreat, seclusion, separateness, sequestration, solitude

private *adj* clandestine, closet, confidential, in camera, inside, off the record, secret, unofficial; (*Inf*) hush-hush; exclusive, individual, intimate, own, particular, personal, reserved, special; concealed, isolated, not overlooked, retired, secluded, secret, separate, sequestered, solitary, withdrawn

privilege *n* advantage, benefit, birthright, claim, concession, due, entitlement, franchise, freedom, immunity, liberty, prerogative, right, sanction

prize *n* accolade, award, honour, premium, reward, trophy; windfall, winnings; aim, ambition, conquest, desire, gain, goal, hope; booty, capture, loot, pickings, pillage, plunder, spoils, trophy

prize *adj* award-winning, best, champion, first-rate, outstanding, top, winning; (*Inf*) topnotch

prize *v* appreciate, cherish, esteem, hold dear, regard highly, set store by, treasure, value

probability *n* chances, expectation, liability, likelihood, likeliness, odds, presumption, prospect

probable *adj* apparent, credible, feasible, likely, most likely, odds-on, on the cards, ostensible, plausible, possible, presumable, presumed, reasonable, seeming

probably *adv* as likely as not, doubtless, in all likelihood, in all probability, likely, maybe, most likely, perhaps, possibly, presumably

probe *v* examine, explore, go into, investigate, look into, query, scrutinize, search, sift, sound, test, verify; explore, feel around, poke, prod

probe *n* detection, examination, exploration, inquest, inquiry, investigation, research, scrutiny, study

problem *n* complication, difficulty, dilemma, disagreement, dispute, disputed, point, doubt, point at issue, predicament, quandary, trouble; (*Inf*) can of worms, hard nut to crack; conundrum, enigma, poser, puzzle, question, riddle

problem *adj* delinquent, difficult, intractable, uncontrollable, unmanageable, unruly; (*Inf*) brain-teaser

procedure *n* action, conduct, course, custom, form, formula, method, *modus operandi*, operation, performance, plan of action, policy, practice, process, routine, scheme, step, strategy, system, transaction

proceed *v* advance, carry on, continue, get going, get on with, get under way with, go ahead, go on, progress, set in motion; arise, come, derive, emanate, ensue, flow, follow, issue, originate, result, spring, stem

proceeding *n* act, action, course of action, deed, measure, move, occur rence, procedure, process, step, undertaking, venture; account, affairs, annals, archives, business, dealings, doings, matters, minutes, records, report, transactions

proceeds *pl n* earnings, gain, income, produce, products, profit, receipts, returns, revenue, takings, yield

process *n* action, course, course of action, manner, means, measure, method, mode, operation, performance, practice, procedure, proceeding, system, transaction; advance, course, development, evolution, formation, growth, movement, progress, progression, stage, step, unfolding

process *v* deal with, dispose of, fulfil, handle, take care of; alter, convert, prepare, refine, transform, treat

procession *n* cavalcade, column, cortege, file, march, motorcade, parade, train

proclaim *v* advertise, affirm, announce, blaze abroad, blazon abroad, circulate, declare, enunciate, give out, herald, indicate, make known, profess, promulgate, publish, show, trumpets; (*Inf*) shout from the rooftops

proclamation *n* announcement, declaration, decree, edict, manifesto, notice, notification, promulgation, pronouncement, pronunciamento, publication

procrastinate *v* adjourn, be dilatory, dally, defer, delay, gain time, play a waiting game, play for time, postpone, prolong, protract, put off, retard, stall, temporize; (*Inf*) drag one's feet

procure *v* acquire, appropriate, buy, come by, earn, effect, find, gain, get, get hold of, lay hands on, manage to get, obtain, pick up, purchase, secure, win

prod *v* dig, drive, elbow, jab, nude, poke, prick, propel, push, shove; egg on, goad, impel, incite, motivate, move, prompt, rouse, spur, stimulate, stir up, urge

prod *n* boost, dig, elbow, jab, nudge, poke, push shove; goad, poker, spur, stick; boost, cue, prompt, reminder, signal, stimulus

prodigal *adj* excessive, extravagant, immoderate, improvident, intemper ate, profligate, reckless, spendthrift, squandering, wanton, wasteful

prodigal *n* big spender, profligate, spendthrift, squanderer, wastrel

prodigy *n* child genius, genius, mastermind, talent, wizard, wonder child, wunderkind; (*Inf*) whiz, whiz kid; marvel, miracle, one in a million, phenomenon, sensation, wonder; (*Inf*) rare bird

produce *v* compose, construct, create, develop, fabricate, invent, make, manufacture, originate, put together, turn out; afford, bear, beget, breed, bring forth, deliver, engender, furnish, give, render, supply, yield; bring about, cause, effect, generate, give rise to, make for, occasion, provoke, set off; advance, bring forward, bring to light, demonstrate, exhibit, offer, present, put forward, set forth, show; direct, do, exhibit, mount, present, put before the public, put on show, stage; extend, lengthen, prolong, protract

produce *n* crop, fruit and vegetables, greengrocery, greens, harvest, product, yield

producer *n* director, impresario, stage manager; builder, creator, farmer, grower, maker, manufacturer

product *n* artefact, commodity, concoction, creation, goods, invention, merchandise, produce, production, work; consequence, effect, fruit, issue, legacy, offshoot, outcome, result, returns, spin-off, upshot, yield

production *n* assembly, construction, creation, fabrication, formation, making, manufacture, manufacturing, origination, preparation, producing; direction, management, presentation, staging

productive *adj* creative, dynamic, energetic, fecund, fertile, fruitful, generative, inventive, plentiful, producing, prolific, rich, teeming, vigorous

productivity *n* abundance, mass production, output, production, productive capacity, productiveness, work rate, yield

profane *adj* disrespectful, godless, heathen, idolatrous, impious, impure, irreligious, irreverent, pagan, sacrilegious, sinful, ungodly, wicked; lay, secular, temporal, unconsecrated, unhallowed, unholy, unsanctified, worldly; abusive, blasphemous, coarse, crude, filthy, foul, obscene, vulgar

profane *v* abuse, commit sacrilege, contaminate, debase, defile, desecrate, misuse, pervert, pollute, prostitute, violate, vitiate

profanity *n* abuse, blasphemy, curse, cursing, execration, foul language, four-letter word, impiety, imprecation, irreverence, malediction, obscenity, profaneness, sacrilege, swearing, swearword

profess *v* acknowledge, admit, affirm, announce, assert, asseverate, aver, avow, certify, confess, con firm, declare, maintain, own, proclaim, state, vouch

professed *adj* avowed, certified, confirmed, declared, proclaimed, self-acknowledged, self-confessed; alleged, apparent, ostensible, pretended, purported, self-styled, so-called, *soi-disant,* supposed, would-be

profession *n* business, calling, career, employment, line, line of work, métier, occupation, office, position, sphere, vocation, walk of life; acknowledgment, affirmation, assertion, attestation, avowal, claim, confession, declaration, statement, testimony, vow

professional *adj* adept, competent, efficient, experienced, expert, finished, masterly, polished, practiced, proficient, qualified, skilled, slick, trained; (*Inf*) ace, crack

professional *n* adept, authority, expert, maestro, master, past master, specialist, virtuoso, wizard; (*Inf*) dab hand, pro

professor *n* chair, head of department, head of faculty, holder of a chair, Regius professor; (*Inf*) don, fellow, prof

proficiency *n* ability, accomplishment, aptitude, competence, dexterity, expertise, expertness, facility, knack, mastery, skilfulness, skill, talent; (*Inf*) know-how

proficient *adj* able, accomplished, adept, apt, capable, clever, competent, conversant, efficient, experienced, expert, gifted, masterly, qualified, skilful, skilled, talented, trained, versed

profile *n* contour, drawing, figure, form, outline, portrait, shape, side view, silhouette, sketch; biography, characterization, character sketch, sketch, thumbnail sketch, vignette; analysis, chart, diagram, examination, graph, review, study, survey, table

profit *n* bottom line, earnings, emoluments, gain, percentage proceeds, receipts, return, revenue, surplus, takings, winnings, yield; advancement, advantage, avail, benefit, gain, good, interest, use, value

profit *v* aid, avail, benefit, be of advantage to, better, contribute, gain, help, improve, promote, serve, stand in good stead; capitalize on, exploit, learn from, make capital of, make good use of, make the most of, put to good use, reap the benefit of, take advantage of, turn to advantage of, turn to advantage, use, utilize; (*Inf*) cash in on; clear, earn, gain, make money; (*Inf*) clean up, make a good thing of, make a killing

profitable *adj* commercial, cost-effective, fruitful, gainful, lucrative, money-making, paying, renumerative, rewarding, worthwhile; advantageous, beneficial, fruitful, productive, rewarding, serviceable, useful, valuable, worthwhile

profound *adj* abstruse, deep, discerning, erudite, learned, penetrating, philosophical, recondite, sagacious, sage, serious, skilled, subtle, thoughtful, weighty, wise; abysmal, bottomless, cavernous, deep, fathomless, yawning; abject, acute, deeply felt, extreme, great, heartfelt, heart-rending, hearty, intense, keen, sincere

profuse *adj* abundant, ample, bountiful, copious, luxuriant, overflow ing, plentiful, prolific, teeming; excessive, extravagant, exuberant, fulsome, generous, immoderate, lavish, liberal, open-handed, prodigal, unstinting

profusion *n* abundance, bounty, copiousness, cornucopia, excess, extravagance, exuberance, glut, lavishness, luxuriance, multitude, oversupply, plentitude, plethora, prodigality, quantity, riot, superabundance, superfluity, surplus, wealth

programme *n* agenda, curriculum, line-up, list, listing, list of players, order of events, order of the day, plan, schedule, syllabus; broadcast, performance, presentation, production, show; design, order of the day, plan, plan of action, procedure, project, scheme

programme *v* arrange, bill, book, design, engage, formulate, itemize, lay on, line up, list, map out, plan, prearrange, schedule, work out

progress *n* advance, course, movement, onward course, passage, progression, way; advance, advancement, amelioration, betterment, breakthrough, development, gain, gaining ground, growth, headway, improvement, increase, progression, promotion, step forward

progress *v* advance, come on, continue, cover ground, forge ahead, gain ground, gather way, get on, go forward, make headway, make one's way, make strides, move on, proceed, travel; advance, ameliorate, better, blossom, develop, gain, grow, improve, increase, mature

progressive *adj* accelerating, advancing, continuing, continuous, developing, escalating, growing, increasing, intensifying, ongoing; advanced, avant-garde, dynamic, enlightened, enterprising, forward-looking, go-ahead, liberal, modern, radical, reformist, revolutionary, up-and-coming

prohibit *v* ban, debar, disallow, forbid, interdict, outlaw, proscribe, veto; constrain, make impossible, obstruct, preclude, prevent, restrict, rule out, stop

prohibition *n* constraint, exclusion, forbiddance, interdiction, negation, obstruction, prevention, restriction;

ban, bar, disallowance, embargo, injunction, interdict, proscription, veto

project *n* activity, assignment, design, enterprise, job, occupation, plan, programme, proposal, scheme, task undertaking, venture, work

project *v* contemplate, contrive, design, devise, draft, frame, map out, outline, plan, propose, purpose, scheme; cast, discharge, fling, hurl, launch, make carry, propel, shoot, throw, transmit; beetle, bulge, extend, jut, overhang, protude, stand out, stick out

projectile *n* bullet, missile, rocket, shell

prolific *adj* abundant, bountiful, copious, fecund, fertile, fruitful, generative, luxuriant, productive, profuse, rank, rich, teeming

prologue *n* exordium, foreword, introduction, preamble, preface, preliminary, prelude, proem

prolong *v* carry on, continue, delay, drag out, draw out, extend, lengthen, make longer, perpetuate, protract, spin out, stretch

promenade *n* boulevard, esplanade, parade, prom, public walk, walk way; airing, constitutional, saunter, stroll, turn, walk

promenade *v* perambulate, saunter, stretch one's legs, stroll, take a walk, walk

prominence *n* cliff, crag, crest, elevation, headland, height, high point, hummock, mound, pinnacle, projection, promontory, rise, rising ground, spur; bulge, jutting, projection, protrusion, protuberance, swelling; conspicuousness, markedness, outstandingness, precedence, salience, specialness, top billing, weight; celebrity, distinction, eminence, fame, greatness, importance, name, notability, pre-eminence, prestige, rank, reputation, standing

prominent *adj* bulging, jutting, projecting, protruding, protrusive, protuberant, standing out; conspicuous, easily seen, eye-catching, in the foreground, noticeable, obtrusive, obvious, outstanding, pronounced, remarkable, salient, striking, to the fore, unmistakable; celebrated, chief, distinguished, eminent, famous, foremost, important, leading, main, noted, outstanding, popular, pre-eminent, renowned, respected, top, well-known, well-thought-of

promiscuous *adj* abandoned, debauched, dissipated, dissolute, fast, immoral, lax, libertine, licentious, loose, of easy virtue, profligate, unbridled, unchaste, wanton, wild; careless, casual, haphazard, heedless, indifferent, indiscriminate, irregular, irresponsible, random, slovenly, uncontrolled, uncritical, undiscriminating, unfastidious, unselective

promise *v* assure, contract, cross one's heart, engage, give an undertaking, give one's word, guarantee, pledge, plight, stipulate, swear, take an oath, undertake, vouch, vow, warrant; augur, bespeak, bespoken, bid fair, denote, give hope of, hint at, hold a probability, hold out hopes of, indicate, lead one to expect, look like, seem likely to, show signs of, suggest

promise *n* assurance, bond, commitment, compact, covenant, engagement, guarantee, oath, pledge, undertaking, vow, word, word of honour; ability, aptitude, capability, capacity, flair, potential, talent

promising *adj* auspicious, bright, encouraging, favourable. full of promise, hopeful, likely, propitious, reassuring, rosy; able, gifted, likely, rising, talented, up-and-coming

promote *v* advance, aid, assist, back, boost, contribute to, develop, encourage, forward, foster, further help, nurture, stimulate, support; aggrandize, dignify, elevate, exalt, honour, prefer, raise, upgrade; (*Inf*) kick upstairs; advocate, call attention to, champion, endorse, espouse, popularize, push for, recommend, speak for, sponsor, support, urge, work for; advertise, publicize, puff, push, sell; (*Inf*) beat the drum for, hype, plug

promotion *n* advancement, aggrandizement, elevation, ennoblement, exaltation, honour, move up, prefer ment, rise, upgrading, advancement, advocacy, backing, boosting, cultivation, development, encourage ment, espousal, furtherance, progress, support; advertising, advertising campaign, hard sell, propaganda, publicity, pushing; (*Inf*) ballyhoo, hype, media hype, plugging

prompt *adj* early, immediate, instant, instantaneous, on time, punctual, quick, rapid, speedy, swift, timely, unhesitating; alert, brisk, eager, efficient, expeditious, quick, ready, responsive, smart, willing

prompt *adv* exactly, on the dot, promptly, punctually, sharp

prompt *v* cause, impel, incite, induce, inspire, instigate, motivate, move, provoke, spur, stimulate, urge; assist, cue, help out, jog the memory, prod, refresh the memory, remind; call forth, cause, elicit, evoke, give rise to; occasion, provoke

prompt *n* cue, help, hint, jog, jolt, prod, reminder, spur, stimulus

prone *adj* face down, flat, horizontal, lying down, procumbent, prostrate, recumbent, supine; apt, bent, disposed, given, inclined, liable, likely, predisposed, subject, susceptible, tending

pronounce *v* accent, articulate, enunciate, say, sound, speak, stress, utter, vocalize, voice; affirm, announce, assert, declare, decree, deliver, judge, proclaim

pronouncement *n* announcement, declaration, decree, dictum, edict, judgment, manifesto, notification, proclamation, promulgation, pronunciamento, statement

pronunciation *n* accent, accentuation, articulation, diction, elocution, enunciation, inflection, intonation, speech, stress

proof *n* attestation, authentication, certification, confirmation, corroboration, demonstration, evidence, substantiation, testimony, verification; galley, galley proof, page proof, pull, slip, trial impression, trial print

proof *adj* impenetrable, impervious, repellent, resistant, strong, tight, treated

prop *v* bolster, brace, buttress, hold up, maintain, shore, stay, support, sustain, truss, uphold; lean, rest, set, stand

prop *n* brace, buttress, mainstay, stanchion, stay, support, truss

propaganda *n* advertising, agit-prop, brainwashing, disinformation, information, newspeak, promotion, publicity; (*Inf*) ballyhoo, hype

propagate *v* beget, breed, engender, generate, increase, multiply, procreate, produce, proliferate, reproduce; broadcast, circulate, diffuse, disseminate, make known, proclaim, promote, promulgate, publicize, publish, spread, transmit

propel *v* drive, force, impel, launch, push, send, set in motion, shoot, shove, start, thrust

proper *adj* appropriate, apt, becoming, befitting, *comme il faut*, fit, fit ting, legitimate, right, suitable, suited; decent, decorous, de riger, genteel, gentlemanly, ladylike, mannerly, polite, punctilious, refined, respectable, seemly; accepted, accurate, conventional, correct, established, exact, formal, orthodox, precise, right

property *n* assets, belongings, buildings, capital, chattels, effects, estate, goods, holdings, houses, means, possessions, resources, riches, wealth; acres, estate, freehold, holding, land, real estate, real property, realty, title; ability, attribute characteristic, feature, hallmark, idiosyncrasy, mark, peculiarity, quality, trait, virtue

prophecy *n* augury, divination, forecast, foretelling, prediction, prognosis, prognostication, revelation, second sight, soothsaying

prophesy *v* augur, divine, forecast, foresee, foretell, forewarn, predict, presage prognosticate, soothsay

prophet *n* augur, Cassandra, clairvoyant, diviner, forecaster, oracle, prognosticator, prophesier, seer, sibyl, soothsayer

prophetic *adj* augural, divinatory, foreshadowing, mantic, oracular, predictive, presaging, prescient, prognostic, sibylline

proportion *n* distribution, ratio, relationship, relative, amount; agreement, balance, congruity, correspondence, harmony, symmetry; amount, division, fraction, measure, part, percentage, quota, segment, share; (*Inf*) cut; amplitude, breadth, bulk, capacity, dimensions, expanse, extent, magnitude, measurements, range, scope, size, volume

proportional *adj* balanced, commensurate, comparable, compatible, consistent, correspondent, corresponding, equitable, equivalent, even, in proportion, just

proposal *n* bid, design, motion, offer, overture, plan, presentation, proffer, programme, project, proposition, recommendation, scheme, suggestion, tender, terms

propose *v* advance, come up with, present, proffer, propound, put forward, submit, suggest, tender; introduce, invite, name, nominate, present, put up, recommend; aim, design, have every intention, have in mind, intend, mean, plan, purpose, scheme; ask for someone's hand in marriage, offer marriage, pay suit; (*Inf*) pop the question

proposition *n* motion, plan, programme, project, proposal, recommendation, scheme, suggestion

proprietor *n* deed holder, freeholder, landlady, landlord, landowner, owner, possessor, titleholder

propriety *n* appropriateness, aptness, becomingness, correctness, fitness, rightness, seemliness, suitableness; breeding, courtesy, decency, decorum, delicacy, etiquette, good form, good manners, manners, modesty, politeness, protocol, punctilio, rectitude, refinement, respectability, seemliness

prosecute *n* arraign, bring action against, bring suit against, bring to trial, indict, litigate, prefer charges, put in the dock, put on trial, seek redress, sue, summon, take to court, try; (*Inf*) do; carry on, conduct, direct, discharge, engage in, manage, perform, practise, work at

prospect *n* anticipation, calculation, contemplation, expectation, future, hope, odds, opening, outlook, plan, presumption, probability, promise, proposal, thought; landscape, out look, panorama, perspective, scene, sight, spectacle, view, vision, vista; chance, likelihood, possibility

prospect *v* explore, go after, look for, search, seek, survey

prospective *adj* about to be, anticipated, approaching, awaited, coming, destined, eventual, expected, forthcoming, future, hoped-for, imminent, intended, likely, looked-for, possible, potential, soon-to-be, to-be, to come

prospectus *n* announcement, catalogue, conspectus, list, outline, plan, programme, scheme, syllabus, synopsis

prosper *v* advance, be fortunate, bloom, do well, fare well, flourish, flower, get on, grow rich, make good, progress, succeed, thrive; (*Inf*) make it

prosperity *n* affluence, boom, ease, fortune, good fortune, good times, life of luxury, luxury, plenty, prosperousness, riches, success, the good life, wealth, well-being; (*Inf*) life of Riley

prosperous *adj* blooming, booming, doing well, flourishing, fortunate, lucky, palmy, prospering, successful, thriving; (*Inf*) on the up and up; affluent, moneyed, opulent, rich, wealthy, well-off, well-to-do; (*Inf*) in clover, in the money, well-heeled

prostitute *n* call girl, camp follower, cocotte, courtesan, fallen woman, fille de joie, harlot, loose woman, streetwalker, strumpet, trollop, white slave, whore; (*Inf*) brass, hooker, hustler, moll, pro, tart

prostitute *v* cheapen, debase, degrade, demean, devalue, misapply, pervert, profane

prostrate *adj* abject, bowed low, flat, horizontal, kowtowing, procumbent, prone; at a low ebb, dejected, depressed, desolate, drained, exhausted, fallen, inconsolable, overcome, spent, worn out;

brought to one's knees, defenceless, disarmed, helpless, impotent, overwhelmed, paralysed, powerless, reduced

prostrate *v* abase, bend the knee to, bow before, grovel, kneel, kowtow, submit; bring low, crush, depress, disarm, lay low, overcome, overthrow, overturn, overwhelm, paralyse, reduce, ruin

protagonist *n* central character, hero, heroine, lead, leading character, principle

protect *v* care for, chaperon, cover, cover up for, defend, foster, give sanctuary, guard, harbour, keep, keep safe, look after, mount guard over, preserve, safeguard, save, screen, secure, shelter, shield, support, take under one's wing, watch over

protection *n* aegis, care, charge, custody, defence, guardianship, guarding, preservation, protecting, safeguard, safekeeping, safety, security; armour, barrier, buffer, bulwark, cover, guard, refuge, safeguard, screen, shelter, shield

protective *adj* careful, covering, defensive, fatherly, insulating, jealous, maternal, motherly, paternal, possessive, protecting, safeguarding, sheltering, shielding, vigilant, warm, watchful

protector *n* advocate, benefactor, bodyguard, champion, counsel, defender, guard, guardian, guardian angel, knight in shining armour, patron, safeguard, tower of strength

protégé/protégée *n* charge, dependant, discovery, pupil, student, ward

protest *n* complaint, declaration, demur, demurral, disapproval, dissent, formal, complaint, objection, outcry, protestation, remonstrance

protest *v* complain, cry out, demonstrate, demure, disagree, disapprove, expostulate, express, disapproval, object, oppose, remonstrate, say no to, take exception; (*Inf*) kick against

protester *n* agitator, demonstrator, dissenter, dissident, protest marcher, rebel

protocol *n* code of behaviour, conventions, courtesies, customs, decorum, etiquette, formalities, good form, manners, politesse, propriety, rules of conduct; agreement, compact, concordat, contract, convention, covenant, pact, treaty

prototype *n* archetype, example, first, mock-up, model, norm, original, paradigm, pattern, precedent, standard, type

proud *adj* appreciative, content, contented, glad, gratified, honoured, pleased, satisfied, self-respecting, well-pleased; arrogant, boastful, conceited, disdainful, egotistical, haughty, imperious, lordly, narcissistic, overbearing, presumptuous, self-important, self-satisfied, snobbish, snooty, supercilious, vain; (*Inf*) high and mighty, stuck-up, toffee-nosed

prove *v* ascertain, attest, authenticate, bear out, confirm, corroborate, demonstrate, determine, establish, evidence, evince, justify, show, show clearly, substantiate, verify;

analyse, assay, check, examine, experiment, put to the test, put to trial, test, try; be found to be, come out, end up, result, turn out

proverb *n* adage, aphorism, apophtegm, byword, dictum, gnome, maxim, saw, saying

provide *v* accommodate, cater, contribute, equip, furnish, outfit, provision, stock up, supply; add, afford, bring, give, impart, lend, present, produce, render, serve, yield; anticipate, arrange for, forearm, get ready, make arrangements, make plans, plan ahead, plan for, prepare for, take measures, take precautions; care for, keep, look after, maintain, support, sustain, take care of

providence *n* destiny, divine intervention, fate, fortune, God's will, predestination; care, caution, discretion, far-sightedness, foresight, forethought, perspicacity, presence of mind, prudence

provident *adj* canny, careful, cautious, discreet, economical, equipped, far-seeing, far-sighted, forearmed, foresighted, frugal, prudent, sagacious, shrewd, thrifty, vigilant, well-prepared, wise

providing *conj* as long as, contingent upon, given, if and only if, in case, in the event, on condition, on the assumption, subject to, upon these terms, with the proviso, with the understanding

province *n* colony, county, department, dependency, district, decision, domain, region, section, territory, tract, zone; area, business, capacity, charge, concern, duty, employment, field, function, line, orbit, part, post, responsibility, role, sphere; (*Inf*) pigeon

provision *n* accoutrement, catering, equipping, fitting out, furnishing, providing, supplying, victualling; arrangement, plan, prearrangement, precaution, preparation; agreement, clause, condition, demand, proviso, requirement, specification, stipulation, term

provisional *adj* conditional, contingent, interim, limited, pro tem, provisory, qualified, stopgap, temporary, tentative, transitional

provisions *pl n* comestibles, eatables, edibles, fare, food, foodstuff, groceries, provender, rations, stores, supplies, sustenance, viands, victuals; (*Inf*) eats, grub

provocation *n* *casus belli*, cause, grounds, incitement, inducement, instigation, justification, motivation, reason, stimulus; affront, annoy ance, challenge, dare, grievance, indignity, injury, insult, offence, red rag, taunt, vexation

provocative *adj* annoying, challenging, disturbing, galling, goading, incensing, insulting, offensive, outrageous, provoking, stimulating; (*Inf*) aggravating

provoke *v* affront, anger, annoy, chafe, enrage, exasperate, gall, get on one's nerves, incense, infuriate, insult, irk, irritate, madden, make one's blood boil, offend, pique, put out, rile, try one's patience, vex; (*Inf*) aggravate; bring about, bring on or down, call forth, cause, draw forth, elicit, evoke, excite, fire, generate, give rise to, incite, induce, inflame, inspire, instigate, kindle, lead to, motivate, move, occasion, precipitate, produce, promote, prompt, rouse, stimulate, stir

prowess *n* ability, accomplishment, adeptness, adroitness, aptitude, attainment, command, dexterity, excellence, expertise, expertness, facility, genius, mastery, skill, talent

proximity *n* adjacency, closeness, contiguity, juxtaposition, nearness, neighbourhood, propinquity, vicinity

prudent *adj* canny, careful, cautious, circumspect, discerning, discreet, judicious, politic, sagacious, sage, sensible, shrewd, vigilant, wary, wise; canny, careful, economical, far-sighted, frugal, provident, sparing, thrifty

prune *v* clip, cut, cut back, dock, lop, pare down, reduce, shape, shorten, snip, trim

pry *v* be a busy body, be inquisitive, ferret about, interfere, intrude, meddle, nose into, peep, peer, poke; (*Inf*) be nosy, poke one's nose into, snoop

pseudo *adj* artificial, bogus, counterfeit, ersatz, fake, false, imitation, mock, not genuine, pretended, quasi-sham, spurious; (*Inf*) phoney

pseudonym *n* alias, assumed name, false name, incognito, *nom de guerre*, nom de plume, pen name, professional name, stage name

psychic *adj* clairvoyant, extrasensory, mystic, occult, preternatural, supernatural, telekinetic, telepathic

psychopath *n* insane person, lunatic, madman, maniac, mental case, psychotic, sociopath; (*Inf*) nutcase, nutter

pub *n* alehouse, bar, inn, public house, roadhouse, tavern; (*Inf*) boozer, local

puberty *n* adolescence, awkward age, juvenescence, pubescence, teenage, teens, young adulthood

public *adj* civic, civil, common, general, national, popular, social, state, universal, widespread; accessible, communal, community, free to all, not private, open, open to the public, unrestricted; acknowledged, exposed, in circulation, known, notorious, obvious, open, overt, patent, plain, published, recognized; important, prominent, respected, well known

public *n* citizens, commonalty, community, country, electorate, everyone, hoi polloi, masses, multitude, nation, people, populace, population, society, voters; audience, buyers, clientele, followers, following, patrons, supporters, those interested, trade; *coram populo*, for all to see, in full view, openly, publicly

publication *n* book, booklet, brochure, handbill, issue, leaflet, magazine, newspaper, pamphlet, periodical

publicity *n* advertising, attention, boost, build-up, press, promotion, public notice, puff; (*Inf*) ballyhoo, hype, plug

publicize *v* advertise, bring to public notice, broadcast, give publicity to, make known, play up, promote, puff, push, spotlight, spread about, write up; (*Inf*) beat the drum for, hype, plug

publish *v* bring out, issue, print, produce, put out; advertise, announce, broadcast, circulate, communicate, declare, disclose, distribute, divulge, impart, leak, proclaim, promulgate, publicize, reveal, spread

puerile *adj* babyish, childish, foolish, immature, inane, infantile, irresponsible, jejune, juvenile, naive, petty, ridiculous, silly, trivial, weak

puff *n* blast, breath, draught, emanation, flurry, gust, whiff; pull, smoke; (*Inf*) drag; advertisement, commendation, favourable, mention, good word, sales talk; (*Inf*) plug

puff *v* blow, breathe, exhale, gasp, gulp, pant, wheeze; draw, inhale, pull at, smoke, suck; (*Inf*) drag; bloat, dilate, distend, expand, inflate, swell

pull *v* drag, draw, haul, jerk, tow, trail, tug, yank; cull, draw out, extract, gather, pick, pluck, remove, take out, uproot, weed; dislocate, rend, rip, sprain, strain, stretch, tear, wrench; (*Inf*) attract, draw, entice, lure, magnetize; **pull strings** influence, pull wires, use one's influence

pull *n* jerk, tug, twitch, yank; attraction, drawing, power, effort, exertion, force, forcefulness, influence, lure, magnetism, power; advantage, influence, leverage, muscle, weight; (*Inf*) clout

pull out *v* abandon, depart, evacuate, leave, quit, rat on, retreat, stop participating, withdraw

pull through *v* come through, get better, get over, pull round, rally, recover, survive, weather

pull up *v* brake, come to a halt, halt, reach a standstill, stop; admonish, castigate, rebuke, reprimand, reprove, take to task; (*Inf*) carpet, dress down, tell off, tick off

pulp *n* flesh, marrow, soft part; mash, mush, pap, paste, pomace, semi-liquid, semi-solid, triturate

pulp *v* crush, mash, pulverize, squash, triturate

pulp *adj* cheap, lurid, rubbishy, sensational, trashy

pulse *n* beat, beating, oscillation, pulsation, rhythm, stroke, throb, throbbing, vibration

pulse *v* beat, pulsate, throb, tick, vibrate

pump *v* drive, force, inject, pour, push send, supply; cross-examine, give someone the third degree, interrogate, probe, question closely, quiz, worm out of; (*Inf*) grill

pun *n double entendre*, equivoque, paronomasia, play on words, quip, witticism

punch *v* bash, box, hit, pummel, slam, slug, smash, sock, strike; (*Inf*) biff, bop, clout, plug, sock, wallop, whack; bore, cut, drill, perforate, pierce, pink, prick, puncture, stamp

punch *n* bash, blow, hit, jab, knock, hit, jab, knock, thump; (*Inf*) biff, bop, clout, plug, sock, wallop, whack; bite, drive, effectiveness, force, forcefulness, impact, point, verve, vigour

punctual *adj* early, exact, in good time, on the dot, on time, precise, prompt, punctilious, seasonable, strict, timely

punctuate *v* break, interject, interrupt, intersperse, pepper, sprinkle; accentuate, emphasize, lay stress on, mark, point up, stress, underline

puncture *n* break, cut, damage, hole, leak, nick, opening, perforation, rupture, slit; flat, flat tyre

puncture *v* bore, cut, nick, penetrate, perforate, pierce prick, rupture; deflate, go down, go flat

pungent *adj* acid, acrid, aromatic, bitter, highly flavoured, hot, peppery, piquant, seasoned, sharp, sour, spicy, stinging, strong, tangy, tart; acrimonious, acute, barbed, biting, caustic, cutting, incisive, keen, mordant, penetrating, piercing, poignant, pointed, sarcastic, scathing, sharp, stinging, stringent, telling, trenchant

punish *v* beat, castigate, chasten, chastise, correct, discipline, flog, give a lesson to, lash, penalize, rap someone's knuckles, scourge, sentence, slap someone's wrist, whip; (*Inf*) give someone the works; abuse, batter, harm, hurt, injure, knock about, maltreat, manhandle, misuse, oppress, rough up; (*Inf*) give someone a going over

punishment *n* chastening, chastise ment, correction, discipline, just desserts, penalty, penance, punitive measures, retribution, sanction; (*Inf*) comeuppance, what for; abuse, beating, hard work, maltreatment, manhandling, pain, rough treatment, slave labour, torture, victimization

puny *adj* diminutive, dwarfish, fee ble, frail, little, pygmy, sickly, stunted, tiny, underfed, undersized, undeveloped, weak, weakly; (Inf), pint-sized

pupil *n* beginner, catechumen, disciple, learner, neophyte, novice, scholar, schoolboy, schoolgirl, student, tyro

purchase *v* acquire, buy, come by, gain, get, get hold of, invest in, make a purchase; obtain, pay for, pick up, procure, put money into, secure, shop for; achieve, attain, earn, gain, realize, win

purchase *n* acquisition, asset, buy, gain, investment, possession, property

pure *adj* authentic, clear, flawless, genuine, natural, neat, perfect, real, simple, straight, true, unalloyed, unmixed; clean, disinfected, germ-free, immaculate, pasteurized, sanitary, spotless, sterile, sterilized, unadulterated, unblemished, uncontaminated, unpolluted, untainted, wholesome; blameless, chaste, guileless, honest, immaculate, innocent, maidenly, modest, true, uncorrupted, undefiled, unspotted, unstained, unsullied, upright, virgin, virginal, virtuous

purge *v* clean out, dismiss, do away with, eject, eradicate, expel, exterminate, get rid of, kill, liquidate, oust, remove, rid of, rout out, sweep out, wipe out; absolve, cleanse, clear, exonerate, expiate, forgive, pardon, purify, wash

purge *n* cleanup, crushing, ejection, elimination, eradication, expulsion, liquidation, reign of terror, removal, suppression, witch hunt

purify *v* clarify, clean, cleanse, decontaminate, disinfect, filter, fumigate, refine, sanitize, wash; absolve, cleanse, exculpate, exonerate, lustrate, redeem, sanctify, shrive

puritan *n* fanatic, moralist, pietist, prude, rigorist, zealot

puritan *adj* ascetic, austere, hide bound, intolerant, moralistic, narrow, narrow-minded, prudish, puritanical, severe, strait-laced, strict

purpose *n* aim, design, function, idea, intention, object, point, principle, reason; aim, ambition, aspiration, design, desire, end, goal, hope, intention, object, objective, plan, project, scheme, target, view, wish; constancy, determination, firmness, persistence, resolution, resolve, single-mindedness, steadfastness, tenacity, will; on purpose by design, deliberately, designedly, intentionally, knowingly, purposely, wilfully, wittingly

purpose *v* aim, aspire, commit oneself, contemplate, decide, design, determine, have a mind to, intend, make up one's mind, mean, meditate, plan, purpose, propose, resolve, set one's sights on, think to, work towards

purposely *adv* by design, calculatedly, consciously, deliberately, designedly, expressly, intentionally, knowingly, on purpose, wilfully, with intent

purse *n* money-bag, pouch, wallet; coffers, exchequer, funds, means, money, resources, treasury, wealth, wherewithal; award, gift, present, prize, reward

pursue *v* accompany, attend, chase, dog, follow, give chase to, go after, harass, harry, haunt, hound, hunt, hunt down, plague, run after, shadow, stalk, tail, track; aim for, aspire to, desire, have as one's goal, purpose, seek, strive for, try for, work towards; adhere to, carry on, continue, cultivate, hold to, keep on, maintain, persevere in, persist in, proceed, see through; chase after, court, pay attention to, pay court to, set one's cap at, woo; (*Inf*) make up to

pursuit *n* chase, hunt, hunting, inquiry, quest, search, seeking, tracking, trail, trailing; activity, hobby, interest, line, occupation, pastime, pleasure, vocation

push *v* depress, drive, poke, press, propel, ram, shove, thrust; elbow, jostle, male or force one's way, move, shoulder, shove, squeeze, thrust; egg on, encourage, expedite, hurry, impel, incite, persuade, press, prod, speed up, spur, urge; advertise, boost, cry up, make known, promote, propagandize, publicize, puff; (*Inf*) hype, plug

push *n* butt, jolt, nudge, poke, prod, shove, thrust; ambition, determination, drive, dynamism, energy, enterprise, initiative, vigour, vitality; (*Inf*) get-up-and-go, go, gumption; advance, assault, attack, charge, effort, offensive, onset, thrust

pushy *adj* ambitious, determined, driving, dynamic, enterprising, go-ahead, on the go, purposeful, resourceful; assertive, bold, brash, bumptious, forward, impertinent, intrusive, presumptuous, self-assertive; (*Inf*) pushy

put *v* bring, deposit, establish, fix,

lay, place, position, rest, set, settle, situate; assign, constrain, employ, force, induce, make, oblige, require, set, subject to; advance, bring forward, forward, offer, posit, present, propose, set before, submit, tender; cast, fling, heave, hurl, lob, pitch, throw, toss

put across *v* communicate, convey, explain, get across, get through, make clear, make oneself under stood, spell out

put aside *v* cache, deposit, keep in reserve, lay by, salt away, save, squirrel away, stockpile, store, stow away

put away *v* put back, replace, return to its place, tidy away; deposit, keep, lay in, put by, save, set aside, store away

put down *v* enter, inscribe, log, record, set down, take down, transcribe, write down; crush, quash, quell, repress, silence, stamp out, suppress; ascribe, attribute, impute, set down; destroy, do away with, put away, put out of its misery, put to sleep; condemn, crush, deflate, dismiss, disparage, humiliate, mortify, reject, shame, slight, snub

put forward *v* advance, introduce, move, nominate, present, press, proffer, propose, recommend, submit, suggest, tender

put off *v* defer, delay, hold over, postpone, put back, reschedule; abash, confuse, discomfit, disconcert, dismay, distress, nonplus, perturb, unsettle; (*Inf*) rattle, throw; discourage, dishearten, dissuade

put on *v* do, mount, present, produce, show, stage; add, gain, increase by; change into, clothe oneself in, don, dress in, get dressed in, slip into

put out *v* anger, annoy, confound, disturb, exasperate, harass, irk, irritate, nettle, perturb, provoke, vex; blow out, douse, extinguish, quench, smother, snuff out, stamp out; bother, discomfit, discommode, discompose, disconcert, discountenance, disturb, embarrass, impose-upon, incommode, inconvenience, put on the spot, trouble, upset

put up *v* build, construct, erect, fabricate, raise; accommodate, board, entertain, give one lodging, house, lodge, take in; float, nominate, offer, present, propose, put forward, recommend, submit; advance, give, invest, pay, pledge, provide, supply; **put up with** abide, bear, brook, endure, pocket, stand, stand for, stomach, suffer, swallow, take, tolerate

puzzle *v* baffle, beat, bewilder, confound, confuse, flumox, mystify, nonplus, perplex, stump; ask one self, brood, mull over, muse, ponder, rack one's brains, study, think about, think hard, wonder; **puzzle out** clear up, crack, crack the code, decipher, figure put, find the key, get it, get the answer, resolve, see, solve, sort out, think through, unravel, work out

puzzle *n* conundrum, enigma, labyrinth, maze, mystery, paradox, poser, problem, question, question mark, riddle; bafflement, bewilderment, confusion, difficulty, dilemma, perplexity, quandary, uncertainty; (*Inf*) brain-teaser

puzzling *adj* above one's head, abstruse, ambiguous, baffling, bewildering, beyond one, enigmatic, full of surprises, hard, incomprehensible, inexplicable, involved, knotty, labyrinthine, misleading, mystifying, perplexing, unaccountable, unfathomable

pygmy *n* dwarf, midget, small person; (*Inf*) pint-sized person, shrimp, Thom Thumb; cipher, lightweight, nobody, nonentity; (*Inf*) pip-squeak

pyromaniac *n* arsonist, fire-raiser, incendiary

Q

quagmire *n* bog, fen, marsh, mire, morass, quicksand, slough, swamp; difficulty, dilemma, entanglement, imbroglio, impasse, muddle, pass, pinch, plight, predicament, quandary; (*Inf*) fix, jam, pickle, scrape

quaint *adj* bizarre, curious, droll, eccentric, fanciful, fantastic, odd, old-fashioned, original, peculiar, queer, singular, strange, unusual, whimsical

quake *v* convulse, move, pulsate, quail, quiver, rock, shake, shiver, tremble, vibrate, waver, wobble

qualification *n* ability, accomplish ment, aptitude, attribute, capability, capacity, eligibility, endowments, fitness, quality, skill, suitability, suitableness; allowance, caveat, condition, criterion, exception, exemption, limitation, modification, objection, prerequisite, proviso, requirement, reservation, restriction, stipulation

qualified *adj* able, accomplished, adept, capable, certified, competent, efficient, equipped, experienced, expert, fit, knowledgeable, licensed, practised, proficient, skilful, talented, trained; abounded, circumscribed, conditional, confined, contingent, equivocal, guarded, limited, modified, provisional, reserved, restricted

qualify *v* capacitate, certify, commission, condition, empower, endow equip, fit, ground, permit, prepare, ready, sanction, train; abate, adapt, assuage, circumscribe, diminish, ease, lessen, limit, mitigate, moderate, modify, modulate, reduce, regulate, restrain, restrict, soften, temper, vary

quality *n* aspect, attribute, characteristic, condition, feature, mark, peculiarity, property, trait; character, constitution, description, essence, kind, make, nature, sort; calibre, distinction, excellence, grade, merit, position, pre-eminence, rank, standing, status, superiority, value, worth

quandary *n* bewilderment, cleft stick, delicate situation, difficulty, dilemma doubt, embarrassment, impasse, perplexity, plight, predicament, puzzle, strait, uncertainty

quantity *n* aggregate, allotment, amount, lot, number, part, portion, quota, sum, total

quarrel *n* affray, altercation, argument, brawl, breach, broil, commotion, contention, controversy, difference of opinion,disagreement, discord, disputation, dispute, dissension, dissidence, disturbance, feud, fight, fracas, fray, misunderstanding, row, spat, squabble, strife, tiff, tumult, vendetta, wrangle; (*Inf*) scrap

quarrel *v* altercate, argue, bicker, brawl, clash, differ, disagree, dispute, fight, row, spar, squabble, wrangle; (*Inf*) fall out

quarrelsome *adj* argumentative, belligerent, choleric, combative, contentious, cross, disputatious, fractious, hot-tempered, ill-tempered, irascible, irritable, peevish, petulant, pugnacious, querulous, ready for a fight; (*Inf*) fight like cats and dogs

quarry *n* aim, game, goal, objective, prey, prize, victim

quarter *n* area, direction, district, locality, location, neighbourhood, part, place, point position, province, region, side, spot, station, territory, zone

quarter *v* accommodate, billet, board, house, install, lodge, place, post, put up, station

quarters *pl n* abode, accommoda-tion, barracks, billet, cantonment, chambers, digs, domicile, dwelling, habitation, lodging, lodgings, post, residence, rooms, shelter, station; (*Inf*) digs

quash *v* annul, cancel, declare null and void, invalidate, nullify, over-rule, overthrow, rescind, reverse, revoke, set aside, void

queen *n* consort, monarch, ruler, sovereign

queer *adj* abnormal, anomalous, atypical, curious, disquieting, droll, eerie, erratic, extraordinary, funny, odd, outlandish, outré, peculiar, remarkable, singular, strange, uncanny, uncommon, unconven-tional, unnatural, unorthodox, unusual, weird; doubtful, dubious, irregular, mysterious, puzzling, questionable, suspicious; (*Inf*) fishy, shady; crazy, demented, eccentric, idiosyncratic, irrational, mad, odd, touched, unbalanced, unhinged

queer *v* botch, endanger, harm, impair, imperil, injure, jeopardize, mar, ruin, spoil, thwart, wreck

quench *v* check, crush, destroy, douse, end, extinguish, put out, smother, snuff out, squelch, stifle, suppress

query *v* ask, enquire, question; challenge, disbelieve, dispute, distrust, doubt, mistrust, suspect

query *n* demand, doubt, hesitation, inquiry, objection, problem, ques-tion, reservation, scepticism, suspi-cion

question *v* ask, catechize, cross-examine, enquire, examine, interro gate, interview, investigate, probe, quiz, sound out; (*Inf*) grill, pump; call into question, cast doubt upon, challenge, controvert, disbelieve, dispute, distrust, doubt, impugn, mistrust, oppose, query, suspect

question *n* examination, inquiry, interrogation, investigation; argu-ment, confusion, contention, contro-versy, debate, difficulty, dispute, doubt, dubiety, misgiving, problem, query, uncertainty; issue, motion, point, point at issue, proposal, proposition, subject, theme, topic

questionable *adj* arguable, contro-versial, controvertible, debatable, disputable, doubtful, dubious, dubitable, equivocal, moot, para-doxical, problematical, suspect, suspicious, uncertain, unproven, unreliable; (*Inf*) fishy, shady

queue *n* chain, concatenation, file, line, order, progression, sequence, series, string, succession, train

quibble *v* carp, cavil, equivocate, evade, pretend, prevaricate, shift, split hairs

quibble *n* artifice, cavil, complaint, criticism, duplicity, equivocation, evasion, nicety, niggle, objection, pretence, prevarication, protest, quirk, shift, sophism, subterfuge, subtlety

quick *adj* active, brief, brisk, cursory, expeditious, express, fast, fleet, hasty, headlong, hurried, perfunctory, prompt, rapid, speedy, sudden, swift; agile, alert, animated, energetic, flying, keen, lively, nimble, spirited, sprightly, spry, vivacious, winged; able, acute, adept, adroit, apt, astute, bright, clever, deft, dexterous, discerning, intelligent, nimble-witted, perceptive, quick-witted, receptive, sharp, shrewd, skilful, smart; (*Inf*) all there, quick on the uptake

quick-tempered *adj* fiery, hasty, hot-tempered, impatient, irascible, irritable, petulant, quarrelsome, snappish, touchy;

quick-witted *adj* alert, bright, discerning, intelligent, lively, quick, sharp-witted, shrewd, smart; (*Inf*) quick on the uptake

quicken *v* accelerate, dispatch, expedite, hasten, hurry, impel, precipitate, speed; activate, animate, arouse, energize, excite, galvanize, incite, inspire, invigorate, kindle, refresh, reinvigorate, resuscitate, revitalize, revive, rouse, stimulate, strengthen, vitalize, vivify

quid pro quo *n* barter, compensation, exchange, recompense, repsisal, retaliation, substitution, trade-off, trading

quiescent *adj* dormant, idle, inactive, inert, passive, stagnant, still

quiet *adj* dumb, hushed, inaudible, low, low-pitched, noiseless, peaceful, placid, restful, serene, smooth, tranquil, untroubled; isolated, private, retired, secluded, secret, sequestered, undisturbed, unfrequented; conservative, modest, plain, restrained, simple, sober, subdued, unassuming, unobtrusive, unpretentious; collected, docile, even-tempered, gentle, imperturbable, meek, mild, phlegmatic, reserved, retiring, sedate, shy, unexcitable

quiet *n* calmness, ease, hush, peace, quietness, repose, rest, serenity, silence, stillness, tranquillity; (*Inf*) shut up

quieten *v* allay, alleviate, appease, assuage, blunt, calm, compose, deaden dull, hush, lull, mitigate, mollify, muffle, mute, palliate, quell, quiet, silence, soothe, stifle, still, stop, subdue, tranquilize; (*Inf*) shush

quietness *n* calm, calmness, hush, peace, placidity, quiescence, quiet, quietude, repose, rest, serenity, silence, still, stillness, tranquillity

quip *n* badinage, *bon mot*, gibe, jest, joke, pleasantry, repartee, retort, riposte, sally, witticism; (*Inf*) wisecrack

quit *v* abandon, abdicate, decamp, depart, desert, exit, forsake, go, leave, pull out, relinquish, renounce, resign, retire, surrender, withdraw; (*Inf*) take off; abandon, cease, conclude, discontinue, drop, end, give up, halt, stop, suspend

quite *adv* absolutely, completely, considerably, entirely, fully, in all respects, largely, perfectly, precisely, totally, wholly, without, reservation; fairly, moderately, rather, reason ably, relatively, somewhat, to a certain extent, to some degree

quiver *v* agitate, convulse, oscillate, palpitate, pulsate, quake, quaver, shake, shiver, shudder, tremble, vibrate

quiz *n* examination, investigation, questioning, test

quiz *v* ask, catechize, examine, interrogate, investigate, question; (*Inf*) grill, pump

quota *n* allocation, allowance, assignment, part, portion, proportion, ration, share, slice; (*Inf*) cut, whack

quotation *n* citation, cutting, excerpt, extract, passage, reference, selection; (*Inf*) quote; bid, price, charge, cost, estimate, figure, price, rate, tender

quote *v* adduce, attest, cite, detail, extract, instance, name, paraphrase, proclaim, recall, recite, recollect, refer to, repeat, retell

R

rabble *n* canaille, crowd, herd, horde, mob, swarm, throng

race *n* chase, competition, con tention, contest, dash, pursuit, rivalry; blood, bloodline, breed, clan, ethnic group, family, folk, house, issue, kin, kindred, line, lineage, nation, offspring, people, progeny, stock, tribe, type

race *v* career, compete, contest, dart, dash, fly, gallop, hasten, hurry, run, speed, tear, zoom; (*Inf*) hare, run like mad

rack *n* frame, framework, stand, structure; affliction, agony, anguish, misery, pain, pang, persecution, suffering, torment, torture

rack *v* afflict, agonize, crucify, distress, excruciate, harass, harrow, oppress, pain, torment, torture

racket *n* babel, clamour, commotion, din, disturbance, fuss, hubbub, hullabaloo, noise, outcry, pandemonium, row, shouting, tumult, uproar; criminal activity, fraud, illegal enterprise, scheme

racy *adj* animated, buoyant, energetic, entertaining, exciting, exhilarating, heady, lively, sparkling, spirited, stimulating, vigorous, zestful

radiant *adj* beaming, bright, brilliant, effulgent, gleaming, glittering, glorious, glowing, incandescent, luminous, lustrous, resplendent, shining, sparkling, sunny

radiate *v* diffuse, disseminate, emanate, emit, give out, gleam, glitter, pour, scatter, send out, shed, shine, spread; branch out, diverge, issue, spread out

radical *adj* basic, constitutional, deep-seated, essential, fundamental, innate, native, natural, organic, profound, thoroughgoing; complete, entire, excessive, extreme, extremist, fanatical, revolutionary, severe, sweeping, thorough, violent

radical *n.* extremist, fanatic, militant, revolutionary

rage *n* agitation, anger, frenzy, fury, high dudgeon, ire, madness, mania, obsession, passion, rampage, raving, vehemence, violence, wrath

rage *v* be beside oneself, be furious, blow one's top, chafe, foam at the mouth, fret, fume, rant and rave, rave, seethe, storm; (*Inf*) blow up, throw a fit

ragged *adj* contemptible, down at the heel, frayed, in holes, in rags, in tatters, mean, poor, shabby, shaggy, tattered, tatty, threadbare, torn, unkempt, worn-out

raid *n* attach, break-in, descent, foray, hit-and-run attack, incursion, inroad, invasion, irruption, onset, sally, seizure, sortie, surprise attack

raid *v* assault, attack, break into, descend on, fall upon, forage foray, invade, pillage, plunder, rifle, sack, sally forth, swoop down upon

raider *n* attacker, forager, invader, marauder, plunderer, robber, thief

rain *n* cloudburst, deluge, downpour, drizzle, fall, precipitation, rain drops, rainfall, showers; deluge, flood, hail, shower, spate, stream, torrent, volley

rain *v* drizzle, fall, shower, teem; (*Inf*) bucket down, come down in buckets, rain cats and dogs

raise *v* build, construct, elevate, erect, exalt, heave, hoist, lift, move up, promote, put up, rear, set upright, uplift; advance, aggravate, amplify, augment, boost, enhance, enlarge, escalate, exaggerate, heighten, increase, inflate, intensify, jack up, magnify, put up, reinforce, strengthen; (*Inf*) hike up; advance, aggrandize, elevate, exalt, prefer, promote, upgrade; bring about, cause, create, engender, give rise to, occasion, originate, produce, provoke, start; advance, bring up, broach, introduce, moot, put forward, suggest; assemble, collect, form, mobilize, muster, obtain, rally, recruit; breed, bring up, cultivate, develop, grow, nurture, produce, propagate, rear

rake *v* collect, gather, remove, scrape up; break up, harrow, hoe, scour, scrape, scratch;

rake *n* debauchee, dissolute man, lecher, libertine, playboy, profligate, roué, sensualist, voluptuary

rally *v* bring or come to order, reassemble, re-form, regroup, reorganize, unite; assemble, bond together, bring together, collect, convene, gather, get together, marshal, mobilize, muster, organize, round up, summon, unite; come round, get better, get one's second wind, improve, perk up, pick up, pull through, recover, recuperate, regain one's strength, revive, take a turn for the better

rally *n* regrouping, reorganization, reunion, stand; assembly, conference, congregation, convention, convocation, gathering, mass meet ing, meeting, muster; improvement, recovery, recuperation, renewal, resurgence, revival, turn for the better; (*Inf*) comeback

ram *v* butt, collide with, crash, dash, drive, force, hit, impact, run into, slam, smash, strike

ramble *v* amble, drift, perambulate, peregrinate, range, roam, rove, saunter, straggle, stray, stroll, walk, wander; (*Inf*) traipse; babble, chat ter, digress, expatiate, maunder, rattle on, wander, witter on; (*Inf*) rabbit on

ramble *n* excursion, hike, perambu lation, peregrination, roaming, roving, saunter, stroll, tour, trip, walk; (*Inf*) traipse

ramification *n* branch, development, divarication, division, excrescence, extension, forking, offshoot, outgrowth, subdivision; complication, consequence, development, result, sequel, upshot

rampage *v* go berserk, rage, run amuck, run riot, run wild, storm, tear

rampage *n* destruction, frenzy, fury, rage, storm, tempest, tumult, uproar, violence

rampant *adj* aggressive, dominant, excessive, flagrant, on the rampage, out of control, out of hand, outrageous, raging, rampaging, riotous, unbridled, uncontrollable, ungovernable, unrestrained, vehement, violent, wanton, wild

rampart *n* barricade, bastion, breastwork, bulwark, defence, earthwork, embankment, fence, fort, fortification, guard, parapet, security, stronghold, wall

ramshackle *adj* broken-down, crumbling, decrepit, derelict, dilapidated, flimsy, jerry-built, rickety, shaky, tottering, tumble-down, unsafe, unsteady

random *adj* accidental, adventitious, aimless, arbitrary, casual, chance, desultory, fortuitous, haphazard, hit or miss, incidental, indiscriminate, purposeless, spot, stray, unplanned, unpremeditated

range *n* amplitude, area, bounds, compass, confines, distance, domain, extent, field, latitude, limits, orbit, province, purview, radius, reach, scope, span, sphere, sweep; (*Inf*) parameters

range *v* align, arrange, array, dispose, draw up, line up, order; cruise, explore, ramble, roam, rove, straggle, stray, stroll, sweep, traverse, wander

rank *n* caste, class, classification, degree, dignity, division, echelon, grade, level, nobility, order, position, quality, sort, standing, station, status, stratum, type; column, file, formation, group, line, range, row, series, tier

rank *v* align, arrange, array, class, classify, dispose, grade, line up, locate, marshal, order, position, range, sort

rank *adj* abundant, dense, exuberant, flourishing, lush, luxuriant, productive, profuse, strong, growing, vigorous; bad, disagreeable, disgusting, fetid, foul, fusty, gamy, mephitic, musty, noisome, noxious, off, offensive, pungent, putrid, rancid, revolting, stale, stinking, strong-smelling

ransack *v* comb, explore, go through, rake, rummage, scour, search, turn inside out; despoil, gut, loot, pillage, plunder, raid, ravage, rifle, sack, strip

ransom *n* deliverance, liberation, redemption, release, rescue; money, payment, payoff, price

ransom *v* buy the freedom of, deliver, liberate, obtain *or* pay for the release of, redeem, release, rescue, set free; (*Inf*) buy someone out

rant *v* bellow, bluster, cry, declaim, rave, roar, shout, vociferate, yell; (*Inf*) spout

rape *n* outrage, ravishment, sexual assault, violation; depredation, despoilment, despoliation, pillage, plundering, rapine, sack, spoliation; abuse, defilement, desecration, maltreatment, perversion, violation;

rape *v* outrage, ravish, sexually assault, violate; despoil, loot, pillage, plunder, ransack, sack, spoliate

rapid *adj* brisk, expeditious, express, fast, fleet, flying, hasty, hurried, precipitate, prompt, quick, speedy, swift

rapt *adj* absorbed, carried away, engrossed, enthralled, entranced, fascinated, gripped, held, intent, preoccupied, spellbound

rapture *n* beatitude, bliss, delectation, delight, ecstasy, enthusiasm, euphoria, exaltation, felicity, happiness, joy, ravishment, rhapsody, seventh heaven, spell, transport; (*Inf*) cloud nine

rare *adj* exceptional, few, infrequent,

out of the ordinary, recherché, scarce, singular, sparse, sporadic, strange, thin on the ground, uncommon, unusual; admirable, choice, excellent, exquisite, extreme, fine, great, incomparable, peerless, superb, superlative

rarely *adv* almost never, hardly, hardly ever, infrequently, little, once in a blue moon, once in a while, only now and then, on rare occasions, scarcely ever, seldom

rarity *n* curio, curiosity, find, gem, one-off, pearl, treasure; infrequency, scarcity, shortage, singularity, sparseness, strangeness, uncom monness, unusualness

rascal *n* blackguard, devil, disgrace, good-for-nothing, imp, miscreant, ne-er-do-well, rake, rapscallion, reprobate, rogue, scamp, scoundrel, villain, wastrel, wretch; (*Inf*) scally wag, varmint

rash *adj* adventurous, audacious, brash, careless, foolhardy, hare-brained, harum-scarum, hasty, headlong, headstrong, heedless, helter-skelter, hot-headed, ill-advised, ill-considered, impetuous, imprudent, impulsive, incautious, indiscreet, injudicious, madcap, precipitate, premature, reckless, thought less, unguarded, unthinking, unwary, venturesome

rash *n* eruption, outbreak, epidemic, flood, outbreak, plague, series, spate, succession, wave

rate *n* degree, percentage, proportion, ratio, relation, scale, standard; charge, cost, dues, duty, fee, figure, hire, price, tariff, tax, toll; gait, measure, pace, speed, tempo, time, velocity; class, classification, degree, grade, position, quality, rank, rating, status, value, worth; **at any rate** anyhow, anyway, at all events, in any case, nevertheless

rate *v* adjudge, appraise, assess, class, classify, consider, count, esteem, estimate, evaluate, grade, measure, rank, reckon, regard, value, weigh

rather *adv* a bit, a little, fairly, moderately, quite, relatively, slightly, somewhat, to some degree, to some extent; (*Inf*) kind of, pretty, sort of; a good bit, noticeably, significantly, very; instead, more readily, more willingly, preferably, sooner

ratify *v* affirm, approve, authenticate, authorize, bear out, bind, certify, confirm, consent, consent to, corroborate, endorse, establish, sanction, sign, uphold, validate

ratio *n* arrangement, correlation, correspondence, equation, fraction, percentage, proportion, rate, relation, relationship

ration *n* allotment, allowance, dole, helping, measure, part, portion, provision, quota, share; commons, food, provender, provisions, stores, supplies

ration *v* allocate, allot, apportion, conserve, deal, distribute, dole, give out, issue, measure out, mete, par - cel out; budget, conserve, control, limit, restrict, save

rational *adj* enlightened, intelligent, judicious, logical, lucid, realistic, reasonable, sagacious, sane, sensible, sound, wise

rationalize *v* account for, excuse,

explain away, extenuate, justify, make allowance for, make excuses for, vindicate; apply logic to, elucidate, reason out, resolve, think through

rattle *v* bang, clatter, jangle; bounce, jar, jiggle, jolt, jounce, shake, vibrate; discompose, disconcert, discountenance, disturb, frighten, perturb, put someone off his stride, put someone out of countenance, scare, shake, upset; (*Inf*) discomfit, faze

raucous *adj* grating, harsh, hoarse, husky, loud, noisy, rasping, rough, strident

ravage *v* demolish, desolate, despoil, destroy, devastate, gut, lay waste, leave in ruins, loot, pillage, plunder, ransack, raze, ruin, sack, shatter, spoil, wreak havoc on, wreck

rave *v* babble, be delirious, fume, go mad, rage, rant, roar, run amuck, splutter, storm, talk wildly, thunder

ravenous *adj* famished, starved, starving, very hungry

ravine *n* canyon, defile, flume, gap, gorge, gully, pass

raw *adj* bloody, fresh, natural, uncooked, undressed, unprepared; basic, coarse, crude, green, natural, organic, rough, unfinished, unprocessed, unrefined, unripe, untreated; abraded, chafed, grazed, open, scratched, sensitive, skinned, sore, tender; callow, green, ignorant, immature, inexperienced, new, undisciplined, unpractised, unseasoned, unskilled, untrained, untried; biting, bitter, bleak, chill, chilly, cold, damp, freezing, harsh, piercing, unpleasant, wet

ray *n* bar, beam, flash, gleam, shaft; flicker, glimmer, hint, indication, scintilla, spark, trace

reach *v* arrive at, attain, get as far as, get to, land at, make; contact, extend to, get a hold of, go as far as, grasp, stretch to, touch; amount to, arrive at, attain, climb to, come to, drop, fall, move, rise, sink

reach *n* ambit, capacity, command, compass, distance, extension, extent, grasp, influence, jurisdiction, mastery, power, range, scope, spread, stretch, sweep

react *v* acknowledge, answer, reply, respond; act, behave, conduct oneself, function, operate, proceed, work

reaction *n* acknowledgment, answer, feedback, reply, response; compensation, counterbalance, counterpoise, recoil; conservatism, counter-revolution, obscurantism, the right

reactionary *adj* blimpish, conservative, counter-revolutionary, obscurantist, rightist

reactionary *n* Colonel Blimp, conservative, counter-revolutionary, die-hard, obscurantist, rightist, right-winger

read *v* glance at, look at, peruse, pore over, refer to, run one's eye over, scan, study; announce, declaim, deliver, recite, speak, utter; comprehend, construe, decipher, discover, interpret, perceive the meaning of, see, understand; display, indicate, record, register, show

read *n* browse, future, perusal, study,

readily *adv* cheerfully, eagerly,

freely, gladly, promptly, quickly, voluntarily, willingly, with good grace, with pleasure; a once, easily, effortlessly, in no time, quickly, right away, smoothly, speedily, straight away, unhesitatingly, without delay, without demur, without difficulty, without hesitation

reading *n* examination, inspection, perusal, review, scrutiny, study; homily, lecture, lesson, performance, recital, rendering, rendition, sermon; conception, construction, grasp, impression, interpretation, treatment, understanding, version; book-learning, edification, education, erudition, knowledge, learning, scholarship

ready *adj* all set, arranged, completed, fit, in readiness, organized, prepared, primed, ripe, set; agreeable, apt, disposed, eager, glad, happy, inclined, keen, minded, predisposed, prone, willing; (*Inf*) game; acute, adroit, alert, apt, astute, bright, clever, deft, dexter ous, expert, handy, intelligent, keen, perceptive, prompt, quick, quick-witted, rapid, resourceful, sharp, skilful, smart; accessible, at hand, at one's fingertips, at the ready, available, close to hand, convenient, handy, near, on call, present; (*Inf*) on tap

real *adj* absolute, actual, authentic, *bona fide*, certain, essential, existent, factual, genuine, heartfelt, honest, intrinsic, legitimate, positive, right, rightful, sincere, true, unaffected, unfeigned, valid, veritable

realistic *adj* businesslike, common-sense, down-to-earth, hard-headed, level-headed, matter-of-fact, practical, pragmatic, rational, real, sensible, sober, unromantic, unsentimental; authentic, faithful, genuine, graphic, lifelike, natural, naturalistic, representational, true, true to life, truthful

reality *n* actuality, authenticity, certainty, corporeality, fact, genuineness, materiality, realism, truth, validity, verisimilitude, verity

realization *n* appreciation, apprehension, awareness, cognizance, comprehension, conception, consciousness, grasp, imagination, perception, recognition, understanding; accomplishment, achievement, carrying-out, completion, consummation, effectuation, fulfilment

realize *v* appreciate, apprehend, be cognizant of, become aware of, become conscious of, comprehend, conceive, grasp, imagine, recognize, take in, understand; (*Inf*) catch on, twig; accomplish, actualize, bring about, bring off, bring to fruition, carry out, complete, consummate, do, effect, effectuate, fulfil, make concrete, make happen, perform, reify; acquire, bring in, clear, earn, gain, get, go for, make, net, obtain, produce, sell for;

reap *v* acquire, bring in, collect, cut, derive, gain, garner, gather, get, harvest, obtain, win

rear *n* back, back end, end, rear guard, stern, tail, tail end

rear *adj* aft, after, back, following, hind, hindmost, last, trailing

rear *v* breed, bring up, care for,

cultivate, educate, foster, grow, nurse, nurture, raise, train; build, construct, erect, fabricate, put up

reason *n* apprehension, brains, comprehension, intellect, judgment, logic, mentality, mind, ratiocination, rationality, reasoning, sanity, senses, sound mind, soundness, understand ing; aim, basis, cause, design, end, goal, grounds, impetus, incentive, inducement, intention, motive, object, occasion, purpose, target, warrant; (*Inf*) why and wherefore; bounds, limits, moderation, propri ety, reasonableness, sense, sensible ness, wisdom

reason *v* conclude, deduce, draw conclusions, infer, make out, ratiocinate, resolve, solve, syllogize, think, work out

reasonable *adj* advisable, arguable, believable, credible, intelligent, judicious, justifiable, logical, plausible, practical, rational, reasoned, sane, sensible, sober, sound, tenable, well-advised, well-thought-out, wise; acceptable, average, equitable, fair, fit, honest, inexpensive, just, moderate, modest, proper, right, tolerable, within reason; (*Inf*) OK

reasoning *n* analysis, cogitation, deduction, logic, ratiocination, reason, thinking, thought; argument, case, exposition, hypothesis, interpretation, proof, train of thought

reassure *v* bolster, buoy up, cheer up, comfort, encourage, hearten, inspirit, put or set one's mind at rest, relieve someone of anxiety, restore confidence to

rebel *v* man the barricades, mutiny, resist, revolt, rise up, take to the streets, take up arms; come out against, defy, disobey, dissent, refuse to obey; flinch, recoil, show repugnance, shrink, shy away

rebel *n* insurgent, insurrectionary, mutineer, resistance fighter, revolutionary, revolutionist, secessionist; apostate, dissenter, heretic, nonconformist, schismatic

rebel *adj* insubordinate, insurgent, insurrectionary, mutinous, rebellious, revolutionary

rebellion *n* insurgence, insurgency, insurrection, mutiny, resistance, revolt, revolution, rising, uprising; apostasy, defiance, disobedience, dissent, heresy, insubordination, nonconformity, schism

rebellious *adj* contumacious, defiant, disaffected, disloyal, disobedient, disorderly, insubordinate, insurgent, insurrectionary, intractable, mutinous, rebel, recalcitrant, revolutionary, seditious, turbulent, ungovernable, unruly; difficult, incorrigible, obstinate, recalcitrant, refractory, resistant, unmanageable

rebound *v* bounce, recoil, resound, return, ricochet, spring back; backfire, boomerang, misfire, recoil

rebound *n* bounce, comeback, kickback, repercussion, return, ricochet

rebuff *v* check, cold-shoulder, cut, decline, deny, discourage, put off, refuse, reject, repulse, resist, slight, snub, spurn, turn down; (*Inf*) brush off

rebuff *n* check, cold shoulder,

defeat, denial, discouragement, opposition, refusal, rejection, repulse, slight, snub, thumbs down

rebuke *v* admonish, berate, blame, castigate, censure, chide, lecture, reprehend, reprimand, reproach, reprove, scold, take to task, upbraid; (*Inf*) bawl out, carpet, dress down, haul someone over the coals, tear someone off a strip, tell off, tick off

rebuke *n* admonition, blame, castigation, censure, lecture, reprimand, reproach, reproof, reproval, row, tongue-lashing; (*Inf*) dressing down, telling-off, ticking-off, wigging

recall *v* bring or call to mind, call up, evoke, look back to, recollect, remember, reminisce about; abjure, annul, call back, call in, cancel, countermand, nullify, repeal, rescind, retract, revoke, take back, withdraw

recall *n* annulment, cancellation, nullification, recision, repeal, rescindment, rescission, retraction, revocation, withdrawal; memory, recollection, remembrance

recede *v* abate, draw back, ebb, fall back, go back, regress, retire, retreat, retrogress, return, subside, withdraw; decline, diminish, dwindle, fade, lessen, shrink, sink, wane

receipt *n* acknowledgment, counterfoil, proof or purchase, sales slip, stub, voucher; acceptance, delivery, receiving, reception, recipient

receive *v* accept, accept delivery of, acquire, be given, be in receipt of, collect, derive, get, obtain, pick up, take; apprehend, be informed of, be told, gather, hear, perceive; bear, be subjected to, encounter, experience, go through, meet with, suffer, sustain, undergo; accommodate, admit, be at home to, entertain, greet, meet, take in, welcome

recent *adj* contemporary, current, fresh, late, latter, latter-day, modern, new, novel, present-day, up-to-date, young

reception *n* acceptance, admission, receipt, receiving, recipient; acknowledgment, greeting, reaction, recognition, response, treatment, welcome; entertainment, function, levee, party, soirée; (*Inf*) do

receptive *adj* alert, bright, perceptive, responsive, sensitive; (*Inf*) quick on the uptake

recess *n* alcove, bay, cavity, corner, depression, hollow, indentation, niche, nook, oriel; break, cessation of business, closure, holiday, intermission, interval, respite, rest, vacation

recession *n* decline, depression, downturn, slump

recipe *n* directions, ingredients, instructions; formula, methos, *modus operandi*, prescription, procedure, process, programme, technique

reciprocate *v* barter, exchange, feel in return, interchange, reply, requite, respond, return, return the compliment, swap, trade

recital *n* account, description, detailing, enumeration, narration, narrative, performance, reading, recapitulation, recitation, rehearsal, relation, rendering, repetition, statement, story, tale, telling

recite *v* declaim, deliver, describe, detail, enumerate, itemize, narrate, perform, recapitulate, recount, rehearse, relate, repeat, speak, tell; (*Inf*) do one's party piece

reckless *adj* careless, daredevil, devil-may-care, foolhardy, hare-brained, harum-scarum, hasty, headlong, heedless, ill-advised, imprudent, inattentive, incautious, indiscreet, irresponsible, madcap, mindless, negligent, overventuresome, precipitate, rash, regardless, thoughtless, wild

reckon *v* add up, calculate, compute, count, enumerate, figure, number, tally, total; account, appraise, consider, count, deem, esteem, estimate, evaluate, gauge, hold, judge, look upon, rate, regard, think of; assume, believe, be of the opinion, conjecture, expect, fancy, imagine, suppose, surmise, think; (*Inf*) guess

reckoning *n* adding, addition, calculation, computation, count, counting, estimate, summation, working; account, bill, charge, due, score, settlement

reclaim *v* get back, recapture, recover, redeem, reform, regain, regenerate, reinstate, rescue, restore, retrieve, salvage

recline *v* be recumbent, drape one self over, lay something down, lean, lie down, loll, lounge, repose, rest, sprawl, stretch out

recluse *n* anchoress, anchorite, ascetic, eremite, hermit, monk, solitary

recognition *n* detection, discovery, identification, recall, recollection, remembrance; acceptance, acknowledgment, admission, allowance, appreciation, avowal, awareness, cognizance, concession, confession, notice, perception, realization, respect, understanding

recognize *v* identify, know, know again, make out, notice, place, recall, recollect, remember, spot; accept, acknowledge, admit, allow, appreciate, avow, be aware of, concede, confess, grant, own, perceive, realize, see, understand

recoil *v* jerk back, kick, react, rebound, resile, spring back; balk at, draw back, falter, flinch, quail, shrink, shy away; backfire, rebound

recoil *n* backlash, kick, reaction, rebound, repercussion

recollect *v* call to mind, place, recall, remember, reminisce, summon up

recollection *n* impression, memory, mental image, recall, remembrance, reminiscence

recommend *v* advance, advise, advocate, counsel, enjoin, exhort, propose, put forward, suggest, urge

recommendation *n* advice, counsel, proposal, suggestion, urging; advocacy, approbation, approval, blessing, commendation, endorse ment, favourable, mention, good word, praise, reference, sanction, testimonial; (*Inf*) plug

reconcile *v* accept, accommodate, get used, make the best of, resign, submit, yield; (*Inf*) put up with; appease, bring to terms, conciliate, make peace between, pacify, placate, propitiate, re-establish, friendly relations between, restore harmony between, reunite; adjust, compose, harmonize, patch up, put to rights, rectify, resolve, settle, square

reconnaissance *n* exploration, inspection, investigation, oberservation, patrol, reconnoitering, scan, scouting, scrutiny, survey; (*Inf*) recce

reconnoitre *v* explore, get the lie of the land, inspect, investigate, make a reconnaissance of, observe, patrol, scan, scout, scrutinize, see how the land lies, spy out, survey; (*Inf*) recce

reconsider *v* change one's mind, have second thoughts, reassess, re-evaluate, re-examine, rethink, review, revise, take another look at, think again, think better of, think over, think twice

reconstruct *v* reassemble, rebuild, recreate, re-establish, reform, regenerate, remake, remodel, renovate, reorganize, restore; build up, build up a picture of, deduce, piece together

record *n* account, annals, archives, chronicle, diary, document, entry, file, journal, log, memoir, memorandum, memorial, minute, register, report; documentation, evidence, memorial, remembrance, testimony, trace, witness; background, career, curriculum vitae, history, performance; (*Inf*) track record; album, black disc, cassettes, CD, compact disc, disc, EP, forty-five, gramophone record, LP, mini-disc, platter, recording, release, single, vinyl; off the record confidential, confidentially, in confidence, in private, not for publication, private, *sub rosa*, under the rose, unofficial, unofficially

record *v* chronicle, document, enrol, enter, inscribe, log, minute, note, preserve, put down, put on file, put on record, register, report, set down, take down, transcribe, write down; (*Inf*) chalk up

recount *v* delineate, depict, describe, detail, enumerate, give an account of, narrate, portray, recite, rehearse, relate, repeat, report, tell, tell the story of

recover *v* find again, get back, make good, recapture, reclaim, recoup, redeem, regain, repair, repossess, restore, retake, retrieve, take back; bounce back, come round, convalesce, feel oneself again, get back on one's feet, get better, get well, heal, improve, mend, pick up, pull through, rally, recuperate, regain one's health or strength revive, take a turn for the better

recovery *n* convalescence, healing, improvement, mending, rally, recuperation, return to health, revival, turn for the better; amelioration, betterment, improvement rally, rehabilitation, restoration, revival, upturn

recreation *n* amusement, distraction, diversion, enjoyment, enter tainment, exercise, fun, hobby, leisure activity, pastime, play, pleasure, refreshment, relaxation, relief, sport

recruit *v* draft, enlist, enrol, impress, levy, mobilize, muster, raise, strengthen; engage, enrol, gather, obtain, procure, proselytize, round up, take on, win over; augment, build up, refresh, reinforce, renew, replenish, restore, strengthen, supply;

recruit *n* apprentice, beginner, convert, helper, initiate, learner, neophyte, novice, proselyte, trainee, tyro; (*Inf*) greenhorn, rookie

rectify *v* adjust, amend, correct, emend, fix, improve, make good, mend, put right, redress, reform, remedy, repair, right, square

recuperate *v* convalesce, get back on one's feet, get better, improve, mend, pick up, recover, regain one's health

recur *v* come again, come and go, come back, happen again, persist, reappear, repeat, return, revert

recurrent *adj* continued, cyclical, frequent, habitual, periodic, recurring, regular, repeated, repetitive

red *adj* cardinal, carmine, cherry, coral, crimson, gules, maroon, pink, rose, ruby, scarlet, vermeil, vermilion, wine; bay, carrot, chestnut, flame-coloured, flaming, foxy, red dish, sandy, titan; blushing, embarrassed, florid, flushed, rubicund, shamefaced, suffused; bloodstained, bloody, ensanguined, gory, sanguine

redeem *v* buy back, reclaim, recover possession of, regain, repossess, repurchase, retrieve, win back; cash in, change, exchange, trade in; abide by, acquit, adhere to, be faithful to, carry out, discharge, fulfil, hold to, keep, keep faith with, make good, meet, perform, satisfy; buy the freedom of, deliver, emancipate, extricate, free, liberate, pay the ransom of, ransom, rescue, save, set free

redress *v* compensate for, make amends for, make up for, pay for, put right, recompense for; adjust, amend, balance, correct, ease, even up, mend, put right, rectify, reform, regulate, relieve, remedy, repair, restore the balance, square

reduce *v* abate, abridge, contract, curtail, cut down, debase, decrease, depress, dilute,diminish, impair, lessen, lower, moderate, shorten, slow down, tone down, truncate, turn down, weaken, wind down; bring, bring to the point of, conquer, drive, force, master, overpower, subdue, vanquish; bring down the price of, cheapen, cut, discount, lower, mark down, slash; break, bring low, degrade, demote, downgrade, humble, humiliate, lower in rank, lower the status of; (*Inf*) take down a peg

redundant *adj de trop*, excessive, extra, inessential, inordinate, supererogatory, superfluous, supernumer ary, surplus, unnecessary, unwanted; diffuse, padded, periphrastic, pleonastic, prolix, repetitious, tautological, verbose, wordy

reek *v* smell, smell to high heaven, stink; (*Inf*) hum, pong

reek *n* effluvium, fetor, mephitis, odour, smell, stench, stink; (*Inf*) pong

reel *v* falter, lurch, pitch, rock, roll, stagger, stumble, sway, totter, waver, wobble; go round and round, revolve, spin, swim,swirl, twirl, whirl

refer *v* advert, allude, bring up, cite,

hint, invoke, make mention of, make reference, mention, speak of, touch on; direct, guide, point, recommend, send; apply, consult, go, have recourse to, look up, seek information from, turn to; apply, be directed to, belong, be relevant to, concern, pertain, relate

referee *n* adjudicator, arbiter, arbitrator, judge, umpire; (*Inf*) ref

referee *v* adjudicate, arbitrate, judge, umpire

reference *n* allusion, citation, mention, note, quotation, remark; applicability, bearing, concern, connection, consideration, regard, relation, respect; certification, character, credentials, endorsement, good word, recommendation, testimonial

refine *v* clarity, cleanse, distil, filter, process, purify, rarefy; civilize, cultivate, elevate, hone, improve, perfect, polish, temper

refined *adj* civil, civilized, courtly, cultivated, cultured, elegant, genteel, gentlemanly. gracious, ladylike, polished, polite, sophisticated, urbane, well-bred, well-mannered; cultured, delicate, discerning, discriminating, exact, fastidious, fine, nice, precise, punctilious, sensitive, sublime, subtle

refinement *n* clarification, cleans ing, distillation, filtering, process ing, purification, rarefaction, rectification; fine point, fine tuning, nicety, nuance, subtlety; civility, civilization, courtesy, courtliness, cultivation, culture, delicacy, discrimination, elegance, fastidiousness, fineness, finesse, finish, gentility, good breeding, good manners, grace, graciousness, polish, politeness, politesse, recision, sophistication, style, taste, urbanity

reflect *v* echo, give back, imitate, mirror, reproduce, return, throw back; cogitate, consider, contem plate, deliberate, meditate, mull over, muse, ponder, ruminate, think, wonder

reflection *n* counterpart, echo, image, mirror image; cerebration, cogitation, consideration, contemplation, deliberation, idea, impression, meditation, musing, observation, opinion, pondering, rumination, study, thinking, thought, view

reform *v* ameliorate, amend, better, correct, emend, improve, mend, rebuild, reclaim, reconstitute, reconstruct, rectify, regenerate, rehabilitate, remodel, renovate, reorganize, repair, restore, revolutionize

reform *n* amelioration, amendment, betterment, correction, improvement, rectification, rehabilitation, renovation

refrain *v* abstain, avoid, cease, desist, do without, eschew, forbear, give up, leave off, renounce, stop

refresh *v* brace, breathe new life into, cheer, cool, enliven, freshen, inspirit, reanimate, reinvigorate, rejuvenate, revitalize, revive, revivify, stimulate; jog, prod, prompt, renew, stimulate; (*Inf*) brush up

refreshing *adj* bracing, cooling, different, fresh, inspiriting, invigorating, new, novel, original, revivi-

fying, stimulating, thirst-quenching
refreshment *n* enlivenment, freshening, reanimation, renewal, renovation, repair, restoration, revival, stimulation; drinks, food and drink, snacks, titbits
refuge *n* asylum, bolt hole, harbour, haven, hide-out, protection, resort, retreat, sanctuary, security, shelter
refugee *n* displaced person, émigré, escapee, exile, fugitive, runaway
refund *v* give back, make good, pay back, reimburse, repay, restore, return; *n.* reimbursement, repayment, return
refusal *n* defiance, denial, negation, no, rebuff, rejection, repudiation, thumbs down; (*Inf*) knockback; choice, consideration, opportunity, option
refuse *v* decline, deny, reject, repel, repudiate, say no, spurn, turn down, withhold
regain *v* get back, recapture, recoup, redeem, repossess, retake, retrieve, take back, win back
regard *v* behold, eye, gaze at, look closely at, mark, notice, observe, remark, scrutinize, view, watch; account, adjudge, believe, consider, deem, esteem, estimate, hold, imagine, judge, look upon, rate, see, suppose, think, treat, value, view; attend, heed, listen to, respect, take into consideration, take notice of
regard *n* attention, heed, mind, notice; account, affection, attachment, care, concern, consideration, deference, esteem, honour, love, note, reputation, repute, respect, store, sympathy, thought
regardless *adj* disregarding, heedless, inattentive, inconsiderate, indifferent, neglectful, negligent, rash, reckless, remiss, unconcerned, unmindful
regardless *adv* anyway, come what may, despite everything, for all that, in any case, in spite of everything, nevertheless, no matter what, nonetheless
regime *n* administration, establishment, government, leadership, management, reign, rule, system
region *n* area, country, district, division, expanse, land, locality, part, place, province, quarter, section, sector, territory, tract, zone
regional *adj* district, local, parochial, provincial, sectional, zonal
register *n* annals, archives, catalogue, chronicle, diary, file, ledger, list, log, memorandum, record, roll, roster, schedule
register *v* catalogue, check in, chronicle, enlist, enrol, enter, inscribe, list, note, record, set down, sign up, take down; be shown, be speak, betray, display, exhibit, express, indicate, manifest, mark, read, record, reflect, reveal, say, show
regret *v* bemoan, be upset, bewail, deplore, feel remorse for, feel sorry for, grieve, lament, miss, mourn, repent, rue, weep over
regret *n* bitterness, compunction, contrition, disappointment, grief, lamentation, pang of conscience, penitence, remorse, repentance, ruefulness, self-reproach, sorrow
regrettable *adj* deplorable, disappointing, distressing, ill-advised, lamentable, pitiable, sad, shameful,

unfortunate, unhappy, woeful, wrong

regular *adj* common, commonplace, customary, daily, everyday, habitual, normal, ordinary, routine, typical, unvarying, usual; consistent, constant, established, even, fixed, ordered, periodic, rhythmic, set, stated, steady, systematic, uniform; balanced, even, flat, level, smooth, straight, symmetrical, uniform

regulate *v* adjust, administer, arrange, balance, conduct, control, direct, fit, govern, guide, handle, manage, moderate, modulate, monitor, order, organize, oversee, rule, run, settle, superintend, supervise, systematize, tune

regulation *n* adjustment, administration, arrangement, control, direction, governance, government, management, modulation, supervision, tuning; commandment, decree, dictate, direction, edict, law, order, ordinance, precept, procedure, requirement, rule, standing order, statute

rehearsal *n* drill, going-over, practice, practice session, preparation, reading, rehearsing, run-through

rehearse *v* act, drill, go over, practise, prepare, ready, recite, repeat, run through, study, train, try out

reign *n* ascendancy, command, control, dominion, empire, hegemony, influence, monarchy, power, rule, sovereignty, supremacy, sway

reign *v* administer, be in power, command, govern, hold sway, influ ence, occupy the throne, rule, wear the crown, wield the sceptre

reinforce *v* augment, bolster, buttress, emphasize, fortify, harden, increase, prop, shore up, stiffen, strengthen, stress, supplement, support, toughen, underline

reinforcement *n* addition, amplification, augmentation, enlargement, fortification, increase, strengthening, supplement; brace, buttress, prop, shore, stay, support; additional troops, auxiliaries, reserves, support

reinstate *v* bring back, recall, re-establish, rehabilitate, replace, restore, return

reject *v* bin, cast aside, decline, deny, despise, disallow, discard, eliminate, exclude, jettison, jilt, rebuff, refuse, renounce, repel, repudiate, repulse, say no to, scrap, spurn, throw out, turn down, veto

reject *n* castoff, discard, failure, flot sam, second

rejection *n* denial, dismissal, elimi nation, exclusion, rebuff, refusal, renunciation, repudiation, thumbs down, veto; (*Inf*) brush-off

rejoice *v* be glad, be happy, be over joyed, celebrate, delight, exult, glory, joy, jump for joy, make merry, revel, triumph

relapse *v* backslide, degenerate, fail, fall back, lapse, regress, retrogress, revert, slip back, weaken; deteriorate, fade, fail, sicken, sink, weaken, worsen

relapse *n* backsliding, fall from grace lapse, recidivism, regression, retrogression, reversion; deteriora tion, recurrence, setback, turn for the worse, weakening, worsening

relate *v* chronicle, describe, detail, give an account of, impart, narrate, preset, recite, recount, rehearse, report, set forth, tell; ally, associate, connect, coordinate, correlate, couple, join, link; appertain, apply, bear upon, be relevant to, concern, have reference to, have to do with, pertain, refer

related *adj* accompanying, affiliated, agnate, akin, allied, associated, cognate, concomitant, connected, correlated, interconnected, joint, linked; agnate, akin, cognate, consanguineous, kin, kindred

relation *n* affiliation, affinity, consanguinity, kindred, kinship, propinquity, relationship; kin, kinsman, kinswoman, relative; application, bearing, bond, comparison, connection, correlation, interdependence, link, pertinence, reference, regard, similarity, tie-in

relations *pl n* affairs, associations, communications, connections, contact, dealings, interaction, intercourse, liaison, meetings, rapport, relationship, terms; clan, family, kin, kindred, kinsmen, relatives, tribe

relationship *n* affair, association, bond, communications, conjunction, connection, correlation, exchange, kinship, liaison, link, parallel, proportion, rapport, ratio, similarity, tie-up

relative *adj* allied, associated, comparative, connected, contingent, corresponding, dependent, proportionate, reciprocal, related, respective; applicable, apposite, appropriate, appurtenant, apropos, germane, pertinent, relevant

relative *n* connection, kinsman, kinswoman, member of one's *or* the family, relation

relatively *adv* comparatively, in comparison, rather, somewhat, to some extent

relax *v* abate, diminish, ease, ebb, lessen, let up, loosen, lower, mitigate, moderate, reduce, relieve, slacken, weaken; be at ease, calm, laze, loosen up, put one's feet up, rest, soften, take one's ease, tran quillize, unbend, unwind; (*Inf*) let oneself go, let one's hair down, take it easy

relaxation *n* amusement, enjoyment, entertainment, fun, leisure, pleasure, recreation, refreshment, rest

relay *n* relief, shift, turn; communication, dispatch, message, transmission

relay *v* broadcast, carry, communi cate, hand on, pass on, send, spread, transmit

release *v* deliver, discharge, disen gage, drop, emancipate, extricate, free, let go, let out, liberate, loose, manumit, set free, turn loose, unchain, undo, unfasten, unfetter, unloose, unshackle, untie; absolve, acquit, dispense, excuse, exempt, exonerate, let go, let off; break, circulate, disseminate, distribute, issue, launch, make known, make public, present, publish, put out, unveil

release *n* acquittal, deliverance, delivery, discharge, emancipation, freedom, liberation, liberty, manu mission, relief

relent *v* acquiesce, be merciful, capitulate, change one's mind, come round, forbear, give in, give quarter, give way, have pity, melt, show mercy, soften, unbend, yield

relentless *adj* cruel, fierce, grim, hard, harsh, implacable, inexorable, inflexible, merciless, pitiless, remorseless, ruthless, uncompromising, undeviating, unforgiving, unrelenting, unstoppable, unyielding

relevant *adj* admissible, *ad rem*, applicable, apposite, appropriate, appurtenant, apt, fitting, germane, material, pertinent, proper, related, relative, significant, suited, to the point, of the purpose

reliable *adj* certain, dependable, faithful, honest, predictable, regular, responsible, safe, sound, stable, sure, tried and true, true, trustworthy, trusty, unfailing, upright

relic *n* fragment, keepsake, memento, remembrance, remnant, scrap, souvenir, survival, token, trace, vestige

relief *n* abatement, alleviation, assuagement, balm, comfort, cure, deliverance, ease, easement, mitigation, palliation, release, remedy, solace; aid, assistance, help, succour, support, sustenance; break, diversion, refreshment, relaxation, remission, respite, rest; (*Inf*) breather, let-up

relieve *v* abate, alleviate, appease, assuage, calm, comfort, console, cure, diminish, dull, ease, mitigate, mollify, palliate, relax, salve, soften, solace, soothe; aid, assist, bring aid to, help, succour, support, sustain; give someone a rest, stand in for, substitute for, take over from, take the place of

religious *adj* churchgoing, devotional, devout, divine, doctrinal, faithful, god-fearing, godly, holy, pious, pure, reverent, righteous, sacred, scriptural, sectarian, spiritual, theological

relish *v* appreciate, delight in, enjoy, fancy, like, look forward to, luxuriate in, prefer, revel in, savour, taste

relish *n* appetite, appreciation, enjoyment, fancy, fondness, gusto, liking, love, partiality, penchant, predilection, stomach, taste, zest; appetizer, condiment, sauce, seasoning; flavour, piquancy, savour, smack, spice, tang, taste, trace

reluctant *adj* averse, backward, disinclined, grudging, hesitant, indisposed, loath, recalcitrant, slow, unenthusiastic, unwilling

rely *v* bank, be confident of, be sure of, bet, count, depend, have confidence in, lean, reckon, repose, trust in, swear by, trust

remain *v* abide, be left, cling, continue, delay, dwell, endure, go on, last, linger, persist, prevail, rest, stand, stay, stay behind, survive, tarry, wait; (*Inf*) stay put

remainder *n* balance, dregs, excess, leavings, relic, remains, remnant, residue, residuum, rest, surplus, trace, vestiges

remains *pl n* balance, crumbs, debris, detritus, dregs, fragments, leavings, leftovers, oddments, odds and ends, pieces, relics, remainder, remnants, residue, rest, scraps, traces, vestiges

remark *v* animadvert, comment, declare, mention, observe, pass, comment, reflect, say, state; espy, heed, make out, mark, note, notice, observe, perceive, regard, see, take note or notice of

remark *n* assertion, comment, declaration, observation, opinion, reflection, statement, thought, utterance, word

remarkable *adj* conspicuous, distinguished, extraordinary, famous, impressive, miraculous, notable, noteworthy, odd, outstanding, phenomenal, pre-eminent, prominent, rare, signal, singular, strange, striking, surprising, uncommon, unusual, wonderful

remedy *n* antidote, counteractive, cure, medicament, medicine, nostrum, panacea, relief, restora tive, specific, therapy, treatment

remedy *v* alleviate, assuage, control, cure, ease, heal, help, mitigate, palliate, relieve, restore, soothe, treat

remember *v* bear in mind, call to mind, call up, commemorate, keep in mind, look back on, recall, recognize, recollect, reminisce, retain, summon up, think back

remind *v* awaken memories of, bring back to, bring to mind, call to mind, call up, jog one's memory, make someone remember, prompt, put in mind, refresh one's memory

reminiscence *n* anecdote, memoir, memory, recall, recollection, reflection, remembrance, retrospection, review

reminiscent *adj* evocative, redo lent, remindful, similar, suggestive

remission *n* absolution, acquittal, amnesty, discharge, excuse, exemption, exoneration, forgiveness, indulgence, pardon, release, reprieve; abatement, abeyance, alle viation, amelioration, decrease, diminution ebb, lessening, lull, moderation, reduction, relaxation, respite, suspension; (*Inf*) let-up

remit *v* dispatch, forward, mail, post, send, transmit; cancel, desist, forbear, halt, repeal, rescind, stop;

remit *n* authorization, brief, guide lines, instructions, orders, terms of reference

remorse *n* anguish, bad conscience, compassion, compunction, contri tion, grief, guilt, pangs of con science, penitence, pity, regret, repentance, ruefulness, self-reproach, shame, sorrow

remorseless *adj* inexorable, relent less, unrelenting, unremitting, unstoppable; callous, cruel, hard, hardhearted, harsh, implacable, inhumane, merciless, pitiless, ruthless, savage, uncompassionate, unforgiving, unmerciful

remote *adj* backwoods, distant, far, faraway, far-off, godforsaken, inaccessible, isolated, lonely, off the beaten track, outlying, out-of-the-way, secluded; alien, extraneous, extrinsic, foreign, immaterial, irrelevant, outside, removed, unconnected, unrelated; abstracted, aloof, cold, detached, distant, faraway, indifferent, introspective, introverted, removed, reserved, standoffish, unapproachable, uncommunicative

removal *n* abstraction, dislodgment, dismissal, displacement, dispossession, ejection, elimination, eradication, erasure, expulsion, expunction, extraction, purging, stripping, subtraction, taking off, uprooting, with drawal; departure, move, relocation, transfer

remove *v* abolish, abstract, amputate, carry away, delete, depose, detach, dethrone, discharge, dislodge, dismiss, displace, do away with, doff, efface, eject, eliminate, erase, expel, expunge, extract, get rid of, move, oust, purge, relegate, shed, strike out, take away, take off, take out, throw out, transfer, transport, unseat, wipe out, withdraw; depart, move, move away, quit, relocate, shift, transfer, transport, vacate

render *v* contribute, deliver, furnish, give, make available, pay, present, provide, show, submit, supply, tender, turn over, yield; display, evince, exhibit, manifest, show; exchange, give, return, swap, trade; cause to become, leave, make; act, depict, do, give, interpret, perform, play, portray, present, represent; construe, explain, interpret, put, reproduce, restate, transcribe, trans late; give back, make restitution, pay back, repay, restore, return

renew *v* begin again, breathe new life into, bring up to date, continue, extend, fix up, mend, modernize, overhaul, prolong, reaffirm, recommence, recreate, re-establish, refit, refresh, refurbish, regenerate, rejuvenate, renovate, reopen, repair, repeat, replace, replenish, restate, restock, restore, resume, revitalize, transform

renounce *v* abandon, abdicate, abjure, abnegate, abstain from, cast off, decline, deny, discard, disclaim, disown, eschew, forgo, forsake, forswear, give up, leave off, quit, recant, reject, relinquish, repudiate, resign, spurn, swear off, throw, waive, wash one's hands of

renovate *v* modernize, overhaul, recondition, reconstitute, recreate, refit, reform, refurbish, rehabilitate, remodel, renew, repair, restore, revamp; (*Inf*) do up, fix up

renowned *adj* acclaimed, celebrated, distinguished, eminent, esteemed, famed, famous, illustrious, notable, noted, well-known

rent *n* fee, hire, lease, payment, rental, tariff

rent *v* charter, hire, lease, let

repair *v* compensate for, fix, heal, make good, make up for, mend, patch, patch up, put back together, put right, recover, rectify, redress, renew, renovate, restore to working order, retrieve, square

repair *n* adjustment, darn, mend, overhaul, patch, restoration

repay *v* compensate, make restitution, pay back, recompense, refund, reimburse, remunerate, requite, restore, return, reward, settle up with, square; avenge, even *or* settle the score with, make reprisal, reciprocate, retaliate, return the compliment, revenge; (*Inf*) get back at, get even with, get one's own back on

repeal *v* abolish, abrogate, annul, cancel, countermand, declare null and void, invalidate, nullify, recall, rescind, reverse, revoke, set aside, withdraw

repeal *n* abolition, abrogation, annulment, cancellation, invalidation, nullification, rescinding, rescindment, rescission, revocation, withdrawal

repeat *v* duplicate, echo, iterate, quote, recapitulate, recite, redo, rehearse, reiterate, relate, renew, replay, reproduce, rerun, reshow, restate, retell

repeat *n* duplicate, echo, recapitulation, reiteration, repetition, replay, reproduction, rerun, reshowing

repeatedly *adv* again and again, frequently, many a time and oft, many times, often, over and over, time after time, time and time again

repel *v* beat off, check, confront, decline, drive off, fight, hold off, keep at arms length, oppose, parry, put to flight, rebuff, refuse, reject, repulse, resist, ward off; disgust, make one shudder, make one sick, nauseate, offend, put one off, revolt, sicken, turn one's stomach; (*Inf*) give one the creeps, turn one off

repent *v* atone, be ashamed, be contrite, be sorry, deplore, feel remorse, lament, regret, relent, reproach oneself, rue, seethe error of one;s ways, show penitence, sorrow

repentant *adj* apologetic, shamed, chastened, contrite, penitent, regret ful remorseful, rueful, self-reproachful, sorry

repercussion *n* backlash, consequence, echo, rebound, recoil, result, reverberation, side effect

repetition *n* duplication, echo, iteration, reappearance, recapitulation, recital, recurrence, redundancy, rehearsal, reiteration, relation, renewal, repeat, repetitiousness, replication, restatement, return, tautology

replace *v* follow, oust, put back, re-establish, reinstate, restore, stand in lieu of, substitute, succeed, supersede, supplant, supply, take over from, take the place of

replacement *n* double, fill-in, proxy, stand-in, substitute, succes sor, surrogate, understudy

replenish *v* fill, furnish, make up, provide, refill, reload, renew, replace, restock, restore, stock, supply, top up

replica *n* carbon copy, copy, duplicate, facsimile, imitation, model, reproduction

reply *v* acknowledge, answer, come back, counter, echo, make answer, react, reciprocate, rejoin, respond, retaliate, retort, return, riposte, write back

reply *n* acknowledgment, answer, counter, echo, reaction, reciprocation, rejoinder, response, retaliation, retort, return, riposte; (*Inf*) come back

report *n* account, announcement, article, communication, communiqué, declaration, description, detail, dispatch, information, message, narrative, news, note, paper, piece, recital, record, relation, statement, story, summary, tale, tidings, version, word, write-up; gossip, hearsay, rumour, talk; bang, blast, boom, crack, crash, detonation, dis charge, explosion, noise, reverbera tion, sound

report *v* air, announce, bring word, broadcast, circulate communicate, cover, declare, describe, detail, document, give an account of, inform of, mention, narrate, note, notify, pass on, proclaim, publish, recite, record, recount, relate, relay, state, tell, write up; appear, arrive, be present, clock in or on, come present oneself, turn up; (*Inf*) show up

reporter *n* announcer, correspondent, hack, journalist, newscaster, newspaperman, newspaperwoman, pressman, writer; (*Inf*) newshound

reprehensible *adj* bad, blamewor thy, censurable, condemnable, cul pable, delinquent, discreditable, disgraceful, errant, erring, ignoble, objectionable, opprobrious, remiss, shameful, unworthy

represent *v* act for, be, betoken, correspond to, equal, equate with, express, mean, serve as, speak for, stand for, substitute for, symbolize; embody, epitomize, exemplify, personify, symbolize, typify; delineate, denote, depict, describe, designate, evoke, express, illustrate, outline, picture, portray, render, reproduce, show, sketch; act, appear as, assume the role of, enact, exhibit, perform, play the part of, produce, put on, show, stage

representation *n* account, delineation, depiction, description, illustration, image, likeness, model, narration, narrative, picture, portrait, portrayal, relation, resemblance, sketch; account, argument, explanation, exposition, expostulation, remonstrance, statement

representative *n* agent, commer cial traveller, rep, salesman, traveller; archetype, embodiment, epitome, exemplar, personification, type, typical, example; agent, commissioner, councillor, delegate, deputy, member, member of parliament, MP, proxy, spokesperson

representative *adj* archetypal, characteristic, emblematic, evocative, exemplary, illustrative, symbolic, typical; chosen, delegated, elected, elective

repress *v* bottle up, chasten, check, control, crush, curb, hold back, hold in, inhibit, keep in check, master, muffle, overcome, overpower, quash, quell, restrain, silence, smother, stifle, subdue, subjugate, suppress, swallow

reprieve *v* abate, allay, alleviate, mitigate, palliate, relieve, respite

reprieve *n* abeyance, amnesty, deferment, pardon, postponement, remission, stay of execution, suspension

reprimand *n* admonition, blame, castigation, censure, lecture, rebuke, reprehension, reproach, reproof, row, tongue-lashing; (*Inf*) dressing-down, flea in one's ear, talking-to, telling-off, ticking-off, wigging

reprimand *v* admonish, blame, castigate, censure, check, chide, lecture, rebuke, reprehend, reproach, reprove, scold, take to task, tongue-lash, upbraid; (*Inf*) dress down, have a row with someone, haul over the coals, rap over the knuckles, send one away with a flea in one's ear, tell off, tick off

reproach *v* abuse, blame, censure, chide, condemn, criticize, defame, discredit, disparage, find fault with, rebuke, reprehend, reprimand, reprove, scold, take to task, upbraid

reproach *n* abuse, blame, blemish, censure, condemnation, contempt, disapproval, discredit, disgrace, dishonour, disrepute, ignominy, indignity, obloquy, odium, opprobrium, scorn, shame, slight, slur, stain, stigma

reproduce *v* copy, duplicate, echo, emulate, imitate, match, mirror, parallel, print, recreate, repeat, replicate, represent, transcribe; breed, generate, multiply, procreate, produce young, proliferate, propagate, spawn

reproduction *n* breeding, generation, increase, multiplication, procreation, proliferation, propagation; copy, duplicate, facsimile, imitation, picture, print, replica

repulsive *adj* abhorrent, abominable, disagreeable, disgusting, distasteful, forbidding, foul, hateful, hideous, horrid, loathsome, nauseating, objectionable, obnoxious, odious, offensive, repellent, revolting, sickening, ugly, unpleasant, vile

reputable *adj* creditable, estimable, excellent, good, honourable, honoured, legitimate, of good repute, reliable, respectable, trustworthy, upright, well-thought-of, worthy

reputation *n* character, credit, distinction, esteem, estimation, fame, honour, name, opinion, renown, repute, standing, stature

reputed *adj* accounted, alleged, believed, considered, deemed, estimated, held, ostensible, putative, reckoned, regarded, rumoured, said, seeming, supposed, thought

request *v* appeal for, apply for, ask for, beg, beseech, call for, demand, desire, entreat, petition, pray, put in for, requisition, seek, solicit, sue for, supplicate

request *n* appeal, application, asking, begging, call, demand, desire, entreaty, petition, prayer, requisition, solicitation, suit, supplication

require *v* crave, depend upon, desire, have need of, lack, miss, need, stand in need of, want, wish; ask, beg, beseech, bid, call upon, command, compel, constrain, demand, direct, enjoin, exact, insist upon, instruct, oblige, order, request

requirement *n* demand, desideratum, essential, lack, must, necessity, need, precondition, prerequisite, qualification, requisite, *sine qua non*, specification, stipulation, want

rescue *v* deliver, extricate, free, get out, liberate, recover, redeem, release, salvage, save, save the life of, set free

rescue *n* deliverance, extrication, liberation, recovery, redemption, release, relief, salvage, salvation, saving

research *n* analysis, delving, examination, experimentation, exploration, fact-finding, ground work, inquiry, investigation, probe, scrutiny, study

research *v* analyse, consult the archives, do tests, examine, experiment, explore, investigate, look into, make inquiries, probe, scruti nize, study

resemblance *n* affinity, analogy, closeness, comparability, comparison, conformity, correspondence, counterpart, facsimile, image, kinship, likeness, parallel, parity, same ness, semblance, similarity, simili - tude

resemble *v* bear a resemblance to, be like, be similar to, duplicate, echo, look like, mirror, parallel, put one in mind of, remind one of, take after; (*Inf*) favour

resent *v* be angry about, bear a grudge bout, begrudge, be in a huff about, be offended by, dislike, feel bitter about, grudge, harbour a grudge against, have hard feelings about, object to, take amiss, take as an insult, take exception to, take offence at, take umbrage at

resentful *adj* aggrieved, angry, bit ter, embittered, exasperated, grudg ing, huffish, huffy, hurt, in huff, incensed, indignant, in high dudgeon, irate, jealous, offended, piqued, put out, revengeful, unfor giving, wounded; (*Inf*) miffed, peeved

resentment *n* anger, animosity, bitterness, displeasure, fury, grudge, huff, hurt, ill feeling, ill will, indignation, ire, irritation, malice, pique, rage, rancour, umbrage, vexation, wrath

reservation *n* condition, demur, doubt, hesitancy, proviso, qualification, scepticism, scruple, stipulation; enclave, homeland, preserve, reserve, sanctuary, territory, tract

reserve *v* conserve, hang on to, hoard, hold, husband, keep, keep back, lay up, preserve, put by, retain, save, set aside, stockpile, store, withhold; bespeak, book, engage, prearrange, pre-engage, retain, secure; defer, delay, keep back, postpone, put off, withhold

reserve *n* backlog, cache, capital, fund, hoard, reservoir, savings, stock, stockpile, store,supply; park, preserve, reservation, sanctuary, tract; aloofness, constraint, coolness, formality, modestly, reluctance, reservation, restraint, reticence, secretiveness, shyness, silence, taciturnity

reserve *adj* alternate, auxiliary, extra, secondary, spare, substitute

reserved *adj* aloof, cautious, close-mouthed, cold, cool, demure, formal, modest, prim, restrained, reticent, retiring, secretive, shy, silent, standoffish, taciturn, unapproachable, uncommunicative, undemonstrative, unforthcoming, unresponsive, unsociable

reside *v* abide, dwell, have one's home, inhabit, live, lodge, remain, settle, sojourn, stay; (*Inf*) hang out

residence *n* abode, domicile, dwelling, habitation, home, house, household, lodging, place, quarters; hall, manor, mansion, palace, seat, villa; (*Inf*) pad

resident *n* citizen, denizen, indweller, inhabitant, local, lodger, occupant, tenant

resign *v* abandon, abdicate, cede, forgo, forsake, give in ones notice, give up, and over, leave, quit, relinquish, renounce, surrender, turn over, vacate, yield

resignation *n* abandonment, abdication, departure, leaving, notice, relinquishment, renunciation, retirement, surrender; acceptance, acquiescence, compliance, endurance, forbearing, fortitude, nonresistance, passivity, patience, submission, suf ferance

resigned *adj* acquiescent, compliant, long-suffering, patient, stoical, subdued, submissive, unprotesting, unresisting

resist *v* battle, be proof against, check, combat, confront, contend with, counteract, countervail, curb, defy, dispute, fight back, hinder, hold out against, oppose, put up a fight against, refuse, repel, stand up to, struggle against, thwart, weather, withstand

resolute *adj* bold, constant, determined, dogged, firm, fixed, inflexible, obstinate, persevering, purposeful, relentless, set, staunch, steadfast, strong-willed, stubborn, tenacious, unbending, undaunted, unflinching, unshakable, unshaken, unwavering

resolution *n* boldness, constancy, courage, dedication, determination, doggedness, earnestness, energy, firmness, fortitude, obstinacy, perseverance, purpose, relentless ness, resoluteness, resolve, sincerity, staunchness, staying power, steadfastness, stubbornness, tenacity, willpower; aim, decision, declara tion, determination, intent, intention, judgement, motion, purpose, resolve, verdict

resolve *v* agree, conclude, decide, design, determine, fix intend, make up one's mind, purpose, settle, undertake; answer, clear up crack, elucidate, fathom, find the solution to, work out; analyse, anatomize, break down, clear, disentangle, dissect, dissolve, liquefy, melt, reduce, separate, solve, split up, unravel

resolve *n* conclusion, decision, design, intention, objective, project, purpose, resolution, undertaking; boldness, courage, determination, earnestness, firmness, resoluteness, resolution, steadfastness, willpower

resort *v* avail oneself of, bring into play, employ, exercise, fall back on, have recourse to, look to, make use of, turn to, use, utilize; frequent, go, haunt, head for, repair, visit

resort *n* haunt, holiday centre, refuge, retreat, spot, tourist centre, watering place

resound *v* echo, fill the air, re-echo, resonate, reverberate, ring

resourceful *adj* able, bright, capable, clever, creative, imaginative, ingenious, inventive, quick-witted, sharp, talented

resources *adj* assets, capital, funds, holdings, materials, means, money, property, reserves, riches, supplies, wealth, wherewithal

respect *n* admiration, appreciation, approbation, consideration, deference, esteem, estimation, honour, recognition, regard, reverence, veneration; aspect, characteristic, detail, facet, feature, matter, particular, point, sense, way; bearing, connection, reference, regard, relation

respect *v* admire, adore, appreciate, defer to, esteem, have a high opinion of, honour, look up to, recognize, regard, revere, reverence, set store by, show consideration for, think highly of, value, venerate; abide by, adhere to, attend, comply with, follow, heed, honour, notice, obey, observe, pay attention to, regard, show consideration for

respectable *adj* admirable, decent, decorous, dignified, estimable, good, honest, honourable, proper, reputable, respected, upright, venerable, worthy; ample, appreciable, considerable, decent, fair, fairly good, goodly, presentable, reasonable, sizable, substantial, tolerable; (*Inf*) tidy

respective *adj* corresponding, individual, own, particular, personal, relevant, separate, several, specific, various

respite *n* break, breathing space, cessation, halt, hiatus, intermission, interruption, interval, lull, pause, recess, relaxation, relief, rest; (*Inf*) breather, let-up

respond *v* acknowledge, act in response, answer, come back, counter, react, reciprocate, rejoin, reply, retort, return

response *n* acknowledgment answer, counterblast, feedback, reaction, rejoinder, reply, retort, riposte; (*Inf*) comeback

responsibility *n* accountability, amenability, answerability, care, charge, duty, liability, obligation, onus, trust; authority, importance, power; blame, burden, culpability, fault, guilt

responsible *adj* at the helm, in authority, in charge, in control; accountable, amenable, answerable, bound, chargeable, duty-bound, liable, subject, under obligation; (*Inf*) carrying the can; authoritative, decision-making, executive, high, important; at fault, culpable, guilty, to blame

rest *n* calm, doze, idleness, inactivity, leisure, lie-down, motionlessness, nap, refreshment, relaxation, relief, repose, siesta, sleep, slumber, som nolence, standstill, stillness, tran quillity; (*Inf*) forty winks, snooze; break, breathing space, cessation, halt, holiday, interlude, intermis sion, interval, lull, pause, stop, time off, vacation; (*Inf*) breather; base, holder, prop, shelf, stand, support, trestle

rest *v* be at ease, be calm, doze, idle, laze, lie down, lie still, nap, put one's feet up, refresh oneself, relax, sit down, sleep, slumber, take a nap, take one's ease; (*Inf*) have a snooze, have forty winks, snooze, take it easy; be supported, lay, lean, lie, prop, recline, repose, sit, stand, stretch out

rest *n* balance, excess, leftovers, others, remainder, remains, remnants, residue, residuum, rump, surplus

restful *adj* calm, calming, comfortable, languid, pacific, peaceful, placid, quiet, relaxed, relaxing, serene, sleepy, soothing, tranquil, tranquillizing, undisturbed, unhurried

restless *adj* active, bustling, change able, footloose, hurried, inconstant, irresolute, moving, nomadic, roving, transient, turbulent, unsettled, unstable, unsteady, wandering; agitated, anxious, disturbed, edgy, fidgeting, fidgety, fitful, fretful, ill at ease, jumpy, nervous, on edge, restive, sleepless, tossing and turning, troubled, uneasy, unquiet, unruly, unsettled, worried

restore *v* fix, mend, rebuild, recondition, reconstruct, recover, refurbish, rehabilitate, renew, renovate, repair, retouch, set to rights, touch up; bring back to health, build up, reanimate, refresh, rejuvenate, revitalize, revive, revivify, strengthen; bring back, give back, hand back, recover, re-establish, reinstate, replace, return, send back

restrain *v* bridle, check, confine, constrain, contain, control, curb, curtail, debar, govern, hamper, handicap, harness, hinder, hold, hold back, inhibit, keep, keep under control, limit, muzzle, prevent, repress, restrict, subdue, suppress

restrained *adj* calm, controlled, mild, moderate, muted, reasonable, reticent, self-controlled, soft, steady, temperate, undemonstrative; discreet, quiet, subdued, tasteful, unobtrusive

restraint *n* coercion, command, compulsion, confines, constraint, control, curtailment, grip, hindrance, hold, inhibition, limitation, moderation, prevention, restriction, self-control, self-discipline, self-possession, self-restraint, suppression; arrest, bondage, bonds, captivity, chains, confinement, detention, fetters, imprisonment, manacles, pinions, straitjacket; ban, bridle, check, curb, embargo, interdict, limit, limitation, rein, taboo

restrict *v* bound, circumscribe, confine, contain, cramp, demarcate, hamper, handicap, hem in, impede, inhibit, keep within bounds, limit, regulate, restrain

restriction *n* check, condition, confinement, constraint, containment, control, curb, demarcation, handicap, inhibition, limitation, regulation, restraint, rule, stipulation

result *n* conclusion, consequence, decision, development, effect, end, event, fruit, issue, outcome, prod uct, reaction, sequel, termination, upshot

result *v* appear, arise, derive, develop, emanate, ensue, eventuate, flow, follow, happen, issue, spring, stem, turn out; **result in** culminate, end, finish, terminate; (*Inf*) wind up

resume *v* begin again, carry on, continue, go on, proceed, recommence, reinstitute, reopen, restart, take up where one left off

resurrect *v* breathe new life into, bring back, raise from the dead, reintroduce, renew, restore to life, revive

resurrection *n* raising from the dead, reappearance, rebirth, renais sance, renascence, renewal, restora tion, resurgence, resuscitation, return, return from the dead, revival; (*Inf*) comeback

retain *v* absorb, contain, detain, grasp, grip, hang onto, hold, hold back, hold fast, keep, keep possession of, maintain, preserve, reserve, restrain, save; bear in mind, impress on the memory, keep in mind, memorize, recall, recollect, remember; commission, employ, engage, hire, pay reserve

retainer *n* attendant, dependant, domestic, flunky, footman, lackey, servant, supporter, valet, vassal;

advance, deposit, fee

retaliate *v* even the score, exact, retribution, give one a taste of one's own medicine, give tit for tat, make reprisal, pay one back in one's own coin, reciprocate, return like for like, strike back, take an eye for an eye, take revenge, wreak vengeance; (*Inf*) get back at, get even with, get one's own back, give as good as one gets

retaliation *n* an eye for an eye, a taste of one's own medicine, counterblow, counterstroke, reciprocation, repayment, reprisal, requital, retribution, revenge, tit for tat, vengeance

reticent *adj* close-mouthed, mum, quiet, reserved, restrained, secretive, silent, taciturn, tight-lipped, uncommunicative, unforthcoming, unspeaking

retire *v* be pensioned off, give up work, stop working; absent oneself, betake oneself, depart, exit, go away, leave, remove, withdraw; go to bed, go to one's room, go to sleep, turn in; (*Inf*) be put out to grass, hit the sack, kip down

retiring *adj* bashful, coy, demure, diffident, humble, meek, modest, quiet, reclusive, reserved, reticent, self-effacing, shrinking, shy, timid, timorous, unassertive, unassuming

retract *v* draw in, pull back, pull in, sheathe; abjure, cancel, deny, disavow, disclaim, disown, recall, recant, renounce, repeal, repudiate, rescind, reverse, revoke, take back, unsay, withdraw

retreat *v* back away, depart, draw back, ebb, fall back, give ground, go back leave, pull back, recede, recoil, retire, shrink, turn tail, withdraw

retreat *n* departure, ebb, evacuation, flight, retirement, withdrawal; asylum, den, haunt, haven, hideaway, privacy, refuge, resort, retirement, sanctuary, seclusion, shelter

retribution *n* fetch back, get back, recall, recapture, recoup, recover, redeem, regain, repair, repossess, rescue, restore, salvage, save, win back

return *v* come back, come round again, go back, reappear, rebound, recoil, recur, repair, retreat, revert, turn back; carry back, convey, give back, put back, re-establish, reinstate, remit, render, replace, restore, send, send back, take back, transmit; give back, pay back, reciprocate, recompense, refund, reimburse, repay, requite; bring in, earn, make, net, repay, yield; choose, elect, pick, vote in

return *n* homecoming, reappearance, rebound, recoil, recrudescence, recurrence, retreat, reversion; re-establishment, reinstatement, replacement, restoration; advantage, benefit, gain, income, interest, proceeds, profit, revenue, takings, yield; compensation, reciprocation, recompense, reimbursement, reparation, repayment, requital, retaliation, reward; account, form, list, report, statement, summary; answer, rejoinder, reply, response, retort, riposte; (*Inf*) comeback

reveal *v* announce, betray, broadcast, communicate, disclose, divulge, give away, give out, impart, leak, let on, let out, let slip, make known, make public, proclaim, publish, tell; bare, bring to light, display, exhibit, expose to view, lay bare, manifest, open, show, uncover, unearth, unmask, unveil

revel *v* carouse, celebrate, go on a spree, make merry, roister; (*Inf*) live it up, paint the town red, push the boat out, rave, whoop it up

revel *n* bacchanal, carousal, carouse, celebration, debauch, festivity, gala, jollification, merrymaking, party, saturnalia

revel in *v* bask, crow, delight, gloat, indulge, joy, lap up, luxuriate, rejoice, relish, savour, take pleasure, thrive on, wallow

revelation *n* announcement, betrayal, broadcasting, communication, disclosure, discovery, display, exhibition, exposé, exposition, exposure, giveaway, leak, manifestation, news, proclamation, publication, telling, uncovering, unearthing, unveiling

revenge *n* an eye for an eye, reprisal, requital, retaliation, retribution, satisfaction vengeance, vindictiveness

revenge *v* avenge, even the score for, make reprisal for, repay, requite, retaliate, take an eye for an eye for, take revenge for, vindicate; (*Inf*) get one's own back for

revenue *n* gain, income, interest, proceeds, profits, receipts, returns, rewards, takings, yield

reverberate *v* echo, rebound, recoil, resound, ring, vibrate

revere *v* adore, be in awe of, defer to, exalt, have a high opinion of, honour, look up to, put on a pedestal, respect, reverence, think highly of, venerate, worship

reverence *n* admiration, adoration, awe, deference, devotion, high esteem, homage, honour, respect, veneration, worship

reverent *adj* adoring, awed, decorous, deferential, devout, humble, loving, meek, pious, respectful, rev erential, solemn, submissive

reverse *v* invert, transpose, turn back, turn over, turn round, turn upside down, upend; alter, annul, cancel, change, countermand, declare null and void, invalidate, negate, overrule, overset, over throw, overturn, quash, repeal, rescind, retract, revoke, set aside, undo, upset; back, backtrack, back up go backwards, move backwards, retreat

reverse *n* antithesis, contradiction, contrary, converse, inverse, opposite; adversity, affliction, blow, check, defeat, disappointment, failure, hardship, misadventure, misfortune, mishap, repulse, reversal, setback, trial, vicissitude

reverse *adj* back to front, backward, contrary, converse, inverse, inverted, opposite

review *v* go over again, look at again, reassess, recapitulate, recon sider, re-evaluate, re-examine, rethink, revise, run over, take another look at, think over; call to mind, look back on, recall, recollect, reflect on, remember, summon up; assess, criticize, discuss, evaluate, examine, give one's opinion of, inspect, judge, read through, scruti-

nize, study, weigh, write a critique of
review *n* analysis, examination, report, scrutiny, study, survey; commentary, critical assessment, criticism, critique, evaluation, judgment, notice, study; journal, magazine, periodical; another look, fresh look, reassessment, recapitulation, reconsideration, re-evaluation, re-examination, rethink, retrospect, revision, second look; display, inspection, march past, parade, procession
revise *v* alter, amend, change, correct, edit, emend, modify, reconsider, redo, re-examine, revamp, review, rework, rewrite, update
revision *n* alteration, amendment, change, correction, editing, emendation, modification, re-examination, review, rewriting, updating; homework, memorizing, rereading, studying; (*Inf*) swotting
revival *n* awakening, quickening, reanimation, reawakening, rebirth, recrudescence, renaissance, renascence, renewal, restoration, resurgence, resurrection, resuscitation, revitalization, revivification
revive *v* animate, awaken, breathe, new life into, bring back to life, bring round, cheer, come round, comfort, invigorate, quicken, rally, reanimate, recover, refresh, rekindle, renew, renovate, restore, resuscitate, revitalize, rouse, spring up again
revoke *v* abolish, abrogate, annul, call back, cancel, countermand, declare null and void, disclaim, invalidate, negate, nullify, quash, recall, recant, renounce, repeal, repudiate, rescind, retract, reverse, set aside, take back, withdraw
revolt *n* defection, insurgency, insurrection, mutiny, putsch, rebellion, revolution, rising, sedition, uprising
revolt *v* defect, mutiny, rebel, resist, rise, take to the streets, take up arms against; disgust, make one's flesh creep, nauseate. offend, repel, repulse, shock, sicken, turn one's stomach; (*Inf*) give one the creeps, turn off
revolting *adj* abhorrent, abominable, appaling, disgusting, dis tasteful, foul, horrible, horrid, loathsome, nasty, nauseating, nauseous, noisome, obnoxious, obscene, offensive, repellent, repugnant, repulsive, shocking, sickening
revolution *n* coup, coup d'état, insurgency, mutiny, putsch, rebellion, revolt, rising, uprising; drastic change, innovation, metamorphosis, reformation, sea change, shift, transformation, upheaval; circle, circuit, cycle, gyration, lap, orbit, rotation, round, spin, turn, wheel, whirl
revolutionary *n* insurgent, insurrectionary, insurrectionist
revolutionary *adj* extremist, insurgent, insurrectionary, mutinous, radical, rebel, seditious, subversive; avant-garde, different, drastic, experimental, fundamental, innovative, new, novel, progressive, radical, thoroughgoing
revolve *v* circle, go round, gyrate, orbit, rotate, spin, turn, twist, wheel, whirl
revulsion *n* abhorrence, abomina

tion, aversion, detestation, disgust, distaste, loathing, recoil, repug nance, repulsion

reward *n* benefit, bonus, bounty, compensation, gain, honour, merit, payment, premium, prize, profit, recompense, remuneration, repayment, requital, return, wages; dessert, just desserts, punishment, requital, retribution; (*Inf*) comeuppance

reward *v* compensate, honour, make it worth one's while, pay, recom pense, remunerate, repay, requite

rewarding *adj* advantageous, beneficial, edifying, enriching, fruitful, fulfiling, gainful, gratifying, pleasing, productive, profitable, remunerative, satisfying, valuable, worthwhile

rhyme *n* ode, poem, poetry, song, verse

rhyme *v* chime, harmonize, sound like

rhythm *n* accent, beat, cadence, flow, lilt, measure, metre, movement, pattern, periodicity, pulse, swing, tempo, time

rich *adj* affluent, moneyed, opulent, propertied, prosperous, wealthy, well-off, well-to-do; (*Inf*) filthy rich, flush, loaded, made of money, rolling, stinking rich, well-heeled; abounding, full, productive, well-endowed, well-provided, well-stocked, well-supplied; abounding, abundant, ample, copious, exuberant, fecund, fertile, fruitful, full, lush, luxurious, plenteous, plentiful, productive, prolific; beyond price, costly, elaborate, elegant, expensive, exquisite, fine, gorgeous, lavish, palatial, precious, priceless, splendid, sumptuous, superb, valuable; creamy, delicious, fatty, flavoursome, full-bodied, heavy, highly-flavoured, juicy, luscious, savoury, spicy, succulent, sweet, tasty

riches *pl n* abundance, affluence, assets, fortune, gold, money, opulence, plenty, property, resources, richness, substance, treasure, wealth

rid *v* clear, deliver, disabuse, disburden, disembarrass, disencumber, free, make free, purge, relieve, unburden; **get rid of** dispense with, dispose of, do away with, dump, eject, eliminate, expel, jettison, remove, shake off, throw away or out, unload, weed out

riddle *n* Chinese puzzle, conundrum, enigma, mystery, poser, problem, puzzle, rebus; (*Inf*) brain-teaser

ride *v* control, handle, manage, sit on; be borne (carried, supported), float, go, journey, move, progress, sit, travel

ride *n* drive, jaunt, journey, lift, out ing, trip; (*Inf*) spin, whirl

ridicule *n* banter, chaff, derision, gibe, irony, jeer, laughter, mockery, raillery, sarcasm, satire, scorn, sneer, taunting

ridicule *v* banter, caricature, chaff, deride, humiliate, jeer, lampoon, laugh at, laugh out of court, laugh to scorn, make a fool of, make fun of, make one a laughing stock, mock, parody, poke fun at, pooh-pooh, satirize, scoff, sneer, take the mickey out of taunt; (*Inf*) send up, take the mickey out of

ridiculous *adj* absurd, comical,

contemptible, derisory, farcical, foolish, funny, hilarious, incredible, laughable, ludicrous, nonsensical, outrageous, preposterous, risible, silly, stupid, unbelievable

rift *n* breach, break, chink, cleavage, cleft, crack, cranny, crevice, fault, fissure, flaw, fracture, gap, opening, space, split; alienation, breach, difference, disagreement, division, estrangement, quarrel, schism, separation, split; (*Inf*) falling out

rig *v* accoutre, equip, fit out, furnish, kit out, outfit, provision, supply, turn out; arrange, doctor, engineer, fake, falsify, gerrymander, juggle, manipulate, tamper with, trump up (*Inf*) fiddle with, fix

rig *n* accoutrements, apparatus, equipage, equipment, fitments, fittings, fixtures, gear, machinery, outfit, tackle

right *adj* equitable, ethical, fair, good, honest, honourable, just, lawful, moral, proper, righteous, true, upright, virtuous; accurate, admissible, authentic, correct, exact, factual, genuine, precise, satisfactory, sound, true, unerring, valid, veracious; (*Inf*) spot-on; advantageous, appropriate, becoming, *comme il faut*, convenient, deserved, desirable, done, due, favourable, fit, fitting, ideal, opportune, proper, propitious, rightful, seemly, suitable; balanced, *compos mentis*, fine, fit, healthy, in good health, in the pink, lucid, normal, rational, reasonable, sane, sound, unimpaired, up to par, well; conser vative, reactionary, Tory; (*Inf*) all there; absolute, complete, out-and-out, pure, real, thorough, thorough going, utter

right *adv* accurately, alright, correctly, exactly, factually, genuinely, pre cisely, truly; appropriately, aptly, befittingly, fittingly, properly, satisfactorily, suitably; directly, immediately, instantly, promptly, quickly, straight, straightaway, without delay; bang, exactly, precisely, squarely; (*Inf*) slap-bang; absolutely, all the way, altogether, completely, entirely, perfectly, quite, thoroughly, totally, utterly, wholly; ethically, fairly, honestly, honourably, justly, morally, properly, righteously, virtuously; advantageously, beneficially, favourably, for the better, fortunately, to advantage, well

right *n* authority, business, claim, due, freedom, interest, liberty, licence, permission, power, prerogative, priviledge, title; equity, good, goodness, honour, integrity, justice, lawfulness, legality, morality, propriety, reason, rectitude, righteousness, truth, uprightness, virtue; by rights equitably, in fairness, justly, properly

right *v* compensate for, correct, fix, put right, rectify, redress, repair, settle, set upright, sort out, straighten, vindicate

rigid *adv* adamant, austere, exact, fixed, harsh, inflexible, intransigent, invariable, rigorous, set, severe, stern, stiff, strict, stringent, unalter able, unbending, uncompromising, undeviating, unrelenting, unyielding

rigorous *adj* austere, challenging, demanding, exacting, firm, hard, harsh, inflexible, rigid, severe, stern, strict, stringent, tough; bad, bleak, extreme, harsh, inclement, inhospitable, severe

rigour *n* asperity, austerity, firmness, hardness, hardship, harshness, inflexibility, ordeal, privation, rigidity, sternness, stringency, suffering, trial

rim *n* border, brim, brink, circumference, edge, lip, margin, verge

ring *n* band, circle, circuit, halo, hoop, loop, round; arena, circus, enclosure, rink; association, band, cable, cartel, cell, circle, clique, combine, coterie, gang, group, junta, knot, mob, organization, syn dicate; (*Inf*) crew

ring *v* circumscribe, encircle, enclose, encompass, grid, girdle, hem in, seal off, surround

ring *v* chime, clang, peal, resonate, resound, reverberate, sound, toll; call, phone, telephone

ring *n* chime, knell, peal; call, phone call; (*Inf*) buzz

riot *n* anarchy, commotion, confu sion, disorder, disturbance, donny brook, fray, lawlessness, mob violence, quarrel, row, street fighting, strife, tumult, turbulence, turmoil, uproar; boisterousness, carousal, excess, festivity, frolic, high jinks, jollification, merrymaking, revelry, romp; display, extravaganza, flour ish, show, splash; **run riot** be out of control, break or cut loose, go wild, let oneself go, raise hell, rampage, throw off all restraint; grow like weeds, grow profusely, luxuriate, spread like wild fire

riot *v* carouse, cut loose, frolic, go on a binge, make merry, revel, roister, romp; (*Inf*) paint the town red

riotous *adj* anarchic, disorderly, insubordinate, lawless, mutinous, rampageous, rebellious, refractory, rowdy, tumultuous, ungovernable, unruly, uproarious, violent; boister ous, loud, luxurious, noisy, orgiastic, roisterous, rollicking, side-split ting, unrestrained, uproarious, wanton, wild; (*Inf*) rambunctious

ripe *adj* fully developed, fully, grown, mature, mellow, ready, ripened, seasoned; auspicious, favourable, ideal, opportune, right, suitable, timely

ripen *v* burgeon, come of age, come of fruition, develop, get ready, grow ripe, make ripe, mature, prepare, season

rise *v* arise, get out of bed, get to one's feet, get up, rise and shine, stand up, surface; arise, ascend, climb, enlarge, go up grow, improve, increase, intensify, levitate, lift, mount, move up, soar, swell, wax; advance, be promoted, climb the ladder, get on, get some where, progress, prosper, work one's way up; (*Inf*) go places; appear, become apparent, crop up, emanate, emerge, eventuate, flow, happen, issue, occur, originate, spring, turn up; mount the barricades, mutiny, rebel, resist, revolt, take up arms; ascend, climb, get steeper, go uphill, mount, slope upwards

rise *n* advance, scent, climb, improvement, increase, upsurge, upswing, upturn, upward turn; advancement, aggrandizement, climb, progress, promotion; acclivity, ascent, elevation, hillock, incline, rising ground, upward slope; increment, pay increase, raise

risk *n* chance, danger, gamble, hazard, jeopardy, peril, possibility, speculation, uncertainty, venture

risk *v* chance, dare, endanger, expose to danger, gamble, hazard, imperil, jeopardize, put in jeopardy, take a chance on, venture

rival *n* adversary, antagonist, challenger, competitor, contender, contestant, emulator, opponent, opposing

rival *v* be a match for, bear comparison with, come up to, compare with, compete, contend, emulate, equal, match, measure up to, oppose, seek to, displace, vie with

rivalry *n* antagonism, competition, competitiveness, conflict, contention, contest, duel, emulation, opposition, struggle, vying

road *n* avenue, course, direction, highway, lane, motorway, path, pathway, roadway, route, street, thoroughfare, track, way

roam *v* drift, meander, peregrinate, prowl, ramble, range, rove, stray, stroll, travel, walk, wander

roar *v* bawl, bay, bellow, clamour, crash, cry, howl, rumble, shout, thunder, vociferate, yell; guffaw, hoot, laugh, heartily; (*Inf*) split one's sides

roar *n* bellow, clamour, crash, cry, howl, outcry, rumble, shout, thunder, yell

rob *v* bereave, burgle, cheat, defraud, deprive, despoil, dispossess, hold up, loot, pillage, plunder, raid, ransack, rifle, sack, strip, swindle; (*Inf*) con, do out of, gyp, mug, rip off, steam

robber *n* bandit, brigand, burglar, cheat, fraud, highwayman, looter, pirate, plunderer, raider, stealer, swindler, thief; (*Inf*) con man, mugger

robbery *n* burglary, depredation, embezzlement, filching, fraud, hold-up larceny, pillage, plunder, raid, rapine, spoliation, stealing, swindle, theft, thievery; (*Inf*) mugging, rip-off, steaming, stick-up

robe *n* costume, gown, habit, vestment

robe *v* apparel, attire, clothe, drape, dress, garb

robust *v* able-bodied, athletic, brawny, fit, hale, hardy, healthy, hearty, in fine fettle, in good health, lusty, muscular, powerful, Ramboesque, rude, rugged, sinewy, sound, staunch, stout, strapping, strong, sturdy, tough, vigorous, well; (*Inf*) husky; boisterous, coarse, earthly, indecorous, raw, roisterous, rollicking, rough, rude, unsubtle

rock *n* lurch, pitch, reel, roll, sway, swing, toss, wobble; astonish, astound, daze, dumbfound, jar, shake, shock, stagger, stun, surprise; (*Inf*) set one back on one's heels

rod *n* bar, baton, birch, cane, dowel, mace, pole, sceptre, shaft, staff, stick, switch, wand

rogue *n* blackguard, charlatan, cheat, deceiver, devil, fraud, mountebank, ne-er-do-well, rapscallion, rascal, reprobate, scamp, scoundrel, sharper, swindler, villain; (*Inf*) con man, crook

role *n* character, impersonation, part, portrayal, representation; capacity, duty, function, job, part, position, post, task

roll *v* elapse, flow, go past, go round, gyrate, pass, pivot, reel, revolve, rock, rotate, run, spin, swivel, trundle, turn, twirl, undulate, wheel, whirl; bind, coil, curl, enfold, entwine, envelop, furl, swathe, twist, wind, wrap; even, flatten, level, press, smooth, spread; boom, drum, echo, grumble, resound, reverberate, roar, rumble, thunder; billow, lurch, reel, rock, sway, swing, toss, tumble, wallow, welter; lumber, lurch, reel, stagger, swag ger, sway, waddle

roll *n* cycle, gyration, reel, revolution, rotation, run, spin, turn, twirl, undulation, wheel, whirl; annals, catalogue, census, chronicle, directory, index, inventory, list, record, register, roster, schedule, scroll, table; boom, drumming, growl, resonance, reverberation, roar, rumble, thunder

romance *n* affair, *affaire du coeur*, affair of the heart, amour, attach ment, intrigue, liaison, love affair, passion, relationship; adventure, charm, colour, excitement, exoticness, fascination, glamour, mystery, nostalgia, sentiment; fairy tale, fan tasy, fiction, idyll, legend, love story, melodrama, novel, story, tale; (*Inf*) tear-jerker

romantic *adj* amorous, fond, lovey-dovey, loving, passionate, sentimental, tender; (*Inf*) mushy, sloppy, soppy; charming, colourful, exciting, exotic, fascinating, glamourous, mysterious, nostalgic, picturesque; dreamy, high-flown, idealistic, impractical, quixotic, starry-eyed, unrealistic, utopian, visionary, whimsical

romantic *n* Don Quixote, dreamer, idealist, romancer, sentimentalist, utopian, visionary

room *n* allowance, area, capacity, compass, elbowroom, expanse, extent, latitude, leeway, margin, play, range, scope, space, territory, volume; apartment, chamber, office; chance, occasion, opportunity, scope

root *n* radicle, radix, rhizome, stem, tuber; base, beginnings, bottom, cause, core, crux, derivation, essence, foundation, fountainhead, fundamental, germ, heart, main spring, nub, nucleus, occasion, origin, seat, seed, source, starting point; birthplace, cradle, family, heritage, home, origins, sense of belonging; completely, entirely, finally, radically, thoroughly, totally, to the last man, utterly, wholly, without exception

root *v* anchor, become established, become settled, embed, entrench, establish, fasten, fix, ground, implant, moor, set, stick, take root

rope *n* cable, cord, hawser, line, strand

rope *v* bind, fasten, hitch, lash, lasso, moor, pinion, tether, tie

roster *n* agenda, catalogue, inventory, list, listing, register, roll, rota, schedule, scroll, table

rosy *adj* pink, red, roseate, rose-coloured; blooming, blushing, flushed, fresh, glowing, healthy-looking, reddish, roseate, rubicund, ruddy; auspicious, bright, cheerful, encouraging, favourable, hopeful, optimistic, promising, reassuring, roseate, rose-coloured, sunny

rot *v* corrode, corrupt, crumble, decay, decompose, degenerate, deteriorate, disintegrate, fester, go bad, moulder, perish, putrefy, spoil, taint; decline, degenerate, deteriorate, languish, waste away wither away

rot *n* blight, canker, corrosion, corruption, decay, decomposition, deterioration, disintegration, mould, putrefaction, putrescence

rotate *v* go round, gyrate, pirouette, pivot, reel, revolve, spin, swivel, turn, wheel; alternate, follow in sequence, interchange, switch, take turns

rotation *n* gyration, orbit, pirouette, reel, revolution, spin, spinning, turn, turning, wheel; alternation, cycle, interchanging, sequence, succession, switching

rotten *adj* bad, corroded, corrupt, crumbling, decayed, decaying, decomposed, decomposing, disintegrating, festering, fetid, foul, mouldering, mouldy, perished, putrescent, putrid, rank, sour, stinking, tainted, unsound; corrupt, deceitful, degenerate, dishonest, dishonourable, disloyal, faithless, immoral, mercenary, perfidious, treacherous, untrustworthy, venal, vicious; (*Inf*) bent, crooked; bad, deplorable, disappointing, regrettable, unfortunate, unlucky

rotter *n* bad lot, blackguard, cur, swine; (*Inf*) blighter, bounder, cad, louse, rat, scumbag, stinker

rough *adj* broken, bumpy, craggy, irregular, jagged, rocky, rugged, stony, uneven; bristly, bushy, coarse, dishevelled, disordered, fuzzy, hairy, shaggy, tangled, tousled, uncut, unshaven, unshorn; agitated, boisterous, choppy, inclement, squally, stormy, tempestuous, turbulent, wild; bearish, bluff, blunt, brusque, churlish, coarse, curt, discourteous, ill-bred, ill-mannered, impolite, inconsiderate, indelicate, loutish, rude, unceremonious, uncivil, uncouth, uncultured, ungracious, unmannerly, unpolished, unrefined, untutored; boisterous, cruel, curt, drastic, extreme, hard, harsh, nasty, rowdy, severe, sharp, tough, unfeeling, unjust, unpleasant, violent; cacophonous, discordant, grating, gruff, harsh, husky, inharmonious, jarring, rasping, raucous, unmusical; arduous, austere, hard, rugged spartan, tough, uncomfortable, unpleasant, unrefined; basic, crude, cursory, formless, hasty, imperfect, incomplete, quick, raw, rough-and-ready, rough-hewn, rudimentary, shapeless, sketchy, unfinished, unpolished, unrefined, untutored; amorphous, approximate, estimated, foggy, general, hazy, imprecise, inexact, sketchy, vague

rough *n* bully boy, casual, lager lout, rowdy, ruffian, thug, tough; (*Inf*) bruiser, ned, roughneck,

round *adj* annular, ball-shaped, bowed, bulbous, circular, curved, curvilinear, cylindrical, discoid, disc-shaped, globular, orbicular, ring-shaped, rotund, rounded, spherical; ample, fleshy, full, full-fleshed, plump, roly-poly, rotund, rounded; full, mellifluous, orotund, resonant, rich, rotund, sonorous

round *n* ball, band, circle, disc, globe, orb, ring, sphere; bout, cycle, sequence, series, session, succession; division, lap, level, period, session, stage, turn; ambit, beat, circuit, compass, course, routine, schedule, series, tour, turn; bullet, cartridge, discharge, shell, shot

round *v* bypass, circle, circumnavigate, encircle, flank, go round, skirt, turn

round off *v* bring to a close, cap, close, complete, conclude, crown, finish off, put the finishing touch to, settle

rouse *v* arouse, awaken, call, get up, rise, wake, wake up; agitate, anger, animate, arouse, bestir, disturb, excite, exhilarate, galvanize, get going, incite, inflame, instigate, move, provoke, startle, stimulate, stir, whip up

rout *n* beating, debacle, defeat, disorderly, retreat, drubbing, headlong, flight, overthrow, overwhelm ing defeat, ruin, shambles, thrash ing; (*Inf*) hiding, licking

rout *v* beat, chase, conquer, crush, cut to pieces, defeat, destroy, dispel, drive off, drub, overpower, overthrow, put to flight put to rout, scatter, thrash, throw back in confusion, worst; (*Inf*) lick

route *n* avenue, bet, circuit, course, direction, itinerary, journey, passage, path, road, round, run, way

routine *n* custom, formula, groove, method, order, patter, practice, procedure, programme, usage, way, wont; (*Inf*) grind

routine *adj* conventional, customary, everyday, familiar, habitual, normal, ordinary, standard, typical, usual, wonted, workaday; boring, clichéd, dull, hackneyed, humdrum, predictable, run-of-the-mill, tedious, tiresome, unimaginative, unin spired, unoriginal

row *n* bank, column, file, line, queue, range, rank, sequence, series, string, tier; altercation, brawl, commotion, controversy, dispute, disturbance, fracas, fay, fuss, noise, quarrel, racket, rumpus, squabble, tiff, trouble, tumult, uproar; (*Inf*) falling-out, ruckus, ruction, scrap, shouting match, slanging match

row *v* argue, brawl, dispute, fight, squabble, wrangle; (*Inf*) scrap

rowdy *adj* boisterous, disorderly, loud, loutish, noisy, obstreperous, rough, unruly, uproarious, wild

royal *adj* imperial, kinglike, kingly, monarchical, princely, queenly, regal, sovereign; august, grand, impressive, magnificent, majestic, splendid, stately, superb, superior

rub *v* abrade, caress, chafe, clean, fray, grate, knead, massage, polish, scour, scrape, shine, smooth, stroke, wipe; apply, put, smear, spread

rub *n* caress, kneading, massage, polish, shine, stroke, wipe

rubbish *n* debris, dregs, dross, flot sam and jetsam, garbage, junk, litter, lumber, offal, refuse, scrap, trash, waste; (*Inf*) crap; balderdash, bunkum, drivel, garbage, gibberish, hogwash, moonshine, nonsense, rot, stuff and nonsense, tommy-rot, twaddle; (*Inf*) bosh, claptrap, codswallop, crap, flapdoodle, guff, piffle, poppycock, tosh

rub out *v* cancel, delete, efface, erase, expunge, obliterate, remove, wipe out

rude *adj* abrupt, abusive, blunt, brusque, cheeky, churlish, curt, discourteous, disrespectful, ill-mannered, impertinent, impolite, impudent, inconsiderate, insolent, insult ing, offhand, peremptory, short, uncivil, unmannerly; barbarous, boorish, brutish, coarse, crude, graceless, gross, ignorant, illiterate, loutish, low, oafish, obscene, rough, savage, scurrilous, uncivilized, uncouth, uncultured, uneducated, ungracious, unpolished unrefined, untutored, vulgar; artless, crude, inartistic, inelegant, makeshift, primitive, raw, rough, rough-hewn, roughly-made, simple; abrupt, harsh, sharp, startling, sudden, unpleasant, violent

rudiments *pl n* basics, beginnings, elements, essentials, first principles, foundation, fundamentals

ruffle *v* derange, disarrange, discom pose, dishevel, disorder, mess up, rumple, tousle, wrinkle; agitate, annoy, confuse, disconcert, disquiet, disturb, fluster. harass, irritate, nettle, perturb, put out, stir, torment, trouble, unsettle, upset, vex, worry; (*Inf*) peeve, rattle, shake up

rugged *adj* broken, bumpy, craggy, difficult, irregular, jagged, ragged, rocky, rough, stark, uneven; furrowed, leathery, lined, rough-hewn, strong-featured, weather-beaten, weathered, worn, wrinkled

ruin *n* bankruptcy, breakdown, collapse, crash, damage, decay, defeat, destitution, destruction, devastation, disintegration, disrepair, dissolution, downfall, failure, fall, havoc, insolvency, nemesis, overthrow, ruination, subversion, the end, undoing, Waterloo, wreck, wreckage; (*Inf*) crackup

ruin *v* bankrupt, break, bring down, bring to nothing, bring to ruin, crush, defeat, demolish, destroy, devastate, impoverish, lay in ruins, lay waste, overthrow, overturn, overwhelm, pauperize, raze, shatter, smash, wreak havoc upon, wreck

rule *n* axiom, canon, criterion, decree, direction, guide, guideline, law, maxim, order, ordinance, precept, principle. regulation, ruli ing, standard, tenet; administration, ascendancy, authority, command, control, direction, domination, dominion, empire, government, influence, jurisdiction, leadership, mastery, power, regime, reign, supremacy, sway; condition, con vention, custom, form, habit, order of things, practice, procedure, routine, wont; course, formula, methos, policy, procedure, way

rule *v* administer, be in authority, be in power, command, control, direct, dominate, govern, guide hold sway, lead, manage, preside over, regulate, reign, wear the crown; (*Inf*) be number one; adjudge, adjudicate, decide, decree, determine, establish, find, judge, lay, down, pronounce, resolve, settle

ruler *n* commander, controller, crowned head, emperor, empress, governor, head of state, king, leader, lord, monarch, potentate, prince, princess, queen, sovereign; measure, rule, straight edge, yardstick

ruling *n* adjudication, decision, decree, finding, judgment, pronouncement, resolution, verdict

ruling *adj* commanding, controlling, dominant, governing, leading, regnant, reigning, upper; chief, current, dominant, main, predominant, pre-eminent, pre-ponderant, prevailing, prevalent, principle, reg nant, supreme

rumour *n* buzz, canard, gossip, hearsay, news, report, story, talk, tidings, whisper, word

run *v* bolt, career, dart, dash, gallop, hasten, hie, hotfoot, hurry, jog, lope, race, rush, scamper, scramble, scud, scurry, speed, sprint; (*Inf*) leg it; abscond, beat a retreat, bolt, clear out, decamp, depart, escape, flee, make a run for it, make off, show a clean pair of heels, take flight, take to one's heels; (*Inf*) beat it, cut and run, leg it, scarper, skedaddle, take off; go, operate, ply; function, perform, tick, work; administer, be in charge of, carry on, conduct control, coordinate, direct, head, lead, look after, manage, mastermind, operate, oversee, own, regulate, superintend, supervise, take care of; (*Inf*) boss; continue, extend, go, last, lie proceed, spill, spout, steam; dissolve, fuse, go soft, liquefy, melt, turn to liquid; come apart, come undone, ladder, tear, unravel; be current, circulate, climb, creep, go round, spread, trail; display, feature, print, publish; be a candidate, challenge, compete, contend, put oneself up for, stand, take part; bootleg, deal in, ship, smuggle, sneak, traffic in

run *n* dash, gallop, jog, race, rush, sprint, spurt; drive, excursion, jaunt, journey, lift, outing, ride, round, trip; (*Inf*) joy ride, spin; chain, course, cycle, passage, period, round, season, sequence, series, spell, streak, stretch, string; ladder, rip, snag, tear; coop, enclosure, pen; **in the long run** at the end of the day, eventually, in the end, in the final analysis, in time, ultimately, when all is said and done; **on the run** at liberty, escaping, fugitive, in flight, on the loose; defeated, falling back, fleeing, in flight, in retreat, retreating, running away; at speed, hastily, hurriedly, hurrying, in a hurry, in a rush, in haste

runaway *n* absconder, deserter, escapee, escaper, fugitive, refugee, truant

runaway *adj* escaped, fleeing, fugitive, loose, out of control, uncontrolled, wild; easily won, easy, effortless

run away *v* abscond, bolt, clear out, decamp, escape, flee, make a run for it, run off, show a clean pair of heels, take flight, take off, take to one's heels; (*Inf*) beat it, cut and run, do a bunk, scarper, scram, skedaddle

run-down *adj* below par, debilitated, drained, enervated, exhausted, fatigued, out of condition, peaky, tried, unhealthy, weak, weary, worn-out; (*Inf*) under the weather; broken-down, decrepit, dilapidated, dingy, ramshackle, seedy, shabby, tumbledown, worn-out

run into *v* bump into, collide with, crash into, dash against, hit, ram, strike; be best by, be confronted by, bump into, chance upon, come across, come upon, encounter, meet, meet with, run across

running *adj* constant, continuous, incessant, in succession, perpetual, together, unbroken, unceasing, uninterrupted; flowing, moving, streaming; (*Inf*) on the trot; administration, charge, conduct, control, coordination, direction, leadership, management, organization, regulation, superintendency, supervision; functioning, maintenance, operation, performance, working; competition, contention, contest

run-of-the-mill *adj* average, common, commonplace, fair, mediocre, middling, modest, middling, mod est, ordinary, passable, tolerable, undistinguished, unexceptional, unexciting, unimpressive

run over *v* hit, knock down, knock over, run down, strike; brim over, overflow, spill, spill over; check, examine, go over, go through, rehearse, reiterate, review, run through, survey

rupture *n* breach, break, burst, cleavage, cleft, crack, fissure, fracture, rent, split, tear; altercation, breach, break, contention, disagreement, disruption, dissolution, estrangement, feud, hostility, quarrel, rift, schism, split; (*Inf*) bust-up, falling out

rupture *v* break, burst, cleave, crack, fracture, puncture, rend, separate, sever, split, tear; break off, cause a breach, come between, disrupt, dissever, divide, split

rural *adj* agrarian, agricultural, Arcadian, bucolic, countrified, country, pastoral, rustic, sylvan, upcountry

rush *v* accelerate, bolt, career, dart, dash, dispatch, expedite, fly, hasten, hotfoot, hurry, hustle, lose no time, make haste, make short work of, press, push, quicken, race, run, scramble, curry, shoot, speed, speed up, sprint, tear

rush *n* charge, dash, dispatch, expedition, haste, hurry, race, scramble, speed, surge, swiftness, urgency

rust *n* corrosion, oxidation; blight, mildew, mould, must, rot

rust *v* oxidize

rustic *adj* Arcadian, bucolic, countrified, country, pastoral, rural, sylvan, upcountry; artless, homely, homespun, plan, simple, unaffected, unpolished, unrefined, unsophisticated; awkward, boorish, churlish, cloddish, clownish, coarse, crude, graceless, loutish, lumpish, maladroit, rough, uncouth, uncultured, unmannerly; (*Inf*) clodhopping

rustic *n* boor, bumpkin, clod, clown, country boy, country cousin, countryman, countrywoman, hillbilly, Hodge, peasant, son of the soil, yokel

rustle *v* crackle, crepitate, crinkle, swish, whish, whisper, whoosh

rustle *n* crackle, crepitation, crinkling, whisper

rut *n* furrow, gouge, groove, indentation, pothole, score, track, trough, wheelmark; dead end, groove, habit, humdrum, existence, pattern, routine, system

ruthless *adj* adamant, barbarous, brutal, callous, cruel, ferocious, fierce, hard, hard-hearted, harsh, heartless, inexorable, inhuman, merciless, pitiless, relentless, remorseless, savage, severe, stern, unfeeling, unmerciful, unpitying, unrelenting, without pity

S

sabotage *v* cripple, damage, destroy, disable, disrupt, incapacitate, sap the foundations of, subvert, under mine, vandalize, wreck; (*Inf*) throw a spanner in the works

sabotage *n* damage, destruction, disruption, subversion, treachery, treason, wrecking

sack *v* axe (*Inf*), discharge, dismiss, give someone his cards, give some one his marching orders; (*Inf*) axe; give someone his books, give someone the boot, give someone the elbow; (*Inf*) fire

sacred *adj* blessed, consecrated, divine, hallowed, holy, revered, sanctified, venerable; inviolable. inviolate, invulnerable, protected, sacrosanct, secure; ecclesiastical, holy, religious, solemn

sacrifice *v* forego, forfeit, give up, immolate, let go, lose, offer, offer up, surrender

sacrifice *n* burnt offering, destruction, hecatomb, holocaust, immolation, loss, oblation, renunciation, surrender, votive offering

sacrilege *n* blasphemy, desecration, heresy, impiety, irreverence, mockery, profanation, profaneness, profanity, violation

sad *adj* blue, cheerless, dejected, depressed, disconsolate, dismal, doleful, down, downcast, gloomy, glum, grief-stricken, grieved, heavy-hearted, low, low-spirited, lugubrious, melancholy, mournful, pensive, sick at heart, sombre, unhappy, wistful, woebegone, wretched; (*Inf*) down in the dumps, down in the mouth; calamitous, dark, depressing, disastrous, dismal, grievous, heart-rending, lachrymose, moving, pathetic, pitiable, pitiful, poignant, sorry, tearful, tragic, upsetting; bad, deplorable, dismal, distressing, grave, lamentable, miserable, regrettable, serious, shabby, sorry, to be deplored, unfortunate, unhappy, unsatisfactory, wretched

sadden *v* aggrieve, bring tears to one's eyes, cast a gloom upon, cast down, dash, depress, desolate, dispirit, distress, grieve, make blue, make one's heart bleed, upset

saddle *v* burden, charge, clog, encumber, load

sadistic *adj* barbarous, beastly, brutal, cruel, fiendish, inhuman, perverse, perverted, ruthless, savage, vicious

sadness *n* bleakness, cheerlessness, dejection, depression, despondency, dolefulness, gloominess, grief, heavy heart, melancholy, misery, mournfulness, poignancy, sorrow, sorrowfulness, the blues, tragedy, unhappiness, wretchedness; (*Inf*) the dumps

safe *adj* all right, free from harm, guarded, impregnable, in safety, intact, out of danger, out of harm's way, protected, safe and sound, secure, undamaged, unharmed, unhurt, unscathed; harmless, innocuous, nonpoisonous, nontoxic, pure, tame, unpolluted, wholesome; (*Inf*) OK, okay; cautious, circumspect, conservative, dependable, discreet, on the safe side, prudent, realistic, reliable,sure, tried and true, trustworthy, unadventurous

safe *n* coffer, deposit box, repository, safe-deposit box, strongbox, vault

safeguard *v* defend, guard, look after, preserve, protect, screen, shield, watch over

safeguard *n* aegis, armour, bulwark, convoy, defence, escort, guard, protection, security, shield, surety

safety *n* assurance, cover, immunity, impregnability, protection, refuge, sanctuary, security, shelter

sage *adj* acute, discerning, intelligent, prudent, sagacious, sapient, sensible, shrewd, wise; prudent, judicious, well-judged; grave, serious, solemn

sage *n* philosopher, pundit, savant

sail *v* cast anchor, embark, get under way, hoist the blue peter, put to sea, set sail, weigh anchor; captain, cruise, go by water, navigate, pilot, ride the waves, skipper, steer, voy age; drift, float, fly, guide, scud, shoot, skim, skirr, soar, sweep, wing; **sail into** assault, attack, begin, belabour, fall upon, get going, get to work on, lambaste, set about; (*Inf*) tear into

sailor *n* Jack Tar, lascar, marine, mariner, navigator, salt, sea dog, seafarer, seafaring man, seaman; (*Inf*) leatherneck, matelot, tar

saintly *adj* devout, godly, holy, pious, religious

sake *n* account, advantage, behalf, benefit, consideration, gain, good, interest, profit, regard, respect, welfare, wellbeing

salary *n* earnings, emolument, income, pay, remuneration, stipend, wage, wages

sale *n* auction, deal, disposal, marketing, selling, transaction, vending; buyers, consumers, customers, demand, market, outlet, purchasers; **for sale** available, in stock, obtainable, on offer, on sale, on the market

salt *n* flavour, relish, savour, seasoning, taste

salt *adj* brackish, briny, saline, salted, salty

salute *v* accost, acknowledge, address, doff one's cap to, greet, hail, kiss, pay one's resects to, salaam, welcome; acknowledge, honour, pay tribute to, present arms, recognize; (*Inf*) take one's hat off to

salute *n* address, greeting, kiss, obeisance, recognition, salaam, salutation, tribute

salvage *v* glean, recover, redeem, rescue, restore, retrieve, save

salvation *n* deliverance, escape, lifeline, preservation, redemption, rescue, restoration, saving

same *adj* aforementioned, aforesaid, selfsame, very; alike, corresponding, duplicate, equal, equivalent, identical, indistinguishable, interchangeable, synonymous, twin

sameness *n* identicalness, identity, monotony, oneness, resemblance, selfsameness, uniformity

sample *n* cross section, example, exemplification, illustration, indication, instance, model, pattern, representative, sign, specimen

sample *v* experience, inspect, partake of, taste, test, try

sample *adj* illustrative, pilot, representative, specimen, test, trial

sanctimonious *adj* canting, false, holier-than-thou, hypocritical, pharisaical, pietistic, pious, priggish, self-righteous, self-satisfied, smug, Tartuffian, too good to be true, unctuous; (*Inf*) goody-goody

sanction *n* allowance, approbation, approval, authority, authorization, backing, confirmation, countenance, endorsement, ratification, stamp of approval, support; ban, boycott, coercive measures, embargo, penalty; (*Inf*) OK, okay

sanction *v* allow, approve, authorize, back, countenance, endorse, lend one's name to, permit, support, vouch for

sanctity *n* devotion, godliness, goodness, grace, holiness, piety, purity, religiousness, saintliness

sanctuary *n* altar, church, Holy of Holies, sanctum, shrine, temple; asylum, haven, protection, refuge, retreat, shelter

sane *adj compos mentis*, in one's right mind, in possession of all one's faculties, lucid, mentally sound, normal, of sound mind, rational; balanced, judicious, level-headed, moderate, reasonable, sensible, sober, sound; (*Inf*) all there

sanitary *adj* clean, germ-free, healthy, hygienic, salubrious, unpolluted, wholesome

sanity *n* mental health, normality, rationality, reason, sameness, stability; common sense, good sense, judiciousness, level-headedness, rationality, sense, soundness of judgment; (*Inf*) right mind

sap *n* animating, force, essence, lifeblood, vital fluid; fool, idiot, nincompoop, ninny, nitwit, noddy, noodle, Simple Simon, simpleton, weakling; (*Inf*) charlie, chump, drip, jerk, mugins, nurd, plonker, prat, twit, wally, wet

sarcasm *n* bitterness, causticness, contempt, cynicism, derision, irony, mockery, mordancy, satire, scorn, sneering, venom, vitriol

sarcastic *adj* acerbic, acid, acrimonious, backhanded, bitchy, citing, caustic, contemptuous, cutting, cynical, derisive, disparaging, ironical, mocking, mordant, sardonic, satirical, sharp, sneering, taunting; (*Inf*) sarky

sardonic *adj* bitter, derisive, ironical, malevolent, malicious, malignment, sarcastic

satanic *adj* accursed, black, demoniac, demoniacal, demonic, devilish, diabolic, evil, fiendish, hellish, infernal, inhuman, iniquitous, malevolent, malignant, wicked

satiate *v* cloy, glut, gorge, jade, nauseate, overfill, stuff; sate, satisfy, slake, surfeit

satire *n* burlesque, caricature, irony, lampoon, parody, pasquinade, raillery, ridicule, sarcasm, skit, travesty, wit; (*Inf*) send-up, spoof, takeoff

satirical *adj* biting, bitter, burlesque, caustic, censorious, cutting, cynical, incisive, ironical, mocking, mordant, pungent, Rabelaisian, sarcastic, sardonic, taunting

satisfaction *n* comfort, complacency, content, contentedness, contentment, ease, enjoyment, gratification, happiness, peace of mind, pleasure, pride, repletion, satiety, well-being; achievement, appeasing, assuaging, fulfilment, gratification, resolution, settlement; amends, atonement, compensation, damages, indemnification, justice, recompense, redress, reimbursement, remuneration, reparation, requital, restitution, vindication

satisfactory *adj* acceptable, adequate, all right, average, competent, fair, good enough, passable, sufficient, suitable, up to standard, up to the mark

satisfy *v* appease, assuage, content, fill, gratify, indulge, mollify, pacify, please, quench, sate, satiate, slake, surfeit; answer, be enough, come up to expectations, do, fulfil, meet, qualify, serve, serve the purpose, suffice; (*Inf*) fit the bill; assure, convince, dispel someone's doubts, persuade, put someone's mind at rest, quiet, reassure; answer, comply with, discharge, fulfil, meet, pay off, settle, square up; atone, compensate, indemnify, make good, make reparation for, recompense, renumerate, requite, reward

saturate *v* douse, drench, imbue, impregnate, soak, souse, steep, suffuse, waterlog, wet through

saunter *v* amble, dally, linger, loiter, meander, ramble, roam, rove, stroll, take a stroll, tarry, wander; (*Inf*) mosey

saunter *n* airing, amble, breather, constitutional, perambulation, promenade, ramble, stroll, turn, walk

savage *adj* feral, rough, rugged, uncivilized, uncultivated, undomesticated, untamed, wild; barbarous, beastly, bestial, bloodthirsty, bloody, brutal, brutish, cruel, devilish, diabolical, ferocious, fierce, harsh, inhuman, merciless, murderous, pitiless, ravening, ruthless, sadistic, vicious; in a state of nature, nonliterate, primitive, rude, unspoilt

savage *n* aboriginal, aborigine, autochthon, barbarian, heathen, indigene, native, primitive; barbarian, bear; (*Inf*) boor, beast, brute, fiend, monster

savage *v* attach, lacerate, mangle, maul; (*Inf*) tear into

save *v* bail someone out, come to someone's rescue, deliver, free, liberate, recover, redeem, rescue, salvage, set free; be frugal, be thrifty, collect, economize, gather, hide away, hoard, hold, husband, keen, lay by, put aside for a rainy day, put by, reserve, retrench, salt away, set aside, store, treasure up; (*Inf*) keep up one's sleeve, tighten one's belt; conserve, guard, keep safe, look after, preserve, protect, safeguard, shield, take care of

saving *adj* compensatory, extenuating, qualifying, redeeming

saving *n* bargain, discount, economy, reduction

saviour *n* defender, deliverer, friend in need, Good Samaritan, guardian, knight in shining armour, liberator, preserver, protector, redeemer, rescuer, salvation

savour *n* flavour, piquancy, relish, smack, smell, tang, taste, zest; distinctive, qualify, excitement, flavour, interest, salt, spice, zest

savour *v* appreciate, delight in, enjoy, enjoy to the full, gloat over, like, luxuriate in, partake, relish, revel in, smack one's lips over

savoury *adj* agreeable, appetizing, dainty, delectable, delicious, full-flavoured, good, luscious, mouthwatering, palatable, piquant, rich, spicy, tangy, tasty, toothsome; (*Inf*) scrumptious; decent, edifying, honest, reputable, respectable, wholesome

say *v* add, affirm, announce, assert, declare, give voice to, maintain, mention, pronounce, put into words, remark, speak, state, utter, voice; (*Inf*) come out with; answer, disclose, divulge, give as one's opinion, make known, reply, respond, reveal, tell; allege, claim, noise abroad, put about, report, rumour, suggest; deliver, do, orate, perform, read, recite, rehearse, render, repeat; assume, conjecture, dare say, estimate, guess, hazard a guess, imagine, judge, presume, suppose, surmise; communicate, convey, express, give the impression that, imply

say *n* authority, influence, power, sway, weight; (*Inf*) clout

saying *n* adage, aphorism, axiom, byword, dictum, gnome, maxim, proverb, saw, slogan

scale *n* calibration, degrees, gamut, gradation, graduated, system, graduation, hierarchy, ladder, progression, ranking, register, seniority system, sequence, series, spectrum, spread, steps; proportion, ratio; degree, extent, range, reach, scope, way; (*Inf*) pecking order

scale *v* ascend, clamber, climb, escalade, mount, surmount

scamper *v* dart, dash, fly, hasten, hurry, romp, run, scoot, scurry, scuttle, sprint

scan *v* check, examine, glance over, investigate, look one up and down, look through, run one's eye over, run over, scour, scrutinize, search, skim, survey, sweep, take stock of; (*Inf*) size up

scandal *n* crime, disgrace, embarrassment, offence, sin, wrongdoing; calumny, defamation, detraction, discredit, disgrace, dishonour, ignominy, infamy, obloquy, offence, opprobrium, reproach, shame, stigma; (*Inf*) crying shame; abuse, aspersion, backbiting, dirt, gossip, rumours, skeleton in the cupboard, slander, talk, tattle; (*Inf*) dirty linen

scandalous *adj* atrocious, disgraceful, disreputable, highly improper, infamous, monstrous, odious, opprobrious, outrageous, shameful, shocking, unseemly; defamatory, gossiping, libellous, scurrilous, slanderous, untrue

scanty *adj* bare, deficient, exiguous, inadequate, insufficient, meagre, narrow, poo, restricted, scant, short, skimpy, slender, sparing, sparse, thin

scar *n* blemish, cicatrix, injury, mark, wound

scar *v* brand, damage, disfigure, mark, traumatize

scar *n* bluff, cliff, crag, precipice

scarce *adj* at at premium, deficient, few, few and far between, infrequent, in short supply, insufficient, rare, seldom met with, uncommon, unusual, wanting

scarcely *adv* barely, hardly, only just; by no means, definitely not, hardly, not at all, on no account, under no circumstances

scarcity *n* dearth, deficiency, infrequency, insufficiency, lack, paucity, poverty, rareness, shortage, undersupply, want

scare *v* alarm, daunt, dismay, frighten, give someone a fright, intimidate, panic, shock, startle, terrify, terrorize; (*Inf*) give someone a turn, put the wind up someone

scare *n* alarm, alert, fright, panic, shock, start, terror

scathing *adj* belittling, biting, brutal, caustic, critical, cutting, harsh, mordant, sarcastic, savage, scornful, searing, trenchant, vitriolic, withering

scatter *v* broadcast, diffuse, disseminate, fling, litter, shower, sow, spread, sprinkle, strew; disband, dispel, disperse, dissipate, disunite, put to flight, separate

scene *n* display, drama, exhibition, pageant, picture, representation, show, sight, spectacle, tableau; area, locality, place, position, setting, site, situation, spot, whereabouts; backdrop, background, location, *mise en scène*, set, setting; act, division, episode, incident, part, stage; commotion, confrontation, display of emotion, drama, exhibition, fuss of emotion, performance, row, tantrum, to-do, upset; (*Inf*) carry-on; landscape, panorama, prospect, view, vista

scenery *n* landscape, surroundings, terrain, view, vista; backdrop, décor, flats, *mise en scéne*, set, setting, stage set

scent *n* aroma, bouquet, fragrance, odour, perfume, redolence, smell; spoor, track, trail

scent *v* be on the track, detect, discern, get wind of, nose out, recognize, sense, smell, sniff, sniff out

sceptic *n* agnostic, cynic, disbeliever, doubter, doubting Thomas, Pyrrhonidt, scoffer, unbeliever

sceptical *adj* cynical, disbelieving, doubtful, dubious, hesitating, incredulous, mistrustful, questioning, quizzical, scoffing, unbelieving, unconvinced

schedule *n* agenda, calendar, catalogue, inventory, itinerary, list, list of appointments, plan, programme, timetable

schedule *v* appoint, arrange, be due, book, organize, plan, programme, slot, time

scheme *n* contrivance, course of action, design, device, plan, programme, project, proposal, strategy, system, tactics, theory; arrangement, blueprint, chart, codification, diagram, disposition, draft, layout, outline, pattern, schedule, schema, system;conspiracy, dodge, intrigue, machinations, manoeuvre, plot, ploy, ruse, shift, stratagem, subterfuge; (*Inf*) game

scheme *v* contrive, design, devise, frame, imagine, lay plans, plan, project, work out; collude, conspire, intrigue, machinate, manoeuvre, plot; (*Inf*) wheel and deal

scholar *n* academic, bookworm, intellectual, man of letters, savant;

disciple, learner, pupil, schoolboy, schoolgirl, student; (*Inf*) egghead

scholarship *n* accomplishments, attainments, book-learning, education, erudition, knowledge, learning, lore; bursary, exhibition, fellowship

school *n* academy, *alma mater*, college, department, discipline, faculty, institute, institution, seminary; adherents, circle, class, clique, denomination, devotees, disciples, faction, followers, following, group, pupils, sect, set; creed, faith, outlook, persuasion, school of thought, stamp, way of life

school *v* coach, discipline, drill, educate, indoctrinate, instruct, prepare, prime, train, tutor, verse

schooling *n* book-learning, education, formal education, teaching, tuition; coaching, drill, grounding, guidance, instruction, preparation, training

science *n* body of knowledge, branch of knowledge, discipline; art, skill, technique

scientific *adj* accurate, controlled, exact, mathematical, precise, systematic

scintillate *v* coruscate, flash, gleam, glisten, glitter, sparkle, twinkle

scoff *v* belittle, deride, despise, flout, gibe, jeer, laugh at, make light of, make sport of, mock, poke fun at, pooh-pooh, revile, ridicule, scorn, sneer, taunt; (*Inf*) knock, slag off

scold *v* berate, blame, bring some one to book, castigate, censure, chide, find fault with, lecture, nag, rate, rebuke, remonstrate with, reprimand, reproach, reprove, take someone to task, upbraid, vituperate; (*Inf*) bawl out, give someone a dressing-down, go on at, haul someone over the coals, have some one on the carpet, tell off, tick off

scoop *n* dipper, ladle, spoon; coup, exclusive, exposé, inside story, revelation, sensation

scoop *v* bail, dig, dip, empty, excavate, gouge, hollow, ladle, scrape, shovel

scope *n* area, capacity, compass, confines, elbowroom, extent, field of reference, freedom, latitude, liberty, opportunity, orbit, outlook, purview, range, reach, room, space, span, sphere

scorch *v* blacken, blister, burn, char, parch, roast, sear, shrivel, singe, wither

score *n* grade, mark, outcome, points, record, result, total; account, basis, cause, ground, grounds, reason; a bone to pick, grievance, grudge, inquiry, injustice, wrong; account, amount due, bill, charge, debt, obligation, reckoning, tab, tally, total

score *v* achieve, amass, gain, make, win; (*Inf*) chalk up, notch up, count, keep a tally of, keep count, record, register, tally; crosshatch, cut, deface, gouge, graze, indent, mar, mark, nick, notch, scrape, scratch, slash; **score through** cancel, cross out, delete, obliterate, put a line through, strike out; adapt, arrange, orchestrate, set; gain an advantage, go down well with someone, impress, make an impact, make a point, put oneself across, triumph

scorn *n* contempt, contemptuousness, contumely, derision, despite, disdain, disparagement, mockery, sarcasm, scornfulness, slight, sneer

scorn *v* be above, consider beneath one, contemn, curl one's lip at, deride, disdain, flout, hold in contempt, look down on, make fun of, reject, scoff at, slight, sneer at, spurn; (*Inf*) turn up one's nose at

scornful *adj* contemptuous, contumelious, defiant, derisive, disdainful, haughty, insolent, insulting, jeering, mocking, sarcastic, sardonic, scathing, scoffing, slighting, sneering, supercilious, withering

scoundrel *n* blackguard, cheat, good-for-nothing, incorrigible, miscreant, ne'er-do-well, rascal, reprobate, rogue, scamp, scape grace, vagabond, villain, wretch; (*Inf*) heel, rotter, swine

scour *v* abrade, buff, burnish, clean, cleanse, flush, furbish, polish, purge, rub, scrub, wash, whiten

scour *v* beat, comb, forage, go over with a fine-tooth comb, hunt, look high and low, rake, ransack, search

scourge *n* affliction, bane, curse, infliction, misfortune, penalty, pest, plague, punishment, terror, torment, visitation; cat, cat-o'-nine-tails, lash, strap, switch, thong, whip

scourge *v* beat, belt, cane, castigate, chastise, discipline, flog, horse whip, lash, leather, punish, take a strap to, thrash, trounce, whale, whip; (*Inf*) tan someone's hide, wallop

scout *v* check out, investigate, make a reconnaissance, observe, probe, reconnoitre, see how the land lies, spy, spy out, survey, watch; (*Inf*) case

scout *n* advance guard, escort, look out, outrider, precursor, reconnoitre, vanguard; recruiter, talent scout

scowl *v* frown, glower, grimace, look-daggers at, lower

scowl *n* black look, dirty look, frown, glower, grimace

scramble *v* clamber, climb, crawl, move with difficulty, push, scrabble, struggle, swarm; contend, hasten, jockey for position, jostle, make haste, push, run, rush, strive, vie; (*Inf*) look snappy

scramble *n* climb, trek; commotion, competition, confusion, hustle, melee, muddle, race, rat race, rush, struggle, tussle; (*Inf*) free-for-all, hassle

scrap *n* atom, bit, bite, crumb, fragment, grain, iota, mite, modicum, morsel, mouthful, part, particle, piece, portion, sliver, snatch, snippet, trace; junk, off cuts, waste; bits, leavings, leftovers, remains, scrapings

scrap *v* abandon, break up, demolish. discard, dispense with, drop, get rid of, jettison, shed, throw away, throw on the scrapheap, toss out, write off; (*Inf*) ditch, junk, trash

scrape *v* abrade, bark, graze, rub, scratch, scuff, skin; grate, grind, rasp, scratch, screech, set one's teeth on edge, squeak; clean, erase, file, remove, rub, scour; pinch, save, scrimp, skimp, stint

scratch *v* claw, cut, damage, etch, grate, graze, incise, lacerate, make a mark on, mark, rub, score, scrape; annul, cancel, delete, eliminate, erase, pull out, stand down, strike off, withdraw

scratch *n* blemish, claw, gash, graze, laceration, mark, scrape

scratch *adj* haphazard, hastily prepared, impromptu, improvised, rough, rough-and-ready

scream *v* bawl, cry, screech, shriek, shrill, sing out, squeal, yell; be conspicuous, slash, jar, shriek; (*Inf*) holler

scream *n* wail, yell, yelp

screen *v* cloak, conceal, cover, hide, mask, shade, shut out, veil; defend, guard, protect, safeguard, shelter, shield; cull, evaluate, examine, filter, gauge, grade, process, riddle, scan, sieve, sift, sort, vet; broadcast, present, put on, show

screen *n* awning, canopy, cloak, concealment, cover, guard, hedge, mantle, shade, shelter, shield, shroud; mesh, net, partition, room divider

screw *v* tighten, turn, twist, work in; bring pressure to bear on, coerce, constrain, force, hold a knife to someone's throat, oppress, pressurize, squeeze; (*Inf*) put the screws on

scrimp *v* contract, curtail, limit, pinch, reduce, scant, shorten, straiten

script *n* calligraphy, hand, handwriting, letters, longhand, penmanship, writing; book, copy, dialogue, libretto, lines, manuscript, text, words

scrounge *v* beg, cadge, forage for, hunt around for, wheedle; (*Inf*) bum, freeload, sponge

scrounger *v* cadger, parasite; (*Inf*) bum, freeloader, sponger

scrub *v* clean, cleanse, rub, scour; abandon, abolish, call off, cancel, delete, discontinue, do away with, drop, forget about, give up

scruffy *adj* disreputable, ill-groomed, mangy, messy, ragged, run-down, seedy, shabby, slatternly, slovenly, sluttish, squalid, tattered, tatty, ungroomed, unkempt, untidy

scrupulous *adj* careful, conscientious, exact, fastidious, honourable, meticulous, minute, moral, nice, painstaking, precise, principled, punctilious, rigorous, strict, upright

scrutinize *v* analyse, dissect, examine, explore, inquire into, inspect, investigate, peruse, pore over, probe, scan, search, sift, study

scrutiny *n* analysis, close study, examination, exploration, inquiry, inspection, investigation, perusal, search, sifting, study

scud *v* flee, fly, haste, hie, post, run, scamper, speed, trip

scuffle *v* clash, come to blows, contend, exchange blows, fight, grapple, jostle, struggle, tussle

scuffle *n* affray, brawl, commotion, disturbance, fight, fray, rumpus, tussle; (*Inf*) scrap, set-to

scum *n* algae, crust, dross, film, froth, impurities, offscourings, scruff; *canaille*, dregs of society, dross, lowest of the low, rabble, riff-raff, rubbish, trash

scurrilous *adj* abusive, coarse, defamatory, foul, foul-mouthed, gross, indecent, infamous, insulting, low, obscene, offensive, Rabelaisian, ribald, salacious, scabrous, scand-

dalous, slanderous, vituperative
scurry *v* bustle, dash, hasten, hurry, scamper, scud, scutter
scurry *n* burst, bustle, dash, flurry, haste, hurry, scamper, scud, spurt
sea *n* main, ocean, the deep, the waves; (*Inf*) the briny, the drink; abundance, expanse, mass, multitude, plethora, profusion, sheet, vast number
sea *adj* aquatic, briny, marine, maritime, ocean, ocean-going, oceanic, pelagic, salt, saltwater, seagoing
seal *v* close, cork, enclose, fasten, make airtight, plug, secure, shut, stop,stopper, stop up, waterproof; assure, attest, authenticate, confirm, establish, ratify, stamp, validate; clinch, conclude consummate, finalise, settle; **seal off** board up, fence off, isolate, put out of bounds, quarantine, segregate
seal *n* assurance, attestation, authen tication, confirmation, imprimatur, insignia, notification, ratification, stamp
sear *v* blight, brand, cauterize, dry, scorch, wither
sear *adj* dried up, dry, sere, withered
search *v* cast around, check, comb, examine, explore, ferret, go over with a finetooth comb, inquire, inspect, investigate, leave no stone unturned, look, look high and low, probe, pry, ransack, rifle through, rummage through, scour, scrutinize, seek, sift, turn inside out, turn upside down; (*Inf*) frisk
search *n* examination, exploration, hunt, inquiry, inspection, investigation, pursuit, quest, researches, rummage, scrutiny; (*Inf*) going-over **in search of** hunting for, in need of, in pursuit of, looking for, making enquiries concerning, on the look out for, on the track of, seeking
searching *adj* close, keen, penetrating, trying; examining, exploring, inquiring, investigating, probing, seeking
season *n* division, interval, juncture, occasion, opportunity, period, spell, term, time, time of year
season *v* colour, enliven, flavour, lace, leave, pep up, salt, salt and pepper, spice; acclimatize, accustom, anneal, discipline, habituate, harden, inure, mature, prepare, toughen, train
seasonable *adj* appropriate, convenient, fit, opportune, suitable, timely
seasoned *adj* battle-scarred, experienced, hardened, long-serving, mature, old, practised, time-served, veteran, weathered, well-versed
seat *n* bench, chair, pew, settle, stall, stool, throne; axis, capital, centre, cradle, headquarters, heart, hub, location, place, site, situation, source, station; base, bed, bottom, cause, footing, foundation, ground, groundwork; abode, ancestral hall, house, mansion, residence; chair, constituency, incumbency, membership, place
seat *v* accommodate, cater for, contain, have room or capacity for, hold, sit, take; deposit, fit, install, locate, place, set, settle, sit
secluded *adj* cloistered, cut off, isolated, lonely, off the beaten track,

out-of-the-way, private, reclusive, remote, retired, sequestered, sheltered, solitary, tucked away, unfrequented

seclusion *n* obscurity, privacy, retirement, secrecy, separation, solitude, withdrawal

second *adj* following, next, subsequent, succeeding; additional, alternative, extra, further, other, repeated; inferior, lesser, lower, secondary, subordinate, supporting; double, duplicate, reproduction, twin

second *n* assistant, attendant, backer, helper, right-hand man, right-hand woman, supporter

second *v* advance, aid, approve, assist, back, encourage, endorse, forward, further, give moral support to, go along with, help, promote, support

second *n* flash, instant, minute, moment, split second, trice, twinkling, twinkling of an eye; (*Inf*) jiffy, sec, tick, two shakes of a lamb's tail

secondary *adj* derivative, derived, indirect, resultant, resulting, second-hand; consequential, contingent, inferior, lesser, lower, minor, second-rate, subordinate, unimportant; alternate, auxiliary, backup, extra, relief, reserve, second, subsidiary, supporting

second-hand *adj* handed down, nearly new, used; (*Inf*) hand-me-downs

second-hand *adv* at second-hand, indirectly; (*Inf*) on the grapevine

second-rate *adj* cheap, commonplace, inferior, low-grade, low-quality, mediocre, poor, rubbishy, shoddy, substandard, tawdry; (*Inf*) tacky

secret *adj* backstairs, camouflaged, cloak-and-dagger, close, concealed, conspiratorial, covered, covert, disguised, furtive, hidden, reticent, shrouded, under wraps, undisclosed, unknown, unpublished, unrevealed, unseen; (*Inf*) closet, hush-hush; abstruse, arcane cabbalistic, clandestine, classified, cryptic, esoteric, mysterious, occult, recondite; hidden, out-of-the-way, private, retired, secluded, unfrequented, unknown; close, deep, discreet, reticent, secretive, sly, stealthy, underhand

secret *n* code, confidence, enigma, formula, key, mystery, recipe, skeleton in the cupboard

secretive *adj* clamlike, close, cryptic, deep, enigmatic, playing one's cards close to one's chest, reserved, reticent, tight-lipped, uncommunicative, unforthcoming, with drawn; (*Inf*) cagey

secretly *adv* behind closed doors, behind someone's back, clandestinely, confidentially, covertly, furtively, in camera, in confidence, in one's heart, in one's inmost thoughts, in secret, on the sly, privately, quietly, stealthily, surreptitiously, unobserved; (*Inf*) on the q.t.

sect *n* denomination, faction, schism, school

sectarian *adj* bigoted, clannish, cliquish, doctrinaire, dogmatic, exclusive, factional, fanatic, fanatical, hidebound, insular, limited, narrow-minded, parochial, partisan, rigid

section *n* component, cross section, division, fraction, fragment, installment, part, passage, piece, portion, sample, segment, slice, subdivision

secular *adj* civil, earthly, laic, laical, lay, non-spiritual, profane, state, temporal, worldly

secure *adj* immune, impregnable, out of harm's way, protected, safe, sheltered, shielded, unassailable, undamaged, unharmed; dependable, fast, fastened, firm, fixed, fortified, immovable, stable, steady, tight; assured, certain, confident, easy, reassured, sure; absolute, conclusive, definite, reliable, solid, steadfast, tried and true, well- founded; (*Inf*) in the bag

secure *v* acquire, come by, gain, get, get hold of, make sure of, obtain, pick up, procure, win, possession of; (*Inf*) land; attach, batten down, bolt, chain, fasten, fix, lash, lock, lock up, make fast, moor, padlock, rivet, tie up

security *n* asylum, care, cover, custody, immunity, preservation, protection, refuge, sanctuary; defence, guards, precautions, protection, safeguards, safety measures, surveillance; assurance, certainty, confidence, conviction, ease of mind, freedom from doubt, positiveness, reliance, sureness; collateral, gage, guarantee, hostage, insurance, pawn, pledge

sedate *adj* calm, collected, composed, cool, decorous, deliberate, demure, dignified, earnest, grave, imperturbable, middle-aged, placid, proper, quiet, seemly, serene, serious, slow-moving, sober, solemn, staid, tranquil, unruffled

sedative *adj* allaying, anodyne, calmative, calming, lenitive, relaxing, sleep-inducing, soothing, soporific, tranquillizing

sedative *n* anodyne, calmative, downer, narcotic, opiate, sleeping pill, tranquillizer

sediment *n* dregs, grounds, lees, precipitate, residue, residuum, settlings

seduce *v* betray, corrupt, debauch, deflower, deprave, dishonour; allure, attract, beguile, deceive, decoy, ensnare, entice, inveigle, lead astray, lure, mislead, tempt

seductive *adj* alluring, attractive, beguiling, bewitching, captivating, enticing, flirtatious, inviting, irresistible, provocative, ravishing, sexy, siren, specious, tempting

see *v* behold, catch a glimpse of, catch sight of, descry, discern, distinguish, espy, glimpse, heed, identify, look, make out, mark, note, notice, observe, perceive, recognize regard, sight, spot, view, witness; (*Inf*) get a load of; appreciate, comprehend, fathom, feel, follow, get, get the drift of, grasp, know, make out, realize, take in, understand; (*Inf*) catch on to, get the hang of; ascertain, determine, discover, find out, investigate, learn, make enquiries, refer to; ensure, guarantee, make certain, make sure, mind, see to it, take care; consider, decide, deliberate, give some thought to, judge, make up one's mind, mull over, reflect, think over; confer with, consult, encounter, interview, meet, receive, run into, speak to, visit; accompany, attend, escort, lead, show, usher, walk; anticipate, divine, envisage, foresee, foretell, imagine, picture, visualize

seed *n* egg, egg cell, embryo, germ, grain, kernal, ovule, ovum, spore; beginning, germ, inkling, nucleus, source, start, suspicion

seedy *adj* decaying, dilapidated, down at heel, faded, grubby, mangy, old, run-down, shabby, sleazy, slovenly, squalid, tatty, unkempt, worm; (*Inf*) crummy, grotty, scruffy

seek *v* be after, follow, go gunning for, go in search of, hunt, inquire, look for, pursue, search for; aim, aspire to, attempt, endeavour, essay, strive, try; ask, beg, entreat, inquire, invite, petition, request, solicit

seem *v* appear, assume, give the impression, have the appearance of, look, look as if, look like, look to be, pretend, sound like, strike one as being

seemly *adj* appropriate, becoming, befitting, *comme il faut,* decent, decorous, fit, fitting, in good taste, nice, proper, suitable, suited, the done thing

seethe *v* boil, bubble, churn, ferment, fizz, frith; be livid, breathe fire and slaughter, foam at the mouth, fume, rage, simmer, storm; be alive with, swarm, teem; (*Inf*) get hot under the collar

see through *v* be undeceived by, be wise to, fathom, get to the bottom of, not fall for, penetrate

segment *n* bit, division, part, piece, portion, section, sector

segregate *v* discriminate, against, dissociate, isolate, separate, set apart, single out

seize *v* clutch, fasten, grab, grasp, grip, lay hands on, snatch, take; apprehend, catch, get, grasp; (*Inf*) collar; abduct, annex, appropriate, arrest, capture, commandeer, confiscate, hijack, impound, take by storm, take captive, take possession of

seizure *n* abduction, annexation, apprehension, arrest, capture, commandeering, confiscation, grabbing, taking; attack, convulsion, fit, paroxysm, spasm

seldom *adv* hardly ever, infrequently, not often, occasionally, rarely, scarcely ever; (*Inf*) once in a blue moon

select *v* choose, opt for, pick, prefer, single out, sort out

select *adj* choice, excellent, first-class, first-rate, hand-picked, picked, preferable, prime, rare, recherché, selected, special, superior; (*Inf*) posh, topnotch

selection *n* choice, choosing, option, pick, preference; anthology, assortment, choice, collection, line-up, medley, miscellany, potpourri, range, variety

selective *adj* careful, discerning, discriminating, discriminatory, eclectic, particular

self-centred *adj* egotistic, inward looking, narcissistic, self-absorbed, selfish, self-seeking, wrapped up in oneself

self-confidence *n* aplomb, composure, confidence, high morale, nerve, poise, self-assurance, self-dependence, self-reliance, self-respect

self-confident *adj* assured, confident, fearless, poised, secure, self-assured, self-reliant, sure of oneself

self-conscious *adj* affected, awkward, bashful, diffident, embarrassed, ill at ease, insecure, nervous, out of countenance, shamefaced, sheepish, uncomfortable

self-control *n* calmness, cool, coolness, restraint, self-discipline, self-mastery, self-restraint, strength of mind, willpower

self-evident *adj* axiomatic, clear, incontrovertible, inescapable, manifestly true, obvious, undeniable, written all over something

self-important *adj* assuming, consequential, proud, haughty, lordly, overbearing, overweening

self-indulgence *n* dissipation, excess, extravagance, incontinence, intemperance, self-gratification, sensualism

selfish *adj* egoistic, egoistical, ego tistic, egotistical, greedy, mean, mercenary, narrow, self-centred, self-interested, self-seeking, ungenerous; (*Inf*) looking out for number one

self-possessed *adj* collected, confident, cool, poised, self-assured, sure of oneself, unruffled; (*Inf*) cool as a cucumber, together

self-respect *n amour-propre,* dignity, faith in oneself, morale, one's own image, pride, self-esteem

self-righteous *adj* complacent, holier-than-though, hypocritical, pharisaic, pietistic, pious, priggish, sanctimonious, self-satisfied, smug, superior, too good to be true; (*Inf*) goody-goody

self-sacrifice *n* altruism, generosity, self-abnegation, self-denial, selflessness

self-satisfied *adj* complacent, flushed with success, like a cat that has swallowed the cream, pleased with oneself, proud of oneself, puffed up, self-congratulatory, smug, well-pleased

self-willed *adj* contumacious, dogged, headstrong, obstinate, pig-headed, stubborn, uncompliant, wilful

sell *v* barter, dispose of, exchange, put up for sale, trade; be in the business of, deal in, handle, hawk, market, merchandise, peddle, retail, stock, trade in, traffic in, vend

seller *n* agent, dealer, merchant, rep, representative, retailer, salesman, saleswoman, shopkeeper, tradesman, traveller, vendor

semblance *n* likeness, resemblance, similarity; air, appearance, aspect, bearing, exterior, figure, form, mien, seeming, show; image, like ness, representation, similitude

send *v* communicate, consign, convey, direct, dispatch, forward, remit, transmit; cast, deliver, fire, fling, hurl, let fly, propel, shoot

send for *v* call for, order, request, summon

sendoff *n* departure, farewell, going-away party, leave-taking, start, valediction

senile *adj* decrepit, doddering, doting, failing, imbecile in one's dotage, in one's second childhood

senior *adj* elder, higher ranking,

older, superior

seniority *n* eldership, longer service, precedence, priority, rank, superiority

sensation *n* awareness, consciousness, feeling, impression, perception, sense, tingle; (*Inf*) vibes; agitation, commotion, excitement, furore, scandal, stir, surprise, thrill, wow; (*Inf*) crowd puller, hit

sensational *adj* amazing, astounding, breathtaking, dramatic, electrifying, exciting, hair-raising, horrifying, lurid, melodramatic, revealing, scandalous, sensationalistic, shocking, spectacular, staggering, startling, thrilling

sense *n* faculty, feeling, sensation, sensibility; appreciation, atmosphere, aura, awareness, consciousness, feel, impression, intuition, perception, premonition, presentiment, sentiment; definition, denotation, drift, gist, implication, import, interpretation, meaning, message, nuance, purport, significance, signification, substance; clear-headedness, cleverness, common sense, discernment, discrimination, intelligence, judgment, mother wit, quickness, reason, sagacity, sanity, sharpness, tact, understanding, wisdom, wits; (*Inf*) brains, gumption, nous

sense *v* appreciate, apprehend, be aware of, discern, divine, feel, get the impression, grasp, have a hunch, just know, notice, observe, perceive, pick up, realize, suspect, understand; (*Inf*) have a feeling in one's bones

senseless *adj* absurd, asinine, crazy, fatuous, foolish, halfwitted, idiotic, illogical, imbecilic, inane, incongruous, inconsistent, irrational, ludicrous, mad, meaningless, mindless, moronic, nonsensical, pointless, ridiculous, silly, simple, stupid, unintelligent, unreasonable, unwise; (*Inf*) daft; anaesthetized, cold, deadened, insensate, insensible, numb, numbed out, out cold, stunned, unconscious, unfeeling

sensible *adj* canny, discreet, discriminating, down-to-earth, far-sighted, intelligent, judicious, matter-of-fact, practical, prudent, rational, realistic, reasonable, sagacious, sage, sane, shrewd, sober, sound, well-reasoned, well-thought-out, wise

sensitive *adj* acute, delicate, easily affected, fine, impressionable, keen, perceptive, precise, reactive, responsive, sentient, susceptible; delicate, easily upset, irritable, temperamental, tender, thin-skinned, touchy

sensual *adj* animal, bodily, carnal, epicurean, fleshly, luxurious, physical, unspiritual, voluptuous; erotic, lascivious, lecherous, lewd, libidinous, licentious, lustful, raunchy, sexual, sexy

sensuous *adj* epicurean, gratifying, hedonistic, lush, pleasurable, rich, sensory, sumptuous

sentence *n* condemnation, decision, decree, doom, judgment, order, pronouncement, ruling, verdict

sentence *v* condemn, doom, mete out justice to, pass judgment on, penalize

sentiment *n* emotion, sensibility,

soft-heartedness, tender feeling, tenderness; attitude, belief, feeling, idea, judgment, opinion, persuasion, saying, though, view, way of thinking; emotionalism, mawkishness, over-emotionalism, romanticism, sentimentality; (*Inf*) slush

sentimental *adj* dewy-eyed, emotional, impressionable, maudlin, mawkish, nostalgic, over-emotional, pathetic, romantic, simpering, soft-hearted, tearful, tender, touching (*Inf*) corny, gushy, mushy, schmaltzy, sloppy, slushy, tear-jerking, weepy

sentimentality *n* emotionalism, mawkishness, nostalgia, play on the emotions, romanticism, tenderness; (*Inf*) corniness, mush, schmaltz, sloppiness, slush

separate *v* break off, cleave, come apart, come away, come between, detach, disconnect, disentangle, disjoin, divide, keep apart, remove, sever, split, sunder, uncouple; discriminate between, isolate, put on one side, segregate, single out, sort out; bifurcate, break up, disunite, diverge, divorce, estrange, go different ways, part, part company, set at odds, split up

separate *adj* detached, disconnected, discrete, disjointed, divided, divorced, isolated, unattached, unconnected; alone, apart, autonomous, distinct, independent, individual, particular, single, solitary

separately *adv* alone, apart, independently, individually, one at a time, one by one, personally, severally, singly

separation *n* break, detachment, disconnection, disengagement, disjunction, dissociation, disunion, division, gap, segregation, severance; break-up, divorce, estrangement, farewell, leave-taking, parting, rift, split, split-up

sequel *n* conclusion, consequence, continuation, development, end, follow-up, issue, outcome, result, upshot

sequence *n* arrangement, chain, course, cycle, order, procession, progression, series, succession

serene *adj* calm, composed, imperturbable, peaceful, placid, tranquil, undisturbed, unruffled, untroubled; bright, clear, cloudless, fair, halcyon, unclouded

serenity *n* calm, calmness, collectedness, composure, coolness, imperturbability, peace, peacefulness, sedateness, tranquillity; brightness, calmness, clearness, fairness, peace, quietness, stillness

series *n* arrangement, chain, course, line, order, progression, run, sequence, set, string, succession, train

serious *adj* grave, humourless, long-faced, pensive, sedate, sober, solemn, stern, thoughtful, unsmiling; deliberate, determined, earnest, genuine, honest, in earnest, resolute, resolved, sincere; crucial, deep, difficult, far-reaching, fateful, grim, important, momentous, no laughing matter, of consequence, pressing, significant, urgent, weighty, worrying; acute, alarming, critical, dangerous, grave, severe

seriously *adv* all joking aside, earnestly, gravely, in all conscience, in earnest, sincerely, solemnly, thoughtfully, with a straight face; (*Inf*) no joking; acutely, badly, critically, dangerously, distressingly, gravely, grievously, severely, sorely

sermon *n* address, exhortation, homily; harangue, lecture; (*Inf*) dressing-down, talking-to

servant *n* attendant, domestic, drudge, help, helper, lackey, maid, menial, retainer, skivvy, slave, vassal

serve *v* aid, assist, attend to, be in the service of, be of assistance, be of use, help, minister to, oblige, succour, wait on, work for; act, attend, complete, discharge, do, fulfil, go through, observe, officiate, pass, perform; answer, answer the purpose, be acceptable, be ade quate, be good enough, content, do, do duty as, do the work of, function as, satisfy, suffice, suit; (*Inf*) fit the bill; arrange, deal, deliver, dish up, distribute, handle, present, provide, set out, supply

service *n* advantage, assistance, avail, benefit, help, ministrations, supply, use, usefulness, utility; check, maintenance, overhaul, servicing; business, duty, office, work; ceremony, function, observance, rite, worship

service *v* check, fine tune, go over, maintain, overhaul, recondition, repair, tune up

servile *adj* dependent, menial; abject, base, beggarly, cringing, fawning, grovelling, low, mean, obsequious, slavish, sneaking, supple, sycophantic, truckling

session *n* assembly, conference, discussion, hearing, meeting, period, sitting, term; (*Inf*) get together

set *v* aim, apply, deposit, direct, embed, fasten, fix, install, lay, locate, lodge, mount, park, place, plant, plonk, plump, position, put, rest, seat, situate, station, stick, turn; agree upon, allocate, appoint, arrange, assign, conclude, decide upon, designate, determine, establish, fix, fix up, name, ordain, regulate, resolve, schedule, settle, specify; arrange, lay, make ready, prepare, spread; adjust, coordinate, rectify, regulate, synchronize; cake, condense, congeal, crystallize, gelatinize, harden, jell, solidify, stiffen, thicken; allot, decree, impose, lay down, ordain, prescribe, specify; decline, dip, disappear, go down, sink, subside, vanish

set *n* attitude, bearing, carriage, fit, hang, position, posture, turn; *mise-en-scène*, scene, scenery, setting, stage set, stage setting

set *adj* agreed, appointed, arranged, customary, decided, definite, established, form, fixed, prearranged predetermined, prescribed, regular, scheduled, settled, usual; entrenched, firm, hard and fast, hardened, hide bound, immovable, inflexible, rigid, strict, stubborn

set *n* band, circle, class, clique, company, coterie, crowd, faction, gang, group, sect; (*Inf*) crew, outfit, assemblage, assortment, batch, collection, compendium, coordinated group, kit, outfit, series

setback *n* bit of trouble, blow, check, defeat, disappointment, hindrance, hitch, hold-up, impediment, misfortune, obstruction, rebuff, reversal, reverse, stumbling block, upset

set off *v* depart, embark, leave, sally forth, set out, start out; detonate, explode, ignite, light, set in motion, touch off, trigger off

setting *n* backdrop, background, context, frame, locale, location, *mise en scéne,* mounting, perspective, scene, scenery, set, site, surround, surroundings

settle *v* adjust, dispose, order, put into order, regulate, set to rights, straighten out, work out; choose, clear up, complete, conclude, decide, dispose of, put an end to, reconcile, resolve; calm, compose, lull, pacify, quell, quiet, quieten, reassure, relax, relieve, sedate, soothe, tranquillize; alight, bed down, come to rest, descend, land, light, make oneself comfortable; dwell, inhabit, live, make one's home, move to, put down roots, reside, set up home, take up residence; colonize, found, people, pioneer, plant, populate; acquit oneself of, clear, discharge, liquidate, pay, quit, square up; decline, fall, sink, subside

settlement *n* adjustment, agreement, arrangement, completion, conclusion, confirmation, disposition, establishment, resolution, termination, working out; clearance, clearing, defrayal, discharge, liquidation, payment, satisfaction; colonization, colony, community, encampment, hamlet, outpost

settler *n* colonist, colonizer, frontiersmen, frontierswoman, immigrant, pioneer, planter

set up *n* arrange, begin, compose, establish, found, initiate, install, institute, make provision for, organize, prearrange, prepare; assemble, build, construct, elevate, erect, put together, put up, raise

server *v* divide, part, rend, separate, sunder; detach, disconnect, disjoin, disunite

several *adj* assorted, different, disparate, distinct, diverse, indefinite, individual, many, particular, respective, single, some, sundry, various

severe *adj* austere, cruel, Draconian, hard, harsh, inexorable, iron-handed, oppressive, pitiless, relentless, rigid, strict, unbending, unrelenting; cold, disapproving, dour, flinty, forbidding, grave, grim, serious, sober, stern, strait-laced, tight-lipped, unsmiling; acute, bitter, critical, dangerous, distressing, extreme, fierce, grinding, inclement, intense, violent; ascetic, austere, chaste, classic, forbidding, functional, plain, restrained, simple, Spartan, unadorned, unembellished, unfussy; arduous, demanding, difficult, exacting, fierce, hard, punishing, rigorous, stringent, taxing, tough, unrelenting

sew *v* baste, bind, embroider, hem, machine stitch, stitch, tack

sex *n* gender; coition, coitus, copula tion, fornication, intimacy, lovemaking, sexual chemistry, sexual desire, sexual intercourse, sexual relations; desire, facts of life, libido, reproduction, sexuality; (*Inf*) the birds and the bees

shabby *adj* dilapidated, down at heel, faded, frayed, having seen better days, men, neglected, poor, ragged, run-down, scruffy, seedy, tattered, tatty, the worse for wear, threadbare, worn, worn-out; contemptible, despicable, dirty, dishonourable, ignoble, low, mean, scurvy, shameful, shoddy, ungentlemanly, unworthy; (*Inf*) low-down, rotten

shackle *v* chain, fetter, hamper, handcuff, manacle; bind, check, clog, confine, cumber, curb, embarrass, encumber, impede, limit, obstruct, restrain, restrict, tether

shackles *pl n* bonds, chains, fetters, handcuffs, irons, manacles, ropes, tethers

shade *n* coolness, dimness, dusk, gloom, gloominess, obscurity, screen, semi-darkness, shadiness, shadow, shadows; blind, canopy, cover, covering, curtain, hue, stain, tinge, tint, tone; apparition, ghost, manes, phantom, shadow, spectre, spirit

shade *v* cast a shadow over, cloud, conceal, cover, darken, dim, hide, mute, obscure, protect, screen, shadow, shield, shut out the light, veil

shadow *n* cover, darkness, dimness, dusk, gathering darkness, gloaming, gloom, obscurity, protection, shade, shelter; hint, suggestion, suspicion, trace; ghost, image, phantom, remnant, representation, spectre, vestige; blight, cloud, gloom, sadness; cast a shadow over, darken, overhang, screen, shade, shield; dog, follow, spy on, stalk, trail; (*Inf*) tail

shadowy *adj* crepuscular, dark, dim, dusky, gloomy, indistinct, murky, obscure, shaded shady, tenebrous, tenebrous; dim, dreamlike, faint, ghostly, illusory, imaginary, impalpable, intangible, nebulous, obscure, phantom, spectral, undefined, unreal, unsubstantial, vague, wraithlike

shady *adj* bowery, cool, dim, dark, leafy, shaded, shadowy, umbrageous; disreputable, dubious, questionable, shifty, slippery, suspect, suspicious, unethical, unscrupulous, untrustworthy; (*Inf*) crooked, fishy

shaft *n* handle, pole, rod, shank, stem, upright; beam, gleam, ray, streak; barb, cut, dart, gibe, sting, thrust

shake *v* bump, fluctuate, jar, joggle, jolt, jounce, oscillate, quake, quiver, rock, shiver, shudder, sway, totter, tremble, vibrate, waver, wobble; brandish, flourish, wave; discompose, distress, disturb, frighten, intimidate, move, shock, unnerve, upset; (*Inf*) rattle

shake *n* agitation, convulsion, disturbance, jar, jerk, jolt, jounce, pulsation, quaking, shiver, shock, shudder, trembling, tremor, vibration

shaky *adj* faltering, insecure, precar ious, quivery, rickety, tottering, trembling, tremulous, unstable, unsteady, weak, wobbly; (*Inf*) all of a quiver; dubious, questionable, suspect, uncertain, undependable, unreliable, unsound, unsupported

shallow *adj* empty, flimsy, foolish, frivolous, idle, ignorant, meaningless, puerile, simple, skin-deep, slight, superficial, surface, trivial, unintelligent

sham *n* counterfeit, feint, forgery, fraud, hoax, humbug, imitation, impostor, imposture, pretence, pretender, wolf in sheeps clothing; (*Inf*) phoney, pseudo

sham *adj* artificial, bogus, counterfeit, ersatz, false, feigned, imitation, mock, pretended, simulated, spuri - ous synthetic; (*Inf*) phoney, pseudo

sham *v* affect, assume, counterfeit, fake, feign, imitate, play possum, pretend, put on, simulate

shame *n* blot, contempt, degradation, derision, discredit, disgrace, dishonour, disrepute, ill repute, infamy, obloquy odium, opprobrium, reproach, scandal, skeleton in the cupboard, smear; abashment, chagrin, compunction, embarrassment, humiliation, humiliate, ignominy, loss of face, mortification, shamefacedness

shame *v* abash, confound, disconcert, disgrace, embarrass, humble, humiliate, mortify, reproach, ridicule; blot, debase, defile, degrade, discredit, dishonour, smear, stain

shameful *adj* atrocious, base, dastardly, degrading, disgraceful, dishonourable, ignominious, indecent, infamous, low, mean, outrageous, reprehensible, scandalous, unbecoming, unworthy, vile, wicked; degrading, embarrassing, humiliating, mortifying, shaming; (*Inf*) blush-making

shameless *adj* abandoned, audacious, barefaced, brash, brazen, corrupt, depraved, dissolute, flagrant, hardened, immodest, improper, impudent, incorrigible, indecent, insolent, profligate, reprobate, unabashed, unashamed, unblushing, unprincipled, wanton

shape *n* build, configuration, contours, cut, figure, form, lines, make, outline, profile, silhouette; frame, model, mould, pattern; appearance, aspect, form, guise, likeness, semblance; condition, fettle, health, kilter, state, trim

shape *v* create, fashion, form, make, model, mould, produce; accommodate, adapt, define, develop, devise, frame, guide, modify, plan, prepare, regulate, remodel

share *v* apportion, assign, deal out, distribute, divide, dole out, go halves in, parcel out, par take, participate, receive, split, use in common; (*Inf*) go Dutch, go fifty-fifty

share *n* allotment, allowance, contribution, division, due, lot, part, portion, proportion, quota, ration; (*Inf*) cut, whack

sharp *adj* acute, cutting, honed, jagged, keen, knife-edged, knifelike, pointed, razor-sharp, serrated, sharpened, spiky; abrupt, distinct, extreme, marked, sudden; alert, apt, astute, bright, clever, discerning, knowing, long-headed, observant, penetrating, perceptive, quick, quick-witted, ready, subtle; acute, distressing, excruciating, fierce, intense, painful, piercing, severe, shooting, sore, stabbing, stinging, violent; clear, clear-cut, crisp, distinct, well-defined; acrimonious, barbed, biting, bitter, caustic, cutting, harsh, hurtful, sarcastic, sardonic, scathing, severe, trenchant, vitriolic; acerbic, acid, acrid, burning, hot, piquant, pungent, sour, tart, vinegary

sharp *adv* exactly, on the dot, on time, precisely, promptly, punctually

sharpen *v* edge, grind, hone, put an edge on, strop, whet

shatter *v* break, burst, crack, crush, crush to smithereens, demolish, explode, implode, pulverize, shiver, smash, split; blast, blight, bring to nought, demolish, destroy, disable, exhaust, impair, overturn, ruin, torpedo, wreck; break someone's heart, crush, devastate, dumbfound, upset; (*Inf*) knock the stuffing out of someone

shave *v* crop, cut off, mow, pare; slice; graze, skim, touch

sheen *n* brightness, gloss, glossiness, shine, splendour

sheepish *adj* bashful, diffident, overmodest, shamefaced, timid, timorous

sheer *adj* abrupt, perpendicular, precipitous, steep; absolute, arrant, complete, downright, out-and-out, pure, rank, thoroughgoing, total, unadulterated, unalloyed, unmitigated, unqualified, utter

sheet *n* coat, film, folio, lamina, layer, leaf, membrane, overlay, pane, panel, piece, plate, slab, stratum, surface, veneer; area, blanket, covering, expanse, stretch, sweep

shell *n* carapace, case, husk, pod; chassis, frame, framework, hull, skeleton, structure

shell *v* husk, shuck; attack, barrage, blitz, bomb, bombard, strafe, strike

shelter *v* cover, defend, guard, harbour, hide, protect, safeguard, seek refuge, shield, take in, take shelter

shelter *n* asylum, cover, covert, defence, guard, haven, protection, refuge, retreat, roof over one's head, safety, sanctuary, screen, security, umbrella

sheltered *adj* cloistered, conventual, ensconced, hermetic, isolated, protected, quiet, reclusive, retired, screened, secluded, shaded, shielded, withdrawn

shelve *v* defer, dismiss, freeze, hold in abeyance, hold over, lay aside, mothball, pigeonhole, postpone, put aside, put off, put on ice, suspend, table

shield *n* buckler; escutcheon; targe; aegis, bulwark, cover, defence, guard, protection, rampart, safe guard, screen, shelter, support, ward

shield *v* cover, defend, guard, protect, safeguard, screen, shelter

shift *v* alter, budge, change, displace, fluctuate, move, move around, rearrange, relocate, remove, reposition, swerve, switch, transfer, transpose, vary, veer

shift *n* about-turn, alteration, change, displacement, fluctuation, modification, move, permutation, rearrangement, removal, shifting, switch, transfer, veering; artifice, contrivance, craft, device, dodge, equivocation, evasion, expedient, move, resource, ruse, strategy, subterfuge, trick, wile

shiftless *adj* improvident, imprudent, negligent, slack, thriftless, unresourceful

shifty *adj* crafty, deceitful, devious,

dishonest, duplicitious, evasive, scheming, sly, tricky, undependable, underhand, wily
shimmer *v* dance, gleam, glisten, phosphoresce, scintillate, twinkle
shine *v* beam, emit light, flash, give off light, glare, gleam, glimmer, glisten, glitter, glow, radiate, scintil late, shimmer, sparkle, twinkle; be conspicuous, be distinguished, be outstanding, excel, stand out, stand out in the crowd, star
shine *n* brightness, glare, gleam, lambency, light, luminosity, radiance, shimmer, sparkle
shining *adj* beaming, bright, bril liant, effulgent, gleaming, glisten ing, glittering, luminous, radiant, resplendent, shimmering, sparkling; brilliant, celebrated, conspicuous, distinguished, eminent, glorious, illustrious, leading, outstanding, splendid
shipshape *adj* neat, orderly, tidy, trim, well-arranged
shirk avoid, dodge, evade, get out of, shun, sidestep, slack; (*Inf*) duck out of, skive
shiver *v* break, shatter, splinter
shiver *n* bit, fragment, piece, slice, sliver, splinter
shiver *v* quake, quiver, shake, shudder, tremble
shiver *n* shaking, shivering, shuddering, tremor
shock *v* agitate, appal, astound, disgust, disquiet, horrify, jar, jolt, nauseate, numb, offend, outrage, paralyse, revolt, scandalize, shake, shake out of one's complacency, sicken, stagger, stun, stupefy, tramatize, unsettle; (*Inf*) give someone a fright, shake up
shock *n* blow, bolt from the blue, bombshell, breakdown, collapse, consternation, distress, disturbance, prostration, state of shock, stupefaction, stupor, trauma, upset; (*Inf*) turn
shocking *adj* abominable, appaling, atrocious, detestable, disgraceful, disgusting, disquieting, distressing, dreadful, foul, frightful, ghastly, hideous, horrible, horrifying, loathsome, monstrous, nauseating, odious, offensive, outrageous, repulsive, revolting, scandalous, sickening, stupefying, unspeakable
shoddy *adj* inferior, junky, poor, rubbishy, second-rate, slipshod, tatty, tawdry, trashy; (*Inf*) cheapskate, cheapo, tacky
shoot *v* bag, bring down, hit, kill, open fire, pick off, zap; (*Inf*) blast; plug, punpfull of lead; discharge, emit, fire, fling, hurl, launch, let fly, project, propel; bolt, charge, dart, dash, flash, fly, hurtle, race, rush, scoot, speed, spring, streak, tear, whisk
shoot *n* branch, bud, offshoot, scion, slip, sprig, sprout, twig
shoot *v* bud, burgeon, germinate, put forth new growth, sprout
shore *n* beach, coast, foreshore, lakeside, sands, seaboard, seashore, strand, waterside
shore *v* brace, buttress, prop, stay, support
shore *n* beam, brace, buttress, prop, stay, support
short *adj* abridged, brief, compendious, compressed, concise, curtailed, laconic, pithy, sententious,

succinct, summary, terse; diminutive, dumpy, little, low, petite, small, squat, wee; brief, fleeting, momentary, short-lived, short-term; deficient, inadequate, insufficient, lacking, limited, low on, meagre, poor, scant, scanty, scarce, shothanded, slender,slim, sparse, tight, wanting

short *adv* abruptly, by surprise, suddenly, unaware, without warning

shortage *n* dearth, deficiency, deficit, failure, inadequacy, insufficiency, lack, leanness, paucity, poverty, scarcity, shortfall, want

shortcoming *n* defect, drawback, failing, fault, flaw, foible, frailty, imperfection, weakness, weak point

shorten *v* abbreviate, abridge, curtail, cut, cut back, cut down, decrease, diminish, dock, lessen, prune, reduce, trim, truncate, turn up

shot *n* discharge, lob, pot shot, throw; ball, bullet, projectile, slug; marksman, shooter; chance, conjec ture, effort, endeavour, essay, go, guess, opportunity, stab, surmise, try, turn; (*Inf*) attempt, crack; **have a shot** (*Inf*) have a bash, have a crack, have a stab, tackle, try, try one's luck; **like a shot** at once, eagerly, immediately, like a flash, quickly, unhesitatingly

shoulder *v* accept, assume, bear, be responsible for, carry, take on, take upon oneself; elbow, jostle, press, push, shove, thrust

shout *n* bellow, call, cry, roar, scream, yell

shout *v* bawl, bay, bellow, call out, cry out, raise one's voice, roar, scream, yell

shove *v* crowd, drive, elbow, impel, jostle, press, propel, push, shoulder, thrust

show *v* appear, be visible, disclose, display, divulge, evidence, evince, exhibit, indicate, make known, manifest, present, register, reveal, testify to; assert, clarify, demonstrate, elucidate, evince, explain, instruct, point out, present, prove, teach; accompany, attend, conduct, escort, guide, lead

show *n* array, demonstrate, display, exhibition, exposition, fair, manifestation, pageant, pageantry, parade, representation, sight, spectacle, view; affectation, air, appearance, display, illusion, likeness, ostentation, parade, pose, pretence, pretext, profession, semblance

showdown *n* breaking point, clash, climax, confrontation, crisis, culmination, face-off, moment of truth

shower *n* barrage, deluge, fusillade, plethora, rain, stream, torrent, volley

shower *v* deluge, heap, inundate, lavish, load, pour, rain, spray, sprinkle

show-off *n* advertise, demonstrate, display, exhibit, flaunt, parade, spread out; boast, brag, make a spectacle of oneself, swagger

show up *v* expose, highlight, lay bare, pinpoint, put the spotlight on, reveal, unmask; appear, be conspicuous, be visible, catch the eye, stand out; embarrass, let down, mortify, put to shame, shame, show in a bad light; appear, arrive, come, make an appearance, put in an appearance, turn up

showy *adj* bedizened, dressy, fine, flashy, flaunting, garish, gaudy, glaring, gorgeous, loud, ornate, smart, swanky, splendid, grand, magnificent, ostentatious, pompous, pretentious, stately, sumptuous

shred *v* cut up, rip, tear up

shred *n* bit, fragment, piece, rag, scrap, strip, tatter

shrewd *adj* acute, artful, astute, calculated, calculating, canny, clever, crafty, cunning, discerning, discriminating, far-seeing, far-sighted, intelligent, keen, knowing, long-headed, perceptive, perspicacious, sagacious, sharp, sly, smart, wily; (*Inf*) fly

shriek *v* scream, screech, squeal, yell, yelp

shriek *n* cry, scream, screech, yell

shrill *adj* acute, ear-piercing, ear-splitting, high, high-pitched, penetrating, piercing, piping, screeching, sharp

shrink *v* contract, decrease, deflate, diminish, drop off, dwindle, fall off, grow smaller, lessen, narrow, shorten, shrivel, wither, wrinkle; cower, cringe, draw back, flinch, hang back, quail, recoil, retire. shy away, wince, withdraw

shrivel *v* burn, dry up, parch, scorch, sear; dehydrate, desiccate, dwindle, shrink, wilt, wither, wizen, wrinkle

shroud *v* bury, cloak, conceal, hide, mask, muffle, protect, screen, shelter, veil

shroud *n* covering, garment; grave clothes, winding sheet

shudder *v* convulse, quake, quiver, shake, shiver, tremble

shudder *n* convulsion, quiver, spasm, trembling, tremor

shuffle *v* drag, scrape, scuff, scuffle, shamble; confuse, disarrange, disorder, intermix, jumble, mix, rearrange, shift

shun *n* avoid, cold-shoulder, elude, eschew, evade, fight shy of, give someone a wide berth, have no part in, keep away from, shy away from, steer clear of

shut *v* bar, close, draw to, fasten, push to, seal, secure, slam

shut out *v* bar, debar, exclude, keep out, lock out, ostracize

shut up *v* bottle up, box in, cage, confine, coop up, immure, imprison, incarcerate, intern, keep in; fall silent, gag, hold one's tongue, hush, muzzle, silence; (*Inf*) be quiet, keep one's trap shut, pipe down

shy *adj* backward, bashful, cautious, chary, coy, diffident, distrustful, hesitant, modest, mousy, nervous, reserved, reticent, retiring, self-conscious, self-effacing, shrinking, suspicious, timid, wary

sick *adj* ill, nauseated, nauseous, qualmish, queasy; (*Inf*) green around the gills, puke, throw up; ailing, diseased, feeble, indisposed, under par, unwell, weak; (*Inf*) laid up, on the sick list, poorly, under the weather; black, cruel, ghoulish, gruesome, macabre, morbid, perverted, sadistic

sicken *v* disgust, nauseate, revolt, shock; become ill with, contract; (*Inf*) come down with; become bored with, feel jaded, tire, weary; (*Inf*) be fed up with

sickly *adj* ailing, bilious, bloodless,

delicate, faint, feeble, indisposed, infirm, in poor health, lacklustre, languid, pallid, peaky, pining, unhealthy, wan, weak; cloying, mawkish, nauseating, slushy, syrupy; (*Inf*) schmaltzy, soppy

sickness *n* affliction, ailment, complaint, disease, disorder, illness, indisposition, infirmity, malady; (*Inf*) bug; nausea, queasiness, retching, vomiting; (*Inf*) puking, throwing up

side *n* border, boundary, division, edge, limit, margin, part, perimeter, periphery, rim, sector, verge; aspect, face, facet, flank, hand, part, surface, view; angle, light, opinion, point of view, position, slant, stand, standpoint, viewpoint; camp, cause, faction, party, sect, team; airs, arrogance, insolence, pretentiousness; (*Inf*) snootiness

side *adj* flanking, lateral; ancillary, incidental, indirect, lesser, marginal, minor, oblique, roundabout, secondary, subordinate, subsidiary

sidetrack *v* deflect, distract, divert, lead off the subject

sideways *adv* crabwise, edgeways, laterally, obliquely, sidelong, sidewards, to the side

sideways *adj* oblique, side, side long, slanted

siege *n* beleaguerment, blockade, investment

sift *v* bolt, filter, pan, part, riddle, separate, sieve; analyse, examine, fathom, go through, investigate, pore over, probe, screen, scrutinize

sigh *v* breathe out, complain, exhale, grieve, lament, mourn; rustle, whisper; long for, mourn for, pine for, weep for, yearn for

sight *n* eye, eyes, eyesight, seeing, vision; appearance, apprehension, eyeshot, field of vision, ken, perception, range, of vision, view, viewing, visibility; display, exhibition, pageant, scene, show, spectacle, vista; catch sight of descry, espy, glimpse, recognize, spot, view

sight *v* behold, discern, distinguish, make out, observe, perceive, see, spot

sign *n* clue, evidence, gesture, giveaway, hint, indication, manifestation, mark, note, proof, signal, spoor, suggestion, symptom, token, trace, vestige; board, notice, placard, warning; badge, character, cipher, device, emblem, ensign, figure, logo, mark, representation, symbol; augury, auspice, foreboding, forewarning, omen, portent, presage, warning, writing on the wall

sign *v* autograph, endorse, initial, inscribe, set one's hand to, subscribe; beckon, gesticulate, gesture, indicate, signal, use sign language, wave

signal *n* beacon, cue, flare, gesture, green light, indication, indicator, mark, sign, token; (*Inf*) go ahead

signal *v* beckon, communicate, gesticulate, gesture, give a sign to, indicate, motion, nod, sign, wave

significance *n* force, implications, import, meaning, message, point, purport, sense, signification; consequence, consideration, importance, impressiveness, matter, moment, relevance, weight

significant *adj* denoting, eloquent, expressing, expressive, indicative, knowing, meaning, meaningful, pregnant, suggestive; critical, important, material, momentous, noteworthy, serious, vital, weighty

signify *v* betoken, communication, express, indicate, intimate; denote, imply, import, mean, purport, suggest; announce, declare, give notice of, impart, make known, manifest, proclaim, utter; augur, foreshadow, indicate, portend, represent, suggest; import, matter, weigh

silence *n* calm, hush, lull, noiselessness, peace, stillness; dumbness, muteness, reticence, speechlessness, taciturnity, uncommunicativeness

silence *v* cut off, cut short, deaden, extinguish, gag, muffle, quell, quiet, quieten, stifle, still, strike dumb, subdue, suppress

silent *adj* hushed, mute, noiseless, quiet, soundless, still; dumb, mum, mute, nonvocal, not talkative, speechless, taciturn, tongue-tied, uncommunicative, unspeaking, voiceless, wordless; (*Inf*) struck dumb; aphonic, implicit, implied, tacit, understood, unexpressed, unpronounced, unspoken

silhouette *n* delineation, form, outline, profile, shape

silhouette *v* delineate, etch, outline, stand out

silly *adj* absurd, asinine, brainless, childish, fatuous, foolhardy, foolish, frivolous, giddy, idiotic, immature, imprudent, inane, inappropriate, irresponsible, meaningless, pointless, preposterous, puerile, ridiculous, senseless, stupid, unwise; (*Inf*) dopy, dozy; benumbed, dazed, groggy, in a daze, muzzy, stunned, stupefied

similar *adj* alike, analogous, close, comparable, congruous, corresponding, homogeneous, in agreement, much the same, resembling, uniform

similarity *n* affinity, agreement, analogy, closeness, comparability, concordance, congruence, corre spondence, likeness, point of comparison, relation, resemblance, sameness, similitude

simmer *v* boil, bubble, seethe, stew

simple *adj* clear, easy, elementary, intelligible, lucid, manageable, plain, straightforward, uncomplicated, understandable, uninvolved; classic, clean, natural, plain, spartan, unadorned, uncluttered, unembellished, unfussy; elementary, pure, single, unalloyed, unblended, uncombined, undivided, unmixed; artless, childlike, frank, green, guileless, ingenuous, innocent, naive, natural, simplistic, sincere, unaffected, unpretentious, unsophisticated; bald, basic, direct, frank, honest, naked, plain, sincere, stark, undeniable, unvarnished; homely, humble, lowly, modest, rustic, unpretentious; brainless, credulous, dense, feeble, feeble-minded, foolish, half-witted, moronic, obtuse, shallow, silly, slow, stupid, think; (*Inf*) dumb

simplicity *n* absence of complications, clarity, clearness, ease, easiness, elementariness, obviousness, straightforwardness; clean lines, lack of adornment, modesty, naturalness, plainness, purity, restraint; artlessness, candour, directness, guilelessness, innocence, lack of sophistication, naivety, openness

simplify *v* abridge, decipher, disentangle, facilitate, make intelligible, reduce to essentials, streamline

simultaneous *adj* coeval, coincident, concomitant, concurrent, contemporaneous, synchronous

sin *n* crime, damnation, error, evil, guilt, iniquity, misdeed, offence, sinfulness, transgression, trespass, ungodliness, unrighteousness, wickedness, wrong, wrongdoing

sin *v* err, fall, fall from grace, go astray, lapse, offend, transgress,

since *conj* as, because, considering, seeing that

since *adv* ago, before this; from that time

since *prep* after, from the time of, subsequently to

sincere *adj* artless, *bona fide*, candid, earnest, frank, genuine, guileless, heartfelt, honest, natural, no-nonsense, open, real, serious, straightforward, true, unaffected, unfeigned, wholehearted

sincerity *n* artlessness, candour, frankness, genuineness, good faith, guilelessness, honesty, probity, seriousness, straightforwardness, truth, wholeheartedness

sinful *adj* bad, corrupt, criminal depraved, erring, guilty, immoral, iniquitous, irreligious, morally wrong, ungodly, unholy, unrighteous, wicked

sing *v* carol, chant, chirp, croon, make melody, pipe, trill, vocalize

singe *v* burn, scorch, sear yodel

single *adj* distinct, individual, lone, one, only, particular, seperate, singular, sole, solitary, unique; free, unattached, unmarried, unwed; exclusive, individual, separate, simple, unblended, uncompounded, undivided, unmixed, unshared

single-minded *adj* dedicated, determined, dogged, fixed, monomaniacal, steadfast, stubborn, tireless, undeviating, unswerving, unwavering; (*Inf*) hellbent

singular *adj* conspicuous, eminent, exceptional, noteworthy, outstanding, prodigious, rare, remarkable, uncommon, unique, unparalleled; atypical, curious, eccentric, extraordinary, odd, out-of-the-way, peculiar, puzzling, queer, strange, unusual; individual, separate, single, sole

sinister *adj* dire, disquieting, evil, injurious, malevolent, malign, malignant, menacing, ominous, threatening

sink *v* cave in, decline, descend, dip, disappear, droop, drop, drown, ebb, engulf, fall, founder, go down, go under, lower, merge, plummet, plunge, sag, slope, submerge, subside; abate, collapse, retrogress, slip, slump, subside; decay, decline, decrease, degenerate, depreciate, deteriorate, die, diminish, dwindle, fade, fail, flag, lessen, weaken, worsen; bore, dig, drill, drive, excavate, lay, put down; be in the ruin of, defeat, destroy, finish, over whelm, ruin, seal the doom of; (*Inf*) go downhill, scupper; be reduced to, debase oneself, lower oneself, stoop, succumb

sinless *adj* faultless, guiltless, immaculate, impeccable, innocent, spotless, unblemished, undefiled, unspotted, unsullied, untarnished

sinner *n* criminal, delinquent, evildoer, offender, reprobate, wrongdoer

sip *v* sample, sup, taste

sip *n* drop, swallow, taste, thimbleful

sire *v* father, reproduce, author, breed, conceive, create, father, generate, originate, produce, propagate

sire *n* father, male parent, progenitor; man, male person; sir, sirrah; author, begetter, creator, father, generator, originator

sit *v* be seated, perch, rest, settle, take a seat, take the weight off one's feet; assemble, be in session, convene, deliberate, meet, officiate, preside

site *n* ground, location, place, plot, position, setting, spot

site *v* install, locate, place, position, set, situate

situation *n* environment, locale, locality, location, place, position, seat, setting, site; case, circumstances, condition, plight, scenario, state of affairs, status quo; (*Inf*) ball game, kettle of fish; rank, sphere, station, status; employment, job, office, place, position, post

size *n* amount, bigness, bulk, dimensions, extent, greatness, hugeness, immensity, largeness, magnitude, mass, measurements, proportions, range, vastness, volume

size *v* categorize, classify, sort; **size up** appraise, assess, estimate, evaluate, gauge, judge, rate

sketch *v* block out, delineate, depict, draft, draw, outline, paint, plot, portray, represent, rough out;

sketch *n* delineation, design, draft, drawing, outline, plan, skeleton

sketchy *adj* bitty, cobbled together, crude, cursory, inadequate, incomplete, outline, perfunctory, rough, scrappy, skimpy, slight, superficial, unfinished, vague

skilful *adj* able, accomplished, adept, droit, apt, clever, competent, dexterous, experienced, expert, handy, masterly, practised, professional, proficient, quick, ready, skilled, trained

skill *n* ability, accomplishment, adroitness, aptitude, art, cleverness, competence, dexterity, experience, expertise, expertness, facility, finesse, handiness, knack, proficiency, quickness, readiness, skillfulness, talent, technique

skilled *adj* able, accomplished, experienced, expert, masterly, practised, professional, proficient, skillful, trained; (*Inf*) a dab hand at

skim *v* brush, glance, graze, kiss, scrape, scratch, sweep, touch lightly; coast, flow, fly, glide, sail, scud, whisk; dip into, glance at, scan, skip, thumb over, touch upon

skin *n* fell, hide, integument, pelt, tegument; casing, coating, crust, film, husk, membrane, outside, peel, rind

skinny *adj* emaciated, lean, scraggy,

skeletal, thin, thin as a rake, twiggy, undernourished; (*Inf*) skin and bone

skip *v* bob, bounce, caper, cavort, dance, flit, frisk, gambol, hop, prance, trip; eschew, give something a miss, leave out, miss out, omit, pass over, skim over

skirmish *n* affair, affray, battle, brush, clash, combat, conflict, encounter, engagement, fracas, incident, scrimmage, spat, tussle; (*Inf*) dust up, scrap, set-to

skirmish *v* clash, collide, come to blows, tussle; (*Inf*) scrap

skirt *v* border, edge, flank, lie alongside

slack *adj* baggy, easy, flaccid, flexible, lax, limp, loose, not taut, relaxed; easy-going, idle, inactive, inattentive, lax, lazy, neglectful, negligent, permissive, remiss, tardy; (*Inf*) asleep on the job; dull, inactive, quiet, slow, slow-moving, sluggish

slack *n* excess, leeway, looseness, play, room; (*Inf*) give

slack *v* dodge, flag, idle, neglect, relax, shirk, skive, slacken

slacken (off) abate, decrease, diminish, drop off, ease off, lessen, let up, loosen, moderate, reduce, release, slack off, slow down, tire

slacker *n* dawdler, dodger, do-noth ing, good-for-nothing, idler, layabout, loafer, malingerer, passenger, shirker, work-dodger; (*Inf*) skiver

slam *v* bang, rash, dash, fling, hurl, smash, throw, thump

slander *n* aspersion, backbiting, calumny, defamation, detraction, libel, misrepresentation, muckracking, obloquy, scandal, smear

slander *v* backbite, blacken someone's name, calumniate, decry, defame, detract, disparage, libel, malign, muckrake, slur, smear, traduce, vilify

slant *v* angle off, bend, bevel, incline, lean, list, shelve, skew, slope, tilt; angle, bias, colour, dis tort, twist, weight

slant *n* camber, declination, diagonal, gradient, incline, pitch, rake, ramp, slope, tilt; angle, attitude, bias, emphasis, leaning, one-sidedness, point of view, prejudice, viewpoint

slanting *adj* angled, aslant, asymmetrical, at an angle, bent, canted, diagonal, inclined, oblique, on the bias, sideways, slanted, slantwise, sloping, tilted, tilting

slap *n* bang, blow, cuff, punch, smack, spank; (*Inf*) belt, clip, clout, swipe, wallop

slap *v* bang, blow, cuff, punch, smack, spank; (*Inf*) belt, clip, clout, sock, swipe, wallop; bang, fling, hurl, plonk, slam, throw, toss; daub, plaster, spread; add, append, put on, tack on

slap *adv* directly, headlong, plumb, right, straight, suddenly; (*Inf*) slap-bang

slapdash *adj* careless, clumsy, disorderly, haphazard, hasty, hurried, last-minute, messy, negligent, perfunctory, slipshod, slovenly, thoughtless, thrown-together, untidy; (*Inf*) sloppy

slash *v* cut, gash, hack, lacerate, rend rip, score, slit

slash *n* cut, gash, incision, laceration, rent, rip, slit

slate *v* berate, blame, castigate, censure, criticize, lambaste, pitch into, rail against, rebuke, scold, slang, take to task; (*Inf*) haul over the coals, lay into, pan, rap some one's knuckles, roast, slam, tear someone off a strip

slaughter *n* blood bath, bloodshed, butchery, carnage, extermination, holocaust, killing, liquidation, massacre, murder, slaying

slaughter *v* butcher, destroy, do to death, exterminate, kill, liquidate, massacre, murder, put to the sword, slay

slave *n* bondservant, bondsman, drudge, serf, servant, vassal; scullion; (*Inf*) skivvy

slave *v* drudge, grind, labour, slog, sweat, toil, work one's fingers to the bone, work like a Trojan; (*Inf*) skivvy

slavery *n* bondage, captivity, enslavement, serfdom, servitude, subjugation, thraldom, thrall, vassalage

sleep *v* be in the land of Nod, catnap, doze, drowse, hibernate, rest in the arms of Morpheus, slumber, snore, take a nap; (*Inf*) drop off, nod of, snooze, take forty winks

sleep *n* dormancy, doze, hibernation, nap, repose, rest, siesta, slumber; (*Inf*) beauty sleep, forty winks, shuteye, snooze

sleepless *adj* disturbed, insomniac, restless, unsleeping, wakeful

sleepy *adj* drowsy, dull, heavy, inactive, lethargic, sluggish, slumbersome, somnolent, torpid; dull, hypnotic, inactive, quiet, sleep-inducing, slow, slumberous, somnolent, soporific

slender *adj* lean, narrow, slight, slim, svelte, sylphlike, willowy; inadequate, inconsiderable, insufficient, little, meagre, scanty, small, spare; faint, feeble, flimsy, fragile, poor, remote, slight, slim, tenuous, thin, weak

slice *n* cut, helping, piece, portion, segment, share, sliver, wedge

slice *v* carve, cut, divide, sever

slick *adj* glib, meretricious, plausible, polished, smooth, sophistical, specious; adroit, deft, dexterous, polished, professional, sharp, skilful

slide *v* coast, glide, glissade, skim, slip, slither, toboggan, veer

slight *adj* feeble, inconsiderable, insignificant, insubstantial, meagre, minor, modest, negligible, paltry, scanty, small, superficial, trifling, trivial, unimportant, weak; delicate, feeble, fragile, lightly-built, slim, small, spare

slight *v* affront, cold-shoulder, despise, disdain, give offence to, ignore, insult, neglect, scorn, show disrespect for, snub, treat with contempt

slight *n* affront, cold shoulder, contempt, discourtesy, disdain, disregard, disrespect, inattention, indifference, insult, neglect, rebuff, snub; (*Inf*) slap in the face

slightly *adv* a little, marginally, on a small scale, somewhat, to some extent

slim *adj* lean, narrow, slender, slight

slim *v* diet, go on a diet, lose

pounds, lose weight, reduce, shed weight, slenderize

slimy *adj* clammy, glutinous, miry, mucous, muddy, oozy, vicious; creeping, grovelling, obsequious, oily, servile, soapy, sycophantic, toadying, unctuous; (*Inf*) smarmy

slip *v* glide, skate, slide, slither; fall, lose one's balance, lose one's foot ing, skid, trip over; conceal, creep, hide, insinuate oneself, sneak, steal; **slip up** blunder, err, go wrong, made a mistake, miscalculate, misjudge, mistake; (*Inf*) boob

slip *n* error, failure, fault, faux pas, imprudence, indiscretion, mistake, omission, oversight, slip of the tongue; (*Inf*) bloomer, slip-up

slippery *adj* glassy, greasy, icy, perilous, smooth, unsafe, unstable, unsteady; (*Inf*) skiddy, slippy; crafty, cunning, devious, dishonest, duplicitous, evasive, false, foxy, shifty, sneaky, treacherous, tricky, two-faced, unpredictable, unreliable, untrustworthy

slit *v* cut open, gash, knife, lance, pierce, rip, slash, split open

slit *n* cut, fissure, gash, incision, opening, rent, split, tear

sliver *n* chip, flake, fragment, scrap, shred, splinter

slogan *n* catch-phrase, catchword, jingle, logo, motto, rallying cry

slope *v* drop away, fall, incline, lean, pitch, rise, slant, tilt

slope *n* declination, declivity, descent, gradient, inclination, incline, ramp, rise, scarp, slant, tilt

sloppy *adj* sludgy, slushy, splashy, watery, wet; careless, clumsy, inattentive, messy, slipshod, slovenly, unkempt, untidy, weak; (*Inf*) amateurish, hit-or-miss

slot *n* aperture, channel, crack, groove, hole, notch, slit; niche, opening, period, place, position, space, time, vacancy

slovenly *adj* careless, disorderly, heedless, loose, negligent, slack, slapdash, slatternly, slipshod, unkempt, untidy; (*Inf*) sloppy

slow *adj* creeping, dawdling, deliberate, easy, lackadaisical, laggard, lagging, lazy, leaden, leisurely, loitering, measured, plodding, ponderous, slow-moving, sluggardly, sluggish, snail-like, tortoise-like, unhurriedly; backward, behindhand, delayed, dilatory, late, long-delayed, tardy, unpunctual; gradual, lingering, long-drawn-out, prolonged, protracted, time-consuming; behind the times, boring, conservative, dead, dull, inactive, quiet, slack, sleepy, sluggish, stagnant, tame, tedious, uneventful, uninteresting, unproductive, unprogressive, wearisome; (*Inf*) dead-and-alive, one-horse; blockish, bovine, dense, dim, dull, dull-witted, obtuse, retarded, slow-witted, stupid, thick, unresponsive; (*Inf*) dopey, dumb

slowly *adv* at a snail's pace, at one's leisure, by degrees, gradually, in one's own good time, leisurely, ploddingly, steadily, taking one's time, unhurriedly, with leaden steps

sluggish *adj* dull, heavy, inactive, indolent, inert, lethargic, lifeless, listless, phlegmatic, slothful, slow, slow-moving, torpid, unresponsive

slump *v* collapse, crash, decline, deteriorate, fall, fall off, plummet, plunge, reach a new low, sink, slip; *(Inf)* go downhill

slump *n* collapse, crash, decline, depreciation, depression, downturn, failure, fall off, falling-off, low, recession, reverse, stagnation, trough

slur *n* affront, aspersion, blot, brand, calumny, discredit, disgrace, innuendo, insinuation, insult, reproach, smear, stain, stigma

sly *adj* artful, astute, clever, conniving, covert, crafty, cunning, devious, foxy, furtive, guileful, insidious, scheming, secret, shifty, stealthy, subtle, underhand, wily

sly *n* on the sly, behind someone's back, covertly, on the quiet, privately, secretly, surreptitiously, underhandedly; (*Inf*) on the q.t, under the counter

small *adj* diminutive, immature, Lilliputian, little, mini, miniature, minute, minuscule, petite, pocket-sized, puny, slight, teeny, teensy-weensy, tiny, under-sized, wee, young; (*Inf*) pint-sized; insignificant, lesser, minor, negligible, paltry, petty, slight, trifling, trivial, unimportant; inadequate, inconsiderable, insufficient, limited, meagre, scanty; humble, modest, small-scale, unpretentious; base, grudging, illiberal, mean, narrow, petty, selfish

small-minded *adj* bigoted, envious, grudging, hidebound, intolerant, mean, narrow-minded, petty, rigid, ungenerous

smart *adj* acute, adept, agile, apt, astute, bright, brisk, canny, clever, ingenious, intelligent, keen, nimble, quick, quick-witted, ready, sharp, shrewd; chic, elegant, fashionable, fine, modish, neat, snappy, spruce, stylish, trim, well turned-out; (*Inf*) natty, trendy; effective, impertinent, nimble-witted, pointed, ready, saucy, witty; (*Inf*) smart-aleck

smart *v* burn, hurt, pain, sting, throb, tingle

smash *v* break, collide, crash, crush, demolish, disintegrate, pulverize, shatter, shiver; defeat, destroy, lay waste, overthrow, ruin, wreck

smash *n* accident, collision, crash, (*Inf*) pile-up, smash-up; collapse, defeat, destruction, disaster, downfall, failure, ruin, shattering; blot, blotch, daub, smudge, splotch, streak; calumny, defamation, libel, mudslinging, slander, vilification, whispering campaign

smear *v* bedaub, bedim, besmirch, blur, coat, cover, daub, dirty, patch, plaster, rub on, smudge, soil, spread over, stain, sully; asperse, blacken, calumniate, malign, tarnish, traduce, vilify; (*Inf*) drag someone's name through the mud

smell *v* aroma, bouquet, fragrance, odour, perfume, redolence, scent, whiff

smell *n* get a whiff of, nose, scent, sniff; be malodorous, reek, stink; (*Inf*) hum, niff, pong, stink to high heaven, whiff

smooth *adj* even, flat, flush, horizontal, level, plain, plane, unwrinkled; glossy, polished, shiny, silky, sleek, soft, velvety; calm, equable, glassy, mirror-like, peace ful, serene, tranquil, undisturbed, unruffled; agreeable, bland, mellow, mild, pleasant, soothing; facile, glib, ingratiating, persuasive, silky, slick, suave, unctuous, urbane; (*Inf*) smarmy; easy, effortless, flowing, fluent, frictionless, regular, rhythmic, steady, unbroken, uneventful, uniform, uninterrupted, untroubled, well-ordered

smooth *v* flatten, iron, level, plane, polish, press; allay, alleviate, appease, assuage, calm, ease, extenuate, facilitate, iron out the difficulties of, mitigate, mollify, palliate, pave the way, soften

smother *v* choke, extinguish, snuff, stifle, strangle, suffocate; conceal, hide, keep back, muffle, repress, stifle, suppress

smug *adj* complacent, conceited, holier-than-thou, priggish, self-opinionated, self-righteous, self-satisfied, superior

smuggler *n* bootlegger, contraban dist, gentleman, moonshiner, rum-runner, runner, trafficker, wrecker

snack *n* bite, bite to eat, break, elevenses, light meal, little some thing, nibble, refreshments, titbit

snack *v* munch, nibble; (*Inf*) graze

snap *v* break, come apart, crack, give way, separate; bite, bite at, catch, grip, nip, seize, snatch; bark, flare out, flash, growl, lash out at, retort, snarl, speak sharply; (*Inf*) fly off the handle at, jump down some one's throat; click, crackle, pop

snap *adj* abrupt, immediate, instant, on-the-spot, sudden, unpremeditated

snappy *adj* cross, crotchety, grouchy, grumpy, irritable, touchy; chic, fashionable, smart, stylish; (*Inf*) natty, trendy; hurry up, look lively; (*Inf*) get a move on, get one's skates on, move it, step on it

snare *v* catch, entrap, net, seize, springe, trap, wire; capture, ensnare

snare *n* catch, gin, net, noose, pitfall, springe, trap, wire

snatch *v* clutch, gain, grab, grasp, grip, make off with, pluck, pull, rescue, seize, take, win, wrench, wrest

snatch *n* bit, fragment, part, piece, smattering, snippet, spell

sneak *v* cower, lurk, paid, sidle, skulk, slink, slip, smuggle, spirit, steal; inform on, tell tales

sneak *n* informer, snake in the grass, telltale; (*Inf*) grass on, peach, tell on

sneaking *adj* hidden, private, secret, suppressed, unavowed, unconfessed, undivulged, unexpressed, unvoiced; intuitive, nagging, niggling, persistent, uncomfortable, worrying

sneer *v* curl one's lip, deride, disdain, gibe, hold in contempt, hold up to ridicule, jeer, laugh, look down on, mock, ridicule, scoff, scorn, sniff at, snigger; (*Inf*) turn one's nose up at

sneer *n* derision, disdain, gibe, jeer, mockery, ridicule, scorn, snidery, snigger

sniff *v* breathe, inhale, smell, snuff, snuffle

snigger *n* giggle, laugh, smirk, sneer, snicker, titter

snip *v* clip, crop, cut, nick, nip off, notch, shave, trim

snip *n* bit, clipping, fragment, piece, scrap, shred, snippet; (*Inf*) bargain, giveaway, good buy

snobbish arrogant, condescending, patronizing, pretentious, superior, uppity; (*Inf*) high and mighty, high-hat, hoity-toity, snooty, stuck-up, toffee-nosed, uppish

snooze *v* catnap, doze, drowse, nap; (*Inf*) drop off, kip, nod off

snooze *n* catnap, doze, nap, siesta; (*Inf*) drop off, forty winks, kip, nod off

snub *v* cold-shoulder, humble, humiliate, mortify, rebuff, shame, slight; (*Inf*) cut dead, give someone the brush-off, give someone the cold shoulder

snub *n* affront, humiliation, insult, put-down, lap in the face; (*Inf*) brushoff

snug *adj* comfortable, comfy, cosy, homely, intimate, sheltered, warm

soak *v* bathe, damp, drench, immerse, infuse, marinate, moisten, penetrate, permeate, saturate, steep, wet

soaking *adj* drenched, dripping, saturated, soaked, soaked to the skin, sodden, sopping, streaming, water logged, wet through, wringing wet

sob *v* bawl, blubber, boohoo, cry, howl, shed tears, snivel, weep

sober *adj* abstemious, abstinent, moderate, temperate; calm, clear-headed cold, composed, cool, dispassionate, grave, level-headed, lucid, peaceful, practical, rational, realistic, reasonable, sedate, serene, serious, solemn, sound, staid, steady, unexcited, unruffled; (*Inf*) on the wagon; dark, drab, plain, quiet, severe, sombre, subdued

sociable *adj* accessible, affable, approachable, companionable, conversable, convivial, cordial, familiar, friendly, genial, gregarious, neighbourly, outgoing, social, warm

social *adj* collective, common, communal, community, general, group, organized, public, societal

social *n* gathering, party; (*Inf*) do, get-together

society *n* civilization, culture, humanity, mankind, people, population, social order, the community, the general public, the public, the world at large; camaraderie, companionship, company, fellowship, friendship; association, brotherhood, circle, club, corporation, fellowship, fraternity, group, guild, institute, league, organization, sisterhood, union; beau monde, elite, gentry, haut monde, high society, polite society, the country set, the smart set, the top drawer, upper classes; (*Inf*) the toffs, upper crust

soft *adj* creamy, cushioned, cushiony, doughy, elastic, gelatinous, pulpy, quaggy, spongy, squashy, swampy, yielding; bendable, ductile, elastic, flexible, impressible, malleable, mouldable, plastic, pliable, supple; downy, feathery, fleecy, flowing, fluid, furry, rounded, silky, smooth, velvety; balmy, bland, caressing, delicate, diffuse, dim, dimmed, dulcet, faint, gentle, light, low, mellifluous, mellow, melodious, mild, murmured, muted, pale, pastel, pleasing, quiet, restful, shaded, soft-toned, soothing, subdued, sweet, temperate, twilight, understated, whispered; compas sionate, gentle, kind, pitying, sensitive, sentimental, sympathetic, tender, tenderhearted; effeminate, flabby, flaccid, limp, namby-pamby, out of condition, out of training, overindulged, pampered, podgy, weak

soften *v* abate, allay, alleviate, appease, assuage, calm, cushion, diminish, ease, lessen, lighten, lower, melt, mitigate, moderate, modify, mollify, muffle, palliate, quell, relax, soothe, still, subdue, temper, tone down, turn down

soil *n* clay, dirt, dust, earth, ground, loam

soil *v* bedraggle, befoul, begrime, besmirch, defile, dirty, foul, muddy, pollute, smear, spatter, spot, stain, sully, tarnish

soldier *n* enlisted man, fighter, GI, man at arms, military man, redcoat, serviceman, squaddy, Tommy trooper, warrior

solemn *adj* earnest, glum, grave, portentous, sedate, serious, sober, staid, thoughtful; august, awe-inspiring, ceremonial, ceremonious, dignified, formal, grand, grave, imposing, impressive, majestic, momentous, stately

solid *adj* compact, concrete, dense, firm, hard, massed, stable, strong, sturdy, substantial, unshakable; genuine, good, pure, real, reliable, sound; constant, decent, dependable, estimable, law-abiding, level-headed, reliable, sensible, serious, sober, trusty, upright, upstanding, worthy

solidarity *n* accord, camaraderie, cohesion, community of interest, concordance, *esprit de corps*, harmony, like-mindedness, singleness of purpose, soundness, stability, team spirit, unanimity, unification, unity

solidify *adj* cake, coagulate, cohere, congeal, harden, jell, set

solitary *adj* concealed, desolate, hidden, isolated, lonely, out-of-the-way, remote, retired, secluded, sequestered, unfrequented, unvisited; alone, lone, single, sole; cloistered, companionless, friendless, hermetical, lonely, lonesome, reclusive, unsociable, unsocial, withdrawn

solitary *n* introvert, hermit, loner, lone wolf, recluse

solitude *n* isolation, loneliness, privacy, reclusiveness, retirement, seclusion

solution *n* answer, clarification, elucidation, explanation, explication, key, resolution, result, solving, unfolding, unravelling; blend, compound, emulsion, mix, mixture, solvent, suspension

solve *v* answer, clarify, clear up, crack, decipher, disentangle, elucidate, explain, expound, get to the bottom of, interpret, resolve, unfold, unravel, work out

sombre *adj* dark, dim, dismal, dole ful, drab, dull, dusky, funereal, gloomy, grave, joyless, lugubrious, melancholy, mournful, obscure, sad, sepulchral, shadowy, shady, sober

somebody *n* celebrity, dignitary, household name, luminary, name, notable, personage, person of note, public figure, star, superstar, VIP;

(*Inf*) big noise, big shot, big wheel, bigwig, celeb, heavyweight

sometimes *adv* at times, every now and then, every so often, from time to time, now and again, now and then, occasionally, off and on, once in a while, on occasion

soon *adv* any minute now, before long, in a little while, in a minute, in a moment, in a short time, in the near future, shortly

soothe *v* allay, alleviate, appease, assuage, calm, calm down compose, ease, hush, lull, mitigate, mollify, pacify, quiet, relieve, settle, smooth down, soften, still, tranquillize

sophisticated *adj* blasé, citified, cosmopolitan, cultivated, cultured, jet-set, refined, seasoned, urbane, worldly, worldly-wise, world-weary; advanced, complex, complicated, delicate, elaborate, highly-developed, intricate, multifaceted, refined, subtle

soporific *adj* hypnotic, sedative, sleep-inducing, sleepy, somniferous, somnolent, tranquillizing

soporific *n* anaesthetic hypnotic, narcotic, opiate, sedative, sleeping pill, tranquillizer

sorcerer *n* enchanter, magician, magus, necromancer, sorceress, witch, wizard

sordid *adj* dirty, filthy, foul, mean, seamy, seedy, sleazy, slovenly, slummy, squalid, unclean, wretched; backstreet, base, debauched, degenerate, degraded, despicable, disreputable, low, shabby, shameful, vicious, vile; avaricious, corrupt, covetous, grasping, mercenary, miserly, niggardly, selfish, self-seeking, ungenerous, venal

sore *adj* angry, burning, chafed, inflamed, irritated, painful, raw, reddened, sensitive, smarting, tender; annoying, distressing, grievous, harrowing, severe, sharp, troublesome; acute, critical, desperate, dire, extreme, pressing, urgent; afflicted, aggrieved, angry, annoyed, grieved, hurt, irked, irritated, pained, resentful, stung, upset, vexed; (*Inf*) peeved

sorrowful *n* affliction, anguish, distress, grief, heartache, heartbreak, misery, mourning, regret, sadness, unhappiness, woe

sorrowful *v* agonize, bemoan, be sad, bewail, grieve, lament, moan, mourn, weep

sorrowful *adj* affecting, afflicted, dejected, depressed, disconsolate, distressing, doleful, grievous, heartbroken, heart-rending, heavy-hearted, lamentable, lugubrious, melancholy, miserable, mournful, painful, piteous, rueful, sad, sick at heart, sorry, tearful, unhappy, woe begone, woeful, wretched

sorry *adj* apologetic, conscience-stricken, contrite, guilt-ridden, in sackcloth and ashes, penitent, regretful, remorseful, repentant, self-reproachable, shamefaced; disconsolate, distressed, grieved, melancholy, mournful, sad, sorrowful, unhappy; commiserative, compassionate, full of pity, moved, pitying, sympathetic; abject, base, deplorable, dismal, distressing, mean, miserable, paltry, pathetic, piteous, pitiable, pitiful, poor, sad, shabby, vile wretched

sort *n* brand, breed, category, character, class, denomination, description, family, genus, group, ilk, kind, make, nature, order, quality, race, species, stamp, style, type, variety

sort *v* arrange, assort, catalogue, categorize, choose, class, classify, distribute, divide, file, grade, group, order, put in order, rank, select, separate, systematize

sort out *v* clarify, clear up, organize, put straight, resolve, tidy up; pick out, put on one side, segregate, select, separate, sift

soul *n* animating, principle, essence, intellect, life, mind, psyche, reason, spirit, vital force; being, body, creature, individual, man, mortal, person, woman; embodiment, essence, incarnation, personification, quintessence, type

sound *n* din, noise, report, resonance, reverberation, tone, voice; drift, idea, implications, impression, look, tenor; earshot, hearing, range

sound *v* echo, resonate, resound, reverberate; appear, give the impression of, look, seem, strike one as being; announce, articulate, declare, enunciate, express, pronounce, signal, utter

sound *adj* complete, entire, firm, fit, hale and hearty, healthy, intact, perfect, robust, solid, sturdy, substantial, undamaged, unhurt, unimpaired, uninjured, vigorous, well-constructed, whole; correct, fair, just, level-headed, logical, orthodox, proper, prudent, rational, reasonable, reliable, responsible, right, right-thinking, sensible, true, trustworthy, valid, well-founded, well-grounded, wise; established, orthodox, proven, recognized, reliable, reputable, safe, secure, solid, stable, tried-and-true; deep, peaceful, unbroken, undisturbed, untroubled

sound *v* fathom, plumb, probe

sour *adj* acetic, acid, acidulated, bitter, pungent, sharp, tart, unpleasant; acrid, acrimonious, churlish, crabbed, cynical, disagreeable, disconnected, embittered, grudging, ill-natured, ill-tempered, jaundiced, peevish, tart, ungenerous

source *n* author, begetter, begin ning, cause, commencement, derivation, fountainhead, origin, originator, rise, spring, wellspring; authority, informant

souvenir *n* keepsake, memento, memorabilia, relic, reminder, token

sovereign *n* chief, emperor, empress. king, monarch, potentate, prince, queen, ruler, shah, supreme ruler, tsar

sovereign *adj* absolute, chief, dominant, imperial, kingly, monarchal, paramount, predominant, principle, queenly, regal, royal, ruling, supreme, unlimited

sow *v* broadcast, disseminate, implant, inseminate, lodge, plant, scatter, seed

space *n* amplitude, capacity, elbowroom, expanse, extension, extent, leeway, margin, play, room, scope, spaciousness, volume; blank, distance, gap, interval, lacuna, omission; duration, interval, period, span, time, while

spacious *adj* ample, broad, capacious, comfortable, commodious, expansive, extensive, huge, large, roomy, sizeable, uncrowded, vast

span *n* amount, distance, extent, length, reach, spread, stretch; duration, period, spell, term

span *v* arch across, bridge, cover, cross, extend across, link, range over, traverse, vault

spank *v* cuff, slap, smack; (*Inf*) belt, give someone a good hiding, tan, wallop, whack

spare *adj* additional, emergency, extra, free, in excess, leftover, reserve, odd, over, superfluous, supernumerary, surplus, unoccupied, unused, unwanted; (*Inf*) going begging; gaunt, lank, lean, meagre, slender, light, slim, wiry; economical, frugal, meagre, modest, scanty, sparing

spare *v* afford, allow, bestow, dispense with, do without, give, grant, let someone have, manage without, part with, relinquish; be merciful to, deal leniently with, have mercy on, leave, pardon, refrain from, release, relieve from, save from; (*Inf*) go easy on, let off

sparing *adj* careful, chary, economical, frugal, money-conscious, prudent, saving, thrifty

spark *n* flare, flash, flicker, gleam, glint, scintillation, spit; atom, hint, jot, scintilla, scrap, trace, vestige

sparkle *v* beam, coruscate, dance, flash, gleam, glint, glow, scintillate, shimmer, shine, spark, twinkle, wink; bubble, effervesce, fizz, fizzle

sparkle *n* brilliance, coruscation, dazzle, flash, flicker, gleam, glint, radiance, shimmer, spark, twinkle; animation, dash, élan, gaiety, life, panache, spirit, vitality, vivacity; (*Inf*) pizzazz, vim, zing, zip

spasm *n* contraction, convulsion, paroxysm, twitch; access, burst, eruption, fit, frenzy, outburst, seizure

speak *v* articulate, communicate, converse, discourse, enunciate, express, make known, pronounce, say, state, talk, tell, utter, voice; address, argue, declaim, deliver an address, descant, discourse, harangue, hold forth, lecture, plead, speechify; (*Inf*) spiel

speaker *n* lecturer, mouthpiece, orator, public speaker, spokesman, spokesperson, spokeswoman, word-spinner

special *adj* distinguished, especial, exceptional, extraordinary, festive, gala, important, memorable, momentous, out of the ordinary, red-letter, significant, uncommon, unique, unusual; appropriate, certain, characteristic, distinctive, especial, individual, particular, peculiar, precise, specialized, specific; chief, main, major, particular, primary

species *n* breed, category, class, collection, description, genus, group, kind, sort, type, variety

specific *adj* clear-out, definite, exact, explicit, express, limited, particular, precise, unambiguous, unequivocal; characteristic, distinguishing, especial, peculiar, special

specify *v* be specific about, cite, define, designate, detail, enumerate, indicate, individualize, itemize, mention, name, particularize, spell out, stipulate

specimen *n* copy, embodiment, example, exemplar, exemplification, exhibit, individual, instance, model, pattern, proof, representative, sample, type

speckled *adj* brindled, dappled, dotted, flecked, freckled, mottled, speckledy, spotted, spotty, sprinkled, stippled

spectacle *n* display, event, exhibition, extravaganza, pageant, parade, performance, show, sight; curiosity, laughing stock, marvel, phenomenon, scene, sight, wonder

spectacular *adj* astonishing, breathtaking, daring, dazzling, dramatic, eye-catching, glorious, grand, impressive, magnificent, marked, picturesque, remarkable, sensational, splendid, staggering, striking; (*Inf*) fantastic, out of this world, stunning

spectator *n* beholder, bystander, eyewitness, looker-on, observer, onlooker, viewer, watcher, witness

speculate *v* cogitate, conjecture, consider, contemplate, deliberate, hypothesize, meditate, muse, scheme, suppose, surmise, theorize, wonder; gamble, play the market, risk, take a chance with, venture; (*Inf*) have a flutter

speech *n* communication, conversation, dialogue, discussion, inter course, talk; address, discourse, disquisition, harangue, homily, lecture, oration

speechless *adj* dumb, inarticulate, mute, silent, tongue-tied, wordless; aghast, amazed, astounded, dazed, dumbfounded, dumbstruck, shocked, thunderstruck

speed *n* acceleration, celebrity, expedition, fleetness, haste, hurry, momentum, pace, precipitation, quickness, rapidity, rush, swiftness, velocity

speed *v* bowl along, career, dispatch, exceed the speed limit, expedite, flash, gallop, go like the wind, hasten, hurry, lose no time, make haste, press on, quicken, race, rush, sprint, tear, urge, zoom; (*Inf*) belt along, bomb along, go hell for leather, go like a bat out of hell, put one's foot down, step on it; advance, aid, assist, boost, expedite, facilitate, further, help, impel, promote

speedy *adj* expeditious, express, fast, fleet, fleet of foot, hasty, head long, hurried, immediate, nimble, precipitate, prompt, quick, rapid, summary, swift, winged

spell *v* add up to, amount to, cause, denote, result in; clarify, detail, itemize, set out, stipulate

spell *n* bout, course, interval, patch, period, season, stint, stretch, term, time, tour of duty, turn; abracadabra, bewitch, charm, conjuration, exorcism, incantation, sorcery, witchery

spend *v* disburse, expend, lay out, pay out; (*Inf*) dish out, fork out, shell out, splash out, spurge; consume, deplete, dispense, dissipate, drain, empty, exhaust, fritter away, run through, squander, use up, waste; (*Inf*) blow the money; fill, occupy, pass, while away

sphere *n* ball, circle, globe, globule, orb; capacity, compass, department, domain, employment, field, function, pale, province, range, rank, realm, scope, station, stratum, territory, walk of life

spherical *n* globe-shaped, globular, orbicular, rotund, round

spice *n* relish, savour, seasoning; colour, excitement, gusto, pep, piquancy, tang; (*Inf*) kick, zap, zip

spike *n* barb, point, prong, spine

spike *v* impale, spear, spit, stick

spill *v* discharge, disgorge, overflow, overturn, scatter, shed, slop over, spill over, throw off, upset

spin *v* gyrate, pirouette, reel, revolve, rotate, turn, twirl, twist, wheel, whirl; be giddy, be in a whirl

spin *n* gyration, revolution, roll, twist, whirl

spiral *adj* circular, cochlear, cochleate, coiled. corkscrew, helical, scrolled, voluted, whorled, ending

spiral *n* coil, corkscrew, curlicue, helix, screw, twist, volute, whorl

spirit *n* air, breath, life, life force, psyche, soul, vital, spark; attitude, character, complexion, disposition, essence, humour, outlook, quality, temper, temperament; animation, ardour, backbone, courage, dauntlessness, earnestness, energy, enterprise, enthusiasm, fire, force, gameness, grit, life, liveliness, mettle, resolution, sparkle, stoutheartedness, vigour, warmth, zest; (*Inf*) guts, spunk; motivation, resolution, resolve, will, willpower; atmosphere, feeling, gist, humour, tenor, tone; essence, intent, intention, meaning, purport, purpose, sense, substance; feelings, frame of mind, humour, mood, morale; apparition, ghost, phantom, shade shadow, spectre, sprite, vision; (*Inf*) spook

spiritual *adj* devotional, divine, ethereal, ghostly, holy, immaterial, incorporeal, nonmaterial, sacred

spit *v* discharge, eject, expectorate, hiss, spew, splutter, putter, throw out

spit *n* dribble, drool, saliva, slaver, spittle, sputum

spite *n* animosity, gall, grudge, hate, hatred, ill will, malevolence, malice, malignity, pique, rancour, spitefulness, spleen, venom; **in spite of** despite, in defiance of, notwithstanding, regardless of

spiteful *adj* barbed, cruel, ill-disposed, ill-natured, malevolent, malicious, malignant, nasty, rancorous, snide, splenetic, venomous, vindictive; (*Inf*) bitchy, catty

splash *v* bespatter, shower, slop, spatter, splodge, spray, spread, sprinkle, squirt, strew, wet; bathe, dabble, paddle, plunge, wade, wallow; batter, break, buffet, dash, plash, plop, smack, strike, surge, wash; blazon, broadcast, flaunt, headline, plaster, publicize, tout, trumpet

splash *n* burst, dash, patch, spattering, splodge, touch; display, effect, impact, sensation, splurge, stir

splendid *adj* admirable, brilliant, exceptional, glorious, grand, heroic, illustrious, magnificent, outstanding, rare, remarkable, renowned, sterling, sublime, superb, supreme; costly, dazzling, gorgeous, imposing, impressive, lavish, luxurious, magnificent, ornate, resplendent, rich, sumptuous, superb; excellent, fine, first-class, glorious, marvellous, wonderful; (*Inf*) fab, fantastic, great, terrific; beaming, bright, brilliant, glittering, glowing, lustrous, radiant, refulgent

splendour *n* brightness, brilliance, ceremony, dazzle, display, effulgence, glory, gorgeousness, grandeur, lustre, magnificence, majesty, pomp, radiance, refulgence, renown, resplendence, richness, show, solemnity, spectacle, stateliness, sumptuousness

splinter *n* chip, flake, fragment, needle, paring, shaving, sliver

splinter *v* break into smithereens, disintegrate, fracture, shatter, shiver, split

split *v* bifurcate, branch, break, break up, burst, cleave, come apart, come undone, crack, disband, disunite, diverge, fork, gape, give away, go separate ways, open, part, pull apart, rend, rip, separate, slash, slit, snap, splinter; allocate, allot, apportion, carve up, distribute, divide, dole out, halve, parcel out, partition, share out, slice up; (*Inf*) divvy up

split *n* breach, crack, damage, division, fissure, gap, rent, rip, separation, slash, slit, tear; breach, break, break-up, difference, discord, disruption, dissension, disunion, divergence, division, estrangement, partition, rift, rupture, schism

split *adj* ambivalent, bisected, broken, cleft, cracked, divided, dual, fractured, ruptured, twofold

split-up *n* break up, disband, divorce, go separate ways, part, part company, separate

spoil *v* blemish, damage, debase, deface, destroy, disfigure, harm, impair, injure, mar, mess up, ruin, upset, wreck; baby, coddle, cosset, indulge, kill with kindness, mollycoddle, overindulge, pamper, spoon-feed; addle, become tainted, curdle, decay, decompose, go ad, mildew, putrefy, rot, turn; (*Inf*) go off

spoken *adj* expressed, oral, phonetic, put into words, said, told, unwritten, uttered, verbal, viva, voice, voiced, by word of mouth

sponsor *n* backer, godparent, guarantor, patron, promoter; (*Inf*) angel

sponsor *v* back, finance, fund, guarantee, lend one's name to, patronize, promote, put up the money for, subsidize

spontaneous *adj* extempore, free, impromptu, impulsive, instinctive, natural, unbidden, uncompelled, unconstrained, unforced, unpremed itated, unprompted, voluntary, willing

sport *n* amusement, diversion, entertainment, exercise, game, pastime, physical activity, play, recreation; badinage, banter, frolic, fun, jest, joking, kidding (*Inf.*), merriment, mirth, raillery, teasing; buffoon, butt, derision, fair game, game, laughing stock, mockery, plaything, ridicule

sport *v* amuse oneself, caper, cavort,

entertain oneself, display, exhibit, frolic, gambol, have on show, romp, show off, wear

spot *n* blemish, blot, boil, botch, daub, discolouration, flaw, mark, pimple, pustule, smudge, speck, speckle, stain, taint, zit; locality, location, place, point, position, scene, site, situation; difficulty, mess, plight, predicament, quandary, tight corner, trouble; (*Inf*) fix, hot water, jam; bit, bite, morsel, smidgen; little, splash

spot *v* catch sight of, descry, detect, discern, espy, identify, make out, observe, pick out, recognize, see, sight; besmirch, blot, dirty, dot, fleck, mark, mottle, soil, spatter, speckle, splodge, splotch, stain, sully, taint, tarnish

spotted *adj* dappled, dotted, flecked, mottled, pied, polka-dot, pecked, speckled

spouse *n* companion, consort, help mate, husband, mate, partner, wife; (*Inf*) better half

spout *v* discharge, emit, erupt, gush, jet, shoot, spray, spurt, squirt, stream, surge

sprawl *v* flop, loll, lounge, ramble, slouch, slump, spread, straggle, trail

spray *v* atomize, diffuse, scatter, shower, sprinkle

spray *n* drizzle, droplets, fine mist, moisture, spindrift, spoondrift; aerosol, atomizer, sprinkler

spread *v* be displayed, bloat, broaden, dilate, expand, extend, fan out, open, open out, sprawl, stretch, swell, unfold, unfurl, unroll, widen; escalate, multiply, mushroom, proliferate

spread *n* advance, advancement, development, diffusion, dispersion, dissemination, escalation, expansion, increase, proliferation, spreading, suffusion, transmission; compass, extent, period, reach, span, stretch, sweep, term

spree *n* bacchanalia, carouse. debauch, fling, junketing, orgy, revel, splurge; (*Inf*) bender, binge, jag

sprightly *adj* active, agile, airy, alert, animated, blithe, brisk, cheerful, energetic, frolicsome, gay, jaunty, joyous, lively, nimble, perky, playful, spirited, sportive, spry, vivacious

spring *v* bounce, bound, hop, jump, leap, rebound, recoil, vault; **spring from** arise, be derived, be descended, come, derive, descend, emanate, emerge, grow, issue, originate, proceed, start, stem; **spring up** appear, burgeon, come into existence or being, develop, mushroom, shoot up

spring *n* bound, buck, hop, jump, leap, saltation, vault; bounce, buoyancy, elasticity, flexibility, recoil, resilience, springiness; (*Inf*) give beginning, cause, fountainhead, origin, root, source, well, wellspring

sprinkle *v* dredge, dust, pepper, powder, scatter, shower, spray, strew

sprout *v* bud, develop, germinate, grow, push, shoot, spring, vegetate

spur *v* animate, drive, goad, impel, incite, press, prick, prod, prompt, prick, rowel; impetus, impulse, incentive, incitement, inducement, motive, stimulus

spurious *adj* artificial, bogus, contrived, counterfeit, deceitful, fake, false, feigned, forged, imitation, mock, pretended, sham, simulated, specious, unauthentic; (*Inf*) phoney, pseudo

spurn *v* cold-shoulder, contemn, despise, disdain, disregard, rebuff, reject, repulse, scorn, slight, snub, (*Inf*) turn one's nose up at

spy *n* double agent, fifth columnist, foreign agent, mole, secret agent, secret service agent, undercover agent

spy *v* catch sight of, descry, espy, glimpse, notice, observe, set eyes on, spot

squabble *v* argue, bicker, brawl, clash, dispute, fight, have words, quarrel, row, wrangle; (*Inf*) fall out, scrap

squabble *n* argument, difference of opinion, disagreement, dispute, fight, row, spat, tiff; (*Inf*) barney, scrap, set-to

squad *n* band, company, crew, force, gang, group, team, troop

squalid *adj* broken-down, decayed, dirty, disgusting, fetid, filthy, foul, low, nasty, poverty-stricken, repulsive, run-down, seedy, sleazy, slovenly, slummy, sordid, unclean

squalor *n* decay, filth, foulness, meanness, sleaziness, slumminess, squalidness, wretchedness

squander *v* be prodigal with, consume, dissipate, expend, fritter away, frivol away, lavish, misspend, misuse, run through, scatter, spend, spend like water, throw away, waste; (I*nf*) blow

square *adj* aboveboard, decent, equitable, ethical, fair, fair and square, genuine, honest, just, straight, straightforward, upright; (*Inf*) on the level; bourgeois, conservative, conventional, old-fashioned, out of date, straight strait-laced, stuffy; (*Inf*) behind the times

square *n* market square, quadrangle, town square, village square; conservative, conventionalist, die-hard, old fogy, traditionalist; (*Inf*) fuddy-duddy, old buffer, stick-in-the-mud

squash *v* compress, crush, distort, flatten, mash, pound, press, pulp, smash, stamp on, trample down; annihilate, crush, humiliate, quash, quell, silence, suppress; (*Inf*) put down, put someone in their place, sit on

squeak *v* peep, pipe, shrill, squeal, whine, yelp

squeal *n* scream, screech, shriek, wail, yell, yelp, yowl

squeal *v* scream, screech, shout, shriek, shrill, wail, yelp

squeamish *adj* nauseous, qualmish, queasy, queer, sick, sickish; fastidious, finicky, particular, prudish, punctilious, scrupulous, strait-laced; (*Inf*) prissy

squeeze *v* clutch, compress, crush, grip, nip, pinch, press, squash, wring; cram, crowd, force, jam, jostle, pack, press, ram, stuff, thrust, wedge; clasp, cuddle, embrace, enfold, hold tight, hug; bring pressure to bear on, extort, milk, oppress, pressurize, wrest; (*Inf*) bleed, lean on, put the screws on, put the squeeze on

squeeze *n* clasp, embrace, hand clasp, hold, hug; congestion, crowd, crush, jam, press, squash
stab *v* bayonet, cut, gore, injure, jab, knife, pierce, puncture, run through, spear, stick, thrust, transfix, wound
stab *n* gash, incision, injury, jab, puncture, thrust, wound; ache, pang, spasm, throb, twinge; attempt, endeavour, try, venture
stable *adj* abiding, constant, deep-rooted, durable, enduring, established, fast, firm, fixed, immutable, invariable, lasting, permanent, reliable, secure, sound, steadfast, steady, strong, sturdy, sure, unalterable, unchangeable, unwavering, well-founded
stack *n* cock, hayrick, haystack, rick, shock; accumulation, collection, heap, hoard, load, mass, mound, mountain, pile, stockpile, store; abundance, amplitude; (*Inf*) bags, heaps, lots, oodles, tons
stack *v* accumulate, amass, bank up, collect, heap up, load, pile up, stockpile, store
staff *n* employees, lecturers, officers, organization, personnel, teachers, team, workers, work force; cane, pole, prop, rod, stave, wand
stage *n* division, juncture, lap, leg, length, level, period, phase, point, step
stagger *v* falter, hesitate, lurch, reel, sway, teeter, totter, vacillate, waver, wobble; amaze, astonish, astound, confound, dumbfound, flabbergast, give someone a shock, nonplus, overwhelm, shake, shock, stun, stupefy, surprise, take someone aback, take someone's breath away, throw off balance; (*Inf*) bowl over, strike someone dumb; alternate, overlap, step, zigzag
stagnant *adj* brackish, motionless, quiet, sluggish, stale, standing, still
stagnate *v* decay, decline, deterio rate, fester, go to seed, idle, languish, lie fallow, rot, rust, stand still, vegetate
staid *adj* calm, composed, decorous, demure, grave, quiet, sedate, self-restrained, serious, sober, solemn, steady
stain *v* blemish, blot, colour, dirty, discolour, dye, mark, soil, spot, tarnish, tinge; besmirch, blacken, contaminate, corrupt, defile, deprave, disgrace, drag through the mud, sully, taint
stain *n* blemish, blot, discolouration, dye, spot, tint; blemish, blot on the escutcheon, disgrace, dishonour, infamy, reproach, shame, slur, stigma
stale *adj* decayed, dry, faded, fetid, flat, fusty, hard, insipid, musty, old, sour, stagnant, tasteless
stalk *v* creep up on, follow, haunt, hunt, pursue, shadow, track; (*Inf*) tail
stamina *n* energy, force, indefatigability, lustiness, power, power of endurance, resilience, resistance, staying power, strength, vigour; (*Inf*) grit
stammer *v* falter, hem and haw, hesitate, pause, splutter, stumble, stutter
stamp *v* beat, crush, trample; engrave, fix, impress, imprint,

inscribe, mark, mould, print

stamp *n* brand, cast, earmark, hallmark, imprint, mark, mould, signature; breed, cast, character, cut, description, fashion, form, kind, sort, type

stampede *n* charge, flight, rout, rush, scattering

stamp out *v* crush, destroy, eliminate, eradicate, extinguish, extirpate, extinguish, extirpate, put down, put out, quell, quench, scotch, suppress

stance *n* bearing, carriage, deportment, posture; attitude, position, stand, standpoint, viewpoint

stand *v* be erect, be upright, be vertical, rise; erect, mount, place, position, put, rank, set; be in force, belong, be situated or located, be valid, continue, exist, halt, hold, obtain, pause, prevail, remain, rest, stay, stop; abide, allow, bear, brook, cope with, countenance, endure, experience, handle, stomach, submit to, suffer, support, sustain, take, tolerate, undergo, weather, with stand; (*Inf*) put up with, wear

stand *n* halt, rest, standstill, stay, stop, stopover; attitude, determination, form, stand, opinion, position, stance, standpoint

standard *n* average, benchmark, canon, criterion, example, gauge, grade, guide, guideline, measure, model, norm, pattern, principle, requirement, rule, sample, specification, touchstone, type, yardstick

standard *adj* accepted, average, basic, customary, normal, orthodox, popular, prevailing, regular, set, staple, stock, typical, usual

standardize *v* assimilate, bring into line, institutionalize, mass-produce, regiment, stereotype

stand out *v* attract attention, be highlighted, be prominent, be conspicuous, be thrown into relief, catch the eye, leap to the eye, project; (*Inf*) stare one in the face, stick out a mile

standpoint *n* angle, point of view, position, post, stance, station, vantage point, viewpoint

stand up for *v* champion, come to the defence of, defend, side with, support, uphold; (*Inf*) stick up for

star *n* asteroid, planet, planetoid; celebrity, dignitary, idol, lead, leading lady, leading man, luminary, main attraction, name, principal, somebody, superstar, VIP; (*Inf*) celeb, draw

star *adj* brilliant, celebrated, illustrious, leading, major, paramount, principal, prominent, talented, well-known

stare *v* gape, gaze, goggle, look, ogle, watch; (*Inf*) gawk, gawp, rubberneck; be blatant, be obvious, be prominent, stand out

start *v* appear, arise, begin, come into being, come into existence, commerce, depart, first see the light of day, get on the road, get under way, issue, leave, originate, saly forth, set off, set out; (*Inf*) go ahead, hit the road, pitch in; activate, embark upon, engender, enter upon, get going, initiate, instigate, make a beginning, open, originate, set about, set in motion, start the ball rolling, take the first step, turn on; (*Inf*) kick off, take the plunge; begin, create, establish, father, found, inaugurate, initiate, institute, introduce, launch, lay the foundations of, pioneer, set up; blench, flinch, jerk, jump, recoil, shy, twitch

start *n* beginning, birth, commencement, dawn, first steps, foundation, inauguration, inception, initiation, inset, opening, outset; (*Inf*) kickoff; advantage, edge, head start, lead; convulsion, jar, jump, spasm, twitch

startle *v* agitate, alarm, amaze, astonish, astound, frighten, make someone jump, scare, shock, surprise, take someone aback; (*Inf*) give someone a turn

starving *adj* faint from lack of food, famished, hungering, hungry, ravenous, sharp-set, starved; (*Inf*) able to eat a horse

state *v* affirm, articulate, assert, asseverate, aver, declare, enumer ate, explain, expound, express, present, propound, express, present, propound, put, report, say, specify, voice

state *n* case, category, circumstances, condition, mode, pass, plight, position, predicament, shape, situation, state of affairs; attitude, frame of mind, humour, mood, spirits; ceremony, dignity, display, glory, grandeur, majesty, pomp, splendour, style

state *n* body politic, commonwealth, country, federation, government, kingdom, land, nation, republic, territory

stately *adj* august, ceremonious, deliberate, dignified, elegant, grand, imperial, imposing, impressive, lofty, majestic, measured, noble, pompous, regal, royal, solemn

statement *n* account, announcement, communication, communiqué, declaration, explanation, proclamation, recital, relation, report, testimony, utterance

station *n* base, depot, headquarters, location, place, position, post, seat, situation; appointment, business, calling, employment, grade, occupation, position, post, rank, situation, sphere, standing, status

station *v* assign, establish, fix, garrison, install, locate, post, set

stationary *adj* at a standstill, fixed, inert, moored, motionless, parked, standing, static, stock-still, unmoving

status *n* condition, consequence, degree, distinction, eminence, grade, position, prestige, rank, standing

stay *v* abide, continue, delay, establish, oneself, halt, hover, linger, loiter, pause, put down roots, remain, reside, settle, sojourn, stand, stay put, stop, tarry, wait; (*Inf*) hang around; adjourn, defer, discontinue, hold in abeyance, hold over, prorogue, put off, suspend

stay *n* holiday, sojourn, stop, stopover, visit

steadfast *adj* constant, dedicated, dependable, established, faithful, fast, firm, fixed, intent, loyal, persevering, reliable, resolute, single-minded, stable, staunch, steady, unfaltering, unflinching, unswerving, unwavering

steady *adj* firm, fixed, immovable, safe, stable, substantial, unchangeable, uniform; balanced, calm, dependable, equable, having both feet on the ground, imperturbable, level-headed, reliable, sedate, sensible, serene, serious-minded, settled, sober, staid, steadfast; ceaseless, conformed, consistent, constant, continuous, even, faithful, habitual, incessant, nonstop, persistent, regular, rhythmic, unbroken, unfaltering, unfluctuating, uninterrupted, unremitting unvarying, unwavering

steady *v* balance, brace, secure, stabilize, support

steal *v* appropriate, be light-fin gered, embezzle, filch, heist, make off with, misappropriate, peculate, pilfer, pirate, plagiarize, poach, purloin, shoplift, take, thieve, walk off with; (*Inf*) lift, nick, pinch, swipe; creep, flit, insinuate oneself, slink, slip, sneak, tiptoe

stealth *n* furtiveness, secrecy, slyness, sneakiness, stealthiness, surreptitiousness, unobtrusiveness

stealthy *adj* clandestine, covert, furtive, secret, secretive, skulking, sly, sneaking, sneaky, surreptitious, underhand

steep *adj* abrupt, headlong, precipitous, sheer; excessive, exhorbitant, extortionate, extreme, high, over priced, stiff; (*Inf*) over the top, OTT; uncalled-for, unreasonable

steer *v* be in the driver's seat, conduct, control, direct, govern, guide, pilot; **steer clear of** avoid, circumvent, eschew, evade, give a wide berth to, sheer off, shun

stem *n* axis, branch, peduncle, shoot, stalk, stock, trunk

stem *v* ring to a standstill, check, contain, curb, dam, hold back, oppose, resist, restrain, stanch, stop, withstand

step *n* footfall, footprint, footstep, gait, impression, pace, print, stride, trace, track, walk; act, action, deed, expedient, manoeuvre, means, measure, move, procedure, proceeding; **take steps** act, intervene, move in, prepare, take action, take measures, take the initiative; advance, advancement, move, phase, point, process, progression, stage; degree, level, rank, remove; **in step** coinciding, conforming, in harmony in line; **out of step** erratic, incongruous, in disagreement, out of harmony, out of line, out of phase, pulling different ways

step *v* move, pace, tread, walk

stereotype *n* formula, mould, pattern, received idea

stereotype *v* categorize, conventionalize, dub, pigeonhole, standardize, take to be, typecast

sterile *adj* abortive, bare, barren, dry, empty, fruitless, infecund, unfruitful, unproductive, unprofitable, unprolific; antiseptic, aseptic, disinfected, germ-free, sterilized

stern *adj* austere, authoritarian, bitter, cruel, flinty, forbidding, frowning, grim, hard, hard, inflexible, relentless, rigid, rigorous, serious, severe, steely, strict, unrelenting, unsparing, unyielding

stick *v* adhere, affix, attach, bind, bond, cement, cleave, cling, fasten, fix, fuse, glue, hold, hold on, join, paste, weld; dig, gore, insert, jab, penetrate, pierce, pin, poke, prod, puncture, spear, stab, thrust, transfix; **stick out** bulge, extend, jut, obtrude, poke, project, protrude, show; be bogged down, become, immobilized, be embedded, catch, clog, come to a standstill, jam, lodge, snag, stop; linger persist, remain, stay; **stick up for** champion, defend, stand up for, support, take the part of side of, uphold

stick *n* baton, birch, cane, pole, rod, staff, stake, switch, twig, wand

sticky *adj* adhesive,clinging, gluey, glutinous, gummy, syrupy, tacky, tenacious, viscid, viscous; (*Inf*) gooey; awkward, delicate, difficult, discomforting, embarrassing, nasty, painful, thorny, tricky, unpleasant; (*Inf*) hairy

stiff *adj* brittle, form, hard, hardened, inelastic, inflexible, rigid, solid, solidified, taut, tense, tight, unbending, unyielding; artificial, austere, ceremonious, chilly, cold, constrained, forced, formal, laboured, mannered, pompous, priggish, prim, punctilious, standoffish, stilted, uneasy, unnatural, unrelaxed, wooden; arthritic, awkward, clumsy, crude, graceless, inelegant, jerky, ungainly, ungraceful, unsupple; (*Inf*) rheumaticky

stiffen *v* brace, coagulate, congeal, crystallize, harden, jell, reinforce, set, solidify, starch, tauten, tense, thicken

stifle *v* asphyxiate, choke, smother, strangle, suffocate; check, choke back, cover up, curb, extinguish, hush, muffle, prevent, repress, restrain, silence, smother, stop, suppress

still *adj* at rest, calm, hushed, inert, lifeless, motionless, noiseless, pacific, peaceful, placid, quiet, restful, serene, silent, smooth, stationary, tranquil, undisturbed, unruffled, unstirring

still *v* allay, alleviate, appease, calm, hush, lull, pacify, quiet, quieten, settle, silence, smooth, smooth over, soothe, subdue, tranquillize

still *conj* but, for all that, however, nevertheless, notwithstanding, yet

stimulant *n* analeptic, energizer, excitant, restorative, reviver, tonic; (*Inf*) bracer, pep pill, pick-me-up, upper

stimulate *v* animate, arouse, encourage, fan, fire, foment, goad, impel, incite, inflame, instigate, prompt, provoke, quicken, rouse, spur, urge; (*Inf*) turn on

sting *v* burn, hurt, pain, smart, tingle, wound

stint *n* assignment, bit, period, quota, share, shift, spell, stretch, term, time, tour, turn

stipulate *v* agree, contract, covenant, engage, guarantee, impose conditions, insist upon, lay down, make a point of, pledge, postulate, promise, require, settle, specify

stipulation *n* agreement, clause, condition, contract, engagement, precondition, prerequisite, provision, proviso, qualification, requirement, restriction, settlement, *sine qua non,* specification, term

stir *v* agitate, beat, disturb, flutter, mix, move, quiver, rustle, shake, tremble; **stir up** animate, arouse, awaken, excite, incite, inflame, instigate, kindle, prompt, provoke, quicken, raise, spur, stimulate, urge;

budge, exert oneself, hasten, make an effort, mill about, move; (*Inf*) be up and about, get a move on, get moving, look lively, shake a leg

stir *n* activity, ado, agitation, bustle, commotion, disorder, disturbance, excitement, ferment, flurry, fuss, movement, to-do, tumult, uproar

stock *n* array, assets, assortment, cache, choice, commodities, funds, goods, hoard, inventor, merchandise, range reserve, reservoir, selection, stockpile, store, supply, variety, wares; beasts, cattle, domestic animals, flocks, herds, horses, livestock, sheep; capital, funds, investment, property; **take stock** appraise, estimate, review the situation, see how the land lies, size up, weigh up; (*Inf*) size up

stock *adj* banal, basic, commonplace, conventional, customary, for mal, hackneyed, ordinary, overused, regular, routine, run-of-the-mill, set, standard, staple, stereotyped, traditional, trite, usual, worn-out

stock *v* deal in, handle, keep, sell, supply, trade in; **stock up** accumulate, amass, buy up, gather, hoard, lay in, put away, replenish, save, store up, supply

stomach *n* abdomen, belly, paunch, potbelly; (*Inf*) breadbasket, corporation, gut, insides, pot, spare tyre, tummy; appetite, desire, inclination, mind, relish, taste

stomach *v* abide, bear, endure, reconcile oneself to, submit to, suffer, swallow, take, tolerate; (*Inf*) put up with

stony *adj* adamant, blank, callous, chilly, expressionless, frigid, hard, heartless, hostile, icy, indifferent, inexorable, merciless, obdurate, pitiless, unfeeling, unforgiving, unresponsive

stoop *v* be bowed, round-shouldered, bend, bow, crouch, descend, suck, hunch, incline, kneel, lean

stop *v* be over, break off, bring to a halt, bring or come to a standstill, cease, come to an end, conclude, cut short, desist, discontinue, draw up, end, finish, halt, leave off, pause, peter out, pull up, put an end to, quit, refrain, run down, run its course, shut down, stall, terminate; (*Inf*) call it a day, cut out, pack in; arrest, bar, block, break, check, close, forestall, frustrate, hinder, hold back, impede, intercept, interrupt, obstruct, plug, prevent, rein in, repress, restrain, seal, silence, staunch, stem, suspend; break one's journey, lodge, put up, rest, sojourn, stay, tarry

stop *n* cessation, conclusion, discontinuation, end, finish, halt, stand still; break, rest, sojourn, stay, stopover, visit; bar, block, break, check, control, hindrance, impediment, plug, stoppage; depot, destination, halt, stage, station, termination, terminus

stoppage *n* abeyance, arrest, close, closure, shut-off, deduction, discontinuance, halt, hindrance, lay-off, shutdown, standstill, stopping

store *v* accumulate, deposit, garner, hoard, husband, keep in reserve, lay by, lock away, put aside, put aside for a rainy day, put by, put in stor age, reserve, salt away, save, stock, stockpile; (*Inf*) stash

store *n* abundance, accumulation, cache, fund, hoard, lot, mine, plenty, plethora, provision, quantity, reserve, reservoir, stock, stockpile, supply, wealth; chain store, department store, emporium, market, mart, outlet, shop, supermarket; depository, storehouse, storeroom, warehouse

storm *n* blast, blizzard, cyclone, gale, gust, hurricane, squall, tempest, tornado, whirlwind; agitation, anger, clamour, commotion, disturbance, furore, hubbub, outbreak, outburst, outcry, passion, roar, row, rumpus, stir, strife, tumult, turmoil, violence

storm *v* assail, assault, beset, charge, rush, take by storm

storm *n* assault, attack, blitz, blitzkrieg, offensive, onset, onslaught, rush

storm *v* bluster, complain, fume, rage, rant, rave, scold, thunder; flounce, fly, rush, stalk, stamp, stomp; (*Inf*) fly off the handle

stormy *adj* blustering, blustery, boisterous, dirty, foul, gusty, raging, rough, squally, tempestuous, turbulent, wild, windy

story *n* account, anecdote, chronicle, fictional account, history, legend, narration, narrative, novel, recital, record, relation, romance, tale, version, yarn; article, feature, news, news item, report, scoop

stout *adj* big, bulky, burly, corpulent, fat, fleshy, heavy. obese, on the large side, overweight, plump, portly, rotund, substantial, tubby; able-bodied, athletic, brawny, hardy, hulking, lusty, muscular, robust, stalwart, strapping, strong, sturdy, substantial, tough, vigorous; (*Inf*) beefy, husky; bold, brave, courageous, dauntless, doughty, fearless, gallant, intrepid, lion-hearted, manly, plucky, resolute, valiant, valourous

straight *adj* direct, near, short, undeviating, unswerving; aligned, erect, eve, horizontal, in line, level, perpendicular, plumb, right, smooth, square, true, upright, vertical; above board, accurate, authentic, decent, equitable, fair, fair and square, honest, honourable, just, law-abiding, reliable, respectable, trustworthy, upright; arranged, in order, neat, orderly, organized, put to rights, ship shape, sorted out, tidy; consecutive, continuous, nonstop, running, solid, successive, sustained, through, uninterrupted, unrelieved; neat, pure unadulterated, undiluted, unmixed

straight *adv* as the crow flies, at once, directly, immediately, instantly

straightaway *adv* at once, directly, immediately, instantly, now, on the spot, right away, straight off, there and then, this instant, without any delay, without more ado

straightforward *adj* above board, candid, direct, forthright, genuine, guileless, honest, open, sincere, truthful; clear-cut, easy, elementary, routine, simple, uncomplicated, undemanding

strain *v* distend, draw tight, extend, stretch, tauten, tighten; drive, exert, fatigue, injure, overexert, overtax, overwork, pull, push to the limit, sprain, tax, tear, tire, twist, weaken, wrench; endeavour, labour, make a supreme effort, strive, struggle; filter, percolate, purify, riddle, screen, seep, separate, sieve, sift

strain *n* effort, exertion, force, injury, pull, sprain, struggle, taut ness, tension, wrench; anxiety, burden, pressure, stress, tension

strained *adj* artificial, awkward, constrained, difficult, embarrassed, false, forced, laboured, put on, self-conscious, stiff, tense, uncomfort able, uneasy, unnatural, unrelaxed

strait-laced *adj* moralistic, narrow, narrow-minded, of the old school, overscrupulous, prim, proper, prudish, puritanical, strict, Victorian

strand *n* fibre, filament, length, lock, rope, string, thread, tress, twist

stranded *adj* aground, ashore, beached, cast away, grounded, marooned, wrecked

strange *adj* abnormal, astonishing, bizarre, curious, eccentric, exceptional, extraordinary, fantastic, funny, irregular, marvellous, mystifying, odd, out-of-the-way, peculiar, perplexing, queer, rare, remarkable, singular, unaccountable, uncanny, uncommon, unheard of, weird, wonderful; alien, exotic, foreign, new, novel, outside one's experience, remote, unexplored, unfamiliar, unknown, untried

stranger *n* alien, foreigner, guest, incomer, new arrival, newcomer, outlander, unknown, visitor

strangle *v* asphyxiate, choke, garrotte, smother, strangulate, suffocate, throttle; gag, inhibit, repress, stifle, suppress

strap *n* belt, leash, thong, tie

strap *v* bind, buckle, fasten, lash, secure, tie, truss

strategy *n* approach, grand design, manoeuvring, plan, planning, policy, procedure, programme, scheme

stray *v* deviate, digress, diverge, get off the point, get sidetracked, go off at a tangent, ramble; be abandoned, drift, err, go astray, lose one's way, meander, range, roam, rove, straggle, wander

stray *adj* abandoned, homeless, lost, roaming, vagrant

streak *n* band, layer, line, slash, smear, strip, stripe, stroke, vein; dash, element, strain, touch, trace, vein

streak *v* dart, flash, fly, hurtle, speed, sprint, sweep, tear, whistle, zoom; (*Inf*) move like greased lightning, whiz

stream *n* beck, brook, burn, course, creek, current, drift, flow, freshet, outpouring, rill, river, rivulet, run, rush, surge, tide, torrent, tributary

stream *v* cascade, course, emit, flood flow, glide, gush, issue, our, run, shed, spill, spout

street *v* avenue, boulevard, lane, road, roadway, row, terrace, thoroughfare

strength *n* backbone, brawn, brawniness, courage, firmness, fortitude, health, lustiness, might, muscle, robustness, sinew, stamina, stoutness, sturdiness, toughness; cogency, concentration, effectiveness, efficacy, energy, force, intensity, potency, power, resolution, spirit, vehemence, vigour; advantage, anchor, asset, mainstay, security, strong point, succour, tower of strength

strengthen *v* animate, brace up, consolidate, encourage, fortify, give new energy to, harden, hearten, invigorate, nerve, nourish, rejuve nate, restore, stiffen, toughen; bolster, brace, build up, buttress, confirm, corroborate, enhance, establish, give a boost to, harden heighten, increase, intensify, justify, reinforce, steel, substantiate, support

strenuous *adj* arduous, demanding, exhausting, hard, laborious, taxing, toilsome, tough, tough going, unrelaxing, up hill; active, bold determined, eager, earnest, energetic, persistent, resolute, spirited, strong, tireless, vigorous, zealous

stress *n* emphasis, force, importance, significance, urgency, weight; anxiety, burden, nervous, tension, oppression, pressure, strain, tautness, tension, trauma, worry; (*Inf*) hassle; accent, accentuation, beat, emphasis

stress *v* accentuate, belabour, dwell on, emphasize, harp on, lay emphasis upon, point up, repeat, rub in, underline, underscore

stretch *v* cover, extend, put forth, reach, spread, unfold, unroll; distend, draw out, elongate, expand, inflate, lengthen, pull, pull out of shape, rack, strain, swell, tighten

stretch *n* area, distance, expanse, extent, spread, sweep, tract

strict *adj* austere, authoritarian, firm, harsh, no-nonsense, rigid, rigorous, severe, stern, stringent; accurate, close, exact, faithful, meticulous, particular, precise, religious, scrupulous, true; absolute, complete, perfect, total, utter

strike *v* bang, beat, box, buffet, chastise, cuff, hammer, hit, knock, pound, punish, slap, smack, smite, thump; (*Inf*) clobber, clout, lay a finger on, sock, wallop; be in collision with, bump into, clash, collide with, come into contact with, dash, hit, knock into, run into, smash into, touch; drive, force, hit, impel, thrust; affect, assail, assault, attack, deal a blow to, devastate, fall upon, hit, invade, set upon, smite; achieve, arrange, arrive at, attain, effect, reach; down tools, mutiny, revolt, walk out

striking *adj* astonishing, conspicu ous, dazzling, extraordinary, forcible, impressive, memorable, noticeable, out of the ordinary, out standing, stunning, wonderful; (*Inf*) great, smashing

string *n* cord, fibre, twine; chain, file, line, procession, queue, row, sequence, series, strand, succession

strip *v* bare, denude, deprive, despoil, dismantle, divest, empty, gut, lay bare, loot, peel, pillage, plunder, ransack, rob, sack, skin, spoil; disrobe, unclothe, uncover, undress

strip *n* band, belt, bit, fillet, piece, ribbon, shred, slip, swathe, tongue

strive *v* attempt, compete, contend, do all one can, do one's best, do one's utmost, endeavour, exert one self, fight, labour, leave no stone unturned, make every effort, strain, struggle, toil, try, try hard; (*Inf*) go all out

stroke *n* accomplishment, achievement, blow, feat, flourish, hit, knock, move, movement, pat, rap, thump; apoplexy, attack, collapse, fit, seizure, shock

stroke *v* caress, fondle, pat, pet, rub

stroll *v* amble, make one's way, promenade, ramble, saunter, stretch one's legs, take a turn, toddle, wander; (*Inf*) mooch, mosey

stroll *n* airing, breath of air, constitutional, excursion, promenade, ramble, turn, walk

strong *adj* athletic, brawny, burly, capable, hale, hardy, healthy, Herculean, lusty, muscular, powerful robust, sinewy, sound, stalwart, stout, strapping, sturdy, tough, virile; aggressive, brave, courageous-determined, firm in spirit, forceful, hard as nails, high-powered, plucky, resilient, resolute, resourceful, self-assertive, steadfast, stouthearted, tenacious, tough, unyielding; (*Inf*) gutsy; acute,dedicated, deep, deep-rooted, eager, fervent, fervid, fierce, firm, intense, keen, severe, staunch, vehement, violent, zealous; clear, clear-cut, cogent, compelling, convincing, distinct, effective, formidable, great, marked, over powering, persuasive, potent, redoubtable, sound, telling, trenchant, unmistakable, urgent, weighty, well-established, well-founded; Draconian, drastic, extreme, force ful, severe; durable, hard-wearing, heavy-duty, on a firm foundation, reinforced, sturdy, substantial, well-armed, well-built, well-protected; biting, concentrated, heady, highly-flavoured, highly-seasoned, hot, intoxicating, piquant, pungent, pure, sharp, spicy, undiluted

struggle *v* exert oneself, labour, make every effort, strain, strive, toil, work, work like a Trojan; battle, compete, contend, fight, grapple, lock horns, scuffle, wrestle

struggle *n* effort, exertion, grind labour, long haul, pains, scramble, toil, work; battle, brush, clash, combat, conflict, contest, encounter, hostilities, skirmish, strife, tussle

stubborn *adj* bull-headed, contumacious, cross-grained, dogged, dour, fixed, headstrong, inflexible, intractable, mulish, obdurate, obstinate, opinionated, persistent, pig-headed, recalcitrant, refractory, self-willed, stiff-necked, tenacious, unbending, unmanageable, unshakable, unyielding, wilful

stuck *adj* cemented, fast, fastened form, fixed, glued, joined; at a loss, at a standstill, at one's wits end, baffled, beaten, bereft of ideas, nonplussed, stumped; (*Inf*) up against a brick wall

student *n* apprentice, disciple, learner, observer, pupil, scholar, undergraduate

studied *adj* calculated, conscious, deliberate, intentional; planned, premeditated, purposeful, well-considered, wilful

studious *adj* academic, assiduous, attentive, bookish careful, diligent, eager, earnest, hard-working, intellectual, meditative, reflective, scholarly, sedulous, serious, thoughtful

study *v* apply oneself to, burn the midnight oil, cogitate, consider, contemplate, examine, go into, hammer away at, learn, meditate, ponder, pore over, read, read up; (*Inf*) cram, mug up, swot; analyse, deliberate, examine, investigate, look into, peruse, research, scrutinize, survey

study *n* academic work, application, book work, learning, lessons, reading, research, school work, thought; (*Inf*) cramming, swotting; analysis, attention, cogitation, consideration, contemplation, examination, inquiry, inspection, investigation, review, scrutiny, survey

stuff *v* compress, cram, crowd, fill, force, jam, load, pack, pad, push, ram, shove, squeeze, stow, wedge; gobble, gorge, guzzle, overindulge, sate, satiate; (*Inf*) make a pig of oneself

stuff *n* belongings, bits and pieces, effects, equipment, gear, goods and chattels, impedimenta, junk, kit, luggage, materials, objects, paraphernalia, possessions, tackle, things, trappings; (*Inf*) clobber; cloth, fabric, material, raw material, textile; essence, matter, pith, quintessence, staple, substance

stuffy *adj* airless, close, fetid, frowsty, fuggy, heavy, muggy, oppressive, stale, stifling, suffocating, sultry, unventilated; conventional, deadly, dreary, dull, fusty, humourless, musty, old-fashioned, old-fogyish, pompous, priggish, prim, prim and proper, staid, stilted, stodgy, strait-laced, uninteresting

stumble *v* blunder about, fall, falter, flounder hesitate, lose one's balance, lurch, reel, slip, stagger, trip; (*Inf*) come a cropper; **stumble upon** blunder upon, chance upon, come across, discover, encounter, find, happen upon, light upon, run across, turn up

stun *v* amaze, astonish, astound, bewilder, confound, confuse, daze, dumbfounded, knock out, over come, overpower, shock, stagger, stupefy; (*Inf*) flabbergast, hit some one like a ton of bricks, knock someone for six, strike someone dumb, take someone's breath away

stunning *adj* beautiful, brilliant, dazzling, gorgeous, heavenly, impressive, lovely, marvellous, ravishing, remarkable, sensational, spectacular, striking, wonderful; (*Inf*) devastating, great, out of this world, smashing

stunt *n* act, deed, exploit, feat, feature, *tour de force,* trick

stupendous *adj* amazing, astounding, breathtaking, colossal, enormous, gigantic, huge, marvellous, overwhelming, phenomenal, prodigious, staggering, superb, surpassing belief, surprising, vast, wonderful; (*Inf*) fabulous, fantastic, mega, mind-blowing, mind-boggling, out of this world, stunning, tremendous

stupid *adj* brainless, deficient, dense, dim, doltish, dull, foolish, gullible, half-witted, moronic, naive, obtuse, simple, simple-minded, slow, slow-witted, sluggish, stolid, thick, thick-headed, unintelligent, witless; (*Inf*) dopey, dozy, dumb, slow on the uptake; crack-brained, daft, futile, idiotic, ill-advised, imbecilic, inane, indiscreet, irrelevant, irresponsible, laughable, ludicrous, meaningless, mindless, nonsensical, pointless, short-sighted, trivial, unintelligent, unthinking; (*Inf*) half-baked; dazed, groggy, in a daze, punch drunk, semiconscious, senseless, stunned, stupefied

stupidity *n* asininity, brainlessness, denseness, dimness, dullness, feeble-mindedness, imbecility, lack of brain, lack of intelligence, naivety, obtuseness, puerility, simplicity, slowness, thick-headeness, thick ness; (*Inf*) dopiness, doziness, dumbness; absurdity, fatuity, fatuousness, folly, foolhardiness, foolishness, futility, idiocy, impracticality, inanity, indiscretion, ineptitude, irresponsibility, ludicrousness, lunacy, madness, pointlessness, rashness, senselessness, silliness

sturdy *adj* athletic brawny, built to last, determined, durable, firm, flourishing, hardy, hearty, lusty, muscular, powerful, resolute, robust, secure, solid, stalwart, staunch, steadfast, stouthearted, substantial, vigorous, well-built, well-made

style *n* cut, design, form, hand, manner, technique; fashion, mode, rage, trend, vogue; approach, custom, manner, method, mode, way; *bon ton,* chic, cosmopolitanism, dash, élan, elegance, fashionableness, flair, race, panache, polish, refinement, *savoir-faire*, smartness, sophistication, stylishness, taste, urbanity; affluence, comfort, ease, elegance, gracious living, grandeur, luxury; appearance, category, characteristic, genre, kind, pattern, sort, spirit, strain, tenor, tone, type, variety

style *v* adapt, arrange, cut, design, dress, fashion, shape, tailor; address, call, christen, denominate, designate, dub, entitle, label, name, term

stylish *adj* à la mode, chic, dapper, fashionable, in fashion, in vogue, modish, polished, smart, snappy, urbane, voguish, well turned-out; (*Inf*) classy, dressy, natty, snazzy, trendy

subconscious *adj* hidden, inner, innermost, intuitive, latent, repressed, subliminal, suppressed

subdue *v* beat down, break, conquer, control, crush, defeat, discipline, gain ascendancy over, get the better of, get the upper hand over, get under control humble, master, overcome, overpower, overrun, put down, quell, tame, trample, triumph over, vanquish; check, control, mellow moderate, quieten down, repress, soften, suppress, tone down

subject *n* affair, business, field of enquiry, issue, matter, object, point, question, subject matter, substance, theme, topic; case, client, participant, patient, victim; citizen, dependant, liegeman, national, subordinate, vassal; (*Inf*) guinea pig

subject *adj* at the mercy of, disposed, exposed, in danger of, liable, open, prone, susceptible, vulnerable; conditional, contingent, dependent; answerable, bound by, captive, dependent, enslaved, inferior, obedient, satellite, subjugated, submissive, subordinate, subservient

subject *v* expose, lay open, make liable, put through, submit, treat

subjective *adj* biased, emotional, idiosyncratic, instinctive, intuitive, nonobjective, personal, prejudiced

submerge *v* deluge, dip, drown, duck, engulf, flood, immerse, inundate, overflow, overwhelm, plunge sink, swamp

submission *n* acquiescence, assent, capitulation, giving in, surrender yielding; compliance, deference, docility, meekness, obedience, passivity, resignation, submissiveness, tractability, unassertiveness; argument, contention, proposal; entry, handing in, presentation, submitting, tendering

submit *v* accede, acquiesce, agree, bend, bow, capitulate, comply, defer, endure, give in, hoist the white flag, knuckle under, lay down arms, resign oneself to, stoop, succumb, surrender, throw in the sponge toe the line, tolerate, yield; (*Inf*) put up with, commit, hand in, present, proffer, put forward, refer, table, tender

subordinate *adj* dependent, inferior, junior, lesser, lower, minor, secondary, subject, subservient; ancillary, auxiliary, subsidiary, supplementary

subordinate *n* aide, assistant, attendant, dependant, inferior, junior, second, subaltern, underling

subscribe *v* contribute, donate, give, offer, pledge, promise; (*Inf*) chip into

subscription *n* annual payment, contribution, donation, dues, gift, membership fee, offering

subsequent *adj* after, consequent, consequential, ensuing, following, later, succeeding, successive

subside *v* abate, decrease, de-esculate, diminish, dwindle, ease, ebb, lessen, let up, level off, melt away, moderate, peter out, quieten, recede, slacken, wane

subsidiary *adj* aiding, ancillary, assistant, auxiliary, contributory, cooperative, helpful, lesser, minor, secondary, serviceable, subordinate, subservient supplemental, supplementary, useful

subsidize *v* finance, fund, promote, put up the money for, sponsor, support, underwrite

subsidy *n* aid, allowance, assistance, contribution, financial aid, grant, help, subvention, support

substance *n* body, element, fabric, material, stuff, texture; burden, essence, gist, import, main point, matter, meaning, pith, significance, subject, sum and substance, theme; actuality, concreteness, entity, force, reality; affluence, assets, estate, means, property, resources, wealth

substantial *adj* ample, big, considerable, generous, goodly, important, large, significant, sizable, worthwhile; (*Inf*) tidy

substantiate *v* affirm, attest to, authenticate, bear out, confirm, corroborate, establish, prove, support, validate, verify

substitute *v* change, commute, exchange, interchange, replace, switch; (*Inf*) swap

substitute *n* agent, deputy, equivalent, expedient, locum, locumtenens, makeshift, proxy, relief, replacement, representative, reserve, stand-by, stopgap, sub, supply, surrogate, temporary; (*Inf*) temp

substitute *adj* acting, additional, alternative, proxy, replacement, reserve, second, surrogate, temporary

subtle *adj* deep, delicate, discriminating, ingenious, nice, penetrating, profound, refined, sophisticated; delicate, faint, implied, indirect, insinuated, slight, understated; artful, astute, crafty, cunning, designing, devious, intriguing, keen, Machiavellian, scheming, shrewd, sly, wily

subtlety *n* acumen, acuteness, cleverness, delicacy, discernment, fine point,intricacy, nicety, refinement, sagacity, skill, sophistication; artfulness, astuteness, craftiness, cunning, deviousness, guile, slyness, wiliness

subtract *v* deduct, detract, diminish, remove, take away, take from, take off, withdraw

suburbs *pl n* dormitory area, environs, neighbourhood, outskirts, residential areas, suburbia

subversive *adj* destructive, incendiary, inflammatory, insurrectionary, overthrowing, perversive, riotous, seditious, treasonous, underground, undermining

succeed *v* be successful, flourish, gain one's end, make good, proper, thrive, triumph, turn out well, work; (*Inf*) arrive, do all right for oneself, do the trick, get to the top, make it; be subsequent, come next, ensue, follow, result, supervene

success *n* ascendancy, eminence, fame favourable outcome, fortune, happiness, luck, prosperity, triumph; best seller, big name, celebrity, market leader, sensation, somebody, star, VIP, winner; (*Inf*) hit, smash hit

successful *adj* acknowledged, at the top of the tree, best-selling, booming, efficacious, favourable, flourishing, fortunate, fruitful, lucky, lucrative, moneymaking, paying, profitable, prosperous, rewarding, thriving, top, unbeaten, victorious, wealthy

succession *n* chain, continuation, course, cycle, flow, order, procession, progression, run, sequence, series, train; accession, assumption, elevation, entering upon, inheritance, taking over

successive *adj* consecutive, following, in a row, in succession, sequent, succeeding

succinct *adj* brief, compact, compendious, concise, condensed, gnomic, in a few well-chosen words, laconic, pithy, summary, tense, to the point

succulent *adj* juicy, luscious, lush, mellow, moist, mouthwatering, rich

succumb *v* capitulate, die, fall, fall victim to, give in, give way, go under, knuckle under, submit, surrender, yield

sudden *adj* abrupt, hasty, hurried, impulsive, quick, rapid, rash, swift, unexpected unforeseen, unusual

sue *v* bring an action against someone, charge, indict, institute legal proceedings against someone, prefer charges against someone, prosecute, summon, take someone to court; appeal for, beg, beseech, entreat, petition, plead, solicit, supplicate

suffer *v* ache, agonize, be affected, be in pain, be racked, feel wretched, grieve, have a thin or bad time, hurt; bear, endure, experience, feel, go through, support, sustain, tolerate, undergo; (*Inf*) go through a lot, put up with; appear in a poor light, be handicapped, be impaired, deteriorate, fall of, show to disadvantage

suffering *n* affliction, agony, anguish, discomfort, distress, hardship, martyrdom, misery, ordeal, pain, torment, torture

sufficient *adj* adequate, competent, enough, satisfactory

suggest *v* advise, advocate, move, offer a suggestion, propose, put forward, recommend; bring to mind, connote, evoke, put one in mind of; hint, imply, indicate, insinuate, intimate, lead one to believe

suggestion *n* motion, plan, proposal, proposition, recommendation; breathe hint, indication, insinuation, intimation, suspicion, trace, whisper

suit *v* agree, agree with, answer, be acceptable to, become, befit, be seemly, conform to, correspond, do, go with, gratify, harmonize, match, please, satisfy, tally; accommodate, adapt, adjust, fashion, fit, modify, proportion, tailor

suit *n* action, case, cause, lawsuit, proceeding, prosecution, trial; clothing, costume, dress, ensemble, habit, outfit; accord with, copy, emulate, follow suit, run with the herd, take one's cue from

suitable *adj* acceptable, applicable, apposite, appropriate, apt, becoming, befitting, convenient, cut out for, due, fit, fitting, in character, in keeping, opportune, pertinent, proper, relevant, right, satisfactory, seemly, suited

sulk *n* be in a huff, be put out, brood, ill humour, look sullen, pique, pout; (*Inf*) take the hump

sulky *adj* aloof, churlish, cross, disgruntled, ill-humoured, in the sulks, moody, morose, perverse, petulant, put out, querulous, resentful, sullen, vexed

sullen *adj* brooding, cheerless, cross, dismal, dull, gloomy, glowering, heavy, moody, morose, obstinate, out of humour, perverse, silent, sombre, sour, stubborn, surly, unsociable

sulky *adj* aloof, churlish, cross, disgruntled, ill-humoured, in the sulks, moody, morose, perverse, petulant, put out, querulous, resentful, sullen, vexed

sullen *adj* brooding, cheerless, cross, dismal, dull, gloomy, glowering, heavy, moody, morose, obstinate, out of humour, perverse, silent, sombre, sour, stubborn, surly, unsociable

sultry *adj* close, hot, humid, muggy, oppressive, sticky, stifling, stuffy, sweltering

sum *n* aggregate, amount, entirety, quantity, reckoning, score, sum total, tally, total, totality, whole

summarize *v* abridge, condense,

encapsulate, epitomize, give a rundown of give the main points of, outline, précis, put in a nutshell, review, sum up

summary *n* abridgment, abstract, compendium, digest, epitome, essence, extract, outline, précis, recapitulation, résumé, review, rundown, summing-up, synopsis

summit *n* acme apex, crown, crowning point, culmination, head, height, peak, pinnacle, top, zenith

summon *v* arouse, assemble, bid, call, call together, cite, convene, convoke, invite, rally, rouse, send for

sumptuous *adj* costly, dear, de-luxe, expensive, extravagant, gorgeous, grand, lavish, luxurious, magnificent, opulent, rich, splendid, superb; (*Inf*) plush, posh, ritzy

sum up *v* close, conclude, put in a nutshell, recapitulate, review, summarize; estimate, form an opinion of, get the measure of; (*Inf*) size up

sundry *adj* assorted, different, miscellaneous, several, some, varied, various

sunny *adj* bright, brilliant, clear, fine, luminous, radiant, summary, sunlit, sunshiny, unclouded, without a cloud in the sky; beaming, blithe, buoyant, cheerful, cheery, genial, happy, joyful, light-hearted, optimistic, pleasant, smiling

superb *adj* admirable, breathtaking, choice, excellent, exquisite, fine, first-rate, gorgeous, grand, magnificent, marvellous, of the first order, splendid, superior, unrivalled

superficial *adj* exterior, external, on the surface, peripheral, shallow, skin-deep, slight, surface; casual, cosmetic, cursory, desultory, hasty, hurried, inattentive, nodding, passing, perfunctory, sketchy, slapdash

superfluous *adj* excess, excessive, extra, in excess, left over, needless, on one's hands, redundant, remaining, residuary, spare, superabundant, supererogatory, supernumerary, surplus, surplus to requirements, uncalled-for, unnecessary, unneeded, unrequired

superhuman *adj* Herculean, heroic, phenomenal, prodigious, stupendous, valiant; divine, paranormal, preternatural, supernatural

superintendent *n* administrator, chief, conductor, controller, director, governor, inspector, manager, overseer, supervisor

superior *adj* better, grander, greater, higher, more advanced paramount, predominant, preferred, prevailing, surpassing, unrivalled; admirable, choice, de luxe, distinguished, excellent, exceptional, exclusive, fine, first-class, first-rate, good, good quality, high calibre, high-class, of the first order; (*Inf*) a cut above; airy, condescend ing, disdainful, haughty, lofty, lordly, patronizing, pretentious, snobbish, supercilious; (*Inf*) stuck-up

superior *n* boss, chief, director, manager, principle, senior, supervisor

superiority *n* advantage, ascendancy, excellence, lead, predominance, pre-eminence, preponderance, prevalence, supremacy

supernatural *adj* abnormal, dark, ghostly, hidden, miraculous, mysterious, mystic, occult, paranormal, phantom, preternatural, psychic, spectral, supernatural, uncanny, unearthly, unnatural

supervise *v* administer, be on duty at, be responsible for conduct, control, direct, handle, have charge of, inspect, keep an eye on, look after, manage, over see, preside over, run, superintend

supervision *n* administration, auspices, care, charge, control, direction, guidance, instruction, management, oversight, stewardship, superintendence, surveillance

supervisor *n* administrator, boss chief, foreman, inspector, manager, overseer, steward, superintendent; (*Inf*) gaffer

supple *adj* bending, elastic, flexible, limber, lithe, loose-limbed, plastic, pliable, pliant

supplement *n* added feature, addendum, addition, appendix, codicil, complement, extra, insert, postscript, pull-out, sequel

supplement *v* add, augment, complement, extend, fill out, reinforce, supply, top up

supplementary *adj* accompanying, additional, ancillary, auxiliary, complementary, extra, secondary, supplemental

supply *v* afford, cater for, come up with, contribute, endow, fill, fur nish, give, grant, minister, outfit, produce, provide, purvey, replenish, satisfy, stock, store, victual, yield

supply *n* cache, fund, hoard, quantity, reserve, reservoir, source, stock, stockpile, store; equipment, food, foodstuff, items, materials, necessities, provender, provisions, rations, stores

support *v* bear, bolster, brace, buttress, carry, hold, hold up, prop, reinforce, shore up, sustain, underpin, uphold; be a source of strength to, buoy up, cherish, finance, foster, fund, keep, look after, maintain, nourish, provide for, strengthen, subsidize, succour, sustain, take care of, underwrite; advocate, aid, assist, back, boost someone's morale, champion, defend, forward, go along with, help, promote, second, side with, stand behind, stand up for, take someone's part, uphold; bear, brook, countenance, endure, stand for, stomach, submit, suffer, tolerate, undergo; (*Inf*) put up with

support *n* abutment, back, brace, foundation, lining, pillar, post, prop, underpinning; aid, approval, assistance, backing, blessing, championship, comfort, encouragement, friendship, furtherance, help, loyalty, moral support, patronage, protection, relief, succour, sustenance; keep, livelihood, maintenance, subsistence, sustenance, upkeep; backbone, backer, comforter, mainstay, prop, second, stay, supporter, tower of strength

supporter *n* adherent, advocate, ally, apologist, champion, co-worker, defender, fan, follower, friend, helper, patron, sponsor, upholder, well-wisher

suppose *v* assume, calculate, conjecture, dare say, expect, imagine, infer, judge, opine, presume, presuppose, surmise, take as read, take for granted, think; believe, conceive, conclude, conjecture, consider, fancy, hypothesize, imagine, pretend

supposition *n* conjecture, doubt, guess, guesswork, hypothesis, idea, notion, postulate, presumption, speculation, surmise, theory

suppress *v* beat down, check, clamp down on, conquer, crack down on, extinguish, overpower, overthrow, put an end to, quash, quell, quench, snuff out, stamp out, stop, subdue, trample on; censor, conceal, contain, cover up, curb, hold back, hold in check, keep secret, muffle, muzzle, repress, restrain, silence, smother, stifle, withhold

supremacy *n* absolute rule, ascendancy, dominance, domination, dominion, lordship, mastery, paramountly, predominance, preeminence, primacy, sovereignty, supreme authority, sway

supreme *adj* cardinal, chief, crowning, culminating, extreme, final, first, foremost, greatest, head, highest, incomparable, leading, matchless, paramount, peerless, predominant, pre-eminent, prevailing, prime, principal, sovereign, superlative, surpassing, top, ultimate, unsurpassed, utmost

sure *adj* assured, certain, clear, confident, convinced, decided, definite, free from doubt, persuaded, positive, satisfied; accurate, dependable, effective, foolproof, honest, indisputable, infallible, neverfailing, precise, reliable, tried and tested, trustworthy, trusty, undeniable, undoubted, unerring, unfailing, unmistakable, well-proven; assured, bound, guaranteed, inescapable, inevitable, irrevocable

surface *n* covering, exterior, façade, face, facet, outside, plane, side, skin, top, veneer

surface *v* appear, come to light, come up, merge, materialize, rise, transpire

surfeit *n* excess, glut, overindulgence, plethora, satiety, superabundancy, superfluity

surfeit *v* cram, fill, glut, gorge, over feed, overfill, satiate, stuff

surge *v* billow, eddy, gush, heave, rise, roll, rush, swell, swirl, tower, undulate, well forth

surly *adj* bearish, brusque, churlish, crabbed, cross, crusty, gruff, ill-natured, morose, perverse, sulky, sullen, testy, uncivil, ungracious; (*Inf*) grouchy

surpass *v* beat, best, eclipse, exceed, excel, outdo, outshine, out strip, override, overshadow, top, tower above, transcend; (*Inf*) go one better than

surplus *n* balance, excess, remainder, residue, superabundance, superfluity, surfeit

surplus *adj* excess, extra, in excess, left over, odd, remaining, spare, superfluous, unused

surprise *v* amaze, astonish, astound, bewilder, confuse, disconcert, leave open-mouthed, nonplus, stagger, stun, take aback; burst in on, catch napping, catch red-handed, catch unawares, come down like a bolt from the blue, discover, spring upon, startle; (*Inf*) bowl over, flabbergast

surprise *n* amazement, astonishment, bewilderment, incredulity, stupefaction, wonder; bolt from the blue, bombshell, jolt, revelation, shock; (*Inf*) eye-opener, start

surprised *adj* amazed, astonished, at a loss, disconcerted, incredulous, nonplussed, open-mouthed, speechless, startled, taken aback, taken by surprise, thunderstruck, unable to believe one's eyes; (*Inf*) caught on the hop, caught on the wrong foot

surprising *adj* amazing, astonishing, astounding, extraordinary, incredible, marvellous, remarkable, staggering, startling, unexpected, unlooked-for, unusual, wonderful

surrender *v* abandon, cede, concede, deliver up, forego, give up, part with, relinquish, renounce, resign, waive, yield; capitulate, give in, give oneself up, give way, lay down arms, quit, show the white flag, submit, succumb, throw in the towel, yield

surrender *n* capitulation, delivery, relinquishment, renunciation, resignation, submission, yielding

surreptitious *adj* clandestine, covert, fraudulent, furtive, secret, sly, sneaking, stealthy, unauthorized, underhand, veiled

surround *v* close in on, encircle, enclose, encompass, envelop, environ, fence in, girdle, hem in, ring

surroundings *pl n* background, environment, environs, location, milieu, neighbourhood, setting

surveillance *n* care, control, direction, inspection, observation, scrutiny, superintendence, supervision, vigilance, watch

survey *v* contemplate, examine, inspect, look over, observe, reconnoitre, research, review, scan, scrutinize, study, supervise, view; appraise, assess, estimate, measure, plan, plot, prospect, size up, take stock of, triangulate

survey *n* examination, inquiry, inspection, overview, perusal, random sample, review, scrutiny, study

survive *v* be extant, endure, exist, hold out, last, live on, outlast, outlive, pull through, remain alive, subsist; (*Inf*) keep body and soul together

suspect *v* distrust, doubt, harbour, suspicions about, have one's doubts about, mistrust; believe, conclude, conjecture, consider, fancy, feel, guess, have a sneaking suspicion, hazard a guess, speculate, suppose. surmise, think probable; (*Inf*) smell a rat

suspect *adj* doubtful, dubious, open to suspicion, questionable; (*Inf*) fishy

suspend *v* append, attach, dangle, hang, swing; adjourn, arrest, cease, cut short, debar, defer, delay, discontinue, hold off, interrupt, lay aside, pigeonhole, postpone, put off, shelve, stay, withhold

suspense *n* anticipation, anxiety, apprehension, doubt, expectancy, expectation, indecision, insecurity, irresolution, tension, uncertainty, wavering

suspicion *n* chariness, distrust, doubt, jealousy, lack of confidence, misgiving, mistrust, qualm, scepticism, wariness; (*Inf*) bad vibes, funny feeling, gut feeling; conjecture, guess, hunch, idea, impression, notion, supposition, surmise; glimmer, hint, shade, shadow, soupçon, strain, streak, suggestion, tinge, touch, trace

suspicious *adj* apprehensive, distrustful, doubtful, jealous, mistrustful, sceptical, suspecting, unbelieving, wary; doubtful, dubious, funny, irregular, of doubtful honesty, open to doubt or misconstruction, queer, questionable, suspect; (*Inf*) fishy, shady

sustain *v* bear, carry, keep from falling, keep up, support, uphold; bear, bear up under, endure, experience, feel, suffer, undergo, withstand; aid, assist, comfort, foster, help, keep alive, nourish, nurture, provide for, relieve; approve, confirm, continue, keep alive, keep going, keep up, maintain, prolong, protract, ratify; endorse, uphold, validate, verify

swallow *v* absorb, consume, devour, drink, eat, gulp, ingest, swill, wash down; (*Inf*) down, swig

swamp *n* bog, everglades, fen, marsh, mire, morass, moss, quagmire, slough

swamp *v* capsize, drench, engulf, flood, inundate, overwhelm, sink, submerge, swallow up, upset, wash over, waterlog

swap *v* bandy, barter, exchange, interchange, switch, trade, traffic

swarm *n* army, bevy, concourse, crowd, drove, flock, herd, horde, host, mass, multitude, myriad, shoal, throng

swarm *v* congregate, crowd, flock, mass, stream, throng; abound, be alive, be infested, be overrun, bristle, crawl, teem

sway *v* bend, fluctuate, incline, lean, lurch, oscillate, rock, roll, swing, wave; affect, control, direct, dominate, govern, guide, induce, influence, persuade, prevail on, win over

sway *n* ascendancy, authority, command, control, dominion, government, influence, jurisdiction, power, predominance, rule, sovereignty; (*Inf*) clout

swear *v* affirm, assert, attest, avow, declare, depose, give one's word, pledge oneself, promise, state under oath, take an oath, testify, vow, warrant; be foul-mouthed, blaspheme, curse, imprecate, take the Lord's name in vain, turn the air blue, utter profanities

sweat *n* diaphoresis, exudation, perspiration, sudor; agitation, anxiety, distress, panic, strain, worry; (*Inf*) agitation, flap; backbreaking task, chore, drudgery, effort, labour, toil

sweat *v* break out in a sweat, exude moisture, glow, perspire; agonize, be on tenderhooks, chafe, dither, fluster, fret, lose sleep over, suffer, torture oneself, worry; (*Inf*) be in a lather, be in a stew, be in a tiz woz, be on pins and needles

sweep *v* brush, clean, clear, remove; career, flounce, fly, glance, glide, hurtle, pass, sail, scud, skim, tear, zoom

sweep *n* arc, bend, curve, gesture,

move, movement, stroke, swing; compass, extent, range, scope, span, stretch, vista

sweet *adj* cloying, honeyed, luscious, melting, saccharine, sugary, sweetened, syrupy, toothsome; affectionate, agreeable, amiable, appealing, attractive, beautiful, charming, delightful, engaging, fair, gentle, kind, lovable, sweet-tempered, taking, tender, unselfish, winning, winsome; beloved, cherished, darling, dear, dearest, pet, precious, treasured; aromatic, balmy, clean, fragrant, fresh, new, perfumed, pure, redolent, sweet-smelling, wholesome

sweet *n* bonbon, candy, confectionery, sweetie, sweetmeats

sweeten *v* honey, sugar, sugar-coat; alleviate, appease, mollify, pacify, soften up soothe, sugar the pill

sweetheart admirer, beau, beloved, boyfriend, darling, dear, girlfriend, inamorata, inamorato, love, lover, suitor, truelove, valentine; (*Inf*) flame, steady, sweetie

swell *v* balloon, become bloated, become distended, become larger, be inflated, belly, billow, bloat, bulge, dilate, distend, enlarge, expand, extend, increase, protrude, puff up, rise, round out, tumefy, well up; add to, aggravate, augment, enhance, heighten, intensify, mount, surge

swell *n* billow, rise, surge, undulation, wave

swelling *n* blister, bruise, bulge, bump, dilation, distention, enlargement, inflammation, lump, protuberance, puffiness, tumescence

swerve *v* bend, deflect, depart from, deviate, diverge, incline, sheer off, shift, skew, stray, swing, turn, turn aside, veer, wander, wind

swift *adj* abrupt, expeditious, express, fast, fleet, fleet-footed, flying, hurried, nimble, prompt, quick, rapid, ready, short, short-lived, spanking, speedy, sudden, winged; (*Inf*) nippy

swindle *v* cheat, deceive, defraud, dupe, fleece, overcharge, trick; (*Inf*) bamboozle, con, diddle, do, pull a fast one, put one over some one, rip someone off, take someone for a ride, take to the cleaners

swindle *n* deceit, deception, double-dealing, fraud, imposition, racket, roguery, sharp practice, trickery; (*Inf*) con trick, fiddle, rip-off, swizz

swindler *n* charlatan, cheat, confidence man, fraud, impostor, mountebank, rascal, rogue, shark, sharper, trickster; (*Inf*) con man, rook

swing *v* be pendent, be suspended, dangle, hang, move back and forth, suspend; fluctuate, oscillate, rock. sway, vary, veer, vibrate, wave

swing *n* fluctuation, oscillation, stroke, sway, swaying, vibration

swirl *v* agitate, boil, churn, eddy, spin, surge, twirl, twist, whirl

switch *v* change, change course, deflect, deviate, divert, exchange, interchange, rearrange, replace by, shift, substitute, trade, turn aside; (*Inf*) swap

switch *n* about-turn, alteration, change, change of direction, exchange, reversal, shift, substitution; (*Inf*) swap

swollen *adj* bloated, distended, dropsical, edematous, enlarged, inflamed, oedematous, puffed up, puffy, tumescent, tumid

swoop *v* descend, dive, pounce, rush, stoop, sweep

swoop *n* descent, drop, lunge, plunge, pounce, rush, stoop, sweep

syllabus *n* course of study, curriculum

symbol *n* badge, emblem, figure, image, logo, mark, representation, sign, token, type

symmetrical *adj* balanced, in proportion, proportional, regular, well-proportioned

symmetry *n* agreement, balance, correspondence, evenness, form, harmony, order, proportion, regularity

sympathetic *adj* affectionate, caring, commiserating, compassionate, concerned, condoling, feeling, interested, kind, kindly, pitying, responsive, supportive, tender, understanding, warm, warm-hearted; agreeable, appreciative, companionable, compatible, congenial, friendly, like-minded, responsive, well-intentioned

sympathize *v* bleed for, commiserate, condole, empathize, feel for, feel one's heart go out to, grieve with, have compassion, offer consolation, pity, share another's sorrow; agree, be in accord, be in sympathy, go along with, identify with, side with, understand

sympathizer *n* condoler, fellow traveller, partisan, supporter, well-wisher

sympathy *n* commiseration, compassion, condolences, empathy, pity, tenderness, thoughtfulness, understanding; affinity, agreement, congeniality, correspondence, fellow-feeling, harmony, rapport, union, warmth

symptom *n* expression, indication, mark, note, sign, syndrome, token, warning

synthetic *adj* artificial, ersatz, fake, man-made, manufactured, mock, pseudo, sham, simulated

system *n* arrangement classification, combination, coordination, organization, scheme, structure; fixed order, frame of reference, method, methodology, *modus operandi*, practice, procedure, routine, technique, theory, usage; definite plan, logical process, method, methodicalness, orderliness, regularity, systematization; (*Inf*) set-up

systematic *adj* businesslike, efficient, methodical, orderly, organized, precise, standardized, systemized, well-ordered

T

table *n* bench, board, counter, slab, stand; board, diet, fare, food, victuals; (*Inf*) spread; agenda, catalogue, chart, diagram, digest, graph, index, inventory, list, plan, record, register, roll, schedule, synopsis, tabulation

table *v* enter, move, propose, put forward, submit, suggest

taboo *adj* anathema, banned, beyond the pale, disapproved of, forbidden, frowned on, not allowed, not permitted, outlawed, prohibited, proscribed, ruled out, unacceptable, unmentionable, unthinkable

taboo *n* anathema, ban, disapproval, interdict, prohibition, proscription, restriction

tacit *adj* implicit, implied, inferred, silent, taken for granted, undeclared, understood, unexpressed, unspoken, unstated, wordless

taciturn *adj* aloof, antisocial, close-lipped, cold, distant, dumb, mute, quiet, reserved, reticent, silent, tight-lipped, uncommunicative, unforthcoming, withdrawn

tack *n* drawing pin, nail, pin, staple, thumbtack, tintack; approach, bearing, course, direction, heading, line, method, path, plan, procedure, tactic, way

tack *v* affix, attach, fasten, fix, nail, pin, staple; baste, stitch

tackle *n* accoutrements, apparatus, equipment, gear, implements, outfit, paraphernalia, rig, rigging, tools, trappings; block, challenge, stop

tackle *v* apply oneself to, attempt, begin, come to grips with, deal with, embark upon engage in, essay, get to grips with, set about, take on, try, turn one's hand to, undertake, wade into; (*Inf*) get stuck into, have a go at; block, bring down, challenge, clutch, confront, grab, grasp, halt, intercept, seize, stop, take hold of, throw

tact *n* address, adroitness, consideration, delicacy, diplomacy, discretion, finesse, judgment, perception, *savoir-faire*, sensitivity, skill, thoughtfulness, understanding

tactful *adj* careful, considerate, delicate, diplomatic, discreet, judicious, perceptive, polished, polite, politic, prudent, sensitive, subtle, thoughtful, understanding

tactic *n* approach, course, device, line, manoeuvre, means, method, move, ploy, policy, scheme, stratagem, tack, trick, way; campaign, generalship, manoeuvres, plans, strategy

tactical *adj* adroit, artful, clever, cunning, diplomatic, foxy, politic, shrewd, skilful, smart, strategic

tactless *adj* blundering, boorish, careless, clumsy, discourteous, gauche, harsh, impolite, impolitic, imprudent, inconsiderate, indelicate, indiscreet, inept, injudicious, insensitive, maladroit, rough, rude, sharp, thoughtless, uncivil, undiplomatic, unfeeling, unkind, unsubtle

tail *n* appendage, conclusion, empennage, end, extremity, rear end, tailpiece, train; file, line, queue, tail back, train

tail *v* dog the footsteps of, follow, keep an eye on, keep under surveillance, shadow, stalk, track, trail; decrease, drop off, dwindle, fade, fall away, peter out

taint *v* adulterate, blight, contaminate, corrupt, dirty, foul, infect, poison, pollute, soil, spoil

taint *n* black mark, blemish, blot, blot on one's escutcheon, defect, disgrace, dishonour, fault, flaw, shame, smear, spot, stain, stigma

take *v* abduct, acquire, arrest, capture, carry off, catch, clutch, ensnare, entrap, gain possession of, get, get hold of, grasp, grip, have, help oneself to, lay hold of, obtain, receive, secure, seize, win; abstract, appropriate, carry off, misappropriate, pocket, purloin, run off with, steal, walk off with; (*Inf*) filch, nick, pinch, swipe; book, buy, engage, hire, lease, pay for, pick, purchase, rent, reserve, select; abide, bear, brave, brook, endure, go through, pocket, stand, stomach, submit to, suffer, swallow, tolerate, undergo, weather, withstand; consume, drink, eat, imbibe, ingest, inhale, swallow; accept, adopt, assume, enter upon, undertake; assume, believe, consider, deem, hold, interpret as, perceive, presume, receive, regard, see as, think of as, understand; bear, bring, carry, cart, convey, ferry, fetch, haul, transport; accompany, bring, conduct, convoy, escort, guide, lead, usher; deduct, eliminate, remove, subtract; accept, accommodate, contain, have room for, hold

take back *v* disavow, disclaim, recant, renounce, retract, unsay, withdraw

take down *v* make a note of, minute, note, put on record record, set down, transcribe, write down

take in *v* absorb, assimilate, comprehend, digest, grasp, understand; comprise, contain, cover, embrace, encompass, include; accommodate, admit, let in receive; bilk, cheat, deceive, dupe, fool, hoodwink, mislead, swindle, trick; (*Inf*) con, do, pull the wool over someone's eyes

take-off *n* departure, launch, lift off; caricature, imitation, lampoon, mocking, parody, satire, travesty; (*Inf*) send up, spoof

take off *v* discard, divest oneself of doff, drop, peel off, remove, strip off; become airborne, leave the ground, lift off, take to the air; decamp, depart, disappear, go, leave, set out, strike out; (*Inf*) hit the road, split

take on *v* employ, engage, enlist, enroll, hire, retain; accept, address oneself to, agree to do, tackle, try, undertake; compete against, contend with, enter the lists against, face, fight, match oneself against, oppose, pit oneself, against, vie with

take up *v* adopt, assume, become involved in, engage in, start; begin again, carry

take up *n* continue, follow on, go on, pick up, proceed, recommence, restart, resume; absorb, consume, cover, extend over, fill, occupy, use up

taking *adj* attractive, beguiling,

captivating, charming, compelling, delightful, enchanting, engaging, fascinating, intriguing, pleasing, prepossessing, winning; (*Inf*) fetching

takings *pl n* earnings, gain, gate money, income, pickings, proceeds, profits, receipts, returns, revenue, take, yield

tale *n* account, anecdote, conte, fable, fiction, legend, narration, narrative, novel, relation, report, romance, saga, short story, spiel, fabrication, falsehood, fib, lie, rigmarole, rumour, untruth; (*Inf*) cock-and-bull story, tall story

talent *n* ability, aptitude, bent, capacity, endowment, faculty, flair, forte, genius, gift, knack, parts, power

talented *adj* able, artistic, brilliant, gifted, well-endowed

talk *v* articulate, chat, chatter, communicate, converse, crack, express oneself, give voice to, gossip, nat ter, prate, prattle, say, speak, utter, verbalize; (*Inf*) gab, gos, witter; confabulate, confer, hold discussions, negotiate, palaver, parley; blab, crack, give the game away, inform, reveal information; (*Inf*) have a confab, grass, sing, spill the beans, squeak, squeal

talk *n* address, discourse, disquisition, dissertation, harangue, lecture, oration, sermon, speech; blather, blether, chat, chatter, chit chat, conversation, crack, gossip, hearsay, natter, rumour, tittle-tattle; (*Inf*) gab, jaw, rap; colloquy, conclave, confabulation, conference, consultation, dialogue, discussion, meeting, negotiation, palaver, parley, seminar, symposium; (*Inf*) confab; argot, dialect, jargon, language, patois, slang, speech, words; (*Inf*) lingo

talkative *adj* chatty, communicative, garrulous, loquacious, voluble

talking-to *n* criticism, lecture, rebuke, reprimand, reproach, reproof, row, scolding; (*Inf*) dressing-down, rap on the knuckles, slating, telling-off, ticking-off, wigging

tall *adj* big, elevated, giant, high, lanky, lofty, soaring, towering; demanding, difficult, exorbitant, hard, unreasonable, well-nigh impossible

tally *v* accord, agree, coincide, concur, conform, correspond, fit, harmonize, match, parallel, square, suit; compute, count up, keep score, mark, reckon, record, register, total

tally *n* count, mark, reckoning, record, running total, score, total

tame *adj* amenable, broken, cultivated, disciplined, docile, domesticated, gentle, obedient, tractable; compliant, docile, manageable, meek, obedient, spiritless, subdued, submissive, unresisting; bland, boring, dull, flat, humdrum, insipid, lifeless, prosaic, tedious, unexciting, uninspiring, uninteresting, vapid, wearisome

tame *v* break in, domesticate, gentle, house-train, make tame, pacify, train; break the spirit of, bridle, bring to heel, conquer, curb, discipline, enslave, humble, master, repress, subdue, subjugate, suppress

tamper *v* alter, damage, interfere, intrude, meddle, mess about, monkey around, tinker; bribe, corrupt, get at, influence, manipulate, rig; (*Inf*) muck about, poke one's nose into, fix

tang *n* aftertaste, flavour, relish, savour, smack, taste; keenness, nip, sting

tangible *adj* corporeal, material, palpable, tactile, touchable; actual, certain, embodied, evident, obvious, open, perceptible, plain, positive, real, sensible, solid, stable, substantial

tangle *n* coil, confusion, entangle ment, jam, jungle, knot, mass, mat, mesh, snarl, twist, web; complication, entanglement, imbroglio, labyrinth, maze, mess, mix-up; (*Inf*) fix

tangle *v* coil, confuse, entangle, interlace, interlock, intertwist, interweave, jam, kink, knot, mat, mesh, snarl, twist

tangled *adj* entangled, jumbled, knotted, knotty, matte, messy, scrambled, snarled, tousled, twisted; complex, complicated, confused, convoluted, involved, knotty, messy, mixed-up

tantalize *v* baffle, balk, disappoint, entice, frustrate, keep someone hanging on, lead on, make someone's mouth water, provoke, taunt, tease, thwart, titillate, torment, torture

tantrum *n* fit, flare-up, hysterics, ill humour, outburst, paroxysm, storm, temper; (*Inf*) paddy

tap *v* beat, drum, knock, pat, rap, strike, touch; bleed, broach, drain, draw off, open, pierce, siphon off, unplug; draw on, exploit, make use of, milk, mine, put to use, turn to account, use, utilize

tap *n* beat, knock, light blow, pat, rap, touch; faucet, spigot, spout, stopcock, valve; bung, plug, spile, stopper

tape *n* band, ribbon, strip

tape *v* bind, seal, secure, stick, wrap; record, tape-record, video

taper *v* come to a point, narrow, thin

tardy *adj* slow, sluggish, snail-like; backward, behindhand, dilatory, late, loitering, overdue, slack

target *n* aim, ambition, bull's eye, end, goal, intention, mark, object, objective; butt, quarry, scapegoat, victim

tariff *n* assessment, duty, excise, impost, levy, rate, tax, toll; bill of fare, charges, menu, price list, schedule

tarnish *v* befoul, blacken, blemish, blot, darken, dim, discolour, drag through the mud, dull, lose lustre, rust, soil, spot, stain, sully, taint

tart *n* pastry, pie, quiche, strudel, tartlet; call girl, fallen women, fille de joie, harlot, loose woman, prostitute, slut, streetwalker, strumpet, trollop, whore, woman of easy virtue; (*Inf*) floozy, hooker

tart *v* dress up, make oneself up, smarten up

tart *adj* acid, acidulous, astringent, bitter, piquant, pungent, sharp, sour, tangy, vinegary; acrimonious, astringent, barbed, biting, caustic, crusty, cutting, harsh, nasty, scathing, sharp, short, snappish, testy, trenchant, wounding

task *n* assignment, business, charge,

chore, duty employment, enterprise, exercise, job, labour, mission, occupation, toil, undertaking

taste *n* flavour, relish, savour, smack, tang; bit, bite, dash, drop, morsel, mouthful, nip, sample, sip, soupçon, spoonful, swallow, titbit, touch; appetite, bent, desire, fancy, fondness, inclination, leaning, liking, palate, partiality, penchant, predilection, preference, relish; appreciation, cultivation, culture, discernment, discrimination, elegance, grace, judgment, perception, polish, refinement, style

taste *v* differentiate, discern, distinguish, perceive; assay, nibble, relish, sample, savour, sip, test, try; come up against, encounter, experience, feel, have knowledge of, know, meet with, partake of, undergo

tasteful *adj* aesthetically pleasing, artistic, beautiful, charming, cultivated, cultured, delicate, discriminating, elegant, exquisite, fastidious, graceful, handsome, harmonious, in good taste, polished, refined, restrained, smart, stylish

tasteless *adj* bland, boring, dull, flat, flavourless, insipid, mild, stale, tame, thin, uninspired, uninteresting, vapid, watered-down, weak; cheap, coarse, crass, crude, flashy, garish, gaudy, graceless, gross, impolite, improper, indecorous, indelicate, indiscreet, inelegant, low, rude, tactless, tawdry, uncouth, unseemly, vulgar

tasty *adj* appetizing, delectable, delicious, flavourful, flavoursome, full-flavoured, good-tasting, luscious, palatable, sapid, savoury, toothsome; (*Inf*) scrumptious, yummy

taunt *v* deride, flout, gibe, insult, jeer, mock, provoke, reproach, revile, ridicule, sneer, tease, torment, twit, upbraid

taunt *n* barb, censure, cut, derision, dig, gibe, insult, jeer, provocation, reproach, ridicule, sarcasm, teasing

taut *adj* flexed, rigid, strained, stressed, stretched, tense, tight

tawdry *adj* Brummagem, flashy, gaudy, glittering, meretricious, raffish, showy, tasteless, tatty, tinsel, tinselly, vulgar; (*Inf*) cheapskate, flash, kitsch, plastic, tacky

tax *n* assessment, charge, contribution, customs, duty, excise, imposition, impost, levy, rate, tariff, tithe, toll, tribute; burden, demand, drain, load, pressure, strain, weight

tax *v* assess, charge, demand, exact, extract, impose, levy a tax on, rate, tithe; burden, drain, enervate, exhaust, load, make heavy demands on, overburden, push, put pressure on, sap, strain, stretch, task, try, weaken, wear out, weary, weigh heavily on; accuse, arraign, blame, charge, impeach, impugn, incriminate, lay at one's door

teach *v* advise, coach, demonstrate, direct, discipline, drill, edify, educate, enlighten, give lessons in, guide, impart, implant, inculcate, inform, instill, instruct, school, show, train, tutor

teacher *n* coach, dominie, don, educator, guide, guru, instructor, lecturer, master, mentor, mistress, pedagogue, professor, schoolmaster, schoolmistress, schoolteacher, trainer, tutor

team *n* band, body, bunch, company, crew, gang, group, line-up, set, side, squad, troupe

team up *v* band together, cooperate, couple, get together, join, link, unite, work together

tear *v* claw, divide, lacerate, mangle, mutilate, pull apart, rend, rip, rive, run, rupture, scratch, server, shred, split, sunder; bolt, career, charge, dart, dash, fly, gallop, hurry, race, run, rush, shoot, speed, sprint, zoom; (*Inf*) belt; grab, pluck, pull, rip, seize, snatch, wrench, wrest, yank

tear *n* hole, laceration, mutilation, rent, rip, run, rupture, scratch, split

tease *v* annoy, badger, bait, bedevil, chaff, gibe, goad, lead on, mock, needle, pester, plague, provoke, rag, ridicule, tantalize, taunt, torment, twit, vex, worry; (*Inf*) aggravate, have on, kid, rib

technique *n* approach, course, fashion, manner, means, method, mode, *modus operandi*, procedure, style, system, way; address, adroitness, art, artistry, craft, craftsmanship, delivery, execution, facility, knack, performance, proficiency, skill, touch; (*Inf*) know-how

tedious *adj* annoying, banal, boring, deadly, dull, drab, dreary, dull, fatiguing, humdrum, irksome, laborious, lifeless, long-draw-out, monotonous, prosaic, prosy, soporific, tiring, unexciting, uninteresting, vapid, wearisome

tedium *n* banality, boredom, deadness, drabness, dreariness, dullness, ennui, lifelessness, monotony, routine, sameness, tediousness, the doldrums

teem *v* abound, be abundant, bear, be crawling with, be full of, be prolific, brim, bristle, burst at the seams, overflow, produce, pullulate, swarm

telepathy *n* mind-reading, sixth sense, though transference

telephone *n* handset, line, phone; (*Inf*) blower

telephone *v* call call up, dial, give someone a call, phone, put a call through to; (*Inf*) buzz, get on the blower, give someone a buzz, give someone a ring, give someone a tinkle, ring

telescope *n* glass, spyglass

telescope *v* concertina, crush, squash; abbreviate, abridge, capsulize, compress, condense, consolidate, contract, curtail, cut, shorten, shrink, squash, squeeze, tighten, trim, truncate

tell *v* acquaint, announce, apprise, communicate, confess, disclose, divulge, express, impart, inform, let know, make known, mention, notify, proclaim, reveal, say, speak, state, utter; authorize, bid, call upon, command, direct, enjoin, instruct, order, require, summon; chronicle, depict, describe, give an account of, narrate, portray, recount, rehearse, relate, report; comprehend, discern, discover, make out, see, understand; differentiate, discern, discriminate, distinguish, identify; carry weight, count, have effect, have force, make its presence felt, register, take its toll, weigh; calculate, compute, count, enumerate, number, reckon, tally

temper *n* attitude, character, constitution, disposition, frame of mind, humour, mind, mood, nature, temperament, tenor, vein; bad mood, fit of pique, fur, passion, rage, tantrum; (*Inf*) paddy; anger, annoyance, heat, hot-headedness, ill-humour, irascibility, irritability, irritation, passion, peevishness, petulance, resentment, surliness; calm, calmness, composure, cool ness, equanimity, good humour, moderation, self-control, tranquillity; (*Inf*) cool

temper *v* abate, admix, allay, assuage, calm, lessen, mitigate, moderate, mollify, palliate, restrain, soften, soothe, tone down; (*Inf*) soft pedal

temperament *n* bent, cast of mind, character, complexion, constitution, disposition, frame of mind, humour, make-up, mettle, nature, outlook, personalty, quality, soul, spirit, stamp, temper, tendencies, tendency

temperamental *adj* capricious, easily upset, emotional, erratic, excitable, explosive, fiery, highly strung, hot-headed, hypersensitive, impatient, irritable, mercurial, moody, neurotic, passionate, petulant, sensitive, touchy, volatile; erratic, inconsistent, undependable, unpredictable, unreliable

temperance *n* continence, discretion, forbearance, moderation, restraint, self-control, self-discipline, self-restraint; abstemiousness, abstinence, prohibition, sobriety, teetotalism

temperate *adj* agreeable, balmy, calm, clement, cool, fair, gentle, mild, moderate, pleasant, soft; calm, composed, dispassionate, equable, even-tempered, mild, moderate, reasonable, self-controlled, self-restrained, sensible, stable; abstemious, abstinent, continent, moderate, extreme

temple *n* church, holy place, place of worship, sanctuary, shrine

temporarily *adv* briefly, fleetingly, for a little while, for a moment, for a short while, for now, for the moment, for the time being, momentarily, pro tem

temporary *adj* brief, ephemeral, evanescent, fleeting, fugacious, fugitive, here today and gone tomorrow, impermanent, interim, momentary, passing, pro tem, *pro tempore,* provisional, short-lived, transient, transitory

tempt *v* allure, appeal to, attract, coax, decoy, draw, entice, inveigle, invite, lead on, lure, make one's mouth water, seduce, tantalize, whet one's appetite, woo; bait, dare, fly in the face of, provoke, risk, test, try

temptation *n* allurement, appeal, attraction, attractiveness, bait, blandishment, coaxing, decoy, draw, enticement, inducement, invitation, lure, pull, seduction, snare, tantalization; (*Inf*) come-on

tempting *adj* alluring, appetizing, attractive, enticing, inviting, mouth-watering, seductive, tantalizing

tenacious *adj* clinging, fast, firm, forceful, iron, strong, tight, unshakable; retentive, unforgetful;

adamant, determined, dogged, firm, inflexible, intransigent, obdurate, obstinate, persistent, pertinacious, resolute, staunch, steadfast, strong-willed, stubborn, sure, unswerving, unyielding

tenancy *n* holding, lease, occupancy, occupation, possession, renting, residence

tenant *n* holder, inhabitant, leaseholder, lessee, occupant, occupier, renter, resident

tend *v* be apt, be biased, be disposed, be inclined, be liable, be likely, gravitate, have a leaning, have an inclination, have a tendency, incline, lean, trend; attend, care for, cater to, control, cultivate, feed, guard, handle, keep, keep an eye on, look after, maintain, manage, minister to, nurse, nurture, protect, see to, serve, take care of, wait on, watch, watch over

tendency *n* bent, disposition, inclination, leaning, liability, partiality, enchant, predilection, predisposition, proclivity, proneness, propensity, readiness, susceptibility

tender *adj* breakable, delicate, feeble, fragile, frail, soft, weak; callow, green, immature, impressionable, inexperience, new, raw, sensitive, unripe, vulnerable, young, youthful; (*Inf*) wet behind the ears; affectionate, amorous, benevolent, caring, compassionate, considerate, fond, gentle, humane, kind, loving, merciful, pitiful, sentimental, softhearted, sympathetic, tenderhearted, warm, warm-hearted; complicated, dangerous, difficult, risky, sensitive, ticklish, touchy, tricky; aching, acute, bruised, inflamed, irritated, painful, raw, sensitive, smarting, sore

tender *v* bid, offer, present, proffer, propose, suggest, volunteer

tender *n* bid, offer, proffer, proposal; currency, money

tenderness *n* delicateness, feebleness, fragility, frailness, sensitiveness, sensitivity, softness, vulnerability, weakness; callowness, greenness, immaturity, impressionableness, inexperience, newness, rawness, sensitivity, vulnerability, youth, youthfulness; affection, amorousness, attachment, benevolence, care, compassion, consideration, devotion, fondness, gentleness, humaneness, humanity, kindness, liking, love, mercy, pity, sentimentality, softheartedness, sympathy, tender-heartedness, warm-hearted ness, warmth; ache, aching, bruising, inflammation, irritation, pain, painfulness, rawness, sensitiveness, sensitivity, smart, soreness

tense *adj* rigid, strained, stretched, taut, tight; anxious, apprehensive, edgy, fidgety, jumpy, keyed up, nervous, on edge, overwrought, restless, strained, under pressure, wrought up; (*Inf*) jittery, strung up, uptight, wound up; exciting, moving, nerve-wracking, stressful, worrying

tension *n* pressure, rigidity, stiff ness, straining, stress, stretching, tautness, tightness; anxiety, apprehension, edginess, hostility, ill-feeling, nervousness, pressure, restlessness, strain, stress, suspense, unease; (*Inf*) the jitters

tentative *adj* conjectural, experimental, indefinite, provisional, speculative, unconfirmed, unsettled; backward, cautious, diffident, doubtful, faltering, hesitant, timid, uncertain, undecided, unsure

tepid *adj* lukewarm, slightly warm, warmish; apathetic, cool, half-hearted, indifferent, lukewarm, unenthusiastic

term *n* appellation, denomination, designation, expression, locution, name, phrase, title, word; duration, interval, period, season, space, span, spell, time, while; course, session; bound, boundary, close, conclusion, confine, culmination, end, finish, fruition, limit, terminus

term *v* call, denominate, designate, dub, entitle, label, name, style

terminal *adj* bounding, limiting; final, terminating, ultimate

terminal *n* end, extremity, termination; bound, limit; airport, depot, station, terminus

terminate *v* abort, bring to an end, cease, close, complete, conclude, cut off, discontinue, end, expire, finish, issue, lapse, put an end to, result, run out, stop, wind up

termination *n* abortion, cessation, close, completion, conclusion, consequence, cut-off point, discontinuation, effect, end, ending, expiry, finale, finis, finish, issue, result; (*Inf*) wind-up

terms *pl n* language, manner of speaking, phraseology, terminology; conditions, particulars, premises, provisions, provisos, qualifications, specifications, stipulations; charges, fee, payment, price, rates

terrible *adj* bad, dangerous, desperate, extreme, intolerable, serious, severe; appaling, awful, dreadful, fearful, frightful, gruesome, harrowing, horrendous, horrible, horrid, horrifying, monstrous, shocking, terrifying, unspeakable; awful, bad, beastly, foul, frightful, hateful, hideous, loathsome, nasty, obnoxious, odious, offensive, poor, repulsive, revolting, unpleasant, vile; (*Inf*) dire, dreadful, duff, rotten

terrific *adj* awesome, awful, dreadful, enormous, excessive, extreme, fearful, fierce, gigantic, great, harsh, horrific, huge, intense, monstrous, severe, terrible, tremendous; amazing, breathtaking, excellent, fine, magnificent, marvellous, outstanding, stupendous, superb, very good, wonderful; (*Inf*) ace, fabulous, fantastic, great, sensational, smashing, super

terrify *v* alarm, appal, awe, dismay, fill with terror, frighten, frighten out of one's wits, horrify, intimidate, make one's blood run cold, make one's flesh creep. make one's hair stand on end, petrify, put the fear of God into, scare, scare to death, shock, terrorize

territory *n* area, bailiwick, country, district, domain, land, province, region, sector, state, terrain, tract, zone

terror *n* alarm, anxiety, awe, consternation, dismay, dread, fear and trembling, fright, horror, intimidation, panic, shock

terrorize *v* browbeat, bully, coerce, intimidate, menace, oppress, threaten; (*Inf*) strong-arm; alarm, appal, awe, dismay, fill with terror, frighten, frighten out of ones wits, horrify, inspire, panic in, intimidate, make one's flesh creep, make one's hair stand on end, petrify, put the fear of God into, scare, scare to death, shock, strike terror into, terrify

terse *adj* aphoristic, brief, clipped, compact, concise, condensed, crisp, elliptical, epigrammatic, gnomic, incisive, laconic, neat, pithy, sententious, short, succinct, summary, to the point; abrupt, brusque, curt, short, snappy

test *v* analyse, assay, assess, check, examine, experiment, investigate, prove, put to the proof, put to the test, try, try out, verify

test *n* analysis, assessment, attempt, catechism, check, evaluation, examination, investigation, ordeal, probation, proof, trial

testify *v* affirm, assert, attest, bear witness, certify, corroborate, declare, evince, give testimony, show, state, swear, vouch, witness

testimonial *n* certificate, character, commendation, credential, endorsement, recommendation, reference, tribute

testimony *n* affidavit, affirmation, attestation, avowal, confirmation, corroboration, declaration, deposition, evidence, information, profession, statement, submission, witness

testy *adj* captious, choleric, cross, fretful, hasty, irascible, irritable, quick, peevish, peppery, pettish, petulant, querilous, snappish, splenetic, touch, waspish

tête-à-tête *n* chat, conversation, dialogue; (*Inf*) confab, rap

text *n* body, contents, main body, matter; wording, words; argument, matter, motif, subject, theme, topic

texture *n* character, composition, consistency, constitution, fabric, feel, grain, make, quality, structure, surface, tissue, weave

thankful *adj* appreciative, beholden, grateful, indebted, obliged

thanks *pl n* acknowledgment, appreciation, credit, gratefulness, gratitude, recognition, thanksgiving

thaw *v* defrost, dissolve, liquefy, melt, soften, unfreeze, warm

theatrical *adj* affected, artificial, ceremonious, dramatic, exaggerated, histrionic, mannered, ostentatious, overdone, pompous, showy, stagy, stilted, unreal; (*Inf*) hammy, showbiz

theft *n* embezzlement, fraud, larceny, pilfering, purloining, robbery, stealing, swindling, thievery, thieving; (*Inf*) rip-off

theme *n* argument, burden, idea, keynoted, matter, subject, subject matter, text, thesis, topic; leitmotif, motif, recurrent, image, unifying, idea; composition, dissertation, essay, exercise, paper

theoretical *adj* abstract, academic, conjectural, hypothetical, ideal, impractical, pure, speculative

theorize *v* conjecture, formulate, guess, hypothesize, project, propound, speculate, suppose

theory *n* assumption, conjecture, guess, hypothesis, presumption, speculation, supposition, surmise, thesis; philosophy, plan, proposal, scheme, system

therapeutic *adj* ameliorative, analeptic, beneficial, corrective, curative, good, healing, remedial, restorative, salubrious, salutary, sanative

therefore *adv* accordingly, afterward, consequently, hence, so, subsequently, then, thence, whence

thick *adj* broad, bulky, deep, fat, solid, substantial, wide; close, clotted, coagulated, compact, concentrated, condensed, crowded, deep, dense, heavy, impenetrable, opaque; abundant, brimming, bristling, bursting, chock-a-block, chock-full, covered, crawling, frequent, full, numerous, packed, replete, swarming, teeming; block-headed, brainless, dense, dull, insensitive, moronic, obtuse, slow, slow-witted, stupid, thick headed; (*Inf.*) dimwitted, dopey; dense, heavy, impenetrable, soupy; distorted, guttural, hoarse, husky, inarticulate, indistinct, throaty; road, decided, distinct, marked, pronounced, rich, strong; close, confidential, devoted, familiar, friendly, hand in glove, inseparable, intimate, on good terms, well in; (*Inf*) chummy, matey, pally

thicken *v* cake, clot, coagulate, condense, congeal, deepen, gel, jell, set

thief bandit, burglar, cheat, crook, embezzler, housebreaker, larcenist, pickpocket, pilferer, plunderer, purloiner, robber, shoplifter, stealer, swindler; (*Inf*) mugger, swiper

thieve *v* cheat, embezzle, peculate, pilfer, plunder, purloin, rob, run off with, shoplift, steal, swindle

thin *adj* attenuate, attenuated, fine, narrow, threadlike; delicate, diaphanous, filmy, fine, flimsy, gossamer, see-thorugh, sheer, translucent, transparent, unsubstantial; bony, emaciated, lank, lanky, lean, light, meagre, scraggy, scrawny, skeletal, skinny, slender, slight, slim, spare, spindly, thin as a rake, undernourished, underweight; deficient, meagre, scanty, scarce, scattered, skimpy, sparse, wispy; dilute, diluted, rarefied, runny, watery, weak; (*Inf*) wishy-washy; feeble, flimsy, inadequate, insufficient, lame, poor, scant, scanty, shallow, slight, superficial, unconvincing, unsubstantial, weak

thing *n* affair, article, being, body, circumstance, concept, entity, fact, matter, object, part portion, some thing, substance; act, deed, event, eventuality, feat, happening, incident, occurrence, phenomenon, proceeding; apparatus, contrivance, device, gadget, implement, instrument, machine, means, mechanism, tool; aspect, detail, facet, factor, feature, item, particular, point, statement, thought; baggage, belongings, bits and pieces, clothes, effects, equipment, goods, impediments, luggage, odds and ends, paraphernalia, possessions, stuff; (*Inf*) clobber, gear

think *v* believe, conceive, conclude, consider, deem, determine, esteem, estimate, hold, imagine, judge, reckon, regard, suppose, surmise; brood, cerebrate, cogitate, consider, contemplate, deliberate, have in mind, meditate, mull over, muse, ponder, reason, reflect, revolve, ruminate, turn over in one's mind, weigh up; (*Inf*) chew over; call to mind, recall, recollect, remember; anticipate, envisage, expect, foresee, imagine, plan for, presume, suppose

thinking *adj* contemplative, cultured, intelligent, meditative, philosophical, ratiocinative, rational, reasoning, reflective, sophisticated, thoughtful

think over *v* consider the pros and cons of, contemplate, give thought to, mull over, ponder, reflect upon, turn over in one's mind, weigh up; (*Inf*) chew over

third-rate *adj* bad, cheap-skate, indifferent, inferior, low-grade, mediocre, poor, poor-quality, shoddy; (*Inf*) duff, ropy

thirst *n* craving to drink, drought, dryness, thirstiness; appetite, craving, desire, eagerness, hankering, hunger, keenness, longing, lust, passion, yearning,

thirsty *adj* arid, dehydrated, dry, parched

thorny *adj* barbed, bristling with thorns, bristly, pointed, prickly, sharp, spiky, spinous, spiny; awk ward, difficult, harassing, hard, irksome, problematic, ticklish, tough, troublesome, trying, unpleasant, upsetting, vexatious, worrying; (*Inf*) sticky

thorough *prep* all-embracing, all-inclusive, assiduous, careful, complete, comprehensive, conscientious, efficient, exhaustive, full, in-depth, intensive, leaving no stone unturned, meticulous, painstaking, scrupulous, sweeping, absolute, arrant, complete, downright, entire, out-and-out, perfect, pure, sheer, total, unmitigated, unqualified, utter

though *conj* albeit, allowing, although, despite the fact that, even if, even supposing, granted, notwithstanding, while

thought *n* brainwork, cerebration, cogitation, consideration, contemplation, deliberation, introspection, meditation, musing, reflection, regard, rumination, thinking; assessment, belief, concept, conception, conclusion, conjecture, conviction, estimation, idea, judgment, notion, opinion, thinking, view; attention, consideration, heed, regard, scrutiny, study; aim, design, idea, intention, notion, object, plan, purpose; anticipation, aspiration, dream, expectation, hope, prospect; anxiety, attentiveness, care, compassion, concern, kindness, regard, solicitude, sympathy, thoughtfulness

thoughtful *adj* attentive, caring, considerate, helpful, kind, kindly, solicitous, unselfish; contemplative, deliberative, in a brown study, introspective, lost on thought, meditative, musing, pensive, rapt, reflective, ruminative, serious, studious, thinking, wistful

thoughtless *adj* impolite, inconsiderate, indiscreet, insensitive, rude, selfish, tactless, uncaring, undiplomatic, unkind; absentminded, careless, foolish, heedless, ill-considered, impudent, inadvertent, inattentive, injudicious, mindless, neglectful, negligent, rash, reckless, regardless, remiss, silly, stupid, unmindful, unobservant, unthinking

thrash *v* beat, belt, birch, cane, chastise, drub, flagellate, flog, horsewhip, lambaste, leather, punish, scourge, spank, whip; (*Inf*) give someone a good hiding, hide, paste, take a stick to, tan; beat, crush, defeat, drub, maul, overwhelm, rout, trounce; (*Inf*) clobber, hammer, paste, slaughter, wipe the floor with

thread *v* course, direction, drift, tenor; reeve, trace

thread *n* cord, fibre, filament, hair, line, twist; pile, staple

threadbare *adj* napless, old, seedy, worn; common, commonplace, hackneyed, stale, trite, worn-out

threat *n* comminution, intimidatory remark, menace, threatening, remark, warning; foreboding, foreshadowing, omen, portent, presage, warning, writing on the wall

threaten *v* endanger, imperil, jeopardize, put at risk, put in jeopardy; be imminent, be in the air, be in the offing, forebode, foreshadow, hand over, impend, loom over, portend, presage warn; browbeat, bully, cow, intimidate, make threats to, menace, pressurize, terrorize; (*Inf*) lean on

threshold *n* door, doorsill, doorstep, doorway, entrance, sill; beginning, brink, dawn, inception, opening, outset, start, stating point, verge

thrift *n* carefulness, economy, frugality, good husbandry, parsimony, prudence, saving, thriftiness

thrifty *adj* careful, economical, frugal, provident, saving, sparing; flourishing, prosperous, thriving, vigorous

thrill *n* adventure, flush of excitement, glow, pleasure, sensation, stimulation, tingle, titillation; (*Inf*) buzz, charge, kick; flutter, fluttering, quiver, shudder, throb, tremble tremor, vibration

thrill *v* arouse, electrify, excite, flush, glow, move, stimulate, stir, tingle, titillate; flutter, quake, quiver, shake, shudder, throb, tremble, vibrate

thrilling *adj* electrifying, exciting, griping, hair-raising, rivetting, rousing, sensational, stimulating, stirring; quaking, shaking, shivering, shuddering, trembling, vibrating; (*Inf*) rip-roaring

thrive *v* advance, bloom, boom, burgeon, develop, do well, flourish, get on, grow, grow rich, increase, prosper, succeed, wax

throb *v* beat, palpitate, pound, pulsate, pulse, thump, vibrate

throb *n* beat, palpitation, pounding, pulsating, pulse, thump, thumping, vibration

throng *n* assemblage, concourse, congregation, crowd, crush, horde, host, jam, mass, mob, multitude, pack, press, swarm

throng *v* bunch, congregate, converge, cram, crowd, fill, flock, hem in, herd, jam, mill around, pack, press, swarm around, troop

throttle *v* choke, garrote, strangle, strangulate; control, inhibit, silence, stifle, suppress; (*Inf*) gag

through *prep* between, by, from

end to end of, from one side to the other of, in and out of, past; as a consequence or result of, because of, by mean of, by virtue of, by way of, using, via, with the help of; during, in, in the middle of, throughout

through *adj* completed, done, ended, finished, terminated, (*Inf*) washed-up

throughout *prep* all over, all the time, all through, during the whole of, everywhere, for the duration of, from beginning to end, from start to finish, from the start, over the length and breadth of, right through, the whole time, through the whole of

throw *v* cast, fling, heave, hurl, launch, pitch, project, propel, put, send, shy, sling, toss; (*Inf*) chuck, lob

throw *n* cast, fling, heave, pitch, projection, put, shy, sling, toss; (*Inf*) lob

throw away *adj* cast off, discard, dispense with, dispose of, get rid of, jettison, reject, scrap, throw out; (*Inf*) ditch, dump; fail to exploit, fritter away, lose, make poor use of, squander, waste; (*Inf*) blow

throw off *v* abandon, cast off, discard, drop, free oneself of, rid one self of, shake off; elude, escape from, evade, get away from, give someone the slip. leave behind, lose, outdistance, outrun, shake off, show a clean pair of heels to; confuse, disconcert, disturb, put one off one's stroke, throw one off one's stride, unsettle, upset

throw out *v* cast off, discard, dismiss, dispense, dispense with, eject, evict, expel, get rid of, jettison, reject, scrap, show the door to, throw away, turn down; (*Inf*) ditch, dump, kick out, turf out; confuse, disconcert, disturb, put one off one's stroke, throw one off one's stride, unsettle, upset; (*Inf*) throw

thrust *v* butt, drive, elbow one's way in, force, impel, jam, plunge, poke, press, prod, propel, push, ram, shove, urge; jab, lunge, pierce, stab, stick

thrust *n* drive, lunge, poke, prod, push, shove, stab; impetus, momentum, motive force, motive power, propulsive force

thud *n/v* clonk, clump, clunk, crash, knock, smack, thump, wallop

thug *n* assassin, bandit, bully-boy, gangster, hooligan, killer, mugger, murderer, robber, ruffian, tough, villain; (*Inf*) bovver boy, heavy, hit-man

thump *n* bang, blow, clout (*Inf*), clunk, crash, knock, rap, smack, thud, thwack, wallop (*Inf*), whack

thump *v* bang, batter, beat, belabour, crash, hit, knock, pound, rap, smack, strike, thrash, throb, thud, thwack, whack; (*Inf*) belt, clout, lambaste, wallop

thunder *n* boom, booming, crack ing, crash, crashing, detonation, explosion, pealing, rumble

thunder *v* blast, boom, clap, crack, crash, detonate, explode, peal, resound, reverberate, roar, rumble

thunderstruck *adj* aghast, amazed, astonished, astounded, dazed, dumbfounded, flummoxed, left speechless, nonplussed, open-mouthed, paralysed, petrified, rooted to the spot shocked, staggered, struck dumb, stunned, taken aback; (*Inf*) bowled over, flabbergasted, floored, knocked for six

thus *adv* as follows, in this fashion manner, way, like so, like this, so, to such a degree; accordingly, consequently, ergo, for this reason, hence, on that account, so, then, therefore

tick *n* clack, click, clicking, tap, tapping, ticktock; dash, mark, stroke

tick *v* clack, click, tap, ticktock; check off, choose, indicate, mark, mark off, select

ticket *n* card, certificate, coupon, pass, slip, token, voucher; card, docket, label, marker, slip, sticker, tab, tag

tickle *v* amuse, delight, divert, enliven, gladden, gratify, please, rejoice, titillate

ticklish *adj* dangerous, precarious, risky, tottering, uncertain, unstable, unsteady; critical, delicate, difficult, nice

tide *n* course, current, ebb, flow, stream, tidal flow, tidewater; course, direction, drift, movement, run, tendency, trend

tide *v* aid, assist, help out, keep one going, keep the wolf from the door, see one through

tidy *adj* businesslike, clean, cleanly, methodical, neat, ordered, orderly, shipshape, spick-and-span, spruce, systematic, trim, well-groomed, well-kept, well-ordered

tidy *v* clean, groom, neated, order, put in order, put in trim, put to rights, spruce up, straighten

tie *v* attach, bind, connect, fasten, interlace, join, knot, lash, link, make fast, moor, rope, secure, tether, truss, unite; bind, confine, hamper, hinder, hold, limit, restrain, restrict; be even, be neck and neck, draw, equal, match

tie *n* band, bond, connection, cord, fastening, fetter, joint, knot, ligature, link, rope, string; affiliation, allegiance, bond, commitment, connection, duty, kinship, liaison, obligation, relationship; dead heat, dead lock, draw, stalemate; contest, fixture, game, match

tier *n* bank, echelon, file, layer, level, line, order, rank, row, series, storey, stratum

tight *adj* close, close-fitting, compact, constricted, cramped, fast, firm, fixed, narrow, rigid, secure, snug, stiff, stretched, taut, tense; hermetic, impervious, proof, sealed, sound, watertight; close, grasping, mean, miserly, niggardly, parsimonious, penurious, sparing, stingy, close, even, evenly-balanced, near, well-matched; drunk, intoxicated, inebriated, tipsy; (*Inf*) half-cut, pickled, pie-eyed, plastered, smashed, sozzled, stewed, stoned three sheets to the wind, tiddly, under the influence

tighten *v* close, constrict, cramp, fasten, fix, narrow, rigidify, screw, secure, squeeze, stiffen, stretch, tauten, tense

till *v* cultivate, dig, plough, turn over, work the land

till *n* cash box, cash drawer, cash

register, strong box

till *prep* before, earlier than, previous to, prior to,

tilt *v* cant, incline, lean, list, slant, slope, tip; attack, break a lance, clash, contend, cross swords, duel, encounter, fight, joust, overthrow, spar

tilt *n* angle, cant, inclination, incline, list, pitch, slant, slope

timber *n* beams, boards, forest, logs, planks, trees, wood

time *n* age, chronology, date, duration, epoch, era, generation, hour, interval, period, season, space, span, spell, stretch, term, while; allotted span, day, duration, life, life span, lifetime, season; heyday, hour, peak; beat; **in time** at the appointed time, early, in good time, on schedule, on time, with time to spare; by and by, eventually, one day, some day, sooner or later, ultimately

time *v* clock, control, count, judge, measure, regulate, schedule, set

timely *adj* appropriate, at the right time, convenient, judicious, opportune, prompt, propitious, punctual, seasonable suitable, well-timed

timetable *n* agenda, calendar, curriculum, diary, list, order of the day, programme, schedule

timid *adj* afraid, apprehensive, bashful, cowardly, coy, diffident, faint-hearted, fearful, irresolute, modest, mousy, nervous, pusillanimous, retiring, shrinking, shy, timorous

tinge *v* colour, dye, stain, tincture, tint; imbue, impregnate, impress, infuse

tinge *n* cast, colour, dye, hue, shade, stain, tincture, tint; flavour, smack, spice, quality, taste

tinker *v* dabble, meddle, mess about, monkey, play, potter, toy; (*Inf*) fiddle, muck about

tint *n* cast, colour, hue, shade, tone; dye, rinse, stain, tincture, tinge, wash

tint *v* colour, dye, rinse, stain, tincture, tinge; affect, colour, influence, taint, tinge

tiny *adj* diminutive, dwarfish, infinitesimal, insignificant, Lilliputian, little, microscopic, mini, miniature, minute, negligible, petite, puny, pygmy, slight, small, trifling, wee; (*Inf*) pint-sized

tip *n* apex, cap, crown, end, extremity, head, peak, point, summit, top

tip *v* cant, capsize, incline, lean, list, overturn, slant, spill, tilt, topple over, upend, upset; ditch, dump, empty, pour out, unload; remunerate, reward; tap, touch; cap, crown, top

tip *n* dump, refuse heap, rubbish heap; baksheesh, gift, gratuity, perquisite, *pourboire;* apex, crown, peak, point, summit, top; cap, cover, end, extremity, point; **tip-off** clue, forecast, hint, information, inside information, pointer, sugges tion, warning, word, word of advice

tire *v* drain, droop, enervate, exhaust, fail, fatigue, flag, jade, sink, wear down, wear out, weary; (*Inf*) fag, knacker, take it out of you, whack; annoy, bore, exasperate, harass, irk, irritate, weary

tired *adj* drained, drooping, drowsy, enervated, exhausted, fatigued, flagging, jaded, ready to drop, sleepy, spent, weary, worn out; (*Inf*) all in, asleep on one's feet, dead on one's feet, dog tired, done in, fagged, knackered, whacked

tireless *adj* determined, energetic, indefatigable, industrious, resolute, unflagging, untiring, unwearied, vigorous

tiresome *adj* annoying, boring, dull, exasperating, flat, irksome, irritating, laborious, monotonous, tedious, trying, uninteresting, vexatious, wearing, wearisome

tiring *adj* arduous, demanding, enervative, exacting, exhausting, fatiguing, laborious, strenuous, tough, wearing, wearying

tissue *n* cloth, fabric; membrane, network, structure, texture, web; accumulation, chain, collection, combination, conglomeration, mass, network, series, set

title *n* caption, heading, inscription, label, legend, name, style; appellation, denomination, designation, epithet, name, nickname, *nom de plume*, pseudonym, sobriquet, term; (*Inf*) handle, moniker; championship, crown, laurels; claim, entitlement, ownership, prerogative, privilege, right

title *v* call, designate, label, name, style, term

toady *n* fawner, flatterer, flunkey, groveller, hanger-on, jackal, lackey, lickspittle, minion, parasite, spaniel, sycophant, truckler; (*Inf*) bootlicker, crawler, creep, yes man; be obsequious to, bow and scrape, butter up, crawl, creep, cringe, curry favour with, fawn on, flatter, grovel, kiss the feet of, kowtow to; (*Inf*) lick the boots of, suck up to

toast *v* brown, dry, heat; honour, pledge, propose, salute

toast *n* compliment, drink, pledge, salutation, salute; favourite, pet

together *adv* as a group, as one, cheek by jowl, closely, collectively, hand in glove, hand in hand, in a body, in concert, in cooperation, in unison, jointly, mutually, shoulder to shoulder, side by side; all at once, as one, at one fell swoop, at the same time, concurrently, contemporaneously, *en masse*, in unison, simultaneously, with one accord; consecutively, continuously, in a row, in succession, one after the other, on end, successively, without a break, without interruption

toil *n* application, donkey-work, drudgery, effort, exertion, hard work, industry, labour pains, slog, sweat, travail; (*Inf*) elbow grease, graft

toil *v* drag oneself, drudge, grub, knock oneself out, labour, push oneself, slave, slog, strive, struggle, work, work like a dog, work like a Trojan, work one's fingers to the bone; (*Inf*) graft, grind, sweat

toilet *n* ablutions; dressing, grooming, washing; bathroom, closet, convenience, ladies' room, latrine, lavatory, mens' room, outhouse, powder room, privy, urinal, wash room, water closet, WC; (*Inf*) bog, gents, ladies, loo

token *n* badge, clue, demonstration, earnest, evidence, expression, index, indication, manifestation, mark, note, proof, representation, sign, symbol, warning; keepsake, memento, memorial, remembrance, reminder, souvenir

token *adj* hollow, minimal, nominal, perfunctory, superficial, symbolic

tolerable *adj* acceptable, allowable, bearable, endurable, sufferable, supportable; acceptable, adequate, all right, average, fair, fairly good, fair to middling, good enough, indifferent, mediocre, middling, ordinary, passable, run-of-the-mill, unexceptional; (*Inf*) not bad, OK, so-so

tolerance *n* broad-mindedness, charity forbearance, indulgence, lenity, magnanimity, open-minded ness, patience, permissiveness, sufferance, sympathy; endurance, fortitude, hardiness, hardness, resilience, resistance, stamina, staying power, toughness; fluctuation play, swing, variation

tolerant *adj* broad-minded, catholic, charitable, fair, forbearing, latitudinarian, liberal, long-suffering, magnanimous, open-minded, patient, sympathetic, unbigoted, understanding, unprejudiced; complaisant, easy-going, free and easy, indulgent, lax, lenient, permissive, soft

tolerate *v* abide, accept, admit, allow, bear, brook, condone, countenance, endure, indulge, permit, pocket, receive, sanction, stand, stomach, submit to, suffer, swallow, turn a blind eye to, undergo, wink at; (*Inf*) put up with

toll *v* chime, clang, knell, peal, ring, sound, strike; announce, call, signal, summon, warn; chime, clang, knell, peal, ring, ringing, tolling

toll *n* assessment, charge, customs, demand, duty, fee, impost, levy, payment, rate, tariff, tax, tribute; cost, damage, inroad, loss, penalty

tomb *n* burial, chamber, catacomb, crypt, grave, mausoleum, sepulchre, vault

tombstone *n* gravestone, headstone, marker, memorial, monument

tone *n* accent, emphasis, force, inflection, intonation, modulation, pitch, strength, stress, timbre, tonality, volume; air, approach, aspect, attitude, character, drift, effect, feel, frame, grain, manner, mood, note, quality, spirit, style, temper, tenor, vein; cast, colour, hue, shade, tinge, tint

tone *v* blend, go well with, harmo nize, match, suit

tongue *n* argot, dialect, idiom, language, parlance, patois, speech, talk, vernacular; (*Inf*) lingo; articulation, speech, utterance, verbal expression, voice

tongue-tied *adj* lost for words, mute, silent, speechless, struck dumb, wordless

tonic *n* analeptic, boost, cordial, fill lip, livener, refresher, restorative, roborant, stimulant; (*Inf*) bracer, pick-me-up, shot in the arm

too *adv* also, as well, besides, further, in addition, into the bargain, likewise, moreover, to boot; exces sively, exorbitantly, extremely, immoderately, inordinately, overly, unduly, unreasonably, very

tool *n* apparatus, appliance, contraption, contrivance, device, gadget, implement, instrument, machine, utensil; agency, agent, intermediary, means, medium, vehicle, wherewithal; cat's-paw, creature, dupe, flunkey, hireling, jackal, lackey, minion, pawn, puppet

top *n* acme, apex, apogee, crest, crown, culmination, head, height, high point, meridian, peak, pinnacle, summit, vertex, zenith; cap, cork, cover, lid, stopper; first place, head, highest rank, lead; a bit too far, immoderate, inordinate, over the limit, over the top, too much, uncalled-for

top *adj* best, chief, crowning, culminating, dominant, elite, finest, first, foremost, greatest, head, highest, lead, leading, pre-eminent, prime, principal, ruling, sovereign, superior, topmost, upper, uppermost; (*Inf*) crack

top *v* be first, be in charge of, command, head, lead, rule; beat, best, better, eclipse, exceed, excel, go beyond, outdo, outshine, outstrip, surpass, transcend

topic *n* issue, matter, point, question, subject, subject matter, text, theme, thesis

topical *adj* contemporary, current, newsworthy, popular, up-to-date, up-to-the-minute

topple *v* fall, overturn, tumble, upset

topsy-turvy *adj/adv* chaotic, confused, disarranged, disorderly, disorganized, inside-out, jumbled, messy, mixed-up, untidy, upside-down, wrong side up

torment *v* afflict, agonize, crucify, distress, excrutiate, harrow, pain, rack, torture; annoy, bedevil, bother, chivvy, harass, harry, hound, irritate, nag, persecute, pester, plague, provoke, tease, trouble, vex, worry; (*Inf*) devil

torn *n* agony, anguish, distress, hell, misery, pain, suffering, torture; affliction, annoyance, bane, bother, harassment, irritation, nag, nagging, nuisance, persecution, pest, plague, provocation, scourge, thorn in one's flesh, trouble, vexation, worry; (*Inf*) pain in the neck

tornado *n* cyclone, gale, hurricane, squall, storm, tempest, typhoon, whirlwind, windstorm; (*Inf*) twister

torrent *n* cascade, deluge, down pour, effusion, flood, flow, gush, outburst, rush, spate, stream, tide

torture *v* afflict, agonize, crucify, distress, excrutiate, harrow, lacerate, martyr, pain, persecute, put on the rack, rack, torment

torture *n* affliction, agony, anguish, distress, hell, laceration, martyrdom, misery, pain, pangs, persecution, rack, suffering, torment

toss *v* cast, fling, flip, hurl, pitch, project, propel, shy, sling, throw; agitate, disturb, jiggle, joggle, jolt, rock, roll, shake, thrash, tumble, wriggle, writhe; (*Inf*) chuck, lob

toss *n* cast, fling, pitch, shy, throw; (*Inf*) lob

total *n* aggregate, all, amount, entirety, full amount, mass, sum, totality, whole

total *adj* absolute, all-out, complete, comprehensive, consummate, downright, entire, full, gross, integral, out-and-out, outright, perfect, sheer, sweeping, thorough, thoroughgoing, unconditional, undisputed, undivided, unmitigated, unqualified, utter, whole

tool *v* add up, amount to, come to, mount up to, reach, reckon, sum up, tot up

touch *n* feel, feeling, handling, palpation, physical contact, tactility; blow, brush, caress, contact, fondling, hit, pat, push, stroke, tap; bit, dash, detail, drop, hint, intimation, jot, pinch, smack, small amount, smattering, *soupçon,* speck, spot, suggestion, suspicion, taste, tinc ture, tinge, trace, whiff; approach, characteristic, handiwork, manner, method, style, technique, trademark, way; ability, adroitness, art, artistry, command, deftness, facility, flair, knack, mastery, skill, virtuosity

touch *v* brush, caress, contact, feel, finger, fondle, graze, handle, hit, lay a finger on, palpate, pat, push, strike, stroke, tap; abut, adjoin, be in contact, border, brush, come together, contact, converge, graze, impinge upon, meet; affect, disturb, get through to, have an effect on, impress, influence, inspire, make an impression on, mark, melt, move, soften, stir, strike, upset; (*Inf*) get to; be a match for, be in the same league as, be on par with, come near, come up to, compare with, equal, match, parallel, rival; (*Inf*) hold a candle to

touching *adj* affecting, emotive, heartbreaking, melting, moving, pathetic, piteous, pitiable, pitiful, poignant, sad, stirring, tender

touchy *adj* choleric, cross, fretful, hot-tempered, irascible, irritable, peevish, petulant, quick-tempered, snappish, splenetic, tetchy, testy, waspish

tough *adj* cohesive, durable, firm, hard, inflexible, leathery, resilient, resistant, rigid, rugged, solid, stiff, strong, sturdy, tenacious; brawny, fit, hard as nails, hardened, hardy, resilient, seasoned, stalwart, stout, strapping, strong, sturdy, vigorous; hard-bitten, pugnacious, rough, ruffianly, ruthless, vicious, violent; adamant, callous, exacting, form, hard, inflexible, intractable, merciless, obdurate, obstinate, refractory, resolute, severe, stern, strict, stubborn, unbending, unforgiving, unyielding; (*Inf*) hard-boiled, hard-nosed; arduous, baffling, difficult, exacting, exhausting, hard, intractable, irksome, knotty, laborious, perplexing, puzzling, strenuous, thorny, troublesome, uphill; hard luck, lamentable, regrettable, unfortunate; (*Inf*) bad, hard cheese, hard lines, too bad, unlucky

tough *n* bravo, brute, bully, bully-boy, hooligan, rowdy, ruffian, thug; (*Inf*) bruiser, rough, roughneck

tour *n* excursion, expedition, jaunt, journey, outing, peregrination, progress, trip; circuit, course, round

tour *v* explore, go on the road, go round, holiday in, journey, sightsee, travel round, travel through, visit

tourist *n* excursionist, globetrotter, holiday-maker, journeyer, sightseer, traveller, tripper, voyager

tow *v* drag, draw, haul, lug, pull,

trail, trawl, tug

towards *prep* en route for, for, in the direction of, in the vicinity of, on the road to, on the way to, to; about, concerning. for, regarding, with regard to, with respect to; almost, close to, coming up to, getting on for, just before, bearing, nearly, not quite, shortly before

tower *n* belfry, column, obelisk, pillar, skyscraper, steeple, turret; castle, citadel, fort, fortification, fortress, keep, refuge, stronghold

tower *v* ascend, be head and shoulders above, dominate, exceed, loom, mount, overlook, overtop, rear, rise, soar, surpass, top, transcend

toy *n* doll, game, plaything

toy *v* amuse oneself, dally, flirt, play, sport, trifle, wanton; (*Inf*) idle

trace *n* evidence, indication, mark, record, relic, remains, remnant, sign, survival, token, vestige; bit, dash, drop, hint, iota, jot, shadow, soupçon, suggestion, suspicion, tincture, tinge, touch, trifle, whiff

trace *v* ascertain, detect, determine, discover, ferret out, find, follow, hunt down, pursue, search for, seek, shadow, talk, track, trail, unearth; chart, copy, delineate, depict, draw, map, mark out, outline, record, show, sketch

track *n* footmark, footprint, footstep, mark, path, scent, slot, spoor, trace, trail, wake; course, flight, path, line, orbit, path, pathway, road, track, trajectory, way; line, permanent way, rail, rails; keep track of follow, keep an eye on, keep on sight, keep in touch with, keep up to date with, keep up with, monitor, oversee, watch; lose track of lose, lose sight of, misplace

track *v* chase, dog, follow, follow the trail of, hunt down, pursue, shadow, stalk, tail, trace, trail

tracks *pl n* footprints, impressions, imprints, tyremarks, tyreprints, wheelmarks

trade *n* barter, business, buying and selling, commerce, dealing, exchange, traffic, transactions, truck; avocation, business calling, craft, employment, job, line, line of work, métier, occupation, profes sion, pursuit, skill; deal, exchange, interchange, swap; clientele, custom, customers, market, patrons, public

trade *v* bargain, barter, buy and sell, deal, do business, exchange, have dealings, peddle, traffic, transact, truck; barter, exchange, swap, switch

tradesperson *n* dealer, merchant, retailer, seller, shopkeeper, vendor; artisan, craftsman, journeyman, skilled worker, workman

tradition *n* convention, custom, customs, established, practice, folklore, habit, institution, lore, praxis, ritual, unwritten law, usage

traditional *adj* accustomed, ancestral, conventional, customary, established, fixed, folk, historic, long-established, old, oral, time-honoured, transmitted, unwritten, usual

traffic *n* coming and going, freight, movement, passengers, transport, transportation, vehicles; barter, business, buying and selling, commerce, communication, dealing, dealings, doings, exchange, intercourse, peddling, relations, trade, truck

traffic *v* bargain, barter, buy and sell, deal, do business, exchange, have dealings, have transactions, market, peddle, trade, truck

tragedy *n* adversity, affliction, calamity, catastrophe, disaster, grievous blow, misfortune

tragic *adj* anguished, appaling, awful, calamitous, catastrophic, deadly, dire, disastrous, doleful, dreadful, fatal, grievous, heart-breaking, heart-rending, ill-fated, ill-starred, lamentable, miserable, mournful, pathetic, pitiable, ruinous, sad, shocking, sorrowful, unfortunate, woeful, wretched

trail *v* dangle, drag, draw, hang down, haul, pull, stream, tow; chase, follow, hunt, pursue, shadow, stalk, tail, trace, track; bring up the rear, dawdle, drag oneself, fall behind, follow, hang back, lag, linger, loiter, straggle; (*Inf*) traipse

trail *n* footprints, footsteps, mark, marks, path, scent, spoor, trace, track, wake; beaten track, footpath, path, road, route, track, way

train *v* coach, discipline, drill, educate, guide, improve, instruct, prepare, rear, rehearse, school, teach, tutor; aim, bring to bear, direct, focus, level, line up, point

train *n* chain, concatenation, course, order, progression, sequence, series, set, string, succession; caravan, column, convoy, file procession; appendage, tail, trail; attendants, cortege, court, entourage followers, following, household, retinue, staff, suite

training *n* coaching, discipline, education, groundling, guidance, instruction, schooling, teaching, tuition, tutelage, upbringing; body building, exercise, practice, preparation, working-out

trait *n* attribute, characteristic, feature, idiosyncrasy, lineament, mannerism, peculiarity, quality, quirk

traitor *n* apostate, back-stabber, betrayer, deceiver, defector, deserter, double-crosser, fifth columnist, informer, Judas, miscreant, quisling, rebel, renegade, turncoat; (*Inf*) snake-in-the-grass, two-timer

traitorous *adj* faithless, false, perfidious, recreant, treacherous; insidious, perfidious, treasonable

tramp *v* footslog, hike, march, ramble, range, roam, rove, slog, trek, walk, yomp; march, plod, stamp, stump, toil, trudge, walk heavily; (*Inf*) traipse; crush, stamp, stomp, trample, tread, walk over

tramp *n* derelict, down-and-out, drifter, vagabond, vagrant; (*Inf*) dosser, hobo; hike, march, ramble, slog, trek

trample *v* crush, flatten, run over, squash, stamp, tread, walk over; do violence to, encroach upon, hurt, infringe, ride roughshod over, show no consideration for, violate

trance *n* abstraction, daze, dream, ecstasy, hypnotic state, muse, rapture, reverie, spell, stupor, unconsciousness

tranquil *adj* at peace, calm, composed, cool, pacific, peaceful, placid, quiet, restful, sedate, serene, still, undisturbed, unexcited, unperturbed, unruffled, untroubled

tranquillizer *n* barbiturate, bromide, opiate, sedative; (*Inf*) downer, red

transact *v* conduct, dispatch, enact, execute, do, manage, negotiate, perform, treat

transaction *n* action, affair, bargain, business, coup, deal, deed, enterprise, event, matter, negotiation, occurrence, proceeding, undertaking

transcend *v* exceed, overlap, overstep, pass, transgress; escel, outstrip, outrival, outvie, overtop, surmount, surpass

transcribe *v* copy out, engross, note, reproduce, rewrite, set out, take down, transfer, write out; inter pret, render, translate, transliterate; record, tape, tape-record

transfer *v* carry, change, consign, convey, displace, hand over, make over, move, pass on, relocate, remove, shift, translate, transmit, transplant, transport, transpose, turn over

transfer *n* change, displacement, handover, move, relocation, removal, shift, transference, translation, transmission, transposition

transform *v* alter, change, convert, make over, metamorphose, reconstruct, remodel, renew, revolutionize, transfigure, translate, transmute; (*Inf*) transmogrify

transformation *n* alteration, change, conversion, metamorphosis, radical change, renewal, revolution, revolutionary change, sea change, transfiguration, transmutation, (*Inf*) transmogrification

transgress *v* break, break the law, contravene, defy, disobey, do wrong, encroach, err, exceed, fall from grace, go astray, go beyond, infringe, lapse, misbehave, offend, overstep, sin, trespass, violate

transient *adj* brief, ephemeral, evanescent, fleeting, flying, fugacious, fugitive, here today and gone tomorrow, impermanent, momentary, passing, short, short-lived short-term, temporary, transitory

transit *n* carriage, conveyance, crossing, motion, movement, passage, portage, shipment, transfer, transport, transportation, travel, traverse; alteration, change, changeover, conversion, shift, transition

transition *n* alteration, change, changeover, conversion, development, evolution, flux, metamorphosis, metastasis, passage, passing, progression, shift, transit, transmutation, upheaval

transitional *adj* changing, developmental, fluid, intermediate, passing, provisional, temporary, transitionary, unsettled

transitory *adj* brief, ephemeral, evanescent, fleeting, flying, fugacious, here today and gone tomorrow, impermanent, momentary, passing, short, short-lived, short-term, temporary, transient

translate *v* construe, convert, decipher decode, interpret, paraphrase, render, transcribe, transliterate; elucidate, explain, make clear, paraphrase, put in plain English, simplify, spell out, state in layman's language; alter, change, convert, metamorphose, transfigure, transform, transmute, turn; carry, convey, move, remove, send, transfer, transplant, transport, transpose

translation *n* construction, decoding, gloss, interpretation, paraphrase, rendering, rendition, transcription, transliteration, version; elucidation, explanation, paraphrase, rephrasing, rewording, simplification; alteration, change, conversion, metamorphosis, transfiguration, transformation, transmutation; conveyance, move, removal, transference, transposition

transmission *n* carriage, communication, conveyance, diffusion, dispatch, dissemination, remission, sending, shipment, spread, transfer, transference, transport; broadcast, programme, show

transmit *n* bear, carry, communicate, convey, diffuse, dispatch, disseminate, forward, hand down, hand on, impart, pass on, remit, send, spread, take, transfer, transport; broadcast, disseminate, put on the air, radio, relay, send, send out

transparent *adj* clear, crystal clear, crystalline, diaphanous, filmy, gauzy, limpid, lucent, lucid, pellucid, see-through, sheer, translucent, transpicious; apparent, distinct, easy, evident, explicit, manifest, obvious, patent, perspicuous, plain, recognizable, unambiguous, understandable, undisguised, visible; (*Inf*) as plain as the nose on one's face; candid direct, forthright, frank, open, plain-spoken, straight, straightforward, unambiguous, unequivocal

transpire *v* arise, befall, chance, come about, come to pass, happen, occur, take place, turn up; become known, be disclosed, be discovered, be made public, come out, come to light, emerge

transport *v* bear, bring, carry, convey, fetch, haul, move, remove, run, ship, take transfer; banish, deport, exile, sentence to transportation; captivate, carry away, delight, electrify, enchant, enrapture, entrance, move, ravish, spell bind

transport *n* conveyance, transportation, vehicle; carriage, conveyance, removal, shipment, shipping, transference, transportation; enchantment, euphoria, heaven, rapture, seventh heaven; (*Inf*) bliss, cloud nine, delight, ecstasy, happiness, ravishment

transpose *v* alter, change, exchange, interchange, move rearrange, relocate, reorder, shift, substitute, switch, transfer; (*Inf*) swap

trap *n* ambush, gin, net, noose, pitfall, snare, springe, toils; ambush, artifice, deception, device, ruse, stratagem, subterfuge, trick, wile

trap *v* catch, corner, enmesh, ensnare, entrap, snare, take; ambush, beguile, deceive, dupe, inveigle, trick

trappings *pl n* accoutrements, adornments, decorations, dress, equipment, finery, fittings, fixtures, fripperies, furnishings, gear, livery, ornaments, panoply, paraphernalia, things, trimmings

trash *n* balderdash, drivel, foolish talk, hogwash, inanity, nonsense, rot, rubbish, trumpery, twaddle; (*Inf*) tripe; dregs, dross, garbage, junk, litter, offscourings, refuse, rubbish, sweepings, waste

travel *v* cross, go, journey, make a journey, make one's way, move, proceed, progress, ramble, roam, rove, take a trip, tour, traverse, trek, voyage, walk, wander, wend

traveller *n* excursionist, explorer, globetrotter, gypsy, hiker, holiday-maker, journeyer, migrant, nomad, passenger, tourist, tripper, voyager, wanderer, wayfarer

travelling *adj* itinerant, migrant, migratory, mobile, moving, nomadic, peripatetic, restless, roaming, roving, touring, unsettled, wandering, wayfaring

travesty *n* burlesque, caricature, distortion, lampoon, mockery, parody, perversion, sham; (*Inf*) send up, spoof, take off

travesty *v* burlesque, caricature, deride, distort, lampoon, make a mockery of, make fun of, mock, parody, pervert, ridicule, sham; (*Inf*) send up, spoof, take off

treacherous *adj* deceitful, disloyal, double-dealing, duplicitous, faithless, false, perfidious, traitorous, treasonable, unfaithful, unreliable, untrue, untrustworthy; (*Inf*) dicey, double-crossing; dangerous, deceptive, hazardous, icy, perilous, precarious, risky, slippery, tricky, unreliable, unsafe, unstable; (*Inf*) slippy

treachery *n* betrayal, disloyalty, double-dealing, duplicity, faithlessness, infidelity, perfidiousness, perfidy, stab in the back, treason; (*Inf*) double-cross

tread *v* hike, march, pace, plod, stamp, step, stride, tramp, trudge, walk; crush underfoot, squash, trample; bear down, crush, oppress, quell, repress, ride roughshod over, subdue, subjugate, suppress

tread *n* footfall, footstep, gait, pace, step, stride, walk

treason *n* disaffection, disloyalty, duplicity, faithlessness, lese-majesty, mutiny, perfidy, sedition, subversion, traitorousness, treachery; high treason

treasonable *adj* disloyal, traitorous, treacherous

treasure *n* cash, fortune, funds, gold, jewels, money, riches, valuables, wealth; apple of one's eye, darling, gem, jewel, nonpareil, paragon, pearl, precious, pride and joy, prize

treasure *v* adore, cherish, dote upon, esteem, hold dear, idolize, love, prize, revere, value, venerate, worship

treasury *n* bank, cache, hoard, repository, store, storehouse, vault; assets, capital, coffers, exchequer, finances, funds, money, resources, revenues

treat *n* banquet, celebration, entertainment, feast, gift, party, refreshment; delight, enjoyment, fun, gratification, joy, pleasure, satisfaction, surprise, thrill

treat *v* act towards, behave towards, consider, deal with, handle, look upon, manage, regard, use; apply treatment to, attend to, care for, doctor, medicate, nurse; buy for, entertain, feast, foot or pay the bill, give, lay on, pay for, provide, regale, take out, wine and dine; (*Inf*) stand; be concerned with, contain, deal with, discourse upon, discuss, go into, touch upon

treatise *n* disquisition, dissertation, essay, exposition, monograph, pamphlet, paper, study, thesis, tract, work, writing

treatment *n* care, cure, healing, medication, medicine, remedy, surgery, therapy; action towards, behaviour towards, conduct, dealing, handling, management, manipulation, reception, usage

treaty *n* agreement, alliance, bargain, bond, compact, concordat, contract, convention, covenant, entente, pact

trek *n* expedition, footslog, hike, journey, long haul, march, odyssey, safari, slog, tramp

trek *v* footslog, hike, journey, march, plod, range, roam, rove, slog, tramp, trudge, (*Inf*) traipse, yomp

tremble *v* oscillate, quake, quiver, rock, shake in one's shoes, shiver, shudder, teeter, totter, vibrate, wobble

tremble *n* oscillation, quake, quiver, shake, shiver, shudder, tremor, vibration, wobble

tremendous *adj* appaling, awesome, awful, colossal, deafening, dreadful, enormous, fearful, formidable, frightful, gargantuan, gigantic, great, huge, immense, mammoth, monstrous, prodigious, stupendous, terrible, terrific, titanic, towering, vast; (*Inf*) whopping; amazing, excellent, exceptional, extraordinary, great, incredible, marvellous, wonderful; (*Inf*) ace, fabulous, fantastic, super, terrific

tremor *n* agitation, quaking, quivering, shaking, trembling, trepidation, tremulousness, vibration

trench *n* channel, cut, ditch, drain, earthwork, entrenchment, excavation, fosse, furrow, gutter, pit, trough, waterway

trend *n* bias, course, current, direction, drift, flow, inclination, leaning, tendency; craze, fashion, look, mode, rage, style, thing, vogue; (*Inf*) fad

trespass *v* encroach, infringe, intrude, invade, obtrude, poach

trespass *n* encroachment, infringement, intrusion, invasion, poaching, unlawful entry, wrongful entry

trial *n* assay, audition, check, examination, experience, experiment, probation, proof, test, testing, test-run; (*Inf*) dry run; contest, hearing, judicial, examination, litigation, tribunal; attempt, effort, endeavour, go, stab, try, venture; (*Inf*) crack, shot, whack; adversity, affliction, burden, cross to bear, distress, grief, hardship, hard times, load, misery, ordeal, pain, suffering, tribulation, trouble, unhappiness, vexation, woe, wretchedness; bane, bother, irritation, nuisance, pest, thorn in one's flesh, vexation; (*Inf*) hassle, pain in the neck, plague

trial *adj* experimental, exploratory, pilot, probationary, provisional, testing

tribe *n* blood, caste, clan, class,

division, dynasty, ethnic group, family, gens, house, people, race, seed, sept, stock

tribulation *n* adversity, affliction, distress, grief, misery, pain, sorrow, suffering, trial, trouble, unhappiness, woe, wretchedness

tribute *n* accolade, acknowledgment, applause, commendation, compliment, encomium, esteem, eulogy, gift, gratitude, honour, laudation, panegyric, praise, recognition, respect, testimonial; charge, contribution, customs, duty, excise, homage, impost, offering, payment, ransom, subsidy, tax, toll

trice *n* flash, instant, jiffy, moment, second, twinkling

trick *n* artifice, deceit, deception, device, dodge, feint, fraud, gimmick, hoax, imposition, imposture, manoeuvre, ploy, ruse, stratagem, subterfuge, swindle, trap, wile; (*Inf*) con; antic, caper, device, feat, frolic, gambol, jape, joke, juggle, legerdemain, practical joke, prank, slight of hand, stunt; (*Inf*) gag, leg-pull, put-on; art, command, craft, device, expertise, gift, knack, secret, skill, technique; (*Inf*) hang, know-how

trick *v* cheat, deceive, defraud, delude, dupe, fool, have someone on, hoax, hoodwink, impose upon, mislead, pull the wool over someone's eyes, swindle, trap; (*Inf*) bamboozle, con, put one over on someone, take in

trickle *v* crawl, creep, dribble, drip, drop, exude, ooze, percolate, run, seep, stream

trickle *n* dribble, drip, seepage

tricky *adj* complicated, delicate, difficult, knotty, problematic, risky, thorny, ticklish, touch-and-go; (*Inf*) sticky

trifle *n* bagatelle, bauble, child's play, gewgaw, knick-knack, nothing, plaything, toy, triviality; bit, dash, drop, jot, little, pinch, spot, touch, trace

trifle *v* amuse oneself, coquet, dally, dawdle, flirt, fritter, idle, mess about, palter, play, toy, wanton, waste, waste time

trifling *adj* empty, frippery, frivolous, inconsiderable, insignificant, nugatory, petty, piddling, shallow, slight, small, trivial, unimportant, worthless

trill *v* shake, quaver, warble

trill *n* quaver, shake, tremolo, warbling

trim *adj* compact, dapper, neat, nice, orderly, shipshape, smart, soigné, soignée, spick-and-span, spruce, tidy, well-groomed, well-ordered, well turned-out; fit, shapely, sleek, slender, slim, streamlined, svelte, willowy; (*Inf*) natty

trim *v* barber, clip, crop, curtail, cut, cut back, dock, even up, lop, pare, prune, shave, shear, tidy; adorn, array, beautify, bedeck, deck out, decorate dress, embellish, embroider, garnish, ornament, trick out; adjust, arrange, balance, distribute, order, prepare, settle

trimming *v* adornment, border, braid, decoration, edging, embellishment, frill, fringe, garnish, ornamentation, piping; accessories, accompaniments, appurtenances, extras, frills, garnish, ornaments, paraphernalia, trappings

trinket *n* bagatelle, bauble, bibelot, gewgaw, gimcrack, kickshaw, knick-knack, nothing, ornament, piece of bric-a-brac, toy, trifle

trio *n* threesome, triad, trilogy, trine, trinity, triple, triplet, triptych, triumvirate, triune

trip *n* errand, excursion, expedition, foray, jaunt, journey, outing, ramble, run, tour, travel, voyage; blunder, error, fall, false move, false step, faux pas, indiscretion, lapse, misstep, slip, stumble; (*Inf*) boob

trip *v* blunder, err, fall, go wrong, lapse, lose one's balance, lose one's footing, make a false move, make faux pas, miscalculate, misstep, slip, stumble, tumble; (*Inf*) boob, slip up; catch out, confuse, discon cert, put off one's stride, throw off, trap, unsettle

triple *adj* threefold, three times as much, three-way, tripartite

triple *n* threesome, triad, trilogy, trine, trinity, trio, triplet, triumvirate, triune

trite *adj* banal, bromidic, clichéd, common, commonplace, dull, hack, hackneyed, ordinary, pedestrian, routine, run-of-the-mill, stale, stereotyped, stock, threadbare, tired, uninspired, unoriginal, worn; (*Inf*) corny

triumph *n* elation, exultation, happiness, joy, jubilation, pride, rejoicing; accomplishment, achievement, ascendancy, attainment, conquest, coup, feat, mastery, sensation, success, *tour de force,* victory; (*Inf*) hit, smash, smash-hit, walkover

triumph *v* celebrate, crow, exult, gloat, glory, jubilate, rejoice, revel, swagger

triumphant *adj* boastful, celebratory, cock-a-hoop, conquering, dominant, elated, exultant glorious, jubilant, proud, rejoicing, successful, swaggering, triumphal, undefeated, victorious, winning

trivial *adj* commonplace, everyday, frivolous, incidental, inconsequential, inconsiderable, insignificant, little, meaningless, minor, negligible, paltry, petty, puny, slight, small, trifling, trite, unimportant, valueless, worthless

troop *n* assemblage, band, body, company, contingent, crowd, drove, flock, gang, gathering, group, herd, horde, multitude, pack, squad, swarm, team, throng, unit; (*Inf*) bunch, crew; armed forces, army, fighting men, men, military, servicemen, soldiers, soldiery;

troop *v* crowd, flock, march, parade, stream, swarm, throng, (*Inf*) traipse

trophy *n* award, bays, booty, cup, laurels, memento, prize, souvenir spoils

tropical *adj* hot, humid, lush, steamy, stifling, sultry, sweltering, torrid

trot *v* canter, go briskly, jog, lope, run, scamper

trot *n* brisk pace, canter, jog, lope, run

trouble *n* agitation, annoyance, anxiety, disquiet, distress, grief, heartache, irritation, misfortune, pain, sorrow, suffering, torment, tribulation, vexation, woe, worry; (*Inf*) hassle; agitation, commotion, discontent, discord, disorder, dissatisfaction, disturbance, row, strife, tumult, unrest; (*Inf*) bother; ailment, complain, defect, disability, disease, disorder, failure, illness, malfunction, upset; bother, concern, danger, difficulty, dilemma, dire straits, mess, nuisance, pest, predicament, problem; (*Inf*) hot water, pickle, scrape, spot; attention, bother, care, effort, exertion, inconve nience, labour pains, struggle, thought, work

trouble *v* afflict, agitate, annoy, bother, discompose, disconcert, disquiet, distress, disturb, fret, grieve, harass, inconvenience, pain, perplex, perturb, pester, plague, sad den, torment, upset, vex, worry; be concerned, bother, burden, discomfort, discommode, disturb, impose upon, incommode, inconvenience, put out; exert oneself, go to the effort of, make an effort, take pains take the time

troublesome *adj* annoying, arduous, bothersome, burdensome, demanding difficult, harassing, hard, importunate, inconvenient, irksome, irritating, laborious, oppressive, pestilential, taxing, tiresome, tricky, trying, upsetting, vexatious, wearisome, worrisome, wor rying; disorderly, insubordinate, rebellious, recalcitrant, refractory, rowdy, turbulent, uncooperative, undisciplined, unruly, violent

truant *n* absentee, delinquent, deserter, dodger, malingerer, runaway, shirker, straggler; (*Inf*) skiver

truce armistice, break, ceasefire, cessation, cessation of hostilities, intermission, interval, lull, moratorium, peace, respite, rest, stay, treaty; (*Inf*) let-up

truck *v* barter, deal, exchange, trade, traffic; lorry, van, wagon

trudge *v* clump, drag oneself, footslog, hike, lumber, march, plod, slog, stump, tramp, trek, walk heavily; (*Inf*) traipse, yomp

trudge *n* footslog, haul, hike, march, slog, tramp, trek; (*Inf*) traipse, yomp

true *adj* accurate, actual, authentic, bona fide, correct, exact, factual, genuine, legitimate, natural, precise, pure, real, right, truthful, valid, veracious, veritable; confirmed, constant, dedicated, devoted, dutiful, faithful, fast, firm, honest, honourable, loyal, pure, reliable, sincere, staunch, steady, true-blue, trustworthy, trusty, unswerving, upright; accurate, correct, exact, on target, perfect, precise, proper, unerring; (*Inf*) spot-on

true *adv* honestly, rightly, truthfully, veraciously, veritable; accurate, correctly, on target, perfectly, precisely, properly, unerringly

truly *adv* absolutely, accurately, actually, authentically, beyond doubt, beyond question, correctly, decidedly, definitely, exactly, factually, genuinely, in actuality, in fact, in reality, in truth, legitimately, precisely, really, rightly, surely, truthfully, unquestionably, veraciously, veritably, without a doubt; confirmedly, constantly, devotedly, dutifully, faithfully, firmly, honestly, honourably, loyally, sincerely, steadily, with all one's heart, with dedication, with devotion; exceptionally, extremely, greatly, indeed, of course, really, to ensure, verily, very

trunk *n* bole, stalk, stem, stock; body, torso; proboscis, snout; bin, box, case, chest, coffer, crate, kist, locker, portmanteau

trust *n* assurance, belief, certainty, certitude, confidence, conviction, credence, credit, expectation, faith, hope, reliance; duty, obligation, responsibility; care, charge, custody, guard, guardianship, protection, safekeeping, trusteeship

trust *v* assume, believe, expect, hope, presume, suppose, surmise, think likely; bank on, believe, count on, depend on, have faith in, lean on, pin one's faith on, place confidence in, place one's trust in, place reliance on, rely upon, swear by, take at face value; assign, command, commit, confide, consign, delegate, entrust, give, put into the hands of, sign over, turn over

trustworthy *adj* dependable, ethical, honest, honourable, levelheaded, mature, principled, reliable, responsible, righteous, sensible, steadfast, to be trusted, true, trusty, truthful, upright

truth *n* accuracy, actuality, exactness, fact, factuality, factualness, genuineness, legitimacy, precision, reality, truthfulness, validity, veracity, verity; candour, constancy, dedication, devotion, dutifulness, faith, faithfulness, fidelity, frankness, honesty, integrity, loyalty, naturalism, realism, uprightness; axiom, certainty, fact, law, maxim, proven principle, reality, truism, verity

truthful adj accurate, candid, correct, exact, faithful forthright, frank, honest literal, naturalistic, plainspoken, precise, realistic, reliable, sincere, straight, straightforward, true, trustworthy, veracious, veritable

try *v* aim, attempt, do one's best, endeavour, essay, exert oneself, have a go, have a crack, shot, stab, whack; make an attempt, make an effort, seek, strive, struggle, undertake; appraise, check out, evaluate, examine, experiment, inspect, investigate, prove, put to the test, sample, taste, test; afflict, annoy, inconvenience, irk, irritate, pain, plague, strain, stress, tax, tire, trouble, upset, vex, weary; adjudge, adjudicate, examine, hear

try *n* attempt, effort, endeavour, essay, shot, stab, whack (*Inf*) crack, whack

trying *adj* difficult, fatiguing, hard, irksome, tiresome, wearisome; afflicting, afflictive, calamitous, deplorable, dire, distressing, grievous, hard, painful, sad, severe

try out *v* appraise, check out, evaluate, experiment with, inspect, put into practice, put to the test, sample, taste, test

tuck *v* fold, gather, insert, push, stuff; pleat, ruffle tuck; cover up, put to bed, tuck up, wrap up; eat heartily, gobble up, wolf down; (*Inf*) get stuck into

tuck *n* fold, gather, pinch, pleat; food, victuals; (*Inf*) comestible, eats, grub, nosh, scoff

tuck in *v* bed down, enfold, fold under, make snug, put to bed, swaddle, wrap up; eat heartily, get; (*Inf*) stuck in

tug *v* drag, draw, haul, heave, jerk, lug, pull, tow, wrench, yank

tug *n* drag, haul, heave, jerk, pull, tow, traction, wrench, yank

tuition *n* education, instruction, lessons, schooling, teaching, training, tutelage, tutoring

tumble *v* drop, fall, fall end over end, fall headlong, fall head over heels, flop, lose one's footing, pitch, plummet, roll, stumble, topple, toss, trip up

tumble *n* collapse, drop, fall, flop, headlong fall, plunge, roll, spill, stumble, toss, trip

tumult *n* ado, affray, agitation, alter cation, bedlam, brawl, brouhaha, clamour, commotion, din, disorder, disturbance, excitement, fracas, hubbub, hullabaloo, outbreak, pandemonium, quarrel, racket, riot, row, stir, strife, turmoil, unrest, upheaval, uproar; (*Inf*) ruction

tumultuous *adj* blustery, breezy, bustling, confused, disorderly, disturbed, riotous, turbulent, unruly

tune *n* air, melody, melody line, motif, song, strain, theme; agreement, concert, concord, consonance, euphony, harmony, pitch, sympathy, unison

tune *v* adapt, adjust, attune, bring into harmony, harmonize, pitch, regulate

tuneful *adj* dulcet, harmonious, melodious, musical

tunnel *n* burrow, channel, hole, passage, passageway, shaft, subway, underground passage, underpass

tunnel *v* burrow, dig, dig one's way, excavate, mine, penetrate, scoop out, undermine

turbulence *n* agitation, boiling, commotion, confusion, disorder, instability, pandemonium, roughness, storm, tumult, turmoil, unrest, upheaval

turbulent *adj* agitated, blustery, boiling, choppy, confused, disordered, foaming, furious, raging, rough, tempestuous, tumultuous, unsettled, unstable; agitated, anarchic, boisterous, disorderly, insubordinate, lawless, mutinous, obstreperous, rebellious, refractory, riotous, rowdy, seditious, tumultuous, ungovernable, unruly, uproarious, violent, wild

turf *n* clod, divot, grass, green, lawn, sod, sward; horse-racing, racing; race-courses

turf *v* grass, lay grass; dispose of, fling out, scrap, throw out; (*Inf*) chuck away, dump; discharge, dismiss, eject, evict, expel; (*Inf*) show someone the door

turmoil *n* agitation, bedlam, brouhaha, bustle, chaos, commotion, confusion, disorder, disturbance, ferment, flurry, hubbub, noise, pandemonium, row, stir, strife, trouble, tumult, turbulence, uproar, violence

turn *v* circle, go round, gyrate, move in a circle, pivot, revolve, roll, rotate, spin, swivel, twirl, twist, wheel, whirl; change course, change position, go back, move, return, reverse, shift, swerve, switch, veer, wheel; arc, come round, corner, go round, negotiate, pass, pass around, take a bend; adapt, alter, become, change, convert, divert, fashion, fit, form, metamorphose, mould, mutate, remodel, shape, transfigure, transform, transmute; become rancid, curdle, go bad, go sour, make rancid, sour, spoil, taint; (*Inf*) go off; appeal, apply, approach, go, have recourse, look, resort; nauseate, sicken, upset; apostalize, change one's mind, change sides, defect, desert, go over, influence, persuade, prejudice, prevail upon, renege, retract, talk into; (*Inf*) bring round; construct, deliver, execute, fashion, frame, make, mould, perform, shape, write; turn tail beat a hasty retreat, bolt, flee, run away, run off, show a clean pair of heels, take to one's heels; (*Inf*) cut and run, take off

turn *n* bend, change, circle, curve, cycle, gyration, pivot, reversal, revolution, rotation, spin, swing, turning, twist, whirl; bias, direction, drift, heading, tendency, trend; bend, change of course, change of direction, curve, departure, deviation, shift; chance, fling, go, opportunity, period, round, shift, spell, stint, succession, time, try, whack; (*Inf*) crack, shot; affinity, aptitude, bent, bias, flair, gift, inclination, knack, leaning, propensity, talent; act, action, deed, favour, gesture, service; bend, distortion, twist, warp; by turns alternately, in succession, one after another, reciprocally, turn and turn about

turning-point *n* change, climacteric, crisis, critical moment, crossroads, crux, decisive moment, moment of decision, moment of truth

turn off *v* branch off, change direction, depart from, deviate, leave, quit, take another road, take a side road; cut out, kill, put out, shut down, stop, switch off, turn out, unplug

turn on *v* activate, energize, ignite, put on, set in motion, start, start up, switch on; balance, be contingent on, be decided by, depend, hang, hinge, pivot, rest; assail, assault, attack, fall on, lose one's temper with, round on

turn up *v* appear, arrive, attend, come, put in an appearance, show one's face; (*Inf*) show, show up; appear, become known, be found, bring to light, come to light, come to pass, come up with, dig up, disclose, discover, expose, find, pop up, reveal, transpire, unearth; (*Inf*) crop up

tussle *v* conflict, contend, contest, scuffle, struggle, wrestle

tussle *n* conflict, contest, fight, scuffle, struggle

tutor *n* coach, educator, governor, guardian, guide, guru, instructor, lecturer, master, mentor, preceptor, schoolmaster, teacher

tutor *v* coach, direct, discipline, drill, edify, educate, guide, instruct, lecture, school, teach, train

tweak *n* jerk, pinch, pull, twinge, twitch

twilight *n* dimness, dusk, evening, half-light, sundown, sunset; decline, ebb, last phase

twilight *adj* crepuscular, darkening. dim, evening

twin *n* clone, corollary, counterpart, double, duplicate, fellow, likeness, lookalike, match, mate; (*Inf*) ringer

twin *adj* corresponding double, dual, duplicate, germinate, identical, matched, matching, paired, parallel, twofold

twine *n* cord, string, tarn; coil, convolution, interlacing, twist, whorl; knot, snarl, tangle

twine *v* braid, entwine, interlace, interweave, knit, plait, splice, twist together, weave; bend, coil, curl, encircle, loop, meander, spiral, surround, twist, wind, wrap, wreathe

twinge *v* pinch, tweak, twitch

twinge *n* pinch, tweak, twitch; gripe, pang, spasm, stitch, tingle

twinkling *n* blink, coruscation, flash, flashing, flicker, gleam, glimmer, glistening, glittering, scintillation, shimmer, shining, sparkle, twinkle, wink; flash, instant, moment, second, split second, trice, twinkle; (*Inf*) jiffy, shake, tick, two shakes of a lamb's tail

twirl *v* gyrate, pirouette, pivot, revolve, rotate, spin, turn, turn on one's heel, twiddle, twist, wheel, whirl wind

twirl *n* gyration, pirouette, revolution, rotation, spin, turn, twist, wheel, whirl

twist *v* coil, corkscrew, curl, encircle, entwine, intertwine, screw, spin, swivel, twine, weave, wind, wrap, wreathe, wring; contort, distort, screw up; rick, sprain, turn, wrench; alter, change, distort, falsify, garble, misquote, misrepresent, pervert, warp

twist *n* coil, curl, spin, swivel, twine, wind; braid, coil, curl, hank, plug, quid, roll; change, development, revelation, slant, surprise, turn, variation; arc, bend, convolution, curve, meander, turn, undulation, zigzag; defect, deformation, distortion, flaw, imperfection, kink, warp; jerk, pull, sprain, turn, wrench; aberration, bent, characteristic, crotchet, eccentricity, fault, foible, idiosyncrasy, oddity, peculiarity, proclivity, quirk, trait; confusion, entanglement, kink, knot, mess, mix-up, snarl, tangle

twitch *v* blink, flutter, jerk, jump, pluck, pull, snatch, squirm, tug, yank

twitch *n* blink, flutter, jerk, jump, pull, spasm, tic, tremor, twinge

tycoon *n* baron, capitalist, captain of industry, financier, industrialist, magnate, merchant, prince, mogul, plutocrat, potentate, wealthy, businessman; (*Inf*) big cheese, big noise, fat cat

type *n* breed, category, class, classification, form, genre, group, ilk, kidney, kind, order sort, species, strain, subdivision, variety; case, characters, face, fount, print, printing; archetype, epitome, essence, example, exemplar, model, original, paradigm, pattern, personification, prototype, quintessence, specimen, standard

typical *adj* archetypal, average, characteristic, classic, conventional, essential, illustrative, in character, indicative, in keeping, model, normal, orthodox, representative, standard, stock, true to type, usual

typify *v* characterize, embody, epitomize, exemplify, illustrate, incarnate, personify, represent, sum up, symbolize

tyrannical *adj* absolute, arbitrary, authoritarian, autocratic, coercive, cruel, despotic, dictatorial, domineering, high-handed, imperious, inhuman, magisterial, oppressive, overbearing, overweening, peremptory, severe, tyrannous, unjust, unreasonable

tyranny *n* absolutism, authoritarian ism, autocracy, coercion, cruelty, despotism, dictatorship, harsh, discipline, high-handedness, imperiousness, oppression, peremptoriness, reign or terror, unreasonableness

tyrant *n* absolutist, authoritarian, autocrat, bully, despot, dictator, martinet, oppressor, slave-driver

U

ubiquitous *adj* all-over, all over the place, ever-present, everywhere, omnipresent, pervasive, present, universal

ugly *adj* hard-favoured, hard-featured, homely, ill-favoured, misshapen, plain, unattractive, unlovely, unprepossessing, unsightly; (*Inf*) not much to look at disagreeable, disgusting, distasteful, frightful, hideous, horrid, hostile, monstrous, objectionable, offensive, repugnant, repulsive, revolting, shocking, sickening, terrible, unpleasant, vile; dangerous, forbidding, menacing, ominous, sinister, threatening; angry, bad-tempered, dark, evil, malevolent, nasty, spiteful, sullen, surly

ulterior *adj* concealed, covert, hidden, personal, secondary, secret, selfish, undisclosed, unexpressed

ultimate *adj* conclusive, decisive, end, eventual, extreme, final, furthest, last, terminal; extreme, greatest, highest, maximum, most significant, paramount, superlative, supreme, topmost, utmost

umbrage *n* shadow, shade, anger, displeasure, dissatisfaction, dudgeon, injury, offence, pique, resentment

umpire *n* adjudicator, arbiter, arbitrator, judge, moderator, referee; (*Inf*) ref

umpire *v* adjudicate, arbitrate, judge, moderate, referee

unable *adj* impotent, inadequate, incapable, ineffectual, no good, not able, not equal to, not up to, powerless, unfit, unfitted, unqualified

unabridged *adj* complete, full-length, uncondensed, uncut, unexpurgated, unshortened, whole

unacceptable *adj* disagreeable, distasteful, improper, inadmissible, insupportable, objectionable, offensive, undesirable, unpleasant, unsatisfactory, unwelcome

unaccommodating *adj* disoblig ing, noncompliant, uncivil, ungracious

unaccompanied *adv* a cappella, alone, by oneself, lone, on one's own, solo, unescorted

unaccustomed *adj* a newcomer to, a novice at, green, inexperienced, new to, not given to, not used to, unfamiliar with, unpracticed, unused to, unversed in

unaffected *adj* artless, genuine, honest, ingenuous, naive, natural, plain, simple, sincere, straightforward, unassuming, unpretentious, unsophisticated, unspoilt, unstudied, without airs

unanimity *n* accord, agreement, concert, concord, harmony, union, unity

unanimous *adj* agreed, agreeing, at one, common, concerted, concordant, harmonious, in agreement, in complete accord, like-minded, of one mind, united

unanswerable *adj* absolute, conclusive, incontestable, incontrovertible, indisputable, irrefutable, unarguable, undeniable

unapproachable *adj* aloof, chilly, cool, distant, frigid, remote, reserved, standoffish, unfriendly, unsociable, withdrawn; inaccessible, out of reach, out-of-the-way, remote, unreachable; (*Inf*) off the beaten track, unget-at-able

unarmed *adj* assailable, defenceless, exposed, helpless, open, open to attack, unarmoured, unprotected, weak, weaponless, without arms

unassailable *adj* impregnable, invincible, invulnerable, secure, well-defended

unassuming *adj* diffident, humble, meek, modest, quiet, reserved, retiring, self-effacing, simple, unassertive, unobtrusive, unostentatious, unpretentious

unattached *adj* autonomous, free, independent, nonaligned, unaffiliated, uncommitted; a free agent, available, by oneself, footloose and fancy free, not spoken for, on one's own, single, unengaged, unmarried

unattended *adj* abandoned, disregard, ignored, left alone, not cared for, unguarded, unwatched; alone, on one's own, unaccompanied, unescorted

unauthorized *adj* forbidden, illegal, prohibited, unaccredited, unapproved, uncertified, unconstitutional, unlawful, unlicensed, unofficial, unsanctioned, unwarranted

unavoidable *adj* bound to happen, certain, compulsory, fated, ineluctable, inescapable, inevitable, inexorable, necessary, obligatory, sure

unaware *adj* heedless, ignorant, incognizant, oblivious, unconscious, unenlightened, uninformed, unknowing, unmindful, unsuspecting

unawares *adv* aback, abruptly, by surprise, off guard, suddenly, unexpectedly, unprepared, without warning; (*Inf*) on the hop; accidentally, by accident, by mistake, inadvertently, mistakenly, unconsciously, unintentionally, unknowingly, unwittingly

unbalanced *adj* asymmetrical, irregular, lopsided, not balanced, shaky, unequal, uneven, unstable, unsymmetrical, wobbly; crazy, demented, deranged, disturbed, eccentric, erratic, insane, irrational, lunatic, mad, *non compos mentis*, not all there, touched, unhinged, unsound, unstable

unbearable *adj* insufferable, insupportable, intolerable, oppressive, unacceptable, unenduring; (*Inf*) too much

unbeatable *adj* indomitable, invincible, more than a match for, unconquerable, unstoppable, unsurpassable

unbecoming *adj* ill-suited, inappropriate, incongruous, unattractive, unbeffiting, unfit, unflattering, unsightly, unsuitable, unsuited; discreditable, improper, indecorous, indelicate, offensive, tasteless, unseemly

unbelievable *adj* astonishing, beyond belief, far-fetched, implausible, impossible, improbable, inconceivable, incredible, out landish, preposterous, questionable, staggering, unconvincing, unimaginable, unthinkable

unbeliever *n* agnostic, deist, disbeliever, doubter, heathen, infidel, sceptic
unbending *adj* aloof, distant, formal, inflexible, reserved, rigid, stiff; firm, hard-line, intractable, resolute, severe, strict, stubborn, tough, uncompromising, unyielding; (*Inf*) uptight
unbiased *adj* disinterested, dispassionate, equitable, even-handed, fair, impartial, just, neutral, objective, open-minded, unprejudiced
unblemished *adj* flawless, immaculate, perfect, pure, spotless, unflawed, unspotted, unstained, unsullied, untarnished
unborn *adj* awaited, embryonic, expected, in utero; coming, future, hereafter, latter, subsequent, to come
unbreakable *adj* armoured, durable, indestructible, infrangible, lasting, nonbreakable, resistant, rugged, shatterproof, solid, strong, toughened
unbridled *adj* excessive, intemperate, licentious, rampant, riotous, unchecked, unconstrained, uncontrolled, uncurbed, ungovernable, ungoverned, unrestrained, unruly, violent, wanton
unbroken *adj* complete, entire, intact, solid, total, undamaged, unimpaired, whole; untamed; continuous, endless, incessant, nonstop; sound, undisturbed; unbeaten, unrivalled, unsurpassed
unburden *v* disburden, discharge, disencumber, ease the load; confess, confide, disclose, divulge, expose, lay bare, make a clean break of, reveal, tell all; (*Inf*) come clean, get something off one's chest
uncalled-for *adj* gratuitous, inappropriate, needless, unasked, undeserved, unjust, unjustified, unnecessary, unprompted, unprovoked, unrequested, unsolicited, unsought, unwarranted, unwelcome
uncanny *adj* eerie, mysterious, preternatural, queer, strange, supernatural, unearthly, unnatural, weird; (*Inf*) creepy, spooky; astonishing, astounding, exceptional, extraordinary, fantastic, incredible, inspired, miraculous, prodigious, remarkable, singular, unheard-of, unusual
unceremonious *adj* abrupt, hasty, hurried, impolite, rude, sudden, uncivil; casual, easy, informal, relaxed, simple, without ritual
uncertain *adj* ambiguous, chancy, conjectural, doubtful, incalculable, indefinite, indeterminate, indistinct, questionable, risky, speculative, undetermined, unforeseeable, unpredictable; (*Inf*) iffy; ambivalent, doubtful, dubious, hazy, in two minds, irresolute, unclear, unconfirmed, undecided, undetermined, unfixed, unresolved, unsettled, unsure, up in the air, vacillating, vague
uncertainty *n* ambiguity, bewilderment, confusion, dilemma, doubt, hesitancy, hesitation, inconclusiveness, indecision, irresolution, lack of confidence, misgiving, mystification, perplexity, puzzlement, qualm, quandary, scepticism, state of suspense, unpredictability, vagueness
unchangeable *adj* changeless, constant, fixed, immutable,

inevitable, invariable, irreversible, permanent, stable, steadfast, strong, unalterable

unchecked *adj* uncurbed, unhampered, unhindered, unobstructed, unrestrained, untrammelled

uncivil *adj* bad-mannered, bearish, boorish, brusque, churlish, discourteous, disrespectful, gruff, ill-bred, ill-mannered, impolite, rude, surly, uncouth, unmannerly

uncivilized *adj* barbarian, barbaric, barbarous, illiterate, primitive, savage, wild; beyond the pale, boorish, brutish, churlish, coarse, gross, philistine, uncouth, uncultivated, uncultured, uneducated, unmannered, unpolished, unsophisticated, vulgar

unclean *adj* contaminated, corrupt, defiled, dirty, evil, filthy, foul, impure, nasty, polluted, soiled, spotted, stained, sullied, tainted

uncomfortable *adj* awkward, causing discomfort, cramped, disagreeable, hard, ill-fitting, incommodious, irritating, painful, rough, troublesome; awkward, confused, discomfited, disquieted, distressed, disturbed, embarrassed, ill at ease, out of place, self-conscious, troubled, uneasy

uncommon *adj* bizarre, curious, few and far between, infrequent, novel, odd, out of the ordinary, peculiar, queer, rare, scarce, singular, strange, unfamiliar, unusual; distinctive, exceptional, extraordi nary, incomparable, inimitable, notable, noteworthy, outstanding, rare, remarkable, singular, special, superior, unparalleled, unprecedented

uncommonly *adv* hardly ever, infrequently, not often, occasionally, only now and then, rarely, scarcely ever, seldom; exceptionally, extremely, particularly, peculiarly, remarkable, strangely, unusually, very

uncommunicative *adj* close, curt, guarded, reserved, reticent, retiring, secretive, short, shy, silent, taciturn, tight-lipped, unforthcoming, unresponsive, unsociable, withdrawn

uncomplaining *adj* long-suffering, meek, patient, resigned, tolerant

uncompromising *adj* decided, die-hard, form, hard-line, inexorable, inflexible, intransigent, obdurate, obstinate, rigid, steadfast, strict, stubborn, tough, unbending, unyielding

unconcerned *adj* aloof, apathetic, callous, cool, detached, dispassionate, distant, incurious, indifferent, oblivious, uninterested, uninvolved, unmoved, unsympathetic

unconditional *adj* absolute, categorical, complete, downright, entire, explicit, full out-and-out, outright, plenary, positive, thoroughgoing, total, unlimited, unqualified, unreserved, unrestricted, utter

unconnected *adj* detached, disconnected, divided, independent, separate; disconnected, disjointed, illogical, incoherent, irrelevant, meaningless, nonsensical, not related, unrelated

unconscious *adj* comatose, dead to the world, insensible, knocked out, numb out, out cold, senseless, stunned; (*Inf*) blacked out; blind to, deaf to, heedless, ignorant, in ignorance, lost to, oblivious, unaware, unknowing, unmindful, unsuspecting; accidental, inadvertent, unintended, unintentional, unpremeditated, unwitting; automatic, inherent, innate, instinctive, involuntary, latent, reflex, repressed, subconscious, subliminal, suppressed, unrealized; (*Inf*) gut

uncontrollable *adj* beside oneself, carried away, frantic, furious, irrepressible, irresistible, like one possessed, mad, strong, ungovernable, unmanageable, ruly, violent, wild

uncontrolled *adj* boisterous, furious, lacking self-control out of control, out of hand, rampant, riotous, running wild, unbridled, unchecked, uncurbed, undisciplined, ungoverned, unrestrained, unruly, unsubmissive, untrammelled, violent

unconventional *adj* atypical, bizarre, bohemian, different, eccentric, idiosyncratic, individual, individualistic, informal, irregular, nonconformist, odd, offbeat, original, out of the ordinary, unorthodox, unusual; (*Inf*) far-out, freakish, way-out

uncouth *adj* awkward, barbaric, boorish, clownish, clumsy, coarse, crude, gawky, graceless, gross, ill-mannered, loutish, lubberly, oafish, rough, rude, rustic, uncivilized, uncultivated, ungainly, unre fined, unseemly, vulgar

uncover *v* bare, lay open, lift the lid, open, show, strip, take the wraps off, unwrap; bring to light, disclose, discover, divulge, expose, lay bare, make known, reveal, unearth, unmask

unctuous *adj* adipose, greasy, oily, fat, fatty, oleaginous, pinguid, sebacious; bland, lubricous, smooth, slippery, bland, fawning, glib, obsequious, oily, plausible, servile, suave, smooth, sycophantic, fervid, gushing

undaunted *adj* bold,, brave, courageous, intrepid, plucky, resolute, unafraid, unfaltering, unflagging, valiant; (*Inf*) spunky

undecided *adj* ambivalent, dithering, doubtful, dubious, equivocating, hesitant, in two minds, irresolute, torn, uncertain, unclear, uncommitted, unsure, vacillating, wavering; debatable, hazy, indefinite, in the balance, moot, open, pending, tentative, unconcluded, undetermined, unknown, unresolved, unsettled, up in the air, vague

undefined *adj* formless, hazy, indefinite, indistinct, shadowy, tenuous, vague; imprecise, indeterminate, inexact, unclear, unexplained, unspecified

undeniable *adj* beyond a doubt, beyond question, certain, clear, evident, incontestable, incontrovert ible, indisputable, indubitable, irrefutable, manifest, obvious, patent, proven, sound, sure, unassailable, undoubted, unquestionable

under *prep* below, beneath, on the bottom of, underneath; directed by, governed by, inferior to, junior to, reporting to, secondary to, subject to, subordinate to, subservient to; belonging to, compromised in, included in, subsumed under; less than, smaller than; in the process of, receiving, undergoing; drowned by, engulfed by, flooded by, immersed in, inundated by, sunk in; bound by, liable to, subject to

under *adv* below, beneath, down, downward, lower, to the bottom

underclothes *pl n* lingerie, underclothing, undergarments, underlinen, underwear; (*Inf*) smalls, under things, undies

undercover *adj* clandestine, concealed, confidential, covert, hidden, intelligence, private, secret, spy, surreptitious, underground; (*Inf*) hush-hush

undercurrent *n* crosscurrent, rip, rip current, riptide, underflow, undertow; atmosphere, aura, drift, feeling, flavour, hidden feeling, hint, murmur, overtone, sense, suggestion, tendency, tenor, tinge, trend, undertone, vibrations; (*Inf*) vibes

underestimate *v* belittle, hold cheap, minimize, miscalculate, misprize, not do justice to, rate too low, set no store by, think too little of, underrate, undervalue; (*Inf*) sell short

undergo *v* bear, be subjected to, endure, experience, go through, stand, submit to, suffer, sustain, weather, withstand

underground *adj* below-ground, below the surface, buried, covered, hypogean, subterranean, sunken; clandestine, concealed, covert, hidden, secret, surreptitious, undercover; alternative, avant-garde, experimental, radical, revolutionary, subversive, unorthodox

underground *n* **the underground** the metro, the subway, the tube; opposition, resistance; partisans

undergrowth *n* bracken, brambles, briars, brush, brushwood, scrub, underbrush, underbush, underwood

underhand *adj* clandestine, crafty, deceitful, deceptive, devious, dishonest, dishonourable, fraudulent, furtive, secret, secretive, sly, sneaky, stealthy, surreptitious, treacherous, underhanded, unethical, unscrupulous; (*Inf*) crooked

underline *v* italicize, mark, rule a line under, underscore; accentuate, bring home, draw attention to, emphasize, give emphasis to, highlight, point up, stress

underling *n* deputy, junior, inferior, lackey, minion, servant, subordinate

underlying *n* concealed, hidden, latent, lurking, veiled; basal, basic, elementary, essential, fundamental, intrinsic, primary, prime, root

undermine *v* dig out, eat away at, erode, excavate, mine, tunnel, undercut, wear away; debilitate, disable, impair, sabotage, sap, subvert, threaten, weaken

underprivileged *adj* badly off, deprived, destitute, disadvantaged, impoverished, in need, in want, needy, poor

underrate *v* belittle, discount, disparage, fail to appreciate, misprize, not do justice to, set too little store by, underestimate, undervalue

undersized *adj* atrophied, dwarfish, miniature, pygmy, runtish, runty, small, squat, stunted, tiny, underdeveloped, underweight

understand *v* appreciate, apprehend, be aware, comprehend, conceive, discern, fathom, follow, get, get to the bottom of, grasp, know, make out, penetrate, receive, realize, recognize, see, take in; (*Inf*) catch on, cotton on, get the hang of, make head or tail of, get to the bottom of, savvy, tumble to, twig; assume, be informed, believe, conclude, gather, hear, learn, presume, suppose, take it, think; accept, appreciate, be able to see, commiserate, show compassion for, sympathize with, tolerate

understanding *n* appreciation, awareness, comprehension, discernment, grasp, insight, intelligence, judgment, knowledge, penetration, perception, sense; belief, conclusion, estimation, idea, conclusion, estimation, idea, interpretation, judgement, notion, opinion, perception, view, viewpoint; accord, agreement, common view, gentlemen's agreement, meeting of minds, pact;

understanding *adj* accepting, compassionate, considerate, discerning, forbearing, forgiving, kind, kindly, patient, perceptive, responsive, sensitive, sympathetic, tolerant

understate *v* down-play, make light of, minimize, play down

understudy *n* double, fill-in, replacement, reserve, stand-in, sub, substitute

undertake *v* agree, bargain, commit oneself, contract, covenant, engage, guarantee, pledge, promise, stipulate, take upon oneself; attempt, begin, commence, embark on, endeavour, enter upon, set about, tackle, take on, try

undertone *n* low tone, murmur, subdued voice, whisper; atmosphere, feeling, flavour, hint, suggestion, tinge, touch, trace, undercurrent

underwater *adj* submarine, submerged, sunken, undersea

underwear *n* lingerie, underclothes, underclothing, undergarments, underlinen, unmentionables; (*Inf*) smalls, undies

underworld *n* criminal element, criminals, gangsters, organized crime; (*Inf*) gangland, mog; abode of the dead, Hades, hell, internal region, nether regions, nether world, the inferno

underwrite *v* back, finance, fund, guarantee, insure, provide, security, sponsor, subsidize; countersign, endorse, initial, sign, subscribe; agree to, approve, consent, sanction; (*Inf*) okay

undesirable *adj* disagreeable, disliked, distasteful, dreaded, objectionable, obnoxious, offensive, out of place, repugnant, (*to be*) avoided, unacceptable, unattractive, unpleasing, unpopular, unsavoury, unsuitable, unwanted, unwelcome, unwished-for

undeveloped *adj* embryonic, immature, inchoate, in embryo, latent, potential, primordial

undignified *adj* beneath one, beneath one's dignity, improper, inappropriate, indecorous, inelegant, lacking dignity, unbecoming, ungentlemanly, unladylike, unrefined, seemly, unsuitable

undisciplined *adj* disobedient, erratic, fitful, obstreperous, uncontrolled, unpredictable, unreliable, unrestrained, unruly, unschooled, unsteady, unsystematic, untrained, wayward, wild, wilful

undisguised *adj* complete, evident, explicit, genuine, manifest, obvious, open, out-and-out, overt, patent, thoroughgoing, transparent, unconcealed, unfeigned, unmistakable, utter, wholehearted

undisputed *adj* accepted, acknowledged, beyond question, certain, conclusive, freely admitted, incontestable, incontrovertible, indisputable, irrefutable, not disputed, recognized, sure, unchallenged, uncontested, undeniable, undoubted, unquestioned

undistinguished *adj* commonplace, everyday, indifferent, mediocre, indifferent, ordinary, pedestrian, plain, prosaic, run-of-the-mill, simple, unexceptional, unexciting, unimpressive, unremarkable; (*Inf*) no great shakes, nothing to write home about, so-so

undisturbed *adj* not moved, quiet, uninterrupted, untouched, without interruption; calm, collected, composed, equable, even, motionless, placid, serene, tranquil, unagitated, unbothered, unperturbed, unruffled, untroubled

undivided *adj* combined, complete, concentrated, concerted, entire, exclusive, full, solid, thorough, unanimous, undistracted, united, whole, wholehearted

undo *v* disengage, disentangle, loose, loosen, open, unbutton, unfasten, unlock, untie, unwrap; annul, cancel, invalidate, neutralize, nullify, offset, reverse, wipe out; bring to naught, defeat, destroy, impoverish, invalidate, mar, overturn, quash, ruin, shatter, subvert, undermine, upset, wreck

undoing *n* collapse, defeat, destruction, disgrace, downfall, humiliation, overthrow, overturn, reversal, ruin, ruination, shame; affliction, blight, curse, fatal flaw, misfortune, the last straw, trial, trouble, weakness

undone *adj* incomplete left, neglected, not completed, not done, omitted, outstanding, passed over, unattended to, unfinished, unfulfilled, unperformed

undoubtedly *adv* assuredly, beyond a shadow of a doubt, beyond question, certainly, definitely, doubtless, of course, surely, undeniably, unmistakably, unquestionably, without doubt

undress *v* disrobe, divest oneself of, shed, strip, take off one's clothes; (*Inf*) peel off

undress *n* disarray, dishabille, nakedness, nudity

undue *adj* disproportionate, excessive, extravagant, extreme, moderate, improper, inordinate, intemperate, needless, overmuch, too great, too much, uncalled-for, undeserved, unnecessary, unseemly, unwarranted

unduly *adv* disproportionately, excessively, extravagantly, immoderately, improperly, inordinately, out of all proportion, overly, over much, unjustifiably, unnecessarily, unreasonably

undying *adj* deathless, endless, immortal, imperishable

unearth *v* dig up, disinter, dredge up, excavate, exhume; bring to light, come across, discover, expose, ferret out, find, hit upon, reveal, root up, turn up, uncover

unearthly *adj* eerie, ghostly, haunted, nightmarish, phantom, spectral, strange, uncanny, weird; ethereal, heavenly, not of this world, preternatural, sublime, supernatural; (*Inf*) spooky; abnormal, absurd, extraordinary, ridiculous, strange, unreasonable; (*Inf*) ungodly, unholy

uneasy *adj* agitated, anxious, apprehensive, discomposed, disturbed, edgy, ill at ease, impatient, nervous, on edge, perturbed, restive restless, troubled, uncomfortable, unsettled, upset, worried; (*Inf*) jittery; awkward, constrained, insecure, precarious, shaky, strained, tense, uncomfortable, unstable

uneconomic *adj* lossmaking, nonpaying, non-profit-making, nonviable, unprofitable

unemotional *adj* apathetic, cold, cool, impassive, indifferent, listless, passionless, phlegmatic, reserved, undemonstrative, unexciteable, unfeeling, unimpressionable, unresponsive

unemployed *adj* idle, jobless, laid off, out of a job, out of work, redundant, workless; (*Inf*) on the dole, resting

unending *adj* ceaseless, constant, continual, endless, eternal, everlasting, incessant, interminable, never-ending, perpetual, unceasing, unremitting

unenthusiastic *adj* apathetic, blasé, bored, half-hearted, indifferent, lukewarm, neutral, nonchalant, unimpressed, uninterested, unmoved, unresponsive

unenviable *adj* disagreeable, painful, thankless, uncomfortable, undesirable, unpleasant

unequal *adj* disproportionate, disproportioned, ill-matched, inferior, irregular, insufficient, not alike, uneven

unequalled *adj* beyond compare, incomparable, inimitable, matchless, nonpareil, paramount, peerless, pre-eminent, second to none, supreme, transcendent, unmatched, unparalleled, without equal

unethical *adj* dirty, dishonest, dishonourable, disreputable, illegal, immoral, improper, underhand, unfair, unprincipled, unprofessional, unscrupulous, wrong; (*Inf*) shady

uneven *adj* bumpy, not flat, not level, not smooth, rough; broken, intermittent, irregular, jerky, patchy, spasmodic, unsteady, variable; asymmetrical, lopsided, not parallel, odd, out of true, unbalanced; disparate, ill-matched, one-sided, unequal, unfair

uneventful *adj* boring, commonplace, dull, humdrum, monotonous, ordinary, quiet, routine, tedious, unexceptional, unexciting, uninteresting, unmemorable, unremarkable, unvaried

unexpected *adj* abrupt, accidental, astonished, chance, fortuitous, not bargained for, out of the blue, startling, sudden, surprising, unanticipated, unforeseen, unpredictable

unfailing *adj* bottomless, boundless, ceaseless, continual, continuous, endless, inexhaustible, never-failing, persistent, unflagging, unlimited; certain, constant, dependable, faithful, infallible, loyal, reliable, staunch, steadfast, sure, tried and true, true

unfair *adj* arbitrary, biased, bigoted, discriminatory, inequitable, one-sided, partial, partisan, prejudiced, unjust; dishonest, dishonourable, uncalled-for, unethical, unprincipled, unscrupulous, unsporting, unwarranted, wrongful; (*Inf*) crooked

unfaithful *adj* deceitful, disloyal, faithless, false, false-hearted, perfidious, traitorous, treacherous, treasonable, unreliable, untrustworthy; adulterous, faithless, fickle, inconstant, unchaste, untrue; (*Inf*) two-timing

unfamiliar *adj* alien, curious, different, little known, new, novel, out-of-the-way, strange, unaccustomed, uncommon, unknown, unusual

unfashionable *adj* antiquated, behind the times, dated, démodé, obsolete, old-fashioned, old-hat, out, outmoded, out of date, out of fashio, passé, square, unpopular

unfasten *v* detach, disconnect, let go, loosen, open, separate, uncouple, undo, unlace, unlock, untie

unfavourable *adj* adverse, bad, contrary, disadvantageous, hostile, ill-suited, infelicitous, inimical, low, negative, poor, unfortunate, unfriendly, unsuited; inauspicious, inopportune, ominous, threatening, unlucky, unpromising, unpropitious, unseasonable, untimely, untoward

unfeeling *adj* apathetic, callous, heartless, insensible, numb, obdurate, torpid, unconscious, unimpressionable, adamantine, cold-blooded, cruel, hard, merciless, pitiless, stony, unkind, unsympathetic

unfit *adj* ill-equipped, inadequate, incapable, incompetent, ineligible, no good, not cut out for, not equal-to, not up to, unprepared, unqualified, untrained, useless; ill-adapted, inadequate, inappropriate, ineffective, not designed, not fit, unsuitable, unsuited; debilitated, decrepit, feeble, flabby, in poor condition, out of kelter, out of shape, out of trim, unhealthy

unflattering *adj* blunt, candid, critical, honest, uncomplimentary, warts and all; not shown in the best light, not shown to advantage, plain, unattractive, unbecoming, unprepossessing

unfold *v* disentangle, expand, flatten, open, spread out, straighten, stretch out, undo, unfurl, unravel, unroll, unwrap; clarify, describe, disclose, divulge, explain, illustrate, make known, present, reveal, show, uncover

unforeseen *adj* abrupt, accidental, out of the blue, startling, sudden, surprise, surprising, unanticipated, unexpected, unlooked-for, unpredicted

unforgettable *adj* exceptional, extraordinary, fixed in the mind, impressive, memorable, never to be forgotten, notable

unforgivable *adj* deplorable, disgraceful, indefensible, inexcusable, shameful, unjustifiable, unpardonable, unwarrantable

unfortunate *adj* adverse, calamitous, disastrous, ill-fated, ill-starred, inopportune, ruinous, unfavourable, untoward; cursed, doomed, hapless, hopeless, luckless, out of luck, poor, starcrossed, unhappy, unlucky, unprosperous, unsuccessful, wretched; deplorable, ill-advised, inappropriate, infelicitous, lamentable, regrettable, unbecoming, unsuitable

unfounded *adj* baseless, fabricated, false, groundless, idle, spurious, trumped up, unjustified, unproven, unsubstantiated, vain, without basis, without foundation

unfriendly *adj* aloof, antagonistic, chilly, cold, disagreeable, distant, hostile, ill-disposed, inhospitable, not on speaking terms, quarrelsome, sour, surly, uncongenial, unneighbourly, unsociable; alien, hostile, inauspicious, inhospitable, inimical, unfavourable, unpropitious

ungainly *adj* awkward, clumsy, gangling, gawky, inelegant, loutish, lubberly, lumbering, slouching, uncoordinated, uncouth, ungraceful

ungodly *adj* blasphemous, corrupt, depraved, godless, immoral, impious, irreligious, profane, sinful, vile, wicked

ungracious *adj* bad-mannered, churlish, discourteous, ill-bred, impolite, offhand, rude, uncivil, unmannerly

ungrateful *adj* heedless, impolite, selfish, thankless, unappreciative, unmindful, unthankful

unguarded *adj* careless, foolhardy, heedless, ill-considered, impolitic, imprudent, incautious, indiscreet, rash, thoughtless, uncircumspect, undiplomatic, unthinking, unwary; defenceless, open to attack, undefended, unpatrolled, unprotected, vulnerable

unhappy *adj* blue, crestfallen, dejected, depressed, despondent, disconsolate, dispirited, down, downcast, gloomy, long-faced, melancholy, miserable, mournful, sad, sorrowful; cursed, hapless, ill-fated, ill-omened, luckless, unfortunate, unlucky, wretched; awkward, ill-advised, ill-timed, inappropriate, inept, infelicitous, injudicious, malapropos, tactless, unsuitable, untactful

unharmed *adj* intact, safe, safe and sound, sound, undamaged, unhurt, uninjured, unscarred, unscathed, untouched, whole, without a scratch; (*Inf*) in one piece

unhealthy *adj* ailing, debilitated, delicate, feeble, frail, ill, infirm, in poor health, invalid, poorly, sick, sickly, unsound, unwell, weak; deleterious, detrimental, harmful, insalubrious, insanitary, noisome, noxious, unwholesome

unheard-of *adj* little known, obscure, undiscovered, unfamiliar, unknown, unregarded, unremarked, unsung; inconceivable, never before encountered, new, novel, singular, unbelievable, undreamed of, unexampled, unique, unprecedented, unusual; disgraceful, extreme, offensive, outlandish, outrageous,

shocking, unacceptable, unthinking
unhesitating *adj* implicit, resolute, steadfast, unfaltering, unquestion ing, unreserved, unswerving, unwavering, wholehearted; immediate, instant, instantaneous, prompt, ready, without delay
unholy *adj* base, corrupt, depraved, dishonest, evil, heinous, immoral, iniquitous, irreligious, profane, sinful, ungodly, vile, wicked
unhurried *adj* calm, deliberate, easy, easy-going, leisurely, sedate, slow, slow and steady, slow-paced
unidentified *adj* anonymous, mysterious, nameless, unclassified, unfamiliar, unknown, unremarked, unnamed, unrecognized, unrevealed
uniform *n* costume, dress, garb, habit, livery, outfit, regalia, regimentals, suit
uniform *adj* consistent, constant, equable, even, regular, smooth, unbroken, unchanging, undeviating, unvarying; alike, equal, identical, like, same, selfsame, similar
unimaginable *adj* beyond one's wildest dreams, fantastic, impossible, inconceivable, incredible, indescribable, ineffable, unbelievable, unheard-of, unthinkable; (*Inf*) mind-boggling
unimaginative *adj* barren, commonplace, derivative, dry, dull, hackneyed, lifeless, matter-of-fact, ordinary, pedestrian, predictable, prosaic, routine, tame, uncreative, uninspired, unoriginal, unromantic, usual
unimportant *adj* immaterial, inconsequential, insignificant, irrelevant, low-ranking, minor, not worth mentioning, nugatory, of no account, of no consequence, of no moment, paltry, petty, slight, trifling, trivial, worthless
uninhabited *adj* abandoned, barren, desert, deserted, desolate, empty, unoccupied, inpopulated, unsettled, untenanted, vacant, waste
uninspired *adj* commonplace, dull, humdrum, indifferent, ordinary, prosaic, stale, stock, unexciting, unimaginative, uninspiring, uninteresting, unoriginal
unintelligent *adj* brainless, dense, dull, empty-headed, foolish, obtuse, slow, stupid, thick, unreasoning, unthinking
unintelligible *adj* illegible, inarticulate, incoherent, incomprehensible, indecipherable, indistinct, jumbled, meaningless, muddles, unfathomable; (*Inf*) double Dutch
unintentional *adj* accidental, casual, fortuitous, inadvertent, involuntary, unconscious, undesigned, unintended, unpremeditated, unthinking, unwitting
uninterested *adj* apathetic, blasé, bored, distant, impassive, incurious, indifferent, listless, unconcerned, uninvolved, unresponsive
uninteresting *adj* boring, commonplace, drab, dreary, dry, dull, flat, humdrum, monotonous, tedious, tiresome, unenjoyable, uneventful, unexciting, uninspiring, wearisome
uninterrupted *adj* constant, continual, continuous, nonstop, peaceful, steady, sustained, unbroken, undisturbed, unending
union *n* amalgamating, amalgamation, blend, combination, confedera-

tion, conjunction, fusion, junction, mixture, synthesis, uniting; alliance, association, Bund, coalition, confederacy, confederation, federation, league; accord, agreement, concord, concurrence, harmony, unanimity, unison, unity

unique *adj* lone, one and only, only, single, solitary, *sui generis*; incomparable, inimitable, matchless, nonpareil, peerless, unequalled, unexampled, unmatched, unparalleled, unrivalled, without equal

unison *n* accord, accordance, agreement, concert, concord, cooperation, harmony, unanimity, unity

unit *n* assembly, detachment, entity, group, section, system, whole; component, constituent, element item, member, module, part, piece, portion, section, segment

unite *v* amalgamate, blend, coalesce, combine, confederate, consolidate, couple, fuse, incorporate, join, link, marry, merge, unify, wed; ally, associate, band, close ranks, club together, cooperate, join forced, join together, league, pool, pull together

united *adj* affiliated, allied, banded together, collective, combined, concerted, in partnership, leagued, pooled, unified; agreed, in accord, in agreement, like-minded, of like mind, of one mind, of the same opinion, one, unanimous

unity *n* entity, integrity, oneness, singleness, undividedness, unification, union, wholeness; accord, agreement, concord, concurrence, consensus, harmony, peace, solidarity, unanimity

universal *adj* all-embracing, catholic, common, ecumenical, entire, general, omnipresent, total, unlimited, whole, widespread, worldwide

universally *adv* always, everywhere, in all cases, in every instance, invariably, uniformly, without exception

universe *n* cosmos, creation, everything, macrocosm, nature, the natural world

unjust *adj* biased, inequitable, one-sided, partial, partisan, prejudiced, undeserved, unfair, unjustified, unmerited, wrong, wrongful

unkind *adj* cruel, hardhearted, harsh, inconsiderate, inhuman, insensitive, malicious, mean, nasty, spiteful, thoughtless, uncaring, uncharitable, unchristian, unfeeling, unfriendly, unsympathetic

unknown *adj* alien, concealed, dark, hidden, mysterious, new, secret, strange, unrecognized, unrevealed, untold; anonymous, nameless, uncharted, undiscovered, unexplored, unidentified, unnamed; humble, little known, obscure, undistinguished, unfamiliar, unheard-of, unrenowned, unsung

unlawful *adj* actionable, against the law, banned, criminal, forbidden, illegal, illegitimate, illicit, outlawed, prohibited, unauthorized, unlicensed

unlike *adj* contrasted, different, dissimilar, distinct, divergent, diverse, ill-matched, incompatible, not alike, opposite, unequal, unrelated

unlike *prep* differently from, not

like, not typical of

unlikely *adj* doubtful, faint, improbable, not likely, remote, slight, unimaginable; implausible, incredible, questionable, unbelievable, unconvincing

unlimited *adj* boundless, countless, endless, extensive, great, illimitable, immeasurable, immense, incalculable, infinite, limitless, unbounded, vast; absolute, all-encompassing, complete, full, total, unconditional, unconstrained, unfettered, unqualified, unrestricted

unload *v* disburden, discharge, dump, empty, off-load, relieve, unburden, unlade, unpack

unloved *adj* disliked, forsaken, loveless, neglected, rejected, spurned, uncared-for, uncherished, unpopular, unwanted

unlucky *adj* cursed, disastrous, hapless, luckless, miserable, unfortunate, unhappy, unsuccessful wretched; doomed, ill-fated, ill-omened, ill-starred, inauspicious, ominous, unfavourable, untimely

unmanageable *adj* awkward, cumbersome, inconvenient, unwieldy; intractable, unruly, unworkable, vicious; difficult, impractical

unmarried *adj* bachelor, celibate, maiden, single, unattached, unwed, unwedded, virgin

unmentionable *adj* disgraceful, disreputable, forbidden, frowned on, immodest, indecent, scandalous, shameful, shocking, taboo, unspeakable, unutterable

unmerciful *adj* brutal, cruel, hard, heartless, implacable, merciless, pitiless, relentless, remorseless, ruthless, uncaring, unfeeling, unsparing

unmistakable *adj* certain, clear, conspicuous, decided, distinct, evident, glaring, indisputable, manifest, obvious, palpable, patent, plain, positive, pronounced, sure, unambiguous, unequivocal

unmitigated *adj* grim, harsh, intense, oppressive, persistent, relentless, unabated, unalleviated, unbroken, undiminished, unmodified, unqualified, unredeemed, unrelieved; absolute, arrant, complete, consummate, downright, out-and-out, outright, perfect, rank, sheer, thorough, thoroughgoing, utter

unmoved *adj* fast, firm, in place, in position, steady, unchanged, untouched; cold, dry-eyed, impassive, indifferent, unaffected, unfeeling, unimpressed, unresponsive, unstirred, untouched; determined, firm, inflexible, resolute, resolved, steadfast, undeviating, unshaken, unwavering

unnatural *adj* aberrant, abnormal, anomalous, irregular, odd, perverse, perverted, unusual; bizarre, extraordinary, freakish, outlandish, queer, strange, supernatural, unaccountable, uncanny; affected, artificial, assumed, contrived, factitious, false, feigned, forced, insincere, laboured, mannered, self-conscious, stagy, stiff, stilted, strained, studied, theatrical; (*Inf*) phoney

unnecessary *adj* dispensable, expendable, inessential, needless, nonessential, redundant, superogatory, superfluous, surplus to require ments, uncalled-for, unneeded, unrequired, useless

unnerve *v* confound, daunt, demoralize, disarm, disconcert, discourage, dishearten, dismay, dispirit, fluster, frighten, intimidate, shake, throw off balance, unhinge, unman, upset; (*Inf*) rattle

unobtrusive *adj* humble, inconspic uous, keeping a low profile, low-key, meek, modest, quiet, restrained, retiring, self-effacing, subdued, unassuming, unnoticeable, unostentatious, unpretentious

unoccupied *adj* empty, tenantless, uninhabited, untenanted, vacant

unofficial *adj* informal, personal, private, unauthorized, unconfirmed, wildcat

unorthodox *adj* abnormal, heterodox, irregular, unconventional, uncustomary, unusual, unwonted

unpaid *adj* due, not discharged, outstanding, overdue, owing, payable, unsettled; honourary, unsalaried, voluntary

unpalatable *adj* bitter, disagreeable, displeasing, distasteful, offensive, repugnant, unappetizing, unattractive, uneatable, unpleasant, unsavoury

unpardonable *adj* deplorable, disgraceful, indefensible, inexcusable, outrageous, scandalous, shameful, unforgivable, unjustifiable

unperturbed *adj* calm, collected, composed, cool, placid, poised, self-possessed, tranquil, undismayed, unflustered, unruffled, untroubled, unworried

unpleasant *adj* abhorrent, bad, disagreeable, displeasing, distasteful, ill-natured, irksome, nasty, objectionable, obnoxious, repulsive, troublesome, unattractive, unlikable, unlovely, unpalatable

unpopular *adj* avoided, detested, disliked, not sought out, out in the cold, out of favour, rejected, shunned, unattractive, undesirable, unloved, unwanted, unwelcome

unprecedented *adj* abnormal, exceptional, extraordinary, freakish, new, novel, original, remarkable, singular, unexampled, unheard-of, unparalleled, unrivalled, unusual

unpredictable *adj* chance, changeable, doubtful, erratic, fickle, inconstant, random, unforeseeable, unreliable, unstable, variable; (*Inf*) iffy

unprejudiced *adj* balanced, even-handed, fair, fair-minded, impartial, just, nonpartisan, objective, open-minded, unbiased, uninfluenced

unpremeditated *adj* extempore, impromptu, impulsive, offhand, spontaneous, spur-of-the-moment, unplanned, unprepared; (*Inf*) off the cuff

unprepared *adj* ill-considered, incomplete, not thought out, unfinished, unplanned; (*Inf*) half-baked; caught napping, surprised, taken aback, taken off guard, unaware, unready, unsuspecting; (*Inf*) caught on the hop; ad-lib, extemporaneous, improvised, spontaneous; (*Inf*) off the cuff

unpretentious *adj* homely, honest, humble, modest, plain, simple, straightforward, unaffected, unassuming, unimposing, unobtrusive, unostentatious, unspoiled

unprincipled *adj* amoral, corrupt, crooked, deceitful, devious, dishonest, immoral, tricky, unconscionable, underhand, unethical, unprofessional, unscrupulous

unproductive *adj* bootless, fruitless, futile, idle, ineffective, inefficacious, otiose, unavailing, unprofitable, unremunerative, unrewarding, useless, vain, valueless, worthless; barren, dry, fruitless, sterile, unprolific

unprofessional *adj* improper, lax, negligent, unethical, unfitting, unprincipled, unseemly, unworthy; amateur, amateurish, incompetent, inefficient, inexperienced, inexpert, untrained

unprotected *adj* defenceless, exposed, helpless, naked, open, open to attack, pregnable, unarmed, undefended, unguarded, unsheltered, unshielded, vulnerable

unqualified *adj* ill-equipped, incapable, incompetent, ineligible, not equal to, not up to, unfit, unprepared; categorical, downright, out right, unconditional, unmitigated, unreserved, unrestricted, without reservation; absolute, complete, consummate, downright, out-and-out, thorough, thoroughgoing, total, utter

unquestionable *adj* absolute, beyond a shadow of doubt, certain, clear, conclusive, definite, faultless, incontestable, incontrovertible, indisputable, indubitable, irrefutable, manifest, patent, perfect, self-evident, sure, undeniable, unequivocal, unmistakable

unravel *v* disentangle, extricate, free, separate, straighten out, undo, unknot, untangle, unwind

unreal *adj* chimerical, dreamlike, fabulous, fanciful, fictitious, illusory, imaginary, make-believe, phantasmagoric, storybook, visionary; hypothetical, immaterial, impalpable, insubstantial, intangible, mythical, nebulous; artificial, fake, false, insincere, mock, ostensible, pretended, seeming, sham

unrealistic *adj* impracticable, impractical, improbable, quixotic, romantic, starry-eyed, theoretical, unworkable; (*Inf*) half-baked

unreasonable *adj* excessive, exorbitant, extortionate, extravagant, immoderate, too great, uncalled-for, undue, unfair, unjust, unwarranted; (*Inf*) steep; arbitrary, biased, blinkered, capricious, erratic, headstrong, inconsistent, opinionated, quirky

unrelated *adj* different, dissimilar, not kin, not kindred, not related, unconnected, unlike; beside the point, extraneous, inapplicable, inappropriate, irrelevant, not germane, unassociated

unreliable *adj* disreputable, irresponsible, not conscientious, treacherous, undependable, unstable, untrustworthy; deceptive, delusive, erroneous, fake, fallible, false, implausible inaccurate, mistaken, specious, uncertain, unconvincing, unsound

unreserved *adj* demonstrative, extrovert, forthright, frank, free, open, open-hearted, outgoing, outspoken, uninhibited, unrestrained, unreticent; absolute, complete, entire, full, total, unconditional, unlimited, unqualified, wholehearted, without reservation

unresolved *adj* doubtful, moot, open to question, pending, problem atical, unanswered, undecided, undetermined, unsettled, unsolved, up in the air, vague, yet to be decided

unrest *n* agitation, disaffection, discontent, discord, dissatisfaction, dissension, protest, rebellion, sedition, strife, tumult, turmoil; agitation, anxiety, disquiet, distress, perturbation, restlessness, uneasiness, worry

unrestrained *adj* abandoned, boisterous, free, immoderate, inordinate, intemperate, natural, unbounded, unbridled, unchecked, unconstrained, uncontrolled, unhindered, uninhibited, unrepressed

unrestricted *adj* absolute, free, open, unbounded, uncircumscribed, unhindered, unlimited, unregulated; (*Inf*) free-for-all, no holds barred; clear, open, public, unobstructed, unopposed

unrighteous *adj* evil, sinful, ungodly, unholy, vicious, wicked, wrong; heinous, inequitable, iniquitous, nefarious, unfair, unjust

unripe *adj* crude, green, hard, immature, premature, sour; incomplete, unfinished

unrivalled *adj* beyond compare, incomparable, matchless, nonpareil, peerless, supreme, unequalled, unexcelled, unmatched, unparal leled, unsurpassed, without equal

unroll *v* develop, discover, evolve, open, unfold; display, lay open

unruly *adj* disobedient, disorderly, fractious, headstrong, insubordinate, intractable, lawless, mutinous, obstreperous, rebellious, refractory, riotous, rowdy, turbulent, uncontrol lable, ungovernable, unmanageable, wayward, wild, wilful

unsafe *adj* dangerous, hazardous, insecure, perilous, precarious, risky, threatening, treacherous, uncertain, unreliable, unsound, unstable

unsaid *adj* tacit, unmentioned, unspoken, unuttered

unsatisfactory *adj* deficient, disappointing, displeasing, inadequate, insufficient, mediocre, not good enough, not up to par, poor, unacceptable, unsuitable, unworthy, weak; (*Inf*) not up to scratch

unsavoury *adj* distasteful, nasty, objectionable, obnoxious, offensive, repellent, repugnant, repulsive, revolting, unpleasant; disagreeable, distasteful, nauseating, sickening, unappetizing, unpalatable

unsay *v* recall, recant, retract, take back

unscrupulous *adj* conscienceless, corrupt, dishonest, dishonourable, exploitative, immoral, improper, roguish, ruthless, unconscionable, unethical, unprincipled; (*Inf*) crooked

unseasonable *adj* ill-timed, inappropriate, inopportune, untimely; late, too late; ill-timed, inappropriate, unfit, ungrateful, unsuitable, untimely, unwelcome; premature, too early

unseasoned *adj* inexperienced, unaccustomed, unqualified, untrained; immoderate, inordinate, irregular; green; fresh, unsalted

unseeing *adj* blind, sightless

unseemly *adj* discreditable, disreputable, improper, inappropriate, indecorous, indelicate, in poor taste, out of keeping, out of place, unbecoming, unbefitting, undignified, unrefined, unsuitable

unseen *adj* concealed, hidden, invisible, lurking, obscure, undetected, unnoticed, unobserved, unobtrusive, unperceived, veiled

unselfish *adj* altruistic, charitable, devoted, disinterested, generous, humanitarian, kind, liberal, magnanimous, noble, self-denying, selfless, self-sacrificing

unsettle *v* agitate, bother, confuse, discompose, disconcert, disorder, disturb, fluster, perturb, throw into confusion, throw off balance, trouble, unbalance, upset; (*Inf*) rattle, throw

unsettled *adj* disorderly, insecure, shaky, unstable, unsteady; change able, changing, inconstant, uncertain, unpredictable, variable; agitated, anxious, confused, disturbed, flustered, on edge, perturbed, restive, restless, shaken, tense, troubled, uneasy, unnerved; debatable, doubtful, moot, open, undecided, undetermined, unresolved; due, in arrears, outstanding, owing, payable, pending

unshaken *adj* constant, firm, resolute, steadfast, steady, unmoved

unshrinking *adj* firm, determined, persisting, resolute, unblenching, unflinching

unsightly *adj* disagreeable, distasteful, hideous, horrible, offensive, repulsive, ugly, unattractive, unpleasant, unprepossessing; (*Inf*) revolting

unskilled *adj* amateurish, inexperienced, uneducated, unprofessional, unqualified, untalented, untrained

unsociable *adj* chilly, cold, distant, hostile, inhospitable, introverted, reclusive, retiring, standoffish, uncongenial, unforthcoming, unfriendly, unneighbourly, unsocial, withdrawn

unsolicited *adj* free-will, gratuitous, spontaneous, unasked for, uncalled-for, unforced, uninvented, unrequested, unsought, unwelcome, voluntary, volunteered

unsophisticated *adj* artless, childlike, guileless, inexperienced, ingenuous, innocent, naive, natural, unaffected, untutored, unworldly; plain, simple, straightforward, uncomplex, uncomplicated, uninvolved, unrefined, unspecialized

unsound *adj* ailing, defective, delicate, deranged, diseased, frail, ill, in poor health, unbalanced, unhealthy, unhinged, unstable, unwell, weak; defective, erroneous, fallacious, false, faulty, flawed, ill-founded, illogical, invalid, shaky, specious, unreliable, weak

unsparing *adj* bountiful, generous, lavish, liberal, profuse, ungrudging, harsh, inexorable, relentless, rigorous, ruthless, severe, uncompromising, unforgiving

unspeakable *adj* beyond description, beyond words, inconceivable, indescribable, ineffable, inexpressible, overwhelming, unbelievable, unimaginable, unutterable, wonderful; abominable, appaling, awful, bad, dreadful, evil, execrable, frightful, heinous, horrible, loathsome, monstrous, odious, repellent, shocking, too horrible for words

unspoilt *adj* intact, perfect, preserved, unaffected, unblemished, unchanged, undamaged, unharmed, unimpaired, untouched; artless, innocent, natural, unaffected, unassuming, unstudied, wholesome

unspoken *adj* assumed, implicit, implied, left to the imagination, not put into words, not spelt out, tacit, taken for granted, undeclared, understood, unexpressed, unspoken, unstated

unstable *adj* infirm, insecure, precarious, top-heavy, tottering, unbalanced, unballasted, unsafe, unsettled, unsteady; changeable, erratic, fickle, inconstant, irresolute, mercurial, mutable, unsteady, vacillating, variable, wavering, weak, volatile

unsteady *adj* infirm, insecure, precarious, reeling, rickety, shaky, tottering, treacherous, unsafe, unstable, wobbly; changeable, erratic, flickering, flighty, fluctuating, inconstant, irregular, unreliable, unsettled, vacillating, variable, volatile, wavering

unstrung *adj* overcome, shaken, unnerved, weak

unsuccessful *adj* abortive, bootless, failed, fruitless, futile, ineffective, ineffectual, nugatory, unavailing, unproductive, unprofitable, useless, vain; defeated, foiled, frustrated, hapless, ill-starred, losing, luckless, unfortunate, unlucky

unsuitable *adj* improper, inapposite, inappropriate, inapt, incompatible, incongruous, ineligible, infelicitous, out of character, out of keep ing, out of place, unacceptable, unbecoming, unbefitting, unfitting, unseasonable, unseemly, unsuited

unsuited *adj* unadapted, unfitted, unqualified

unsure *adj* insecure, lacking in confidence, unassured, unconfident; distrustful, doubtful, dubious, hesitant, in a quandary, irresolute, mistrustful, sceptical, suspicious, unconvinced, undecided

unsurpassed *adj* matchless, peerless, unequalled, unexampled, unexcellent, unmatched, unparagoned, unparalleled, unrivalled

unsuspecting *adj* confiding, credulous, gullible, inexperienced, ingenuous, innocent, naive, off guard, trustful, trusting, unconscious, unsuspicious, unwarned, unwary

unswerving *adj* direct, straight, undeviating; constant, determined, firm, resolute, staunch, steadfast, steady, stable, unwavering

unsympathetic *adj* apathetic, callous, cold, cruel, hard, harsh, heartless, indifferent, insensitive, pitiless, soulless, stony-hearted, uncaring, uncompassionate, unconcerned, unfeeling, unkind, unmoved, unpitying, unresponsive; against, anti, opposed to,

untamed *adj* fierce, unbroken, wild

untangle *v* clear up, disentangle, explain, extricate, solve, straighten out, unravel, unsnarl

untenable *adj* indefensible,

unmaintainable, unsound; fallacious, hollow, illogical, indefensible, insupportable, injustifiable, weak

unthinkable *adj* absurd, illogical, impossible, improbable, out of the question, preposterous, unlikely, unreasonable; (*Inf*) not on; beyond belief, beyond the realms of possibility, implausible, inconceivable, incredible, insupportable, unbelievable, unimaginable

untidy *adj* bedraggled, chaotic, cluttered, disorderly, jumbled, littered, messy, muddled, muddly, rumpled, shambolic, slatternly, slip-shod, slovenly, topsy-turvy, unkempt; (*Inf*) higgledy-piggledy, sloppy

untie *v* free, loosen, release, unbind, undo, unfasten, unknot, unlace

untimely *adj* awkward, badly timed, early, ill-timed, inappropriate, inauspicious, inconvenient, inopportune, mistimed, premature, unfortunate, unseasonable, unsuitable

untiring *adj* constant, dedicated, determined, devoted, dogged, incessant, indefatigable, patient, persevering, persistent, staunch, steady, tireless, unflattering, unflagging, unremitting, unwearied

untold *adj* countless, incalculable, innumerable, uncounted, unnumbered; unrelated, unrevealed

untouched *adj* intact, safe and sound, undamaged, unharmed, unhurt, uninjured, unscathed, with out a scratch; dry-eyed, indifferent, unaffected, unconcerned, unimpressed, unmoved, unstirred

untoward *adj* annoying, awkward, disastrous, ill-timed, inconvenient, inimical, irritating, troublesome, unfortunate, vexatious; adverse, contrary, inauspicious, inopportune, unfavourable, unlucky, untimely; improper, inappropriate, indecorous, out of place, unbecoming, unfitting, unseemly, unsuitable

untrained *adj* amateur, green, inexperienced, raw, uneducated, unpractised, unqualified, unschooled, unskilled, untaught, untutored

untroubled *adj* calm, composed, cool, peaceful, placid, serene, steady, tranquil, unagitated, unconcerned undisturbed, unflustered, unperturbed, unrifled, unstirred, unworried; (*Inf*) unflappable

untrue *adj* deceptive, dishonest, erroneous, fallacious, false, inaccurate, incorrect, lying, misleading, mistaken, sham, spurious, untruthful, wrong; deceitful, disloyal, faithless, false, forsworn, inconstant, perfidious, traitorous, treacherous, two-faced, unfaithful, untrustworthy; deviant, distorted, inaccurate, off, out of line, out of true, wide

untrustworthy *adj* capricious, deceitful, devious, dishonest, disloyal, fair-weather, faithless, false, fickle, not to be depended on, slippery, treacherous, tricky, two-faced, undependable, unfaithful, unreliable, untrue, untrusty; (*Inf*) fly-by-night

untruth *n* deceit, fabrication, falsehood, falsification, fib, fiction, lie, prevarication, story, tale, trick; (*Inf*) whopper

untruthful *adj* deceitful, deceptive, dishonest, dissembling, false, fibbing, hypocritical, lying, mendacious; (*Inf*) crooked

unusual *adj* abnormal, atypical, bizarre, curious, different, exceptional, extraordinary, odd, out of the ordinary, phenomenal, queer, rare, remarkable, singular, strange, surprising, uncommon, unconventional, unexpected, unfamiliar, unwonted

unutterable *adj* incommunicable, indescribable, ineffable, inexpressible, unspeakable

unvarnished *adj* unpolished; candid, plain, simple, true, unadorned, unembellished

unveil *v* bare, bring to light, disclose, divulge, expose, lay bare, lay open, make known, make public, reveal, uncover

unversed *adj* inexperienced, raw, undisciplined, undrilled, uneducated, unpractised, unprepared, unschooled; unskilled

unwanted *adj de trop,* going begging, outcast, rejected, superfluous, surplus to requirements, unasked, undesired, uninvited, unneeded, unsolicited, unwelcome, useless

unwary *adj* careless, hasty, heedless, imprudent, incautious, indiscreet, precipitate, rash, reckless, remiss, uncircumspect, unguarded

unwavering *adj* consistent, dedicated, determined, resolute, single-minded, staunch, steadfast, steady, undeviating, unfaltering, unflagging, unshakable, unshaken, unswerving, untiring

unwelcome *adj* excluded, rejected, unacceptable, undesirable, uninvited, unpopular, unwanted, unwished for; disagreeable, displeasing, distasteful, undesirable, unpleasant

unwell *adj* ailing, ill, indisposed, in poor health, off colour, out of sorts, sick, sickly, unhealthy; (*Inf*) poorly, under the weather

unwholesome *adj* deleterious, harmful, insalubrious, noxious, poisonous, tainted, unhealthy, unnourishing; (*Inf*) junk; bad, corrupting, degrading, demoralizing, depraving, evil, immoral, perverting, wicked

unwieldy *adj* awkward, burdensome, cumbersome, inconvenient, unhandy, unmanageable; bulky, clumsy, hefty, massive, ponderous, ungainly, weighty

unwilling *adj* averse, demurring, disinclined, grudging, indisposed, loath, not in the mood, opposed, reluctant, resistant, unenthusiastic

unwind *v* disentangle, slacken, uncoil, undo, unravel, unreel, unroll, untwine, untwist; calm down, let oneself go, loosen up, quieten down, relax, sit back, slow, down, take a break, wind down; (*Inf*) take it easy

unwise *adj* foolhardy, foolish, ill-advised, ill-considered, ill-judged, impolitic, improvident, imprudent, inadvisable, indiscreet, injudicious, irresponsible, rash, reckless, senseless, short-sighted, silly, stupid

unwitting *adj* ignorant, innocent, unaware, unconscious, unknowing, unsuspecting; accidental, chance, inadvertent, involuntary, undesigned, unintended, unintentional, unmeant, unplanned

unworldly *adj* abstract, celestial, metaphysical, nonmaterialistic, religious, spiritual, transcendental; green, idealistic, inexperienced, innocent, naive, raw, trusting, unsophisticated; ethereal, extraterrestrial, otherworldly, unearthly

unworthy *adj* base, contemptible, degrading, discreditable, disgraceful, dishonourable, disreputable, ignoble, shameful; ineligible, not deserving of, not fit for, not good enough, not worth, undeserving

unwrap *v* open, unfold

unwrinkled *adj* smooth, unforrowed

unwritten *adj* oral, unrecorded, vocal, word-of-mouth; accepted, conventional, customary, tacit, traditional, understood, unformulated

unyielding *adj* adamant, determined, form, hardline, immovable, inexorable, inflexible, intractable, loyal, obdurate, obstinate, relentless, resolute, rigid, staunch, steadfast, stubborn, tough, unbending, uncompromising, unwavering

upbringing *n* breeding, bringing up, care, cultivation, education, nurture, raising, rearing, tending, training

upgrade *v* advance, ameliorate, better, elevate, enhance, improve, promote, raise

upheaval *n* cataclysm, disorder, disruption, disturbance, eruption, overthrow, revolution, turmoil, violent change

uphill *adj* ascending, climbing, mounting, rising; arduous, difficult, exhausting, gruelling, hard, Herculean, laborious, punishing, Sisyphean, strenuous, taxing, tough, wearisome

uphold *v* advocate, aid, back, champion, defend, encourage, endorse, hold to, justify, maintain, promote, stand by, support, sustain, vindicate

upkeep *n* conservation, keep, maintenance, preservation, repair, running costs, subsistence, support, sustenance; expenditure, expenses, operating costs, outlay, overheads, running costs

uplift *v* elevate, heave, hoist, lift up, raise; advance, ameliorate, better, civilize, cultivate, edify, improve, inspire, raise, refine, upgrade

uplift *n* advancement, betterment, cultivation, edification, enhancement, enlightenment, enrichment, improvement, refinement

upon *prep* on, on top of, over; about, concerning, on the subject of, relating to; immediately after, with

upper *adj* high, higher, loftier, top, topmost; elevated, eminent, greater, important, superior

upper hand *n* advantage, ascendancy, control, dominance, edge, mastery, superiority, supremacy, sway, whip hand

uppermost *adj* highest, loftiest, most elevated, top, topmost, upmost; chief, dominant, foremost, greatest, leading, main, paramount, predominant, pre-eminent, primary, principal, supreme

upright *adj* erect, on end, perpendicular, straight, vertical; above board, conscientious, ethical, faithful, good, high-minded, honest, honourable, incorruptible, just, principled, righteous, straightforward, true, trustworthy, unimpeachable, virtuous

uproar *n* brawl, brouhaha, clamour, commotion, confusion, din, furore, hubbub, hullabaloo, hurly-burly, mayhem, noise, outcry, pandemonium, racket, riot, rumpus, turbulence, turmoil; (*Inf*) ruckus, ruction

uproarious *adj* boisterous, clamorous, loud, noisy, obstreperous, riotous, tumultuous

uproot *v* eradicate, extirpate, root out

upset *v* capsize, knock over, overturn, spill, tip over, topple over; change, disorder, disorganize, disturb, mess up, put out of order, spoil, turn topsy-turvy; agitate, bother, discompose, disconcert, dismay, disquiet, distress, disturb, fluster, grieve, perturb, ruffle, throw someone off balance, trouble; be victorious over, conquer, defeat, get the better of, overcome, overthrow, triumph over, win against the odds

upset *n* defeat, reverse, sudden change, surprise; (*Inf*) shake-up; complaint, disorder, disturbance, illness, indisposition, malady, queasiness, sickness; (*Inf*) bug; agitation, bother, discomposure, disquiet, distress, disturbance, shock, trouble, worry

upset *adj* capsized, overturned, spilled, tipped over, toppled, tumbled, upside down; disordered, disturbed, ill, queasy, sick; (*Inf*) gippy, poorly; agitated, bothered, confused, disconcerted, dismayed, disquieted, distressed, disturbed, frantic, grieved, hurt, overwrought, put out, ruffled, troubled worried; at sixes and sevens, chaotic, confused, disordered in disarray of disorder, messed up, muddled, topsy-turvy; beaten, conquered, defeated; beaten, conquered, defeated, overcome, overthrown, vanquished

upshot *n* conclusion, consequence, culmination, end, end result, event, finale, issue, outcome, result; (*Inf*) payoff

upside down *adj* bottom up, inverted, on its head, overturned, upturned, wrong side up; chaotic, confused, disordered, in confusion, in chaos, in disarray, in disorder, jumbled, muddled, topsy-turvy; (*Inf*) at sixes and sevens, higgledy-piggledy,

upstart *n arriviste*, nobody, *nouveau riche,* parvenu, social climber, status seeker, would-be

upturned *adj* raised, uplifted; retroussé

upward *adj* ascending, climbing, mounting, rising, uphill

upward *adv* above, aloft, overhead, up; heavenwards, skywards, up

urban *adj* city, citified, civic, inner-city, metropolitan, municipal, oppidan, town

urbane *adj* civil, complaisant, courteous, courtly, elegant, mannerly, polished, polite, refined, smooth, sauve, well-mannered

urchin *n* brat, gamin, guttersnipe, imp, ragamuffin, stray, waif, young rogue

urge *v* appeal to, beg, beseech, entreat, exhort, implore, plead, press, solicit; advise, advocate, champion, counsel, insist on, push for, recommend, support; compel, constrain, drive, egg on, encourage, force, goad, hasten, impel, incite, induce, instigate, press, propel, push, spur, stimulate

urge *n* compulsion, desire, drive, fancy, impulse, itch, longing, wish, yearning; (*Inf*) yen

urgency *n* exigency, extremity, gravity, hurry, imperativeness, importance, importancy, importunity, necessity, need, pressure, seriousness, stress

urgent *adj* compelling, critical, crucial, immediate, imperative, important, instant, not to be delayed, pressing, top-priority; clamourous, earnest, importunate, insistent, intense, persistent, persuasive

usable *adj* at one's disposal, available, current, fit for use, functional, in running order, practical, ready for use, serviceable, utilizable, valid, working

usage *n* control, employment, handling, management, operation, regulation, running, treatment, use; convention, custom, form, habit, matter of course, method, mode, practice, procedure, regime, routine, rule, tradition, wont

use *v* apply, avail oneself of, bring into play, employ, exercise, find a use for, make use of, operate, ply, practice, profit by, put to use, turn to account, utilize, wield, work; act towards, behave towards, deal with, exploit, handle, manipulate, misuse, take advantage of, treat; consume, exhaust, expend, run through, spend, waste

use *n* application, employment, exercise, handling, operation, practice, service, treatment, usage, wear and tear; advantage, application, avail, benefit, good, help, point, profit, service, usefulness, utility, value, worth; (*Inf*) mileage; custom, habit, practice, usage, way, wont

used *adj* cast-off, nearly new, not new, second-hand, shopsoiled, worn; (*Inf*) hand-me-down

useful *adj* advantageous, all-purpose, beneficial, capable, competent, convenient, effective, effectual, fruitful, general-purpose, helpful of help, of service, of use, practical, productive, profitable, salutary, serviceable, valuable, worthwhile

useless *adj* abortive, bootless, disadvantageous, fruitless, futile, hopeless, idle, impractical, ineffective, ineffectual, of no use, pointless, profitless, unavailing, unproductive, unworkable, vain, valueless, worthless; hopeless, incompetent, ineffectual, inept, no good, stupid, weak

use up *v* absorb, burn up, consume, deplete, devour, drain, exhaust, finish, fritter away, run through, squander, swallow up, waste

usher *n* attendant, doorkeeper, escort, guide, usherette

usher *v* conduct, direct, escort, guide, lead, pilot, show in, show out, steer

usual *adj* accustomed, common, constant, customary, everyday, expected, familiar, fixed, general, habitual, normal, ordinary, regular, routine, standard, stock, typical, wonted

usually *adv* as a rule, as is the custom, as is usual, by and large, commonly, for the most part, generally, habitually, in the main, mainly, mostly, most often, normally, on the whole, ordinarily, regularly, routinely

usurp *v* appropriate, arrogate, assume, seize

utility *n* advantageousness, avail, benefit, convenience, efficacy, fitness, point, practicality, profit, service, serviceableness, use, usefulness

utilize *v* employ, exploit, make use of, put to use, turn to account, use

utmost *adj* chief, extreme, greatest, highest, maximum, paramount, pre-eminent, supreme; extreme, farthest, final, last, most distant, outermost, remotest, uttermost

utmost *n* best, greatest, hardest, highest, most

utter *v* articulate, enunciate, express, pronounce, put into words, say, speak verbalize, vocalize, voice; declare, divulge, give expression to, make known, proclaim, promulgate, publish, reveal, state

utter *adj* absolute, arrant, complete, consummate, downright, entire, out-and-out, perfect, sheer, stark, thorough, thoroughgoing, total, unmitigated, unqualified

utterance *n* articulation, delivery, disclosure, emission, expression, pronouncement, pronunciation, publication, speech

utterly *adv* absolutely, completely, entirely, extremely, fully perfectly, thoroughly, totally, to the core, wholly

V

vacancy *n* job, opening, opportunity, position, post, room, situation; absent-mindedness, abstraction, blankness, inanity, inattentiveness, incomprehension, incuriousness, lack of interest, vacuousness

vacant *adj* available, disengaged, empty, free, idle, not in use, to let, unemployed, unengaged, unfilled, unoccupied, untenanted, void; absent-minded, abstracted, blank, dreaming, dreamy, expressionless, idle, inane, incurious, thoughtless, unthinking, vacuous

vacate *v* abandon, evacuate relinquish, surrender, abolish, abrogate, annul, cancel, disannul, invalidate, nullify, over-rule, quash, rescind

vacuum *n* emptiness, free space, gap, nothingness, space, vacuity, void

vagabond *adj* footloose, idle, meandering, rambling, roving, roaming, strolling, vagrant, wandering

vagabond *n* beggar, castaway, landloper, loafer, lounger, nomad, outcast, tramp, vagrant, wanderer

vagrant *adj* erratic, itinerant, roaming, roving, nomadic, strolling, unsettled, wandering

vagrant *n* beggar, castaway, landloper, loafer, lounger, nomad, outcast, tramp, vagrant, wanderer

vague *adj* amorphous, blurred, dim, doubtful, fuzzy, generalized, hazy, ill-defined, imprecise, indefinite, indeterminate, indistinct, lax, loose, nebulous, obscure, shadowy, uncertain, unclear, unknown, unspecified, woolly

vain *adj* arrogant, cocky, conceited, egotistical, inflated, narcissistic, ostentatious, overweening, peacockish, pleased with oneself, proud, self-important, swaggering, vainglorious; (*Inf*) big-headed, stuck-up, swollen-headed, swanky; abortive, empty, fruitless, futile, hollow, idle, nugatory, pointless, senseless, timewasting, trifling, trivial, unavailing, unimportant, unproductive, unprofitable, useless, worthless; fruitlessly, ineffectually, to no avail, to no purpose, unsuccessfully, uselessly, vainly, wasted, without success

valiant *adj* bold, brave, courageous, dauntless, doughty, fearless, gallant, heroic, indomitable, intrepid, lionhearted, plucky, redoubtable, stouthearted, valourous, worthy

valid *adj* authentic, bona fide, genuine, in force, lawful, legal, legally binding, legitimate, official

valley *n* coomb, coom, dale, dell, depression, dingle, glen, hollow, strath, vale

valour *n* boldness, bravery, courage, daring, gallantry, heroism, prowess, spirit

valuable *adj* costly, dear, expensive, high-priced, precious; beneficial, cherished, esteemed, estimable, held dear, helpful, important, prized, profitable, serviceable, treasured, useful, valued, worthwhile, worthy

value *n* cost, equivalent, market

price, monetary worth, rate; advantage, benefit, desirability, help, importance, merit, profit, serviceableness, significance, use, usefulness, utility, worth; code of behaviour, ethics, standards, principles

value *v* account, appraise, assess, compute, estimate, evaluate, price, put a price on, rate, set at, survey; appreciate, cherish, esteem, hold dear, hold in high esteem, prize, regard highly, respect, set store by, treasure

vanguard *n* advance guard, cutting edge, forefront, forerunners, front, front line, front rank, leaders spearhead, trailblazers, trendsetters, van

vandal *n* barbarian, destroyer, savage

vandalism *n* barbarism, barbarity, savagery

vanish *v* become invisible, be lost to sight, die out, disappear, disappear from sight or from the face of the earth, dissolve, evanesce, evaporate, exit, fade away, melt away

vanity *n* affected ways, airs, arrogance, conceit, conceitedness, egotism, narcissism, ostentation, pretension, pride, self-admiration, self-conceit, self-love, vainglory; (*Inf*) big-headedness, showing off, swollen-headedness; emptiness, frivolity, fruitlessness, futility, hollowness, inanity, pointlessness, profitlessness, triviality, unproductiveness, unreality, unsubstantiality, uselessness, worthlessness

vanquish *v* conquer, defeat, outwit, overcome, overpower, overthrow, subdue, subjugate, crush, discomfit, foil, master, quell, rout, worst

vapour *n* breath, dampness, exhalation, fog, fumes, haze, miasma, mist, smoke, steam

variable *adj* capricious, chameleonic, changeable, fickle, fitful, flexible, fluctuating, inconstant, mercurial, mutable, protean, shifting, temperamental, unstable, unsteady, vacillating, wavering

variance *n* difference, difference of opinion, disagreement, discord, discrepancy, dissension, dissent, divergence inconsistency, lack of harmony, strife, variation

variation *n* alteration, break in routine, change departure, departure from the norm, deviation, difference, discrepancy, diversification, diversity, innovation, modification, novelty, variety

varied *adj* assorted, different, diverse, heterogeneous, miscellaneous, mixed, motley, sundry, various

variety *n* change, difference, discrepancy, diversification, diversity, many-sideness, multifariousness, variation; array, assortment, collection, cross section, intermixture, medley, miscellany, mixture, multiplicity, range; brand, breed, category, class, kind, make, order, sort, species, strain, type

various *adj* assorted, different, differing, disparate, distinct, diverse, diversified, heterogeneous, many, many-sided, miscellaneous, several, sundry, varied, variegated

varnish *v* adorn, decorate, embellish, gild, glaze, gloss, japan, lacquer, polish, shellac

vary *v* alter, alternate, be unlike, change, depart, differ, disagree, diverge, diversify, fluctuate, intermix, modify, permutate, reorder, transform

vast *adj* astronomical, boundless, colossal, enormous, extensive, gigantic, great, huge, illimitable, immeasurable, immense, limitless, mammoth, massive, measureless, monstrous, monumental, never-ending, prodigious, sweeping, tremendous, unbounded, unlimited, voluminous, wide; (*Inf*) ginormous, mega

vault *v* bound, clear, hurdle, jump, leap, spring; arch, bend, bow, curve, overarch, span

vault *n* arch, ceiling, roof, span; catacomb, cellar, crypt, mausoleum, tomb, undercroft; depository, repository, strongroom

veer *v* be deflected, change, change course, change direction, sheer, shift, swerve, tack, turn

vegetate *v* be inert, deteriorate, exist, go to seed, idle, languish, loaf, moulder, stagnate, veg out

vehemence *n* ardour, eagerness, earnestness, emphasis, energy, enthusiasm, fervency, fervour, fire, force, forcefulness, heat, impetuosity, intensity, keenness, passion, verve, vigour, violence, warmth, zeal

vehement *adj* ardent, eager, earnest, emphatic, enthusiastic, fervent, fervid, fierce, forceful, forcible, impassioned, impetuous, intense, passionate, powerful, strong, violent, zealous

veil *v* cloak, conceal, cover, dim, disguise, hide, mantle, mask, obscure, screen, shield

veil *n* blind, cloak, cover, curtain, disguise, film, mask, screen, shade, shroud

vein *n* blood vessel, course, current, lode, seam, stratum, streak, stripe; dash, hint, strain, streak, thread, trait; attitude, bent, character, faculty, humour, mode, mood, note, style, temper, tenor, tone, turn

velvety *adj* delicate, downy, smooth, soft

vend *v* dispose, flog, hawk, retail, sell

vendetta *n* bad blood, blood feud, feud, quarrel

veneer *n* appearance, façade, false front, finish, front, gloss, guise, mask, pretence, semblance, show

venerable *adj* august, esteemed, grave, honoured, respected, revered, reverenced, sage, sedate, wise, worshiped

veneration *n* adoration, devotion, esteem, respect, reverence, worship

vengeance *n* an eye for an eye, avenging, reprisal, requital, retaliation, retribution, revenge, settling of scores

venom *n* bane, poison, toxin; acidity, acrimony, bitterness, gall, grudge, hate, ill will, malevolence, malice, maliciousness, malignity, rancour, spite, spitefulness, spleen, virulence

venomous *adj* deadly, poisonous, septic, toxic, virulent; caustic, malicious, malignant, mischievous, noxious, spiteful

vent *n* aperture, duct, hole, opening, orifice, outlet, split

vent *v* air, come out with, discharge, emit, empty, express, give expression to, give vent to, pour out, release, utter, voice
ventilate *v* air, bring out into the open, broadcast, debate, discuss, examine, make known, scrutinize, sift, talk about
venture *v* chance, endanger, hazard, imperil, jeopardize, put in jeopardy, risk, speculate, stake, wager; advance, dare, dare say, hazard, make bold, presume, take the liberty, volunteer; (*Inf*) stick one's neck out
venture *n* adventure, chance, endeavour, enterprise, fling, gamble, hazard, jeopardy, project, risk, speculation, undertaking
verbal *adj* literal, oral, spoken, unwritten, verbatim, word-of-mouth
verbatim *adj* exactly, precisely, to the letter, word for word
verdict *n* adjudication, conclusion, decision, finding, judgment, opinion, sentence
verge *n* border, boundary, brim, brink, edge, extreme, limit, lip, margin, roadside, threshold
verge *v* approach, border, come near
verification *n* authentification, confirmation, corroboration, proof, substantiation, validation
verify *v* attest, attest to, authenticate, bear out, check, confirm, corroborate, prove, substantiate, support, validate
vernacular *adj* colloquial, common, indigenous, informal, local, mother, native, popular, vulgar
vernacular *n* argot, cant, dialect, idiom, jargon, native language, parlance, patois, speech, vulgar tongue
versatile *adj* adaptable, adjustable, all-purpose, all-round, flexible, functional, handy, many-sided, multifaceted, protean, resourceful, variable
versed *adj* able, accomplished, acquainted, clever, conversant, practised, proficient, qualified, skilful, skilled, trained
version *n* account, adaptation, exercise, interpretation, portrayal, reading, rendering, side, translation
vertical *adj* erect, on end, perpendicular, upright
vertigo *n* dizziness, giddiness, lightheadedness, loss of equilibrium, swimming of the head
verve *n* animation, ardour, energy, enthusiasm, force, rapture, spirit
very *adv* absolutely, acutely, decidedly, deeply, eminently, exceedingly, excessively, extremely, greatly, highly, noticeably, particularly, profoundly, really, remarkably, superlatively, surpassingly, truly, uncommonly, unusually, wonderfully; (*Inf*) awfully, jolly, terribly
vessel *n* barque, boat, craft, ship; container, pot, receptacle, utensil
vest in *v* authorize, be developed upon, bestow, confer, consign, empower, endow, entrust, furnish, invest, lodge, place, put in the hands of, settle
vestige *n* evidence, footprint, footstep, mark, record, relic, sign, token
vet *v* appraise, check, check out, examine, investigate, look over,

pass under review, review, scan, scrutinize; (*Inf*) give someone the once over, size up

veteran *n* master, old hand, old stager, old-timer, past master, past mistress, trouper, warhorse; (*Inf*) pro

veteran *adj* adept, battle-scarred, expert, long-serving, old, proficient, seasoned

veto *v* ban, disallow, forbid, give the thumbs down to, interdict, negative, prohibit, refuse permission, reject rule out, turn down; (*Inf*) kill, put the kibosh on

veto *n* ban, embargo, interdict, non-consent, prohibition

vex *v* afflict, agitate, annoy, bother, displease, distress, disturb, exasper ate, fret, gall, grate on, harass, irritate, molest, nettle, offend, perplex, pester, pique, plague, provoke, put out, rile, tease, torment, trouble, upset, worry; (*Inf*) aggravate, bug, needle, peeve

vexed *adj* afflicted, agitated, annoyed, bothered, confused, displeased, distressed, disturbed exasperated, fed up harassed, irritated, nettled, out of countenance, perplexed, provoked, put out, riled, ruffled, tormented, troubled, upset, worried; (*Inf*) aggravated, miffed, peeved

vibrant *adj* aquiver, oscillating, palpitating, pulsating, quivering, trembling; alive, animated, colourful, dynamic, electrifying, responsive, sensitive, sparkling, spirited, vivacious, vivid; (*Inf*) full of pep

vibrate *v* fluctuate, oscillate, pulsate, pulse, quiver, resonate, reverberate, shake, shiver, sway, swing, throb, tremble, undulate; (*Inf*) judder

vibration *n* oscillation, pulsation, pulse, quiver, resonance, reverberation, shaking, throb, throbbing, trembling, tremor; (*Inf*) juddering

vice *n* corruption, degeneracy, depravity, evil, evildoing, immorality, iniquity, profligacy, sin, venality, wickedness

vicinity *n* nearness, proximity, locality, neighbourhood, vicinage

vicious *adj* abandoned, abhorrent, atrocious, bad, barbarous, corrupt, cruel, dangerous, debased, degenerate, degraded, depraved, diabolical, ferocious, fiendish, foul, heinous, immoral, infamous, monstrous, profligate, savage, sinful, unprincipled, vile, violent, wicked, worthless, wrong; backbiting, cruel, defamatory, malicious, mean, rancorous, slanderous, spiteful, venomous, vindictive; (*Inf*) bitchy

victim *n* casualty, fatality, injured party, martyr, sacrifice, scapegoat, sufferer; dupe, easy prey, innocent, sitting target; (*Inf*) fall guy, patsy, sitting duck, sucker

victimize *v* discriminate against, have one's knife into someone, persecute, pick on; cheat, deceive, defraud, dupe, exploit, fool, hood wink, prey on, swindle, take advantage of, use; (*Inf*) have it in for someone

victor *n* champion, conquering hero, conqueror, first, prizewinner, vanquisher, winner; (*Inf*) champ, number one, top dog

victorious *adj* champion, conquering, first, prizewinning, successful, triumphant, vanquishing, winning

victory *n* conquest, laurels, mastery, success, superiority, the palm, the prize, triumph, win

view *n* aspect, landscape, outlook, panorama, perspective, picture, prospect, scene, spectacle, vista; range *or* field of vision; attitude, belief, conviction, feeling, impression, judgment, notion, opinion, point of view, sentiment, thought, way of thinking

view *v* behold, contemplate, examine, explore, eye, gaze at, inspect, look at, observe, regard, scan, spectate, stare at, survey, watch, witness; consideration, deem, judge, look on, regard, think about

viewer *n* observer, one of an audience, onlooker, spectator, TV watcher, watcher

viewpoint *n* angle, frame of reference, perspective, point of view, position, slant, stance, standpoint, vantage point, way of thinking

vigilant *adj* alert, Argus-eyed, attentive, careful, cautious, circumspect, on one's guard, on one's toes, on the alert, on the lookout, on the qui vive, on the watch, sleepless, unsleeping, wakeful, watchful, wideawake; (*Inf*) keep one's eyes peeled

vigorous *adj* active, brisk, dynamic, effective, efficient, energetic, enterprising, flourishing, forceful, full of energy, hale, hale and hearty, hardy, healthy, intense, lively, powerful, red-blooded, robust, sound, spank ing, spirited, strenuous, strong, virile, vital; (*Inf*) zippy

vigour *n* activity, animation, dash, dynamism, energy, force, forcefulness, gusto, health, liveliness, might, pep, power, robustness, soundness, spirit, strength, verve, virility, zip; (*Inf*) balls, oomph, punch, snap, vim

vile *adj* abandoned, abject, appaling, bad, base, coarse, contemptible, corrupt, debased, degenerate, degrading, depraved, despicable, disgraceful, evil, humiliating, ignoble, impure, loathsome, low, mean, miserable, nefarious, perverted, shocking, sinful, ugly, vicious, vulgar, wicked, worthless, wretched; disgusting, foul, horrid, loathsome, nasty, nauseating, noxious, offensive, repellent, repugnant, repulsive, revolting, sickening

vilify *v* abuse, asperse, backbite, berate, blacken, blemish, brand, calumniate, decry, defame, disparage, lampoon, libel, malign, revile, scandalize, slander, slur, traduce, vituperate

villain *n* blackguard, criminal, evildoer, libertine, malefactor, miscreant, profligate, rapscallion, reprobate, rogue, scoundrel, wretch

villainous *adj* atrocious, bad, base, blackguardly, criminal, cruel, debased, degenerate, depraved, detestable, diabolical, evil, fiendish, hateful, heinous, ignoble, infamous, inhuman, mean, nefarious, outrageous, ruffianly, scoundrelly, sinful, terrible, vicious, vile, wicked

vindicate *v* absolve, acquit, clear, defend, do justice to, exculpate, excuse, exonerate, free from blame, justify, rehabilitate

vindication *n* apology, assertion, defence, exculpating, exculpation, excuse, exoneration, justification, maintenance, plea, rehabilitation, substantiation, support

vindictive *adj* full of spleen, implacable, malicious, malignant, rancorous, relentless, resentful, revengeful, spiteful, unforgiving, unrelenting, vengeful, venomous

vintage *n* collection, crop, epoch, era, generation, harvest, origin, year

vintage *adj* best, choice, classic, mature, prime, rare, ripe, select, superior, venerable

violate *v* break, contravene, disobey, disregard, encroach upon, infract, infringe, transgress; abuse, assault, befoul, debauch, defile, desecrate, dishonour, invade, outrage, pollute, profane, rape, ravish

violence *n* bestiality, bloodshed, bloodthirstiness, brutality, brute force, cruelty, destructiveness, ferocity, fierceness, fighting, force, frenzy, fury, murderousness, passion, rough handling, savagery, terrorism, thuggery, vehemence, wildness; (*Inf*) strong-arm tactics

violent *adj* berserk, bloodthirsty, brutal, cruel, destructive, fiery, forcible, furious, headstrong, homicidal, hot-headed, impeturious, intemperate, maddened, maniacal, murderous, passionate, powerful, Ramboesque, raging, riotous, rough, savage, strong, tempestuous, uncontrollable, ungovernable, unrestrained, vehement, vicious, wild; blustery, boisterous, devastating, full of force, gale force, powerful, raging, ruinous, strong, tempestuous, tumultuous, turbulent, wild

virgin *n* girl, immaculate, pure, spotless, unblemished, untainted, untouched, vestal

virginal *adj* chaste, pure, snowy, uncorrupted, undefiled, unsullied, untouched, unused, virtuous

virile *adj* all-male, forceful, manly, masculine, powerfully built, robust, rugged, strapping, vigorous

virtual *adj* constructive, equivalent, essential, implicit, implied, indirect, practical, substantial

virtually *adv* as good as, effectually, for all practical purposes, in all but name, in effect, in essence, nearly, practically, to all intents and purposes

virtue *n* ethicalness, excellence, goodness, high-mindedness, incorruptibility, integrity, justice, morality, probity, quality, rectitude, righteousness, uprightness, worth, worthiness; advantage, asset, attribute, credit, good point, good quality, merit, strength; chastity, honour, innocence, morality, purity, virginity

virtuoso *n* artist, expert, genius, grandmaster, maestro, magician, master, wizard

virtuoso *adj* bravura, brilliant, dazzling, impressive, masterly, outstanding, skilful,

virtuous *adj* blameless, ethical, excellent, exemplary, good, high-principled, honest, honourable, incorruptible, moral, praiseworthy, pure, righteous, upright, worthy; celibate, chaste, clean-living, innocent, pure, spotless, virginal

virulent *adj* deadly, infective, injurious, lethal, malignant, pernicious, poisonous, septic, toxic, venomous; acrimonious, bitter, envenomed, hostile, malevolent, malicious, rancorous, resentful, spiteful, splenetic, venomous, vicious, vindictive

visible *adj* anywhere to be seen, apparent, clear, conspicuous, detectable, discernible, discoverable, distinguishable, evident, in sight, in view, manifest, not hidden, noticeable, observable, obvious, palpable, patent, perceivable, perceptible, plain, to be seen, unconcealed, unmistakable

vision *n* eyes, eyesight, perception, seeing, sight, view; breadth of view, discernment, farsightedness, foresight, imagination, insight, intuition, penetration, insight, intuition, penetration, prescience; castle in the air, concept, conception, daydream, dream, fantasy, idea, ideal, image, mental picture, pipe dream; apparition, chimera, delusion, ghost, hallucination, illusion, mirage, phantasm, phantom, revelation, spectre

visionary *adj* dreaming, dreamy, idealistic, quixotic, romantic, starry-eyed, with one's head in the clouds

visionary *n* daydreamer, Don Quixote, dreamer, enthusiast, idealist, mystic, prophet, romantic, seer, theorist, utopian, zealot

visit *v* be the guest of, call in, call on, go to see, inspect, look someone up, pay a call on, stay at, stay with, stop by; (*Inf*) drop in on, pop in, take in; afflict, assail, attack, befall, descend upon, haunt, smite, trouble

visit *n* call, sojourn, stay, stop

visitation *n* examination, inspection, visit; bane, blight, calamity, cataclysm, catastrophe, disaster, infliction, ordeal, punishment, scourge, trial

visitor *n* caller, company, guest, visitant

visual *adj* ocular, optic, optical; discernable, observable, perceptible, visible

visualize *v* conceive of, conjure up a mental picture of, envisage, imagine, picture, see in the mind's eye

vital *adj* basic, cardinal, essential, fundamental, imperative, indispensable, necessary, requisite; critical, crucial, decisive, important, key, life-or-death, significant, urgent; animated, dynamic, energetic, forceful, full of the joy of living, lively, sparky, spirited, vibrant, vigorous, vivacious, zestful; alive, animate, generative, invigorate, life-giving, live, living, quickening

vitality *n* animation, energy, exuberance, life, liveliness, lustiness, pep, robustness, sparkle, stamina, strength, vigour, vivacious, vivacity; (*Inf*) go, vim

vivacious *adj* animated, bubbling, cheerful, ebullient, effervescent, frolicsome, full of life, gay, high-spirited, jolly, light-hearted, lively, merry, scintillating, sparkling, sparky, spirited, sportive, sprightly

vivid *adj* bright, brilliant, clear, colourful, glowing, intense, rich; distinct, dramatic, graphic, highly-coloured, lifelike, memorable, powerful, realistic, sharp, sharply-etched, stirring, strong, telling, true to life

vocabulary *n* dictionary, glossary, language, lexicon, wordbook, word hoard, words, word stock

vocal *adj* articulate, articulated, oral, put into words, said, spoken, uttered, voiced; articulate, blunt, clamourous, eloquent, expressive, forthright, frank, free-spoken, strident, vociferous

vocation *n* business, calling, career, employment, job, life's work, life work, métier, mission, office, post, profession, pursuit, role, trade

vociferous *adj* clamant, clamourous, loud, noisy, obstreperous, outspoken, ranting, shouting, strident, uproarious, vehement, vocal; (*Inf*) loudmouthed

vogue *n* craze, custom, *dernier cri,* fashion, last word, mode, style, the latest, the rage, trend, way; acceptance, currency, fashionableness, favour, popularity, prevalence, usage, use; (*Inf*) the thing

voice *n* articulation, language, power of speech, sound, tone, utterance, words; decision, expression, part, say, view, vote, will, wish; agency, instrument, medium, mouthpiece, organ, spokesman, spokesperson, spokeswoman, vehicle

voice *v* air, articulate, assert, declare, divulge, enunciate, express, give expression to, put into words, say, utter, ventilate; (*Inf*) come out with

void *adj* bare, clear, drained, emptied, empty, free, tenantless, unfilled, unoccupied, vacant; destitute, devoid, lacking, without; dead, ineffective, ineffectual, inoperative, invalid, nonviable, nugatory, null and void, unenforcable, useless, vain, worthless

void *n* blank, blankness, emptiness, gap, lack, opening, space, vacuity, vacuum, want

void *v* discharge, drain, eject, eliminate, emit, empty, evacuate

volatile *adj* airy, changeable, erratic, explosive, fickle, flighty, gay, giddy, inconstant, lively, mercurial, sprightly, unsettled, unstable, unsteady, variable, whimsical; (*Inf*) up and down

volley *n* barrage, blast, bombardment, burst, cannonade, discharge, explosion, fusillade, hail, salvo, shower

volume *n* aggregate, amount, body, bulk, capacity, compass, cubic, content, dimensions, mass, quantity, total; book, publication, tome, treatise

voluminous *adj* ample, big, bulky, full, great, large; copious, diffuse, discursive, flowing

voluntarily *adv* by choice, freely, of one's own will, on one's own initiative, willingly, without being asked, without prompting

voluntary *adj* discretionary, free, gratuitous, honourary, intended, intentional, optional, spontaneous, uncompelled, unconstrained, unforced, unpaid, volunteer, willing

volunteer *v* advance, need no invitation, offer, offer one's serviced, present, proffer, propose, put forward, put oneself at someone's disposal, step forward, suggest, tender

vomit *v* belch forth, be sick, bring up, disgorge, eject, emit, heave, regurgitate, retch, spew up; (*Inf*) barf, puke, sick up, throw up

voracious *adj* avid, devouring, glutinous, greedy, hungry, insatiable, omnivorous, prodigious, rapacious, ravening, ravenous, uncontrolled, unquenchable

vote *n* ballot, franchise, plebiscite, poll, referendum, right to vote, show of hands, suffrage

vote *v* ballot, cast one's vote, elect, go to the polls, opt, return

vouch for *v* affirm, answer for, assert, asseverate, attest to, back, certify, confirm, give assurance of, go bail for, guarantee, stand witness, support, swear to, uphold

vow *v* affirm, consecrate, dedicate, devote, pledge, promise, swear, undertake solemnly

vow *n* oath, pledge, promise

voyage *n* crossing, cruise, journey, passage, travels, trip

vulgar *adj* blue, boorish, cheap and nasty, coarse, common, crude, dirty, flashy, gaudy, gross, ill-bred, impolite, improper, indecent, indecorous, indelicate, low, nasty, naughty, off colour, ribald, risqué, rude, suggestive, tasteless, tawdry, uncouth, unmannerly, unrefined; general, native, ordinary, unrefined, vernacular

vulgarity *n* bad taste, coarseness, crudeness, crudity, gaudiness, grossness, indecorum, indelicacy, lack of refinement, ribaldry, rudeness, suggestiveness, tasteless, tawdriness

vulnerable *adj* accessible, assailable, defenceless, exposed, open to attack, sensitive, susceptible, tender, thin-skinned, unprotected, weak, wide open

W

wade *v* ford, paddle, splash, walk through; **wade into** assail, attack, go for, launch oneself at, set about, tackle; (*Inf*) get stuck in, light into, tear into

waft *v* bear, be carried, carry, convey, drift, float, ride, transmit, transport

wag *v* bob, flutter, nod, oscillate, quiver, rock, shake, stir, sway, vibrate, waggle, wave, wiggle

wag *n* bob, flutter, nod, oscillation, quiver, shake, toss, vibration, waggle, wave, wiggle; advance, move, progress, stir

wag *n* humourist, jester, joker, wit

wage *n* allowance, compensation, earnings, emolument, fee, hire, pay, payment, recompense, renumeration, reward, stipend

wager *n* bet, flutter, gamble, pledge, punt, stake, venture

wager *v* bet, chance, gamble, hazard, lay, pledge, punt, put on, risk, speculate, stake, venture

waif *n* foundling, orphan, stray

wail *v* bemoan, bewail, cry, deplore, grieve, howl, keen, lament, ululate, weep, yowl

wail *n* complaint, cry, grief, howl, keen, lament, lamentation, moan, ululation, weeping, yowl

wait *v* abide, bide one's time, cool one's heels, dally, delay, hang fire, hold back, linger, mark time, pause, remain, rest, stand by, stay, tarry; (*Inf*) hold on

wait *n* delay, halt, hold-up, interval, pause, rest, stay

waiter, waitress *n* attendant, server, steward, stewardess

wait on *v* attend, minister to, serve, tend

waive *v* abandon, defer, dispense with, forgo, give up, postpone, put off, refrain from, relinquish, remit, renounce, resign, set aside, surrender

wake *v* arise, awake, awaken, bestir, come to, get up, rouse, rouse from sleep, stir; activate, animate, arouse, awaken, enliven, excite, fire, galvanize, kindle, provoke, quicken, stimulate, stir up

wake *n* aftermath, backwash, path, track, trail, train, wash, waves

wakeful *adj* insomniac, restless, sleepless, unsleeping; alert, alive, attentive, heedful, observant, on guard, on the alert, on the lookout, on the qui vive, unsleeping, vigilant, wary, watchful

waken *v* activate, animate, arouse, awake, awaken, be roused, come awake, come to, enliven, fire, galvanize, get up, kindle, quicken, rouse, stimulate, stir

walk *v* advance, amble, foot it, go, go on foot, hike, march, move, pace, perambulate, promenade, saunter, step, stride, stroll, tramp, travel on foot, trek, trudge; (*Inf*) go by shank's pony, hoof it, traipse; accompany, convoy, escort, take

walk *n* constitutional, hike, march, perambulation, promenade, ramble, saunter, stroll, tramp, trek, trudge, turn; (*Inf*) traipse; carriage, gait, manner of walking, pace, step, stride; aisle, alley, avenue, esplanade, footpath, lane, path, pathway, pavement, promenade, sidewalk, trail; area, arena, calling, career, course, field, line, métier, profession, sphere, trade, vocation

walker *n* footslogger, hiker, pedestrian, rambler, wayfarer

walk-out *n industrial* action, protest, stoppage, strike

wall *n* divider, enclosure, panel, partition, screen; barricade, breastwork, bulwark, embankment, fortification, palisade, parapet, rampart, stockade; barrier, block, fence, hedge, impediment, obstacle, obstruction

wallet *n* case, holder, notecase, pocketbook, pouch, purse

wallow *v* lie, roll about, splash around, tumble, welter; flounder, lurch, stagger, stumble, wade; bask, delight, glory, indulge oneself, luxuriate, relish, revel, take pleasure

wan *adj* ashen, bloodless, cadaverous, colourless, haggard, pale, pallid

wand *n* baton, rod, sprig, stick, twig, withe, withy

wander *v* cruise, drift, knock about, knock around meander, peregrinate, ramble, range, roam, rove, straggle, stray, stroll;(*Inf*) mooch around, traipse; depart, deviate, digress, diverge, err, get lost, go astray, go off at a tangent, go off course, lapse, lose concentration, lose one's train of thought, lose one's way, swerve, veer; babble, be delirious, be incoherent, ramble, rave, speak incoherently, talk nonsense

wander *n* cruise, excursion, meander, peregrination, ramble, (*Inf*) traipse

wanderer *n* bird of passage, drifter, gypsy, itinerant, nomad, rambler, ranger, rolling stone, rover, stroller, traveller, vagabond, vagrant, voyager

wandering *adj* drifting, homeless, itinerant, migratory, nomadic, peripatetic, rambling, rootless, roving, strolling, travelling, vagabond, vagrant, voyaging, wayfaring

wane *v* abate, atrophy, decline, decrease, die out, dim, diminish, draw to a close, drop, swindle, ebb, fade, fade away, fail, lessen, sink, subside, taper off, weaken, wind down, wither

wane *n* at its lowest ebb, declining, dropping, dwindling, dying out, ebbing, fading, lessening, obsolescent, on its last legs, on the decline, on the way out, subsiding, tapering off, weakening, withering

want *v* covet, crave, desire, feel a need for, hanker after, have a fancy for, hunger for, long for, need, pine for, require, thirst for, wish, yearn for; (*Inf*) have a yen for; be able to do with, be deficient in, be short of, be without, call for, demand, fall short in, have need of, lack, miss, need, require, stand in need of

want *n* appetite, craving, demand, desire, fancy, hankering, hunger, longing, necessity, need, requirement, thirst, wish, yearning; (*Inf*) yen; absence, dearth, default, deficiency, famine, insufficiency, lack, paucity, scantiness, scarcity, shortage; destitution, indigence, need, neediness, pauperism, penury, poverty, privation

wanting *adj* absent, incomplete, lacking, less, missing, short, shy; defective, deficient, disappointing, faulty, imperfect, inadequate, inferior, leaving much to be desired, not good enough, not up to expectations, not up to par, patchy, poor, sketchy, substandard, unsound

wanton *adj* abandoned, dissipated, dissolute, fast, immoral, lecherous, lewd, libertine, libidinous, licentious, loose, lustful, of easy virtue, promiscuous, rakish, shameless, unchaste; arbitrary, cruel, evil, gratuitous, groundless, malevolent, malicious, motiveless, needless, senseless, spiteful, uncalled-for, unjustifiable, unjustified, unprovoked, vicious, wicked, wilful

wanton *n* Casanova, debauchee, Don Juan, gigolo, harlot, lecher, loose woman, profligate, prostitute, rake, slut, strumpet, trollop, voluptuary, whore, woman of easy virtue; (*Inf*) tart

war *n* armed, conflict, battle, blood shed, combat, conflict, contention, contest, enmity, fighting, hostility, strife, struggle, warfare

war *v* battle, campaign against, carry on hostilities, clash, combat, conduct a war, contend, contest, fight, make war, strive, struggle, take up arms, wage war

ward *n* area, district, division, precinct, quarter, zone; charge, dependant, minor, protégé, pupil; care, charge, custody, guardianship, keeping, protection, safekeeping

warden *n* administrator, caretaker, curator, custodian, guardian, janitor, keeper, ranger, steward, superintendent, warder, watchman

warder, wardress *n* custodian, gaoler, guard, jailer, keeper, prison officer; (*Inf*) screw

ward off *n* avert, avoid, beat off, block, deflect, fend off, forestall, keep at arm's length, keep at bay, parry, repel, stave off, thwart, turn aside, turn away

wardrobe *n* closet, clothes cupboard, clothes-press; apparel, attire, clothes, collection of clothes, outfit

warehouse *n* depository, depot, stockroom, store, storehouse

wares *pl n* commodities, goods, lines, manufactures, merchandise, produce, products, stock, stuff

warfare *n* armed conflict, armed struggle, arms, battle, blows, campaigning, clash of arms, combat, conflict, contest, discord, fighting, hostilities, passage of arms, strategy, strife, struggle, war

warily *adv* carefully, cautiously, charity, circumspectly, distrustfully, gingerly, vigilantly, watchfully, with care; (*Inf*) cagily

warlike *adj* aggressive, bellicose, belligerent, bloodthirsty, combative, hawkish, hostile, inimical, jingoistic, martial, militaristic, military, pugnacious, sabre-rattling, unfriendly, warmongering

warm *adj* balmy, heated, lukewarm, moderately hot, pleasant, sunny, tepid, thermal; affable, affectionate, amiable, amorous, cheerful, cordial, friendly, genial, happy, heart, hospitable, kindly, loving, pleasant, tender; animated, ardent, cordial, earnest, effusive, emotional, enthusiastic, excited, fervent, glowing, heated, intense, keen, lively, passionate, spirited, stormy, vehement, vigorous, violent, zealous; irascible, irritable, passionate, quick, sensitive, short, touchy

warm *v* heat, heat up, melt, thaw, warm up; animate, awaken, excite, interest, make enthusiastic, put some life into, rouse, stimulate, stir; (*Inf*) get going, turn on

warmth *n* heat, hotness, warmness; animation, ardour, eagerness, earnestness, effusiveness, enthusiasm, excitement, fervency, fervour, fire, heat, intensity, passion, spirit, transport, vehemence, vigour, violence, zeal, zest; affability, affection, amorousness, cheerfulness, cordiality, happiness, heartiness, hospitableness, kindliness, love, tenderness

warn *v* admonish, advise, alert, apprise, caution, forewarn, give fair warning, give notice, inform, make someone aware, notify, put one on one's guard, summon, tip off

warning *n* admonition, advice, alarm, alert, augury, caution, caveat, foretoken, hint, notice, notification, omen, premonition, presage, sign, signal, threat, tip, tip-off, token, word, word to the wise

warrant *n* assurance, authority, authorization, carte blanche, commission, guarantee, license, permission, permit, pledge, sanction, security, warranty

warrant *v* affirm, answer for, assure, attest, avouch, certify, declare, guarantee, pledge, secure, stand behind, underwrite, uphold, vouch for; approve, authorize, call for, commission, demand, empower, entitle, excuse, give ground for, justify, license, necessitate, permit, require, sanction

warrior *n* champion, combatant, fighter, fighting man, man-at-arms, soldier

wary *adj* alert, attentive, careful, cautious, chary, circumspect, distrustful, guarded, heedful, on one's guard, on the lookout, on the qui vive, prudent, suspicious, vigilant, watchful, wide-awake; (*Inf*) cagey, leery

wash *v* bath, bathe, clean, cleanse, launder, moisten, rinse, scrub, shampoo, shower, wet; bear away, carry off, erode, move, sweep away, wash off; bear scrutiny, be convincing, be plausible, carry weight, hold up, hold water, stand up; (*Inf*) stick; abandon, accept no responsibility for, give up on, have nothing to do with, leave to one's own devices

wash *n* ablution, bath, bathe, clean ing, cleansing, laundering, rinse, scrub, shampoo, shower, washing; ebb and flow, flow, roll, surge, sweep, swell, wave

waste *v* dissipate, fritter away, lavish, misuse, run through, squander, throw away; (*Inf*) blow, frivol away; atrophy, consume, corrode, crumble, debilitate, decay, decline, deplete, disable, drain, swindle, eat away, ebb, emaciate, enfeeble, exhaust, fade, gnaw, perish, sap the strength of, sink, undermine, wane, wear out, wither; despoil, destroy, devastate, lay waste, pillage, rape, ravage, raze, ruin, sack, spoil, wreak havoc upon

waste *n* dissipation, expenditure, extravagance, frittering away, loss, lost opportunity, misapplication, misuse, prodigality, squandering, unthriftiness, wastefulness; desolation, destruction, devastation, havoc, ravage, ruin; debris, dregs, dross, garbage, leavings, leftovers, litter, offal, offscourings, refuse, rubbish, scrap, sweepings, trash; desert, solitude, void, wasteland, wild, wilderness

waste *adj* leftover, superfluous, supernumerary, unused, unwanted, useless, worthless; bare, barren, desolate, devastated, dismal, dreary, empty, uncultivated, uninhabited, unproductive, wild

wasteful *adj* extravagant, improvident, lavish, prodigal, profligate, ruinous, spendthrift, thriftless, uneconomical, unthrifty

watch *v* contemplate, eye, gaze at, loo, look at, look on, mark, note, observe, pay attention, peer at, regard, see, stare at, view; attend, be on the alert, be on the lookout, be vigilant, be wary, be watchful, keep an eye open (*Inf*), look out, take heed, wait; guard, keep, look after, mind, protect, superintend, take care of, tend

watch *n* chronometer, clock, pocket watch, timepiece, wristwatch; alert ness, attention, eye, heed, inspection, lookout, notice, observation, supervision, surveillance, vigil, vigilance, watchfulness

watchdog *n* guard dog; custodian, guardian, inspector, monitor, protector, scrutineer

watchful *adj* alert, attentive, circumspect, guarded, heedful, observant, on one's guard, on the lookout, on the qui vive, on the watch, suspicious, vigilant, wary, wide awake

watchword *n* battle cry, byword, catchword, catch-phrase, motto, password, slogan

water *n* Adam's ale; aqua, H_2O

water *v* damp, dampen, douse, drench, flood, hose, irrigate, moisten, soak, souse, spray, sprinkle; add water to, adulterate, dilute, put water in, thin, water down, weaken

waterfall *n* cascade, cataract, chute, fall

watertight *adj* sound, waterproof; airtight, firm, flawless, foolproof, impregnable, inconvertible, sound, unassailable

watery *adj* aqueous, damp, fluid, humid, liquid, marshy, moist, soggy, squelchy, wet; adulterated, dilute, diluted, flavourless, insipid, runny, tasteless, thin, washy, watered-down, waterish, weak; (*Inf*) wishy-washy

wave *v* brandish, flap, flourish, flutter, move to and fro, oscillate, quiver, ripple, shake, stir, sway, swing, undulate, wag, waver, wild; beckon, direct, gesticulate, gesture, indicate, sign, signal

wave *n* billow, breaker, comber, ridge, ripple, roller, sea, surf, swell, undulation, unevenness; current, drift, flood, ground swell, movement, outbreak, rash, rush, stream, surge, sweep, tendency, trend, upsurge

waver *v* be indecisive, be irresolute, be unable to decide, be unable to make up one's mind, dither, falter, fluctuate, hesitate, hum and haw, seesaw, swither, vacillate; (*Inf*) bow hot and cold, shillyshally; flicker, fluctuate, quiver, reel, hake, sway, totter, tremble, undulate, vary, wave, weave, wobble

wax *v* become fuller, become larger, develop, dilate, enlarge, expand, fill out, get bigger, grow, increase, magnify, mount, rise, swell

way *n* approach, course of action, fashion, manner, means, method, mode, plan, practice, procedure, process, scheme, system, technique; access, avenue, channel, course, direction, highway, lane, path, pathway, road, route, street, thoroughfare, track, trail; elbowroom, opening, room, space; distance, journey, length, stretch, trail; advance, approach, journey, march, passage, progress; characteristic, conduct, custom, habit, idiosyncrasy, manner, nature, personality, practice, style, trait, usage, wont; aspect, detail, feature, particular, point, respect, sense; by the way by the bye, en passant, incidentally, in parenthesis, in passing; **give way** collapse, crack, crumple, fall, fall to pieces, give, go to pieces, subside; accede, acknowledge, defeat, acquiesce, back down, concede, make concessions, withdraw, yield; **under way** afoot, begun, going, in motion, in progress, moving, on the move, started; (*Inf*) on the go

wayfarer *n* bird of passage, globetrotter, Gypsy, itinerant, journeyer, nomad, rover, traveller, trekker, voyager, walker, wanderer

wayward *adj* capricious, change able, contrary, contumacious, cross-grained, disobedient, erratic, fickle, flighty, froward, headstrong, inconstant, incorrigible, insubordinate, intractable, mulish, obdurate, obstinate, perverse, rebellious, refractory self-willed, stubborn, undependable, ungovernable, unmanageable, unpredictable, unruly, wilful

weak *adj* anaemic, debilitated, decrepit, delicate, effete, enervated, exhausted, faint, feeble, fragile, frail, infirm, languid, puny, shaky, sickly, spent, tender, unsound, unsteady, wasted, weakly cowardly, impotent, indecisive, ineffectual, infirm, irresolute, namby-pamby, powerless, soft, spineless, timorous; (*Inf*) weak-kneed; distant, dull, faint, imperceptible, low, muffled, poor, quiet, slight, small, soft; deficient, faulty, inadequate, lacking, poor, substandard, understrength, wanting; feeble, flimsy, hollow, inconclusive, invalid, lame, pathetic, shallow, slight, unconvincing, unsatisfactory; defenceless, exposed, helpless, unguarded, vulnerable, wide open; diluted, insipid, milk-and-water, runny, tasteless, thin, understrength, waterish, watery; (*Inf*) wishy-washy

weaken *v* abate, debilitate, depress, diminish, droop, dwindle, ease up, enervate, fade, fail, flag, give way, impair, invalidate, lessen, lower, mitigate, moderate, reduce, sap, sap the strength of, soften up, temper, tire, undermine, wane; adulterate, cut, debase, dilute, thin, thin out, water down

weakness *n* debility, decrepitude, enervation, faintness, feebleness, fragility, frailty, impotence, infirmity, irresolution, powerlessness, vulnerability; Achilles heel, blemish, chink in one's armour, defect, deficiency, failing, fault, flaw, imperfection, lack, shortcoming; fondness, inclination, liking, passion, penchant, predilection, proclivity, proneness, soft spot

wealth *n* affluence, assets, capital, cash, estate, fortune, funds, goods, lucre, means, money, opulence, pelf, possessions, property, prosperity, resources, riches, substance; abundance, bounty, copiousness, cornucopia, fullness, plenitude, plenty, profusion, richness, store

wealthy *adj* affluent, comfortable, moneyed, opulent, prosperous, rich, well-off, well-to-do; (*Inf*) filthy rich, flush, in the money, loaded, loads of money, made of money, on easy street, quids in, rolling in it, stinking rich, well-heeled

wear *v* bear, be clothed in, be dressed in, carry, clothe oneself, don, dress in, have on, put on, sport; display, exhibit, fly, show; abrade, consume, corrode, deteriorate, erode, fray, grind, impair, rub, use, wash away, waste; bear up, be durable, endure, hold up, last, stand up; annoy, drain, enervate, exasperate, fatigue, harass, irk, pester, tax, undermine, vex, weaken, weary

wear *n* employment, service, use, usefulness, utility; (*Inf*) mileage; apparel, attire, clothes, costume, dress, garb, garments, gear, habit, outfit, things; abrasion, attrition, corrosion, damage, depreciation, deterioration, erosion, friction, use, wear and tear

weariness *n* drowsiness, enervation, exhaustion, fatigue, languor, lassitude, lethargy, listlessness, prostration, tiredness

wearisome *adj* annoying, boring, bothersome, burdensome, dull, exasperating, exhausting, fatiguing, humdrum, irksome, monotonous, oppressive, pestilential, prosaic, tedious, troublesome, trying, uninteresting, vexatious, wearing

wear off *v* abate, decrease, diminish, disappear, dwindle, ebb, fade, lose effect, lose strength, peter out, subside, wane, weaken

wear out *v* become useless, become worn, consume, deteriorate, erode, fray, impair, use up, wear through; enervate, exhaust, fatigue, prostrate, sap, tire, weary; (*Inf*) fag out, frazzle, knacker

weary *adj* drained, drooping, drowsy, enervated, exhausted, fatigued, flagging, jaded, ready to drop, sleepy, spent, tired, wearied, worn out; (*Inf*) al in, dead on one's feet, dead beat, dog tired, done in, fagged, knackered, whacked; arduous, enervative, irksome, laborious, taxing, tiresome, tiring, wearing, wearisome

weary *v* burden, debilitate, drain, droop, enervate, fade, fail, fatigue, grow tired, sap, tax, tire, tire out, wear out; (*Inf*) take it out of; annoy, become bored, bore, exasperate, have had enough, irk, jade, make discontented, plague, sicken, try the patience of, vex

weather *n* climate, conditions; **under the weather** ailing, below par, ill, indisposed, nauseous, not well, off-colour, out of sorts; (*Inf*) poorly, seedy, sick; crapulent, crapulous, drunk, inebriated, intoxicated, the worse for drink; (*Inf*) groggy, hung over, one over the eight, three sheets in the wind, under the influence

weather *v* expose, harden, season, toughen; bear up against, brave, come through, endure, get through, love through, resist, ride out, rise above, stand, suffer, surmount, survive, withstand; (*Inf*) stick it out

weave *v* blend, braid, entwine, fuse, incorporate, interlace, intermingle, intertwine, introduce, knit, mat, merge, plait, twist, unite; build, construct, contrive, create, fabricate, make, make up, put together, spin; crisscross, move in and out, weave one's way, wind, zigzag

web *n* cobweb, spider's web; interlacing, lattice, mesh, net, netting, network, screen, tangle, toils, weave, webbing

wed *v* become a man and wife, be married to, espouse, get married, join, make one, marry, take as one's husband, take as one's wife, take to wife, unite; (*Inf*) get hitched, splice, tie the knot

wedding *n* espousals, marriage, marriage ceremony, nuptial rite, nuptials, wedlock

wedge *n* block, chock, chunk, lump; (*Inf*) wodge

wedge *v* block, cram, crowd, force, jam, lodge, pack, ram, split, squeeze, stuff, thrust

weep *v* bemoan, bewail, blubber, boohoo, complain, cry, keen, lament, moan, mourn, shed tears, snivel, sob, ululate, whimper; (*Inf*) blub, whinge

weigh *v* consider, contemplate, deliberate upon, evaluate, examine, give thought to, meditate upon, mull over, ponder, reflect upon, study, think over; be influential, carry weight, count, have influence, impress, matter, tell; (*Inf*) cut any ice; bear down, burden, oppress, prey

weight *n* avoirdupois, burden, gravity, heaviness, load, mass, poundage, pressure, tonnage; ballast, heavy object, load, mass; burden, load, millstone, oppression, pressure, strain; greatest force, main force, onus, preponderance; (*Inf*) heft; authority, consequence, consideration, efficacy, emphasis, impact, import, importance, influence, moment, persuasiveness, power, significance, substance, value; (*Inf*) clout

weight *v* add weight to, ballast, charge, freight, increase the load on, increase the weight of, load, make heavier; burden, encumber, handicap, impede, oppress, overburden, weigh down; bias, load, unbalance

weighty *adj* burdensome, cumbersome, dense, heavy, massive, ponderous; (*Inf*) hefty; consequential, considerable, critical, crucial, forcible, grave, important, momentous, portentous, serious, significant, solemn, substantial; backbreaking, burdensome, crushing, demanding, difficult, exacting, onerous, oppressive, taxing, worrisome, worrying

weird *adj* bizarre, eerie, freakish, ghostly, grotesque, mysterious, odd, outlandish, queer, strange, supernatural, uncanny, unearthly, unnatural; (*Inf*) creepy, far-out, spooky

welcome *adj* acceptable, accepted, agreeable, appreciated, delightful, desirable, gladly received, gratify ing, pleasant, pleasing, pleasurable, refreshing, wanted; at home, free, invited, under no obligation

welcome *n* acceptance, entertainment, greeting, hospitality, reception, salutation

welcome *v* accept, gladly, bid welcome, embrace, greet, hail, meet, offer hospitality to, receive, receive with open arms, roll out the red carpet for, usher in

welfare *n* advantage, benefit, good, happiness, health, interest, profit, prosperity, success, wellbeing

well *adv* agreeable, capitally, happily, in a satisfactory manner, nicely, pleasantly, satisfactorily, smoothly, splendidly, successfully; (*Inf*) famously; ably, adeptly, adequately, admirable, conscientiously, correctly, effectively, efficiently, expertly, proficiently, properly, skillfully, with skill; accurately, attentively, carefully, closely; comfortably, flourishingly, prosperously; correctly, easily, fairly, fittingly, in all fairness, justly, properly, readily, rightly, suitably; closely, completely, deeply, fully, intimately, personally, profoundly, thoroughly; approvingly, favourable, glowingly, graciously, highly, kindly, warmly; abundantly, amply, completely, considerably, fully, greatly, heartily, highly, substantially, sufficiently, thoroughly, very much

well *adj* able-bodied, fit, hale, healthy, hearty, in fine fettle, in good health, robust, sound, strong, up to par

well *n* fountain, pool, source, spring, waterhole; bore, hole, pit, shaft

well *v* flow, gush, jet, ooze, pour, rise, run, seep, spout, spring, spurt, stream, surge, trickle

well-balanced *adj* graceful, harmonious, proportional, symmetrical, well-proportioned

well-being *n* comfort, good, happiness, prosperity, welfare

well-known *adj* celebrated, familiar, famous, illustrious, notable, noted, popular, renowned, widely known

well-off *adj* comfortable, flourishing, fortunate, lucky, successful, thriving

wet *adj* aqueous, damp, dank, drenched, dripping, humid, moist, moistened, saturated, soaked, soaking, sodden, soggy, sopping, waterlogged, watery, wringing wet; clammy, dank, drizzling, humid, misty, pouring, raining, rainy, showery, teeming

wet *n* clamminess, condensation, damp, dampness, humidity, liquid, moisture, water, wetness

wet *v* damp, dampen, dip, douse, drench, humidify, irrigate, moisten, saturate, soak, splash, spray, sprinkle, steep, water

wharf *v* dock, jetty, landing stage, pier,quay

wheel *n* circle, gyration, pivot, revolution, roll, rotation, spin, turn, twirl, whirl

wheel *v* circle, gyrate, orbit, pirouette, revolve, roll, rotate, spin, swing, swivel, turn, twirl, whirl

wheeze *v* breathe roughly, catch one's breath, cough, gasp, hiss, rasp, whistle

wheeze *n* cough, gasp, hiss, rasp, whistle; idea, plan, ploy, ruse, scheme, stunt, trick, (*Inf*) expedient, wrinkle

whereabouts *n* location, position, site, situation

whet *v* edge, file, grind, hone, sharpen, strop

whiff *n* aroma, blast, breath, draught, gust, hint, odour, puff, scent, smell, sniff

whiff *v* breathe, inhale, puff, smell, smoke, sniff, waft

whim *n* caprice, conceit, craze, crotchet, fancy, freak, humour, impulse, notion, passing thought, quirk, sport, sudden notion, urge, vagary, whimsy; (*Inf*) fad

whimper *v* blubber, cry, mewl, moan, snivel, sob, weep, whine, whinge; (*Inf*) blub, grizzle;

whimper *n* moan, snivel, sob, whine

whimsical *adj* capricious, crotchety, eccentric, erratic, fanciful, frolic some, odd, peculiar, quaint, singular

whine *n* cry, moan, plaintive, cry, sob, wail, whimper; complaint, grouse, grumble, moan; (*Inf*) beef, gripe

whine *v* carp, complain, cry, grouse, grumble, moan, sob, wail, whimper; (*Inf*) beef, bellyache, gripe, grizzle, whinge

whip *v* beat, birch, cane, castigate, flagellate, flog, lash, leather, punish, scourge, spank, strap, switch; (*Inf*) give a hiding to, tan, thrash; exhibit, flash, jerk, produce, pull, remove, seize, show, snatch, whisk; beat, whisk

whip *n* birch, bullwhip, cane, cat-o'-nine-tails, crop, horsewhip, lash, rawhide, riding crop, scourge, switch, thong

whirl *v* circle, gyrate, pirouette, pivot, reel, revolve, roll, rotate, spin, swirl, turn, twirl, twist, wheel; feel dizzy, reel, spin

whirl *n* circle, gyration, pirouette, reel, revolution, roll, rotation, spin, swirl, turn, twirl, twist, wheel; confusion, daze, dither, flurry, giddiness, spin

whirlwind *n* dust devil, tornado, waterspout

whirlwind *adj* hasty, headlong, impetuous, impulsive, lightning, quick, rapid, rash, short, speedy, swift

whisper *v* breathe, murmur, say softly, speak in hushed tones, utter under the breath; gossip, hint, insinuate, intimate, murmur, spread rumours; hiss, murmur, rustle, sigh, sough, susurrate, swish

whisper *n* hushed tone, low voice, murmur, soft voice, undertone; hiss, murmur, rustle, sigh, sighing, susurration, swish; breath, fraction, hint, shadow, suggestion, suspicion, tinge, trace, whiff; gossip, innuendo, insinuation, report, rumour, word; (*Inf*) buzz

white *adj* ashen, bloodless, ghastly, grey, pale, pallid, pasty, wan, waxen, whey-faced; grey, grizzled, hoary, silver, snowy; clean, immaculate, innocent, pure, spotless, stainless, unblemished, unsullied

whiten *v* blanch, bleach, blench, etiolate, fade, go white, pale, turn pale

whitewash *n* camouflage, concealment, cover-up, deception, extenuation

whitewash *v* camouflage, conceal, cover up, extenuate, gloss over, make light of, suppress

whole *adj* complete, entire, full, in one piece, integral, total, unabridged, uncut, undivided; faultless, flawless, good, in one piece, intact, inviolate, mint, perfect, sound, unbroken, undamaged, unharmed, unhurt, unimpaired, uninjured, unmutilated, unscathed, untouched; able-bodied, better, cured, fit, hale, healed, healthy, in fine fettle, in good health, recovered, robust, sound, strong, well

whole *n* aggregate, all, everything, lot, sum total, the entire amount, total; ensemble, entirety, entity, full ness, piece, totality, unit, unity

wholehearted *adj* committed, complete, dedicated, determined, devoted, earnest, emphatic, enthusiastic, genuine, heartfelt, hearty, real, sincere, true, unqualified, unreserved, unstinting, warm, zealous

wholesale *adj* all-inclusive, broad, comprehensive, extensive, far-reaching, indiscriminating, mass, sweeping, wide-ranging

wholesale *adv* all at once, comprehensively, extensively, indiscriminately, on a large scale, without exception

wholesome *adj* healthy, healthful, helpful, invigorating, nourishing, nutritious, salubrious, salutary; fresh, sound, sweet

wicked *adj* abandoned, abominable, amoral, atrocious, bad, black-hearted, corrupt, debased, depraved, devilish, dissolute, egregious, evil, fiendish, flagitious, foul, guilty, heinous, immoral, impious, iniquitous, irreligious, nefarious, scandalous, shameful, sinful, unprincipled, unrighteous, vicious, vile, villainous, worthless; arch, impish, incorrigible, mischievous, naughty, rascally, roguish; bothersome, difficult, distressing, galling, offensive, troublesome, trying, unpleasant

wide *adj* ample, broad, catholic, comprehensive, distended, encyclopedic, expanded, expansive, far-reaching, general, immense, inclusive, large, sweeping, vast; away, distant, off, off course, off target, remote; dilated, distended, expanded, fully open, outspread, outstretched; ample, baggy, capacious, commodious, full, loose, roomy, spacious

wide *adv* as far as possible, completely, fully, right out, to the furthest extent; astray, nowhere near, off course, of target, off the mark, out

widen *v* broaden, dilate, enlarge, expand, extend, open up, open wide, spread, stretch

widespread *adj* broad, common, epidemic, extensive, far-flung, far-reaching, general, pervasive, popular, prevalent, rife, sweeping, universal, wholesale

width *n* breadth, compass, diameter, extent, girth, measure, range, reach, scope, span, thickness, wideness

wield *v* brandish employ, flourish, handle, manage, manipulate, ply, swing, use; apply, be possessed of, command, control, exercise, exert, have, have at one's disposal, hold, maintain, make use of, manage, possess, put to use, utilize

wife *n* bride, helpmate, mate, partner, spouse, woman; (*Inf*) better half, little woman, old lady, old woman, the missus

wild *adj* feral, ferocious, fierce, savage, unbroken, undomesticated, untamed; free, indigenous, native, natural, uncultivated; desert, deserted, desolate, empty, godforsaken, trackless, uncivilized, uncultivated, uninhabited, unpopulated, virgin; barbaric, barbarous, brutish, ferocious, fierce, primitive, rude, savage, uncivilized; boisterous, chaotic, disorderly, impetuous, law less, noisy, riotous, rough, rowdy, self-willed, turbulent, unbridled, uncontrolled, undisciplined, unfettered, ungovernable, unmanageable, unrestrained, unruly, uproarious, violent, wayward; at one's wits' end, berserk, beside oneself, crazed, crazy, delirious, demented, excited, frantic, frenzied, hysterical, irrational, mad, maniacal, rabid, raving

wilderness *n* desert, jungle, waste, wasteland, wild

wile *n* artfulness, artifice, cheating, chicanery, craft, craftiness, cunning, fraud, guile, slyness, trickery

wilful *adj* adamant, bull-headed, determined, dogged, froward, headstrong, inflexible, intractable, intransigent, mulish, obdurate, obstinate, persistent, perverse, pig-headed, refractory, self-willed, stubborn, uncompromising, unyielding; conscious, deliberate, intended, intentional, purposeful, volitional, voluntary, willed

will *n* choice, decision, determination, discretion, option, prerogative, volition; declaration, last wishes, testament; choice, decision, decree, desire, fancy, inclination, mind, pleasure, preference, wish; aim, determination, intention, purpose, resolution, resolve, willpower; attitude, disposition, feeling

will *v* bid, bring about, cause, command, decree, determine, direct, effect, ordain, order, resolve; choose, desire, elect, opt, prefer, see fit, want, wish; bequeath, confer, give, leave, pass on, transfer

willing *adj* agreeable, amenable, compliant, consenting, content, desirous, disposed, eager, enthusiastic, favourable, happy, inclined, in favour, in the mood, nothing, loath, pleased, prepared, ready, so-minded; (*Inf*) game

willingly *adv* by choice, cheerfully, eagerly, freely, gladly, happily, of one's own accord, of one's own free will, readily, voluntarily, without hesitation, with pleasure

willingness *n* agreeableness, agreement, consent, desire, disposition, enthusiasm, favour, good will, inclination, volition, will, wish

will-power *n* determination, drive, firmness of purpose, fixity of purpose, force of will, grit, resolution, resolve, self-control, self-discipline, single-mindedness

wily *adj* arch, artful, crafty, crooked, cunning, deceitful, designing, diplomatic, foxy, insiduous, intriguing, politic, sly, subtle, treacherous, tricky

win *v* achieve first place, achieve mastery, be victorious, carry all before one, carry the day, come first, conquer, finish first, gain victory, overcome, prevail, succeed, take the prize, triumph; accomplish, achieve, acquire, attain, catch, collect, come away with, earn, gain, get, net, obtain, pick up, procure, receive, secure; (*Inf*) bag

win *n* conquest, success, triumph, victory

wind *n* air, air-current, blast, breath, breeze, current of air, draught, gust, zephyr; babble, blather, bluster, boasting, empty talk, hot air, humbug, idle talk, talk, verbalizing; (*Inf*) gab; breath, puff, respiration; about to happen, approaching, close at hand, coming, imminent, impending, in the offing, near, on the way; (*Inf*) on the cards

wind *v* coil, curl, encircle, furl, loop, reel, roll, spiral, turn around, twine, twist, wreathe; bend, curve, deviate, meander, ramble, snake, turn, twist, zigzag

wind *n* bend, curve, meander, turn, twist, zigzag

windfall *n* bonanza, find, godsend, jackpot, manna from heaven, stroke of luck

winding *n* bending, convolution, curve, meander, turn, twist, undulation

winding *adj* anfractuous, bending, circuitous, convoluted, crooked, curving, flexuous. indirect, meandering, roundabout, serpentine, sinuous, spiral, tortuous, turning, twisting

wind up *v* bring to a close, close, close down, conclude, end, finalize, finish, liquidate, settle, terminate, wrap up; (*Inf*) tie up the loose ends

windy *adj* blowy, blustering, blustery, boisterous, breezy, gusty, squally, stormy, tempestuous, wild, windswept

wing *n* organ of flight, pinion; arm, branch, circle, clique, coterie, faction, group, grouping, section, segment, set, side; adjunct, annexe, cell, extension

wing *v* fly, glide, soar; fleet, fly, hasten, hurry, race, speed, zoom; clip, hit, nick, wound

wink *v* bat, blink, flutter, nictitate; flash, gleam, glimmer, sparkle, twinkle

wink *n* blink, flutter, nictation; flash, gleam, glimmering, sparkle, twinkle; instant, moment, second, split second, twinkling; (*Inf*) jiffy

winner *n* champion, conquering hero, conqueror, first, master, vanquisher, victor; (*Inf*) champ

winning *adj* alluring, amiable, attractive, bewitching, captivating, charming, delectable, delightful, disarming, enchanting, endearing, engaging, fascinating, fetching, lovely, pleasing, prepossessing, sweet, taking, winsome

winnow *v* comb, cull, divide, fan, part, screen, select, separate, separate the wheat from the chaff, sift, sort out

wintry *adj* chilly, cold, freezing, frosty, frozen, harsh, hibernal, hiemal, icy, snowy; bleak, cheerless, sold, desolate, dismal

wipe *v* brush, clean, dry, dust, mop, rub, sponge, swab; clean off, erase, get rod of, remove, rub off, take away, take off

wipe *n* brush, lick, rub, swab

wipe out *v* annihilate, blot out, destroy, efface, eradicate, erase, expunge, exterminate, extirpate, kill to the last man, massacre, obliterate

wisdom *v* astuteness, circumspection, comprehension, discernment, enlightenment, erudition, foresight, insight, intelligence, judgment, judiciousness, knowledge, learning, penetration, prudence, reason, sagacity, sapience, sense, sound judgment, understanding

wise *adj* aware, clever, discerning, enlightened, erudite, informed, intelligent, judicious, knowing, perceptive, politic, prudent, rational, reasonable, sagacious, sage, sapient, sensible, shrewd, sound, understanding, well-advised, well-informed

wisecrack *n* barb, jest, jibe, joke, pithy, remark, quip, sardonic, remark, smart remark, witticism; (*Inf*) funny, gag

wish *v* aspire, covet, crave, desiderate, desire, hanker, hope, hunger, long, need, set one's heart on, sigh for, thirst, want, yearn; bid, greet with; ask, bid, command, desire, direct, instruct, order, require

wish *n* aspiration, desire, hankering, hope, hunger, inclination, intention, liking, longing, thirst, urge, want, whim, will, yearning

wistful *adj* contemplative, disconsolate, dreaming, dreamy, forlorn, longing, meditative, melancholy, mournful, musing, pensive, reflective, sad, thoughtful, yearning

wit *n* badinage, banter, drollery, facetiousness, fun, humour, jocularity, levity, pleasantry, raillery, repartee, wordplay; comedian, epigrammatist, *farceur,* humourist, joker, punster, wag; (*Inf*) card; acumen, brains, cleverness, common sense, comprehension, discernment, ingenuity, insight, intellect, judgment, mind, perception, practical intelligence, reason, sense, understanding, wisdom; (*Inf*) nous

witch *n* enchantress, magician, necromancer, occultist, sorceress

witchcraft *n* enchantment, incantation, magic, necromancy, occultism, sorcery, sortilege, spell, the black art, the occult, voodoo, witchery, witching, wizardry

withdraw *n* draw back, draw out, extract, pull out, remove, take away, take off; abjure, disavow, disclaim. recall, recant, rescind, retract, revoke, take back, unsay; absent oneself, back out, depart, detach oneself, disengage, drop out, fall back, go, leave, pull back, pull out, retire, retreat, secede; (*Inf*) make oneself scarce

withdrawal *n* extraction, removal; abjuration, disavowal, disclaimer, recall, recantation, repudiation, rescission, retraction, revocation; departure, disengagement, exit, exodus, retirement, retreat, secession

withdrawn *adj* aloof, detached, distant, introverted, quiet, reserved, retiring, shrinking, shy, silent, taciturn, timorous, uncommunicative, unforthcoming

wither *v* blast, blight, decay, decline, desiccate, disintegrate, droop, dry, fade, languish, perish, shrink, shrivel, wane, waste, wilt; abash, blast, humiliate, mortify, shame, snub; (*Inf*) put down

withering *adj* blasting, blighting, devastating, humiliating hurtful, mortifying, scornful, snubbing; deadly, death-dealing, destructive, devastating, killing, murderous, slaughterous

withhold *v* check, conceal, deduct, hide, hold back, keep, keep back, keep secret, refuse, repress, reserve, resist, restrain, retain, suppress; (*Inf*) sit on

witness *n* beholder, bystander, eyewitness, looker-on, observer, onlooker, spectator, viewer, watcher; attestant, corroborator, deponent, testifier; depone, depose, give evidence, give testimony, testify; attest to, bear out, be evidence of, be proof of, betoken, confirm, constitute proof of, corroborate, demonstrate, evidence, prove, show, testify to, vouch for

witness *v* attend, be present at, look on, mark, note, notice, observe, perceive, see, view, watch; attest, authenticate, bear out, bear witness, confirm, corroborate, depose, give evidence, give testimony, testify

wits *pl n* acumen, astuteness, cleverness, comprehension, faculties, ingenuity, intelligence, judgment, reason, sense, understanding; (*Inf*) brains, nous

witty *adj* amusing, brilliant, clever, droll, epigrammatic, facetious, fanciful, funny, gay, humourous, ingenious, jocular, lively, original, piquant, sparkling, waggish, whimsical

wizard *n* conjurer, enchanter, mage, magician, magus, necromancer, occultist, shaman, sorcerer, warlock, witch; adept, expert, genius, maestro, master, prodigy, star, virtuoso; (*Inf*) ace, hotshot, whiz, whizz kid

wizened *adj* dried up, gnarled, lined, shrivelled, shrunken, withered, worn, wrinkled

woe *n* adversity, affliction, agony, anguish, burden, curse, dejection, depression, disaster, distress, gloom, grief, hardship, heartache, heartbreak, melancholy, misery, misfortune, pain, sadness, sorrow, suffering, trial, tribulation, trouble, unhappiness, wretchedness

woman *n* female, girl, lady, lass, lassie, miss, she; (*Inf*) bird, chick, dame; chambermaid, charwoman, domestic, female servant, house keeper, lady-in-waiting, maid, maidservant; (*Inf*) char

wonder *n* admiration, amazement,

astonishment, awe, bewilderment, curiosity, fascination, stupefaction, surprise, wonderment; curiosity, marvel, miracle, nonpareil, phenomenon, portent, prodigy, rarity, sight, spectacle, wonderment

wonder *v* ask oneself, be curious, be inquisitive, conjecture, doubt, inquire, meditate, ponder, puzzle, query, question, speculate, think; (*Inf*) cudgel one's brains; be amazed, be astonished, be awed, be dumbstruck, boggle, gape, marvel, stand amazed, stare; (*Inf*) be flabbergasted, boggle, gawk

wonderful *adj* amazing, astonishing, astounding, awe-inspiring, awesome, extraordinary, fantastic, incredible, marvellous, miraculous, odd, peculiar, phenomenal, remarkable, staggering, startling, strange, surprising, unheard-of, wondrous; admirable, brilliant, excellent, magnificent, marvellous, outstanding, sensational, stupendous, superb, terrific, tiptop, tremendous; (*Inf*) ace, fabulous, fantastic, great, smashing, super

woo *v* chase, court, cultivate, importune, pay court to, pay one's addresses to, pay suit to, press one's suit with, pursue, seek to win, solicit the good will of

wooden *adj* ligneous, made of wood, of wood, timber, woody; awkward, clumsy, gauche, gawky, graceless, inelegant, maladroit, rigid, stiff, ungainly; blank, colourless, deadpan, dull, emotionless, empty, expressionless, glassy, lifeless, spiritless, unemotional, unresponsive, vacant; dense, dim, dull, dull-witted, obtuse, slow, stupid, thick, witless; (*Inf*) dim-witted, dull, muf fled, wooden headed,

woolly *adj* fleecy, flocculent, hairy, made of wool, shaggy, woollen; blurred, clouded, confused, foggy, fuzzy, hazy, ill-defined, indefinite, indistinct, muddled, nebulous, unclear, vague

word *n* brief conversation, chat, chitchat, colloquy, confabulation, consultation, discussion, talk, tête-à-tête; (*Inf*) chit-chat, confab, pow-wow; brief statement, comment, declaration, expression, remark, utterance; expression, locution, name, term, vocable; account, advice, bulletin, communication, communiqué, dispatch, information, intelligence, intimation, message, news, notice, report, tidings; (*Inf*) gen, low-down; command, green light, order, signal; affirmation, assertion, assurance, go-ahead, guarantee, oath, parole, pledge, promise, solemn oath, solemn word, undertaking, vow, word of honour; (*Inf*) green light; bidding, command, commandment, decree, edict, mandate, order, will; countersign, password, slogan, watchword

word *v* couch, express, phrase, put, say, state, utter

words *pl n* lyrics, text; altercation, angry exchange, angry speech, argument, bickering, disagreement, dispute, quarrel, row; (*Inf*) barney, falling out, run-in, set-to, squabble

wordy *adj* diffuse, discursive, garrulous, long-winded, loquacious, pleonastic, prolix, rambling, verbose, windy

work *n* drudgery, effort, exertion, industry, labour, slog, sweat, toil; (*Inf*) elbow grease, grind; business, calling, craft, duty, employment, job, line, livelihood, métier, occupation, office, profession, pursuit, trade; assignment, chore, commission, duty, job, stint, task, undertaking; achievement, composition, creation, handiwork, *oeuvre,* opus, performance, piece, production; art, craft, skill, workmanship; **out of work** idle, jobless, on the street, out of a job, unemployed; (*Inf*) on the dole

work *v* drudge, exert oneself, labour, peg away, slave, slog away, sweat, toil; be employed, be in work, do business, earn a living, have a job; act, control, direct, drive, handle, manage, manipulate, move, operate, ply, use, wield; function, go, operate, perform, run; cultivate, dig, farm, till; arouse, excite, move, prompt, provoke, rouse, stir

worker *n* artisan, craftsman, employee, hand, labourer, proletarian, tradesman, wage earner, working man, working woman, workman

working *n* action, functioning, manner, method, mode of operation, operation, running; diggings, excavations, mine, pit, quarry, shaft

working *adj* active, employed, in a job, in work, labouring; function ing, going, operative, running; effective, practical, useful, viable

workman, workwoman *n* artificer, artisan, craftsman, employee, hand, journeyman, labourer, mechanic, operative, tradesman, worker

work out *v* accomplish, achieve, attain, win; calculate, clear up, figure out, find out, puzzle out, resolve, solve; arrange, construct, contrive, develop, devise, elaborate, evolve, form, formulate, plan, put together; be effective, flourish, go as planned, go well, prosper, prove satisfactory, succeed; add up to, amount to, come to, reach. reach a total of

work-out *n* drill, physical exercise, training; aerobics, exercises, gymnastics; training session

works *pl n* factory, mill, plant, shop, workshop; canon, oeuvre, output, productions, writings; actions, acts, deeds, doings; action, machinery, mechanism, movement, moving parts, parts, workings; (*Inf*) guts, innards, insides

workshop *n* atelier, factory, mill, plant, shop, studio, workroom, works

work up *v* agitate, animate, arouse, enkindle, excite, foment, generate, incite, inflame, instigate, move, rouse, spur, stir up; (*Inf*) get some one all steamed up, wind up

world *n* earth, earthly, fleshly, lay, mundane, physical, profane, secular, sublunary, temporal, terrestrial; avaricious, covetous, grasping, greedy, materialistic, selfish, worldly-minded; blasé, cosmopolitan, experienced, knowing, politic, sophisticated, urbane, well versed in the ways of the world, worldly-wise

worldwide *adj* general, global, international, omnipresent, pandemic, ubiquitous, universal

worldly *adj* common, earthly, human, mundane, sublunary, terrestrial, carnal, fleshly, profane, secular, temporal; ambitious, grovelling, irreligious, selfish, proud, sordid, unsanctified, unspiritual

worn *adj* frayed, ragged, shabby, shiny, tattered, tatty, the worse for wear, threadbare; careworn, drawn, haggard, lined, pinched, wizened; exhausted, fatigued, jaded, spent, tired, tired out, wearied, weary, worn-out; (*Inf*) played-out

worried *adj* afraid, anxious, apprehensive, bothered, concerned, distracted, distraught, distressed, disturbed, fearful, fretful, frightened, ill at ease, nervous, on edge, overwrought, perturbed, tense, tormented troubled, uneasy, unquiet, upset

worry *v* agonize, annoy, badger, be anxious, bother, brood, disquiet, distress, disturb, feel uneasy, fret, harass, harry, hector, importune, irritate, make anxious, perturb, pester, plague, tantalize, tease, torment, trouble, unsettle, upset, vex; (*Inf*) hassle

worry *n* annoyance, care, irritation, pest, plague, problem, torment, trial, trouble, vexation

worsen *v* aggravate, damage, decay, decline, degenerate, deteriorate, exacerbate, get worse, go from bad to worse, retrogress, sink, take a turn for the worse; (*Inf*) go downhill

worship *v* adore, adulate, deify, exalt, glorify, honour, idolize, laud, love, praise, pray to, put on a pedestal, respect, revere, reverence, venerate

worship *n* adoration, adulation, deification, devotion, exaltation, glorification, glory, homage, honour, laudation, love, praise, prayers, regard, respect, reverence

worst *v* beat, best, conquer, crush, defeat, gain the advantage over, get the better of, master, overcome, overpower, overthrow, subdue, subjugate, vanquish

worth *n* aid, assistance, avail, benefit, credit, deserts, estimation, excellence, goodness, help, importance, merit, quality, usefulness, utility, value, virtue, worthiness; cost, price, rate, valuation, value

worthless *n* futile, ineffectual, insignificant, inutile, meaningless, miserable, no use, nugatory, paltry, pointless, poor, rubbishy, trashy, trifling, trivial, unavailable, unimportant, unusable, useless, valueless, wretched; abandoned, abject, base, contemptible, depraved, despicable, good-for-nothing, ignoble, useless, vile

worthwhile *adj* beneficial, constructive, gainful, good, helpful, justifiable, productive, profitable, useful, valuable, worthy

worthy *adj* admirable, commendable, creditable, decent, dependable, deserving, estimable, excellent, good, honest, honourable, laudable, meritorious, praiseworthy, reliable, reputable, respectable, righteous, upright, valuable, virtuous, worth while

worthy *n* dignitary, luminary, notable, personage; (*Inf*) big shot, big wig

wound *n* cut, damage, gash, harm, hurt, injury, laceration, lesion, slash;

anguish, distress, grief, heartbreak, injury, insult, offense, pain, pang, sense of loss, shock, slight, torment, torture, trauma

wound *v* cut, damage, gash, harm, hit, hurt, injure, irritate, lacerate, pierce, slash, wing; annoy, cut someone to the quick, distress, grieve, hurt, hurt the feelings of, mortify, offend, pain, shock, sting, traumatize

wrangle *v* altercate, argue, bicker, brawl, contend, disagree, dispute, fight, have words, quarrel, row, scrap, squabble; (*Inf*) fall-out

wrangle *n* altercation, angry exchange, bickering, brawl, clash, contest, controversy, dispute, quar rel, row, squabble, tiff; (*Inf*) argy-bargy, barney, falling out, set-to, slanging match

wrap *v* absorb, bind, bundle up, cloak, cover, encase, enclose, enfold, envelop, fold, immerse, muffle, pack, package, roll up, sheathe, shroud, surround, swathe, wind

wrapper *n* case, cover, envelope, jacket, packaging, paper, sheath, sleeve, wrapping

wrath *n* anger, choler, displeasure, exasperation, fury, indignation, ire, irritation, passion, rage, resentment, temper

wreath *n* band, chaplet, coronet, crown, festoon, garland, loop, ring

wreathe *v* adorn, coil, crown, encircle, enfold, entwine, envelop, enwrap, festoon, intertwine, interweave, surround, twine, twist, wind, rap, writhe

wreck *v* break, dash to pieces, demolish, destroy, devastate, mar, play havoc with, ravage, ruin, shatter, smash, spoil; founder, go aground, run onto the rocks, shipwreck, strand

wreck *n* derelict, hulk, shipwreck, sunken vessel

wreckage *n* debris, fragments, hulk, pieces, remains, rubble, ruin, wreck

wrench *v* force, jerk, pull, rip, tear, tug, twist, wrest, wring, yank; distort, rick, sprain, strain

wrench *n* jerk, pull, rip, tug, twist; ache, blow, pain, pang, shock, upheaval, uprooting

wrest *v* force, pull, strain, twist, wrench, wring

wrestle *v* battle, combat, contend, fight, grapple, scuffle, strive, struggle, tussle

wretch *n* blackguard, cur, good-for-nothing, miscreant, outcast, profligate, rascal, rogue, ruffian, scoundrel, swine, vagabond, villain, worm; poor thing, unfortunate; (*Inf*) rat, rotter, rotter

wretched *adj* abject, brokenhearted, cheerless, comfortless, crestfallen, dejected, deplorable, depressed, disconsolate, distressed, doleful, downcast, forlorn, gloomy, hapless, hopeless, melancholy, miserable, pathetic, pitiable, pitiful, poor, sorry, unfortunate, unhappy, woe begone, woeful, worthless; calamitous, deplorable, inferior, miserable, paltry, pathetic, poor, sorry, worthless

wriggle *v* jerk, jiggle, squirm, turn, twist, wag, waggle, wiggle, writhe; crawl, slink, snake, twist and turn, worm, zigzag; crawl, dodge,

extricate oneself, manoeuvre, sneak, talk one's way out, worm
wriggle *n* jerk, jiggle, squirm, turn, twist, wag, waggle, wiggle
wring *v* coerce, extort, extract, force, screw, squeeze, twist, wrench, wrest; distress, hurt, lacerate, pain, pierce, rack, rend, stab, tear at, wound
wrinkle *n* corrugation, crease, crimp, crinkle, crow's-foot, crumple, fold, furrow, gather, line, plait, pucker, ridge, ruck, rumple
wrinkle *v* corrugate, crease, crumple, fold, furrow, gather, line, pucker, ruck, rumple
writ *n* court order, decree, document, summons
write *v* commit to paper, compose, copy, correspond, create, dash off, draft, draw up, indite, inscribe, jot down, list, pen, put down in black and white, put in writing, record, scribble, set down, take down, tell, transcribe; (*Inf*) drop a line
write-off *n* annul, cancel, cross out, disregard, forget about, give up for lost, score out, shelve, wipe out; crash, damage beyond repair, demolish, destroy, smash up, wreck; (*Inf*) total; disregard, dismiss
writer *n* author, biographer, columnist, essayist, hack, novelist, penman, penpusher, scribbler, scribe, scriptwriter, wordsmith
writhe *v* contort, distort, jerk, squirm, struggle, thrash, thresh, toss, twist, wiggle, wriggle
writing *n* calligraphy, chirography, hand, handwriting, penmanship, print, scrawl, scribble, script; book, composition, document, letter, opus, publication, work
wrong *adj* erroneous, fallacious, false, faulty, inaccurate, incorrect, in error, mistaken, off target, out, unsound, untrue, wide of the mark; (*Inf*) off-beam; bad, blameworthy, criminal, crooked, dishonest, dishonourable, evil, felonious, illegal, illicit, immoral, iniquitous, repre hensible, sinful, unethical, unfair, unjust, unlawful, wicked, wrongful; funny, improper, inappropriate, inapt, incongruous, incorrect, indecorous, infelicitous, malapropos, not done, unacceptable, unbecoming, unconventional, undesirable, unfitting, unhappy, unseemly, unsuitable; amiss, askew, awry, defective, faulty, not working, out of commission, out of order; inside, inverse, opposite, reverse
wrong *adv* amiss, askew, astray, awry, badly, erroneously, inaccurately, incorrectly, mistakenly, wrongly; **go wrong** come to nothing, fail, fall through, miscarry, misfire; (*Inf*) come to grief, flop; err, go astray, make a mistake; (*Inf*) boob, slip up; break down, cease to function, fail, malfunction, misfire; (*Inf*) conk out, go kaput, go on the blink, go phut; err, fall from grace, go astray, go to the bad, lapse, sin; (*Inf*) go off the straight and narrow
wrong *n* abuse, bad deed, crime, error, evil deed, grievance, immorality, inequity, infraction, infringement, iniquity, injury, injustice, misdeed, offense, sin, sinfulness, transgression, trespass, unfairness, wickedness
wrong *v* abuse, cheat, discredit, dis-

honour, harm, hurt, ill-treat, ill-use, impose upon, injure, malign, maltreat, misrepresent, mistreat, oppress, take advantage of

wrongdoer *n* criminal, culprit, delinquent, evildoer, felon, law breaker, malefactor, miscreant, offender, sinner, transgressor, villain

wrongful *adj* blameworthy, criminal, dishonest, dishonourable, evil, felonious, illegal, illegitimate, illicit, immoral, improper, reprehensible, unethical, unfair, unjust, unlawful, unwarranted, wicked

wry *adj* askew, aslant, awry, contorted, crooked, deformed, distorted, lopsided, off the level, twisted, uneven, warped; droll, dry, humor ous, ironic, mocking, sarcastic, sardonic, witty

XYZ

xerox *v* copy, duplicate, photocopy, photostat, reproduce
X-rays *n* image, radiogram, radiograph
xylograph *n* cut, woodcut, wood engraving
yank *v* jerk, pull, tug, wrench
yap *v* bark, cry, yelp
yard *n* close, compound, court, courtyard, enclosure, garden
yardstick *n* benchmark, criterion, gauge, guideline, measure, model, pattern, scale, standard, touchstone
yarn *n* fibre, strand, thread; anecdote, fable, story, tale, traveller's tale; (*Inf*) cock-and-bull story, tall story
yawn *v* dehisce, gape, open wide
yawn *n* gap, gape, gulf
yawning *adj* cavernous, chasmal, gaping, vast, wide, wide-open
yearly *adj* annual, every year, once a year
yearly *adv* annually, once a year, per annum
yearn *v* ache, covet, crave, desire, fancy, hanker after, hunger for, itch, languish, long, lust, pant, pine, set one's heart upon, thirst for, want, wish for; (*Inf*) have a yen for
yell *v* bawl, cry out, howl, roar, scream, screech, shout, shriek, squeal, whoop; (*Inf*) holler
yell *n* cry, howl, scream, screech, shout, shriek, squeal, whoop; (*Inf*) holler
yelp *v* bark, howl, yap; complain, bitch, grouse
yelp *n* bark, howl, sharp cry
yes *adv* all right, certainly, sure
yet *adv* as yet, so far, thus far, until now, up to now; despite that, for all that, however, just the same, never the less, notwithstanding, still; additionally, as well, besides, further, in addition, into the bargain, more over, over and above, still, to boot, too; already, just now, right now, so soon, too
yield *v* afford, bear, bring forth, bring in, earn, furnish, generate, give, net, pay, produce, provide, return, supply
yield *n* crop, earnings, harvest, income, output, produce, profit, return, revenue, takings
yield *v* bear, give, give forth, provide, supply; bring in, earn, fetch, generate, abandon, abdicate, admit defeat, bow, capitulate, cede, cry quits, give in, give up the struggle, give way, knuckle under, lay down one's arms, part with, raise the white flag, relinquish, resign, resign oneself, submit, succumb, surrender throw in the towel; (*Inf*) cave in, throw in the towel; accede, agree, allow, bow, comply, concede, consent, go along with, grant, permit
yielding *adj* accommodating, acquiescent, biddable, compliant, docile, easy, flexible, obedient, pliant, submissive, tractable; elastic, pliable, quaggy, resilient, soft, spongy, springy, supple, unresisting
yoke *n* bond, chain, coupling, ligament, link, tie; bondage, burden, enslavement, oppression, serfdom, service, servility, servitude, slavery,

thraldom, vassalage

yoke *v* couple, harness, hitch up, join up; bond, join, link, tie, unite

yokel *n* boor, bucolic, (country) bumpkin, country cousin, country man, hillbilly, rustic; (*Inf*) clod-hopper, hick, hill-billy, peasant

young *adj* adolescent, callow, green, growing, immature, infant, in the springtime of life, junior, juvenile, little, unfledged, youthful; at an early stage, early, fledgling, new, newish, not far advanced, recent, undeveloped

young *n* family, issue, offspring, progeny; babies, little ones; (*Inf*) sprogs

youngster *n* boy, cub, girl, juvenile, lad, lass, teenager, urchin, young adult, young hopeful, young person, youth; (*Inf*) kid, pup, young shaver, young 'un; (*Sl*) teenybopper

youth *n* adolescence, boyhood, early life, girlhood, immaturity, juvenescence, salad days, young days; adolescent, boy, lad, stripling, teenager, young man, youngster; (*Inf*) kid, young shaver

youthful *adj* boyish, childish, immature, inexperienced, juvenile, pubescent, puerile, young; active, fresh, spry, vigorous, young at heart, young looking

zany *adj* comic, comical, crazy, droll, eccentric, funny, imaginative, scatterbrained; clownish, foolish, ludicrous, silly; (*Inf*) daft, screwy, wacky, weird

zap *v* destroy, kill, murder, slay; strike; beat, conquer, crush, defeat, overcome, overpower, overthrow, trounce, vanquish; dash, fly, pelt, rush, shoot, sprint, tear, zoom

zeal *n* ardour, devotion, eagerness, earnestness, enthusiasm, fanaticism, fervency, fervour, fire, gusto, keenness, militancy, passion, spirit, verve, warmth, zest

zealot *n* bigot, enthusiast, extremist, fanatic, militant, radical

zealous *adj* ardent, burning, devoted, eager, earnest, energetic, enthusiastic, fanatical, fervent, fervid, impassioned, intense, keen, militant, passionate, rabid, spirited, vigorous

zenith *n* acme, apex, climax, crown ing point, culmination, height, heyday, meridian, pinnacle, prime, summit, top, utmost, vertex

zero *n* cipher, naught, nil, nothing, nought; (*Inf*) not a sausage, zilch; lowest point, nadir, rock bottom

zest *n* appetite, delectation, eagerness, energy, enjoyment, enthusiasm, gusto, keenness, liveliness, relish, vigour, zeal; (*Inf*) oomph, zing; charm, flavour, interest, piquancy, pungency, relish, savour, smack, spice, tang, taste; (*Inf*) kick

zing *n* brio, energy, enthusiasm, live liness, pep, sparkle, vigour, vitality; (*Inf*) go, pizzazz, zip

zip *n* eagerness, life, liveliness, pep

zip *v* dash, fly, hasten, hurry, rush, scurry, shoot, speed, tear; (*Inf*) hare, whiz, zoom

zone *n* area, belt, district, province, region, section, sector, sphere

zoom *v* buzz, fly; dash, hurry, pelt, race, rush, shoot, tear; (*Inf*) hare, whiz, zip

APPENDICES

PALINDROMES

3
AHA
BIB
BOB
DAD
DID
DUD
ERE
EVE
EWE
EYE
GAG
GIG
HAH
HEH
HUH
MAM
MOM
MUM
NUN
OHO
PAP
PEP
PIP
POP
PUP
SIS
SOS
TAT
TIT
TNT
TOT
TUT
WOW
4
BOOB
DEED
KOOK
MA'AM
NOON
PEEP
POOP
SEES
TOOT
5
CIVIC
KAYAK
LEVEL
MADAM
MINIM
RADAR
REFER
ROTOR
SAGAS
SEXES
SOLOS
TENET
6
DENNED
HALLAH
HANNAH
REDDER
TERRET
TUT-TUT
9
MALAYALAM
ROTAVATOR

BACK WORDS

2
AH - HA
AM - MA
AT - TA
EH - HE
HA - AH
HE - EH
HO - OH
IT - TI
MA - AM
MP - PM
NO - ON
OH - HO
ON - NO
PM - MP
TA - AT
TI - IT
3
AND -DNA
BAD - DAB
BAG - GAB
BAN - NAB
BAT - TAB
BIN - NIB
BOG - GOB
BOY - YOB
BUD - DUB
BUN - NUB
BUS - SUB
BUT - TUB
DAB BAD
DAM - MAD
DEW - WED
DIM - MID
DNA - AND
DOG - GOD
DOH - HOD
DON - NOD
DOT - TOD
DUB - BUD
EEL - LEE
GAB - BAG
GAL - LAG
GAS - SAG
GEL - LEG
GOB - BOG
GOT - TOG
GOD - DOG
GUM - MUG
GUT - TUG
HOD - DOH
JAR - RAG
LAG - GAL
LAP - PAL
LEE - EEL
LEG - GEL
MAD - DAM
MAR - RAM
MAY - YAM
MID - DIM
MUG - GUM
NAB - BAN
NAP - PAN
NET - TEN
NIB - BIN
NIP - PIN
NIT - TIN
NOD - DON
NOT - TOD
NOW - WON
NUB - BUN
PAL - LAP
PAN - NAP
PAR - RAP
PAT - TAP
PAY - YAP
PER - REP
PIN - NIP
PIT - TIP
POT - TOP
PUS - SUP
RAJ - JAR
RAM - MAR
RAT - TAR
RAW - WAR
REP - PER
ROT - TOR
SAG - GAS
SUB - BUS
SUP - PUS
TAB - BAT
TAP - PAT
RAT - TAR
TEN - NET
TIN - NIT
TIP - PIT
TOD - DOT
GOT - TOG
TON - NOT
TOP - POT
TOR - ROT
TUB - BUT
TUG - GUT
WAR RAW
WAY - YAW
WED - DEW
WON - NOW
YAM - MAY
YAP - PAY
YAW - WAY
YOB - BOY
4
ABLE - ELBA
ABUT - TUBA
BARD - DRAB
BATS - STAB
BRAG - GARB
BUNS - SNUB
BUTS - STUB
DEER - REED

DIAL - LAID
DOOM - MOOD
DOOR - ROOD
DRAB - BARD
DRAW - WARD
DRAY - YARD
DUAL - LAUD
EDAM - MADE
EDIT - TIDE
ELBA - ABLE
EMIR -RIME
EMIT -TIME
ERGO - ORGE
ET AL - LATE
EVIL - LIVE
FLOG - GOLF
FLOW - WOLF
GALS - SLAG
GARB - BRAG
GNAT - TANG
GOLF - FLOG
GULP - PLUG
GUMS - SMUG
HOOP POOH
KEEL - LEEK
KEEP - PEEK
LAID - DAIL
LAIR - RIAL
LATE -ET AL
LAUD -DUAL
LEEK - KEEL
LEER - REEL
LIAR - RAIL
LIVE - EVIL
LOOP - POOL
LOOT - TOOL
MACS - SCAM
MADE - EDAM
MAPS - SPAM
MAWS - SWAM
MEET - TEEM
MOOD - DOOM -
NAPS - SPAN
NIPS - SPIN
NUTS - STUN
OGRE - ERGO
PALS - SLAP
PANS - SNAP
PART - TRAP
PAWS - SWAP
PEEK - KEEP
PETS - STEP
PINS - SNIP
PLUG - GULP
POOH - HOOP
POOL - LOOP
POTS - STOP
RAIL - LIAR
RAPS - SPAR
RATS - STAR
REED - DEER
REEL - LEED
RIAL - LAIR
RIME - EMIR
ROOD - DOOR
SCAM - MACS
SLAG - GALS
SLAP - PALS
SMUG - GUNS
SPAM - MAPS
SPAN - NAPS
SPAR - RAPS
SPAT - TAPS
SPAY -YAPS
SPIN -TIPS
SPOT - TOPS
STAB - BATS
STAR - RATS
STEP - PETS
STEW - WETS
STOP - POTS
STUB - BUTS
STUN - NUTS
SWAM - MAWS
SWAP - PAWS
SWAY -YAWS
SWOT - TOWS
TANG - GNAT
TAPS - SPAT
TEEM - MEET
TIDE - EDIT
TIME - EMIT
TIPS - SPIT
TONS - SNOT
TOOL - LOOT
TOPS - SPOT
TORT - TROT
TOWS - SWOT
TRAP - PART
TROT - TROT
TUBA - ABUT
WARD - DRAW
WETS - STEW
WOLF - FLOW
YAPS - SPAY
YARD - DRAY
YAWS - SWAY

5

ANNAM - MANNA
ATLAS - SALTA
CARES - SERAC
DARAF - FARED
DECAL - LACED
DENIM - MINED
DEVIL - LIVED
FARAD - DARAF
FIRES - SERIF
KEELS - SLEEK
LACED - DECAL
LAGER - REGAL
LEPER - REPEL
LEVER - REVEL
LIVED - DEVIL
LOOPS - SPOOL
MANNA - ANNAM
MINED - DENIM
PACER - RECAP
PARTS --STRAP
POOLS - SLOOP
PORTS - STROP
REBUT - TUBER
RECAP - PACER
REGAL - LAGER
REMIT - TIMER
REPEL - LEPER
REVEL - LEVER
SALTA - ATLAS
SERAC - CARES
SERIF - FIRES
SLEEK - KEELS
SLOOP - POOLS
SMART - TRAMS
SNIPS - SPINS
SPINS - SNIPS
SPOOL - LOOPS
SPOTS - STOPS
STRAP - PARTS
STRAW - WARTS
STROP - PORTS
TIMER - REMIT
TRAMS - SMART
TUBER - REBUT
WARTS - STRAW

6

ANIMAL - LAMINA
DELIAN - NAILED
DENIER - RENIED
DIAPER - REPAID
DRAWER - REWARD
HARRIS - SIRRAH
LAMINA - ANIMAL
LOOTER - RETOOL
NAILED - DELIAN
PUPILS - SLIP-UP
RECAPS - SPACER
REINED - DENIER
RENNET - TENNER
REPAID - DAIPER
RETOOL - LOOTER
REWARD - DRAWER
SERVES - SEVRES
SEVRES - SERVES
SIRRAH - HARRIS
SLIP-UP - PUPILS
SNOOPS - SPOONS
SPACER - RECAPS
SPOONS - SNOOPS
TENNER - RENNET

8

DESSERTS - STRESSED
STRESSED - DESSERTS

HOMOPHONES

ALE - AIL
ALL - AWL, ORLE
ALMS - ARMS
ALTAR - ALTER
ALTER - ALTAR
AMAH - ARMOUR
ANTE - ANTI
ANTI - ANTE
ARC - ARK
ARMOUR - AMAH
ARMS - ALMS
ASCENT - ASSENT
ASSENT - ASCENT
ATE - AIT, EIGHT
AUK - ORC
AUNT - AREN'T
AURAL - ORAL
AUSTERE - OSTIA
AWAY - AWEUGH
AWE - OAR, O'ER, ORE
AWEIGH - AWAY
AWL - ALL, ORLE
AXEL - AXLE
AXLE - AXEL
AY - AYE, EYE, I
AYAH - IRE
AYE - AY, EYE, I
AYES - EYES
BAA - BAH, BAR
BAAL - BASLE
BAH - BAA, BAR
BAIL - BALE
BALL - BAWL
BALM - BARM
BAR - BAA, BAH
BARE - BEAR
BARM - BALM
BARMY - BALMY
BARON - BARREN
BARREN - BARON
BASE - BASS
BASLE - BAAL
BASS - BASE
BAUD - BAWD, BOARD
BAWD - BAUD, BOARD
BAWL - BALL
BAY - BEY
BEACH - BEECH
BEAN - BEEN
BEAR - BARE
BEAT - BEET
BEATER - BETA
BEAU - BOH, BOW
BEECH - BEACH
BEEN - BEAN
BEER - BIER
BEET - BEAT
BEL - BELL,BELLE
BELL - BEL, BELLE
BELLE - BEL, BELL
BERRY -BURY
BERTH - BIRTH
BETA - BEATER
BEY - BAY
BHAI - BI, BUY, BY, BYE
BI - BHAI, BUY, BY, BYE
BIER - BEER
BIGHT -
BITE, BYTE
BIRTH - BERTH
BITE - BYTE, BIGHT
BLEW - BLUE
BLUE - BLEW
BOAR - BOER, BOOR, BORE
BOARD - BAUD, BAWD
BOARDER - BORDER
BOART - BOUGHT
BOER - BOAR, BOOR, BORE
BOOTIE - BOOTY
BOOTY - BOOTIE
BORDER - BOARDER
BORE - BOAR, BOER, BOOR
BORN - BORNE
BORNE - BORN
BOUGH -BOW
BOUGHT - BOART
BOULT - BOLT
BOW - BEAU,BOH
BOW - BOUGH
BOWL - BOLE
BOY - BOUY
BRAKE - BREAK
BREAD - BRED
BREAK - BRAKE
BRED - BREAD
BREDE - BREED, BREID
BREED - BREDE, BREID
BREID - BREDE, BREED
BRIDAL - BRIDLE
BRIDLE - BRIDAL
BROACH - BROOCH
BROOCH - BROACH
BUNION - BUNYAN
BUNYAN - BUNION

BUOY - BOY
BURGER - BURGHER
BURGHER - BURGER
BURY - BERRY
BUS - BUSS
BUSS - BUS
BUY - BHAI, BI, BY, BYE
BUYER - BYRE
BY - BHAI, BI, BUY, BYE
BYE - BHAI, BI, BUY, BY
BYRE - BUYER
CACHE - CASH
CACHOU - CASHEW
CAIN - CANE, KAIN
CALL - CAUL
CALLAS - CALLOUS, CALLUS
CALLOUS - CALLAS, CALLUS
CALLUS - CALLAS, CALLOUS
CANAPÉ - CANOPY
CANE - CAIN, KAIN
CANOPY - CANAPÉ
CARAT - CARROT, KARAT
CARROT - CARAT, KARAT
CART - CARTE, KART
CARTE - CART, KART
CASH - CACHE
CASHEW - CACHOU
CASHMERE - KASHMIR
CAST - CASTE, KARST
CASTE - CAST, KARST
CAUGHT - COURT
CAUL - CALL
CAW - COR, CORE, CORPS
CEDAR - SEEDER
CEDE - SEED
CEIL - SEEL, SEAL
CELL - SELL, SZELL
CELLAR - SELLER
CENSER - CENSOR, SENSOR
CENSOR - CENSER, SENSOR
CENT - SCENT, SENT
CERE - SEAR, SEER
CEREAL - SERIAL
CESSION - SESSION
CHAW - CHORE
CHEAP - CHEEP
CHECK - CZECH
CHEEP - CHEAP
CHOIR - QUIRE
CHOLER - COLLAR
CHORD - CORD
CHORE - CHAW
CHOTT - SHOT, SHOTT
CHOU - SHOE, SHOO
CHOUGH - CHUFF
CHUFF - CHOUGH
CHUTE - SHOOT, SHUTE
CITE - SIGHT, SITE
CLACK - CLAQUE
CLAQUE - CLACK
CLIMB - CLIME
CLIME - CLIMB
COAL - COLE - KOHL
COARSE - CORSE, COURSE
COLE - COAL, KOHL
COLLAR - CHOLER
COLONEL - KERNEL
COLOUR - CULLER
COME - CUM
COMPLEMENTARY - COMPLIMENTARY
COO - COUP
COOP - COUPE
COR - CAW, CORE, CORPS
CORD - CHORD
CORE - CAW, COR, CORPS
CORNFLOUR - CORNFLOWER
CORNFLOWER - CORNFLOUR
CORPS - CAW, COR, CORE
CORSE - COARSE, COURSE
COUNCIL - COUNSEL
COUNSEL - COUNCIL
COUP - COO
COUPE COOP
COURSE - COARSE, CORSE
COURT - CAUGHT
CREAK - CREEK
CREEK - CREAK
CULLER - COLOUR
CUM - COME
CURB - KERB
CURRANT - CURRENT
CURRENT - CURRANT
CYGNET - SIGNET
CYMBAL - SYMBOL
CZECH - CHECK
DAM - DAMN
DAMN - DAM
DAW - DOOR, DOR
DAYS - DAZE
DAZE - DAYS
DEAR - DEER
DEER - DEAR
DESCENT - DISSENT
DESERT - DESSERT
DEW - DUE
DINAH - DINER
DINE - DYNE
DINER - DINAH
DISSENT - DESCENT
DOE - DOH, DOUGH
DOH - DOE, DOUGH
DONE - DONNE, DUN

DONNE - DONE, DUN
DOOR - DAW, DOR
DOR - DAW, DOOR
DOST - DUST
DOUGH - DOE, DOH
DRAFT - DRAUGHT
DROOP - DRUPE
DRUPE - DROOP
DUAL - DUEL
DUCKS - DUX
DUE - DEW
DUEL - DUAL
DUN - DONE, DONNE
DUST - DOST
DUX - DUCKS
DYEING - DYING
DYING - DYEING
DYNE - DINE
EARN - URN
EATEN - ETON
E'ER - AIR, AIRE, ERE, EYRE, HEIR
EERIE - EYRIE
EIDER - IDA
EIGHT - AIT, ATE
EIRE - EYRA
ELATION - ILLATION
ELICIT - ILLICIT
ELUDE - ILLUDE
ELUSORY - ILLUSORY
EMERGE - IMMERGE
EMERSED - IMMERSED
EMERSION - IMMERSION
ERE - AIR, AIRE, E'ER, EYRE, HEIR
ERK - IRK
ERR - UR
ESTER - ESTHER
ESTHER - ESTER
ETON - EATEN
EWE - YEW, YOU
EYE - AY, AYE, I
EYED - I'D, IDE
EYELET - ISLET
EYES - AYES
EYRA - EIRE
EYRE - AIR, AIRE, E'ER, ERE, HEIR
EYRIE - EERIE
FA - FAR
FAIN - FANE, FEIGN
FAINT - FEIGNT
FAIR - FARE
FANE - FAIN, FEIGN
FAR - FA
FARE - FAIR
FARO - PHARAOH
FARTHER - FATHER
FATE - FÊTE
FATHER - FARTHER
FAUGH - FOR, FOUR, FORE
FAUN - FAWN
FWN - FAUN
FAZE - PHASE
FEAT - FEET
FEET - FEAT
FEIGN - FAIN, FANE
FEIGNT - FAINT
FELLOE - FELLOW
FELLOW - FELLOE
FELT - VELD, VELDT
FETA - FETTER
FÊTE - FATE
FETTER - FETA
FEU - FEW, PHEW
FEW - FEU, PHEW
FIR - FUR
FISHER - FISSURE
FISSURE - FISHER
FIZZ - PHIZ
FLAIR - FLARE
FLARE - FLAIR
FLAW - FLOOR
FLEA - FLEE
FLEE - FLEA
FLEW - FLU, FLUE
FLOE - FLOW
FLOOR - FLAW
FLOUR - FLOWER
FLOW - FLOE
FLOWER - FLOUR
FLU - FLEW, FLUE
FLUE - FLEW, FLU
FOR - FAUGH, FOUR, FORE
FORE - FAUGH, FOR, FOUR
FORT - FOUGHT
FORTE - FORTY
FORTH - FOURTH
FORTY - FORTE
FOUGHT - FORT
FOUL - FOWL
FOUR - FAUGH, FOR, FORE
FOURTH - FORTH
FOWL - FOUL
FRIAR - FRIER
FRIER - FRIAR
FUR - FIR
GAIL - GALE
GAIT - GATE
GALE - GAIL
GALLOP - GALLUP
GALLUP - GALLOP
GAMBLE - GAMBOL
GAMBOL - GAMBLE
GATE - GAIT

GAWKY - GORKY
GENE - JAEN
GIN - JINN
GLADDEN - GLADDON
GLADDON - GLADDEN
GNASH - NASH
GNAT - NAT
GNAW - NOR
GORKY - GAWKY
GRATER - GREATER
GREATER - GRATER
GROAN - GROWN
GROWN - GROAN
HAE - HAY, HEH, HEY
HAIL - HALE
HAIR - HARE
HALE - HAIL
HALL - HAUL
HANDEL - HANDLE
HANDLE - HANDEL
HANGAR - HANGER
HANGER - HANGAR
HARE - HAIR
HART - HEART
HAUD - HOARD, HORDE
HAUL - HALL
HAW - HOARE, WHORE
HAY - HAE, HEH, HEY
HEIR - AIR, AIRE, E'ER, ERE, EYRE
HEIRSHIP - AIRSHIP
HERE - HEAR
HEROIN - HEROINE
HEROINE - HEROIN
HEW - HUE
HEY - HAE, HAY, HEH
HIE - HIGH
HIGH - HIE
HIGHER - HIRE
HIM - HYMN
HIRE - HIGHER
HO - HOE
HOAR - HAW, WHORE
HOARD - HAUD, HORDE
HOARSE - HORSE
HOE - HO
HOLE - WHOLE
HOO - WHO
HORDE - HAUD, HOARD
HORSE - HOARSE
HOUR - OUR
HOURS - OURS
HUE - HEW
HYMN - HIM
I - AY, AYE, EYE
I'D - EYED, IDE
IDA - EIDER
IDE - EYED, I'D
IDLE - IDOL
IDOL - IDLE
I'LL - AISLE, ISLE
ILLAATION - ELATION
ILLICIT - ELICIT
ILLUDE - ELUDE
ILLUSIONARY - ELUSORY
IMMERGE - EMERGE
IMMERSED - EMERSED
IMMERSION - EMERSION
IN - INN
INCITE - INSIGHT
INDICT - INDITE
INDITE - INDICT
INN - IN
INSIGHT - INCITE
INSOLE - INSOUL
INSOUL - INSOLE
ION - IRON
IRE - AYAH
IRK - ERK
IRON - ION
ISLE - AISLE, I'LL
ISLET - EYELET
JAM - JAMB, JAMBE
JAMB - JAM, JAMBE
JAMBE - JAM, JAMB
JEAN - GENE
JINKS - JINX
JINN - GIN
JINX - JINKS
KAIN - CAIN, CANE
KARAT - CARAT, CARROT
KARST - CAST, CASTE
KART - CART, CARTE
KASHMIR - CASHMERE
KERB - CURB
KERNEL - COLONEL
KEW - KYU, QUEUE
KEY - QUAY
KNAVE - NAVE
KNEAD - NEED
KNEW - NEW, NU
KNIGHT - NIGHT
KNIGHTLY - NIGHTLY
KNIT - NIT
KNOW - NOH, NO
KNOWS - NOES, NOSE
KOHL - COAL, COLE
KYU - KEW, QUEUE
LACKER - LACQUER
LACQUER - LACKER
LAIN - LANE
LANCE - LAUNCE
LANE - LAIN

LAUD - LORD
LAUNCE - LANCE
LAW - LORE
LAY - LEI,LEY
LAYS - LAZE
LAZE - LAYS
LEAD - LED
LEAF - LIEF
LEAH - LEAR, LEER, LEHR
LEAK - LEEK
LEANT - LENT
LEAR - LEAH, LEER, LEHR
LED - LEAD
LEEK - LEAK
LEER - LEAH, LEAR, LEHR
LEHR - LEAH, LEAR, LEER
LEI - LAY, LEY
LEMAN
LEMON
LEMON - LEMAN
LENT - LEANT
LESSEN - LESSON
LESSON - LESSEN
LEY - LAY, LEI
LIAR - LYRE
LIEF - LEAF
LINCS - LINKS, LYNX
LINKS - LINCS, LYNX
LOAD - LODE
LOAN - LONE
LODE - LOAD
LONE - LOAN
LORD - LAUD
LORE - LAW
LUMBAR - LUMBER
LUMBER - LUMBAR
LYMX - LINCS, LINKS
LYRE - LIAR
MA - MAAR, MAR
MADE - MAID
MAID - MADE
MAIL - MALE
MAIN - MAINE , MANE
MAINE - MAIN, MANE
MAIZE - MAZE
MALE - MAIL
MALL - MAUL
MANE - MAIN, MAINE
MANNA - MANNER, MANOR
MANNER - MANNA, MANOR
MANOR - MANNA, MANNER
MAR - MA, MAAR
MARC - MARK, MARQUE
MARQUE - MARC, MARK
MARQUEE - MARQUIS
MARQUIS - MARQUEE
MAUL - MALL
MAW - MOR, MORE, MOOR
MAYOR - MARE
MAZE - MAIZE
MEAN - MESNE, MIEN
MEAT - MEET, METE
MEDAL - MEDDLE
MEDDLE - MEDAL
MEET - MEAT, METE
MESNE - MIEN, MEAN
METAL - METTLE
METE - MEAT, MEET
METTLE - METAL
MEWS - MUSE
MIEN - MESNE, MEAN
MIGHT - MITE
MINER - MINOR
MINOR - MINER
MITE - MIGHT
MOAN - MOWN
MOAT - MOTE
MOCHA - MOCKER
MOCKER - MOCHA
MOOR - MAW, MOR, MORE
MOOSE - MOUSSE
MOR - MAW, MORE, MOOR
MORE - MAW, MORE, MOOR
MORN - MOURN
MORNING - MOURNING
MOTE - MOAT
MOURN - MORN
MOURNING - MORNING
MOUSSE - MOOSE
MOWN - MOAN
MUSCLE - MUSSEL
MUSE - MEWS
MUSSEL - MUSCLE
NAE - NAY, NEAGH, NEIGH, NEY
NEAGH - NAE, NAY, NEIGH, NEY
NEED - KNEAD
NEIGH - NAE, NAY, NEAGH
NEY
NEUK - NUKE
NEW - KNEW, NU
NEY - NAE, NAY, NEAGH, NEIGH
NIGH - NYE
NIGHT - KNIGHT
NIGHTLY - KNIGHTLY
NIT - KNIT
NO - KNOW, NOH
NOES - KNOWS, NOSE
NOH - KNOW, NO
NONE - NUN
NOR - GNAW
NOSE - KNOWS, NOES
NOUGHT - NAUGHT

NU - KNEW, NEW
NUKE - NEUK
NUN - NONE
NYE - NIGH
OAR - AWE, O'ER, ORE
O'ER - AWE, OAR, ORE
OFFA - OFFER
OFFER - OFFA
OH - OWE
ORAL - AURAL
ORC - AUK
ORE - AWE, OAR, O'RE
ORLE - ALL, AWL
OSTIA - AUSTERE
OUR - HOUR
OURS - HOURS
OUT - OWT
OVA - OVER
OWE - OH
OWT - OUT
PA - PAH, PAR, PARR, PAS
PACKED - PACT
PAH - PA, PAR, PARR, PAS
PAIL - PALE
PAIR - PARE, PEAR
PALATE - PALETTE, PALLET
PANDA - PANDER
PANDER - PANDA
PAR - PA, PAH, PARR, PAS
PARE - PEAR, PAIR
PARR - PA, PAH, PAR, PAS
PAS - PA, PAH, PAR, PARR
PAW - POOR, PORE, POUR
PAWKY - PORKY
PAWN - PORN
PEA - PEE
PEACE - PIECE
PEAK - PIQUE
PEAKE - PEEK, PEKE
PEAL - PEEL
PEAR - PARE, PAIR
PEARL - PURL
PEARLER - PURLER
PEDAL - PEDDLE
PEDDLE - PEDAL
PEE - PEA
PEEK - PEAKE, PEKE
PEEL - PEAL
PEKE - PEAKE, PEEK
PER - PURR
PETREL - PETROL
PETROL - PETREL
PHARAOH - FARO
PHASE - FAZE
PHEW - FEU, FEW
PHIZ - FIZZ
PI - PIE, PYE
PIE - PI, PYE
PIECE - PEACE
PILATE - PILOT
PILOT - PILATE
PIQUE - PEAK
PLACE - PLAICE
PLAICE - PLACE
PLAIN - PLANE
PLANE - PLAIN
POLE - POLL
POLL - POLE
POMACE - PUMICE
POMMEL - PUMMEL
POOR - PAW, PORE, POUR
PORKY - PAWKY
PORN - PAWN
POUR - PAW, POOR, PORE
PRAY - PREY
PREY - PRAY
PRINCIPAL - PRINCIPLE
PRINCIPLE - PRINCIPAL
PROFIT - PROPHET
PROPHET - PROFIT
PSALTER - SALTER
PUCKA - PUCKER
PUCKER - PUCKA
PUMICE - POMACE
PUMMEL - POMMEL
PURL - PEARL
PURLER - PEARLER
PURR - PER
PYE - PI, PIE
QUAY - KEY
QUEUE - KEW, KYU
QUIRE - CHOIR
RACK - WRACK
RACKET - RACQUET
RACQUET - RACKET
RAIN - REIGN, REIN
RAINS - REINS
RAISE - RASE
RAW - ROAR
READ - REDE, REED
REED - READ, REED
REEK - WREAK
REIGN - RAIN, REIN
REIN - RAIN, REIGN
REINS - RAINS
RENNES - WREN
RETCH - WRETCH
REVERE - REVERS
REVERS - REVERE
RHEUM - ROOM
RHEUMY - ROOMY
RHO - ROW, ROE

RHÔNE - ROAN, RONE
RIGHT - RITE, WRIGHT, WRITE
RING - WRING
RINGER - WRINGER
RITE - RIGHT, WRIGHT, WRITE
ROAM - ROME
ROAN - RHÔNE, RONE
ROAR - RAW
ROE - RHO, ROW
ROLE - ROLL
ROLL - ROLE
ROME - ROAM
RONE - RHÔNE, ROAN
ROOD - RUDE
ROOM - RHEUM
ROOMY - RHEUMY
ROOSE - RUSE
ROOT - ROUTE
RORT - WROUGHT
ROTE - WROTE
ROUGH - RUFF
ROUTE - ROOT
ROW - RHO, ROE
RUDE - ROOD
RUFF - ROUGH
RUNG - WRUNG
RUSE - ROOSE
RYE - WRY
SAIL - SALE
SAIN - SANE, SEINE
SALE - SAIL
SALTER - PSALTER
SANE - SAIN, SEINE
SAUCE - SOURCE
SAUT - SORT, SOUGHT
SAW - SOAR, SORE
SAWN - SORN
SCENE - SEEN
SCENT - CENT, SENT
SCULL - SKULL
SEAM - SEEM
SEAR - CERE, SEER
SEED - CEDE
SEEDER - CEDAR
SEEK - SEIK, SIKH
SEEL - CEIL, SEAL
SEEM - SEAM
SEEN - SCENE
SEER - CERE, SEAR
SEIK - SEEK, SIKH
SEINE - SAIN, SANE
SELL - CELL, SZELL
SELLER - CELLAR
SENSOR - CENSER, CENSOR
SENT - CENT, SCENT
SERF - SURF
SERGE - SURGE
SERIAL - CEREAL
SESSION - CESSION
SEW - SO, SOH, SOW
SEWN - SONE, SOWN
SHAKE - SHEIK
SHEIK - SHAKE
SHIER - SHYER, SHIRE
SHIRE - SHIER, SHYER
SHOE - CHOU, SHOO
SHOO - CHOU, SHOE
SHOOT - SHUTE, CHUTE
SHOT - SHOTT, CHOTT
SHOTT - SHOT, CHOTT
SHUTE - SHOOT, CHUTE
SHYER - SHIER, SHIRE
SIGHT - CITE, SITE
SIGN - SYN
SIGNET - CYGNET
SIKH - SEEK, SEIK
SIOUX - SOU
SITE - CITE, SIGHT
SKULL - SCULL
SKY - SKYE
SKYE - SKY
SLAY - SLEIGH
SLEAVE - SLEEVE
SLEEVE - SLEAVE
SLEIGH - SLAY
SLOE - SLOW
SLOW - SLOE
SO - SEW, SOH, SOW
SOAR - SAW, SORE
SOH - SEW, SO, SOW
SOLE - SOUL
SOME - SUM
SON - SUN, SUNN
SONE - SEWN, SOWN
SONNY - SUNNI, SUNNY
SORE - SAW, SOAR
SORN - SAWN
SORT - SAUT, SOUGHT
SOU - SIOUX
SOUGHT - SAUT, SORT
SOUL - SOLE
SOURCE - SAUCE
SOW - SEW, SO, SOH
SOWN - SEWN, SONE
STAIR - STARE
STAKE - STEAK
STALK - STORK
STARE - STAIR
STEAK - STAKE
STEAL - STEEL
STEEL - STEAL
STOREY - STORY

STORK - STALK
STORY - STOREY
SUITE - SWEET
SUM - SOME
SUN - SON, SUNN
SUNDAE - SUNDAY
SUNDAY - SUNDAE
SUNN - SON, SUN
SUNNI - SONNY, SUNNY
SUNNY - SONNY, SUNNI
SURF - SERF
SURGE - SERGE
SWAT - SWOT
SWEET - SUITE
SWOT - SWAT
SYMBOL - CYMBAL
SYN - SIGN
SZELL - CELL, SELL
TACIT - TASSET
TAI - TAILLE, THAI, TIE
TAIL - TALE
TAILLE - TAI, THAI, TIE
TALE - TAIL
TALK - TORC, TORQUE
TARE - TEAR
TASSET - TACIT
TAUGHT - TAUT, TORT, TORTE
TAUT - TAUGHT, TORT, TORTE
TEA - TEE, TI
TEAM - TEEM
TEAR - TARE
TEE - TEA, TI
TEEM - TEAM
TENNER - TENOR
TENOR - TENNER
TERNE - TURN
THAI - TAI, TAILLE, TIE
THAW - THOR
THEIR - THERE, THEY'RE
THERE - THEIR, THEY'RE
THEY'RE - THEIR, THERE
THOR - THAW
THREW - THOUGH, THRU
THROE - THROW
THRONE - THROWN
THROUGH - THREW, THRU
THROW - THROE
THROWN - THRONE
THRU - THREW, THROUGH
THYME - TIME
TI - TEA, TEE
TIC - TICK
TICK - TIC
TIDE - TIED
TIE - TAI, TAILLE, THAI
TIED - TIDE
TIER - TIRE, TYRE
TIGHTEN - TITAN
TMBER - TIMBRE
TIMBRE - TIMBER
TIME - THYME
TIRE - TIER, TYRE
TITAN - TIGHTEN
TO - TOO, TWO
TOAD - TOED, TOWED
TOO - TO, TWO
TOR - TORE
TORC - TALK,TORQUE
TORE - TOR
TORQUE - TALK, TORC
TORT - TAUGHT, TAUT, TORTE
TORTE - TAUGHT, TAUT, TORT
TOW - TOE
TOWED - TOAD, TOED
TROOP - TOUPE
TROUPE - TROOP
TUNA - TUNER
TUNER - TUNA
TURN - TERNE
TWO - TO, TOO
TYRE - TIER, TIRE
UR - ERR
URN - EARN
VAIL - VALE, VEIL
VAIN - VANE, VEIN
VALE - VAIL, VEIL
VANE - VAIN, VEIN
VELD - FELT, VELDT
VELDT - FELT, VELD
WAE - WAY, WHEY
WAIL - WHALE
WAIN - WANE, WAYNE
WAR - WAUGH, WAW, WORE
WARE - WEAR, WHERE
WARN - WORN
WASTE - WAIST
WATT - WHAT, WOT
WAUGH - WAR, WAW, WORE
WAVE - WAIVE
WAW - WAR, WAUGH, WORE
WAY - WAE, WHEY
WAYNE - WAIN, WANE
WEAK - WEEK
WEAKLY - WEEKLY
WEAR - WARE, WHERE
WEAVE - WE'VE
WHALE - WAIL
WHAT - WATT, WOT
WHEAL - WEEL, WE'LL, WHEEL
WHEEL - WEEL, WE'LL, WHEAL
WHEN - WEN
WHERE - WARE, WEAR

WHEY - WAE, WAY
WHICH - WITCH
WHINE - WINE
WHIRR - WERE
WHITE - WIGHT, WITE
WHITHER - WITHER
WHO - HOO
WHOA - WO, WOE
WHOLE - HOLE
WHORE - HAW, HOAR
WIGHT - WHITE, WITE
WINE - WHINE
WITCH - WHICH
WITE - WHITE, WIGHT
WITHER - WHITHER
WO - WHOA, WOE
WOE - WHOA, WO
WORE - WAR, WAUGH, WAW
WORN - WARN
WOT - WATT, WHAT
WRACK - RACK
WRAP - RAP
WRAPPED - RAPT
WREAK - REEK
WRECK - RECK
WREN - RENNES
WRETCH - RETCH
WRIGHT - RIGHT, RITE, WRITE
WRING - RING
WRINGER - RINGER
WRITE - RIGHT, RITE, WRIGHT
WROTE - ROTE
WROUGHT - RORT
WRUNG - RUNG
WRY - RYE
YAW - YORE, YOUR
YAWS - YOURS
YEW - EWE, YOU
YOKE - YOLK
YORE - YAW, YOUR
YOU - EWE, YEW
YOU'LL - YULE
YOUR - YAW, YORE
YOURS - YAWS
YULE - YOU'LL

TWO-WORD PHRASES

FIRST WORD

A

ABERDEEN - ANGUS, TERRIER
ABLE - BODIED, RATING, SEAMAN
ABSOLUTE - ALCOHOL, HUMIDITY, JUDGEMENT, MAGNITUDE, MAJORITY, MONARCHY, MUSIC, PITCH, TEMPERATURE, THRESHOLD, UNIT, VALUE, ZERO
ABSTRACT - EXPRESSIONISM, NOUN
ACCESS - ROAD, TIME
ACCOMMODATION - ADDRESS, BILL, LADDER, PLATFORM
ACHILLES - HEEL, TENDON
ACID - DROP, RAIN, ROCK, SOIL, TEST, VALUE,
ACT - AS, FOR, ON, OUT, UP
ACTION - COMMITTEE, GROUP, PAINTING, POTENTIAL, REPLAY, STATIONS
ACTIVE - CENTRE, LIST, SERVICE, TRANSPORT, VOCABULARY, VOLCANO
ADMIRALITY - BOARD, HOUSE, ISLANDS, MILE, RANGE
ADVANCE - BOOKING, COPY, GUARD, MAN, NOTICE, POLL, RATIO
AEOLIAN - DEPOSITS, HARP, ISLANDS, MODE
AFRICAN - LILY, MAHOGANY, VIOLET, TIME
AGONY - AUNT, COLUMN
AIR - ALERT, BAG, BED, BLADDER, BRAKE, BRIDGE, COMMODORE, CONDITIONING, CORRIDOR, COVER CURTAIN, CUSHION, CYLINDER, DAM, EMBOLISM, FORCE, GAS, GUN, HARDENING, HOLE, HOSTESS, JACKET, LETTER, MAIL, MARSCHAL, MASS, MILE, OFFICER, PLANT, POCKET, POWER, PUMP, RAID, RIFLE, SAC, SCOOP, SCOUT, SHAFT, SHOT, SOCK, SPRAY, SPRING, STATION, TERMINAL, TRAFFIC, TURBINE, VALVE, VICE-MARSHAL
ALL - BLACK, CLEAR, FOURS, HAIL, IN, ONE, OUT, RIGHT, SQUARE, THERE, TOLD
ALPHA - CENTAURI, HELIX, IRON, PARTICLE, PRIVATIVE, RAY, RHYTHM
ALTAR - BOY, CLOTH, PIECE
AMERICAN - ALOE, CHAMELEON, CHEESE, CLOTH, EAGLE, FOOTBALL, INDIAN, PLAN, REVOLUTION
ANCHOR - MAN, PLATE, RING
ANCIENT - GREEK, HISTORY, LIGHTS, MONUMENT
ANGEL - CAKE, DUST, FALLS, FOOD, SHARK
ANGLE - BRACKET, DOZER, IRON, PLATE
ANIMAL - HUSBANDRY, KINGDOM, MAGNETISM, RIGHTS, SPIRITS, STARCH
ANT - BEAR, BIRD, COW, EATER, HEAP, HILL
APPLE - BLIGHT, BOX, BRANDY, BUTTER, GREEN, ISLE, JACK, MAGGOT, POLISHER, SAUCE
ARCTIC - CHAR, CIRCLE, FOX, HARE, OCEAN, TERN, WILLOW
ART - DECO, FORM, NOUVEAU, PAPER
ARTIFICIAL - INSEMINATION, INTELLIGENCE, RESPIRATION
ASH - BLOND, CAN, WEDNESDAY, TRAY
ATOMIC - AGE, CLOCK, COCKTAIL, ENERGY, HEAT, MASS, NUMBER, PILE, POWER, STRUCTURE, THEORY, VOLUME, WEIGHT
AUTOMATIC - CAMERA, PILOT, REPEAT, TRANSMISSION, TYPESETTING

B

BABY - BOOM, BUGGY, CARRIAGE, GRAND, SNATCHER, TALK, TOOTH
BACK - BOILER, BURNER, COUNTRY, DOOR, DOWN, END, LIGHT, LIST, MARKER, MATTER, OUT, PASSAGE, PAT, REST, ROOM, SEAT, STRAIGHT, UP, YARD
BAD - BLOOD, FAITH, LANDS, NEWS
BALL - BEARING, BOY, COCK, GAME, VALVE
BANANA - OIL, REPUBLIC, SKIN, SPLIT
BANK - ACCEPTANCE, ACCOUNT, ANNUITIES, BILL, CARD, CLERK, DISCOUNT, HOLIDAY, MANAGER, ON RATE, STATEMANT
BAR - BILLIARDS, CHART, CODE, FLY, GIRL, GRAPH, MITZVAH, SINISTER

BARLEY - SUGAR, WATER, WINE
BARN - DANCE, DOOR, OWL, SWALLOW
BASE - LOAD, METAL, RATE
BASKET - CASE, CHAIR, HILT, MAKER, WEAVE
BATH - BUN, CHAIR, CHAP, CUBE, SALTS, STONE
BATTLE - CRUISER, CRY, FATIGUE, ROYAL
BAY - LEAF, LYNX, RUM, STREET, TREE, WINDOW
BEACH - BALL, BOYS, BUGGY, FLEA, PLUM
BEAR - DOWN, GARDEN, HUG, OFF, OUT, UP, WITH
BEAUTY - QUEEN, SALON, SLEEP, SPOT
BED - JACKET, LINEN
BELL - BRONZE, BUOY, GLASS, HEATHER, JAR, MAGPIE, METAL, MOTH, PULL, PUNCH, PUSH, SHEEP, TENT
BELLY - DANCE, FLOP, LANDING, LAUGH
BERMUDA - GRASS, RIG, SHORTS, TRIANGLE
BEST - BOY, END, GIRL, MAN, SELLER
BICYCLE - CHAIN, CLIP, PUMP
BIG - APPLE, BAND, BANG, BEN, BERTHA, BROTHER, BUSINESS, CHEESE, CHIEF, DEAL, DIPPER, END, SCREEN, SHOT, STICK, TIME, TOP, WHEEL
BINARY - CODE, DIGIT, FISSION, FORM, NOTATION, NUMBER, STAR, WEAPON
BIRD - CALL, CHERRY, DOG, PEPPER, SPIDER, STRIKE, TABLE
BIRTH - CERTIFICATE, CONTROL, RATE
BIRTHDAY - HONOURS, SUIT,
BIT - PART, RATE, SLICE
BITTER - APPLE, END, LAKES, ORANGE, PRINCIPLE
BLACK - ART, BEAN, BEAR, BEETLE, BELT, BILE, BODY, BOOK, BOTTOM, BOX, COUNTRY, DEATH, DIAMOND, ECONOMY, EYE, FLY, FOREST, FRIAR, FROST, HILLS, HOLE, ICE, MAGIC, MARIA, MARK, MARKET, MASS, MONK, MOUNTAINS, PANTHER, PEPPER, PRINCE, PUDDING, ROD, ROT, SEA, SHEEP, SPOT, SWAN, TIE, TREACLE, VELVET,WATCH, WIDOW
BLANK - CARTRIDGE, CHEQUE, ENDORSEMENT, VERSE
BLANKET - BATH, FINISH, STITCH
BLIND - ALLEY, DATE, FREDDIE, GUT, SNAKE, SPOT, STAGGERS, STAMPING
BLISTER - BEETLE, COPPER, PACK, RUST
BLOOD - BANK, BATH, BROTHER, CELL, COUNT, DONOR, FEUD, GROUP, HEAT, MONEY, ORANGE, POISONING, PRESSURE, PUDDING, RED, RELATION, SPORT, STONE, TEST, TYPE, VESSEL
BLUE - BABY, BAG, BILLY, BLOOD, CHEESE, CHIP, DEVILS, ENSIGN, FUNK, GUM, JAY, MOON, MOUNTAINS, MOVIE, MURDER, NILE, PENCIL, PETER, RIBAND, RIBBON, VEIN
BOARDING - HOUSE, OUT, SCHOOL
BOAT - DECK, DRILL, NECK, PEOPLE, RACE, TRAIN
BOBBY - CALF, PIN, SOCKS
BODY - BLOW, BUILDING, CAVITY, CORPORATE, IMAGE, LANGUAGE, POPPING, SHOP, SNACHER, STOCKING, WARMER
BOG - ASPHODEL, COTTON, DEAL, DOWN, IN, MOSS, MYRTLE, OAK, ORCHID, RUSH, STANDARD
BON - MOT, TON, VIVANT, VOYAGE
BONE - ASH, CHINA, IDLE, MEAT, OIL, UP
BOOBY - HACH, PRIZE, TRAP
BOOK - CLUB, END, IN, INTO, OUT, SCORPIAN, TOKEN, UP
BOTTLE - GOURD, GREEN, OUT, PARTY, TREE, UP
BOTTOM - DRAWER, END, HOUSE, LINE, OUT
BOW - LEGS, OUT, TIE, WINDOW
BOWLING - ALLEY, CREASE, GREEN
BOX - CAMERA, COAT, ELDER, GIRDER, JELLYFISH, NUMBER, OFFICE, PLEAT, SEAT, SPANNER, SPRING
BRAIN - CORAL, DEATH, DRAIN, FEVER, STEM, WAVE
BRAKE - BAND, DRUM, FLUID, HORSE POWER, LIGHT, LINING, PARACHUTE, SHOE, VAN
BRAND - IMAGE, LEADER, NAME
BRANDY - BOTTLE, BUTTER, SNAP
BRASS - BAND, FARTHING, HAT, NECK, RUBBING, TACKS
BREAK - DANCE, DOWN, EVEN, IN, INTO, OFF, OUT, THROUGH, UP, WITH
BRING - ABOUT, DOWN, FORWARD, IN, OFF, ON, OUT, OVER, ROUND, TO, UP
BRISTOL - BOARD, CHANNEL, FASHION
BROAD - ARROW, BEAN, CHURCH, GAUGE, JUMP, SEAL
BROWN - BEAR, BOMBER, BREAD, FAT,

OWL, PAPER, RICE, SAUCE, SHIRT, SNAKE, STUDY, SUGAR
BRUSSEL - CARPET, LACE, SPROUT
BUBBLE - BATH, CAR, CHAMBER, FLOAT, GUM, MEMORY, PACK, WRAP
BUCK - FEVER, RABBIT, UP
BUILDING - BLOCK, LINE, PAPER, SOCIETY
BULL - MASTIFF, NOSE, RUN, SESSION, SNAKE, TERRIER, TONGUE, TROUT
BURNT - ALMOND, OFFERING, SHALE, SIENNA, UMBER
BUS - BOY, LANE, SHELTER, STOP
BUTTER - BEAN, MUSLIN, UP
BUZZ - BOMB, OFF, SAW, WORD

C
CABBAGE - BUG, LETTUCE, MOTH, PALM, PALMETTO, ROSE, TREE, WHITE
CABIN - BOY, CLASS, CRUISER, FEVER
CABLE - CAR, RAILWAY, RELEASE, STITCH, TELEVISION
CALL - ALARM, BOX, DOWN, FORTH, GIRL, IN, LOAN, MONEY, NUMBER, OFF, OUT, RATE, SIGN, SLIP, UP
CAMP - DAVID, FOLLOWER, MEETING, OVEN, SITE
CANARY - CREEPER, GRASS, ISLANDS, SEED, YELLOW
CANTERBURY - BELL, LAMB, PILGRIMS
CAPE - BUFFALO, CART, COD, COLONY, COLOURED, DOCTOR, DUTCH, FLATS, GOOSEBERRY, HORN, JASMINE, PENINSULA, PIGEON, PRIMROSE, PROVINCE, SPARROW, TOWN, VERDE, YORK
CAPITAL - ACCOUNT, ALLOWANCE, ASSETS, EXPENDITURE, GAIN, GOODS, LEVY, MARKET, PUNISHMENT, SHIP, STOCK, SURPLUS
CARD - FILE, INDEX, PUNCH, READER, VOTE
CARDINAL - BEETLE, FLOWER, NUMBER, POINTS, SPIDER, VIRTUES
CARPET - BEETLE, KNIGHT, MOTH, PLOT, SHARK, SLIPPER, SNAKE, TILES
CARRIAGE - BOLT, CLOCK, DOG, LINE, TRADE
CARRIER - BAG, PIGEON, WAVE
CARRY - AWAY, BACK, FORWARD, OFF, ON, OUT, OVER, THROUGH
CARTRIDGE - BELT, CLIP, PAPER, PEN
CASH - CROP, DESK, DISCOUNT, DISPENSER, FLOW, IN, LIMIT, RATIO, REGISTER, UP
CAST - ABOUT, BACK, DOWN, IRON, ON, OUT, STEEL, UP
CAT - BURGLAR, DOOR, HOLE, LITTER, RIG, SCANNER
CATCH - BASIN, CROP, ON, OUT, PHRASE, PIT, POINTS, UP
CAULIFLOWER - CHEESE, EAR
CENTRE - BIT, FORWARD, HALF, PUNCH, SPREAD, THREE-QUARTER
CHAIN - DRIVE, GANG, GRATE, LETTER, LIGHTENING, MAIL, PRINTER, REACTION, RULE, SAW, SHOT, STITCH, STORE
CHAMBER - COUNSEL, MUSIC, ORCHESTRA, ORGAN, POT
CHARGE - ACCOUNT, DENSITY, HAND, NURSE, SHEET
CHEESE - CUTTER, MITE, SKIPPER, STRAW
CHICKEN - BREAST, FEED, LOUSE, OUT, WIRE
CHILD - ABUSE, BENEFIT, CARE, GUIDANCE, LABOUR, MINDER
CHIMNEY - BREAST, CORNER, STACK, SWALLOW, SWEEP, SWIFT
CHINA - ASTER, BARK, CAY, INK, ROSE, TREE
CHINESE - BLOCK, CABBAGE, CHEQUERS, CHIPPENDALE, EMPIRE, GOOSEBERRY, INK, LANTERN, LEAVES, PUZZLE, WALL, WAX, WHITE, WHISPERS, WINDLASS
CHIP - BASKET, HEATER, IN, LOG, PAN, SHOT
CHRISTMAS - BEETLE, BOX, CACTUS, CAKE, CARD, DISEASE, EVE, ISLAND, PUDDNG, ROSE, STOCKING, TREE
CIGARETTE - BUTT, CARD, END, HOLDER, LIGHTER, PAPER
CIRCUIT - BINDING, BOARD, BREAKER, JUDGE, RIDER, TRAINING
CITY - BLUES, COMPANY, DESK, EDITOR, FATHER, HALL, MANAGER, PLANNER, SLICKER
CIVIL - DEFENCE, DISOBEDIENCE, ENGINEER, LAW, LIBERTY, LIST, MARRIAGE, RIGHTS, SERVANT, SERVICE, WAR
CLAW - BACK, HAMMER, HATCHET, OFF, SETTING
CLOCK - GOLF, OFF, ON, UP

CLOSE - CALL, COMPANY, DOWN, HARMONY, IN, OUT, PUNCTUATION, QUARTER, SEASON, SHAVE, WITH
CLOSED - BOOK, CHAIN, CIRCUIT, CORPORATION, GAME, PRIMARY, SCHOLARSHIP, SENTENCE, SET, SHOP
CLOTHES - MOTH, PEG, POLE, PROP
CLUB - FOOT, HAND, MOSS, ROOT, SANDWICH
COAL - CELLAR, GAS, HEATER, HOLE, MEASURE, OIL, POT, SACK, SCUTTLE, TAR, TIT
COCONUT - BUTTER, ICE, MATTING, OIL, PALM, SHY
COFFEE - BAG, BAR, BEANS, CUP, GROUNDS, HOUSE, MACHINE, MILL, MORNING, NUT, PERCOLATOR, SHOP, TABLE, TREE
COLD - CALL, CHISEL, CREAM, CUTS, DUCK, FEET, FRAME, FRONT, SHOULDER, SNAP, SORE, STORAGE, SWEAT, TURKEY, WAR, WARRIOR, WAVE, WORK
COLLECTIVE - AGREEMENT, BARGAINING, FARM, FRUIT, NOUN, OWNERSHIP, SECURITY, UNCONSCIOUS
COLORADO - BEETLE, DESERT, FALLS, SPRINGS
COLOUR - BAR, CODE, CONTRAST, FILTER, GUARD, INDEX, LINE, PHASE, SCHEME, SERGEANT, SUPPLEMENT, TEMPERATURE
COME - ABOUT, ACROSS, ALONG, AT, AWAY, BETWEEN, BY, FORWARD, IN, INTO, OFF, OUT, OVER, ROUND, THROUGH, TO UP, UPON
COMIC - OPERA, STRIP
COMMAND - GUIDANCE, MODULE, PAPER, PERFORMANCE, POST
COMMERCIAL - ART, BANK, COLLEGE, PAPER, TRAVELLER, VEHICLE
COMMON - COLD, DENOMINATOR, ENTRANCE, ERA, FACTOR, FEE, FRACTION, GOOD, GROUND, KNOWLEDGE, LAW, MARKET, NOUN, ROOM, SENSE, STOCK, TIME
COMMUNITY - CARE, CENTRE, CHEST, SERVICE, SINGING
COMPOUND - EYE, FLOWER, FRACTION, FRACTURE, INTEREST, LEAF, NUMBER, SENTENCE, TIME
CON - AMORE, BRIO, DOLORE, ESRESSIONE, FUOCO, MAN, MOTO, ROD, SORDINO, SPIRITO, TRICK
CONTINENTAL - BREAKFAST, CLIMATE, DIVIDE, DRIFT, QUILT, SHELF, SYSTEM
CORAL - FERN, REEF, SEA, SNAKE, TREE
CORN - BORER, BREAD, BUNTING, DOLLY, EXCHANGE, FACTOR, LAWS, LILY, MARIGOLD, MEAL,OIL, PONE, POPPY, ROSE, ROW, SALAD, SHOCK, SHUCK, SILK, WHISKY
CORONA - AUSTRALIS, BOREALIS, DISCHARGE
COTTAGE - CHEESE, FLAT, HOSPITAL, INDUSTRY, LOAF, PIANO, PIE
COTTON - BELT, BUSH, CAKE, CANDY, FLANNEL, GRASS, ON, PICKER, SEDGE, STAINER, TO, WASTE, WOOL
COUGH - DROP, MIXTURE, UP
COUNTRY - CLUB, CODE, COUSIN, DANCE, HOUSE, MUSIC, SEAT
COURT - CARD, CIRCULAR, DRESS, MARTIAL, ROLL, ROOM, SHOE
COVER - CROP, GIRL, NOTE, PONT, STORY, VERSION
CRASH - BARRIER, DIVE, DUMMY, HELMET, OUT, PAID, VICTIM
CREAM - CHEESE, CRACKER, PUFF, SAUCE, SODA, TEA
CREDIT - ACCOUNT, CARD, LINE, RATING, SQUEEZE, STANDING
CROCODILE - BIRD, CLIP, RIVER, SHOES, TEARS
CRYSTAL - BALL, GAZING, MICROPHONE, PALACE, PICK-UP, SET, VIOLET
CUCKOO - BEE, CLOCK, SHRIKE, SPIT
CURTAIN - CALL, LECTURE, SPEECH, WALL
CUSTARD - APPLE, PIE, POWDER
CUT - ACROSS, ALONG, DOWN, GLASS, IN, OFF, OUT, STRING, UP
CUTTY - GRASS, SARK, STOOL

D

DANISH - BLUE, LOAF, PASTRY
DARK - AGES, CONTINENT, GLASSES, HORSE, LANTERN, REACTION, STAR
DAVY - JONES, LAMP
DAY - BED, LILY, NAME, NURSERY, RELEASE, RETURN, ROOM, SCHOOL, SHIFT, TRIP
DE - FACTO, FIDE, LUXE, PROFUNDIS, RIGEUR, TROP,
DEAD - BEAT, CENTRE, DUCK, END,

FINISH, HAND, HEART, HEAT, LETTER, LOSS, MARCH, SEA, SET, WEIGHT
DEATH - ADDER, CAMP, CAP, CELL, CERTIFICATE, DUTY, GRANT, KNELL, MASK, PENALTY, RATE, RATTLE, RAY, ROW, SEAT, VALLEY, WARRANT, WISH
DECIMAL - CLASSIFICATION, CURRENCY, FRACTION, PLACE, POINT, SYSTEM
DECK - CHAIR, HAND, OVER, TENNIS
DENTAL - CLINIC, FLOSS, HYGIENE, HYGIENIST, NURSE, PLAQUE, SURGEON
DESERT - BOOTS, COOLER, ISLAND, LYNX, OAK, PEA, RAT, SOIL
DIAMOND - ANNIVERSARY, BIRD, JUBILEE, POINT, SNAKE, WEDDING, WILLOW
DINNER - BREAK, JACKET, LADY, SERVICE, TIME
DIPLOMATIC - BAG, CORPS, IMMUNITY, SERVICE
DIRECT - ACCESS, ACTION, EVIDENCE, LABOUR, METHOD, OBJECT, QUESTION, SPEECH
DISC - BRAKE, FLOWER, HARROW, JOCKEY, PLOUGH, WHEEL
DISPATCH - BOX, CASE, RIDER
DOG - BISCUIT, BOX, COLLAR, DAYS, FENNEL, HANDLER, HOUSE, LATIN, PADDLE, ROSE, STAR, TAG, VIOLET
DONKEY - DERBY, ENGINE, JACKET, VOTE
DOUBLE - AGENT, BACK, BAR, BASS, BASSOON, BILL, BOND, CHIN, CREAM, CROSS, DUTCH, ENTENDRE, ENTRY, EXPOSURE, FAULT, FIRST, GLAZING, GLOUCESTER, KNIT, KNITTING, NEGATION, NEGATIVE, PNEUMONIA, STANDARD, TAKE, TALK, TIME, UP
DOWN - PAYMENT, TIME, UNDER
DRAWING - BOARD, CARD, PIN, ROOM
DRESS - CIRCLE, COAT, DOWN, PARADE, REHERSAL, SHIELD, SHIRT, SUIT, UNIFORM, UP
DRESSING - CASE, GOWN, ROOM, STATION, TABLE
DROP - AWAY, CANNON, CURTAIN, FORGE, GOAL, HAMMER, KICK, LEAF, OFF, OUT, SCONE, SHOT, TANK
DRUM - BRAKE, MAJOR, MAJORETTE, OUT, UP
DRY - BATTERY, CELL, DISTILLATION, DOCK, ICE, MARTINI, MEASURE, NURSE, OUT, ROT, RUN, UP
DUST - BOWL, COAT, COVER, DEVIL, DOWN, JACKET, SHOT, STORM
DUTCH - AUCTION, BARN, CAP, CHEESE, COURAGE, DOLL, DOOR, ELM, MEDICINE, OVEN, TREAT, UNCLE

E

EAR - LOBE, PIERCING, SHELL, TRUMPET
EARLY - BIRD, CLOSING, WARNING
EARTH - CLOSET, MOTHER, PILLAR, RETURN, SCIENCE, UP, WAX
EASTER - CACTUS, EGG, ISLAND, LILY
EASY - CHAIR, GAME, MEAT, MONEY, STREET
EGG - CUP, ROLL, SLICE, SPOON, TIMER, TOOTH, WHITE
ELECTRIC - BLANKET, BLUE, CHAIR, CHARGE, CONSTANT, CURRENT, EEL, EYE, FIELD, FIRE, FURNACE, GUITAR, HARE, NEEDLE, ORGAN, POTENTIAL, RAY, SHOCK, STORM
ELEPHANT - BIRD, GRASS, SEAL, SHREW
EVENING - CLASS, DRESS, PRIMROSE, STAR
EX - CATHEDRA, DIVIDEND, GRATIA, LIBRIS, OFFICIO
EYE - CONTACT, DOG, RHYME, SHADOW, SOCKET, SPLICE

F

FACE - CLOTH, OUT, PACK, POWDER, VALUE
FAIR - COPY, GAME, ISLE, PLAY, RENT, SEX
FAIRY - CYCLE, GODMOTHER, LIGHTS, PENGUIN, RING, SHRIMP, SWALLOW, TALE
FALL - ABOUT, AMONG, AWAY, BACK, BEHIND, DOWN, FOR, GUY, IN, OFF, ON, OVER, THROUGH, TO
FALSE - ALARM, COLOURS, DAWN, IMPRISONMENT, PRETENCES, STEP, TEETH
FAMILY - ALLOWANCE, BENEFIT, BIBLE, CIRCLE, DOCTOR, MAN, NAME, PLAN NING, SKELETON, TREE
FAN - BELT, CLUB, DANCE, HEATER, MAIL, VAULTING
FANCY - DRESS, GOODS, MAN, WOMAN
FAST - FOOD, LANE, MOVER, TALK
FATHER - CHRISTMAS, CONFESSOR, TIME

FIELD - ARMY, ARTILLERY, BATTERY, CENTRE, DAY, EMISSION, EVENT, GLASSES, HOSPITAL, MARSHALL, OFFICER, SPORTS, STUDY, TRIP, WORK
FIGURE - ON, OUT, SKATING
FILM - BUFF, LIBRARY, PACK, SET, STAR, STRIP
FILTER - BED, OUT, PAPER, PRESS, PUMP, TIP
FINGER - BOWL, PAINTING, POST, WAVE
FIRE - ALARM, ANT, AWAY, BRIGADE, CLAY, CONTROL, DEPARTMENT, DOOR, DRILL, ENGINE, ESCAPE, EXIT, HYDRANT, INSURANCE, IRONS, RAISER, SCREEN, SHIP, STATION, WALKING, WALL, WATCHER
FIRING - LINE, ORDER, PARTY, PIN, SQUAD
FIRST - AID, BASE, CLASS, FLOOR FRUITS, LADY, LANGUAGE, LIEUTENANT, LIGHT, MATE, NAME, NIGHT, OFFENEDER, OFFICER, PERSON, POST, PRINCIPLE, READING, REFUSAL, SCHOOL, WATER
FIVE - HUNDRED, NATIONS, STONES, TOWNS
FLAKE - OUT, WHITE
FLASH - BURN, CARD, ELIMINATOR, FLOOD, GUN, PHOTOGRAPHY, PHOTOLYSIS, POINT, SET, SMELTING
FLAT - CAP, KNOT, RACING, SPIN, TUNING
FLIGHT - ARROW, DECK, ENGINEER, FEATHER, FORMATION, LIEUTENANT, LINE, PATH, PLAN, RECORDER, SERGEANT, SIMULATOR, STRIP SURGEON
FLYING - BOAT, BOMB, BRIDGE, BUTTRESS, CIRCUS, COLOURS, DOCTOR, DUTCHMAN, FISH, FOX, FROG, JIB, LEMUR, LIZARD, MARE, OFFICER, PICKET, SAUCER, SQUAD, SQUIRREL, START, START, WING
FOLK - DANCE, MEDICINE, MEMORY, MUSIC, SINGER, SONG, TALE, WEAVE
FOOD - ADDITIVE, CHAIN, POISONING, PROCESSOR
FOOT - BRAKE, FAULT, ROT, RULE, SOLDIER
FOREIGN - AFFAIRS, AID, BILL, CORRESPONDANT, EXCHANGE, LEGION, MIISTER, MISSION, OFFICE, SERVICE
FOUL - PLAY, SHOT, UP
FOURTH - DIMENSION, ESTATE, INTERNATIONAL, REPUBLIC, WORLD
FREE - AGENT, ASSOCIATION, CHURCH, COUNTRY, ELECTRON, ENERGY, ENTERPRISE, FALL, FLIGHT, FORM, GIFT, HAND, HOUSE, KICK, LOVE, SPACE, SPEECH, STATE, THOUGHT, THROW, TRADE, VERSE, WILL, ZONE
FRENCH - ACADEMY, BEAN, BREAD, CHALK, CRICKET, CUFF, CURVE, DOORS, DRESSING, HORN, KISS, KNICKERS, KNOT, LEAVE, LETTER, MUSTARD, PLEAT, POLISH, SEAM, STICK, TOAST, WINDOWS
FRONT - BENCH, DOOR, LINE, MAN, DOOR
FRUIT - BAT, BODY, COCKTAIL, CUP, FLY, KNIFE, MACHINE, SALAD, SUGAR, TREE
FULL - BLOOD, BOARD, DRESS, HOUSE, MOON, NELSON, PITCH, STOP, TIME, TOSS

G

GALLEY - PROOF, SLAVE
GALLOWS - HUMOUR, TREE
GAME - BIRD, CHIPS, FISH, FOWL, LAWS, PARK, POINT, THEORY, WARDEN
GARDEN - CENTRE, CITY, CRESS, FLAT, FRAME, PARTY, SNAIL, SUBURB, WARBLER
GAS - BURNER, CHAMBER, CONSTANT, COOKER, ENGINE, EQUATION, FIRE, FIXTURE, GANGRENE, LAWS, LIGHTER, MAIN, MANTLE, MASK, METER, OIL, POKER, RING, STATION, TURBINE
GENERAL - ANAESHHETIC, ASSEMBLY, DELIVERY, ELECTION, HOSPITAL, PRACTITIONER, STAFF, STRIKE, SYNOD, WILL
GIN - PALACE, RUMMY, SLING
GINGER - ALE, BEER, GROUP, SNAP, UP, WINE
GIRL - FRIDAY, GUIDE, SCOUT
GIVE - AWAY, IN, OFF, ONTO, OUT, OVER, UP
GLAD - EYE, HAND, RAGS
GLOVE - BOX, COMPARTMENT, PUPPET
GOLD - BASIS, BEETLE, BRICK, CERTIFICATE, COAST, DUST, FOIL, LEAF, MEDAL, MINE, NOTE, PLATE, POINT, RECORD, RESERVE, RUSH, STANDARD, STICK
GOLDEN - AGE, ASTER, CALF, CHAIN,

DELICIOUS, EAGLE, FLEECE, GATE, GOOSE, HANDSHAKE, NUMBER, OLDIE, RETRIEVER, RULE, SECTION, SYRUP

GOLF - BALL, CLUB, COURSE, LINKS

GOOD - AFTERNOON DAY, EVENING, FRIDAY, MORNING, NIGHT, SAMARITAN, SORT, TURN

GOOSE - BARNACLE, BUMP, FLESH, STEP

GRAND - CANARY, CANYON, DUCHESS, DUCHY, DUKE, FINAL, GUIGNOL, JURY, LARCENY, MAL, MARINER, MASTER, NATIONAL, OPERA, PIANO, PRIX, SEIGNEUR, SIÈCLE, SLAM, TOUR

GRANNY - BOND, FLAT, KNOT, SMITH

GRASS - BOX, CLOTH, COURT, HOCKY, MOTH, ROOTS, SNAKE, TREE, WIDOW

GRAVY - BOAT, TRAIN

GREASE - CUP, GUN, MONKEY

GREAT - AUK, BEAR, BRITAIN, DANE, DIVIDE, LAKES, OUSE, PLAINS, SEAL, TIT, TREK, WAR

GREEN - BEAN, BELT, BERET, CARD, DRAGON, FINGERS, LIGHT, MONKEY, MOULD, PAPER, PEPPER, PLOVER, THUMB, TURTLE, WOODPECKER

GREGORIAN - CALENDER, CHANT, TELESCOPE, TONE

GREY - AREA, EMINENCE, FOX, FRIAR, MARKET, MATTER, SQUIRREL, WARBLER, WHALE, WOLF

GREGORIAN - CALENDER, CHANT, TELESCOPE, TONE

GROUND - CONTROL, COVER, ENGINEER, FLOOR, GLASS, ICE, IVY, PLAN, PLATE, PROVISIONS, RENT, RULE, SWELL

GROW - BAG, INTO, ON, UP

GUIDE - DOG, ROPE, WIRE

H

HAIR - DRYER, FOLLICLE, GEL, LACQUER, RESTORER. SHIRT, SLIDE, SPRAY, TRIGGER

HAPPY - EVENT, HOUR, MEDIUM, RELEASE

HARD - CASH, CHEESE, COPY, CORE, COURT, DISK, FEELING, HAT, HITTER, LABOUR, LINES, ROCK, SELL, SHOULDER, STANDING

HARVEST - HOME, MITE, MOON, MOUSE

HAT - STAND, TRICK

HATCHET - JOB, MAN

HEALTH - CENTRE, FOOD, VISITOR

HIGH - ALTAR, CHURCH, COMEDY, COMMAND, COMMISIONER, COUNTRY, COURT, DAY, EXPLOSIVE, FASHION, FIDELITY, GERMAN, HAT, HOLIDAYS, JINKS, JUMP, POINT, PRIEST, SCHOOL, SEAS, SEASON, SOCIETY, SPOT, STREET, TABLE, TEA, TECH, TECHNOLOGY, TIDE, TIME, TREASON, WATER, WIRE, WYCOMBE

HIGHLAND - CATTLE, DRESS, FLING, REGION

HIP - BATH, FLASK, HOP, JOINT, POCKET

HIT - LIST, MAN, OFF, ON, OUT, PARADE

HOLD - BACK, DOWN, FORTH, IN, OFF, ON, OUT, OVER, TOGETHER, WITH

HOLY - BIBLE, CITY, COMMUNION, DAY, FATHER, GHOST, GRAIL, ISLAND, JOE, LAND, MARY, OFFICE, ORDERS, PLACE, ROLLER, ROOD, SCRIPTURE, SEE, SEPULCHRE, SPIRIT, WAR, WTAER, WEEK, WRIT

HOME - AID, COUNTIES, ECONOMICS, FARM, GROUND, GUARD, HELP, LOAN, OFFICE, PLATE, RANGE, RULE, RUN, SECRETARY, STRAIGHT, TEACHER, TRUTH, UNIT

HORSE - AROUND, BEAN, BRASS, CHEST NUT, GUARD, LAUGH, MACKERAL, MARINE, MUSHROOM, NETTLE, OPERA, PISTOL, SENSE, TRADING

HOT - AIR, DOG, LINE, METAL, MONEY, PEPPER, POTATO, ROD, SEAT, SPOT, SPRING, STUFF, UP, ZONE

HOUSE - ARREST, GUEST, LIGHTS, MARTIN, MOTH, ORGAN, PARTY, PHYSICIAN, PLANT, SARROW, SPIDER

HUMAN - BEING, CAPITAL, INTEREST, NATURE, RESOURCES, RIGHTS

HURRICANE - DECK, LAMP

I

ICE - AGE, AXE, BAG, BLOCK, CREAM, FISH, HOCKEY, HOUSE, LOLLY, MACHINE, MAN, PACK, PICK, PLANT, POINT, SHEET, SHELF, SHOW, SKATE, STATION, WATER, YACHT

ILL - FEELING, HUMOUR, TEMPER, WILL

IN - ABSENTIA, AETERNUM, CAMERA, ESSE, EXTENSO, EXTREMIS, MEMORI AM, NOMINE, PERPETUUM, PERSONAM, RE, REM, SITU, TOTO, VACUO, VITRO, VIVO

INDIA - PAPER, PRINT, RUBBER

INDIAN - CLUB, EMPIRE, FILE, HEMP, INK, MALLOW, MILLET, MUTINY, OCEAN, RED, RESERVE, ROPE-TRICK, SUMMER
INNER - CITY, EAR, HEBRIDES, LIGHT, MAN, MONGOLIA ,TUBE
INSIDE - JOB, FORWARD, LANE, TRACK
IRISH - COFFEE, MOSS, POTATO, REPUBLIC, SEA, SETTER, STEW, TERRIER, WHISKEY, WOLFHOUND
IRON - AGE, CHANCELLOR, CROSS, CURTAIN, FILINGS, GUARD, HAND, HORSE, LUNG, MAIDEN, MA, OUT, PYRITES, RATIONS

J
JACK - FROST, IN, PLANE, RABBIT, ROBINSON, RUSSELL, TAR, UP
JAM - FULL, JAR, PACKED
JOB - CENTRE, DESCRIPTION
JUMPING - JACK
JUNK - BOX, MAIL

K
KICK - ABOUT, IN, OFF, OUT, PLEAT, TURN, UP, UPSTAIR
KID - AROUND, GLOVES
KIDNEY - BEAN, MACHINE, STONE, VETCH
KING - CUP, FISHER, PENGUIN, PIN, SIZED
KNIFE - EDGE, GRINDER, PLEAT, SWITCH

L
LADY - BOUNTIFUL, CHAPEL, DAY, FERN, MAYORESS, MUCK, ORCHID
LAND - AGENT, BANK, BRIDGE, CRAB, FORCES, GIRL, GRANT, LINE, MINE, OFFICE, RAIL, REFORM, TAX, UP, WITH
LAST - JUDGMENT, NAME, OUT, POST, QUARTER, RITES, STRAW, SUPPER, THING
LATIN - AMERICA, CROSS, QUARTER, SQUARE
LAY - ASIDE, AWAY, BROTHER, DAYS, DOWN, FIGURE, IN, INTO, OFF, ON, OUT, OVER, READER, TO, UP
LEADING - AIRCRAFTMAN, ARTICLE, DOG, EDGE, LIGHT, MAN, NOTE, QUESTION, REINS
LEAVE - BEHIND, OFF, OUT
LEFT - BANK, BEHIND, WING,
LEMON - BALM, CHEESE, CURD, DROP, FISH, GERANIUM, GRASS, JUICE, SOLE, SQUASH, SQUEEZER, VERBENA
LETTER - BOMB, BOX, CARD
LIBERTY - BELL, BODICE, CAP, HALL, HORSE, ISLAND, SHIP
LIE - DETECTOR, DOWN, IN, TO
LIFE - AMBITION, ASSURANCE, BELT, BUOY, CYCLE, EXPECTANCY, FORM, GUARDS, HISTORY, INSURANCE, INTEREST, JACKET, PEER, PRESERVER, RAFT, SCIENCE, SPAN, STYLE
LIGHT - BULB, FAC, FLYWEIGHT, HEAVY WEIGHT, HORSE, INTO, METER, MIDDLEWEIGHT, MUSIC, OPERA, OUT, SHOW, UP, WELTERWEIGHT, YEAR
LIVER - FLUKE, SALTS, SAUSAGE
LIVING - DEATH, FOSSIL, PICTURE, ROOM, WAGE
LOBSTER - MOTH, NEWBURG, POT, THERMIDOR
LOCAL - ANAESTHETIC, AUTHORITY, COLOUR, GOVERNMENT, TIME
LONE - HAND, WOLF
LONG - ARM, BEACH, FACE, HAUL, HOP, ISLAND, JENNY, JOHNS, JUMP, PLAYING, SHOT, SIGHTED, STANDING, SUIT, SUFFERING, TERM, TOM, VACATION, WEEKEND, WINDED
LOOK - AFTER, BACK, DOWN, ON, OVER, THROUGH, UP
LOOSE - CHANGE, COVER, END
LORD - ADVOCATE, CHAMBERLAIN, CHANCELLOR, LIEUTENANT, MAYOR, MUCK, PROTECTOR, PROVOST,
LOUNGE - LIZARD, SUIT
LOVE - AFFAIR, APPLE, CHILD, FEAST, GAME, KNOT, LETTER, LIFE, MATCH, NEST, POTION, SEAT, SET
LOW - CHURCH, COMEDY, COUNTRIES, FREQUENCY, PROFILE, TECH, TECHNOLOGY, TIDE
LUNAR - CAUSTIC, ECLIPSE, MODULE, MONTH, YEAR
LUNCHEON - CLUB, MEAT, VOUCHER

M
MACHINE - BOLT, GUN, HEAD, SHOP, TOOL
MACKERAL - BREEZE, SHARK, SKY
MAGIC - CARPET, EYE, LANTERN, MUSHROOM, NUMBER, SQUARE
MAGNETIC - CIRCUIT, COMPASS,

CONSTANT, DISK, EQUATOR, FIELD, FLUX, INDUCTION, INK, LENS, MOMENT, NEEDLE, NORTH, PICK-UP, POLE, STORM, TAPE
MAIDEN - NAME, OVER, VOYAGE
MAIL - DROP, ORDER
MAKE - AFTER, AWAY, BELIEVE, FOR, OF, OFF, OUT, OVER, WITH
MALT - EXTRACT, LIQUOR, WHISKY
MANDARIN - CHINESE, COLLAR, DUCK
MARCH - BROWN, HARE, PAST
MARKET - GARDEN, GARDENING, ORDER, PLACE, PRICE, RENT, RESEARCH, SHARE, TOWN, VALUE
MARRIGE - BUREAU, GUIDANCE
MARSH - ELDER, FERN, FEVER, GAS, HARRIER, HAWK, HEN, MALLOW,
MARIGOLD, ORCHID, TIT
MASTER - BUILDER, CYLINDER, KEY, RACE, SERGEANT
MATINÉE - COAT, IDOL, SHOW
MAUNDY - MONEY, THURSDAY
MAY - APPLE, BEETLE, BLOBS, BLOSSOM, DAY, QUEEN, TREE
MECHANICAL - ADVANTAGE, DRAWING, ENGINEERING, INSTRUMENT
MEDICAL - CERTIFICATE, EXAMINATION, EXAMINER, JURISPRUDENCE
MEDICINE - BALL, CHEST, LODGE, MAN
MELBA - SAUCE, TOAST
MEMORY - BANK, MAPPING, SPAN, TRACE
MENTAL - AGE, BLOCK, CRUELTY, DISORDER, HANDICAP
MERCHANT - BANK, NAVY, PRINCE, SHIP
MERCY - FLIGHT, KILLING, SEAT
MESS - ABOUT, HALL, JACKET, KIT
MICHAELMAS - DAISY, TERM
MICKEY - FINN, MOUSE
MIDDLE - AGE, AGES, C, CLASS, EAR, EAST, MANAGEMENT, NAME, SCHOOL, TEMPLE
MIDNIGHT - BLUE, SUN
MIDSUMMER - DAY, MADNESS
MILITARY - ACADEMY, HONOURS, LAW, ORCHID, PACE, POLICE
MILK - BAR, CHOCOLATE, FEVER, FLOAT, LEG, PUDDING, PUNCH, ROUND, RUN, SHAKE, STOUT, TOOTH
MINT - BUSH, JULEP, SAUCE,
MINUTE - GUN, HAND, MARK, STEAK
MIRROR - CANON, CARP, FINISH, IMAGE, LENS, SYMMETRY, WRITING
MITRE - BLOCK, BOX, GEAR, JOINT, SQUARE
MIXED - BAG, BLESSING, DOUBLES, ECONOMY, FARMING, GRILL, MARRIAGE, METAPHOR
MONEY - MARKET, ORDER, SPIDER, SUPPLY
MONKEY - BREAD, BUSINESS, CLIMB, FLOWER, JACKET, NUT, ORCHID, PUZZLE, SUIT, TRICKS, WRENCH
MORNING - COAT, DRESS, SICKNESS, STAR, TEA, WATCH
MOSQUITO - BITE, BOAT, HAWK, NET
MOSS - AGATE, LAYER, PINK, ROSE, STITCH
MOTHER - COUNTRY, GOOSE, HUBBARD, LODE, SHIP, SHIPTON, SUPERIOR, TONGUE, WIT
MOTOR - CARAVAN, DRIVE, GENERATOR, SCOOTER, VEHICLE, VESSEL
MOUNTAIN - ASH, CAT, CHAIN, DEVIL, COAT, LAUREL, LION, RANGE, SHEEP, SICKNESS
MUD - BATH, DAUBER, FLAT, HEN, MAP, PIE, PUPPY, TURTLE
MUSTARD - GAS, OIL, PLASTER, SEED
MYSTERY - PLAY, TOUR

N

NARROW - BOAT, GAUGE, SEAS
NATIONAL - ACCOUNTING, AGREEMENT, ANTHEM, ASSEMBLY, ASSISTANCE, DEBT, FRONT, GALLERY, GRID, SERVICE, TRUST
NERVE - CELL, CENTRE, FIBRE, GAS, IMPULSE
NEW - BROOM, FOREST, GUINEA, LOOK, MATHS, MOON, PENNY, TESTAMENT, TOWN, WAVE, WORLD, YEAR, YORK, ZEALAND
NEWS - AGENCY, CONFERENCE, FLASH, VENDOR
NIGHT - BLINDNESS, DANCER, FIGHTER, NURSE, OWL, ROBE, SAFE, SCHOOL, SHIFT, WATCH, WATCHMAN
NINETEETH - HOLE, MAN
NOBLE - ART, GAS, SAVAGE
NORFOLK - ISLAND, JACKET, TERRIOR
NOSE - CONE, DIVE, OUT, RAG, RING
NUCLEAR - BOMB, ENERGY, FAMILY, FISSION, FUEL, FUSION, ISOMER, PHYSICS, POWER, RESCTIO, REACTOR, THRESHOLD, WINTER

NURSERY - RHYME, SCHOOL, SLOPES, STAKES

O

OFF - CHANCE, COLOUR, KEY, LIMITS, LINE, SEASON

OIL - BEETLE, CAKE, DRUM, HARDENING, PAINT, PAINTING, PALM, RIG, RIVERS, SHALE, SLICK, VARNISH, WELL

OLD - BAILEY, BILL, BIRD, BOY, CONTEMPTIBLES, COUNTRY, GIRL, GOLD, GUARD, HAND, HAT, LADY, MAID, MAN, MOON, NICK, PRETENDER, SCHOOL, STYLE, TESTAMENT, WORLD

OLIVE - BRANCH, BROWN, CROWN, DRAB, GREEN, OIL, SKIN

ON - OFF, KEY, LINE

OPEN - AIR, BOOK, CHAIN, CIRCUIT, COURT, DAY, DOOR, HOUSE, LETTER, MARKET, PRISON, PUNCTUATION, QUESTION, SANDWICH, SESAME, UNIVERSITY, UP, VERDICT

OPERA - BUFF, CLOAK, GLASSES, HAT, HOUSE, SERIA

OPIUM - DEN, POPPY, WARS

ORANGE - BLOSSOM, PEEL, PEKOE, STICK

ORDINARY - LEVEL, RATING, RAY, SEAMAN, SHARES

OXFORD - ACCENT, BAGS, BLUE, ENGLISH, FRAME, GROUP, MOVEMENT, UNIVERSITY

OYSTER - BED, CRAB, PINK, PLANT, WHITE

P

PACK - ANIMAL, DRILL, ICE, IN, RAT, UP

PALM - BEACH, CIVET, OFF, OIL, SUGAR, SUNDAY, VAULTING, WINE

PANAMA - CANAL, CITY, HAT

PANIC - ATTACK, BOLT, BUTTON, BUYING, STATIONS

PAPER - CHASE, FILIREE, MONEY, MULBERRY, NAUTILUS, OVER, TAPE, TIGER

PAR - AVION, EXCELLENCE, VALUE

PARISH - CHURCH, CLERK, COUNCIL, PUMP, REGISTER

PARTY - BAG, DRESS, LINE, MAN, POLITICS, WALL

PASSING - BELL, NOTE, PLACE, SHOT

PASSION - FRUIT, PLAY, SUNDAY, WEEK

PATCH - BOARD, POCKET, QUILT, TEST

PAY - BACK, BED, DIRT, DOWN, FOR, IN, OFF, OUT, PACKET, TELEVISION, UP

PEACE - CORPS, OFFERING, PIPE, RIVER, SIGN

PEG - CLIMBING, DOWN, LEG, OUT, TOP

PEN - FRIEND, NAME, PAL

PENNY - ARCADE, BLACK, FARTHING, TRAY, WHISTLE

PER - ANNUM, CAPITA, CENT, CONTRA, DIEM, MENSEM, MILL, PRO, SE

PERSIAN - BLINDS, CARPET, CAT, EMPIRE, GREYHOUND, GULF, LAMB, MELON, RUG

PETIT - BOURGEOIS, FOUR, JURY, LARCENY, MAL, POINT

PETROL - BOMB, CAN, PUMP, STATION

PETTY - CASH, JURY, LARCENY, OFFICER, SESSIONS

PICTURE - CARD, FRAME, HAT, HOUSE, MOULDING, PALACE, WINDOW, WRITING

PIECE - GOODS, OUT, RATE

PILLOW - BLOCK,.FIGHT, LACE, LAVA, SHAM, TALK

PILOT - BALLOON, BIRD, BISCUIT, CLOTH, ENGINE, FILM, FISH, HOUSE, LAMP, LIGHT, OFFICER, PLANT, STUDY, WHALE

PIN - CURL, DOWN, JOINT, MONEY, RAIL, TUCK, WRENCH

PINE - CONE, END, MARTEN, NEEDLE, TAR

PINK - ELEPHANTS, GIN, NOISE, SALMON, SLIP

PIPE - CLEANER, DOWN, DREAM, MAJOR, ORGAN, ROLL, UP

PLACE - CARD, KICK, NAME, SETTING

PLAIN - CHOCOLATE, CLOTHES, FLOUR, SAILING, TEXT

PLAY - ALONG, DOWN, OFF, ON, OUT, UP, WITH

PLYMOUTH - BRETHEREN, COLONY, ROCK

POCKET - BATTLESHIP, BILLIARDS, BOROUGH, GOPHER, MONEY, MOUSE

POETIC - JUSTICE, LICENCE

PONY - EXPRESS, TREKKING

POOR - BOX, LAW, MOUTH, RELATION, WHITE

POP - ART, OFF, SHOP, SOCKS, STAR

POST - CHAISE, HOC, HORN, HOUSE, MERIDIEM, OFFICE

POT - CHEESE, LIQOUR, MARIGOLDON, PLANT, ROAST, SHOT, STILL

POTATO - BEETLE, BLIGHT, CHIP, CRISP
POWDER - BLUE, BURN, COMPACT, FLASK, HORN, KEG, MONKEY, PUFF, ROOM
POWER - CUT, DIVE, DRILL, FACTOR, LINE, PACK, PLANT, POINT, POLITICS, STATION, STEERING, STRUCTURE
PRARIE - DOG, OYSTER, PROVINCES, SCHOONER, SOIL, TURNIP, WOLF
PRAYER - BEADS, BOOK, MEETING, RUG, SHAWL,WHEEL
PRESS - AGENCY, AGENT, BOX, CONFERENCE, GALLERY, GANG, RELEASE, STUD
PRESSURE - CABIN, COOKER, DRAG, GAUGE, GRADIENT, GROUP, HEAD, POINT, SUIT
PRICE - COMMISSION, CONTROL, DIS CRIMINATION, RING, SUPPORT, TAG, WAR
PRICKLY - ASH, HEAT, PEAR, POPPY
PRIME - COST, MERIDIAN, MINISTER, MOVER, NUMBER, RATE, TIME, VERTICAL
PRIVATE - BAR, BILL, COMPANY, DETECTIVE, ENTERPRISE, EYE, HOTEL, INCOME, LANGUAGE, LIFE, MEMBER, PARTS, PATIENT, PRACTICE, PRESS, PROPERTY, SCHOOL, SECRETARY, SECTOR
PRIVY - CHAMBER, COUNCIL, PURSEM, SEAL
PRIZE - COURT, MONEY, RING
PRO - FORMA, PATRIA, RATA, TEMPORE
PUBLIC - BAR, BILL, COMPANY, CONVENIENCE, CORPORATION, DEBT, DEFENDER, ENEMY, ENTERPRISE, EXPENDITURE, FOOTPATH, GALLERY, HOLIDAY, HOUSE, LAW, NUISANCE, OPINION, OWNERSHIP, PROSECUTOR, RELATIONS, SCHOOL, SECTOR, SERVANT, SERVICE, SPEAKING, SPENDING, TRANSPORT
PUFF - ADDER, PASTRY
PULL - ABOUT, BACK, DOWN, IN, OFF, ON, OUT, THROUGH, TOGETHER, UP
PURPLE - EMPEROR, GALLINULE, HEART, MEDIC, PATCH
PUSH - ABOUT, ALONG, BUTTON, IN, OFF, ON, THROUGH
PUT - ACROSS, ASIDE, AWAY, BACK, BY, DOWN, FORTH, FORWARD, IN, OFF, ON, OUT, OVER, THROUGH, UP, UPON

Q

QUANTUM - LEAP, MECHANICS, NUMBER, STATE, STATISTICS, THEORY
QUARTER - CRACK, DAY, GRAIN, HORSE, NOTE, PLATE, ROUND, SECTION, SESSIONS, TONE
QUEEN - BEE, CONSORT, DOWAGER, MAB, MOTHER, OLIVE, POST, REGENT, REGNANT, SUBSTANCE
QUEER - FISH, STREET
QUESTION - MARK, MASTER, TIME

R

RAIN - CHECK, GAUGE, SHADOW, TREE
REAL - ALE, ESTATE, LIFE, NUMBER, PART, PRESENCE, PROPERTY, TENNIS, WAGES
RED - ADMIRAL, ALGAE, BAG, BARK, BEDS, BIDDY, CARPET, CEDAR, CROSS, DUSTER, DWARF, ENSIGN, FLAG, HAT, HEAT, HERRING, INDIAN, MEAT, MULLET, PEPPER, RAG, RIVER, ROSE, SALMON, SEA, SETTER, SHANK, SHIFT, SNAPPER, SPIDER, SQUIRREL, TAPE
RES - ADJUDICATA, GESTAE, JUDICATA, PUBLICA
RIGHT - ABOUT, ANGLE, ASCENTION, AWAY, HAND, HONOURABLE, OFF, ON,
REVEREND, WING
ROCK - BOTTOM, CAKE, CLIMBING, GARDEN, PLANT, SALT, STEADY
ROLLER - BEARING, CAPTION, COASTER, DERBY, SKATE, TOWEL
ROMAN - ARCH, CALENDAR, CANDLE, CATHOLIC, CATHOLICISM, COLLAR, EMPIRE, HOLIDAY, LAW, MILE, NOSE, NUMERALS
ROOF - GARDEN, RACK
ROOM - SERVICE, TEMPERATURE
ROOT - BEER, CANAL, CROP, NODULE, OUT, POSITION, UP
ROTARY - CLOTHSLINE, CLUB, ENGINE, PLOUGH, PRESS, PUMP
ROUGH - COLLIE, DIAMOND, OUT, PASSAGE, SPIN, STUFF, UP
ROUND - ANGLE, CLAM, DANCE, DOWN, HAND, OFF, IN, OUT, ROBIN, TABLE, TOP, TRIP, UP
ROYAL - ACADEMY, ASSENT, BLUE, BURGH, COMMISSION, ENGINEERS, FLUSH, HIGHNESS, ICING, JELLY, MARINES, NAVY, PURPLE, STANDARD, TENNIS, WARRANT, WORCESTER

RUBBER - BAND, BRIDGE, CEMENT, CHEQUE, GOODS, PLANT, STAMP, TREE
RUN - ACROSS, AFTER, ALONG, AROUND, AWAY, DOWN, IN, INTO, OFF, ON, OUT, OVER, THROUGH, TO, UP
RUNNING - BOARD, COMMENTARY, HEAD, LIGHT, MATE, REPAIRS, RIGGING, STITCH
RUSSIAN - DRESSING, EMPIRE, REVOLUTION, ROULETTE, SALAD, WOLFHOUND

S

SAFETY - BELT, CATCH, CHAIN, CURTAIN, FACTOR, FILM, FUSE, GLASS, LAMP, MATCH, NET, PIN, RAZOR, VALVE
SALAD - BOWL, DAYS, DRESSING
SALLY - ARMY, FORTH, LUNN
SALT- AWAY, BATH, CAKE, DOME, FLAT, LAKE, LICK, MARSH, OUT, PORK
SAND - BAR, CASTLE, DUNE, EEL, FLEA, HOPPER, LANCE, LEEK, LIZARD, MARTIN, PAINTING, SHRIMP, TABLE, TRAP, VIPER, WASP, WEDGE, YACHT
SANDWICH - BOARD, CAKE, COURSE, ISLANDS, MAN
SAUSAGE - DOG, ROLL
SCARLET - FEVER, HAT, LATTER, PIMPERNEL, RUNNER, WOMAN
SCATTER - CUSHIONS, DIAGRAM, PIN, RUG
SCOTCH - BROTH, EGG, MIST, PANCAKE,SNAP, TAPE, TERRIER
SCRAPE - IN, THROUGH, TOGETHER
SCRATCH - PAD, SHEET, TEST, TOGETHER, VIDEO
SECOND - CHILDHOOD, CLASS, COMING, COUSIN, FIDDLE, FLOOR, GENERATION, GROWTH, HAND, LANGUAGE, LIEUTENANT, MATE, NAME, NATURE, READING, SIGHT, STRING, THOUGHT, WIND
SEONDARY - COLOUR, EMISSION, PICKET, PROCESSES, QUALITIES, SCHOOL, STRESS
SECRET - AGENT, POLICE, SERVICE, SOCIETY
SEE - ABOUT, INTO, OF, OFF, OUT, OVER, THROUGH
SENIOR - AIRCRAFTMAN, CITIZEN, MANAGEMENT, SERVICE
SERVICE - AREA, CHARGE, INDUSTRY, MODULE, ROAD, STATION
SET - ABOUT, AGAINST, ASIDE, BACK, DOWN, FORTH, IN, OFF, ON, OUT, PIECE, POINT, SQUARE, THEORY, TO, UP, UPON
SETTLE - DOWN, FOR, IN, WITH
SHAKE - DOWN, OFF, UP
SHEET - ANCHOR, BEND, DOWN, LIGHTNING, METAL, MUSIC
SHOP - AROUND, ASSISTANT, FLOOR, STEWARD
SHORE - BIRD, LEAVE, PATROL
SHORT - CIRCUIT, CUT, USE, HEAD, LIST, ODDS, SHRIFT, STORY, STRAW, TIME, WAVE
SHOW - BILL, BUSINESS, CARD, COPY, OFF, STOPPER, TRIAL, UP
SIAMESE - CAT, TWINS
SICK - LEAVE, LIST, NOTE, PAY
SIGN - AWAY, IN, LANGUAGE, MANUAL, OFF, ON, OUT, UP
SINGLE - BOND, CREAM, DENSITY, ENTRY, FILE, TAX, THREAD, TICKET
SIT - BACK, DOWN, ON, OUT, OVER, UNDER, UP
SITTING - BULL, ROOM, TARGET, TENANT,
SKI - JUMP, LIFT, PANTS, RUN, STICK, TOW
SKIN - CREAM, DIVING, EFFECT, FLICK, FOOD, FRICTION, GAME, GRAFT, TEST
SLAVE - ANT, COAST, CYLINDER, DRIVER, SHIP, STATE, TRADE,
SLIDE - FASTENER, GUITAR, OVER, REST, RULE, TROMBONE, VALVE
SLIP - GAUGE, RAIL, RING, ROAD, STEP, STITCH, UP
SLOW - BURN, HANDCLAP, MARCH, MOTION, TIME
SMALL - ARMS, BEER, CHANGE, FRY, HOURS, INTESTINE, SLAM, TALK
SMART - ALECK, CARD, MONEY, SET
SMOKE - ALARM, BOMB, OUT, SCREEN, TREE
SNEAK - PREVIEW, THIEF
SOB - SISTER, STORY, STUFF
SOCIAL - CLIMBER, SCIENCE, SECRETARY, SECURITY, SERVICES, STUDIES, WELFARE, WORK
SODA - ASH, BISCUIT, BREAD, FOUNTAIN, JERK, LIME, NITRE, POP, SIPHON, WATER
SOFT - DRINK, FRUIT, FURNISHINGS, GOODS, LANDING, LINE, OPTION,

PORN, SELL, SELL, SOAP, SPOT, TOP, TOUCH
SOLAR - ECLIPSE, FLARE, FURNACE, HEATING, MONTH, MYTH, PANEL, PLEXUS, POWER, SYSTEM, WIND, YEAR
SOUND - BARRIER, BOW, CHECK, EFFECT, HEAD, HOLE, MIXER, OFF, OUT, WAVE
SOUR - CHERRY, CREAM, GOURD, GRAPES, GUM, MASH
SPACE - AGE, BLANKET, CADET, CAPSULE, CHARACTER, HEATER, INVADERS, OPERA, PLATFORM, PROBE, SHUTTLE, STATION
SPAGHETTI - JUNCTION, WESTERN
SPARK - CHAMBER, COIL, EROSION, GAP, OFF, PLUG, TRANSMITTER
SPEAK - FOR, OUT, TO, UP
SPECIAL - ASSESSMENT, BRANCH, CASE, CONSTABLE, DELIVERY, EFFECTS, JURY, LICENCE, PLEADING, PRIVILEGE, SCHOOL, SORT
SPEED - LIMIT, TRAP, UP
SPINNING - JENNY, MULE, TOP, WHEEL
SPIRIT - GUM, LAMP, LEVEL, VARNISH
SPLIT - CANE, DECISION, INFINITIVE, PEA, PERSONALITY, SECOND, SHIFT, TIN, UP
SPONGE - BAG, BATH, CAKE, CLOTH, DOWN
SPORTS - CAR, COAT, JACKET, SHIRT
SPRING - BALANCE, BOARD, CHICKEN, FEVER, LOCK, MATTRESS, ONION, ROLL, TIDE
SPUN - SILK, SUGAR, YARN
SQUARE - AWAY, BRACKET, DANCE, LEG, MEAL, NUMBER, OFF, ROOT, UP
STABLE - DOOR, FLY, LAD
STAFF - ASSOSIATION, COLLEGE, CORPORAL, NURSE, OFFICER, SERGEANT
STAG - BEETLE, PARTY
STAGE - DIRECTION, DOOR, EFFECT, FRIGHT, LEFT, MANAGER, RIGHT, WHISPER
STAMP - ACT, COLLECTING, DUTY, MILL, OUT
STAND - BY, DOWN, FOR, IN, OIL, ON, OUT, OVER, PAT, TO, UP
STAR - CHAMBER, CONNECTION, FISH, GRASS, LIGHT, SAPPHIRE, SHELL, STREAM, SYSTEM, THISTLE, WARS
STATUS - QUO, SYMBOL
STEEL - BAND, BLUE, GREY, GUITAR, WOOL
STICK - AROUND, AT, BY, DOWN, INSECT, OUT, TO, TOGETHER, WITH
STICKEY - END, WICKET
STIRRUP - BONE, CUP, PUMP
STOCK - CAR, CERTIFICATE, COMPANY, EXCHANGE, FARM, MARKET
STOCKING - CAP, FILLER, FRAME, MASK, STITCH
STORAGE - BATTERY, CAPACITY, DEVICE, HEATER
STORM - BELT, CENTRE, CLOUD, COLLAR, CONE, DOOR, GLASS, LANTERN, PETREL, WARNING, WINDOW
STRAIGHT - BAT, FACE, FIGHT, FLUSH, MAN, OFF, UP
STRAWBERRY - BLONDE, BUSH, MARK, TOMATO, TREE
STREET - ARAB, CREDIBILITY, CRY, DOOR, PIANO, THEATRE, VALUE
STRIKE - DOWN, FAULT, NOTE, OFF, OUT, PAY, THROUGH, UP
STRING - ALONG, BAND, BASS, BEAN, COURSE, LINE, ORCHESTRA, QUARTET, TIE, VARIABLE
STRIP - CARTOON, CLUB, CROPPING, LIGHTING, MILL, MINING, OUT, POKER
SUGAR - BEET, CANDY, CANE, CORN, DADDY, DIABETES, LOAF, MAPLE
SUMMER - HOLIDAY, PUDDING, SCHOOL, SOLSTICE, TIME
SUN - BATH, BEAR, BED, BITTERN, BLIND, BLOCK, DANCE, DECK, DISK, KING, LAMP, LOUNGE
SUPRREME - BEING, COMMANDER, COURT, SACRIFICE
SURFACE - MAIL, NOISE, PLATE, STRUCTURE, TENSION
SWAN - DIVE, MAIDEN, NECK, SONG
SWEAT - GLAND, OFF, OUT, SHIRT, SUIT
SWEET - BASIL, BAY, CHERRY, CHESTNUT, CICELY, CIDER, CLOVER, CORN, FERN, FLAG, GALE, GUM, MARJORAM, MARTEN, OIL, PEA, PEPPER, POTATO, SHOP, TOOTH, WILLIAM, WOODRUFF
SWISS - CHARD, CHEESE, GUARD, MUSLIN, ROLL, TOURNAMENT

T

TABLE - BAY, D'HOTE, LICENCE, MONEY, MOUNTAIN, NAPKIN, SALT, TALK, TENNIS, WINE

TAIL - COAT, COVERT, END, FAN, GATE, OFF, OUT

TAKE - ABACK, AFTER, APART, AWAY, BACK, DOWN, FOR, IN, OFF, ON, OUT, OVER, TO, UP

TALK - ABOUT, AT, BACK, DOWN, INTO OUT, ROUND, SHOW

TANK - ENGINE, FARMING, TOP, TRAP, UP, WAGON

TAX - AVOIDANCE, DISC, EVASION, EXILE, HAVEN, RATE, RETURN, SHELTER

TEA - BAG, BISCUIT, CLOTH, COSY, GARDEN, GOWN, LEAF, PARTY, ROSE, SERVICE, TOWEL, TROLLEY

TEAR - AWAY, DOWN, DUCT, GAS, INTO, OFF, SHEET

TELEPHONE - BOX, DIRECTORY, NUMBER

TERRA - ALBA, COTTA, FIRMA, INCOGNITA, SIGIATA

TEST - ACT, BAN, CASE, CRICKET, MARKETING, MATCH, PAPER, PILOT, TUBE

THIRD - CLASS, DEGREE, DIMENSION, ESTATE, EYELID, MAN, PARTY, PERSON, REICH, WORLD

THROW - ABOUT, IN, OFF, OUT, OVER, TOGETHER, UP, WEIGHT

TIME - BOMB, CAPSULE, LOCK, IMMEMORIAL, MACHINE, SERIES, SHARING, SHEET, SIGNATURE, SWITCH, TRAVEL, TRIAL, ZONE

TIN - CAN, GOD, HAT, LIZZIE, PLATE, SOLDIER, WHISTLE

TITLE - DEED, PAGE, ROLE

TOILET - PAPER, SET, SOAP, TRAINING, WATER

TONE - CLUSTER, COLOUR, CONTROL, DOWN, LANGUAGE, POEM, ROW, UP

TORQUE - CONVERTER, METER, SPANNER, WRENCH

TOUCH - FOOTBALL, JUDGE, OFF, UP

TOWN - CLERK, CRIER, GAS, HALL, HOUSE, MEETING, PLANNING

TRACK - DOWN, EVENT, MEET, RECORD, ROD, SHOE

TRADE - ACCEPTANCE, CYCLE, DISCOUNT, GAP, JOURNAL, NAME, ON, PLATE, SCHOOL, SECRET, UNION, WIND

TRAFFIC - COP, COURT, ISLAND, JAM, LIGHT, OFFICER, PATTERN, WARDEN

TREASURY - BENCH, BILL, BOND, CERTIFICATE, NOTE, TAG

TRENCH - COAT, FEVR, FOOT, KNIFE, MORTAR, MOUTH, WARFARE

TRIPLE - ALLIANCE, BOND, ENTENTE, JUMP, POINT, TIME

TURKISH - BATH, COFFEE, DELIGHT, EMPIRE, TOBACCO, TOWEL

TURN - AGAINST, AWAY, BRIDGE, DOWN, IF, ON, OUT, OVER, TO, UP

TWELFTH - DAY, MAN, NIGHT

TWIN - BED, BILL, TOWN

U

UMBRELLA - BIRD, PINE, PLANT, STAND, TREE

UNION - CARD, JACK

UNIT - COST, FACTOR, PRICE, TRUST

UNITED - KINGDOM, NATIONS, PARTY, PROVINCES

V

VACCUM - CLEANER, FLASK

VALUE - ADDED, DATE, JUDGEMENT

VENETIAN - BLIND, GLASS, RED

VENTURE - CAPITAL, SCOUT

VICAR - APOSTOLIC, FORANE, GENERAL

VICE - ADMIRAL, CHANCELLOR, PRESIDENT, SQUAD, VERSA

VIDEO - CASSETTE, GAME, NASTY, TAPE

VIRGIN - BIRTH, ISLANDS, MARY, WOOL

VIRGINIA - BEACH, CREEPER, DEER, REEL, STOCK

VOX - ANGELICA, HUMANA, POP, POPULI

VULGAR - FRACTION, LATIN

WALK - AWAY, INTO, OFF, OUT

W

WAR - BABY, BONNET, BRIDE, CHEST, CORRESPONDANT, CRIME, CRY, DANCE, GAME, MEMORIAL, OFFICE, PAINT, WHOOP

WASHING - MACHINE, POWDER, SODA

WATCH - CAP, CHAIN, COMMITTEE, FIRE, NIGHT, OUT

WEATHER - EYE, HOUSE, MAP, STATION, STRIP, VANE, WINDOW

WEDDING - BREAKFAST, CAKE, DRESS, RING

WEIGH - DOWN, IN, UP

WELSH - CORGI, DRESSER, HARP, MOUNTAIN, POPPY, RABBIT, TERRIER

WET - BLANKET, CELL, DREAM, FISH, FLY, LOOK, NURSE, PACK, ROT, STEAM, SUIT

WHITE - ADMIRAL, AREA, BEAR, BIRCH, ELEPHANT, ENSIGN, FEATHER, FISH, FLAG, GOLD, HEAT, HORSE, HOUSE, KNIGHT, LADY, LEAD, LIE, LIGHT, MEAT, OUT, PAPER, PEPPER, SLAVE, SPIRIT, STICK, TIE, WHALE

WINDOW - BOX, ENVELOPE, SASH, SEAT, TAX

WINE - BAR, BOX, CELLAR, COOLERER, TASTING

WING - CHAIR, COLLAR, COMMANDER-COVERT, LOADING, NUT, SHOT, TIP

WITCH - DOCTOR, HAZEL

WOLF - CUB, SPIDER, WHISTLE

WORD - ASSOCIATION, BLINDNESS, ORDER, PICTURE, PROCESSING, PROCESSOR, SQUARE

WORK - BACK,CAMP, ETHIC, FUNCTION, IN, OFF, ON,OUT, OVER, SHEET, STA TION, THROUGH, UP

WORKING - BEE, CAPITAL, CLASS, DAY, DOG, DRAWING, PAPERS, PARTY, SUBSTANCE, WEEK

WRITE - DOWN, IN, ON, OFF, UP

Y

YELLOW - BELLY, CANARY, CARD, FEVER, JACKET, PAGES, PERIL, RIVER, STREAK

YORKSHIRE - DALES, FOG, PUDDING, TERRIER

YOUNG - BLOOD, FOGEY, LADY, MAN, PRETENDER, TURK

YOUTH - CLUB, CUSTODY, HOSTEL

TWO-WORD PHRASES

SECOND WORD

ABOUT - BRING, CAST, COME, FALL, HANG, KICK, KNOCK, MESS, MUCK, PUSH, PUT, RIGHT, SET, TALK, THROW
ABSOLUTE - ABLATIVE, DECREE
ACADEMY - FRENCH, MILITARY, ROYAL
ACCESS - DIRECT, RANDOM, SEQUENTIAL
ACCOUNT - BANK, BUDGET, CAPITAL, CHARGE, CONTROL, CREDIT, CURRENT, DEPOSIT, DRAWING, EXPENSE, JOINT, SAVIMGS, SHORT, SUSPENSE, TRUST,
ACCOUNTANT - CHARTERED, TURF
ACROSS - COME, CUT, GET, PUT, RUN
ACT - ENABLING, HOMESTEAD, JURISTIC, LOCUTIONARY, RIOT, SPEECH, STAMP, TEST
ADMIRAL - FLEET, REAR, RED, VICE, WHITE
ADVOCATE - DEVIL'S, JUDGE, LORD
AGAINST - COUNT, GO, SET, STACK, TURN
AGENCY - ADVERTISING, EMPLOYMENT, MERCANTILE, NEWS, PRESS, TRAVEL
AGENT - CROWN, DISCLOSING, DOUBLE, ESTATE, FORWARDING, FREE, HOUSE, LAND, LAW, OXIDIZING, PRESS, REDUCING, SECRET, SHIPPING, WETTING
AGREEMENT - COLLECTIVE, GENTLE MEN'S, NATIONAL, PROCEDURAL, STANDSTILL, TECHNOLOGY
AID - ARTIFICIAL, FIRST, FOREIGN, HEARING, HOME, LEGAL, TEACHING
ALARM - CALL, FALSE, FIRE
ALCOHOL - ABSOLUTE, ALLYL, AMYL, BUTYL, ETHYL, GRAIN, LAURYL, MENTYL, RUBBING, WOOD
ALE - GINGER, REAL
ALLEY BLIND, BOWLING
ALLIANCE - DUAL, HOLY, TRIPLE
ALONG - COME, CUT, GET, GO, MUDDLE,, PLAY, PUSH, RUB, RUN, SING, STRING
ANGEL - DESTROYING, FALLEN, HELL'S, RECORDING
ANGLE - ACUTE, CENTRAL, COMPLIMENTARY, CRITICAL, EXTERIOR, FACIAL, HOUR, INTERIOR, OBLIQUE, PLANE, RIGHT, STRAIGHT
ANT - AMAZON, ARMY, BULLDOG, DRIVER, FIRE, LEAFCUTTER, LEGIONARY, PHARAOH, SLAVE, VELVET, WHITE, WOOD
APPLE - ADAM'S, BALSAM, BIG, BITTER, CRAB, CUSTARD, LOVE, MAY, OAK, ROSE, SUGAR, THORN
ARCADE - AMUSEMENT, PENNY
ARCH - ACUTE, FALLEN, GOTHIC, HORSE SHOE, KEEL, LANCET, NORMAN, OGEE, POINTED, ROMAN, SKEW, TRIUMPHAL, ZYGOMATIC
AREA - CATCHMENT, DEVELOPMENT, GOAL, GREY, MUSH, NO-GO, PENALTY, SERVICE
ARMS - CHANTING, ORDER, SIDE, SMALL
ARMY - CHURCH, FIELD, SALLY, SALVATION, STANDING, TERRITORIAL
AROUND - BAT, GET, GO, HORSE, RUN, SHOP, SLEEP, SLOP, STICK
ART - BLACK, COMMERCIAL, FINE, NOBLE, OP, PERFORMANCE, POP
ARTS - GRAPHIC, LIBERAL, PERFORMING, VISUAL
ASH - BONE, FLY, MOUNTAIN, PEARL, PRICKLY, SODA
ASIDE - BRUSH, LAY, PUT, SET
ASSEMBLY - GENERAL, LEGISLATIVE, NATIONAL, UNLAWFUL
ATTORNEY - CROWN, DISTRICT, PROSECUTING
AWAY - BLOW, BOIL, CARRY, CLEAR, COME, EXPLAIN, FALL, FIRE, GET, GIVE, GO, KEEP, LAUGH, LAY, MAKE, PUT, RIGHT, RUN,SALT, SIGN, SOCK, SQUARE, TAKE, TEAR, TRAIL, TUCK, TURN, WALK, WHILE

B

BABY - BLUE, FOOD, JELLY, PLUNKET, RHESUS, TEST-TUBE, WAR
BACK - ANSWER, BITE, BOUNCE, CARRY, CAST, CHOKE, CLAW, DOUBLE, FALL, FIGHT, GET, GO, HANG, HARK, HOLD, KEEP, KNOCK, LADDER, LOOK, PAY, PULL, PUT, RING, SET, SIT, TAKE, TALK

BAG - AIR, BLUE, BODY, CARRIER, COFFEE, COOL,DIPLOMATIC, DOGGY, DUFFEL, GLADSTONE, GROW, ICE, JELLY, JIFFY, LAVENDER, MIXED, SAG, SLEEPING, SPONGE, TEA, TOTE

BALLOON - BARRAGE, HOT-AIR, PILOT, TRIAL

BAND -BIG, BRAKE, BRASS, CITIZENS', CONDUCTION, ELASTIC, ENERGY, FREQUENCY, RUBBER, STEEL

BANK - BLOOD, CNTRAL, CLEARIN, COMMERCIAL, COOPERATIVE, DATA, DOGGER, FOG, JODRELL, LAND, LEFT, MEMORY, MERCHANT, NATIONAL, PIGGY, RESERVE, SAVINGS, SOIL, SPERM

BAR - CAPSTAN, COFFEE, COLOUR, DOUBLE, HEEL, HORIZONTAL, INNER, MILK, OUTER, PINCH, PRIVATE, PUBLIC, SAND, SINGLES, SNACK, TORSION, WINE

BARRIER - CRASH, CRUSH, HEAT, SONIC, SOUND, THERMAL, TRANSONIC

BASE - AIR, DATA, FIRST, LEWIS, PRISONER'S, PYRIMIDINE

BASKET - CHIP, MOSES, POLLEN, WASTEPAPER

BASS - BLACK, DOUBLE IGURED, GROUND, LARGEMOUTH, ROCK, SEA, SMALLMOUTH, STONE, STRING, THOROUGH, WALKING

BAT - FRUIT, HORSESHOE, INSECTIVOROUS, STRAIGHT, VAMPIRE

BATH - BLANKET, BLOOD, BUBBLE, HIP, MUD, SALT, SPONGE, STEAM, SUN, SWIMMING, TURKISH

BEACON - BELISHA, LANDING, RADAR, RADIO

BEAN - ADSUKI, ADZUKI, BLACK, BROAD, BUTTER, CALABAR, CASTOR, COCOA, DWARF, FRENCH, GREEN, HORSE, JACK, JUMPING, KIDNEY, LIMA, MUNG, PINTO, RUNNER, SHELL, SNAP, SOYA, STRING, TONKA, WAX

BEAR - ANT, BLACK, BROWN, CINNAMON, GREAT, GRIZZLY, HONEY, KOALA, KODIAK, LITTLE, NAIVE, POLAR, SLOTH, SUN, TEDDY, WATER, WHITE, WOOLLY

BEAT - DEAD, MERSEY, WING

BEAUTY - BATHING, CAMBERWELL, SPRING

BED - AIR, BUNK, FEATHER, OYSTER, PAY, SOFA, TRUCKLE, TWIN, WATER

BEE - CARPENTER, CUCKOO, HIVE, LEAFCUTTER, MASON, MINING, QUEEN, SPELLING, WORKING

BEER - BOCK, GINGER, KAFFIER, ROOT, SMALL, SPRUCE

BELL - CANTERBURY, DIVING, LUTINE, PASSING, SACRING, SANCTUS, SHARK, SILVER

BELT - BIBLE, BLACK, CARTRIDGE, CHASTITY, CONVEYOR, COPPER, COTTON, FAN, GREEN, LIFE, LONSDALE, SAFETY, SEAT, SHELTER, STOCKBROKER, STORM, SUSPENDER, SWORD

BENCH - FRONT, KING'S, OPTICAL, TREASURY

BENEFIT - CHILD, DISABLEMENT, FAMILY, FRINGE, HOUSING, INJURY, INVALIDITY, MATERNITY, SICKNESS, SUPPLEMENTARY, UNMPLOYMENT, WIDOW'S

BILL - ACCOMMODATION, BUFFALO, DEMAND, DOUBLE, FINANCE, FOREIGN, OLD, PRIVATE, PUBLIC, REFORM, TRESURY, TRUE, TWIN

BIRD - ADJUTANT, ANT, BRAIN-FEVER, CROCODILE, DIAMOND, EARLY, ELEPHANT, GAALLOWS, GAME, PARSON, WATER

BISCUIT - BOURBON, CAPTAIN'S, DIGESTIVE, DOG, PILOT, SEA, SHIP'S, SODA, TARARUA, TEA, WATER,

BLACK - ALL, CARBON, GAS, IVORY, JET, LARGE, PENNY, PLATINUM

BLOCK - BREEZE, BUILDING, CAVITY, CYLINDER, HEART, ICE, MENTAL, OFFICE, PSYCHOLOGICAL, SADDLE, STARTING, STUMBLING, SUN, WOOD

BLOOD - BAD, BLUE, BULL'S, DRAGON'S, FULL, WHOLE, YOUNG

BOARD - ABOVE, ADNIRALITY, BULLETIN, CATCHMENT, CIRCUIT, CRIBBAGE, DIVING, DRAFT, DRAINING, DRAWING, EMERY, FULL, HALF, IDIOT, IRONING, NOTICE, PATCH, RUNNING, SANDWICH SCHOOL, NOTICE, SOUNDING, WOBBLE

BOAT - CANAL, FLYING, GRAVY, JOLLY, MOSQUITO, NARROW, ROWING, SAILING, SAUCE, SWAMP, TORPEDO

BOMB - ATOM, BUZZ, CLUSTER, FISSION, FLYING, FUSION, HYDROGEN, LETTER, NEUTRON, NUCLEAR, PETROL, SMOKE, STINK, TIME, VOLCANIC

BOND - BAIL, CHEMICAL, COORDINATE, COVALENT, DATIVE, DOUBLE, ELECTROVALENT, ENGLISH, FLEMISH, GRANNY, HERRINGBONE, HYDROGEN, INCOME, IONIC, METALLIC, PAIR, PEPTIDE, SINGLE, TREASURY, TRIPLE

BONE - CANNON, CARTILAGE, COFFIN, CRAZY, FETTER, FRONTAL, FUNNY, HAUNCH, HEEL, INNOMINATE, MEMBRANE, OCCIPITAL, PARIETAL, SPEHENOID, SPLINT, STIRRUP, TEMPORAL, TYMPANIC, ZYGOMATIC

BOOK - BLACK, CLOSED, COMMON PLACE, COOKERY, DOMESDAY, DOOMSDAY, HYMN, OPEN, PHRASE, PRAYER, REFERANCE, STATUTE, TALKING

BOTTLE - BRANDY, FEEDING, HOT-WATER, KLEIN, NANSEN, WATER

BOWL - BEGGING, DUST, FINGER, GOLDFISH, RICE

BOX - APPLE, BALLOT, BLACK, CHRISTMAS, COIN, DEED, DISPATCH, DEFUSE, FUZZ, GLOVE, JUNCTION, JURY, LETTER, MUSIC, PENALTY, PILLAR, POOR, PRESS, SENTRY, SHOOTING, SIGNAL, TELEPHONE, VOICE, WINDOW, WINE, WITNESS

BOY - ALTER, BALL, BARROW, BEST, BEVIN, BLUE-EYED, CABIN, ERAND, OFFICE, OLD, PRINCIPLE, RENT, TAR, TEDDY, WHIPPING

BRAKE - AIR, CENTRIFUGAL, DISC, DRUM, FOOT, HYDRAULIC, SHOOTING

BRETHREN - BOHEMIAN, ELDER, EXCLUSIVE, OPEN, PLYMOTH, TRINITY

BRIDGE - AIR, AUCTION, BAILEY, BALANCE, BOARD, CABLE-STAYED, CANTILEVER, CLAPPER, CONTRACT, COUNTERPOISE, DUPLICATE, FLYING, FOUR-DEAL, LAND, PIVOT, RAINBOW, RUBBER, SNOW, SUSPENSION, SWING, TRANSPORTER, TRUSS, TURN, WHEATSTONE

BRIGADE - BOYS', FIRE, FUR, INTERNATIONAL

BROTHER - BIG, BLOOD, LAY

BUG - ASSASSIN, CABBAGE, DAMSEL, DEBRIS, FLOWER, GROUND, HARLE-QUIN, KISSING, LACE, LIGHTNING, MAORI, MEALY, PILL, RHODODENDRON, SHIELD, SQUASH, WATER, WHEEL

BUGGY - BABY, BEACH, SWAMP

BUOY - BELL, BREECHES, CAN, LIFE, NUN, SPAR

BURNER - BACK, BUNSEN, GAS, LIME, WELSBACH

BUSH - BURNING, BUTTERFLY, CALICO, COTTON, CRANBERRY, CREOSOTE, DAISY, EMU, GOOSEBERRY, MINT, NATIVE, NEEDLE, ORCHARD, STRAWBERRY, SUGAR

BUSINESS - BIG, MONKEY, SHOW

BY - COME, DO, GET, PASS, PUT, STAND, STICK

C

CAKE - ANGEL, BANBURY, BARN, COTTON, DUNDEE, ECCLES, FISH, FRUIT, GENOA, JOHNNY, LARDY, LAYER, MADERIA, MARBLE, OIL, PONTEFRACT, POUND, ROCK, SALT, SANDWICH, SIMNEL, SPONGE, TIPSY, UPSIDE-DOWN, WEDDING

CALL - BIRD, CLOSE, COLD., CURTAIN, LINE, PHOTO, ROLL, TOLL, TRUNK

CAMERA - AUTOMATIC, BOX, CANDID, CINE, COMPACT, GAMMA, IN, MINATURE, MOVIE, PINHOLE, REFLEX

CAMP - CANCENTRATION, HEALTH, HIGH, HOLIDAY, LABOUR, LOW, MOTOR, TRANSIT, WORK,

CANAL - ALIMENTARY, ANAL, CALEDONIAN, ERIE, GRAND, HAVERSIAN, MITTLELLAND, PANAMA, ROOT, SEMICIRCULAR, SPINAL, SUEZ, WELLAND

CAP - BATHING, CLOTH, CROWN, DEATH, DUNCE, DUTCH, FILLER, FLAT, FOOL'S, FUNNEL, JOCKEY, JULIET, LEGAL, LIBERTY, MILK, PERCUSSION, ROOT, SHAGGY, STOCKING, WATCH, WAX

CAPITAL - BLOCK, HUMAN, RISK, SMALL, VENTURE, WORKING

CAPSULE - SEED, SPACE, TIME

CARD - BANK, BANKER'S, BIRTHDAY, CALLING, CHEQUE, CHRISTMAS, CIGARETTE, COURT, CREDIT, DONOR, DRAWING, FLASH, GREEN, GREETING, ID,LASER, PICTURE, PLACE, PLAYING, POSTAL, PUNCHED, RED, SHOW, SMART, UNION, VISITING, YELLOW

CASE - ATTACHÉ, BASKET, DOT, DISPATCH, DRESSING, LOWER,

SPECIAL, SPORE, STATED, TEST, UPPER, WARDIAN, WORST, WRITING

CELL - BLOOD, CADIMUN, CLARK, COLLAR, CONDEMNED, DANIELL, DEATH, DRY, ELECTROYLTIC, FLAME, FUEL, GERM, GRAVITY, GUARD, LYMPH, MAST, NERVE, PADDED, PERIETAL, PHOTOELECTRIC, PRIMARY, SECONDARY, SELENIUM, SOLAR, SOMATIC, STANDARD, STEM, SWARM, UNIT, VOLTAIC, WET

CENTRE - ACTIVE, ATTENDANCE, CIVIC, COMMUNITY, COST, DAYCARE, DEAD, DETENTION, GARDEN, HEALTH, MUSIC, NERVE, REMAND, SHOPPING, STORM

CHAIN - BICYCLE, BRANCHED, CLOSED, DAISY, FOOD, GOLDEN, GRAND, GUNTER'S, LEARNER'S, MARKOV, MOUNTAIN, OPEN, SAFETY, SIDE, SNIGGING, STRAIGHT, SURVEYOR'S, WATCH

CHAIR - BATH, BOATSWAIN'S, DECK, EASY, ELECTRIC, ROCKING, SEDAN, STRAIGHT, SWIVEL, WINDSOR, WING

CHAMBER - BUBBLE, CLOUD, COMBUSTION, DECOMPRESSION, ECHO, FLOAT, GAS, INSPECTION, IONIZATION, LOWER, MAGMA, PRESENCE, PRIVY, SECOND, SPARK, STAR, UPPER

CHART - BAR, BREAKEVEN, CONTROL, FLOW, ORGANIZATION, PIE, PLANE

CHASE - PAPER, WILD-GOOSE

CHEST - COMMUNITY, HOPE, MEDICINE, SEA, SLOP, WAR, WIND

CHILD - FOSTER, LATCHKEY, LOVE, MOON

CHINA - BONE, COCHIN, COMMUNIST, DRESDEN, NATIONALIST, RED, WORCESTER

CHIP - BLUE, LOG, POTATO, SILICON

CIRCLE - ANTARCTIC, ARCTIC, DIP, DRESS, EQUINOCTICAL, FAMILY, GREAT, HOUR, HUT, MERIDIAN, PARQET, PITCH, POLAR, TURNING, VERTICAL, VICIOUS

CLASS - CABIN, CRYSTAL, EVENING, FIRST, LOWER, MIDDLE, SECOND, THIRD, UNIVERSAL, UPPER, WORKING

CLAY - BOULDER, CHINA, FIRE, PORCELAIN

CLEF - ALTO, BASS, C, F, G, SOPRANO, TENOR, TREBLE, VIOLA

CLERK - ARTICLED, BANK, DESK, FILING, PARISH, SHIPPING, TALLY, TOWN

CLIP - BICYCLE, BULLDOG, CARTRIDGE, CROCODILE, WOOL

CLOCK - ALARM, ANALOGUE, ATOMIC, BIOLOGICAL, CAESIUM, CARRIAGE, CUCKOO, DIGITAL, GRANDFATHER, GRANDMOTHER, LONGCASE, QUARTZ, SETTLER'S, SPEAKING, TIME, TOWN HALL, WATER

CLOTH - AEROPLANE, AIRCRAFT, ALTER, BARK, COVERT, FACE, GRASS, MONK'S, NUN'S, SPONGE, TEA, WIRE

CLUB - BOOK, CHARTERED, COUNTRY, GLEE, GOLF, INDIAN, JOCKEY, LIONS, LUNCHEON, MONDAY, PROVIDENT, PUDDING, ROTARY, STRIP, SUPPER, TRAMPING, YOUTH

COAL - BITUMINOUS, BROWN, CANNEL, GAS, HARD, SOFT, STEAM, WHITE, WOOD

COCKTAIL - ATOMIC, FRUIT, MOTOLOV

CODE - AREA, BAR, BINARY, CHARACTER, CLARENDON, COLOUR, COUNTRY, DIALLING, GENETIC, GRAY, HIGHWAY, JUSTINIAN, MORSE, NAPOLEONIC, NATIONAL, PENAL, STD, TIME, ZIP

COLLAR - CLERICAL, DOG, ETON, HEAD, MANDARIN, ROMAN, SHAWL, STORM, VANDYKE, WING

COLOUR - ACHROMATIC, CHROMATIC, COMPLEMENTARY, CROSS, LOCAL, OFF, PRIMARY, SECONDARY, TONE

COLUMN - AGONY, CORRESPONDENCE, FIFTH, PERSONAL, SPINAL, STEERING, VERTEBRAL

COMPANY - CLOSE, FINANCE, FIRE, FREE, HOLDING, JOINT-STOCK, LIMITED, PARENT, PRIVATE, PUBLIC, REPERTORY, STOCK

COMPLEX - ELECTRA, INFERIORITY, LAUNCH, OEDIPUS, PERSECUTION, SUPERIORITY

CONE - ICE-CREAM, NOSE, PINE, STORM, STORM, WIND

CORD - COMMUNICATION, SASH, SPERMATIC, SPINAL, UMBILICAL

COUNTER - CRYSTAL, GEIGER, PROPORTIONAL, REV, SCINTILLATION

COURSE - ASSAULT, BARGE, GOLF, MAGNETIC, MAIN, REFRESHER, SANDWICH

COURT - CLAY, COUNTY, CROWN, DISTRICT, DOMESTIC, GRASS, HARD, HIGH, INFERIOR, JUSTICE, JUVENILE, KANGAROO, MAGISTRATES', MOOT, OPEN, POLICE, PRIZE, PROVOST, SHERIFF, SUPERIOR, SUPREME, TENNIS, TERRITORIAL, TOUT, TRAFFIC, TRIAL, WORLD

COVER - AIR, DUST, EXTRA, FIRST-DAY, GROUND, LOOSE

CREAM - BARRIER, BAVARIAN, CLOTTED, COLD, DEVONSHIRE, DOUBLE, GLACIER, ICE, PASTRY, SINGLE, SOUR, VANISHING, WHIPPING

CROP - CASH, CATCH, COVER, ETON, RIDING, ROOT

CROSS - CALVARY, CELTIC, CHARING, DOUBLE, FIERY, GORGE, GREEK, IRON, JERUSALUM, LATIN, LORRAINE, MALTESE, NORTHERN, PAPAL, PATRIARCHAL, RED, SOUTHERN, TAU, VICTORIA

CROSSING - LEVEL, PEDESTRIAN, PELICAN, ZEBRA

CROW - CARRION, HOODED, JIM

CUP - AMERICA'S, CLARET, COFFEE, DAVIS, EGG, FA, FRUIT, GRACE, GREASE, LOVING, MOUSTACHHE, STIRRUP, WORLD

CURRENCY - DECIMAL, FRACTIONAL, MANAGED, RESERVE

CURRENT - ALTERNATING, CROMWELL, DARK, DIRECT, EDDY, ELECTRIC, FOUCAULT, HUMBOLDT, JAPAN, LABRADOR, PERU, THERMIONIC, TURBIDITY

CURTAIN - AIR, BAMBOO, DROP, IRON, SAFETY

CUT - CREW, CULEBRA, GAILLARD, NAVY, OPEN, POWER, SHORT

D

DASH - EM, EN, PEBBLE, SWUNG

DAYS - DOG, EMBER, HUNDRED, JURIDICAL, LAY, ROGATION, SALAD

DEATH - BLACK, BRAIN, CIVIL, COT, CRIB, HEAT, LIVING, SUDDEN

DECK - 'TWEEN, BOAT, FLIGHT, HURRICANE, LOWER, MAIN, POOP, PROMENADE, SUN, TAPE

DELIVERY - BREECH, FORWARD, GENERAL, JAIL, RECORDED, RURAL, SPECIAL

DERBY - CROWN, DONKEY, KENTUCKY, ROLLER, SAGE

DESK - CASH, CITY, COPY, ROLL-TOP, WRITING

DEVIL - DUST, MOUNTAIN, PRINTER'S, SNOW, TASMANIAN

DIAGRAM - BAR, BLOCK, INDICATOR, RUSSELL, SCATTER, VENN

DIVE - CRASH, NOSE, POWER, SWALLOW, SWAN

DOCTOR - ANGELIC, BAREFOOT, CAPE, FAMILY, FLYING, SAW, WITCH

DOG - BACKING, BIRD, CARRIAGE, COACH, ESKIMO, EYE, GREAT, GUIDE, GUN, HEADING. HOT, KANGAROO, LEADING, LITTLE, NATIVE, PARIAH, PIG, POLICE, PRARIE, RACCOON, SAUSAGE, SEA, SHEPHERD, SLED, SNIFFER, SPOTTED, TOP, TRACKER, WORKING

DOOR - BACK, BARN, CAT, DUTCH, FIRE, FOLDING, FRONT, NEXT, OPEN, OVER HEAD, REVOLVING, STABLE, STAGE, STORM, STREET, SWING, TRAP

DOWN - BACK, BEAR, BEAT, DOG, BOIL, BREAK, BRING, BUCKET, BUCKLE, CALL, CAST, CHANGE, CLAMP, CLIMB, CLOSE, CRACK, CRY, CUT, DIE, DO, DRAG, DRESS, DUST, FALL, GET, GO, HAND, HOLD, HUNT, KEEP, KNOCK, LAY, LET, LIE, LIVE, LOOK, MOW, NAIL, PAY, PEG, PIN, PIPE, PLAY, PULL, PUT, RIDE, ROND, RUB, RUN, SEND, SETM SETTLE, SHAKE, SHOOT, SHOUT, SIMMER, SIT, SLAP, SPONGE, STAND, STEP, STICK, STOP, STRIKE, TAKE, TALK, TEAR, TONE, TRACK, TURN, UPSIDE, VOTE, WASH, WEAR, WEIGH, WIND, WRITE

DRESS - ACADEMIC, COAT, COURT, EVENING, FANCY, FULL, HIGHLAND, MORNING, PINAFORE, TENT

DRESSING - FRENCH, ORE, RUSSIAN, SALAD, TOP, WELL

DRILL - BOAT, FIRE, HAMMER, KERB, PACK, POWER, TWIST

DRIVE - BEETLE, CHAIN, DISK, FLUID, FOUR-WHEEL, MOTOR, WHILST

DROP - ACID, COUGH, DELAYED, DOLLY, KNEE, LEMON, MAIL

DUCK - BLUE, BOMBAY, COLD, DEAD, HARLEQUIN, LAME, MANDARIN, MUS COVY, MUSK, PARADISE, RUDDY, SEA, TUFTED, WOOD

DUST - ANGEL, BULL, COSMIC, GOLD

DUTY- DEATH, ESTATE, POINT, STAMP

E

EDGE - DECKLE, KNIFE, LEADING, TRAILING

EGG - CURATE'S, DARNING, EASTER, NET, SCOTCH,

END - BACK, BEST, BIG, BIGGER, BOOK, BOTTOM, BUSINESS, CIGARETTE, COD, DEAD, EAST, AG, GABLE,LAND'S, LOOSE, ROPE'S, STICKY, TAG, TAIL, TOP, WEST

ENGINE - AERO, BEAM, BYPASS, DIESEL, DONKEY, EXTERNAL-COMBUSTION, ION, JET, LIGHT, OVERRHEAD-VALVE, PILOT, PLASMA, RADIAL, REACTION, RECIPROCATING, ROCKET, ROTARY, SIDE-VALVE, STATIONARY, STIRLING, TANK, TRACTION,TURBOJET, V-TYPE, VALVE-IN-HEAD, WANKEL

ENSIGN - BLUE, RED, WHITE

EVENT - FIELD, HAPPY, MEDIA, THREE-DAY, TRACK

EVIDENCE - CIRCUMSTANTIAL, CUMULATIVE, DIRECT, HEARSAY, KING'S, PRIMA-FACIE, QUEEN'S, STATE'S

EXCHANGE - CORN, EMPLOYMENT, FOREIGN, ION, LABOUR, PART, POST, STOCK

EYE - BEADY, BLACK, COMPOUND, ELECTRIC, EVIL, GLAD, MAGIC, MIND'S, PHEASANT'S, PINEAL, POPE'S, PRIVATE, RED, SCREW, WEATHER

F

FACE - BOLD, EN, LIGHT, LONG, OLD, POKER, STRAIGHT

FACTOR - COMMON, CORN, GROWTH, HOUSE, LOAD, POWER, QUALITY, RH, RHESUS, SAFETY, UNIT

FEATHER - COCK, CONTOUR, FLIGHT, SHAFT, SICKLE, WHITE

FILE - CARD, CROSSCUT, INDIAN, SINGLE

FINGER - INDEX, LADY'S, RING

FINISH - BLAKET, DEAD, MIRROR, PHOTO

FIRE - BRUSH, ELECTRIC,GREEK, LIQUID, QUICK, RAPID, RED, WATCH

FLAT - ABODE, ALKALI, COTTAGE, DOUBLE, GARDEN, GRANNY, MUD, SALT, STUDIO

FOOD - CONVENIENCE, FAST, HEATLH, JUNK, SKIN, SOUL

FORTH - CALL, GO, HOLD, PUT, SET

FORWARD - BRING, CARRY, CENTRE, COME, INSIDE, PUT

FRACTION - COMMON, COMPLEX, COMPOUND, CONTINUED, DECIMAL, IMPROPER, PACKING, PARTIAL, PROPER, SIMPLE, VULGAR

FRACTURE - COLLES', COMMINUTED, COMPOUND, GREENSTICK, POTT'S, SIMPLE

FRAME - CLIMBING, COL, GARDEN, HALF, OXFORD, PORTAL, SAMPLING, STILL, STOCKING

FRIDAY - GIRL, GOOD, MAN

FRONT - COLD, EYES, NATIONAL, OCCLUDED, PEOPLE'S, POLAR, POPULAR, RHODESIAN, WARM, WAVE

FROST - BLACK, JACK, SILVER, WHITE

FRUIT - ACCESSORY, COLLECTIVE, FALSE, FORBIDDEN, KEY, KIWI, MULTIPLE, PASSION, SIMPLE, SOFT, STONE,WALL

G

GALLERY - LADIES', NATIONAL, PRESS, PUBLIC, ROUGES, SHOOTING, STRANGER'S, TATE, WHISPERING, WINNING

GAP - CREDIBILITY, DEFLATIONARY, ENERGY, GENERATION, INFLATIONARY, SPARK, TRADE, WATER, WIND

GARDEN - BEAR, BOTANICAL, COVERT, KITCHEN, KNOT, MARKET, PEBBLE, ROCK, ROOF, TEA, WINTER, ZOOLOGICAL

GAS - AIR, BOTTLED, CALOR, COAL, CS, ELECTROLYTIC, IDEAL, INERT, LAUGHING, MARSH, MUSTARD, NATURAL, NERVE, NOBLE, NORTH-SEA, PERFECT, POISON, PRODUCER, RARE, SEWAGE, TEAR, TOWN, WATER

GATE - GOLDEN, HEAD, IRON, KISSING, LICH, LYCH, MORAVIAN, STARTING, TAIL, TARANAKI, WATER

GIRL - BACHELOR, BAR, BEST, CALL, CAREER, CHORUS, CONTINUITY, COVER, DANCING, FLOWER, GIBSON, LAND, MARCHING, OLD, SWEATER

GLASS - BELL, BURNING, CHEVAL, CROWN, CUPPING, CUT, FAVRILLE, FIELD, FLINT, FOAT, GREEN, GROUND, HAND, LEAD, LIQUID, LOOKING,

MAGNIFYING, MILK, MURRHINE, OBJECT, OPTICAL, PIER, PLATE, QUARTZ, REDUCING, RUBY, SAFETY, SILIC, SOLUBLE, STAINED, STORM, TIFFANY, VENETIAN, VOLCANIC, WATER, WIRE,

GLASSES - DARK, FIELD, OPERA

GOAT - ANGORA, BILLY, KASHMIR, MOUNTAIN, NANNY

GOLD - FILLED, FOOL'S, FREE, MOSAIC, OLD, ROLLED, WHITE

GREEN - APPLE, BACK, BOTTLE, BOWLING, CHROME, CROWN, GRETNA, JADE, KENDAL, LIME, LINCOLN, NILE, OLIVE, PARIS, PEA, PUTTING, RIFLE, SEA

GROUND - BURIEL, CAMPING, COMMON, HOME, HUNTING, MIDDLE, PROVING, RECREATION, STAMPING, VANTAGE

GUARD - ADVANCE, COLOUR, HOME, IRON, NATIONAL, OLD, PRAETORIAN, PROVOST, RED, SECURITY, SWISS

GUIDE - BROWNIE, GIRL, HONEY, QUEEN'S

GUM - ACAROID, BLUE, BUBBLE, CHEWING, COW, FLOODED, GHOST, KAURI, RED, NOW, SOUR, SPIRIT, SUGAR, SWEET, WATER, WHITE

H

HALF - BETTER, CENTRE, FLY, SCRUM

HALL - CARNEGIE, CITY, FESTIVAL, LIBERTY, MESS, MUSIC, TAMMANY, TOWN

HAND - CHARGE, CLUB, COURT, DAB, DEAD, DECK, FARM, FREE, GLAD, HELPING, HOUR, IRON, LONE, MINUTE, OLD, ROUND, SECOND, SHED, SWEEP, UPPER, WHIP

HAT - BRASS, COCKED, COSACK, HARD, HIGH, OLD, OPERA, PANAMA, PICTURE, PORKPIE, RED, SAILOR, SCARLET, SHOVEL, SILK, SLOUCH, TEN-GALLON, TIN, TOP

HEART - BLEEDING, BULLOCK'S, DEAD, FLOATING, PURPLE, SACRED

HEAT - ATOMIC, BLACK, BLOOD, DEAD, LATENT, PRICKLY, RADIANT, RED, TOTAL, WHITE

HISTORY - ANCIENT, CASE, LIFE, NATURAL, ORAL

HITCH - BLACKWALL, CLOVE, HARNESS, MAGNUS, ROLLING, TIMBER, WEAVER'S

HOLE - AIR, BEAM, BLACK, BOLT, COAL, FUNK, GLORY, KETTLE, LUBBER'S, NINETEENTH, SOUND, SPIDER SWALLOW, WATER, WATERING

HOLIDAY - BANK, BUSMAN'S, HALF, LEGAL, PUBLIC, ROMAN, SUMMER

HOME - EVENTIDE, HARVEST, MOBILE, NURSING, REMAND, REST, STATELY, VILLA

HORSE -- CHARLEY, DARK, IRON, LIBERTY, LIGHT, NIGHT, POLE, POST, QUARTER, RIVER, ROCKING, SADDLE, SEA, SHIRE, TROJAN, WHEEL, WHITE, WILLING, WOODEN

HOUR - ELEVENTH, HAPPY, LUNCH, RUSH, SIDEREAL, WITCHING, ZERO

HOUSE - ACCEPTING, ADMIRALITY, BOARDING, BROILER, BUSH, CHARNEL, CHATTEL, CLEARING, COACH, COFFEE, COUNTING, COUNTRY, CUSTOM, DISCOUNT, DISORDERLY, DOWER, FASHION, FORCING, FREE, FULL, HALFWAY, ICE, ISSUING, LODGING, MANOR, MANSION, MEETING, OPEN, OPERA, PICTURE, POST, PUBLIC, ROOMING, SAFE, SOFTWARE, SPORTING, STATE, STATION, STOREY, TERRACED, THIRD, TOWN, TRINITY, UPPER WASH, WENDY, WHITE

HUMOUR - AQUEOUS, GALLOWS, ILL, VITREOUS

HUNT - DRAG, FOX, SCAVENGER, STILL, TREASURE

I

ICE - BLACK, CAMPHOR, COCONUT, DRIFT, DRY, GLAZE, GROUD, PACK, PANCAKE, SHELF, SLOB, WATER

IN - ALL, BLOCK, BLOW, BOOK, BREAK, BRING, BUILD, BURN, BUY, CALL, CASH, CAVE, CHECK CHIP, CLOSE, COME, DIG, DO, DRAG, DRAW, FALL, FILL, FIT, GET, GIVE, GO, HAND, HANG, HOLD HORN, INK, JACK, KEEP, KEY, KICK, LAY, LET, LIE, LISTEN, LIVE, LOG, MOVE, MUCK, PACK, PAY, PHASE, PITCH, PLUG, PULL, PUSH, PUT, RAKE, REIN, RING, ROLL, ROPE, RUB, RUN, SCRAPE, SET, SETTLE, SIGN, SINK, SLEEP, STAND, START, STEP, SUCK, SWEAR, TAKE, THROW, TIE, TUCK, TUNE, TURN, WEIGH, WELL, WHIP, WORK, WRITE, ZERO, ZOOM

INTEREST - COMPOUND, CONTROLLING, HUMAN, LIFE, SIMPLE, VESTED

IRON - ALPHA, ANGLE, BETA, CAST, CHANNEL, CORRUGATED, DELTA, GAMMA, GEM, GRAPPLING, GROZING, INGOT, LILY, MALLEABLE, PIG, PUMP, SHOOTING, SMOOTHING, SOLDERING, STEAM, TOGGLE, WROUGHT

IVY - BOSTON, GRAPE, ROUND, JAPANESE, POISON, WEEPING

J

JACK - JUMPING, MAN, SCREW, UNION, YELLOW

JACKET - AIR, BED, BOMBER, BUSH, DINNER, DONKEY, DUST, ETON, FLAK, HACKING, LIFE, MESS, MONKEY, NORFOLK, PEA, REEFING, SAFARI, SHELL, SMOKING, SPORTS, STEAM, WATER, YELLOW

JELLY - CALF'S FOOT, COMB, MINERAL, PETROLEUM,ROYAL

JOE - GI, HOLY, SLOPPY

JUDGEMENT - ABSOLUTE, COMPARATIVE, LAST, VALUE

JUMP - BROAD, HIGH, LONG, SKI, TRIPLE, WATER

K

KEY - ALLEN, CHROMA, CHURCH, CONTROL, DEAD, FUNCTION, IGNITION, MASTER, MINOR, NUT, OFF, ON, PRONG, SHIFT, SKELETON, TUNING

KICK - DROP, FLUTTER, FREE, FROG, GOAL, PENALTY, PLACE, SCISSORS, STAB

KNIFE - BOWIE, CARVING, CASE, CLASP, FLICK, FRUIT, HUNTING, PALLET, SHEATH, TRENCH

KNOT - BLACK, FISHERMAN'S, FLAT, FRENCH, GORDIAN, GRANNY, LOOP, LOVE, OVERHAND, REEF, SQUARE, STEVEDORE'S, SURGEON'S, SWORD, THUMB, TRUELOVE, WALL, WINDSOR

L

LACE - ALENCON, BOBBIN, BRUSSELS, CHANTILLY, CLUNY, MECHLIN, PILLOW, POINT, SEA, TORCHON

LADY - BAG, DINNER, FIRST, PAINTED

LAMP - ALDIS, DAVY, FLUORESCENT, GLOW, HURRICNE, INCANDESCENT, NEON, PILOT, SAFETY, SPIRIT, SUN, TUNGSTEN

LANGUAGE - BODY, COMPUTER, FIRST, FORMAL, MACHINE, NATURAL, PROGRAMMING, SECOND, SIGN,

LANTERN - CHINESE, DARK, FRIAR'S, JAPANESE, MAGIC, STORM

LEAVE - FRENCH, MASS, MATERNITY, SHORE, SICK

LETTER - AIR, BEGGING, BLACK, CHAIN, COVERING, DEAD, DOMINICAL, FORM, FRENCH, LOVE, OPEN, POISON-PEN, SCARLET

LIBRARY - CIRCULATING, FILM, LENDING, MOBILE, SUBSCRIPTION

LICENCE - DRIVING, OCCASIONAL, POETIC, SPECIAL, TABLE

LIFE - FUTURE, LOVE, MEAN, PRIVATE, REAL, SHELF, STILL

LIGHT - ARC, BACK, BACK-UP, BEGNAL, BRAKE, COURTESY, FIRST, GREEN , INNER, KLIEG, LEADING, PILOT, REAR, RED, REVERSING, TRAFFIC, WHITE

LIGHTING - INDIRECT, STRIP, STROBE

LIGHTNING - CHAIN, FORKED, HEAT, SHEET

LIGHTS - ANCIENT, BRIGHT, FAIRY, HOUSE, NORTHERN, POLAR, SOUTHERN

LINE - ASSEMBLY, BAR, BOTTOM, BRANCH, CLEW, CONTOUR, DATE, FALL, FIRING, FLIGHT, FRONT, GOAL, HARD, HINDENBURG, HOT, LAND, LEAD, LEDGER, MAGINOT, MAIN, MASON-DIXON, NUMBER, OFF, ON, PARTY, PICKET, PLIMSOLL, PLUMB, POWER, PRODUCTION, PUNCH, SIEGFRIED, SNOW, STORY, TIMBER, WATER

LINK - CUFF, DRAG, MISSING

LION - MOUNTAIN, NEMEAN, SEA

LIST - BACK, CHECK, CIVIL, CLASS, HIT, HONOURS, MAILING, RESERVED, SHORT, SICK, TRANSFER, WAITING

LOCK - COMBINATION, FERMENTATION, MAN, MORTISE, PERCUSSION, SCALP, SPRING, STOCK, VAPOUR, WHEEL, YALE

LOVE - CALF, COURTLY, CUPBOARD, FREE, PUPPY

M

MACHINE - ADDING, ANSWERING, BATHING, FRUIT, KIDNEY, SEWING, SLOT, TIME,VENDING, WASHING

MAIL - AIR, CHAIN, ELECTRONIC, FAN, SURFACE

MAIN - RING, SPANISH, WATER

MAN - ADVANCE, ANCHOR, BEST, COMPANY, CON, CONFIDENCE, ENLISTED, FAMILY, FANCY, FRONT, HATCHET, HIT, ICE, INNER, IRON, LADIES, LEADING, MEDICINE, MUFFIN, NEANDERTHAL, PALAEOLITHIC, PARTY, PILTDOWN, RAG-AND-BONE, SANDWICH, STRAIGHT, TWELFTH, YES

MARCH - DEAD, FORCED, HUNGER, LONG, QUICK, SLOW

MARIA - AVE, BLACK, HENRIETTA, SANTA, TIA

MARK - BENCH, BLACK, EXCLAMATION, KITE, PUNCTUATION, QUESTION, QUOTATION

MARKET - BLACK, BUYERS' CAPITAL, CAPTIVE, COMMON, FLEA, KERB, MONEY, OPEN, SELLERS', SPOT, STOCK

MARRIAGE - CIVIL, COMMON-LAW, GROUP, MIXED

MASK - DEATH, GAS, LIFE, LOO, OXYGEN, SHADOW, STOCKING

MASTER - CAREERS, GRAND, HARBOUR, INTERNATIONAL, OLD, PAST, QUESTION

MATCH - FRICTION, LOVE, SAFETY, SHIELD, SLANGING, SLOW, TEST

MATE - FIRST, FOOL'S, RUNNING, SCHOLAR'S, SECOND, SOUL

MATTER - BACK, END, FRONT, GREY, SUBJECT, WHITE

MEDICINE - ALTERNATIVE, COMPLEMENTARY, DUTCH, FOLK, FORENSIC, PATENT

MILE - ADMIRALITY, AIR, GEORAPHICAL, NAUTICAL, ROMAN, SEA, STATUE, SWEDISH

MILL - COFFEE, PEPPER, ROLLING, SMOCK, STAMP, STRIP, WATER

MITE - BULB, CHEESE, DUST, FLOUR, FOWL, GALL, HARVEST, ITCH, SPIDER, WATER

MONEY - BLOOD, CALL, CONSCIENCE, DANGER, EASY, FOLDING, GATE, HEAD, HOT, HUSH, KEY, MAUNDY, NEAR, PAPER, PIN, PLASTIC, POCKET, PRIZE, READY, SEED, SHIP

MOON - BLUE, FULL, HARVEST, HUNTER'S, MOCK, NEW, OLD

MOTHER - EARTH, FOSTER, NURSING, QUEEN, REVEREND, SOLO

MOTION - FAST, HARMONIC, LINK, PERPETUAL, PROPER, SLOW

N

NAME - BRAND, CHRISTIAN, DAY, FAMILY, FIRST, GIVEN, HOUSEHOLD, LAST, MAIDEN, MIDDLE, PEN, PLACE, PROPRIETARY, SECOND, STREET, TRADE

NECK - BOAT, BRASS, CREW, SCOOP, SWAN, V

NEEDLE - CLEOPATRA'S, DARNING, DIP, ELECTRIC, ICE, MAGNETIC, PINE, SHEPHERD'S

NET - DRIFT, GILL, LANDING, MOSQUITO, POUND, SAFETY, SHARK

NIGHT - FIRST, GOOD, TWELFTH, WALPURGIS, WATCH,

NOTE - ADVICE, AUXILIARY, BLUE, COVER, CURRENCY, DEMAND, EIGHTH, GOLD, GRACE, LEADING, PASSING, POSTAL, PROMISSARY, QUARTER, SICK, TREASURY, WHOLE

NUMBER - ACCESSION, ALGEBRAIC, ATOMIC, BACK, BINARY, BOX, CALL, CARDINAL, COMPLEX, COMPOSITE, COMPOUND, CONCRETE, E, GOLDEN, INDEX, MACH, MAGIC, OPPOSITE, ORDINAL, PERFECT, PRIME, REAL, REGISTRATION, SERIAL, SQUARE, TELEPHONE, WHOLE, WRONG

O

OFFERING - BURNT, PEACE

OFFICE - BOX, CROWN, DIVINE, ELECTRONIC, EMPLOYMENT, FOREIGN, HOLY, HOME, LAND, LEFT-LUGGAGE, PATENT, POST, REGISTER, WAR

OIL - CAMPHORATED, CASTOR, COCONUT, COD-LIVER, CORN, CRUDE, DIESEL, ESSENTIAL, FATTY, GAS, LINSEED, MACASSAR, MINERAL, MUSTARD, NUT, OLIVE, PALM, PEANUT, RAPE, SASSAFRAS, SHALE, SPERM, VEGETABLE, WHALE

OPERA - BALLAD, COMIC, GRAND, HORSE, LIGHT, SOAP, SPACE

ORANGE - AGENT, BITTER, BLOOD, MOCK, NAVEL, OSAGE, SEVILLE

ORDER - AFFILATION, APPLE-PIE, ATTIC, BANKER'S, COMMUNITY-SERVICE, COMPENSATION, ENCLOSED, FIRING, LOOSE, MAIL, MARKET, MONEY, PICKING, POSSESSIN, POSTAL RECIEVING, SHORT, STANDING, SUPERVISION, TEUTONIC, THIRD, WORD

ORDERS - HOLY, MAJOR, MARCHING, MINOR, SEALED

ORGAN - BARREL, ELECTRIC, ELECTRONIC, END, GREAT, HAMMOND, HOUSE, MOUTH, PIPE, PORTATIVE, REED, SENSE, STEAM

OVER - BIND, BLOW, BOIL, BOWL, BRING, CARRY, CHEW, DO, FALL, GET, GIVE, GLOSS, GO, HAND, HOLD, KEEL, LAY, LOOK MAIDEN, MAKE, PAPER, PASS, PUT, ROLL, RUN, SEE, SKATE, SLIDE, SMOOTH, SPILL, STAND, TAKE, THINK, THROW, TICK, TIDE, TURN, WARM, WORK

OYSTER - BUSH, PEARL, PRARIE, SAUCE, SEED, VEGETABLE

P

PACK - BLISTER, BUBBLE, COLD, FACE, FILM, ICE, POWER, WET

PAD - CRASH, HARD, LAUNCHING, LILY, SCRATCH, SHOULDER

PAINT - GLOSS, OIL, POSTER, WAR

PALACE - BUCKINGHAM, CRYSTAL, GIN, PICTURE

PAPER - ART, BALLOT, BLOTTING, BOND, BROMIDE, BROWN, BUILDING, CARBON, CARTRIDGE, CIGARETTE, COMMERCIAL, CREPE, FILTER, FLOCK, GRAPH, GREEN, INDIA, LAVATORY, LINEN, MANILA, MERCANTILE, MUSIC, ORDER, RICE, TISSUE, TOILET, TRACING, WAX, WRITING,

PARK - AMUSEMENT, CAR, COUNTRY, FOREST, GAME, HYDE, NATIONAL, SAFARI, SCIENCE, THEME

PARTY - BOTTLE, COMMUNIST, CONSERVATIVE, FIRING, GARDEN, HEN, HOUSE, LABOUR, LIBERAL,NATIONAL, NATIONALIST, PEOPLE'S, REPUBLICAN, SEARCH, STAG, TEA, THIRD, WORKING

PASSAGE - BACK, BRIDGE, DRAKE, MIDDLE, MONA, NORTHEAST, NORTH WEST, ROUGH, WINDWARD

PATH - BRIDLE, FLARE, FLIGHT, GLIDE, PRIMROSE, TOWING

PAY - BACK, EQUAL, SEVERANCE, SICK, STRIKE, TAKE-HOME

PEA - BLACK-EYED, DESERT, PIGEON, SLIT, SUGAR, SWEET

PEAR - ALLIGATOR, ANCHOVY, CONFERENCE, PRICKLY, WILLIAMS

PEN - CARTRIDGE, CATCHING, DATA, FELT-TIP, FOUNTAIN, QUILL, SEA

PENSION - EN, OCCUPATIONAL, RETIREMENT

PIANO - COTTAGE, CUSTARD, GRAND, PLAYER, PREPARED, SQUARE, STREET, UPRIGHT

PIE - APPLE, COTTAGE, CUSTARD, FISH, HUMBLE, MINCE, MUD, PORK, SHEPHERD'S

PIN - BOBBY, COTTER, DRAWING, END, FIRING, GUDGEON, PANEL, ROLLING, SAFETY, SCATTER, SHEAR, STICK, SWIVEL, TAPER, WREST, WRIST

PIPE - CORNCOB, ESCAPE, FLUE, INDIAN, JET, PEACE, PITCH, RAINWATER, REED, SOIL, WATER

PITCH - ABSOLUTE, CONCERT, FEVER, PERFECT, WOOD

PLACE - DECIMAL, HIGH, HOLY, RESTING, WATERING

PLASTER - COURT, MUSTARD, STICKING

PLATE - ANGLE, ARMOUR, BATTEN, BUTT, ECHO, FASHION, FUTTOCK, GLACIS, GOLD, GROUND, HOME, LICENSE, NICKEL, QUARTER, REGISTRATION, SCREW, SILVER, SOUP, SURFACE, SWASH, TIN, TRADE, WALL, WOBBLE

PLAY - CHILD'S, DOUBLE, FAIR, FOUL, MATCH, MIRICLE, MORTALITY, MYSTERY, PASSION, SHADOW, STROKE

PLEAT - BOX, FRENCH, INVERTED, KICK, KNIFE

POCKET - AIR, HIP, PATCH, SLASH, SLIT

POINT - BOILING, BREAKING, BROWNIE, CHANGE, CLOVIS, CLOVER, CRITICAL, CURIE, DEAD, DECIMAL, DEW, DIAMOND, DRY, END, EQUINOCTIAL, FESSE, FIXED, FLASH, FOCAL, FREEZING, GALLINAS, GAME, GOLD, HIGH, ICE, LIMIT, MATCH, MELTING, OBJECTIVE, PETIT, POWER, PRESSURE, SAMPLE, SATURATION, SET, SPECIE, STEAM, STRONG, SUSPENSION, TRANSITION, TRIG,

TRIPLE, TURNING, VANISHING VANTAGE, WEST, YIELD
POLE - BARBER'S, CELESTIAL, MAGNETIC, NORTH, SOUTH, TOTEM
POLL - ADVANCE, DEED, GALLUP, OPINION, RED, STRAW
POST - COMMAND, FINGER, FIRST, GOAL, GRADED, GRADIENT, HITCHING, LAST, LISTENING, NEWEL, OBSERVATION, REGISTERED, STAGING, TOOL, TRADING, WINNING
POT - CHAMBER, COAL, LOBSTER, MELTING, PEPPER, WATER
POTATO - HOT, IRISH, SEED, SWEET, WHITE
POWDER - BAKING, BLACK, BLEACHING, CHILLI, CURRY, CUSTARD, FACE, GIANT, TALCUM, TOOTH, WASHING
PRESS - DRILL, FILTER, FLY, FOLDING, GUTTER, HYDRAULIC, PRINTING, PRIVATE, RACKET, STOP,
PRESSURE - ATMOSPHERIC, BAROMETRIC, BLOOD, CRITICAL, FLUID, OSMOTIC, PARTIAL, VAPOUR
PRICE - ASKING, BIDDING, BRIDE, INTERVENTION, LIST, MARKET, OFFER, RESERVE, STARTING, UNIT,
PROFESSOR - ASSISTANT, ASSOCIATE, FULL, REGIUS, VISITING
PUDDING - BLACK, CLOOD, CABINET, CHRISTMAS, COLLEGE, EVE'S, HASTY, MILK, PEASE, PLUM, SUET, SUMMER, WHITE, YORKSHIRE
PUMP - AIR, BICYCLE, CENTRIFUGAL, ELECTROMAGNETIC, FILLER, FORCE, HEAT, LIFT, PARISH, PETROL, ROTARY, STIRRUP, STOMACH, SUCTION, VACUUM
PUNCH - BELL, CARD, CENTRE, HOLE, KEY, MILK, PLANTER'S, RABBIT, SUFFOLK, SUNDAY
PURSE - LONG, MERMAID'S, PRIVY, SEA
PUZZLE - CHINESE, CROSSWOR, JIGSAW, MONKEY

Q

QUARTER - EMPTY, FIRST, LAST, LATIN
QUESTION - DIRECT, INDIRECT, LEADING, OPEN, RHETORICAL

R

RABBIT - ANGORA, BUCK, JACK, ROCK, WELSH
RACE - ARMS, BOAT, BUMPING, CLAIMING, DRAG, EGG-AND-SPOON, GREYHOUND, HORSE, HUMAN, MASTER, OBSTACLE, PIGEON, RAT, RELAY, SACK, THREE-LEGGED
RACK CLOUD, ROOF, TOAST
RATE - BANK, BASE, BASIC, BIRTH, BIT, DEATH, EXCHANGE, LAPSE, MORTALITY, MORTGAGE, PIECE, POOR, PRIME, TAX
RECORDER - FLIGHT, INCREMENTAL, TAPE, WIRE
RED - BLOOD, BRICK, CHINESE, CHROME, CONGO, INDIAN, TURKEY, VENETIAN
RELATIONS - COMMUNITY, INDUSTRIAL, LABOUR, PUBLIC, RACE
RELIEF - HIGH, LOW, OUTDOOR, PHOTO
RENT - COST, ECONOMIC, FAIR, GROUND, MARKET, PEPPERCORN
RESERVE - CENTRAL, GOLD, INDIAN, NATURE, SCENIC
REVOLUTION - AMERICAN, BLOODLESS, CHINESE, CULTURAL, FEBRUARY, FRENCH, GLORIOUS, GREEN, INDUSTRIAL, OCTOBER, PALACE, RUSSIAN
RING - ANCHOR, ANNUAL, BENZENE, ENGAGEMENT, ETERNITY, EXTENSION FAIRY, GAS, GROWTH, GUARD, KEEPER. NOSE, PISTON, PRICE, PRIZE, RETAINING, SEAL, SIGNET, SLIP, SNAP, TEETHING, TREE, VORTEX, WEDDING
ROAD - ACCESS, CLAY, CONCESSION, DIRT, ESCAPE, POST, RING, SERVICE, SLIP, TRUNK
ROD - AARON'S, BLACK, BLUE, CON, CONNECTING, CONTROL, DIVINING, DOWSING, DRAIN, FISHING, FLY, IRON, HOT, PISTON, STAIR, TIE, TRACK, WELDING
ROLL - BARREL, BRIDGE, COURT, DANDY, EGG, FORWARD, MUSIC, MUSTER, PIANO, PIPE, SAUSAGE,SNAP, SPRING, SWISS, VICTORY, WESTER,
ROOM - BACK, BED, COMMON, CONSULTING, DAY, DINING, DRAWING, DRESSING, ENGINE, FRONT, GUN, LIVING, MEN'S, OPERATIONS, POWDER, PUMP, RECEPTION, RECREATION, REST, ROBING, RUMPUS, SITTING, SMOKING, STILL, TIRING, UTILITY, WAITING, WITHDRAWING

ROOT - BUTTRESS, CLUB, CUBE, CULVER'S, MALLEE, PLEURISY, PROP, SQUARE
ROT - BACK, BROWN, DRY, FOOT, SOFT, WET
ROUND - BRING, CHANGE, COME, MILK, PAPER, RALLY, SCRUB, TALK
ROW - CORN, DEATH, NOTE, SKID, TONE
ROYAL - ANNAPOLIS, BATTLE, PAIR, PORT, PRINCE, PRINCESS, RHYME
RUBBER - COLD, CREPE, HARD, INDIA, PARA, SMOKED, SORBO, SYTHETIC, WILD
RULE - CHAIN, FOOT, GLOBAL, GOLDEN, GROUND, HOME, PARALLELOGRAM, PHASE, PLUMB, SETTING, SLIDE
RUN - BOMBING, BULL, DRY, DUMMY, GROUND, HEN, HOME, MILK, MOLE, SKI, TRIAL

S
SALAD - CAESAR, CORN, FRUIT, GREEN, RUSSIAN, WALDORF
SALE - BOOT, BRING-AND-BUY, CAR-BOOT, JUMBLE, RUMMAGE, WHITE
SALTS - BATH, EPSOM, HEALTH, LIVER, SMELLING
SAUCE - APPLE, BÉCHAMEL, BREAD, BROWN, CHILLI, CRANBERY, CREAM, HARD, HOLLANDAISE, MELBA, MINT, MOUSSELINE, SOY, TARTAR, TOMATO, WHITE, WORCESTER
SAW - BACK, BAND, BUZZ, CHAIN, CIRCULAR, COMPASS, COPING, CROSSCUT, CROWN, FLOORING, FRET, GANG, HACK, PANEL, SCROLL, STONE, TENON
SCHOOL - APPROVED, BOARDING, CHOIR, COMPREHENSIVE, CORRESPONDENCE, DAME, DAY, DIRECT-GRANT, ELEMENTARY, FINISHING, FIRST, GRAMMAR, HIGH, INDEPENDENT, INFANT, JUNIOR, LOWER, MEDICAL, MIDDLE, NIGHT, NURSEY, PREP, PREPARATORY, PRIMARY, PRIVATE, PUBLIC, RESIDENTIAL, SECONDARY, STAGE, STATE, SUMMER, SUNDAY, UPPER
SCIENCE - BEHAVIOURAL, CHRISTIAN, COGNATIVE, DOMESIC, EARTH, HARD, INFOMATION, LIFE, NATURAL, PHYSICAL, POLICY, POLITICAL, RURAL, SOCIAL, VETERINARY
SCOUT - AIR, BOY, CUB, GIRL, KING'S, QUEEN'S, SEA,TALENT, VENTURE
SCREEN - BIG, FIRE, ORGAN, ROOD, SILVER, SMALL, SMOKE
SCREW - ARCHIMEDES', CAP, COACH, GRUB, ICE, INTERRUPTED, LAG, LEAD, LEVELLING, LUG, MACHINE, MICROMETER, PHILLIPS
SEASON - CLOSE, HIGH, OFF, SILLY
SEAT - BACK, BOX, BUCKET, COUNTRY, COUNTY, DEATH, EJECTION, HOT, JUMP, LOVE, MERCY, RUMBLE, SAFE, SLIDING, WINDOW
SECRETARY - COMPANY, HOME, PARLIAMENTARY, PRIVATE, SOCIAL
SERVICE - ACTIVE, CIVIL, COMMUNITY, DINNER, DIPLOMATIC, DIVINE, FOREIGN, LIP, NATIONAL, PUBLC, ROOM, SECRET, SENIOR, SILVER, TEA
SET - CLOSED, CMPAION, CRYSTAL, DATA, DEAD, FILM, FLASH, JET, LOVE, NAIL, OPEN, ORDERED, PERMANENT, POWER, SAW, SMART, SOLUTION, TOILET, TRUTH
SHAFT - AIR, BUTT, DRIVE, ESCAPE, PROPELLER
SHEET - BALANCE, CHARGE, CRIME, DOPE, FLOW, FLY, ICE, SCRATCH, SWINDLE, TEAR, THUNDER, TIME, WINDING, WORK
SHIFT - BACK, BLUE, DAY, EINSTEIN, FUNCTION, NIGHT, RED, SOUND, SPLIT, SWING
SHIRT - BOILED, BROWN, DRESS, HAIR, SPORTS, STUFFED, SWEAT, TEE
SHOE - BLOCKED, BRAKE, COURT, GYM, HOT, LAUNCHING, PILE, TENNIS, TRACK
SHOP - BETTING, BODY, BUCKET, CLOSED, COFFEE, DUTY-FREE, FISH-AND-CHIP, JUNK, MACHINE, OPEN, PRINT, SEX, SWAP, SWEET, TALKING, TEA, TUCK, UNION
SHOT - APPROACH, BIG, BOOSTER, DIRECT-MAIL, DROP, FOUL, JUMP, LONG, PARTHIAN, PASSING, POT
SHOW - CHAT, DUMB, FLOOR, ICE, LIGHT, MINISTREL, ROAD, TALK, VARIETY
SICKNESS - ALTITUDE, BUSH, DECOMPRESSION, FALLING, MILK, MORNING,, MOTION, MOUNTAIN, RADIATION, SEA, SERUM, SLEEPING, SWEATING
SIDE - FLIP, PROMPT, SPEAR, SUNNY

SLEEVE - BALLOON, BATWING, BISHOP, DOLMAN, RAGLAN

SOAP - CASTILE, GREEN, JOE, METALLIC, SADDLE, SOFT, SUGAR, TOILET

SODA - CAUSTIC, CREAM, ICE-CREAM, WASHING

SOLDIER - FOOT, GALLANT, OLD, RETURNED, TIN, UNKNOWN, WAGON, WATER

SONG - FOLK, PART, PATTER, PRICK, SWAN, THEME, TORCH

SPEECH - CURTAIN, DIRECT, FREE, INDIRECT, KING'S, QUEEN'S, REPORTED

SPIRIT - HOLY, PROOF, SURGICAL, TEAM, WHITE, WOOD

SPOT - BEAUTY, BLACK, BLIND, HIGH, HOT, LEAF, SOFT, TROUBLE

SQUAD - FIRING, FLYING, FRAUD, SNATCH, VICE

SQUARE - ALL, BEVEL, LATIN, MAGIC, MITRE, SET, TIMES, WORD

STAMP - DATE, POSTAGE, RUBBER, TRADING

STAND - HALL, HAT, MUSIC, ONE-NIGHT, UMBRELLA

STANDARD - DOUBLE, GOLD, LAMP, ROYAL, SILVER

STAR - BINARY, BLAZING, DARK, DOG, DOUBLE, DWARF, EVENING, EXPLODING, FALLING, FEATHER, FILM, FIXED, FLARE, GIANT, MORNING, MULTIPLE, NEUTRON, NORTH, POLE, PULSATING, RADIO, SHOOTING

START - BUMP, FLYING, HEAD

STEAK - MINUTE, T-BONE, TARTAR

STICK - BIG, CANCER, COCKTAIL, CONTROL, FRENCH, JOSS, POGO, SHOOTING, SKI, SWAGGER, SWIZZLE, WALKING, WHITE

STITCH - BLANKET, BUTTONHOLE, CABLE, CHAIN, GARTER, LOCK, MOSS, RUNNING, SATIN, SLIP, STOCKING, TENT

STOCK - CAPITAL, COMMON, DEAD, JOINT, LAUGHING, PREFERRED, ROLLING, VIRGINIA

STONE - BATH, BLARNEY, COPING, FOUN DATION, IMPOSING, KIDNEY, OAMARU, PAVING, PRECIOUS, ROSETTA, STEPPING

STOOL - CUCKING, CUTTY, DUCKING, MILKING, PIANO

STRAW - CHEESE, LAST, SHORT

STRIKE - BIRD, GENERAL, HUNGER, OFFICIAL, SIT-DOWN, SYMPATHY, TOKEN, WILDCAT

STUDY - BROWN, CASE, FEASIBILITY, FIELD, MOTION, NATURE, PILOT, TIME

STUFF - HOT, KIDS', ROUGH, SMALL, SOB

SUGAR - BARLEY, BEET, BROWN, CANE, CASTER, CONFECTIONERS', FRUIT, GRANULATED, GRAPE, ICING, INVERT, LOAF, MAPLE, MILK, PALM, SPUN, WOOD

SUIT - BATHING, BIRTHDAY, BOILER, DIVING, DRESS, JUMP, LONG, LOUNGE, MAJOR, MAO, MINOR, MONKEY, PARENITY, PRESSURE, SAFARI, SAILOR, SLACK, TROUSER, WET, ZOOT

T

TABLE - BIRD, COFFEE, DRESSING, GATE-LEG, GLACIER, HIGH, LEAGUE, LIFE, MULTIPLICATION, OCCASIONAL, OPERATING, PEMBROKE, PERIODIC, POOL, REFECTORY, ROUND, SAND, TIDE, TIMES, WATER, WOOL, WRITING

TALK - BABY, DOUBLE, PEP, PILLOW, SALES, SMALL

TAPE - CHROME, FRICTION, GAFFER, GRIP, IDIOT, INSULATING, MAGNETIC, MASKING, PAPER, PERFORATED, PUNCHED, RED, SCOTCH, TICKER, VIDEO

TAR - COAL, JACK, MINERAL, PINE, WOOD,

TENNIS - COURT, DECK, LAWN, REAL, ROYAL, TABLE,

TERM - HALF, HILARY, INKHORN, LAW, LENT, MICHAELMAS, TRINITY

THROUGH - BRAK, CARRY, COME, FOLLOW, MUDDLE, PULL, PUSH, PUT, ROMP, RUN, SCRAPE, SEE, WALK, WORK

TICKET - BUS, MEAL, ONE-WAY, PARKING, PAWN, PLANE, PLATFORM, RETURN, ROUND-TRIP, SEASON, SINGLE, TRAIN,

TIDE - HIGH, LOW, NEAP, RED, SPRING

TIE - BLACK, BOW, CUP, ENGLISHMAN'S, STRING, WHITE, WINDSOR

TIME - BIG, BORROWED, CLOSING, COMMON, COMPOUND, CORE, DAYLIGHT-SAVING, DOUBLE, DOWN, DRINKING-UP, EXTRA, FATHER, FOUR-FOUR, FULL, HIGH, IDLE, INJURY,

LIGHTING-UP, LOCAL, MEAN, OPENING, PRIME, QUADRUPLE, QUESTION, QUICK, RESPONCE, SHORT, SIX-EIGHT, SLOW, STANDARD, SUMMER, THREE-FOUR, TRIPLE, TWO-FOUR, UNIVERSAL

TO - BRING, COME, FALL, GO, HEAVE, KEEP, RISE, RUN, SET, SPEAK, STAND, STICK, TAKE, TUMBLE, TURN

TOGETHER - GO, HANG, HOLD, LIVE, PULL, SCRAPE, SCRATCH, STICK, THROW

TOM - LONG, PEEPING, UNCLE

TOOTH - BABY, EGG, MILK, SWEET, WISDOM

TOP - BIG, DOUBLE, FIGHTING, HUMMING, PEG, ROUND, SCREW, SOFT, SPINNING, TANK

TOWN - BOOM, CAPE, COUNTY, GEORGE, GHOST, MARKET, NEW, POST, TWIN

TRADE - CARRIAGE, FREE, RAG, SLAVE

TRAIN - BOAT, DOG, GRAVY, WAGON, WAVE

TRAP - BOOBY, LIVE, POVERTY, RADAR, SAND, SPEED, STEAM, STENCH, STINK, TANK

TRIANGLE - BERMUDA, CIRCULAR, ETERNAL, PASCAL'S, RIGHT, RIGHT-ANGLED, SPHERICAL

TRICK - CON, CONFIDENCE, DIRTY, HAT, THREE-CARD

TRIP - DAY, EGO, FIELD, ROUND

TROT - JOG, RISING, SITTING, TURKEY

TUBE - CAPILLARY, CATHODE-RAY, DRIFT, ELECTRON, EUSTACHIAN, FALLOPIAN, GEISSLER, INNER, NIXIE, PICTURE, PITOT, POLLEN, SHOCK, SIEVE, SPEAKING, STATIC, TELEVISION, TEST, VACUUM

TURN - ABOUT, GOOD, KICK, LODGING, PARALLEL, STEM, THREE-POINT

U

UNDER - DOWN, GO, KEEP, KNUCKLE, SIT

W

WALL - ANTONINE, CAVITY, CELL, CHINESE, CLIMBING, CURTAIN, FIRE, HADRIAN'S, HANGING, PARTY, RETAINING, SEA, WAILING, WESTERN

WATCH - BLACK, MIDDLE, MORNING, NIGHT

WAVE - BRAIN, ELECTROMAGNETIC, FINGER, GROUND, HEAT, LONG, LONGTIUDINAL, MEDIUM, NEW, PERMANENT, RADIO, SEISMIC, SHOCK, SHORT, SKY, SOUND, STANDING, STATIONARY, TIDAL

WAX - CHINESE, COBBLER'S, EARTH, JAPAN, MINERAL, MONTAN, PARAFFIN, SEALING, VEGETABLE

WAY - APPIAN, EACH, FLAMINIAN, FLY, FOSSE, MILKY, PENNINE, PERMANANT, UNDER

WHEEL - BALANCE, BIG, BUFFING, CATHERINE, CROWN, DISC, DRIVING, EMERY, ESCAPE, FERRIS, GRINDING, PADDLE, POTTER'S, PRAYER, SPINNING, STEERING, STITCH, TAIL, WATER, WIRE

WHISKEY - CORN, IRISH, MALT, SCOTCH

WHISTLE - PENNY, STEAM, TIN, WOLF

WINDOW - BAY, BOW, COMPASS, GABLE, JESSE, LANCET, LAUNCH, PICTURE, RADIO, ROSE, SASH, STORM, WATHER, WHEEL

WIRE - BARBED, CHICKEN, FENCING, HIGH, LIVE, RAZOR

WITH - BEAR, BREAK, CLOSE, DEAL, GO, LIVE, PLAY, SETTLE, SLEEP, STICK

WOMAN - FANCY, LITTLE, LOOSE, OLD, PAINTED, SCARLET, WIDOW

WORK - FIELD, NUMBER, OUTSIDE, SOCIAL

Y

YARD - BACK, MAIN, SCOTLAND

YEAR - ASTRONOMICAL, CALENDAR, CIVIL, EQUINOCTIAL, FINANCIAL, FISCAL, GREAT, HOLY, LEAP, LIGHT, LUNAR, NEW, SABBATICAL, SCHOOL, SIDEREAL, SOLAR, TROPICAL

Z

ZONE - ECONOMIC, ENTERPRISE, FREE, FRIGID, HOT, NUCLEAR-FREE, SKIP, SMOKELESS, TEMPERATE, TIME, TORRID, TWILIGHT

ABBREVIATIONS

A

AA (Alcoholics Anonymous; Automobile Association)
AAA (Amateur Athletics Association)
AB (able-bodied seaman)
ABA (Amateur Boxing Association)
ABP (archbishop)
ABTA (Association of British Travel Agents)
AC (alternating current)
a/c (account)
ACA (Associate of the Institute of Chartered Accountants)
ACAS (Advisory Conciliation and Arbitration Service)
ACIS (Associate of the Chartered Institute of Secretaries)
AD (Anno Domini)
ADC (aide-de-camp; amateur dramatic club)
ADJ (adjective)
ADM (admiral)
ADV (adverb)
AD VAL (ad valorem)
AF (Admiral of the Fleet)
AFA (Amateur Football Association0
AFC (Air Force Cross)
AFM (Air Force Medal)
AG (Adjutant-General)
AGM (annual eneral meeting)
AI (artificial insemination; artificial intelli gence)
AIB (Associate of the Institute of Bankers)
AIDS (Acquired Immune Deficiency Syndrome)
AK (Alaska)
AL (Alabama)
ALA (American Library Association)
AM (ante meridiem)
AMU (atomic mass unit)
ANON (anonymous)
AOB (any other business)
AOC (Air Officer Commanding)
AP (Associated Press)
APEX (Association of Professional, Executive, Clerical and Computer Staff)
APOCR (Apocrypha)
APPROX (approximate)
APT (Advanced Passenger Train)
AR (Arkansas)
ARA (Associate of the Royal Academy)
ARAM (Associate of the Royal Academy of Music)
ARCS (Associate of the Royal College of Science)
ARIBA (Associate of the Royal Institute of British Architects)
ASA (Advertising Standards Agency)
ASAP (as soon as possible)
ASH (Action on Smoking and Health)
ASLEF (Associated Society of Locomotive Engineers and Firemen
AT (atomic)
ATC (air traffic control; Air Training Corps)
ATS (Auxiliary Territorial Service)
ATTN (for the attention of)
ATTRIB (attributive)
AT WT (atomic weight)
AU (Angström unit; astronomical unit)
AUEW (Amalgamated Union of Engineering Workers)
AUG (August)
AV (ad valoem; Authorized Version, average)
AVDP (avoirdupois)
AVE (avenue)
AWOL (absent without leave)
AZ (Arizona)

B

BA (Bachelor of Arts; British Academy; British Airways; British Association)
BAA (British Airports Association)
BAFTA (British Academy of Film and Television Arts)
B ARCH (Bachelor of Architecture)
BART (baronet)
BB (Boys' Brigade)
BBC (British Broadcasting Corporation)
BC (Before Christ; British Columbia)
BCH (Bachelor of Surgery)
BCL (Bachelor of Civil Law)
BCOM (Bachelor of Commerce)
BD (Bachelor of Divinity)
BDA (British Dental Association)
BDS (Bachelor of Dental Surgery)
BE (bill of exchange)
B Ed (Bachelor of Education)
B ENG (Bachelor of Engineering)
BHP (brake horsepower)
BIM (British Institute of Management)
BL (bill of lading)
B LITT (Bachelor of Letters)
BM (British Museum)
BMA (British Medical Association)
BMC (British Medical Council)
BMJ (British Medical Journal)
BMUS (Bachelor of Music)

BN (billion)
BOC (British Oxygen Company)
BP (bishop, boiling point; British Petroleum; British Pharmacopoeia)
BPAS (British Pregnancy Advisory Centre)
BPHARM (Bachelor of Pharmacy)
BPHIL (Bachelor of Philosophy)
BR (British Rail)
BRCS (British Red Cross Society)
BROS (brothers)
BSC (Bachelor of Science)
BSI (British Standards Institution)
BST (British Standard Time; British Summer Time)
BT (Baronet; British Telecom)
BTA (British Tourist Authority)
BVA (British Veterinary Association)

C

C (centigrade, circa)
CA (chartered accountant; California)
CAA (Civil Aviation Athority)
CAD (computer-aided design)
CADCAM (computer-aided design and manufacture)
CAL (calorie)
CAM (computer-aided manufacture)
CAMRA (Campaign for Real Ale)
C and G (City and Guilds)
C and W (country and western)
CANT (canticles)
CANTAB (of Cambridge - used with academic awards)
CAP (capital)
CAPT (captain)
CARD (carinal)
CB (Citizens' Band; Companion of the Order of Bath; confined to barracks)
CBE (Commander of the British Empire)
CBI (Confederationof British Industry)
CC (County Council; City Council; Cricket Club; Chamber of Commerce; cubic centimetre; carbon copy)
CD (compact disc; civil defence; corps diplomatique)
CDR (Commander)
CDRE (Commodore)
CE (Church of England; civil engineer)
CEGB (Central Electricity Generating Board)
C ENG (Chartered Engineer)
CENTO (Central Treaty Organization)
CERT (certificate, certified, certify)
CET (Central European Time)
CF (compare; Chaplain to the Forces)
CFE (College of Further Education)
CFI (cost, freight, and insurance)
CGM (Conspicuous Gallantry Medal)
CH (chapter; church; Companion of Honour)
CHAS (Charles)
CI (Channel Islands; Lady of Imperial Order of the Crown of India)
CIA (Central Intelligence Agency)
CID (Criminal Investigation Depatment)
CIE (Companion of the Indian Empire)
CIF (cost, insurance, and freight)
CII (Chartered Insurance Institute)
C in C (Commander in Chief)
CIS (Chartered Institute of Secretaries)
CJ (Chief Justice)
CL (centilitre; clause; class; Companion of Literature)
CLLR (councillor)
cm (centimetre)
CMG (Companion of Saint Michael and Saint George)
CNAA (Council for National Academic Awards)
CND (Campaign for Nuclear Disarmament)
CO (commanding officer; company; county; Colorado; concientious objector)
c/o (care of)
COD (cash on delivery)
C of E (Church of England)
C of S (Church of Scotland)
COHSE (Confederation of Health Service Employees)
COL (colonel; Colossians)
CONT (continued)
COR (Corinthians)
COS (cosine)
CP (Communist Party)
CR (credit)
CRO (cathode ray oscilloscope; Criminal Records Office)
CSE (Certificate of Secondary Education)
CSI (Companion of the Star of India)
CSM (Company Segeant Major)
CT (Connecticut; Civic Trust
CU (cubic; Cambridge University)
CV (curriculum vitae)
CVO (Commander of the Victorian Order)
CWT (hundredweight)

D

D (daughter; died; penny)
DA (District Attorney)
dB (decibel)
DAN (Daniel)
DBE (Dame Commander of the British Empire)
DC (Detective Constable; direct current; from the beginning; District of Columbia)

DCB (Dame Commander of the Bath)

DCL (Doctor of Civil Law)

DCM (Distinguished Conduct Medal)

DCMG (Dame Commander of Saint Michael and Saint George)

DCVO (Dame Commander of the Victorian Order)

DD (direct debit; Doctor of Divinity)

DDS (Doctor of Dental Surgery)

DE (Delaware)

Dept (department)

DES (Department of Education and Science)

Deut (Deuteronomy)

DF (Defender of the Faith)

DFC (Distinguished Flying Cross)

DFM (Distinguished Flying Medal)

DG (Dei gratia - by the Grace of God; Deo gratias – thanks be to God)

DHSS (Department of Health and Socal Security)

DI (Detective Inspector)

DIAL (dialect)

DIP (Diploma)

DIP ED (Diploma in Education)

DIY (do it yourself)

DK (Dakota)

DL (Deputy Lieutenant)

D LITT (Doctor of Literature)

DM (Deutschmark; Doctor of Medicine)

D MUS (Doctor of Music)

DNB (Dictionary of National Biography)

DO (ditto)

DOA (dead on arrival)

DOB (date of birth)

DOD (date of death

DOE (Department of the Enviroment)

DOM (to God, the best and the greatest)

DOZ (dozen)

DPHIL (Doctor of Philosophy)

DPP (Director of Public Prosecutions)

DHSS (Department of Health and Socal Security)

DI (Detective Inspector)

DIAL (dialect)

DIP (Diploma)

DIP ED (Diploma in Education)

DIY (do it yourself)

D LITT (Doctor of Literature)

DM (Doctor of Medicine)

D MUS (Doctor of Music)

DNB (Dictionary of National Biography)

DO (ditto)

DOA (dead on arrival)

DOB (date of birth)

DOE (Department of the Enviroment)

DOM (to God, the best and the greatest)

DOZ (dozen)

DPHIL (Doctor of Philosophy)

DPP (Director of Public Prosecutions)

DR (debter; doctor; drive; Drachma)

DSC (Distinguished Service Cross; Doctor of Science)

DSM (Distinguished Service Medal)

DSO (Distinguished Service Order)

DT (delirium tremens)

DV (Deo volente – God willing)

DVLC (Driver and Vehicle Licencing Centre)

E

E (East; Easterly, Eastern)

EA (each)

EC (East Central London postal district; European Community; electricity council)

ECCLES (Ecclesiastes)

ECCLUS (Ecclesiasticus)

ECG (electrocardiogram)

ECS (European Communicating Satellite)

Ed (editor)

EE (Early English; Electrical engineer; errors accepted

EEC (European Economic Community)

EEG (electroencephalogram)

EFTA (European Free Trade Association)

EG (exempli gratia – for example)

EMA (Europen Monetry Agreement)

EMF (electromotive force)

ENC (enclosed; enclosure)

ENE (east-northeast)

ENSA (Entertainments National Service Association)

ENT (ear, nose and throat)

EOC (Equal Opportunities Commission)

EOF (end of file)

EP (electroplatde; epistle' extended play)

EPH (Ephesians)

EPNS (electropated nickel silver)

EPROM (erasable programmable read only memory)

eq (equal)

ER (Edward Rex; Elizabeth Regina)

ERNIE (Electronic Random Number Indicator Equipment

ESE (east-southeast)

ESN (educationally subnormal)

ESQ (esquire)

ETA (estimated time of arrival)

ETC (etctera)

ETD (estimated time of departure)

ET SEQ (and the following one)

EU (European Union)

EX DIV (without dividend)

EX LIB (from the books)

EXOD (Exodus)
EZEK (Ezekiel)

F

F (Fahrenheit; franc)
FA (Football Association)
FAS (free alongside ship)
FBA (Fellow of the British Academy)
FBI (Federal Bureau of Investigation)
FC (Football Club)
FCA (Fellow of the Institute of Chartered Accountants)
FCII (Fellow of the Chartered Insurance Institute)
FCIS (Fellow of the Chartered Institute of Secretaries)
FCO (Foreign Commonwealth Office)
ff (fortissimo)
FH (fire hydrant)
FIFA (International Football Federation)
FL (flourished; Florida)
FM (Field Marshall; frequency modulation)
FO (Field Officer; Flying Officer; Foreign Office; folio)
FOB (free on board)
FOC (Father of the Chapel; free of charge)
fp (freezing point)
FPA (Family Planning Association)
Fr (French)
FRAM (Fellow of the Royal Academy of Music)
FRAS (Fellow of the Royal Astronomical Society)
FRCM (Fellow of the Royal College of Music)
FRCO (Fellow of the Royal College of Organists)
FRCOG (Fellow of the Royal College of Obstetricians and Gynaecologists)
FRCP (Fellow of the Royal College of Physicians)
FRCS (Fellow of the Royal College of Surgeons)
FRCVS (Fellow of the Royal College of Veterinary Surgeons)
FRGS (Fellow of the Royal Geographical Society)
FRIBA (Fellow of the Royal Institute of British Architects)
FRIC (Fellow of the Royal Institute of Chemistry)
FRICS (Fellow of the Royal Institute of Chartered Surveyers)
FRPS (Fellow of the Royal Photographic Society)
FRS (Fellow of the Royal Society)
FRSA (Fellow of the Royal Society of Arts)
FSA (Fellow of the Society of Antiquaries)
ft (feet; foot)
FZS (Fellow of the Zoological Society)

G

G (gram)
GA (Georgia)
GAL (Galatians)
GATT (General Agreement on Tarrifs and Trade)
GB (Great Britain)
GBE (Knight/Dame Grand Cross of the British Empire)
GBH (grievous bodily harm)
GC (George Cross)
GCB (Knight/Dame Grand Cross of the Bath)
GCE (General Certificate of Education)
GCHQ (Government Communication Head Quarters)
GCIE (Grand Commander of the Indian Empire)
GCMG (Knight/Dame Grand Cross of Saint Michael and Saint George)
GCSE (Ge
neral Certificate of Secondary Education)
GCVO (Knight/Dame Grand Cross of the Victorian Order)
GDNS (gardens)
GDP (gross domestic product)
GDR (German Democratic Republic)
GEO (George)
GER (German)
GHQ (General Head Quarters)
GI (governement issue; US soldier)
GIB (Gibralter)
GLC (Greater London Council)
gm (gram
GM (George Medal; Grand Master)
GMT (Greenwich Mean Time)
GNP (gross national product)
GOM (grand old man)
GP (general practitioner)
GPO (general post office)

H

H (hour)
HCF (highest common factor)
HEB (Hebrews)
HF (high frequency)
HGV (heavy goods vehicle)
HI (Hawaii)
HIH (His/Her Imperial Highness)
HIM (His/Her Imperial Majesty)
HM (headmaster/headmistress; His Her Majesty)

HMI (His/Her Majesty's Inspector)
HMS (His/Her Majesty's Ship)
HMSO (His/Her Majesty's Stationary Office)
HND (Higher National Diploma)
HO (Home Office; house)
HON (honorary; honour; honourable)
HONS (honours)
HON SEC (Honorary Secretary)
HOS (Hosea)
HP (hire purchase; horsepower)
HQ (headquarters)
HR (holiday route; hour)
HRH (His/Her Royal Highness)
HSH (His/Her Serene Highness)
HT (height)
HV (high velocity; high voltage)

I
IA (Institute of Actuaries; Iowa)
IAAF (International Amateur Athletic Federation)
IABA (International Amateur Boxing Association)
IATA (International Air Transport Association)
IB (ibidem; Institute of Bankers)
IBA (Independent Broadcasting Authority)
IBID (ibidem)
IC (in charge; intergrated circuit)
ICE (Institution of Civil Engineers)
ICHEME (Institute of Chemical Engineers)
ID (idem; identification; Idaho)
IE (that is)
IEE (Institute of Electrical Engineers)
IHS (Jesus)
IL (Illinois)
I MECH E (Institution of Mechanical Engineers)
IMF (International Monetary Fund)
IN (Indiana)
INC (incorporated)
INCL (included; including; inclusive)
INST (instant)
IOM (Isle of Man)
IOW (Isle of Wight)
IPA (International Phonetic Alphabet)
IQ (intelligence quotient)
IR (Inland Revenue)
IRA (Irish Republican Army)
IS (Isaiah)
ISO (Imperial Service Order)
ITA (initial teaching alphabet)
ITAL (italic; italicized)
ITV (Independent Television)

J
JAM (James)
JC (Jesus Christ; Julius Caesar)
JER (Jeremiah)
JNR (junior)
JP (Justice of the Peace)
JR (junior)

K
KB (King's Beach)
KBE (Knight Commander of the British Empire)
KC (King's Council)
KCB (Knight Commander of the Bath)
KCIE (Knight Commander of the Indian Empire)
KCMG (Knight Commander of Saint Michael and Saint George)
KCSI (Knight Commander of the Star of India)
KCVO (Knight Commander of the Victorian Order)
KG (kilogram; Knight of the Garter)
KGB (Soviet State Security Commitee)
KKK (Ku Klux Klan)
KM (kilometre)
KO (knock out)
KP (Knight of Saint Patrick)
KS (Kansas)
KSTJ (Knight of Saint John)
KT (Knight of the Thistle)
KY (Kentucky)

L
L (Latin; learner; pound)
LA (Louisiana; Los Angeles)
LAT (latitude)
LB (pound)
LBW (leg before wicket)
lc (lower case)
LCD (liquid crystal display; lowest common denominator)
LCJ (Lord Chief Justice)
LEA (Local Education Authority)
LEV (leviticus)
LF (low frequency)
LIEUT (Lieutenant)
LITT D (Doctor of Letters; Doctor of Literature)
LJ (Lord Justice)
LLB (Bachelor of Laws)
LLD (Doctor of Laws)
LLM (Master of Laws)
LOC CIT (in the place cited)
LOQ (he/she speaks)
LP (long playing)

LPG (liquefied petroleum gas)
LPO (London Philharmonic Orchestra)
LPS (London Privy Seal)
LRAM (Licentiate of the Royal Academy of Music)
LRCM (Licentiate of the Royal College of Music)
LRCP (Licentiate of the Royal College of Physicians)
LRCS (Licentiate of the Royal College of Surgeons)
LS (locus sigilli)
LSD (pounds, shillings, pence)
LSE (London School of Economics)
LSO (London Symphony Orchestra)
LTD (limited)
LW (long wave)

M

M (male; married; motorway; thousand)
MA (Master of Arts; Massachusetts)
MAJ (Major)
MAL (Malachi)
MASH (moblie army surgical hospital)
MATT (Matthew)
MB (Bachelor of Medicine)
MBE (Member of the British Empire)
MC (Master of Ceremonies)
MCC (Marylebone Cricket Club)
MCP (male chauvinist pig)
MD (Doctor of Medicine; Managing Director, Maryland)
ME (Maine)
MEP (Member of the European Parliament)
MET (meteorological; meteorology; metropolitan)
MF (medium frequency)
mg (milligram)
MI (Michigan)
MICE (Member of the Institution of Civil Engineers)
MIEE (Member of the Institution of Mechanical Engineers)
ML (millilitre)
M LITT (Master of Letters)
MLR (minimum lending rate)
mm (millimetre)
MN (Minnesota)
MO (Medical Officer; Missouri)
MOC (Mother of the Capel)
MOD (Ministry of Defence)
MOH (Medical Officer of Health)
MP (Member of Parliament; Metropolitan Police; Military Police)
MPG (miles per gallon)
MPH (miles per hour)
MPHIL (Master of Philosophy)
MR (Master of the Rolls)
MRCOG (Member of the Royal College of Obstetricians and Gynacologists)
MRCP (Member of the Royal College of Physicians)
MRCS (Member of the Royal College of Surgeons)
MRCVS (Member of the Royal College of Veterinary Surgeons)
MS (manuscript; multiple sclerosis; Mississippi)
MSC (Master of Scienec)
MSM (Meritorious Service Medal)
MSS (manuscripts)
MT (Mount; Montana)
MVO (Memeber of the Victorian Order)

N

N (north)
NA (North America; not applicable)
NAAFI (Navy, Army, and Air Force Institutes)
NALGO (National and Local Government Officers Association)
NATO (North Atlantic Treaty Organisation)
NATSOPA (National Society of Operative Printers, Graphical, and Media Personnel)
NB (note well)
NC (North Carolina)
NCB (National Coal Board)
NCO (non-commissioned officer)
NCP (National Car Parks)
NCT (National Childbirth Trust)
NCV (no commercial value)
ND (North Dakota)
NE (northeast; Nebraska)
NEC (National Executive Commitee)
NF (National Front)
NFU (National Farmers' Union)
NGA (National Geographical Association)
NH (New Hampshire)
NHS (National Health Service)
NI (National Insurance; Northern Ireland)
NJ (New Jersey)
NM (New Mexico)
NNE (north-northeast)
NNW (north-northwest)
NO (not out; number)
NORM (normal)
NOS (numbers)
NP (new paragraph)
NR (near; Northern Region)
NRA (National Rifle Association)
NSB (National Savings Bank)
NSPCC (National Society fot the Provention of Cruelty to Children)
NSW (New South Wales)

NT (National Trust; New Testament)
NUBE (National Union of Bank Employees)
NUGMW (National Union of General and Municipal Workers)
NUJ (National Union of Journaists)
NUM (National Union of Mineworkers)
NUPE (National Union of Public Employees)
NUR (National Union of Railwaymen)
NUS (National Union of Seamen; National Union of Students)
NUT (National Union of Teachers)
NV (Nevada)
NW (northwest)
NY (New York)
NZ (New Zealand)
O
OAP (old-age pensioner)
OB (outside broadcast)
OBE (Officer of the British Empire)
OCTU (Officer Cadets Training Unit)
OECD (Organization for Economic Co-operation and Development)
OFM (Order of Friars Minor)
OH (Ohio
OHMS (On His/Her Majesty's Service)
OK (okay; Oklahoma)
OM (Order of Merit)
ONC (Ordinary National Certificate)
OND (Ordinary National Diploma)
ONO (or near offer)
OP (opus)
OP CIT (in the work cited)
OPEC (Organisation of Petroleum Exporting Countries)
OPS (operations)
OR (Oregon)
OS (ordinary seamen; Ordanace Survey)
OSA (Order of Saint Augustine)
OSB (Order of Saint Benedict)
OSF (Order of Saint Francis)
OT (occupational therapy; Old Testament)
OTC (Officers' Training Corps)
OU (Open University)
OUDS (Oxford University Dramatic Society)
OXFAM (Oxford Commitee for Famine Relief)
OZ (ounce)

P
P (page; penny; purl)
PA (Pennsylvania; per annum; personal assistant; public address system)
PAYE (pay as you earn)
PC (per cent; personal computer; police constable; politically correct)
PD (paid)
PDSA (Peaple's Dispensary for Sick Animals)
PE (physical education)
PEI (Prince Edward Island)
PER PRO (by the agency of)
PG (paying guest; post graduate)
PHD (Doctor of Philosophy)
PHIL (Philippians)
PL (place; plural)
PLC (public limited company)
PLO (Palestine Liberation Organisation)
PM (post meridiem; Prime Minister0
PO (Petty Office; Pilot Officer; postal order; Post Office)
POW (prisoner of war)
PP (pages; per pro)
PPS (further postscript; Parliamentary Private Secretary)
PR (public relations)
PRAM (programmable random access memory)
PRO (Public Records Office; public relations officer)
PROM (programmable read-only memory)
PROV (Proverbs)
PS (postscript; private secretary)
PT (physical training)
PTA (Parent-Teacher Association)
PTO (please turn over)
PVA (polyvinyl acetate)
PVC (polyvinyl chloride)
Q
QB (Queen's Bench)
QC (Queen's Council)
QUD (which was to be demonstrated)
QM (quartermaster)
QR (quarter; quire)
QT (quart)
QV (which see)

R
R (king; queen; right; river)
RA (Royal Academy; Royal Artillery)
RAC (Royal Automoile Club)
RADA (Royal Academy of Dramatic Art)
RAF (Royal Air Force)
RAM (random access memory; Royal Academy of Music)
RAMC (Royal Army Medical Corps)
RAOC (Royal Army Ordnance Corps)
R and D (research and development)
RBA (Royal Society of British Arts)
RBS (Royal Society of British Sculpters)
RC (Roman Catholic)
RCA (Royal College of Art)
RCM (Royal College of Music)
RCN (Royal College of Nursing)

RCP (Royal College of Physicians)
RCS (Royal College of Surgeons)
RCVS (Royal College of Veterinary Surgeons)
RD (road)
RE (religious education; Royal Engineers)
REME (Royal Electrical and Mechanical Engineers)
REV (Reverend)
RFC (Royal Flying Corps)
RH (Royal Highness; right hand)
RHA (Royal Horse Artillery)
RI (religious instruction; Rhode Island)
RIBA (Royal Institute of British Architects)
RIC (Royal Institute of Chemistry)
RICS (Royal Institution of Chartered Surveyors)
RIP (may he rest in peace)
RK (religious knowledge)
RM (Resident Magistrate; Royal Mail; Royal Marines)
RMA (Royal Military Academy)
RN (Royal Navy)
RNIB (Royal National Institute for the Blind)
RNLI (Royal National Lifeboat Association)
ROM (read only memory)
ROSPA (Royal Society for the Prevention of Accidents)
RPM (revolutions per minute)
RSA (Royal Society of Arts)
RSC (Royal Shakespeare Company)
RSM (Regimental Sereant Major; Royal Society of Medicine)
RSPB (Royal Society for the Protection of Birds)
RSPCA (Royal Society for the Prevention of Cruelty to Animals)
RSVP (please answer)
RT HON (Right Honorable)
RT REV (Right Reverend)
RU (Rugby Union)
RUC (Royal Ulster Constabulary)

S

S (second; shilling; South)
SA (Salvation Army; Sex Appeal; South Africa)
SAE (stamped addressed envelope)
SALT (Strategic Arms Limitation Talks)
SAS (Special Air Service)
SATB (soprano, alto, tenor, bass)
SAYE (save as you earn)
SC (South Carolina)
SCD (Doctor of Science)
SD (South Dakota)
SE (southeast)
SEATO (South-East Asia Treaty Organization)
SEC (second; secretary)
SEN (senior; State Enrolled Nurse)
SEQ (the following)
SF (science fiction)
SGT (Sergeant)
SHAPE (Supreme Headquarters Allied Powers in Europe)
SI (Internatiuonal System of Units)
SINE (sine)
SLADE (Society of Lithographic Artists, Designers, and Etchers)
SLR (single lens reflex)
SNCF (French National Railways)
SNP (Scottish National Party)
SNR (senior)
SOGAT (Society of Graphical and Allied Trades)
SOP (soprano)
SQ (square)
SRN (State Registered Nurse)
SSE (south-southeast)
SSW (south-southwest)
ST (saint; street)
STD (sexually transmitted disease; subscriber trunk dialling)
SW (southwest)

T

TA (Territorial Army)
TAN (tangent)
TASS (official news agency of the Soviet Union)
TB (tubercle bacillus)
TCCB (Test and County Cricket Board)
TEFL (teaching English as a foreign language)
TGWU (Transport and General Workers' Union)
THOS (Thomas)
TM (tademark; transcendental meditation)
TN (Tennesee)
TOPS (Training Opportunities Scheme)
TSB (Trustee Savings Bank)
TT (teetotal; teetotaller; time trials)
TU (trade union)
TUC (Trades Union Congress)
TV (television)
TX (Texas)

U

UC (upper case)
UCAS (University and Colleges Admissions Service)
UCATT (Union of Construction, AlliedTrades, and Technicians)

UCCA (Universities Central Council on Admissions)
UCL (University College, London)
UDI (unilateral declaration of independence)
UEFA (Union of European Football Assosiations)
UHF (ultrahigh frequency)
UHT (ultrahigh temperature)
UK (United Kingdom)
ULT (ultimo)
UN (United Nations)
UNCTAD (United Nations Commission for Trade and Development)
UNESCO (United Nations Educational, Scientific, and Cultural Organisation)
UNICEF (United Nations International Children's Emergency Fund)
UNO (United Nations Organisation)
UPOW (Union of Post Office Workers)
US (United States)
USA (United States of America)
USDAW (Union of Shop, Distributive, and Allied Workers)
UT (Utah)

V

V (verse; versus; volt)
VA (Order of Victoria and Albert; Virginia)
VAT (value-added tax)
VB (verb)
VC (Vice Chancellor; Victoria Cross)
VD (venereal disease)
VDU (visual display unit)
VE (Victory in Europe)
VG (very good)
VHF (very high frequency)
VIP (very important person)
VIZ (namely)
VLF (very low frequency)
VR (Victoria Regina; Volunteer Reserve)
VS (veterinary surgeon; vital statistics)
VSO (Voluntary Service Overseas)
VT (Vermont)

W

W (west)
WA (Washington)
WAAC (Woman's Army Auxiliary Corps)
WAAF (Woman's Auxiliary Air Force)
WC (water closet; West Central)
WI (West Indies; Wisconsin; Woman's Institute)
WK (week)
WM (William)
WNW (west-northwest)
WO (Warrent Officer)
WP (word processor)
WPC (Woman Police Constable)
WPM (words per minute)
WRAC (Woman's Royal Army Corps)
WRAF (Woman's Royal Air Force)
WRNS (Woman's Royal Naval Service)
WRVS (Woman's Royal Voluntary Service)
WSW (west-southwest)
WT (weight)
WV (West Virginia)
WW (World War)
WWF (World Wildlife Fund)
WY(Wyoming)

X

XL (extra large)

Y

YHA (Youth Hostels Association)
YMCA (Young Men's Christian Association)
YR (year)
YWCA (Young Woman's Christian Association)

GAZETTEER OF COUNTRIES

AFGHANISTAN
Capital: Kabul
Currency: afghani (pul)
Language: Pushtoo, Dari Persian

ALBANIA
Capital: Tirana
Currency: lek (qindar)
Language: Albanian

ALGERIA
Capital: Algiers
Currency: dinar (centime)
Language: Arabic, French

ANGOLA
Capital: Luanda
Currency: kwanza (lweis)
Language: Portuguese

ANTIGUA AND BARBUDA
Capital: St Johns
Currency: dollar (cent)
Language: English

ARGENTINA
Capital: Buenos Aires
Currency: austral (centavo)
Language: Spanish

ARMENIA
Capital: Erevan
Currency: rouble (kopek)
Language: Armenian

AUSTRALIA
Capital: Canberra
Currency. dollar (cent)
Language: English

AUSTRIA
Capital: Vienna
Currency: schilling (groschen)
Language: German

AZERBAIJAN
Capital: Baku
Currency: rouble (kopek)/manat(gopik)
Language: Turkish

BAHAMAS
Capital: Nassau
Currency: dollar (cent)
Language: English

BAHRAIN
Capital: Manama
Currency: dinar (fils)
Language: Arabic

BANGLADESH
Capital: Dhaka
Currency taka (poisha)
Language: Bengali, English

BARBADOS
Capital: Bridgetown
Currency: dollar (cent)
Language: English

BELARUS
Capital: Minsk
Currency: rouble (kopeks)
Language: Russian

BELGIUM
Capital: Brussels
Currency: dollar (cent)
Language: English

BELIZE
Capital: Belmopan
Currency: franc (centime)
Language: French, Flemish, German

BOLIVIA
Capital: La Paz
Currency: boliviano (centavo)
Language: Spanish

BOSNIA-HERZEGOVINA
Capital: Sarajevo
Currency: dinar (para)
Language: French, Flemish, German

BOTSWANA
Capital: Gaborone
Currency: pula (thebe)
Language: English

BRAZIL
Capital: Brasilia
Currency: cruzado (centavo)
Language: Portuguese

BRUNEI
Capital: Bandar Seri Begawan
Currency: dollar (sen)
Language: Malay

BULGARIA
Capital: Sofia
Currency:lev (stotinka)
Language: Bulgarian

CAMBODIA
Capital: Phnom Penh
Currency: riel (sen)
Language: Khmer

CAMEROON
Capital: Yaounde
Currency: franc CFA (centime)
Language: French, English

CANADA
Capital: Ottowa
Currency: dollar (cent)
Language: English, French

CENTRAL AFRICAN REBUBLIC
Capital: Bangui
Currency: franc CFA (centime)
Language: French, Sango

CHAD
Capital: Ndjamena
Currency: franc CFA (centime)
Language: French

CHILE
Capital Santiago
Currency: peso (centavo)
Language: Spanish

CHINA
Capital: Peking
Currency: yuan (fen)
Language: Mandarin Chinese

COLOMBIA
Capital: Bogota
Currency: peso (centavo)
Language: Spanish

CONGO
Capital: Brazzaville
Currency: franc CFA (centime)
Language: French

COSTA RICA
Capital: San Jose
Currency: colon (centimo)
Language: Spanish

COTE D'IVOIRE
Capital: Abidjan
Currency: franc CFA (centime)
Language: French

CROATIA
Capital: Zagreb
Currency: dinar (para)
Language: Serbo-Croat

CUBA
Capital: Havana
Currency: peso (centavo)
Language: Spanish

CYPRUS
Capital: Nicosia
Currency: pound (cent)
Language: Greek, Turkish

CZECH REPUBLIC
Capital: Prague
Currency: koruna (heller)
Language: Czech

DENMARK
Capital: Copenhagen
Currency: krone (ore)
Language: Danish

DOMINICA
Capital: Roseau
Currency: dollar (cent)
Language: English

DOMINICAN REPUBLIC
Capital: Santo Domingo
Currency: peso (centavo)
Language: Spanish

ECUADOR
Capital: Quito
Currency: sucre (centavo)
Language: Spanish

EGYPT
Capital: Cairo
Currency: pound (piastre)
Language: Arabic

EL SALVADOR
Capital: San Salvador
Currency: colon (centavo)
Language: Spanish

ESTONIA
Capital: Tallinn
Currency: kroon (sent)
Language: Estonian, Russian

ETHIOPIA
Capital: Addis Ababa
Currency: birr (cent)
Legislature: Shengo (National Assembly)

FIJI
Capital: Suva
Currency: dollar (cent)
Language: English

FINLAND
Capital: Helsinki
Currency: markka (penni)
Language: Finnish, Swedish

FRANCE
Capital: Paris
Currency: franc (centime)
Language: French

THE GABON
Capital: Libreville
Currency: Franc CFA (centime)
Language: French

GAMBIA
Capital: Banjul
Currency: dalasi (butut)
Language: English

GERMANY
Capital: Bonn
Currency: Deutsche Mark (Pfennig)
Language: German

GHANA
Capital: Accra
Currency: cedi (pesewa)
Language: English

GREECE
Capital: Athens
Currency: drachma (lepton)
Language: Greek

GUATEMALA
Capital: Guatemala City
Currency: quetzal (centavo)
Language: Spanish

HAITI
Capital: Port-au-Prince
Currency: gourde (centime)
Language: French, Creole

HONDURAS
Capital: Tegucigalpa
Currency: lempira (centavo)
Language: Spanish

HONG KONG
Capital: Victoria
Currency: dollar (cent)
Language: Mandarin Chinese

HUNGARY
Capital: Budapest
Currency: forint (filler)
Language: Hungarian

ICELAND
Capital: Reykjavik
Currency: krona (eyrir)
Language: Icelandic

INDIA
Capital: New Delhi
Currency: rupee (paisa)
Language: Hindi, English

INDONESIA
Capital: Jakarta
Currency: rupiah (sen)
Language: Bahasa Indonesian

IRAN
Capital: Tehran
Currency: rial (dinar)
Language: Farsi (Persian)

IRAQ
Capital: Baghdad
Currency: dinar (fils)
Language: Arabic

IRELAND, REPUBLIC OF
Capital: Dublin
Currency: pound (pence)
Language: Irish Gaelic, English

ISRAEL
Capital: Jerusalem
Currency: shekel (agora)
Language: Hebrew, Arabic

ITALY
Capital: Rome
Currency: lira (centesimo)
Language: Italian

JAMAICA
Capital: Kingston
Currency: dollar (cent)
Language: English

JAPAN
Capital: Tokyo
Currency: yen
Language: Japanese

JORDAN
Capital: Amman
Currency: dinar (fils)
Language: Arabic

KAZAKHSTAN
Capital: Alma-Ata
Currency: rouble (kopek)
Language: Russian, Kazakh

KENYA
Capital: Nairobi
Currency: shilling (cent)
Language: English, Swahili

KOREA, DEMOCRATIC PEOPLE'S REPUBLIC OF (North Korea)
Capital: P'yongyang
Currency: won (chon)
Language: Korean

KOREA, REPUBLIC OF (South Korea)
Capital: Seoul
Currency: won (jeon)
Language: Korean

KUWAIT:
Capital: Kuwait
Currency: dinar (fils)
Language: Arabic

LAOS
Capital: Vientiane
Currency: kip (at)
Language: Lao

LATVIA
Capital: Riga
Currency: lats
Language: Latvian, Russia

LEBANON
Capital: Beirut
Currency: pound (piastre)
Language: Arabic

LIBERIA
Capital: Monrovia
Currency: dollar (cent)
Language: English

LIBYA
Capital: Tripoli
Currency: dinar (dirham)
Language: Arabic

LITHUANIA
Capital: Vilnius
Currency: lita
Language: Lithuanian

LUXEMBOURG
Capital: Luxembourg
Currency: franc
Language: Letzeburgesch

MACEDONIA
Capital: Skopje
Currency: dinar (para)
Language: Macedonian

MADAGASCAR
Capital: Antananaivo
Currency: franc (centime)
Language: French

MALAWI
Capital: Lilongwe
Currency: kwacha (tambala)
Language: English

MALAYSIA
Capital: Kuala Lumpur
Currency: dollar (cent)
Language: Malay

MALTA
Capital: Valletta
Currency: Lira (cent)
Language: Maltese

MEXICO
Capital: Mexico City
Currency: peso (centavo)
Language: Spanish

MONGOLIA
Capital: Ulan Bator
Currency: tugrik (mongo)
Language: Khalkha Mongolian

MONTENEGRO
Capital: Podgorica
Currency: dinar (paras)
Language: Serbo-Croat

MOROCCO
Capital: Rabat
Currency: dirham (centime)
Language: Arabic

MOZAMBIQUE
Capital: Maputo
Currency: metical (centavo)
Language: Portuguese

MYANMAR (FORMERLY BURMA)
Capital: Yangon (Rangoon)
Currency: kyat (pya)
Language: Burmese

NAMIBIA
Capital: Windhoek
Currency: dollar (cent)
Language: English

NEPAL
Capital: Kathmandu
Currency: rupee (paisa)
Language: Nepali

NETHERLANDS
Capital: Amsterdam
Currency: florin (cent)
Language: Dutch

NEW ZEALAND
Capital: Wellington
Currency: dollar (cent)
Language: English

NICARAGUA
Capital: Managua
Currency: cordoba (centavo)
Language: Spanish

NIGERIA
Capital: Abuja
Currency: naira (kobo)
Language: English

NORWAY
Capital: Oslo
Currency: krone (ore)
Language: Norwegian

PAKISTAN
Capital: Islamabad
Currency: rupee (paisa)
Language: English

PANAMA
Capital:Panama City
Currency: balboa (cent)
Language: Spanish

PAPUA NEW GUINEA
Capital: Port Moresby
Currency: kina (toea)
Language: English, French

PARAGUAY
Capital: Asuncion
Currency: guarani (centimo)
Language: Spanish

PERU
Catpital: Lima
Currency: inti (centimo)
Language: Spanish

PHILIPPINES
Capital: Manila
Currency: peso (centavo)
Language: Filipino, English

POLAND
Capital: Warsaw
Currency: zioty (grosz)
Language: Polish

PORTUGAL
Capital: Lisbon
Currency: escudo (centavo)
Language: Portuguese

ROMANIA
Capital: Bucharest
Currency: leu (ban)
Language: Romanian

RUSSIA
Capital: Moscow
Currency: rouble (kopek)
Language: Russian

RWANDA
Capital: Kigali
Currency: franc (centime)
Language: Kinyarwanda, English

SAUDI ARABIA
Capital: Riyadh
Currency: riyal (halalas)
Language: Arabic

SERBIA
Capital: Belgrade
Currency: dinar (paras)
Language: Serbo-Croat

SIERRA LEONE
Capital: Freetown
Currency: leone (cent)
Language: English

SINGAPORE
Capital: Singapore City
Currency: dollar (cent)
Language: Malay, English, Tamil, Chinese

SLOVAKIA
Capital: Bratislava
Currency: karuna (haleru)
Language: Slovak

SOUTH AFRICA
Capital: Pretoria
Currency: rand (cent)
Language: Afrikaans

SPAIN
Capital: Madrid
Currency: peseta (centimo)
Language: Cortes: Spanish

SRI LANKA
Capital: Colombo
Currency: rupee (cent)
Language: Sinhalese, Tamil, English

SUDAN
Capital: Khartoum
Currency: pound (piastre)
Language: Arabic

SWEDEN
Capital: Stockholm
Currency: krona (ore)
Language: Swedish

SWITZERLAND
Capital: Bern
Currency: franc (centime)
Language: French, German, Italian

SYRIA
Capital: Damascus
Currency: pound (piastre)
Language: Arabic

TAIWAN
Capital: Taipei
Currency: dollar (cent)
Language: Mandarin Chinese

TANZANIA
Capital: Dodoma
Currency: shilling (cent)
Language: Swahili, English

THAILAND
Capital: Bangkok
Currency: baht (stangs)
Language: Thai

TUNISIA
Capital: Tunis
Currency: dinar (millieme)
Language: Arabic

TURKEY
Capital: Ankara
Currency: lira (kurus)
Language: Turkish

UGANDA
Capital: Kampala
Currency: shilling (cent)
Language: Swahili, English

UKRAINE
Capital: Kiev
Currency: karbovanet
Language: Ukrainian

UNITED KINGDOM
Capital: London
Currency: pound (pence)
Language: English

UNITED STATES OF AMERICA
Capital: Washington,DC
Currency: dollar (cent)
Language: English

URUGUAY
Capital: Montevideo
Currency: peso (centesimos)
Language: Spanish

UZBEKISTAN
Capital: Tashkent
Currency: rouble (kopek)
Language: Uzbek

VENEZUELA
Capital: Caracas
Currency: bolivar (centimos)
Language: Spanish

VIETNAM
Capital: Hanoi
Currency: dong (hao/xu
Language: Vietnamese

YEMEN
Capital: Sana'a
Currency: dinar (fils/riyal)
Language: Arabic

ZAIRE
Capital: Kinshasa
Currency: zaire (makuta/senghi)
Language: French

ZAMBIA
Capital: Lusaka
Currency: kwacha (ngwee)
Language: English

ZIMBABWE
Capital: Harare
Currency: dollar (cent)
Language: English, Shona, Ndebele

PORTS OF THE WORLD

ALGERIA
4
ORAN
6
SKIKDA
7
ALGIERS
9
PORT ARZEW

ANGOLA
6
LOBITO
LUANDA

ARGENTINA
7
LA PLATA
11
BUENOS AIRES

AUSTRALIA
6
SYDNEY
7
DAMPIER
GEELONG
8
ADELAIDE
BRISBANE
9
MELBOURNE
NEWCASTLE
10
FREEMANTLE
11
PORT JACKSON
12
PORT ADELAIDE

AZERBAIJAN
4
BAKU
BELGIUM
6
OSTEND
7
ANTWERP
9
ZEEBRUGGE

BENIN
7
COTONOU
9
PORTO NOVO

BRAZIL
4
PARA
5
SELEM
6
RECIFE
SANTOS
7
TOBARAO

10
PERNAMBUCO
RIO DE JANEIRO

BULGARIA
5
VARNA

BURMA
5
AKYAB
6
SITTWE
7
RANGOON
8
MOULMEIN

CAMEROON
6
DOUALA

CANADA
7
HALIFAX
KITIMAT
8
MONTREAL
9
CHURCHILL
ESQUIMALT
OWEN SOUND
VANCOUVER
11
THREE RIVERS

CHANNEL ISLANDS
8
ST HELIER
11
SAINT HELIER
ST PETER PORT

CHILE
5
ARICA
8
COQUIMBO
10
VALPARAISO

CHINA
4
AMOY
6
CHEFOO
HANKOW
SWATOW
WEIHAI
7
FOOCHOW
YINGKOW
8
SHANGHAI
TIENTSIN
10
PORT ARTHUR
COLUMBIA
9
CARTAGENA
12
BARRANQUILLA
BUENAVENTURA

CORSICA
6
BASTIA
AJACCIO

CROATIA
6
RIJEKA

CUBA
6
HAVANA
14
SANTIAGO DE CUBA

CYPRUS
7
LARNACA
8
LIMASSOL

DENMARK
6
ODENSE
7
AALBORG
HORSENS
8
ELSINORE
HELSINGOR
10
COPENHAGEN
13
FREDERIKSHAVN

ECUADOR
9
GUAYAQUIL

EGYPT
4
SUEZ
8
DAMIETTA
PORT SAID
10
ALEXANDRIA

ENGLAND
4
HULL
5
DOVER
6
LONDON
7
CHATHAM
GRIMSBY
HARWICH
TILBURY
8
FALMOUTH
NEWHAVEN
PENZANCE
PLYMOUTH
PORTLAND
SANDWICH
WEYMOUTH
9
AVONMOUTH
DEVONPORT
GRAVESEND
KING'S LYNN
LIVERPOOL
NEWCASTLE
SHEERNESS
10
BARNSTABLE
COLCHESTER
FELIXSTOWE
FOLKESTONE
HARTLEPOOL
PORTSMOUTH
SUNDERLAND
TEIGNMOUTH
WHITSTABLE
11
CINQUE PORTS
SOUTHAMPTON
12
NORTH SHIELDS
PORT SUNLIGHT
13
MIDDLESBROUGH

ESTONIA
7
TALLINN

FINLAND
8
HELSINKI

FRANCE
5
BREST
6
CALAIS
CANNES
DIEPPE
TOULON
7
DUNKIRK
LE HAVRE
8
BORDEAUX
BOUEOGNE
HONFLEUR
9
CHERBOURG
FOS-SUR-MER
MARSEILLE
10
LA ROCHELLE
MARSEILLES

FRENCH GUIANA
7
CAYENNE

GERMANY
4
KIEL
5
EMDEN
6
BREMEN
WISMAR
7
HAMBURG
ROSTOCK
8
CUXHAVEN
9
FLENSBURG
10
TRAVEMUNDE
11
BREMERHAVEN
13
WILHELMSHAVEN

GHANA
4
TEMA
8
TAKORADI

GREECE
5
CANEA
CORFU
6
PATRAS
RHODES
7
PIRAEUS
NAVARINO
10
HERMOPOLIS
11
HERMOUPOLIS

HAWAII
8
HONOLULU
11
PEARL HARBOUR

HUNGARY
8
BUDAPEST

INDIA
6
BOMBAY
COCHIN
HALDIA
KANDLA
MADRAS
8
CALCUTTA
COCANADA
KAKINADA
11
MASULIPATAM
PONDICHERRY
12
MASULIPATNAM

INDONESIA
6
PADANG
7
JAKARTA
8
MACASSAR
MAKASSAR
PARADEEP

IRAN
6
ABADAN
7
BUSHIRE

IRAQ
5
BASRA

IRELAND
4
COBH
CORK
7
DONEGAL
DUNDALK
YOUGHAL
8
DUNLEARY
12
DUN LAOGHAIRE

ISRAEL
4
ACRE
AKKO
ELAT
5
EILAT
HAIFA
6
ASHDOD

ITALY
4
BARI
5
GAETA
GENOA
OSTIA
TRANI
6
ANCONA
NAPLES
VENICE
7
LEGHORN

MARSALA
MESSINA
PALERMO
SALERNO
TRAPANI
TRIESTE
8
BRINDISI

IVORY COAST
7
ABIDJAN

JAMAICA
8
KINGSTON
9
PORT ROYAL
10
MONTEGO BAY

JAPAN
4
KOBE
5
KOCHI
OSAKA
8
HAKODATE
NAGASAKI
YOKOHAMA
9
HIROSHIMA
KAGOSHIMA
11
SHIMONOSEKI

KENYA
7
MOMBASA

KUWAIT
12
MINA AL-AHMADI

LATVIA
4
RIGA

LEBANON
6
BEIRUT

LIBYA
7
TRIPOLI
8
BENGHAZI

MADAGASCAR
8
TAMATAVE

MALAYSIA
6
PENANG
9
PORT KLANG
10
GEORGE TOWN
12
KOTAKINABALU

MAURITIUS
9
PORT LOUIS

MEXICO
7
GUAYMAS
8
VERA CRUZ

MOROCCO
4
SAFI
5
CEUTA
RABAT
6
AGADIR
TETUAN
7
MELILLA
MOGADOR
TANGIER
9
ESSAOUIRA
10
CASABLANCA

MOZAMBIQUE
5
BEIRA
6
MAPUTO

NETHERLANDS
5
DELFT
8
FLUSHING
9
AMSTERD AM
EUROPOORT
ROTTERDAM
10
VLISSINGEN

NEW ZEALAND
6
NELSON
8
AUCKLAND
GISBORNE
9
LYTTELTON

NIGERIA
5
LAGOS
PORT HARCOURT

NORTHERN IRELAND
7
BELFAST

NORWAY
4
OSLO
6
BERGEN
LARVIK
NARVIK
TROMSO
9
STAVANGER
TRONDHEIM
10
CHRISTIANA
HAMMERFEST
13
CHRISTIANSUND

PAKISTAN
6
CHALNA
7
KARACHI

PANAMA
5
COLON
6
BALBOA
9
CRISTOBAL

PAPUA NEW GUINEA
11
PORT MORESBY

YEMEN
4
ADEN

PERU
3
ILO
6
CALLAO
MATARINI
10
SAN JUAN BAY

PHILIPPINES
4
CEBU
6
MANILA

POLAND
6
DANZIG
GDANSK
GDYNIA
7
STETTIN
8
SZCZECIN
9
KOLOBRZEG

PORTUGAL
6
LISBON
OPORTO

PUERTO RICO
7
SAN JUAN

ROMANIA
10
CONSTANTSA

RUSSIA
9
ARCHANGEL
LENINGRAD
11
VLADIVOSTOK
13
PETROPAVLOVSK

SAUDI ARABIA
6
JEDDAH

SCOTLAND
4
TAIN
WICK
5
LEITH
SCAPA
6
DUNBAR
DUNDEE
8
GREENOCK
ARDROSSAN
SCAPA FLOW
STORNAWAY
11
GRANGEMOUTH
PORT GLASGOW

SENEGAL
5
DAKAR

SIERRA LEONE
8
FREETOWN

SOUTH AFRICA
6
DURBAN
8
CAPE TOWN
9
MOSSEL BAY
PORT NATAL
10
EAST LONDON
SIMONSTOWN
RICHARD'S BAY
13
PORT ELIZABETH

SOUTH KOREA
5
PUSAN

SPAIN
5
PALMA
PALOS
BILBAO
FERROL
MALAGA
7
CORUNNA
FUNCHAL
8
ALICAME
ARRECIFE
LA CORUNA
9
ALGECIRAS
BARCELONA
CARTAGENA
LAS PALMAS

SRI LANKA
5
GALLE
7
COLOMBO

SUDAN
6
SUAKIN
9
PORT SUDAN

SWEDEN
5
LULEA
MALMO
WISBY
YSTAD
6
KALMAR
8
GOTEBORG
HALMSTAD
NYKOPING
9
STOCKHOLM
10
GOTHENBURG
11
HELSINGSORG

TAIWAN
6
TAINAN
7
KEELUNG
KAOHSIUNG

TANZANIA
6
MTWARA
11
DAR ES SALAAM

TRINIDAD AND TOBAGO
11
PORT-OF-SPAIN

TURKEY
5
IZMIR
6
SMYRNA
8
ISTANBUL
14
CONSTANTINOPLE

URUGUAY
10
MONTEVIDEO

USA
4
ERIE
7
DETROIT
HOUSTON
NEW YORK
NORFOLK
SEATTLE
8
NEW HAVEN
9
BALTIMORE
GALVESTON
NANTUCKET
PENSACOLA
10
BRIDGEPORT
CHARLESTON
JERSEY CITY
LOS ANGELES
NEW BEDFORD
NEW ORLEANS
PERTH AMBOY
PORTSMOUTH
11
ROCK HARBOUR
SAN FRANCISCO

VENEZUELA
8
LA GUIARA
12
PUERTO HIERRO
13
PUERTO CABELLO

WALES
7
CARDIFF
SWANSEA
HOLYHEAD
LLANELLI
PEMBROKE
9
PORTMADOC
12
MILFORD HAVEN

YUGOSLAVIA
3
BAR
5
KOTOR
7
CATTARO
9
DUBROVNIK

ZAIRE
6
MATADI
9
MBUJI-MAYI

BIBLICAL CHARACTERS

3
Abe
Asa
Eli
Eve
God
Ham
Job
Lot

4
Abel
Adam
Ahab
Amos
Baal
Boaz
Cain
Esau
Joab
John
Jude
Leah
Levi
Like
Magi (The)
Mark
Mary
Moab
Noah
Paul
Ruth
Saul
seth
Shem

5
Aaron
Annas
Caleb
David
Devil (The)
Enoch
Herod
Hiram
Hosea
Isaac
Jacob
James
Jesse
Jesus
Jonah
Judah
Judas
Laban
Linus
Lydia
Micah
Moses
Nahum
Naomi
Peter
Sarah
Satan
Silas
Simon
Titus
Uriah

6
Andrew
Christ
Daniel
Darius
Dorcas
Elijah
Elisha
Esther
Gideon
Haggai
Isiah
Jairus
Joseph
Joshua
Martha
Miriam
Naboth
Nathan
Philip
Pilate
Rachel
Reuben
Salome
Samson
Samuel
Simeon
Thomas

7
Abraham
Absalom
Delilah
Ephraim
Ezekiel
Gabriel
Goliath
Ishmael
Jehovah
Jezebel
Lazarus
Lucifer
Malachi
Matthew
Michael

7
Obadiah
Pharoh
Raphael
Rebecca
Rebekah
Shallum
Solomon
Stephen
Zebulon

8
Barabbas
Barnabas
Benjamin
Caiaphas
Herodias
Hezekiah
Jeremiah
Jeroboam
Jonathan
Matthias
Mordecai
Nehemiah
Philemon

9
Abimelech
Bathsheba
Nathaniel
Nicodemus
Zachariah
Zacharias

10
Belshazzar
Methuselah

11
Bartholomew
Jehoshaphat

13
Judas Iscariot
Mary Magdalene
Pontius Pilate

14
John the Baptist
Nebuchadnezzar

BOOKS OF THE BIBLE

OLD TESTAMENT
GENESIS
EXODUS
LEVITICUS
NUMBERS
DEUTERONOMY
JOSHUA
JUDGES
RUTH
I SAMUEL
II SAMUEL
I KINGS
II KINGS
I CHRONICLES
II CHRONICLES
EZRA
NEHEMIAH
ESTHER
JOB
PSALMS
PROVERBS
ECCLESIASTES
THE SONG OF SOLOMON
ISIAH
JEREMIAH
LAMENTATIONS
EZEKIEL
DANIEL
HOSEA
JOEL
AMOS
OBADIAH
JONAH
MICAAH
NAHUM
HABAKKUK
ZEPHANIAH
HAGGAI
ZECHARIAH
MALACI

NEW TESTAMENT
MATTHEW
MARK
LUKE
JOHN
THE ACTS OF THE APOSTLES
ROMANS
I CORINTHIANS
II CORINTHIANS
GALATIANS
EPHESIANS
PHILIPPIANS
COLOSSIANS
I THESSALONIANS
II THESSALONIANS
I TIMOTHY
II TIMOTHY
TITUS
PHILEMON
HEBREWS
JAMES
I PETER
II PETER
I JOHN
II JOHN
III JOHN
JUDE
REVELATION

APOCRYPHA
I ESDRA
II ESDRA
TOBIT
JUDITH
THE REST OF ESTHER
WISDOM
ECCLESIASTICUS
BARUCH, WITH EPISTLE OF JEREMIAH
SONG OF THE THREE CHILDREN
SUSANNA
BEL AND THE DRAGON
PRAYER OF MANASSES
I
MACCABEES
II MACCABEES

COLLECTIVE NAMES AND GROUP TERMS

APES (SHREWDNESS)
ASSES (HERD; PACE)

BABOONS (TROOP)
BADGERS (CETE)
BEARS (SLOTH)
BEES (ERST; SWARM)
BIRDS (FLOCK)
BISHOPS (BENCH)
BISON (HERD)
BITTERNS (SEDGE)
BOARS (SOUNDER)
BUFFALOES (HERD)

CATERPILLARS (ARMY)
CATTLE (DROVE; HERD)
CHOUGHS (CHATTERING)
COLTS (RAG)
COOTS (COVERT)
CRANES (HERD)
CROWS (MURDER)

DEER (HERD)
DOGS (KENNEL)
DOVES (FLIGHT)
DUCKS (PADDLING)

ELEPHANTS (HERD)
ELK (GANG)
FERRETS (BUSINESS)
FISH (SHOAL)
FLIES (SWARM)
FOXES (SKULK)

GEESE (GAGGLE; SKEIN)
GIRAFFES (HERD)
GOATS (HERD; TRIBE)
GOLDFINCHES (CHARM)
GROUSE (COVEY; PACK)
GULLS (COLONY)

HARES (DOWN; HUSK)
HENS (BROOD)
HERONS (SEDGE; SIEGE)
HORSES (HARRAS; STABLE; STUD)
HOUNDS (MUTE; PACK)
HUNTERS (BLAST)

KANGAROOS (TROOP)
KITTENS (KINDLE; LITTER)

LAPWINGS (DESERT)
LARKS (EXALTATION)
LEOPARDS (LEAP; LEPE)
LIONS (PRIDE; SAWT; SOUSE; TROOP)
LOCUSTS (SWARM)

MAGPIES (SORD; SUTE)
MARES (STUD0
MARTENS (RICHESSE)
MICE (NEST)
MOLES (LABOUR)
MONKEYS(TROOP)
MULES (BARREN; SPAN)

NIGHTINGALES (WATCH)

OWLS (PARLIAMENT; STARE)
OXEN (HERD; YOKE)

PARTRIDGES (COVEY)
PEACOCKS (MUSTER)
PIGEONS (FLIGHT; FLOCK)
PIGS (HERD; LITTER)
PLOVERS (WING)
PORPOISES (SCHOOL)
PUPS (LITTER)

RABBITS (BURY; NEST)
RACEHORSES (STRING)
RHINOCEROS (CRASH)
ROOKS (BUILDING; CLAMOUR)

SHEEP (FLOCK)
SNIPE (WISP)
STARLINGS (MURMURATION)
SWINE (DOYLT; SOUNDER)

TEAL (SPRING)
TURKEYS (RAFTER)

WASPS (NEST)
WHALES (SCHOOL)
WHITING (POD)
WIDGEON (COMPANY; KNOB)
WILDFOWL (PLUMP; SORD; SUTE)
WITCHES 9COVEN)
WOLVES (PACK; ROUT)
WOODCOCKS (FALL)
WOODPECKERS (DESCENT)